MAJOR PRINCIPLES OF MEDIA LAW

2023 EDITION

Genelle I. Belmas
University of Kansas

Jason M. Shepard
California State University, Fullerton

CENGAGE

Australia • Brazil • Mexico • Singapore • United Kingdom • United States

Table of Contents

Preface

Welcome to the 30th edition of *Major Principles of Media Law*. This edition includes new developments through the U.S. Supreme Court's 2020-2021 term, and the two prior terms since the last update. It also includes major revisions to several chapters.

At the Supreme Court, the most important development since the last edition was the transformation of the Court's makeup as a result of President Donald Trump's three appointments of Justice Neil Gorsuch, Justice Brett Kavanaugh, and Justice Amy Coney Barrett. In terms of public access to the Supreme Court, in 2021, the Court for the first time in its history provided live streaming of its audio arguments, prompted by closure of the Supreme Court building during the COVID-19 pandemic.

In the last three years, the Supreme Court handed down several cases with First Amendment precedent. In two cases, the Court restricted public access to government records by broadly construing exemptions to the federal Freedom of Information Act. In *NCAA v. Alston*, the Court used antitrust law to strike down a ban on compensation for college athletes, likely spurring a new age of college athletes to exercise to their right of publicity. Antitrust is also a hotter topic than it's been in many years, with Congress and the Biden administration poised to issue new rules and orders reforming it.

The Court also handed down a bumper crop of intellectual property decisions, including the highly anticipated *Google v. Oracle* case about fair use in software APIs, several trademark cases (such as *Iancu v. Brunetti*, overturning yet another Lanham Act content restriction), and other opinions clarifying IP damages and procedures. A federal appeals court refused to stop states from passing their own net neutrality laws, and Section 230 continues to be on the minds of both politicians and the public as the power of Big Tech grows.

Also in 2021, the justices handed down one of their rare decisions about student expression, saying that a high school cheerleader's profane Snap, sent off-campus and on a Saturday, shouldn't have resulted in administrative punishment.

The Court expanded religious freedom in several decisions about the establishment and free exercise clauses (*American Legion v. American Humanist Association, Our Lady of Guadalupe v. Morrissey-Berru*, and *Tandon v. Newsom*.) And the the 1964 *New York Times v. Sullivan* libel case, considered by many as one of the most important cases in all media law jurisprudence, has gained more critics, including Justice Neil Gorsuch, who expressed concern about how "actual malice" has developed since the case was handed down.

In reviewing issues of press freedom during the past three years, former President Donald Trump looms large. Trump rhetorical attacks on the press, calling them "fake news" and "the enemy of people," was matched by widespread legal actions, including subpoenaing journalists' phone and email records, banning credentialed reporters from the House, filing libel lawsuits against the press, and suing social media companies for blocking his access after he was accused of inciting violence that led to the Jan. 6 insurrection at the Capitol. While president, Trump even directed his aides to investigate whether he had the power to punish *Saturday Night Live* for making fun of him, according to reports. Joe Biden's election as president brought signs of greater respect—or at least reduced hostility —for press freedom from the federal executive branch.

Given these and many other developments, it is an especially important time to understand the principles and history of free speech and press rights. The 30th edition of *Major Principles* notes many other changes in the law since 2018.

Here are a few of the highlights of what's new in this edition.

Chapter One (The American Legal System) discusses:
- Appointments of Brett Kavanaugh and Amy Coney Barrett to U.S. Supreme Court.
- The legacy of Ruth Bader Ginsburg.
- Synthesis on First Amendment jurisprudence by the Roberts Court.
- Expanded "Focus On" box about "The Whole First Amendment" to include new religious establishment and free exercise precedents.

Chapter Two (The Legacy of Freedom) discusses:
- New "Focus On" boxes on John Stuart Mill and First Amendment values.
- Updated legal theorists to include critical approaches.
- Updated developments in the Wikileaks and Snowden cases.
- Issues related to incitement regarding Jan. 6, 2021 insurrection at the U.S. Capitol.

Chapter Three (Modern Prior Restraints) discusses:
- Several state statutes prohibiting "deepfake" videos.
- *Nieves v. Bartlett,* in which the Court clarified its doctrine on First Amendment retaliation when probable cause exists to justify an arrest.
- *Pennsylvania v. Knox,* in which the Pennsylvania Supreme Court upheld the conviction of a rap singer for a song called "Fuck the Police."
- First Circuit in *Rideout v. Gardner* strikes down state law prohibiting ballot selfies.

Chapter Four (Libel and Slander) discusses:
- Anti-*Sullivan* takes from two Supreme Court justices and an appellate judge.
- A reorganized and updated Section 230 section (and a 2021 case involving Snapchat).
- The "Carlson defense" for libel defendants.
- Updates to libel suits filed by women against former president Trump.

Chapter Five (The Right to Privacy) discusses:
- Digital privacy developments, including new laws in response to new controversies, including social media practices, data breaches, and hackings.
- Two Supreme Court decisions about gay rights applying the Civil Rights Act of 1964's ban on employment discrimination to gay and transgender individuals and balancing religious freedom claims against non-discrimination laws.
- Updates to the Court's abortion-rights jurisprudence, including *June Med. Svc. v. Russo.*
- Implications of *NCAA v. Alston* on college athletes' rights of publicity.

Chapter Six (Copyrights and Trademarks) discusses:
- A host of new Supreme Court IP cases (eight decided, one future) providing guidance on topics from software APIs copyright to procedures such as registration and damages, from domain names as trademarks to the registrability of profane marks, and more.
- New "Focus On boxes:" Blackbeard and copyright, the Amen Break, parody pet toys.
- Developments in music copyright: a Led Zeppelin win for "Stairway to Heaven" and a new law to manage royalty payments.
- The CASE Act, setting up a voluntary system to address "small" infringement cases.

Chapter Seven (Fair Trial-Free Press) discusses:
- Derek Chauvin trial as the latest example involving prejudicial publicity claims.
- U.S. Supreme Court allows live audio streaming of its oral arguments.
- DC Circuit upholds the use of a "husher" to prevent hearing of *voir dire* proceedings.
- Colorado Supreme Court rules no qualified right of access to court documents.

Chapter Eight (Newsgatherer's Privilege) discusses:
- Update on leak prosecutions by the Trump administration, including details of eight convictions of individuals accused of leaking information to journalists.
- President Biden's pledge to not go after journalists' phone and email records.
- A police raid on a freelance journalist's house violated California's shield law.

Chapter Nine (Freedom of Information) discusses:
- Two Supreme Court decisions limiting the scope of FOIA.
- Updated statistics on FOIA backlog and delays with FOIA compliance.
- A Ninth Circuit Court of Appeals decision finding that requests can't be denied on the theory that running a database query is creating a "new record."
- Two journalists' suits to have their press credentials restored after the White House revoked them (*CNN v. Trump* and *Karem v. Trump*).

Chapter 10 (Obscenity and Pornography) discusses:
- Update on legal challenges to FOSTA/SESTA, a law aimed at curbing sex trafficking.
- New "revenge porn" laws in some states, and four state high courts uphold laws.

Chapter 11 (Regulation of the Electronic Media) discusses:
- Five new cases from the Supreme Court: three involving the Telephone Consumer Protection Act and one interpreting the 1986 Computer Fraud and Abuse Act.
- "Focus On" boxes featuring new FCC rules for spoofing/robocalls, "FrankenFM" broadcasters, and a justice's ideas for regulating private social media companies.
- Updates in net neutrality, Section 230, and KidVid rules.

Chapter 12 (Antitrust and Media Ownership Issues) discusses:
- The high court upholds FCC's ownership regulations in the latest *Prometheus* case.
- "Big Tech" antitrust cases in the United States and European Union—against Google, Apple, and Facebook.
- New mergers and new antitrust laws on the horizon.

Chapter 13 (Advertising and the Law) discusses:
- Supreme Court cases on campaign finance, disclosure rules, and the FTC Act.
- Updates to e-cigarette regulation and FDA cigarette graphic warnings mandated by the Tobacco Control Act.
- New "Focus On" box: almond "milk."

Chapter 14 (Freedom of the Student Press) discusses:
- *Mahanoy Sch. Dist. v. B.L.*, a 2021 Supreme Court case about off-campus speech.
- Other developments in student expression involving dress codes and professionalism.
- Haskell Indian Nation University's conflict with its paper's editor-in-chief.

* * *

Genelle's thanks: Even during a pandemic, free speech rocks. First Amendment issues are everywhere once you start looking, and this work lets me find, explore, and write about them. To Jason Shepard, my partner on this wild ride, for his knowledge, generosity, and critical editorial eye. To my parents, Gene and Gin, for their constant love and support and for continuing to encourage my curiosity and creativity. To Reshi, who keeps me honest and grounded. To my KU journalism students and colleagues, who challenge me to learn more, teach better, and keep loving what I do. To Michael, who listens, suggests, and hears me (and who isn't scared to tell me I'm wrong). And, always, to Douglas Bornemann, Ph.D., J.D., upon whom for 24 years (and then some) I have relied for, well, everything, and whom I can never thank or love enough. I wouldn't want to be stuck in a house for months upon months with anyone else.

Jason's thanks: Writing this textbook is a labor of love. I am thankful to work with Genelle Belmas on this adventure in our shared passion for the First Amendment. I got hooked on media law early in life thanks to a run-in with a prior restraint over a middle school student council newsletter. I am thankful for my Mom, Dad, and Grandma, who never let meager means stop me from being the first in my family to graduate college and dream big things. My former journalism and media law mentors taught me much: in high school, Roxanne Biffert, Loni Lown, and Gail Gunderson; in college, Don Downs and Robert Drechsel; at *The Capital Times*, Dave Zweifel, Ron McCrea, and Anita Weier; and at *Isthmus*, Marc Eisen and Bill Lueders. And lastly, I am grateful to my students at California State University, Fullerton, where I serve as the chair of the Department of Communications. The student journalists I work with, including as publisher of the *Daily Titan* student newspaper, and those in my Communications Law classes, remind me each time I step into the newsroom and the classroom how amazing it is that my job is to bring to life the principles found in this textbook.

We both offer gratitude to Wayne Overbeck, who has trusted us with this work that he so ably shepherded through so many editions, and to Rick Pullen of California State University, Fullerton (now also retired), who was co-author of the first two editions of this book. Much of the credit should go to the many reviewers who have offered so many helpful suggestions since the first edition was written years ago, and to others who have contributed to the design and content over the years.

Genelle I. Belmas, Ph.D.
Jason M. Shepard, Ph.D.
July 1, 2021

For updates during the academic year, access to archives of material not published in this year's print edition, and contact information, please visit our websites:
www.genellebelmas.com
www.jasonmshepard.com

A test bank for each chapter is available with an instructor account at login.cengage.com.

Table of Cases

1 *The American Legal System*

America has become a nation of laws, lawyers, and lawsuits. Both the number of lawsuits being filed and the number of lawyers have skyrocketed in recent generations. Nationwide, 1.3 million lawyers practiced law in the United States in 2020, three times as many as one generation ago. For good or ill, more people with grievances are suing somebody.

The media have not escaped this flood of litigation. The nation's broadcasters, cable and satellite television providers, newspapers, magazines, wire services, entertainment companies, internet services, and advertising agencies are constantly fighting legal battles. Today, few media executives can do their jobs without consulting lawyers. Moreover, legal problems are not just headaches for top executives. Working media professionals run afoul of the law regularly, facing lawsuits and even jail sentences. Million-dollar verdicts against the media are no longer unusual. For example, the internet company Gawker was bankrupted out of business after a Florida jury in 2016 ordered the company to pay $140 million in damages for invasion of privacy for posting a sex tape of professional wrestler Hulk Hogan.

Big national media are by no means the only targets. The growth of social media has provided ample examples of individuals being sued for posting comments on Facebook, Twitter, Instagram and Yelp. Likewise, anyone who works in journalism, public relations, advertising, entertainment or digital media may risk lawsuits, and threats of lawsuits, for anything from libel to copyright infringement to invasion of privacy.

More than ever before, a knowledge of media law is essential for a successful career in mass communications. This textbook was written for communications students and media professionals, not for lawyers or law students. We will begin by explaining how the American legal system works.

■ THE KEY ROLE OF THE COURTS

Mass media law is largely based on court decisions. Even though Congress and the 50 state legislatures have enacted many laws affecting the media, the courts play the decisive role in interpreting those laws. For that matter, the courts also have the final say in interpreting the meaning of our most important legal document, the U.S. Constitution. The courts have the power to modify or even overturn laws passed by state legislatures and Congress, particularly when a law conflicts with the Constitution. In so doing, the courts have the power to establish legal precedent, handing down rules that other courts must ordinarily follow in deciding similar cases.

Chapter Objectives:

- Explain the role of courts in media law.
- Describe the structure of the U.S. court system.
- Identify the sources of law.
- Compare and contrast criminal law and civil law.

Essential Questions:

- What is law? Where do laws come from? How are they enforced?
- What is federalism and why is it important?
- What is the role of the Supreme Court of the United States in determining the law?
- How does the Supreme Court work?
- What is the difference between civil and criminal law? What are torts?
- What are the basic steps of a lawsuit?
- What are the basic elements of a court decision?

precedent:
a case that other courts rely on when deciding future cases with similar facts or issues.

appellate court:
a court to which a finding from a lower court may be appealed.

questions of fact:
resolutions of factual disputes that are decided by a jury.

remand:
to send back to a lower court for evaluation based on new legal rules.

But not all court decisions establish legal *precedents*, and not all legal precedents are equally important as guidelines for later decisions. The Supreme Court of the United States is the highest court in the country; its rulings are generally binding on all lower courts. On matters of state law the highest court in each of the 50 states (usually called the state supreme court) has the final say—unless one of its rulings somehow violates the U.S. Constitution. On federal matters the U.S. Courts of Appeals rank just below the U.S. Supreme Court. All of these courts are *appellate* courts; cases are appealed to them from trial courts.

Trial vs. appellate courts. There is an important difference between trial and appellate courts. While appellate courts make precedent-setting decisions that interpret the meaning of law, trial courts are responsible for deciding factual issues such as the guilt or innocence of a person accused of a crime. This fact-finding process does not normally establish legal precedents. The way a judge or jury decides a given murder trial, for instance, sets no precedent for the next murder trial. The fact that one alleged murderer may be guilty doesn't prove the guilt of the next murder suspect.

In civil (i.e., non-criminal) lawsuits, this is also true. A trial court may have to decide whether a newspaper or broadcaster libeled the local mayor by falsely accusing the mayor of wrongdoing. Even if the media did—and if the mayor wins his or her lawsuit—that doesn't prove the next news story about a mayoral scandal is also libelous. Each person suing for libel—like each person charged with a crime—is entitled to his or her own day in court.

Finding facts. The trial courts usually have the final say about these *questions of fact*. An appellate court might rule that a trial court misapplied the law to a given factual situation, but the appellate court doesn't ordinarily reevaluate the facts on its own. Instead, it sends the case back (*remands*) to the trial court with instructions to reassess the facts under new legal rules written by the appellate court. For instance, an appellate court might decide that a certain piece of evidence was illegally obtained and cannot be used in a murder trial. It will order the trial court to reevaluate the factual issue of guilt or innocence, this time completely disregarding the illegally obtained evidence. The appellate court's ruling may well affect the outcome of the case, but it is still the job of the trial court to decide the factual question of guilt or innocence, just as it is the job of the appellate court to set down rules on such legal issues as the admissibility of evidence.

This is not to say trial courts never make legal (as opposed to fact-finding) decisions: they do so every time they apply the law to a factual situation. But when a trial court issues an opinion on a legal issue, that opinion usually carries little weight as legal precedent.

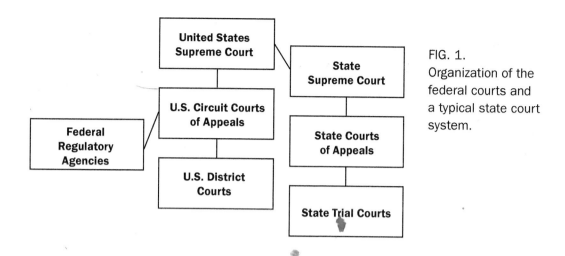

FIG. 1.
Organization of the federal courts and a typical state court system.

Sometimes there is high drama in the trial courtroom, and that may result in extensive media coverage. One trial verdict may even inspire (or discourage) more lawsuits of the same kind. Still, the outcome of a trial rarely has long-term legal significance. On the other hand, a little-noticed appellate court decision may fundamentally alter the way we live. That is why law textbooks such as this one concentrate on appellate court decisions, especially U.S. Supreme Court decisions.

■ STRUCTURE OF THE U.S. COURT SYSTEM

Because the courts play such an important role in shaping the law, the structure of the court system itself deserves some explanation. Fig. 1 shows how the state and federal courts are organized. In the federal system, there is a nationwide network of trial courts at the bottom of the structure. Next higher are 12 intermediate appellate courts serving various regions of the country, with the Supreme Court at the top of the system.

U.S. District Courts

In the federal system there is at least one trial court called the U.S. District Court in each of the 50 states and the District of Columbia. Some of the more populous states have more than one federal judicial district, and each district has its own trial court or courts. As trial courts, the U.S. District Courts have limited precedent-setting authority. Nevertheless, a U.S. District Court decision occasionally sets an important precedent. The primary duty of these courts, however, is to serve as *trial courts* of general jurisdiction in the federal system; that is, they handle a variety of federal civil and criminal matters, ranging from civil disputes over copyrights to criminal trials of persons accused of acts of terrorism against the United States.

U.S. Courts of Appeals

At the next level up in the federal court system, there are U.S. Courts of Appeals, often called the *circuit courts* because the nation is divided into geographic *circuits*. That term, incidentally, originated in an era when all federal judges (including the justices of the Supreme Court) were required to be "circuit riders." They traveled from town to town, holding court

FIG. 2.
Geographic
boundaries of
United States
Courts of Appeals
and United States
District Courts.

U.S. Courts, http://www.
uscourts.gov/sites/de-
*fault/files/u.s._federal_*
courts_circuit_map_1.
pdf

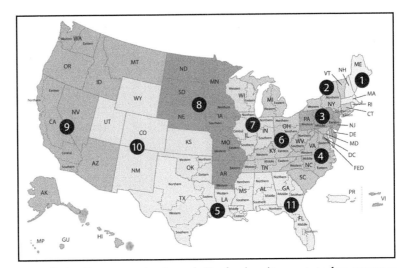

D.C. Circuit
Court

sessions wherever there were federal cases to be heard. Each circuit court today serves a specific region of the country, and most still hear cases in various cities within their regions.

There are 11 regional circuit courts. Fig. 2 shows how the United States is divided into judicial circuits. In addition, a separate circuit court (the U.S. Court of Appeals for the D.C. circuit) exists solely to serve Washington, D.C.; it often hears appeals of decisions by federal agencies, many of them involving high-profile issues. Many "D.C. circuit" judges have been promoted to the Supreme Court. There is also a U.S. Court of Appeals for the Federal Circuit. Unlike the other circuit courts, this one serves no single geographic area. Instead, it has nationwide jurisdiction over certain special kinds of cases, including patent and customs appeals and some claims against the federal government. This court is the product of a merger of the old Court of Claims and the Court of Customs and Patent Appeals. This book will generally refer to these courts by their numbers (e.g., First Circuit, Ninth Circuit).

Some of the circuits have been divided over the years as the population grew. Until 1981, the Fifth Circuit included Alabama, Georgia, and Florida, the states that now comprise the Eleventh Circuit. Legislation has been proposed repeatedly to divide the far-flung Ninth Circuit, which serves Alaska, Hawaii, and the entire West Coast (nine states with a total population of about 60 million people). Although critics say it is too large and too California-oriented because California's huge population has resulted in many of the Ninth Circuit's judges coming from one state, Congress has never agreed upon a plan to divide it. The Ninth Circuit has 29 active judges, by far the largest number of any circuit. The second largest circuit is the Fifth, which has 17 active judges. Each court also has *senior judges* who are officially retired but volunteer to continue hearing cases.

Appeals process. The losing party in most U.S. District Court trials may appeal the decision to the circuit court serving that region of the country. The decisions of the circuit courts produce many important legal precedents; on federal questions the rulings of these courts are second in importance only to U.S. Supreme Court decisions. Although each circuit court has a large number of judges, most cases are heard by panels of three judges. Two of the three constitute a majority and may issue the *majority opinion*, which sets forth the court's legal reasoning. Sometimes a case is considered so important or controversial that a larger panel of judges decides the case, usually reconsidering an earlier decision by a three-judge panel. When that happens, it is called deciding a case *en banc*. Ordinarily, an *en banc* panel consists of all of the judges serving on a particular circuit court. As the circuit courts grew larger, Congress authorized smaller *en banc* panels in some instances. The Ninth Circuit used panels of 15 judges to hear cases *en banc* for a time and now uses panels of 11.

Since these appellate courts decide only matters of law, there are no juries in these courts. Juries serve only in trial courts, and even there juries only decide factual issues (such as the guilt or innocence of a criminal defendant), not legal issues. Appellate cases are decided by judges alone, unassisted by a jury—both in the federal and state court systems.

Circuit splits. One point should be explained about the significance of the legal precedents established by the U.S. circuit courts. As long as the decision does not conflict with a U.S. Supreme Court ruling, each circuit court is free to arrive at its own conclusions on issues of law, which are then binding on lower courts in that circuit. A circuit court is not required to follow precedents established by other circuit courts around the country, although precedents from other circuits usually carry considerable weight and are often followed.

Occasionally two different circuit courts will rule differently on the same legal issue, called a *circuit split*. When that happens, the trial courts in each region have no choice but to follow the local circuit court's ruling. Trial courts located in other circuits may choose to follow either of the two conflicting precedents, or they may follow neither. Since this kind of uncertainty about the law is obviously bad for everyone, the U.S. Supreme Court often intervenes, establishing a uniform rule of law all over the country.

As well as hearing appeals of federal trial court decisions, the circuit courts also hear appeals from special-purpose courts and federal administrative agencies. For instance, decisions of both the Federal Trade Commission and the Federal Communications Commission may be appealed to the federal circuit courts. Such cases are often heard by the U.S. Court of Appeals for the D.C. circuit, giving that court a major role in communications law.

It bears noting that even though there are many judges serving in federal courts below the Supreme Court, some empty judicial seats go unfilled for months. Sometimes appointments to these seats are politically charged. A snapshot of current vacancies in the federal judiciary, in mid-2021, showed a total of 890 federal judge positions. Of those, there were 81 judicial vacancies and 16 pending nominees (including 5 in the appellate courts). This information is tracked by the Administrative Office of the U.S. Courts (www.uscourts.gov).

en banc:
Latin/French for "in the bench," a session where all judges on a court participate in the hearing and resolution of a case, rather than just a small panel. Pronounced "on bonk."

circuit split:
when two or more circuit courts have different rules on the same issue of law; often the Supreme Court will step in to resolve the split.

writ of certiorari:
the order issued by the Supreme Court when it agrees to hear a case.

rule of four:
four justices must agree to grant *certiorari* to hear a case before the case is permitted to be argued before the Court.

The U.S. Supreme Court

The U.S. Supreme Court is the highest court in the country. Its nine justices are the highest-ranking judges in the nation, and its decisions represent the most influential legal precedents, binding on all lower courts.

Limited caseload. Because of this court's vast authority, it is common for people involved in a lawsuit to threaten to "fight this all the way to the Supreme Court." However, very few cases have any real chance to make it that far. The U.S. Supreme Court is, after all, only one court, and it can decide only a limited number of cases each year. The Supreme Court accepts at most a few hundred cases annually for review—out of about 10,000 petitions for a hearing. In the end, the justices issue formal signed opinions in no more than about 100 cases each year. In recent years the Court has produced even fewer: often only 80 or 90 per term. Obviously, some screening is required to determine which cases will get that far.

In doing the screening, the Supreme Court tries to hear those cases that raise the most significant legal issues, those where the lower courts have flagrantly erred, and those where conflicting lower court decisions must be reconciled. However, the fact that the Supreme Court declines to hear a given case does not mean it necessarily agrees with the decision of a lower court. To the contrary, the Supreme Court may disagree with it, but it may choose to leave the decision undisturbed because it has a heavy caseload of more important matters.

The fact that the Supreme Court declines to review a lower court decision establishes no precedent: for the Supreme Court to refuse to hear a case is not the same as the Supreme Court taking up the case and then affirming the lower court's ruling. When the Supreme Court declines to take a case, the lower court ruling on that case remains in force—but it is still just the decision of a lower court. There are occasions, however, when the Supreme Court accepts a case and then affirms the opinion of a lower court instead of issuing its own opinion, giving the lower court's opinion the legal weight of a Supreme Court decision.

The nine justices vote to decide which cases they will hear of the many appealed to them. Under the Supreme Court's rules of procedure, it takes four votes to get a case on the high court's calendar (commonly called "*the rule of four*").

Getting to the Court. Cases reach the U.S. Supreme Court by several routes. The Constitution gives the Supreme Court *original jurisdiction* over a few types of cases (the first court to hear those cases). Disputes between states and cases involving ambassadors of foreign countries are examples of cases in which the Supreme Court has original jurisdiction. Even these cases may sometimes be heard in lower courts instead—with the blessing of the Supreme Court's nine overworked justices. In disputes between states, the Court may appoint Special Masters to hear evidence and prepare factual findings prior to oral argument.

Then there are a few cases in which the losing party in the lower courts has an automatic right to appeal to the Supreme Court. For example, when a lower federal court or the highest court in a state rules an Act of Congress unconstitutional, the U.S. Supreme Court must hear an appeal if asked to do so by the government. The Supreme Court is required to accept these cases for review.

Finally, there are a vast number of cases that the Supreme Court may or may not choose to review; it is not required to hear these cases, but some raise very important questions. In these cases the losing party in a lower court asks the Supreme Court to issue a *writ of certiorari* (often abbreviated *cert*). Technically, a writ of *certiorari* is an order from the Supreme Court to a lower court to send up the records of the case. *Certiorari granted* means the Court has agreed to hear an appeal, while *certiorari denied* means the Court has decided not to hear the

FIG. 3.
The Supreme
Court of the United
States, 2020–2021.

*Fred Schilling, Collection
of the Supreme Court of
the United States.*

*Front, L-R: Justice Samuel
Alito, Justice Clarence
Thomas, Chief Justice John
Roberts, Justice Stephen
Breyer, and Justice Sonia
Sotomayor. Back, L-R:
Justice Brett Kavanaugh,
Justice Elena Kagan,
Justice Neil Gorsuch, and
Justice Amy Coney Barrett.*

case. (This book will use the terms "*cert* granted" or "*cert* denied.") For the Court to grant *cert*, according to the *rule of four*, four of the nine justices must vote to hear the case.

This *certiorari* procedure is by far the most common way cases reach the Supreme Court, although many more petitions for *cert* are denied than granted. Cases may reach the Supreme Court in such appeals from both lower federal courts and from state courts. The Supreme Court often hears cases that originated in a state court, but only when an important federal question, such as the First Amendment's guarantee of freedom of the press, is involved. Most of the Supreme Court decisions on libel and invasion of privacy that will be discussed later reached the high court in this way.

The Supreme Court will consider an appeal of a state case only when the case has gone as far as possible in the state court system. That normally means the state's highest court must have either ruled on the case or refused to hear it.

The justices. It would be difficult to overstate the importance of the nine justices of the U.S. Supreme Court in shaping American law. Like all federal judges, they are appointed by the president and confirmed by the Senate. They have lifetime appointments, subject to retirement, death, or removal by impeachment.

Nomination hearings of justices can be controversial. Clarence Thomas' nomination hearings in 1991 were broadcast live on television after he was accused of sexually harassing former employee Anita Hill. President George W. Bush was forced to withdraw one his nominees, Harriet Miers, in 2005 after senators from both parties questioned her qualifications. In 2016, the Republican-controlled U.S. Senate refused to hold confirmation hearings for President Barack Obama's nomination of Merrick Garland, the chief judge on the District of Columbia Court of Appeals. Senate Republicans aimed to delay Garland's nomination hearings until after the end of Obama's second term, hoping that a Republican president, if elected, would nominate a justice more to their liking. Their strategy worked. After Donald J. Trump was sworn into office in 2017, he nominated Neil Gorsuch, a judge on the Tenth Circuit Court of Appeals, to fill Antonin Scalia's seat. Gorsuch, a native of Colorado with a law degree from Harvard and a doctorate from Oxford University, was confirmed by the Senate in April 2017. President Trump's second nomination to the court, Brett Kavanaugh,

The newest associate justices of the U.S. Supreme Court.

(L) FIG. 4. Justice Brett Kavanaugh.

(R) FIG. 5. Justice Amy Coney Barrett.

Collection of the Supreme Court of the United States.

then a judge on the District of Columbia Court of Appeals, also faced significant scrutiny during his confirmation hearings over allegations of past sexual misconduct. He was confirmed in 2018 by a vote of 50–48. President Trump's third nomination, of Amy Coney Barrett, then a judge on the Seventh Circuit Court of Appeals, was tame in comparison. She was confirmed on a vote of 52–48 in 2020.

While Supreme Court justices are appointed through a political process, justices do not always vote in the traditional liberal-conservative mold of the presidents who nominated them. For example, as Chapter Five explains, in 1992 the Supreme Court upheld the basic principle of *Roe v. Wade*, the landmark abortion decision, by a 5-4 vote. Three justices appointed by presidents who opposed abortions joined the majority that upheld *Roe v. Wade*. Had any of them voted as the president who nominated them probably expected, Roe v. Wade would have been overturned. Furthermore, in the context of First Amendment decisions, the liberal-conservative labels don't often predict how justices will rule on cases.

The "Roberts Court." The Supreme Court is sometimes closely identified with its chief justice, who often sets the tone for the entire court.

For example, the "Warren Court," named for Earl Warren, who served as chief justice from 1953 to 1969, had an enormous influence on the modern interpretation of the First Amendment. Later in this chapter and in Chapter Four there are references to the Warren Court's major role in reshaping American libel law. But the Warren Court did far more than that: it also rewrote American obscenity law and greatly expanded the rights of those who are accused of crimes, to cite just two examples. Since the era of the liberal Warren Court ended, more conservative justices have dominated the Court. Under Chief Justice William Rehnquist from 1869 to 2005, the Court began to overturn some of the precedents established by the Warren Court, particularly in such fields as criminal law.

The current court is known as the "Roberts Court," named for Chief Justice John G. Roberts Jr., appointed by President George W. Bush to replace Rehnquist as chief justice when Rehnquist died in 2005. Chief Justice Roberts is one of two Bush appointees, the other being Samuel A. Alito, who replaced Sandra Day O'Connor in 2006. Roberts' record during

Focus on...
The legacy of Justice Ruth Bader Ginsburg

Justice Ruth Bader Ginsburg, a leading women's rights advocate who served on the U.S. Supreme Court for 27 years before her death in September 2020, left a lasting legacy.

Justice Ginsburg was pioneer for equal rights for women. She was one of only nine women in a class of 500 at Harvard Law School in the 1950s, and she faced gender discrimination throughout her early career as a lawyer and law professor. Before becoming a judge, Ginsburg represented many clients in gender discrimination lawsuits, and she argued six cases before the U.S. Supreme Court. President Jimmy Carter appointed her to a seat on the U.S. Court of Appeals for the District of Columbia in 1980, and in 1993, President Bill Clinton appointed her to the U.S. Supreme Court. She became the second woman to be appointed to the Court (following Sandra Day O'Connor).

FIG. 6. Justice Ruth Bader Ginsburg.

Steve Petteway, Collection of the Supreme Court of the United States.

Among her most significant written opinions was *U.S. v. Virginia* (518 U.S. 515), a 1996 decision that struck down the males-only admission policy of the Virginia Military Institute as violating the Equal Protection Clause of the Fourteenth Amendment.

While Ginsburg was often seen as a leader of the Court's liberal wing, for many years her closest personal friend was the conservative justice Antonin Scalia.

In her later years on the Court, she became the most recognized justice, celebrated in popular culture as the "Notorious RBG." She was portrayed affectionately on "Saturday Night Live," and her life was made into a feature film, *On the Basis of Sex*, starring Felicity Jones.

After surviving several bouts of cancer and appearing in frail health in her later years, Ginsburg was criticized by some liberals for not retiring during President Barack Obama's term to allow a Democratic president to appoint her successor. She died on September 18, 2020, and President Donald J. Trump's appointment of Amy Coney Barrett was a major issue in the final days of the 2020 presidential election. The U.S. Senate confirmed Barrett's appointment days before Joe Biden defeated Trump on November 3, 2020.

his first years as chief justice seemed to mark him more as a consensus builder than a doctrinaire conservative. Until he retired in 2018, Justice Anthony Kennedy was often described as the "swing vote" on a 5-4 court during the Roberts court. Chief Justice Roberts has also been described as a moderate and swing vote, and he stressed the importance of an independent and nonpartisan judiciary in many public comments.

Today, the court's conservative leaning justices include Roberts, Alito, and Thomas, along with President Donald Trump's appointments of Gorsuch, Kavanaugh, and Coney Barrett. The high court's three liberal leaning members include President Obama's appointees, Sonia Sotomayor, a former judge on the Second Circuit Court of Appeals, and Elena Kagan, the former dean of Harvard Law School and Obama's solicitor general, as well as President Bill Clinton appointee Stephen G. Breyer.

original jurisdiction:
the first court with jurisdiction to hear a case; in the case of the Supreme Court, its findings in original jurisdiction cases are final.

residual jurisdiction:
the Tenth Amendment gives all powers to the states that are not granted to the federal government or prohibited to the states by the Constitution.

federal question:
an area in which the federal government has subject jurisdiction, including interpretation of the Constitution and acts of Congress and international treaties.

Chief Justice Roberts has supported strong First Amendment protections in many cases during his tenure on the Court, and he has described himself as "probably the most aggressive defender of the First Amendment." One study found that the Supreme Court decided 56 First Amendment free speech cases between 2005 and 2020. The Court was unanimous in about one-third of the cases, while the Court split 5-4 about 25% of the time. Chief Justice Roberts sided with the majority in 95% of those cases.

The State Courts

Each of the 50 states has its own court system, as already indicated. Larger states such as California, New York, Ohio, Pennsylvania, Texas, Illinois, and Michigan have two levels of state appellate courts plus various trial courts, duplicating the federal structure.

In these states, the intermediate appellate courts (usually called simply "courts of appeal") handle cases that the state supreme court has no time to consider. The state supreme court reviews only the most important cases. Worth special note is the New York system, which is structurally similar to the systems in other populous states, but with opposite nomenclature. In New York, the "supreme court" is a trial court that also has intermediate appellate jurisdiction; there are many such courts in the state. New York's highest court is called the Court of Appeals. Maryland also calls its highest court the Court of Appeals.

In smaller states, the trial courts send cases directly to the state supreme court, which may have from three to nine or more justices to hear all state appeals. As both the population and the volume of lawsuits increase, more and more states are adding intermediate appellate courts. The states tend to have a greater variety of trial courts than does the federal government, since the state courts must handle many minor legal matters that are of no concern to the federal courts. A typical state court system includes some kind of local court that handles minor traffic and civil matters and perhaps minor crimes. Such courts are sometimes called municipal courts, county or city courts, justice courts, or the like.

In some states the highest trial courts not only hear the most important trials but also perform some appellate functions, reviewing the verdicts of the lower trial courts.

State and Federal Jurisdiction

It may seem inefficient to have two complete judicial systems operating side by side. Wouldn't it be simpler and less expensive to consolidate the state and federal courts that operate in each state? Perhaps it would, but one of our strongest traditions is power sharing between the federal government and the states. We'll have separate state and federal laws—and separate court systems—throughout the foreseeable future.

How then is authority divided between the federal and state courts? State jurisdiction and federal jurisdiction sometimes overlap, but basically the state courts are courts of *residual jurisdiction*; that is, they have authority over all legal matters that are not specifically placed under federal control. Anything that isn't a *federal question* automatically falls within the jurisdiction of the state courts. In addition, the state courts may also rule on some issues that are federal questions (for instance, First Amendment rights).

Federal questions. What makes an issue a federal question? The Constitution declares that certain areas of law are inherently federal questions. For instance, the Constitution specifically authorized Congress to make copyright law a federal question. And Congress, acting under the authority of the Constitution, has declared copyrights and many other matters to be federal questions. Congress has used its constitutional power to regulate interstate commerce as a basis for federal regulation of broadcasting, for instance. Legal issues such as copyrights and broadcast regulation are federal questions because of their subject matter.

In addition, federal courts may intervene in state cases if a state court ruling conflicts with the U.S. Constitution. Much of mass communications law is based on cases of this type. In almost every area of state law discussed in this textbook, the U.S. Supreme Court has intervened at one time or another, interposing federal constitutional requirements on the states. Most often, of course, the constitutional issue is freedom of expression as protected by the First Amendment; the Supreme Court has often overruled state laws and court decisions that violated the First Amendment.

Diversity issues. In addition to these federal questions, there is another reason the federal courts will sometimes agree to hear a case: *diversity of citizenship.* This principle applies only when a citizen of one state sues a citizen of another state. For example, if a New Yorker and a Pennsylvanian are involved in a serious auto accident, each may be able to avoid a lawsuit in the other's state courts under the diversity principle. If there is a lawsuit, it may well be removed to a federal court instead of being heard in a state court.

The framers of the Constitution felt it would be unfair to force anyone to fight a lawsuit on someone else's "home turf," so they ordered the federal courts to provide a neutral forum to hear these disputes involving citizens of two different states. The theory is that a state court might be biased in favor of its own citizens and against outsiders. When a federal court hears a case that would be a state matter if it involved two citizens of the same state, the federal court's right to hear the case is based on *diversity jurisdiction* rather than *federal question jurisdiction*. In diversity lawsuits, the trial may still occur in the home state of one of the litigants, but in a federal rather than a state court.

diversity of citizenship/ diversity jurisdiction: when one party to a lawsuit is from one state and the other is from another state; diversity jurisdiction gives the federal courts jurisdiction over such lawsuits.

complete diversity: a state where no plaintiff in a case is from the same state as any defendant in the same case.

federal preemption: when the federal government has sole jurisdiction over a subject area.

concurrent jurisdiction: when the federal government and the states share jurisdiction.

There are limits on diversity jurisdiction. If there were not, the federal courts might be overwhelmed by minor cases. To avoid that problem, federal courts accept diversity-of-citizenship cases only when the dispute involves more than $75,000. This jurisdictional threshold has been increased repeatedly over the years. Until it was raised from $10,000 to $50,000 in 1988, the federal courts had to handle many relatively minor civil lawsuits—cases that federal judges felt should rightfully be left to the state courts.

Another limitation on diversity jurisdiction is the requirement of *complete diversity*. That is, all of the parties on one side of a lawsuit must come from a different state than anyone on the other side. That means, for instance, that a suit by a New Yorker against both an individual from Pennsylvania and an insurance company in New York would *not* usually qualify as a diversity case.

Sometimes there is considerable legal maneuvering when a case does qualify for federal jurisdiction, either because a federal question is involved or because there is diversity of citizenship. One side may want the case kept in state court, while the other prefers a federal court. Such a case may be filed in a state court, removed to federal court, and eventually sent back to a state court.

Federal preemption. One more point about federal-state relationships bears explaining. Certain legal matters are exclusively federal concerns, either under the Constitution or an act of Congress. In those areas, the federal government is said to have *preempted the field*. That is, no state law in this area is valid; the federal government has exclusive jurisdiction. Copyright law is one such area.

In certain other areas of law, Congress has enacted some federal laws without preempting the field. The states may also enact laws in these areas, providing that the state laws do not conflict with any federal laws. These are called areas of *concurrent jurisdiction*. Examples in media law include the regulation of advertising, antitrust law, and trademark regulation. A typical dividing line in such an area of law is the one that exists in trademark regulation, where the federal Lanham Act protects trademarks of businesses engaged in interstate commerce, while many states have laws to protect the trademarks of local businesses.

In addition to the areas of law preempted by the federal government and areas of concurrent jurisdiction, of course, a large number of legal matters are left to the states—unless a state should violate some federal principle in the exercise of that authority. Libel and invasion of privacy are two areas of media law that are essentially state matters. Recently the U.S. Supreme Court has been refining the concept of federalism by limiting the power of Congress to curtail the traditional authority of the states, a trend that is discussed later.

Judicial Behavior

In recent years, the public has cast a far more suspicious eye on the judiciary than it once did. Because in three-quarters of the states, judges are elected rather than appointed, considerations about judicial impartiality and electoral processes have arisen.

Recusal. The Supreme Court has paid more attention in recent years to questions about whether judges should *recuse* (remove) themselves from cases. Campaign donations to judicial elections are on the rise, and in 2009 the Supreme Court said that a judge's failure to recuse himself from a case in which he received significant campaign donations from one litigant violated the due process rights of the other litigant. At issue in *Caperton v. A.T. Massey Coal Company Inc.* (556 U.S. 868) was the decision of West Virginia Supreme Court of Appeals chief justice Brent Benjamin not to recuse himself in a case in which one of the litigants, Massey Coal, had given him $3 million in campaign donations. Justice Benjamin had refused several times to remove himself from the case, and his court reversed a $50 million award against Massey Coal. In a 5-4 decision, the U.S. Supreme Court said that the due process clause of the Fourteenth Amendment was violated by Justice Benjamin's participation in this case. The Supreme Court has applied the *Caperton* holding to other cases. In 2016, the Court ruled that judges must recuse themselves if they played a significant role in the prosecution of the case before they became judges. In *Williams v. Pennsylvania* (136 S. Ct. 1899), the Court ruled that Pennsylvania Supreme Court Justice Ronald Castille should have recused himself from an appeal involving Terrence William's death penalty conviction because Castille was the district attorney at the time Williams was prosecuted.

Judicial elections. Judicial elections continue to raise questions beyond recusal. How are judges to raise money for campaigning when many state bar rules forbid direct solicitations by the candidate? In 2015, the Court took on this question of whether the state bar rules that forbid a judge from soliciting contributions passed First Amendment muster. Lanell Williams-Yulee, a candidate for judicial office, posted online and mailed a letter asking for financial contributions for her campaign. She was censured by the Florida Bar under Canon 7C(1) of the bar rules, which states that candidates "shall not personally solicit campaign funds, or solicit attorneys for publicly stated support" but allows committees formed for that purpose to do so. Yulee alleged that this canon violated the First Amendment, but the Supreme Court said no (*Williams-Yulee v. Fla. Bar,* 575 U.S. 433). Writing for the Court, Chief Justice John Roberts said that there is a compelling interest for states to ensure that their judges are unbiased and fair.

Other judicial appointments. Who has say over other elements of judgeships? Often commissions or councils either make recommendations or appointments to state judicial positions (a process called *merit selection*); sometimes the governor has appointment power. In 2012, the Tenth Circuit declined to grant a group of non-lawyer citizens the power to directly affect this method in Kansas (*Dool v. Burke,* 497 Fed. Appx. 782). In Kansas, a commission, made up mostly of attorneys, gives recommendations to the governor, who ultimately makes the appointment decision. Non-attorneys filed suit, saying that the 5-4 majority of attorneys on the commission was an equal protection violation. The Tenth Circuit, in a *per curiam* (unsigned) opinion, said there was no violation.

■ TYPES OF LAW

Although the courts play a major role in shaping the law, the other branches of government also have the power to make laws in various ways. In fact, the term law refers to several different types of rules and regulations, ranging from the bureaucratic edicts of administrative agencies to the unwritten legal principles we call the *common law*. This section explains how the courts interact with other agencies of government in shaping the various kinds of law that exist side by side in America.

The Constitution

The most important foundation of modern American law is the U.S. Constitution. No law that conflicts with the Constitution is valid. The U.S. Constitution is the basis for our legal system: it sets up the structure of the federal government and defines federal-state relationships. It divides authority among the three branches of the federal government and limits their powers, reserving a great many powers for the states and their subdivisions (such as cities and counties).

The First Amendment to the Constitution is vital to the media. In just 45 words, it sets forth the principles of freedom of the press, freedom of speech, and freedom of religion in America. The First Amendment says:

> Congress shall make no law respecting an establishment of religion, or prohibiting the free exercise thereof; or abridging the freedom of speech, or of the press; or the right of the people peaceably to assemble, and to petition the government for a redress of grievances.

What do those words mean? The job of interpreting what they mean has fallen to the appellate courts, which have written millions of words in attempting to explain those 45 words. For instance, the First Amendment sounds absolute when it says "Congress shall make no law...." However, the courts have repeatedly ruled that those words are not absolute, and that freedom of expression must be balanced against other rights. In practice, the First Amendment should really be read more like this: "Congress shall make *almost* no laws..." or "Congress shall make *as few laws as possible*...abridging freedom of speech, or of the press...." The chapters to follow will discuss the many other rights that the courts have had to balance against the First Amendment.

The First Amendment (as well as the other amendments in the Bill of Rights) originally applied only to Congress and to no one else. It was written that way because its authors did not think it was their place to tell the state governments not to deny basic civil liberties; their purpose was to reassure those citizens who feared that the new federal government might deny basic liberties. They felt that many basic liberties were so firmly rooted in the common law that no written declaration was needed to ensure that the states would safeguard these liberties. However, it became clear over the years that state and local governments, like the federal government, may violate the rights of their citizens from time to time. Hence, the Supreme Court eventually ruled that the First Amendment's safeguards should apply to state and local governments as well, a concept called *incorporation* that will be discussed later.

Constitutional supremacy. The U.S. Constitution plays the central role in American law. No law may be enacted or enforced if it violates the Constitution. The courts—particularly the U.S. Supreme Court—play the central role in interpreting what the Constitution means, often in practical situations that the founders never dreamed of when they wrote the document more than 200 years ago. Perhaps the Constitution has survived for so long because the courts do adapt it to meet changing needs, and because it can be amended when there is strong support for this step. The Sixteenth Amendment, for example, was approved in 1913, authorizing the federal income tax at a time when the federal government needed to find a way to bring in more revenue. And the Twenty-first Amendment, approved in 1933, abolished prohibition (thus ending an era that began when the Eighteenth Amendment was enacted to ban alcoholic beverages). The normal procedure for amending the Constitution is for each house of Congress to approve a proposed amendment by a two-thirds vote, after which it must be ratified by three-fourths of the states.

State and local constitutions and rules. In addition to the federal Constitution, each state has its own constitution, and that document is the basic legal charter for the state.

No state law may conflict with either the state's own constitution or the federal Constitution. Each state's courts must interpret the state constitution, overturning laws that conflict with it. Likewise, many cities and counties have *home rule charters* that establish the fundamental structure and powers of local government. Like the state and federal constitutions (which local governments must also obey), local charters are basic sources of legal authority. On the other hand, many local governments operate under the general laws enacted by state legislatures instead of having their own local charters.

In these circumstances, the courts must decide when a government action—be it an act of Congress or the behavior of the local police department—violates one of these basic government documents. When that happens, it is the job of the courts to halt the violation.

The Common Law

The common law, which began to develop out of English court decisions hundreds of years ago, is our oldest form of law. It is an amorphous collection of legal principles based on thousands of court decisions handed down over the centuries. It is *unwritten* law in the sense that you cannot sit down and read it all in one place as you can with the statutory laws enacted by Congress. Starting nearly 1,000 years ago, English judges began to follow *legal precedents* from previous cases. Each new decision added a little bit to this accumulated body of law. As it grew, the common law came to include rules concerning everything from crimes such as murder and robbery to non-criminal matters such as breach of contract.

When the American government took its present form with the ratification of the Constitution in 1789, the entire English common law as it then existed became the basis for the American common law. Since then, thousands of additional decisions of American courts have expanded and modified the common law in each state.

It should be emphasized that the Supreme Court has ruled that the common law is mainly state law and not federal law. Each state's courts have developed their own judicial traditions, and those traditions form the basis for that state's common law, which may vary from the common law of other states.

Sovereign immunity. Several controversial U.S. Supreme Court decisions underscored the continuing power of the common law as a force that even Congress cannot ignore. In *Alden v. Maine* (527 U.S. 706, 1999) and several other cases, the high court looked back to the status of the common law before the Constitution was ratified in 1789 and concluded that a concept called *sovereign immunity* was firmly entrenched in the law then—and was not abrogated by the Constitution. Sovereign immunity exempts the "sovereign"

statute:
any law that is adopted by a legislature of a federal, state or local governmental body.

sovereign immunity:
the ability of a government to limit lawsuits against it.

stare decisis:
Latin for "let the law or the decision stand," the policy of courts to rely on precedents.

distinguishing a case:
declining to follow a precedent based on the precedential case differing from the case being decided.

reversing/overruling a precedent:
choosing not to follow precedent even if the facts of the case being decided are very similar.

Focus on...
The whole First Amendment

This book focuses on just two of the five rights enshrined in the First Amendment—the free speech and press clauses. But there are three more rights in that amendment: the religion clause (establishment and exercise), the free assembly clause, and the freedom to petition clause. It's sometimes hard to disentangle the clauses from each other.

Here are a few examples: It's clear how closely freedom to speak (or to refrain from speaking) is tied to the establishment clause, which says, in effect, that government can't create a state religion. Michael Newdow, an atheist, medical doctor, and attorney most noted for repeated suits against the federal government for actions including "In God We Trust" on American currency, faced the Supreme Court in 2004 (and lost), arguing that making school children say the Pledge of Allegiance, including "under God," was an establishment of religion (*Elk Grove Unified Sch. Dist. v. Newdow*, 542 U.S. 1).

FIG. 7. Canterbury Cathedral, Kent, circa 1910.

Library of Congress Digital prints and photographs [LC-DIG-det-4a24699]

More recently, the Roberts Court has issued several decisions redefining the meaning of the establishment and free exercise clauses. For example, the Supreme Court ruled 7-2 that a 93-year-old government-funded memorial of World War I shaped like a cross does not violate the Establishment Clause of the First Amendment. The Court's majority ruled that historical monuments on public property with secular meanings have a presumption of constitutionality, even if they have religious overtones (*Am. Legion v. Am. Humanist Ass'n*, 139 S. Ct. 2067). In other cases, the Roberts Court has upheld laws that exempt religious institutions from employment discrimination laws based on the Free Exercise Clause (*Our Lady of Guadalupe School v. Morrissey-Berru*, No. 19-267, 2020). During the COVID pandemic, the Supreme Court also struck down laws that limited religious gatherings on public health grounds, ruling such laws violated the Free Exercise Clause (*Tandon v. Newsom*, No. 20-A151, 2021).

Finally, the rise of public protests about police violence against Black Americans in recent years underscore the relevance of the free assembly and petition clauses. As several states considered new legislation to regulate mass assembly and protests, concerns were raised about whether such new laws would survive legal challenges under First Amendment precedents.

from being sued in the courts. In eighteenth-century England, the sovereign was the king or queen. In the pre-constitutional United States, the individual states had sovereign immunity.

How does sovereign immunity affect modern America? In these decisions, a 5-4 majority of the Supreme Court said the states still enjoy sovereign immunity, and Congress does not have the right to authorize lawsuits against the states either in federal courts or in state courts. The result: the Court held that states are largely exempt from various federal laws that purport to allow private parties (such as individuals and corporations) to sue a state. The Court has said the states (but not private parties) are exempt from many patent and copyright infringement lawsuits, for example, and also to some actions brought by federal regulatory agencies. These decisions were widely criticized in the media. They are based on an expansive view of common law concepts that are routinely taught in law school and that still apply today—in the opinion of the Supreme Court majority. However, the states have all *voluntarily* agreed to limit their own sovereign immunity by enacting laws to allow lawsuits against themselves under various circumstances.

Evolution of the common law. Like federal constitutional law, the common law can grow and change without any formal act of a legislative body precisely because it is based on court decisions. When a new situation arises, the appellate courts may establish new legal rights, acting on their own authority. A good example of the way the common law develops a little at a time through court decisions is the emergence of the right of privacy. As Chapter Five explains, there was no legal right of privacy until the twentieth century. But as governments and the media (and eventually, the internet) became more powerful and pervasive, the need for such a right became apparent. The courts in a number of states responded by allowing those whose privacy had been invaded to sue the invader, establishing precedents for other courts to follow.

In addition to privacy law, several other major areas of mass media law had their beginnings in common law, among them libel, slander, and the earliest copyright protections.

If this all happens through judicial precedent, with the courts expected to follow the example set by earlier decisions, how can the common law correct earlier errors?

The importance of precedent. The common law system has survived for nearly a thousand years precisely because there are mechanisms to allow the law to change as the times change. Courts don't always follow legal precedent; they have other options.

When a court does adhere to a previous decision, it is said to be observing the rule of *stare decisis*. That Latin term, roughly translated, means "Let the precedent stand." However, courts need not always adhere to *stare decisis*. Instead, a court faced with a new situation may decide that an old rule of the common law should not apply to the new facts. The new case may be sufficiently different to justify a different result. When a court declines to follow a precedent on the ground that the new case is different, that is called *distinguishing* the previous case. When an appellate court does that, the common law keeps up with changing times.

Another option, of course, is for a court to decline to follow precedent altogether, even though the factual circumstances and issues of law may be virtually identical. That is called *reversing* or *overruling* a precedent; it is considered appropriate when changing times or changing conditions have made it clear that the precedent is unfair or unworkable.

A good example of the way this process works is the 1954 ruling of the U.S. Supreme Court in the famous school desegregation case, *Brown v. Board of Education* (347 U.S. 483). Although this case is based on an interpretation of the Constitution and is therefore an example of the development of constitutional law rather than the common law, it provides a good illustration of how law develops over time.

When the Court took the *Brown* case, there was a precedent, an 1896 Supreme Court decision called *Plessy v. Ferguson* (163 U.S. 537). In that earlier case, racial segregation had been ruled constitutionally permissible as long as the facilities provided for different races were "separate but equal." But in 1954 the Supreme Court pointed out that more than half a century's experience proved that the "separate but equal" approach didn't work. The Court noted that segregated facilities were almost always unequal—and ruled that the public schools must be desegregated. As a result of that new decision, the precedent from the 1896 case was no longer binding, and a new precedent replaced it. In the end, the *Brown* case became one of the most important court decisions of the twentieth century.

Statutory Law

The third major type of law in America is the one most people think of when they hear the word *law*. It is statutory law, a sweeping term that encompasses acts of Congress, laws enacted by state legislatures and even ordinances adopted by city and county governments.

If constitutional and common law are largely unwritten (or at least uncodified) forms of law because they are the result of accumulated court decisions, statutory law is just the opposite. It is law written down in a systematic way. Statutory laws are often organized into *codes*. A *code* is a collection of laws on similar subjects, indexed and arranged by subject matter. Much federal law is found in the *United States Code*. Each title of the U.S. Code deals with a particular subject or group of related subjects. Title 17, for example, deals with copyright law, discussed in Chapter Six. On the state level, statutory law is similarly organized, although not all states refer to their compilations of statutory laws as codes.

Judicial interpretation of statutes. Although statutory law is created by legislative bodies, the courts have an important place in statutory lawmaking just as they do in other areas of law. That is true because the courts have the power to interpret the meaning of statutory laws and apply them to practical situations. For this reason, law books containing statutory laws are often *annotated*. This means each section of the statutory law is followed by brief summaries of the appellate court decisions interpreting it. Thus, one can quickly learn whether a given statutory law has been upheld or if it has been partially or totally invalidated by the courts. Annotated codes also contain cross-references to other relevant analyses of the statutory law, such as attorney general's opinions or articles in law reviews.

Why would a court invalidate a statutory law? It can happen for several reasons. First, of course, if the statute conflicts with any provision of the appropriate state or federal constitution, it is invalid. In addition, there are sometimes conflicts between two statutory laws enacted by the same state legislature or by Congress. When that happens, the differences must be reconciled, and that may mean reinterpreting or even invalidating one of the laws. In addition, courts may void laws that conflict with well-established (but unwritten) common law principles.

There is considerable interplay between the courts and legislative bodies in the development of statutory law. As already indicated, often a new legal concept is recognized first by the courts, whose decisions will make it a part of the common law. At some point, a legislature may take note of what the courts have been doing and formally codify the law by enacting a statute. The courts may then reinterpret the statute, but the legislature may respond by passing yet another statute intended to override the court decision.

We will see precisely this sort of interplay between a legislative body and the courts in several areas of media law, particularly in such areas as copyright, shield laws, and broadcasting. For example, the Supreme Court once ruled that most private, at-home videotaping of television shows is legal under the U.S. Copyright Act, explained in Chapter Six. Congress then considered legislation that would have revised the Copyright Act to overturn that decision and outlaw home videotaping. That legislation was rejected because most members of Congress believed public opinion supported the court's interpretation of the law.

On the other hand, if the Supreme Court had said a constitutional principle (such as the First Amendment) protected the right to make home videotapes of TV shows for personal use, the only way to reverse that ruling would have been by amending the Constitution—or waiting for the Court to reverse its own earlier decision. Congress cannot pass a statutory law to overrule a Supreme Court decision *interpreting the meaning of the Constitution*. Congress can, of course, propose a constitutional amendment and submit it to the states for ratification. Short of that, the most Congress can do when a statutory law is ruled unconstitutional is to revise it to bring it into compliance with the Constitution.

Administrative Law

Another important kind of law in America is administrative law. Within the vast bureaucracies operated by the federal government and by the states, there are numerous agencies with the power to adopt and enforce administrative regulations, and these regulations have the force of law. The term "administrative law" may seem contradictory, but these agencies do have law-making powers.

In fact, agencies often have so much authority that it would seem to violate the traditional concept of separation of powers. They may write and enforce rules and try alleged violators, handing out *de facto* criminal penalties to those convicted. The Federal Communications Commission (FCC) is a regulatory body with that kind of authority over the electronic media. The Federal Trade Commission (FTC) exercises similar authority over the advertising industry.

Checks and balances. While these agencies have considerable power, there are important checks and balances that limit their authority. For example, their decisions may be appealed to the courts, and that gives the appellate courts a veto power over the rules adopted by these agencies. In addition, many of these agencies were created by legislation, and in recent years Congress and the various state legislatures have proven that they can take back some of the authority they handed out, either directly by rewriting the enabling legislation or indirectly by making budget cuts.

Also, while the policy-making boards and commissions of these administrative agencies are rarely elected, the commissioners are usually appointed by the president or by the governor of a state, who is elected. Their appointments must usually be confirmed by a legislative body. Among the thousands of agencies with administrative rule-making powers, some of the most important (in addition to the FCC and FTC) are the Interstate Commerce Commission, the Federal Aviation Administration and the Federal Elections Commission on the federal level, and the state regulatory bodies that determine rates charged by public utilities.

Actions in Equity: When Money Won't Do

One final kind of "law" that should be mentioned here is not really a form of law at all but an alternative to the law: a remedy for legal wrongs called *equity.*

History. The concept of equity is an old one: it developed in medieval times. Hundreds of years ago in England, it became obvious that courts sometimes caused injustices while acting in the

burden of proof:
the party who has this burden must present evidence to support the claim.

beyond a reasonable doubt:
the level of certainty required for a criminal conviction and the highest level of proof; does not mean absolute certainty but only a remote possibility of another reasonable explanation.

preponderance of the evidence:
the level of certainty required for a civil decision, a lower burden than for criminal cases; means that the facts support one side more than the other.

tort:
a civil wrong creating a right for a victim to sue a perpetrator.

tortfeasor:
person who commits a wrong.

defendant:
the tortfeasor in a civil lawsuit or accused in a criminal lawsuit.

plaintiff:
person who brings a lawsuit.

name of justice. There are some circumstances in which faithfully applying the law simply does not result in a fair decision. For example, the common law has always held that *damages* (money) would right a wrong, and that the courts should not act until an injury actually occurred—and even then they could only order a payment of money to compensate the injured party. Obviously there are times when letting a court sit back and wait for an injury to occur just isn't satisfactory. The harm might be so severe that no amount of money would make matters right. In those situations, courts have the power to act in equity: they can issue an *injunction* to prevent a wrong from occurring.

In English common law, people facing irreparable injuries appealed to the king, since he was above the law and could mete out justice when the courts could or would not. As the volume of such appeals increased, kings appointed special officers to hear appeals from those who could not get justice in the courts of law. These officers came to be known as *chancellors* and their court as the *court of the chancery*. This brand of justice, based on the dictates of someone's conscience, came to be known simply as equity.

Equity today. In America, the same courts that apply the law usually entertain actions in equity, too. Unlike the law, which has elaborate and detailed rules, equity is still a system that seeks to offer fairness based on the dictates of the judge's conscience. Equity is only available in situations where there is no adequate remedy under the law, and only then if the person seeking *equitable relief* is being fair to the other parties.

A good example of an occasion when an action in equity would be appropriate is when highway builders are about to excavate and thus destroy an important archeological site. Those seeking to preserve the site cannot wait until after an injury occurs and sue for damages. The artifacts that would be destroyed might be priceless.

There are legal actions that are based on equity rather than law. Probably the most important for our purposes are *injunctions*, which are court orders requiring people to do something they are supposed to do (or to refrain from doing something that would cause irreparable harm). Chapter Three discusses several attempts by the federal government to prevent the publication of information that officials felt would cause irreparable harm to national security. When a court orders an editor not to publish something, that is ordinarily an example of an action in equity.

■ CRIMINAL LAW AND CIVIL LAW

Another major distinction in the law is between criminal and civil law. Although criminal and civil law are not categories comparable to statutory law, the common law, or administrative law, there are important differences between civil and criminal cases.

Different standards of proof. In a criminal case, someone is accused of committing an act that is considered to be an offense against society as a whole—a crime such as murder, rape, or robbery. Therefore, society as a whole ("the people," if you will) brings charges against this individual, with the taxpayers paying the bill for the people's lawyer, often called the district attorney (or U.S. attorney in federal cases). If the person accused of the crime *(the defendant)* is impoverished, the taxpayers will also pay for his or her defense by providing a lawyer from the local (or federal) public defender's office. Defendants who are more financially secure will hire their own defense lawyers, but the basic point to remember is that the legal dispute is between the defendant and "the people"—society as a whole. Moreover, because the defendant's life or liberty may be at stake, the prosecution must prove *guilt beyond a reasonable doubt*. That is a difficult standard of proof.

In a civil case, it is a different matter. Here, one party claims another party injured him/her individually, without necessarily doing something so bad it is considered a crime against society as a whole. It's just a dispute between two individuals (or two corporations, or two government agencies, etc.). The courts simply provide a neutral forum to hear a private dispute. The burden of proof is correspondingly lower in civil cases: to win, litigants must usually prove their cases by the *preponderance of the evidence,* but not necessarily beyond a reasonable doubt, as in criminal cases.

Don't assume that all legal matters are either criminal or civil matters—some are both. The same series of events may lead to both civil and criminal litigation. For instance, someone who has an auto accident while intoxicated may face criminal prosecution for drunk driving as well as civil lawsuits by the victims for personal injuries and property damage, among other things.

■ TORTS AND DAMAGES

Two other legal concepts that should be explained here are the concepts of *torts and damages.* Most civil lawsuits not based on a breach of contract are tort actions. A *tort* is any civil wrong that creates a right for the victim to sue the perpetrator. Almost any time one party injures another, the resulting lawsuit is a tort action.

Examples of torts. For example, if you are walking across the street and you're struck by a car driven by a careless driver, you have a right to sue for your personal injuries in a tort action for *negligence.* Suppose you need surgery as a result of the accident. If the doctor at the hospital should forget to remove a sponge from your body after the emergency surgery, you could sue for the tort of *medical malpractice.*

On the other hand, if you could prove that the car struck you not because the driver was careless but because a manufacturing defect caused the steering to fail, you could sue the manufacturer for the tort of *products liability.*

Finally, you could sue for *libel* if the local newspaper falsely reported that you had just committed a crime and were fleeing from the crime scene when you were hit by the car.

All of these legal actions and dozens of others fall into the broad category called torts. The person who commits the wrong is called the *tortfeasor;* he or she becomes the *defendant* in the lawsuit while the victim is the *plaintiff.*

Several of the important legal actions affecting the media are tort actions. Examples include libel and slander, invasion of privacy, and unfair competition. To win a tort lawsuit the plaintiff generally has to show that there was some sort of wrongful act on the part of

types of damages:

general: compensation for non-monetary loss.

special: compensation that requires proof of monetary losses.

actual/compensatory: can include both general and special damages.

presumed: awarded without any proof.

statutory: damages set by statute.

treble: three times the actual damages.

punitive: damage award, often high, intended to punish a wrongdoer.

the tortfeasor, often either negligence or a malicious intent. The plaintiff also has to show some kind of *damages*, although courts are sometimes permitted to presume damages when certain kinds of wrongful acts have occurred.

Types of damages. This brings us to the definition of damages, which is a central point in this introduction to media law. In many states, there are three basic kinds of damages: general damages, special damages, and punitive damages.

General damages are monetary compensation for losses incurred under circumstances in which the injured party cannot place a specific dollar amount on the loss. In an auto accident where you suffer personal injuries, for instance, you may win general damages to compensate you for your pain and suffering, which are obviously intangible. In a libel suit, the plaintiff seeks general damages for embarrassment or loss of prestige in the community.

Special damages are a little different. Here, the plaintiff must prove out-of-pocket monetary losses. In the auto accident we've been using as an example, you can show that your doctor and hospital bills came to a certain amount of money. Maybe you can also show that you were unable to work for several months or years, or maybe you needed in-home nursing care or rehabilitation. These are all things for which courts can establish specific dollar values. Special damages are intended to compensate for these kinds of provable losses.

Sometimes other terms are used to describe the various types of damages. *Actual damages* or *compensatory damages* means provable losses, including out-of-pocket losses (special damages) and, in some instances, some intangible but nonetheless real losses (i.e., general damages). *Presumed damages* are damages that a court assumes occurred without any proof. For many years, libel plaintiffs were awarded presumed damages without having to prove the defamation actually caused any injury. In some kinds of lawsuits, such as copyright infringement cases, *statutory damages* may be awarded by a court without proof of a tangible or intangible loss. Instead, the damage award is based on legal rules set forth in a statutory law such as the Copyright Act. In some areas of law, *treble damages* (three times the actual damages) are awarded as a means of discouraging improper behavior. For example, federal antitrust and advertising fraud laws allow treble damages.

In contrast to general and special damages, *punitive damages* are not based on any tangible or intangible loss. Instead, they are intended as a punishment for a person (or company) that commits a maliciously wrongful act. For the victim, they constitute a windfall profit—and the Internal Revenue Service taxes them as such. For the wrongdoer, they're a form of non-criminal punishment, imposed by the court to deter such wrongful actions.

Punitive damages are only awarded in those tort actions where the victim can prove there was malice on the part of the tortfeasor. As we'll see in Chapter Four, the term *malice* has more than one meaning in law. For the purpose of winning punitive damages in most tort actions, it means ill will or evil intentions toward the victim. In libel cases, it usually has a different meaning, but either way, it is difficult to show malice—unless the tortfeasor actually set out to injure someone deliberately.

In recent years, juries have awarded millions (or billions) of dollars in punitive damages to victims of alleged corporate misconduct who could only prove that they were entitled to modest general and special damage awards. The Supreme Court has responded to this trend by overturning large punitive damage awards as a violation of the corporate defendant's due process rights. In a 2003 decision, the Court ruled that punitive damages should not ordinarily exceed 10 times the general and special damages (*State Farm v. Campbell*, 538 U.S. 408).

This decision is likely to benefit the media by reducing the tendency of jurors to impose very large punitive damage awards in libel cases. It also brings U.S. law closer to the law in other countries. Even in countries with a common law heritage, such as England, courts generally limit punitive damages to relatively small sums. In many other countries, punitive damages are not allowed at all. The highest courts in Italy and Germany, for example, have refused to enforce judgments of American courts that involved a punitive damage award.

As we'll see later, keeping track of the various kinds of damages is important in several areas of media law. Sometimes one type of damages is available but not another. It is not unusual for a plaintiff in a libel suit, for example, to be denied a right to sue for anything but special damages because a newspaper has printed a retraction.

■ THE STORY OF A LAWSUIT

Perhaps the best way to illustrate how the legal system works is to follow a lawsuit through the courts, step by step. We'll trace a civil case called *New York Times v. Sullivan* (376 U.S. 254), a libel suit that is usually remembered for the very important legal precedent it established. Its effect on libel law is discussed in Chapter Four. However, it is also an excellent case to illustrate court procedures, since the case was carried through almost every step that occurs in civil lawsuits.

People who think a newspaper story has injured their reputations have a right to sue the newspaper for monetary damages. This case involved a lawsuit between an individual named L. B. Sullivan and the company that publishes the *New York Times*.

The case began after the *New York Times* published an advertisement from a group of African-American civil rights leaders that described instances of alleged police brutality in the South. Some of the incidents occurred in Montgomery, Alabama. The ad was accurate for the most part, but it did contain several errors of fact. It did not name any individual as responsible for the alleged police misconduct. Nevertheless, Sullivan, who was one of three elected commissioners in Montgomery and the man in charge of police and fire services there, contended that his reputation had been damaged by the ad, so he hired a lawyer and sued the *New York Times* for libel. He contended that to criticize the police was to criticize the city commissioner who oversees the police department. The result was a lawsuit that went all the way to the U.S. Supreme Court after a variety of intermediate steps.

Initiating the Lawsuit

When Sullivan's lawyer filed the papers required to initiate the lawsuit (a document called the *complaint*), the clerk of the trial court assigned the case a number for record-keeping purposes, and the case became known as *Sullivan v. New York Times*. In our legal

complaint:
the document that initiates a lawsuit.

answer:
the defendant's response to the complaint; no answer results in *default*, where the court rules for the other side.

to serve:
to deliver a copy of the complaint to the appropriate party.

to quash:
to invalidate or void.

liability:
responsibility for an alleged wrong.

demurrer/motion to dismiss:
a pretrial motion that requests that the case be dismissed based on the lack of legal basis to support it.

summary judgment:
a pretrial motion in which the parties agree on the facts and one party is entitled to a judgment as a matter of law.

discovery:
the pretrial process by which the parties share information and evidence, including *depositions* and *interrogatories*.

system, court cases are identified by the names of the parties to the dispute, with a lowercase "v." (for versus) between the two names. When there are multiple parties on either side, the case is popularly identified by the name of the first person listed on each side. The name of the party bringing the lawsuit (the *plaintiff*) appears first, followed by the name of the party defending (the *defendant*). When the defendant loses the case in the trial court and then appeals, the two names are sometimes reversed. Hence, this case later became known as *New York Times v. Sullivan.*

As the plaintiff, Sullivan was seeking an award of monetary damages. The *New York Times,* of course, wanted to convince the court it had done nothing to injure Sullivan and that damages should therefore not be awarded.

Sullivan could have chosen to sue the *New York Times* in the New York state courts or even in the federal courts (based on diversity of citizenship). However, at that point in history many southerners bitterly resented northern efforts to promote the civil rights of African-Americans in the South. To many in Alabama, the *New York Times* symbolized all that they disliked. Thus, Sullivan's lawyer knew his client would have a much more sympathetic jury in Alabama than in New York. Besides, it would certainly be more convenient for them (but not for the *Times*) to try the case there.

Serving papers. Having filed the complaint in the Alabama trial court, the next step was to *serve* the *New York Times.* That is, a *process server* had to deliver a copy of the papers announcing the lawsuit to an appropriate representative of the paper. Some states permit the plaintiff to simply mail a copy to the defendant, depending on the nature of the case. Serving the *New York Times* was a bit of a problem for Sullivan, since the paper didn't have any offices or regular employees in Alabama. Shortly after Sullivan initiated his lawsuit, a *Times* reporter visited the state to cover a civil rights demonstration, but *Times* lawyers in New York advised the reporter to leave the state before Sullivan's process servers could catch him, and he did so. Sullivan ultimately served the papers on an Alabama resident who was a "stringer" (a part-time correspondent) for the *Times.* The *Times* immediately filed a motion in the Alabama courts to *quash* (invalidate) the service of process. Anxious to gain jurisdiction, the Alabama court denied the motion—and then found a technicality in the *Times'* legal petition that enabled Alabama courts to hear the case.

Given the sentiments of many Alabama residents toward the *New York Times,* this would seem to have been an ideal case to be tried in federal court on a diversity of citizenship basis. However, the Alabama courts ruled that the *Times* had voluntarily consented to Alabama jurisdiction by the manner in which the motion to quash the process service was worded. Although it had a daily circulation of only 390 in the entire state and about 35 in the Montgomery area, the *New York Times* was forced to submit to the jurisdiction of the Alabama state courts due to a legal technicality.

Once the Alabama court established jurisdiction, the paper was obliged to respond. The *Times* filed a reply (called the *answer*), denying Sullivan's claims. If no answer had been filed, the *New York Times* would have *defaulted.* That means the court would have been free to award Sullivan whatever he asked for, without the paper having any say in the matter. But the *Times* did file an answer, denying any *liability* (responsibility for the alleged wrong).

Pretrial Motions

The *Times* also initiated a series of legal motions designed to get the case thrown out of court before trial by saying, in effect, "Look, this is nothing but a harassment lawsuit, and we shouldn't be put to the expense of a full trial."

Motions to dismiss. Two kinds of pretrial motions can lead to a dismissal of the case before trial. One is called a *demurrer* (or simply a *motion to dismiss*) and it contends that there is no *legal basis* for a lawsuit, even if every fact the plaintiff alleges is true. The other kind is a motion for *summary judgment,* and it is often based on the defendant's contention that there is no *factual basis* for the lawsuit to proceed further even if all the facts that the plaintiff alleges are completely true. A summary judgment motion may also be made when either side contends that there is no real disagreement between the parties about the facts, and that the judge should simply decide the case without further proceedings. The *Times* filed a series of demurrers to argue that, among other things, the ad in no way referred to Sullivan and thus there was no legal basis for Sullivan to sue. (Someone must be identified and defamed before that person can sue for libel, as Chapter Four explains.)

Demurrers and motions for summary judgment are particularly important for the media, because the media are often sued by people who may be embittered over unfriendly coverage but who have no valid basis for a lawsuit. The media may be entitled to a dismissal without the expense of a full trial. However, pretrial dismissals deny plaintiffs their day in court. Thus, a court reviewing such a request must give the plaintiff the benefit of every doubt. A pretrial dismissal is improper if there is any reasonable possibility the plaintiff could win at a trial. This point is important because a number of Supreme Court decisions affecting the media have come on appeals of motions to dismiss a case before trial. When a newspaper or television station, for instance, is denied a pretrial dismissal and the U.S. Supreme Court affirms the denial, that does not mean the Court thinks the plaintiff will eventually win the lawsuit. Rather, it merely says that the plaintiff might have some slight chance to win and, in our system of justice, has a right to try.

Returning to the *Sullivan* case, the Alabama court denied all of the *Times*' motions to dismiss the case before trial, and a trial was eventually scheduled.

Discovery

After the legal maneuvering over motions for summary judgment and demurrers, there is another very important pretrial procedure: the process of *discovery.* It is a process that allows each side to find out a great deal about the strengths and weaknesses of the other side's case. *Subpoenas,* or court orders compelling testimony or information, can be part of this process. Each *litigant* (party to the lawsuit) is permitted to ask the opposition a variety of oral questions (at *depositions*) and written questions (*interrogatories*). During depositions, each side is permitted to meet and question hostile witnesses who are under oath (i.e., the witness has taken an oath promising to tell the truth).

appellant:
party that appeals a case to a higher court.

respondent:
party on the other side of an appealed case.

subpoena:
Latin for "under penalty"; an order to an individual to appear before a body at a particular time to give testimony.

majority opinion:
the opinion of the court that gets the most votes and carries the weight of legal precedent.

dissenting opinion:
an opinion written by a judge disagreeing with part or all of the majority or another judge's opinion.

concurring opinion:
an opinion written by a judge agreeing with part or all of the majority or another judge's opinion.

As a result of discovery, a defendant might find out how substantial the plaintiff's losses really were, for instance. A plaintiff who says the wrong thing during a deposition can devastate his or her own case. And each litigant can size up the other's witnesses to see whether they will be credible in court. Much important information is revealed during discovery.

Why do courts allow discovery? Allowing discovery encourages many out-of-court settlements of lawsuits that would otherwise clog up the courts. If you find out that your opponent has a good case against you, you'll be much more likely to make a generous settlement offer. Taking a case to trial costs time and money, so it is in everybody's interest to see cases settled out of court whenever possible. The more each side knows about the other's case, the more likely they are to reach an agreement on their own.

However, Sullivan and the *New York Times* were hopelessly far apart; no settlement was possible. Sullivan was suing for half a million dollars, and the *Times* was contending that this was ridiculous. With a circulation of only 35 in Sullivan's county, and with him never mentioned either by name or title, the *Times* felt there was simply no way the ad could have done $500,000 worth of damage to the man's reputation.

The Trial

Sullivan and the *New York Times* faced off in a courtroom for trial. The first step in the trial was the selection of a jury, a process that raises an interesting point about civil cases.

Juries. Jury rights in civil cases differ somewhat from those in criminal cases. A defendant's right to a trial by a jury is one of the cornerstones of our criminal justice system, but no such stringent constitutional safeguards are involved in civil cases. There is a growing trend toward reducing the size of civil juries from the traditional panel of 12 to as few as six persons, and to allow verdicts to be rendered by nonunanimous civil juries. Only a few states allow nonunanimous juries or juries of fewer than 12 persons to decide major criminal cases.

In fact, many civil cases are tried without any jury because the losing side could be stuck with a bill for the jury, a risk neither side wishes to take. (By contrast, the defendant never has to pay for asserting his constitutional right to a jury trial in a criminal case.) Moreover, some civil litigants avoid jury trials because they feel they will fare better if a judge decides the facts as well as the law. But on the other hand, there are instances where a civil plaintiff may insist on a jury trial in the hope that the jurors will become emotional and award a big judgment. That happened in the *Sullivan* case. Sullivan's lawyers were not unaware of the hostility many white southerners felt toward both the civil rights movement and the *New York Times* in the early 1960s when this case was tried. Blacks were still rare on Alabama juries at that point. The lawyers felt—correctly—that their client would do well before a jury.

Process of the trial. Thus, the trial began. Sullivan, as the plaintiff, presented his evidence first, and then the *New York Times* responded. The plaintiff always goes first, the defendant last. A variety of witnesses testified for each side, with Sullivan's witnesses saying that they indeed associated him with the actions of the Montgomery police, and that they would think less of him if they believed the charges in the *New York Times* advertisement. Other witnesses testified about what they claimed were inaccuracies in the ad. In its response, the *Times* contended that publishing the ad was protected by the First Amendment and that the ad in no way referred to Sullivan. The significance of these arguments will become more clear in Chapter Four, which discusses what one must prove to win a libel suit and what the media can do to defend such a lawsuit.

After all of the evidence was in, the judge instructed the jury on the law. He told the jurors the material was libelous as a matter of law. Thus, their job was to decide only whether the *Times* was responsible for the publication and whether, in fact, the ad referred to Sullivan. The judge ruled that Sullivan did not need to prove any actual monetary losses due to the ad, since damages could be presumed from any libelous statement under Alabama law.

Eventually the jurors adjourned to a private room and arrived at a verdict: a judgment of half a million dollars (the full amount requested) for Sullivan. They would see to it that the *Times* would pay for its decision to publish an ad alleging police brutality in Montgomery. After that verdict was rendered, the *New York Times* took two important procedural steps.

The first was to file a motion for a new trial, citing what it claimed were errors and irregularities in the original trial. That motion was promptly denied in this case, but that doesn't always happen. If a trial court judge feels the jury improperly weighed the evidence or was not impartial, or if improper evidence was presented at the trial, or if various other procedural errors occurred during the trial, the losing side may be entitled to a new trial. In this case, the motion for a new trial was denied. Then the *Times* exercised its other option, appealing the verdict to the Alabama Supreme Court.

The Appeals

When a case is appealed, the nomenclature changes a little. The party that appeals the case becomes the *appellant*, while the other party becomes the *respondent*. When the losing side at the trial level appeals, the names may be reversed, as we already suggested would happen in this case. Hence, the *New York Times* became the appellant and Sullivan the respondent: the case became known as *New York Times v. Sullivan*.

The Alabama Supreme Court agreed to hear the *New York Times v. Sullivan* case. When an appellate court grants an appeal such as this one, several things occur. First, each side submits a *brief*, which is an elaborate argument of the legal issues involved in the case: a brief is not always brief. The appellant's brief must argue that the trial court erred in applying the law to the facts at hand, while the respondent must defend the trial court's decision.

Process of the appeal. After the briefs are filed and read by the appellate justices, oral arguments are usually scheduled. At oral arguments the lawyers for each side are given a short period of time to highlight their main points. The justices may ask them questions, sometimes on obscure points, perhaps forcing the lawyers to use up their time allotment without ever getting to their most important arguments. Sometimes the lawyers (and knowledgeable spectators such as journalists who regularly cover the court) can guess which side will win from the kind of questions the justices are asking. Appellate court justices sometimes reveal their own sympathies by the nature of their questions.

After the oral arguments, the justices informally vote on the case to see how they will rule. Once the positions of the various justices are clear, one justice will be assigned to write the *majority opinion*—the opinion that will prevail and become a legal precedent. If other justices disagree with this opinion, they may write *dissenting opinions* in which they argue that the majority is in error. Or a justice may agree with the result reached by the majority but disagree with some of the reasoning. When that happens, the result is a *concurring opinion*. A justice may also concur with another's concurring or dissenting opinion. Dissenting and concurring opinions are important, because as times change it is not unusual for a new majority to coalesce around what was once a minority viewpoint. A dissenting opinion may become the foundation for a later majority opinion.

When the appellate opinion is then *published*—that is, printed in a law book that provides a verbatim record of all published decisions of the particular court—that decision officially becomes a legal precedent, adding a little more to the ever-growing body of law.

Not all appellate opinions are published in law books. Many courts publish only their most important opinions. For many years the unpublished ones had little or no weight as legal precedents. But because appellate court opinions are usually accessible via computer databases today, more and more appellate courts are allowing all of their decisions to be treated as legal precedents, largely eliminating the legal distinction between published and unpublished decisions. There are other occasions when an appellate court decision will lose its significance as a legal precedent. For instance, that occurs when a higher court decides to review the decision and issue its own ruling on the case.

Outcome and appeal to high court. In *New York Times v. Sullivan*, the Alabama Supreme Court affirmed the judgment of the trial court in full, upholding the half-million-dollar libel award to Sullivan. In an elaborate legal opinion, the Alabama Supreme Court defended the trial court's finding that it had jurisdiction over the *New York Times*. Then the court upheld the trial judge's controversial jury instructions, in which he told the jurors Sullivan didn't need to prove any actual losses to win his case. Finally, the state supreme court affirmed all other aspects of the decision, including the large award of damages.

After this setback, the *New York Times* had one hope left: the chance that the U.S. Supreme Court might agree to hear the case in spite of the fact that civil libel had traditionally been purely a matter of state law. The *Times* petitioned for a *writ of certiorari*, contending that this kind of a libel judgment violated the First Amendment because it would inhibit public discussion of controversial issues such as civil rights.

To the amazement of some legal experts, the Supreme Court agreed to hear the case.

The U.S. Supreme Court Ruling

When the *New York Times v. Sullivan* case reached the U.S. Supreme Court, all of the steps just described happened again. Elaborate briefs were filed by both sides, and oral arguments were heard by the nine Supreme Court justices. Then the justices conferred privately and Justice William J. Brennan was selected to write a majority opinion in what was destined to become the most famous court decision of all time on libel law.

Chapter Four describes the legal reasoning of the Supreme Court in this landmark decision. At this point, we'll simply say the *New York Times* won. The decisions of the Alabama courts were *reversed and remanded*. That means the Supreme Court invalidated the lower court decisions and ordered the Alabama trial court to reconsider the facts of the case under new legal rules set down by the Supreme Court. As a practical matter, sometimes a decision like this one terminates the case. Sullivan's lawyers knew they could not win a trial conducted under the new legal ground rules. When the U.S. Supreme Court reversed and remanded the Alabama court's decision, this case was terminated—in fact if not in legal theory.

Other Options

In addition to reversing and/or remanding a lower court ruling, there are several other options open to an appellate court. The decision can be upheld (*affirmed*) or it can be affirmed in part and reversed in part. Then a new trial may be scheduled later. But whatever the ultimate outcome of the case at trial, often *the most important aspect is the precedent-setting ruling of an appellate court*. In the study of media law, you will encounter cases where the discussion centers on a major legal issue—and the final disposition of the lawsuit isn't discussed at all. After a landmark appellate ruling, it may take many more years to complete all of the various legal maneuvers at the trial court level and conclude a lawsuit—or the matter may be terminated as soon as a high appellate court rules.

Certainly valid criticisms of the American legal system are the time and money it takes to get a case to trial, up through the appellate courts and then back to trial again if necessary. If "justice delayed is justice denied," as critics of the system suggest, the expensive route through the American court system often includes enough detours to deny justice to many.

■ HOW TO FIND THE LAW

Once you understand the various kinds of law and how the American legal system fits together, it isn't difficult to learn the law on any given subject. Legal research (i.e., the process of finding out what the law is on a subject) involves nothing more than knowing how to use some basic online reference tools or books that every well-stocked law library keeps on its shelves. Most larger county courthouses either have a law library or are located near one since judges need ready access to the laws on which to base their decisions. Also, every accredited law school has an extensive law library. Most of these law libraries are open to the public. You can go in and look up the law for yourself.

More than ever before, it is also possible to use the internet, or a computer database such as Lexis-Nexis or Westlaw, to do legal research. These computer databases, once so costly that only the best-heeled law firms could afford them, are now accessible online via many university libraries. The amount of legal information available on the internet is enormous and growing daily—a trend that is revolutionizing legal research.

Free legal research tools. The internet itself is a powerful legal research tool, as state and federal courts, as well as other government agencies, post the full text of their decisions, regulations, and other documents on their websites. For example, there is a wealth of regulatory information about advertising on the Federal Trade Commission's website (www.ftc.gov) and about the electronic media on the Federal Communications Commission's website (www.fcc.gov). Popular general online legal resources include Thomas (thomas.loc.gov), the Library of Congress legislative information website; FindLaw (www.findlaw.com), a comprehensive privately maintained website; the Cornell Legal Information Institute site (www.law.cornell.edu), widely regarded as one of the best law sites; and Oyez (www.oyez.org), Chicago-Kent College of Law's U.S. Supreme Court site that has audio of oral arguments before the Court. The official website of the federal court system (www.uscourts.gov) has the full text of most recent federal court decisions, including those of the Supreme Court (www.supremecourt.gov) and the U.S. Courts of Appeals. Many specialty law firms have websites and electronic newsletters highlighting important cases or legal developments. Google Scholar (scholar.google.com) contains legal documents and patents.

Court Decisions: Citations

Precedent-setting appellate court decisions are not difficult to look up, because there's a citation system that will tell you where to find each case. Throughout each chapter in this book you'll find citations to important court decisions in that area of media law. After the names of the two parties in the case, you'll see the case *citation* (a series of numbers and letters). We've already discussed the landmark libel decision *New York Times v. Sullivan*.

When you look up that case in this or any other law-oriented book, you'll see this legal citation after the name of the case: 376 U.S. 254. The letters and numbers tell you exactly where to find the full text of the Supreme Court's ruling in a law book.

The "U.S." in the middle tells you which court ruled on the case because it stands for *United States Reports,* a series of books carrying the official text of Supreme Court decisions. Thus, to find the decision in print, you'd ask the law librarian where the "U.S. Supreme Court Reports" are kept. When you find this large collection of identical-looking volumes, the rest is simple. The first number in the citation (376) refers to the volume number of the law book in which the *New York Times v. Sullivan* case appears. You would look down the row, find the volume labeled "376" on the binding and pull it out.

Now you're there. The number after the "U.S." is the page number where the text of the case begins. Turn to page 254 in volume 376 of the *United States Reports,* and there's *New York Times v. Sullivan.* Before the actual text, there are introductory notes explaining the decision, designed to facilitate a quick review of the case highlights. Some citations end with the year of the decision. For example, *New York Times v. Sullivan* is cited as 376 U.S. 254, 1964.

When doing online research using Lexis-Nexis or Westlaw, for example, it's possible to search by the case name, the citation, or both—or to search for key words in the text of the case. Many case citations have letters in the middle such as "F.2d" or "F.3d." "F.2d" means *Federal Reporter, second series,* which is a set of law books containing decisions of the various U.S. Courts of Appeals. Why *second series?* The publisher of these books began producing them many years ago, and after a time the original editorial treatment and even the style of the binding seemed old-fashioned. Thus, the publisher modernized the book and started a second series, beginning again with volume number one in the new series. In 1993, the publisher launched a *third series,* once again starting with volume number one. If you see a citation to "F.3d," the case is a 1993 or later decision of a U.S. Court of Appeals.

In this textbook you will see a variety of legal citations to court decisions, and in each instance the letters in the middle tell you which court decided the case. Those decisions of the federal district courts published as legal precedents (many are not) appear in the *Federal Supplement* (abbreviated "F.Supp."). There are also second and third series for the Federal Supplement ("F.Supp 2d" and "F.Supp 3d").

The citation system works much the same way in the state courts. Chapter Eight cites a case on reporter's privilege named *Zelenka v. Wisconsin,* 266 N.W.2d 279. It's a decision of the Wisconsin Supreme Court, but the citation refers to the *Northwestern Reporter, second series.* That series carries important court decisions from a number of midwestern states. It is a part of the *National Reporter System,* one publishing house's collection of regional reports that cover all 50 states. Most law libraries have the National Reporter system and other sets of volumes reporting major cases of the state appellate courts around the country. Lexis-Nexis and Westlaw both have the full text of cases from all 50 states.

In many instances, law libraries have more than one set of law books reporting the most important court decisions. This is true in part because there are competing legal publishing houses, each offering a full set of reports of major appellate cases. To illustrate by returning once again to *New York Times v. Sullivan,* here is a more complete set of citations to that case: 376 U.S. 254, 84 S. Ct. 710, 11 L.Ed.2d 686 (1964). Don't be intimidated by all those numbers. You already know what "376 U.S. 254" means. But suppose that volume is unavailable when you visit the law library. No problem. Just go to the next citation. "S. Ct." means *Supreme Court Reporter,* and if you pull down volume 84 and look on page 710, there's your case. Or you could go to "L.Ed.2d", which means *Lawyer's Edition, U.S. Supreme Court Reports, second series,* and pull down volume 11 and look on page 686. The text of the decisions is exactly the same, but the introductory matter and editorial treatment may vary in these privately published books. Many law libraries keep all three sets of Supreme Court rulings, because the privately published versions are in print long before the official *U.S. Reports.*

In the mass communications field, another convenient way to look up court decisions is to check the *Media Law Reporter.* One volume is published each year, and it carries the full text of most precedent-setting court decisions on media law, including Supreme Court decisions, lower federal court rulings, and state cases. In this book there are several citations to the *Media Law Reporter* (abbreviated in citations as Media L. Rep.).

"Shepardizing" cases. The courts frequently interpret and reinterpret previous decisions. You should make sure the key cases in any given topic are still *good law* and have not been reversed by a higher court or a later decision of the same court. A good way to do that is to consult a cross-reference index called *Shepard's Citator.* Most law libraries have *Shepard's* covering state and federal appellate courts, and many online databases let you perform this function with a few clicks. By "Shepardizing" cases before citing them, you can avoid writing 10 pages about a court decision that has been overturned.

Legal Encyclopedias

What happens if you don't know the names of any court decisions and you want to learn something about the law on a particular topic? One place you might look is a legal encyclopedia. These are just like regular encyclopedias—except that they discuss only legal subjects. There are two leading legal encyclopedias in America, produced by different publishing houses: *American Jurisprudence,* or "Am. Jur." for short, and *Corpus Juris Secundum,* or "CJS."

Legal encyclopedias are not difficult to use. The many legal topics they treat are listed in alphabetical order with brief summaries of the major legal principles in each area. The only trick is knowing where to look for a particular subject, and for that there's a comprehensive index at the end of each set. If you want to know more about libel law, for instance, you would look up the word "libel." It's not always that straightforward, because the name you have in mind may not be the key word under which that subject is indexed; you may have to think of some synonyms. Once you find the right word, the index will lead you directly to a summary of the law, whether it's bankruptcy or crimes, unfair competition or medical malpractice. Some of these encyclopedias are available online as well. There are also legal encyclopedias that specifically summarize the laws of one state. Most of the populous states have such encyclopedias, such as Florida, California, Texas, and New York.

One thing you need to be aware of when you consult a physical legal encyclopedia is the existence of *pocket parts.* What a legal encyclopedia says in its main text is supplemented by annual updates that are tucked into a pocket at the back of each volume.

Because there have been thousands of important court decisions, and because many have reached inconsistent conclusions, the American Law Institute has commissioned groups of legal scholars to write summaries of the law as it has developed over the years. These are called *Restatements* of the law, and the courts give them considerable weight. The *Restatement of Torts* summarizes libel, privacy, and other areas of tort law and is an important reference work in these fields. The *Restatements* carry far more legal weight than the legal encyclopedia, although they might seem less user-friendly to those doing their first legal research.

Annotated Codes

Once you have read a survey of your subject in a legal encyclopedia, you might want to learn more about the subject by reading some of the decisions and statutory laws summarized in the encyclopedia. We've already described the method of finding court decisions by working from the case citations. Looking up the text of a statutory law is often even easier.

Many important state and federal laws are organized by subject matter. To look up a statutory law, locate the appropriate book of state or federal statutes: a legal encyclopedia will refer you to statutory laws as well as court decisions that pertain to your subject. If you wanted to read the federal Copyright Act, for instance, you would use its legal citation, which is "17 U.S.C. § 100 *et seq.*" That means Title 17 of the *United States Code*, Section 100 and following sections. To find the text of the Copyright Act, you would ask the law librarian where the U.S. Code volumes are kept, and then look up Section 100 in Title 17. The number before the name of a state or federal code is always the title, book, or volume number, and the number after the name will lead you to the correct chapter and section.

There are two things to remember in looking up statutory laws. One is that the most complete sets are annotated; they contain brief summaries of court decisions interpreting the statutory laws as well as the text of the laws themselves. It's important to make sure the law you're learning has not been overruled by a court decision. And be sure to check the pocket parts if you're using physical volumes of the law. Second, like encyclopedias, the annotated collections of statutory laws are extensively indexed. If you want to learn what the law of libel is in West Virginia, for instance, you can simply look up libel in the index to the *West Virginia Code* and turn to the appropriate sections to find statutes and case summaries.

Administrative Regulations

Administrative law is such a vast and amorphous thing that we will not devote much space to it here. However, students with interest in broadcasting, for instance, should be aware that the regulations of the Federal Communications Commission (FCC) are organized to facilitate research. Title 47 of a legal work called *The Code of Federal Regulations*, or "CFR" for short, contains the FCC's rules and regulations. Working from the table of contents, you can quickly look up the rules on a particular point of broadcast regulation in CFR. CFR is updated frequently, since administrative agencies constantly change their rules.

There are also published summaries of actions taken by major administrative agencies. Major law libraries keep complete sets of specialized legal reference materials such as *Pike & Fischer's Communications Regulation*, and these are now available online by subscription. And, of course, regulatory agencies have their own websites that include compilations of their regulations, news releases, and reports.

WHAT SHOULD I KNOW ABOUT MY STATE?

- What federal circuit is my state in?
- Where is my closest federal district court?
- How is my state judicial system structured?
- Where is my closest state trial court?
- How are my state's judges chosen (elected, appointed)?
- What does my state constitution say about free speech and press rights?
- How do criminal and civil procedures work in my state?

2 *The Legacy of Freedom*

Americans are sometimes accused of taking freedom for granted. It is easy to talk about the First Amendment almost as if it were a universal law of nature, a principle that always existed and always will.

That, of course, is not the case. The kind of freedom of expression that is permitted today in the United States and a few dozen other democracies is unique in world history. Our freedoms were won through centuries of struggle, and they could easily be lost. Even today, fewer than half of the world's people live in countries that fully recognize such basic freedoms as freedom of speech, freedom of the press, and freedom of religion.

Many leaders see the media as tools of propaganda or national development—weapons to be used against their rivals, both foreign and domestic. The rise of social media use across the globe, including the 2011 use of Facebook and Twitter to create governmental and societal change by Egyptian protesters, vividly demonstrated the "mass media" are less easy to control in the age of the internet than in the age of newspapers. Yet, investigations into Russian influence in the 2016 U.S. presidential election underscored the fears of government propaganda in an era of digital mass communications. Moreover, as information can easily be manipulated in digital format, what challenges will sites like WikiLeaks offer to those who wish to keep certain information secret?

As we will see in a review of the history of freedom of speech and press in the United States to the present day, some of the same issues, albeit using different technologies, face Americans in the twenty-first century as faced those Americans who experienced its founding.

■ CENSORSHIP IN ENGLAND

A summary of the evolution of freedom of expression could begin in the ancient world, were this chapter a survey of the philosophical underpinnings of modern civilization. Powerful arguments for freedom of expression were made thousands of years ago in ancient Greece and several other places around the globe. But our tradition of freedom of expression traces its roots most directly to England about 400 years ago.

English traditions. In the 1600s, England was caught up in a battle that mixed politics and religion. The monarchy and the government-sponsored Church of England were determined to silence dissenters, many of them Puritans. The religious and political struggle was closely linked with an economic battle between the aristocracy and the rising middle class.

Chapter Objectives:

- Locate America's free expression history in English traditions.
- Examine the early understandings of the First Amendment.
- Describe the evolution of free expression rights in the nineteen and twentieth centuries.
- Explain how First Amendment principles are applied in legal analysis.
- Critique the role of extremism in today's First Amendment controversies.

Essential Questions:

- What are the early influences and original understandings of the First Amendment?
- What values do the First Amendment's free speech and press clauses serve?
- When has the Court ruled it is appropriate to punish people for expressing radical or inciting ideas, and how has that changed over time?

Leaders on both sides of this ideological battle understood the importance of the printing press and sometimes resorted to heavy-handed efforts to censor ideas they considered dangerous. In those days more than one Englishman was jailed, tortured, and eventually executed for expressing ideas unacceptable to those in power. Brutality that would be shocking to Americans—or Britons—today was fairly commonplace in England in that period.

Official censorship was enforced through a licensing system for printers that had been introduced as early as 1530. The licensing denied access to printing presses to those with unacceptable ideas, but it also enabled government representatives to preview and pre-censor materials before publication. By making the possession of a license to print a coveted privilege, the government was often able to control underground printing. The licensed printers themselves helped to ferret out bootleg presses to protect their own self-interests.

Milton and the Puritans

By the early 1600s censorship was being used to suppress all sorts of ideas that threatened the established order. This inspired leading political philosophers of the day to write eloquent appeals for freedom of expression as a vital adjunct to the broader freedom from religious and political oppression they sought. An early apostle of freedom of expression was John Milton, who in 1644 wrote his famous argument against government censorship, *Areopagitica*. Milton's appeal for freedom contained this statement:

> Though all the winds of doctrine were let loose to play upon the earth, so Truth be in the field, we do injuriously by licensing and prohibiting to misdoubt her strength. Let her and Falsehood grapple; who ever knew Truth put to the worse in a free and open encounter?

Out of this passage several modern ideas emerged, including the concept that a *self-righting* process would occur through open debate of controversial issues. In effect, Milton said censorship was unnecessary because true ideas would prevail over false ones. He advocated something of a *marketplace of ideas.* That was a revolutionary idea: almost no one in Milton's

(L) FIG. 8.
John Milton
(1608–1674).

(R) FIG. 9.
John Locke
(1632–1704).

*Library of Congress
Prints and
Photographs Division,
[LC-USZ62-48596]*

*Library of Congress
Prints and
Photographs Division,
[LC-USZ62-59655]*

time believed that freedom of expression should be universal. But even to Milton, freedom had its limits. Although he favored far more freedom than most of his contemporaries, Milton did not think these rights should be extended to those who advocated ideas he considered subversive. In fact, after the Puritan movement led by Oliver Cromwell gained control of England and executed King Charles I in 1649, Milton accepted a government appointment that required him to act as something of a government censor. One of his duties was to license and oversee the content of an official newssheet, *Mercurius Politicus*. By 1651—only seven years after he appealed to the government to allow true and false ideas to struggle for popular acceptance—Milton was engaged in censorship. And he was serving in a government that imposed strict Puritan beliefs and showed little tolerance for other religious groups.

Other advocates of free expression. There were some who went further than Milton did in advocating freedom of expression. Roger Williams, a onetime Puritan minister in the Massachusetts Bay colony who was exiled to Rhode Island for his controversial religious ideas, later returned to England and wrote *Bloudy Tenent of Persecution for Cause of Conscience* in the same year as Milton's *Areopagitica*. Williams urged freedom of expression even for Catholics, Jews, and Muslims—people Milton would not have included.

Perhaps even more emphatic in their arguments for freedom from censorship in the 1640s were the Levellers, a radical Puritan group. Their tracts consistently contained passages condemning censorship and the licensing system. In their view, free expression was essential to the religious freedom and limited government authority they so fervently sought.

In a 1648 petition to Parliament, the Levellers appealed for a free press. When "truth was suppressed" and the people ignorant, this ignorance "fitted only to serve the unjust ends of tyrants and oppressors." For a government to be just "in its constitution" and "equal in its distributions," it must "hear all voices and judgments, which they can never do, but by giving freedom to the press."

Despite the Puritans' rhetoric, England restored the monarchy in 1660 and the licensing of printers continued. It was also a time of religious repression. A 1662 act of Parliament, for instance, limited printing presses and prohibited the printing of books contrary to the Christian faith as well as seditious or anti-government works.

John Locke and Natural Rights

As the struggle between the monarchy and Parliament intensified in the late 1600s, new philosophers of free expression emerged. Chief among them was John Locke. While his ideas were not necessarily original, he presented them so eloquently that he is remembered as one of the great political theorists of his time.

marketplace of ideas:
the notion that there should be freedom of speech so that all ideas would have a chance to be heard, considered, and compete for attention and believers.

social contract theory:
a theory of government where the people give up some rights to enjoy other rights, moving from a state of nature to a state of cooperation for self-governance; Locke's version of the social contract said that people have natural rights such as life, liberty, and property rights.

sedition:
incitement of resistance to or revolt against the government.

Social contract theory. Locke's famous *social contract theory* said that governments were the servants of the people, not the other way around. Locke believed men were endowed with certain natural rights, among them the right to life, liberty, and property ownership. In effect, Locke said the people make a deal with a government, giving it the authority to govern in return for the government's promise to safeguard these natural rights.

Central to these natural rights, Locke felt, was freedom of expression. Thus, when the English licensing system came up for review in 1694, Locke listed 18 reasons why the act should be terminated. The act was allowed to expire, primarily because of "the practical reason arising from the difficulties of administration and the restraints on trade."

Other forces in English society were also providing impetus for freedom of expression. For one, Parliament gained a major victory over the monarchy in the Glorious Revolution of 1688. James II, an avowedly Catholic king so offensive that several warring factions united against him, fled the country that year. Then in 1689 Parliament enacted a Bill of Rights and invited William of Orange and his consort, Mary, James' Protestant daughter, to assume the throne with limited powers. In the Declaration of Rights, William and Mary accepted these conditions, ending England's century-long struggle between Parliament and the monarchy. In addition, a two-party system was emerging in England; the times were ready for open, robust political debate. The two parties, the Whigs and Tories, both relied extensively on the printing press in taking their views to the people.

Seditious Libel as a Crime

If official censorship by licensing the press was a thing of the past as England moved into the 1700s, the crime of seditious libel (i.e., the crime of criticizing the government or government officials) remained a viable deterrent to those who publish defamatory tracts.

A good illustration of this problem was the 1704 case of John Tuchin, who was tried for "writing, composing and publishing a certain false, malicious, seditious and scandalous libel, entitled, *The Observator*" (*Rex v. Tuchin*, 14 Howell's State Trials 1095). Tuchin was convicted, and in the process the judge defined the common law on seditious libel:

> If people would not be called to account for possessing the people with an ill opinion of the government, no government can subsist. For it is very neces-
> sary for all governments that the people should have a good opinion of it. And nothing can be worse to any government, than to endeavor to procure animosi-
> ties, as to the management of it; this has been always looked upon as a crime, and no government can be safe without it be punished.

This common law rule did not go unchallenged for long. Free press advocates, perhaps strengthened by their success in abolishing licensing, opened the eighteenth century with a flurry of writings advocating greater freedom. Nevertheless, criticism of the government remained a crime throughout the century, with the truthfulness of the criticism not a defense against the charge. The prevailing legal maxim was "the greater the truth, the greater the libel."

Fox Libel Act. Parliament itself recognized the abuses possible under the common law of seditious libel, and in 1792 the Fox Libel Act was passed. That act permitted juries, rather than judges, to decide whether a statement was libelous. Prior to that, the law allowed the jury to determine only whether the defendant was guilty of *printing* the libelous publication. The judge ruled on the legal question of whether the material was actually libelous. This reform did not eliminate seditious libel prosecutions, but it did make it more difficult for a government to punish its critics because a jury, whose members might well sympathize with the defendant's allegedly libelous statements, could decide if the statements were libelous.

An additional reform came in 1843, further strengthening the rights of those who would criticize the government in England. In that year, Parliament passed Lord Campbell's Act, establishing truth as a defense in all seditious libel cases. Thus, the old maxim, "the greater the truth, the greater the libel," was at last abolished.

While the struggle for freedom of expression was being fought in England, a parallel battle was under way in the American colonies.

■ FREEDOM IN A NEW NATION

Although many of the early colonists in North America left England or the European continent to escape religious or political oppression, they found (or created) an atmosphere of less than total freedom in some of the colonies here. As the Puritans gained control in New England, they established close church-state ties, and persons with unpopular religious or political ideas were hardly more welcome here than they had been in England.

In fact, the first laws that restricted freedom of the press in North America preceded the first newspaper here by some 30 years. Even without any specific authority, colonial rulers often simply assumed they had the right to censor dissenting publications because the authorities had that right in England. Even after licensing was abolished in England, colonial leaders continued to act as if they had licensing powers, and several colonial newspapers carried the phrase "published by authority" in their mastheads years after the right to publish without government permission was won in England.

Moreover, in North America as in England, seditious libel prosecutions were used to control the press, as were laws that placed special tax burdens on newspapers. The Stamp Act of 1765, for instance, taxed newspapers by forcing publishers to purchase revenue stamps to attach to each copy. The result was such blatant defiance of British authority by colonial publishers that it helped inspire the eventual revolution against the mother country.

The Zenger Libel Trial

Early in the colonial publishing experience there was a seditious libel case that became a *cause célèbre* on both sides of the Atlantic: the trial of John Peter Zenger in 1735 (*Attorney General v. John Peter Zenger*, 17 Howell's State Trials 675).

Zenger, a German immigrant, was the publisher and printer of the *New York Weekly Journal*. His paper became a leading voice for the opposition to a particularly unpopular royal governor, William Cosby. After some legal maneuvering, the governor was able to have Zenger jailed and charged with "printing and publishing a false, scandalous and seditious libel, in which...the governor...is greatly and unjustly scandalized, as a person that has no regard to law nor justice."

Andrew Hamilton. Zenger was fortunate enough to have Andrew Hamilton of Philadelphia, one of the most respected lawyers in the colonies, make the trip to New York for his defense. And Hamilton, ignoring the orders of Cosby's hand-picked judge, appealed directly to the jury. He urged the jurors to ignore the maxim of "the greater the truth, the greater the libel" and to decide for themselves whether the statements in question were actually true, finding them libelous only if they were false.

FIG. 10.
The John Peter
Zenger trial in
1735 captured
the attention of
the New York law
community, packing
the courtroom in
City Hall.

*Marsha J. Lamb, Wall
Street in History, 1883.*

"Nature and the laws of our country have given us a right—and the liberty—both of exposing and opposing arbitrary power ...by speaking and writing truth," Hamilton said.

In urging the jurors to ignore the judge's instructions and acquit Zenger if they decided the statements were true, Hamilton was clearly overstepping the bounds of the law. A less prestigious lawyer might have been punished for an action so clearly in contempt of the court's authority. However, Hamilton was not cited, and his eloquent appeal to the jury worked: the jury returned a not-guilty verdict even though there was little question that Zenger was the publisher of the challenged statements.

The impact. It would be difficult to overstate the importance of the Zenger trial in terms of its psychological impact on royal governors in America. Still, its direct effect on the common law was minimal in America and England itself. Even in those days, a criminal trial verdict established no binding legal precedent. English courts continued to punish truthful publications that were critical of government authority. Nevertheless, the argument was made again and again that mere words critical of the government—and especially truthful words—should not be a crime. In 1773 the Rev. Philip Furneaux wrote that only overt acts against a government should be punished: "The tendency of principles, tho' it be unfavourable, is not prejudicial to society, till it issues in some overt acts against the public peace and order; and when it does, then the magistrate's authority to punish commences; that is, he may punish the overt acts, but not the tendency which is not actually harmful; and therefore his penal laws should be directed against overt acts only."

Declaration of Independence

When a series of incidents strained relations between England and the colonies past the breaking point, the colonists declared their independence in 1776. Yet even in breaking with England, the Americans borrowed heavily from the mother country. Thomas Jefferson's ideas and even some of his language in the Declaration of Independence were borrowed from English political philosophers, notably John Locke. Locke's natural rights and social contract ideas appear repeatedly in the declaration.

After independence was won on the battlefield, the new nation briefly experimented with a weak central government under the Articles of Confederation and then became a unified nation under the Constitution, ratified by the states in 1788. Despite its ratification, many Americans feared the new federal government, particularly because the Constitution had no guarantees that basic civil liberties would be respected. Although the defenders of the Constitution argued that these civil liberties were firmly entrenched in the common law we had inherited from England, many were wary. Some states ratified the Constitution only after they received assurances that it would be amended quickly to add a Bill of Rights.

Early First Amendment Questions

That promise was kept. In the first session of Congress, the Bill of Rights was drawn up and submitted to the states to ratify. It was declared in force late in 1791. Of our paramount concern, of course, is the First Amendment. Taken literally, it is almost everything that a free press advocate might hope for, but phrases such as "Congress shall make no law" have not always been taken literally. In fact, the exact meaning of the First Amendment has been vigorously debated for more than 200 years. The record of the discussions when the Bill of Rights was drafted is sketchy: it is impossible to be certain what Congress had in mind. Constitutional scholars have advanced various theories, but most doubt that the majority of the framers of the Constitution intended the First Amendment to be an absolute prohibition on all government actions that might in any way curtail freedom of the press.

The crucial question, then, and the one that is the focus of the rest of this chapter, is this: which restrictions on freedom of expression are constitutionally permissible and which ones are not?

Alien and Sedition Acts. Whatever the first Congress intended in drafting those words, it was only a few years later that Congress passed laws that seemed to be a flagrant violation of the First Amendment. In 1798 Congress hurriedly approved the *Alien and Sedition Acts*, designed to silence political dissent in preparation for a war with France, a war that was never declared. The Sedition Act made it a federal crime to speak or publish seditious ideas. The law had one safeguard: truth was recognized as a defense. Nevertheless, a fine of up to $2,000 or two years' imprisonment was prescribed for any person who dared to:

> ...[W]rite, print, utter or publish, or ...knowingly and willingly assist or aid in writing, printing, uttering or publishing any false, scandalous and malicious writing or writings against the government of the United States, or either house of the Congress of the United States, or the President of the United States, with intent to defame the said government, or either house of said Congress, or the said President, or to bring them, or either of them, into contempt or disrepute; or to excite against them, or either or any of them, the hatred of the good people of the United States, or to stir up sedition within the United States.

There were about 25 arrests and 15 indictments under the Act. All were aimed at opponents of President John Adams and the Federalist Party, which then controlled Congress and had enacted the law over the opposition of Jefferson and his followers. Even though the Federalist press was often guilty of vicious attacks on Thomas Jefferson and other non-Federalist government officials, no Federalist was ever prosecuted under the Sedition Act. A two-party system was emerging, and the Jeffersonian, or anti-Federalist, opposition party was the real target of the Sedition Act.

Jefferson, by then vice president, strenuously opposed the Alien and Sedition Acts. The Kentucky and Virginia legislatures passed resolutions, backed by Jefferson, that purported to "nullify" these laws, thus raising questions about states' rights that would not be resolved until the Civil War. James Madison, later to be Jefferson's secretary of state and then the fourth president, made it clear in drafting the Virginia Resolution that he felt the Sedition Act was a violation of the First Amendment. Madison believed the First Amendment was supposed to be an absolute prohibition on all actions of the federal government that restricted freedom of the press. Jefferson probably agreed. In one letter to a friend, he wrote: "I am...for freedom of the press and against all violations of the Constitution to silence by force and not by reason the complaints or criticisms, just or unjust, of our citizens against the conduct of their agents." When Jefferson ran for president in 1800, he made the Alien and Sedition Acts a major issue; public discontent over these laws was certainly an important factor in his victory. Immediately after his inauguration, Jefferson ordered the pardon of those who had been convicted under the Sedition Act.

Jefferson's record as a champion of a free press was not entirely unblemished. During his presidency he was subjected to harsh personal attacks by opposition newspapers. Although he usually defended the right of his foes to express their views, he eventually became so annoyed that he encouraged his backers to prosecute some of his critics in state courts.

The Sedition Act expired in 1801, and it was more than 100 years before Congress again attempted to make criticism of the government a federal crime. However, this does not prove the First Amendment was intended to eliminate sedition as a crime, and debates over sedition and the First Amendment continue even today.

The Supreme Court and Judicial Review

In 1803, the Supreme Court gained the power to declare acts of Congress unconstitutional and thereby invalidate them. In the landmark case of *Marbury v. Madison* (1 Cranch 137), what the Court really did was simply to declare that it had the power to overturn acts of Congress. Perhaps the Court got away with it mainly because President Jefferson and his followers were happy with the outcome of the case.

Just before his term expired, John Adams, the lame-duck Federalist president, had appointed a number of federal judges. Because of their belated appointments, they came to be called "midnight judges." The new judges were Federalists, and the Jeffersonians were anxious to keep them from taking office. James Madison, Jefferson's secretary of state, refused to give William Marbury, one of the would-be judges, his signed commission (the document appointing him to office). Marbury sued to get the commission. The Jeffersonians were not displeased when the Court, under its famous chief justice, John Marshall, dismissed Marbury's claim by overturning the Judicial Act of 1789, on which the would-be judge had based his lawsuit. In the convoluted politics of the day, Marshall—a Federalist— had sided with the Jeffersonians on a small matter (Marbury's commission), but in so doing Marshall had prevailed on the larger issue: the right of the courts to review actions of other branches of government for compliance with the Constitution.

Other Marshall decisions. Ironically, Chief Justice Marshall had himself been appointed by John Adams during the final year of his presidency. Although the Federalist Party faded away, never winning another national election, Marshall served as chief justice for 34 years, allowing the Federalist philosophy to have an ongoing impact on American law long after the Federalist Party disappeared from the scene. Marshall's Supreme Court asserted its

Focus on...
Marbury v. Madison, 5 U.S. 137 (1803)

Chief Justice John Marshall realized that the political clout of the Supreme Court was low in 1803. This case, which many legal scholars recognize as a legal *tour de force*, provided him the opportunity to make the judiciary a full partner in the country's governance.

Marshall's solution was both a brilliant legal tradeoff and a smart political move. In exchange for giving up a fairly minor right, Marshall claimed for the judiciary the power of ***judicial review***—the power to invalidate a law when it's in conflict with the Constitution.

Marshall, a Federalist, was also able to give President Thomas Jefferson, a Republican, a slap on the wrist for not having delivered Marbury's commission in the first place. But had Marshall tried to force the delivery of the commission, Jefferson may have refused, creating a situation where a direct order of the Supreme Court was ignored.

FIG. 11. John Marshall, third chief justice.

John B. Martin, Collection of the Supreme Court of the United States.

authority in many other areas, attempting to define the scope and limits of federal power. In 1812, the Court ruled that the federal courts had no authority to entertain actions involving common law crimes such as criminal libel. In *U.S. v. Hudson and Goodwin* (7 Cranch 32), the Court said this area of law fell within the exclusive domain of the states, a philosophy that has remained largely unchanged ever since. On the other hand, in *McCulloch v. Maryland* (4 Wheat. 316), an 1819 decision among Marshall's most famous, the Court upheld the right of Congress to create a national bank and regulate the economy even though a narrow, literal reading of the Constitution might not permit it. Having so ruled, Marshall then declared once and for all that the states may not tax agencies of the federal government.

State powers. When the Bill of Rights was added to the U.S. Constitution, its authors wanted to be certain that the federal government's powers would be strictly limited to avoid usurping the powers of the states. The Tenth Amendment reads, "The powers not delegated to the United States by the Constitution, nor prohibited by it to the states, are reserved to the states respectively, or to the people." While the federal government stayed out of mass communications law during much of the nineteenth century, the states filled that void. Throughout the century, the states were expanding the common law and adopting statutory laws in such areas as libel and slander.

One of the best-known state cases was the 1804 libel trial of Harry Croswell in New York (*People v. Croswell*, 3 Johnson's Cases 336). Croswell attacked President Thomas Jefferson in print and was prosecuted for criminal libel. He was convicted and appealed to a higher state court. His defense attorney, Federalist leader Alexander Hamilton, argued that truth plus "good motives for justifiable ends" should be a defense in such cases.

Although Croswell lost when the appellate panel of four judges deadlocked 2-2, the concept that truth should be a libel defense was sometimes called the *Hamilton Doctrine* and was adopted in a number of states during that era. For instance, the New York legislature recognized the truth defense by statute in 1805—and added a provision empowering the jury to determine whether the statement in question was actually libelous. Some states had recognized truth as a libel defense even before that time and, of course, the 1798 Sedition Act had recognized it on the federal level. Nevertheless, what Andrew Hamilton, the distinguished Philadelphia lawyer, had argued for in the Zenger trial 70 years earlier gained general acceptance in American law only after another distinguished lawyer named Hamilton made it his cause as well.

Alexander Hamilton, of course, didn't live long enough to enjoy whatever recognition the Hamilton Doctrine might have brought him: a newspaper account of something he purportedly said during the Croswell trial led to the infamous duel in which he was killed by Aaron Burr, then the vice president of the United States.

Slavery and Free Expression

Aside from the gradual evolution of libel law, probably the most significant conflict over American freedom of expression in the 1800s resulted from the struggle over slavery and the War Between the States.

As the national debate over slavery intensified in the early 1800s, a number of southern states enacted "gag laws" that prohibited the circulation of newspapers and other materials advocating the abolition of slavery. Although these laws were clearly acts of prior censorship and violated the spirit of the First Amendment, the First Amendment had not yet been made applicable to the states, and these laws were never tested for their constitutionality.

Some northern states also attempted to curb abolitionist literature through various laws; these laws too escaped constitutional scrutiny because the Bill of Rights did not yet apply to the states. Even Congress adopted rules to suppress debate about slavery that violated the spirit of the First Amendment. When anti-slavery groups submitted petitions to Congress asking that the slave trade in Washington, D.C., be abolished, the House of Representatives adopted internal "gag rules" to prevent these petitions from being introduced and considered. These rules not only censored anti-slavery members of Congress but also took direct aim at the First Amendment's provision guaranteeing the right to petition the government.

Rep. John Quincy Adams of Massachusetts, who returned to Congress after serving as the nation's sixth president, led the fight against these gag rules. At one point he arrived in Washington with anti-slavery petitions signed by more than 50,000 persons. When he was barred from presenting them formally, he left the petitions stacked high on his desk in the House of Representatives as a silent protest against the gag rules. In 1844, Adams—by then 77 years old—finally garnered enough support to have the gag rules eliminated.

Copperheads and Lincoln. During the Civil War, a vigorous antiwar movement emerged in the North, and antiwar editors came to be known as Copperheads. Some of them tested freedom of the press in wartime to the limit, openly advocating a southern victory. The Copperheads' rhetoric often hindered recruiting for the Union Army. On several occasions, military commanders in the North acted against Copperheads, creating a difficult dilemma for President Abraham Lincoln, who was deeply committed to the First Amendment but also wanted to end the war quickly. He is generally credited with exercising restraint in the face of vicious criticism from Copperhead editors. On one occasion he countermanded a general's decision to occupy the offices of the *Chicago Times* to halt that paper's attacks on the war effort.

However, in 1864 Lincoln reached his breaking point when two New York newspapers published a false story claiming there was to be a massive new draft call—an announcement sure to stir violent anti-draft riots. The president allowed the editors to be arrested and their papers occupied by the military until it was learned the newspapers got the story from a forged Associated Press dispatch that they had every reason to believe was authentic. As it

Focus on...
John Stuart Mill and the "marketplace of ideas"

John Stuart Mill, an English political philosopher, refined theoretical concepts of freedom of expression during the nineteenth century.

Mill's *On Liberty*, first published in 1859, defined the limits of freedom and authority in the modern state. He said that by the mid-1800s the important role of the press as one of "the securities against corrupt or tyrannical government" was well recognized—at least in such countries as England and the United States.

Mill stressed that any attempt to silence expression, even that of a one-person minority, deprives the people of something important. He said that "if the opinion is right, they (the people) are deprived of the opportunity of exchanging error for truth; if wrong, they lose what is almost as great a benefit, the clearer perception and livelier impression of truth, produced by its collision with error."

FIG. 12. John Stuart Mill (1806–1873).

Library of Congress Prints and Photographs Division, [LC-USZ62-76491]

Mill presented four basic propositions in defense of freedom of expression. First, an opinion may contain truth, and if one silences the opinion, the truth may be lost. Second, there may be a particle of truth within a wrong opinion; if the wrong opinion is suppressed, that particle of truth may be lost. Third, even if an accepted opinion is the truth, the public tends to hold it not on rational grounds but as a prejudice unless forced to defend it. And fourth, a commonly held opinion loses its vitality and its effect on conduct and character if it is not contested from time to time.

In these terms, Mill expanded upon John Milton's "marketplace of ideas" concept. The impact of these ideas on the evolution of free expression became evident in the twentieth century.

turned out, the story was fabricated by an unscrupulous journalist who hoped to reap large profits in the stock market during the panic he expected the story to produce.

The Fourteenth Amendment and due process. After the end of the Civil War, the Fourteenth Amendment was approved, requiring the states to safeguard the basic civil liberties of all of their residents. The relevant part of the Fourteenth Amendment reads as follows:

> No state shall make or enforce any law which shall abridge the privileges or immunities of citizens of the United States; nor shall any State deprive any person of life, liberty or property, without due process of law; nor deny to any person within its jurisdiction the equal protection of the laws.

Like the First Amendment, this amendment had far-reaching consequences that were not fully understood when it was adopted. Its immediate impetus came from the desire to protect the former slaves from oppressive legislation in southern states. But during the twentieth century the "liberty" clause of the Fourteenth Amendment was relied upon repeatedly to make the various federal rights guaranteed in the Bill of Rights—including the First Amendment—applicable to the states. Under a modern understanding of constitutional law, no state could enforce a gag law of the sort adopted by many states before the Civil War.

■ SEDITION IN THE TWENTIETH CENTURY

Wars and the threat of wars tend to make lawmakers worry more about national security and less about such ideals as freedom of speech. The Alien and Sedition Acts of 1798 were passed at a time when war with France seemed imminent, and the Civil War created pressures for censorship of those who opposed that war effort.

Espionage and Sedition Acts. Early in the twentieth century, the nation became involved in what many Americans thought would be the war to end all wars: World War I. In preparation, Congress again decided that domestic freedom would have to be curtailed. The result was the Espionage Act in 1917, which was expanded by the Sedition Act in 1918.

In passing these laws, Congress was not merely expressing its own collective desire to suppress unpopular views. In fact, there was a growing worldwide movement for fundamental social change, a movement many Americans found threatening. Already, Marxist revolutionaries were on the move in Russia, and socialists, anarchists, and Marxists were also highly visible in this country. Moreover, we were about to undertake a war against Germany, and yet there were millions of persons of German descent living in America. In addition, labor unions such as the Industrial Workers of the World (the "Wobblies") were gaining wide support and calling for basic changes in the capitalist system.

The Espionage Act was passed shortly after the United States entered World War I. It prohibited seditious expression that might hurt the war effort. This federal law was particularly aimed at those who might hamper armed forces recruiting, and it was written so broadly that it was once used to prosecute a grandmother who wrote a letter urging her grandson not to join the army.

Unlike the 1798 Sedition Act, which resulted in only a handful of prosecutions, the 1918 Sedition Act was vigorously enforced. About 2,000 persons were arrested for violating the Espionage and Sedition acts and nearly 1,000 were convicted. Several of the convictions were appealed to the U.S. Supreme Court, which upheld every conviction it reviewed.

Early Free Expression Decisions

The first Espionage Act or Sedition Act case to reach the Supreme Court was *Schenck v. U.S.* (249 U.S. 47) in 1919. Charles T. Schenck, general secretary of the Socialist Party, and another socialist were convicted under the Espionage Act and state anarchy and sedition laws for circulating about 15,000 leaflets to military recruits and draftees. The tracts denounced the draft as an unconstitutional form of involuntary servitude, banned by the Thirteenth Amendment. They urged the draftees not to serve and called the war a cold-blooded venture for the profit of big business.

Clear and present danger rule. When their conviction was reviewed by the Supreme Court, the socialists argued that their speech and leaflets were protected by the First Amendment. The Court was thus compelled to rule on the scope and meaning of the First Amendment. In a famous opinion written by Justice Oliver Wendell Holmes Jr., the Court rejected the socialists' argument:

> We admit that in many places and in ordinary times the defendants in saying
> all that was said in the circular would have been within their constitutional
> rights. But the character of every act depends upon the *circumstances in which it
> is done.* The question in every case is whether the words used are used in such

FIG. 13.
Supreme Court of the United States, 1924.

Library of Congress Prints and Photographs Division, [LC-USZ62-91090]

Front, L-R: Justice Willis Van Devanter, Justice Joseph McKenna, Chief Justice William Howard Taft, Justice Oliver Wendell Holmes, Justice James McReynolds. Back, L-R: Justice Pierce Butler, Justice Louis Dembitz Brandeis, Justice George Sutherland, Justice Edward Sanford.

circumstances and are of such a nature as to create *a clear and present danger* that they will bring about the substantive evils that Congress has a right to prevent (emphasis added).

In short, the Supreme Court said the First Amendment is not absolute. Congress may abridge freedom of speech whenever that speech presents a "clear and present danger" to some other national interest that is more important than freedom of speech at the moment.

In reaching this conclusion, Holmes made his famous analogy: "free speech would not protect a man in falsely shouting fire in a theatre and causing a panic." Thus, he wrote, free speech can never be considered absolute. Instead, each abridgment of freedom must be weighed against its purpose to decide if it is an appropriate or inappropriate one.

Although the *clear and present danger* test has proved to be vague and difficult to administer, it replaced a common law test for allegedly dangerous speech that was even more difficult to administer without unduly inhibiting freedom. The old common law test, known as the *reasonable tendency* or *bad tendency test,* was established in England in the 1700s and adopted as American common law along with the rest of the English common law.

This test could be used to forbid any speech that might tend to create a low opinion of public officials, institutions or laws. It gave prosecutors wide latitude to prosecute anyone charged with seditious libel. Whatever its limitations, the clear and present danger test was more precise and offered more protection for unpopular speech than the old reasonable tendency test.

After *Schenck.* Following *Schenck,* the Supreme Court quickly upheld the convictions of two others charged with violating the Espionage Act: Jacob Frohwerk, a German language newspaper editor, and Eugene V. Debs, the famous leader of the American Socialist Party, who later received nearly a million votes for president of the United States while in jail.

Eight months after the *Schenck, Frohwerk v. U.S.* (249 U.S. 204) and *Debs v. U.S.* (249 U.S. 211) decisions, the Supreme Court ruled on another Espionage Act case, *Abrams v. U.S.* (250 U.S. 616). The convictions of Jacob Abrams and four others who had published antiwar leaflets were upheld, but this time the Court had a new dissenter: Justice Holmes had rethought his position and wrote an eloquent defense of freedom of expression that was joined by Justice Louis Brandeis. In the majority opinion that affirmed the convictions, Justice John Clarke said the primary goal of Abrams and his co-defendants was to aid the enemy. That constituted a clear and present danger to national interests. But Holmes and Brandeis replied in dissent: "Congress certainly cannot forbid all effort to change the mind of the country. Now nobody can suppose that the surreptitious publishing of a silly leaflet by an unknown man, without more, would present any immediate danger that its opinions would hinder the success of the government aims or have any appreciable tendency to do so." This opinion was very influential in later years, but at the time it was a minority view. Neither the country nor the Court was in a mood to be tolerant toward political radicals.

In the Court's last reviewed Espionage Act, it affirmed a lower court ruling that denied second-class mailing privileges to the *Milwaukee Leader,* the best known Socialist paper in the country. The Court found that articles in the *Leader* "sought to convince readers...that soldiers could not be legally sent outside the country," and thus the sanctions were appropriate *(U.S. ex rel. Milwaukee Social Democratic Publ'g Co. v. Burleson,* 255 U.S. 407, 1921).

By today's standards, these Supreme Court decisions seem repressive. The expression of views that would have been considered well within the protection of the First Amendment in more recent times led to criminal prosecutions during World War I. Obviously, First Amendment law was in its infancy at that point. The courts felt little obligation to observe the niceties of constitutional law at a time when leftists seemed threatening to many Americans.

Incorporation: The First Amendment and the States

During the first part of the twentieth century, at least 20 states enacted laws against various kinds of political radicalism, motivated by fear of groups that sought to change the American political and social system and advocated force as a means of accomplishing their goals. The constitutionality of these laws was soon challenged by those convicted under them, and it wasn't long before some of these cases reached the U.S. Supreme Court.

Probably the most important of these state sedition cases was *Gitlow v. New York* (268 U.S. 652), which reached the Supreme Court in 1925. Benjamin Gitlow, a New York socialist, and three others were convicted of violating a state criminal anarchy law by writing a document called the "Left Wing Manifesto." They were also convicted of distributing a paper called *The Revolutionary Age.* Gitlow argued that the New York law violated his freedom of expression as guaranteed under the First Amendment. In so doing, he was asking the high court to reverse an 1833 decision that said the Bill of Rights only applied to the federal government *(Barron v. Baltimore,* 7 Peters 243). Gitlow contended that the Fourteenth Amendment's requirement that the states safeguard the "liberty" of their residents meant the civil liberties guaranteed in the Bill of Rights could no longer be violated by the states.

Enacted after the Civil War and intended to safeguard the civil rights of the former slaves, the Fourteenth Amendment applies specifically to the states. Among other things, it has a provision known as the *due process clause,* which says, "...nor shall any state deprive any person of life, liberty or property, without due process of law...." Gitlow argued that "liberty," as the term is used in the Fourteenth Amendment, includes all of the freedoms guaranteed in the First Amendment.

By making this argument, Gitlow won a tremendous long-term victory for freedom of expression, but he lost his own appeal. In an amazingly brief passage, the Supreme Court

(L) FIG. 14.
Eugene Debs, circa 1921.
The socialist leader received
8 million votes for president
while jailed.

(R) FIG. 15.
Charlotte Anita Whitney, circa
1910–1920. The California
socialist was convicted of
criminal syndicalism.

*Library of Congress Prints and
Photographs Division*

*Library of Congress Prints and
Photographs Division, [LC-DIG-
hec-41847]*

completely rewrote the rules on constitutional law, acknowledging that the Fourteenth Amendment had indeed made the First Amendment applicable to the states (known as the *incorporation doctrine*). But then the Court said the First Amendment did not protect Gitlow's activities, upholding the New York conviction: "A state in the exercise of its police power may punish those who abuse this freedom by utterances inimical to the public welfare, tending to corrupt public morals, incite to crime, or disturb the public peace."

Although Gitlow's conviction was affirmed, the Supreme Court had almost offhandedly rewritten the basic rules governing free expression rights at the state and local level. By requiring the states (and their political subdivisions such as city and county governments) to respect freedom of speech, press and religion, the Supreme Court had vastly expanded the rights of Americans. In 2010 the Supreme Court by a 5-4 vote incorporated the Second Amendment, the right to keep and bear arms (*McDonald v. City of Chicago*, 561 U.S. 742).

"More speech, not enforced silence." Two years after *Gitlow*, the Court affirmed another state conviction in a case that produced a famous opinion defending freedom of expression. In that case (*Whitney v. California*, 274 U.S. 357), Charlotte Anita Whitney was prosecuted for violating a California criminal syndicalism law, a law that made it a felony to belong to a group that advocated forcible change. She was a member of the Communist Labor Party, but she had argued against its militant policies at a meeting just before her prosecution.

Despite these mitigating circumstances, the Supreme Court affirmed Whitney's conviction. For technical reasons, Justice Brandeis concurred in the Court's decision, but his concurring opinion (which Justice Holmes joined) was a powerful appeal for freedom:

> Those who won our independence by revolution were not cowards. They did not fear political change. They did not exalt order at the cost of liberty. To courageous self-reliant men, with confidence in the power of free and fearless reasoning applied through the processes of popular government, no danger flowing from speech can be deemed clear and present, unless the incidence of the evil apprehended is so imminent that it may befall before there is opportunity for full discussion. If there be time to expose through discussion the falsehood and fallacies, to avert the evil by the processes of education, the remedy to be applied is more speech, not enforced silence.

clear and present danger:
a judicial test to determine whether speech should be suppressed; only when speech poses a clear and present danger should it be stopped.

due process:
a constitutional guarantee, contained in the Fifth and Fourteenth Amendments, that the government may not take away anyone's life, liberty, or property arbitrarily or unfairly, and that legal proceedings will be fair and include notice to those affected.

incorporation doctrine:
a constitutional doctrine by which many of the rights contained in the first eight amendments of the Bill of Rights are applied to the states using the due process clause of the Fourteenth Amendment; the First, Second, Fourth, and Sixth Amendments, as well as parts of the Fifth and Eighth Amendments, have been incorporated.

Brandeis said he believed that free speech should be suppressed only in times of emergency and that it was always "open to Americans to challenge a law abridging free speech and assembly by showing that there was no emergency justifying it." Brandeis' concurrence in *Whitney* is often described as the most influential judicial opinion on the values of the First Amendment.

Post-War Sedition and Dissent

The 1918 Sedition Act, like its 1798 predecessor, was only in force a short time: most of its provisions were repealed in 1921. Major portions of the 1917 Espionage Act were not repealed, but that law was specifically written so that it only applied in wartime. Thus, for nearly two decades after 1921, there was no federal law prohibiting seditious speech. But as World War II approached, those who felt the need to curtail freedom in the interest of national security again gained support in Congress.

The Smith Act. Finally, a sedition law was attached to the Alien Registration Act of 1940, popularly known as the Smith Act because one of its sponsors was Congressman Howard Smith of Virginia. Among other things, the new sedition law made it a crime to advocate the violent overthrow of the government or even to belong to a group that advocated overthrowing the government by force. In addition, there were provisions making it a crime to proselytize for groups having such goals. The law did not require proof that the group might actually carry out any of those goals before its members could be prosecuted; mere advocacy was sufficient. Nor did this law apply only during wartime.

The 1940 law was rarely used at first. In fact, compared to other wars, World War II elicited little domestic opposition, perhaps because of the manner in which the United States became involved in that war as well as the widely publicized atrocities of the Nazis. However, during the tense "cold war" era that followed World War II, the Smith Act was used to prosecute numerous members of the American Communist Party. The Smith Act's constitutionality was first tested before the U.S. Supreme Court in a 1951 case involving 12 alleged Communists, *Dennis v. U.S.* (341 U.S. 494). Eugene Dennis and the others were tried on charges of willfully and knowingly conspiring to overthrow the U.S. government by force. After a controversial nine-month trial, they were convicted and the Supreme Court eventually upheld the convictions.

"Gravity of the evil" rule. Chief Justice Fred Vinson's opinion, in which three other justices joined, didn't specifically apply the clear and present danger test to the defendants' activities. Instead, the Court adopted a test formulated by Learned Hand, a famous appellate court judge who heard the case before it reached the Supreme Court. Hand's test is this: "In each case (courts) must ask whether the gravity of the 'evil,' discounted by its improbability, justifies such invasion of free speech as is necessary to avoid the danger." By using Judge Hand's *modified version of the clear and present danger test*, it was possible for the Supreme Court to sustain the convictions without any evidence that there was a real danger that the Communists could achieve their stated goals.

Justice Vinson ruled that the American Communist movement, tiny though it was, constituted a sufficient "evil" to justify the limitations on freedom of speech in the Smith Act. For the moment, it would be unlawful even to belong to an organization that advocated the violent overthrow of the government. Chief Justice Vinson wrote, "Certainly an attempt to overthrow the Government by force, even though doomed from the outset because of inadequate numbers or power of the revolutionists, is sufficient evil for Congress to prevent."

After winning the *Dennis* case, the U.S. Justice Department began a new series of prosecutions under the Smith Act. During the early 1950s at least 121 persons were prosecuted under the act's conspiracy provisions, and others were prosecuted under the provisions outlawing mere membership in organizations advocating violent overthrow of the government.

This may seem to be an alarming violation of the American tradition of free speech, but it was in keeping with the mood of the times. The early 1950s were the heyday of McCarthyism, a time when prominent Americans were accused of pro-Communist sympathies, often with little or no proof. For example, a number of well-known writers and motion picture celebrities were blacklisted in the entertainment industry after undocumented charges were made against them. In Congress, the House Committee on Un-American Activities conducted investigations that its critics felt were little more than witch-hunts designed to harass those with unpopular ideas.

However, the times were changing, and so was the makeup of the Supreme Court. Senator Joseph McCarthy of Wisconsin, the man whose name is synonymous with the red scare, was censured by his Congressional colleagues, and public disapproval of his tactics increased notably by the time of his death in 1957. Meanwhile, the Court gained several new members, most notably Chief Justice Earl Warren, who led the Court into an unprecedented period of judicial liberalism. Warren was appointed in 1953 after the death of Chief Justice Vinson.

"Advocacy to action" rule. In 1957 the Supreme Court responded to these changes by modifying the *Dennis* "gravity of the evil" rule in another case involving the prosecution of alleged Communists under the Smith Act, *Yates v. U.S.* (354 U.S. 298). In this case, the Supreme Court reversed convictions or ordered new trials for 14 people charged with Communist activities. In so ruling, the Court focused on the distinction between teaching the desirability of violently overthrowing the government as an abstract theory and actually *advocating* violent action. The Court said the convictions had to be invalidated because the jury instructions did not require a finding that there was any tendency of the advocacy to produce forcible action.

The Supreme Court said the Smith Act could only be used against "the advocacy and teaching of concrete action for the forcible overthrow of the Government, and not of principles divorced from action." The justices did not return to the clear and present danger test as such, and the Court insisted it was not abandoning the *Dennis* rule. But the new requirement of proof that the defendant was calling for action rather than teaching an abstract doctrine made it very difficult to convict anyone under the Smith Act. As a result, this controversial law was almost never used against political dissidents after that time.

the current incarnation of the clear and present danger test; speech can be suppressed if it causes or results in immediate violence or other lawlessness.

Incitement to Imminent Lawless Action

Perhaps it was fortuitous timing that the Smith Act was rarely used against radicals after 1957, because in the 1960s there was a period of political dissent unprecedented in twentieth-century America. Eventually millions of Americans came to disagree with their government's handling of the Vietnam War, and countless numbers of them vociferously demanded changes in the political system that led to this unpopular war. Had that happened at a time when the government was prepared to vigorously enforce the Smith Act (and when the courts were willing to brush aside the First Amendment and let it happen) far more people than were jailed under the World War I Sedition Act might have been imprisoned for opposing the government during the Vietnam War.

Brandenburg v. Ohio. The First Amendment protection for those accused of seditious speech was again expanded in a controversial 1969 Supreme Court decision involving a Ku Klux Klansman. In that case, *Brandenburg v. Ohio* (395 U.S. 444), a man convicted of violating an Ohio criminal syndicalism law contended that his conduct was protected under the First Amendment. Brandenburg spoke at a Klan rally that was filmed. Part of the film was later televised nationally. Much of what was said was incomprehensible, but the meaning of other remarks was quite clear. Brandenburg urged sending Blacks to Africa and Jews to Israel, and also talked of the need for "revengeance."

Was this a call for action that could be prosecuted under the *Yates* rule, or was it merely the teaching of abstract doctrine? The Supreme Court went beyond the constitutional protection it had given speech in the *Yates* decision. In *Brandenburg*, the justices said the First Amendment even protects speech that is a call for action, as long as the speech is not likely to produce *imminent lawless action*. Thus, the point at which the First Amendment ceases to protect seditious speech is not when there is a call for action, but when that call for action is persuasive and effective enough that it is likely to produce imminent results. The Court said:

> [T]he constitutional guarantees of free speech do not
> permit (state regulation) ...except where the speech
> is directed to inciting or producing imminent lawless
> action, and is likely to incite or produce such action.

Brandenburg's criminal conviction was reversed, and the Supreme Court invalidated the Ohio criminal syndicalism law itself. In so doing, the Court reversed the 1927 *Whitney v. California* decision, in which a state law virtually identical to Ohio's had been upheld. This provides an interesting illustration of the way a dissenting or concurring opinion of one generation can inspire a majority opinion in another. Justice Brandeis' concurring opinion in *Whitney* argued for an imminent danger requirement: Brandeis said the First Amendment should not permit sanctions for political speech unless it threatens to provoke imminent lawless action. More than 40 years later, the Supreme Court adopted that view in the *Brandenburg* decision, repudiating the majority opinion in *Whitney*.

Even now—many years after the *Brandenburg* decision—millions of Americans feel passionately that the Supreme Court was wrong: the Ku Klux Klan and other racist organizations do not deserve First Amendment protection, they believe. Debates over "hate speech" rage on today.

■ INTERPRETING THE FIRST AMENDMENT

In moving from the "clear and present danger" test in the 1920s to the "incitement" test of the 1960s, the Supreme Court's decisions underscored different visions and philosophies about the First Amendment. Following, we will look at some scholarly interpretations of before turning to some of the specific doctrines and rules of interpreting the First Amendment.

Scholarly Views

Leonard Levy. Historian Leonard Levy, a leading scholar of constitutional history, once wrote, "What is clear is that there exists no evidence to suggest an understanding that a constitutional guarantee of free speech or press meant the impossibility of future prosecutions of seditious utterances...." Levy argued that most likely the framers of the First Amendment weren't certain what its full implications were, but that most of the framers believed future prosecutions for seditious utterances were possible. His early research supported the idea that while the First Amendment was suspicious of prior restraints, it did not necessarily preclude subsequent punishment.

However, later in his life Levy rethought that conclusion based on extensive additional research into the content of early American newspapers. He ultimately decided that the framers must have intended for the First Amendment to provide "a right to engage in rasping, corrosive, and offensive discussions on all topics of public interest." His earlier, more narrow view of the First Amendment was presented in a 1960 book, *Legacy of Suppression: Freedom of Speech and Press in Early American History*. In 1985, he published a revised and enlarged edition of the book retitled *Emergence of a Free Press*. In the Preface, Levy wrote: "Some states gave written constitutional protection to freedom of the press after Independence; others did not. Whether they did or not, their presses operated as if the law of seditious libel did not exist." Levy's work remains important in assessing the original intent of the First Amendment.

Zechariah Chafee. In revising his views, Levy came much closer to agreeing with several other noted legal historians. For example, Harvard Professor Zechariah Chafee wrote that the First Amendment was indeed intended to eliminate the common law crime of seditious libel "and make further prosecutions for criticism of the government, without any incitement to law-breaking, forever impossible in the United States."

Chafee, in his 1941 work, argued that freedom of expression is essential to the emergence of truth and advancement of knowledge. The quest for truth "is possible only through absolutely unlimited discussion," Chafee said. Yet, he noted that there are other purposes of government, such as order, the training of the young, and protection against external aggression. Those purposes, he said, must be protected too, but when open discussion interferes with those purposes, there must be a balancing against freedom of speech, "but freedom of speech ought to weigh heavily on that scale."

Chafee argued against prior restraint of expression unless it was very clear that such expression imperiled the nation. He wrote:

> The true boundary line of the First Amendment can be fixed only when Congress and the courts realize that the principle on which speech is classified as lawful or unlawful involves the balancing against each other of two very important social interests, in public safety and in the search for truth. Every reasonable attempt should be made to maintain both interests unimpaired, and the great interest in free speech should be sacrificed only when the interest in public safety is really imperiled, and not, as most men believe, when it is barely conceivable that it may be slightly affected.

Chafee's boundary line, then, is that point where words will incite unlawful acts. That is precisely where the Supreme Court has drawn the line on the meaning of the First Amendment.

Alexander Meiklejohn. A third noted constitutional scholar, Alexander Meiklejohn, agreed for the most part with Chafee's interpretation of the First Amendment. He said only expression that incites unlawful acts should be punishable. Further, incitement does not occur unless an illegal act is actually performed and the prior words can be directly connected to the act. Then, and only then, can words be punished in spite of the First Amendment.

Meiklejohn said that the First Amendment was written during a time when large sections of the population were hostile to the form of government then being adopted. Thus, the framers knew full well that a program of political freedom was a dangerous thing. Yet, Meiklejohn said, the framers chose to write the First Amendment as it is and not the way the courts have rewritten it during the twentieth century. He said that if the framers had wanted the federal government to control expression, the First Amendment could have read: "Only when, in the judgment of the legislature, the interests of order and security render such action advisable shall Congress abridge the freedom of speech."

Both Chafee and Meiklejohn felt that the voters must be well informed to make wise decisions. Both endorsed the "marketplace of ideas" concept, and Meiklejohn supported Milton's view that truth will prevail in this clash of ideas:

No one can deny that the winning of the truth is important for the purposes of self-government. But that is not our deepest need. Far more essential, if men are to be their own rulers, is the demand that whatever truth may become available shall be placed at the disposal of all the citizens of the community.

Much of what we have just discussed is quite theoretical, but the views of scholars such as Chafee, Meiklejohn, and Levy have often influenced the U.S. Supreme Court when it was forced to make difficult decisions about the scope and meaning of the First Amendment in the real world.

Critical theorists. In recent decades, scholars have offered critical theories about the First Amendment, suggesting that free expression has undermined gender and racial equality, for example. Law professor Catharine MacKinnon and writer Andrea Dworkin are scholars who have argued that pornography is a form of sex discrimination and a civil rights violation of women because of its tendency to dehumanize women as sex objects of men. Their scholarship draws from radical feminist theory and media effects research, among other fields. Their advocacy led the city of Indianapolis in 1984 to pass an ordinance allowing individuals to sue for civil rights violations over the effects of pornography, which was ultimately struck down by the courts as a violation of the First Amendment (see Chapter Ten).

Critical race theorists have also argued that the First Amendment protects speech that is harmful and racist, to the detriment of racial equality. In one groundbreaking book, *Words That Wound: Critical Race Theory, Assaultive Speech and the First Amendment*, scholars Mari J. Matsuda, Charles R. Lawrence III, Richard Delgado, and Kimberlé Williams Crenshaw argued that traditional ideas about the First Amendment have preserved societal inequities by protecting racist speech that targets oppressed minorities. These scholars have criticized First Amendment protections for "hate speech" that allow individuals to express ideas deemed to be racist without punishment.

The First Amendment as Legal Rules

In tracing the development of First Amendment freedoms, we have noted several philosophies and "tests" that have been proposed to aid in interpreting what the First Amendment means. Because interpreting the Constitution is so central to the study of media law, we will summarize some basic principles of constitutional interpretation.

Balancing tests. Almost every dispute about constitutional rights involves some kind of a *balancing* test. The courts must weigh conflicting rights and decide which is the most important. That means sometimes one constitutional principle must give way to another: there are few absolutes in constitutional law. That fact, of course, is unfortunate for the media. Were the First Amendment an absolute, many of the legal problems the media face would not exist. Given an absolute First Amendment, there would be no such thing as sedition or prior restraint, and it is doubtful the media could even be held accountable for libel, invasions of privacy, or copyright infringements. Certainly there would be no obscenity law and no limits on media coverage of the criminal justice system. But if that were the case, many of society's other interests would be forced to yield to freedom of speech and freedom of the press.

First Amendment absolutism. Fortunately or unfortunately, depending on your point of view, the *absolutist theory* of the First Amendment has never been the majority view on the U.S. Supreme Court. Some of the founding fathers, such as James Madison, may have

absolutist theory:
a reading of the First
Amendment which
takes literally the
phrase "Congress shall
make no law," suggest-
ing an absolute protec-
tion for speech.

preferred position theory:
a theory of the First
Amendment which
favors the rights of
free speech and press
over other rights when
balanced against those
rights.

rational relationship:
a theory that gives
high deference to
government regula-
tion; if government
provides a legitimate
objective and the regu-
lation is reasonably
related to that objec-
tive, the regulation will
stand.

compelling state interest:
a right that is funda-
mental to society, like
voting or national
security, receives the
highest level of judicial
review.

considered it something of an absolute safeguard for free speech,
and two well-known Supreme Court justices who served during the
1950s and 1960s (Hugo Black and William O. Douglas) took an
almost absolutist position. However, the majority view has always
been that the First Amendment must be weighed against other
rights and social needs. Thus, the courts' task over the years has
been to develop guidelines to assist in this balancing process.

One of the best known of these guidelines for balancing the
First Amendment against other interests has been the clear and
present danger test. As already noted, it was first cited by Justice
Oliver Wendell Holmes in the 1919 *Schenck* decision. In the years
since, it has sometimes been applied to political speech cases,
although in recent years the Supreme Court has not mentioned it
in the leading decisions on free speech. As Chapter Eight explains,
the Court has also applied the clear and present danger test in
resolving conflicts between the media and the courts, weighing the
First Amendment guarantee of a free press against judges' rights to
exercise their contempt of court powers.

Preferred position. Some constitutional scholars argue for a
preferred position test as an alternative to balancing the First Amendment against other rights and interests. In their view, the amendment
should occupy a preeminent place in constitutional law and should
rarely give way to other interests. Some believe that during the era
when Earl Warren was chief justice, the Supreme Court leaned toward
that view of the First Amendment. Indeed, many of the decisions most
favorable to the media were handed down by the Warren Court.

In a more general way, the Supreme Court always uses a kind of
preferred position test in weighing constitutionally protected interests against other values. In *U.S. v. C.I.O.* (335 U.S. 106), a 1948
case, Justice Wiley Rutledge articulated this view. The normal rule
of judicial interpretation requires the courts to adopt a presumption in *favor* of the validity of legislative acts. However, he said, when
a legislative act restricts First Amendment rights, the presumption
must be reversed so that there is a presumption against the validity
of the law rather than in favor of its validity. Thus, he advocated a
"reverse presumption of constitutionality" when a statutory law is
challenged on constitutional grounds.

The concept that the rights protected by the Bill of Rights
occupy a preferred position compared to other interests has been
mentioned in a number of other Supreme Court decisions. However, on a practical level that bias in favor of constitutional rights
does not necessarily translate into tangible results. What the Court
still does is balance the competing interests—albeit with the scales
tipped slightly toward constitutional rights.

Rational relationship versus compelling state interest. The
Supreme Court has also developed a series of more specific guidelines

to use in evaluating claims that a statutory law or government action violates a constitutional right. When a statute (or a state's application of the common law) is challenged, the Court normally looks for nothing more than a *rational relationship* between the law and a legitimate government goal. When a state law is challenged, the state may try to defend it by showing that the law bears a rational relationship to its police power or its duty to promote health and welfare of its citizens.

However, when the claim is that the statute violates a fundamental right protected by the Constitution, the state must show a *compelling state interest* to justify the statute. The state must, in effect, convince the court that its objective in enacting this statute is of such overriding importance that a fundamental right (such as freedom of expression) must give way.

Content-based vs. content-neutral laws. Many laws can potentially impact freedom of expression. One framework used by the courts to assess the constitutionality of these laws is to look at whether the law singles out expression based on its content, or if the laws are "content-neutral."

Content-based laws are laws that target speech based on its communicative content. "(I)f a law applies to particular speech because of the topic discussed or the idea or message expressed," it is a content-based regulation, the court wrote in *Reed v. Town of Gilbert*, discussed further in Chapter Three. Laws that are content based are presumed to be an unconstitutional violation of the First Amendment. The courts will only uphold content-based laws if they meet the standards of "strict scrutiny."

A content-neutral law may regulate expression, but it does so in a neutral way regardless of the content of the regulated speech. One example of a content-neutral regulation of expression are noise ordinances in city parks (see a discussion of *Ward v. Rock Against Racism* in Chapter Three). Content-neutral regulations of expression are evaluated under "intermediate scrutiny."

Strict scrutiny and intermediate scrutiny. The courts apply strict scrutiny to content-based restrictions. Under a strict scrutiny analysis, the court analyzes where there is a "compelling government interest in the regulation and whether the law is narrowly tailored by "the least restrictive means for addressing" the government's interest. For content-neutral laws, the courts apply intermediate scrutiny. Under intermediate scrutiny analysis, the courts generally require the government to establish an "important or substantial government interest" in the regulation and that the regulation is no more restrictive than necessary. Chapter Three explores many cases that apply these standards.

Vagueness and overbreadth. Another way the courts, and particularly the Supreme Court, evaluate state and federal statutes is to

content-based laws: laws target speech based on its communicative content.

content-neutral laws: laws may regulate expression but in a neutral way regardless of the content of the communication.

strict scrutiny: standard used to evaluate content-based laws that requires a compelling government interest and narrow tailoring.

intermediate scrutiny: standard used to evaluate content-neutral laws that requires an important government interest that is no more restrictive than necessary.

vagueness: unclear or subject to several interpretations by reasonable individuals; laws that are vague are often overturned on that basis.

overbreadth: regulating too much protected speech in regulating unprotected speech; laws must be written so as not to proscribe protected speech.

decide whether they are *vague* or *overly broad*. If a law limiting constitutionally protected rights is so broad that it inhibits freedom more than necessary to achieve a legitimate government purpose, or so vague that it is difficult to know exactly what speech or conduct is prohibited, it may be invalidated for overbreadth or vagueness. If a court is going to invalidate a statutory law, it has two options: (1) to find that the law is unconstitutional and thus void under all circumstances; or (2) to find that it is unconstitutional only as it has been applied to the person challenging the law. Moreover, given an ambiguous law, the courts have an obligation to resolve the ambiguity in such a way as to avoid a constitutional conflict if possible.

Who has final say? The U.S. Supreme Court has the final say in construing the language in federal statutes, but the *state* courts have the final say in interpreting *state* laws. The Court can only decide whether a state law is unconstitutional as interpreted by the state courts; it cannot reinterpret a state statute. This means the U.S. Supreme Court sometimes has to send a case back to a state court to find out what a state law means. Once the state court spells out the meaning, the nation's highest court can then decide whether the law—as interpreted by the state court—violates the U.S. Constitution. If it does, it is invalid, of course. But if the state court can interpret the law in a way to avoid a conflict with the U.S. Constitution, the law is valid. Obviously, determining whether a given statute or government action violates the Constitution is a difficult and subjective job. The Supreme Court has a variety of guidelines that it may choose to follow (or choose to ignore) in any given situation.

Critics of the process suspect that whatever test is or isn't applied in a particular case, the ultimate outcome of the case depends more on the values and priorities of the nine justices than on how the facts measure up against one or another set of guidelines. In short, whatever other test may be applied, cases are decided on the basis of a rather subjective balancing process in which various competing values, interests, and social objectives are weighed.

Against this backdrop of historical and legal developments, we can argue that the more things change, the more they stay the same. That is, many of the issues facing American society today reflect similar concerns for the law of free speech and press as have been faced throughout the decades. Yet technological developments and new forms of war have put a new face on these issues.

■ EXTREMISM AND THE FIRST AMENDMENT

In this chapter, we have traced nearly 400 years of struggles for freedom of expression. Of the total history of humanity, that is but a tiny portion. Where, then, is freedom going in the next 400 years? Perhaps more to the point, what will be the future of freedom in the near future—an era that may be dominated by the threat of terrorism and extremism in many parts of the world? Obviously, no one can answer these questions. Freedom in America may depend on who runs the country—and the world. It also depends on who is appointed to the Supreme Court, the federal appellate courts, and the appellate courts of the 50 states. And it depends on who is elected to national, state, and local offices. It is those people who shape the law. In a larger sense, the future of freedom is always decided by the changing mood of the times. As several later chapters explain, there has been a growing sentiment in America today in favor of more restrictions on free expression. In the United States, the threat of terrorism has given rise to new developments in law and the spread of information in a free society. Some of that stems from the threats of international terrorism, including after the Sept. 11, 2001 terrorism attacks in the United States. In recent years, so-called "homegrown" terrorism, including violence motivated by white nationalism, has also increased concerns about how communications have radicalized individuals.

9/11 Terrorism Attacks

In America in the aftermath of the terrorist attacks of Sept. 11, 2001, the threat of terrorism prompted new restrictions on civil liberties unseen in generations. The USA PATRIOT Act, passed shortly after the attacks, created a new crime of domestic terrorism, broadened the federal government's power to monitor telephone and internet communications, and authorized the attorney general to detain any foreigner believed to threaten national security, among other things. The law's name is an acronym for "Uniting and Strengthening America by Providing Appropriate Tools Required to Intercept and Obstruct Terrorism."

Congressional reauthorizations. Despite concerns about the USA PATRIOT Act's implications for the civil liberties of Americans, Congress has reauthorized the law several times. New versions made permanent many provisions of the act that had originally been temporary measures with a four-year sunset clause. Many controversial provisions set to expire have been were renewed with some modifications. One is the "library provision" that allows government investigators to obtain records from libraries and businesses that would reveal an individual's financial or medical information or even private reading habits. A second provision extends the authorization for "national security letters"—subpoenas issued by a government agency such as the FBI instead of a court. Other provisions extended include a "lone wolf" provision that allows the government to track a non-U.S. person who has no discernible affiliation to a foreign power; a "business records provision" that allows the government to compel third parties, such as financial services and travel and telephone companies, to turn over business records of a terrorism suspect without that suspect's knowledge; and a "roving wiretaps" provision which allows the government to monitor phone lines or internet accounts of terrorism suspects, regardless of whether non-suspects regularly use those lines or accounts. After a showdown in 2015, Congress passed a compromise bill that restricted the government's access to American citizens' phone "metadata" that the National Security Agency (NSA) had been secretly collecting. The law still required that phone companies keep the data but required that the (NSA) get approval from a court before it can access the information.

"Material support." In 2010, the Supreme Court took up the question of whether some attempts to monitor terrorism activity conflict with the First Amendment. In *Holder v. Humanitarian Law Project* (561 U.S. 1), the Court upheld the constitutionality of 18 U.S.C. §2339B, a statute that criminalizes providing "material support" or resources to any foreign terrorist organization designated by the secretary of state, including "training," "expert advice and assistance," "service," and "personnel," even to support peaceful actions. Under the most stringent level of review applied to laws that regulate speech based on its content, the government had met its burden. Subsequent lower court rulings have generally been deferential to the government.

The government also pursued illegal disclosures of war-related classified information discussed in the two following cases.

WikiLeaks

The website WikiLeaks has played a controversial role in several major political events in recent years, raising complicated legal questions about national security and freedom in a terrorism era. Touting itself as a publisher of "material of ethical, political and historical significance while keeping the identity of our sources anonymous," WikiLeaks and its eccentric spokesperson and editor-in-chief, Julian Assange, not only made government officials nervous but invited criminal investigations and calls for new legislation to prevent such unauthorized releases of information.

Assange created WikiLeaks in 2006, but it catapulted to international prominence in 2010 after publishing scores of U.S. government secrets: a group of over 76,000 documents entitled "Afghan War Diary" about the war in Afghanistan; over 40,000 documents called "Iraq War Logs;" and most dramatically, over 250,000 U.S. embassy cables, some of which proved humiliating to U.S. diplomats. The source of the leaks was Chelsea Manning, a U.S. Army soldier who worked during the Iraq War as an intelligence analyst. Manning had become morally opposed to the war and smuggled the classified documents on compact discs labeled "Lady Gaga." She first tried to pass the material to the *Washington Post* and *New York Times*, but neither seemed interested, so she contacted WikiLeaks.

International reactions to the leaks were varied, with some foreign officials laughing it off to others expressing concern about the information contained in the documents. The White House issued a strong statement of condemnation, and President Barack Obama in 2011 issued an executive order to limit classified information leaks. Manning was sentenced to 35 years after being convicted in 2013 of 21 charges, including violation of the Espionage Act. She was found not guilty of the most serious charge of aiding the enemy, which could have resulted in a death sentence. In one of his last acts in office, President Obama commuted her sentence after she had served seven years. Manning was released in May 2017.

While Manning's leaks gave WikiLeaks its claim to fame, the website has continued to disclose highly sensitive materials under the direction of Assange, who remained living for years in the Ecuadorian embassy in London after jumping bail on a rape charge in Sweden. Other disclosures include over 700 files related to prisoner interrogations at Guantánamo Bay released in 2011. During the 2016 U.S. presidential election, questions arose about WikiLeaks' role in disclosing hacked emails from Democratic Party officials and whether the website colluded with Russia or the Trump campaign.

(L) FIG. 16.
WikiLeaks editor-in-chief
Julian Assange, 2010.

Espen Moe, "IMG_4739,"
March 20, 2010, via Flickr,
Creative Commons attribution
license.

(R) FIG. 17.
Chelsea Manning, 2017.

Tim Travers Hawkins, May 18,
2017, via Wikimedia Commons,
Creative Commons attribution
license.

FIG. 18.
Whistleblower
Edward Snowden
speaking at
Websummit 2019 in
Lisbon, Portugal.

*Random Institute, Nov.
7, 2019, via Unsplash.*

In 2019, after a falling out with his Ecuadorian hosts, Assange was arrested by British authorities. The U.S. government unsealed a criminal indictment against him and sought his extradition. Assange faced 18 counts of computer crimes and violating the Espionage Act for publishing Manning's leaks. Press freedom advocates accused the U.S. government of overreach, suggesting that Assange's actions in publishing government secrets were not that different from what U.S. news organizations do routinely. The Department of Justice argued that Assange was not a journalist and aided Manning in stealing the secret documents. In January 2021, a British judge denied Assange's extradition to the United States, although Assange remained jailed while the United States appealed in the long-running case.

Edward Snowden Leaks

Chelsea Manning's leaks to the website WikiLeaks made public many significant wartime documents, much to the consternation of the U.S. government. But an even bigger leak occurred when Edward Snowden provided journalists with 1.7 million documents exposing government terrorist-surveillance programs, some of which had questionable legal bases.

In 2013, Snowden, a contractor with the firm Booz Allen Hamilton, smuggled the confidential information out of NSA offices in Hawaii on flash drives. Using encrypted email and instant messaging, Snowden contacted several journalists to provide them with the documents while he fled to Hong Kong in fear of arrest by the American government. The 2014 film *Citizenfour* dramatically documents the events.

Snowden has said his motive for the leaking was to let the public know what the government was doing in their name. He said he was careful to give the documents directly to trusted journalists and asked them to evaluate what information should be made public and what information would be too harmful to be made public. He was charged with theft of government property and two counts of violating the Espionage Act, including "unauthorized communication of national defense information" and "willful communication of classified communications intelligence information to an unauthorized person."

One of the first major stories from the Snowden documents was reported by Glenn Greenwald, a freelance journalist working for the British newspaper *The Guardian*. Greenwald worked with Snowden to break the news in June 2013 that the United States and Great Britain were engaged in a mass surveillance program called PRISM. The justification for this surveillance came from Section 215 of the USA PATRIOT Act, which allows the FBI to compel the overturning of "any tangible things" to help in its investigations regarding national security. *The Guardian* also posted a copy of a PowerPoint document that outlined how PRISM was supposed to work. Nine companies, including Microsoft, Yahoo!, Facebook, Google, Skype, YouTube, and Apple, were mentioned as participants in PRISM. The disclosure led Rep. James Sensenbrenner, an author of the PATRIOT Act and a Republican House member from Wisconsin, to say the program far exceeded its legal basis.

PRISM was just one of many programs made public by the Snowden leaks. Other programs of mass surveillance had names such as Tempora, Boundless Informant, and XKeyscore. In an ominous quote underscoring the reach of these programs, Snowden said, "I, sitting at my desk, [could] wiretap anyone, from you or your accountant, to a federal judge or even the president, if I had a personal email [address]."

Snowden has been hailed a traitor as well as a hero for his leaks. President Obama said Snowden's leaks laid bare to other countries and terrorists some of the United States' most important national security efforts. U.S. Secretary of State John Kerry said Snowden's leaks "damaged his country very significantly." Conversely, Daniel Ellsberg, who leaked the famous Pentagon Papers (discussed in Chapter Three), said in 2014, "Edward Snowden has done more for our Constitution in terms of the Fourth and First Amendment than anyone else I know." Two newspapers, *The Guardian* and the *Washington Post*, were awarded the 2014 Pulitzer Prize for Public Service for their reporting on the Snowden leaks.

At the time of this writing, Snowden remains in Russia, where he has been living with temporary asylum. In 2013, Attorney General Eric Holder announced that Snowden would not face the death penalty or torture if he returned to the United States to face charges of espionage. Snowden has said he would return to the United States only if he were allowed to make a "public interest defense" in his prosecution.

In 2019, Macmillan Publishers published a memoir by Snowden titled *Permanent Record*. Immediately, the U.S. government filed a civil lawsuit seeking all profits from the book and other money Snowden received from more than 50 speaking engagements. U.S. law requires that government employees who have signed non-disclosure disagreements submit manuscripts for pre-publication review to ensure classified information is not disseminated (for more on this, see Chapter Three). Because Snowden failed to submit his book and speeches for pre-publication review, a U.S. district court ruled the U.S. government was entitled to $5.2 million in profits (*U.S. v. Snowden*, Case 1:19-cv-01197, 2019).

Domestic Terrorism and White Nationalism

So-called "homegrown" domestic terrorism is also a growing concern, including how media and communications have fueled extremism. In 2017, after Heather Heyer was killed and nearly two dozen were injured by white nationalist protestors in Charlottesville, Virginia, white supremacist and "alt-right" websites were scrutinized for potentially inciting violence. Among them were the Daily Stormer, a website espousing white supremacist, neo-Nazi views named after a favorite publication of Adolf Hitler. The Southern Poverty Research Center reported that Dylann Roof, the man who killed nine African Americans at a church in Charleston, South Carolina, in 2015, regularly read and posted to the site. After Charlottesville, several web-hosting companies cut off service to the website for violating terms of service agreements. However, the website moved to other hosting services to continue operations, with a disclaimer on its home page saying it does not advocate violence.

(L) FIG. 19. Newspaper coverage of the 2021 Capitol insurrection.

little plant, Jan. 8, 2021, via Unsplash.

(R) FIG. 20. Capitol rioter identified (and arrested) by the FBI.

fbi.gov.

Capitol Insurrection

Following Joe Biden's defeat of Donald Trump in the 2020 presidential election, Trump and his allies pushed false claims of widespread voter fraud as part of a "Stop the Steal" conspiracy aimed at thwarting the certification of the election results. Fanned by some right-wing media outlets, thousands of Trump supporters arrived in Washington, D.C., on January 6, 2021, and after attending a heated rally with pitched calls to stop the Congress from voting on the election results, they stormed the U.S. Capitol in a violent raid. Five people died, more than 140 were injured, and the Capitol sustained at least $30 million in damage. More than 500 people were arrested in the subsequent months on charges including trespass, destruction of government property, conspiracy, and assaulting law enforcement officers. Some people arrested were linked to domestic extremist groups, including the Proud Boys, Oath Keepers, Three Percenters, Texas Freedom Force, and QAnon.

The Capitol insurrection stood to many people as one of the clearest examples of how the spread of misinformation in the digital era can lead to deadly consequences. The insurrection also raised questions about whether Trump and his supporters, including his lawyer (and mayor of New York City during the 9/11 terrorist attacks) Rudy Giuliani, were guilty of sedition or illegal incitement, based on the *Brandenburg* test. "If anything is incitement, it's what President Trump and Rudy Giuliani did," Erwin Chemerinsky, dean of the law school at the University of California, Berkeley and a leading First Amendment scholar, said. The insurrection led to Trump's second impeachment, in which a group of 144 constitutional lawyers signed a letter denouncing Trump's First Amendment defense and concluding that Trump's speech and conduct constituted unprotected incitement under the *Brandenburg* test.

In the days following the insurrection, social media companies including Facebook and Twitter blocked Trump and his supporters from posting on their platforms. The companies came under withering criticism for allowing the spread of misinformation with deadly consequences. Many conservatives, meanwhile, accused the companies of censorship and called for reforms to laws governing the liability of website content, including Section 230 of the Communications Decency Act. In many of these debates, social media companies reminded critics that the First Amendment protects them as speakers and allows publishers to govern the content on the websites they own. While the First Amendment protects citizens from government censorship, it does not give them a right to say whatever they want on somebody else's website. In 2021, both Facebook and Instagram said they were extending Trump's ban on their platforms for at least two years, or until the "risk to public safety has receded." These issues will be discussed in more depth in Chapter Eleven.

Censorship in the Twenty-First Century

In much of the world it is still commonplace for governments to censor the media directly. It was not long ago that those who advocated basic civil liberties were brutalized in many other countries that now permit free expression and free elections. The story of how earlier generations won the freedoms we enjoy today is an important part of this summary of mass communications law. Within the United States, however, the overriding factor in determining the status of freedom in the near future is likely to be the progress of the war against terrorism, both foreign and domestic.

Whenever a society feels threatened by subversive forces within or powerful enemies abroad, freedom suffers. Over the past 200 years, constitutional freedoms have been curtailed repeatedly in wartime. Former Chief Justice William Rehnquist wrote a book in 1998, several years before Sept. 11, summarizing some of that history. In *All the Laws but One: Civil Liberties in Wartime*, Rehnquist discussed Supreme Court decisions concerning the constitutionality of military trials for those accused of subversive activities. His conclusion was that the Supreme Court has often interpreted the law differently in wartime than in peacetime, but with each successive war, Americans became *more* protective of civil liberties and less willing to abandon constitutional rights in the name of national security.

For much of the twentieth century, the United States was once something of a beacon to the world in advocating broader human rights. When the United Nations General Assembly approved the Universal Declaration of Human Rights in 1948, the United States was its most prominent advocate. The United States was a leading advocate of the 1975 Helsinki Accords, in which 35 mostly European countries pledged to respect basic human rights. The United States has also been a leading advocate of human rights within the Inter-American Commission on Human Rights, among other international bodies.

Although the limits on First Amendment freedoms within the United States since Sept. 11, 2001 have been minimal compared with those imposed during World War I, for example, there have been growing concerns both in the United States and abroad about the role of freedom in America. In this era of terrorism and extremism, what will the legacy of freedom look like in the twenty-first century?

3 *Modern Prior Restraints*

Censorship. That word has a lot of emotional impact today, just as it has throughout American history. But its meaning has shifted over the years. Today, censorship in a legal sense usually means *prior restraint* of communications by an agency of government, not *subsequent punishment* for disseminating an unlawful form of communication. As Chapter Two explains, the First Amendment is not absolute: the courts have allowed a variety of limitations on freedom of expression. But most of those limitations would be classified as subsequent punishments, not prior restraints. For example, lawsuits that charge someone with libel or invasion of privacy involve the threat of subsequent punishments, not prior restraints. The media are free to disseminate the information, but they must be prepared to face the legal consequences—afterward.

However, there are some occasions when prior restraints are permitted—times when an agency of government actually engages in some form of prior censorship. And prior restraints are usually considered a far greater threat to freedom than subsequent punishments. If the media are free to publish controversial or unpopular facts and opinions without government interference beyond the threat of punishment afterward, at least a few courageous publishers and broadcasters (or bloggers) will take the risk and make the questionable material public. If the material turns out to be of social importance, the publisher may still be punished, but at least people will have the information and a public dialogue can begin.

Only a few forms of prior restraint are permitted in America today; many communications that are highly offensive to someone (or perhaps to almost everyone) are protected by the First Amendment and may not be censored. Nevertheless, there are times when prior censorship does occur, or is attempted, at least. For example, sometimes government officials attempt to censor the news media to prevent the dissemination of information they see as a threat to national security. Another form of prior restraint involves laws that have been enacted to forbid "hate speech" that expresses hostility on the basis of ethnicity, religion, gender, or sexual orientation. And there are other examples of prior restraints: government censorship of controversial films, bureaucratic attempts to regulate stock market newsletters, and rules that forbid the media to publish confidential court information such as the names of juvenile offenders or rape victims. In all of these diverse situations, there is one common element: a government agency or official is attempting to censor some kind of communication that is considered unacceptable—and that action raises First Amendment questions. In this chapter, we look at these and a few other forms of prior restraint.

Chapter Objectives:

- Explain the prior restraint doctrine.
- Describe key prior restraint precedents.
- Identify examples of prior restraints.
- Define categories of expression unprotected by the First Amendment.
- Evaluate when speech restrictions are reasonable as time, place, and manner regulations.

Essential Questions:

- Why are prior restraints considered to be repugnant to First Amendment values?
- Under what narrow circumstances may prior restraints be warranted, based on Supreme Court precedents?
- What are the categories of unprotected expression?
- Why does it matter if a law is content neutral or content based, and what level of scrutiny do the courts use for each?

■ PRIOR RESTRAINT FOUNDATIONS

Near v. Minnesota

A good place to begin any discussion of prior restraints is the landmark Supreme Court that resolved some of the most basic issues in this field of law. In the 1931 case of *Near v. Minnesota ex rel. Olson* (283 U.S. 697), the U.S. Supreme Court made it clear that prior restraints are generally improper in America. While there have been occasional prior restraints upheld by courts, the *Near* precedent remains a foundational precedent if the government tries to prevent the publication of newsworthy information by the media.

The case resulted from a challenge to a Minnesota state statute that allowed government officials to treat a "malicious, scandalous and defamatory newspaper" as a public nuisance and forbid its publication. Under this law, a county attorney brought suit to shut down *The Saturday Press,* a small weekly newspaper produced by Howard Guilford and J. M. Near.

Guilford and Near had published several articles critical of certain public officials over a period of two months. In their attacks, they charged that a gangster controlled gambling, bootlegging, and racketeering in Minneapolis. They claimed law enforcement agencies did little to stop this corruption. In particular, they accused the police chief of gross neglect of duty, illicit relations with gangsters, and participation in corruption.

A trial court ruled the paper a public nuisance under the Minnesota law and banned its further publication. The Minnesota Supreme Court affirmed the ruling, and Near appealed to the U.S. Supreme Court.

Rare prior restraints. In a decision that made constitutional history, the Court overturned the lower courts and allowed Near to continue publishing. In a 5-4 decision, the Court traced the history of prior restraints and concluded that a newspaper may not be censored before publication except under very exceptional circumstances. Chief Justice Charles Evans Hughes wrote:

FIG. 21.
Chief Justice Charles Evan Hughes, who served as associate justice from 1910 to 1916 and chief justice from 1930 to 1941. The last justice to resign from the Court to run for political office, running for president in 1916. After losing, he served as secretary of state under President Warren G. Harding and was nominated to the Court for a second time, as chief justice, by President Herbert Hoover.

Library of Congress Prints and Photographs Division, [LC-USZ62-67935]

The fact that for approximately one hundred and fifty years there has been almost an entire absence of attempts to impose previous restraints upon publications relating to the malfeasance of public officers is significant of the deep-seated conviction that such restraints would violate constitutional rights. The general principle that the constitutional guaranty of the liberty of the press gives immunity from previous restraints has been approved in many decisions under the provisions of state constitutions.

The Court cited James Madison's interpretation of the First Amendment as well as the views of William Blackstone, a highly respected British jurist of the eighteenth century. Blackstone argued against prior restraints but in favor of punishments afterward for those whose publications turn out to be unlawful.

The Supreme Court also pointed to *Schenck v. U.S.* (discussed in Chapter Two) as an example of an exceptional circumstance in which prior restraint might be proper. Chief Justice Hughes said that, in addition to prior censorship in the interest of national security, prior restraints might be proper to control obscenity and incitements to acts of violence. The Court said, "The constitutional guaranty of free speech does not protect a man from an injunction against uttering words that may have all the effect of force."

In the decades since the landmark *Near v. Minnesota* decision, the closeness of the Supreme Court's vote against prior restraints has often been overlooked. The dissenters in *Near*, who needed just one more Supreme Court justice on their side to prevail, would have allowed prior restraints under many more circumstances. In fact, their reading of history led them to believe that the only form of prior restraint the First Amendment was actually intended to prohibit was licensing of the press by the executive branch of government.

Despite the decision's closeness, the *Near* case established a pattern that the Supreme Court has followed ever since. The Court has often invalidated prior restraints on the media, declaring that censorship would be possible under the right conditions but usually failing to find those conditions.

New York Times v. U.S. (Pentagon Papers case)

One of the most controversial forms of prior restraint has involved government efforts to censor the news media to prevent potential breaches of national security. In 1971 the Supreme Court decided a very significant case involving censorship in the name of national security, a case that pitted then-President Richard Nixon against two leading newspapers, the *New York Times* and the

---

**Focus on...
Near exceptions**

While the Supreme Court rejected a prior restraint in *Near v. Minnesota,* the Court left the door open for prior restraints in some circumstances:

"[T]he protection even as to previous restraint is not absolutely unlimited. But the limitation has been recognized only in exceptional cases ... No one would question but that a government might prevent actual obstruction to its recruiting service or the publication of the sailing dates of transports or the number and location of troops. On similar grounds, the primary requirements of decency may be enforced against obscene publications. The security of the community life may be protected against incitements to acts of violence and the overthrow by force of orderly government. The constitutional guaranty of free speech does not protect a man from an injunction against uttering words that may have all the effect of force. These limitations are not applicable here."

Washington Post. The case came to be known as the "Pentagon Papers" case, although its official name is *New York Times v. U.S.* (403 U.S. 713). For the first time in U.S. history, the federal government sought to censor major newspapers to prevent them from publishing secret documents that would allegedly endanger national security.

Background. A secret Defense Department study of American policy during the Vietnam war was surreptitiously photocopied and portions of it given to several newspapers. It revealed questionable decisions by four presidents (Truman, Eisenhower, Kennedy, and Johnson) that led the country into war. Although the "Pentagon Papers" only covered the period through 1968, and thus did not cover Nixon's presidency (he took office in 1969), the *Times'* and *Post's* editors knew Nixon would be outraged if these documents were published. But after consulting with First Amendment lawyers, the *Times* and *Post* went ahead.

When the first installment of a planned series based on the "Pentagon Papers" appeared in each newspaper, the Nixon administration demanded that the *Times* and *Post* halt all further stories on the subject. When they refused, the Justice Department secured a temporary order from a federal district judge forbidding the *Times* to publish any more articles on the Pentagon Papers. The judge then changed his mind and *vacated* (set aside) the order, but a federal appellate court reinstated it. The case was immediately appealed to the U.S. Supreme Court. Meanwhile, another federal appellate court refused to stop the *Post* from publishing more stories about the Pentagon Papers.

In view of the flagrant censorship inherent in the order against the *Times*, the Supreme Court decided the case only two weeks after the controversy arose, during what might otherwise have been its summer recess. The Nixon administration argued that publication of the Pentagon Papers would endanger national security and damage U.S. foreign relations.

The newspapers replied that this was a clear-cut First Amendment issue involving information of great importance to the American people. Further, the newspapers contended that the entire classification system under which these documents were declared secret should be revised. The system existed only by presidential order; it was not established by an act of Congress. And at least one Pentagon official had conceded in Congressional testimony that

FIG. 22.
An exhibit at the Newseum shows printers at the *New York Times* preparing to go to press after the Supreme Court overturned a prior restraint against publishing the Pentagon Papers.

Author's collection.

FIG. 23.
An exhibit at the Newseum shows the front page of the *New York Times* on the day of the Pentagon Papers decision and also displays the physical copies of the Pentagon Papers that were leaked to the newspaper.

Author's collection.

only a few of the millions of classified documents actually dealt with *bona fide* military secrets or other material affecting national security.

The decision. The Supreme Court voted 6-3 to set aside the prior restraint and allow the publication of articles based on the Pentagon Papers. Journalists proclaimed the victory as if it were the outcome of the Super Bowl. *Newsweek,* for instance, put "Victory for the Press" in bold yellow type on its cover. But unfortunately, it wasn't that clear cut. In a brief opinion, the Court had simply said the government had failed to prove that the articles would endanger national security sufficiently to justify prior restraint of the nation's press. In the majority were Justices Hugo Black, William Brennan, William O. Douglas, Thurgood Marshall, Potter Stewart, and Byron White. The minority consisted of Justices John Harlan II and Harry Blackmun and Chief Justice Warren Burger.

In addition to the brief opinion by the Court, the nine justices wrote their own separate opinions explaining their views. When legal scholars began analyzing those opinions, they realized the decision was no decisive victory for the press. Only two of the justices (Black and Douglas) took the absolutist position that prior restraints such as the government sought would never be constitutionally permissible. Justice Marshall said the courts should not do by injunction what Congress had refused to do by statute (i.e., authorize prior censorship). Justice Brennan said the government simply hadn't satisfied the very heavy burden of proof necessary to justify prior censorship in this case.

However, the other five made it clear they either favored censorship in this case or would at least condone criminal sanctions against the nation's leading newspapers after publication of the documents. At least two justices (Harlan and Blackmun) favored prior restraint in this case, while Chief Justice Burger voted to forbid publication at least until the lower courts had more time to consider the matter, although he didn't really address the substantive issue of prior restraint. Justice White, in an opinion joined by Justice Stewart, said the government had not justified prior censorship but also suggested (as did Burger) that the editors could face criminal prosecution after publication for revealing the secret documents.

FIG. 24.
Daniel Ellsberg
speaking at the
2012 Whistleblower
Conference in
Berkeley.

*Carol Leigh AKA Scarlot
Harlot, "Daniel Ellsberg
at Whistleblower Confer-
ence Berkeley 2012,"
Feb. 17, 2012 via Flickr,
Creative Commons attri-
bution license.*

Thus, the Pentagon Papers case was not a clear-cut victory for freedom of expression, but at least the nation's press was allowed to publish stories based on the documents. No journalist was ever prosecuted in connection with the Pentagon Papers, although the government unsuccessfully prosecuted Daniel Ellsberg, the social scientist who copied the documents in the first place. In June 2011, the federal government finally released the entire 7,000-page report, 40 years after the *Times* published its stories.

U.S. v. Progressive

The question of prior restraint in the interest of national security also arose in a controversial 1979 case, *U.S. v. The Progressive* (467 F. Supp. 990). This case was never given full consideration even by a court of appeals, let alone by the Supreme Court, so it has limited value as a legal precedent. Nevertheless, it did dramatize the conflict between freedom of the press and the need for national security.

The Progressive, a liberal magazine, was planning to publish an article entitled "The H-bomb Secret: How We Got It, Why We're Telling It." The author, Howard Morland, had assembled an apparently accurate description of a hydrogen bomb through library research. The magazine sent the article to the federal government prior to publication, requesting that its technical accuracy be verified. The U.S. Department of Energy responded by declaring that publication of the article would violate the secrecy provisions of the 1954 Atomic Energy Act. The U.S. Justice Department sought a court order prohibiting publication.

Federal Judge Robert Warren issued an order forbidding the magazine to publish the article. He said the article could "accelerate the membership of a candidate nation in the thermonuclear club." He distinguished this case from the Pentagon Papers case in that he said the H-bomb article posed a current threat to national security. Also, he ruled, a specific statute prohibited the article's publication, whereas there was no statutory authorization to censor the Pentagon Papers.

Ultimately, however, Judge Warren offered a pragmatic rationale for censorship: "Faced with a stark choice between upholding the right to continued life and the right to freedom of the press, most jurists would have no difficulty in opting for the chance to continue to breathe and function as they work to achieve perfect freedom of expression."

Doubting that the issue was quite that black and white, *The Progressive* appealed Warren's ruling. However, before a federal appellate court could decide the case, articles describing an H-bomb in similar detail appeared in other publications, rendering the case *moot* (beyond the law's reach). Once the information was published elsewhere, the government dropped its attempt to censor the magazine article.

Therefore, the *Progressive* case left many important issues unresolved. One of the most troubling is that the information for the article was gleaned from non-classified sources, yet when it was put into an article questioning the classification system, the U.S. government tried to censor it. Also, Judge Warren's abandonment of the First Amendment invited appellate review. In reviewing Warren's order, a higher court might have clarified the extent to which the national security classification system overrides the First Amendment.

Other Key Prior Restraint Precedents

One form of prior restraint results from laws and court orders forbidding the media to publish confidential information, often concerning crimes and court proceedings. This creates legal problems that fall into several areas, including fair trial-free press (discussed in Chapter Seven) and the privacy of crime victims (discussed in Chapter Five). Here, we will briefly discuss the cases as they relate to the censorship questions. Primarily, the cases all ask: when does the government prevent the publication of truthful information?

Names of crime victims. One of the most difficult problems in this area involves laws forbidding the media to reveal the names of crime victims and juvenile offenders. Although a good case can be made for protecting the privacy of crime victims, the Supreme Court has held that the media have a right to publish their identities if the information was lawfully obtained from court records. The Court so ruled in 1975, overturning a Georgia privacy judgment against a broadcaster who published a rape victim's name. In that case (*Cox Broadcasting v. Cohn*, 420 U.S. 469), a television reporter had obtained the victim's name from a court record, and the station later faced a civil invasion of privacy suit for broadcasting it. The Court said the First and Fourteenth Amendments do not permit either criminal sanctions or civil invasion of privacy lawsuits for the publication of truthful information lawfully obtained from court records. However, the states can keep victims' names secret if they wish.

In 1989, the Court again addressed this issue in *Florida Star v. B.J.F.* (491 U.S. 524). Under Florida law in effect then, the media were forbidden to publish the names of sex crime victims. However, a reporter for the *Florida Star* copied the name of a rape victim from a police report that was posted in the Jacksonville Sheriff's pressroom. The name was published, and the crime victim sued. She won a $97,000 judgment from the newspaper, but the Supreme Court overturned the verdict, ruling that the newspaper could not be penalized for publishing the name when it was lawfully obtained from a police record— even though the police may have violated the Florida law by making the information available to a reporter. However, the 6-3 majority declined to rule that the media are *always* exempt from liability for publishing information that they lawfully obtain. The Court said that *Cox Broadcasting* and other earlier cases had stopped short of ruling out all liability for the truthful publication of lawfully obtained information. But when judicial records are involved, the Court seemed to say that the media are free to publish information they lawfully obtain.

An interesting footnote to the *Florida Star* case is that the state law forbidding the media to publish the names of sex crime victims was eventually ruled unconstitutional by the Florida Supreme Court. In *Florida v. Globe Communications Corp.* (648 So.2d 110, 1994), the state court ruled that the Florida law was too broad because it banned the publication of victims' names without any consideration of the circumstances—and also too narrow because it applied only to the media. This case arose when the *Globe,* a tabloid newspaper, published the name of the woman who accused William Kennedy Smith, a nephew of former President John F. Kennedy and Sen. Edward Kennedy, of rape. As was true in the *Florida Star* case, the *Globe* lawfully obtained the alleged victim's name, and the woman eventually agreed to the release of her name—even appearing on national TV after Smith was acquitted. When the *Globe* was criminally prosecuted for publishing the name, a trial court, a state appellate court, and the Florida Supreme Court all agreed that the state law was unconstitutional.

Names of juveniles. The Supreme Court overturned an Oklahoma court order that banned publication of the name of an 11-year-old boy allegedly involved in a fatal shooting, in *Oklahoma Publishing v. District Court* (430 U.S. 377, 1977). Reporters attended the boy's initial hearing and learned his name there. Local media carried the name, but a judge ordered them not to publish the boy's name or picture again. The Oklahoma Publishing Company appealed the order to the state supreme court, which upheld it. The U.S. Supreme Court reversed, ruling that the order amounted to prior censorship in violation of the First and Fourteenth Amendments. The Court relied on *Cox Broadcasting* and said there was no evidence that the press got the information unlawfully or without the state's permission.

In 1979, the Supreme Court overturned a West Virginia law that imposed criminal sanctions on newspapers for publishing the names of juvenile offenders. In *Smith v. Daily Mail* (443 U.S. 97), a newspaper published the name of a student who killed another student at a junior high school. Reporters learned his name by monitoring police radio broadcasts and talking to eyewitnesses. The Supreme Court again ruled that the media cannot be punished for publishing truthful information that was lawfully obtained.

Judges' performance records. The publication of another kind of confidential information produced a 1978 U.S. Supreme Court decision, *Landmark Communications v. Virginia* (435 U.S. 829). The case involved the *Virginian Pilot's* coverage of the proceedings of a state commission reviewing a judge's performance in office. The paper published the name of the judge and other information. Virginia had a law making these proceedings confidential. The paper was criminally prosecuted and fined for publishing, and the state supreme court upheld the judgment. But the Supreme Court ruled that the law violated the First Amendment. The Court said judges have no greater immunity from criticism than other persons or institutions. When a newspaper lawfully obtains information about a proceeding such as the one in question, the paper may not be criminally punished for publishing what it learns.

Grand jury testimony. The Supreme Court ruled on another case involving the right to publish lawfully obtained information in *Butterworth v. Smith* (494 U.S. 624, 1990). A reporter who had testified before a grand jury wanted to write about the things he told the grand jury—including alleged wrongdoing by a local public official. But under Florida law, it was illegal for grand jury witnesses to disclose their testimony *ever.* In overturning the Florida law, the Court ruled that it is an unconstitutional prior restraint to prohibit a witness from disclosing his own testimony even after the grand jury investigation ends. Chief Justice William Rehnquist said this case did not involve the reporter disclosing *anything he learned from a secret grand jury investigation.* Instead, it was merely a journalist forbidden to publish information already in his possession before he testified. That violates the First Amendment.

One noteworthy limitation on the media's right to publish lawfully obtained information involves the pretrial discovery process when a news organization is involved in a lawsuit. The Supreme Court has held that a judge can forbid a newspaper to publish information it obtains during discovery. In *Seattle Times v. Rhinehart* (467 U.S. 20, 1984), the Court said the *Seattle Times* and another paper *could* be forbidden to publish information they learned while defending a libel suit against a religious group. During discovery, the plaintiff was ordered to provide membership lists, tax returns, and other information. The Court upheld the trial judge's order forbidding the newspapers to publish this material, saying they would be free to publish if they learned of it independently, but when a plaintiff is compelled to hand it over, the judge may require that it remain confidential. This may be a prior restraint, but the Court said that it was legitimate. The *Seattle Times* case is a rare exception to the rule that the media may not be forbidden to publish court documents that they lawfully obtain.

■ OFFENSIVE EXPRESSION AND "HATE SPEECH"

While the *Near* and Pentagon Papers decisions represent the Supreme Court's repugnance toward prior restraints, the government regulates expression in many ways that might be viewed as "censorship" by some. The fault lines between protected and unprotected expression are certainly messy when it comes to offensive expression and so-called "hate speech." On college campuses, for example, debates over free speech versus "hate speech" have raged since the 1980s. In the last several decades, hundreds of colleges and universities adopted rules forbidding hostile remarks toward persons of any racial or ethnic group, gender or sexual orientation. These rules are intended to foster a campus environment that is not perceived as hostile by members of any group. But because many of these rules were written so broadly that they could be used to prohibit expression of unfashionable viewpoints on social issues, critics charged that they really enforced "politically correct" speech. Meanwhile, more than 40 states adopted laws criminalizing "hate speech" in various forms. Like many of the campus rules, some laws banned the expression of ideas, rather than forbidding violent acts. However, the Supreme Court has regularly made it clear that offense alone does not justify censorship, and while "hate speech" may be a description used by many to define unacceptable speech, "hate speech" is not a category of unprotected expression.

Chaplinsky and the "Categorical Approach"

One important concept in Supreme Court First Amendment decision-making is the categorical approach. The Court has long said that some "categories" of expression are not protected by the First Amendment. In recent years, the Supreme Court has rejected attempts to add new categories of unprotected expression.

Fighting words. The Supreme Court first articulated the categorical approach in *Chaplinsky v. New Hampshire* (315 U.S. 568, 1942). In that case, the high court upheld the criminal conviction of a man who used words likely to produce an immediate violent response—a breach of the peace. Thus, speech likely to cause a fight, such as calling someone a "damned fascist" during the heyday of Hitlerism (as happened in *Chaplinsky*), may be prohibited, the Court ruled. For expression to be defined as fighting words not protected by the First Amendment, it typically must be made in a context that is directed at a specific individual and automatically provoke violence and/or emotional harm.

In explaining why some categories of expression do not justify First Amendment protection, Justice Murphy said they "are no essential part of any exposition of ideas, and are of such slight social value as a step to truth that any benefit that may be derived from them is clearly outweighed by the social interest in order and morality." Writing for the majority, Justice Murphy wrote:

> [I}t is well understood that the right to free speech is not absolute at all times and under all circumstances. There are certain well-defined and narrowly limited classes of speech, the prevention and punishment of which have never been thought to raise any Constitutional problem. These include the lewd and obscene, the profane, the libelous, and the insulting or 'fighting' words – those which by their very utterance inflict injury or tend to incite an immediate breach of the peace.

In essence, the Court said categories of unprotected expression don't convey meaningful ideas, and that any modicum of value is outweighed by social norms. Chapter Two discussed incitement to violence as a category of unprotected speech. Subsequent chapters will focus on other unprotected categories, including libel and obscenity. In this chapter, we will explore the nuances of the categorical approaches and related issues.

Racial epithets as fighting words. In 2020, the Connecticut Supreme Court upheld the conviction of David Liebenguth for breach of the peace after he called a parking enforcement officer a "fucking n*****" in a dispute over a parking ticket (*Connecticut v. Liebenguth*, SC 20145, 2020). Liebenguth was arrested and convicted, but a state appellate court found his expression to be protected by the First Amendment. The state supreme court reversed, finding that Liebenguth's expression was unprotected fighting words. The court's fighting words analysis had two components: the nature of the words themselves and the circumstances in which they were used. In uttering the words "fucking n******" twice in an aggressive manner in an angry, one-on-one confrontation, the defendant was "asserting his own perceived racial dominance and superiority" and "evoking a history of racial violence, brutality and subordination." The court's decision reviewed a history of fighting words cases that limited the category to words that "touch the raw nerves" of a person's "sense of dignity, decency and personality" that is likely to "trigger an immediate violent reaction." The court found "this to be the rare case in which that demanding standard has been met." The court recognized that while some jurisdictions hold police officers to a higher standard of expected restraint when met with hostile words, it distinguished a parking enforcement officer from that standard. "[W]e conclude that the language the defendant used to demean, intimidate and anger [the parking officer] were fighting words likely to provoke a violent response from a reasonable person under the circumstances."

"Fuck the Draft." Offensiveness alone is not a good enough reason to punish individuals for using provocative language. In *Cohen v. California* (403 U.S. 15, 1971), Paul R. Cohen was criminally prosecuted for appearing in a Los Angeles courthouse wearing a leather jacket emblazoned with the motto "Fuck the Draft." At the time, several people who had demonstrated against the Vietnam-era military draft were standing trial. The U.S. Supreme Court ultimately held that this was a constitutionally protected expression of opinion, despite the offensiveness of the word. Writing for the Court, Justice John Marshall Harlan said:

> While the particular four-letter word being litigated here is perhaps more distasteful than most others of its genre, it is nevertheless often true that one

Focus on...
The law of flags

The flag is a revered symbol in America. For many, there is no more precious symbol of democracy and freedom. So when it's burned or there are issues with its display, lawmakers get involved.

FIG. 25. American flag.

Author's collection.

Burning the flag is an acceptable way to dispose of a damaged or old flag, and it is currently constitutional to burn one in protest. Interestingly, even after flag desecration laws were struck down in 1989 in *Texas v. Johnson*, legal blogger and First Amendment scholar Eugene Volokh found at least a dozen flag desecration prosecutions since 1992 (post-*R.A.V.*) in Florida, North Carolina, Pennsylvania, Texas, and Washington State (he reported that most were dismissed but two led to convictions).

In 2006, President George W. Bush signed the Freedom to Display the American Flag Act, which prohibits condominium associations from denying their members the ability to display the flag. Associations can put reasonable time, place and manner restrictions on the display, such as size and flag pole placement, but cannot ban American flag display altogether. Several states have similar laws.

man's vulgarity is another's lyric. Indeed, we think it is largely because governmental officials cannot make principled distinctions in this area that the Constitution leaves matters of taste and style so largely to the individual.

Speech and Conduct

The *Chaplinsky* and *Cohen* cases raised questions not only about offensiveness but also about the line between free expression and impermissible conduct — a line the U.S. Supreme Court has struggled to draw. While the First Amendment prohibits undue regulation of expression, it does not prohibit regulations of conduct. However, some speech and conduct are so intertwined, the Court has created special considerations for so-called expressive conduct or symbolic speech.

The *O'Brien* test. In *U.S. v. O'Brien* (391 U.S. 367, 1968), the Court ruled that expressive conduct may be regulated if the government meets certain standards, referred to as intermediate scrutiny. The case involved the arrest of David Paul O'Brien for burning his Selective Service Registration Certificate, or draft card, during the Vietnam War in violation of U.S. law. O'Brien burned the card publicly on the steps of the South Boston Courthouse during a protest and claimed the act of protest was protected by the First Amendment. The Court said in cases "when 'speech' and 'nonspeech' elements are combined in the same course of conduct, a sufficiently important governmental interest in regulating the nonspeech elements can justify incidental limitations on First Amendment freedoms." The Court ruled against O'Brien, finding the government's need to raise and support armies allows it to establish appropriate draft procedures that include prohibiting destruction of draft cards.

While O'Brien lost his case, the *O'Brien* test, as the standards are often called, have over time protected free expression in many expressive conduct cases. The *O'Brien* test requires that laws regulating expressive conduct must: 1) further an important or substantial government interest, 2) be unrelated to the suppression of free expression, and 3) burden free expression no greater than is essential to the furtherance of the government interest.

Flag burning. Americans have been bitterly divided over the idea that burning the American flag is a protected form of expression. Flag burning stirs strong feelings in many people—and they find it hard to see the value of permitting this kind of symbolic speech. When this issue gained national attention, it became clear that many Americans believed the American flag was a national symbol that deserved special protection. But those who desecrate the flag were given First Amendment protection by the Supreme Court. The Court concluded that there is a higher principle involved in these cases, and that a truly democratic society must extend free expression rights even to those whose ideas or political activities are reprehensible to most people.

In 1989 and 1990, the Supreme Court handed down two separate decisions on flag burning as symbolic speech protected by the First Amendment. In 1989, *Texas v. Johnson* (491 U.S. 397), the Court declared that Gregory Lee Johnson could not be punished for burning an American flag during the 1984 Republican National Convention to protest then-President Reagan's policies. In a decision that produced strong dissenting opinions by four justices, the majority ruled that flag desecration is a protected form of symbolic speech, particularly when it occurs in a clearly political context (as it did in this case).

The ruling brought vehement objections from many people. President George H.W. Bush, for example, called for a constitutional amendment to overturn the Johnson ruling and restore flag desecration as a crime. On the other hand, many civil libertarians feared that such a constitutional amendment would end up including restrictions on other First Amendment freedoms such as the right to express controversial views on racial issues and the right of consenting adults to possess erotic but non-obscene literature. After a major public debate over this question, Congress enacted the Flag Protection Act of 1989, a federal law that carried penalties of up to a year in jail and a $1,000 fine for flag desecration. President George H.W. Bush allowed this act to go into effect without his signature, declaring that he still favored a constitutional amendment instead of a statutory law that could be overturned by the courts. Predictably, the new law was challenged in court as soon as it went into effect. Recognizing the importance of this question, the Supreme Court agreed to hear this new case on an expedited schedule.

In 1990, just a year after *Texas v. Johnson*, the Court declared the new flag protection law to be unconstitutional. Ruling in *U.S. v. Eichman* (496 U.S. 310), the same 5-4 majority reaffirmed its earlier holding that flag desecration is a form of symbolic political speech protected by the First Amendment. While the four dissenting justices again advanced legal arguments to explain why they felt that the First Amendment should *not* protect those who desecrate the flag—as they did a year earlier—in the later decision they also took the unusual step of criticizing public officials who exploited the popular emotions on this issue for their own partisan gain. Writing for the four dissenters, Justice John Paul Stevens said the integrity of the flag is tarnished "by those leaders who seem to advocate compulsory worship of the flag even by individuals it offends, or who seem to manipulate the symbol of national purpose into a pretext for partisan disputes about meaner ends."

Nevertheless, the *Eichman* decision triggered a new campaign for a constitutional amendment that would modify the First Amendment to exclude flag desecration from its scope. Congress took up the issue immediately. But this time, much of the debate centered on the question of whether it was wise to amend the First Amendment for the first time in American history. In June 1990, only days after the *Eichman* ruling, the proposed anti-flag-burning amendment was killed when the House of Representatives failed to give it the two-thirds majority required for constitutional amendments. As the debate reached its conclusion, many members of Congress argued that the flag is a symbol of American freedom—including even the freedom to burn the flag itself as a political protest. Repeated attempts at such an amendment have failed in Congress.

"Hate Speech"

In recent generations, rules and laws prohibiting racist, sexist, or homophobic speech, often referred to as "hate speech," have proliferated. However, in 1992 the Supreme Court ruled that "hate speech" cannot be banned on the basis of its content—although violent action can, of course, be prohibited.

R.A.V. and content neutrality. Ruling in the case of *R.A.V. v. St. Paul* (505 U.S. 377), the high court overturned a St. Paul, Minnesota, ordinance intended to punish those who burn crosses, display swastikas, or express racial or religious hatred in other ways. The case involved a Caucasian youth who burned a homemade cross in the front yard of an African-American family's home. He could have been prosecuted for a variety of other offenses, including arson and trespassing, but city officials chose to prosecute him under the "hate speech" law. Because he was a juvenile, "R.A.V." was originally identified only by his initials. Later he was widely identified in the media as Robert A. Viktora.

In ruling against the St. Paul law, Justice Antonin Scalia said, "Let there be no mistake about our belief that burning a cross in someone's yard is reprehensible. But St. Paul has sufficient means at its disposal to prevent such behavior without adding the First Amendment to the fire." In an opinion that was a wide-ranging defense of the First Amendment right to express unpopular and offensive ideas, Scalia said that governments may not punish those who "communicate messages of racial, gender or religious intolerance" merely because those ideas are offensive and emotionally painful to those in the targeted group.

The Supreme Court was unanimous in overturning the St. Paul "hate speech" ordinance, but the justices disagreed about the legal rationale for doing so. Four justices (Byron White, Harry Blackmun, Sandra Day O'Connor, and John Paul Stevens) argued that the ordinance was unconstitutional only because it was overbroad—not limited to expressions that could lead to violence under the fighting words doctrine.

The other five joined in a majority opinion taking a much broader view of the First Amendment rights of those who engage in "hate speech." They said that any law is unconstitutional if it singles out expressions of "bias-motivated hatred" for special punishment. While the majority did not specifically overturn *Chaplinsky*, they made it clear that the fighting words doctrine cannot be used to suppress the expression of racial, religious, or gender-based hostilities. That kind of viewpoint discrimination violates the First Amendment.

The *R.A.V. v. St. Paul* decision stirred a new national controversy about the meaning of the First Amendment—and it created deep rifts among traditional allies. The St. Paul youth was represented by the American Civil Liberties Union, which argued that St. Paul's "hate speech" law violates the First Amendment. But other traditionally liberal, pro-civil-liberties groups such as People for the American Way criticized the Supreme Court ruling.

The *R.A.V.* ruling raised serious doubts about the constitutionality of many other "hate speech" laws as well as many of the campus speech codes adopted in recent years. However, this was by no means the first time the courts had held that "hate speech" is protected by the First Amendment. Several universities' speech codes had been overturned by lower courts prior to the Supreme Court's ruling in the *R.A.V.* case.

Hate crimes. On the other hand, when an act of violence is motivated by hatred based on race, religion, national origin, gender, or sexual orientation, the First Amendment does *not* protect the violent act. Indeed, a state may impose harsher penalties for violent acts motivated by hatred than it would otherwise for the same violent acts. The Supreme Court so held in a unanimous 1993 decision, *Wisconsin v. Mitchell* (508 U.S. 476). The case arose when several African-American youths watched the movie *Mississippi Burning* and then attacked a white youth. After seeing the movie, Todd Mitchell, then 19, asked his friends, "Do you feel all hyped up to move on some white people?" Then Mitchell saw a 14-year-old youth across the street and said, "There goes a white boy. Go get him." The victim spent several days in a coma, but survived. Mitchell was convicted of aggravated battery, and his sentence was increased under a state hate-crime law.

Writing for a unanimous Court, Chief Justice William Rehnquist said, "A physical assault is not by any stretch of the imagination expressive conduct protected by the First Amendment." In so ruling, the Court upheld the law in Wisconsin—and similar laws in many other states—that treat hate crimes as more serious offenses than crimes in which hate cannot be proven to be the motivation. In 2000, the Supreme Court added a proviso to this: if there is a sentence enhancement for a hate crime (i.e., a crime is punished more severely if motivated by hate), that extra sentence must be imposed by the jury—not added later by the judge (*Apprendi v. New Jersey*, 530 U.S. 466).

New Categories of Unprotected Expression?

In recent years, the Supreme Court has refused to add new categories of unprotected speech in First Amendment law.

Animal cruelty videos. The Supreme Court declined to do that in 2010 in *U.S. v. Stevens* (559 U.S. 460), in a case involving the sale of videos depicting animal cruelty. Robert Stevens sold videos of pit bulls engaged in dogfighting to law enforcement and was charged under a 1999 federal animal cruelty law, the first person to be charged. A divided *en banc* Third Circuit struck down the law, saying that it did not advance the government's interest in reducing animal cruelty but merely punished its depiction. Nor could the government demonstrate a compelling interest in regulating the speech. The Supreme Court overturned the law as overbroad. Chief Justice John Roberts, writing for an 8-1 majority, rejected the notion that animal cruelty speech should be outside the protection of the First Amendment based on "an *ad hoc* balancing of relative social costs and benefits." However, Roberts did leave open the notion that a more carefully crafted animal cruelty law might be constitutional. Justice Samuel Alito dissented, saying that he did not think the law overbroad; it contains "a substantial core of constitutionally permissible applications."

After the *Stevens* decision, Congress passed and President Barack Obama signed a narrower law specifically banning crush videos. Called the Animal Crush Video Prohibition Act of 2010, it criminalizes the creation, sale, and marketing of these videos. The law labels the videos "obscene," which may result in challenges because no sexual acts usually take place in these videos.

Violent video games. The Supreme Court has also resisted adding violence as a special category of unprotected speech, at least in the context of violence in video games. In 2011, the Court in *Brown v. Entertainment Merchants Assoc.* (564 U.S. 786) voted 7-2 to strike down a California law that regulated the sale or rental of violent video games to minors. The state asked the court to use the "variable obscenity" (obscenity to minors) standard discussed in Chapter Ten, but the court rejected that approach, saying that the Supreme Court's obscenity standards have been limited to sexual, not violent, content. The state, the court added, had not provided evidence to demonstrate harm, and there were less restrictive means available to address the state's concerns.

Justice Antonin Scalia, writing for the majority, rejected the application of variable obscenity to violent video games. The state, he wrote, "wishes to create a wholly new category of content-based regulation that is permissible only for speech directed at children"—and that is not acceptable. Nor does the state have "a free-floating power to restrict the ideas to which children may be exposed." In fact, Scalia noted, citing stories from Hansel and Gretel to Snow White to Homer's *Odyssey*, children are regularly exposed from childhood to violence and violent imagery. And the fact that the violence in video games is unlike that in classical literature or fairy tales does not make it unprotected, said Scalia: "Reading Dante is unquestionably more cultured and intellectually edifying than playing Mortal Kombat. But these cultural and intellectual differences are not *constitutional* ones."

Basically, Scalia said, the law was both too narrow *and* too broad:

> As a means of protecting children from portrayals of violence, the legislation is seriously underinclusive, not only because it excludes portrayals other than video games, but also because it permits a parental or avuncular veto. And as a means of assisting concerned parents it is seriously overinclusive because it abridges the First Amendment rights of young people whose parents (and aunts and uncles) think violent video games are a harmless pastime. And the overbreadth in achieving one goal is not cured by the underbreadth in achieving the other.

Justice Samuel Alito, joined by Chief Justice John Roberts, concurred in the outcome, but they thought that the law "fails to provide the fair notice that the Constitution requires" and would have overturned it on those grounds. Justices Clarence Thomas and Stephen Breyer dissented. Thomas relied on the intent of the founders, claiming that history demonstrates that parents were expected to have full control over their children. Breyer, while agreeing that video games are expressive content deserving of First Amendment protection, would restrict access by those under 17 to video games that are "highly realistic" and "violent." He also believed that the language of the statute was clear. "Why are the words 'kill,' 'maim,' and 'dismember' any more difficult to understand than the word 'nudity?'" he asked. Breyer also attached two lengthy appendices to the opinion containing citations of academic articles on the psychological harm that could result from playing violent videogames.

■ TRUE THREATS

The Supreme Court has ruled that "true threats" are an unprotected category of speech. In *Watts v. U.S.* (394 U.S. 705, 1969), the Court upheld the constitutionality of a federal statute that makes it a crime to threaten to kill or inflict bodily harm against the president of the United States. But as applied to the facts in the case, the Court overturned the conviction of an 18-year-old who made inflammatory remarks at a political rally in 1966. The basis for the man's arrest included him saying the following: "If they ever make me carry a rifle the first man I want to get in my sights is LB.J.," referring to U.S. President Lyndon B. Johnson. The Court said the context of the man's remarks needed to be taken into consideration. While it was a "very crude offensive method of stating a political opposition to the President," the Court said, the context of the remarks, the conditional nature of the statement, and the reaction of the listeners should lead a reasonable person not to take the remarks as intended to convey a true threat.

The challenge, then, is when does incendiary, provocative speech that suggests violence against another person cross the line between protected expression and true threats?

"The Nuremburg Files" website. In the late 1990s, anti-abortion advocates created a macabre website named "The Nuremburg Files" that called abortion doctors "baby butchers" and included names, home addresses, and license plate numbers as well as names of spouses and children of some doctors who performed abortions. If such a doctor was killed, as three who were depicted in "wanted" posters on the website had been, the site showed a line through the doctor's name. A group of abortion providers sued the website's operators under a federal law signed into law by President Bill Clinton in 1994 called the Freedom of Access to Clinic Entrances (FACE) Act. The law made it a federal crime to make threats at abortion providers, among other things. After a trial, a federal jury awarded $107 million in actual and punitive damages.

Ruling in *Planned Parenthood of the Columbia/Willamette v. American Coalition of Life Activists* (290 F.3d 1058), the Ninth Circuit ruled on a 6-5 vote that the judgment did not violate the First Amendment rights of anti-abortion activists. Over the objections of five dissenters, the six-judge majority on the Ninth Circuit upheld the actual damages but ordered the trial court to reconsider the amount of the punitive damages. The majority also upheld an injunction by the trial judge ordering some of the "wanted" posters taken down, an order that was undisputedly a prior restraint of communications on a controversial public issue.

Eleven judges participated instead of the usual panel of three because the court was reconsidering the case *en banc*. Earlier, a three-judge panel of the Ninth Circuit had upheld the website and posters as protected speech in a ruling that was set aside by the *en banc* decision. The *en banc* majority ruled that the language of the website constituted "true threats" to health care workers even though there were no explicit threats on the site. Writing for the majority, Judge Pamela Rymer said a true threat is one "where a reasonable person would foresee that the listener will believe he will be subjected to physical violence upon his person, (and) is unprotected by the First Amendment." She added, "It is not necessary that the defendant intend to, or be able to carry out the threat; the only requirement for a true threat is that the defendant intentionally or knowingly communicate the threat."

In three separate opinions, the dissenters said the majority was weakening the First Amendment by its dismissal of the free expression rights of abortion foes. Judge Alex Kozinski, joined by four judges, wrote: "While today it is abortion protesters who are singled out for punitive treatment, the precedent set by this court... will haunt dissidents of all political stripes for many years to come."

Cross-burning. In 2003, the Supreme Court again addressed the conflict between the First Amendment and legislative attempts to curb expressions of hate such as cross-burning. The Court again said cross-burning is protected by the First Amendment—but not when the act is an attempt to intimidate someone rather than an expression of symbolic speech. In *Virginia v. Black* (538 U.S. 343, 2003), the Court reviewed Virginia's across-the-board ban on cross-burning. The Court upheld its use to prosecute those who burn a cross on a neighbor's property with the intent to intimidate those who live there—or the intent to intimidate anyone else. But a majority of the Court also held that burning a cross in an open field at a political rally is protected by the First Amendment as symbolic speech unless the specific intent to intimidate can be proven.

Writing for the Court, Justice Sandra Day O'Connor said that the Ku Klux Klan's history of using burning crosses to intimidate African-Americans, Jews, and others justified Virginia's law against cross-burning that is intended to intimidate someone. "Threats of violence are outside the First Amendment," she wrote, adding, "The burning cross often serves as a message of intimidation, designed to inspire in the victim a fear of bodily harm." She said this history justifies Virginia's decision (and that of many other states) to ban cross-burning as a "signal of impending violence."

However, the Court overturned the conviction of the lead defendant in the case, Barry Elton Black, a Klansman who led a rally in an open field at a Virginia farm. The Court said there was insufficient proof that this political rally, which featured a verbal attack on "the Blacks and Mexicans" and on former President Bill Clinton and his wife, Hillary Clinton, was specifically intended to intimidate anyone. Instead, the Court saw it as a form of protected symbolic speech. The rally concluded with the singing of "Amazing Grace," and the symbolic burning of a 30-foot cross. The Court said two other defendants who had burned a cross in an African-American neighbor's yard could be prosecuted for that.

Justice O'Connor reconciled the case with *R.A.V. v. St. Paul* by interpreting that decision narrowly to protect only symbolic speech but not cross-burning intended to intimidate someone. "A ban on cross-burning carried out with the intent to intimidate is fully consistent with our holding in *R.A.V.* and is proscribable under the First Amendment," she explained.

The 2003 decision led several justices to issue separate concurring or dissenting opinions. Perhaps most notable was Justice Clarence Thomas' opinion. Thomas, the Court's only African-American justice, said he would uphold the Virginia law and other anti-cross-burning laws in full. During oral arguments in this case, Thomas had called cross-burning "a symbol of a reign of terror." In his separate opinion when the case was decided, he said cross-burning should never be regarded as symbolic speech protected by the First Amendment.

On the other hand, Justices David Souter, Ruth Bader Ginsburg, and Anthony Kennedy said they would not uphold any law forbidding cross-burning. In an opinion joined by Ginsburg and Kennedy, Souter said any ban on cross burning is a "content-based" ban on a symbolic message and could not survive First Amendment scrutiny. One irony in *Virginia v. Black* is that Virginia rewrote its cross-burning law after a lower court invalidated the version of the law under review by the Supreme Court. The new law requires proof of intent to intimidate and would probably be upheld in full under the Court majority's rationale.

Facebook threats. With the explosive growth of social media, authorities have wrestled with difficult cases involving threats on social media websites. The Supreme Court took up the question of online threats in 2015 in *Elonis v. U.S.* (135 S. Ct. 2001). The case involved the arrest and conviction of Anthony Elonis, who was arrested for his violent posts on Facebook about his estranged wife, his co-workers, a local school, and an FBI agent. (One example about his ex-wife: "If I only knew then what I know now, I would have smothered your ass with a pillow, dumped your body in the back seat, dropped you off in Toad Creek, and made it look like a rape and murder.") Elonis said his posts were merely a way to vent and let off steam, and that he did not mean to threaten anyone. Elonis was convicted and served 44 months in prison. The Third Circuit upheld the conviction, writing, "Limiting the definition of true threats to only those statements where the speaker subjectively intended to threaten would fail to protect individuals from the fear of violence."

However, in a closely watched case, the U.S. Supreme Court reversed, ruling that authorities must show an intent to cause harm rather than merely show that the words could be reasonably interpreted by listeners to be threatening. Chief Justice John Roberts, writing for the majority, said that the Third Circuit's standard was not sufficient to uphold a conviction against Elonis. "Elonis's conviction ... was premised solely on how his posts would be understood by a reasonable person. Such a 'reasonable person' standard is a familiar feature of civil liability in tort law, but is inconsistent with 'the conventional requirement for criminal conduct—*awareness* of some wrongdoing,'" the chief justice wrote. "The jury was instructed that the Government need prove only that a reasonable person would regard Elonis's communications as threats, and that was error. Federal criminal liability generally does not turn solely on the results of an act without considering the defendant's mental state," said Roberts.

Justice Clarence Thomas dissented. He wrote that nine circuits had adopted the position that a general intent was sufficient to convict as a true threat, and two circuits had used the "intent-to-harm" standard. But now, he said, instead of resolving the circuit split, lower courts "can safely infer that a majority of this Court would not adopt an intent-to-threaten requirement, as the opinion carefully leaves open the possibility that recklessness may be enough." Thomas added, "Because the Court of Appeals properly applied the general-intent standard, and because the communications transmitted by Elonis were 'true threats' unprotected by the First Amendment, I would affirm the judgment below." Justice Samuel Alito, concurring in part and dissenting in part, said that the Court had not given appropriate guidance to courts and Facebook users as to what type of intent would be necessary for hate speech to qualify as a true threat.

The Supreme Court remanded the case back to the Third Circuit. In 2016, the appellate court affirmed Elonis's conviction, saying there was ample evidence provided to the jury that Elonis intended his remarks to be threats. Elonis again appealed to the Supreme Court. This time, the Court declined to take the case, ultimately upholding his conviction under the true threats doctrine.

Rap video is a true threat. In 2018, the Pennsylvania Supreme Court found that a rap song constituted a true threat. The case (*Commonwealth v. Knox*, 190 A.3d 1146) began when two men, Jamal Knox and Rashee Beasley, were arrested following a traffic stop that police said resulted in a crash and the discovery of heroin, cash, and a stolen gun. While facing charges, the men wrote and recorded a rap video called "Fuck the Police" that police deemed to be terrorist threats. The lyrics described in detail the killing of the police officers involved in the case, while the video included photos of the arresting officers. A trial court convicted the defendants, finding the video specifically intended to intimidate the officers and obstruct justice by intimidating potential witnesses. The Pennsylvania Supreme Court upheld the conviction, finding that the defendants intended the video to threaten and intimidate, while court proceedings were occurring, the officers who arrested them. The lyrics and video were not merely artistic expression but "both threatening and highly personalized to the victims," the court wrote. Several high-profile rap artists and civil liberties groups urged the Supreme Court to consider whether Pennsylvania proved all of the elements of the true threat doctrine, including whether the state must prove both a subjective intent of the speaker to threaten and whether a "reasonable person" would regard the statement as a true threat of violence, but the Court declined to do so, denying *cert* in 2019. The conviction stood.

"Not quite right" speech. What about speech that federal authorities feel is "not quite right" but isn't an outright threat, or bumper stickers with a contrary political message at a president's public speech? Steven Howards and his son were at a Colorado mall when then-Vice President Richard Cheney was making a public appearance there. Secret Service agents heard Howards tell someone on his cell phone, "I'm going to ask him [the Vice President] how many kids he's killed today." The agents watched as Howards approached Cheney, asked him a question, and then laid a hand on his shoulder. The agents arrested Howard and turned him over to state law enforcement; those charges were dropped but Howards sued the agents under the First and Fourth Amendments. The Tenth Circuit said that agents violated Howards' First Amendment rights by retaliating against him.

But the Supreme Court in 2012 unanimously said that the agents did not violate Howards' First Amendment rights (*Reichle v. Howards*, 566 U.S. 658). Justice Clarence Thomas wrote that the question was not one of First Amendment retaliation, but rather the "right to be free from a retaliatory arrest that is otherwise supported by probable cause"—and there is no such right, he said. Justice Ruth Bader Ginsburg, concurring in the result, added that the agents "were duty bound to take the content of Howards' statements into account in determining whether he posed an immediate threat to the Vice President's physical security."

Similarly, the Court in *Wood v. Moss* (572 U.S. 744, 2014), clearly wanting to err on the side of precaution, unanimously said that the Secret Service did not have to treat a president's supporters differently from his detractors when it came to ensuring his safety. Secret Service agents had moved a protesting group of individuals down the road from President George W. Bush as he ate dinner on a patio outside a restaurant in Jacksonville, Oregon, putting the detractors about a block farther from the president than the supporters. The detractors sued, saying that the move was an unconstitutional viewpoint-based decision.

Expressing concern for direct lines of fire to President Bush, Justice Ruth Bader Ginsburg wrote for the Court, "No decision of which we are aware, however, would alert Secret Service agents engaged in crowd control that they bear a First Amendment obligation 'to ensure that groups with different viewpoints are at comparable locations at all times.'" The unusual addition of an area map, with an arrow added by the Court showing a direct line of fire from the first position to which the protestors were moved, further dramatized the Court's holding in this very fact-based holding.

In a case that drew two Supreme Court justices' dissent from denial of *cert*, a divided panel of the Tenth Circuit affirmed qualified immunity for Secret Service agents who refused to allow two individuals to attend a 2005 speech given by President George W. Bush at a Colorado museum because the bumper sticker on their car read "No More Blood For Oil" (*Weise v. Casper*, 593 F.3d 1163). Leslie Weise and Alex Young were removed from the event in accordance with a White House Advance Office policy of excluding those who disagree with the president from his official public appearances. The court said that the law was not clearly established at the time of the event, and "no specific authority instructs this court … how to treat the ejection of a silent attendee from an official speech based on the attendee's protected expression outside the speech area." The dissent pointed out that the speech in question "is unquestionably protected, or more accurately, entitled to be protected under the First Amendment."

Weise and Young appealed to the Supreme Court, which declined to hear the case. However, Justice Ruth Bader Ginsburg, joined by Justice Sonia Sotomayor, took the unusual step of issuing a dissent from the denial of *cert*: "I cannot see how reasonable public officials, or any staff or volunteers under their direction, could have viewed the bumper sticker as a permissible reason for depriving Weise and Young of access to the event."

Retaliatory arrests. The court has dealt with many cases in which plaintiffs have argued they were wrongfully arrested based on expression otherwise protected by the First Amendment. In the 2019 case *Nieves v. Bartlett* (139 S. Ct. 1715), the Supreme Court ruled that a citizen did not have a valid First Amendment retaliatory-arrest claim because police had probable cause when they arrested him. The case involved the arrest of an Alaskan man at a festival who claims the officers intended to suppress his protected speech by arresting him. Police said the man, Russell Bartlett, was drunk, yelling at police, and refusing to identify himself. Because the case was the third since 2006 to reach the Court raising similar questions, the Court's opinion provides some clarity to lower courts. Writing for the majority, Justice John Roberts said plaintiffs in retaliatory arrest cases must prove the absence of probable cause to proceed with a First Amendment claim. In this case, Bartlett's intoxication and threatening behavior were enough to justify an arrest. Roberts created a "narrow qualification" for cases where someone was arrested when similarly situated individuals were not.

■ TIME, PLACE, AND MANNER REGULATIONS

If the First Amendment does not permit the direct censorship of such offensive forms of expression as "hate speech" or flag burning that do not rise to the level of incitement, fighting words, or true threats, are there other ways governments can control those who want to engage in these forms of expression? Could a local government simply refuse to let a group like the Ku Klux Klan or the Nazi Party hold rallies or distribute literature on public property? What about other groups whose views are controversial, such as anti-abortion groups known for confrontational demonstrations?

Over the years, there have been hundreds of court decisions about questions such as these. The basic answer is that federal, state, and local governments may adopt *content-neutral time, place, and manner restrictions* on First Amendment activities—but groups wishing to express controversial views cannot be censored through the use of laws governing public assemblies or literature distribution. For example, a government agency may require that all groups obtain a permit before holding a parade on the public streets or a large rally in a public park. And the permit could impose reasonable time limits or noise limits for such events. Similarly, a government agency may set reasonable limits on the places where groups hand out their literature or collect signatures on petitions. However, no government may issue permits for rallies, parades, and literature distribution to groups with which it agrees while denying permits to groups with which it disagrees unless there is a *compelling state interest that justifies such a content-based restriction* on First Amendment activities.

The Supreme Court has repeatedly ruled on cases involving these issues, holding that governments may not arbitrarily deny controversial or unpopular groups the right to distribute literature or hold rallies or demonstrations in a *public forum*—a public place where First Amendment activities are regularly permitted. Governments can, however, also declare certain areas to be *nonpublic forums* and control literature distribution in that way. In this section, we highlight major principles and precedents of time, place, and manner regulations.

Early Controls on Pamphleteering

In early cases, the U.S. Supreme Court ruled on the constitutionality of restrictions on public literature distribution in cases involving the proselytizing activities of the Jehovah's Witness movement.

Since this religious group engages in door-to-door and street-corner soliciting that is unpopular with many Americans, its efforts led to restrictive ordinances in a number of cities by the late 1930s. The Witnesses challenged these limits on their First Amendment rights in a series of lawsuits, several of which reached the Supreme Court and established new free expression safeguards that benefitted not only Jehovah's Witnesses but also the advocates of many other religious and political causes. In 2002, the Supreme Court revisited these issues again in still another Jehovah's Witness case, illustrating the timelessness of these issues.

The first of these Jehovah's Witness cases was *Lovell v. City of Griffin* (303 U.S. 444), decided in 1938. Alma Lovell, a Witness, circulated pamphlets in Griffin, Georgia, without the city manager's permission, something a local law required. She was fined $50, but she took her case all the way to the Supreme Court and won. The Supreme Court found the ordinance invalid, saying it "strikes at the very foundation of the freedom of the press by subjecting it to license and censorship." The city claimed the First Amendment applied only to newspapers and magazines and not to Lovell's pamphlets. The Supreme Court disagreed: "The liberty of the press is not confined to newspapers and periodicals. It necessarily embraces pamphlets and leaflets. These indeed have been historic weapons in the defense of liberty, as the pamphlets of Thomas Paine and others in our own history abundantly attest." Moreover, the Court emphasized that the First Amendment protects the right to distribute literature as well as the right to publish it.

Elsewhere, a number of communities attempted to curb Jehovah's Witnesses by using anti-littering ordinances against them. Several of these laws were considered by the Supreme Court in a 1939 case, *Schneider v. State of New Jersey* (308 U.S. 147).The Court said a city indeed has the right to prevent littering, but it must do so by punishing the person who actually does the littering, not by punishing someone who hands literature to willing recipients. The person handing out a pamphlet cannot be punished even if the recipient later throws it away, the high court said. In *Schneider*, the Supreme Court also invalidated a city ordinance that required anyone seeking to distribute literature door-to-door to get police permission first. The Court said giving the police discretion to decide which ideas may and may not be advanced by neighborhood canvassing is a violation of the First Amendment. A city may limit the hours of door-to-door soliciting, but requiring an advance

time, place, and manner regulation:
a content-neutral regulation that regulates the time, place, and/or manner of speech acts.

public forum:
a place in which free speech activities traditionally take place.

permit is unconstitutional when the permit system gives police discretion to approve or deny permits for causes they like or don't like.

In 1942, the Supreme Court first approved and then invalidated another city ordinance that had been used against a Jehovah's Witness, this one simply requiring a $10 "book agent" license for all solicitors. In this case (*Jones v. Opelika*, 316 U.S. 584), the high court initially upheld the license requirement. But some 11 months later, the Court vacated its decision and adopted what had been a dissenting opinion as the majority view. The court's final decision was based on the fact that the ordinance gave city officials discretion to grant or revoke these licenses without explaining why the action was taken.

To the amazement of many, 60 years later the same kind of questions were addressed again in still another Supreme Court decision involving Jehovah's Witnesses, *Watchtower Bible and Tract Society v. Village of Stratton* (536 U.S. 150, 2002). Stratton, a small town in Ohio, adopted an ordinance that made it a misdemeanor for door-to-door "canvassers" to promote "any cause" without first obtaining a permit from the mayor's office. The ordinance also made it a misdemeanor for anyone to go to a private home where a "no solicitors" sign was posted—a provision the Jehovah's Witnesses did not challenge. After lower courts largely upheld the Stratton ordinance, the Supreme Court overturned its permit requirement on an 8-1 vote. Writing for the Court, Justice John Paul Stevens said extending such a permit requirement to religious and political advocates and other non-commercial canvassers violates the First Amendment. The Court did not rule out permit systems that apply only to commercial solicitors. Stevens said the Stratton ordinance is overbroad and "offensive—not only to the values protected by the First Amendment, but to the very notion of a free society." He condemned laws that require citizens, "in the context of everyday public discourse," to first inform the government of their desire to speak "and then obtain a permit to do so."

As a result of these and other Jehovah's Witness cases, it is now a settled principle of constitutional law that government authorities may not arbitrarily grant solicitation permits to those advocating popular ideas while denying permits to advocates of unpopular ideas. Even a *content-neutral* permit system that merely controls the time, place, and manner of free expression raises constitutional questions because it precludes anonymous religious or political speech and forces those who want to engage in this kind of activity to ask a government for prior permission.

FIG. 26.
New York City's Central Park. In *Ward v. Rock Against Racism*, the U.S. Supreme Court upheld regulations on noise controls for groups that use the park's facilities.

Author's collection.

Access to Public Places

The principles of content neutrality and the government's interest in reasonable time, place, and manner restrictions govern the rights to distribute materials and hold events in public and private places.

Parks. Public parks may be a quintessential forum for the public to gather and interact, but when do government regulations concerning the use of a public park become a form of censorship? For example, may a city restrict the sound levels at rock concerts in a city park without violating the First Amendment?

In 1989, the Supreme Court ruled on this question in *Ward v. Rock Against Racism* (491 U.S. 781). For a number of years a group called Rock Against Racism sponsored annual concerts at a bandshell in New York City's Central Park. The group drew repeated complaints from other park-goers and nearby residents about the sound level at RAR concerts. Eventually the city set limits on the sound level and placed monitors to measure the sound. When the prescribed volume was repeatedly exceeded during a RAR concert, city officials ordered the sound turned down. The concert promoters refused and were cited for excessive noise several times as the concert continued. The city finally cut off power to the bandshell to halt the concert—and refused to allow RAR to hold future concerts in Central Park. RAR sued the city.

The Court acknowledged that rock music is a form of expression protected by the First Amendment. However, the city's limits on sound level were a reasonable time, place, and manner restriction. The majority said the city's policy has "no material impact on any performer's ability to exercise complete artistic control over sound quality." The Court conceded that the city's use of its own technician to control sound levels was not the least intrusive means of achieving the goal (i.e., keeping the volume down). The city could have continued to monitor sound levels, issue citations, and halt concerts if the sound level remained too high. In earlier cases, governments had been required to use the least intrusive means of regulating time, place, and manner. However, the Court dropped that requirement and said that it is no longer necessary that time, place, and manner restrictions on First Amendment freedoms be as non-intrusive as possible.

Dissenting, Justices Marshall, Brennan, and Stevens objected to the broad sweep of the Court's decision: "Until today, a key safeguard of free speech has been government's obligation to adopt the least intrusive restriction necessary to achieve its goals. By abandoning the requirement that time, place and manner regulations must be narrowly tailored, the majority replaces constitutional scrutiny with mandatory deference (to local officials' decisions)."

The Court's decision settled the question of regulation of sound levels at rock concerts: the sound level may be limited—and government employees may be placed in charge of the equipment to make sure the limits are observed—without that violating the First Amendment.

In another case, the Supreme Court upheld Chicago's rules governing the use of its parks. In *Thomas v. Chicago Park District* (534 U.S. 316), the high court in 2002 upheld the reasonableness of Chicago's rules for deciding whether to grant permits to demonstrators seeking to stage an event in a public park. The Court ruled unanimously that the city's 13-point guidelines, which require groups of more than 50 people to prove they have insurance, among other requirements, do not violate the First Amendment because it applies equally to all groups regardless of their viewpoint. Chicago officials defended the policy as necessary to ensure fair access to local parks by individuals as well as large groups. Writing for the Court, Justice Antonin Scalia said, "The licensing scheme at issue here is not subject-matter censorship but content-neutral time, place and manner regulation of the use of a public forum." He added, "The picnicker and soccer player, no less than the political activist or parade marshal, must apply for a permit if the 50-person limit is to be exceeded."

Access to public airports. The Supreme Court has addressed the question of solicitation laws at airports in two cases inspired by the activities of Hare Krishna believers.

In a 1987 case, *Board of Airport Commissioners v. Jews for Jesus* (482 U.S. 569), the Court overturned a rule adopted by the government agency in charge of Los Angeles International Airport that flatly prohibited all First Amendment activities at this government-owned facility. After lower courts overruled several earlier attempts by the airport commissioners to ban literature distribution by Hare Krishna believers, the board adopted a complete ban on all First Amendment activities at the airport. Under this rule a clergyman associated with Jews for Jesus, an evangelical Christian organization, was barred from distributing leaflets there. The Jews for Jesus organization decided to challenge the validity of the ban on First Amendment grounds. The high court unanimously held that the regulation was so sweeping as to be unconstitutional on its face. Writing for the Court, Justice Sandra Day O'Connor said almost any traveler might violate such an all-encompassing ban on First Amendment activities—by doing something as commonplace as talking to a friend or reading a newspaper, for instance. However, the Court did not rule out the possibility that more narrowly drawn regulations limiting the time, place, and manner of literature distribution might pass constitutional muster. Nonetheless, federal judges repeatedly rejected later ordinances intended to regulate soliciting at Los Angeles International Airport. After Sept. 11, 2001, however, very little space at the airport was left open to the general public, and in 2006 a federal judge upheld post-Sept. 11 regulations that limited soliciting to only a few areas. In 2010 the California Supreme Court declined to say whether the Los Angeles airport was a public forum (*Int'l Society for Krishna Consciousness of California, Inc. v. City of Los Angeles*, 48 Cal. 4th 446).

In 1992, the Supreme Court ruled on another case resulting from Hare Krishna members' First Amendment activities at airports. This time the Court ruled that soliciting donations can be banned, although handing out literature must be permitted at appropriate places in public airports. Ruling in *Lee v. Int'l Society for Krishna Consciousness* (505 U.S. 830), a 6-3 majority of the Court held that Hare Krishna members could be barred from fund-raising at the New York area's public airports. Five of the justices also agreed that unlike city streets and parks, airports are not traditional public forums for First Amendment activities. However, in a separate opinion the Court ruled by a 5-4 vote that airports must still be open for First Amendment activities that are less intrusive than soliciting money (for example, handing out free literature).

As a result of these cases, fund-raising can be prohibited not just at airports and post offices but also at many other government-owned facilities that are open to the public but are not traditional public forums. However, governments must allow other First Amendment activities such as literature distribution at many of these same places. And there is still a First Amendment right to solicit donations at places that *are* traditional public forums—subject only to the authorities' right to impose reasonable restrictions on the time, place, and manner of free expression activities.

College campuses. The Supreme Court ruled on another access issue in 2006, upholding the Solomon Amendment, a federal law requiring colleges and universities to allow military recruiting if they receive federal funds and allow other recruiters. On many campuses,

FIG. 27.
The Jefferson Memorial
in Washington, D.C.
Courts have ruled
that the government
can require permits
for demonstrations at
national landmarks, even
for things such as "silent
expressive dancing."

Author's collection.

military recruiters had been barred because of the military's "don't ask, don't tell" policy toward homosexual service personnel. A coalition of law schools and professors argued that they have a First Amendment right to decide who recruits on campus, and to bar recruiters who will not sign a non-discrimination pledge. In *Rumsfeld v. Forum for Acad. & Inst'l Rights* (547 U.S. 47), Chief Justice John Roberts offered a three-part analysis of the First Amendment question. Writing for a unanimous Court, he said the Solomon Amendment does not require law schools or their faculties to speak in favor of military service. Nor does it prevent them from speaking against military service. Roberts wrote: "Nothing about recruiting suggests that law schools agree with any speech by recruiters, and nothing in the Solomon Amendment restricts what the law schools may say about the military's policies."

Military bases. In *U.S. v. Apel* (571 U.S. 359, 2014), the Court ruled unanimously that the military, once it sets up a base, fully controls the use of all base property, even if it allows some public use of some of the base. John Apel, an antiwar activist, demonstrated at Vandenberg Air Force Base beyond the designated protest area and threw blood on a sign. He was convicted of trespass but argued that the military should not have full control over public roads on an easement. Chief Justice John Roberts wrote that it would not require judges to evaluate military sites on a case-by-case basis, adding, "The use-it-or-lose-it rule that Apel proposes would frustrate the administration of military facilities and raise difficult questions for judges, who are not expert in military operations." Apel did, however, have the right to continue a First Amendment claim, as the ruling was just on the law, not on its application to him. In 2015 the Court denied *cert* on Apel's appeal on remand.

National landmarks. Courts have also struggled with balancing the rights of users and protestors of national parks and landmarks. The key takeaway is that courts have often upheld content-neutral laws that are narrowly tailored to serve legitimate government interests.

One religious protestor, Michael Marcavage, litigated several cases with mixed results. In 2010, the Third Circuit threw out Marcavage's conviction after he refused to move away from the Liberty Bell at a National Park Service ranger's request. Applying strict scrutiny, the court found that the government had not narrowly tailored its response to him, particularly given that there were other groups gathered at the Bell, and did not exercise the least restrictive means of dealing with his speech(*U.S. v. Marcavage*, 609 F.3d 264). Marcavage made an appearance in the Seventh Circuit in 2011 as well, as part of a protest he organized in Chicago during the 2006 Gay Games (*Marcavage v. City of Chicago*, 659 F.3d 626). He alleged that he was restricted from entering three areas during the Games because he did not obtain a permit. The court threw out two of the three complaints and remanded the third back to the lower court to evaluate whether Marcavage's First Amendment rights had been violated. In 2012, Marcavage also showed up at the Republican National Convention in New York to protest, and he was arrested after failing to comply with police orders to move to a place where protests were approved (*Marcavage v. City of New York*, 689 F.3d 98, 2012). In upholding the arrest, the Second Circuit said the restrictions were content neutral and narrowly tailored, and "the record amply establishes non-security reasons for banning protesters from occupying a crowded sidewalk" as well as sufficient security reasons.

Similarly, the D.C. Circuit struck down as overbroad the rules governing protests in national parks in 2010 (*Boardley v. U.S. Dept. of the Interior*, 615 F.3d 508). Michael Boardley and his group distributed free religious tracts in a "free speech zone" in Mount Rushmore National Park, and they were told by a ranger that they needed a permit; they left and applied for one but never received a response. When he filed suit, he then received the permit, but continued the suit on the grounds that the speech rules were too broad. The appellate court agreed: "The Constitution does not tolerate regulations that, while serving their purported aims, prohibit a wide range of activities that do not interfere with the Government's objectives," the court wrote. The court listed a number of speech acts, ranging from Girl Scout meetings to teachers taking students on field trips, that would require permits even though they do not interfere with government interests.

On the other hand, a regulation prohibiting chalking messages on the street in front of the White House was found to be constitutional because it was intended to prohibit defacement of public and private property in a content-neutral way, said the D.C. Circuit in 2011 (*Mahoney v. Doe*, 642 F.3d 1112). Rev. Patrick Mahoney requested permission for a chalk demonstration against abortion in 2008. He was allowed to bring banners and signs but was prohibited from chalking 1600 Pennsylvania Avenue NW, in front of the White House. The appellate court said that the chalking ban was a reasonable time, place, and manner restriction because it was content neutral and served an important government interest in preserving the aesthetics of public property. Judge Brett Kavanaugh, concurring in the judgment, further noted, "No one has a First Amendment right, for example, to spray-paint the Washington Monument or smash the windows of a police car."

How about silent dancing in the Jefferson Memorial rotunda? No, said the D.C. Circuit in 2011. Mary Brooke Oberwetter and her friends refused to stop "silent expressive dancing" inside the Jefferson Memorial, saying they were observing Thomas Jefferson's birthday. She was arrested under National Park Service regulations that prohibit demonstrations without a permit. The court pointed out that of course she could dance to honor Jefferson, but "the question this case presents is whether she had the right to perform her dance inside the Jefferson Memorial." The court said she did not, because the Jefferson Memorial is "a space with a solemn commemorative purpose that is incompatible with the full range of free expression that is permitted in public forums" (*Oberwetter v. Hilliard*, 639 F.3d 545).

In 2012, President Obama signed the Federal Restricted Buildings and Grounds Improvement Act of 2011. The law criminalizes impeding or disrupting the conduct of government business or official functions in or near "any restricted buildings or grounds"—including the White House and vice president's residence, anywhere the president or others protected by Secret Service are or will be temporarily visiting, or an event of national significance. Critics call it the "anti-Occupy law" and allege that the breadth and vagueness of the law may well render it unconstitutional.

In addition, the Supreme Court issued regulations for its building in June 2013. The language says: "No person shall engage in a demonstration within the Supreme Court building and grounds. The term 'demonstration' includes demonstrations, picketing, speechmaking, marching, holding vigils or religious services and all other like forms of conduct that involve the communication or expression of views or grievances, engaged in by one or more persons, the conduct of which is reasonably likely to draw a crowd or onlookers."

Newsrack ordinances. Another First Amendment issue concerns newsracks on public property. Many states and cities have adopted laws regulating the size and placement of newsstands on sidewalks, for instance. Some banned newsracks altogether. This has produced a variety of conflicting court rulings. In 1988, the Supreme Court squarely addressed this issue for the first time, and in so doing handed the news media a significant victory.

In *City of Lakewood v. Plain Dealer Publishing Co.* (486 U.S. 750), the Court voted 4-3 to overturn a Lakewood, Ohio, ordinance that gave the town's mayor broad discretion to grant or deny publishers' requests to place newsstands on public sidewalks. The Court ruled that newsracks are a legitimate form of expression in a public forum protected by the First Amendment, and a city may not base decisions to grant or deny newsrack space on the content of the publication. The mayor of Lakewood, a suburb of Cleveland, rejected the *Cleveland Plain Dealer's* request to place newsracks at 18 locations in the town. The newspaper argued that the decision was arbitrary and violated the First Amendment. Writing for the majority, Justice William Brennan acknowledged that a city could flatly prohibit all newsracks, but he said a city may not ban some while permitting others based on arbitrary decisions about their content.

In 1993, the Supreme Court went even further in upholding the right to distribute literature in newsracks on public property. In *Cincinnati v. Discovery Network* (507 U.S. 410), the Court said the city of Cincinnati could not flatly ban newsracks for commercial literature while allowing newspaper vending machines. Voting 6-3, the Court rejected the city's contention that the free flyers could be banned because they were merely commercial speech. The Court ruled that commercial speech enjoys considerable First Amendment protection and cannot be banned by a government agency unless the agency has a reasonable basis for doing so. The Court rejected Cincinnati's argument that banning the 62 commercial newsracks would enhance the appearance of the city at a time when the city was not acting to remove 2,000 newspaper stands. The commercial speech aspects of this case are discussed in Chapter Thirteen.

Numerous lower courts have addressed these issues. In 2010, for instance, the Fourth Circuit found a public airport's total ban on newsracks to be a significant harm to newspaper publishers' protected expression (*News and Observer v. Raleigh-Durham Airport Auth.*, 597 F.3d 570). In 2012, the Fifth Circuit upheld the city of Houston's newsrack ordinance against a First Amendment challenge, saying it was content-neutral and tailored to meet city aesthetic concerns (*Lauder, Inc. v. City of Houston*, 670 F.3d 664).

City council meetings. The First Amendment does not protect unlawful conduct such as acts of intimidation, violence, arson, or trespass. But the line is not bright between free expression and disruptive behavior at government meetings. The Ninth Circuit in 2010 overturned a city council's expulsion of a man who gave the Nazi salute at a council meeting. Robert Norse, a homeless advocate, performed the salute at two Santa Cruz city council meetings and was ejected. A panel of the Ninth Circuit found that the ejections did not violate Norse's rights because his salutes were not "on account of any permissible expression of a point of view" but rather in response to the council enforcing its own rules. The Ninth Circuit reheard the case *en banc* and ruled for Norse on procedural grounds, and the Supreme Court denied *cert.* Norse lost in a federal jury trial in 2012, and his appeal for a new trial was rejected in 2013. But part of another Southern California city council's policy was rejected in 2012 as overbroad in *Acosta v. City of Costa Mesa* (694 F.3d 960). Benito Acosta was ejected from a Costa Mesa city council meeting because, he alleged, he expressed an opinion contrary to the mayor's. The Ninth Circuit found the city council policy, which included a prohibition on "disorderly, insolent, or disruptive behavior" to include a significant amount of "non-disruptive, protected speech." Instead of being limited to only actual disturbances, the policy, the court said, was facially overbroad.

Prison inmates. What about access to prison inmates? The Ninth Circuit addressed the question in 2011 in *Hrdlicka v. Reniff* (631 F.3d 1044). Ray Hrdlicka wanted to distribute his magazine, *Crime, Justice & America*, free but unsolicited, to prison inmates in California county jails. Several jails had policies that did not allow the distribution. Relying on a test from an earlier Supreme Court case (*Turner v. Safley*, 482 U.S. 78, 1987), the district court had issued summary judgment in favor of the jails. But a divided panel of the Ninth Circuit said that the *Turner* test was more nuanced than the district court had thought and reversed and remanded the case; the fact that the publication was not solicited by the prisoners did not, for the majority, matter: "A First Amendment interest in distributing and receiving information does not depend on a recipient's prior request for that information."

Many of these cases discussed above generally involve the acts of government agencies that attempted to control the dissemination of ideas in public forums or by door-to-door canvassing. Is the rule different if the activity occurs in a company-owned town or a private shopping center?

Access to Private Places

The Supreme Court first addressed the question of literature distribution on private property in a 1946 case, *Marsh v. Alabama* (326 U.S. 501). The case arose in Chickasaw, Alabama, a company town owned by Gulf Shipbuilding. The distribution of literature without permission of the town's authorities was forbidden. The case arose when a Jehovah's Witness tried to pass out tracts there. She was told that permission was required before solicitation was allowed, and she would not be given permission. She was ordered to leave, and when she refused she was prosecuted for trespassing.

Even though the entire town was privately owned, the high court stood by its earlier decisions in the *Marsh* case. Noting that for all practical purposes this company town was a city, the Court applied the same rules to it as had been applied to other cities. The Court pointed out that the town was in fact open to the public and was immediately adjacent to a four-lane public highway. Even though the streets were privately owned, the public used them as if they were public streets.

Shopping centers. More than 20 years later, the Supreme Court applied the same kind of logic to a private shopping center in *Amalgamated Food Employees Local 590 v. Logan Valley Plaza* (391 U.S. 308, 1968). This case involved union picketing, which had been forbidden on shopping center premises. The union challenged this rule and won.

The Supreme Court compared the private shopping center to the private town in *Marsh* and said the same right to distribute literature existed here. However, the Court said a factor in its decision was that the case involved a labor dispute to which a merchant in the shopping center was a party. The Court did not say whether the First Amendment would have applied if there had not been this close relationship between the picketing and the merchant. That question was addressed by the Supreme Court in 1972 in *Lloyd Corp. v. Tanner* (407 U.S. 551). In that case there was no relationship between the material being distributed and any merchant in a shopping center. This decision allowed a large shopping center in Portland, Oregon, to ban anti–Vietnam War protesters who wanted to pass out literature.

In the years between the *Logan Valley* and *Lloyd* decisions, the Court backed away from previous rulings about literature distribution on private property. In 1976 the Supreme Court came full circle, expressly reversing the *Logan Valley* decision as it decided another shopping center case, *Hudgens v. NLRB* (424 U.S. 507). This case involved warehouse employees of the Butler Shoe Company who were on strike. When they picketed a Butler store in an Atlanta shopping center, the center's management ordered them out of the mall. The National Labor Relations Board held this to be an unfair labor practice, and the shopping center owner appealed. The *Hudgens* majority made it clear that there is no longer any constitutional right to distribute literature at a private shopping center, even if the literature specifically involves a labor dispute with a merchant doing business there. The Court said that, if First and Fourteenth Amendment rights are involved, the content of the material should be irrelevant; it shouldn't matter whether the literature has anything to do with the business being conducted at the shopping center or not. Whatever the subject matter of the literature, there is no constitutional right to distribute it at a private shopping center, the *Hudgens* majority ruled.

In 1980, the Supreme Court made another sharp turn in its circuitous route through this area of law in the case of *PruneYard Shopping Center v. Robins* (447 U.S. 74). This case presented the conservative majority on the Supreme Court with a classic confrontation between private property rights and states' rights, two causes that have sometimes been rallying cries of conservatives. At a shopping center near San Jose, California, a group of high school students tried to distribute literature opposing a United Nations resolution against "Zionism." They were refused permission, and they sued in California's state courts. The state supreme court said that the California Constitution provides a broader guarantee of free expression than the federal Constitution. The California court said there is a right to distribute literature in private shopping centers in California, even if no such right is guaranteed by the federal Constitution. The center's owners appealed to the U.S. Supreme Court, contending that this ruling denied their property and due process rights under the federal Constitution. The respondents replied, of course, in states' rights terms, asserting the right of a state to afford its citizens more free speech rights than the federal Constitution mandates. In a 7-1 opinion, Justice William Rehnquist chose states' rights over property rights, ruling that the California Supreme Court decision violated no federal right of the shopping center owners that was as important as a state's right to define freedom for its citizens. Rehnquist said the U.S. Supreme Court's earlier rulings on access to shopping centers were not intended to "limit the authority of the state to exercise its police power or its sovereign right to adopt in its own Constitution individual liberties more expansive than those conferred by the Federal Constitution."

In short, the Supreme Court affirmed California's right to create broader rights than the federal Constitution requires. The effect of the *PruneYard* decision is to leave it up to other state legislatures and courts to decide whether to grant literature distribution rights in private places similar to those recognized in California. In the years since the *PruneYard* decision, the highest courts in a few other states have recognized at least a limited right to engage in various forms of free expression at private shopping malls. These decisions have been based on several different legal grounds, including general free expression provisions in state constitutions and the right to circulate petitions for ballot measures, also recognized in some state constitutions.

Las Vegas Strip. In Nevada, a major legal controversy has involved literature distribution and picketing on the heavily used sidewalks along the Las Vegas Strip.

When the iconic street was widened in the early 1990s, local authorities allowed several large hotels to retain ownership of the new sidewalks as their private property. Hotel owners then banned leafletting on the new sidewalks for "erotic" entertainment, arguing that as private property, the sidewalks are not a public forum. The county also restricted commercial leafletting along the Strip in general. In 2001, a divided Nevada Supreme Court upheld the right of the casinos to ban leafletting for outcall services and similar businesses. Three justices joined in an opinion saying the sidewalks are not a public forum. Two others said that even if the sidewalks are a public forum, the leafletting in question is not protected by the First Amendment because it represents a commercial message for an apparently illegal activity (*S.O.C. v. The Mirage*, 23 P.3d 243, 2001). However, the hotel owners quickly learned that it wouldn't be that easy to control the privatized, once-public sidewalks. Two months later the Ninth Circuit held that the sidewalks along the Strip are in fact a public forum to which the First Amendment applies (*Venetian Casino Resort v. Local Joint Executive Board of Las Vegas*, 257 F.3d 937). In a case involving picketing by a labor union, the court rejected The Venetian's attempt to render the sidewalks off-limits to free expression. The U.S. Supreme Court declined to hear the hotel's appeal, leaving the Ninth Circuit decision as a binding precedent and protecting the right to engage in traditional First Amendment activities such as union picketing along the Strip. In 2004, local officials, casinos owners, and civil libertarians reached an agreement that would allow many forms of free expression on Las Vegas Strip sidewalks, including the privatized ones in front of leading hotels on the Strip.

Mormon Temple Square. Another controversy concerning privatized once-public sidewalks arose in Salt Lake City. In 2002, the Tenth Circuit held that the sidewalks along a recently closed portion of Main Street in Salt Lake between the Mormon Temple Square and the church's administrative complex is still a public forum. Ruling in *First Unitarian Church et al. v. Salt Lake City Corp.* (308 F.3d 1114), the court held that the Church of Jesus Christ of Latter-day Saints could not ban expressive activities on the sidewalks even though the city sold the street to the church. After buying that block of Main Street, the church converted it into an "ecclesiastical park." The city retained a pedestrian easement to ensure that the sidewalks would remain open to the public. The church left the sidewalks open but banned traditional free-expression activities such as leafletting, soliciting, picketing, and demonstrating. The ban was challenged by local organizations, backed by the ACLU. The court agreed, concluding that the area within the public sidewalk easement retained its status as a free-speech zone: "The city cannot create a 'First Amendment-free zone.'"

Later the city and the church reached an agreement under which the city abandoned the public sidewalk easement altogether, allowing the church to control or forbid expressive activities there, while the city received two acres of land elsewhere in return. The church agreed to build a $5 million recreation center on the two acres. That arrangement was upheld by the Tenth Circuit (*Utah Gospel Mission v. Salt Lake City Corp.*, 425 F.3d 1249, 2005).

Signage. Still another aspect of the problem of First Amendment rights on private property led to an important Supreme Court decision in 1994: the question of local ordinances that forbid property owners to place signs containing political messages on their own property. In *City of Ladue v. Gilleo* (512 U.S. 43), the Court overturned an ordinance in Ladue, Missouri (a suburb of St. Louis) that barred almost all signs in the front yards of private homes. The case arose when a Ladue woman, Margaret Gilleo, put up a sign in her yard protesting the Persian Gulf War in 1990. It was stolen, so she put up another sign. Someone knocked that sign down, and she reported this vandalism to police. She was then told her signs were illegal, and she sued, alleging that the city was violating her First Amendment rights. After a lower court ordered the city not to enforce its sign ordinance, Gilleo placed a sheet of paper in a window that read, "For Peace in the Gulf." That, too, was probably a violation of Ladue's rules, but it didn't matter: the Supreme Court ruled that the town's strict sign ordinance was unconstitutional. The court said this ban on almost all yard signs precluded an entire category of speech, thereby violating the First Amendment. The court conceded that Ladue could ban most commercial signs in front yards (but not "for sale" signs: see Chapter Thirteen for a discussion of that issue). However, this ordinance went too far by censoring all political and religious messages that might be conveyed in yard signs.

The Supreme Court overturned the Ninth Circuit's finding that a town's sign code was content-neutral in 2015 (*Reed v. Town of Gilbert*, 576 U.S. 155). Writing for the majority, Justice Clarence Thomas applied strict scrutiny to the town's sign policy and found it wanting. Three of the categories exempted from display without a license were "ideological signs," "political signs," and "temporary directional signs relating to a qualifying event." Pastor Clyde Reed and the Good News Community Church wished to advertise Sunday services at locations where they were to be held (the church had no building of its own). Church members put up such signs early on Saturdays and removed them midday on Sundays. But this ran afoul of the sign policy. The Ninth Circuit said that the sign code was content-neutral. However, Thomas wrote, the code "is content based on its face. It defines 'Temporary Directional Signs' on the basis of whether a sign conveys the message of directing the public to church or some other 'qualifying event.' It defines 'Political Signs' on the basis of whether a sign's message is 'designed to influence the outcome of an election.' And it defines 'Ideological Signs' on the basis of whether a sign 'communicat[es] a message or ideas' that do not fit within the Code's other categories." Thus, the code must undergo strict scrutiny. Because the town's interests were at best weak (not compelling), and the code "hopelessly underinclusive," it was deemed a violation of the First Amendment.

Access to Parades and Organizations

Another issue that stirred controversy in recent years has been whether privately sponsored parades and fairs on public property are First Amendment forums open to all viewpoints, or whether the sponsors have a First Amendment right to decide who will participate.

Gays in parades. A focal point of this debate has been the efforts of gay groups to participate in St. Patrick's Day parades. In New York, the Ancient Order of Hibernians, a Roman

Catholic fraternal organization, sponsors the nation's oldest formal St. Patrick's Day parade: it was first held in 1762. Based on their religious beliefs, the Hibernians have refused to allow gay and lesbian groups to join the parade, which annually attracts as many as 150,000 participants and two million spectators. In 1993, a federal judge ruled that the Hibernians have a First Amendment right to exclude groups with whom they disagree.

On the other hand, the largest St. Patrick's Day parade in Boston has been sponsored by veterans' groups rather than a religious group, and in 1994 the veterans were ordered by a Massachusetts court to include a gay and lesbian group in the parade under a state law guaranteeing gay men and lesbians equal access to public facilities. The Massachusetts Supreme Court upheld the lower court's order, but in 1995 the U.S. Supreme Court disagreed and ruled in favor of the veterans. In *Hurley v. Irish-American Gay, Lesbian and Bisexual Group of Boston* (515 U.S. 557), the Court ruled unanimously that the veterans' groups have a First Amendment right to choose which other groups they will include in their parade. Justice David Souter said the state could not use its public accommodations law to force a private group to admit anyone with whom it disagreed to a parade. He wrote, "One important manifestation of the principle of free speech is that one who chooses to speak may also decide what not to say." Souter noted the "enlightened purpose" of the public accommodations law (to prevent discrimination against gay men and lesbians), but said the state cannot force a private organization to alter its own message. Souter also added that individual gay men and lesbians are entitled to march in the parade as members of any group that is admitted to the parade, and that gay men and lesbians are certainly free to conduct their own parade on city streets (and presumably, to exclude veterans' groups if they wish).

Gay scoutmasters. A related issue has arisen concerning groups such as the Boy Scouts of America, an organization that has traditionally barred gays from being scoutmasters. Do state laws guaranteeing equal access to public facilities or forbidding discrimination against lesbians and gay men by business enterprises apply to private organizations? How can those laws be reconciled with a private organization's First Amendment freedom of association rights? Also, do these laws require the Boy Scouts to admit members who are unwilling to take the Scouts' oath affirming a belief in God?

The U.S. Supreme Court ruled on this issue in a 2000 decision, *Boy Scouts of America v. Dale* (530 U.S. 640). The 5-4 majority ruled that the Boy Scouts may exclude gays as troop leaders, declaring that a private organization has the right to set its own moral code and espouse a viewpoint. In so ruling, the high court overturned a New Jersey Supreme Court decision that said the Boy Scouts had to allow gay scoutmasters under that state's law banning discrimination in public accommodations. Writing for the Court, Chief Justice William Rehnquist said the Boy Scouts have a First Amendment right to freedom of association, including the right to include or exclude persons based on their beliefs or their sexual orientation. Thus, the Scouts could exclude James Dale, a one-time Eagle Scout and assistant scoutmaster who was dismissed after Scout leaders learned he was gay. "It appears that homosexuality has gained greater societal acceptance. But this is scarcely an argument for denying First Amendment protection to those who refuse to accept those views," Rehnquist wrote.

Abortion Clinics and Military Funerals

Congress, the courts, and state and local governments have all become involved in the emotion-charged debate not only about abortion itself but also about the methods used by demonstrators who oppose abortions. There are several related questions involved. Under what circumstances may demonstrations near medical clinics be restricted? When may demonstrations that target the homes of doctors and other clinic workers be restricted?

The government has latitude to regulate protests and picketing using content-neutral, reasonable time, place, and manner regulations. This section will focus on two key areas of Supreme Court law from cases involving protesters at abortion clinics and military funerals.

Abortion clinics. The activities of protesters near abortion clinics led to four U.S. Supreme Court decisions, all of which required the Court to balance the rights of protesters against those of clinic patrons and staff.

In a 1994 case, the Supreme Court upheld a Florida court's injunction ordering demonstrators to stay 36 feet away from the entrances to an abortion clinic (*Madsen v. Women's Health Center,* 512 U.S. 753). In that case, the Supreme Court's 6-3 majority, in an opinion by Chief Justice William Rehnquist, said the 36-foot buffer zone was not an undue restriction on demonstrators' First Amendment rights. However, the Supreme Court overturned several other parts of the Florida court order, including a provision that barred demonstrators from approaching patients anywhere within 300 feet of the clinic. The Court also overturned a portion of the Florida order that banned demonstrations within 300 feet of the residences of clinic workers. Rehnquist said that was too broad a restriction on the First Amendment rights of anti-abortion demonstrators, although a smaller buffer zone around workers' homes, coupled with limits on the time and duration of residential demonstrations, might be acceptable. The Supreme Court also overturned a portion of the Florida court order that prohibited demonstrators from displaying "images observable" by patients in the clinic. Rehnquist said the complete ban on signs was overly broad, although a ban on signs carrying threats might be acceptable. On the other hand, Rehnquist's opinion upheld a part of the Florida order that banned excessive noise during abortion protests.

In 1997, the Supreme Court went further to protect the First Amendment rights of anti-abortion demonstrators, overturning a New York judge's order that required them to stay 15 feet away from clinic patrons and workers. Ruling in *Schenck v. Pro-Choice Network* (519 U.S. 357), an 8-1 majority of the Court held that demonstrators have a right to approach patrons on public sidewalks. The Court overruled the judge's order establishing a 15-foot "floating bubble" around patrons that abortion protesters could not enter. But the Court upheld another part of the judge's order that created a 15-foot no-demonstration zone around clinic entrances. Again writing for the Court, Chief Justice Rehnquist emphasized that picketing, leafletting, and even loud protesting are "classic forms of speech that lie at the heart of the First Amendment." Rehnquist noted that sidewalk protesters have no right to grab, push, or stand in the way of persons going to abortion clinics, but he also said the New York judge's ban on approaching patrons or workers was overly broad: "We strike down the floating buffer zones around people entering and leaving clinics because they burden more speech than is necessary" to protect the free flow of traffic and public safety.

In ruling on all of these specific restrictions on demonstrations, the Supreme Court held that they were *content neutral* (that is, they would apply to everyone, regardless of the issue addressed by demonstrators). Therefore, the restrictions were valid unless they imposed a greater burden on First Amendment freedoms than was necessary to serve a *significant government interest.* The Court's majority concluded that there was a significant government interest in protecting the safety of clinic workers and patients, and in ensuring that they could enter and leave the clinic freely. The Court held that small buffer zones around clinic entrances are sufficient to accomplish those goals, and that larger buffer zones or floating buffer zones around clinic patrons or workers create an undue burden on free expression.

In 2000, however, the Supreme Court *upheld* a Colorado state law that included an eight-foot floating buffer zone. Ruling in *Hill v. Colorado* (530 U.S. 703), the Court's 6-3 majority said the Colorado law was narrowly tailored enough to pass constitutional muster. The law established a 100-foot zone around every health care facility's entrance. Inside that perimeter, no one could distribute leaflets, display signs, or engage in sidewalk counseling within eight feet of another person unless that person consented to being approached. Displaying signs within the perimeter, but not within eight feet of any person, was legal.

After first ruling that the Colorado law was content neutral, the Court held that it was a valid time, place, and manner regulation of speech. The Court noted that protest signs can be read, and normal conversations can occur, at a distance of eight feet. The Court called that distance a "normal conversational distance." The Court said the ban on approaching people does not prevent leafletting because a protester can stand in one place and hand out leaflets as people approach the person doing the leafletting. "This statute simply empowers private citizens entering a health care facility with the ability to prevent a speaker, who is within eight feet and advancing, from communicating a message they do not wish to hear," Justice John Paul Stevens wrote for the Court. In short, the majority in *Hill* said this floating buffer zone is sufficiently different from the one overturned in *Schenck* to be constitutional.

But in 2014, the Court struck down a Massachusetts buffer zone in *McCullen v. Coakley* (573 U.S. 464). The 2007 law had made it a crime for anyone to stand on a public road or sidewalk within 35 feet of any abortion clinic. Anti-abortion protestors had argued that this rule made it difficult for them to counsel women as they approached the clinic. While all nine justices agreed that the law was unconstitutional, they came to no clear consensus as to why. Chief Justice John Roberts wrote the majority opinion, saying that the law does not regulate what is said, but where it is said. Thus, strict scrutiny does not apply. But the law still must be narrowly tailored to meet the government's goals, and it is not.

During the 1990s many cities and states—and eventually Congress—passed laws to curtail demonstrations near clinics where abortions are performed. In 1994, Congress enacted the Freedom of Access to Clinic Entrances (FACE) Act, which prohibits protesters from blocking access to abortion clinics or intimidating patients and employees. First offenses carry fines of up to six months in prison and $10,000 fines. Those convicted of repeated violations of the law could face life imprisonment and fines of up to $250,000.

Almost as soon as the new federal law went into effect, anti-abortion demonstrators challenged it in court. Among other things, they contended that it unduly restricts their First Amendment freedoms and violates the ban on cruel and unusual punishments in the Eighth Amendment by imposing such severe sentences on persons who are doing nothing more than civil rights and antiwar demonstrators did in the 1960s: engaging in civil disobedience as an act of conscience. In 1995, those arguments were rejected in two federal appellate court decisions, *Woodall v. Reno* (47 F.3d 656) and *American Life League v. Reno* (47 F.3d 642). Deciding the cases together, the Fourth Circuit ruled the FACE Act does *not* violate the First Amendment because it targets unprotected acts such as obstructing doorways, not activities protected by the First Amendment such as peaceful picketing.

Anti-abortion images and children. In 2008, the Ninth Circuit held that the First Amendment rights of anti-abortion activists were infringed when they were ordered to leave the site of a middle school they were circling with a truck emblazoned with enlarged images of aborted fetuses. In *Center for Bio-Ethical Reform v. Los Angeles County Sheriff Dept.* (533 F.3d 780), the court said that police violated the First Amendment when they required the activists to remove their truck from an area adjacent to the middle school. There was some disruption to normal school activities, but the court said that it was not acceptable to remove the speakers just when they started to get reactions from their intended audience.

But a Colorado appeals court upheld an injunction that forbid the display of "gruesome" images near a church in *Saint John's Church in the Wilderness v. Scott* (296 P.3d 273, 2012). Protestors had displayed graphic anti-abortion posters near a Denver church. Citing the compelling interest in protecting children from harm from seeing these images, the court said the injunction was narrowly tailored: "identifying the prohibited content as 'gruesome images of mutilated fetuses' is the least restrictive means available to protect young children who are attending worship services."

Abortion providers' homes. What about protests outside private homes? The Supreme Court first addressed the question of whether a town may ban demonstrations near the homes of doctors and other abortion workers in a 1988 case, *Frisby v. Schultz* (487 U.S. 474). In this case the town of Brookfield, Wisconsin, a suburb of Milwaukee, banned demonstrations near private homes after anti-abortion protesters picketed several times in front of a doctor's home. Sandra Schultz and other demonstrators sued Russell Frisby and other officials, charging that the ordinance violated their First Amendment rights. The Court affirmed Brookfield's right to ban targeted picketing at a specific private home. In essence, the majority held that while residential streets in general are a public forum, the space in front of a specific home is not. That means a city must allow protesters to walk down residential streets carrying signs, but if they stop and linger too long near one particular residence, that is not protected by the First Amendment. If a local government wishes to do so, it may forbid targeted picketing at someone's home. The Court based its decision largely on the idea that a person is entitled to a certain amount of privacy and freedom from harassment in his or her own home. In the years since *Frisby v. Schultz* was decided, many cities adopted restrictions on picketing individual homes patterned after the Brookfield ordinance.

Funeral protests. While protests at abortion clinics resulted in many court decisions, so too have protests at funerals—largely as a result of one man.

Fred Phelps (1929–2014) was the leader of the Westboro Baptist Church (WBC) in Topeka, Kansas, an organization comprised largely of his family. For years, they have led public protests over their belief that God hates the United States for its acceptance of homosexuality, and that the Lord is punishing servicemembers by death as a result. In more recent years, they have targeted military funerals for their protests.

Several states have passed laws limiting protests at funerals in response to the WBC activities. At the federal level, the Respect for America's Fallen Heroes Act was passed in 2006 and prohibits protests within 300 feet of the entrance of any cemetery under the control of the National Cemetery Administration from an hour before to an hour after a funeral.

When Missouri passed its law banning protests at funerals, members of the church filed suit, claiming that their First Amendment rights were infringed. In 2008, the Eighth Circuit found that the church would likely prove that even though the Missouri law was content neutral, it was also likely to be overbroad, and enjoined the enforcement of the law, permitting the church's funeral pickets to continue until the law is fully evaluated. In *Phelps-Roper v. Nixon* (545 F.3d 685), the court said that the church "presents a viable argument that those who protest or picket at or near a military funeral wish to reach an audience that can only

FIG. 28.
Shirley Phelps-Roper
of the Westboro
Baptist Church
surrounded by
counterprotestors
in Long Beach,
California,
Feb. 2010.

*Photo by
Christine Amarantus.
Used with permission.*

be addressed at such occasion and to convey to and through such an audience a particular message." The Eighth Circuit's decision conflicts with the Sixth Circuit's 2008 conclusion in *Phelps-Roper v. Strickland* (529 F.3d 356), where that court said that a similar Ohio funeral protest law was content neutral, sufficiently narrowly tailored, and served an important governmental interest; the Supreme Court declined to hear an appeal in *Nixon.*

The church continued to appear in court to challenge funeral protest ordinances. Finally, the Supreme Court stepped into the fray in 2011.

In *Snyder v. Phelps* (562 U.S. 443) the Supreme Court ruled 8-1 that the WBC's funeral picketing activities and website (www.godhatesfags.com) were protected under the First Amendment. Albert Snyder's son, Marine Lance Cpl. Matthew A. Snyder, was killed in Iraq in the line of duty, and the members of the church picketed his Maryland funeral. The picketers complied with regulations and police directions, and Snyder did not see the protest until after the funeral when it was shown on local television.

Chief Justice John Roberts wrote that the content of the signs displayed by WBC protestors related to matters of public, rather than private, interest, as those signs focused on political and moral questions, and the protest was not intended as a private assault on the Snyder family, as WBC had been protesting funerals for some time. Because the WBC members followed all police rules as to where they protested and did not interfere with the funeral itself, the distress felt by the family was a result of the content of the signs. "What Westboro said, in the whole context of how and where it chose to say it, is entitled to 'special protection' under the First Amendment, and that protection cannot be overcome by a jury finding that the picketing was outrageous," wrote Roberts. He wrote:

> Speech is powerful. It can stir people to action, move them to tears of both joy and sorrow, and—as it did here—inflict great pain. On the facts before us, we cannot react to that pain by punishing the speaker. As a Nation we have chosen a different course—to protect even hurtful speech on public issues to ensure that we do not stifle public debate. That choice requires that we shield Westboro from tort liability for its picketing in this case.

Justice Samuel Alito, writing in dissent, pointed out that the WBC could have chosen anywhere in Maryland or Washington, D.C., in which to protest, and the fact that they chose Snyder's funeral made the protest personal and was done to increase publicity. He concluded, "In order to have a society in which public issues can be openly and vigorously debated, it is not necessary to allow the brutalization of innocent victims like [the Snyder family]."

Access and Expression in Polling Places

Several states have laws that forbid campaigning near polling places as well as political expression inside polling places. Some states prohibit the wearing of the wearing of electioneering materials (t-shirts, hats, buttons, stickers) inside polling places. Some states also prohibit activities in polling places such as taking photos. In the digital age, is a ban on selfies a violation of an individual's First Amendment rights?

Apparel bans. The Supreme Court struck down Minnesota's ban on political apparel inside polling places. Several election-reform groups challenged the law after members were delayed in voting by having to remove buttons or t-shirts, even though these materials did not advocate to vote for or against anyone or anything on the ballot. They argued that polling places were public fora. The Eighth Circuit disagreed and found that the policy was viewpoint neutral. However, in 2018, the Supreme Court struck down the Minnesota law (*Minnesota Voters Alliance v. Mansky*, 138 S. Ct. 1876). The Court said polling places are nonpublic forums and that some prohibitions on expression and behavior in polling places are appropriate. However, the Minnesota law banning clothing with "political insignia" was not "reasonable" in light of the broad meanings of the word "political."

Media access. Is there an access right for the media to enter a polling place during an election? There is now a circuit split about that question. The Third Circuit upheld a Pennsylvania law restricting access in 2013 (*PG Publ'g Co. v. Aichele*, 705 F.3d 91). Saying that the media is not "entitled to any greater protection under this [newsgathering] right than is the general public," the court drew an interesting distinction, saying that it was not concerned with limitations on access to a forum, but rather on access to information. Because "the matter here concerns information about government bodies, their processes, and their decisions," the court did not use forum analysis. This decision contrasts with a Sixth Circuit 2004 decision, *Beacon Journal Publ'g Co. Inc. v. Blackwell* (389 F.3d 683), in which that court used traditional forum analysis and ruled that the state was required to allow media access to polling places so long as the access doesn't interfere with voting.

Ballot selfies. What about selfies in polling places? One survey found that at least 35 states had laws prohibiting photographs in polling places. Many of these laws were motivated by protecting the security of polling places and the privacy of voting. Several individuals have filed lawsuits challenging these laws. Federal courts struck down a New Hampshire law that banned digital photography of marked ballots. The state said the law was necessary to avoid vote buying or voter coercion. In *Rideout v. Gardner* (123 F. Supp. 3d 218, 2015), a federal judge ruled that the law was an invalid content-based law that failed to meet strict scrutiny standards. The judge said the state failed to show that vote buying was a significant problem that a selfie ban would in fact solve. The First Circuit of Appeals agreed with the outcome, finding the law a violation of the First Amendment (*Rideout v. Gardner*, 838 F.3d 65, 2016). "There is an increased use of social media and ballot selfies in particular in service of political speech by voters," the Court wrote. "A ban on ballot selfies would suppress a large swath of political speech, which 'occupies the core of protection afforded by the First

Amendment.'" The court, even applying intermediate scrutiny standards, found the state's justification did not serve a significant government interest nor was it narrowly tailored to that interest.

■ OTHER RELATED QUESTIONS

The twentieth century was a time of government regulation, an era when many forms of activity were brought under government supervision and regulation for the first time. When the targeted activity involved the communication of ideas or information, however, the regulation has often been challenged as a violation of the First Amendment. This has forced the nation's courts—and ultimately the Supreme Court—to look at government control of expressive activities of many kinds. This section summarizes some key questions and precedents.

False Speech

Can a person be punished for publishing or saying things he or she knows to be false but that aren't defamatory? Does the First Amendment protect liars? In recent years there have been a number of cases, including two high court decisions, dealing with false speech.

Stolen Valor Act. In 2005, Congress passed the Stolen Valor Act. This act criminalizes the false representation of having been awarded "any decoration or medal authorized by Congress for the Armed Forces of the United States, any of the service medals or badges awarded to the members of such forces, the ribbon, button, or rosette of any such badge, decoration, or medal, or any colorable imitation of such item." Courts' reactions to the law were mixed. The Ninth Circuit struck down the act by a 2-1 vote as overbroad, while the Tenth Circuit upheld it.

The U.S. Supreme Court granted *cert* in the Ninth Circuit case and overturned the Stolen Valor Act by a 6-3 vote in 2012 (*U.S. v. Alvarez*, 567 U.S. 709). Calling Xavier Alvarez's lies "but a pathetic attempt to gain respect that eluded him," Justice Anthony Kennedy wrote that there is no "general exception to the First Amendment for false statements." Quoting Justice Oliver Wendell Holmes' dissent in *Abrams v. U.S.* (see Chapter Two), that "the best test of truth is the power of the thought to get itself accepted in the competition of the market," Kennedy said that the power of the American people to ferret out and refute false claims like those covered in the Act was preferable. "Truth needs neither handcuffs nor a badge for its vindication," he added. Justice Samuel Alito, joined by Justices Antonin Scalia and Clarence Thomas, dissented. Alito accused the majority of a departure from "a long line of cases recognizing that the right to free speech does not protect false factual statements that inflict real harm and serve no legitimate interest."

In two related cases, federal courts upheld a law that criminalizes knowingly wearing unauthorized military uniforms or insignia. In *U.S. v. Hamilton* (699 F.3d 356, 2012), the Fourth Circuit said, "We conclude that the insignia statutes are drawn sufficiently narrowly to satisfy the 'most exacting scrutiny' standard. By preventing the unauthorized wearing of military uniforms and honors, the insignia statutes seek to ensure that the individuals displaying these honors to the general public are those who actually have received such honors." The Ninth Circuit agreed in *U.S. v. Perelman* (695 F.3d 866, 2012), saying that the law "reaches only intentionally deceptive acts, thus limiting the statute's reach to a narrow range of conduct similar to that prohibited by impersonation statutes."

Political campaigns. The Stolen Valor Act is not the only instance of knowingly false speech to be punishable under state or federal law, and the outcomes are decidedly varied. Several cases have struck down laws punishing false speech in political campaigns.

The Eighth Circuit relied on the Ninth Circuit's analysis in *Alvarez* to overturn a part of the Minnesota Fair Campaign Practices Act that criminalizes knowingly making a false statement about a proposed ballot initiative. The court applied strict scrutiny and said, "Prior decisions that have discussed the worthlessness of speech categorically excepted from the First Amendment are descriptive not prescriptive—they tell us something about the speech that is exempt but not about what other types of speech may be exempt from First Amendment scrutiny" (*281 Care Committee v. Arneson*, 638 F.3d 621, 2011). The Washington Supreme Court in 2007 overturned a state law that allowed a government agency to punish political candidates for making what the agency deemed to be false statements in campaign materials. Marilyn Rickert, a Green Party candidate for state legislature, was fined $1,000 for making statements determined to be false about a candidate. She challenged the fine. In *Rickert v. Public Disclosure Commission* (168 P.3d 826, 2007), the 5-4 majority said, "The notion that the government, rather than the people, may be the final arbiter of truth in political debate is fundamentally at odds with the First Amendment." The dissenters said the decision was an "invitation to lie with impunity."

In *Susan B. Anthony List v. Driehaus* (573 U.S. 149), the Supreme Court in 2014 unanimously said that state laws making it a crime to issue false statements during a campaign are open to constitutional challenge. Sixteen states have such laws, and the Ohio law (up to six months in jail and a fine of up to $5,000) was at issue here, by Susan B. Anthony List (SBA), a pro-life group that had criticized members of Congress who voted for the Patient Protection and Affordable Care Act ("Obamacare"). Steve Driehaus, a former Congressman, brought suit because an SBA press release said he had "voted FOR taxpayer-funded abortion." After the Supreme Court ruled that the Susan B. Anthony List had standing to sue, the Sixth Circuit Court of Appeals in 2016 struck down the law based on the *Alvarez* precedent. The Court said the Ohio statute did not meet the standards of strict scrutiny. "Ohio's political false-statements laws are content-based restrictions targeting core political speech that are not narrowly tailored to serve the state's admittedly compelling interest in conducting fair elections," the Sixth Circuit said (*Susan B. Anthony List v. Driehaus*, 814. F.3d 466).

Deepfakes. Collins Dictionary created a new entry for "deepfakes" in 2019—defined as digitally altered videos depicting real people doing and saying things they did not do. Because people tend to believe audio and video recordings, experts say sophisticated deepfake videos are more pernicious than other types of disinformation. Several states passed laws prohibiting different kinds of deepfakes. At least four states have passed laws targeting fake sex videos, in which people's faces are digitally transposed in sex scenes, Deepfake pornography is by far the most common form of deepfake videos, according to experts. (This would be an example of "revenge porn," discussed further in Chapter 10.)

Some states, including California and Texas, also passed laws targeting political deepfakes. The California law prohibits the distribution of "materially deceptive audio or visual media" done with "actual malice" and "with the intent to injure a candidate's reputation or to deceive a voter in voting for or against a candidate." California's law prohibits deepfakes 60 days prior to an election, while Texas law prohibits deepfakes 30 days before an election. The California law requires that videos subject to the law must falsely appear to be authentic and that they cause reasonable people to have a "fundamentally different understanding" than the original, unedited footage. The law exempts materials that are identified as having been manipulated, videos shared by news organizations, and videos that constitute satire or parody. Candidates subject to deepfakes can seek injunctions barring distribution, and they can seek damages, attorney's fees, and court costs. Lawmakers in other states, as well as in Congress, have also introduced bills prohibiting deepfakes. Because these laws create prior restraints for political speech, some experts say the violate First Amendment rights of the video's creators. It remains to be seen whether these laws will be held to be constitutional upon court challenges.

Government Employee Speech

Should government employees have the same First Amendment rights as other citizens? What about employees of agencies such as the Central Intelligence Agency (CIA), who have access to government secrets and are required to sign agreements that they will not disclose these secrets? What about other government employees—people who have no particular access to government secrets?

Problematic books. A major challenge to the national security classification system came from two former employees of the CIA, both of whom published books on their CIA experiences. In both instances, the agency attempted to censor the ex-employees' writings under a provision of their employment contracts that prohibited them from publishing information they gained as CIA agents without the agency's prior approval. Both employees said these provisions violated their First Amendment rights.

The first case, *U.S. v. Marchetti* (466 F.2d 1309, 1972), arose after Victor L. Marchetti left the CIA and published a book and a magazine article critical of CIA activities. When the agency learned he was about to publish another book, it got a court order temporarily halting the project. After a secret trial (much of the testimony was classified), the court ordered Marchetti to submit everything he might write about the CIA to the agency for approval. Marchetti appealed that decision, but it was largely affirmed by the U.S. Court of Appeals.

However, the appellate court said the CIA could only censor classified information, and after further legal maneuvering a district court allowed the agency to censor only 27 of 166 passages in the new book that the agency wanted to suppress.

Although the U.S. Supreme Court refused to review the *Marchetti* case, in 1980 it did rule on a similar case, *Snepp v. U.S.* (444 U.S. 507). Former CIA agent Frank Snepp resigned in 1976 and wrote a book alleging CIA ineptness in Vietnam. He did not submit it for prior CIA approval, as required by his employment contract. After its publication, the U.S. government filed a breach of contract suit against Snepp. Snepp contended the contract violated his First and Fifth Amendment rights. A trial court ordered Snepp to turn over all his profits from the book to the government and submit any future manuscripts about the CIA to the agency for prior approval. An appellate court reversed that ruling in part, prompting the Supreme Court to hear the case.

The Supreme Court reinstated the trial court's order against Snepp without even hearing full arguments from both sides: the Court never let Snepp present his case. But the high court upheld the validity of the contract, ignoring the prior censorship implications of such contracts. The Court said: "He (Snepp) deliberately and surreptitiously violated his obligation to submit all material for prepublication review. Thus, he exposed the classified information with which he had been entrusted to the risk of disclosure."

Focus on...
Is it protected? First Amendment oddities

Courts have construed many activities to have expressive components and thus to be under the First Amendment's purview. Here are a few of the odder freedom of expression questions in the past few years that courts have been asked to address.

FIG. 29. Itinerant preacher, Marshall, Texas, April 1939.

Library of Congress Prints and Photographs Division, [LC-USF33-012122-M2]

Using a shofar to preach on the street. Not in Houston, at least not unless it's a small one. A shofar is "a trumpet-like instrument made from a ram's horn," and David Allen liked to use it in his street preaching. The size of Allen's shofar (six inches in width) ran afoul of Houston's demonstration ordinance, which disallowed objects that "exceed three-quarters inch in their thickest dimension." Because the shofar clearly violated the ordinance, officers had the right to detain Allen, said the Fifth Circuit (*Allen v. Cisneros*, 815 F.3d 239, 2016).

Sending a "strongly worded" political email to a senator. Protected as long as it's not blackmail. Al Gerhart sent an email to his Oklahoma state senator, Cliff Branan, that read: "Get that bill heard or I will make sure you regret not doing it. I will make you the laughing stock of the Senate if I don't hear that this bill will be heard and passed. We will dig into your past, yoru [sic] family, your associates and once we start on you there will be no end to it. This is a promise." Although the state appellate court acknowledged that Gerhart was "somewhat of an irritant" to state lawmakers and that he was "crude and uncivil," his right to correspond with lawmakers in this kind of hyperbolic way was protected. One judge disagreed, saying that the email should be considered blackmail and that it "crosses the line from 'irritant' to criminal conduct" (*Gerhart v. Oklahoma*, 360 P.3d 1194, 2015).

Messing up Grant Park in Chicago and not allowing park staff time alone to clean it up. No. An Illinois appellate court found that Occupy Chicago protestors, when ordered to vacate Grant Park when told they were violating a park safety and use code, were not protected by the First Amendment. The code was content neutral and allowed for the park to be closed for any reason for seven hours each day for maintenance (*City of Chicago v. Alexander*, 46 N.E.3d 1207, 2015).

Exposing another person to HIV without that person's knowledge and consent. Not in Missouri, said the Missouri Supreme Court. Appellant S.F. said it was a denial of her First Amendment rights to have to disclose her HIV status to her sexual partners, one of whom notified authorities. She was convicted of a class A felony, to which her free speech rights were no defense (*Missouri v. S.F.*, 483 S.W.3d 385, 2016).

The *Snepp* case, then, was decided according to the provisions of Snepp's employment contract and would not be applicable to persons who had not signed such contracts. However, thousands of present and former CIA employees are subject to such contracts—and the CIA has now reviewed and censored many other manuscripts written by former employees.

In light of *Snepp*, many former government employees have been entangled in pre-publication review. In 2007, former CIA operative Valerie Plame Wilson and her publisher sued the CIA for forbidding her to publish such basic facts as the dates of her CIA employment in her memoir. Plame became newsworthy because the former top aide to Vice President Dick Cheney, I. Lewis "Scooter" Libby, was convicted of perjury for denying his role in revealing Plame's CIA status to the media after her husband wrote a newspaper column critical of the Bush administration. She lost, even though those dates had been reported online because the government had not declassified them. In 2009, the Second Circuit ruled that the CIA's refusal to allow Wilson to publish information about her possible pre-2002 CIA service, even though the information had been previously publicly disclosed, did not violate the First Amendment (*Wilson v. CIA*, 586 F.3d 171).

Honoraria and political activity. Another controversy over restrictions on the speech rights of government employees occurred in 1989 when Congress amended the Ethics in Government Act to bar not only members of Congress but virtually all federal workers from receiving "honoraria"—payments for writing articles or giving speeches—even if the subject has little to do with their official duties. Few would question the wisdom of telling federal officials they cannot be paid for giving talks about job-related subjects to special interest groups that they regulate. But the federal regulations written to implement the law did not stop there. One Internal Revenue Service worker pointed out that she had been supplementing her $22,000 annual salary by earning about $3,000 a year as a freelance writer. Her articles were about camping and the outdoors, a subject that had nothing to do with her job, but the new rules prohibited her from being paid for her writing. Other workers who wrote or gave talks about subjects such as African-American history, the Quaker religion, and dance performances also objected to the rules. Several lawsuits were filed by government workers who had been paid for writing or speaking about subjects unrelated to their work, contending that they should have the same right as other citizens to be paid for writing and speaking.

In 1995, the Supreme Court ruled on this question in *U.S. v. National Treasury Employees Union* (513 U.S. 454). The Court said the ban on federal employees receiving pay for writing articles or giving speeches was excessively broad and a violation of the First Amendment. The Court's 6-3 majority held that Congress had gone too far by banning payments for speeches and articles not only by senior government officials but also by rank and file employees of the executive branch. The Court ruled that lower-level employees could not be barred from accepting payments for speeches and articles.

In 1993 Congress expanded the free expression rights of federal workers by amending the Hatch Act, which prohibited most partisan political activities by federal employees for more than 50 years. Under the 1993 amendments, most federal workers may now work in political campaigns, do political fund-raising and hold positions in political parties—as long as it's on their own time. Federal workers are still barred from holding partisan elective offices, however. About 85,000 workers in sensitive federal jobs, such as many law enforcement and national security-related positions, are not covered by the 1993 Hatch Act amendments and are still barred from partisan political activities, even on their own time.

Political activity by government employees continues to raise First Amendment questions. In 2016, the Supreme Court ruled that a police officer had a right to challenge a demotion he received as a result of a mistaken belief that he had engaged in political activity in a local mayor's campaign. The officer was demoted after he was seen with a yard sign for a mayoral candidate, and word spread that the officer was overtly supporting the candidate. In fact, the officer was picking up the sign for his bedridden mother. While the First Amendment generally allows government employees to engage in political activity, does a demotion based on false information give rise to a constitutional challenge? In a 6-2 decision, the

Court ruled the officer had a right to challenge his demotion and remanded the case for further proceedings (*Heffernan v. City of Paterson*, 136 S. Ct. 1412, 2016).

Speech acts. Although many public employees now have a right to speak publicly about controversial issues, the First Amendment does not necessarily protect their right to report alleged wrongdoing to superiors inside a government agency. In *Garcetti v. Ceballos* (547 U.S. 410), a 2006 decision, the Supreme Court ruled that the First Amendment does not protect a government attorney who allegedly faced retaliation after reporting suspicions of police misconduct to a supervisor. Writing for a 5-4 majority, Justice Anthony Kennedy said, "We hold that when public employees make statements pursuant to their official duties, the employees are not speaking as citizens for First Amendment purposes, and the Constitution does not insulate their communications from employer discipline." The First Amendment applies if certain conditions are met: the employee is speaking as a private citizen, not as a public employee, and the speech is a matter of public concern.

Then, in 2011, the Court handed down a pair of decisions that provided additional guidance regarding the First Amendment's protections on speech or petition acts by government employees. The first case, *Nevada Comm'n on Ethics v. Carrigan* (564 U.S. 117), saw the Court uphold a Nevada law that prohibited government employees from voting on or debating matters in which they have a conflict of interest. Sparks city council member Michael Carrigan was censured for failing to recuse himself from a vote for a casino project whose developer retained a close friend of Carrigan's. Writing for a unanimous Court, Justice Antonin Scalia noted that voting by a lawmaker should not be considered a personal speech act. "[A] legislator's vote is the commitment of his apportioned share of the legislature's power to the passage or defeat of a particular proposal" and not his own speech act, unlike those of voters, which are their own symbolic speech acts, said Scalia. Moreover, he added, the United States has had a long history of conflict-of-interest rules that require recusal.

In the second 2011 case, *Borough of Duryea v. Guarnieri* (564 U.S. 379), the Court placed additional limits on government employees' First Amendment protections for workplace grievances. Charles Guarnieri filed a union grievance when he was fired as chief of police in Duryea, Pennsylvania, and when he was rehired, orders were issued that governed his return to the position. He argued that the grievance was a petition protected by the First Amendment (by the petition clause, not the free speech clause), and these orders were in retaliation for that protected grievance. The Third Circuit said that the public concern test does not limit public employees' petition clause claims, but the Supreme Court disagreed, ruling unanimously that government retaliation against an employee does *not* create liability under the First Amendment's petition clause unless the petition deals with a public concern.

In 2014, the Court unanimously said that the First Amendment protects a public employee's subpoenaed testimony (*Lane v. Franks*, 573 U.S. 228). Here, Edward Lane, who worked for a community college program, was protected for his testimony in a criminal case examining fraud in that program. But the protection did not extend to personal liability for Lane's firing, because the law was not sufficiently settled. Justice Sonia Sotomayor wrote bluntly for the Court, "[T]he First Amendment protects a public employee who provided truthful sworn testimony, compelled by subpoena, outside the course of his ordinary job responsibilities," calling this speech "speech as a citizen for First Amendment purposes." The case, she said, was "a straightforward application of *Garcetti.*"

Whistleblowers and state laws. *Garcetti* does not affect federal and state laws that protect whistleblowers. However, said the Court, if no such law protects an employee in a particular situation, the First Amendment does not fill the gap. On the other hand, if an employee's allegation of wrongdoing by superiors is not related to the employee's official duties, such speech is still protected by the First Amendment, according to a 2007 Ninth Circuit decision (*Marable v. Nitchman*, 511 F.3d 924). Ken Marable, an engineer for the Washington State Ferry system, complained that his superiors were engaged in corrupt practices that wasted public funds and endangered public safety. He said he faced disciplinary actions and sued, alleging his First Amendment rights had been violated. The court said Marable had a right to pursue his case because his speech had nothing to do with his official duties and had "all the hallmarks that we normally associate with constitutionally protected speech."

State law can also control whether an employee's speech is protected. In *Huppert v. City of Pittsburg* (574 F. 3d 696, 2009), the Ninth Circuit said that a police officer who talks to FBI agents about police corruption outside his normal job and is allegedly punished by the police department for doing so is actually pursuing his official duties, and therefore that speech is not protected. Relying on *Garcetti*, the court said that Ron Huppert's speech "owes its existence to [his] professional responsibilities" and was not protected—even though Huppert had been told by the FBI that his inquiries were not part of his official duties. The court added that police officers' official duties under California law include crime detection and prevention, so Huppert's conversations with the FBI were part of his job.

A related question that often arises among journalists and public relations practitioners is whether government employees can be forbidden to talk to a reporter without first seeking approval of a public affairs officer or other government official. The Second Circuit held that such a requirement violates the First Amendment in *Harman v. City of New York* (140 F.3d 111, 1998). A radio station interviewed a child-welfare worker about the death of a young child. When the interview was aired, the employee was suspended for speaking to the media without first getting approval from New York's Media Relations Office as required by city policy. The worker sued, and the appellate court held that the city could not justify such censorship of government workers. Even though the city contended that the policy did not prevent city employees from speaking to the media, the court rejected it because it allowed city officials to delay until the employee's comments were no longer newsworthy.

The "Like" button. Is clicking "Like" on a Facebook page protected speech? Six employees of the Hampton, Va. sheriffs' office "Liked" the Facebook campaign page of Jim Adams, the sheriff's opponent, before a 2009 election. When the incumbent, B.J. Roberts, won, he let the employees go. The employees sued for retaliation, claiming that the reason they were fired is because they supported Roberts' opponent with a click on the "Like" button on his Facebook page. The district judge said that a "Like" was not really speech.

But the Fourth Circuit overturned in 2013 (*Bland v. Roberts*, 730 F.3d 368). "On the most basic level, clicking on the 'like' button literally causes to be published the statement that the User 'likes' something, which is itself a substantive statement. In the context of a political campaign's Facebook page, the meaning that the user approves of the candidacy whose page is being liked is unmistakable," the court said, adding, "That a user may use a single mouse click to produce that message that he likes the page instead of typing the same message with several individual key strokes is of no constitutional significance."

Interestingly, another government agency is getting involved with social media usage by employees: the National Labor Relations Board (NLRB). As the *New York Times* put it, the NLRB "says workers have a right to discuss work conditions freely and without fear of retribution, whether the discussion takes place at the office or on Facebook." In one NLRB holding of note, *Hispanics United of Buffalo, Inc. and Carlos Ortiz* (Case 03-CA-027872, 2012), in response to one co-worker's allegations that others were not doing their work, several co-workers discussed workload, conditions, and complaints over the weekend on their Face-book pages and were subsequently fired. The NLRB said the firing was unlawful.

Compelled speech and union dues. In recent years, courts have heard First Amendment challenges to laws that require individuals to join unions and pay union dues. Individuals have made arguments that compulsory union dues are a form of compelled speech, requir-ing individuals to pay money to organizations they don't support. Unions have argued that requiring individuals to pay dues for the costs of collective bargaining benefits all workers through "labor peace" that comes from one common bargaining unit, and without compul-sory dues, "free riders" would still benefit from the work of the unions without having to pay their fair share to support the work.

The Supreme Court ruled in 1977 that forcing non-union members of a Detroit public school district to pay for collective bargaining did not violate the First Amendment (*Abood v. Detroit Bd. of Educ.*, 431 U.S. 209). However, as a result of recent litigation, the Supreme Court sent signals that it might be open to revisiting that precedent.

Over three decades later, in 2012, the Court ruled that fee-paying non-union member workers cannot be forced to pay dues to support causes with which they don't agree. In *Knox v. SEIU* (567 U.S. 298), the justices said the First Amendment does not permit a union to make a special assessment without notice and consent of those it affects. "To respect the limits of the First Amendment, the union should have sent out a new notice allowing nonmembers to opt in to the special fee rather than requiring them to opt out," Justice Samuel Alito wrote for the majority. Then, in 2014, in *Harris v. Quinn* (573 U.S. 616), the Court on a 5-4 vote said that the First Amendment does not allow some types of employ-ees (here, home health care providers who didn't want to join a union) to be forced to pay an agency fee. Calling into question the *Abood* precedent, Alito (again writing for the majority) said that "*Abood* failed to appreciate the difference between the core union speech involuntarily subsidized by dissenting public-sector employees and the core union speech involuntarily funded by their counterparts in the private sector." He also declined to expand *Abood's* reach: "If we allowed *Abood* to be extended to those who are not full-fledged public employees, it would be hard to see just where to draw the line."

On the heels of *Knox* and *Harris*, the Supreme Court granted *cert* for its 2015 Term a case in which the constitutionality of requiring government workers to pay fees to support labor union activity would be at issue. Rebecca Friedrichs, a teacher from Orange County, California, filed the lawsuit funded by the Center for Individual Rights, challenging laws that required her to pay monthly dues to the teachers union that represented her in collec-tive bargaining. The case was a direct challenge to *Abood* at its inception, and the lower courts decided it without opinions to clear the way for it to go to the Supreme Court. At oral arguments in January 2016, it seemed that a majority of the Court was ready to strike down mandatory dues payments to public employee unions as a form of "compelled speech" that violates the First Amendment. But then, in February 2016, Justice Antonin Scalia died. A month after his death, the Supreme Court issued a *per curiam* statement affirming the judgment of the Ninth Circuit Court of Appeals by an equally divided Court (*Friedrichs v. California Teachers Assoc.*, 136 S. Ct. 1083, 2016). The appellate court had upheld the union dues requirement, so mandatory union dues for public employees remained in effect in California and in other states with similar laws.

Then, in 2018, another case raising the same question finally made its way to a full Court. This time, Neil Gorsuch had replaced Scalia, and by a 5-4 vote, the majority struck down mandatory union dues and overruled *Abood*. In *Janus v. Am. Fed'n of State, County, & Mun. Employees* (AFSCE) (138 S. Ct. 2448), Justice Alito again wrote for the Court, "We conclude that this arrangement violates the free speech rights of nonmembers by compelling them to subsidize private speech on matters of substantial public concern." He said that freedom of speech "includes both the right to speak freely and the right to refrain from speaking at all," and "the right to eschew association for expressive purposes is likewise protected." In dissent, Justice Elena Kagan was sharply critical. "The majority overthrows a decision entrenched in this nation's law—and in its economic life—for over 40 years," she wrote. "As a result, it prevents the American people, acting through their state and local officials, from making important choices about workplace governance. And it does so by weaponizing the First Amendment, in a way that unleashes judges, now and in the future, to intervene in economic and regulatory policy."

Government Money, Government Views?

Under what circumstances may the government use its money to control what is said by those organizations and individuals who accept that money? The Supreme Court has ruled on this question several times (in abortion speech, in *Rust v. Sullivan*, in Chapter Five, and in arts speech in *NEA v. Finley*, in Chapter Ten).

In 2013, in *Agency for Int'l Dev. v. Alliance for Open Society Int'l* (570 U.S. 205) the Court said that what organizations say that does not align with governmental goals must be paid for with their own money. The Alliance, an organization that combats HIV/AIDS overseas, got funding from the government that came with the requirement that it must be "opposed to 'prostitution and sex trafficking because of the psychological and physical risks they pose for women, men, and children.'" The Alliance said that explicitly opposing prostitution may make host countries less likely to work with them and could result in self-censorship and less ability to carry out its goals. Chief Justice John Roberts, writing for a 6-2 Court (Justice Elena Kagan did not participate), said that the case was "about compelling a grant recipient to adopt a particular belief as a condition of funding." The policy, said Roberts, mandates that the Alliance "pledge allegiance to the Government's policy of eradicating prostitution." And that is in violation of the First Amendment. Justice Antonin Scalia, with Justice Clarence Thomas, dissented, saying that it was common sense that "the Constitution does not prohibit government spending that discriminates against, and injures, points of view to which the government is opposed; every government program which takes a position on a controversial issue does that."

License plates. A "Focus On" box in this chapter contains discussions of state license plate controversies. But in 2015 the Supreme Court settled the question of whether speech on license plates constituted private or governmental speech in *Walker v. Texas Div., Sons of Confederate Veterans, Inc.* (576 U.S. 200). Texas offers for sale over 350 license plate designs, ranging from school logos to Mothers Against Drunk Driving to private organizations. The Sons of Confederate Veterans wanted approved a specialty plate featuring a Confederate flag. The Texas Division of Motor Vehicles Board denied the application, and the Sons appealed. The Fifth Circuit said that license plates were private speech and thus the board engaged in unlawful content-based regulation. But the Supreme Court reversed.

Justice Stephen Breyer, writing for a 5-4 majority, relied on the reasoning in *Pleasant Grove City v. Summum*, discussed later in this chapter. "First, the history of license plates shows

Focus on...
The law of license plates

You might not think that license plates would generate much First Amendment law, but surprisingly, there have been several cases in the appeals courts, and two that made it all the way to the Supreme Court. In *Wooley v. Maynard* (430 U.S. 705, 1977) the Court said that New Hampshire could not require its citizens to display the state motto, "Live Free or Die," on their license plates if they have moral objections to that sentiment. And, as discussed in this chapter, the Supreme Court in 2015 answered the question of whether license plates are government speech in the affirmative in *Walker v. Sons of Confederate Veterans.* But this decision does not mean that all such cases are moot. Here are a few cases from the past on which *Walker* might

FIG. 30. License plates, Ardovino's Desert Crossing, New Mexico.

Photo by Lourdes Cueva Chacón. Used with permission.

shed some light. Which might turn out differently under the Court's *Walker* rationale?

In *Cressman v. Thompson* (719 F.3d 1139, 2013), plaintiff Keith Cressman said the standard Oklahoma license plate image of a Native American shooting an arrow skyward was religious speech he did not want to display. The Tenth Circuit found that Cressman had a "plausible compelled speech claim" and remanded the case.

In 2008, the Seventh Circuit held in *Choose Life Illinois v. White* (547 F.3d 853) that Illinois could constitutionally exclude *all* points of view on abortion from its plates. But in other venues, the outcome was different. In 2004, the Fourth Circuit in *Rose v. Planned Parenthood of SC* (361 F.3d 786) said that South Carolina could not issue "Choose Life" plates without allowing the pro-choice side a similar forum; the same court said the same thing about North Carolina in 2014 (*ACLU of NC v. Tata*, 742 F.3d 563). A federal district court in South Carolina said that a state law requiring "I Believe" license plates violated the constitutional separation of church and state (*Summers v. Adams*, 669 F. Supp. 2d 637, 2009). The Sixth Circuit held in 2006 that Tennessee could issue "Choose Life" but not pro-choice plates in *ACLU of Tenn. v. Bredesen* (441 F.3d 370).

The Eighth Circuit said in 2009 in *Roach v. Stouffer* (560 F.3d 860) that Missouri could not discriminate based on the viewpoint of the speaker when approving applications for specialty plates. The Ninth Circuit agreed in 2008 and said that Arizona had created a public forum in its plates and could not discriminate in that forum in *Ariz. Life Coalition v. Stanton* (515 F.3d 956). The Third Circuit said in 2010 that New Jersey's rejection of the plates may be unconstitutional viewpoint discrimination in *Children First Foundation Inc. v. Legreide* (373 Fed. Appx. 156) and remanded the case. In 2010, the Second Circuit overturned Vermont's ban on plates that referred to religion or deities as unconstitutional viewpoint discrimination (*Byrne v. Rutledge*, 623 F.3d 46). The Supreme Court declined to review any of these decisions.

that, insofar as license plates have conveyed more than state names and vehicle identification numbers, they long have communicated messages from the States," he noted, adding that "Texas license plates are, essentially, government IDs. And issuers of ID 'typically do not permit' the placement on their IDs of 'message[s] with which they do not wish to be associated.'" Texas' ability to control the messages makes the speech on the plates governmental; Texas can choose to promote the various schools its residents attend but need not, for example, allow an anti-schooling plate.

Arts funding. As will be discussed in Chapter Ten, the Supreme Court upheld the requirement that National Endowment of the Arts recipients sign anti-obscenity pledges and that grantors of federal funding for artistic endeavors take into account "general standards of decency" in the *Finley* case below. Several appellate decisions have addressed other issues of artistic freedom.

In 1998 the Supreme Court ruled in *Nat'l Endowment for the Arts v. Finley* that it does not violate the First Amendment for those who award government grants for the arts to consider "general standards of decency and respect for the diverse beliefs and values of the American people." The Court was ruling on a challenge to standards Congress directed the National Endowment for the Arts (NEA) to adopt in 1990. The new rules were a reaction to a public outcry over the funding of several controversial artists by the NEA. Four performance artists who were initially denied federal grants under the new standards, including New York performance artist Karen Finley, challenged the rules.

In upholding the grant criteria, Justice Sandra Day O'Connor said, "Congress has wide latitude to set spending priorities." She noted that libraries routinely choose to spend tax dollars to buy certain books while rejecting others, including those considered indecent or unsuitable for children. She said that the grant system is not unconstitutional on its face. She emphasized the system could be implemented in a way that would be unconstitutional viewpoint discrimination, but there was no evidence of that before the Court. The lone dissenter, Justice David Souter, argued that the NEA criteria inevitably involve viewpoint discrimination that violates the First Amendment because the federal government has not justified it.

As a practical matter, the decision had little effect on the arts: the four artists who challenged the rules received grants early in the litigation, and the NEA no longer gives much money to individual artists. Instead, arts-oriented groups and organizations receive most of the grant money, and they are screened by panels of experts and community representatives.

Monuments as government speech. A different kind of access issue is presented by the permanent installation of monuments in public parks. The Supreme Court entered the controversy in a 2009 case *Pleasant Grove City v. Summum* (555 U.S. 460). At issue was whether Corky Ra, founder of Summum, a religion whose goal it is "to help you liberate and emancipate you from yourself," could force Pleasant Grove City, Utah, to display a monument containing the "Seven Aphorisms of Summum" because the city had already accepted other monuments, including one of the Ten Commandments. The Supreme Court said that the city did not have to display the Summum monument because the placement of a permanent monument in a city park was a form of *government speech* and not subject to the First Amendment. Relying on cases involving government-sponsored speech like *Johanns v. Livestock Marketing Association* (discussed in Chapter Thirteen), Justice Samuel Alito, speaking for a unanimous Court, said, "Permanent monuments displayed on public property typically represent government speech." Government need not maintain neutrality when it speaks, and government speech does not receive First Amendment scrutiny. Even if the monuments that Pleasant Grove City accepted were funded privately, the city engaged in selectivity in the choice of those monuments and did not open the park in which they were installed to all monuments. A federal judge in 2010 dismissed a follow-up lawsuit against Pleasant Grove alleging an establishment clause violation by the city for allowing the Ten Commandments monument.

FIG. 31.
A Newseum
display of a Ten
Commandments
monument at
the Texas Capitol
Building, similar to
the one in Pleasant
Grove City, Utah.

Author's collection.

Censorship and Financial Information

Does the federal government have the right to prohibit the publication of newsletters offering advice to stock market investors by people with questionable backgrounds, or does the First Amendment protect the right to publish such newsletters? How about lawyers giving bankruptcy advice to clients; can that be regulated?

The newsletter question was raised in a 1985 Supreme Court decision, *Lowe v. SEC* (472 U.S. 181). Under the federal Investment Advisers Act, the Securities and Exchange Commission (SEC) is empowered to regulate the dissemination of investment advice, even when the advice is in the form of a publication that would seem to be protected by the First Amendment. The act exempts *bona fide* newspapers and magazines. Christopher Lowe was convicted of mishandling a client's funds, and the SEC canceled his registration as an investment adviser. However, he continued to publish a financial newsletter. When the SEC tried to stop him from publishing his newsletter, he argued that he had a First Amendment right to publish it. The Court ruled that Lowe's newsletter was in fact a *bona fide* publication and therefore exempt from regulation by the SEC. But writing for the majority, Justice John Paul Stevens noted that Lowe's newsletter contained disinterested investment advice intended for numerous readers, not personalized advice for specific individual clients. The Court said the SEC *could* regulate those who give individualized advice, as opposed to publishers who offer their analyses of various investments to a general audience.

In short, the Court liberally interpreted the Investment Advisers Act's exemption for *bona fide* publications, and thereby avoided the First Amendment implications of the act's restrictions on giving investment advice. The Court did not resolve the question of when the right to communicate opinions about the stock market is protected by the First Amendment.

However, a year after it lost *Lowe* at the Supreme Court, the SEC abandoned many of its efforts to regulate publications and broadcasts that give investment advice or discuss economic issues. Nevertheless, the SEC continued to act against financial publications that allegedly published misleading information that might affect the stock market. In 1988, the SEC lost such a case in the U.S. Court of Appeals, *SEC v. Wall Street Publ'g Institute Inc.* (851 F.2d 365). That firm, the publisher of *Stock Market Magazine,* was accused of publishing articles that were little more than corporate "flackery" (as a federal judge put it)—uniformly flattering articles that were written by the companies or their public relations agencies.

The appellate court ruled that neither the SEC nor the courts can delve into the sources or origins of magazine articles without violating the First Amendment. However, the appellate court did send the case back to a trial judge to determine whether some of the articles might have been paid advertising disguised as news. The court said that if the magazine was accepting payment for publishing the articles, the SEC might have the authority to force the magazine to disclose that fact. Accepting payment to publish an article would make the article a form of advertising; it should be identified as such.

In contrast, the government can constitutionally put limitations on bankruptcy advice. In 2010 the Supreme Court decided *Milavetz, Gallop & Milavetz v. U.S.* (559 U.S. 229), holding that prohibitions on bankruptcy advisers giving certain types of advice to their clients contained in the Bankruptcy Abuse Prevention and Consumer Protection Act (BAPCPA) did not run afoul of the First Amendment. At issue was BAPCPA's provision barring debt relief services from advising clients to incur more debt for filing for bankruptcy; a law firm filed a pre-enforcement suit to request that the court say that it was not a debt relief agency and could advise its clients to incur additional debt. Justice Sonia Sotomayor, writing for the Court, said that attorneys who provide bankruptcy advice are considered debt relief agencies for the purpose of BAPCPA. Moreover, the law does not overburden speech, as it regulates only one form of legal advice: recommending that clients incur more debt in advance of filing for bankruptcy. She added, "[I]t is hard to see how a rule that narrowly prohibits an attorney from affirmatively advising a client to commit this type of abusive prefiling conduct could chill attorney speech or inhibit the attorney-client relationship."

Anonymous Speech

Increasing numbers of litigants have been willing to go to court to protect their anonymity—or to discover others' identities to sue them for libel or copyright infringement. In the 1990s and beyond, courts, including the Supreme Court, have been asked to wrestle with whether and when to unmask anonymous speakers.

The Supreme Court's first precedent regarding anonymous speech is *McIntyre v. Ohio Elections Commission*, in 1995, in which the Court struck down laws that prohibited the dissemination of anonymous campaign literature. But how does this endorsement of the right to remain anonymous apply to the online environment, particularly when there is a lawsuit at stake? Recent cases address anonymity in several online and offline contexts.

The case that is often considered to be the lead case in whether to require an online anonymous speaker to be revealed is the 2001 case of *Dendrite Int'l, Inc. v. Doe* (775 A.2d 756). Dendrite, a pharmaceutical sales and support company, wanted the identity of an anonymous online poster to a Yahoo! message board so that the company could sue the person for libel. The New Jersey court denied Dendrite's claim and provided a five-part test for revealing the identity of an anonymous entity: First, the plaintiff must attempt to notify the anonymous poster, including by posting on the original message board. Second, the plaintiff must identify allegedly actionable statements made by the defendant. Third, the plaintiff must provide a basis on which to bring suit, such as libel. Fourth, the plaintiff must provide evidence for that claim, and finally, the court should "balance the defendant's First Amendment right of anonymous free speech against the strength of the *prima facie* case presented and the necessity for the disclosure of the anonymous defendant's identity to allow the plaintiff to properly proceed." (*Prima facie* is Latin for "at first sight," and it means obvious or self-evident.) In this case, the court said there was no evidence to suggest that Dendrite had been harmed or its stock prices reduced due to the false anonymous postings.

The *Dendrite* test. In the first such ruling by a state's highest court, the Delaware Supreme Court in 2005 upheld the right of internet bloggers to speak anonymously. In *John Doe No. 1 v. Cahill* (884 A.2d 451), the court, using a modified version of the *Dendrite* test, said bloggers have a First Amendment right to anonymity unless someone suing a blogger has a clearly valid case, rejecting a local official's attempt to identify bloggers who criticized him on a newspaper-sponsored blog site. The Delaware court likened bloggers to the political pamphleteers who won Supreme Court decisions protecting their anonymity. Other courts are adopting or adapting this approach; for example, in 2008, a Maryland appeals court said a plaintiff had not made a strong enough defamation case against five anonymous bloggers to compel their identification (*Independent Newspapers Inc. v. Brodie*, 966 A.2d 432).

In the late 2000s, the number of cases dealing with anonymous online speech exploded, with courts adapting elements from tests in cases like *Dendrite* and *Cahill*. A few cases are offered here, but there are many more. In 2009, the District of Columbia appeals court added a requirement that plaintiffs make the case that the information they are seeking is truly important for their cases in *Solers, Inc. v. Doe* (977 A.2d 941). A software industry association investigated Solers, a defense industry software company, in response to an anonymous tip to determine whether it was using pirated software. Although the industry association found no wrongdoing, Solers filed a complaint against the anonymous tipster. The court dismissed Solers' claim and said that the plaintiff must "determine that the information sought is important to enable the plaintiff to proceed with his lawsuit." Also in 2009, model Liskula Cohen was able to discover the identity of an anonymous blogger whom she wanted to sue for defamation for writing about her on a blog entitled "Skanks of NYC" (*Cohen v. Google, Inc.*, 887 N.Y.S.2d 424). The New York court said that to unmask an anonymous defendant, the plaintiff must make a *prima facie* showing of a "meritorious cause of action." (This case's libel actions will be discussed in Chapter Four.)

In 2010, the New Hampshire Supreme Court also explicitly endorsed the *Dendrite* test in a case involving an online service that gathers and posts online information about mortgage lenders, saying that it did not have to reveal the identity of an anonymous poster. The court said in *Mortgage Specialists Inc. v. Implode-Explode Heavy Industries Inc.* (999 A.2d 184), "We hold that the qualified privilege to speak anonymously requires the trial court to 'balanc[e]…the equities and rights at issue,' thus ensuring that a plaintiff alleging defamation has a valid reason for piercing the speaker's anonymity." The court remanded the case to the trial court to apply the *Dendrite* standard.

But courts differ in their willingness to apply these emerging tests. In 2010, a divided Illinois appeals court reversed a lower court's dismissal of a plaintiff's petition to reveal an anonymous source, ordering a news organization to reveal the anonymous poster. In *Maxon v. Ottawa Publishing Co.* (929 N.E.2d 666), the majority said that an Illinois rule made the application of the *Dendrite/Cahill* test unnecessary. The dissent claimed that the *Dendrite/Cahill* test "adds a crucial extra layer of protection to anonymous speech" and is "designed to protect the identity of those participating in non-actionable anonymous speech." And the Second Circuit adopted a test from a New York federal district court in determining whether to reveal the identity of an anonymous filesharer: "(1) [the] concrete[ness of the plaintiff's] showing of a prima facie claim of actionable harm… (2) [the] specificity of the discovery request… (3) the absence of alternative means to obtain the subpoenaed information… (4)

[the] need for the subpoenaed information to advance the claim, …and (5) the [objecting] party's expectation of privacy" (*Arista Records LLC v. Doe 3*, 604 F.3d 110, 2010).

Revealing anonymous sources? But what if a news organization decides to *reveal* the identity of an anonymous online commenter? A Cleveland newspaper settled with an Ohio judge after it revealed her identity in 2010. Cuyahoga County Court of Common Pleas Judge Shirley Strickland-Saffold and her daughter, Sydney, sued the *Cleveland Plain Dealer* for defamation, breach of contract, and invasion of privacy after the *Plain Dealer* divulged that the pseudonym "lawmiss" connected to the judge's email address was the source of comments about cases currently before her court (the Ohio Supreme Court removed the judge from one of those, a serial murder case). The judge claimed that her daughter and ex-husband were the authors of those comments.

However, the Ninth Circuit applied a reduced level of protection to anonymous commercial communication in 2011. In what was primarily a procedural case between Amway (formerly Quixtar) and Signature Management TEAM, a company that provides support materials like books and motivational speaker appearances to those who sell Amway products, the court said that the district court's application of the strict standard established in *Cahill* (a political speech case) went too far in protecting anonymous commercial speech. "[W]e suggest that the nature of the speech should be a driving force in choosing a standard by which to balance the rights of anonymous speakers in discovery disputes," the court said (*In re Anonymous Online Speakers*, 661 F.3d 1168).

Could this be the start of a trend in which courts evaluate different types of online anonymous speech differently? If so, the anonymity of participants on sites like Yelp! and Urbanspoon, in which users review restaurants and shops, could be in danger. At least one district court in the Ninth Circuit has applied the distinction (*Cornelius v. DeLuca*, 39 Media L. Rep. 1660, 2011) but protected the anonymity of an online poster, saying that the post "is deserving of more protection than mere commercial speech but less than speech that lies at the heart of First Amendment values, such as religious or political speech."

Not every court follows the *Dendrite/Cahill* standard, believing it to be an unnecessary addition to the law. In considering whether clothing company Façonnable could obtain the identities of anonymous editors of a Wikipedia site that alleged that Façonnable was a supporter of militant group Hezbollah, a federal district court in Colorado said instead that "existing procedures, applied with a heightened sensitivity to any First Amendment implications, is the correct approach" to determine when anonymous speakers can be unmasked. The court ordered online service provider Skybeam to provide the identities; however, Skybeam was granted an emergency stay to avoid the disclosure. Then Façonnable voluntarily dismissed the case. The court later vacated the original order so as not to prejudice Skybeam in other cases (*Façonnable USA Corp. v. John Does 1-10*, 799 F. Supp. 2d 1202, 2011).

Some states are considering bills to combat anonymous online posting. In New York, such a bill, introduced in 2012, would mandate that website administrators, if asked, "shall remove any comments posted on his or her web site by an anonymous poster unless such anonymous poster agrees to attach his or her name to the post and confirms that his or her IP address, legal name, and home address are accurate."

Offline anonymity. While offline anonymity is not nearly as hot a legal topic as its online counterpart, the Supreme Court in 2010 again stepped into the debate in *Doe v. Reed* (561 U.S. 186). At issue was whether the First Amendment is violated when a state compels public release of identifying information about petition signers—in this case, those who had signed an anti–gay rights petition in Washington State. The Court said that as a general rule, disclosure of names under the Washington public records act is not a free speech violation, but disclosure could be problematic in some cases. The plaintiffs in this case brought their case to the lower court again. The case is discussed in more depth in Chapter Nine; other anonymity issues as they relate to political advertising are discussed in Chapter Thirteen.

Discriminatory Taxation as Censorship

One of the oldest forms of government control over the media is discriminatory taxation. Authorities in seventeenth- and eighteenth-century England used taxes to control the press. One of the major grievances of the colonists before the revolutionary war was the Stamp Act, which singled out newspapers and legal documents for heavy taxation. Taxes may be burdensome for everyone, but if governments can levy high taxes on the news media and exempt other kinds of businesses, governments can force crusading news organizations into bankruptcy—or force them to become docile to avoid punitive taxation.

For many years after independence, attempts to single out newspapers for special taxes were rare in America, but a classic example of such a tax cropped up in the 1930s.

In 1936, just five years after its landmark *Near v. Minnesota* decision, the Supreme Court decided *Grosjean v. Am. Press* (297 U.S. 233). This case arose because Louisiana, dominated by Governor Huey "Kingfish" Long's political machine, had imposed a special tax on the 13 largest papers in the state, 12 of which opposed Long. The tax applied to total advertising receipts of all papers and magazines with a circulation over 20,000 copies per week.

The newspapers challenged the tax and a federal court issued an order barring the tax as a violation of the First Amendment. The Supreme Court heard the case on appeal and unanimously affirmed the lower court. In an opinion by Justice George Sutherland, the Court said the First Amendment was intended to prevent prior restraints in the form of discriminatory taxes. Sutherland noted that the license tax acted as a prior restraint in two ways. First, it would curtail advertising revenue, and second, it was designed to restrict circulation. The Louisiana tax, Sutherland said, was "not an ordinary form of tax, but one single in kind, with a long history of hostile misuse against the freedom of the press."

The Supreme Court has overturned three other state tax systems that improperly singled out the media for unconstitutional taxation. In 1983, the Court overturned a Minnesota plan that taxed some—but not all—newspapers. Minnesota created a "use" tax on the ink and newsprint used by newspapers in 1971. But after some of the smaller papers complained of the economic hardship the tax caused, the legislature rewrote the law to exempt the first $100,000 in newsprint and ink each newspaper purchased annually. Thus, the law in effect exempted small newspapers or, to put it another way, singled out large newspapers for a special tax. By 1974, one newspaper company—the *Minneapolis Star & Tribune*—was paying about two-thirds of the total amount the state collected from all Minnesota newspapers through this tax. Citing the *Grosjean* precedent, the *Star & Tribune* company challenged the constitutionality of the tax.

In *Minneapolis Star & Tribune v. Minnesota Commissioner of Revenue* (460 U.S. 575, 1983), the Supreme Court voted 8-1 to overturn Minnesota's tax on ink and newsprint. Justice Sandra Day O'Connor, writing for the Court, warned that because such a tax "targets a small group of newspapers," it "presents such a potential for abuse that no interest suggested by Minnesota can justify the scheme." Justice William Rehnquist dissented, arguing that the use tax in question was less of a burden than the normal sales tax paid by other businesses.

(Minnesota had exempted newspapers from the state sales tax, a practice that was then common in other states as well.) Rehnquist said the state was actually conferring a benefit on the press, something the states may do without violating the First Amendment.

In 1987 the Supreme Court overturned another state taxation scheme that singled out some media for taxes not paid by others. This case involved an Arkansas sales tax that applied to general interest magazines but not to newspapers or to specialized magazines (e.g., religious, professional, trade, and sports publications). In *Ark. Writers' Project v. Ragland* (481 U.S. 221), the Supreme Court ruled the tax unconstitutional, relying on much the same rationale as in the *Minneapolis Star & Tribune* case.

In fact, the Court said the Arkansas tax was even more flagrantly unconstitutional than the one in Minnesota because it required government officials to base a tax break on the *content of the media.* "[O]fficial scrutiny of the content of publications as the basis for imposing a tax is entirely incompatible with the First Amendment's guarantee of freedom of the press," Justice Thurgood Marshall wrote for the majority. Thus, any tax giving some media favorable treatment while not extending the benefit across the board is unconstitutional. However, the Court did not rule out the possibility that a state could impose a tax on *entire categories of media,* taxing all newspapers while exempting all magazines, for instance.

The ruling produced a strong dissent from Justices Antonin Scalia and William Rehnquist (by then the Chief Justice). Scalia said that instead of promoting press freedom, the ruling would actually undermine other government tax breaks based on content, such as subsidies of public broadcasting, educational publications, and the arts in general.

In 1989, the Supreme Court continued in this pattern by overturning a Texas tax system that granted sales tax exemptions to religious books, magazines, and newspapers but not to secular publications. In *Texas Monthly v. Bullock* (489 U.S. 1), the majority ruled that the Texas tax scheme was unconstitutional because it violated the First Amendment's requirement of separation of church and state. In effect, the tax break was an unconstitutional state action to subsidize religion, they ruled.

But, in 1991 the Supreme Court again made it clear that the media are subject to the same taxes as other businesses—as long as the tax does not improperly single out the media. Ruling in *Leathers v. Medlock* (499 U.S. 439), the Court voted 7-2 to uphold an Arkansas sales tax that applied to cable and satellite television services—as well as to utilities, hotels, and other businesses. Writing for the Court, Justice Sandra Day O'Connor said this tax was not like the taxes on the media that the Court had previously overturned: "There is no indication in this case that Arkansas has targeted cable television in a purposeful attempt to interfere with its First Amendment activities." Justices Thurgood Marshall and Harry Blackmun dissented, arguing that this kind of sales tax could be used to inhibit freedom of expression.

A week after it upheld the Arkansas cable tax, the Supreme Court disposed of three other cases involving taxes on the media. The Court declined to review state court decisions on media taxes in Tennessee and Iowa. But in the third case, *Miami Herald v. Dep't of Revenue* (499 U.S. 972), the high court issued an order directing the Florida Supreme Court to reconsider the validity of a sales tax on magazines but not newspapers. The state court complied with the U.S. Supreme Court's order—and again ruled that the state cannot tax just magazines. Such a tax is improper because it is based on the content, the court ruled in 1992 (*Dep't of Revenue v. Magazine Publishers of America,* 604 So.2d 459).

To summarize, these decisions on media taxation basically say that the media may not be taxed in a discriminatory fashion. If some media must pay a tax that does not apply to others based on their content or their size, the tax is unconstitutional. But if the tax applies across the board to similar media—and especially if it applies to other businesses—it is valid.

Seizing Criminals' Royalties

Is it an unlawful form of censorship for a state to seize profits or royalties criminals receive for telling or writing about their crimes? Many states and the federal government have laws allowing the authorities to take criminals' publishing profits and give them to the victims of their crimes. These laws are often called *"Son of Sam"* laws because New York's pioneering law of this type was enacted after serial killer David Berkowitz, who called himself by that name, received lucrative offers to tell his story.

The Supreme Court addressed this issue in 1991. The Court held that New York's Son of Sam law was unconstitutional because it imposed a special financial burden on communications—based on the content of the message. In *Simon & Schuster v. New York State Crime Victims Board* (502 U.S. 105), the Court said New York would have to show a compelling state interest to justify a law that burdened First Amendment activities in this way—and that the state had failed to do so.

Writing for the Court, Justice Sandra Day O'Connor said the law was "overinclusive" and therefore unconstitutional because it would apply to many legitimate literary works. Had it been in effect in an earlier era, the law would have allowed the state to seize the profits from works such as Henry David Thoreau's *Civil Disobedience*, she wrote. Under the New York law, criminals were required to give up the royalties and profits from books and other communications that in any way concerned their crimes. The money was placed in a fund for crime victims. It was challenged by publisher Simon & Schuster, which paid Henry Hill, a former mafia figure, nearly $100,000 for his story about his life as a mobster who became a government informant. The resulting book, *Wiseguy*, became a best-seller and was made into the movie *Goodfellas*. Simon & Schuster was holding another $27,000 that it owed to him when the Crime Victims Board demanded the money. Instead of complying, the publisher challenged the Son of Sam law—and prevailed when the Supreme Court declared the law to be unconstitutional.

In the years since the *Simon & Schuster* Supreme Court decision, several states have enacted narrower laws to give crime victims any money earned by convicted felons for telling the stories of their crimes. These laws generally apply only to persons convicted of a crime and are limited to money earned for a specific, detailed account of the crime.

Liability for Inspiring Crimes

Another troubling First Amendment question involves holding the media accountable for crimes committed by readers or viewers who were allegedly inspired by a movie, website, television show, book, news story, magazine article, or an advertisement. Although such cases may involve subsequent punishments rather than prior restraints, the issues they raise should be discussed here.

In 1998, the Supreme Court refused to intervene in a case where a book allegedly facilitated a crime: *Rice v. Paladin Enterprises* (128 F.3d 233, 1997). In this case, the publisher of a book called *Hit Man: A Technical Manual for Independent Contractors* was sued by the families of three people who were killed by a man who followed the detailed instructions in *Hit Man*. The publisher sought to have the lawsuit dismissed on First Amendment grounds, but a federal appellate court held that this book, with its "extraordinary comprehensiveness, detail and clarity" in describing how to commit murder, is not exempted from civil lawsuits by the First Amendment. The court held that a publisher can be sued by those who are injured (or the families of those who are killed) in this situation. The Fourth Circuit called the 130-page book a "step-by-step murder manual, a training book for assassins." Because it was intended to train potential murderers and not merely to entertain, it falls outside the scope of the First Amendment, the court ruled.

After the Supreme Court refused to hear an appeal, Paladin settled. However, the case caused alarm among media organizations. Publishers, broadcasters, and filmmakers, among others, had urged the Supreme Court to hear the case, arguing that the same rationale could be used in lawsuits alleging that books, magazines, scientific and military manuals, movies, and other media might have inspired or assisted someone who committed a crime.

Similar issues were also raised in several other widely publicized recent cases, including one in which an Oakland, Michigan, jury ordered the producers of the *Jenny Jones* television talk show to pay almost $30 million in damages to the family of a man who was killed by another man who had appeared with him on the show. The victim said (on camera) that he had a gay interest in the man who later shot and killed him. In 2002, a Michigan appellate court overturned the jury verdict, holding that the show's producers "had no duty to anticipate and prevent the act of murder committed by [a guest] three days after leaving defendants' studio and hundreds of miles away" (*Graves v. Warner Bros.*, 656 N.W.2d 195).

In 1999, the U.S. Supreme Court declined to intervene in a similar case where a Louisiana appellate court held that the family of a shooting victim could sue the producers of the movie *Natural Born Killers* if they could prove that the producers intended to inspire others to commit violent acts. In *Byers v. Edmonson* (712 So.2d 681), the Supreme Court refused to hear an appeal of the Louisiana court's ruling, which cleared the way for a lawsuit by the family of Patsy Byers, a convenience store clerk who was wounded by a couple who had repeatedly watched *Natural Born Killers* and then went on a crime spree.

The Byers family never proved that filmmaker Oliver Stone and others involved in producing this movie actually *intended* to inspire violent acts by viewers, and a Louisiana judge eventually dismissed the case. However, this legal victory, coming only after lengthy (and costly) litigation, does little to protect the media from other lawsuits by crime victims or their families when a crime is committed by someone who watched a movie or television program—or read a book, a news story, or a magazine article—about a similar crime.

Lawsuits alleging that the media inspired a crime are not a new phenomenon. Nearly a decade before these cases arose, a family sued *Soldier of Fortune* magazine and won a large award because the magazine published an advertisement that led to a murder for hire. The Eleventh Circuit eventually upheld the award and dismissed the magazine's First Amendment arguments (*Braun v. Soldier of Fortune Magazine*, 968 F.2d 1110, 1992). In 1985, the magazine carried an ad from an unemployed Vietnam veteran who described himself as a "37-year-old professional mercenary [who] is discrete [sic] and very private.

Body guard, courier and other special skills. All jobs considered." He accepted an assignment to kill a man in Atlanta and was later caught and convicted of the crime. The family sued the magazine for wrongful death; a jury awarded the family $4.3 million. Publishers and industry groups asked the Supreme Court to grant *cert*, arguing that the case could have a serious chilling effect on First Amendment freedoms, but to no effect.

■ AN OVERVIEW OF MAJOR ISSUES

If the First Amendment stands for anything, it is the proposition that the government generally cannot censor expression based on its content. But as this chapter shows, there are very few absolutes. Prior restraints of expression are generally unconstitutional, especially when they are based on the content on the speech. The 1931 precedent of *Near v. Minnesota* set forth the basic rationales for why prior restraints are generally unconstitutional, and not even the publication of leaked, classified documents was reason for the Supreme Court to support a prior restraint against publication in *New York Times v. U.S.* Subsequent precedents found that the government could not meet its very burden in justifying a prior restraint in cases of publication of the names of crime victims and juvenile offenders, for example.

Generally, the Supreme Court has ruled that laws that target expression based on their content are subject to strict scrutiny standards. In order to be upheld as constitutional under strict scrutiny, laws must be narrowly tailored to serve a compelling government interest. Laws that are content neutral are subject to intermediate scrutiny standards, requiring that the law furthers an important government interest.

Still, there are categories of expression that can be prohibited or punished. In *Chaplinksy v. New Hampshire*, the Supreme Court noted that some categories of speech do not convey meaningful ideas and that the interests in social morality and order outweigh any minimal social value. These include fighting words, obscenity, libel, and true threats, for example.

General offensiveness, however, is usually not a good enough reason to justify prior restraints or subsequent punishment. As the Court noted in *Cohen v. California*, "one man's vulgarity is another's lyric." The Court has rejected laws prohibiting flag burning, for example, and it has never ruled that so-called "hate speech" is unprotected by the First Amendment.

Still, not all expression is permissible in all circumstances. The government has latitude to regulate expression based on reasonable "time, place and manner regulations." This allows for reasonable rules and permitting schemes for the use of public places like parks and city streets, for example. This chapter has outlined some of the major principles that guide government regulations of expression in a wide variety of contexts and situations.

WHAT SHOULD I KNOW ABOUT MY STATE?

- What are my state and local rules regulating public parks and streets?
- Does my state have hate crime or penalty enhancement laws? If so, what do they cover?
- What regulations do my state, city, or municipality put on newsracks, billboards, and public transportation shelter signs?
- Are there ordinances that regulate how and where protests may take place? What do they specify? Are there fees?
- What has my state and federal circuit said about anonymity?

A SUMMARY OF PRIOR RESTRAINTS

What Is a Prior Restraint, and Is It Permitted in America?

A prior restraint is an act of government censorship to prevent facts or ideas that the government considers unacceptable from being disseminated. It is a far greater abridgment of freedom of expression than a subsequent punishment system, which allows publication but punishes the publisher afterward for any harm. Prior restraints are permitted only under extremely compelling circumstances, with the government agency that wishes to censor required to carry a very heavy burden of proof to justify it.

When Would a Direct Prior Restraint Be Constitutional?

In the "Pentagon Papers" case, the Supreme Court ruled that prior censorship of the news media would be permissible if the government could prove that irreparable harm to national security would otherwise occur. However, the government was unable to prove national security was sufficiently endangered to justify prior restraint in that case.

What Is a Time, Place, and Manner Regulation?

Governments may lawfully regulate the *time, place, and manner* in which First Amendment activities occur, provided the rules are *content neutral*. Rules are content neutral if they treat all speech the same, regardless of its content. Rules that are content based, that treat different content of speech differently, must undergo increased judicial scrutiny. They may be found constitutional but the burden on the government is much higher to justify them.

Are There Other Rules Concerning Prior Restraints Today?

Laws that unduly restrict literature distribution or other free expression activities on public property may be prior restraints. Private property owners, on the other hand, may usually prohibit First Amendment activities on their property, although some states recognize limited free expression rights at *quasi-public* places such as large shopping malls. Discriminatory taxes that single out some media have also been declared unconstitutional. Laws forbidding racial and religious "hate speech" have been overturned on First Amendment grounds. However, material that is found to be a threat to individuals is not protected. Laws or court orders forbidding the media to publish information they lawfully obtain are usually unconstitutional, even if the information is legally confidential (e.g., some crime victims' names). While the media may not have a right of access to this kind of news, governments cannot ordinarily prevent its publication once the media have it—particularly if obtained from a public record. The law on anonymous speech, particularly online, is still developing.

4 *Libel and Slander*

Ever since American journalists won their basic First Amendment freedoms, their most serious ongoing legal problem has been the danger of being sued for *defamation*—libel or slander. Other threats to journalistic freedom arise from time to time, but over the past two centuries libel has been a continuing legal problem, with thousands of lawsuits resolved by the courts—and thousands more settled out of court. Even the fear of libel suits often leads journalists to suppress newsworthy stories they would otherwise publish, thus engaging in a form of self-censorship that may not be in the public interest.

The landmark *New York Times v. Sullivan* decision, which set national standards for libel litigation, is over a half-century old. Not everyone loves it. Justice Antonin Scalia called the decision "wrong" at a 2014 National Press Club event celebrating the case's 50th anniversary, saying the framers would have been "appalled" at this revision of the Constitution. While there is little serious debate about whether *Sullivan* should be the law, several judges—including two sitting Supreme Court justices—agree with Scalia, as will be discussed later in this chapter.

A libel is a *written defamatory statement*; a slander is a *spoken* one. Libel and slander laws exist to protect people whose reputations have been *wrongfully* damaged. Clearly, there is a need for that kind of protection. However, many libel suits are filed by persons who were not actually libeled but who are angry about unfavorable but true (thus non-libelous) publicity. And hostile juries sometimes hand out enormous punitive damage awards against the media without worrying much about the validity of the libel claim itself.

Libel is a lot about money. A single libel suit can be financially devastating, even to a powerful media corporation. Multimillion-dollar libel judgments have become commonplace in recent years. Although most large libel judgments are eventually overturned by appellate courts, the cost of defending such a lawsuit often runs into millions of dollars. And if small local newspapers are targets in libel suits, which can easily put them out of business, well-known national media are even bigger targets for angry jurors. A jury once awarded a former "Miss Wyoming" beauty contest winner $26.5 million for a *Penthouse* magazine article about a fictitious "Miss Wyoming" who resembled her. An appellate court eventually set aside the verdict and dismissed the case, but by then *Penthouse* had spent more than a million dollars on legal fees (*Pring v. Penthouse*, 695 F.2d 438, 1983).

The *Pring* judgment seems small compared to a 1997 verdict in which a Houston jury ordered the *Wall Street Journal* to pay *$222.7 million* (including $200 million in punitive damages) to an investment

Chapter Objectives:

- Describe the definitions and elements of libel in First Amendment jurisprudence.
- Trace the historic development of libel law in the United States.
- Identify defenses to allegations of libel.
- Compare how libel actions and defenses vary among jurisdictions and media forms.

Essential Questions:

- What is libel? How has the law in this area changed over the years, particularly in the wake of the 1964 *Sullivan* case?
- Do the characteristics of online speech change how libel law functions? Should they?
- To what extent has Section 230 of the Communications Decency Act changed the face of libel law?
- How should media professionals ensure that their work is free of potentially libelous content? How should they defend themselves against claims of libel?

defamation:
a false intentional written or spoken communication that injures a person's reputation.

libel:
a written defamation.

slander:
a spoken defamation.

actual malice:
in libel, a statement made with knowing falsity or reckless disregard for the truth; a high burden of proof for fault that falls on plaintiffs who are public officials or public figures.

negligence:
in libel, a statement made carelessly or without exercise of normal care in verification; a lower burden of proof for fault that falls on plaintiffs who are private figures.

brokerage that went out of business shortly after the *Journal* reported on the firm's alleged difficulties. However, the judge later threw out the $200 million punitive damage award and eventually set aside the rest of the judgment as well, ruling that the brokerage withheld crucial evidence that would have corroborated the *Journal* story. But by then the *Journal* had spent several years and several million dollars defending itself in court.

Even this award pales in comparison to the *billions* that voting companies Dominion Voting Systems and Smartmatic USA Corp. demanded in libel suits filed in 2021 against Fox News and others. Dominion sued Fox News for $1.6 billion in Delaware, alleging that the network used false claims against it to keep viewers who were "fleeing Fox in favor of media outlets endorsing the lie" that the election was stolen from former president Donald Trump. Smartmatic's suit, filed in New York for $2.7 billion, outlined 16 defamation claims against Fox News, and the company pulled no punches in its complaint: "Defendants engaged in a conspiracy to spread disinformation about Smartmatic. They lied. And they did so knowingly and intentionally. Smartmatic seeks to hold them accountable for those lies and for the damage that their lies have caused." The suits are ongoing; stay tuned.

How does all of this affect smaller media organizations—the ones that couldn't begin to write a $15 million check to get out of a lawsuit? Libel insurance is available, but it can be prohibitively expensive. Not even bloggers are safe—in 2009, a South Carolina judge awarded $1.8 million to the owner of an advertising agency who claimed that he had been libeled in a post on a Myrtle Beach blog; the alleged author of the blog said he was unaware of the proceedings and did not appear in court. A settlement was negotiated, and the appeal was dropped. Clearly those who prepare content for the media, online or offline, need to be aware of the legal hazards of libel.

■ LIBEL DEFINED

Just what are libel and slander?

Libel versus slander. They are legal actions to compensate the victims of defamatory communications—communications that tend to injure someone's reputation. The legal distinction between a libel—a *written* defamatory statement—and slander—a *spoken* defamation—is perhaps less important today than it once was as a result of the convergence of the media as well as several important Supreme Court decisions. Often, this chapter refers to all kinds of lawsuits for defamation under the term libel. In many (but not all) states, broadcast defamation is treated as libel rather than slander.

Libel and slander suits are almost as old as the English common law from which they emerged. Even before this country was colonized,

(L) FIG. 32.
Clarence Thomas,
current U.S. Supreme
Court justice.

(R) FIG. 33.
Antonin Scalia, former
U.S. Supreme Court
justice (1936-2016).

Both justices expressed
distaste for *New York
Times v. Sullivan*, the
famous 1964 libel case.

*Collection of the Supreme
Court of the United States.*

libel and slander were recognized legal actions in much of the world. In fact, the concept that a person's good name is something of value, and that anyone who damages it has committed a wrong, can be traced back to the time of the ancient Romans—and on back to the Ten Commandments.

Most libel cases today are handled as civil tort actions, private disputes between two parties in which the courts merely provide a neutral forum. In earlier times, libel was often treated as a criminal matter: the prevailing view was that defamatory words might lead to a breach of the peace and should be regarded as a crime. This was especially true in the case of *seditious libel* (the crime of criticizing the government), for reasons explained in Chapter Two. While some states still have criminal libel laws on their books, these laws are rarely enforced today. Some have been ruled unconstitutional. Thus, the bulk of this chapter will be devoted to civil rather than criminal libel.

Usually state actions. Libel suits are ordinarily state cases, not federal ones. The U.S. Supreme Court has intervened in some state libel cases, reminding the states that their libel laws can have a chilling effect on freedom of the press. But aside from the Supreme Court's role in setting constitutional limits for libel suits, this remains a field of law reserved primarily for the *states*. However, that does not mean that libel suits are never tried in federal courts. State libel cases are sometimes heard in federal courts when the two parties live in different states, but even then, the federal courts apply state law rather than federal law.

Although libel is a matter of state law, its basic principles are much the same all over the United States, as is true of many kinds of law that grew out of the English common law. Moreover, the Supreme Court's rulings have tended to make libel law more uniform among the states. Nevertheless, there are still important state-to-state variations; you may wish to supplement this national overview by reading your own state's libel statute. The state codes section of Westlaw, Nexis UNI, and other online research services can be searched by keywords such as defamation, libel, or slander. And, as mentioned earlier and will be discussed in more depth later, *New York Times v. Sullivan*, the Supreme Court decision that set the standard in 1964, isn't universally revered. It is possible that more judges will join Justices Thomas, Gorsuch, and Scalia in calling for *Sullivan's* demise.

■ AN OVERVIEW OF LIBEL

In studying a complex legal subject such as libel, it is easy to get lost in the details, overlooking some of the major principles. This section summarizes the basics of libel law.

Technically, a libel occurs whenever the *elements* of libel are present. As you look at the list of these elements, you will realize that many libelous statements are published and broadcast every day. But that doesn't mean numerous libel suits are filed against the media every day. Instead, most libelous publications and broadcasts are unlikely to produce lawsuits because they are covered by one or more of the legal *defenses* that apply in libel law. There's a difference between a libel and an *actionable* libel—one that's likely to get someone sued. To decide whether a given item is likely to produce a libel suit, you have to determine not only whether the elements of libel are present but also whether there is a viable defense.

Elements of libel. For a libel to occur, at least four elements must be present—with a fifth one required in most cases. The elements are: (1) *defamation* (a message that tends to hurt someone's reputation); (2) *identification* of a victim (and potential plaintiff), either by name or some other designation that is understood by someone other than the victim and the perpetrator; (3) *publication, communication, or dissemination* of the defamatory message to someone other than the victim and perpetrator; (4) an element of *fault* on the part of the communicator, usually by communicating a provably *false* message (sometimes considered a separate element) with *actual malice* or *negligence*, and (5) usually *damages* (tangible or intangible losses that may be compensated in money).

Once these elements are present, a libel has occurred. It doesn't matter whether the defamatory statement is in a direct quote, a letter to the editor, an advertisement, a broadcast interview, or whatever. With few exceptions, anyone who contributes to the libel's dissemination may be sued for it, even if the libel was originated by someone else. That means the reporter who writes a story, the editor who reviews it, and everyone else in the production process may be named as a defendant in a libel suit. Of course, the normal legal strategy is to go after the "deep pocket"—the person with enough money to make it worthwhile. Therefore, the prime defendant is usually a corporate owner or publisher, not the hired hands who actually processed the libelous material. If you were defamed in a letter to the editor, you might want to sue the letter writer and the editor who chose to print it, but your prime defendant would probably be the parent company.

Internet services that do not edit materials placed on their servers are generally exempt from liability for postings by third parties, even though those who actually post libelous messages (and ARE liable) may be anything but "deep pockets." Section 230 of the federal Communications Decency Act *generally* exempts internet services from liability for content created by others (more on this later). But that is not true for the traditional media.

Possible defenses. After you determine whether the elements of libel are present in a given communication, the next crucial question is whether any of the defenses apply. Three major defenses developed under common law and have been recognized for many years. In addition, defenses of lesser importance are also recognized in some instances; they will be noted later. The major defenses are: (1) *truth* that can be proven in court; this classic common law defense is stronger than ever because plaintiffs usually have the *burden of proving falsity* now; (2) *privilege*, which protects fair and accurate accounts of what occurs during many government proceedings or appears in many public records; (3) *fair comment*, a statement of *opinion* as opposed to provably false facts.

If one or more of these defenses is present, the media may publish libelous material without fear of losing a libel suit. However, many lawsuits are filed by people who know they have little chance of ultimately winning. The mere opportunity to force the media into court may seem inviting to someone who feels he or she has been subjected to unfair publicity. Thus, the cost of defending a libel suit is itself a deterrent to publishing some controversial stories, no matter how strong the defenses are. This is especially true in states that do not have a procedure for dismissing frivolous libel suits quickly (see anti-SLAPP laws later in this chapter). In addition to the *elements of libel and defenses*, there are other factors to consider in deciding if a particular defamatory statement is risky.

Who May Sue for Libel?

The first step in analyzing any potentially libelous item is to determine whether there is a *plaintiff*—a party who may sue for libel. Generally, the rule is that any living person or other private legal entity (such as a corporation or an unincorporated business) may sue for libel. The right to sue for libel is what is called *a personal right, not a property right.* This means that the right dies with the individual: most states follow the common law rule that the heirs cannot sue on behalf of a deceased person unless they were also personally libeled. New Jersey and Pennsylvania do allow a libel victim's heirs to sue under certain circumstances, but that is the exception. However, a number of states allow the heirs to *continue an existing lawsuit* if a libel victim dies before the case is resolved.

On the other hand, corporations are not limited by the life span or tenure in office of any individual. They may pursue a lawsuit for decades, regardless of the departure of individual officers. But for a corporation to sue for libel, the organization itself must have been defamed, not just an individual officer.

It may seem surprising that a big company can sue for libel. Nevertheless, courts have often ruled that a corporation has the same right as an individual to sue for libel when its reputation is besmirched. However, special rules may apply when the defamation is directed at a product rather than the company itself. Many states allow a special legal action called *product disparagement* or *trade libel*. In a trade libel suit, the company usually has to prove that the libelous statement actually damaged its business, sometimes difficult to prove. These laws were rarely used for many years, but they enjoyed a new surge in popularity during the 1990s, when at least 13 states passed laws to protect perishable food products from negative publicity. These "veggie libel" laws are discussed later.

If companies can sue for libel, what about nonprofit associations and other unincorporated organizations? They, too, may sue for libel in some states, but the rule on this point varies somewhat

Elements of libel:

defamation: false intentional communication that injures a person's reputation.

identification: can be accomplished by a name or any other information that sufficiently identifies a person.

publication/communication: to someone other than the perpetrator or the victim.

fault: includes falsity and is measured as *actual malice* or *negligence.*

damages: tangible or intangible losses that can be financially compensated.

Defenses to libel:

truth: a strong defense because the burden of proof is on the plaintiff to prove falsity.

privilege: also known as *qualified privilege*, given to accurate accounts of proceedings of public meetings or materials in public records.

fair comment: a statement of actual opinion (not provably false facts).

around the country. And what about government agencies? On this question, the law does not vary: governments may not sue for libel anywhere. However, government officials may sue *as individuals* if their personal reputations are damaged by a libel.

Group Libel

What about a libel of a group of people? May the individuals sue? A long-recognized rule of law is that individuals may sue for libel when a group to which they belong has been defamed, but only if one of two conditions is met: (1) the group must be small enough that the libel affects the reputations of the individual members; or (2) the libelous statement must refer particularly to the individual who is suing.

A libel of a five-member city council could very well hurt the reputations of all the individual members. But what about a libel directed against a big organization, such as the U.S. Army? Would it be legally safe to say something like "all soldiers are criminals"?

The courts settled that sort of group libel question long ago. No individual may sue for libel when the libelous statement is directed toward such a large group. The cutoff seems to be somewhere between five and 100 people, depending on which court you listen to. A court once allowed individual football players to sue when the University of Oklahoma football team was libeled. But other courts have refused to allow individuals to sue when groups considerably smaller than a college football team were libeled. In general, the bigger the group is, the less the chance an individual may be able to sue for libel.

Rolling Stone and "small group" defamation. In 2014, *Rolling Stone* published a story entitled "A Rape on Campus" about an alleged rape on the University of Virginia (UVA) campus at the Phi Kappa Psi fraternity house. While "Jackie's" story was gritty, disturbing, and full of brutal details, it was also fabricated—and a report conducted by Columbia Graduate School of Journalism revealed that the reporter and staff at *Rolling Stone* had failed to perform many of the most basic journalistic fact-checking routines that could have stopped the publication.

Beyond its ethical problems, however, the magazine suffered several libel losses. In 2017, the Second Circuit reversed and remanded a lower court's dismissal of two fraternity members' libel claims (*Elias v. Rolling Stone*, 872 F.3d 97). Key to the determination was the New York libel law's requirement that the defamation be "of and concerning" the plaintiffs, and the court said that the article was directed at all members of the "sufficiently small" fraternity at the time, so under the theory of *small group defamation* (as defined in New York, "an individual belonging to a small group may maintain an action for individual injury resulting from a defamatory comment about the group, by showing that he is a member of the group") the two men's suits could continue. *Rolling Stone* settled for an undisclosed amount, and it also paid the Virginia chapter of Phi Kappa Psi $1.65 million in 2017. A federal jury in Virginia had awarded a former UVA associate dean of students $3 million in damages in 2016, after finding that *Rolling Stone* acted with actual malice.

To summarize: any living individual may sue if he or she is libeled, as may a corporation. Unincorporated organizations may sue in some states but not in others. Government agencies may not sue for libel, although government officials may if they are personally libeled. Individuals may sue for libel if they belong to a sufficiently small group that has been libeled.

In analyzing an item for possible libel, the next step after deciding there is a potential plaintiff is to check off the elements of libel and see if all are present. If so, then you should check off the defenses and see if any will protect you. That kind of analysis requires a more detailed summary of the elements of libel and the defenses.

■ THE ELEMENTS OF LIBEL

Defamation

Of the various elements of a libel case, the one that is sometimes the hardest to remember is the most obvious: the requirement that a statement actually *be* libelous (i.e., defamatory). Without defamation there is no libel, so the first step in analyzing a statement for potential libel is to decide whether there really is a defamation.

Per se* versus *per quod. Over the years courts have recognized a wide variety of statements as defamatory, dividing them into two categories: libel *per se* and libel *per quod.* Libel *per se* is the classic kind of defamation where the words themselves will hurt a person's reputation. Words such as "murderer," "rapist," "racist," and "extortionist" are obvious examples, but there are thousands of others. Any word or phrase is likely to be libelous if it falsely accuses a person of a heinous crime, public or private immorality, insanity or infection by loathsome disease (e.g., HIV/AIDS), or professional incompetence. Even words that don't fall into these categories may be ruled libelous if they cause others to shun and avoid the person.

When the words themselves communicate the defamation with no additional explanation needed (as the words would in the examples), you have libel *per se.* But when, on the other hand, it is not immediately apparent that the words are libelous, or when one must know additional facts to understand that there is defamation, it is called libel *per quod.*

A classic example of libel *per quod* arose in a case called *Fellows v. National Enquirer* (42 C.3d 234, 1986). The *Enquirer* reported that television director Arthur Fellows was "steady dating" a famous actress. That statement would not ordinarily be libelous—except for the fact that he had been married to someone else for many years. The paper didn't mention that he was married, and few readers knew this additional fact that made the statement libelous *per quod.* If the *Enquirer* had said he was committing adultery, that would probably qualify as libel *per se.* But merely to say he was dating an actress without mentioning his marriage would only be libel *per quod* (unless the fact that he was married was widely known).

When Fellows sued, he presented evidence that he was not dating the famous actress or anyone else besides his wife, but he lost because he could not prove *special damages* (any provable monetary loss). Many states require a showing of special damages in libel *per quod* cases, whereas only general damages (pain and suffering or merely embarrassment due to the loss of reputation) are typically required in cases of libel *per se.* Fellows may have been embarrassed by the article in the *Enquirer,* but he didn't suffer any significant financial losses (if anything, the libelous story might have helped his career).

The distinction between libel *per se* and libel *per quod* is becoming less important today. For many years, courts generally ruled that libel *per se* was automatically actionable; that is, the plaintiff didn't even have to prove general damages. Instead, courts would presume damages merely because a libelous statement had been published. But on the other hand, if it was only a matter of libel *per quod,* the plaintiff had to prove special damages.

However, the *Gertz v. Welch* (418 U.S. 323) decision, a landmark 1974 Supreme Court decision that we will return to later, prohibited presumed damages in many libel suits against the media. The plaintiff today must be prepared to prove that he or she suffered at least general damages whether the defamatory statement was libel *per se* or libel *per quod.* The only time damages may be *presumed* in cases involving the media is when the plaintiff proves *actual malice* (i.e., that a falsehood was published knowingly or with reckless disregard for the truth). Some states have even eliminated presumed damages in non-media cases.

libel per se:
a statement defamatory on its face; e.g., calling someone a murderer, rapist, or racist; a false accusation of a heinous crime, public or private immorality, insanity or infection by loathsome disease, or professional incompetence (*per se* is Latin for "in itself").

libel per quod:
a statement that requires additional background knowledge to understand that defamation has taken place (*per quod* is Latin for "whereby").

qualified privilege:
a libel defense which covers truthful reports of what was said or done in a public government meeting or what is contained in public records; also called fair reporting.

strict liability:
liability without fault; a standard that puts responsibility on the perpetrator of an event regardless of the party who was actually responsible.

republication rule:
anyone who repeats or republishes a defamatory statement, even if accurately attributed, can be liable for damages.

As a result, there is not much difference between libel *per se* and libel *per quod* today when the media are involved. If a statement is libelous (either on its face or only because of unique circumstances in the context of the statement) the media may have to defend a libel suit, provided the victim of the libel can prove the rest of the elements of libel.

Common plaintiffs. In the American system of justice, a person is presumed innocent until proven guilty: stories that label people as "rapists" or "murderers" before they are convicted by a court are particularly dangerous. The best way to avoid lawsuits is to be as accurate and specific as possible in reporting the news. If someone has been detained for questioning in connection with a crime, say that much and nothing more. If the person has been formally charged, report that but don't go beyond what the facts will support. If the person has been arraigned, indicted, bound over for trial, released on bail, or whatever, be careful to report only what has *actually happened* and no more. If the police are seeking someone for questioning, be wary of a story that identifies him/her as a "suspect" prematurely.

Several other areas of journalism also produce more than their share of libel suits. A number of libel suits have resulted from stories accusing someone of having Mafia or organized crime connections. Another dangerous area—because of the ease with which special damages can be proven—is any statement that reflects upon a professional person's competence. Professionals such as physicians, psychologists, and attorneys rely on public confidence for their continued livelihood to a greater extent than most other persons. Should the local paper publish a story questioning a doctor's or lawyer's integrity or competence and that person's business thereafter declines, special damages can often be proven. A false or misleading statement (or even an innuendo) about a professional person invites a libel suit.

Those seeking public office are another group of people who generate a lot of libel suits. Although the media now have strong constitutional safeguards when sued by a *public official* or *public figure*, public officials are frequently inclined to file libel suits as a means of saving face if nothing else. Even if there is little chance that the politician will ultimately win in court, the cost of defending a libel suit may force some publishers and broadcasters to think twice about carrying a story that reflects upon the character or competence of a politician.

Another problem area is gossip about the private lives of the famous. Some publications that deal in this sort of "news" as their basic commodity expect (and are prepared for) frequent libel suits as a result. Of course, many celebrities would prefer to let the matter drop and thus avoid the cost and additional publicity a libel suit would bring, rather than sue a supermarket scandal sheet. But those who do sue may have a good chance of success: tales about the private lives of celebrities that a publisher knew or should have known to be false are beyond the First Amendment's protection.

What's defamatory now? What counts as defamation today? While this determination is fact-dependent, here are a few recent answers from the courts. The New Jersey Supreme Court said in 2009 that one candidate's truthfully reporting another's criminal background in campaign flyers, even when that conviction had been expunged (removed) from the record, was not libelous, as the expunging didn't make the information false. The expungement statute didn't protect the private facts in the libel case, and "the breadth of the expungement statute—on its face—is limited to those government agencies that are statutorily required to be served with the expungement order" (*G.D. v. Kenny*, 15 A.3d 300, 2011). Defendants may raise truth as a defense, the court said. Neither is it libelous, said the Second Circuit, to truthfully report that an individual is cooperating with law enforcement, even if that individual is in a prison population that might find that information unsavory (*Michtavi v. New York Daily News*, 587 F. 3d 551, 2009).

What about calling someone "gay"? The trend seems to be that this is not defamatory. A New York trial court ruled that the law of New York indicated that calling somone gay is libel *per se*. But the New York appeals court overturned: "Given this state's well-defined public policy of protection and respect for the civil rights of people who are lesbian, gay or bisexual, we now overrule our prior case to the contrary and hold that such statements are not defamatory *per se*"(*Yonaty v. Mincolla*, 2012 NY Slip Op 04248, 2012). Calling someone gay during a talk show where the use of hyperbole and insults is common is also *not* defamatory, according to a New Jersey federal court in 2010; the court said that "it appears unlikely that the New Jersey Supreme Court would legitimize discrimination against gays and lesbians by concluding that referring to someone as homosexual 'tends so to harm the reputation of that person as to lower him in the estimation of the community as to deter third persons from associating or dealing with him'" (*Murphy v. Millennium Radio Group LLC*, 38 Media L. Rep. 2338). The Third Circuit on appeal did not address this issue; it did rule on copyright issues, discussed in Chapter Six.

How about saying someone is "transgender"? Nope. Fitness personality Richard Simmons sued the *National Enquirer* for libel for a 2016 cover story that said that he had undergone a sex change and was now a woman. In 2018, Los Angeles Superior Court judge Gregory Keosian meticulously examined the history of similar labels and determined that in current society, a mistaken label of transgender is no longer *per se* libelous "because such an identification does not expose 'any person to hatred, contempt, ridicule, or obloquy, or which causes him to be shunned or avoided, or which has a tendency to injure him in his occupation.'" He added, "While, as a practical matter, the characteristic may be held in contempt by a portion of the population, the court will not validate those prejudices by legally recognizing them," dismissed the case, and awarded the *Enquirer* $130,000 in attorney's fees.

Is calling someone a communist defamatory? Yes, said the Washington Supreme Court, if you're Vietnamese (*Tan v. Le*, 300 P.3d 356, 2013). Norman Le wrote a series of articles for Vietnamese publications alleging that Duc Tan and the Vietnamese Community of Thurston County (VCTC) were communist sympathizers. A lower court awarded Tan $310,000; the award was overturned by an appeals court but reinstated by the Washington Supreme Court: "Defendants insist that the sting of their allegations is that Tan and the VCTC are communists or communist sympathizers. However, there are no true statements showing

Tan and the VCTC are communists or communist sympathizers." Analyzing these and other statements, the court said the publication contained actual malice.

Is the internet changing what kinds of words are defamatory? Not just yet. In *Cohen v. Google, Inc.* (887 N.Y.S.2d 424) the anonymity elements of which were discussed in Chapter Three, an anonymous blogger writing on a blog called "Skanks of NYC" claimed that using the words "skank," "skanky," "ho," and "whoring" in reference to model Liskula Cohen was merely opinion. Moreover, the blogger (later revealed to be fashion student Rosemary Port) said that those words were no longer really defamatory; they "have become a popular form of 'trash talk' ubiquitous across the Internet ..." The court disagreed and said the words could reasonably be interpreted to suggest that Cohen was sexually promiscuous.

The Identification Element

Another element the plaintiff must prove in a libel suit is *identification*: at least some of the readers or listeners must understand to whom the defamatory statement refers.

Where a person's name is used, there is usually little difficulty in proving identification. However, there are a great many ways a person may be identified other than by name. Any reference—no matter how oblique—is sufficient if the plaintiff can produce witnesses who testify convincingly that they understand the libelous statement to refer to him or her.

Perhaps the classic example of an oblique reference producing a libel suit is the situation that led to the famous *New York Times v. Sullivan* decision from the Supreme Court. As Chapter One indicated, the plaintiff in that case was a city commissioner in Montgomery, Alabama. What prompted the lawsuit was a *New York Times* ad that alleged police misconduct in the South (including Montgomery) but never mentioned Sullivan either by name or as a city commissioner. He was able to convince a jury that the criticism of the conduct of the local police injured his reputation because many people knew that one of his responsibilities as a city commissioner was to oversee the police. In reversing the judgment years later, the Supreme Court expressed doubt that the ad really referred to Sullivan. But the case had gone all the way up through the American legal system at a cost of thousands of dollars.

In short, don't expect to escape a libel suit by using vague identification. If even a few people know who you are talking about, the identification requirement has been met.

Wonderful examples—of negligence. Beyond the dangers inherent in publishing a story with libelous content when more than one person has the same name, there are pitfalls to avoid when two people have similar names, given that journalists make errors. A notable example is the case of Ralph A. Behrend and R. Allen Behrendt, two medical doctors who had worked at the same hospital in Banning, California. The *Los Angeles Times* reported that Dr. Behrendt had been arrested for theft and using narcotics. Sure enough, it was really Dr. Behrend who was arrested—and Dr. Behrendt had a great libel suit against the *Times* as a result of this copy desk error (*Behrendt v. Times Mirror Co.*, 30 C.A.2d 77, 1939). If newspapers of the stature of the *Los Angeles Times* and the *Washington Post* have identification problems and face libel suits as a result, you can see why this sort of thing is a serious problem.

Another problem that leads to many libel suits is an identification so vague that it can refer to more than one person. A famous libel case nearly a century ago proved this point. Two lawyers in the Washington, D.C., area were named Harry Kennedy. One used his middle initials; the other did not. The one who normally used his middle initials was arrested for a serious crime. The *Washington Post* reported the fact, but omitted the middle initials. The other Harry Kennedy sued for libel, claiming that his reputation had been damaged, and he won (*Washington Post v. Kennedy*, 3 F.2d 207, 1924).

The moral of these stories is obvious: when you publish/broadcast a defamatory but true statement, be sure to identify the person or persons involved as completely as possible, lest you inadvertently also identify an innocent party. It is good journalistic practice to identify people by full name, address, and occupation whenever the story involves potential libel.

The Communication Element

A defamatory statement has to be *communicated (published* or *disseminated)* for it to be libelous. The rules in this area are quite liberal: any time someone besides the party making the defamatory statement and the victim sees or hears it, this requirement is met. Actually, the plaintiff in a lawsuit may have a tough time proving damages if only a few people saw or heard the defamatory statement. Nevertheless, there have been cases where communicating a libel to only a handful of people resulted in a lawsuit for the perpetrator of the libel.

In most instances, of course, libel suits against the media result from statements that were *actually* published or broadcast; proving the dissemination element is not difficult.

Accurately quoting someone else's libel doesn't get YOU off the hook! *Under the common law republication rule, everyone who furthers the dissemination of a libel can be sued.* This is important. Even though the defamation first appeared in a letter to the editor, in a public speech, or in a wire service dispatch, with few exceptions every publisher or broadcaster who further disseminates it can be sued (as can the originator of the libel). Unless one of the defenses is available, *the media are at risk even when they accurately report what someone else said.* The speaker may be sued—but in many instances so may everyone who further disseminates the libelous statement. You need not be the originator of a libel to be sued for it.

"Twibel," or libel on Twitter. Can one libel, or be libeled, in just 280 characters? The microblogging service Twitter has shown it's possible. Among the first cases, in 2009, Chicago resident Amanda Bonnen publicly tweeted a friend of hers, inviting a visit—despite the mold she alleged was in her apartment: "You should just come anyway. Who said sleeping in a moldy apartment was bad for you? Horizon realty thinks it's okay." Horizon Realty sued Bonnen for $50,000. A Cook county judge dismissed the case; media reports quoted the judge as saying in court that the tweet was "really too vague" to be actionable.

Also in 2009, singer Courtney Love was sued by fashion designer Dawn Simorangkir for statements Love made on her Twitter and MySpace accounts that allegedly threatened Simorangkir after she sent Love a bill for her Boudoir Queen fashions. According to the complain, among other tweets and posts, Love tweeted (complete with profanity and typos), "oi vey dont fuck with my wradrobe or you willend up in a circle of corched eaeth hunted til your dead." Simorangkir sued for defamation and invasion of privacy, among other actions. In 2011, Love agreed to pay $430,000 to Simorangkir to settle the case. Former president Donald J. Trump was embroiled in a Twibel suit with adult performer Stormy Daniels (Stephanie Clifford); the case is discussed elsewhere in this chapter.

Libel via email. Even email may count as publication. In 2010, a Texas bankruptcy court was among the first courts to find that sending someone an email with a link to an allegedly defamatory site counts as publication for purposes of libel: "An email, just like a letter or a note, is a means for a statement to be published so that third parties are capable of understanding the defamatory nature of the statement" (*In re Perry*, 423 B.R. 215). The email was also part of the context necessary to establish actual malice, said the court.

The Element of Fault

Until 1964, our summary of the things a plaintiff must prove to win a libel suit would have been basically complete at this point. However, in that year the U.S. Supreme Court handed down its landmark *New York Times v. Sullivan* decision. A decade later, the Court announced another very important libel decision, *Gertz v. Welch.* Both cases are discussed in depth in the section "Libel and the First Amendment," but in the interest of offering a logical presentation of the elements of libel, their basic provisions are summarized here.

In *New York Times v. Sullivan,* the Supreme Court ruled that public officials who sue for libel must prove *actual malice,* which is defined as publishing a falsehood with *knowledge of its falsity, or with reckless disregard for the truth.* In the *Gertz* case, the Court extended this principle by ruling that in all libel cases involving matters of public concern, the plaintiff must prove some degree of *fault.* No longer would the media face libel suits under a legal doctrine called *strict liability,* a doctrine assuming that whenever a wrong occurs its perpetrator will be held strictly responsible (no matter whose fault it was). Without this protection, the justices ruled, the fear of libel suits would unduly inhibit the media in covering controversial stories that should be reported in a free society. Therefore, these safeguards were required to protect First Amendment freedoms.

Actual malice versus negligence. The Supreme Court in *Gertz* set up two levels of fault for the media: *negligence* and *actual malice.* The justices said the states could not allow libel suits by public figures and public officials unless they could prove actual malice, something they'd already said in *Sullivan* and other cases before *Gertz.* But the Court also said (for the first time) that private citizens as well as public figures had to prove some fault by the media to win libel cases. The Court ruled that the states could allow private citizens to sue by showing a lower level of fault than actual malice, perhaps just negligence. Alternately, any state that wished to do so could also impose the tough actual malice requirement on private citizens as well as public figures who sue the media for libel. The *Gertz* case raised two legal problems:

1. What is *negligence,* and how does it differ from *actual malice?*
2. Who is a *public figure,* and who is a *private person?*

Negligence is a term that has a long legal history in other kinds of tort actions, but it had not previously been used in libel cases. It refers to a party's failure to do something that they have a duty to do, and that a reasonable person would do. In libel cases, it has come to mean failing to adhere to the standards of good journalism by doing such things as checking the facts. Courts in several states have ruled that private persons must prove something more than negligence—but less than actual malice—in most libel cases against the media.

Plaintiffs cannot simply claim they informed a media organization about information they think could change coverage about them; they must prove that the media organization did not follow up on that information to demonstrate negligence, according to the Fifth Circuit in *Henry v. Lake Charles American Press LLC* (566 F.3d 164, 2009). Mark Henry, the owner of Chennault Jet Center, sued the Lake Charles *American Press* for libel for articles about a government investigation of alleged sales of contaminated fuel for military aircraft. Henry said his attorney had told the *American Press* that some of the information in the stories was wrong and gave the paper contact information for an Air Force official who could clarify the facts, and the newspaper had failed to act on this information. The Fifth Circuit found for the newspaper, saying Henry had provided no evidence that the newspaper had not followed up on the information provided by Henry's attorney.

Malice is another old legal term, but the Supreme Court gave it a special meaning in connection with libel suits in *New York Times v. Sullivan* by saying that it meant publishing a falsehood knowingly or with reckless disregard for the truth. "Reckless disregard" generally means publishing a false story when you strongly suspect it to be false—or should entertain such suspicions. That is very hard to prove in a libel case. But, as will be discussed, some states have common law definitions of "malice" that mean ill will or malicious intent, and one federal appeals court used such a state law to award a win in a libel suit to a plaintiff.

Since it is harder to prove actual malice than negligence, the *Gertz* decision made it important to determine who is a private person (and therefore required to prove only negligence in most states) and who is a public figure (and required to prove actual malice).

Why should it be harder for public figures to win libel cases? The court's rationale for this approach was twofold. First, public officials and public figures have much greater access to the media to reply to libelous charges than do private persons. Second, those who place themselves in the limelight have to expect some adverse publicity, while private persons should not be unduly subjected to publicity they do not seek.

Because winning a libel suit is usually much easier for a private person than a public figure, almost everyone who files a libel suit wants to be classified as a private person. The media, of course, want most plaintiffs classified as public figures. Several Supreme Court decisions since *Gertz* have helped to clarify who is and is not a public figure for libel purposes.

Proving Damages

Another way in which the Supreme Court's *Gertz* decision changed libel law was that, as mentioned earlier, it abolished what were called *presumed* damages except in those cases where the plaintiff was able to prove actual malice.

Special damages. Under the old presumed damage rules, many states allowed plaintiffs in libel suits to simply skip the difficult matter of proving that they were really injured by the libelous publication or broadcast. If there was a libel, the courts would simply presume there were damages, without any proof. The Supreme Court's *Gertz* decision changed all that. Now all plaintiffs who cannot prove the media guilty of actual malice—even private persons—must prove damages to win their cases. Plaintiffs can win *special damages* by proving their out-of-pocket losses, of course. But in addition, the Court ruled that plaintiffs may also collect *general damages* for such intangibles as embarrassment and loss of reputation. Obviously, no dollar amount can be placed on such losses, but if the plaintiff can prove he or she was injured, the court (i.e., the judge or a jury) may then decide how many dollars the plaintiff should be given as compensation.

How is this different from presumed damages? Under the old presumed damages doctrine, plaintiffs didn't have to offer *any* proof of their loss of reputation in the community. The court just *assumed* the bad publicity had a bad effect. Now plaintiffs must *prove* there was harm to their reputation. How? For example, a plaintiff may bring in witnesses to testify about the effect the defamatory statement had on that person's reputation. Often plaintiffs themselves testify that their friends shunned them.

For example, in an interesting turn of the tables in 2011, the Second Circuit determined that a newspaper publisher was unable to show that *per se* defamation by a mayor actually chilled his speech and resulted in damages (*Zherka v. Amicone*, 634 F.3d 642). Selim Zherka was the publisher of the *Westchester Guardian* in Yonkers, New York, and in 2007 the paper criticized Yonkers mayor Philip Amicone's administration, alleging corruption and financial mismanagement. But the *publisher* sued the *mayor*, claiming that the mayor had retaliated against him. The district court dismissed Zherka's claims, and the Second Circuit agreed. Saying that Zherka had failed to demonstrate "actual chilling" of his speech, the court said that simply alleging that the defamation was libel *per se* was not enough to establish chilling. The injury must be *demonstrable*—in other words, the court said, "Hurt feelings or a bruised ego are not by themselves the stuff of constitutional tort." Other forms of tangible harm are required, such as loss of business, the court added.

In the *Gertz* decision, the Supreme Court went a step further in placing limits on damages in libel suits: it also held that punitive damages should *not* be awarded—even to private persons—without *proof* of actual malice (i.e., knowing or reckless publication of a falsehood) by the media. Previously, the courts in some states allowed punitive damage awards (which can involve huge amounts of money) on proof of a different sort of malice. That kind of malice involved showing that the publisher or broadcaster harbored ill will or evil intentions toward the plaintiff. Under that rule, a publisher could face a massive punitive damage award without being guilty of actual malice as the Court defined the term for libel cases.

As indicated earlier, punitive damage awards by no means disappeared in libel cases since the *Gertz* decision, but at least plaintiffs now must prove actual malice under the new definition to win punitive damages.

■ LIBEL DEFENSES

In analyzing a given news item (or advertisement, press release, or whatever) for libel, the next step after determining if the elements are present is to decide whether any of the recognized libel defenses apply. At this point, however, the analysis must be approached a little differently. In order to win a libel case, the plaintiff must convince the court that the elements of libel are present; that is not the defendant's task. The plaintiff bears the burden of proof in that part of the case. But when it comes to building an affirmative defense against a libel suit, it's often the other way around: the defense bears the *burden of proof.* Thus, in many cases it isn't enough for publishers or broadcasters to believe they have a libel defense: they may have to prove it under a court's rules of evidence.

That can be a problem. The rules of evidence make it difficult to prove many things that are discovered through investigative journalism. A reporter may be absolutely convinced of the correctness of a story: the sources may be completely reliable and the reporter may have extensively double-checked the facts. But that doesn't mean the facts can be proven in court. For example, under a court's rules of evidence, hearsay (statements made by one person to another, with the second person testifying about what he was told) is often inadmissible. A good deal of the information a reporter gathers would be considered hearsay.

Another problem arises when journalists promise to keep the identities of sources confidential. Many important stories could not be developed without the use of such sources, but in a libel suit journalists may have to choose between identifying their sources and losing the case. A judge won't take their word that the source exists; the source may have to be identified during the discovery process, or may even have to testify. If the source cannot be produced without compromising journalistic ethics, the case may be forfeited.

With these problems in mind, you should check off the defenses that might apply to a potentially libelous item. Only if there is a defense—and it could be proved in court—should the item be considered safe. There may be times when it is necessary to take a chance and publish an important story without certainty that it could be defended in court, but the decision to gamble in that way should only be made intelligently, after calculating the risks.

Truth

The oldest of all libel defenses—and certainly the most obvious—is *truth* (sometimes called *justification*). Since the early days of American independence, courts have been allowing publishers to prove the truth of what they printed as a means of defending against civil libel suits. For many years, there was a catch: in some states the proof of truth had to be accompanied by proof that the publisher's motives were not improper. For instance, a publisher sometimes could be sued for engaging in character assassination of an enemy (often a rival publisher), even if all of the charges were true.

And, of course, there was the additional catch that only those truthful facts that could be proved under a court's rules of evidence would be considered true in deciding the case. As just suggested, that has been a serious problem for journalists.

However, the U.S. Supreme Court revised the rules on truth as a libel defense, particularly by shifting the burden of proof from the media to the plaintiff. As indicated earlier, in its *Gertz* decision the Court said it was not constitutionally permissible to allow a libel judgment against the media unless the plaintiff could prove fault, with fault meaning the publication of a false statement of fact due to negligence or malice.

Proof of falsity required to win. The Supreme Court reinforced this in a 1986 decision, *Philadelphia Newspapers v. Hepps* (475 U.S. 767). In that case, the *Philadelphia Inquirer* had published several articles linking beverage distributor Maurice Hepps to organized crime. When he sued for libel, he was unable to prove the charges false, but neither could the reporters fully document the charges to prove them true.

Pointing out that conclusively proving that type of charge can be difficult, the Court said that to prevent self-censorship by journalists, those who sue for libel must now bear the burden of proving the story *false*, at least when issues of public concern are involved. In such cases, *no* state may require the media to prove that a statement is true; the person suing must prove that it is false. Justice Sandra Day O'Connor explained, "[W]e hold that the common-law presumption that defamatory speech is false cannot stand when a plaintiff seeks damages against a media defendant for speech of public concern.... There will always be instances when the factfinding process will be unable to resolve conclusively whether the speech is true or false. It is in those instances that the burden of proof is dispositive."

Thus, the rule today is that to win a libel case resulting from the media's coverage of any issue of public concern, the plaintiff always bears the burden of proving that the libelous statement is false. But what about libel cases *not* involving issues of public concern? The Supreme Court left that up to the states: the states are constitutionally required to place the burden of proof on plaintiffs only in cases involving public issues. Some states have completely abandoned the common-law rule that presumed all libelous statements to be false and now require *all* plaintiffs to prove the falsity of every allegedly libelous statement. Also, in most cases the old requirement of truth plus good intentions is no longer valid.

Defamation by implication. Judge Leon Kendall, formerly on the Virgin Islands superior court, sued the *Virgin Islands Daily News* for libel arising from its coverage of several decisions Kendall made while on that court, and the Third Circuit, exercising appellate review over the Virgin Islands Supreme Court, evaluated the issue of *defamation by implication.* The court noted that this "occurs when a defendant juxtaposes a series of facts to imply a defamatory connection between them." But, said the court, Judge Kendall lost as he could not "show something that establishes defendants' intent to communicate the defamatory meaning" (*Hon. Leon A. Kendall v. Daily News Publ'g Co.*, 716 F.3d 82, 2013).

As a general rule, there can be no successful libel suit against the media unless the material is proven false—period. If it cannot be proven false, the publisher's motives no longer matter in most libel suits. However, one federal appeals court revisited this notion in 2009 and said that truthful statements *may* be actionable if the state statute uses a common law definition of malice, which does examine the motivations of the publisher. This case, *Noonan v. Staples*, will be discussed later in this chapter.

If the publisher's motives are irrelevant when a publication is truthful, they are very relevant if a publication turns out to be false. In that circumstance, the key issue may be whether the media organization knew or should have known that the libelous statement was false. If so, a court may find actual malice, which means that even a public official or public figure may win a libel case against the media. And in cases involving private persons rather than public figures, publishing a false statement negligently but unknowingly—because of sloppy fact-checking—may be enough to lose a libel suit.

Also, flatly stating that the First Amendment does not permit libel judgments against the media for truthful publications about public issues does not rule out other potential legal problem for the media. As Chapter Five explains, truth is not always a defense in a privacy suit. The fact that a statement is true may not necessarily win an invasion of privacy lawsuit.

Privilege

The legal concept of *privilege* is an old one, and it creates a strong libel defense for the media. A privilege is an immunity from legal liability, and the term is used in a variety of legal contexts. Chapter Eight discusses *reporter's privilege*, the concept that a journalist should be exempt from being forced to testify about his sources of information and unpublished notes. Other privileges excuse lawyers and doctors from testifying about much of what their clients and patients tell them in confidence.

As the term is used in libel and slander law, "privilege" means an immunity from a lawsuit. The concept was recognized in Article I, Section 6 of the U.S. Constitution, which created an absolute privilege for members of Congress engaged in debates on the floor of Congress. They may never be sued for anything they say there; they have *absolute* freedom of speech during Congressional debates.

Over the years, this absolute privilege has been broadened to encompass many other government officials, government proceedings, and government documents. Today, there is a broad privilege for local, state, and national legislative bodies, and it extends to major officials in the executive branch of government and to court proceedings. When performing their official duties, many government officials now have an absolute privilege; they cannot be sued for libel or slander as a result of what they do while conducting their official duties.

As this privilege for government officials was developing, the courts also recognized that in a democracy the news media need to be free to report to the public on what their elected leaders are doing and saying. This led to the concept of *qualified privilege*, sometimes called *conditional privilege*, or the *fair report privilege*.

Qualified privilege defined. Qualified privilege is a libel defense that allows the media to report on government proceedings and records without fear of a libel suit, provided they give a fair and accurate account. A biased account or one that pulls a libelous quote out of context may not be protected by the qualified privilege defense. However, this defense is broad enough to allow the media to publish many stories based on government documents or statements by government officials—without worrying about whether the statements themselves are true. If a charge of wrongdoing is contained in a government document such as a court record, for example, the media may publish it even if it later turns out to be false. Nevertheless, this defense raises at least two major legal questions:

1. What officials and records are within its scope?
2. Under what circumstances does it apply—when are officials conducting official business, and when are they doing something else?

It would take a detailed state-by-state summary to describe which officials and what records are covered by the qualified privilege defense, but some general rules have developed over the years. First, this defense clearly applies to official legislative proceedings from the local level to Congress, but not necessarily to informal and unofficial functions. What a local government official says during a meeting of a city council or commission is privileged, but what the same official says at a service club meeting or a campaign appearance (or writes in a press release, as will be explained shortly) may sometimes be a different matter.

Exec: Senior officials only (usually). In the executive branch, most states apply the privilege to the official conduct of senior elected officials, but *not necessarily* to lesser officials or appointees. The state attorney general's remarks on an official occasion may be privileged, for example, but not necessarily the statements of her deputies. In general, the less official the occasion and the lower the status of the person making the statement, the less likely it is to be privileged. Many courts recognize the privilege defense even in situations involving unofficial public events where matters of public concern are discussed. On the other hand, in some states the courts are moving in the *opposite* direction, declining to extend the privilege beyond government officials.

Judicial: Public info only (usually). In the judiciary, the privilege applies to public court proceedings and official records. It may not apply to proceedings and records that are not open to the public, however. If a particular type of proceeding is routinely closed to the public (as divorce and juvenile proceedings are in some states), the reporter who surreptitiously covers such a proceeding or publishes information taken from the secret records of the proceeding may not be protected by the privilege defense. Also particularly dangerous are false charges appearing in nonpublic documents that are "leaked" to the press.

Another problem in reporting court news involves documents that have been filed but have not yet received any review by a judge. A number of states recognize a rule that court documents are not privileged (even though they may be available to the public) until they are in some way acted upon by a judge. An additional complication is that a lawyer who sends court documents to the media may not be protected from liability even if the document itself is privileged. It's generally okay if reporters discover public court records on their own and publish them, but if a document is libelous, a lawyer can be sued for giving the document to a reporter.

Police beat. A serious privilege problem involves reporting the police beat. Law enforcement officials sometimes let journalists see files that are not public records. A story based on such reports may not be protected by the qualified privilege defense: if the police privately

Focus on...
Teddy Roosevelt's libel cases

Do American presidents ever sue for libel? Most do not. Prior to
President Donald J. Trump taking office in 2017, the last president
to do so was President Theodore Roosevelt (TR), who filed at least
one libel suit during his presidency (1901–1909) and participated in
at least two thereafter. In the first, TR sued famous publisher Joseph
Pulitzer over coverage of financial improprieties in the building of
the Panama Canal; in February 1909 a grand jury indicted Pulitzer
and some editors. The case was eventually dismissed.

After his presidency, in 1912, Roosevelt sued the publisher of
the *Ishpeming Iron Ore* in the Upper Peninsula of Michigan for a
mean-spirited editorial. Publisher George Newitt wrote, "Roosevelt
lies, and curses in a most disgusting way, he gets drunk too, and
that not infrequently, and all of his intimates know about it."
TR brought all his (considerable) power to bear on the case,
and Newitt, outmaneuvered, eventually apologized and paid the
president the requested damages: six cents.

FIG. 34. Theodore Roosevelt,
c. 1904.

*Library of Congress Prints and
Photographs Division Washington, [LC-USZ62-13026]*

Finally, in 1925, the former president found himself the defendant in a libel case brought by the
publisher of the *Albany Times-Union* for a comment carried by many newspapers that in New York,
"we see at its worst the development of bipartisan boss rule." Publisher William Barnes, Jr. was
the Republican "boss," said TR. The trial was moved to Syracuse to avoid bias toward Barnes in
Albany. Roosevelt won based on his counterclaims: Barnes was guilty of corruption, and probably
also of collusion with the Democrats.

suspect someone of a crime and they're wrong (i.e., guilt isn't proven in court), there is a
danger of libel. Beware of undocumented charges leveled against a potential suspect, charges that may never be substantiated or placed in a public record. Stories about a person's
arrest and booking are almost always privileged; stories quoting police hunches usually are
not. This is not to suggest that journalists should never report the progress of a law enforcement investigation aimed at someone suspected of a serious crime until *charges are formally
filed or an arrest is made.*

There are occasions when this kind of story is important. At times, it may be necessary
to report information not protected by the qualified privilege defense. But it should be
done with a full awareness of the potential for libel that may exist. At that point, the precise
wording of the story may be crucial. To qualify a story by saying someone is only an "alleged"
murderer probably will not help if he has not been charged with the crime, but to say he was
"detained for questioning in connection with" a crime may—if that is what has happened.

Statements beyond official duties. Equally troubling is the problem of government officials who engage in activities beyond the scope of their official duties. A 1979 U.S. Supreme
Court decision provided a classic example of a U.S. senator engaged in a thoroughly newsworthy activity in which he was not—the Court ruled—protected by privilege. The case,
Hutchinson v. Proxmire (443 U.S. 11), involved the "Golden Fleece of the Month Awards,"
presented to various individuals and organizations by Senator William Proxmire (D-Wis.)
because he felt they were wasting taxpayer money in a conspicuous way. One "winner" of
this tongue-in-cheek award was Dr. Ronald Hutchinson, a mental health researcher who had

received nearly a half-million dollars in government grants to study such things as teeth-clenching habits of monkeys under stress. Dr. Hutchinson sued, claiming this satirical award damaged his professional reputation, and won. Inasmuch as Proxmire regularly issued press releases publicizing his selections for the "Golden Fleece" award, Hutchinson showed the elements of libel, including a publication beyond the limits of Proxmire's absolute privilege as a senator. The Court said this government privilege covered the senator's remarks in the *Congressional Record* but did not cover the press release even though it was almost a *verbatim* copy of those remarks. The senator had gone beyond his official capacity in issuing a press release, even if it said the same thing he had said on the floor of Congress.

If a U.S. senator who pokes fun at what he considers wasteful government spending is not protected by the privilege defense in a press release, it should be apparent that this libel defense has its limitations. However, it should be noted that the libel suit was against the *senator* and not against the media that reported the award. Probably no state would entertain (nor would the First Amendment allow) a libel suit against a news medium that accurately reported the contents of the Congressional speech in which Proxmire announced the award. The senator's mistake was *republishing his own remarks* off the floor of Congress.

The *Proxmire* decision troubled many journalists, because the "Golden Fleece" awards were not only newsworthy but also dealt with a matter of great public concern (wasteful government spending). But that case had little effect on the qualified privilege of the media to report on issues of public concern; that privilege has been expanding in recent years. Nor did it affect the right of other public officials to issue press releases. All *Proxmire* really did was to limit the constitutional privilege of those who serve in Congress.

As a means of protecting the media to fairly and accurately report public records and public proceedings, qualified privilege represents an important safeguard. When a public official engages in slander during a government proceeding, or when an official public document carries a libelous charge, the privilege defense enables the media to report this newsworthy item to the public.

Qualified privilege in the states. The privilege remains alive and well as state supreme courts continue to support it. The Supreme Judicial Court of Massachusetts in *Howell v. Enterprise Publ'g Co.* (455 Mass. 641, 2010) said that a Brockton, Massachusetts, newspaper was protected for reports on the firing of James Howell, a sewer department superintendent, after inappropriate sexual materials were found on his work computer. The *Enterprise* used some anonymous sources, and the court said that even those were protected under the fair reporting privilege. Noting a concern that anonymous reports may distort the truth of official actions, the court said, "The privilege to report official actions would mean very little, however, if to qualify for its protection, the media were limited to reporting such actions solely on the basis of on-the-record statements by high-ranking (authorized to speak) officials or published official documents."

In *Salzano v. North Jersey Media Group* (993 A.2d 778, 2010) the New Jersey Supreme Court upheld the privilege after a state appellate court had narrowed it by applying it only to journalists' use of final judgments, not pretrial filings. Thomas Salzano sued two New Jersey newspapers for libel after they reported on his bankruptcy case using information filed in court. The court said initial pleadings "fall squarely within the protective sweep of the privilege," and described the privilege as a hybrid: "It is conditional insofar as it attaches only to full, fair, and accurate reports of government proceedings. It becomes absolute once those prerequisites are met."

But the fair report privilege is far from absolute. In a 2019 case, the Tennessee Supreme Court declined to extend the privilege to a private one-on-one conversation between a reporter and a detective from a county sheriff's department who also served as the department's public information officer. In *Burke v. Sparta Newspapers, Inc.* (592 S.W.3d 116), Jeffrey Todd Burke sued *The Expositor*, a twice-weekly paper, for allegedly defamatory statements published about his arrest and indictment provided by the detective to the reporter in a private conversation. A state trial court found for the news organization, but an appeals court reversed. The Tennessee Supreme Court, in affirming the appellate court's decision, said that the conversation between the detective and the reporter did not constitute "a meeting open to the public that deals with a matter of public concern" as required by the fair report privilege. "We agree with the Court of Appeals that the fair report privilege encompasses only *public* proceedings or official actions of government that have been made *public*," said the court.

Section 315 immunity. In addition to the qualified privilege defense, there is one circumstance under which the media are afforded an absolute privilege defense. Under Section 315 of the Communications Act, broadcasters are required to provide equal opportunities for air time to all candidates for a given public office. And the act denies the broadcaster any control over the content of a candidate's remarks made on the air under this provision. Thus, the broadcaster has no way to prevent a politician from defaming someone during such a broadcast.

In a 1959 decision (*Farmers Educ. & Coop. Union v. WDAY*, 360 U.S. 525), the U.S. Supreme Court afforded broadcasters an absolute immunity from libel and slander suits under these circumstances. Since they are forbidden to censor or otherwise control the content of political speeches required under Section 315, broadcasters are powerless to prevent a defamation and should not be held accountable if one occurs, the Court ruled. Some states exempt broadcasters from liability for defamatory statements made as a part of network programming they are not allowed to edit locally (although the network remains liable).

Fair Comment and Criticism

Another of the classic common law libel defenses is called *fair comment*. Although it has been partially superseded by the constitutional protection for the media created by the Supreme Court in recent years, it remains important in many states.

The fair comment defense protects expressions of opinion about the public performances of persons such as entertainers and politicians who voluntarily place themselves before the public. The courts recognized long ago that reviewing public figures' performances is a legitimate function of the press and should be protected, even if it some-times means excusing defamation.

As this defense was expanded by the courts, it came to protect even hostile expressions of opinion as long as two qualifications were met: the expression had to be based on facts that were correct and accurate, and it had to be a critique of the person's public perfor-mance rather than that person's private life.

In recent years, many states eliminated these requirements, extending libel protection to all expressions of opinion that are clearly labeled as such, while allowing libel suits only for *false statements of fact.* This trend was greatly encouraged by the majority opinion in the Supreme Court's *Gertz* decision, which said, "Under the First Amendment there is no such thing as a false idea. However pernicious an opinion may seem, we depend for its correc-tion not on the conscience of judges and juries but on the competition of other ideas." That language seemed to rule out libel suits for expressions of opinion.

Opinion versus implied fact: the *Milkovich* case. However, in 1990 the Supreme Court added an important qualification in *Milkovich v. Lorain Journal Co.* (497 U.S. 1). The justices allowed Michael Milkovich, a high school wrestling coach, to sue a sports columnist who accused him of lying under oath during an investigation of a melee at a campus wrestling match. A lower court ruled that the entire sports column was an expression of opinion and therefore not libelous. The Supreme Court held that expressions of opinion enjoy no *sepa-rate* constitutional protection in libel suits.

The Court reaffirmed its holding in *Philadelphia Newspapers v. Hepps,* discussed earlier, that libel plaintiffs must prove the falsity of any allegedly libelous statement, at least in cases involving matters of public concern. And because opinions by their nature cannot be proven true or false, pure opinion cannot be the basis for a successful libel suit. But in *Milkovich* there was more than an expression of opinion: there were *potentially false factual allegations.* For example, to accuse a coach of lying under oath is to accuse him of a crime. This was an opinion column—but it also contained factual allegations that might be proven false, and states may allow libel suits in such situations. Chief Justice William Rehnquist gave an example of the difference between fact and opinion: "[U]nlike the statement, 'In my opinion Mayor Jones is a liar,' the statement, 'in my opinion Mayor Jones shows his abysmal ignorance by accepting the teaching of Marx and Lenin,' would not be actionable."

While a pure expression of opinion cannot be the basis for a libel suit, an opinion that carries a false factual implication (like the charge that "Mayor Jones is a liar") is not constitu-tionally protected. If the writer or speaker cannot prove that Mayor Jones actually told a lie on at least one specific occasion, the statement may be an actionable libel, not a protected expression of opinion. To say that someone told a lie is a factual allegation that may be proved or disproved; to say a person is "abysmally ignorant" is just someone's opinion.

The distinction between a fact and an opinion is often very subtle. As a result, it may be necessary to have a full libel trial in which a jury determines whether a given statement is a protected expression of opinion or a false and libelous factual allegation.

Nevertheless, the fair comment defense offers excellent protection for those who dissem-inate pure opinions. Fair comment often protects the media from liability even for vitriolic political rhetoric, social commentary, and criticism of the arts. This defense allows the media to use intemperate language and get away with it as long as a statement is clearly an expression of opinion, and it often protects *rhetorical hyperbole.* For instance, a court allowed the media to refer to a newspaper publisher as a "near-Neanderthal" whose paper is published "by paranoids for paranoids" (*Loeb v. New Times*, 497 F.Supp. 85, 1980).

A legal test for opinion versus fact. Two federal court decisions may help to explain the difference between a statement of fact (which could lead to a successful libel suit if false) and an expression of opinion (which could not). In a 1985 case, *Ollman v. Evans* (750 F.2d 970), and a 1986 case, *Janklow v. Newsweek* (788 F.2d 1300), two different federal circuit courts faced the problem of separating fact from opinion.

The first case arose when syndicated columnists Rowland Evans and Robert Novak accused Bertell Ollman, a political science professor at New York University, of not only being an avowed Marxist but also of wanting to use his teaching position as a platform for political indoctrination. In the second case, William Janklow, the governor of South Dakota, was described in *Newsweek* as having had a long-running feud with Native American activist Dennis Banks. *Newsweek* implied that as South Dakota's attorney general, Janklow prosecuted Banks to get revenge after Banks falsely accused him of raping a Native American girl.

Both Ollman and Janklow sued for libel. In both cases, the courts had to distinguish facts from opinion. In both, the judges found the statements to be opinions and thus not the proper basis for a libel suit. And both decisions are especially significant because they are *en banc* decisions (made by all the judges in the circuit, not just a panel of three).

Adapting and slightly modifying the guidelines developed in the *Ollman* case, the *Janklow* decision listed the following four criteria to be used in determining whether a statement is a potentially libelous fact or a protected expression of opinion:

1. *The precision and specificity of the disputed statement.* Calling someone a "fascist" is indefinite and therefore an opinion; charging someone with a specific wrongful act would be a statement of fact.
2. *The verifiability of the statement.* "If a statement cannot plausibly be verified, it cannot be seen as 'fact,'" the court said.
3. *The literary context in which the statement is made.* A court may look at the type of publication, its style of writing, and intended audience to determine whether a statement is fact or opinion.
4. *The "public context" of the statement.* A statement made in "a public, political arena" or which "implicates core values of the First Amendment" is much more likely to be an expression of opinion than a statement of fact.

This four-part test has been adopted by several federal circuit courts.

Book reviews: fact or opinion? In 1994, a federal court caused near panic among book reviewers and others who write critical reviews by holding that a reviewer could be sued for expressing the opinion that a book contains "too much sloppy journalism." However, the court changed its mind and reversed itself a few months later. In *Moldea v. New York Times Co.* (15 F.3d 1137; 22 F.3d 310, 1994), the D.C. Circuit issued this surprising pair of opinions. The case began when *New York Times* sports writer Gerald Eskenazi reviewed *Interference: How Organized Crime Influences Professional Football,* a book by Dan E. Moldea. The review, published in the *New York Times Book Review,* offered a number of examples from Moldea's book to back up the charge that it contained "sloppy journalism."

Moldea sued for libel, charging that the *New York Times* book review destroyed his career as an author. A trial court dismissed the lawsuit almost immediately and Moldea appealed.

At first, the appellate court reinstated the lawsuit, but then the three-judge panel that ruled on the case took the unusual step of reversing itself.

In the second ruling, the court held that to escape libel, a book reviewer's criticism must be "rationally supportable by reference to the actual text he or she is evaluating." In short, what a book review says about a book need not be more than a *supportable interpretation* of the book. In the context of a book review, a charge such as "sloppy journalism" is not libelous as long as it is backed up with valid examples from the book.

Summary: Fact versus opinion. To summarize the fact-versus-opinion distinction, a false charge that someone committed a crime is likely to be ruled a libelous statement of fact, even if it appears on an "opinion" page of a newspaper, in a direct quote, or in a letter to the editor or an advertisement. However, if the charge is made by a public official or during a government proceeding, the *privilege* defense may apply even though the charge is a false statement of fact and not a protected expression of opinion.

On the other hand, a clearly labeled column or editorial accusing a public figure of incompetence is likely to be ruled an opinion, protected by the fair comment defense. But between the extremes of falsely calling someone a murderer (almost certainly a statement of fact) and accusing a celebrity of lacking talent or accusing a politician of incompetence (which would usually qualify as an expression of opinion), there is a large gray area. In this ill-defined middle ground between fact and opinion, the courts must often decide on a case-by-case basis whether a statement is fact or opinion. If anything, the gray area is a little bigger as a result of the Supreme Court's 1990 decision in the *Milkovich* case.

However, one thing has become clear about the *Milkovich* decision: most states are continuing to dismiss libel cases based on statements that are clearly expressions of opinion as opposed to verifiably true or false statements of fact. When the *Milkovich* case was decided, many journalists feared an avalanche of lawsuits by persons criticized in columns, reviews, editorials, and op-ed pieces. Except where an opinion piece also contains an allegedly false factual statement, that has simply not happened.

In the years since the *Milkovich* decision, most courts have continued to interpret the fair comment defense liberally, extending broad protection to expressions of opinion. A 1998 decision of the Ninth Circuit illustrates the degree to which the courts refuse to allow libel suits based on expressions of opinion. In *Dodds v. American Broad. Co.* (145 F.3d 1053), the court dismissed a lawsuit filed by a judge after ABC's *PrimeTime Live* depicted him as incompetent. The judge said, "Part of our American heritage is the right of all citizens to express their views about politicians, officeholders and umpires, frequently in highly unfavorable terms." He added that the First Amendment protects "statements of opinion concerning whether a person who holds high public office is fit for that office or is competent to serve... whether or not those statements are supportable, verifiable or based on facts or premises that are disclosed."

Personality defenses

In recent years, some of those faced with libel suits have begun employing defenses based on their personality quirks or the media products they create. Although these approaches have met with mixed success, they are making increasingly regular appearances for media provocateurs facing libel suits. Some examples follow.

"Caustic personality" defense. Several courts have extended the opinion defense to radio hosts known for their confrontational styles. The Ninth Circuit interpreted the distinction between fact and opinion in 2009 in *Gardner v. Martino* (563 F.3d 981) to be one

FIG. 35.
Tucker Carlson (then at MSNBC) at a 2007 Dept. of Interior awards gala at the American Museum of Natural History, New York City. His "unbelievable person" libel defense has been gaining traction in recent years.

National Archives.

of public expectations. Plaintiffs John and Susan Gardner brought suit against talk show host Tom Martino for comments made on his nationally syndicated radio show about their personal watercraft business. A caller had complaints about the Gardners' handling of a defective craft, and Martino called the Gardners liars and made other negative comments about their business. The court, in finding against the Gardners, said, in effect, that no one really expects bombastic talk show hosts like Martino to be purveyors of fact: "*The Tom Martino Show* is a radio talk show program that contains many of the elements that would reduce the audience's expectation of learning an objective fact: drama, hyperbolic language, an opinionated and arrogant host, and heated controversy." Thus, said the court, Martino's statements were opinion rather than objective statements of fact.

The "caustic personality as defense" approach also worked for a radio defendant in the Rhode Island Supreme Court in 2013 in *Burke v. Gregg* (55 A.3d 212). The state high court rejected the defamation claims of a restaurant owner, Robert Burke, against *Providence Journal* reporter Katherine Gregg and AM talk-show host Dan Yorke, who, on-air, called Burke a "punk" and a "piece of garbage" (Gregg had written an article about Burke's forbidding journalists to cover a political "roast" at his restaurant, and Yorke commented about it on his show). Nothing the journalists said was defamatory, though some comments were in bad taste. The court said that on-air, "on occasion, tensions flare and these conversations deteriorate from moderate exchanges into heated free-for-all arguments: the tone can become caustic, the comments blunt, unrefined, and downright unfair."

"No one should believe me anyway," or the Carlson defense. An odd libel defense has emerged in recent years based on a related idea. At least three individuals have raised it: no reasonable person is likely to believe what they say, so their information should not be considered factual. Rather, their outlandish claims should be viewed as protected opinion.

An attorney representing Alex Jones of InfoWars first raised this defense in a motion to dismiss a case brought by parents of a Sandy Hook Elementary School shooting victim, writing, "No reasonable reader or listener would interpret Mr. Jones' statements regarding the possibility of a 'blue-screen' being used as a verifiably false statement of fact, and even if it is verifiable as false, the entire context in which it was made discloses that the statements are mere opinions 'masquerading as a fact.'" A "blue screen" (or "green screen") is a technique by which actors perform in front of a blue or green screen which can then be digitally eliminated and replaced with another background. In this case, Jones alleged that Anderson Cooper's live interview with a Sandy Hook parent was faked before a blue screen. Jones' attorney was in essence asserting that because Jones' statements were unbelievable as statements of fact, they should be considered as "opinions masquerading as facts" and thus not actionable as false facts.

A Texas appeals court explicitly rejected Jones' "Carlson defense" in 2019. In *Jones v. Pozner* (2019 Tex. App. LEXIS 9641), the judge said not only had Jones offered no background to support his claim, but the parents provided evidence of the claim's falsity. Moreover, she added, Jones "should have known [his allegation] was false given that the facts and evidence available regarding the shooting at Sandy Hook had been well established" by the time of the broadcast, four years after the tragedy.

Two other libel defendants reprised this approach in later years. Tucker Carlson used a version of the defense—and won—in a case brought by former Playboy model Karen McDougal, who was alleged to have had a year-long affair with former President Donald J. Trump in the mid-2000s. McDougal was allegedly paid $150,000 to keep quiet about that affair before the 2016 presidential election. On a December 2018 edition of "Tucker Carlson Tonight," Carlson showed an image of McDougal on-screen during a segment in which he discussed the payment made to McDougal (and to another woman in a similar situation discussed elsewhere in this chapter, Stephanie Clifford/Stormy Daniels): "Two women approached Donald Trump and threatened to ruin his career and humiliate his family if he doesn't give them money. Now, that sounds like a classic case of extortion. Yet, for whatever reason, Trump caves to it, and he directs Michael Cohen to pay the ransom. Now, more than two years later, Trump is a felon for doing this. It doesn't seem to make any sense."

McDougal sued Fox News for libel. The judge, in finding for Fox, said that the "general tenor" of Carlson's show suggests that Carlson isn't using facts but instead "engaging in 'exaggeration' and 'non-literal commentary'" (*McDougal v. Fox News Network*, 489 F. Supp. 3d 174, 2020). In addition, the judge said, "Given Mr. Carlson's reputation, any reasonable viewer 'arrive[s] with an appropriate amount of skepticism'" about what Carlson says.

More recently, in March 2021, former Trump attorney Sidney Powell, in response to a billion-dollar libel lawsuit filed by Dominion Voting Systems, said that her claims that the 2020 elections were rigged and that the election was stolen by Democrats were classified by Dominion attorneys as "wild accusations" and "outlandish claims." Thus, she claimed, "reasonable people would not accept such statements as fact but view them only as claims that await testing by the courts through the adversary process." Will the "Carlson defense" work for her? Stay tuned.

Minor Defenses

In addition to the generally recognized libel defenses, other defenses have been recognized by some courts. Also, two purely technical defenses should be noted here.

Neutral reportage. Perhaps the most interesting of the less-recognized defenses is one called *neutral reportage*. It got its main impetus from a 1977 Second Circuit decision in *Edwards v. National Audubon Society* (556 F.2d 113). That case involved a *New York Times* story reporting a heated dispute between the National Audubon Society and a group of scientists the society had accused of being "paid to lie" by pesticide companies. The paper attempted to cover both sides on this controversy and was sued by some of the scientists for reporting the charge against them, even though the reporter attempted to present their side of the story too. The Second Circuit recognized a special defense for this situation, pointing out that the paper was attempting to be neutral in reporting both sides of a controversial issue.

Although the idea of a neutral reportage defense is appealing to those who believe the media should be able to cover all sides of a controversy without risking a libel suit, the concept has not been widely accepted by other courts. Some state courts (in Florida, for instance) have recognized neutral reportage, while others (in Kentucky, Michigan, New York, and Pennsylvania, for example) have not. In Illinois, one appellate court recognized neutral reportage but another appellate court rejected the concept.

In short, while neutral reportage has been accepted as a new libel defense in some jurisdictions, it has not yet gained the broad acceptance that many journalists hoped it would.

Technical defenses. Among the technical (as opposed to substantive) libel defenses, two should be mentioned here: *consent* and the *statute of limitations*. Where it can be proved that a plaintiff gave an actual consent to a libelous publication, he or she cannot thereafter sue for libel. If the consent was voluntarily and intelligently given, it precludes a libel suit. Likewise, where the statute of limitations (the time limit during which a law suit must be filed) has run, the defendant is entitled to an easy dismissal without the trouble and expense of a trial.

■ LIBEL AND THE FIRST AMENDMENT

Until 1964 we could have concluded our discussion of libel law with almost no mention of the Supreme Court. For nearly 200 years of American jurisprudence, the nation's highest court took the position that civil libel suits were purely a state matter and none of its business. But in 1964 the historic *New York Times v. Sullivan* decision was handed down, establishing that there are constitutional limits to what states may do in awarding libel judgments.

New York Times v. Sullivan: **a landmark case.** What prompted this landmark Supreme Court decision was a half-million-dollar libel judgment against the *New York Times*. In making this award, an Alabama jury was allowed to presume that a massive injury had occurred simply because it found the wording of an advertisement libelous to L. B. Sullivan, a Montgomery city commissioner. The ad never mentioned Sullivan, and in fact only a few copies of that issue of the *Times* were ever distributed in Sullivan's community.

What did the advertisement say to produce such a large libel judgment? It said, among other things, that the Montgomery police had taken certain actions against civil rights demonstrators that they in fact had not. Chapter One discussed this case to illustrate court procedures, so we'll not repeat the details here. But Sullivan won at the trial level, and the Alabama Supreme Court affirmed the judgment in its full amount.

Meanwhile, other Montgomery public officials filed additional libel suits against the *New York Times*, seeking total damages of $3 million. The *Times* was going to pay dearly for publishing a pro–civil rights advertisement that contained some factual errors and then distributing a few dozen copies of the paper in Montgomery, Ala.

Had the U.S. Supreme Court not chosen to review the case—instead maintaining its long tradition of leaving civil libel law completely up to the states—the threat of censorship via libel suits would have been a serious one. The Supreme Court broke with tradition and agreed to hear the case precisely because lawsuits such as this one were a serious threat to First Amendment freedoms.

New York Times v. Sullivan's **holding.** Writing for a unanimous Court, Justice William Brennan ruled that the huge libel judgment against the *Times* could not stand—for three

FIG. 36.
Justice William J. Brennan, Jr., official Supreme Court portrait, 1976. He wrote the majority opinion in *New York Times v. Sullivan.*

Library of Congress Prints and Photographs Division Washington, D.C. 20540 [LC-USZ62-60138]

reasons. He said to allow such a judgment would in effect sanction a new form of government censorship of the press via civil libel suits. To avoid lawsuits by local officials in various communities to which the nation's major newspapers are mailed, the major papers would have to steer clear of controversial subjects. Moreover, Brennan wrote, the media need some "breathing space" in their handling of controversial issues—including some protection when errors inevitably occur during the "robust" debate of these issues.

Finally, Brennan pointed out that public officials voluntarily move into the public arena when they seek office, subjecting themselves to much more scrutiny than private citizens should have to face. Criticism is something they must expect. In return, public officials gain more access to the media to present their side of the story than a private citizen enjoys. Thus, public officials need less libel protection than other citizens.

The key language. Under this rationale, Brennan wrote that public officials could no longer win libel judgments against the media unless they could prove *actual malice.*

> The constitutional guarantees require, we think, a federal rule that prohibits a public official from recovering damages for a defamatory falsehood relating to his official conduct unless he proves that a statement was made with "actual malice"—that is, with knowledge that it was false or with reckless disregard of whether it was false or not.

This language is among the most important ever written on mass media law in America. If you remember any single concept from this discussion, you should remember that public officials must prove actual malice to win libel suits and remember how actual malice is defined. First, actual malice means *publishing a falsehood.* Second, it means publishing that falsehood either with *knowledge* that it was false *or* with *reckless disregard* for whether it was false or not.

Malice is a legal term that has other meanings in other contexts, often referring to bad intentions. It was given a special meaning in *Sullivan* for libel law. But as we will see, a 2009 development in the First Circuit calls the meaning of "malice" in libel cases into question, allowing state law to define it as ill will.

When a landmark Supreme Court decision is handed down, there are often unanswered questions—issues that must be clarified by additional Supreme Court rulings. The *Sullivan* case had exactly that result. First of all, what public officials are included in its coverage?

FIG. 37.
The March 1960
New York Times
advertisement that gave
rise to *New York Times v.
Sullivan* in 1964. There
were some errors in the
text but the Court did
not believe that should
result in a finding of
actual malice.

*National Archives at Atlanta,
made available on Flickr as
part of the U.S. National
Archives' Documented Rights
Exhibit.*

Does it apply only to elected officials, or does it also apply to public figures who hold no office? And does it apply to all public servants or just to certain prominent ones? And equally important, exactly what does "reckless disregard for the truth" mean?

*Post-*Sullivan *Rulings*

In the years that followed the *Sullivan* decision, the Supreme Court attempted to resolve some of these ongoing questions by handing down a series of additional libel rulings. First, in a 1966 case (*Rosenblatt v. Baer*, 383 U.S. 75) the Court said the actual malice requirement would apply to minor public officials. A. D. Rosenblatt, a New Hampshire newspaper columnist, had accused the former supervisor of a county skiing and recreation area of mishandling public funds. The Court said even a public employee of that rank would henceforth have to prove actual malice to win a libel suit. The "public official" designation would apply to all who have "substantial responsibility for...the conduct of governmental affairs," the Court ruled. (More recent rulings have cast doubts on the applicability of the actual malice requirement to "minor" public employees, however.)

Then in 1967 the Court applied the actual malice rule to public figures who held no office and offered guidance on the meaning of the "reckless disregard" concept in two cases decided together, *Curtis Publishing Co. v. Butts* and *Associated Press v. Walker* (388 U.S. 130).

Butts *and* **Walker.** The *Butts* case arose when the *Saturday Evening Post,* published by Curtis, carried an article entitled "The Story of a College Football Fix." The article claimed that Wally Butts, athletic director at the University of Georgia, had given Alabama coach Paul "Bear" Bryant information in advance about Georgia's game plans for an upcoming football game between the two schools. The story was based on information provided by an insurance agent in Atlanta who said he had overheard a telephone conversation between Butts and Bryant through an electronic error. Although there was no deadline pressure and the article was published some time after the game, the *Post* did not double-check the story with anyone knowledgeable about football to see whether the information the insurance man claimed he overheard would in fact have helped Alabama or hurt Georgia.

The *Walker* case differed in several respects. It resulted from an AP dispatch detailing the activities of former U.S. Army General Edwin Walker, who resigned his command and engaged in conservative political activities, often speaking out against school desegregation. Walker was present at the University of Mississippi during the initial desegregation of the campus. A group of white people attacked the federal marshals who were protecting the first Black student enrolled at the university. Walker had addressed that crowd. The AP dispatch, moved over the wires within minutes after the fast-breaking events occurred, said ex-General Walker led the charge of the white crowd. Walker claimed he called for a peaceful protest, counseled against violence, and denied leading the attack.

Butts and Walker each won a libel judgment of about half a million dollars; both Curtis Publishing and the Associated Press appealed to the U.S. Supreme Court. The Supreme Court voted 5-4 to affirm Butts' libel judgment against the *Saturday Evening Post,* but unanimously overruled Walker's judgment against the AP. The Court took the occasion to compare the two situations as a way of illustrating what reckless disregard for the truth means.

But first, a majority of the Supreme Court justices agreed that both men were public figures and should be subject to the *New York Times v. Sullivan* rule, although neither was a public official at the time of the respective libel suits. Walker was no longer an officer in the U.S. Army, and Butts received his salary from the Georgia Athletic Association, a private corporation, not from the state.

However, both men were involved in issues "in which the public has a justified and important interest." Although the Court was not unanimous in deciding that the *New York Times* rule as such should apply to public figures as well as public officials, the precedent has held up in the years since and is now settled law. Thus, both men had to show reckless disregard for the truth to win their libel suits.

One win, one loss. Why, then, did Butts win while Walker lost? The Court pointed out that there was a big difference between the types of reporting that went into the two stories. The AP was under intense deadline pressure and had no time to double-check its information; the *Post* was not. The AP had a reporter with a good reputation for accuracy on the scene; the *Post* relied on the uncorroborated statements of a non-journalist, a man who was in fact an ex-convict, and the staff never checked the story with anyone with special expertise in football. Further, the conduct AP's reporter attributed to Walker was consistent with Walker's previous statements on school desegregation. In short, because the Court found a substantial difference between the *Saturday Evening Post's* reporting practices and AP's, the libel judgment against the *Post* was affirmed while the one against AP was reversed.

Other libel reversals. The Supreme Court continued its trend of reversing libel judgments against the media with three cases handed down on the same day in 1971: *Monitor-Patriot Co. v. Roy* (401 U.S. 265), *Ocala Star-Banner v. Damron* (401 U.S. 295), and *Time Inc. v. Pape* (401 U.S. 279). The *Monitor-Patriot* case stemmed from a syndicated column that branded a candidate for the U.S. Senate a "small time bootlegger" because of a conviction in the 1920s. The plaintiff contended the publisher was vulnerable to a libel judgment because the conviction involved his private life long ago and had nothing to do with his public performance. The justices said the actual malice requirement had not been met, and the libel case could not be sustained, to no one's surprise. After all, the accusation was basically true.

In *Ocala*, the Supreme Court overruled a libel judgment where a newspaper had confused two brothers, identifying a candidate for office as having been convicted of perjury when in fact it was his brother who had been convicted. The Supreme Court said there was no reckless disregard for the truth in this copy desk error. At the time, this seemed to free the media from liability when a public official or public figure is the victim of an accidental misidentification problem such as those discussed earlier in this chapter.

The *Pape* case involved a libel in a U.S. Commission on Civil Rights report, disseminated in a *Time* magazine article. *Time* changed the reported information somewhat, but the Supreme Court found no reckless disregard for the truth in *Time's* reporting of a statement charging a Chicago police officer with brutality—even though the story did not make it clear these were mere allegations. *Time's* imprecise reporting was forgiven in large part because the report itself was ambiguous and subject to more than one interpretation.

The theme in all three 1971 cases seemed clear: the traditional rules of libel must give way when a public official is the plaintiff, lest the threat of libel suits unduly inhibit the reporting of public affairs.

Almost abolishing libel? Later in 1971 the Supreme Court handed down a decision heralded by some as the ultimate victory for the media over the threat of libel: *Rosenbloom v. Metromedia* (403 U.S. 29). Although there was no majority opinion, the three-justice plurality opinion seemed to foreclose libel judgments against the media whenever the plaintiff was involved in an issue of public interest, no matter how private a citizen he or she might be.

George Rosenbloom, a Philadelphia magazine dealer, was arrested during a police campaign against obscenity, and he was called a "smut distributor" and "girlie-book peddler" on Metromedia radio station WIP. He was never convicted, and a court granted an injunction ordering the police to leave him alone, since the books were not legally obscene. Rosenbloom sued the station and won a $275,000 libel judgment. An appellate court reversed.

The Supreme Court agreed on a 5-3 vote that Rosenbloom should not win a libel judgment, but only three justices (Brennan, Burger, and Blackmun) joined the plurality opinion. Justices Black and White concurred in the result, but on a different rationale. What made *Rosenbloom* memorable was the sweep of the language in that plurality opinion. Justice Brennan, writing for the Court, said the distinction between public officials and public figures on the one hand and private citizens on the other "makes no sense." Rather, in the future the criterion for applying the actual malice requirement should be whether the plaintiff was involved in a matter of *"public or general interest."* Thus, the Court seemed to be saying the media could bootstrap themselves out of libel suits by publicizing a private person's activities so as to generate public interest and then avoid a lawsuit *because* of that interest.

After *Rosenbloom*, it seemed that virtually everyone whose name appeared in a newspaper or in a radio or television newscast might have to prove actual malice. And because proving actual malice turned out to be so difficult, it appeared for a time in the early 1970s that the media were at last virtually free from their most troubling legal problem, the libel suit.

Malice, Negligence, and Gertz

However, three years later the hope that libel was being abolished vanished when the Supreme Court handed down its famous *Gertz v. Welch* decision in 1974. Much has already been said of this decision, which profoundly changed the law of libel—and thus laid the foundation for modern libel law when private persons are involved.

Elmer Gertz, a Chicago lawyer, represented the family of a young Black man who had been killed by a Chicago police officer (the officer was later prosecuted for the act). With Gertz's help, the family was seeking civil damages in a suit for *wrongful death* in the late 1960s.

An article appeared in *American Opinion*, the magazine of the ultraconservative John Birch Society, claiming that Gertz was part of a communist conspiracy to discredit law enforcement. Gertz was called a "communist-fronter" and a "Leninist." The article also falsely accused Gertz of various subversive activities.

Gertz sued Robert Welch Inc., publisher of *American Opinion*, and initially won a $50,000 jury verdict. However, the trial judge set aside the verdict and ruled that Gertz was a public figure who could not win a libel judgment without proving actual malice, something he had not proved during the original trial. Then the Supreme Court's *Rosenbloom* decision was announced, and an appellate court upheld the trial judge's decision that Gertz would have to prove actual malice to win a libel judgment against Welch. Gertz asked the Supreme Court to review the determination that he was a public figure.

In a narrow 5-4 decision that Justice Harry Blackmun said he joined only because the country needed a clear-cut majority opinion on an issue as important as libel, the Supreme Court backed away from *Rosenbloom* and reinstated the distinction between private persons and public figures. He said that Gertz, although he was a prominent Chicago lawyer, had done nothing to seek public figure status in this context. Thus, Gertz should not be constitutionally required to prove actual malice to win a libel suit.

Blackmun said the states should feel free to allow private persons such as Elmer Gertz to win libel suits against the media by proving a level of fault short of actual malice. However, in no case could the media be held on the "strict liability" (or "liability without fault") basis that had been the prevailing rule of law for at least 200 years. The media had to be guilty of something *beyond* merely publishing a falsehood—there had to be some level of fault. Still, the Court didn't say every state had to allow private persons to prove mere negligence, just that the states *could* allow this lesser standard of proof for private plaintiffs if they wished, and any state that wished to could still require private persons to prove actual malice.

As a result, in all 50 states public figures still have to prove actual malice. But in most states, that level of fault is not required of private persons. Most states accepted the Court's invitation and adopted rules under which private persons must prove only some level of negligence to win a libel case against the media. However, some state courts have chosen to require *all* libel plaintiffs—private persons as well as public figures—to prove actual malice in any libel case involving an issue of public or general concern.

Both of these terms—*actual malice* and *negligence*—have special meanings in law. There is no way we can define them in a way that would be applicable in all states. We already indicated that negligence is a less serious breach of the standards of good journalism than reckless disregard for the truth. Negligence may well mean nothing more than publishing a falsehood as a result of sloppy reporting, or perhaps even because an innocent error slipped past the copy desk. Some states say it means failing to do the kind of checking a "reasonable" person would do under the circumstances.

In addition to ruling that private persons could be allowed to sue for libel without proving actual malice, *Gertz* had an important effect on damage awards in libel suits, as already noted: the ruling required most private libel plaintiffs to prove at least *general damages* (sometimes called *actual damages*). The Court said that in the absence of a showing of actual malice, there could be no punitive or presumed damages. Instead, plaintiffs who could only prove negligence and not actual malice could win only such damages as they could prove, although those damages would not be limited to just out-of-pocket losses (special damages).

As a result of these sweeping changes in American libel law, a new period of reassessment occurred, as the courts and legislatures tried to adapt their rules to the new boundaries. It quickly became apparent that the crucial issue in future suits would often be *whether the plaintiff was a public figure or a private person.* To help resolve this question, the *Gertz* ruling offered this observation:

> For the most part those who attain this [public figure] status have assumed roles of especial prominence in the affairs of society. Some occupy positions of such persuasive power and influence that they are deemed public figures for all purposes. More commonly, those classed as public figures have thrust themselves to the forefront of particular public controversies in order to influence the resolution of the issues involved.

Thus, the Court said that many public figures are so classified because they thrust themselves into the vortex of a controversy. These people might be called vortex public figures, and the courts should look mainly at a libel plaintiff's own conduct to see if the definition applied.

There is one ironic footnote to the *Gertz* case: after the landmark decision, Elmer Gertz patiently waited as his remanded case meandered through pretrial procedures and finally went to trial again. Although his Supreme Court decision emphasized that nonpublic figures didn't necessarily have to prove actual malice, during the second trial a jury agreed that Gertz *did* prove actual malice and awarded him $400,000 ($300,000 punitive), which was affirmed by a federal appellate court in 1982—eight years after the Supreme Court decision and 14 years after the shooting that led to the original libel.

Private Persons and Public Figures

In the aftermath of the *Gertz* decision, the Supreme Court had to decide whether libel plaintiffs were public figures (who had to prove actual malice to win) or private persons (who could win by proving just negligence). The first of these cases, *Time Inc. v. Firestone* (424 U.S. 448, 1976), involved a divorce in a wealthy and socially prominent Florida family. Russell Firestone, an heir to the tire company fortune, sued his wife Mary Alice for divorce on the grounds of extreme cruelty and adultery, and the case received extensive publicity. When the divorce was granted after a trial in which there was considerable evidence of marital infidelity on both sides (enough evidence "to make Dr. Freud's hair curl," the judge said), *Time* magazine reported that one of the grounds for the divorce was adultery.

However, the judge was vague about the legal grounds for the divorce, and in fact an obscure provision of Florida law would have prohibited the award of alimony if adultery had been a ground for a divorce. Since Firestone had been granted alimony, her alleged adultery couldn't have been one of the legal grounds on which the divorce was granted. This obscure point of Florida law escaped the *Time* correspondent—but that could hardly be called publishing a falsehood with reckless disregard for the truth. There was evidence that she sought publicity: she held press conferences to discuss the divorce and subscribed to a clipping service. The story was covered in no fewer than 45 articles in one local newspaper.

However, the Supreme Court ruled that Firestone was *not* a public figure. She had not voluntarily thrust herself into any public controversy: "Dissolution of marriage through judicial proceedings is not the sort of 'public controversy' referred to in *Gertz,* even though the marital difficulties of extremely wealthy individuals may be of interest to some portion of the reading public." Firestone had done nothing more than she had to do—avail herself of the courts to terminate a marriage.

The Supreme Court seemed to be saying this: while some celebrities and politicians are so pervasively famous that they are *all-purpose public figures,* most people do not become public figures unless they voluntarily inject themselves into a public debate on a controversial issue. As a result, some relatively well-known persons may not be considered public figures should they sue for libel based on a reference to their personal lives. And when it comes to persons involved in a crime, the Court's *Firestone* ruling made it clear they will *not* ordinarily be classified as public figures: "There appears little reason why these individuals should substantially forfeit that degree of protection which the law of defamation would otherwise afford them simply by virtue of their being drawn into a courtroom."

After the Supreme Court ruled that Firestone was not a public figure, she chose not to pursue her lawsuit further, and the case was eventually dismissed.

It would be difficult to overemphasize the extent to which the thinking in the *Firestone* case is a retrenchment from the libel protection the media enjoyed in the late 1960s and early 1970s. However, the Supreme Court continued the same trend away from classifying newsworthy persons as public figures in a pair of 1979 decisions, *Hutchinson v. Proxmire* (443 U.S. 111) and *Wolston v. Reader's Digest Assn.* (443 U.S. 157).

The *Hutchinson* case (involving Sen. Proxmire's Golden Fleece Award) was discussed earlier in connection regarding its adverse effect on the privilege defense. It offered the media little comfort on the issue of who is a public figure, either. The Court said Dr. Hutchinson was *not* a public figure, despite the fact that he was the research director of a major state-controlled mental health facility—and had won large government grants. The *Wolston* case followed the same policy of narrowing the definition of a public figure. Ilya Wolston had an aunt and uncle who had pleaded guilty to charges of spying for the former Soviet Union, and he had been cited for contempt himself when he failed to comply with a Congressional subpoena. Other than that contempt citation, he was never convicted of any offense. Many years later, a *Reader's Digest* publication included his name in a list of "Soviet agents" in the United States. He sued for libel and a lower court ruled that he was a public figure who could not prove actual malice. The Supreme Court reversed, finding that he had done nothing to inject himself into a public controversy. Once again, a libel plaintiff was ruled to be a private person who did not need to prove actual malice to win, thereby reducing the media's First Amendment protection and making it much easier for the plaintiff to win.

The definition of a public figure or public official was changing. If some of the Court's early libel rulings were decided under the new standards, would Athletic Director Butts be a public figure—or a public official? What about Pape, the Chicago policeman?

General rule? In the decades since the *Firestone, Hutchinson* and *Wolston* decisions, the public figure–private person question has been addressed in literally thousands of lower court cases. If there is a general rule today, it is that many people whose names are in the news are *not* public figures—unless they intentionally inject themselves into a public controversy or take other actions likely to place them in the limelight. Even people who hold newsworthy but non-elective government positions may not be classified as public figures or public officials. So who is a public figure or public official today? The answer depends on which court decides the question.

■ REFINING THE ACTUAL MALICE RULE

Once someone is ruled to be a public official or public figure, that person faces the difficult challenge of proving actual malice—as defined by the Supreme Court—to win a libel case. During the 1980s and 1990s, the high court clarified the scope of the actual malice rule, applying it in several difficult fact situations.

Actual malice as a matter of law. One of the most important of these cases to the media was *Bose v. Consumers Union* (466 U.S. 485). This 1984 case was a strong reaffirmation of the constitutional safeguards journalists enjoy under *New York Times v. Sullivan*, a decision handed down almost exactly 20 years before the *Bose* ruling.

The case began when the Bose Corporation, a manufacturer of high-fidelity speakers, sued *Consumer Reports* magazine for a review that commented negatively and hyperbolically about the performance of Bose speakers. In a 1970 article, the magazine said that with these speakers music "tended to wander about the room." A Consumers Union engineer had written that the speakers made violins seem "about 10 feet wide." The manufacturer sued for product disparagement and won a six-figure damage award. During the trial, the judge concluded that the engineer should have said Bose speakers made music sound as if it wandered "along the wall," not "about the room." This, he said, was evidence of actual malice. (If you're thinking "huh?" you're not alone.) On appeal, the First Circuit reversed that judgment, ruling that the magazine was *not* guilty of actual malice in its product review even if some of the engineer's words and conclusions were debatable.

Normally, appellate courts are not supposed to second-guess a trial court's assessment of the evidence in deciding factual issues (such as whether there was actual malice in this *Consumer Reports* article), but that is exactly what the First Circuit did in this case. The high court upheld that decision, ruling that the media need the additional protection of being able to appeal a trial court's determination of actual malice. To rule otherwise, the Court said, would unduly erode First Amendment freedoms by denying the media the right to challenge libel judgments that are improperly awarded by trial judges or juries.

In finding a lack of actual malice, Justice John Paul Stevens wrote for the majority, "We agree with the Court of Appeals that the difference between hearing violin sounds move around the room and hearing them wander back and forth fits easily within the breathing space that gives life to the First Amendment." Moreover, "an appellate court has an obligation to 'make an independent examination of the whole record' in order to make sure that the judgment does not constitute a forbidden intrusion on the field of free expression."

The *Bose* case represents a *significant* expansion of the protection the media enjoy under the *New York Times v. Sullivan* rule. When a judge or jury finds actual malice in a publication or broadcast with little or no evidence of "reckless disregard for the truth," the media now have a second shot at that verdict.

Narrowing Gertz. In 1985, the Supreme Court took a major step to narrow the scope of the *Gertz* case: it ruled that *Gertz* applies only to issues of public concern, not to libel cases arising from discussions of purely private matters. That happened in the case of *Dun & Bradstreet v. Greenmoss Builders* (472 U.S. 749).

This case began after Dun & Bradstreet (D&B), a credit reporting agency, falsely informed several of its clients that Greenmoss, a Vermont construction company, had filed for bankruptcy. The false credit report resulted from a young worker's negligent (but not malicious) error in record-checking. Although Greenmoss could not prove actual malice, it won a $350,000 libel judgment against D&B, including punitive damages, despite *Gertz's* holding that even nonpublic figures must prove actual malice to win punitive damages. The judgment was upheld by the Supreme Court.

Affirming the libel verdict, three justices ruled that credit rating reports are not a matter of public concern and should not be subject to the actual malice requirement as set forth in *New York Times v. Sullivan* and expanded in *Gertz v. Welch.* This represented a new distinction in libel law: the plurality said the actual malice rule from *Gertz* should to apply to libel cases involving issues of public concern but not to cases involving purely private matters.

While the three justices in the plurality (Lewis Powell, William Rehnquist, and Sandra Day O'Connor) voted to create this new exception to the *Gertz* principle, two others (Chief Justice Warren Burger and Justice Byron White) filed concurring opinions in which they agreed that *Gertz* was inapplicable to this situation. The remaining four justices dissented, arguing that the *Gertz* principle should apply to this case. Justice William Brennan joined Thurgood Marshall, Harry Blackmun, and John Paul Stevens to argue that credit reporting is a legitimate matter of public concern and therefore should be subject to actual malice requirements.

States may choose. Nevertheless, the three justices who carved out this exception to *Gertz*—together with the two justices who would overturn *Gertz* altogether—constituted a majority of the Supreme Court, a majority that said *Gertz* simply does not apply to libel cases involving nonpublic issues. In such cases, the states are free to allow libel plaintiffs to win without proving either actual malice *or* negligence. However, some states have chosen to continue requiring proof of actual malice or negligence in all libel cases, despite this ruling. The five justices were merely saying that the *states are not constitutionally required* to make plaintiffs prove actual malice or negligence in libel cases involving purely private matters.

Actual malice: hard to prove. Proving actual malice is usually so difficult that few libel cases are won by public officials or public figures, the people who must do so to win any libel case that involves an issue of public concern. In 1989, the first time since the 1960s, the Supreme Court upheld a libel decision involving actual malice in *Harte-Hanks Commc'ns v. Connaughton* (491 U.S. 657), unanimously affirming a lower court's finding that the *Hamilton* (Ohio) *Journal-Beacon* was guilty of actual malice. The newspaper falsely reported that Daniel Connaughton, who was running for a judgeship, wrongfully tried to discredit an opponent.

The Court reaffirmed the guidelines it had set down in the 1984 *Bose* case (discussed earlier), requiring appellate courts to independently review the evidence in libel cases involving alleged actual malice. But it then agreed with the appellate court's

Focus on...
Bose v. Consumers Union, 466 U.S. 485 (1984)

The *Bose* case may be confusing without understanding the roles of different courts. Generally, trial courts with juries are triers of fact (establishing the record of facts to be used in an appeal), and appeals courts are arbiters of law. But these roles are not exclusive in libel cases.

Justice John Paul Stevens wrote, "Judges, as expositors of the Constitution, must independently decide whether the evidence in the record is sufficient to cross the constitutional threshold that bars the entry of any judgment that is not supported by clear and convincing proof of 'actual malice.'"

This means that appeals courts must exercise their own judgments, determining for themselves whether there was actual malice or not. A finding of actual malice, then, is a matter of law, not a finding of fact.

conclusion that actual malice *was* present in this case. Justice John Paul Stevens noted the newspaper's failure to check its own news sources—and the fact that an editor declined an opportunity to listen to tape-recorded interviews that could have cast doubts on the accuracy of the story. Those newsroom practices constitute more than just a departure from normal professional standards of journalism; they create evidence of actual malice, the Court said, and affirmed the jury award to Connaughton of $5,000 in compensatory and $195,000 in punitive damages.

Actual Malice, Direct Quotations, and Context

Is it possible to libel people by misquoting them or by taking their words out of context? When a book, newspaper, or magazine uses quotation marks, do readers assume the words inside the quotes are the speaker's exact words? Suppose a reporter knows that a quotation is not precisely what the speaker said. Does that mean the reporter is guilty of actual malice if a libel suit results from the quotation? Or what if a video clip is edited so as to suggest something that isn't true? Does that result in actual malice?

Misquote. In 1991, the Supreme Court ruled on a libel case that raised misquote questions, *Masson v. New Yorker Magazine* (501 U.S. 496). The case began when Jeffrey Masson, a psychoanalyst who once was the archivist for Sigmund Freud's papers, sued freelance writer Janet Malcolm and *New Yorker* magazine for publishing a lengthy article about him containing at least six quoted statements that he denied making. Malcolm conducted 40 hours of tape-recorded interviews with Masson. She also claimed there were additional non-recorded interviews during which she took detailed notes; Masson said she took no notes during most of the non-recorded interviews. Malcolm could not find her notes at the time.

Among other things, Malcolm quoted Masson as calling himself an "intellectual gigolo" and "the greatest analyst who ever lived." Those phrases were not in the taped interviews, but Malcolm claimed Masson did say those things during the non-recorded interviews. Masson flatly denied making those statements, charging that he was seriously misquoted—and that the resulting misrepresentation of his views injured his reputation.

Lower federal courts dismissed Masson's libel suit before trial, ruling that the quoted statements were "rational interpretations" of things Masson did say on tape and therefore not actionable. But the Supreme Court reinstated the case and remanded it to a federal appellate court to determine if the case should go to trial or be dismissed. Writing for the Court, Justice Anthony Kennedy said that journalists could not be expected to be absolutely precise in every direct quote. However, he said that the quoted statements in the article differed *significantly enough* from the taped statements that Masson was entitled to a jury trial (at which he would have to prove that Malcolm did misquote him, did so knowingly or recklessly, and thereby damaged his reputation).

Journalists who make *minor* changes in quotes by public figures are protected by the actual malice rule. But if the meaning is knowingly or recklessly changed in a "material" way, and the change hurts the person's reputation, then the person may have a case. Private persons would only need to prove they were libeled by a *negligent* misquote rather than by a knowing or reckless one under the law of most states.

In short, *Masson* gives journalists some leeway in handling direct quotes while holding them accountable for changing the meaning of a quote in a way that harms the quoted person's reputation. Armed with this holding, Masson got a federal appellate court to refer the case back to a federal trial court. In a 1993 trial, the jury agreed that he was libeled but deadlocked on the damages to award, and a mistrial was declared. In a second jury trial a year later, the jury ruled against Masson. Masson appealed once more, and in 1996 a federal appellate court upheld the jury's verdict, ending a complex and costly 12-year legal battle.

By 1996, Malcolm's legal expenses exceeded $2.5 million. Oddly, in 1995 Malcolm said her two-year-old granddaughter pulled a stack of old papers off a shelf, including a red notebook containing the missing notes from the non-recorded interviews. The notes included several key statements that Masson denied making, including "intellectual gigolo." If she could have produced those notes in 1984, the case might have been resolved much earlier, saving her and her publishers a fortune in legal expenses. Malcolm died in 2021 at age 86.

Context. But what about statements actually made by public figures but presented in a context that changes the viewer's understanding of the statements? The Ninth Circuit in 2010 said it didn't matter that the plaintiff's statement was actually spoken by him because the *context* in which it was presented made it misleading. In *Price v. Stossel* (620 F.3d 992), Dr. Frederick Price, a televangelist, delivered a sermon in which he said, "I live in a 25-room mansion. I have my own $6 million yacht. I have my own private jet, and I have my own helicopter, and I have seven luxury automobiles." ABC's *20/20* program, featuring John Stossel, placed the clip in a context so it appeared as though Price was bragging about his own material wealth—when actually Price was speaking from the perspective of a hypothetical wealthy person who is unhappy despite that wealth. ABC broadcast a retraction, but Price sued.

The district court dismissed the case because Price actually said the words, but the Ninth Circuit reversed. Relying on *Masson,* the court said that "the meaning of the quotation as published and the meaning of the words as uttered" must be compared and concluded that "the video quotation of Price's statement materially changed the meaning of Price's words."

Context was key in a libel case filed by someone whose speech had been heavily edited for political purposes. In 2015, a settlement was reached in the case of Shirley Sherrod's libel claims against conservative blogger Andrew Breitbart, in which an edited speech posted on the conservative commentator's website resulted in Sherrod's losing her job. In 2010, Breitbart posted a video clip of a speech Sherrod made for an NAACP fundraising event while she was Georgia State Director of Rural Development for the U.S. Department of Agriculture. The clip contained quotes that made Sherrod, who is Black, look as if she was discriminating against white farmers by stating that she might not have done all she could to help a white

FIG. 38.
Shirley Sherrod on *The Laura Flanders Show* in a 2016 episode, "Free The Land: Shirley Sherrod and Black Land Struggles in the South." Sherrod was the victim of political context editing by Andrew Breitbart in 2010.

The Laura Flanders Show, via Wikimedia Commons.

farmer who was acting superior to her. Sherrod was forced to resign from Agriculture under pressure from her superiors, and the NAACP and other groups decried her—until it was determined that Breitbart selectively edited out the context of Sherrod's speech, in which her major point was that it was poverty, not race, that was key to rural development.

In 2011, Sherrod sued Breitbart, alleging libel, false light, and infliction of emotional distress. Breitbart moved to use Washington, D.C.'s anti-SLAPP law against Sherrod's suit, and she countered that anti-SLAPP laws don't apply in federal court—a position other states have taken, although several circuits have enforced state anti-SLAPP laws in federal cases (the Fifth in *Lake Charles American Press* discussed earlier, the Ninth in a 1999 case, and in 2010, the First Circuit applied the Maine statute in a case involving an elementary school principal, *Godin v. Schencks*, 629 F.3d 79). Breitbart died in 2012, and his widow was named in the suit. In 2013, the D.C. Circuit dismissed Breitbart's appeal of a denial of an motion under the D.C. anti-SLAPP law, saying that it had not been timely filed (*Sherrod v. Breitbart*, 720 F.3d 932). The parties settled in 2015 under undisclosed terms.

Food Lion. One of the most controversial judgments against a news organization in many years was $5.5 million in punitive damages that a jury awarded to the Food Lion grocery chain in 1997 because ABC's *PrimeTime Live* had two of its staff members obtain jobs at Food Lion under false pretenses. The ABC staffers used hidden cameras to document the mishandling of foods. Although Food Lion did not even allege that ABC's report was libelous, the jury found ABC guilty of trespass, fraud, and other wrongs in connection with its undercover newsgathering. The trial judge later reduced the punitive damage award to $315,000. In 1999, the Fourth Circuit overturned that award, upholding only $2 (yes, two dollars) in damages against ABC for trespass and a breach of the duty of loyalty to an employer by the two ABC staffers who took jobs at Food Lion only to get the story (*Food Lion v. Capital Cities/ABC*, 194 F.3d 505). From the outset, ABC's defenders saw Food Lion's lawsuit as an end run around libel laws by a company that could not prove the ABC report was false but wanted to sue anyway. The appellate court verdict largely vindicated ABC, but only after years of litigation and enormous legal bills for the network.

Recent Developments: The Meaning of "Malice"

As mentioned earlier, the term "malice" has a particular meaning in libel law. When he wrote the Court's opinion in the *Masson* case, Justice Anthony Kennedy offered a suggestion concerning the actual malice rule itself—one that might have been drawn from his experience as a law professor. He said the term "actual malice" is confusing and should not be used in jury instructions. Instead, he said judges should merely tell jurors to decide if a falsehood was published knowingly or with reckless disregard for the truth. The problem, of course, is that many people who have never read a media law textbook assume (with the encouragement of most dictionaries) that "actual malice" means ill will or evil intentions. In libel cases involving public figures or public officials, it doesn't usually mean that at all. But perhaps he was prescient, as the First Circuit suggested exactly that some years later.

That court in 2009 sent shockwaves through media companies and attorneys with its decision in *Noonan v. Staples* (556 F.3d 20) by returning to a state's archaic interpretation of the "actual malice" standard in libel. Usually truth is an absolute defense against a libel claim, but the First Circuit interpreted Massachusetts state law to suggest that even truthful statements could give rise to a libel action if they were published with *malicious intent*.

Plaintiff Alan Noonan was fired from his sales position at office supply company Staples for padding his travel expense accounts. A Staples executive vice president sent a mass email to 1,500 employees informing them that Noonan had been fired for violating the travel and expense policy and warning them that non-compliance would be taken seriously. Noonan sued for libel. The trial court found for Staples, as did the First Circuit initially. However, after a rehearing, the First Circuit reversed. In what some commentators called the most dangerous libel decision in decades, the First Circuit applied a 1902 Massachusetts law that said that even *true* statements can result in libel if the defendant acted with ill will or malevolent intent—a common law interpretation of "actual malice." The court said the 1902 statute, passed before the 1964 *New York Times v. Sullivan* decision that provided the modern interpretation of "actual malice," dealt with defenses under traditional tort law. Noting the traditional truth defense to libel claims, the court then clarified:

> Massachusetts law, however, recognizes a narrow exception to this defense: the truth or falsity of the statement is immaterial, and the libel action may proceed, if the plaintiff can show that the defendant acted with "actual malice" in publishing the statement.

After finding that "malice" in the 1902 statute should mean publication with ill will, the court noted that the sending of an email naming an employee and saying the employee had been fired had never been done before, and it may have been sent to draw attention away from Noonan's supervisor's malfeasance. Many Staples employees who received the email did not travel and would have no reason to be informed of the policy's enforcement. These actions, said the court, could be interpreted by a jury to indicate that the vice president acted with ill will toward Noonan. The court remanded the libel case back to the trial court. The First Circuit declined to rehear the case *en banc*. However, on remand, the jury found for Staples, saying that the company did *not* act with malice in sending the truthful email.

Does this case open the door to plaintiffs' attorneys encouraging courts to apply state statutes' common law definitions of malice as ill will in cases where the publication was true? Some commentators have suggested that Staples lost at the First Circuit because the plaintiff in this case was not a public official. In Massachusetts, at least, the precedent remains.

In the most recent libel case to be decided by the Supreme Court, in 2014, the justices offered an interpretation of malice when they addressed the question of whether a court can deny civil case immunity under an airline security act without first deciding whether the airline's report was true. William Hoeper won a $1.4 million judgment from a Colorado court when it found that Air Wisconsin told Transportation Security Administration (TSA) officials that he was "mentally unstable" and may have a gun. The airline argued that the 2001 Aviation and Transportation Security Act (ATSA) protected it from the civil suit, but Hoeper successfully argued that Air Wisconsin gave up its immunity under ATSA when it made a disclosure "with actual knowledge that the disclosure was false, inaccurate, or misleading" or "with reckless disregard as to the truth or falsity of that disclosure." The Court unanimously reversed the Colorado Supreme Court's holding for Hoeper (*Air Wisconsin Airlines Corp. v. Hoeper*, 571 U.S. 237, 2014).

Justice Sonia Sotomayor noted that the language in ATSA matched that in *New York Times v. Sullivan*. Because of this, she reasoned, and "because we presume that Congress meant to incorporate the settled meaning of actual malice when it incorporated the language of that standard," a statement may not be denied ATSA immunity it was otherwise entitled to get unless it was materially false. It is important to note that Sotomayor used the words "settled meaning" when referring to "actual malice," thus suggesting that in the Court's eyes (or at least in hers), that term does indeed mean what Justice Brennan said it did in 1964.

The Future of New York Times v. Sullivan

Justice Sotomayor and others may think that the approach to libel law established in *New York Times v. Sullivan* is "settled," but not all judges (or Justices) approve of the 1964 landmark case. As noted earlier, the late Justice Antonin Scalia detested it, telling interviewer Charlie Rose in 2012 that it didn't comport with historical libel law: "Nobody thought that libel, even libel of public figures, was permitted, was sanctioned by the First Amendment."

It turns out Scalia was not alone. His colleague on the Supreme Court bench, Justice Clarence Thomas, made his views known in an opinion concurring in the denial of *cert* in a libel case filed against actor Bill Cosby (*McKee v. Cosby*, 139 S. Ct. 675, 2019). Plaintiff Kathrine McKee accused Cosby of raping her 40 years earlier and said that his attorney wrote and leaked a defamatory letter on Cosby's behalf that damaged her reputation and called her honesty into question. While Thomas agreed that the Court should not take on her case, he echoed Scalia's perspective on the *Sullivan* case and its progeny, labeling them "policy-driven decisions masquerading as constitutional law." Calling for the Court to examine the original meanings of the First and Fourteenth Amendments, he added, "If the Constitution does not require public figures to satisfy an actual-malice standard in state-law defamation suits, then neither should we." Thomas' suggestion for libel actions? Leave it up to the states, which are "perfectly capable of striking an acceptable balance between encouraging robust public discourse and providing a meaningful remedy for reputational harm."

A libel case in which two former Liberian officials sued international human rights organization Global Witness for a report that falsely implied that they had accepted bribes from Exxon was dismissed by first a district court and then by the D.C. Circuit in 2021 (*Tah v. Global Witness Publ'g*, 991 F.3d 231). The case would have likely disappeared quietly except for a partial dissent from appellate judge Laurence Silberman, who launched into a vitriolic attack on *Sullivan*, calling it "a threat to American democracy" and insisting, "It must go."

Silberman did not hold back. Arguing that the holding in *Sullivan* has "no relation to the text, history, or structure of the Constitution," he called it "policymaking in constitutional garb." He bemoaned the Democratic-leaning tendencies of the press, accusing the *New York Times*, the *Washington Post*, and "nearly all television" of being arms of the Democratic party. This homogeneity, he said, "risks repressing certain ideas from the public consciousness just as surely as if access were restricted by the government." He concluded that "when the media has proven its willingness—if not eagerness—to so distort [the marketplace], it is a profound mistake to stand by unjustified legal rules that serve only to enhance the press' power."

A second justice signs on. On July 2, 2021, Thomas was joined by his colleague Justice Neil Gorsuch in calling for a fresh look at *Sullivan*. The two justices dissented from the denial of *cert* in *Berisha v. Lawson* (No. 20–1063), a case involving the son of a former Albanian prime minister who alleged he was libeled in the book *War Dogs*—which later became the foundation for that Hollywood movie. Gorsuch's separate opinion offers a perspective different from Thomas' concerns about textual interpretation and states' rights. He pointed out that a "public figure" label on a plaintiff virtually guarantees the plaintiff's loss. "It seems that publishing *without* investigation, fact-checking, or editing has become the optimal legal strategy" because of this change, Gorsuch said, adding, "Not only has the doctrine evolved into a subsidy for published falsehoods on a scale no one could have foreseen, it has come to leave far more people without redress than anyone could have predicted."

Legal commentators have identified a case with the potential to make Thomas' and Silberman's hopes a reality: *Palin v. New York Times* (940 F.3d 804). Former vice-presidential candidate Sarah Palin sued the *Times* for a 2017 editorial that suggested that her political action committee website might have incited gunman Jared Lee Loughner's 2011 Tucson shooting spree that killed six people and wounded Rep. Gabby Giffords (D-Ariz.). The *Times* issued a correction that said there was no evidence of such a connection and originally won.

Palin's attorneys called the *Sullivan* rule "obsolete and unworkable, incapable of consistent application, and [without] footing in the modern speech landscape," to which federal district judge Jed Rakoff shot back, "Binding precedent does not…come with an expiration date," exhorting Palin to take her arguments against actual malice to the Supreme Court. But in 2019 the Second Circuit reinstated her case on an evidentiary procedural rule, offering the possibility that if she loses and appeals, the Supreme Court could take the case. Justices Thomas and Gorsuch would have to be joined by two of their colleagues to hear the case and three additional votes to overturn or change *Sullivan*. Most commentators think that unlikely but with a second justice on board, it's at least possible. Stay tuned.

■ LIBEL AND PROCEDURAL RIGHTS

The details of courtroom procedure often seem to be arcane and irrelevant technicalities—certainly not issues that should concern journalists. However, on several occasions the Supreme Court has ruled against the media on procedural issues that can be vitally important in libel cases. On the other hand, the Court has ruled in favor of the media in several other libel cases decided on legal technicalities.

Journalists on the witness stand. The Supreme Court held in 1979 that libel plaintiffs have the right to inquire into journalists' thought processes at the time when an allegedly libelous story was being prepared. Ruling in the case of *Herbert v. Lando* (441 U.S. 153), the Court said that since libel plaintiffs often have to prove actual malice or at least negligence on the part of journalists, they are entitled to use the *pretrial discovery* process (explained in Chapter One) to check on journalists' attitudes and thought processes.

The *Herbert* case caused considerable alarm among journalists when the Court ruled that the First Amendment does not excuse journalists from providing *state-of-mind evidence* to libel plaintiffs who are looking for proof of actual malice. Actually, though, the decision did little more than uphold a long-recognized principle: each party is permitted to use *discovery* to gather information about the other side's case. Where the plaintiff must prove actual malice to win his case, the rules have allowed plaintiffs to seek evidence of malice.

Anthony Herbert, a military officer, sued the producers of the CBS television program *60 Minutes* for libel and then sought to put journalists on the stand to gather state-of-mind evidence during discovery. The show's producers refused to cooperate, citing the First Amendment, but the high court ruled that the First Amendment provides journalists no special immunity from normal rules of discovery. Since *Herbert*, discovery has been an increasing burden for the media in libel cases. Herbert lost his libel suit when a federal appellate court dismissed most of his case against CBS in 1986—12 years after the suit began.

Where does *Herbert* leave the media? Technically, the media is in the same position they were in before this decision: required to cooperate in the discovery process even if it means responding to questions designed to determine whether there really was actual malice present when an allegedly libelous story was prepared. However, the decision appears to have had an important psychological impact on libel cases. The Supreme Court has in effect endorsed and encouraged the aggressive use of discovery procedures by libel plaintiffs to ferret out evidence of actual malice or negligence.

Retractions. In at least 33 states, publishing (or broadcasting) a retraction or correction of a libelous item reduces the likelihood of a successful lawsuit against the media or at least the risk of a news organization facing large damages. In most states with retraction laws, publishing a timely retraction of a libel (and placing the retraction in as prominent a place as the original libel) limits the damages that may be won. In many states, a retraction restricts the plaintiff to special damages (provable out-of-pocket monetary losses, often difficult to show). So publishing a retraction may effectively preclude a lawsuit in many instances.

The provisions of the retraction laws vary widely from state to state. Some of the strongest ones are found in midwestern and western states, such as Arizona, California, Idaho, Nebraska, and Nevada. These states all have laws that require a potential plaintiff to demand a retraction within a fixed period of time (often 20 days after learning of the libel). After that, the media usually have another 21 days to publish or broadcast the retraction.

Under these retraction statutes, if the plaintiff fails to demand a retraction or if a suitable retraction is published or broadcast, the plaintiff is limited to special damages (provable out-of-pocket monetary losses). In these states a plaintiff may win other damages only if: (1) a retraction was demanded in a timely fashion; *and* (2) a legally adequate retraction was not published or broadcast in a timely fashion. To be legally adequate, a retraction usually must retract all of the libelous charges without further libeling the potential plaintiff and published as prominently as the original libel. On the other hand, some states have retraction laws that simply say a libel defendant can show that a retraction was published as a way to "mitigate" damages, or perhaps to defend against charges of malice.

Not all retraction laws are equally comprehensive in their protection of the media. About half the states with retraction laws specifically include broadcasters within their coverage. Several other states have laws that cover "all libel suits" or "all media." But some have retraction laws that apply *only* to the print media or, more specifically, only to newspapers. California's retraction law is unusual in that respect: it protects newspapers and radio and television stations but *not* magazines. Montana's retraction law, on the other hand, was once so comprehensive that it was ruled unconstitutional (it has since been revised).

Retraction statutes are obviously useful in situations where the media have made an honest error, but they do little good in many of the circumstances that produce lawsuits—situations in which the publisher does not feel he or she made an error and is in no mood to back down. Moreover, there is a natural human tendency to believe the original charge—not anyone's later denial. To accuse someone of a crime in print and then retract, saying it was all a mistake, is certain to leave some readers with a strong suspicion that it really wasn't a mistake. For this reason, some people question whether retraction statutes are really fair to libel victims. Nevertheless, many states have such laws, and they have an important impact on libel litigation in those states.

Long-Arm Jurisdiction

A growing burden for the media—albeit once again not really a new burden—is the cost of defending libel suits in courts thousands of miles from home. Online communication only adds to this issue; digital content can be accessed anywhere. *Long-arm statutes*, both state and federal, allow courts to decide cases regarding those not in their regular jurisdictions.

For many years the law has said persons and companies that engage in interstate commerce may be sued in any state where they have *minimum contacts*. The Supreme Court so ruled in 1945, in a case called *Int'l Shoe v. Washington* (326 U.S. 310). However, some journalists have argued that they should not be forced to defend a libel suit in a faraway state merely because copies of their newspaper or magazine are distributed there or their material is broadcast there. That argument has gotten nowhere with the Supreme Court. Instead, the Court said, lawsuits against journalists should have to meet only the same test of fairness as would a lawsuit against another kind of business.

In short, if it would be fair for a company that makes cars or lawnmowers to be hauled into court in a distant state where its products are sold, the Court said that it is also fair for the media to be sued in that state if their "product" is sold there.

Forum shopping and "libel tourism." In two cases decided on the same day in 1984—*Calder v. Jones* (465 U.S. 783) and *Keeton v. Hustler* (465 U.S. 770)—the high court unanimously rejected the argument that forcing journalists to defend themselves in faraway courts would have any chilling effect on press freedom. The national media may be sued in *any* state, and libel plaintiffs may engage in *forum shopping*: selecting the state with the best laws to file their libel suits, regardless of where prospective defendants live or maintain offices.

In the *Jones* case, the Supreme Court unanimously ruled that the writer and editor were subject to California jurisdiction even though neither went to California to research or write the story. Justice William Rehnquist, who wrote the Court's opinion, pointed out that the *Enquirer* was selling about 600,000 copies of each issue in California—twice as many as in any other state. Although the decision was troubling to some journalists, the *Keeton v. Hustler* case seemed far more so. At least the *Jones* plaintiffs had filed suit in the state where they lived and worked; they could hardly be accused of forum shopping.

But in *Keeton*, the choice of venue was clearly forum shopping: New Hampshire was apparently the only state whose statute of limitations (i.e., the deadline) for filing libel suits was not past. The Court overturned lower courts' rulings in favor of *Hustler*. "[T]here is no unfairness in calling (*Hustler*) to answer for the contents of that publication wherever a substantial number of copies are regularly sold and distributed," Justice Rehnquist wrote.

Libel tourism, related to forum shopping, is often used to describe some U.S. plaintiffs' preferences for filing libel suits in foreign countries with fewer defenses (traditionally England). In 2010, the SPEECH Act (Securing the Protection of our Enduring and Established Constitutional Heritage) was signed by President Barack Obama; this law, which applies to both state and federal courts, invalidates foreign libel judgments against Americans that would fail in the United States under First Amendment or due process protections. Several states have similar laws (California, Florida, Illinois, and New York, as of 2021).

Long-arm jurisdiction online. American courts are split on the issue of applying long-arm statutes online. Some U.S. courts have held that libel cases cannot be filed in a distant court just because a news item appeared online. In *Young v. New Haven Advocate* (315 F.3d 256, 2002), the Fourth Circuit held that the warden of a Virginia prison could not sue Connecticut newspapers in Virginia for posting material that allegedly libeled him on their Connecticut-based websites. The Fourth Circuit held that the articles were aimed at a Connecticut audience, denying Virginia jurisdiction over the Connecticut newspapers' websites. At about the same time, the California Supreme Court held that California cannot take jurisdiction over out-of-state residents merely because their websites are allegedly harmful to Hollywood or Silicon Valley businesses. In *Pavlovich v. Superior Court (DVD Copy Control Assn.)* (29 C.4th 262, 2002), the California court said a Texan could not be sued under California's long-arm jurisdiction law for posting computer code on the internet that allows DVDs to be copied.

Some courts have extended long-arm jurisdiction laws to apply online. The Ohio Supreme Court in 2010 said the state's long-arm statute applied to the internet, making it possible for Ohio businesses to sue individuals from other states who defame them online (*Kauffman Racing Equip. LLC v. Roberts*, 930 N.E.2d 784). The Tenth Circuit allowed an online libel case to proceed in New Mexico (*Silver v. Brown*, 382 Fed. Appx. 723, 2010). Using reasoning from *Calder v. Jones*, the court said the offending blog was intentionally aimed at New Mexico with knowledge that the brunt of the injury would be felt there. And in Florida, a federal district court said that Florida's long-arm statute applied when an allegedly defamatory article was accessible in Florida via mobile app and website and was in fact accessed in Florida (*Gubarev v. Buzzfeed, Inc.*, 253 F. Supp. 3d 1149, 2017).

The *Zippo* scale. A 1997 federal district court decision from Pennsylvania offered a novel way to determine how long-arm statutes should apply to online content. In *Zippo Mfg. Co. v. Zippo Dot Com* (952 F. Supp. 1119), the judge suggested a sliding scale "directly proportionate to the nature and quality of commercial activity that an entity conducts over the Internet." Commercial sites that actively do business online are at one end of the continuum, with sites that merely provide information at the other; the more passive the interaction with visitors, the less likely that long-arm jurisdiction should apply. At least five federal circuits have adopted this scale, giving it a key role in determining online jurisdiction.

■ ONLINE LIBEL: THE RISE OF SECTION 230

Traditionally, most libel lawsuits have resulted from newspaper and magazine articles and radio or television broadcasts. However, many lawsuits are now also filed by people who claim they were defamed by something that appeared online. Online communication has grown explosively: today there are millions of websites with even more millions of users who post literally billions of words of new material online every week. Some of that material is inevitably libelous, and its reach is potentially a lot farther than any traditional medium. When a libelous message is posted on a website, blog, chat room, or comments section, it is obviously disseminated: many persons are likely to see it. But is anyone other than the originator of the message legally responsible?

A 1991 decision (*Cubby, Inc. v. CompuServe, Inc.*, 776 F. Supp. 135) made the initial suggestion that companies running interactive sites whose outside content they did not monitor or edit were to be treated like bookstores rather than newspapers for purposes of libel: as *distributors* (rather than *publishers*) of that content. Under traditional libel law, these companies were not liable for damages caused by material posted by others. The judge foresaw not only the flood of third-party content that would eventually become the interactive internet but also the near-impossibility of trying to screen all that content, noting that "it would be no more feasible for CompuServe to examine every publication it carries for potentially defamatory statements than it would be for any other distributor to do so."

The "Wolf of Wall Street" meets Prodigy. However, in 1995, a New York trial judge ruled that Prodigy, a commercial online service provider, could be sued for libel. A subscriber posted a message on a Prodigy board accusing Stratton Oakmont, an investment firm (and

Focus on...
Publishers versus distributors under Section 230

Courts have interpreted the protections of Section 230 of the Communications Decency Act very broadly. The law says that "No provider or user of an interactive computer service shall be treated as the publisher or speaker of any information provided by another information content provider." This federal law preempts state laws that hold otherwise. But what does that distinction mean?

Publishers have *control over the content* they publish, while distributors are just the *conduits* that bring content to users. For example, if you buy a newspaper from a vendor, and you read an article that you think libels you, you wouldn't sue the vendor—you'd sue the paper. The vendor is thus the distributor, and the newspaper is the publisher.

FIG. 39. Man buying *The Evening Star* from newsboy, Washington, D.C., April 7, 1917 (headline reads "U.S. at War with Germany").

Library of Congress Prints and Photographs Division [LC-USZ62- 69048]

How does this work? If you allow comments on your blog, and someone posts a defamatory comment, Section 230 would likely prevent you from liability for that libel, because you are not the publisher of the comment. You're simply the distributor. You can edit comments to some degree for civility or accuracy as long as you don't change the meaning of the original comment. Section 230 doesn't apply to intellectual property cases, however, or federal criminal liability.

the inspiration for Martin Scorsese's 2013 film *The Wolf of Wall Street*) of criminal conduct—and Prodigy tried to monitor and edit the content posted on those boards.

In *Stratton Oakmont Inc. v. Prodigy Serv. Co.* (23 Media L. Rep. 1794), the judge ruled that Prodigy became the legal equivalent of a publisher by *attempting to monitor the content of incoming messages* with text-scanning software (i.e., software that checks for offensive words or phrases) and removing potentially dangerous content. Therefore, by taking on the mantle of publisher rather than mere distributor, Prodigy could be sued for libel.

Prodigy eventually settled the case by doing nothing more than issuing an apology. Still, the unpublished (non-precedential) *Stratton Oakmont* decision sent shockwaves through the internet community, as it showed how vulnerable nascent interactive internet service companies like Prodigy were to lawsuits brought by individuals or companies aggrieved by content posted by third parties to their sites. If, as the case suggested, companies that hosted these interactive sites were legally responsible for their users' content, they would need to monitor their sites for potentially problematic material and remove it—an expensive proposition, and one that could well put many smaller start-ups out of business and stifle new entries into the industry. Congress agreed.

Enter Section 230

As one recent book title suggests, Section 230 contains "the 26 words that created the internet." These 26 words are "No provider or user of an interactive computer service shall be treated as the publisher or speaker of any information provided by another information content provider." Simply put, Section 230 of the Telecommunications Act of 1996 overruled the the *Stratton Oakmont* decision by declaring that internet service providers *are not to be treated as publishers* and held liable for the content of the messages they carry, regardless of whether they employ a content-filtering system to screen out objectionable material or merely deliver all messages without review. Instead, they are merely *distributors*. In addition, providers may screen out material they consider libelous, obscene, or inappropriate without assuming liability for everything they *don't* screen out, called a "Good Samaritan" clause.

An early 230 test: *Zeran v. AOL*. Even if an online service provider is notified of an allegedly libelous posting and doesn't delete it, the provider is (usually) exempt from liability under Section 230. Ken Zeran's harrowing experience of getting anonymously trolled on an America Online (AOL) message board resulted in the famous 1997 Fourth Circuit decision *Zeran v. America Online* (129 F.3d 327), one of the earliest interpretations of Section 230.

As Zeran told NPR in a 2021 interview, he awoke in April 1995 to repeated angry phone calls that had nothing to do with his Seattle real estate magazine. Instead, the irate callers screamed at him, asking how he "could do such a thing." He eventually determined that he was the victim of an AOL poster known only as "Zen ZZ03." This individual was advertising t-shirts containing tasteless messages about the recent Oklahoma City federal building bombing and was directing viewers to contact "Ken" at Zeran's home office phone number.

Zeran managed to get AOL to delete Zen ZZ03's original posts after a day of effort, but similar messages reappeared, and AOL was slow to respond. Meanwhile, Zeran's phone continued to ring, infuriated callers continued to berate him, and his life ground to a halt. When AOL continued to drag its feet in responding to his pleas, Zeran sued.

As Section 230 had been enacted mere months before, there was virtually nothing to suggest how the law would be interpreted. But the Fourth Circuit, in sweeping terms, held that online services are exempt from liability under state libel laws for any message posted by a third party. "Congress recognized the threat that tort-based lawsuits pose to freedom of speech in the new and burgeoning Internet medium," the judge said, adding, "Section 230 was enacted, in part, to maintain the robust nature of Internet communication and, accordingly, to keep government interference in the medium to a minimum." In 1998, the U.S. Supreme Court denied *cert*. The Ninth Circuit later ruled that a provider is exempt even if it does minor editing before a libelous item is posted *(Batzel v. Smith*, 333 F.3d 1018, 2003).

The *Zeran* case has been cited in thousands of cases since 1997, often protecting online service providers. Zeran told NPR that the decision was a mistake that "created chaos."

A sampling of post-*Zeran* 230 claims. In recent years dozens of courts have dismissed suits against internet providers based on Section 230 protections. A major 2006 California Supreme Court holding said that *only* those who create a libelous internet message may be sued, not internet providers or even users who post a message created by someone else.

This case, *Barrett v. Rosenthal* (40 C.4th 33), is so broad that it seems to exempt traditional newspaper publishers and broadcasters from libel suits for content generated by others on their websites, *even* when they could be held liable if the same material were disseminated in print or broadcast. It arose when Ilena Rosenthal, a San Diego women's health activist, posted materials critical of two medical doctors, including an allegedly libelous email written by *another* critic of the two doctors, on two internet newsgroups. The doctors' libel lawsuit was dismissed because much of what Rosenthal posted was opinion, not provably false statements of fact. But a California appellate court held that certain statements could be seen as false statements of fact and therefore actionable libels. The appellate court declined to apply the federal Section 230 exemption, triggering an appeal to the state supreme court.

The California Supreme Court reversed the lower court, ruling that Rosenthal was protected by Section 230 even though she was only an internet user and not a provider. As long as she did not *create* the allegedly libelous content but merely posted materials created by others, her postings are exempt from liability. The Florida Supreme Court ruled similarly, but not in such sweeping terms, in *Doe v. America Online* (783 So.2d 1010, 2001).

Rosenthal appears to provide internet publishers far broader protection than traditional media. Under the *common law republication rule*, recognized in most states, anyone who republishes libelous material may be sued, not merely the creator. Newspapers can be sued for libelous letters to the editor and for libels contained in direct quotations, among other things. Similarly, broadcasters can be sued for statements made by callers on talk shows. If the material is a defamatory, false, unprivileged statement of fact as opposed to opinion, the media are generally liable for republishing it, regardless of who originated the libel. But under *Barrett v. Rosenthal*, internet providers and users are exempt from liability for republications. Under cases like this one, the internet remains a wide-open forum where messages can be freely forwarded to others, regardless of whether they may be libelous. Only the creator—often someone who is "lawsuit-proof" due to lack of assets—is liable.

The Eighth Circuit's first opinion on Section 230 was in 2010 in *Johnson v. Arden* (614 F.3d 785). Susan and Robert Johnson, owners of Cozy Kittens Cattery in Missouri, sued a number of individuals and service providers after seeing negative comments about their cattery on ComplaintsBoard.com. The court said that ComplaintsBoard.com's online service provider, InMotion, could not be held liable due to Section 230 protection: "InMotion did not originate the material that the Johnsons deem damaging."

In *Shiamili v. The Real Estate Group of New York, Inc.* (17 N.Y.3d 281, 2011), the New York Court of Appeals (the state's highest court) said that Section 230 applied to third-party comments on a blog even if the editorial role by the hosts was unusually active. The CEO of Ardor Realty sued The Real Estate Group for allegedly defamatory comments on a blog the group hosted. Even though The Real Estate Group moved the comments to their own stand-alone post and highlighted them, the court ruled that Section 230 *still* barred liability. The chief judge, while agreeing that this interpretation was generally acceptable, lamented that in its first Section 230 decision, the court "shielded defendants from the allegation that they abused their power as website publishers to promote and amplify defamation targeted at a business competitor." He thought the state high court went too far in this case.

When 230 fails. Given how successful Section 230 is at eliminating liability for online service providers, it is perhaps more instructive to focus on cases in which it fails to do so. In *Barnes v. Yahoo! Inc.* (565 F.3d 560, 2009), the Ninth Circuit said that Section 230 didn't insulate Yahoo from *promissory estoppel* claims. As will be further discussed in Chapter Eight, *promissory estoppel* prevents someone from withdrawing from a promise if the other person has relied upon that promise and acted upon it to their detriment.

After Cecilia Barnes broke up with her boyfriend, he created a Yahoo profile under her name using her actual personal contact information. He posted nude pictures of her, impersonated her in Yahoo chat rooms, and directed interested men to the profile without her permission. Barnes began getting contacted by men interested in sex. She followed Yahoo's instructions to have the profile removed but Yahoo did not act, even after repeated requests—and after Barnes talked to a Yahoo director who promised to "walk over" the removal request personally. She filed suit, alleging a *promissory estoppel* claim.

Calling the case "a dangerous, cruel, and highly indecent use of the internet for the apparent purpose of revenge," the judge found that Barnes had a *promissory estoppel* claim against Yahoo. And, the judge noted, Barnes was not framing Yahoo as a publisher "but rather as the counterparty to a contract as a promissory who has breached." Under these circumstances, Section 230 does not provide immunity. The case also established a three-prong

common law republication rule:
rule that says that anyone who republishes libelous material can be sued, not just the original creator or publisher.

certify a question:
a process by which the highest court in a state can answer a question that would affect the outcome of a case in which there is no controlling legal precedent in that state.

long-arm jurisdiction:
gives a local court jurisdiction over an out-of-state entity whose actions caused damage to a local party as long as the out-of-state entity has minimum contacts with the local party.

test for determining Section 230 protection: immunity will apply only if a defendant is "(1) a provider or user of an interactive computer service (2) whom a plaintiff seeks to treat, under a state law cause of action, as a publisher or speaker (3) of information provided by another information content provider."

Gossip website TheDirty.com was originally *denied* Section 230 protection because it *encouraged* offensive postings that were heavily moderated (the case involved a teacher, Sarah Jones, who was also a Cincinnati Bengals cheerleader allegedly sleeping with the team and her students). But the Sixth Circuit overturned (*Jones v. Dirty World Entm't Recordings*, 755 F.3d 398, 2014). Section 230 barred liability for TheDirty.com, the court said, adding, "Consistent with our sister circuits, we adopt the material contribution test to determine whether a website operator is 'responsible, in whole or in part, for the creation or development of [allegedly tortious] information.'" This test comes from the Ninth Circuit *Roommates.com* case (discussed in Chapter Thirteen) and is defined as "being responsible for what makes the displayed content allegedly unlawful." Under that definition, the mere fact that Dirty World selected statements alleged to be libelous about Jones for publication didn't mean it was "materially contributing" to the defamation.

"Negligent design" and 230. Plaintiffs continue to try to circumvent Section 230 in creative ways. In May 2021, the Ninth Circuit *declined* to extend Section 230 protection to Snap, the owner of the social media company Snapchat, in *Lemmon v. Snap, Inc.* (995 F.3d 1085), a case in which parents of two teens who died in a high-speed car accident alleged that Snap caused their sons' deaths due to Snapchat's "negligent design" of its controversial "Speed Filter." The two teens and another young man were documenting speeds of over 120 miles an hour on a Wisconsin highway using Snapchat's Speed Filter, an overlay that can be added to Snaps (photos/videos generated by the app) when their car veered off the road, hit a tree, and burst into flames, killing all three. The parents sued Snap for negligent design, alleging that Snapchat entices its users to document high speeds using the filter; as the court put it, "Many of Snapchat's users suspect, if not actually 'believe,' that Snapchat will reward them for 'recording a 100-MPH or faster [s]nap' using the Speed Filter." Snap argued that the suit was barred by Section 230, and a trial court agreed. The parents appealed.

Using the three-prong test it had established in *Barnes* (above), the Ninth Circuit said that Snap was the provider of an interactive service and thus satisfied the first prong. But, said the court, the parents' negligent design suit "neither treats Snap as a 'publisher or speaker' nor relies on 'information provided by another information content provider'" under the second and third prongs. As the court put it, the point of the suit is to hold Snap liable for "designing Snapchat in such a way that it allegedly encourages dangerous behavior." Therefore, Section 230 immunity does not apply, and the court remanded the parents' case for additional review. In June 2021, a month after the decision, Snap announced that it was eliminating the Speed Filter, saying that it was "barely used by Snapchatters."

Still, this win doesn't guarantee that the parents will ultimately win: Snap prevailed in a nearly identical situation in Georgia in 2020. A Georgia appeals court in 2018 denied Section 230 protection to Snap for damages allegedly caused by its Speed Filter and remanded the case to a trial court. However, the trial court found Snap not liable for damages, and the appeals court affirmed: "Georgia law does not impose a general duty to prevent people from committing torts while misusing a manufacturer's product" (*Maynard v. Snapchat, Inc.*, 851 S.E.2d 128, 2020). Will the California parents prevail on remand? Stay tuned.

Section 230, meet FOSTA and a (reinstated) lawsuit. In 2018, President Donald J. Trump signed an amendment to Section 230 that some fear will do serious damage to Section 230 protections. *FOSTA-SESTA*, an aggregation of the Senate (*Allow States and Victims to Fight Online Sex Trafficking Act*—the abbreviation generally used) and House (*Stop Enabling Sex Traffickers Act*) was intended to combat sex trafficking by eliminating protection for liability for those sites that knowingly host any material that violates federal sex-trafficking law, and a fuller discussion of that element is provided in Chapter Ten. However, critics of FOSTA suggest that the law, as written, not only opens the door to actions against sites that do not engage in sex trafficking support but also harms sex workers themselves. The Electronic Frontier Foundation and others filed suit in 2018 to block enforcement of FOSTA. The lead plaintiff, Woodhull Freedom Foundation, works to protect the safety of sex workers.

A federal court found against Woodhull in 2018, saying that the plaintiffs lacked standing to sue. But on appeal, the D.C. Circuit in 2020 reversed, finding that two plaintiffs did have standing: the owner of a website providing resources for sex workers called Rate That Rescue who claimed that FOSTA would be used against her, and the owner of a therapeutic massage business who lost 90% of his advertising when, in response to FOSTA, Craigslist shuttered its "Therapeutic Services" section and blocked him from posting ads anywhere else on Craigslist (*Woodhull Freedom Found. v. U.S.*, 948 F.3d 363). Stay tuned.

Online review sites. As consumer review services like Angie's List, Yelp, RateMyProfessor, and various doctor review sites become more popular, those who get poor reviews have taken their claims to court. In a high-profile case, *McKee v. Laurion* (825 N.W.2d 725, 2013), the Minnesota Supreme Court said that negative comments posted by a man about the care given to his ailing father by a hospital neurologist were opinion and not actionable. Kenneth Laurion posted comments about Dr. David McKee's interactions with his father and the family ("Dr. McKee said, 'When you weren't in ICU, I had to spend time finding out if you transferred or died.' When we gaped at him, he said, "Well, 44% of hemorrhagic strokes die within 30 days. I guess this is the better option") on various "rate your doctor" sites, and McKee sued. The state supreme court evaluated each of six statements and found none of them individually or as a whole were defamatory.

The Sixth Circuit said that a list of "dirtiest hotels" published by TripAdvisor was not defamatory to a hotel on the list. In *Seaton v. TripAdvisor, LLC* (728 F.3d 592, 2013), the owner of the first hotel on the list, the Grand Resort Hotel and Convention Center in Tennessee, alleged that TripAdvisor used a "flawed, inconsistent, unsupported, and improper system or method" to create the list and so acted at least with negligence. Calling the word "dirtiest" to describe the hotels a form of hyperbole, the court pointed out that TripAdvisor was clear about the information source: "On the webpage in which the list appears, TripAdvisor states clearly 'Dirtiest Hotels - United States as reported by travelers on TripAdvisor.'"

Similarly, in 2018 the California Supreme Court in *Hassell v. Bird* (420 P.3d 776) refused to order Yelp to remove a negative review, saying that to do so would treat Yelp as a publisher under Section 230 even if the company was not named in the suit. San Francisco attorney Dawn Hassell sued Ava Bird in 2012 for one-star Yelp reviews (Bird wrote, among other things, "STEER CLEAR OF THIS LAW FIRM!"). When Hassell sued, she named only Bird, not Yelp, in her complaint. Bird did not appear in court, so the court awarded a default judgment to Hassell, ordered Bird to remove her negative reviews and also demanded that Yelp take them down. When Yelp was served with that order, the company got involved, refusing to do so. The appeals court affirmed the trial court, claiming that the removal order treated Yelp simply as an "administrator of the forum" used to post the defamatory reviews and thus not entitled to Section 230 protection. The California high court reversed, saying that the appeals court's construction of 230 was too narrow. Noting that "Yelp could have promptly sought and received Section 230 immunity had plaintiffs originally named it as a defendant in this case," the fact that Hassell had not named the company in her original complaint didn't change that. As the court put it, "[W]e must decide whether plaintiffs' litigation strategy allows them to accomplish indirectly what Congress has clearly forbidden them to achieve directly. We believe the answer is no." The Supreme Court denied *cert.*

Yet don't feel free to post negative reviews without fear. Jane Perez found this out the hard way when she posted on Yelp and Angie's List not only that her contractor, Christopher Dietz, had done shoddy work refurbishing her condominium, but she suspected that he had stolen her jewelry. Dietz retaliated with a $750,000 libel suit, and a judge ordered Perez to revise or take down parts of her reviews, including the theft allegations. The Virginia Supreme Court reversed (*Perez v. Dietz Dev., LLC,* 2012 Va. LEXIS 227). In 2014, a jury found that Dietz and Perez had libeled each other and so awarded no damages.

And a state appellate court in Florida found that online complaints against a divorce lawyer were not really opinion, as they were based on provable facts (*Blake v. Giustibelli,* 182 So. 3d 881, 2016). Copia Blake posted online claims that her divorce attorney, Ann-Marie Giustibelli, lied about her fees. Blake said this was protected opinion. But the judges, finding for the lawyer, disagreed: "Two of the reviews contained the allegation that Giustibelli falsified a contract. These are factual allegations, and the evidence showed they were false."

So, if you're unhappy with a service or product, before you rage about it online, be sure you're not basing your tirades on false facts. While the Consumer Review Fairness Act, a 2016 law, offers reviewers some protections for their online comments (see Chapter Thirteen), it's still best to be cautious.

But wait, there's more. Other recent issues surrounding Section 230, a presidential executive order, and the January 6 Capitol insurrection will be discussed in Chapter Eleven.

▪ OTHER ISSUES IN DEFAMATION LAW

Libel and Summary Judgment

As explained in Chapter One, a *summary judgment* is a ruling in which the court decides the case without a trial, saving the expense and trouble of a prolonged lawsuit. However, because such a dismissal denies plaintiffs their day in court, it is only supposed to be granted when it is absolutely certain the plaintiff could not win.

In recent years, some courts have recognized that many libel suits against the media are filed not in the hope of winning but as a means of harassment. Thus, libel suits have sometimes been thrown out of court under summary judgment proceedings. This procedure has been particularly applicable in situations where a public official or public figure is suing but is clearly unable to prove actual malice.

In 1986 the Supreme Court addressed this problem—and endorsed the idea that many of these questionable libel suits should be dismissed on summary judgment. Deciding the case of *Anderson v. Liberty Lobby* (477 U.S. 242), the Court said that public figures must provide "clear and convincing" evidence that a jury could find actual malice on the part of the media—or have their lawsuits dismissed on motions for summary judgment. The high court ruled by a 6-3 majority that if a libel plaintiff cannot show by "clear and convincing" proof that the plaintiff could win the case if it went to a full trial, it should be dismissed without subjecting the media to the expense of a trial.

Both media lawyers and lawyers for libel plaintiffs agreed that this decision would have an enormous dollars-and-cents effect on libel law and that it represented a clear invitation to trial judges to dismiss libel suits on summary judgment instead of letting them go to trial.

In the years since *Anderson*, at least four federal appeals courts have held that the decision requires them to conduct an independent review of the record to decide whether to allow summary judgment in a libel case and to dismiss the case if the plaintiff is someone who must prove actual malice—but cannot do so by clear and convincing evidence.

Getting "SLAPP" Lawsuits Dismissed

A lawsuit can be an intimidating form of harassment, as journalists have sometimes discovered. The whole point of the *Anderson* case was to allow journalists to get harassment libel suits dismissed quickly on summary judgment. In recent years, it has also become commonplace for citizen activists to be sued for libel or slander by wealthy corporations when they speak against a corporate project at public hearings or circulate petitions to oppose a project. These lawsuits are often nothing more than a form of intimidation—an attempt to silence a corporation's critics. An acronym to describe these lawsuits has gained wide acceptance: *SLAPP (strategic lawsuits against public participation).*

Because it is costly to defend a lawsuit, citizens who oppose corporate activities in the public arena may have no choice but to back down in the face of a threatened lawsuit. Sometimes leaders of a citizens' group that opposes a project such as a large real estate development receive letters from the developer's lawyers telling them they will be sued for libel or slander if they don't stop criticizing the project. Such lawsuits have been given the SLAPP acronym because they take aim at the very foundation of democracy: the right to speak out on local issues at public hearings where the whole point is to solicit comments from citizens.

The SLAPP acronym was first used by Penelope Canan and George W. Pring, two University of Denver professors who advocated legislation to curb these lawsuits in a 1990 law review article. They later published a book, *SLAPPs: Getting Sued for Speaking Out,* in 1996. As of 2021, these states/territories have anti-SLAPP laws, according to the Public Participation Project, an advocacy group (www.anti-slapp.org): Arizona, Arkansas, California, Colorado, Connecticut, Delaware, the District of Columbia, Florida, Georgia, Guam, Hawaii, Illinois, Indiana, Kansas, Louisiana, Maine, Maryland, Massachusetts, Missouri, Nebraska, Nevada, New Mexico, New York, Oklahoma, Oregon, Pennsylvania, Rhode Island, Tennessee, Texas, Utah, Vermont, Virginia, and Washington. Some states, while not having laws on their books,

SLAPP suit:
shorthand for "strategic lawsuit against public participation," a suit that is an attempt by a corporation to stop the exercise of First Amendment rights such as petition, assembly, speech, and press by threatening high-cost libel suits based on the content of those exercises.

trade libel laws:
A.K.A. "veggie libel" or product disparagement laws, state statutes that allow recovery of damages for false statements intended to tarnish the quality of goods or services.

have other statutes or common law that acts like an anti-SLAPP law (e.g., West Virginia). There is no federal anti-SLAPP law but several have been considered.

The Washington Supreme Court struck down its state's original anti-SLAPP law in 2015, saying in *Davis v. Cox* (351 P.3d 862) that it gave *too* much deference to speakers by permitting defendants to delay discovery while allowing a *judge* to dismiss the case if the statements were of public concern; juries, not judges, must make determinations of fact in trials. The Minnesota Supreme Court struck down Minnesota's law in 2017 on identical grounds (*Leiendecker v. Asian Women United of Minn.*, 895 N.W.2d 623).

California is widely regarded as having the most sweeping anti-SLAPP law in the country. This law requires anyone who sues someone else for the exercise of free speech in the public arena to show at the outset that there is a "probability" the lawsuit has a valid basis and is not a form of harassment. If a court determines there is no probability of a valid case, the lawsuit is to be dismissed quickly, sparing the defendant the expense of fighting a prolonged legal battle that could have a chilling effect on free speech.

Plaintiffs who file these harassment lawsuits must usually pay defendants' legal expenses if the lawsuit is dismissed before trial. Under California's anti-SLAPP law, defendants must pay plaintiffs' legal expenses incurred in opposing the motion for dismissal if a court rules the lawsuit valid enough to not be dismissed before trial. Those who get a lawsuit dismissed under this anti-SLAPP law are allowed to countersue for malicious prosecution, among other things (sometimes called a "SLAPPback provision").

California's anti-SLAPP law not only protects individuals who face a harassment lawsuit from a corporation but also protects corporate defendants in some lawsuits filed by individuals. For example, it has been held to protect the media from meritless libel suits even if the plaintiff is an individual and the defendant is a corporation. Because corporations using the law against individual plaintiffs is the *opposite* of what its authors envisioned, the California anti-SLAPP law was amended in 2003 to curb its use by defendants in suits filed solely in the public interest and suits alleging false advertising.

State anti-SLAPP laws vary significantly in their scope and strength. Some do not include the provision requiring plaintiffs to pay a defendant's legal expenses in all cases. And the Massachusetts high court in 2010 declined to extend the state's anti-SLAPP law to a reporter who is also an activist in a libel suit filed against her by a real estate developer (*Fustolo v. Hollander*, 455 Mass. 861), saying that the anti-SLAPP law did not apply to paid writing.

Do state anti-SLAPP laws apply in federal cases? The circuits disagree: the Second (making news in 2020 for its decision in *La Liberte v. Reid*, 966 F.3d 79), Fifth, Eleventh and D.C. circuits say no, and the First and Ninth say yes—a split ripe for high court review.

A new uniform anti-SLAPP law. In 2020, the Uniform Law Commission, a non-profit organization established in 1892 that offers model legislation to, as it says, provide "clarity and stability to critical areas of state statutory law," approved a new uniform anti-SLAPP law. In 2021, Washington became the first state to adopt this model law, called the Uniform Public Expression Protection Act (UPEPA), to replace the version overturned in 2015. UPEPA offers courts a way to quickly determine whether a plaintiff's case has merit, striking a balance between the rights of plaintiffs with legitimate cases and those of defendants facing frivolous suits primarily intended to impose financial burden.

In addition, several states have strengthened their anti-SLAPP laws in recent years. New York's statute was amended in 2020 to expand its coverage to "any communication in a place open to the public or a public forum in connection with an issue of public interest" or "any other lawful conduct in furtherance of the exercise of the constitutional right of free speech in connection with an issue of public interest." Colorado added an anti-SLAPP statute in 2019 to excellent common-law protections established in 1984 (*Protect Our Mountain Env't v. Dist. Ct.*, 677 P.2d 136). And in 2019 Tennessee expanded its law's coverage from statements made to governmental agencies to any suit against "a party's exercise of the right of free speech, right to petition, or right of association."

Sandy Hook, Alex Jones, InfoWars, and SLAPP. On December 14, 2012, 26 people at the Sandy Hook Elementary School in Newtown, Connecticut, were killed by a 20-year-old gunman in the deadliest elementary school shooting in U.S. history. Victims included 20 children between six and seven years old. In the wake of the tragedy, Alex Jones began publishing stories denying that the massacre happened on his website InfoWars and on YouTube shortly thereafter. Among other claims, Jones alleged that the individuals seen in Sandy Hook news footage were "crisis actors" employed by the government and that journalists, including Anderson Cooper of CNN, were faking interviews with victims' parents. At least six enraged families sued Jones and InfoWars for libel. Jones has often turned to state anti-SLAPP statutes for support in these challenges.

While litigation is ongoing, several key losses for Jones include a July 2020 decision by the Connecticut Supreme Court (*Lafferty v. Jones*, 246 A.3d 429) declining to employ the Connecticut anti-SLAPP law to invalidate sanctions against Jones for violating discovery orders and engaging in harassment of the plaintiff's attorney and several decisions by a Texas state appellate court refusing to use the Texas anti-SLAPP law to protect Jones in a suit by the father of a child slain at Sandy Hook (*Jones v. Heslin*, 2020 Tex. App. LEXIS 2441, 2020) and again in a suit by the mother of another shooting victim in her claim of intentional infliction of emotional distress (*Jones v. Lewis*, 2019 Tex. App. LEXIS 9016, 2019). In a related case, in March 2021 a Wisconsin appeals court upheld a $450,000 jury award to a shooting victim's father in a case against a retired professor who had written a book entitled *Nobody Died at Sandy Hook: It Was a FEMA Drill to Promote Gun Control* (*Pozner v. Fetzer*, 2021 Wisc. App. LEXIS 123). James Fetzer, a retired professor, wrote that the death certificate of Leonard Pozner's son, Noah, was fake and Pozner himself was a fraud and "complicit in a grand conspiracy to fake the massacre."

And in January 2021, the Texas Supreme Court refused to dismiss four defamation suits against Jones, rejecting Jones' contention that his speech was protected participation in debate about a matter of public concern. One family's lawyer shot back, "[A]ccusing [a parent] of lying about holding the body of his dead son does not amount to a matter of public concern." Jones has also been banned from social media platforms such as YouTube, Facebook, Pinterest, and others. Stay tuned.

Libel and Emotional Distress

Libel is only one of many legal theories on which a lawsuit may be based. When someone sues for libel, he or she may also sue on some other legal theory such as invasion of privacy.

FIG. 40.
A historic political cartoon: "The 'rail splitter' at work repairing the union," depicting Vice President Andrew Johnson and President Abraham Lincoln, 1865. The Court emphasized the importance to political debate of such cartoons in *Hustler v. Falwell*.

Library of Congress Prints and Photographs Division, [LC-DIG-ppmsca-17158]

THE 'RAIL SPLITTER' AT WORK REPAIRING THE UNION.

It is entirely possible to lose a libel case but win on a different legal basis—because the elements and defenses may be different under the two legal theories. A plaintiff may have a weak libel case (because of the truth defense, for example) but a strong invasion of privacy case (truth is not always a defense in those cases). In recent years it has become common for those who sue the media for libel to add other charges, often invasion of privacy or even the intentional infliction of emotional distress, a trend that is discussed in Chapter Five.

That trend led to a 1988 Supreme Court decision that presented about as clear a contrast between plaintiff and defendant as any lawsuit discussed in this book: *Hustler Magazine v. Falwell* (485 U.S. 46). Although widely reported as a libel case, it was primarily an emotional distress case. But in the end, the high court disposed of it by applying the classic *New York Times v. Sullivan* doctrine as if it had been a libel case.

The case began when *Hustler* magazine published a satirical purported advertisement suggesting that the Rev. Jerry Falwell, founder of the Moral Majority and arch-enemy of *Hustler* publisher Larry Flynt, had his first sexual experience in an outhouse with his mother. The Falwell pseudo-ad was a take-off on an advertising campaign for Campari liquor that used "the first time" as its theme. The ad was clearly labeled as fiction, not to be taken seriously. Courts often hold that a satirical statement cannot be libelous even without a disclaimer, provided a reasonable reader would understand that it is satirical.

Nevertheless, Falwell sued *Hustler* on two grounds: libel and the intentional infliction of emotional distress. A jury awarded Falwell $200,000 on the emotional distress rationale and ruled against him in the libel case. Because Falwell was clearly a public figure, he would have had to prove actual malice to win his libel case. And the ad was obviously satirical; it could not be understood as presenting facts that the reader was supposed to take literally. Thus, Falwell could not prove actual malice. However, in affirming the jury verdict, a lower federal court had said Falwell did not need to prove actual malice to win an emotional distress case.

That verdict alarmed many journalists because it suggested that numerous other public figures who could not win libel cases could get around the protection provided by the actual malice rule by suing for intentional infliction of emotional distress instead of libel. However, the Supreme Court voted unanimously to overturn the verdict for Falwell. Writing for the Court, Chief Justice William Rehnquist said that public figures must henceforth prove actual malice to win damages for emotional distress, just as they must in libel cases. To rule otherwise would force political cartoonists, among others, to heavily censor their work. He wrote:

> Lincoln's tall, gangling posture, Teddy Roosevelt's glasses and teeth and Franklin D. Roosevelt's jutting jaw and cigarette holder have been memorialized by political cartoons ...and our political discourse would have been poorer without them. .... "Outrageousness" in the area of political and social discourse has an inherent subjectiveness about it which would allow a jury to impose liability on the basis of the jurors' tastes or views....

What encouraged many journalists the most about the *Falwell* decision was that it was not only a strongly worded defense of freedom of the press, but that it was authored by Rehnquist, who rarely took a broad view of the First Amendment in earlier decisions. Rehnquist often dissented when the high court expanded First Amendment rights.

The media still face many emotional distress lawsuits. In fact, media lawyers sometimes call emotional distress a "tag-along tort" because plaintiffs' lawyers often toss in this claim when they sue for libel. For example, the Kansas Supreme Court in 2010 reversed judgments against a news organization for "outrage" (the same thing as emotional distress in Kansas) and defamation in the reporting that a man had been detained in connection with the famous BTK murder investigation (*Valadez v. Emmis Commc'ns*, 229 P.3d 389). In overturning the awards on appeal, the Kansas Supreme Court said Valadez had not met the burden of proof for outrage. The media's conduct must be reasonably considered to be outrageous, and the plaintiff must have suffered more than discomfort. The court added, "Conduct that rises to the level of tortious outrage must transcend a certain amount of criticism, rough language, and occasional acts and words that are inconsiderate and unkind."

But in the years since the *Falwell* case, as the *Valadez* case shows, it has become clear that a plaintiff must prove that the media engaged in clearly *outrageous* conduct that was either *deliberate* or *reckless* and caused *severe* emotional distress to win this kind of lawsuit. That is not often easy to do. And, of course, public-figure plaintiffs now have to prove actual malice as well if the lawsuit is based on the *content* of something that appeared in the media. (As Chapter Five explains, the media are often sued for *newsgathering torts* based on the *behavior* of media representatives instead of the content of what was published or broadcast.)

Product Disparagement and "Veggie Libel"

During the 1990s, a close relative of libel—*product disparagement*—became a newsworthy topic after many years of obscurity. Farmers and ranchers in some areas became alarmed about what they considered to be overly sensational media accounts of alleged health hazards associated with food products. They cited examples in which food producers suffered large losses when public demand for a perishable product suddenly dwindled after the media reported claims that the product might be unsafe. Food producers lobbied for state laws allowing them to sue in response; these laws are known as "veggie libel" or "trade libel" laws.

This trend began with a case in which Washington state apple growers sued CBS for a *60 Minutes* segment that said Alar, a chemical used by some growers to enhance the growth and appearance of apples, could cause cancer. There was a large decline in apple consumption, and growers claimed the CBS report was false or at least exaggerated—and cost them $130 million. Their lawsuit was eventually dismissed; the Ninth Circuit ruled that the growers could not prove the CBS report was false—as they must to win a product disparagement lawsuit (*Auvil v. CBS 60 Minutes*, 67 F.3d 816, 1995).

In response to the CBS story, a number of states passed new laws that were much tougher than traditional product disparagement laws, authorizing growers to sue whenever false information is published claiming that a perishable food product is unsafe. Such laws were passed in at least 13 states: Alabama, Arizona, Colorado, Florida, Georgia, Idaho, Louisiana, Mississippi, North Dakota, Ohio, Oklahoma, South Dakota, and Texas. Most of these laws define false information as not based on "reliable scientific data." Allowing growers to sue under these circumstances raises First Amendment questions because growers, journalists, and consumer groups are not likely to agree about what is "reliable" scientific data.

Oprah and "mad cow" disease. These laws made national headlines in 1997 when a group of Texas ranchers sued talk show host Oprah Winfrey after a guest on her show discussed mad cow disease, an illness that had caused the death of at least 20 persons in Britain, and raised questions about whether this illness could spread to the United States. Cattle prices dropped sharply, and the ranchers sued Winfrey under Texas' trade libel law.

Amidst what many called a media circus, the case went to trial in Amarillo, Texas. Winfrey moved production of her show there during the trial. The case went badly for the ranchers from the beginning. With no written opinion, the trial judge dismissed the part of the lawsuit based on the "veggie libel" law, allowing the ranchers to continue the case only under a general business defamation law. In the end, the plaintiffs were unable to persuade the jury that Winfrey or her guest intended to harm the Texas cattle industry by making knowingly false statements about it, as required by the business defamation law.

In a case more newsworthy than legally significant, the jury ruled against the ranchers. In 2000, the Fifth Circuit upheld the verdict (*Engler v. Winfrey*, 201 F.3d 680). Nonetheless, media attorneys expressed fears that future "veggie libel" lawsuits could chill the First Amendment right of the media to report legitimate health questions about food products.

"Pink slime" case settled. In another case on "beef libel," a South Dakota beef producer, Beef Products, Inc. (BPI) brought suit against ABC News and its reporters for a March 2012 story on lean finely textured beef. BPI said that ABC's calling the product "pink slime" and passing alleged misinformation about it (like suggesting it wasn't really meat but more like dog food) violated the state trade disparagement law. ABC attempted to move the case into federal court, but BPI successfully fought the move (*Beef Products, Inc. v. ABC News, Inc.*, 949 F. Supp. 2d 936). In 2014 the South Dakota Supreme Court allowed the suit to proceed, rebuffing ABC's attempts to dismiss, and in 2017, ABC paid BPI a whopping $177 million to settle the claim. That was just what the network itself paid: a BPI spokesperson said ABC's insurer would pay the balance. The final terms of the settlement were not disclosed.

Libel and Fiction

The fundamental question in many libel cases is truth or falsity: only if a statement is false can it be the basis for a successful libel case. But what about libelous innuendoes in a work of fiction—which by its very nature is *intended* to be false? Most media organizations didn't worry about this problem until the 1980s, because courts rarely allowed libel suits based on works of fiction. A more serious legal problem was the threat of privacy suits by those who recognized themselves—or thought they did—in fictitious works.

However, in the 1970s and 1980s that began to change. Courts started finding sufficient identification in works of fiction to support libel judgments. The *New York Times v. Sullivan* rule sometimes has been applied—some say misapplied—with disastrous results for the media. In a work of fiction, the characters necessarily differ from real people, but some courts have ruled fictionalization equals knowing or reckless falsehood, thus proving actual malice and opening the door to punitive damages.

The case that initiated this trend toward libel judgments for fictionalization was *Bindrim v. Mitchell* (92 C.A.3d 61, 1979), a California appellate court ruling. As a decision of an intermediate appeals court in a single state, it carries little weight as a precedent, but it encouraged other fiction-based libel cases, including the Wyoming judgment against *Penthouse* in the introduction to this chapter (*Pring v. Penthouse*, 695 F.2d 438, 1983, discussed below).

In *Bindrim*, novelist Gwen Davis Mitchell described a fictitious "nude encounter marathon" similar to therapy sessions conducted by Dr. Paul Bindrim, a psychologist. In fact, Mitchell had attended one of Bindrim's sessions and signed an agreement not to write about it. In Mitchell's book, *Touching*, the psychologist who conducted the sessions had a different name and did not physically resemble Bindrim. The main thing the real man and the fictional character had in common was that they both conducted nude encounters on the theory that nudity made therapy more effective. Nevertheless, a jury found that Bindrim was identified and libeled by the fictional account in the novel, and awarded Bindrim $75,000 in total damages against Mitchell and her publisher, later reduced to $50,000. "The test is whether a reasonable person, reading the book, would understand that the fictional character was, in actual fact, the plaintiff," the appellate majority wrote. Both the California and U.S. Supreme Courts refused to review the decision.

"Fairy tales" immune. However, fiction writers could take comfort in the ultimate decision in the "Miss Wyoming" libel suit. The case stemmed from a *Penthouse* article describing a fictitious "Miss Wyoming" who competed in the Miss America Pageant, a champion baton twirler who had a more interesting talent: oral sex. The story said she performed an act of oral sex at the pageant before a national audience, and the recipient of her favors was levitated—he rose up in the air in defiance of the laws of gravity. Kim Pring, a champion Miss Wyoming baton twirler in a Miss America Pageant, sued, claiming the story was about her and damaged her reputation. A Wyoming jury agreed and awarded $26.5 million in damages. The Tenth Circuit overturned the verdict because it found the story to be "physically impossible in an impossible setting," and not something readers could reasonably understand as describing actual events. The Supreme Court denied *cert.*

The court offered guidance on the murky issue of libel and fiction: "The test is not whether the story is or is not characterized as 'fiction,' 'humor,' or anything else in the publication, but whether the charged portions in context could be reasonably understood as describing actual facts about the plaintiff or actual events in which [Pring] participated." Thus, the court said the *Penthouse* story was too incredible and obviously false to be libelous. However, this decision offers little comfort for serious fiction writers. If a story is an accurate portrayal of life, it may be a more powerful (and artistically sound) literary work—but also more likely to be the basis for a libel suit. In effect, the *Pring v. Penthouse* decision says fairy tales are immune to libel judgments, but realistic literature is not.

Libel and Broadcasting

So far this summary of the principles of libel law has made almost no distinction between the print and electronic media. That was done in the interest of clarity and simplicity—and because it is generally justified. There are, however, some special libel problems when the broadcast media are involved. Not the least of these problems is the question of whether a broadcast defamation is really a libel at all or is in fact a *slander*. Before broadcasting came along, slander (a spoken defamation) was a limited legal action for the obvious reason that an oral statement was a fleeting thing, while a printed one might be read by thousands of people over many years. In view of slander's limited nature, the courts generally ruled that one could only win a slander suit by proving special damages unless the slander fell into one of several particularly offensive categories that were sometimes called slander *per se*. Because of these restrictions, successful slander suits were relatively rare.

But when broadcasting developed, the potential for harm in a spoken defamation became at least as great as in a written one. Recognizing the pervasiveness of a broadcast defamation, some states simply declared that broadcast defamation would be regarded as libel, not slander. Other states such as California classified broadcast defamation as slander but liberalized the requirements for a successful slander suit so there was little difference between libel and slander. Some states even adopted the rule that a defamation contained in a script would be treated as a libel (since it was written down, after all), while an ad-libbed one would be treated as slander. Only a few states still adhere to that rule today.

Whatever its name, broadcast defamation is a viable legal action in all states. As noted, some states exempt local broadcasters from liability for defamation occurring during network programs they have no power to edit, but even then the network remains liable. And, as already noted, the Supreme Court has exempted broadcasters from liability for defamation occurring during political advertising that broadcasters are forbidden to censor under Section 315 of the Communications Act.

Aside from these exceptions, a broadcast defamation is as actionable as a printed one, and perhaps more because of the massive audiences the electronic media attract. In evaluating defamation that was broadcast rather than published, the same rules normally apply.

Criminal Libel

Although some states still have criminal libel laws on the books, they have rarely been enforced since two 1960s Supreme Court decisions. Criminal libel laws generally cover situations in which civil libel law is inapplicable. For instance, some states still make it a crime to libel a dead person—a form of libel rarely actionable in civil suits. In addition, some states forbid distributing literature so defamatory that it may cause a breach of the peace.

Shortly after handing down its landmark *New York Times v. Sullivan* civil libel ruling in 1964, the Supreme Court announced an important criminal libel decision: *Garrison v. Louisiana* (379 U.S. 64). New Orleans prosecutor Jim Garrison had severely criticized a group of judges, calling them sympathetic with "racketeer influences" and "vacation-minded." He was then prosecuted under a Louisiana law that made it a crime to defame public officials. The Court said Garrison's prosecution was not permitted by the First Amendment unless it could be proved that he made false statements either knowingly or with reckless disregard for the truth. In short, the same standards that apply in *civil* libel suits by public officials also apply in *criminal* prosecutions for defamation of public officials: actual malice must be shown. The Court then quickly dealt another blow to criminal libel in *Ashton v. Kentucky* (384 U.S. 195, 1966), ruling a criminal libel law overbroad and in violation of the First Amendment.

As a result of these Supreme Court decisions and parallel rulings by a number of state courts, criminal libel prosecutions constitute a minimal legal threat to the media today. If the remaining criminal libel laws were vigorously enforced, few of them could withstand a constitutional challenge at this point in our history.

Prior Restraint to Prevent Libel

Normally, when someone sues for libel and wins, the court awards monetary damages. But may a court instead engage in prior restraint, ordering the defendant not to make any more defamatory statements about the plaintiff?

In *Balboa Island Village Inn v. Lemen* (156 P.3d 339, 2007), the California Supreme Court said that Anne Lemen could be ordered not to make *future* statements falsely accusing the restaurant of serving tainted food and engaging in child pornography and prostitution. Lemen had run a long campaign against the restaurant, making those and other charges that were proven false when the restaurant owner sued her for libel and won. "A properly limited injunction prohibiting defendant from repeating to third persons statements about the Village Inn that were determined at trial to be defamatory" would not violate Lemen's rights, said the court. The dissenting justices were troubled by this endorsement of prior restraint, saying that the majority opinion "goes beyond chilling speech; it freezes speech."

The Kentucky Supreme Court held in 2010, citing *Lemen*, that a lower court's "broad-sweeping and vaguely worded injunction against future expression, before final adjudication of its defamatory character, constitutes an improper prior restraint on speech" (*Hill v. Petrotech Resources Corp.*, 325 S.W.3d 302). An investor retained an agency owned by H.C. Hill to recover investments made in Petrotech. The lower court enjoined Hill from making defamatory statements about Petrotech throughout the case or until further ordered. The Kentucky high court adopted this rule: "defamatory speech may be enjoined only after the trial court's final determination by a preponderance of the evidence that the speech at issue is, in fact, false, and only then upon the condition that the injunction be narrowly tailored to limit the prohibited speech to that which has been judicially determined to be false."

Libel as a Political Question

Courts may decline to decide cases that implicate issues best left to other branches of government—like questions dealing with national defense or presidential power. A recent example: The Supreme Court in 2019 said that political *gerrymandering* (a technique in which voting districts are contorted to favor one party) is a *political question* that must be handled by Congress. Chief Justice John Roberts said in a combined case (*Rucho v. Common Cause*, 139 S. Ct. 2484), involving Republican districts in North Carolina and Democratic ones in Maryland, that while the Court "does not condone excessive partisan gerrymandering," addressing it is beyond its jurisdiction. So, does libel ever present a political question?

Libel suits against a president: not necessarily political questions. Libel suits against a sitting president, while they may be political by nature, are not necessarily political questions. The allegations brought by plaintiffs against former president Donald J. Trump while he was in office are related to actions he took before he became president and thus are not accorded any special privilege; however, some speech acts took place during his presidency. Most important for this book are libel cases brought by women whom Trump had met prior to his presidency, several of which are ongoing.

FIG. 41.
Stormy Daniels
(Stephanie Clifford)
with photographer
Daniel X. O'Neil.

*Daniel X. O'Neil, "DXO
and Stormy Daniels,
June 2018," June 16,
2018 via Flickr, Creative
Commons attribution
license.*

Stephanie Clifford/Stormy Daniels: resolved. Clifford, a.k.a. "Stormy Daniels" (her screen name), a former adult film actress, first appeared on the national scene when she sought to nullify a confidentiality agreement for which she received $130,000 for her silence about an alleged 2006 sexual affair she had with Trump.

Clifford was going to talk to a tabloid about her story in 2011 but was frightened out of doing so, she told CNN reporter Anderson Cooper in a *60 Minutes* interview in March 2018. She claimed that she and her baby daughter were approached in a gym parking lot. "A guy walked up on me and said to me, 'Leave Trump alone. Forget the story.' And then he leaned around and looked at my daughter and said, 'That's a beautiful little girl. It'd be a shame if something happened to her mom.' And then he was gone," Clifford told Cooper. When the *Wall Street Journal* broke the story that Michael Cohen, an attorney for Trump, had paid $130,000 in "hush money" to her under a non-disclosure agreement, she sued and released a forensic artist's sketch of the man she claimed had threatened her. In her March 2018 complaint, Clifford sought to nullify the contract because the terms were one-sided in Trump's favor and, moreover, he never signed the final document. Her complaint also contained a libel action against Cohen for a public statement he made in February: "Just because something isn't true doesn't mean that it can't cause you harm or damage. I will always protect Mr. Trump." The defamation, Clifford said, occurred because the statement suggested that Clifford was lying about her relationship with Trump. Trump eventually did admit that he reimbursed Cohen for the $130,000 paid to Clifford.

In February 2019, federal judge S. James Otero dismissed Clifford's defamation claims against Cohen with prejudice, meaning that she cannot again bring the case against him.

Clifford filed a second libel suit at the end of April 2018 in New York federal court against Trump himself for a tweet he posted after the news of her original lawsuit about the "hush money" broke. The tweet was a retweet of the sketch of the man Clifford claimed threatened her and her baby daughter in the parking lot in 2011 next to a photo of Clifford and her husband, accompanied by Trump's comment "A sketch years later about a nonexistent man. A total con job, playing the Fake News Media for Fools (but they know it)!"

In the complaint, Clifford's lawyer argued that the tweet was libel *per se* because it "falsely attacks the veracity of Ms. Clifford's account of the threatening incident" and "effectively states that Ms. Clifford falsely accused an individual of committing a crime against her when no such crime occurred." Moreover, the lawyer said that Trump knew the tweet was false and used his huge Twitter platform to widely disseminate that falsehood. Attorneys for Trump argued that the tweet was protected opinion.

In Oct. 2018, Judge Otero dismissed the case under the Texas anti-SLAPP law. "The Court agrees with Mr. Trump's argument because the tweet in question constitutes 'rhetorical hyperbole' normally associated with politics and public discourse in the United States. The First Amendment protects this type of rhetorical statement," said the judge (*Clifford v. Trump*, 339 F. Supp. 3d 915). He also awarded attorneys' fees to the former president, assessed at nearly $300,000, which Clifford has appealed, so stay tuned for that. Clifford did, however, win her case against Trump over the "hush money" agreement signed before the 2016 presidential election in August 2020 and was awarded $44,100 in attorneys' fees.

Why did Judge Otero, a California federal judge, use Texas law? Clifford initially brought the suit in New York federal court because Trump had a residence there. The New York court transferred the case to California. Judge Otero relied on New York rules to determine which state's laws should apply. These rules say that the law of the state with the most significant interest in the litigation should govern—usually where the plaintiff lives. Thus, because Clifford is a resident of Texas, Texas law applies.

The Ninth Circuit affirmed Judge Otero's decision (*Clifford v. Trump*, 818 Fed. Appx. 746, 2020). Clifford then appealed to the Supreme Court over the use of the Texas anti-SLAPP law. She alleged that the law's use in her (federal) case "requires this Court to resolve a conflict among the circuits about whether state anti-SLAPP laws apply in federal courts." As noted earlier, the circuits do disagree on the question. Back in 1938, the Supreme Court held that state law governs *substantive* issues, while federal law directs *procedural* issues, and thus federal courts must apply state laws in diversity cases (*Erie R.R. Co. v. Tompkins*, 304 U.S. 64). Such a rule was intended to stop plaintiffs from forum-shopping for the best possible outcome. While circuit splits like this often entice the high court to take a case, the justices declined to do so here, denying *cert* in 2021.

Summer Zervos: ongoing. The first plaintiff to file suit against the former president, Summer Zervos was a contestant on Trump's reality TV show *The Apprentice*. According to her complaint, Zervos later sought employment with the Trump organization, and Trump agreed to meet with her. Zervos alleged that when she met with Trump, he made unwanted sexual advances toward her, and when she rebuffed him, he lost interest in her but then eventually offered her employment at his golf course at half the salary she sought. She called him and told him she was upset because she felt penalized for not sleeping with him.

According to her complaint, Zervos lost business at her restaurant as a result of Trump's repeated lies and depictions of women who came forward to tell their stories of his inappropriate sexual advances. The suit was filed on Jan. 17, 2017, just prior to Trump's inauguration.

Trump's legal team argued that the Supremacy Clause of the U.S. Constitution barred a sitting president from state lawsuits. In 2018, a New York judge found no reason the case could not go forward, citing the Supreme Court in *Clinton v. Jones* (520 U.S. 681, 1997) that a sitting president could be sued in *federal* court for unofficial acts while leaving open the question of *state* lawsuits. A New York appeals court agreed in 2019, discarding Trump's Supremacy Clause argument; the clause "provides that federal law supersedes state law with which it conflicts, but it does not provide that the President himself is immune from state law that does not conflict with federal law" (*Zervos v. Trump*, 94 N.Y.S.3d 75). Trump appealed to the New York Court of Appeals, the state's highest court, but that court mooted his appeal in March 2021, as he was no longer president. The case continues. Stay tuned.

E. Jean Carroll: ongoing. The most recent of these high-profile libel cases filed against the former president came from *Elle* magazine columnist E. Jean Carroll, who accused Trump of sexual assault in Manhattan department store Bergdorf Goodman in the mid-1990s. When the former president denied the allegations (saying that she was "not his type"), she sued him for defamation. When Justice Department attorneys sought to substitute the United States as a defendant using the Federal Tort Claims Act and the Westfall Act (intended to protect government employees from lawsuits while engaged in their official duties), Carroll's legal team argued that her libel suit was filed against Trump as a private person, not as the then-sitting U.S. president.

DOJ attorneys maintained that under the acts, Trump was an employee of the government, and Carroll's libel suit against him should be treated like, as a New York district court judge put it, "a lawsuit against a Postal Service driver for causing a car accident while delivering the mail." The judge rejected that interpretation in 2020, saying that Westfall did not include sitting presidents, and even if it did, Carroll's libel claim dealt with Trump's behavior *before* he was president (*Carroll v. Trump*, 498 F. Supp. 3d 422).

The case is currently on appeal at the Second Circuit, with President Joe Biden's Justice Department participating in the case—not defending Trump's position in the libel suit but rather arguing that the district court erred in its interpretation of the Federal Tort Claims and Westfall Acts. Why would the Biden administration do this? It's a matter of department reliability and consistency. As a *Vox* commentator puts it, "If Justice Department lawyers get a reputation for changing their arguments every time a new president comes into office, judges across the country could decide that those arguments are not credible, and DOJ risks losing many, many cases." Again, stay tuned.

◼ AN OVERVIEW OF MAJOR ISSUES

Through most of American history, the threat of being sued for libel has been the most serious continuing legal hazard for the media, and that threat has not disappeared. For a time, it appeared that the libel problem was subsiding. After *New York Times v. Sullivan*, the Supreme Court handed down several decisions in the 1960s and early 1970s that made it more difficult for plaintiffs to win. By the time of *Rosenbloom v. Metromedia* in 1971, even private persons involved in public issues were being required to prove actual malice (i.e., that a falsehood was published with knowledge or with reckless disregard for the truth).

However, the 1974 *Gertz v. Welch* decision reversed that trend. While *Gertz* rewrote the common law of libel in all 50 states by forcing even private plaintiffs to prove at least negligence in most cases (something not usually required before), it also reclassified many people as private persons when they were previously considered public figures.

The high cost of defending a libel suit grew even higher after the Supreme Court's *Keeton v. Hustler* and *Calder v. Jones* decisions, which permit *forum shopping* in libel cases. Few people would question the fairness of requiring a major corporation to defend a lawsuit in a state where it injures someone while doing business. Years ago the Supreme Court authorized states to exercise *long-arm jurisdiction* over companies having *minimum contacts* with a particular state. Some of today's questions involve long-arm jurisdiction on the internet and related online issues. Does operating a website constitute minimum contacts sufficient to allow a libel plaintiff to sue anywhere the site can be viewed, including foreign countries?

Section 230 will continue to be a hotly debated legal topic. Calls for its revision or elimination, while certainly not new, reached a fever pitch after the January 6 Capitol riot, where social media provided a forum for its organization. Is the exemption from liability for everyone except the creator of a defamatory online message, enshrined in the law, fair to those who are defamed online, or, as Ken Zeran suggested, are broad interpretations of 230 by judges costly mistakes? What will happen to Section 230 in coming years? Abolished?

The Supreme Court's *Milkovich v. Lorain Journal* decision sent a message to the states to give expressions of opinion less protection in libel cases. While statements of pure opinion are still exempt from libel suits, that is not necessarily true of mixed statements that include false factual allegations within an expression of opinion. Editorials, letters to the editor, columns, reviews, and op-eds often combine factual assertions with expressions of opinion; now they enjoy less protection from libel suits.

But the Court has given the media some help. The *Hepps* case declared the burden of proof in virtually all libel cases involving the media falls on the plaintiff, who must prove the publication false. And the *Bose* decision told appellate courts to review evidence in libel cases to be certain that actual malice was really shown when it was required to be.

The adoption of anti-SLAPP laws in many states to curb *strategic lawsuits against public participation* has been helpful to the media. Although these laws are intended primarily to protect citizen activists who speak out on controversial issues, in some states they also protect the media from harassment lawsuits. Even in states lacking anti-SLAPP laws, of course, media defendants can always seek to have nuisance libel suits dismissed before trial by seeking summary judgment, a tactic encouraged by the Court's *Liberty Lobby* decision. Unfortunately, a summary judgment motion cannot be made until later in a lawsuit than a dismissal motion under most anti-SLAPP laws, running up the legal expenses for both sides.

Another scary development for media organizations is the First Circuit's determination in *Noonan v. Staples* that truth may not always be an absolute defense for libel cases. Will other states follow suit, dredging up old libel statutes? And does the gigantic settlement paid by ABC to BPI for a trade libel suit in South Dakota suggest the start of a trend in which media organizations will be forced to watch their criticisms of food products much more closely for fear of legal penalties? Where does this leave the watchdog role of the press over private companies that control our food supplies?

Libel suits over Twitter have become more common. Questions about the use of this and other social media platforms as political tools will continue to generate both public discussion and additional lawsuits, not just in the libel arena.

Ultimately, the discussion of libel must end where it began: with the observation that the system is costly and cumbersome—and that libel is and will remain a serious legal problem for the media.

WHAT SHOULD I KNOW ABOUT MY STATE?

- What are the elements of my state's libel law; e.g., how, does it define terms like "actual malice" and "negligence"?
- What is my state's statute of limitations for libel?
- What does my state long-arm statute include?
- What defenses does my state recognize for libel? Does my state recognize the neutral reportage defense, for example?
- Does my state have an anti-SLAPP and/or trade libel law? If so, how have these statutes been interpreted?
- Does my state have a retraction law? If so, what does it say?

A SUMMARY OF LIBEL AND SLANDER

What Are Libel and Slander?

Libel and slander are legal actions to compensate someone whose reputation has been wrongfully damaged. Traditionally, a written defamation was called libel and a spoken defamation was called slander, but in many states the two are virtually identical.

Who May Sue or Be Sued for Libel?

Individuals and corporations—but not government agencies—may sue. Unincorporated associations may sue in some states but not in others. An individual may sue for group libel if the group is very small and the libel refers particularly to that individual. Usually anyone who contributes to the publication—or republication—of a libelous statement may be sued, even if the libel is in a direct quote, a live interview, an advertisement, or a letter to the editor.

To Win a Libel Suit, What Must a Plaintiff Prove?

To win, the plaintiff (the person who initiates the lawsuit) must prove all of the elements of libel, which are: (1) *defamation*; (2) *identification*; (3) *publication/communication*; (4) in cases involving issues of public concern, *fault* on the part of the publisher or broadcaster (i.e., dissemination of a falsehood due to either negligence or actual malice); (5) in many instances, *actual damages*.

What Defenses Are There?

Even though all of the elements of libel may be present, the plaintiff will not prevail if the defendant can prove that any of the recognized defenses apply. The major ones are: (1) *truth*; (2) *fair comment and criticism*; (3) *privilege*. The Supreme Court has ruled that the plaintiff usually *bears the burden of proof*; that party must prove the falsity of a libelous statement—the defendant does *not* have the burden of proving truth. In many states, publishing a timely retraction—as prominently as the original libel—limits the plaintiff to special damages (i.e., provable monetary losses). Online, Section 230 may provide distributors with protection.

Are There Different Rules for Public Figures and Private Persons?

The Supreme Court has ruled that public officials and public figures must prove actual malice, meaning the publication of a falsehood with knowledge of its falsity or with reckless disregard for the truth. With the Supreme Court's blessing, most states now permit private persons to win libel cases by proving merely negligence on the part of the media, not actual malice. In cases involving purely private matters rather than issues of public concern, the high court has held that the states may allow private persons to win libel cases without proving any fault at all.

5 | *The Right of Privacy*

The right to privacy has become a legal right in the last century in many different contexts. Some of the most controversial decisions by the Supreme Court, including the right to contraception, the right to abortion, and gay rights, are in part based on a constitutional right to privacy that some Supreme Court justices have never fully embraced.

In the media context, the legal concept called *the right of privacy* has much in common with libel and slander. Like libel, invasion of privacy is usually a *tort* action—a civil lawsuit in which an injured party sues for monetary compensation. Moreover, the privacy torts, like libel, are basically a state legal matter, although the U.S. Supreme Court has sometimes stepped in to place constitutional limits on state actions in this area just as it has in libel law.

Invasion of privacy and libel are so similar that persons offended or embarrassed by media publicity often sue for both, hoping to win on at least one of the two legal theories. Libel and invasion of privacy overlap enough to invite this sort of double-lawsuit strategy, particularly because the two actions can have different defenses. However, there are important differences between libel and invasion of privacy, including their histories. Libel was incorporated into the English common law hundreds of years ago, but invasion of privacy was not widely recognized until the twentieth century.

Although privacy law developed more recently, it has become one of the most important and controversial aspects of communications law. In recent years, much of privacy law is related to *data privacy and security*. The Supreme Court continues to delve into violations of personal privacy in the digital era. Some cases involve the First Amendment. But many cases deal with the scope of the Fourth Amendment, which grants "the right of the people to be secure in their persons, houses, papers, and effects against unreasonable searches and seizures." The ability of our technological gadgets to gather and transmit information, as well as our affection for online social networks, contributes to these new developments.

Also, media practitioners must be aware of the four privacy torts—*intrusion, disclosure of private facts, false light* invasion of privacy, and *misappropriation*. These civil causes of action can result in lawsuits for damages, sometimes with dire consequences.

In this chapter, we provide a brief history of the right to privacy and survey its broader constitutional dimensions, including those inherent in one's body and personal choices. Then, we turn to media issues. We explore the right to privacy in the digital era and issues with protection of data privacy and security. The second half of the chapter examines the four privacy torts in detail, discussing major principles, key precedents, and primary defenses.

Chapter Objectives:

- Summarize the history and scope of the constitutional right to privacy.
- Identify the effects of digital technology on the right to privacy.
- Evaluate the elements of and defenses to the four privacy torts.

Essential Questions:

- What are the ways in which people's privacy can be invaded?
- What are the basic elements a plaintiff must prove for each of the four privacy torts, and what are possible defenses?
- How does the First Amendment provide a defense to some invasion of privacy claims?

■ THE HISTORY OF PRIVACY LAW

The legal concept of a "right of privacy" developed only after the media, corporations, and government agencies became powerful enough—and technically sophisticated enough—to threaten individual privacy. That happened early in the twentieth century.

By 1900, the biggest newspapers had achieved circulations of nearly a million copies a day, and they did it with a heavy emphasis on stories about crime and scandal, stories that were not always truthful and tasteful. It became obvious that the media could destroy someone's reputation, sometimes in a way that did not make a libel suit a good remedy. Suppose, for instance, that a sensational newspaper revealed intimate (but truthful) details of a person's private life. The truth defense would preclude a successful libel suit, but shouldn't there be some way for the injured party to win justice in court?

Brandeis' law review article. In one of the most widely quoted law review articles of all time, Samuel D. Warren and Louis D. Brandeis addressed this issue in 1890. (Brandeis later served on the U.S. Supreme Court and wrote several well-known opinions on freedom of expression in America.) Their essay in the *Harvard Law Review* contended that there should be a right of privacy either under the common law or state statutory law. Such a right, they felt, should protect prominent persons from gossipy reporting of their private affairs. The article was prompted at least in part by the experiences of Warren's family, which had occasionally found its name mentioned in unflattering ways in the Boston press. "The press is overstepping in every direction the obvious bounds of propriety and of decency," they wrote. "Gossip is no longer the resource of the idle and of the vicious, but has become a trade, which is pursued with industry as well as effrontery."

Earliest privacy law. Influential as that law review article became later, it did not create an overnight legal revolution. In fact, it was a dozen years later when a case based on the Warren-Brandeis theory finally reached a New York appellate court, and the court didn't buy the idea. The case (*Roberson v. Rochester Folding Box Co.*, 64 N.E. 442, 1902), was brought by Abigail Roberson, whose picture was used without her permission in a flour advertisement. She sued, but the court ruled that "the so-called 'right of privacy' has not yet found an abiding place in our jurisprudence...." However, Roberson's defeat in court quickly was turned into a victory in the New York legislature, which responded to a public outcry over the court decision by passing the nation's first statutory law on privacy. Acting in 1903, the legislature enacted what are now Sections 50 and 51 of the New York Civil Rights Law, which read in part: "[T]he name, portrait or picture of any living person cannot be used for advertising purposes or for purposes of trade, without first obtaining that person's written consent."

Obviously, this was not a sweeping law: it didn't address the sort of invasion of privacy Warren and Brandeis had in mind. All it did was outlaw commercial exploitation of a person's name or likeness without consent—a separate legal wrong we call *misappropriation* or invasion of the *right of publicity* today. It said nothing about situations in which the media reveal intimate details about a person's private life or engage in intrusive newsgathering.

Two years after the New York privacy law was enacted, a state supreme court judicially recognized a right of privacy in connection with the media for the first time. In that 1905 case (*Pavesich v. New England Life Insurance Co.*, 50 S.E. 68), the Georgia Supreme Court upheld the right of an artist named Paolo Pavesich to sue New England Life for using his likeness in an advertisement without permission. The ad included a photo of Pavesich and a testimonial implying that he endorsed the company's insurance.

FIG. 42.
Justice Louis
Dembitz Brandeis,
between 1905 and
1945. His 1905
article set the stage
for the development
of privacy law.

*Library of Congress
Prints and
Photographs Division,
[LC-DIG-hec-16557]*

Another famous early privacy case raised a different question, one that has plagued the courts (and journalists) ever since: can a public figure return to a private life and then sue for invasion of privacy if the press does a "where-is-he-now" story years later? In *Sidis v. F-R Publishing Co.* (113 F.2d 806, 1940), William J. Sidis sued the publisher of the *New Yorker* magazine for doing an article about him. He was a one-time mathematical genius who graduated from Harvard University at age 16. The article, published some 20 years later, revealed that he was living in a shabby rooming house and working as a low-salaried clerk. It ridiculed him and even included a cartoon with a caption calling him an "April fool."

Should someone like William Sidis be able to sue the *New Yorker* for invading his privacy? A federal appellate court ruled that the case should be dismissed, pointing to the newsworthiness of the story. The court said that someone who becomes a celebrity even involuntarily (as Sidis had) cannot completely avoid publicity later in life.

The *Sidis* case did not settle this issue, of course. Old-but-true-facts cases continue to arise, and the media defend coverage of such stories by citing the continued public interest in the subject and by pointing out that the coverage is often based on truthful reporting of public records. Publicity-shy plaintiffs, of course, argue that they should not be forced to have their past deeds revealed to people who have forgotten (or never knew) about them.

Two key principles. Two legal concepts were emerging from these early privacy cases. First, there is the idea that the news media do not need anyone's consent to do stories about *newsworthy* subjects. But, on the other hand, when a person's name or likeness is used for commercial purposes (as in advertising), it must be with the person's permission. Most states now recognize these aspects of the right of privacy, either by statute or court decision.

A Constitutional Right of Privacy

Meanwhile, the U.S. Supreme Court began to recognize that there is also a *constitutional* right of privacy, although none of those early decisions actually involved the media. Rather, the early cases all involved the right of individuals to be free of excessive *government* intrusions into their private lives. The high court acknowledged the right of privacy in a law enforcement context as long ago as 1886, in *Boyd v. U.S.* (116 U.S. 616). In that case, the Court said the Fourth and Fifth Amendments provide protection against governmental invasions of the "sanctity of a man's home and the privacies of life."

Fourth Amendment:
"The right of the people to be secure in their persons, houses, papers, and effects, against unreasonable searches and seizures, shall not be violated, and no Warrants shall issue, but upon probable cause, supported by Oath or affirmation, and particularly describing the place to be searched, and the persons or things to be seized."

newsgathering tort:
torts that involve how news is gathered rather than what is published; can include wiretapping/phone recordings, ride-alongs, fraud, breach of duty of loyalty, trespass, and other torts.

ride-along:
when a media professional accompanies the police on official duties.

Then in 1928, Louis Brandeis—by then a Supreme Court justice—wrote a famous dissenting opinion in which he urged recognition of the right of privacy in *Olmstead v. U.S.* (277 U.S. 438). That case involved government eavesdropping to gain evidence against suspected bootleggers in the prohibition era, and the majority opinion held that there was no violation of any right of privacy unless the federal agents committed a physical trespass in order to listen in. But in his dissent, Brandeis called for a "right to be let alone." He said the framers of the Constitution intended "to protect Americans in their beliefs, their thoughts, their emotions and their sensations.... They conferred, as against government, the right to be let alone—the most comprehensive of rights and the right most valued by civilized man."

Since then, the Supreme Court has specifically recognized the right of privacy, both in media cases and in other areas. For instance, the *Olmstead* majority opinion, which allowed government eavesdropping as long as there was no physical trespass, was reversed some 40 years later in *Katz v. U.S.* (389 U.S. 347). In that 1967 case, federal agents had used monitoring devices atop a public telephone booth to gather evidence against alleged bookmakers (i.e., persons taking illegal bets on horse races). The Court said a person's right to privacy extends to all areas where there is a justifiable expectation of privacy. Unauthorized law enforcement surveillance activities need not involve a physical trespass to constitute a violation of the Fourth Amendment, the Court ruled.

In the decades since *Katz*, the Supreme Court has repeatedly ruled on the privacy issues raised by the use of other technologies by law enforcement investigators to conduct searches without a search warrant. In 2001, the Court ruled against federal agents who used heat-sensing equipment to detect an indoor marijuana farm. In *Kyllo v. U.S.* (533 U.S. 27), a 5-4 majority declared that the use of thermal imaging equipment violated the right of privacy guaranteed by the Fourth Amendment even though there was no physical intrusion into the home. This was true even though the imaging equipment merely detected heat radiating out from the home and did not involve looking into the house, the Court said.

Birth control. The Supreme Court also relied largely on a privacy rationale in reaching its famous decisions on birth control, abortion, and LGBTQ rights. In the 1965 ruling that overturned state laws against contraceptive devices (*Griswold v. Connecticut*, 381 U.S. 479), Justice William O. Douglas said the various rights listed in the Bill of Rights, taken together, add up to a right of privacy that bars the state from involving itself in individuals' sexual relations in marriage. Although some of the other justices based their decision on a different rationale, Douglas' view was widely quoted later in support of a limited constitutional right of privacy. A couple's

FIG. 43.
Justice Sandra Day O'Connor, the first woman to serve on the U.S. Supreme Court, was personally opposed to abortion. But she wrote in *Casey*, "Our obligation is to define the liberty of all, not to mandate our own moral code."

Library of Congress..

decision to use contraceptives was a private matter and none of the state's business, Douglas claimed. Thus, the Connecticut law banning the use of contraceptives (even by married couples) was ruled unconstitutional.

Abortion law. The right to have an abortion is rooted in the constitutional right to privacy. In the landmark 1973 decision overturning state laws against abortions (*Roe v. Wade*, 410 U.S. 113), the Supreme Court focused on concepts related to personal privacy in ruling that abortions were a private matter between a woman and her physician, at least during the early months of pregnancy. In the years since 1973, *Roe* become the most controversial Supreme Court decision of the twentieth century. Millions of Americans vehemently disagree with the ruling that a state cannot prohibit abortions during the first six months of pregnancy when the fetus is not viable outside the womb. Millions of others strongly support the court's holding that there is a right of privacy in this area. It was inevitable that the Supreme Court would have to revisit the abortion question again and again. The Court has upheld the basic *Roe* frameworks in several controversial opinions since 1973, including the 1992 decision *Planned Parenthood v. Casey* and the 2016 decision in *Whole Woman's Health v. Hellerstedt*.

In the 1992 case *Planned Parenthood of SE Pennsylvania v. Casey* (505 U.S. 833), many on both sides of the abortion controversy expected the Supreme Court to overturn *Roe v. Wade*. Two liberal justices who were strong supporters of *Roe v. Wade* (William Brennan and Thurgood Marshall) had been replaced by more conservative justices (David Souter and Clarence Thomas). But to almost everyone's astonishment, a new coalition of moderate conservatives led the Court in a 5-4 vote to *reaffirm* the basic holding of *Roe.* Justice Sandra Day O'Connor formed a coalition with Justices Anthony Kennedy and David Souter to rule that the states may not place an *undue burden* on a woman's right to choose an abortion during the early months of pregnancy. When the decision was announced, O'Connor said she was personally very opposed to abortions, but she added, "Our obligation is to define the liberty of all, not to mandate our own moral code." In *Casey,* the Court upheld Pennsylvania laws establishing a 24-hour waiting period for adult women who want an abortion and requiring teenagers to get a parent's or a judge's permission for an abortion. But the justices overturned Pennsylvania's requirement that married women had to notify their husbands of their plans. That, they said, *was* an undue burden.

A year before its 1992 *Planned Parenthood* decision, the Supreme Court addressed a related issue: whether the federal government can order health care providers who receive federal funds not to mention abortions to their patients. In *Rust v. Sullivan* (500 U.S. 173), the Court upheld such federal regulations. In so ruling, the Court's 5-4 majority ruled that doctors do *not* have a First Amendment right to inform their patients about abortions. (However, the federal rules were later rewritten to eliminate this ban on federally supported doctors mentioning abortions to their patients.)

States continue to pass laws that test the constitutional limits to abortion rights. For example, in 2000, the Supreme Court ruled that a Nebraska law forbidding "partial birth abortions" placed an undue burden on a woman's constitutional right to terminate a pregnancy and was therefore unconstitutional (*Stenberg v. Carhart*, 530 U.S. 914). The Nebraska law defined partial birth abortion as a procedure in which a person "...intentionally delivers into the vagina a living unborn child, or a substantial portion thereof, for the purpose of performing a procedure" that the person knows "will kill the unborn child." The Court said this law (and laws banning partial-birth abortions in about 30 other states) was too broad, precluding methods that are safer for the mother than alternative methods used in late-term abortions. Four justices dissented, writing four separate opinions. They argued that a state should be free to ban partial-birth abortions for various reasons. Justice Antonin Scalia said, "The method of killing a human child...proscribed by this statute is so horrible that the most clinical description of it evokes a shudder of revulsion."

In 2003, Congress approved a federal Partial Birth Abortion Ban Act, forbidding certain partial-birth abortion procedures. This federal law is similar to the Nebraska state law overturned in the *Stenberg v. Carhart* decision, but legal challenges to it had a very different outcome: the Supreme Court eventually upheld the law. Initially, the federal law was overturned by three different federal appellate courts. However, in 2007 the Court overturned all three appeals court decisions, voting 5-4 to uphold the constitutionality of the Partial Birth Abortion Act. Justice Samuel Alito provided the fifth vote to restrict abortion rights in the new decision, *Gonzales v. Carhart* (550 U.S. 124). A year earlier, he replaced Justice Sandra Day O'Connor, the architect of the "undue burden" test and frequently the fifth vote to uphold abortion rights on the Court. Writing for the majority in upholding the federal law, Justice Anthony Kennedy now took what appeared to be a different approach than he had in joining O'Connor's opinion in the 1992 *Casey* case. This time, he wrote for the court, "The government has a legitimate and substantial interest in preserving and promoting fetal life." He said the government may regulate "the medical profession in order to promote respect for...the life of the unborn." The 5-4 majority in the 2007 decision *upheld* the federal ban on essentially the same procedure that was forbidden in Nebraska in the law *overturned* by a 5-4 majority in *Stenberg v. Carhart* seven years earlier. In this ruling, Kennedy focused more on "the life of the unborn" and not on women's privacy rights or the right of doctors to choose the safest procedure for women. This 2007 decision was applauded by abortion opponents, who launched a campaign to win restrictions on abortions state by state—and condemned by abortion-rights advocates and some doctors.

In another major victory for abortion rights advocates, in 2016 the Supreme Court struck down a Texas law that had the effect of reducing by half the number of abortion clinics in the state. Like more than a dozen states in recent years, Texas had passed a law requiring abortion clinics to have surgical-center standards and doctors with admitting privileges to nearby hospitals—provisions that effectively shut down many abortion clinics that couldn't afford the stringent requirements. In its 5-3 decision in *Whole Woman's Health v. Hellerstedt* (136 S. Ct. 2292), drawing upon the *Casey* precedent, the Court said the Texas law created an undue burden on a woman's right to an abortion. "We conclude that neither of these provisions offers medical benefits sufficient to justify the burdens upon access that each imposes. Each places a substantial obstacle in the path of women seeking a previability abortion, each constitutes an undue burden on abortion access, and each violates the federal Constitution," Justice Stephen Breyer wrote for the majority.

In 2020, the Supreme Court struck down a similar law to that in *Whole Woman's Health*. In *June Medical Services, LLC v. Russo* (No. 18-1323), a split 5-4 Court ruled that a Louisiana law requiring abortion clinic doctors to have hospital admission privileges was unconstitutional. However, Chief Justice John Roberts became the "swing" vote, following Justice Brett Kavanaugh's replacement of Justice Anthony Kennedy. Roberts sided with the majority based on the precedent set by *Whole Woman's Health*, even though he dissented from that opinion.

Following Justice Amy Coney Barrett's replacement of Justice Ruth Bader Ginsburg in 2020, abortion opponents were hopeful they may have a solid majority on the Court to overturn *Roe v. Wade*, or at least significantly weaken its precedent. The newly constituted Court will have an opportunity to review its abortion precedents in an upcoming case, *Dobbs v. Jackson Women's Health Org.*, that reviews the constitutionality of a Mississippi law banning abortions after the first 15 weeks of pregnancy. Lower courts have issued injunctions banning the enforcement of the law, based on the *Roe v. Wade* precedent. Stay tuned.

LGBTQ rights. While the Supreme Court was considering the constitutional right of privacy in connection with abortions, another privacy issue was looming in the background—the issue of gay rights and same-sex marriage. Taking a step back, it is remarkable to see how much legal protections have changed for LGBTQ Americans in just one generation. Much of that is the result of the Court's decisions in two cases involving the constitutional right of privacy and same-sex sexual activity. In 1986, the Court ruled that there was *no* constitutional right of privacy to protect even private, consensual homosexual acts by adults. But in 2003 the Court reversed itself and held that a law banning private homosexual acts by adults violated the constitutional right of privacy.

In 1986 the Supreme Court declined to recognize constitutional privacy rights for homosexuals in *Bowers v. Hardwick* (478 U.S. 186). In *Bowers*, the Court upheld a Georgia law forbidding sex acts such as sodomy, even between consenting adults in private. The Georgia law, similar to laws then in effect in more than 20 other states, made sodomy a crime for everyone including heterosexual married couples, although it was primarily enforced against homosexuals. Georgia officials said there had been few modern prosecutions. In refusing to overturn the Georgia law in 1986, the 5-4 majority said that the authors of the Constitution were surely not trying to protect the rights of gay men and lesbians when they wrote the Bill of Rights. Although the Court earlier had held that the Constitution includes a right of privacy in connection with contraception and abortion, the majority in *Bowers* ruled that the same privacy rights do not exist when the private sex lives of gay people are concerned. Writing for the Court, Justice Byron R. White said, "We think it is evident that none of the rights announced in those cases (involving contraception, abortion, and similar questions) bears any resemblance to the claimed constitutional rights of homosexuals to engage in acts of sodomy." After *Bowers*, a number of states recognized a right of privacy for gay men and lesbians under their own *state* constitutions, ruling that these state constitutions provided broader rights than the U.S. Constitution.

The first signal that the Supreme Court was reconsidering it hard line against LGBTQ rights came in 1996, when the Court ruled that the voters of Colorado could not legalize discrimination against gay men and lesbians by passing a ballot initiative to invalidate existing state and local laws protecting gay rights. In *Romer v. Evans* (517 U.S. 620), the Court overturned a Colorado ballot initiative banning state and local laws giving legal protection to the rights of gay men and lesbians. The initiative was approved by a majority of Colorado voters in 1992. In a 6-3 ruling, the Court said a state cannot single out a group for "disfavored treatment" based on "animosity." Writing for the majority, Justice Anthony Kennedy said that the ballot initiative "classifies homosexuals not to further a proper legislative end but to make them unequal to everyone else. This Colorado cannot do." This decision does not necessarily guarantee gay men and lesbians equal rights in all areas of the law. But it was the first time the Court overturned a law intended to legalize discrimination against them.

In 2003, the U.S. Supreme Court took the highly unusual step of reversing one of its own prior decisions only 17 years later. In *Lawrence v. Texas* (539 U.S. 558), the Court voted 6-3 to overturn a Texas law similar to the Georgia law that it had upheld in *Bowers*. By a narrower 5-4 majority, the Court also voted to overturn *Bowers*. The *Lawrence* case arose when Houston police entered John Lawrence's apartment to investigate what turned out to be a false report of a disturbance. But they found Lawrence and another man engaged in anal sex. The two men were arrested, jailed overnight, and fined $200 each for violating Texas' anti-sodomy law. They challenged the law's constitutionality. Writing for the majority, Justice Anthony Kennedy said the two men "are entitled to respect for their private lives" in upholding their privacy. "The state cannot demean their existence or control their destiny by making their private sexual conduct a crime," he added. The decision overturned not only the Texas sodomy law but also laws in 12 other states that still prohibited acts of anal and oral sex. At the time of *Lawrence*, four states (Texas, Oklahoma, Kansas, and Missouri) banned sodomy only between gay couples. Nine other states had laws banning such acts between any two people. The *Lawrence* decision was widely hailed by gay-rights attorneys as the most important Supreme Court decision in many years, and it led to campaigns for greater LGBTQ rights in other areas of law.

Gays in the military. One long-standing legal issue for LGBTQ citizens was their right to serve openly in the U.S. military. For most of U.S. history, openly LGTBQ individuals were prohibited from service. In 1993, after years of advocacy by LGBTQ rights groups,

FIG. 44.
President Barack Obama signs the Don't Ask, Don't Tell Repeal Act of 2010 at the U.S. Department of Interior in Washington, D.C., Dec. 22, 2010.

Official White House photo by Chuck Kennedy.

FIGS. 45 & 46: Protestors outside the Supreme Court on Mar. 26, 2013, the day of same-sex marriage oral arguments.

Author's collection.

the government created a compromise rule called "Don't Ask, Don't Tell" (DADT), which prohibited the military from discriminating against closeted gay or bisexual service members or applicants, while forbidding openly gay or bisexual persons from serving. The DADT policy had been upheld in four circuit courts. But in 2010 a federal judge said that it violated the First and Fifth Amendments in a case filed by the Log Cabin Republicans, the largest Republican gay organization (*Log Cabin Republicans v. U.S.*, 716 F. Supp. 2d 884), saying that it did not further the government's interests in unit cohesion or military readiness and is a content-based regulation. Before the case made its way to the Supreme Court, in 2010, President Barack Obama signed the Don't Ask, Don't Tell Repeal Act of 2010, allowing gay and bisexual individuals to serve openly in the military.

Same-sex marriage. In the years after the Supreme Court recognized a constitutional right of privacy for LGBTQ citizens in the *Lawrence* case, another question involving their constitutional rights had become a major issue: whether they have a right to same-sex marriage. By 2010, 29 states had enacted laws or constitutional amendments defining marriage as a union of a man and a woman. Several state supreme courts upheld these same-sex marriage bans. However, court challenges over California's Prop 8 and the federal government's 1996 Defense of Marriage Act garnered major attention as the Supreme Court waded into the controversy.

Prop 8. In 2008, the California Supreme Court ruled that gay men and lesbians have broad constitutional rights under the state constitution, including the right to marry (*In re Marriage Cases*, 43 C.4th 757). However, Proposition 8 (Prop 8), a measure to amend the California Constitution to define marriage as a union between a man and a woman, passed in a 2008 election and was promptly challenged in the courts. In 2009 in *Strauss v. Horton* (46 Cal. 4th 364), the California Supreme Court upheld Proposition 8, saying, "Proposition 8 must be understood as creating a limited exception to the state equal protection clause." The court however said the ruling could not be applied retroactively to annul the marriages of 18,000 gay marriages that took place in California prior to the passage of Proposition 8.

In 2010, following a landmark court trial, federal district judge Vaughn Walker struck down Proposition 8 as unconstitutional under the due process and equal protection clauses of the Fourteenth Amendment in *Perry v. Schwarzenegger* (704 F.Supp.2d 921). In a lengthy opinion, the judge noted that marriage is a fundamental right, and fundamental rights cannot be voted upon. Moreover, he said, Prop 8 could not even survive rational basis scrutiny, much less the much stricter test that abridgments of fundamental rights must surmount. Thus, he wrote, "Proposition 8 fails to advance any rational basis in singling out gay men and lesbians for denial of a marriage license. Indeed, the evidence shows Prop 8 does nothing more than enshrine in the California Constitution the notion that opposite-sex couples are superior to same-sex couples." He ordered a permanent injunction against Prop 8.

The case wove a complicated path on appeal, largely on the question of standing because the state of California chose not to defend the law, leaving the supporters of the proposition to represent to defend the law in court. Ultimately, in *Hollingsworth v. Perry* (570 U.S. 693), the U.S. Supreme Court in 2013 left Judge Walker's ruling intact, finding that the appellants lacked standing. The effect was that same-sex marriage was legal in California.

DOMA. Meanwhile, marriage equality advocates were challenging the federal law that prohibited same-sex marriage, the 1996 Defense of Marriage Act (DOMA), which said that no state must recognize a same-sex marriage even if it is recognized in other states and defines marriage as a legal union between a man and a woman for the federal government.

In 2011, Attorney General Eric Holder notified House Speaker John Boehner that the Obama administration believed DOMA to be unconstitutional and so would no longer defend the statute in court. Several courts declared DOMA unconstitutional, including the First Circuit in *Commonwealth of Massachusetts v. U.S. Dep't of Health & Human Services* (682 F.3d 1), in which the court pointed out the impact of DOMA on states like Massachusetts that permit same-sex marriage: "Under current Supreme Court authority, Congress' denial of federal benefits to same-sex couples lawfully married in Massachusetts has not been adequately supported by any permissible federal interest."

The Supreme Court granted *cert*, and in the most awaited decision of that year, struck down DOMA on equal protection grounds and dismissed the case against Prop 8 on standing issues. In the DOMA case, *U.S. v. Windsor* (570 U.S. 744), Justice Anthony Kennedy, writing for a 5-4 majority, said that DOMA created "two contradictory marriage regimes within the same State" but forcing same-sex couples "to live as married for the purpose of state law but unmarried for the purpose of federal law." He said this places "same-sex couples in an unstable position of being in a second-tier marriage." In dissent, Chief Justice John Roberts said that the Court did not have standing to decide the case, and in any case DOMA was constitutional: "Interests in uniformity and stability amply justified Congress's decision to retain the definition of marriage that, at that point, had been adopted by every State in our Nation, and every nation in the world." Justice Antonin Scalia went further in his dissent, calling the majority's opinion "jaw-dropping:" "It is an assertion of judicial supremacy over the people's Representatives in Congress and the Executive."

Constitutional right to same-sex marriage. After the *Windsor* and *Hollingsworth* decisions, dozens of cases flooded the lower courts seeking to strike down same-sex marriage bans. Most lower courts struck down bans, although the Sixth Circuit of Appeals held that states did not have to recognize same-sex marriages.

In a 2015 decision that was immediately described as a landmark Supreme Court decision, *Obergefell v. Hodges* (576 U.S. 644), the Court on a 5-4 vote overturned the Sixth Circuit's ruling and held that same-sex couples have a constitutional right to marriage in all 50 states. Justice Kennedy was again the swing vote between the Court's liberals and conservatives. The majority found that the Fourteenth Amendment's rights of due process

Focus on...
Justice Anthony Kennedy's legacy on LGBTQ rights

Justice Anthony Kennedy, 81, retired from the U.S. Supreme Court in 2018, ending a 30-year career as a conservative and libertarian-leaning associate justice who often was the swing vote in landmark 5-4 decisions.

The California native served on the Ninth Circuit Court of Appeals before President Ronald Reagan appointed him to fill Justice Lewis Powell's seat on the highest court. The Senate unanimously confirmed him in 1988.

To be sure, Kennedy's most lasting legacy will be on gay rights. He was the crucial swing vote and author of majority opinions in three landmark decisions enshrining gay equality as a constitutional right.

FIG. 47. Justice Anthony Kennedy.

Collection of the Supreme Court of the United States.

Kennedy opened the door for gay equality when he wrote the 1996 decision in *Romer v. Evans* (517 U.S. 620), striking down a Colorado law that banned municipalities from passing nondiscrimination laws. The goal was to make homosexuals "unequal to everyone else," Kennedy wrote, and therefore, the law violated the Constitution. In 2003, he authored *Lawrence v. Texas* (539 U.S. 558), a decision that struck down laws that criminalized same-sex sexual activity and reaffirmed the constitutional "right to privacy."

Kennedy also wrote the decisions finding a constitutional right for same-sex marriage. In 2013, he wrote the decision striking down the federal Defense of Marriage Act in *U.S. v. Windsor* (570 U.S. 744). And in 2015, he authored the opinion in *Obergefell v. Hodges* (576 U.S. 644), in which he wrote for a 5-4 Court, "Under the Constitution, same-sex couples seek in marriage the same legal treatment as opposite-sex couples, and it would disparage their choices and diminish their personhood to deny them this right."

and equal protection made it unconstitutional to deny same-sex couples marriage rights that heterosexual couples received. "It is now clear that the challenged laws burden the liberty of same-sex couples, and it must be further acknowledged that they abridge central precepts of equality," Justice Kennedy wrote.

In *Obergefell*, the judicial philosophies of different justices were on stark display over one of the most controversial social issues of their generation. Justice Kennedy's opinion articulated a "living document" view of the Constitution that protects fundamental rights, including liberty, privacy, and equal protection, that are sometimes not obvious without the wisdom of history and experience. "The right to marry is fundamental as a matter of history and tradition, but rights come not from ancient sources alone. They rise, too, from a better informed understanding of how constitutional imperatives define a liberty that remains urgent in our own era," Justice Kennedy wrote. "The right of same-sex couples to marry that is part of the liberty promised by the Fourteenth Amendment is derived, too, from that Amendment's guarantee of the equal protection of the laws."

The four dissenters chastised the majority for inventing a new fundamental right that they said is neither provided in the text or original understanding of the Constitution.

They also said the right to marry should be left to the people and legislative branches to decide, not unelected judges. "Five lawyers have closed the debate and enacted their own vision of marriage as a matter of constitutional law," Chief Justice Roberts wrote in his dissent. "Stealing this issue from the people will for many cast a cloud over same-sex marriage, making a dramatic social change that much more difficult to accept."

Other constitutional issues over LGBTQ rights. As the gay marriage question became settled law, the Supreme Court faced other questions involving the rights of LGBTQ citizens.

One major continuing legal question pits gay rights against religious freedom. In 2018, the Court punted on what could have been a divisive decision. In *Masterpiece Cakeshop, Ltd. v. Colorado Civil Rights Comm'n* (138 S. Ct. 1719), the Court declined to create a religious freedom right for businesses to refuse services to gays and lesbians. Instead, the Court ruled a cake maker did not receive a fair and unbiased hearing by a Colorado administrative panel.

The Court again took a narrow approach in a case involving the Free Exercise Clause and anti-LGBTQ discrimination laws, in its 2021 decision in *Fulton v. City of Philadelphia* (No. 19-123). The case involved a lawsuit filed by Catholic Social Services (CSS) after Philadelphia declined to renew a contract for foster parent screening after CSS announced it would not accept gay couples. In a 9-0 decision, the Supreme Court sided with CSS, finding that the city had violated the group's religious freedom rights. However, the Court's ruling was on narrow grounds: because the city's policy allowed exemptions to its non-discrimination principle, by not doing so in this case showed an intolerance toward religious views. The Court also ruled that CSS's services did not constitute a public accommodation under anti-discrimination laws. Justice Samuel Alito wrote a lengthy concurrence, joined by Justices Clarence Thomas and Neil Gorsuch, that would have used the case to issue a broader ruling expanding free exercise claims and in doing so advocated overturning *Employment Div. v. Smith* (494 U.S. 872), in which the Supreme Court in 1990 held that "neutral and generally applicable" laws do not violate the Free Exercise Clause as long as they don't single out religious activity.

In another case described as a landmark decision for LGBTQ rights, the Supreme Court ruled that LGBTQ citizens are protected from workplace discrimination under federal law. In *Bostock v. Clayton County* (140 S. Ct. 1731, 2020), the Court reviewed three lower court decisions splitting on the question of whether discrimination based on sexual orientation or gender identity was prohibited by Title VII of the Civil Rights Act of 1964, which prohibits discrimination based on an individual's 'race, color, religion, sex, or national origin." In a 6-3 decision written by Justice Neil Gorsuch, the Court ruled that the meaning of "sex" as defined in the statute prohibits disparate treatment of heterosexual and LGBTQ individuals. "An employer who fired an individual for being homosexual or transgender fires that person for traits or actions it would not have questioned in members of a different sex. Sex plays a necessary and undisguisable role in the decision, exactly what Title VII forbids," Gorsuch wrote. The case was heralded as a major victory for LGBTQ equality.

While the Supreme Court's decisions about privacy rights in these controversial areas have generated more headlines, the rights of privacy in other areas more directly affect the media. The rest of this chapter concerns the purely media-related aspects of privacy law. First we'll explore issues related to data privacy and security and then turn to the four privacy torts.

■ PRIVACY IN THE DIGITAL ERA

Perhaps no technical advance of the twentieth and twenty-first centuries created greater concern about personal privacy than the explosive growth of personal computer technology—and especially the internet. Internet privacy has become a major national issue. This led to legislation and calls for legislation in many places. Certain aspects of this question involve the privacy issues of the sort addressed in this chapter, including legislation to protect individuals from hackers and unscrupulous data-gatherers and the legal questions surrounding the use of people's names and images on the internet without consent.

Sometimes, as Chapter Nine discusses in the context of freedom of information requests, the government wants to keep information private that the media wants to be made public, but in many cases, individuals are fighting to retain their informational privacy from the government or from private companies. As we've noted earlier, the area that seems to be growing most quickly in the courts as well as in the minds of legislatures, government regulatory agencies, and the public is data privacy. The internet makes it all too easy for information to be gathered, stored, aggregated, and searched.

A Constitutional Right to Data Privacy?

Is there an actual *constitutional* right to data privacy? Some justices on the U.S. Supreme Court would say no, as they did in a 2011 case. The Court ruled in favor of the National Aeronautics and Space Administration's (NASA) background checks for employees of companies working under contract in *NASA v. Nelson* (562 U.S. 134). Robert Nelson, a contract employee of Jet Propulsion Laboratory (JPL), objected to a background questionnaire intended to eliminate differences between contract employees who had worked at JPL for years without background checks and those newly hired. Two sections, one asking about treatment or counseling for recent illegal drug use and another with open-ended questions for references to answer, were under consideration. Justice Samuel Alito, writing for a unanimous Court, upheld the questions as not violating the constitutional rights of the employees. The government, he said, has "an interest in conducting basic employment background checks." But Alito did *not* address the major question in the case: is there a constitutional right to informational privacy? Alito assumed there was for purposes of the case (without actually ruling that there is) and said that if the right did exist, it was not violated here. But Justices Clarence Thomas and Antonin Scalia in their concurring opinions made no secret of their position on the informational privacy right: there isn't one. Scalia wrote bluntly: "A federal constitutional right to 'informational privacy' does not exist." Thomas, going even further, quoted himself from *Lawrence v. Texas*: "I can find neither in the Bill of Rights nor any other part of the Constitution a general right of privacy."

These justices' opinions notwithstanding, the Supreme Court in recent terms has greatly expanded the right to privacy in the digital era. For example, in 2012, the Court ruled that attaching a global positioning system (GPS) device to a person's car without that person's knowledge counted as a "search" under the Fourth Amendment (*U.S. v. Jones*, 565 U.S. 400). In 2014, the Court ruled in *Riley v. California* (573 U.S. 373) that police may not, "without a warrant, search digital information on a cell phone seized from an individual who has been arrested." And in 2018, in *Carpenter v. U.S.* (138 S. Ct. 2206), the Court ruled that police must get a warrant before accessing cell phone tracking data collected by cell phone companies. Technology has advanced so much that cell phones are "almost a feature of human anatomy" and present many new legal questions, the Court noted. "A cell phone faithfully follows its owner beyond public thoroughfares and into private residences, doctor's offices, political headquarters, and other potentially revealing locales," Chief Justice John Roberts wrote in a 5-4 decision. "Accordingly, when the Government tracks the location of a cell phone it achieves near perfect surveillance, as if it had attached an ankle monitor to the phone's user." The decision was described as an important precedent in ever-evolving privacy law.

Digital Privacy Laws

In the United States, there is no single federal privacy statute, although several laws provide some data privacy protections. In the absence of general privacy legislation, the Federal Trade Commission has become a primary federal agency in privacy enforcement actions. FTC authority in privacy actions falls under its general authority to prohibit unfair and deceptive practices in the marketplace, and also under several statutes in specific areas of law. Some states are stepping in to pass state statutes, creating a headache for companies that might have to comply with different rules in different states. International laws also vary greatly. What might be normal practice for Facebook in the United States might be prohibited in other countries, for example.

No federal statute. In recent years, Congress has been busy drafting laws to protect data privacy, but few of them get out of committee. A few notable examples: Senator Patrick Leahy (D-Vt) announced the Personal Data Privacy and Security Act in 2009. The bill would require some data holders to disclose personal electronic records to individuals for a fee and to include information on how to correct errors in those records. Senator Leahy also proposed the Electronic Communications Privacy Act (ECPA) Amendments Act to update ECPA, a major federal online privacy law. Several online "do not track" bills were also announced: the Do Not Track Me Online Act, to make the FTC "prescribe regulations regarding the collection and use of information obtained by tracking the internet activity of an individual, and for other purposes" and Do Not Track Kids Act, to "extend, enhance, and revise the provisions relating to collection, use, and disclosure of personal information of children." None of those bills advanced to become law. In 2021, Rep. Suzan DelBene (D-Wa.) introduced the Transparency and Personal Data Control Act in the House. The bill would set national standards for data privacy and require companies to provide an opt-in provision for many data collection practices. The bill had the support of several business groups, including the U.S. Chamber of Commerce.

State data privacy laws. As of 2021, three states have passed consumer data privacy laws, and many others were considering their own bills.

California passed a law that went into effect in 2014 that requires websites to disclose all their privacy practices, including how a site "responds to Web browser 'do not track' signals or other mechanisms that provide consumers the ability to exercise choice regarding the collection of personally identifiable information about an individual consumer's online activities over time and across third-party Web sites or online services." In 2018, the California legislature passed the nation's toughest data privacy law. Titled the California Consumer Privacy Act of 2018, the law grants consumers a right to know what information websites collect and share about them. Citizens can also bar websites from selling data about them, although websites can charge more for services to citizens who don't want their data shared. And in 2020, California voters passed an even stricter ballot measure, called the California Consumer Privacy Rights Act, that expands protections further, giving consumers the right to prevent businesses from sharing personal information and creating a Privacy Protection Agency to enforce the laws and impose fines for violators.

Virginia and Nevada have also passed consumer privacy laws with some similar protections as California law.

International law. The European Union passed the General Data Protection Regulation (GDPR) that went into effect in 2018. The GDPR gives citizens of the EU rights to control the uses of their personal information and have personal information collected about them deleted upon their request. It has many provisions. Among them, the law requires that companies have consent to collect personal data and detail how the data is used and stored. Companies that violate the GDPR risk serious fines of up to 2% of their annual revenue in the preceding fiscal year. Most websites that have the possibility of being used by people in Europe have to comply with the law's provisions, so it effectively covers digital communications across the globe.

Internet Privacy on Social Media

As the popularity of social networking sites like Facebook, Twitter, Instagram, and Snapchat continues to rise, lawmakers, the courts and governmental agencies are regularly being asked to address questions of how information on those sites is protected, managed, and used.

Are social media posts considered to be private information? In 2009, a California appeals court said that MySpace is more like a public bulletin board than a private room, at least if the individual page is set to be public. College student Cynthia Moreno posted a hostile "ode" to her hometown of Coalinga, California, on her MySpace page. The high school principal in Coalinga saw the ode and sent it to the editor of the local paper, the *Coalinga Record*, who published it as a letter to the editor with Moreno's full name. Moreno's family, still living in Coalinga, received the brunt of the community's ire; their home was shot at and they had to close the 20-year-old family business. In *Moreno v. Hanford Sentinel Inc.* (172 Cal. App. 4th 1125), the court considered whether Moreno had a cause of action for publication of private facts and intentional infliction of emotional distress. The court said that the posting on MySpace was not private; anyone could see it, and Moreno had her picture and first name on her profile, so her identity was not private, either. Nor did Moreno's family have a cause of action because privacy rights are personal rights. The court did say that a jury should decide whether there was intentional infliction of emotional distress and remanded the case for consideration.

Focus on...
"7 Sins" of Digital Privacy Invasion

In his book *Privacy Lost: How Technology Is Endangering Your Privacy,* author David Holtzman identifies the following ways technology can invade personal privacy. He calls them the "7 sins" against privacy.

Intrusion: uninvited encroachment on a person's physical or virtual space.

Latency: excessive hoarding of personal information.

Deception: using stored data in authorized ways.

Profiling: misusing and categorizing stored data.

Identify theft: thief uses your data as you.

Outing: revealing information a person wants hidden.

Loss of dignity: revelations attacking self-respect.

The Stored Communications Act makes it a crime for anyone who "intentionally accesses without authorization a facility through which an electronic communication service is provided" or "intentionally exceeds an authorization to access that facility," and by doing so "obtains, alters, or prevents authorized access to a wire or electronic communication while it is in electronic storage in such system." Employees of a New Jersey restaurant who were fired after supervisors saw their MySpace "gripe group" page venting about the workplace brought suit in *Pietrylo v. Hillstone Restaurant Group* (29 I.E.R. Cas. 1438, 2009). The supervisor got the password to the group from another employee who said she gave it up because she was afraid of being fired. The fired employees alleged that their participation in the gripe group was private and that their employer violated the Stored Communications Act by accessing the invitation-only group. Hillstone's motion for summary judgment was denied. A jury found that Hillstone managers violated the Stored Communications Act by intentionally accessing the MySpace gripe group without authorization. But the managers prevailed on the privacy claims, as the jury said that the employees had no reasonable expectation of privacy in the MySpace group.

The key takeaway from these early cases is that individuals generally don't have a right of privacy against third-party disclosure of materials they post on social media platforms. Also, most social media companies' terms of service specifically state they own the content uploaded by users, and companies can disclose that information for a variety of purposes. That said, social media companies do have some legal responsibilities to protect its users, including being transparent in their practices and not deceiving consumers about the extent of their privacy protections.

Facebook and FTC actions. The Federal Trade Commission has been very active in privacy issues in recent years. In its early days, Facebook faced two possible class-action lawsuits alleging it disclosed personal information like real names, schools, and friends lists to advertisers. Facebook had said that it revised its code so that personal information in profile tags is no longer sent to advertisers. The social network had already revised its privacy rules once in May 2010, providing new settings to control what information is seen by whom.

In 2011, Facebook settled charges with the FTC that it had made user information public that it had promised to keep private, agreeing, among other things, to 20 years of privacy audits. In 2012, the company also agreed to pay $10 million and make changes to its terms to settle a lawsuit alleging that its "Sponsored Stories" feature violates members' rights of publicity. Now the site's policies state that members' names and likenesses could be used as sponsored stories, as well as provide users with options regarding this use and obtain parental permission to use minors' information in this way.

In 2019, Facebook faced an unprecedented investigation by the FTC and others, including Congress. The investigation began over a Facebook app called "This Is Your Digital Life," in which users completed a personality quiz that unknowingly gave developers access to their personal data and the data of their friends. A political data mining firm, Cambridge Analytica, gained access to the data and matched it with voting records to sell for targeted political advertising in the 2016 presidential election, leading to a major scandal that exposed serious privacy violations at Facebook and elsewhere. Facebook agreed to pay a $5 billion fine, the largest fine in FTC history, and overhaul its privacy rules. "Despite repeated promises to its billions of users worldwide that they could control how their personal information is shared, Facebook undermined consumers' choices," FTC Chairman Joe Simons said in a statement.

"The magnitude of the $5 billion penalty and sweeping conduct relief are unprecedented in the history of the FTC. The relief is designed not only to punish future violations but, more importantly, to change Facebook's entire privacy culture to decrease the likelihood of continued violations."

Cy pres **remedies.** Beyond FTC actions, class-action lawsuits have been a tool for individuals to police privacy violations. A defunct Facebook app, Beacon, which would notify a user's friends of transactions made on third-party websites but without asking users to agree to participate, cost the social network $9.5 million in 2013. One of the plaintiffs who objected to the class action settlement appealed to the Supreme Court after the Ninth Circuit approved the settlement, and the Court denied *cert* (*Marek v. Lane*, 571 U.S. 1003). However, Chief Justice John Roberts issued a statement on the allocation of the settlement money. He wrote, "And while Facebook also agreed to pay $9.5 million, the parties allocated that fund in an unusual way. Plaintiffs' counsel were awarded nearly a quarter of the fund in fees and costs, while the named plaintiffs received modest incentive payments. The unnamed class members, by contrast, received no damages from the remaining $6.5 million." This is called a *cy pres* remedy (from the French, "so near/close"), and Roberts expressed concern that these kinds of awards are becoming common in class action suits, with the large number of class members receiving little or no compensation and the money going into funds or foundations—often managed by the settler. Roberts agreed with the denial of *cert* but said that it may be necessary for the Court to examine future *cy pres* arrangements.

Internet Privacy: Protecting Children

Responding to concerns expressed by many parents and community groups in the early days the internet, Congress passed the 1998 *Children's Online Privacy Protection Act* (COPPA) to limit the collection of information from children under age 13 without parental consent. (This law should not be confused with the Child Online Protection Act [COPA], a different 1998 law intended to curtail access to adult materials by minors. That law is discussed in Chapter Ten.)

COPPA limits the ability of children under 13 to have email accounts without parental consent, and it requires those who gather data to deal with parents before dealing with their children. A website cannot simply have children fill in personal information on an electronic form and then click "send" when they're finished. The act includes federal *preemption*: states may not enact conflicting laws governing the collection of information from children. Websites that collect personal information about children must post their privacy policies prominently. The law also includes

Focus on...
Consumer privacy

The FTC issued a report titled "Protecting Consumer Privacy in an Era of Rapid Change," in 2012. Among the recommendations:

• "privacy by design," meaning that companies need to incorporate principles of privacy into all their baseline practices;

• companies should limit their gathering of information using mobile devices and geolocation data, regularly purging unnecessary information from their records and to give consumers a choice before collecting "sensitive data"

• development of "Do Not Track" mechanisms to let consumers opt out of online tracking; and

• consumers' ability to affirmatively consent (or "opt in") to material changes to privacy regulations and transparency in companies' data practices.

provisions for self-regulation by industry groups that develop their own programs to protect children's privacy.

The Federal Trade Commission is charged with supervising and approving these self-regulation programs. In 1999, the FTC adopted regulations to implement this law.

A company that operated virtual worlds for children agreed to pay a fine of $3 million to the FTC in 2011 to settle charges that they violated COPPA by illegally collecting information about children under 13 without parental consent. Playdom, Inc. operated a number of children's sites, including one called "Pony Stars" on which the FTC said 821,000 children were registered to play.

The FTC proposed updates to COPPA in 2013, including, among other changes, a modification in the list of "personal information" that cannot be collected without parental notice and consent; streamlined, voluntary, and transparent approval processes for companies to get parental consent; closing of a loophole in apps and websites that allowed personal information to be sent through plug-ins; inclusion of "persistent identifiers" that can recognize users over time and across websites; and stronger data security provisions.

In 2019, the FTC and the New York Attorney General fined YouTube and its parent company Google $170 million for collecting children's usage information without their parents' consent in violation of COPPA. The fine was by far the largest in FTC history under COPPA. YouTube also changed its practices in labeling videos as child content to better limit tracking of and targeted advertisements for children.

In 2020, the FTC reported that it had taken action in 34 cases since COPPA had passed and collected $190 million in civil penalties.

Internet Privacy: Email and Text Messages

Other controversial aspects of internet privacy concern the interception and review of email or other electronic communications and surreptitious monitoring of closed discussion groups, often by an employer. Employers have defeated challenges to the practice of monitoring email that passes through a corporate server, and in 2010 the Supreme Court said employees' text messages can be monitored for legitimate work purposes.

Both government and private employers often monitor email, and there is little that employees can do about it, aside from using an outside email server to avoid having their messages read by supervisors. Even if an employer provides a computer to an employee for *home* use, but with the provision that it is to be used for company business only, the employee has no reasonable expectation of privacy that would prevent the employer from getting a court order to examine files on that computer (*TBG Insurance Services v. Superior Court*, 96 C.A.4th 443, 2002).

The Supreme Court in 2010 said that if an employer monitors employees' communications on company equipment pursuant to legitimate work-related concerns, those communications are not private. At issue were sexually explicit text messages sent by a Special Weapons and Tactics team member on his city pager. The Ninth Circuit ruled that the Fourth Amendment's ban on unreasonable searches and seizures protects employees from searches of their email and text messages that are handled by an outside provider, not an in-house system. That court declined to hear the case *en banc*, but the Supreme Court granted *cert*—and disagreed.

In *City of Ontario v. Quon* (560 U.S. 746), the Court said that the search of the text messages was reasonable. Justice Anthony Kennedy, writing for the Court, said that the department's policy made it clear that the text messages were *not* private. Kennedy did, however, acknowledge that new technologies suggest the need for a new examination of how companies deal with unofficial uses.

The federal Electronic Communications Privacy Act (ECPA) was at the center of another controversy in 2006, when *USA TODAY* and other news media reported that several of the largest telephone companies had handed over telephone and email records of millions of Americans to the National Security Agency, in violation of the ECPA's ban on such disclosures. Not only was calling information given to federal investigators, but the content of telephone calls and email was apparently monitored by the federal government on a massive scale without court authorization. The Electronic Frontier Foundation and others sued over this controversial and seemingly unlawful government surveillance. Some defended the surveillance as necessary to fight terrorism—and said revealing that the monitoring program even existed was a crime by journalists. Others said domestic surveillance on this scale is a fundamental violation of American civil liberties. This issue is also discussed in Chapter Two.

The California Supreme Court in 2003 ruled that Intel Corp. could not use a trespass rationale to prevent a former employee from sending email messages hostile to the company to current employees at work, upholding his free expression rights (*Intel. Corp. v. Hamidi,* 30 C.4th 1342). The court held that the company would have a case for trespassing only if the email in some way damaged the company's computer system.

The Eleventh Circuit supported a very limited view of email privacy when it held that emails sent to and received by a third party result in the expectation of privacy being lost (*Rehberg v. Paulk,* 598 F.3d 1268, 2010). Investigators used a state subpoena to an internet service provider to access Charles Rehberg's emails. The court said that "Rehberg's voluntary delivery of emails to third parties constituted a voluntary relinquishment of the right to privacy in that information." The U.S. Supreme Court granted *cert* to address a different question: whether a government official can be sued for causing someone to be wrongly prosecuted by giving false testimony to a grand jury. The justices unanimously ruled in 2012 that a witness in a grand jury proceeding is entitled to the same absolute immunity as a witness who testifies at a trial (*Rehberg v. Paulk,* 566 U.S. 356).

Employee passwords. In 2012, Maryland became the first state to pass a law that forbids employers to demand the passwords for their employees' social network sites as either a requirement for hiring or for staying employed. The Maryland law reads in part: "An employer may not request or require that an employee or applicant disclose any user name, password, or other means for accessing a personal ac-count or service through an electronic communications device." Nor can an employer refuse to hire a potential employee because the applicant refuses to turn over passwords.

In 2021, 26 states have laws that apply to employers, according to the National Conference of State Legislatures. Fifteen states and the District of Columbia have laws that apply protections to educational institutions, and one, Wisconsin, also applies to landlords. In addition, Maine and Vermont have authorized studies.

Data Hacking

Major hacks of personal data have underscored the dangers of computer hacking and the privacy vulnerabilities for people whose data is stored on computers. Sometimes, hacked information appears for sale on the "dark web," leaving individuals vulnerable to identify theft and fraud.

Focus on...
"Pulling plug on privacy"

That's the title of a 2011 essay by Alex Kozinski, former chief judge of the Ninth Circuit, well known for his quotable decisions. He and one of his law clerks, Stephanie Grace, wrote a eulogy for privacy on *The Daily*, an iPad-only magazine.

FIG. 48. Customer loyalty cards.

Public domain image by Mattes, via Wikimedia Commons.

The judge and his clerk blame all of us for the death of the Fourth Amendment, the amendment that guards against unreasonable searches and seizures, as we gave up little bits of our privacy for convenience and a few pennies saved: "It started with the supermarket loyalty programs. They seemed innocuous enough—you just scribble down your name, number and address in exchange for a plastic card and a discount on Oreos. The problem, at least constitutionally speaking, is that the Fourth Amendment protects only what we reasonably expect to keep private." Thus, say Kozinski and Grace, we've forfeited our expectations of privacy by giving away so much of it.

The eulogy concludes: "With so little left private, the Fourth Amendment is all but obsolete. Where police officers once needed a warrant to search your bookshelf for 'Atlas Shrugged,' they can now simply ask Amazon.com if you bought it. ... Someday soon we'll realize that we've lost everything we once cherished as private. And as we grieve the loss of the Fourth Amendment, we'll be forced to look deep in our hearts—and at the little pieces of plastic dangling from our keychains—and ask ourselves if it was all worth it. R.I.P."

In the spring of 2015, personal data of an estimated 18 million current and former government employees and contractors maintained by the Office of Personnel Management was allegedly stolen by Chinese hackers. At the time, officials described the intrusion as the worst ever against the U.S. government. The hackers gained access to highly sensitive personal information, including background check information, addresses, and Social Security numbers.

The unprecedented government hacking followed the 2014 hack of Sony Pictures Entertainment and the release of highly sensitive and embarrassing information about the film studio. In that case, hackers allegedly allied with North Korea stole and then disseminated data from Sony's internal computers to punish Sony for its film *The Interview*, a Seth Rogen and James Franco comedy that ridiculed North Korean leader Kim Jung-un. In addition to personal employment and financial data of employees, the hackers released emails among Sony executives and actors, as well as feature films yet to be released. Sony aggressively policed the pirated films using copyright law, but also threatened news organizations with lawsuits for reporting information disclosed by the hackers. Wikileaks was among the websites to publish the hacked Sony emails.

Hacks have grown exponentially in recent years. In 2019, a major hack of data at Equifax, the credit reporting company, exposed personal financial data of 147 million people, including Social Security numbers, driver's license numbers, and financial information. The FTC and other government agencies reached a $575 million settlement over Equifax's failure to take reasonable steps to secure its data. The hack was included in a 2021 list published by CNET.com of the biggest hacks of the past decade. Among others: data from 500 million LinkedIn profiles published in April 2021; personal information of more than 530 million Facebook users posted online in 2021 allegedly scrapped from Facebook in 2019; information about 5.2 million Marriott guests and 10.7 million MGM resort guests disclosed in 2020; account information of 200 million Words With Friends users hacked in 2019; account information of almost 5 million DoorDash users in 2019; and personal information of 100 million accounts at Capital One hacked in 2019.

Medical Privacy: HIPAA

In 1996, with little fanfare, Congress enacted a privacy law governing medical records: the Health Insurance Portability and Accountability Act (HIPAA). That law, implemented by regulations adopted by the Clinton administration, imposed new restrictions on the release of medical information to protect the privacy of patients' medical records. Some portions of the rules were opposed by health insurers and others in the health care industry who said they were too restrictive and too costly to implement. Privacy advocates also lobbied for changes in the rules, as did media representatives who said information that has been reported for years will now be off-limits to journalists.

The regulations require that doctors and other health care providers obtain written consent from patients before sharing their health records. The rules also allow patients to see their own files and request corrections of errors. Patients must also be told how their health information will be used when possible.

Of most concern to journalists are provisions of the regulations that restrict the release of once-public information such as the identity of well-known hospital patients and the medical condition of those admitted after an accident, natural disaster, crime, or terrorist act. There are *criminal* penalties of up to 10 years in prison and fines of $250,000 for revealing confidential medical information, which may cause potential news sources to avoid taking a chance of revealing information to journalists even when it may not be restricted.

A number of states already had medical privacy laws that included some of these provisions, but HIPAA established *nationwide* standards for medical record privacy. However, HIPAA also has a loophole: it says health information can be disclosed "to the extent that such...disclosure is required by law." In 2006, the Ohio Supreme Court ruled that HIPAA does not preempt the Ohio Public Record Act's provisions requiring disclosure of some health information that HIPAA seemingly made secret (*State ex rel. Cincinnati Enquirer v. Daniels*, 844 N.E.2d 1181).

HIPAA also underwent revisions in 2013, focused primarily on health care providers, health plans, and others that process health insurance claims. The revisions are in three areas: privacy, security, and breach notification policies and procedures; notification of privacy practices; and agreements with business associates.

Does the type of medical condition suffered change the amount of privacy to which someone is entitled? Apparently it does in the Second Circuit. At issue in *Matson v. Bd. of Educ. of the City Sch. Dist. of N.Y.* (631 F.3d 57, 2011) was this question: "[D]oes the Constitution protect Matson's right to maintain the confidentiality of her fibromyalgia?" (This case was *not* brought under HIPAA.) Dorrit Matson, a music teacher, claimed that the board of education violated her privacy rights by disclosing that she suffered from fibromyalgia (chronic pain often brought on by anxiety or stress) in an online report. A divided panel said the interest in privacy varies with the medical condition; for example, HIV/AIDS would require the highest level of confidentiality. But, said the court, "although fibromyalgia is a serious medical condition, it does not carry with it the sort of opprobrium that confers upon those who suffer from it a constitutional right of privacy as to that medical condition."

Other Data Privacy Cases

Other pieces of personal data have had their days in court. The Fourth Circuit found that the First Amendment protected a blogger's right to post Social Security numbers (SSNs) of public officials in Virginia as a protest to the state's postings of land records online without first redacting (removing) SSNs (*Ostergren v. Cuccinelli,* 615 F.3d 263, 2011). Virginia passed a law ordering the redaction of SSNs but did not appropriate enough funds, and many records contained SSNs. In protest, B.J. Ostergren, owner of "The Virginia Watchdog" website, posted public records that contained SSNs she got while searching government records. The Virginia general assembly changed a statute so that Ostergren could be charged with knowingly disseminating SSNs online. She filed suit, alleging that she had a right to engage in protected government criticism. The Fourth Circuit said the district court didn't go far enough to remedy the constitutional problems of Virginia's law. The court relied on the "Pentagon Papers" line of cases (*Cox Broadcasting, Florida Star, Daily Mail,* and others), saying that "the First Amendment does not allow Virginia to punish Ostergren for posting its land records online without redacting SSNs when numerous clerks are doing precisely that." The court was essentially saying that Virginia had to clean up its own act first.

ZIP codes. In *Pineda v. Williams-Sonoma Stores, Inc.* (51 Cal. 4th 524, 2011), the California Supreme Court said that stores could no longer require customers to provide ZIP codes when buying something with a credit card. Jessica Pineda claimed that Williams-Sonoma stored her ZIP code and then used it with her address to engage in marketing. Williams-Sonoma claimed that this practice did not abridge Pineda's privacy under state law because her ZIP code was not unique to her. Justice Carlos Moreno wrote, "The Legislature intended to provide robust consumer protections by prohibiting retailers from soliciting and recording information about the cardholder that is unnecessary to the credit card transaction."

Video Privacy Protection Act. In 2010, Amazon fought off an attempt by the North Carolina Department of Revenue to turn over names, addresses, and transaction data of all North Carolina residents who purchased anything from Amazon between 2003 and 2010—50 million transactions, according to Amazon—in an investigation of Amazon's tax liability. Amazon argued that this would be a serious privacy violation under the First Amendment and the Video Privacy Protection Act (VPPA), a 1988 federal law that prohibits the "wrongful disclosure of video tape rental or sale records" (which also includes DVDs, CDs, and other media). The law had been passed after the failed Supreme Court nomination of Robert Bork, when a newspaper published his video rental history obtained from a video store clerk (which was unremarkable but resulted in the law's passage). A federal judge agreed with Amazon: "Citizens are entitled to receive information and ideas through books, films, and other expressive materials anonymously" (*Amazon.com LLC v. Lay,* 758 F. Supp. 2d 1154). The court also agreed that the VPPA also prohibited the release of the data.

In 2013, President Barack Obama signed the Video Privacy Protection Act Amendments Act of 2012 into law. These amendments to VPPA changed the consent requirements for disclosing consumers' viewing information online. Users of social media sites like Facebook could share information like what songs they were listening to, but they could not share video information under VPPA without the site getting specific information for each shared history. Now users can set their permissions to be good for up to two years of sharing.

■ AN OVERVIEW OF THE PRIVACY TORTS

While the Supreme Court was wrestling with constitutional questions concerning the right of privacy, the states were developing their own concepts, often in cases involving the media.

The four torts. In 1960, William L. Prosser, one of the greatest legal scholars of his era, published an analysis of privacy law in which he said the concept of invasion of privacy breaks down into four different legal rights. His classification has been widely accepted and is the basis for many of the court decisions in this field that have followed. Prosser wrote:

> The law of privacy comprises four distinct kinds of invasion of four different interests of the plaintiff, which are tied together by a common name, but otherwise have almost nothing in common except that each represents an interference with the right of the plaintiff ... "to be let alone." Without any attempt to (write an) exact definition, these four torts may be described as follows:
>
> 1. Intrusion upon the plaintiff's seclusion or solitude, or into his private affairs;
> 2. Public disclosure of embarrassing private facts about the plaintiff;
> 3. Publicity which places the plaintiff in a false light in the public eye;
> 4. Appropriation, for the defendant's advantage, of the plaintiff's name or likeness. (48 *Calif. Law Review* 383, 1960)

Courts in a number of states had recognized these four kinds of invasion of privacy before Prosser wrote his classic analysis; many others have done so in the years since. Even today, though, not all states recognize all four kinds of invasion of privacy as a legal wrong that may be remedied in a civil lawsuit. For example, about 10 states have declined to recognize Prosser's third kind of invasion of privacy, false light. The false light concept closely parallels libel, and some states have chosen not to recognize it as a separate action. But for the most part, Prosser's four-category breakdown of privacy law remains valid.

The *intrusion* concept is based on a journalist's conduct as a newsgatherer. Reporters—and especially photographers or video crews—who pursue someone too aggressively may face this kind of lawsuit. The late 1990s saw an explosion in litigation of this kind.

The four privacy torts:

intrusion: a physical unauthorized entry into a person's private space.

private facts: publication of facts that are actually private that would be embarrassing to the victim.

false light: publication of distorted or fabricated information about a person that would cause others to believe things about that person that were not true.

misappropriation: the unauthorized use of a person's name or likeness for some kind of gain, either financial or otherwise.

Private facts cases usually result from the dissemination of intimate or embarrassing information about a person's private life or past—information that may be factually correct, thus precluding a successful libel suit.

Lawsuits based on holding a person before the public in a *false light* resemble libel suits because there must be an element of falsity in the communication. The basic difference between libel and false light privacy is that the latter does not necessarily require proof that the false statement is defamatory.

The fourth tort occurs most often in advertising and entertainment-related communications. Alternately called *misappropriation* (or *appropriation*) or an invasion of the *right of publicity*, it prohibits the unauthorized use of a person's name, likeness, voice, or some other element of their public persona for someone else's commercial gain.

Defenses. As in libel law, there are defenses that the media may assert to escape liability in lawsuits for invasion of privacy. The two most widely recognized ones are *newsworthiness* (also called the *public affairs* or *public interest* defense) and *consent*. If the media show that the subject matter of a news story or broadcast is newsworthy, the plaintiff in a private facts lawsuit will normally lose in court.

However, the newsworthiness defense is of little help when the alleged invasion of privacy involves an intrusion or holding someone before the public in a false light. Even celebrities have some right to be free of harassment by journalists, although that right is limited. And no amount of newsworthiness will excuse a story that holds someone up before the public in a false light. Newsworthiness is not helpful when the issue is an unauthorized commercial use of a person's name or likeness (in an advertisement, movie, or poster, for instance). In fact, the more newsworthy a person is, the greater the potential injury is likely to be if the name or likeness is used commercially without consent.

The consent defense is most applicable in misappropriation cases: celebrities regularly give their consent to commercial uses of their names and likenesses, but for a fee. The consent defense could also be useful in other kinds of privacy lawsuits, provided it could be shown that the person suing actually gave consent.

In addition to these two common law defenses, the Supreme Court has created constitutional defenses in privacy cases, just as it has in libel cases. In fact, the *New York Times v. Sullivan* principle has been transplanted from libel to privacy law and applies in certain kinds of privacy cases. In addition, the Court has also recognized a constitutional right of the media to publish the contents of many public records that are lawfully obtained, notwithstanding anyone's claim that publishing the information is an invasion of privacy.

Although these defenses often enable the media to defeat invasion of privacy claims in court, the fact remains that serious legal hazards exist in this area. For that reason, the four major categories of invasion of privacy warrant a more detailed summary.

◼ INTRUSION

The concept of *intrusion* is based more on the conduct of a reporter, photographer, or video crew than on the content of the media. It is a legal action to compensate a person when a journalist unduly intrudes into his or her *physical solitude or seclusion* or *private affairs*. It often involves snooping, eavesdropping, using a hidden camera, or simply being in the way when someone has a reasonable right to expect a little peace and quiet.

In general, journalists have a right to ask questions or take pictures in public places without risking a lawsuit for this kind of invasion of privacy. In fact, in this era of miniaturized

Focus on...
"Big Brother is watching you"

If you've spent any time playing with Google Maps (maps.google.com), you know that by using Google's Street View, you can, as Google says, "zoom, rotate and pan through street level photos of cities around the world." Google creates these maps by sending cars through neighborhoods with panoramic cameras to take pictures from public streets. But what if the cameras capture something illegal or private? At least one image has been captured of a drug deal going down, for example. How have the courts responded to privacy claims?

FIG. 49. A circa 1818 map of the city of Washington in the District of Columbia.

Aaron and Christine Boring lived on a private road in Pittsburgh, Pennsylvania. In browsing Google Maps, they found color images of their home, car, and swimming pool that they had given no permission for Google to obtain

Library of Congress.

or use. They sued for trespass, publication of private facts, and intrusion upon seclusion. A lower court found for Google, and the Third Circuit agreed, at least on the privacy claims. The court, in an unpublished (non-precedential) opinion, agreed that the Borings were not entitled to recovery for private facts or intrusion, because Google's conduct "would not be highly offensive to a person of ordinary sensibilities." But the Borings were entitled to pursue the trespass claim, and the case was remanded to the lower court (*Boring v. Google, Inc.*, 38 Media L. Rep. 1306, 2010).

electronic listening devices and long telephoto lenses, technology has created a variety of new newsgathering opportunities (or threats to personal privacy, depending on your point of view). While the law affords journalists a good deal of latitude in gathering the news, there are limits to this right: journalists are sometimes sued for stepping over the bounds of propriety in their pursuit of a story or visual image. The growing popularity of "tabloid television" shows led to a number of new controversies and lawsuits in this area, as video crews aggressively pursued their subjects—often into their own private homes during "ride-alongs" with law enforcement officers. This has led to a series of new court decisions holding that the media may sometimes be sued for intrusive newsgathering, including two notable U.S. Supreme Court decisions in a two-year period.

Early Intrusion Cases

Long before cell phone eavesdropping and media ride-alongs with law enforcement officers became national issues and led to Supreme Court decisions, a number of individuals charged that intrusive newsgathering invaded their privacy. These early cases played a major role in shaping the modern concept of intrusion.

The pioneering case of *Dietemann v. Time Inc.* (449 F.2d 245, 1971) is a good example of an intrusion by journalists that violated someone's privacy. Two reporters for *Life* magazine investigated a man suspected of practicing medicine without a license by posing as a patient and her husband. They visited the man at his home—where he practiced his craft—and surreptitiously took photographs. They also carried a hidden transmitter so law enforcement personnel nearby could monitor and record the conversation. The result was a criminal prosecution and an article in *Life* called "Crackdown on Quackery."

The man accused of medical quackery sued for invasion of privacy and ultimately won $1,000 in general damages. In a 1971 decision the Ninth Circuit agreed that the pictures and story were newsworthy but said the reporters had intruded upon Dietemann's privacy in gathering the information. The magazine had a right to publish the story but did not have the right to use hidden electronic devices in the man's home to get the information.

If the news media may not surreptitiously enter a private home to get a story, may journalists go into a private home that is the scene of a fire and take pictures at the invitation of a public official? The Florida Supreme Court addressed that question in a 1976 case, *Florida Publishing Co. v. Fletcher* (340 So.2d 914). A photographer took a picture of a silhouette left on the floor by a girl's body after a fire, and the girl's mother sued, claiming a trespass and an invasion of privacy, among other things. But the Florida Supreme Court found no actionable trespass or invasion of privacy in the photographer's actions. In fact, a fire marshal had asked the photographer to take the picture when the marshal's own camera ran out of film. The court noted that it was customary for journalists to accompany public officials to the scene of such disasters. The U.S. Supreme Court refused to review this case. However, as noted earlier, in 1999 the high court ruled that when *law enforcement* officials enter private property with a search warrant and allow the media to go along, they are violating the Fourth Amendment and inviting a lawsuit.

Photographers' rights. These cases raise questions about the rights of photographers under privacy law. It is difficult to generalize because the rules vary somewhat from state to state, but in most states photographers who trespass to get a picture may face both civil and criminal sanctions unless they have consent to be there from someone authorized to give it. On the other hand, photographers in public places may generally shoot any subject within view for news purposes—but not for commercial or advertising purposes, for reasons that will be explained later in this chapter. There are occasional exceptions, but the general rule is that anything within camera range of a public place may be photographed for journalistic purposes. If the picture has even a little newsworthiness, and if no false impression is created with a misleading caption, it is usually safe.

Nevertheless, even in public places a photographer may not lawfully be so offensive in taking pictures as to seriously interfere with the subject's right to be left alone. The classic example of harassment by a photographer is the case of *Galella v. Onassis* (487 F.2d 986, 1973). Ron Galella, a freelance photographer who made something of a career of photographing the late Jacqueline Kennedy Onassis and her children in the late 1960s and early 1970s, was ordered by the Second Circuit to stay 25 feet away from Onassis and even farther from her children. This was by no means a typical case: Galella's conduct prior to the court order had been outrageous. He had engaged in a variety of offensive activities, some of which actually endangered the safety of Onassis and her children. He followed her and her children, bumped into other people while taking pictures, spooked a horse her son was riding, and was generally underfoot at all hours.

In fact, a decade after the original lawsuit Onassis again hauled Galella into court for invading her privacy. She contended that he had repeatedly violated the original order by failing to stay far enough away, among other things. The court agreed and found Galella in contempt (*Galella v. Onassis*, 533 F.Supp. 1076, 1982). The court emphasized—again—that Galella had a right to photograph Onassis (or any other celebrity) in public places, or to write articles about her if he wished. But Galella's conduct was so outrageous as to justify some restrictions on his activities, the court said. This was, in short, an unusual situation.

In more typical circumstances, there is little that celebrities can do about those who photograph them in public places, except perhaps to surround themselves with bodyguards whose job is to make it impossible for anyone to get a good shot. (Several state anti-paparazzi laws exist, however, and will be discussed later in this chapter.) Occasionally, in fact, those who try to photograph the famous encounter violence from bodyguards. In those cases, photographers may have grounds to sue—the celebrity's guards. But that does nothing to salvage the pictures that the guards destroyed or prevented the photographer from taking.

In recent years, however, the ability of journalists using powerful microphones and tele-photo lenses to see and hear the activities of people in their own homes and other private places without trespassing has led many to rethink whether journalists should be free to report everything they can see or hear from a public place.

The Hazards of Intrusion: Ride-Alongs

Many lawsuits have been filed in state and federal courts charging journalists— particularly photographers, television crews, and reporters with hidden cameras—with various wrongful acts while gathering the news. These lawsuits often alleged not only an invasion of privacy (intrusive newsgathering) but also an intentional infliction of emotional distress (see Chapter Four). The resulting court decisions have raised questions about the proper line between the First Amendment freedoms of journalists and the privacy rights of celebrities and others who are involved in newsworthy situations such as accidents.

In fact, this area of law has acquired a new name: *newsgathering torts*, a term that encompasses a variety of different legal theories advanced by those who want to sue because of journalists' *newsgathering behavior*—as opposed to suing because of the *content* of what appears in the media. Those who are angry about journalists' newsgathering activities may sue for intrusion, of course, and for the infliction of emotional distress. In addition, the media are being sued for trespass, fraud, and "outrage," which some states recognize as a tort.

The U.S. Supreme Court's *Wilson v. Layne* (526 U.S. 603) decision in 1999 made it clear that the media—and law enforcement officers—risk liability for media ride-alongs that allow journalists to enter a private home, even if the officers have a search warrant. The court held that while a search warrant gives officers the right to enter a private home, it is nevertheless a violation of the Fourth Amendment's ban on illegal searches and seizures for journalists to go into a home without the consent of residents.

The Court reached this conclusion in considering appeals by several people whose homes were invaded by the news media during ride-alongs with officers. The *Wilson* case began when law enforcement officers, armed with an arrest warrant, entered the home of Charles and Geraldine Wilson at 6:45 a.m. to arrest their son, who turned out not to be living there. A *Washington Post* reporter and photographer entered the home with the officers and observed a scuffle between officers and Charles Wilson, who came out of his bedroom wearing only briefs to ask the officers why they were in his home. No photographs of the incident were ever published, but the Wilsons sued the officers for allowing journalists to enter their home. The Supreme Court ruled that law enforcement officials are violating the Fourth Amendment in most instances when they allow the media to accompany them onto private property to conduct a search or make an arrest. Chief Justice William Rehnquist wrote for the Court that the Fourth Amendment's protection against unreasonable searches and seizures "embodies centuries-old principles of respect for the privacy of the home.... It does not necessarily follow from the fact that the officers were entitled to enter (a suspect's) home that they (were) entitled to bring a reporter and a photographer with them."

The Court stopped short of ruling that the *officers* could be sued in *Wilson v. Layne*—as opposed to future cases. Rehnquist noted that the law on ride-alongs may not have been clear before this definitive Supreme Court ruling. But in the future, there can be no doubt that officers who allow the media to accompany them onto private property to conduct searches or make arrests are inviting lawsuits for violating the Fourth Amendment.

Another case that troubled many journalists (and contributed to the Supreme Court's decision to hear *Wilson v. Layne*) was *Berger v. Hanlon* (129 F.3d 505), a 1997 decision of the Ninth Circuit. In the *Berger* case, Cable News Network (CNN) arranged to send a television crew with federal wildlife agents on a raid of a 75,000-acre ranch in Montana. The federal agents suspected that Paul Berger, the elderly owner of the ranch, had killed American bald eagles in violation of the Endangered Species Act. An agent wearing a hidden microphone searched the ranch and questioned Berger and his wife inside their home.

A lower court said that by agreeing to cooperate with CNN, federal agents had "transformed the execution of a search warrant into television entertainment." The judge held that the federal agents and CNN could both be sued for an allegedly unlawful intrusion, adding, "Law enforcement authority was used to assist commercial television, not to assist law enforcement objectives." Berger was later acquitted of charges of killing protected species and convicted only of a misdemeanor pesticide charge. In turn, the Bergers sued the federal agents—and CNN—for $10 million for the alleged invasion of privacy.

The *Berger* case was appealed to the U.S. Supreme Court. The high court considered it along with *Wilson v. Layne* and then sent the *Berger* case back to the appeals court to reconsider the issue of law enforcement liability based on *Wilson v. Layne*. The high court said that the federal officers should be given *qualified immunity* for allowing the *Berger* ride-along because the law was not clear when the ride-along occurred. The appellate court then followed that reasoning, granting legal protection to the officers who authorized the ride-along, while holding that CNN itself was not entitled to qualified immunity, thereby leaving the network in a difficult legal position (*Hanlon v. Berger*, 526 U.S. 808).

Even before *Wilson v. Layne,* media attorneys were warning of the legal hazards of intrusive journalism based on earlier adverse court decisions. In 1998, the California Supreme Court alarmed many media lawyers by ruling that a television producer may be sued when a crew shoots video of an accident victim being freed from a car and receiving emergency medical care in a rescue helicopter. In *Shulman v. Group W Productions* (18 C.4th 200), the court ruled that Ruth Shulman, the accident victim, had a right to go to trial with her claim that the video crew's coverage of her auto accident was unduly intrusive. Although the state high court was deeply divided in its reasoning, five of the seven justices agreed that the media can be sued for intruding on an accident victim's privacy, even if the accident itself is newsworthy. On the other hand, the justices agreed that the media could *not* be sued for the revelation of private facts in a situation as newsworthy as an accident near a major highway.

Writing the court's lead opinion, Justice Kathryn Mickle Werdegar said, "A jury could reasonably believe that fundamental respect for human dignity requires the patient's anxious journey be taken only with those whose care is solely for them and out of sight of the prying eyes of others (via cameras)." What troubled the justices most about the case was that the video crew secretly recorded Shulman's post-accident conversations with emergency workers at the scene and in the helicopter by using microphones hidden on paramedics.

Bottom line. The use of hidden cameras or microphones has been central to several other cases in which the courts have ruled that journalists could be sued for intrusive newsgathering. In the aftermath of these cases, most media attorneys are cautioning their clients that it is legally hazardous *ever* to do photographic or video coverage during a law enforcement ride-along in which journalists accompany officers onto private property, even if the photos are never published and the video is never aired. And now very few officers are willing to risk being sued by allowing ride-alongs that enter private property (unless someone with authority to do so gives consent for the media's presence).

The Hazards of Intrusion: Hidden Cameras and Secret Taping

The courts are also growing impatient with the use of hidden cameras in private or semi-private places. In a widely noted 1999 decision, the California Supreme Court ruled that ABC could be sued for having a reporter pose as a psychic and use a hidden camera to video-tape the conversations of workers who were paid to give psychic advice via telephone. Ruling in *Sanders v. ABC* (20 C.4th 907), the state high court ordered a lower court to consider reinstating $1.2 million in damages and attorney's fees that had been won by two employees of the telepsychic operation who were shown on ABC's *PrimeTime Live.*

Writing for a unanimous court, Justice Kathryn Mickle Werdegar said that even work-ers who talk openly to co-workers can have "a limited, but legitimate, expectation that their conversations and other interactions will not be secretly videotaped by undercover televi-sion reporters." However, she also said that the *Sanders* decision does not preclude all use of hidden cameras by journalists in the state; rather, a violation of privacy only occurs if the intrusion is "highly offensive to a reasonable person," and that the determination of reason-ableness should include consideration of the motives of newsgatherers.

In the *Sanders* case, the telepsychics worked in cubicles in a large room off-limits to nonemployees. Stacy Lescht, the ABC reporter, sometimes stood on her chair and looked around the room. Unbeknownst to other employees, she had a camera hidden in a flower on her hat and a microphone attached to her brassiere. That, the court concluded, was unduly intrusive even though the resulting story revealed the newsworthy fact that the tele-psychics did not always take the advice they were giving to 900-line callers very seriously.

The same ABC undercover investigation also led to a Ninth Circuit decision in 1999. In this case, the court ruled that the subjects of hidden-camera exposés cannot sue for federal wiretap violations unless they can show that a news organization *intended* to commit a crime or a civil wrong. This ruling came in *Sussman v. ABC* (186 F.3d 1200).

In *Sussman,* 12 employees of the telepsychic operation claimed that by surreptitiously recording their conversations and airing them on *PrimeTime Live,* ABC violated the federal anti-wiretapping statute, the Electronic Communications Privacy Act. By adopting this strat-egy, their attorneys hoped to establish a precedent that would permit lawsuits against the media even in states that do not follow the *Sanders* precedent. But it didn't work. Writing for a unanimous panel, Judge Alex Kozinski seemed to be saying that *Sanders* defines the outer limit of media liability for a hidden-camera exposé. He wrote: "Although the ABC taping may well have been a tortious invasion of privacy under state law, plaintiffs have provided no probative evidence that ABC had an illegal or tortious purpose when it made the tape."

The *Sanders* and *Sussman* cases are reminiscent of another case in which ABC was slapped with a $5.5 million jury verdict for having two *PrimeTime Live* staffers take jobs at the Food Lion grocery store chain in North and South Carolina—and use hidden cameras to record alleged health hazards. As noted in Chapter Four, that verdict was reduced to $315,000 by the trial judge and later reduced to a token amount ($2) by a federal appellate court. But ABC spent at least a million dollars for its legal defense.

A mixed bag of outcomes. On the other hand, some recent court decisions have *upheld* the right of journalists to use hidden cameras and microphones. A notable example is *Deteresa v. ABC* (121 F.3d 460), a 1997 decision in which the Ninth Circuit interpreted California privacy law to allow a TV network to secretly tape a conversation between a producer and a reluctant news source on her front porch and then use a small portion on the air. The court dismissed a lawsuit against ABC by Beverly Deteresa, a flight attendant who worked the flight that carried O.J. Simpson to Chicago the night of the murders of Nicole Brown Simpson and Ron Goldman. A week after the murders, an ABC producer went to Deteresa's condominium to ask her to appear on an ABC program and discuss the flight. She declined, but she also volunteered that she was "frustrated" to hear news reports about the flight that she knew were false. After further conversation, she said she would "think about" appearing on ABC. The producer called Deteresa the next day and again asked her to appear. When she declined, the producer told her he had recorded their conversation the previous day on her porch, and that an ABC cameraperson had videotaped them talking from a public street nearby. She hung up on the producer; later her husband called the producer and demanded that the tape not be aired. ABC did air a five-second clip on *Day One*, with a summary of her recollections of Simpson's behavior during the flight.

The Ninth Circuit held that Deteresa had no reasonable expectation of privacy when she talked to a TV producer on her front porch, in plain view of a nearby street. The court said ABC did not violate California's wiretap law, which forbids surreptitious taping of any "confidential communication" because that law applies only when someone reasonably expects the *content* of a conversation to be confidential. Deteresa knew she was talking to a media representative and that others could see and hear the conversation. And she continued to talk to him about what she saw on the flight. Based on these facts, there was no violation of the wiretap law. Nor was there an actionable invasion of privacy by intrusion, the federal appellate court concluded. The U.S. Supreme Court declined to hear an appeal.

Illustrating the complexity of the evolving law of hidden-camera journalism, the same court later ruled against another news organization on similar facts. In 1999, the Ninth Circuit ruled in *Alpha Therapeutic Corp. v. Nippon Hoso Kyokai (NHK)* (199 F.3d 1078) that it may be an invasion of privacy for a broadcaster to secretly tape an interview on someone's doorstep and then air it without consent. This time the court said a medical director and his company could sue because NHK, Japan's government-backed network, did the same thing that ABC did—but aired much *more* of the tape.

In *Alpha Therapeutic*, the appellate court said a jury could conclude under California law that the surreptitious taping was an invasion of privacy because the director knew only that he was talking to a reporter—he did not know the conversation was being taped. (Like *Deteresa*, this was a federal case based on diversity of citizenship, which requires the federal court to apply state law.)

Unlike most state laws and the federal wiretap law, the wiretap laws in California and 12 other states require *all* parties to a "confidential communication" to consent to the taping or monitoring of a conversation by others. Most state laws require the consent of only *one* party, which means a company can record all of its incoming calls in those states. The California Supreme Court in 2002 adopted a very broad definition of the term "confidential communication," increasing the number of conversations that would be considered confidential and therefore off limits for secret taping or monitoring. In *Flanagan v. Flanagan*

(27 C.4th 766, 2002), the Court said a communication is confidential, and therefore cannot be secretly taped, whenever *any* party believes it is not being taped or monitored by anyone else. Under this definition, even a party who knows the *content* of a conversation is not confidential may have a reasonable expectation of privacy that precludes secret taping.

Again illustrating the complexity and contradictions on this area of law, another federal appellate court *upheld* the right of ABC to use hidden cameras for newsgathering in another circuit in a 1995 decision, *Desnick v. American Broadcasting Co.* (44 F.3d 1345). ABC's *PrimeTime Live* equipped seven persons with hidden cameras and had them pose as patients at clinics that did cataract procedures. The resulting story suggested that the Desnick Eye Centers, a chain of 25 eye clinics in the upper Midwest, did unnecessary cataract surgeries for Medicare patients. The Seventh Circuit held that Desnick did not have a right to sue for intrusion even though ABC had people posing as patients enter the clinics with hidden cameras. The *Desnick* decision was notable because the court's opinion was written by Richard A. Posner, one of America's best-known appellate judges and a widely quoted expert on privacy law.

ABC won another hidden-camera case in 2003, when the Ninth Circuit dismissed a lawsuit against the network for using hidden cameras to show questionable procedures in an Arizona medical lab that evaluated pap smear samples (*Medical Laboratory Management Consultants v. ABC*, 306 F.3d 806). The court said ABC did not violate anyone's reasonable expectation of privacy under Arizona state law in the 52-second video clip of the lab that was aired on *PrimeTime Live*. The video revealed only lab procedures and related business matters, not anyone's personal affairs.

The Hazards of Intrusion: A Supreme Court Ruling

The question of surreptitious monitoring and recording of telephone conversations—and then broadcasting them—resulted in a Supreme Court decision in 2001. In *Bartnicki v. Vopper* (532 U.S. 514), the high court ruled that a broadcaster had a First Amendment right to air a newsworthy but pirated tape recording of a private cell phone call. By a 6-3 vote, the Court rejected the argument that airing such a tape is a violation of the federal wiretap law.

In this case, a Pennsylvania broadcaster, Frederick Vopper, was given a tape of a conversation between two teacher's union officials. Whoever made the tape gave it anonymously to a local anti-tax crusader amidst a controversy over teachers' salaries. The anti-tax crusader then passed it on to Vopper, who broadcast it on his talk show several times. The tape included some fiery rhetoric aimed at local school leaders. At one point, one union official said to the other, "we're going to have to go to their homes...to blow off their front porches" if school board members resisted the union's demands for a pay raise. Gloria Bartnicki and another union leader sued Vopper for airing the tape of their conversation.

No one disputed that whoever monitored the phone call and made the tape violated the law. But the court ruled that when such a tape *concerns an issue of public concern and the media lawfully obtain it from a third party without participating in or encouraging the illegal taping*, the media have a First Amendment right to air the tape. Justice John Paul Stevens relied heavily on the "Pentagon Papers" case (*New York Times v. U.S.*, discussed in Chapter Three), in which the Court allowed the *Times* to publish excerpts from the so-called Pentagon Papers even though they had been illegally copied and given to the *Times*. "A stranger's illegal conduct does not suffice to remove the First Amendment shield about a matter of public concern," Stevens said. However, two justices, Stephen Breyer and Sandra Day O'Connor, wrote a concurring opinion in which they took a narrower view of the media's rights in such cases. They said the media wouldn't have the right to air a tape that reveals gossip about someone's private life, as opposed to a discussion of a major local issue such as teachers' salaries. And there were three dissenters, Chief Justice William Rehnquist and Justices Antonin Scalia and Clarence Thomas. They said the media should *not* be free of liability for airing a bootlegged tape of a private phone conversation, even if it addresses an issue of public concern.

Thus, the result was a victory for the media, but a narrow one. The right to air a pirated tape extends only to a tape of a conversation about an issue of public concern—usually a political or social issue. Also, new telephone technologies have made the interception of private phone calls much more difficult in recent years. Media lawyers generally hailed the *Bartnicki* decision as good—while emphasizing that it may have little real impact on personal privacy because of improvements in telephone privacy protection in the digital age.

Limits on *Bartnicki*. But a Dallas television station that played a more active role in illegal taping was liable for intrusion: *Peavy v. WFAA-TV* (221 F.3d 158, 2000). The Fifth Circuit said the station could be held liable because a reporter cooperated with a family that illegally monitored and taped a neighbor's telephone conversations. The neighbor, Carver Dan Peavy, was an elected Dallas school trustee. The tapes led the reporter to believe that Peavy had taken kickbacks on school insurance purchases. They were *not* aired, but they were used by WFAA-TV in preparing stories about alleged wrongdoing by Peavy (a series that won a Peabody award for excellence). Peavy sued, and a trial court dismissed on First Amendment grounds. The appellate court reinstated Peavy's case, and the Supreme Court denied *cert.*

In 2007, the D.C. Court of Appeals also declined to apply *Bartnicki* to a case involving disclosure of an illegally intercepted cell phone conversation. In *Boehner v. McDermott* (484 F.3d 573), the court held that a Congressperson violated the law by giving to the media a recording of a conference call involving other members of Congress, even though he played no part in making the illegal recording. The tape, concerning an ethics probe of then-House Speaker Newt Gingrich, received wide publicity. A divided court said a public official has no First Amendment right to disclose even a newsworthy tape lawfully obtained from someone else (who recorded it illegally); this disclosure is a violation of the public trust.

The Hazards of Intrusion: Other Problems

With only a few exceptions, the trend today is for the courts to take a narrow view of aggressive newsgathering methods that allegedly intrude upon one's physical solitude. After the death of Princess Diana in 1997, journalists began to face laws restricting their right to pursue newsworthy persons or use high-tech hardware to observe people in private places.

Anti-paparazzi laws. A pioneering anti-paparazzi law was enacted in 1998 in California. Under this law, it is a *constructive invasion of privacy* for journalists even to *attempt* to capture images or sounds of "personal or familial activities" on private property where there is a reasonable expectation of privacy if "enhancing devices" such as a boom microphone or telephoto lens are used to capture images or sounds that could not be obtained without these devices. And if journalists trespass to obtain such images or sounds, that is also an invasion of privacy—regardless of whether they use enhancing devices. In either case, victims may sue for *treble damages* (three times the actual damages). The law was expanded in 2005 to allow treble damages and the seizure of profits in lawsuits by celebrities who are assaulted by paparazzi. That provision was signed into law by Governor Arnold Schwarzenegger—who with his wife, Maria Shriver, was once blocked in a car by paparazzi at their son's pre-school.

While the mainstream media try to distance themselves from paparazzi tactics, it doesn't foster journalistic freedom when a celebrity who ends up being the governor has firsthand experience with paparazzi who chase and trap him in a car.

Even in states without this kind of law, aggressive journalists may risk not only civil lawsuits but also criminal sanctions. At various times journalists have been charged with trespassing, assault, and reckless driving, among other things.

A California court in 2013 threw out parts of the anti-paparazzi bill as unconstitutional while considering against a photographer who allegedly chased singer Justin Bieber; Paul Raef, the photographer, was the first person charged under the California law. The judge said the statute was overbroad and could have affected wedding or other non-paparazzi photographers. In Hawaii, Aerosmith lead singer Steven Tyler has pushed a similar anti-paparazzi bill, which flew through the state Senate but stalled in the House.

In 2015, the California state legislature added three new laws to its books aimed at curtailing aggressive activities by paparazzi. One law prohibits individuals from using drones to capture a person engaged in a personal or familial activity. The two other laws expand the definition of stalking to make it a crime to place someone under surveillance in ways that cause emotional distress and make it illegal to block someone from entering public buildings.

Other issues. Some journalists have also been accused of misrepresenting their identity to gain information from news sources. Sometimes they do just that (in violation of most media codes of ethics). But often a source has second thoughts about granting an interview and then claims to have been misled, misquoted, or both. To the alarm of the news media, the California Supreme Court in 2007 allowed an intrusion lawsuit to go to trial where a news source accused a psychology professor and author of misrepresenting her identity, a charge she denied (*Taus v. Loftus*, 40 C.4th 683).

Many tabloid television cases have been litigated, but few are as notable—and troubling— as *Clift v. Narragansett Television* (688 A.2d 805), in which a news person spoke by phone with a man barricaded in his home, threatening to commit suicide. The man apparently watched the television news, which included a taped excerpt from the phone call, at 6:04 p.m. and then killed himself at 6:07—with his television still on and tuned to the station that aired the newscast. His widow sued the station on various grounds, and in late 1996 the Rhode Island Supreme Court denied the station's motion to have the case dismissed.

■ DISCLOSURE OF PRIVATE FACTS

The second widely recognized kind of invasion of privacy is the *public disclosure of private facts*. A legal action for the revelation of private facts provides a remedy for a person who has been embarrassed by a publication but may have little chance to win a libel suit because the facts revealed are accurate. In many states this type of invasion of privacy causes problems for journalists, often because it is hard to anticipate which stories may lead to lawsuits. What may seem clearly newsworthy to journalists may seem to be a flagrant instance of revealing private facts to someone else. Perhaps a summary of some of the situations that have led to lawsuits will help illustrate the problem.

Legal test; state differences. In many states, to win a private facts case, a plaintiff has to prove that (1) there was a public disclosure of a private fact (2) that is not newsworthy and (3) was done in a manner that is offensive or objectionable to a reasonable person. A few states including Oregon allow private facts lawsuits only if the revelation is truly outrageous (*outrage* as a legal concept is discussed later in this chapter). And several, including New York and North Carolina, do not recognize this tort. In 1997, a plurality of the Indiana Supreme Court rejected private facts as a legal action in that state (*Doe v. Methodist Hospital*, 690 N.E.2d 681). On the other hand, in 1998 the Minnesota Supreme Court broke new legal ground by recognizing not only private facts but also intrusion and misappropriation as actionable forms of invasion of privacy in that state (*Lake v. Wal-Mart Stores*, 582 N.W.2d 231).

In some states, publishing or broadcasting information about a person's shady past has produced litigation, especially if the person later changed their way of life. For nearly 75 years California courts allowed those whose unsavory pasts were revealed to sue even if the information was true and in the public record. However, in 2004 the California Supreme Court joined courts in many other states (and the U.S. Supreme Court) in holding that accurate reports of public records are constitutionally protected, even many years later. The earliest—and perhaps still the best known—of these "old-but-true-facts" cases is a 1931 California appellate court ruling, *Melvin v. Reid* (112 C.A. 285).

The case resulted from a motion picture that revealed the past activities of a former prostitute who was charged with murder and acquitted. Her maiden name was used in the movie advertising. However, after the murder trial the woman had moved to another town, married, and adopted a new lifestyle. She said her new friends were unaware of her past. The court ruled that she was entitled to sue for invasion of privacy. In so doing, the court created a *social utility* test to determine whether the newsworthiness defense should apply. In *Melvin* and some later California cases, courts held that if a communication had little social utility or social value, the newsworthiness defense might not apply. In several cases after *Melvin*, California courts reiterated the principle that a person's privacy may sometimes be invaded by the republication of old news if the republication has little social utility.

California courts allowed several other "old-but-true-facts" cases to go to trial; it was not until 2004—long after the U.S. Supreme Court had recognized a constitutional right to publish information lawfully obtained from public records, that California held that the media may publish truthful information obtained even from old public records. In the 2004 case, *Gates v. Discovery Communications* (34 C.4th 679), the California Supreme Court held that the news media and entertainment industry may now disseminate truthful information lawfully obtained from public records even when the information exposes a rehabilitated ex-convict to new hatred or ill will. Steven Gates sued the Discovery Channel for airing a documentary about a San Diego murder in which he had been convicted as an accessory after the fact. The murder occurred 12 years before the television program was broadcast. By then Gates had served his time, moved to a new community, become a successful salesman, and opened a business with his wife. Gates said that the program caused him to lose friends, quit his business and move, and contributed to his divorce.

The state supreme court rejected Gates' claims. "[C]ourts are not freed by the mere passage of time to impose sanctions on the publication of truthful information that is obtained from public official court records," Justice Kathryn Mickle Werdegar wrote for a unanimous court. The media may do reenactments of historical events under this principle. "Any state interest in protecting, for rehabilitative purposes, the long-term anonymity of former convicts" does not justify abridging the First Amendment, she wrote. The court said lawsuits based on the truthful publication of public records should be allowed unless there is a "need to further a state interest of the highest order."

Focus on...
Hulk Hogan v. Gawker

In one of the most significant invasion of privacy trials in recent years, a Florida jury in 2016 awarded $140 million in damages to professional wrestler Hulk Hogan against the website Gawker for publishing a 90-second clip of a sex tape (*Bollea v. Gawker*, No. 12012447-CI-011).

The judgment forced the website into bankruptcy, and in 2017, the media organization shut itself down as part of a settlement.

The case established a worrisome precedent: a wealthy litigant can be successful in shutting down a media company through strategic litigation.

FIG. 50. Hulk Hogan sued the website *Gawker* after it posted a clip of a sex tape.

Mike Kalasnik, "Hulk Hogan," July 27, 2010 via Flickr, Creative Commons attribution license.

The case began in 2012 after Gawker posted a 90-second clip showing Hogan having sex with the wife of his friend, DJ "Bubba the Love Sponge" Clem. Hogan, whose real name is Terry Bollea, sued for invasion of privacy and publicity rights, saying that the disclosure was a "gross and egregious intrusion" into Hogan's privacy.

According to court records, the tape was one of several allegedly stolen from the Clems' house and used in a possible blackmail effort against Hogan. A more damaging tape from the Clems' bedroom, one showing Hogan using racist and homophobic slurs, was later made public, causing World Wrestling Entertainment (WWE) to fire Hogan. Gawker claimed a newsworthiness defense, arguing that the video was related to a newsworthy story, including Hogan's very public boasting of his sexual prowess, and was evidence contradicting the reality star's public comments denying knowing the woman in the video, according to reports.

After the trial, it was revealed that a Silicon Valley billionaire, Peter Thiel, had funded Hogan's lawsuit against Gawker after Gawker had "outed" him as being gay. Thiel said he had funded other lawsuits against the website as well.

Supreme Court resolves the issue. The U.S. Supreme Court made the *Gates* decision inevitable by upholding the constitutional right to publish truthful information lawfully obtained from most public records. In *Cox Broadcasting v. Cohn* (420 U.S. 469), a 1975 case, and in several later cases, the high court rejected lawsuits against the media for publishing such information. The *Cox* decision resulted from a news broadcast that identified a rape victim in Georgia. A Georgia law prohibited publishing or broadcasting the identity of rape victims, but a reporter was given a copy of the court records during criminal proceedings against several young men accused of the rape. The victim, Cynthia Cohn, was identified in these public records, and Cox Broadcasting used the name in its coverage of the trial. The victim's father, Martin Cohn, sued Cox Broadcasting, contending that the broadcasts identifying his daughter invaded his privacy.

The Georgia Supreme Court upheld the law against publishing rape victims' names and also ruled that the father could sue under common law invasion of privacy principles. However, the U.S. Supreme Court reversed that decision. Writing for an 8-1 majority, Justice

Byron White ruled that a state may not impose sanctions against the media for accurately reporting the contents of open court records such as those involved in this case. Quoting an earlier opinion by Justice William O. Douglas, Justice White said: "A trial is a public event. What transpires in the courtroom is public property."

At the time, this decision was viewed as a victory for the media. As noted in Chapter Three, the Court has also applied this principle in some other circumstances. A later Supreme Court decision suggested that the *Cox* rule was *not* limited to court records: "Our holding there (in *Cox*) was that a civil action against a television station for breach of privacy could not be maintained consistently with the First Amendment when the station had broadcast only information which was already in the public domain" (*Landmark Communications v. Virginia*, 435 U.S. 829, 1978). However, in a 1989 decision, *Florida Star v. B.J.F.* (491 U.S. 524), the Supreme Court avoided more broadly interpreting the *Cox* rule, as Chapter Three explains. While the 1989 case also overturned an invasion of privacy judgment against a news organization for publishing a rape victim's name, this decision is more limited in scope. In fact, this time the Court said that the media are not necessarily exempt from all lawsuits even when they accurately report information that they lawfully obtain. If the information is obtained lawfully from court records, it is safe to publish.

But the Court stopped short of saying that the same thing is always true when the information is obtained elsewhere. On the other hand, state laws banning the publication or broadcast of sex crime victims' names have also faced constitutional challenges in state courts. As noted in Chapter Three, the Florida Supreme Court overturned such a law in 1994 in *Florida v. Globe Communications Corp.* (648 So.2d 110).

If the *Cox* and *Florida Star* cases give the media the right to publish information they lawfully obtain from court records, does that mean state laws against publishing the names of juvenile offenders are invalid? The U.S. Supreme Court has also addressed that issue.

Naming Juveniles and Other Ethical Issues

Obviously, there are ethical as well as legal issues involved in publishing the names of sex crime victims and juvenile offenders. But in both areas, many of the legal issues have now been resolved in favor of the media. The Supreme Court in 1979 ruled that no state may impose *criminal sanctions* where the media have disseminated the names of juvenile offenders, even if that information was secured from sources other than public records. The high court didn't rule out *civil* invasion of privacy lawsuits where such information is secured from unofficial sources, but at least criminal prosecution of journalists was forbidden.

The 1979 case (*Smith v. Daily Mail*, 443 U.S. 97) was a test of a West Virginia law making it a crime for a newspaper to publish the name of any young person involved in juvenile court proceedings. The case arose when two newspapers were indicted after they identified a 14-year-old boy charged with fatally shooting a schoolmate. The shooting occurred at a junior high school, and journalists learned the name from eyewitnesses. They also heard the name by monitoring a police band radio.

After the indictments, the West Virginia Supreme Court overturned both the indictments and the state law, and the U.S. Supreme Court agreed. Chief Justice Warren Burger wrote: "At issue is simply the power of a state to punish the truthful publication of an alleged juvenile delinquent's name lawfully obtained by a newspaper."

Burger warned that the Court might uphold a similar law if there were an issue of "unlawful press access to a confidential judicial proceeding" or an issue of "privacy or prejudicial pretrial publicity," or if the publication were false. Still, this represented another instance when the Supreme Court intervened to protect the right of the media to disseminate lawfully obtained information. The *Daily Mail* case did not create a new defense, but it did make it clear that criminal prosecution of the media is not an appropriate way to prevent the dissemination of juvenile names (and presumably other kinds of embarrassing information).

Another important point to remember about *Smith v. Daily Mail* is that it did not prohibit invasion of privacy lawsuits for publication of personal information that is not part of a public record; the Supreme Court only banned *criminal* sanctions. Moreover, the Court has not created any special right of access to the names of rape victims and juvenile offenders. It is still constitutionally permissible for a state to keep that kind of information secret—and many states do so. But if the media do obtain the information lawfully, it may be published without fear of criminal prosecution. And, as just explained, the *Cox* case and several later Supreme Court decisions generally protect the media from civil suits for invasion of privacy when they lawfully obtain the names of sex crime victims from public records. But there are several unresolved problems in this area—particularly where the media obtain the information from confidential sources instead of public records.

There are still other limitations on the right of the media to publish truthful information that was lawfully obtained. For example, there was a troubling 1988 case about the naming of a woman who could identify a murderer: *Times Mirror Co. v. Superior Court of San Diego County* (198 C.A.3d 1420). In this case, a woman returned home just after her roommate had been raped and murdered. As she arrived, she saw the murderer leaving. The *Los Angeles Times* published her name and said she had discovered the body, but did not identify her as the person who also saw the fleeing suspect. Nonetheless, she sued, contending that publishing her name while the suspect was at large endangered her safety.

The *Times* argued that the use of the name was absolutely privileged because the name was in the official coroner's report, a public record. However, a California appellate court declined to order the case dismissed on a 2-1 vote. Although the dissenting judge said the ruling could have a chilling effect on First Amendment freedoms, the other two judges who heard the appeal concluded that the First Amendment does *not* necessarily apply here. They were clearly troubled by the facts of this case: a major newspaper published the name of someone who could identify a suspected murderer who was not in custody. When no higher court was willing to hear the *Times'* appeal, the newspaper settled the case by paying an undisclosed sum of money to the woman.

Bottom line. Given compelling facts such as these, courts are likely to continue creating exceptions to the principles upheld in Supreme Court decisions such as *Cox Broadcasting* and *Florida Star*. But as a general rule, the media may disseminate truthful information lawfully obtained from public records.

Private Facts: Other Contexts

In addition to the kinds of cases discussed so far, there are other situations that produce private facts lawsuits. Often the facts are contemporaneous and correct but simply embarrassing for some reason. In these cases, the crucial issue is usually whether the facts fall within the newsworthiness defense.

There have been many such cases litigated over the years, most of them ultimately won by the media. However, the litigation is often protracted and costly, and the threat of such a lawsuit is often a deterrent to publishing stories containing embarrassing personal information.

A good example is *Virgil v. Time Inc.* (527 F.2d 1122, 1975). This case involved Mike Virgil, a surfing enthusiast who was profiled in an article in *Sports Illustrated*. The writer of the article had interviewed Virgil at great length and had also received Virgil's permission to photograph him. Before the article was published, Virgil revoked all consent for publication of the article and photographs because he feared the article would focus on bizarre incidents in his life that were not directly related to surfing.

Withdrawn consent. The fact that Virgil revoked his consent for the publication did not mean the article could not be published. The news media routinely publish and broadcast stories about people who don't want publicity. When an item is published or broadcast without the subject's consent, it merely means the publisher or broadcaster must be certain it is newsworthy enough to preclude a successful lawsuit for invasion of privacy.

The article about Virgil was published over his objections, and it contained this quotation: "Every summer I'd work construction and dive off billboards to hurt myself or drop loads of lumber on myself to collect unemployment compensation so I could surf at The Wedge." The article also said he had extinguished a cigarette in his mouth and had eaten spiders and insects. Virgil sued for invasion of privacy, and his lawsuit reached the Ninth Circuit on a motion to dismiss the case before trial. The court said that unless a subject is newsworthy, the publicizing of private facts is not protected by the First Amendment. The court said: "In determining what is a matter of legitimate public interest, account must be taken of the customs and conventions of the community, and what is proper becomes a matter of the community mores." The court ruled that Virgil could take his case to trial.

The U.S. Supreme Court denied *cert*, and the case went back to a federal district court, which ruled that *Sports Illustrated* published a "newsworthy" article that in fact generally portrayed Virgil in a positive way in the context of prevailing social mores (424 F.Supp. 1286, 1976). Thus, the magazine eventually won the *Virgil* case, but only after a protracted and expensive legal battle. Moreover, the appellate court's ruling left much room for uncertainty about which stories are protected by the newsworthy defense and which ones are not. Newsworthiness is a broad but vague privacy defense.

Unintendedly public intimate life details. But suppose an ordinary citizen happens to be in the right place at the right time to do something heroic, and as a result the whole world learns intimate details of his or her life. Has that person's privacy been invaded? A good example of this problem is the case of Oliver Sipple, who may have saved former President Gerald Ford's life during an assassination attempt in 1975.

FIG. 51.
The Wedge in
Newport Beach,
California, where
Mike Virgil surfed.

*YoTuT, "The Wedge,
Newport Beach," July 25,
2009 via Flickr, Creative
Commons attribution
license.*

When Sara Jane Moore, the would-be assassin, took aim at the president, Sipple struck her arm and caused her shot to miss. He was hailed as a hero, but soon the media also revealed the fact that he was gay, an active member of the San Francisco gay community. He sued for invasion of privacy, but the California Court of Appeal ruled that the stories about his sexual preferences were newsworthy, given all of the circumstances (*Sipple v. Chronicle Publishing Co.*, 10 Media L. Rep. 1690, 1984). However, the court ordered that its decision in the *Sipple* case not be published in the official reports of California appellate court decisions. Under California law, unpublished decisions may not be cited as legal precedents. This is, nonetheless, an interesting case that raises difficult ethical and legal issues.

Another case that raises troubling ethical as well as legal issues is *Diaz v. Oakland Tribune* (139 C.A.3d 118, 1983). Toni Ann Diaz was originally a male, but she underwent surgery to change her sex. Then she enrolled at a community college and was eventually elected student body president. Apparently no one on campus was aware of the sex change operation until it was revealed in a column in the *Oakland Tribune*. She sued for invasion of privacy and won a jury verdict of $775,000. But an appellate court overturned the verdict and ordered a new trial, ruling that the trial judge erred in requiring the newspaper to prove the story newsworthy. Instead, the burden should have been on Diaz to prove that the story was *not* newsworthy, the appellate court held. As student body president, Diaz had often been in the news; she dropped the case rather than go through a second trial at which she would have to prove that the story was not newsworthy. Nonetheless, the newspaper's decision to reveal the fact of Diaz' sex change raises ethical questions.

Perhaps equally troubling—and a good illustration of the legal hazards of journalistic sensationalism—is an Orlando, Florida, case in which a television station showed a video of a police officer holding the skull of a six-year-old girl who was kidnapped and murdered. The girl's family—and thousands of other viewers—were shocked by the video, shown on the evening news without any warning, even to the family. In *Armstrong v. H&C Communications* (575 So. 2d 280, 1991), a Florida appellate court ruled that showing the skull was not an actionable invasion of privacy because of the public interest in the girl's abduction and the discovery of her remains. On the other hand, the court ruled that the family could sue the station on the legal theory that showing the video was an outrageous act.

Outrage as a tort. Like a number of other states, Florida recognizes *outrage* as a separate basis for a lawsuit—a legal wrong somewhat akin to the *intentional infliction of emotional distress* (see Chapter Four). In states that recognize outrage as a legal wrong, a person may be sued for engaging in a course of conduct that would make a reasonable person angry enough to say, "that is outrageous," even though the wrongful act may not fit into any other category that is recognized as a basis for a lawsuit. In the *Armstrong* case, there was evidence not only that the video angered many viewers but also that it was shown over the objections of some members of the station's staff, and that the station later expressed regrets when it became clear that many viewers were offended. Those facts could form the basis for a lawsuit against the station, the Florida court held. A California appellate court reached a similar conclusion in a case where a television reporter confronted several children and told them two neighborhood children were killed by their mother, who then killed herself. The reporter asked the children for their reaction to this news. The court said the reporter and the television station could be sued for the intentional infliction of emotional distress under these circumstances (*KOVR-TV v. Superior Court of Sacramento County*, 31 C.A.4th 1023, 1995).

Do surviving family members of the dead have privacy rights in outrageous cases? In *Catsouras v. State of California Highway Patrol* (181 Cal. App. 4th 856, 2010), a California appeals court said that they do, at least in some cases. Nikki Catsouras was killed in a terrible car accident in which she was decapitated. Photos of the accident taken by the California Highway Patrol were leaked; those images went viral online, and cruel pranks were played on Catsouras' family (for example, the family received emails with the images with such captions as "Hey Daddy, I'm still alive"). The trial court dismissed the Catsouras' claim, and the appeals court overturned. Saying that there was no press freedom at issue here, the appeals court said, "The dissemination of death images can only affect the living. As cases from other jurisdictions make plain, family members have a common law privacy right in the death images of a decedent, subject to certain limitations." Does this finding elevate the privacy rights of the dead over rights of the living, as some critics have suggested?

These cases involving outrage or emotional distress are often reminiscent of the situations that may lead to lawsuits for *intrusion*. There is clearly an overlap among the various areas of privacy law and some of the similar legal actions that have evolved in recent years.

Bottom line. To summarize, the private facts area of privacy law is by no means clearly defined. Usually the media win private facts lawsuits by asserting the newsworthiness defense, but even then, a court may allow the lawsuit to go to trial on some other legal basis. Also, no one—not the courts, not legal scholars, and not even journalists—can precisely define newsworthiness. Another unresolved issue is when the media may be sued for revealing allegedly private facts contained in public records, given *Cox*'s strong affirmation of the constitutional protection for news reports of information lawfully obtained from public records.

The conflict between the individual's right to keep private facts private and the media's right to report the news raises a number of other ethical questions, too. For instance, should the media be able to make a person a celebrity by intensive coverage and then defend against a privacy lawsuit by citing that celebrity status? Does mere publicity make a person newsworthy, or must one already be newsworthy before publicity is permitted? Moreover, when the media make the judgment that someone is newsworthy and publicize his or her activities, should the First Amendment permit the courts to second-guess that judgment?

■ FALSE LIGHT AND FICTIONALIZATION

The third area of privacy law that has produced litigation for the media is referred to as *false light* invasion of privacy. It involves publicity that places the plaintiff in a false light before the public. This kind of privacy case might be described as a libel case but without the defamation. As noted earlier, false light is recognized in most states, but it has been rejected as a valid basis for a lawsuit in about 10 states. By 2000, appellate courts in Massachusetts, Minnesota, Mississippi, Missouri, Ohio, Virginia, Washington, and Wisconsin had joined the Texas and North Carolina courts in refusing to recognize false light invasion of privacy. In 2002, the Colorado Supreme Court also rejected false light as a basis for a lawsuit (*Denver Publishing Co. v. Bueno*, 54 P.3d 893). But in 2007, the Ohio Supreme Court, which had previously rejected false light, recognized it as a valid legal action as long as the person suing can prove actual malice (*Welling v. Weinfeld*, 866 N.E.2d 1051).

Supreme Court cases. Where it is recognized, a person may sue when (1) portrayed falsely (2) in a manner that would be highly offensive (3) to a reasonable person. Photographers (and those who write captions for photographs) have been especially vulnerable here, but other journalists should also be aware of the pitfalls in this area. Two false light privacy cases stemming from inaccurate reporting reached the U.S. Supreme Court many years ago.

The first of these false light Supreme Court decisions came in 1967. The case, *Time Inc. v. Hill* (385 U.S. 374), involved the James J. Hill family, which gained notoriety when it was taken hostage in its own home by three escaped convicts in 1952. The incident was clearly newsworthy, especially because two convicts were eventually killed in a shoot-out with police.

A year later, novelist Joseph Hayes published *The Desperate Hours*, a story about a family taken hostage by escaped convicts. Later the novel was made into a play and a movie. The story differed in significant ways from the Hills' experiences, although there were similarities. For example, the convicts were not brutal to the Hill family during the real situation, but in the book the escapees did commit acts of violence on the fictional hostage family.

An invasion of privacy suit was filed by the Hill family in 1955 after an article was published in *Life* magazine reviewing the play based on Hayes' book. *Life* directly stated that the play was based on the Hill family incident. The Hills sought damages on grounds that the magazine article "was intended to, and did, give the impression that the play mirrored the Hill family's experience, which, to the knowledge of defendant...was false and untrue."

The Hill family won a $30,000 judgment in the New York state courts, but Time Inc., appealed the case to the U.S. Supreme Court, which in 1967 reversed the New York judgment. Justice William Brennan, writing for a divided court, applied the *New York Times v. Sullivan* libel rule to this kind of privacy lawsuit. Brennan said persons involved in a *matter of public interest* could not win a false light privacy suit unless they could show that the falsehood was published either knowingly or with reckless disregard for the truth. Although some have suggested that the Hills could have proven reckless disregard for the truth if they had opted to pursue the case through a second trial, they dropped the case instead.

In transplanting the *New York Times v. Sullivan* actual malice rule into privacy law, Justice Brennan emphasized that it was to be applied only in the "discrete context of the facts of the *Hill* case." Nevertheless, Brennan's opinion has often been applied by state courts and was cited in a later U.S. Supreme Court ruling on false light invasion of privacy.

That later ruling, *Cantrell v. Forest City Publishing Co.* (419 U.S. 245, 1974), presented the high court with the chance to abandon the *Time Inc. v. Hill* requirement in privacy cases the same year the Court limited application of the *Sullivan* rule to public figures in libel cases, but it didn't address that issue. Instead, the Court upheld an invasion of privacy judgment against a newspaper by saying the paper was guilty of "calculated falsehoods" and "reckless untruth." The justices did not say what the outcome of the case would have been if the newspaper had been guilty of nothing more than negligence.

The *Cantrell* case resulted from coverage of the consequences of the collapse of a bridge across the Ohio River. A man named Melvin Cantrell was among 44 victims, and Joseph Eszterhas, a *Cleveland Plain Dealer* reporter, followed up the tragedy with a feature story about how the man's death affected his widow and children. Several months after the accident, Eszterhas and photographer Richard Conway visited the Cantrell residence to gather information for the follow-up. Margaret Cantrell, the widow, was not home, so Eszterhas talked to the children and Conway took many pictures. The resulting feature appeared as the lead story in the *Plain Dealer's* Sunday magazine. It stressed the family's abject poverty and contained a number of inaccuracies including a description of Margaret Cantrell's mood and attitude, with statements clearly implying that Eszterhas had talked to her.

Mrs. Cantrell brought an action for invasion of privacy against the publisher of the newspaper. When the U.S. Supreme Court reviewed the case in 1974, it upheld a $60,000 judgment in her favor. The Court said the evidence showed that the newspaper "had published knowing or reckless falsehoods about the Cantrells." The Court also said much of what was published consisted of "calculated falsehoods and the jury was plainly justified in finding that...the Cantrells were placed in a false light through knowing or reckless untruth."

Interestingly enough, the Supreme Court ruled that the photographer who took the pictures should not be held liable since there was no misrepresentation inherent in his pictures. In comparison, there was an obvious misrepresentation in the feature story itself.

The *Hill* and *Cantrell* cases are notable because they reached the U.S. Supreme Court— but they are not necessarily representative of all false light privacy suits. As indicated earlier, another common source of false light privacy lawsuits is misleading photo captions. Two California Supreme Court decisions in the 1950s nicely illustrate the problem in this area.

Lower court cases. Both lawsuits were initiated by John and Sheila Gill, a couple who operated a candy and ice cream store at Farmer's Market, a tourist attraction in Los Angeles. Noted photographer Henri Cartier-Bresson caught the couple sitting side by side at the counter in their shop. John had his arm around Sheila, and they were leaning forward with their cheeks touching. The photo, taken without permission on private property open to the public, was published in both *Harper's Bazaar*, a Hearst publication, and *Ladies Home Journal*, a Curtis publication. The Hearst publication used the photo to illustrate an article entitled, "And So the World Goes Round." The couple was described as "immortalized in a moment of tenderness." However, the Curtis publication used the photo in a different context. There, it illustrated an article on the dangers of "love at first sight," with statements such as this one: "Publicized as glamorous, love at first sight is a bad risk." Further, the article went on to condemn this sort of thing as love based on "instantaneous powerful sex attraction—the wrong kind of love."

The Gills sued both publishers, but the two lawsuits produced opposite results. In *Gill v. Hearst Corporation* (40 C.2d 224, 1953), the couple lost. The California Supreme Court found no misrepresentation of their status, and thus no basis for an invasion of privacy lawsuit. But in *Gill v. Curtis Publishing* (38 C.2d 273, 1952), the couple won: the court found that the Gills had been held up before the public in a false light, since there was no basis for saying their relationship was "love at first sight" or based merely on "instantaneous ... sex attraction."

The two *Gill* cases are typical of many others that have been filed since. If there is a general rule in these situations, it is that a photograph is reasonably safe if the caption is not misleading, provided it was taken in a public place and is used in a manner that falls within the newsworthiness defense. However, if the caption creates a false impression about the subjects, or if it is used for a commercial purpose such as advertising (as opposed to a journalistic purpose), the risk of a lawsuit for invasion of privacy is often much greater.

Docudramas. Producers of so-called docudramas—fictionalized films and series based on real people and events—closely watched a lawsuit in California over the acclaimed FX series *Feud: Bette and Joan*. The series, nominated for 18 Emmy awards in 2018, portrayed the frayed relationship between film stars Bette Davis and Joan Crawford and featured Catherine Zeta-Jones portraying the actress Olivia de Havilland, a two-time Oscar winner and star of *Gone with the Wind*. The real life de Havilland, age 101, filed a lawsuit over the series, arguing that FX violated her right of publicity and sued for misappropriation and false light invasion of privacy. The actress said the false portrayal damaged her "professional reputation for integrity, honesty, generosity, self-sacrifice and dignity." She sought damages for emotional distress and harm to her reputation, among other things.

FIG. 52.
The actress Olivia de Havilland accepting an Oscar for the film *To Each His Own*. In 2018, at age 101, de Havilland lost a privacy lawsuit over the FX series *Feud: Bette and Joan*.

Wikimedia Commons, public domain collection, 20th Century Fox, March 13, 1947.

FX sought dismissal under California's anti-SLAPP laws, which require plaintiffs establish the merits of their case early in the legal process to avoid unnecessary chilling of free expression. However, a trial court ruled de Havilland established a meritorious case because her likeness was used without permission and without an attempt to negotiate compensation. The judge also found that de Havilland had a valid false light claim because she was portrayed as saying things she never said. While the producers said they sought to portray the real-life characters as real as possible, de Havilland established that viewers may think her "to be a gossip who uses vulgar terms about other individuals," based on the depictions in the series that included a fictional interview in which she called her sister a "bitch."

But in a decision heralded by entertainment companies (*de Havilland v. FX Networks*, 21 Cal. App. 5th 845), a three-judge California appeals court panel overturned the trial court and dismissed the lawsuit under the anti-SLAPP statute. The appeals court said the trial court decision left authors, filmmakers, playwrights, and television producers with a Catch-22. It would allow individuals depicted in entertainment media to sue for right of publicity and/or misappropriation claims if they were portrayed accurately without permission but sue for false light if not depicted accurately. That would create a chilling effect for entertainment content creators, the court determined.

The *Feud* series "is speech that is fully protected by the First Amendment, which safeguards the storytellers and artists who take the raw materials of life—including the stories of real individuals, ordinary or extraordinary—and transform them into art, be it articles, books, movies or plays," the appeals court wrote. The court said that while filmmakers may negotiate rights with individuals portrayed, "the First Amendment simply does not require such acquisition agreements." In order to succeed on her false light claim, de Havilland as a public figure would have to prove FX maligned her reputation by acting with actual malice—a bar the court said de Havilland could not meet. "Zeta-Jones' portrayal of de Havilland in *Feud* is not highly offensive to a responsible person as a matter of law. Even it were, however, de Havilland has not demonstrated that she can prove actual malice by clear and convincing evidence," the appeals court ruled. Both the California Supreme Court and the

right of publicity:

a form of the misappropriation tort that permits individuals to control the commercial aspects of their names and likenesses; protected differently state by state.

Booth rule:

the media may use previously published newsworthy materials in later advertising of the publication itself as long as no endorsement is implied.

U.S. Supreme Court denied de Havilland's appeal, leaving the California state appellate ruling to stand.

One last example. Perhaps one of the most memorable examples of a false light claim is Linda Duncan's case. Her face was shown in a Washington, D.C. television report on the spread of herpes with a voiceover saying, "for the 20 million Americans who have herpes, it's not a cure." She claimed that a reasonable person would believe she had herpes, and the court said she had a valid false light claim (*Duncan v. WJLA-TV*, 106 F.R.D. 4, DDC 1984).

◼ MISAPPROPRIATION

The fourth type of invasion of privacy protects people from unauthorized commercial use of their names, photographs and other aspects of their "public personas." This concept has been given several names, including *misappropriation* or *commercial appropriation*. Today it is often referred to as a violation of the *right of publicity*. Perhaps it has more than one name because it is a very broad legal concept; no one term really describes all of the kinds of legal issues involved in this field. Whatever its name, this concept is quite different from the other three kinds of privacy law: it involves the *economic* rights of people whose names are well known, not the *personal* rights of private individuals who just want to be left alone.

Misappropriation and right of publicity. Although right of publicity lawsuits are occasionally filed by private persons whose names or photographs were used for someone else's commercial gain, more often the plaintiffs in these lawsuits are celebrities, people whose names have great commercial value. Usually the problem isn't that celebrities object to publicity *per se*; rather, what they object to is not being adequately *paid*—or perhaps having their names or images used commercially in an objectionable way. An endorsement or an appearance by a celebrity may be worth thousands (or even millions) of dollars, and the celebrity's lawyers want to make sure their client collects. There are times, of course, when a celebrity doesn't want to endorse a particular product at all, regardless of what fee may be offered. And some celebrities simply refuse to do *any* endorsements.

The media have the right to do *news stories* and publish newsworthy photographs of celebrities as often as they wish—with or without permission. No celebrity has the right to keep his or her name or picture out of the news media. The newsworthiness or public affairs defense protects the right of the media to cover news about celebrities. What the right of publicity prevents is the unauthorized *commercial exploitation* of the celebrity's name or likeness (in advertising or product endorsements, for example).

The right of publicity is the oldest privacy right to be recognized by the law. The 1902 *Roberson* case, discussed in the section on the history of privacy, would be called a right of publicity case if it were decided today. The New York statutory privacy law that was enacted in response to the *Roberson* decision is fundamentally a right of publicity law—it protects a person's name and likeness from unauthorized commercial exploitation.

In the years since that pioneering New York case, most states have recognized the right of publicity in some form, either by statute or court decision. The concept was given its contemporary name in a 1953 Second Circuit decision, *Haelan Laboratories v. Topps Chewing Gum* (202 F.2d 866, 1953). The case involved the right of baseball players to control the commercial use of their names and photos on baseball trading cards, and the court said:

> ...[I]n addition to an independent right of privacy ... a man has a right in the publicity value of his photograph, i.e., the right to grant the exclusive privilege of publishing his picture.... This right might be called a "right of publicity."

A variety of state laws and court decisions have reiterated the point made in the *Haelan* case: no one may *commercially exploit* a person's name, public persona, or likeness without consent. Various courts have said the right protects sports figures, entertainment celebrities, and even people who would be classified as public figures only because of their involvement in controversial public issues.

Celebrities and advertising. Nor does the right of publicity just protect a person's name and likeness. A number of courts have ruled that the right extends to the commercial exploitation of other aspects of a celebrity's public persona. A memorable illustration of this point is the 1983 federal appellate court decision in *Carson v. Here's Johnny Portable Toilets Inc.*, 698 F.2d 831). The case arose after Here's Johnny Portable Toilets Inc. began marketing its products in 1976. Entertainer Johnny Carson, longtime host of NBC's *Tonight Show*, was introduced to viewers with the phrase "Here's Johnny" from the time he became the host in 1962 until he retired 30 years later. Carson was obviously not amused when the toilet company not only called its product "Here's Johnny" but also added the phrase, "the world's foremost commodian." Carson sued, alleging a violation of his right of publicity, among other things.

Overruling a trial judge who had dismissed Carson's lawsuit, the appellate court held that the use of "Here's Johnny" as a brand name violated Carson's right of publicity. The court emphasized that a person's full name need not be used for the right of publicity to be violated, especially involving a celebrity as well known as Carson. Clearly, the phrase "here's Johnny" was associated with Carson in the minds of millions of TV viewers. In fact, at one point the company conceded that it was trying to capitalize on Carson's reputation.

In deciding the *Here's Johnny* case in this way, the appellate court cited another case it had ruled on about 10 years earlier: *Motschenbacher v. R. J. Reynolds Tobacco* (498 F.2d 821, 1974). In that case, the court held that a race car driver's right of publicity was violated by an advertisement in which R. J. Reynolds used a photo of his car, even though the driver's face was not visible. The car's markings were so distinctive that the car fell within the driver's public persona, the court ruled. Thus, the right of publicity protects celebrities and others from the commercial use of far more than just their names and likenesses. Catch phrases and even tangible objects that are closely associated with a celebrity in the public mind may be off-limits to advertisers (unless permission is negotiated and paid for).

However, there are limits to this rule. Another federal appellate court decision permitted a tire company ad to use actresses dressed in miniskirts and boots, a style that singer Nancy Sinatra had popularized, even though the advertisements also featured a revised version of "These Boots are Made for Walkin'," one of her popular songs. In *Sinatra v. Goodyear* (435 F.2d 711), the court said it was clear that Nancy Sinatra was neither singing the song nor appearing on camera in the ad, which promoted Goodyear's "Wide Boots" tires. The court said Sinatra's right of publicity had therefore not been violated. (Note that the use of the song itself was not an issue. The advertiser had made arrangements with the copyright owner for use of the song.)

A similar question arose in a 1988 right of publicity case much like the *Sinatra v. Goodyear* case—but with a different result. In *Midler v. Ford Motor Company* (849 F.2d 460), singer-actress Bette Midler sued Ford and Young & Rubicam, Ford's ad agency, for using a Midler sound-alike vocalist in advertising for the Mercury Sable. The ad agency asked Ula Hedwig, who was Midler's backup singer for a decade, to sing a Midler hit song, "Do You Wanna Dance," and to "sound as much as possible like the Bette Midler record." Before employing Hedwig, the agency had asked Midler's agent to have Midler sing—and was turned down.

Although the ad agency had obtained permission to use the copyrighted song, Midler contended that the recording sounded so much like her performance that many listeners would believe it was her. Citing *Motschenbacher* as a precedent, a federal appellate court said there were adequate grounds for Midler to pursue her lawsuit. Like the cigarette ad showing the race car driver's auto, this ad campaign might lead many people to conclude that Midler was endorsing the product, the court said. The case was sent back to a trial court to assess damages; in 1989, a jury awarded Midler $400,000. The Supreme Court denied *cert.*

Why was this case decided differently than the *Sinatra* case? Perhaps the most significant reason was that there was more likelihood of the public being deceived into believing there was an endorsement by Midler. In reality, *Midler* was based on the idea that the impersonation itself was wrong; there was no actual misappropriation of Midler's name, likeness, or voice. However, there was no impersonation in the *Sinatra* case: it was obvious in the Goodyear ad that Nancy Sinatra was neither on camera nor doing the singing—although the Goodyear ad used a song closely identified with Sinatra, just as the Ford ad did with Midler.

FIG. 53.
The actress and singer Bette Midler won a right of publicity case in 1988 over a Ford advertisement that used a singer that sounded like her.

Author's collection.

The *Sinatra* and *Midler* cases raise the question of how far an advertiser can go in using celebrity impersonations. Traditionally, the rule has been that celebrity imitations do not violate a celebrity's right of publicity as long as the public is not deceived into thinking the celebrity is actually appearing in the ad or endorsing the product.

Advertisers have often relied on the phrase "celebrity voice impersonated" for protection when they did sound-alike ads. However, the *Midler* decision led many advertising agency lawyers to believe that a disclaimer may not be enough. They are becoming especially wary of celebrity impersonations—with or without a disclaimer—in the aftermath of an even bigger damage award to a celebrity in an impersonation case: more than $2 million. In *Waits v. Frito-Lay* (978 F.2d 1093, 1992), the Ninth Circuit upheld almost all of a $2.5 million jury verdict against the manufacturer of Doritos brand corn chips for doing commercials featuring a song made popular by singer Tom Waits, using a close imitation of his vocal style.

At about the same time as the *Waits* case, the Ninth Circuit also ruled that game show hostess Vanna White could sue Samsung Electronics and its advertising agency, David Deutsch, for ads featuring a blond robot wearing a gown and jewelry reminiscent of White's on-air style, standing in front of a large game board. Although one judge dissented, arguing that there was little likelihood of the public mistaking a mechanical robot for Vanna White, the 2-1 majority ruled that this could be a wrongful commercial exploitation of White's public persona and allowed her to go to trial (*White v. Samsung*, 971 F.2d 1395, 1992).

A Kozinski dissent. Samsung asked the Ninth Circuit to rehear the case *en banc*. That request was denied, but it gave one of the nation's most quotable appellate judges, Alex Kozinski, a chance to issue a colorful opinion objecting to the court's decision not to rehear the case. Kozinski blasted the court for its expansion of the right of publicity:

> Something very dangerous is going on here.... Concerned about what it sees as a wrong done to Vanna White, the panel majority erects a property right of remarkable and dangerous breadth: Under the majority's opinion, it's now a tort for advertisers to *remind* the public of a celebrity. Not to use a celebrity's name, voice, signature or likeness; not to imply the celebrity endorses a product; but simply to evoke the celebrity's image in the public's mind. This Orwellian notion withdraws far more from the public domain than prudence and common sense allow. ... It raises serious First Amendment problems. It's bad law, and it deserves a long, hard second look.

Perhaps encouraged by Kozinski's passionate arguments, Samsung appealed to the Supreme Court, but as in the *Midler* and *Waits* cases, the Court refused to hear an appeal of this case. White then took her case to trial, and in 1994 a jury awarded her $403,000 in damages, which Samsung and its ad agency agreed to pay instead of appealing again. In return, White agreed not to appeal for a chance to seek an even larger judgment.

Another similar dispute led to *Wendt v. Host International* (125 F.3d 806, 1997). George Wendt and John Ratzenberger, the actors who played Norm and Cliff in the *Cheers* television series, sued Host for placing animatronic robotic figures resembling them in airport bars modeled after the set of *Cheers*. They contended that the robots resembled them sufficiently to be a possible misappropriation, and a federal appellate court agreed, ruling that they had a right to take their case to trial. In a series of rulings, various courts held again and again that Host could be sued for invading the two actors' right of publicity even though Host had purchased the right to depict the *Cheers* bar scene from Paramount

Studios, the copyright owner. Eventually the U.S. Supreme Court refused to review this case, clearing the way for a trial. In 2001, Paramount and the actors settled under undisclosed terms.

Separate legal rights. In essence, the courts were saying in *Wendt* that a copyright and the right of publicity are *separate* legal rights: a copyright clearance does not give someone the right to depict the actors who appeared in the copyrighted show. To depict actual people without consent and for commercial gain is a violation of the right of publicity.

Although the *Midler, Waits, Wendt,* and *White* cases were all federal cases, they were based primarily on California state law—either the statutory right of publicity in the California Civil Code or state common law principles. However, the recent trend toward courts refusing to allow celebrity impersonations in advertising began in New York. In 1984 a New York judge ruled that the use of a celebrity look-alike in an ad violated Jackie Onassis' right of publicity, and he ordered an ad agency to stop using an Onassis look-alike to promote Christian Dior clothes. The judge issued this order without finding that anyone was actually deceived into thinking Onassis was appearing in the ad or endorsing the product.

Right of publicity cases still often come before the courts. In a 2012 case, General Motors was sued in California by Hebrew University of Jerusalem, recipient of famed physicist Albert Einstein's "manuscripts, copyrights, publication rights, royalties and royalty agreements" for pasting Einstein's head on the body of a muscled, topless model in an ad for a terrain vehicle, with the caption "Ideas are sexy too." GM won, even though the court thought the ad "tasteless." New Jersey courts had not formally ruled on how long a right of publicity should survive a person's death, but in an earlier state case, a federal court in New Jersey (the state whose laws would govern here) had predicted that the right would last for 50 years after death (shorter than California's, which lasts for 70). So, said the California federal court, under the 50-year limit, Einstein, who died in 1955, would no longer have rights of publicity (*Hebrew Univ. of Jerusalem v. Gen'l Motors LLC,* 903 F. Supp. 2d 932). The court did wax rhapsodic on how important Einstein is to the American public, calling him "the symbol and embodiment of genius" and adding that his "persona should be freely available to those who seek to appropriate it as part of their own expression, even in tasteless ads."

Athletes in video games. One area of ongoing litigation involves the depictions of athletes in video games. The Supreme Court in 2016 declined to hear an appeal from the makers of the video game *Madden NFL*. Athletes sued the video game maker in 2010 over the unlicensed uses of their likenesses. The issue was whether the First Amendment "protects a speaker against a state-law right-of-publicity claim that challenges the realistic portrayal of a person in an expressive work." In *Electronic Arts v. Davis* (775 F. 3d 1172), the Ninth Circuit Court of Appeals ruled that the First Amendment protects only "transformative" depictions from right-of-publicity claims, and therefore ruled that the lawsuit could proceed because the use of the athletes' likenesses were not sufficiently "transformative." The Ninth Circuit adopted similar reasoning as the Third Circuit in 2013. In *Hart v. Electronic Arts, Inc.* (717 F.3d 141), the Third Circuit said it needed to balance the First Amendment against the New Jersey right of publicity. Using a test of transformation usually used in copyright law, the court evaluated the use of Rutgers quarterback Ryan Hart's likeness in the NCAA Football game. Hart and his avatar were very similar: "Not only does the digital avatar match Appellant in terms of hair color, hair style and skin tone, but the avatar's accessories mimic those worn by [Hart] during his time as a Rutgers player." This similarity, plus that of the game-play, in which Hart plays football as he did in real life, was not transformative. Not even

Electronic Arts' attempt to introduce customizability (like changing hair colors and faces) was enough; the court noted that if it found that it were, "acts of blatant misappropriation would count for nothing so long as the larger work, on balance, contained highly creative elements in great abundance."

Student athletes profiting from names and likenesses. The rights of student athletes to profit from their name, image and likeness appeared to be coming to a head in 2021. In *Nat'l Collegiate Athletic Ass'n v. Alston* (No. 20-512), the Supreme Court ruled 9-0 that the NCAA's strict limits on payments to student athletes, in the name of supporting amateurism in collegiate sports, violated antitrust law, at least as it concerns payments for educational benefits like equipment, scholarships, tutoring, and internships. Days after the Supreme Court announced its decision, the NCAA suspended its limits on athletes' profiting from their names, images, and likenesses. This also came as more than a dozen states were poised to implement new state laws giving student athletes the ability to make endorsement deals on their own. A federal bill was also introduced in Congress to set one national standard. The changes will create more opportunities for student athletes to profit from their fame, giving them a right to publicity enjoyed by nearly everyone else. Stay tuned.

Misappropriation and the News

If celebrities have a right to prevent the unauthorized commercial use of their names and likenesses—and sometimes even the right to prevent advertisers from *reminding* the public of them (as Judge Kozinski put it)—where does that leave a journalist who wants to write news stories about the famous?

That is an important issue, and the answer is relatively clear: the right of publicity does not apply to news situations, even though the media are commercial enterprises. The print and broadcast media are free to use a person's name and likeness whenever the situation creates newsworthiness—and the courts have tended to be very liberal in defining newsworthiness for these purposes. Even if a news medium engages in advertising to promote itself and reproduces a photograph of someone famous that appeared in print or on the air, that advertisement does not usually fall within the right of publicity.

Implied endorsement. However, if a newspaper, magazine, or radio or TV station uses the name or photograph of a celebrity in a way that implies an endorsement, it is a different matter. Cher, the singer and actress, was involved in a case that illustrated this point in 1982.

In *Cher v. Forum International* (692 F.2d 634), Cher had granted an interview to a free-lance writer who hoped to write an article for *Us* magazine. The article was rejected by *Us*, and the writer then sold it to the publishers of two other magazines, *Star* and *Forum*. Both published it. *Star* carried the article with a headline that offended Cher. The headline read, "Exclusive Series ...Cher: My life, my husbands, and my many, many men."

Cher disliked the idea that the interview ended up in *Star* instead of *Us*, and she disliked the headline even more. But what apparently offended Cher the most was that *Forum* not only ran the article but also used her name and likeness in advertising that implied she endorsed and read the magazine. One ad in the *New York Daily News* included Cher's photograph and the words, "There are certain things that Cher won't tell *People* and would never tell *Us*. She tells *Forum*.... So join Cher and *Forum's* hundreds of thousands of other adventurous readers today." What *Forum* did was to promote the article in a way that clearly implied an endorsement by Cher. Although *Forum's* publication of the article itself did not violate Cher's right of publicity, the advertising for it did, the court ruled in finding for Cher.

This case illustrates the principle that the media may freely publish stories about news-worthy people—but not advertisements that imply an endorsement—without violating their right of publicity. On the other hand, if the ad had promoted the story by saying something like "Read an interesting article about Cher in *Forum*," it would probably have been safe.

The *Cher v. Forum* decision was based in part on the *Booth Rule*, an old principle of privacy law that says the media may use previously published newsworthy materials in later advertising of the publication itself as long as no endorsement is implied. This concept originated with *Booth v. Curtis Publishing* (182 N.E.2d 812), a 1962 New York Court of Appeals decision that allowed *Holiday* magazine to use a previously published photo of actress Shirley Booth in later advertising for the magazine.

A different legal issue was raised when the Coors brewery did advertising that included a drawing based on a news photograph of baseball star Don Newcombe pitching for the Brooklyn Dodgers in the 1949 World Series. The Ninth Circuit said Newcombe had the right to sue Coors and its ad agency for misappropriation (*Newcombe v. Adolf Coors*, 157 F.3d 686, 1998). A newspaper that published the photo in 1949 could republish it to advertise itself later, but others cannot. Newcombe objected to the use of his image in beer advertising because of his own acknowledged problems with alcoholism.

Another case that raised questions about the boundary between public affairs or news and commercial exploitation of a celebrity's public persona arose soon after Arnold Schwar-zenegger was elected California governor in 2003. An Ohio company that had made "bobble-head" dolls depicting various public officials, including George W. Bush, Bill Clinton, Hill-ary Rodham Clinton, and John Kerry, started selling a doll featuring Schwarzenegger with a gun—an obvious reference to his most famous role in the *Terminator* movies. He sued, alleg-ing a violation of his right of publicity. The product used his name and a photo from his days as an actor without consent. But the company's defenders pointed out that when an actor becomes a public official, the rules change. An actor can prevent someone from using his or her name or image on a product without consent; a politician probably cannot. In the end, the lawsuit was settled with an agreement under which the company could sell bobblehead dolls depicting the California governor, but without the gun.

Although this is unusual, a celebrity won a lawsuit stemming from news coverage in a 1997 case, *Eastwood v. National Enquirer* (123 F.3d 1249): the Ninth Circuit *upheld* a large damage award won by actor Clint Eastwood against the *National Enquirer* for merely publish-ing an article about him when he had not submitted to an interview with that publication. On its face, this seemed very similar to the case Cher lost against the *Star*. The *National Enquirer* billed the story as "exclusive" when in fact it had appeared earlier in a British tabloid, but the *Enquirer* pointed out that it had purchased exclusive U.S. rights to the story from the British author. Eastwood objected to the implication that he would grant an exclusive interview to the *Enquirer* (just as Cher did when she sued the *Star*), but Eastwood won $150,000 in damag-es, plus at least $650,000 in attorney's fees. Eastwood claimed that the purported interview never occurred at all, and that his quotes were fabricated by a British journalist (and then reprinted in the *Enquirer*). Eastwood apparently prevailed because the court thought calling the story "exclusive" was a misappropriation of his name (an argument that the court did not accept in Cher's case). The only real difference between the Cher and Eastwood cases may be the fact that Cher admitted being interviewed by the writer of the article, while Eastwood denied even sitting for an interview. But both publications claimed they had an "exclusive" story when the celebrity never agreed to be interviewed by that publication.

Perhaps the best conclusion here is that anyone can write and publish an article about Cher or Clint Eastwood (or reprint someone else's article with permission of the copyright owner), but saying it's "exclusive" is dangerous—sometimes. And don't even consider using the celebrity's name in an advertisement that implies an endorsement of the publication—that goes beyond what the Booth Rule allows. Virtually every other form of commercial advertising (as opposed to news coverage) falls within the restrictions of the right of publicity. In most advertising, you cannot include photographs of recognizable people, be they famous or unknown, unless you get their consent. This rule applies equally to advertising in the print and electronic media: you can be sued if you use a street scene in a television ad without getting the consent of everyone recognizable on the street.

Digital photo alteration. May a magazine digitally alter a photo? Actor Dustin Hoffman won a $3 million jury verdict against *Los Angeles Magazine* in 1999 after the magazine used a digitally altered photo of Hoffman's head superimposed on a model in a designer dress. The jury concluded that the magazine's use of Hoffman's image was commercial misappropriation, not news coverage, even though it was one of a series of digitally altered photos depicting celebrities in modern, fashionable attire. In 2001 the Ninth Circuit reversed the jury verdict, holding that the magazine had a First Amendment right to publish the altered photograph of Hoffman as news, particularly because he made *Tootsie*, a movie in which his character impersonates a woman (*Hoffman v. Capital Cities/ABC*, 255 F.3d 1180).

The *right of publicity* also applies to the entertainment media. When someone produces a motion picture, all of the people appearing on the screen who are recognizable must give their consent—which is why producers commonly use "extras" who are on the payroll instead of just photographing anyone who happens to be walking past for use in scenes showing public places. These rules do not apply, of course, to most news and public affairs productions. Nor do they ordinarily prevent accurate portrayals of newsworthy persons in docudramas based on news events. But in movies produced for entertainment purposes, the unauthorized use of a person's likeness invites a lawsuit.

Life stories and docudramas. Nonetheless, major television networks routinely broadcast docudramas without obtaining the consent of every single person depicted. Where the story is based on facts that have already been reported by the news media, there is little risk of a successful right of publicity lawsuit by anyone who was involved in the story. This is especially true where the facts are in the public record (in court documents, for example).

A noteworthy 1994 federal court decision reaffirmed the right of authors and motion picture producers to tell a person's life story without violating that person's right of publicity. In *Matthews v. Wozencraft* (15 F.3d 432), the Fifth Circuit upheld the right of author Kim Wozencraft to use a character based on her ex-husband and fellow police officer Creig Matthews in her book, *Rush*. Their story received extensive media publicity: they served as undercover narcotics officers in Texas, became romantically involved, used marijuana and cocaine themselves (but later denied it under oath), and falsified evidence to win a drug conviction. They eventually served time in federal prison and were divorced.

Wozencraft later earned a master's degree at Columbia University and published *Rush*, based on their life stories. She eventually sold the movie rights to *Rush* for $1 million and Matthews sued, alleging that she violated his right of publicity by using his life story without permission. The court held that a person's life story does not fall within Texas' right of publicity and affirmed a lower court dismissal of Matthews' lawsuit. It also held that Wozencraft had a First Amendment right to publish a book about these events without Matthews' consent.

FIG. 54.
A Zacchini family
cannon truck at the
John and Mable
Ringling Museum
of Art in Sarasota,
Florida. Hugo
Zacchini, a "human
cannonball," won
a right of publicity
case at the high
court in 1977.

*Daderot, March 19,
2017, via Wikimedia
Commons, Creative
Commons attribution
licence.*

But, the Eleventh Circuit said, there must actually *be* a news story to qualify for protection. That court found a right to privacy in old nude images of a dead woman. Professional wrestler Chris Benoit killed his wife, Nancy, and their son, and then killed himself in 2007. *Hustler* magazine published stills from a nude video that Nancy had made 20 years earlier, accompanying an article on the deaths. Nancy's mother, Maureen Toffoloni, brought a claim based on her daughter's right of publicity. The trial court dismissed the claim, saying that the images were newsworthy. The Eleventh Circuit disagreed (*Toffoloni v. LFP Publishing Group*, 572 F.3d 1201, 2009). Asking "whether a brief biographical piece can ratchet otherwise protected, personal photographs into the newsworthiness exception," the court answered no, saying the article was "incidental" to the photos. In 2011, a federal judge reduced *Hustler's* penalty to $375,000, down from nearly $20 million awarded by a jury.

The Supreme Court case. On the other hand, even a news presentation may lead to a lawsuit for invasion of the right of publicity under some circumstances. An excellent example is a case that produced a U.S. Supreme Court decision—the only one to date dealing with the right of publicity. The case was *Zacchini v. Scripps-Howard Broadcasting* (433 U.S. 562, 1977), and it involved Hugo Zacchini, who called himself "the human cannonball" and had an "act" in which he was shot from a cannon into a net at fairs and other exhibitions. His entire "act" was filmed and broadcast as news by Scripps-Howard Broadcasting despite his objections to the filming. He sued for invasion of his right of publicity under Ohio law, but the state supreme court said the First Amendment precluded any recovery by Zacchini because the newscast covered a matter of "legitimate public interest."

However, in 1977 the U.S. Supreme Court modified the Ohio ruling by declaring that the First Amendment did *not* protect a broadcaster who took a performer's entire act and showed it without consent as news. The Court didn't rule that Zacchini's rights had necessarily been invaded: that was a matter for Ohio state courts to decide. But the high court did say that Scripps-Howard was *not* constitutionally exempt from being sued if the state courts cared to entertain such a suit. The case was returned to the Ohio courts, and Zacchini won.

To deny him a right to sue when his entire act was broadcast without his consent would deny him the economic value of his performance, the state court said. The *Zacchini* decision is troubling to many journalists, particularly because it seems to suggest that other people whose ability to earn money is somehow damaged by a news story could also sue.

There is obviously a fine line between news coverage of a celebrity's activities and the commercial exploitation of the person's name and likeness. Normally the courts give the news media considerable leeway in this area, but the rule is different in a situation such as the *Zacchini* case where all or most of a performer's act is broadcast without consent.

Copyright versus right of publicity. The test of what is improper commercial exploitation versus legitimate news coverage is somewhat like the test used to determine what is a fair use under copyright law (discussed in Chapter Six). Thus, a purported news story or broadcast that seriously impairs a celebrity's ability to make a profit by exercising their right of publicity is less likely to be considered proper than one using only a small portion of a performance and having little effect on the celebrity's profit.

Even news coverage of people who aren't celebrities sometimes produces right of publicity lawsuits. A number of people whose photographs have been used in newspapers and news programs without their consent have sued for an alleged invasion of their right of publicity, but they have almost always lost in court if the photograph was taken in a public place and the use was even minimally newsworthy. The news media clearly have the right to use people's names and show their likenesses in covering the news—without violating anyone's right of publicity. Of course, there is still the danger that the combination of a photograph and text matter may place someone in a false light. If that happens, a false light invasion of privacy lawsuit may result, even though there may be no basis for a right of publicity lawsuit.

Misappropriation and the Internet

As the internet has become a pervasive medium of communication, many questions have arisen concerning the unauthorized use of the names and images of celebrities and sometimes others. This question has led to many lawsuits but few precedent-setting appellate court decisions. In one of the first cases to be resolved, in 1998 television actress Alyssa Milano won a $238,000 default judgment against a Minnesota man and got several other website operators to pay undisclosed settlements for posting nude photographs of her. In a series of lawsuits, she accused website operators of violating her right of publicity, claiming that they were making thousands of dollars a month in access fees paid by users to view their websites.

The news media have a First Amendment right to use the name and image of anyone, including private persons as well as celebrities. This is true regardless of whether the news medium is delivered to the public at no charge, as is broadcast television, or sold, as are newspapers and magazines. The mere fact that a fee is charged for a newspaper or magazine (or access to a website) does not automatically make its use of someone's name or image a commercial misappropriation. But there have been many lawsuits that questioned where the boundary should be drawn between coverage of the news and commercial misappropriation.

At this point, the few courts that have addressed the unauthorized use of someone's name or likeness on the internet have generally found the uses to be misappropriations, not journalistic uses. However, it remains clear that news coverage is not a form of misappropriation. Where a website is clearly engaged in covering the news, it can use celebrities' (and other people's) names and images without permission. If a website is not covering the news, its owner can be sued for the unauthorized use of peoples' names or images.

Still another factor that must be considered when images are posted on a website is *copyright ownership,* which is discussed in the next chapter. It may not be a misappropriation to publish someone's picture on the internet in a journalistic context. But whoever owns the copyright to the picture may sue for copyright infringement even if the person in the picture has no recourse under privacy law.

A Personal or Property Right?

One unsettled point about the right of publicity is whether it is a *personal right* or an inheritable *property right.* Courts in various regions of the United States have taken conflicting positions on this question.

In a widely noted case involving Bela Lugosi, the star of the original *Dracula* film, the California Supreme Court ruled that the right is a personal right and dies with the person. In the 1979 case, *Lugosi v. Universal Pictures* (25 C.3d 813), the court had to mediate a long-standing dispute between Universal and the widow and son of the late actor. The Lugosis contended that Universal was violating their inherited publicity rights by marketing T-shirts and other "Dracula" souvenirs using the actor's likeness after his death. The state supreme court said they had no right to sue, because the right of publicity could not be inherited. Even if a person builds a business marketing his name or likeness during his lifetime, the court said the most his heirs could inherit would be monies from the use of his name or likeness during his lifetime—not the right to control his right of publicity after his death. The California state legislature later passed the Celebrity Rights Act, a law giving the heirs of deceased celebrities the right to profit from the commercial use of their names and likenesses for 50 years (later extended to 70 years) after their deaths. That law effectively overturned *Lugosi* and made the right of publicity a fully inheritable property right in California.

The death of an even more famous celebrity, singer Elvis Presley, produced conflicting federal appellate court decisions. Almost as soon as Presley died, unauthorized commercial exploitation of his name and likeness began. In a 1978 decision *(Factors v. Pro Arts,* 579 F.2d 215), the Second Circuit ruled that Presley's right of publicity was a property right and survived his death. Moreover, the court said that the right could be transferred to a business, which could maintain its exclusive right to exploit Presley's name after his death.

However, two years later another federal circuit court ruled the opposite regarding Elvis Presley. The Sixth Circuit ruled, in *Memphis Development Foundation v. Factors* (616 F.2d 956, 1980), that Presley's right of publicity did *not* survive his death. Thus, the court said Factors did not have an exclusive right to exploit the rock and roll star's name and likeness. At issue was the foundation's right to sell $25 pewter replicas of a statue of Presley it planned to erect in Memphis. The court said, "After death, the opportunity for gain shifts to the public domain, where it is equally open to all."

Further confusing matters, after the *Memphis Development Foundation* decision was published, the court that decided the case (the Second Circuit) reversed itself. In a 1981 ruling (*Factors v. Pro Arts,* 652 F.2d 278), the court followed the Sixth Circuit's lead, concluding that Presley's right of publicity did *not* survive his death. The Second Circuit made this abrupt switch because it felt obligated to follow the law of Tennessee, Presley's home state, as it had been interpreted by a court in that region (the Sixth Circuit).

The *Factors* decision did not settle the matter: Tennessee and several other states joined California in enacting statutory laws forbidding the unauthorized commercial exploitation of a deceased celebrity's name or likeness for 50 years or longer. In Tennessee, the law has no cutoff date, giving the owners of Presley's right of publicity the exclusive right to exploit his name and likeness in perpetuity. New York, on the other hand, refused to recognize that the right of publicity extends beyond a celebrity's lifetime, although legislation that was proposed in 2007 would change that. California's right of publicity law was amended in 2007 to extend its coverage retroactively to celebrities who died as early as 1915, giving their heirs the right to control and profit from the use of their public personas for 70 years after their deaths.

Copyright is always a property right. The court decisions and laws governing the inheritability of the right of publicity do *not* affect the *copyright* on a celebrity's recordings or motion pictures. As the next chapter explains, copyrights are always property rights rather than personal rights, and they do *not* terminate at the artist's death. Only the inheritability of the right of publicity, not that of copyrights, is at issue here.

Another difference between copyrights and the right of publicity is that the latter does not extend to non-residents, at least under the California law. That became clear when a charity trust fund established to control uses of the late Princess Diana's public persona tried to stop the Franklin Mint from selling a Princess Di commemorative doll. The Ninth Circuit held that the trust fund could not prevent the sale of the dolls, in part because the trust fund is based in Great Britain (*Cairns v. Franklin Mint*, 292 F.3d 1139, 2002).

■ PRIVACY DEFENSES

Throughout this chapter we have repeatedly talked about the legal defenses available to the media in various kinds of privacy cases, but in the interest of completeness we should separately reiterate them here.

Newsworthiness. In most cases where the media are defendants, the best defense is *newsworthiness*, often called *public affairs* or *public interest*. If it is possible to convince a court that a given story, broadcast, or photograph is newsworthy, the plaintiff will not win a private facts lawsuit. The trend just about everywhere is for the courts to define newsworthiness liberally, recognizing that even sensational reporting is permissible as long as it is not inaccurate. Therefore, the media do not often lose private facts cases, although the cost of defending a lawsuit alone may deter coverage of some kinds of stories.

Truth. However, if there are inaccuracies, it is a different matter. False light privacy cases against the media are more often successful, with the constitutional standards first established in libel cases sometimes used to evaluate the media's conduct.

Defenses to invasion of privacy:

newsworthiness: a claim that a story or image is newsworthy is excellent for private facts cases because judges interpret the defense broadly.

plain view: information gathered in plain view in a public place is usually protected from intrusion claims.

consent: permission for the publication of the material, best if written.

truth: may eliminate an actual malice finding in a false light claim.

The Supreme Court created a limited First Amendment defense for false light privacy cases in *Time Inc. v. Hill.* That defense protects the media from false light privacy suits for non-malicious but erroneous publications involving matters of public interest. If a journalist has not been guilty of actual malice, a person involved in a newsworthy event has little chance of winning a false light privacy suit. If, on the other hand, there has been wrongful conduct by the media, plaintiffs fare about as well in false light privacy cases as in libel cases.

Plain view. In intrusion cases, the inquiry focuses on the conduct of the media when a court tries to decide if someone's right of privacy has been invaded. The newsworthiness of a story is not a defense for unscrupulous reporting methods. A journalist who resorts to unlawful acts in getting a story (or otherwise intrudes upon someone's right to be let alone) may face a privacy lawsuit. The use of telephoto lenses, boom microphones, and other enhancing technology can lead to intrusion lawsuits in some states. The fact that someone or something is in *plain view of a public place* is generally a valid defense, although sometimes the use of image or sound enhancement technology may offset that defense.

Consent. In areas other than news-editorial journalism, the best (and often the only) privacy defense is *consent.* Persons who consent to a use of their names or likenesses have no recourse when the use to which they consented occurs. The consent must be legally enforceable, and that means there must be a contract that complies with the formalities of contract law. The person who enters the contract must be of age, and the contract must be supported by some form of consideration. Consideration is often thought of as another way of saying money, but it can be other things, even intangibles. For instance, photo release forms are one of the most common kinds of contracts granting consent, and they sometimes simply say that the person posing gives his or her consent for publication of a picture in return for the free publicity that may result. Publicity is a valid form of consideration. Another caution is that the consent must be all-encompassing enough to apply to all situations in which a person's name/likeness is likely to be used. A consent for one commercial use may not imply any consent for subsequent uses of the same photograph. And a consent to use a picture at one time may not be a consent to use it later. All these problems are contract law problems, and the solution lies in writing a contract that leaves no loopholes.

Public records. In addition to the newsworthiness and consent defenses, the Supreme Court has, in effect, created another separate constitutional defense for publication of information lawfully obtained from court records. The *Cox Broadcasting v. Cohn* and *Florida Star v. B.J.F.* decisions included language ensuring the media's right to report information lawfully obtained from court records and possibly other public records. That right may not include a right to report on rehabilitated criminals' past activities—additional decisions are needed to clarify that issue—but in other respects the right to report the contents of lawfully obtained court records appears to be firmly entrenched.

These, then, are the major defenses in privacy law. Because they differ somewhat from the defenses in libel cases, it is possible to publish something that is safe from a libel standpoint but risky under privacy law (or vice versa). In evaluating stories that may defame or embarrass someone, you should keep that point in mind. Once you have analyzed any sort of material that you plan to publish or broadcast for potential libel and concluded it is safe, you must also run through the possible invasion of privacy problems.

■ AN OVERVIEW OF MAJOR ISSUES

The right to privacy has many dimensions, and legislatures and the courts continue to redefine them. While the word "privacy" does not appear in the Constitution, the Supreme Court has ruled that under various constitutional provisions, a "right to privacy" is included in the liberty and due process rights of citizens. In recent years, the Court has extended privacy protections in the digital era, recognizing that new technologies have significant implications for the protection of personal privacy.

The media are often caught up in these questions but have their own privacy concerns. The trend toward "tabloid television" has produced new ethical and legal dilemmas. When is it acceptable for journalists to go undercover or use hidden cameras to get a story? Does it matter if the story is truthfully reported when the newsgathering is really intrusive?

What about law enforcement ride-alongs? The Supreme Court ruled that it violates the Fourth Amendment for officers to take journalists with them when they enter private property with a search warrant or arrest warrant. Was this decision right? Which should take priority—the right of privacy inside one's own home or the news value of showing people who are suspected of serious crimes at the moment of their arrest?

What about the right of publicity? Where do celebrities' rights to profit from the use of their names or likenesses end? Is there enough First Amendment protection for those who want to use some element of a celebrity's right of publicity? And what about paparazzi? There are media willing to buy these pictures because a large segment of the public wants to see candid pictures of celebrities—and is willing to pay for the privilege. Do celebrities abandon all privacy rights when they become famous?

There are other contexts in which the rules on privacy remain unclear or controversial. When, for example, may a journalist report embarrassing but truthful private facts? Should the media be free to report *any* facts that they lawfully obtain? Do the Court's *Cox Broadcasting* and *Florida Star* decisions go too far, or perhaps not far enough? Should there be any private facts that are off-limits to the press?

Finally, what about internet privacy? When should email or other electronic communications be able to be monitored or obtained by employers or courts? And what precautions should social networking sites like Facebook take when dealing with information on their sites?

To be sure, privacy in the digital era will often involve a clash of rights. While individuals want to protect the use of their personal information and data, other entities have rights to collect and publish information. Privacy law will continue to evolve.

WHAT SHOULD I KNOW ABOUT MY STATE?

- What privacy torts does my state recognize (intrusion, private facts, false light, and misappropriation [and what about right of publicity])? The Reporters Committee for Freedom of the Press has an excellent resource: www.rcfp.org/photographers-guide-privacy
- What are my state's rules about recording conversations on the phone or in person? Who has to know that the recording is taking place? See a Reporters Committee resource: www.rcfp.org/reporters-recording-guide
- Does my state have a law about social media passwords?

SUMMARY

A SUMMARY OF THE RIGHT OF PRIVACY

What Is Invasion of Privacy?

Invasion of privacy is a legal action to compensate persons whose right of privacy has been interfered with. There are four generally recognized types of invasion of privacy: (1) *intrusion* upon a person's physical solitude; (2) publication of *private facts*, causing embarrassment; (3) placing a person before the public in a *false light*; (4) *misappropriation*, or *unauthorized commercial exploitation* of a person's name or likeness.

Are These Rights Universally Recognized?

No. Some states have recognized all four kinds of invasion of privacy, while others allow lawsuits for only some of them. However, statutory laws or court decisions in virtually all states recognize that a person's name or likeness may not be exploited in commercial advertising without permission.

What Is the Right of Publicity?

Misappropriation and violation of the *right of publicity* are terms for the fourth type of invasion of privacy listed above (the commercial exploitation of a person's name or likeness). The right of publicity is fundamentally different from the other types of privacy in that it involves a *property right* that is inheritable in many states rather than a *personal right* that is extinguished when the victim of an invasion of privacy dies. Those who use a person's name, voice, photograph, or any other element of the *public persona* for a commercial purpose must have consent.

What Defenses Are There?

The courts have recognized several defenses as applicable to one or more of the four kinds of invasion of privacy. The primary ones are: (1) *newsworthiness* or public interest (which applies mainly in private facts cases); (2) *consent*; and (3) a constitutional *public record defense* (which also applies mainly in private facts cases).

Is Invasion of Privacy a Serious Legal Problem for the Media?

Compared to libel, invasion of privacy was traditionally a less serious legal problem for the news media. While the media lose privacy lawsuits on occasion, courts have broadly interpreted the newsworthiness defense to protect the media from many types of privacy lawsuits. However, right of publicity lawsuits are an increasingly serious problem for advertisers, the entertainment industry, and others who exploit celebrities' public personas for commercial gain. And "tabloid television" has created new controversies and lawsuits that raise difficult questions about hidden cameras and intrusive or undercover newsgathering.

6   *Copyrights and Trademarks*

Should anyone be able to own words, images, sounds, or ideas? Shouldn't information and ideas belong to everyone in a free society? Why should copyright owners—rarely the actual creators of artistic, musical or literary works—be able to lock up someone else's creative endeavors and treat them as private property, denying their use to others? Specifically, why should record companies, publishing houses, and Hollywood producers be able to buy other people's creative works and then profit from them, depriving even the creators of any say about the future use of their works? Should a television distribution company be able to purchase the rights to classic movies and then change them despite the objections of the people who made those movies into classics in the first place?

Should creative works be locked as they are, without permission for others to transform them, to mix and mash them into new creative works? Some transformations and mixes are more acceptable to the original work's creator than others. Take Pepe the Frog. Created by Matt Furie in 2006 for the comic book series *Boy's Club* as a "chill frog-dude," Pepe initially appeared in mostly benign memes. But by 2018, the frog had a different brand: as Furie's complaint put it, groups "connected with the alt-right attempted to coopt Pepe" by combining him "with images of hate, including white supremacist language and symbols"—succeeding so much that the Anti-Defamation League listed Pepe as a hate symbol and supported Furie's attempts to regain control.

Furie sued Alex Jones and Infowars for copyright infringement based on Pepe's unauthorized appearance on a poster sold by Infowars with former president Trump, Jones, Kellyanne Conway, and others, accompanied by Trump's "Make America Great Again" slogan. A judge in 2019 dismissed Infowar's request for summary judgment (*Furie v. Infowars, LLC*, 401 F. Supp. 3d 95), sending the case to trial. But before that happened, the parties settled, with Infowars agreeing to pay Furie $15,000, destroy any remaining copies of the poster, and not to use Pepe again.

The growth of the internet has created difficult new questions about copyright law. It has become easy for millions of internet users around the world to share copyrighted materials. Even worse, in the view of some copyright owners, the internet also makes it easy to share software that defeats the copy-protection schemes built into some digital audio and video products. There is potential for huge damage awards as well; in 2012, as will be discussed, a court reinstated a case against Google for a $1 billion (yes, *billion*) infringement lawsuit filed by motion picture companies against its video-sharing site YouTube.

Chapter Objectives:

- Define "intellectual property" and its various types.
- Trace the historical development and current application of copyright and other intellectual property laws.
- Describe the rights of creators and the ways that others can legally use protected works.
- Explain the statutes and legal tests that protect creators and users of intellectual property.

Essential Questions:

- How does copyright differ from trademark, patent, and trade secret law? What is protected, and why, and what isn't?
- How can creators protect their own works from infringement?
- What legal avenues exist to allow the use of copyrighted material by others?
- How does the rise of the internet as a (digital) mass medium change how creative products are protected?
- What are parody and satire, and why are they given legal protection?

FIG. 55.
Pepe the Frog
appearing on
protestor signs
condemning police
brutality in Hong
Kong, Aug. 2019.

Joseph Chan, Aug. 31, 2019, via Unsplash.

Copyright law creates a maze of problems for the entire creative community. To make a video and distribute it legally, one must obtain copyright clearances from many sources, including the owner of the underlying story, the author of the script, music composers and publishers, recording artists and record companies, among others.

■ INTELLECTUAL PROPERTY IN GENERAL

Clearly, these are difficult philosophical questions; there are no satisfactory answers to some of them. But the fact remains that creative works, like inventions and trademarks, are often treated as private property—property that can be bought and sold or even rented out, if you will. Collectively, the law governing this kind of property is called *intellectual property law*. It includes copyrights, trademarks, trade secrets, unfair competition, and patent law. Mass communicators are primarily concerned with copyrights (which protect creative works such as books, periodicals, manuscripts, music, film and video productions, computer software, and works of art) and trademarks (which protect words, phrases, and symbols identifying products and services). Unfair competition, a legal concept that sometimes protects works not covered by copyright or trademark law, is also important to some communicators. Patents, on the other hand, typically protect inventions and scientific processes. They are usually more important to scientists and engineers than to mass communicators. Finally, as will be discussed more thoroughly in Chapter Nine, trade secret law protects not just product formulas and business practices but also customer lists and other things that companies keep confidential to maintain their economic advantages.

Intellectual property law exists for a variety of reasons: among them, to encourage creativity by protecting creators' rights to profit from the dissemination of their works, to entice inventors to share their ideas so others may improve on them, and to help buyers distinguish among consumer brands. One fundamental rationale is that creative people are just as entitled to profit from their labors as are the people who make consumer (or "real") goods. However, in practice the creators of intellectual property frequently find it necessary to sell their works to others—often at low prices—just to make a living. As a result, by the time a creative work becomes highly profitable, someone other than the creator is often entitled to the bulk of the profits.

The fact that someone other than the creator often profits from copyrights is troubling to some people. Another troubling aspect of intellectual property law is that it creates monopolistic controls on knowledge. For that reason educators, librarians, scientific researchers, and even newsgatherers sometimes find copyrights and patents to be a major annoyance.

Though intellectual property law may be monopolistic and an abridgment of free expression, it has a long history in the United States, one that, as will be discussed, differs somewhat from that in other countries. It is unlikely this form of monopoly will soon disappear, the First Amendment notwithstanding.

The Constitution. Intellectual property law originally evolved within the English common law, but the framers of the U.S. Constitution considered it so important that they specifically recognized it, making both copyrights and patents federal matters from the time the Constitution was ratified. Article I, Section 8 of the Constitution includes this language:

> The Congress shall have the power to promote the progress of science and the useful arts, by securing for limited times to authors and inventors the exclusive right to their respective writings and discoveries.

Shortly after the Constitution was ratified, Congress accepted that invitation and enacted the first federal copyright law, the Copyright Act of 1790. That law has been revised several times since, as technology created new problems that could not have been anticipated by the framers of the Constitution. The 1976 Copyright Act—the most recent comprehensive revision of the law—attempted (not always successfully) to deal with such troublesome problems as photocopying, audio and video recording, satellite communications, and cable television. More recently, even more difficult questions have arisen because of the growth of the internet and digital filesharing, among other issues.

"Limited times." Critics of modern copyright law point out that the Constitution says copyrights and patents are supposed to be *for limited times*. The 1790 Copyright Act decreed that copyrights would last for 14 years, renewable for another 14—far less than today's 95-year term for corporate copyrights. Because copyright owners have done a better job of lobbying than consumers, librarians, educators, journalists, and others who would benefit from shorter copyright terms, Congress has repeatedly extended the duration of copyrights.

Federal law only for patent and copyright. Whatever the unresolved problems in copyright law, the history of Congressional involvement makes copyright law fundamentally different from some of the other areas of media law: it is an area of federal statutory law, not primarily a form of state statutory or common law. If the problems of copyright law are to be solved at all, they must be resolved mainly by Congress, with help from the federal courts.

There is another way in which copyrights and other kinds of intellectual property law differ from such areas of law as libel and invasion of privacy. As Chapters Four and Five point out, the right to sue for libel, slander, or most kinds of invasion of privacy is a purely personal right; it dies with the aggrieved party. That person's heirs usually have no basis for a lawsuit unless they were also personally injured. Copyrights and trademarks are entirely different in this respect. They create property rights rather than personal rights, rights that may be passed on to one's heirs. In fact, copyright law is specifically written to provide legal rights many years after the death of a work's creator.

Trade secrets were primarily governed by state law. But the *Defend Trade Secrets Act of 2016* created a private right of action that can be brought in either state or federal courts.

■ AN OVERVIEW OF COPYRIGHT LAW

To summarize very briefly, the owner of a copyright has the *exclusive right* to *reproduce* the copyrighted work, to create *derivative works* based on it, and to *distribute* copies, *perform* the work or *display* it to the public. Anyone else who does these things without the copyright owner's permission is guilty of *copyright infringement* unless what that person does qualifies as a *fair use.* To prove an infringement, the copyright owner must show *substantial similarity* between the original work and the allegedly infringing work. The owner must also show that the copyright is *valid* and the infringer had *access* to the original work and had violated one of the exclusive rights just listed. When the copyright eventually expires, the work then falls into the *public domain*; at that point, the once-exclusive rights belong to everyone.

What Copyright Law Covers

The Copyright Act of 1976 continued a tradition begun in earlier U.S. copyright laws, setting up a system under which people may protect their creative works from unauthorized copying. The 1976 law was a major rewrite of the 1909 Copyright Act, and the 1976 law has been amended a number of times since then.

What's copyrightable? Generally, all kinds of creative endeavors may be copyrighted. That includes literary (fiction and non-fiction, prose and poetry), musical (and any accompanying words), and dramatic works (including music), as well as choreographic works and pantomimes, pictorial, graphic and sculptural works (both photographs and paintings), computer software, maps, architectural designs, recordings, motion pictures and radio or television productions (whether dramatic or news/documentary). Just about everything that's printed or broadcast may be copyrighted.

However, there are some very important exceptions to that rule. Probably the most important one for the media is that the news itself cannot be copyrighted, although a *description* of a news event can be. The first reporter to reach the scene of a plane crash, for instance, cannot prevent others from reporting the fact that the plane crashed or the details of how it happened. The most that this reporter can deny to others is his or her account of the event. Others may tell the story in their own words.

Thus, it is commonplace for journalists to rewrite each other's stories. When one reporter scores an important "scoop," others quickly pick up the story, carefully putting it in their own words and perhaps giving credit to the original source. Even though this is permissible under copyright law, it should be emphasized that one news medium cannot systematically purloin all of its news from a competitor to avoid having to employ its own news staff. To do that is called *unfair competition,* and courts have awarded damages for that kind of wrongdoing even though it may not be a copyright infringement. Systematic "news piracy," as it has been called, is not permissible. More will be said of unfair competition later.

What's not copyrightable? There are several important categories of material that cannot be copyrighted. Like news, other forms of factual information cannot be copyrighted. Historical or scientific information, for instance, is available to everyone. (However, remember that a particular description of the facts can be copyrighted, and that a scientific process may be patented.) And ideas, processes, and inventions may not be copyrighted; usually they may be protected only by patent law. Copyright law protects the style of presentation, not the underlying factual information or ideas.

In an important 1991 case, the U.S. Supreme Court emphasized the point that only an *original* arrangement of facts can be copyrighted, not the facts themselves. The court held that the information in a telephone directory lacks the requisite originality and creativity to be copyrightable (*Feist Publ'ns v. Rural Telephone Serv. Co.*, 499 U.S. 340). However, the Copyright Act still protects a compilation of facts when it is an *original* selection and arrangement of facts, even if all of the underlying facts were obtained from public records that are available to all. Someone else could do another compilation, of course, using the same underlying facts. A mere listing of all of the facts (a printout of the information on every gravestone in a cemetery, for example) is not copyrightable.

In addition to facts, another thing that cannot be copyrighted is a word or short phrase, including the words that constitute *trademarks* and *service marks*. As will be explained later, they may be protected under state and federal trademark registration laws, but they cannot be copyrighted. You cannot be sued for copyright infringement for mentioning someone's trademark in a book or news story, for example. However, you may face a trademark infringement lawsuit if you wrongfully exploit a protected trademark as if it were your own. Within the limits of libel law, you can write anything you like about a product with a registered trademark such as Coca-Cola, but you cannot make a soft drink and call it Coca-Cola.

Government works: The government edicts doctrine. Some of the images in this book originated with the federal government. They are free and available for anyone to use in any way. Why? The Copyright Act is explicit: "Copyright protection under this title is not available for any work of the United States Government." The government edicts doctrine grew up around this notion, supported in several nineteenth-century Supreme Court cases (e.g., *Banks v. Manchester*, 128 U.S. 244, 1888, asserting that copyright requires an identified author, and government documents are published impersonally and so are not copyrightable).

State and local laws are also in the public domain, as are court cases and the text of ordinances, legislation, and the like. But there is no similar rule for other work created by state governments, such as annotations to its laws created by legislative commissions. Public. Resource.org, a nonprofit government transparency advocate, put the entire Georgia state code, annotations and all, online for free. The state responded with a copyright lawsuit. A district court said that the annotations were not the actual law, so they could be copyrighted; the Eleventh Circuit disagreed, claiming that the government edicts doctrine applied not only to the law itself but to annotations added by government officials.

In 2019, the Supreme Court affirmed the appellate court on a 5-4 vote (*Georgia v. Public. Resource.Org, Inc.*, 140 S. Ct. 1498). Chief Justice John Roberts, writing for the majority, extended the government edicts doctrine to the legislative annotations. He said that it didn't matter if the annotations had the force of law; in fact, the Court in *Banks* "denied copyright protection to judicial opinions without excepting concurrences and dissents that carry no legal force." He voiced two other fears: that citizens who didn't have access to the entire code and its annotations would get false and out-of-date information; and that states could monetize their laws. "With today's digital tools, states might even launch a subscription or pay-per-law service," he worried.

Justice Clarence Thomas, joined by Justices Samuel Alito and Stephen Breyer, dissented. Thomas thought that the outcome was bound too closely to the facts of the Georgia situation and thus would offer no clear guidance to other states. He also expressed concern that the outcome would work in reverse without that guidance: "Perhaps, to the detriment of all, many States will stop producing annotated codes altogether. Were that to occur, the majority's fear of an 'economy class' version of the law will truly become a reality." Justice Ruth

Bader Ginsburg, also joined by Justice Breyer, dissented on the grounds that the annotations were of an "auxiliary, nonlegislative character."

Separability. An early rule of copyright is if something is copyrightable as a standalone work of art, it would be copyrightable if it was created first as part of a useful object. This rule was confirmed when, in 2017, the Supreme Court provided guidance as to when designs on clothing could be copyrighted. At issue in *Star Athletica, LLC. v. Varsity Brands* (137 S. Ct. 1002) were designs on cheerleader uniforms that were "'combinations, positionings, and arrangements of elements' that include 'chevrons ..., lines, curves, stripes, angles, diagonals, inverted [chevrons], coloring, and shapes.'" The Sixth Circuit said the designs were separate from the clothing in that if they were separated, the designs could be hung on the wall as art.

The Court agreed. Justice Clarence Thomas, writing for the majority, said that "an artistic feature of the design of a useful article is eligible for copyright protection if the feature (1) can be perceived as a two- or three-dimensional work of art separate from the useful article and (2) would qualify as a protectable pictorial, graphic, or sculptural work either on its own or in some other medium if imagined separately from the useful article."

Justice Ruth Bader Ginsburg concurred, saying that the designs were just two-dimensional copyrightable graphics on clothing. Justice Stephen Breyer, joined by Justice Anthony Kennedy, dissented. Breyer said that in his view, the Varsity designs were not copyrightable because they couldn't exist apart from the clothing. In his words, "If the claimed feature could be extracted without replicating the useful article of which it is a part, and the result would be a copyrightable artistic work standing alone, then there is a separable design." Here, the designs could not be removed from the uniforms without copying the uniforms.

Securing a Copyright

Once you have a creative work that is eligible for copyright, obtaining copyright protection is easy. Basically, copyright protection is automatic: you don't have to do anything to copyright a work once it is *fixed in a tangible medium of expression*. You can *register* the copyright, and you should put a *copyright notice* in the work. However, the failure to do those things does not cause you to forfeit your copyright.

Although it is no longer mandatory, you normally announce to the world that your work is copyrighted by inserting a notice in a prominent place that says the work is copyrighted. The notice says something like this: "Copyright © 2021 by J.J. Author." The © is a standard symbol to indicate that a work is copyrighted.

The 1976 Copyright Act was amended in 1988 to make it far more flexible regarding the insertion of this copyright notice. Under the 1909 version of the Copyright Act, the failure to include the notice—or even putting it in the wrong place—generally meant forfeiture of copyright protection. Under the 1988 amendments to the 1976 Act, there was a complete liberalization of the rules on inserting copyright notices. Now even if you should fail to insert the notice, your copyright is valid, although innocent infringers (those who do not know the work is copyrighted) have some legal protection until they are notified of the copyright.

For full copyright protection, it is also desirable to register the copyright. You are still required to register the copyright before filing any lawsuit against an infringer, and if you register within 90 days of publishing the work—or at least *before* an infringement occurs—you have better legal protection than you would otherwise.

What happens to a work if you do not insert the copyright notice or register the copyright? You still have a valid copyright, but you must notify any infringer that the work is copyrighted.

Of course, if you choose not to claim copyright protection, the work falls into the *public domain.* That means the work belongs to everyone, and anyone who wishes may reproduce or perform it as if he or she owned the copyright.

Registration. Copyrighting something yourself is easy; you don't have to pay a lawyer to do it. You can either do so through the mail or online. If you want to do so by mail, it'll cost more, and you must obtain paper forms (available to print online, or by calling or writing the Copyright Office in Washington, D.C.). Some applications must be done on paper, like renewing a copyright or registering a vessel hull design.

But if you want to register your copyright online, here are the basics. Go to copyright.gov and choose the Registration option—that'll take you to copyright.gov/registration. Create a user ID and password for eCO (the electronic Copyright Office). Select the kind of work you want to register and follow those instructions.

Mandatory deposit. To complete the registration, within three months of the work's publication you'll have to send electronic copies or images of that work to the Copyright Office for the use of the Library of Congress. In some cases, a copy of the actual work must be sent. For example, if you're a cartographer registering a globe, the Copyright Office says that you as "an owner of a published three-dimensional cartographic work, such as a globe or relief model, may submit one complete copy of the best edition of the work." (That information, and a lot more, is available via the Copyright Office's *circulars*, which are brief summaries of the elements and processes, at copyright.gov/circs.)

What about online-only works? In 2020, the Copyright Office issued a rule regarding mandatory deposit of electronic works published in the United States and available only online. These works are exempt from mandatory deposit until the Copyright Office asks for them (this also includes books that may be printed on demand but are otherwise only online).

You have to complete these steps for each edition you want to register. Some critics of the system have argued that the deposit requirement allows the Library of Congress to acquire most of the major works published in America—for free. Some have unsuccessfully challenged the validity of the deposit system in court.

By dropping the mandatory registration requirement, the Copyright Act legalized a practice that had become commonplace: merely inserting the copyright notice without doing anything further unless an infringement occurs. The new law legitimized this practice by eliminating copyright registration as a precondition to the validity of a copyright. However, registering either within 90 days of publication or before an infringement occurs still gives you more legal remedies than you would have if you do not register until later, and you still must register before suing an infringer.

Registering a copyright also has other advantages. For example, a copyright must be registered before U.S. Customs will stop infringing goods from being imported. Also, registration creates a rebuttable presumption that the facts in the registration statement are true (i.e, anyone who challenges the validity of a registered copyright bears the burden of proving that the facts are not true). Even if a copyright isn't registered, the *deposit* requirement still applies, with fines and other penalties awaiting those who fail to send the Copyright Office the required copies—if they get caught.

Costs. It's not free to register a copyright. The Copyright Office must by law "establish fees that are fair, equitable, and serve the objectives of the overall copyright system." Every three to five years, the office reviews its registration fees; the most current review was published in March 2020. Key elements of this new fee schedule appear in the chart below.

Registration of a claim in an original work of authorship	
Electronic filing	
Single author, same claimant, one work, not for hire	$45
All other filings	$65
Paper filing (Forms PA, SR, TX, VA, SE)	$125
Registration of a claim in a group of unpublished works	$85
Registration of a claim in a group of published photographs	$55
Registration of a claim in a group of works published on an album of music	$65
Registration of a claim in a group of serials (per issue, minimum two issues)	
Electronic filing	$35
Paper filing	$70
Registration of a claim in a group of newspapers or a group of newsletters	$95
Registration of a claim in a group of contributions to periodicals	$85
Registration of a claim in a group of short online literary works	$65
Registration of a claim in a group of unpublished works	$85

The office can expect to recover at most about 70% of its costs under this schedule. Most of its revenue is "elastic," meaning that a small change in pricing results in a large fluctuation in demand. Because many of its services, including copyright registration, the office's primary offering, are voluntary—remember, a work is copyrighted upon fixation—setting prices too high will likely result in fewer registrations and work against the public interest in copyright registration. So full cost recovery is almost never likely.

Additions to the Copyright Act: CCCCA and CASE. In 2010, the *Copyright Cleanup, Clarification, and Corrections Act (CCCCA)* was signed, which increased the use of electronic communication at the Copyright Office and allowed Copyright Royalty Board decisions to be judicially reviewed. It also eliminated dated clauses in the Copyright Act and applied the phonorecord exemption to all pre-1978 records, amending the law to read "The distribution before January 1, 1978, of a phonorecord shall not for any purpose constitute a publication of *any musical work, dramatic work, or literary work* embodied therein."

In December 2020, a new copyright law, the *Copyright Alternative in Small-Claims Enforcement Act of 2019 (CASE Act)*, was signed into law. It created the Copyright Claims Board (CCB) within the Copyright Office to handle "small" ($15,000 for statutory damages and no more than $30,000 for non-statutory claims) claims that might otherwise be too costly for plaintiffs to bring to federal court. Fees to bring cases to the CCB will be lower than those associated with federal court. The CCB will be made up of three officials, copyright experts who will use federal copyright law and defenses to decide infringement claims, provide declarations of non-infringement, and handle some Digital Millennium Copyright Act (DMCA) issues for both users and copyright holders. The whole process is optional—anyone can opt to file a traditional lawsuit in federal court.

Proponents of the CASE Act (including the Authors Guild, the Copyright Alliance, and several photographer groups) say that it provides an alternative to small creators to protect their rights from infringers. Critics such as the EFF and Public Knowledge claim that the act won't protect small users against large corporations, and the voluntary nature of the process means that big companies will probably go to court as usual. And, they add, the CASE Act itself, setting up a board outside the judicial system, may be unconstitutional. Due to the COVID-19 pandemic, the earliest the CCB will be active is likely June 2022. Stay tuned for future litigation.

Remedies for Infringements

Copyright protection would mean little if the law had no enforcement provisions. Thus, the Copyright Act provides a variety of legal remedies for copyright owners to use against infringers. When a copyright *is* registered, the remedies available include the right to seek an injunction (a court order to stop the infringement), a court order to impound all pirated copies, court-ordered payment of the copyright owner's attorney's fees by the infringer, and either actual or statutory damages. Owners of unregistered copyrights retain some (but not all) of these rights, as will be explained shortly.

Damages. In 1994, the Supreme Court ruled that the provision for attorney's fees cuts both ways: both plaintiffs (those who sue, claiming that someone infringed their copyright) and defendants (those sued for copyright infringement) can ask the court to order the other side to pay their attorney's fees if they win. That ruling came in *Fogerty v. Fantasy* (510 U.S. 517), a case in which singer John Fogerty was sued by his former manager and publisher, who claimed that Fogerty's new songs were so similar to his older songs that they infringed the copyrights on the older songs (owned by the publisher). Fogerty won, and the Supreme Court said the trial court could order the publisher to pay Fogerty's attorney's fees. A trial court later awarded Fogerty over $1.3 million in attorney's fees, and that ruling was upheld by an appellate court in 1996.

Statutory damages are an arbitrary sum of money a court may award when *actual damages* (i.e., the infringer's net profits) are hard to prove or nominal (perhaps because the infringer made little or no profit). Congress increased the amount of statutory damages by 50% in 1999. Now the damages for each infringement may range from $750 to $30,000 at the judge's discretion, although awards as low as $300 are authorized for innocent infringements, with amounts as high as $150,000 permitted in a flagrantly intentional infringement.

In an interpretation of the Copyright Act in 1998, the Supreme Court ruled that the defendant has a constitutional right to a jury trial in copyright infringement lawsuits seeking statutory as well as actual damages (*Feltner v. Columbia Pictures Television*, 523 U.S. 340). Previously, statutory damage cases were decided by judges without juries. Of course, if the infringer made a lot of money, the copyright owner would seek actual, not statutory, damages.

Statutory damages limited to one award. Can a copyright holder get statutory damages from everyone involved with the infringing work in one fell swoop? Not in the Ninth Circuit, where a potentially important 2021 case interpreted the Copyright Act to limit statutory damages. The act says that a copyright holder can recover "an award of statutory damages for all infringements involved in the action, with respect to any one work, for which any one infringer is liable individually, or for which any two or more infringers are liable jointly and severally." ("Joint and several liability" means that legal responsibility is shared among several parties, and a plaintiff may sue any or all of those parties.)

A jury found that Manna Textiles had infringed floral fabric designs owned by Desire, and a lower court awarded five statutory damage awards against Manna and other companies that had willfully or innocently infringed the copyright (these companies made garments from Manna's infringing fabric or sold those garments). Manna appealed, and in *Desire, LLC v. Manna Textiles, Inc.* (986 F. 3d 1253), the Ninth Circuit said that Desire could recover only *one* statutory award from all defendants where *one* work is infringed—not one award from

Copyright Act:
17 U.S. Code § 102: "Copyright protection subsists, in accordance with this title, in original works of authorship fixed in any tangible medium of expression, now known or later developed, from which they can be perceived, reproduced, or otherwise communicated, either directly or with the aid of a machine or device."

protectible elements:
elements of a work that can be copyrighted; does not include elements like facts or common measures.

joint and several liability:
a responsibility shared by two or more parties to a lawsuit.

scènes à faire:
French for "scene to be done," scenes so customary in a genre of work that it is expected that they will be there; e.g., in a western, a saloon scene with a flirtatious female server.

mechanical license:
a license from the holder of the composition or lyrics copyright of a musical work to allow others to make "cover" recordings or sample a portion of the work.

each defendant. The court said that the act's language doesn't allow "multiple statutory damages awards where one infringer is jointly and severally liable with *all* other infringers, but the other infringers are not completely jointly and severally liable with one another." In other words, the other companies didn't share liability with each other, only with Manna, and thus one award was appropriate. The court added that statutory damages were optional, and copyright holders could elect to sue for actual damages. A dissenting judge feared that the case would encourage a flood of separate suits, "peppering the courts with individual cases that would be more efficiently tried together."

Unregistered copyrights. When a copyright is unregistered at the time of an infringement, the copyright owner may still seek remedies. First, however, the owner must register the copyright. Only then may a lawsuit for copyright infringement be initiated. After registering the copyright, the owner may sue the infringer for actual damages—but not statutory damages. That person may also seek an injunction or court-ordered impoundment of the pirated copies, but not attorney's fees.

Still, the viability of an unregistered copyright shouldn't be overlooked. Actual damages alone can be a substantial deterrent because of how they're calculated. To collect actual damages, the copyright owner sues for both losses and the infringer's gross profits, deducting any expenses from that figure. Actual damages are thus supposed to take away all net profit from an infringement.

However, this provision can be so harsh to an infringer that courts have sometimes refused to enforce it fully. For instance, there was a famous 1940 U.S. Supreme Court decision involving a pirated script that was made into a major motion picture, complete with high-priced promotion and big-name stars. The profits for the movie (*Letty Lynton*, starring Joan Crawford and Nils Asther) came to nearly $600,000—a very large sum for the time. A trial court complied with the Copyright Act and awarded that full amount to the author of the pirated script. However, the high court set aside the provisions of the Copyright Act and apportioned the profits, awarding the author only $120,000. Much of the profit was attributable to factors other than the script, the justices said (*Sheldon v. MGM*, 309 U.S. 390).

Despite the *Sheldon* decision, large actual damage awards do occur. Moreover, the infringer could face criminal sanctions. The law was designed to make copyright infringements painful and expensive, whether the copyrighted work is registered or not.

"Full costs." Federal courts may, under the Copyright Act, award successful parties "full costs" from their opponents in copyright litigation; the act specifies six categories of such costs (including fees for court personnel and processes, copying/printing costs, and costs for witnesses and court-appointed experts). In a unanimous opinion in 2019, the Supreme Court said that "full costs" meant *only* costs associated with those six categories and no more (*Rimini St. Inc. v. Oracle USA Inc.*, 139 S. Ct. 873). Justice Brett Kavanaugh's language made his textual approach (as well as his love of sports) clear:

> The word "full" operates in the phrase "full costs" just as it operates in other common phrases: A "full moon" means the moon, not Mars. A "full breakfast" means breakfast, not lunch. A "full season ticket plan" means tickets, not hot dogs. So too, the term "full costs" means *costs*, not other expenses.

Suit timing: registration. Can plaintiffs bring copyright suits after they've submitted an application, or must they wait until the Copyright Office issues the registration? While registering a copyright is voluntary, that must happen before a lawsuit can commence. It can take six months or more for the office to process applications. But when can a copyright holder file suit—when the paperwork is filed, or when the Copyright Office registers the work? The Supreme Court resolved a circuit split in 2019 and unanimously set the official registration date for litigation purposes at the point where the Copyright Office registers or rejects the copyright (*Fourth Estate Public Benefit Corp. v. Wall-Street.com*, 139 S. Ct. 881).

Suit timing: laches. *Laches* is an equity concept, an unreasonable delay in filing a lawsuit. The Supreme Court addressed the question of whether laches, a non-statutory copyright defense, can bar civil copyright remedies filed within the three-year statute of limitations (*Petrella v. Metro-Goldwyn-Mayer, Inc.*, 134 S. Ct. 1962, 2014). Paula Petrella, daughter of the late Frank Petrella, asked the Court to let her prove that her father's 1963 screenplay was the basis for the 1980 *Raging Bull* movie. Petrella did not bring suit until 2009. She could theoretically recover damages for infringements incurred over the last three years prior to that (2006) as well as force agreements with MGM, the movie's owner, for future profits. But MGM said that since Petrella had waited so long to sue, the suit should be barred by laches. Both the district court and the Ninth Circuit agreed with MGM, but the Supreme Court reversed. Justice Ruth Bader Ginsburg wrote for a 6-3 majority. Following a long discussion on copyright terms, statutes of limitations, and changes within the law, she noted that laches' "principal application was, and remains, to claims of an equitable cast for which the Legislature has provided no fixed time limitation." But, she said, "If the rule were, as MGM urges, 'sue soon, or forever hold your peace,' copyright owners would have to mount a federal case fast to stop seemingly innocuous infringements, lest those infringements eventually grow in magnitude." The dissent, by Justice Stephen Breyer and joined by Chief Justice John Roberts and Justice Anthony Kennedy, expressed fear that this ruling would result in a profusion of late copyright claims—something they viewed as not particularly equitable.

Inaccurate copyright filing? Nobody's perfect—and sometimes people intentionally deceive. What happens when there is inaccurate information on a copyright registration application? A section of the Copyright Act says that a copyright registration is invalid if it was acquired using false information, and the false information would have resulted in the registration being denied if it had been known. If inaccurate information is known to have been included in a copyright application, courts must "request the Register of Copyrights to advise ... whether the inaccurate information if known, would have caused the Register of Copyrights to refuse the registration." But is fraudulent intent required? The circuits are split: the Eleventh says yes, but the Ninth says no. To resolve the split, the Supreme

Court granted *cert* in 2021 to a case from the Ninth Circuit (*Unicolors, Inc. v. H&M Hennes & Mauritz, L.P.*, 959 F.3d 1194, 2020) to determine whether courts must refer challenges to the Copyright Office if the misrepresentation in the registration contains no evidence of an intent to defraud. Stay tuned.

Proving an Infringement

Suppose someone publishes a work that you feel was pirated from a similar work that you created. What can you do about it? As already pointed out, there are many remedies available if you sue the infringer and win your lawsuit. But to win a copyright infringement lawsuit, there are several things you have to prove:

(1) your copyright is valid in that it covers a legitimate, original work;
(2) the alleged infringer had access to your work; and
(3) there is substantial similarity between the two works.

There are various ways to amass evidence that could be used in court to prove your original authorship, should a lawsuit be necessary. The classic advice was to mail a copy to yourself before submitting the work to anyone else, retaining the copy in the sealed (and postmarked) envelope. However, the 1976 Copyright Act provided a much more dependable approach: you may now copyright the unpublished work under federal law and register it with the U.S. Copyright Office. Then your copyright is protected, prior to the work's submission to anyone who might be tempted to claim it as his or her own. It is far better to register the copyright than to merely mail yourself a copy and keep it in a sealed envelope. The first element is often the easiest to prove; the second and third are more challenging.

Access to original work. If someone who has never seen nor heard of your copyrighted work creates a similar work or even an identical one, that is not a copyright infringement. If you cannot prove the alleged infringer had opportunity to learn of your work, you can't prove the person copied it. If the second work is truly an independent creation by someone who had no access to your original work, that person can copyright it and go into business reproducing and selling it, as far as copyright law is concerned. However, there may be other legal problems in the unfair competition and trademark areas.

Given the pervasiveness of the media and the internet today, though, it is rare for creative persons to be able to prove that they had no access to any earlier published work substantially similar to theirs. For example, musician George Harrison spent several years in court trying to prove that his 1971 hit song, "My Sweet Lord," was not copied from "He's So Fine," a 1963 song that a group called the Chiffons made into a big hit (*Bright Tunes Music Corp. v. Harrisongs Music, Ltd.*, 420 F.Supp. 177, 1976). The two songs have virtually the same melody, but Harrison vehemently argued that he was not familiar with the earlier song and had no intention to plagiarize it. In the end, a court ruled that he could not have avoided hearing the earlier song at some time, and that he must have been inspired by its catchy tune, *at least at the subconscious level.* (Ironically, during a contract dispute with Harrison, his former managers purchased the rights to "He's So Fine." Because of his managers' resulting conflict of interest, a court later required Harrison to pay a small penalty and then awarded him the ownership rights to both "My Sweet Lord" and "He's So Fine" in several countries!)

In 2008, Joe Satriani, a guitarist who played with Mick Jagger, filed suit against British group Coldplay for alleged copyright violations in Coldplay's song "Viva La Vida." Satriani claimed that "Viva La Vida" infringed on his 2004 song "If I Could Fly." He asked for a jury trial and requested all profits from the alleged infringement—which could be significant, given the success of Coldplay's album *Viva La Vida or Death and All His Friends,* which was 2008's best-selling album, selling 6.8 million copies worldwide. Coldplay's response? They said Satriani didn't write the melody either, and "If I Could Fly" "lacks originality" and should not be copyrighted. In 2009 the case was settled and dismissed *with prejudice,* which means that Satriani cannot bring the suit again.

Substantial similarity. To prevail in an infringement case, there must be proof of *similarity of the protectible elements,* not just underlying historical facts which can't be copyrighted. For example, if someone made a new movie about the 1912 sinking of the *Titanic,* it could include the same historical characters and events depicted in the James Cameron movie *Titanic.* It could *not* use characters and plot lines substantially similar to the film's fictitious aspects, such as the story of the aristocratic Rose DeWitt Bukater falling in love with the free-spirited artist Jack Dawson and fleeing her arrogant, wealthy fiancé, Cal Hockley. Plot ideas aren't protectible.

Sometimes there is only one way to depict something, and then a copyright owner who claims an infringement may have to prove that a later work is not just similar but virtually identical. For example, in 2003 a federal appeals court ruled that a photograph of a vodka bottle used in an advertising campaign did not infringe the copyright on an earlier and similar photograph of the vodka bottle. The court applied the *merger* doctrine, which holds that a work will not be protected from infringement unless a later work is virtually identical when the underlying idea of the work can be expressed in only one way (a merger of the idea and the copyrighted work). The court also cited *scènes à faire,* which says a work isn't protected if the expression embodied in the work necessarily flows from a common idea—in this case an image of a vodka bottle for advertising (*Ets-Hokin v. Skyy Spirits Inc.,* 323 F.3d 763).

After all legal analysis of what constitutes substantial similarity is completed, the original copyright owner ultimately must convince a judge or jury that the *average* person (not an expert) would see the new work as similar enough to have been pirated from the original.

Extrinsic and intrinsic tests. In the case of a *verbatim* copy of a copyrighted work, proving these things is usually not difficult, but what happens if the infringer was skillful enough to modify the original work? At that point, you must prove there is substantial similarity between your work and the allegedly infringing work—not always easy. Where literary works are involved, authorities on literature may be brought in as expert witnesses to testify about the subtle similarities of plot, character development, and theme. For the substantial similarity test to be met, there must be similarity in

extrinsic test:
a test for copyright infringement that depends on specific criteria which can be listed and analyzed.

intrinsic test:
a test for copyright infringement that depends on a reasonable person's subjective evaluation of whether two works are substantially similar.

derivative works:
a whole work based on parts of one or more other works; for example, making a movie from the story in a book.

public domain works:
works that can be freely used by the public because their creators no longer have an exclusive right to restrict or receive a royalty for their reproduction or use.

unfair competition:
to "reap what one has not sown" by taking one's competitor's work and passing it off as one's own.

laches:
from the French for "slackness," an unreasonable delay in bringing a lawsuit, a defense in equity law. A maxim of equity law: "Equity aids the vigilant, not the sleeping ones."

the specific expressive elements of the two works (including plot, themes, dialogue, mood, setting, characters, and sequence of events). The Ninth Circuit calls this the *extrinsic test* for similarity, an objective test. In addition, the Ninth Circuit has said the works must be substantially similar under a more subjective *intrinsic test*, which considers whether an ordinary, reasonable audience would find the works substantially similar in total concept and feel.

"Blurred Lines" and "thin" copyright. Robin Thicke's song "Blurred Lines" was not only a highly controversial song, banned on college campuses for being "rapey" (as one writer put it), but it was the best-selling single in the world in 2013, according to the Ninth Circuit. But the court in 2018 wasn't interested in the song's sales—rather, whether Thicke and his co-writer Pharrell Williams had infringed on legendary R&B artist Marvin Gaye's copyright in the 1977 song "Got to Give It Up" (*Williams v. Gaye*, 885 F.3d 1150). The answer was yes.

In 2013, Gaye's family sued Williams and Thicke for infringement. At the district court, two musicologists offered differing opinions on the similarities between "Blurred Lines" and "Got to Give It Up." The Gaye family's expert argued that there were eight similarities between the songs; Thicke and Williams' expert refuted each of these claims. In 2015, a jury found that Thicke and Williams had infringed on the Gaye family's copyright and awarded the Gaye family $7.3 million. Thicke and Williams appealed.

In finding for the Gaye family, the Ninth Circuit panel by a 2-1 vote differentiated between "broad" and "thin" copyright protection: "'If there's a wide range of expression ... then copyright protection is "broad" and a work will infringe if it's "substantially similar" to the copyrighted work. On the other hand, '[i]f there's only a narrow range of expression ... then copyright protection is "thin" and a work must be "virtually identical" to infringe.'"

The majority offered as a "broad" example an "aliens-attack movie" and as a "thin" one, a painting of "a red bouncy ball on blank canvas" where there are "only so many ways" to paint it. Music is more like a movie than a red-ball painting, the judges said, so broad protection applies. Thus, the extrinsic test for infringement is met "[s]o long as the plaintiff can demonstrate, through expert testimony ... that the similarity was 'substantial' and to 'protected elements' of the copyrighted work."

"Stairway to Heaven." Music copyright infringement cases continue to be filed. In one of the most-watched cases in recent years, Led Zeppelin in 2020 fended off an infringement suit against its famous song "Stairway to Heaven" (*Skidmore v. Led Zeppelin*, 952 F. 3d). Jimmy Page didn't write the iconic introduction to "Stairway," alleged Michael Skidmore, foundation trustee for guitarist Randy Wolfe ("Randy California") of the 1960s psychedelic rock band Spirit—rather, Page stole it from Wolfe's earlier work "Taurus." A trial court affirmed a jury's finding that "Stairway" and "Taurus" weren't substantially similar, failing the extrinsic test (thus not bothering with the intrinsic test). A panel of the Ninth Circuit vacated the decision and remanded the case; the court then agreed to hear the case *en banc*.

The full court found for Zeppelin. The appeal focused on what law should be used and whether certain jury instructions were appropriate. "Taurus" was an unpublished work registered in 1967, with a deposit copy at the Copyright Office that consisted of one page of sheet music. The 1909 Copyright Act was in effect at the time, which doesn't protect sound recordings, and so when the trial judge refused Skidmore's request that a recording of "Taurus" be played for the jury, that was not an error, the court said. The jury had to decide using the "Taurus" deposit copy only (which expert guitar witnesses played live to the jury).

The "Stairway" case is only one of many infringement cases filed in the wake of the "Blurred Lines" decision (including Katy Perry's win for her song "Dark Horse" the same month as "Stairway"). Each case must wind its way through the courts, and that, as *New York Times* pop music critic Jon Caramanica, lamented, may result in a chilling effect. Maybe he's right when he writes, "Originality is a con: Pop music history is the history of near overlap."

The Duration of Copyrights

So once copyright has been established, either formally or informally, how long does it last? The duration of copyright protection has been extended repeatedly. As noted earlier, U.S. copyrights were originally valid for 14 years and could be renewed for another 14. In 1831, Congress extended the term to 28 years, renewable for 14 more. Under the 1909 Copyright Act, copyrights were valid for 28 years and could be renewed for another 28 years. The 1976 Copyright Act extended the basic term of a copyright to the author's life plus 50 years. For works created anonymously or for hire, the term was extended to 75 years from the date of publication. For unpublished "works made for hire" and for unpublished anonymous or pseudonymous works, the term was set at 100 years from the year of creation by the 1976 act.

Bono Act. In 1998, on the urging of Disney and others, Congress added 20 more years to all of these copyright terms in the Sonny Bono Copyright Term Extension Act. The basic term now is the author's life plus 70 years, or 95 years for works created anonymously or for hire, which means most corporate copyrights are valid for 95 years. Unpublished works made for hire or created anonymously are now protected for 120 years from the year of creation. The 20-year extension applies retroactively to all works created after Jan. 1, 1978 as well as to new works. Copyrights now expire on Dec. 31 of the expiration year.

How do these extensions of copyright periods affect works copyrighted earlier? For pre-1978 works that still held a valid copyright when the 1998 law went into effect, the term was extended to 95 years from the original copyright date by granting automatic 67-year renewals to most of these works when their original 28-year term expires. The 1998 act did not restore copyright protection to many works that had fallen into the public domain.

The 1998 Congressional action to extend copyright terms was controversial. Although the Bono Act brought U.S. law into line with many European countries, it was vigorously opposed by law professors, librarians, and others who felt it would deny future generations the right to adapt and expand upon established works by imposing an excessive delay before copyrighted works fall into the public domain. And, they contended, the term extension had a serious downside, preventing *derivative works* (new works based on older works) for 20 more years. To buttress their argument, they

Creative Commons licenses:

Attribution (by) lets others distribute, remix, tweak, and build upon your work, even commercially, as long as they credit you for the original creation.

Attribution Share Alike (by-sa) lets others remix, tweak, and build upon your work even for commercial reasons, as long as they credit you and license their new creations under the identical terms.

Attribution No Derivatives (by-nd) allows for redistribution, commercial and non-commercial, as long as it is passed along unchanged and in whole, with credit to you.

Attribution Non-commercial (by-nc) lets others remix, tweak, and build upon your work noncommercially, and although their new works must also acknowledge you and be noncommercial, they don't have to license their derivative works on the same terms.

All definitions are from the Creative Commons website: creativecommons.org pointed to the U.S. Constitution, which authorized Congress to establish copyright protection for *limited times*. Is 120 years—or even 95 years—what the framers of the Constitution meant by limited times? In response, the recording industry and other copyright owners contended that creative works should not fall into the public domain while they are still popular. Foes of longer copyright terms replied that even popular works *should* become everyone's property *someday*, and that the framers of the Constitution never intended for that "someday" to be 95 or 120 years later.

Bono Act held constitutional. Eventually the coalition opposed to extending copyright terms challenged the constitutionality of the Bono Act. The Supreme Court upheld the Act in *Eldred v. Ashcroft* (537 U.S. 186, 2003), declaring that extending copyrights by another 20 years did not violate either the First Amendment or the constitutional provision for limited copyright terms. The decision was a victory for movie studios, publishers, record labels, and others who own valuable copyrights—and a defeat for historians, journalists, and librarians who need access to older copyrighted works. Writing for the majority, Justice Ruth Bader Ginsburg rejected the argument that the repeated extension of copyright terms by Congress violated the "limited times" provision of the Constitution by creating perpetual copyrights. "Those earlier acts did not create perpetual copyrights, and neither does the [Bono Act]," she wrote. Ginsburg rejected the idea that the monopoly created by copyright violates the First Amendment. She noted that the copyright clause and the First Amendment were written within a few years of each other and concluded that the framers of the Constitution did not intend for the free-expression provisions of the First Amendment to limit copyrights. In essence, Ginsburg said, copyright laws are generally exempt from First Amendment scrutiny.

Focus on...
"Happy Birthday to You"... finally public domain

We've all sung it dozens of times and heard it in dozens of movies, but we've probably never stopped to think who owns the copyright—or if anyone should, for that old a song. Believe it or not, if it was in a movie, a fee was paid for its use. In 2013, a documentary filmmaker filed suit, claiming that the song was in the public domain.

"Happy Birthday to You," cited by Guinness as the most recognized English-language song, was written by schoolteacher Patty Smith Hill and her sister, Mildred Hill, in 1893 with different lyrics. Warner/Chappell Music claims ownership. In 2015, a federal court said that Warner/Chappell did not own the copyright to the song, and Warner/Chappell agreed to relinquish its claim. Warner, the successor to Clayton F. Summy Co., which had claimed the original copyright, would also return $14 million licensing fees to be distributed among those who had paid fees during the last 50 years. Judge George King wrote, "The Hill sisters gave Summy Co. the rights to the [Happy Birthday] melody, and the rights to piano arrangements based on the melody, but never any rights to the lyrics" (*Marya v. Warner/Chappell Music Inc.*, 131 F. Supp. 3d 975). As of July 12, 2016, the song was finally in the public domain—123 years after its creation.

FIG. 56. Poet Robert Frost poses with his birthday cake on his 85th birthday.

Library of Congress Prints and Photographs Division, reproduction number LC-USZ62- 120744

The "unfreezing" of the public domain in 2019. Due to regular extensions of copyright duration, Jan. 1, 2019 marked the first date in years that a mass body of work—works published in 1923—entered the public domain, becoming free for anyone to use without cost. The last time this occurred was in 1998, when works published in 1922 entered the public domain; the Bono Act delayed the next such release for 20 years. Disney has been behind some of these copyright extensions; as *Smithsonian Magazine* put it, "*Steamboat Willie,* featuring Mickey Mouse's first appearance on screen, in 1928, was set to enter the public domain in 2004. At the urging of Disney and others, Congress passed the Sonny Bono Copyright Term Extension Act ... adding 20 years to the copyright term. Mickey would be protected until 2024—and no copyrighted work would enter the public domain again until 2019, creating a bizarre 20-year hiatus between the release of works from 1922 and those from 1923." So, unless another law extending copyright is passed, works will continue to pass into the public domain annually. On Jan. 1, 2021, works published in 1925 became part of the public domain, including F. Scott Fitzgerald's classic novel *The Great Gatsby.*

Creative Commons: Some rights reserved. Many of those who challenged the extension of copyright terms in the *Eldred* case are affiliated with Creative Commons, a worldwide nonprofit organization that is seeking to establish a large body of creative works for others to build upon and share. Its founding chair was Stanford Law School professor Lawrence Lessig, who argued the case against copyright term extensions at the Supreme Court (see www.creativecommons.org). Many of the images in this book are licensed with Creative Commons licenses via the image-sharing sites Flickr or Wikimedia Commons. Other images are from the U.S. government; these images are not entitled to copyright protection under the Copyright Act. Still others come from Unsplash and other sites to which photographers and artists post their work for anyone to use for (nearly) any reason.

The Copyright Owner's Exclusive Rights

Once there is a copyright, the owner has a variety of property rights that are protected by federal law. First of all, the copyright owner has the exclusive right to reproduce the work and sell copies. In addition, the copyright owner may abridge, expand, revise or rearrange the copyrighted work. And the copyright owner has the right to perform or display the copyrighted work. The owner also has the exclusive right to create derivative works based on a previous copyrighted work (for instance, a novelization of a motion picture or a movie script based on a novel). The owner can sell (or give away) any or all of these rights. In practice, many creators of copyrighted works sell their rights to corporations that agree to publish or distribute a work and pay the creator a portion of the income from the work as *royalties.*

Licensing. The creator of a work may also make arrangements that amount to renting out the work by allowing someone else to use the work temporarily in return for royalties. Granting first North American serial rights to a magazine allows the author to earn royalties for an article's initial publication while retaining ownership of the copyright. That allows the author to use the work in a later anthology, for instance. As explained later in this chapter, the republication of printed works in electronic form (by posting them on the internet or an information service such as Nexis UNI, for example) has created new copyright questions. Many publishers routinely republished works in electronic form under contracts granting North American serial rights without paying additional royalties. By 2000, court decisions forced publishers to rewrite contracts to cover the republication republication of works in electronic form.

Compulsory licensing. In some performing arts areas, it is also commonplace to give others the right to arrange and perform a work in return for the payment of royalties. In fact, the law requires those who own the copyrights to musical works to grant anyone permission to make *sound recordings* (i.e., CDs and tapes; since 1996 there is also a limited right for digital recordings) of their music once it has been publicly performed. This is called *compulsory licensing*. The recording artist merely pays the prescribed royalties for each copy of the recording that is sold; the copyright owner cannot allow one performer to record a song while denying that right to others. The amount of these royalties is specified in the Copyright Act, although copyright owners sometimes agree to lower royalties to encourage well-known artists to record their songs. Those who record copyrighted music under the compulsory licensing provision of the Copyright Act must perform it essentially as written; they cannot normally make major changes without the consent of the copyright owner.

There is no similar compulsory licensing system for most other kinds of copyrighted works, such as written materials, audiovisual works, and works of art. Nor does the compulsory license apply to *synchronization rights* (combining music with the visual images in a movie or video). The producer must get specific permission to add music to a movie or video—if the copyright owner is willing to grant it. However, the 1976 Copyright Act did establish a compulsory licensing system in one area: cable television.

In the motion picture, television, and music industries, incredibly complex business arrangements have been developed to compensate the owners of the many copyrights that go into modern productions. Often there are separate arrangements with the authors of an underlying short story or novel; screenwriters who adapt the work; those who write, arrange, and perform the music and lyrics; choreographers; and many others. And these arrangements cover a variety of different rights. For example, the producer of a television show obtains (and pays for) the synchronization rights to include music in the show. However, the *performance rights* for the same music are another matter: ordinarily, each television station must pay for the performance rights, because the producer does not purchase these rights. Most broadcasters obtain *blanket licenses* from music licensing agencies for all of the copyrighted music they put on the air. All-news and talk radio stations often obtain *per-program licenses*, which are less expensive for stations that air little music.

The case of *Stewart v. Abend* (495 U.S. 207), a 1990 Supreme Court decision, illustrates the great complexity of the copyright arrangements in the entertainment industry. This case involved the right of a group headed by actor Jimmy Stewart to re-release an old movie, *Rear Window*. But Sheldon Abend had purchased the rights to the short story on which the movie was based from the heirs of the story's author after the author died. The original 28-year term had expired, and the heirs had renewed the copyright (as permitted under the 1909 copyright law, which was in effect when this movie was made). The Supreme Court supported Abend's contention that Stewart's group had to negotiate again for the rights to the original story after the copyright renewal. The original sale of the rights to the story was valid only during the first copyright term, the Court held.

Lawyers for the major Hollywood studios strenuously objected to this ruling, arguing that it would make it prohibitively expensive to re-release many old movies—or to use old story lines or music in new movies. The Copyright Act now deals with this issue by providing a *derivative works exception*. Under some circumstances, the original author regains ownership of an old copyright when it is renewed, but the owners of derivative works (such as a movie based on a copyrighted story) do not lose their rights when the copyright on the underlying work is renewed and reverts to the original author. However, under the 1976 Copyright Act and more recent laws, copyrights have longer but nonrenewable terms.

Rights retrieval. Current law recognizes *termination rights* for nonrenewable copyrights, allowing authors or their heirs to retrieve copyrights that an author might have signed over to a publisher early in life, when he or she had little bargaining power. Post-1978 copyrights may be terminated by authors or their heirs after 35 to 40 years. Copyrights on earlier works now may be retrieved by heirs at various times from 56 to 75 years after the original copyright term began. This aspect of copyright law was widely discussed in 2006 when the son and granddaughter of author John Steinbeck won a federal court ruling that they, and not Steinbeck's publisher, will eventually control the book publishing rights to novels such as *The Grapes of Wrath* and *Of Mice and Men*. On Jan. 1, 2013, those who transferred copyright rights in the past 35 years have the ability to take back those transfers under the Copyright Act. These creators of copyrights on or after Jan. 1, 1978 can terminate transfers for work at least 35 years old—including musicians like the Rolling Stones and Blondie. The transfer, however, does not apply to works made for hire.

"Works Made for Hire"

There are many instances when those who create artistic and literary works sell some or all of their rights to others instead of retaining those rights themselves. Often the author or creator of a work cannot afford to publish it and promote it properly. Thus, he or she makes a deal with a publisher to get the work into print—and in return the publisher asks for an assignment of the copyright. That means the publisher and not the author then owns the copyright to the work.

That is a common arrangement. However, there are some potential hazards in copyright law that may trap unwary creators of copyrighted works. One is the Copyright Act's *works made for hire* provision. The law says that if a person creates a work within the scope of his or her employment, the copyright belongs to the *employer*, not to the creator of the work. For example, if you are a staff writer for a newspaper, the publisher owns the copyright on the stories you write on the job unless you can negotiate a contract that says otherwise. Any time you create something on the job, that principle applies.

Few people would question the fairness of that part of the "works made for hire" rule, but what about writers and others who do freelance work? What about the composer who accepts a commission to write the score for a new musical production? In many cases the law presumes that such a person is not creating a "work made for hire." However, there can be questions about whether a person is actually an employee or a freelancer. Also, contracts offered by publishers and others who buy creative works are often written to offset this presumption. If your contract says you are doing a "work made for hire," someone else may end up owning all rights to your creative efforts rather than just the first reprint or performance rights you intended.

Independent contractors. In 1989 the Supreme Court ruled on the "works made for hire" provision of the Copyright Act in the case of *Community for Creative Non-Violence v. Reid* (490 U.S. 730). The Court dealt with a situation not uncommon among freelancers, including writers, photographers, artists, and composers. In many instances freelancers agree to produce a work on assignment without having a clear arrangement for copyright ownership. Under the Copyright Act's "works made for hire" provision, such works are presumed to belong to the creator if he or she is truly *independent* but not if the person is more like an employee than an independent contractor. The Court ruled that if the creator of a work is an *independent contractor* as that term is normally defined in other areas of law, he or she is entitled to the copyright—unless the creator and whoever commissioned the work have a contract that says otherwise. Some copyright experts considered the Supreme Court's test for independent contractor status to be so liberal that many media corporations reassessed their policies on copyright ownership. The Court seemingly tipped the scales in favor of those who create works in freelance situations. Many freelance works that corporations assumed they owned may now legally belong to the original creator instead.

The *Reid* case involved a dispute between James Earl Reid and Community for Creative Non-Violence (CCNV), an organization that commissioned Reid to do a sculpture for display at a Christmas pageant in Washington, D.C. His sculpture, "Third World America," depicted a homeless family sleeping on a grate. CCNV contended that because it contracted with Reid to do the sculpture, supervised his work, and paid him, he was really an employee, and therefore CCNV owned the copyright to the sculpture. Reid claimed that he owned the copyright—and therefore had the right to profit from reproductions of the sculpture.

The Court ruled that Reid retained the copyright. The language suggested that those not on an organization's regular payroll almost always retain the ownership of works they create unless there is a contract that spells out some other arrangement. The crucial factor in the entire "works made for hire" area of copyright law at this point appears to be the contract between the freelance creator and the person who commissions the work and pays for it. If the contract clearly says who owns the copyright, that contract is enforceable. If, however, the contract is vague or silent about copyright ownership, or if there isn't any contract, the law will presume that the freelance creator owns the copyright. This does not affect works created by employees rather than freelancers: an employer still owns an employee's job-related creative endeavors unless there is a contract that gives ownership to the employee.

Federal Copyright Law Preemption

One of the most significant changes in copyright law that resulted from the passage of the 1976 Copyright Act is that now both published and unpublished works are protected under the federal system. Previously, the federal law protected only published works, leaving unpublished materials protected only by the varying state laws that developed from what was called *common law copyright*. That meant there were different rules and sometimes two different copyright offices with which to deal because some states set up their own registration systems to protect the copyright on unpublished works.

That dual system of state and federal copyright protection also caused both state and federal courts to stretch their definitions of the word "published" to protect authors. If someone handed out 100 copies of a short story to friends or potential publishers, was it published? If the author remembered to put in the copyright notice, federal courts tended to rule that it was published so the federal copyright system could be used to protect the work from would-be infringers. But if, on the other hand, the author failed to insert the notice, the work would fall into the public domain if "published." Thus, state courts tended to bend the rules to find that such works were really unpublished so they could provide common law copyright protection to otherwise unprotected authors.

The 1976 law eliminated this double standard for new works. As soon as a work is *fixed in a tangible medium of expression*, it is protected by the federal law. This means that as soon as a work is written down on paper, saved on a computer disk, recorded on film or tape, or placed almost anywhere else outside the creator's mind, it can be copyrighted under the federal

Focus on...
Pirates! Shipwrecks! (And copyright law.)

In 1718, Edward Teach (better known as Blackbeard) lost his flagship, *Queen Anne's Revenge*, when it hit a sandbar off a North Carolina coast. Blackbeard and most of his crew escaped, but the ship sank and remained undisturbed until 1996, when Intersal, Inc., a marine salvage company, discovered it. The state of North Carolina, which owns the *Revenge* wreck under marine law, contracted with Intersal to recover it. Intersal, in turn, retained videographer Frederick Allen to document the salvage efforts. Allen registered copyrights for all the videos and images he created. When North Carolina published some of these works without permission, the parties settled for $15,000, but the state used more of Allen's works, passing "Blackbeard's Law" to make "all photographs, video recordings, or other documentary materials of a derelict vessel or shipwreck" public records. Allen then sued the state for infringement or, as Justice Elena Kagan put it, "a modern form of piracy."

FIG. 57. Blackbeard.

Charles Johnson, *A General History of the Lives and Adventures of the Most Famous Highwaymen, Murderers, Street-Robbers, &c.* London: 1736.

Remember from Chapter One the concept of sovereign immunity, which says that the "sovereign" (the king or queen in England, and the states in the United States) cannot be sued in the courts. Under this doctrine the states are exempt from many copyright suits. To combat this, Congress in 1990 enacted the Copyright Remedy Clarification Act (CRCA) to allow copyright suits against the states. North Carolina argued that CRCA was unconstitutional, so Allen could not sue it (or any other state) for copyright infringement.

The Fourth Circuit sided with North Carolina, and in 2020, the high court agreed: Congress could not use CRCA to repeal state sovereign immunity (*Allen v. Cooper*, 140 S. Ct. 994). Neither the Intellectual Property Clause of Article I nor the Fourteenth Amendment's Section 5 (limiting state power) provided the basis for CRCA to stand. Justice Kagan relied on a 1999 case overturning a nearly identical act dealing with sovereign immunity for patent suits (*Florida Prepaid Postsecondary Ed. Expense Bd. v. College Savings Bank*, 527 U.S. 627). Using that reasoning, she said that CRCA also fails the "congruence and proportionality" test (to set aside state sovereign immunity, congruousness and proportionality must exist between the injury to be prevented and the means to prevent it). Congress can try to pass better laws to "stop States from behaving as copyright pirates," she pointed out, though since 1999, Congress hasn't tried again in the patent arena.

For now, states will likely be immune from many copyright suits. So what? As one commentator wryly noted, "it is not ridiculous to posit a state, strapped for cash due to reduced tax revenues, launching a subscription … website with pirated content" as it "would simply be immune" from infringement suits. Copyright holders would publicly and vociferously cry foul over such a stunt, making it unlikely. Blackbeard would probably be amused.

law. One need not wait until the work is published to secure protection—federal copyright protection is immediately available. To secure this protection, you merely include a copyright notice in the draft of the work—and you may register the unpublished work if you want the strongest possible protection. But even without the copyright notice, under 1988 amendments to the Copyright Act the author is protected from all but innocent infringers.

Common law copyright no more. In short, the 1976 Copyright Act completely abolished the state common law copyright system for works published after Jan. 1, 1978 (the effective date for the 1976 law). For new works, state laws relating to copyrights were *preempted*. That is, all such laws were superseded by the federal law and ceased to be valid for new works. Congress always had the authority to abolish state common law copyright protection and assume complete jurisdiction in this field; in the 1976 Copyright Act, Congress finally did so, thus simplifying the American copyright system.

However, a 2005 decision of New York's highest court illustrated that common law copyright is still a powerful tool for controlling earlier works. In *Capitol Records v. Naxos of America* (4 N.Y.3d 540), the New York Court of Appeals (the highest court in the state) held that sound recordings made before copyright law was amended in 1972 to cover recordings are still protected by New York's common law copyright—and will be protected until 2067. The court said several performances by world-renowned musicians recorded in England in the 1930s are still protected by New York's common law, even though they have been in the public domain in England since the 1980s. In 2010, the Second Circuit adopted the New York high court's interpretation (*Arista Records LLC v. Lime Group*, 715 F. Supp. 2d 481).

■ THE FAIR USE DOCTRINE

If there were no exceptions to the hard and fast rules of copyright law, no journalist, historian, or teacher could do his or her job very well. No one could quote even one sentence from a copyrighted work for the purposes of teaching, scholarly criticism, or even reporting the news. Because of these problems, the *fair use doctrine* exists—and creates a major exception to the copyright rules.

Basically, the fair use doctrine is a legal concept originally created by the courts to allow some copying of copyrighted works in spite of the seemingly absolute rules against it in the 1909 Copyright Act. The courts recognized that such things as quoting brief passages for scholarly criticism or satire were reasonable and did not interfere with the copyright owner's financial return. The 1976 Copyright Act specifically recognized the fair use doctrine and established guidelines for determining which uses of copyrighted works are fair ones. Congress even addressed the tough issue of photocopying and attempted to establish some basic rules in that area.

To decide if a given use of a copyrighted work is a fair use, the Copyright Act says these four factors must be considered:

1. The *purpose and character of the use*, including whether it is for profit or a nonprofit/educational purpose and whether it is a *transformative* use;
2. The *nature of the copyrighted work*;
3. The *amount and substantiality of the use*;
4. The *effect the use will have on the market value* or profit potential of the work.

This four-part test is vague and general; it often takes a court decision to determine whether a given use of copyrighted material is an illegal copyright infringement or a legal fair use.

A fair use assessment by the high court. A 1985 Supreme Court case provides an excellent example of how courts evaluate the elements of the fair use test. In this case, pitting journalists against authors and book publishers, the high court ruled that *The Nation* magazine was guilty of copyright infringement for *"scooping"* *Time* magazine and a book publisher by publishing a preview article about former President Gerald Ford's memoirs. In *Harper & Row Publishers v. The Nation Enterprises* (471 U.S. 539), the justices said the unauthorized use of about 300 words of *verbatim* quotations from Ford's memoirs before they were published elsewhere constituted piracy, not a fair use.

Ford contracted with Harper & Row to publish his book, and *Time* magazine agreed to pay $25,000 for the right to publish excerpts. Shortly before the *Time* article was to appear, *The Nation* obtained a copy of Ford's manuscript and published an article based on the memoirs. The article focused on Ford's explanation of his controversial decision to pardon former President Richard Nixon for his role in the Watergate scandal. *Time* then refused to publish (or fully pay for) its article about Ford's book, since *Time* had been "scooped" by another magazine. Harper & Row then sued *The Nation* for copyright infringement.

Reversing a lower court, the Supreme Court ruled that *The Nation's* story went beyond news reporting and was not protected by the fair use doctrine. Justice Sandra Day O'Connor emphasized that journalists are free to publish summaries of copyrighted manuscripts, since neither facts nor ideas can be copyrighted. But publishing 300 words of *verbatim* quotations before the authorized publisher could get the memoirs into print was not a fair use. She implied that a similar article—even one containing 300 words of direct quotations—would be a fair use rather than a copyright infringement once the author's original work was in print. However, by publishing the excerpts as news *before* the original work was published, *The Nation* excessively cut into the profit potential of the work. In ruling as it did, the high court had to strike a balance between the First Amendment right of the media to cover the news and the right of an author to profit from his copyrighted creative efforts. This conflict between freedom of expression and the right of authors to profit from their work has existed as long as there have been copyright laws.

Writing for the Court, Justice O'Connor said, "The obvious benefit to author and public alike of assuring authors the leisure to develop their ideas free from fear of expropriation outweighs any short-term 'news value' to be gained from premature publication of the author's expression." Journalists generally viewed the *Harper & Row* decision as a serious defeat for their interests because it limited their right to quote extensively from the unpublished writings even of a former president. Although it does not prevent them from quoting a public official's writings *after* publication—or perhaps paraphrasing a person's unpublished works—much newsworthy (and historically important) information about the famous is locked up in their unpublished writings.

The *Harper & Row* case doesn't include an evaluation of whether *The Nation* had transformed Ford's work somehow in such a way as to make the use a fair use. The concept of transformation would not appear for nearly another decade.

Transformation

Transformation in fair use is challenging both to understand and to apply. While it is generally considered to be part of the first element of the fair use test, the purpose and character of the use, it has become such a key part of fair use analysis that some legal scholars consider it to be a new fifth element of the test.

Parody as precursor. When composers Marvin Fisher and Jack Segal wrote the song, "When Sunny Gets Blue," it probably never occurred to them that someone might rewrite the lyrics as "When Sonny Sniffs Glue." But the song, a big hit for vocalist Johnny Mathis in the 1950s, was a hit again with those new lyrics in the 1980s. Radio personality Rick Dees included a 30-second excerpt of the tune—with his own lyrics—in a 1984 comedy album. In part, the lyrics went: "When Sonny sniffs glue, her eyes get red and bulgy, then her hair begins to fall." Fisher and Segal weren't amused, and they sued (*Fisher v. Dees*, 794 F.2d 432).

Focus on...
My Kindle ate my homework

Amazon.com's e-book Kindle is the book of the future: you can download what you want immediately, read it on a non-glare screen, annotate it, and carry thousands of books with you anywhere you go. And prices continue to drop on e-book technology. What's not to like?

Well, if you're high school senior Justin Gawronski, you might not be so happy to turn on your Kindle one day and find that Amazon deleted your copies of George Orwell's classics *1984* and *Animal Farm*—along with your notes. Amazon was notified that it did not have a license to distribute particular editions of those books in the United States, so it simply removed copies on users' Kindles without telling them.

FIG. 58. Amazon's Kindle.

Perfecto Capucine, Jult 18, 2018, via Unsplash.

In 2009, Gawronski and Amazon settled. The court awarded attorney's fees and established a rule for Amazon's e-books: customers have a "non-exclusive right to keep a permanent copy" of each work and view it an unlimited number of times for personal, noncommercial use. Moreover, Amazon cannot remotely delete or modify books *unless* the user consents or requests a refund for the book, a judicial order mandates deletion, or there is a virus or other harm posed by the book (*Gawronski v. Amazon.com, Inc.*, No. 09-CV-01084).

The Ninth Circuit said the unauthorized revision of the lyrics was unmistakably a *parody*. It was not intended to tap the same market as the original song about a woman's depression after a love affair turned sour, the court ruled. The judge wrote, "Although we have no illusions of musical expertise, it was clear to us that Dees' version was intended to poke fun at the composers' song, and at Mr. Mathis' rather singular vocal range." The court reaffirmed that someone may do a parody of a copyrighted work without infringing the copyright.

"Transformative value" in parody: *Campbell v. Acuff-Rose*. In 1994 the Supreme Court finally clarified that even a highly profitable parody may still be a fair use rather than a copyright infringement. The case involved a parody of a Roy Orbison song from the 1960s, "Oh, Pretty Woman," by the rap group 2 Live Crew.

In a very important fair use decision, *Campbell v. Acuff-Rose Music Co.* (510 U.S. 569), the Supreme Court held that 2 Live Crew's commercial purpose in recording a parody did not necessarily make the new song (called "Pretty Woman") a copyright infringement rather than a fair use of the material borrowed from Orbison's original hit. The new song took the opening bass notes and the first line of the lyrics before launching into new material.

Writing for a unanimous Court, Justice David Souter adopted an idea from a 1990 law journal article written by Judge Pierre Leval and declared that the 2 Live Crew song had sufficient "transformative value" to permit a trial court to find that it was a fair use rather than an infringement despite its commercial intent. Souter emphasized that the other parts of the fair use test must still be applied: the fact that a work is a parody with "transformative value" does not automatically make it a fair use. But he did weight transformation heavily in the analysis, writing that "the more transformative the new work, the less will be the significance of other factors, like commercialism, that may weigh against a finding of fair use."

In short, the Supreme Court said that even a commercially successful parody of a copyrighted song may be a fair use rather than a copyright infringement, depending on how the other fair use criteria are weighed and how transformative the new song is. And, as always in copyright infringement lawsuits, fair use questions must be decided on a case-by-case basis.

Parody litigation

Parody vs. satire. Another point that should be noted about "Pretty Woman" is that the Supreme Court treated the 2 Live Crew recording as a parody, as opposed to a satire. A *parody* (borrowing from a copyrighted work *to poke fun at that particular work*) is more likely to be a fair use than a *satire* (borrowing from a copyrighted work *to lampoon someone or something else* rather than the copyrighted work itself). This distinction was illustrated by a 1997 Ninth Circuit ruling against the publishers of a rhyming summary of the O.J. Simpson murder trial, using a style obviously borrowed from the classic Dr. Seuss book *The Cat in the Hat.* The court halted distribution of the new work, called *The Cat NOT in the Hat, A Parody by Dr. Juice (Dr. Seuss Enter. v. Penguin Books*, 109 F.3d 1394). Holding that *Dr. Juice* mimics but does not parody Dr. Seuss' style, the court mused, perhaps the use was "to get attention or maybe even to avoid the drudgery in working up something fresh." The work must be truly parodic, not simply a close copy, for protection. (A similar outcome with different reasoning for a Dr. Seuss–inspired book is discussed elsewhere in this chapter.)

Gone With the Wind. Another widely publicized case involving a parody—this one of a famous novel and motion picture—arose in 2001. Author Alice Randall wrote a book for Houghton Mifflin that is an African-American retelling of *Gone With the Wind*. Entitled *The Wind Done Gone*, it includes characters who closely resemble those in the Civil War classic. But it also introduced new characters, including Scarlett O'Hara's half sister—the daughter of plantation owner Gerald O'Hara (simply called "Planter" in the new novel) and a slave, thus putting a new spin on the story.

The estate of Margaret Mitchell, author of *Gone With the Wind*, sued to halt publication of the new work, contending that it was an unauthorized derivative and therefore a copyright infringement. A federal judge issued an injunction to prevent the new work's publication, but the Eleventh Circuit set it aside, saying that a work would be considered a parody "if its aim is to comment upon or criticize a prior work by appropriating elements of the original in creating a new artistic, as opposed to scholarly or journalistic, work" (*Suntrust Bank v. Houghton Mifflin Co.*, 268 F.3d 1257). That left the Mitchell estate free to pursue its lawsuit for monetary damages. The dispute was settled in 2002 when the estate agreed to drop the lawsuit in return for Randall's publisher agreement to make a donation to Morehouse College, a historically Black college in Atlanta.

The Catcher in the Rye. In 2009, J.D. Salinger got a temporary injunction against publication of an "unauthorized sequel" to his classic novel *The Catcher in the Rye.* The "sequel," *60 Years Later: Coming Through the Rye*, by "John David California" (the pen name of Fredrik Colting, living in Sweden) purports to tell the further story of Salinger's famous character, Holden Caulfield, at age 76, wandering around New York after having escaped a retirement home. Salinger alleged that the publication "is a ripoff pure and simple."

A judge agreed, saying that she did not see any criticism or comment at all in the sequel (unlike *The Wind Done Gone*) and enjoined the publication, noting that Colting's work was not sufficiently transformative. However, in 2010 the Second Circuit said that the judge had erred in issuing the preliminary injunction (*Salinger v. Colting*, 607 F.3d 68) and sent the case back for reconsideration, saying that "the district court presumed irreparable harm without discussion." Such a misapplication was understandable, the court said, because the Second Circuit's rules in this area conflicted with the Supreme Court's rules, established in a 2006 case, *eBay, Inc. v. MercExchange* (547 U.S. 388). The *eBay* case dealt with patent law, but the Second Circuit said it applied equally to copyright law. Those rules said that injunctions could be issued if (i) the plaintiff suffered irreparable injury that (ii) remedies like money wouldn't compensate, and (iii) balancing the hardships between the parties warranted a remedy in equity (from Chapter One) that (iv) wouldn't disserve the public interest.

Salinger died in 2010. He fiercely defended the character of Holden Caulfield over the years and refused offers to make a movie based on his book. In 2011, the Salinger estate settled with Colting, reluctantly permitting the sequel to be published in countries other than the United States and Canada, and there when the copyright on *Catcher in the Rye* runs out.

Fair use without a trial: "What What..." Can a court determine fair use *without* discovery and trial? The Seventh Circuit said yes in 2012, particularly when the work is a clear parody. The court took on a claim by Samwell, creator of the internet viral video "What What (In the Butt)," against *South Park's* character Butters' parody of the video. In finding for Comedy Partners, the company behind *South Park*, the court said, "When a defendant raises a fair use defense claiming his or her work is a parody, a court can often decide the merits of the claim without discovery or a trial. When the two works in this case are viewed side-by-side, the *South Park* episode is clearly a parody of the original WWITB video, providing commentary on the ridiculousness of the original video and the viral nature of certain YouTube videos" (*Brownmark Films, LLC v. Comedy Partners*, 682 F.3d 687).

Moreover, since there is no "Internet money" for the original video on YouTube, there could be no monetary damages, said the court, as Brownmark had provided no evidence "that the *South Park* parody has cut into any real market (with real, non-internet dollars) for derivative uses of the original WWITB video."

■ SELECTED FAIR USE LITIGATION

Many problems have arisen as courts have tried to apply the fair use doctrine, and particularly in the wake of *Campbell v. Acuff-Rose*. A sample of past and recent applications of the doctrine demonstrates the breadth of its interpretation by courts and juries.

Fair use and the classroom. As Congress was completing its revision of copyright law in 1976, representatives of educators, authors, and publishers met to decide what would be a fair use of copyrighted work in a classroom. Under their agreement, teachers are permitted to photocopy as much as a chapter of a book, an article from a newspaper or magazine, a short story, an essay or poem, and charts, graphs, drawings or similar materials—but only for their own use. Showing a DVD only licensed for home use, much less a pirated copy, is not a fair use. During the 1990s, another issue involving classroom copying became controversial: the use of course packages in college classes. In 1991, a federal court ruled that Kinko's Graphics, a major producer of these course packets, had to pay royalties for virtually all of the copyrighted materials (such as magazine or journal articles and book chapters) included in these custom anthologies of previously published materials (*Basic Books v. Kinko's Graphics Corp.*, 758 F.Supp. 1522). The court held that such large-scale copying was *not* a fair use. The result is that companies and college bookstores charge higher prices for course packets so royalties can be paid to each copyright owner.

In 1996, the advocates of free copying for classroom use thought they had won a great victory when a panel of the Sixth Circuit refused to follow the *Kinko's* decision in *Princeton University Press v. Michigan Document Services* (74 F.3d 1528). In this case, the court's 2-1 majority seemingly gave teachers and copying services *carte blanche* to copy magazine and journal articles as well as large parts of books for inclusion in course packets by holding that such copying is a fair use, not a copyright infringement.

Armed with this decision, many copying services geared up for a bonanza of royalty-free copying. But then the celebration ended: the full panel of judges on the Sixth Circuit voted to rehear the case *en banc* (all judges participating). The judges then voted 8-5 to overturn the earlier decision and ruled that large-scale copying for course packets is an infringement, not a fair use (*Princeton Univ. Press v. Michigan Document Serv.*, 99 F.3d 1381).

Another fair use question concerns photocopying by libraries. The Copyright Act is rather specific about this because an important court decision had allowed wholesale reproduction of copyrighted works by libraries—something Congress wished to curtail. That case (*Williams & Wilkins v. U.S.*, 487 F.2d 1345) was initiated by a publishing house whose medical journals were being photocopied on a massive scale by federally funded medical libraries so the libraries could avoid purchasing additional copies. The publishing house lost: in 1973 a federal court said the dissemination of medical knowledge was so important that this copying was a fair use. The case was appealed to the Supreme Court, but because the high court divided 4-4 (with one justice not participating), the judgment of the lower court stood.

Alarmed at the *Williams & Wilkins* case, publishers got another compromise from Congress, with rules for photocopying by libraries spelled out in considerable detail. Basically, the law now says it is a fair use for a librarian to make copies of damaged or deteriorating works that cannot be replaced at a reasonable cost, and to provide single copies to those who request them, provided the request is for only a small portion of a work. An entire work that cannot be purchased at a reasonable price may also be copied at a patron's request.

These rules contain other qualifications and restrictions that will not be summarized here. Significantly, however, they apply only to copying done by library staff members, not copying by members of the public who use coin-operated machines. The Copyright Act exempts librarians from liability for copyright infringements by unsupervised library patrons, as long as a warning about infringements is posted near the self-service copy machine.

Obviously, the law on photocopying was written in this fashion in tacit recognition that there is simply no way to prevent private individuals from engaging in coin-operated infringements—just as there is no way to prevent private audio or videotaping of copyrighted broadcast materials (a separate problem discussed elsewhere).

Fair use continues to be an issue with university reserves. In a whopping 350-page decision, a federal district court said that only 5 of 99 alleged infringements by Georgia State University in its electronic reserves violated the plaintiffs' copyrights. The judge said in *Cambridge Univ. Press v. Becker* (863 F. Supp. 2d 1190, 2012) that the plaintiffs, Cambridge University Press, Oxford University Press, and SAGE Publications, had not demonstrated that they lost significant amounts of money from the electronic reserves after engaging in a case-by-case evaluation of all alleged infringements. The court acknowledged what teachers, scholars, and others who wish to use copyrighted materials already know: fair use principles are notoriously difficult to apply.

In the classroom: Turnitin. If you have ever been asked to submit a paper to Turnitin.com for evaluation of plagiarism, the Fourth Circuit has said that you have no infringement claim against its owner, iParadigms, if your paper is kept and added to the anti-plagiarism database. In *A.V. v. iParadigms LLC* (562 F.3d 630, 2009), the court applied the four-part fair use test and said that iParadigm's use of students' work is transformative and unconnected to any creative elements in the work. Moreover, the fact that iParadigms makes money with this use does not affect the students' abilities to sell their unpublished works, even to so-called "paper mills" for resale—iParadigms does not replace these paper mills; it simply suppresses demand for them. Thus, iParadigms' use of student work is a fair use.

Fair use and appropriation art. Appropriation art uses existing art to comment on or criticize society, like Andy Warhol's Campbell Soup Can art and his famous portraits of Marilyn Monroe. In a broad interpretation of the fair use doctrine and the transformation principle as applied to appropriation artwork, the Second Circuit in 2013 overturned a narrow interpretation of fair use in *Cariou v. Prince* (714 F.3d 694). Richard Prince, an appropriation artist, used parts of Patrick Cariou's book *Yes Rasta*, a study of Jamaican Rastafarians, in his work, *Canal Zone*. Prince cut up images from *Yes Rasta* and pasted them onto other images and painted over them. The *Canal Zone* works were shown in a gallery; this association caused Cariou to lose a gallery show, and he sued. The district court said that Prince's were not fair uses. But the Second Circuit overturned, saying, "The law imposes no requirement that a work comment on the original or its author in order to be considered transformative, and a secondary work may constitute a fair use even if it serves some purpose other than those (criticism, comment, news reporting, teaching, scholarship, and research) identified in the preamble to the statute." The court, in finding that 25 of the 30 alleged infringements were fair uses, focused instead on "how the artworks may 'reasonably be perceived' in order to assess their transformative nature."

In another Second Circuit appropriation art case, the court in 2021 found that pop artist Warhol had infringed the copyright of a photographer in one of her images of the artist Prince (*Andy Warhol Found. for the Visual Arts, Inc. v. Goldsmith*, 992 F.3d 99). Photographer Linda Goldsmith took black-and-white photos of Prince in 1981, and the magazine *Vanity Fair* licensed one photo as an "artistic reference" for Warhol's use to "create a work of art based on [the] image reference." Warhol created an image of Prince that appeared in the Nov. 1984 issue of *Vanity Fair*—an image strikingly similar to Goldsmith's photo. When Goldsmith became aware of the Warhol piece, after Prince's 2016 death, she sued.

Infringement or fair use? The district court said it was a fair use, a transformation of the photo by Warhol into a new work. However, the Second Circuit disagreed. Calling the Warhol piece "substantially similar" to Goldsmith's photo as a matter of law, the court said that the addition of "a new aesthetic or new expression to its source material" doesn't necessarily make a secondary work transformative. But it's not over: this case came down a mere 10 days before the Supreme Court released a significant fair use interpretation in *Google v. Oracle*. That decision caused the Andy Warhol Foundation to quickly challenge the Second Circuit's finding of infringement. On the foundation's petition for rehearing, the court asked Goldsmith to provide a brief describing "what impact, if any, [*Oracle*] may have on the appropriate disposition of the appeal." Stay tuned.

Fair use and the public "right to know." One of the most important involves the conflict between copyright law and the public's right to know. Several court decisions have addressed these questions. One of the best-known of these cases came from the Second Circuit in 1966, *Rosemont Enterprises v. Random House* (366 F.2d 303). In that case, Rosemont (a company set up by billionaire industrialist Howard Hughes) was trying to prevent publication of a biography about Hughes, who intensely disliked publicity. Rosemont learned that the biographer was relying heavily on information from several old *Look* magazine articles. The company quickly bought the copyright on those articles and then sought an injunction to prevent publication of the biography as an infringement of the copyrighted articles.

A trial court ruled in Rosemont's favor, but the Second Circuit reversed that decision, holding that a copyright owner has no right to, in effect, copyright history. The appellate court noted that the magazine articles were only a fraction of the length of the book and that there had been extensive independent research for the book. The court brushed aside the argument that the book, like the original copyrighted magazine articles, was aimed at a popular market and was not merely an instance of scholarly criticism (something that earlier court decisions had recognized as a fair use).

Ultimately, the appellate court ruled that there is a legitimate public interest in the doings of the rich and powerful, and that this interest outweighs the copyright consideration in a case such as this one. Random House was allowed to publish its book about Howard Hughes without incurring liability for a copyright infringement.

Right to know: The Zapruder film. Another fair use case involving an issue of even greater public interest arose a few years later (*Time Inc. v. Bernard Geis Assoc.*, 293 F.Supp. 130, 1968). That case involved amateur photographer Abraham Zapruder's film of the assassination of President John F. Kennedy in 1963—"the most important 26 seconds of film in history." The highly unusual and revealing film was purchased by Time Inc., and published in *Life* magazine. Of course, it was copyrighted.

Later, author Thomas Thompson was publishing a book advocating a new theory about the assassination, *Six Seconds in Dallas*. Bernard Geis, the publisher, offered to pay *Life* a royalty equal to the entire net profits from the book in return for permission to use *Life's* still photographs made from the copyrighted film, which was central to Thompson's theory. *Life* refused. The book publisher then hired an artist to make charcoal sketches from the copyrighted photographs, and these appeared in the book. Time Inc. sued for copyright infringement. The federal court said the use of charcoal drawings instead of the photographs themselves did not eliminate the copyright infringement, but the court also pointed to the legitimate public interest in the assassination of a president and said this was a fair use of the copyrighted pictures. To rule otherwise would prevent a full public discussion of the controversial issues raised by President Kennedy's assassination.

In 1992, the Assassination Records Review Board declared the Zapruder film to be U.S. government property and an arbitration panel ordered the government to pay Zapruder's heirs $16 million for the film in 1999. Critics said that sum was outrageous, especially since the government was buying only the physical film, not its copyright. The copyright eventually reverted to the Zapruder family, which has since donated it to the Sixth Floor Museum in Dallas. The original footage, said to be too fragile to be run through a projector, is housed at the National Archives.

Right to know: "I Have A Dream" speech. A somewhat similar copyright dispute arose in the late 1990s, when the estate of Dr. Martin Luther King, Jr. sued CBS for using 9 minutes of Dr. King's famous 16-minute-long "I Have a Dream" speech in a documentary history of the twentieth century. The estate contended that CBS was guilty of copyright infringement for including the segment. CBS responded by arguing that the speech, which was heard live by an enormous audience and has been quoted widely ever since it was delivered in 1963, is such an important public event that no one should be able to prevent others from using it for journalistic purposes. However, a federal appellate court overturned a judge's decision to dismiss the lawsuit and said the King estate could pursue its claim against the network (*Estate of Martin Luther King v. CBS*, 194 F.3d 1211). The network settled the case by agreeing to make a donation to the Martin Luther King Center.

Fair use and unpublished works. Journalists, historians, and others with an interest in the unpublished works of the famous became more alarmed when federal appellate courts began expanding on the *Harper & Row* ruling to limit the right to quote from the unpublished works of famous people. Among the most controversial of these cases involved the works of the late L. Ron Hubbard, founder of the Church of Scientology. In that case, *New Era Publ'ns v. Henry Holt & Co.* (873 F.2d 576, 1989), the court allowed a firm affiliated with Scientology to prevent the use of 41 unpublished writings of Hubbard in Russell Miller's biography, *Bare-Faced Messiah*. The biography offended Scientologists by portraying Hubbard as a bizarre and sometimes dishonest messianic figure—and quoted his own correspondence with government agencies to back up those charges. By ruling that those quotations were not protected by the fair use doctrine, the court in effect allowed Scientologists to censor an unflattering portrayal of Hubbard.

Copyright Act amendment supporting use of unpublished works. Organizations representing book publishers, historians, and journalists began urging Congress to amend the Copyright Act to re-legalize the use of quotations from the unpublished works of important historical figures. After several years of discussion—and several appellate court decisions—many journalists and scholars were even more uncertain of when they could and couldn't quote the unpublished writings of famous persons. In 1992, Congress responded to this problem by adding this sentence to the Copyright Act: "The fact that a work is unpublished shall not itself bar a finding of fair use if such finding is made upon consideration of all the above factors" (i.e., the four-part test that is used to determine whether the fair use doctrine applies). The purpose of this language was to overcome the uncertainty among journalists and scholars by confirming that the fair use doctrine does indeed apply to unpublished works when the four-part test is met. Given this message from Congress, courts have been more sympathetic to the use of quotations from the unpublished works of the famous by journalists and scholars in recent years.

Fair use, news, and clipping services. Another controversial application of the fair use doctrine has involved *video clipping services*—businesses that make videotapes (now, digital copies) of television news and public affairs programs for sale to individuals and organizations that are mentioned on TV. The idea of a clipping service is nothing new: for years newspaper clipping services have monitored the print media for stories that mention their clients. Originally, these firms literally clipped stories from newspapers and sent them to public relations practitioners and others who needed to see what the media were saying about them or their clients.

Modern clipping services monitor mass media outlets for mentions of their clients, copying physical and digital publications as well as video mentions, social media coverage, and more, for their customers. During the 1980s, the video clipping business enjoyed enormous growth. Everyone from prominent politicians to the Library of Congress used video clipping services to keep track of television news coverage. As a result, several video clipping services that started out as small businesses in somebody's basement mushroomed into million-dollar operations. The growth of the video clipping industry led to lawsuits by TV stations objecting to someone else taping their material, repackaging it, and selling it for a profit. In the early 1990s, several federal courts ruled that video clipping services are not protected by the fair use doctrine—they are guilty of copyright infringement.

Focus on...
Sampling music: The Amen Break

It's been called the most important six seconds in modern music, and even if you don't know its name, you've doubtless heard it. Dubbed the "Amen Break," by 2020 the four-bar drum solo has been sampled over 4,500 times by artists as diverse as Salt 'N Pepa, David Bowie, Slipknot, and Oasis.

FIG. 59. Drum notation for the Amen break.

忍者猫, *"Notation for the Amen break notated as tab in the article Amen break," Wikimedia Commons, May 20, 2021.*

The break appeared in the song "Amen, Brother," the B-side of the single "Color Him Father," a 1969 Grammy-winning single by R&B band The Winstons. Drummer Gregory Coleman added the solo to pad the length of the song. The break consists of a two-bar repeat, followed by a snare and the syncopated crash of a cymbal. When sampling became a trend for rap and hiphop artists in the 1980s, the break appeared on a compilation album entitled *Ultimate Breaks and Beats*, where it took off. Most commentators trace the earliest sampling of the Amen Break to Salt 'N Pepa's use in "I Desire" in 1986.

Sampling law was murky in the 1980s; it wasn't clear whether or how permission should be gotten for sampled works. As a result, neither Coleman nor any other member of The Winstons got a dime for the multiple uses of the break. The Winstons, a mixed-race group, found it difficult to get bookings or advertising and disbanded; Coleman died homeless in 2006, and lead singer Richard Spencer left the music business and became a teacher and writer. In 2015, two British DJs created a GoFundMe campaign for donations to Spencer, the owner of the copyright, raising £24,000 (over $33,000). Spencer died in December 2020. Want to learn more? Check out Nate Harrison's 2004 brief but elegant documentary on YouTube, entitled *Can I Get An Amen?*

After several defeats in court, video clipping services sought legislation to exempt them from copyright liability. Although many members of Congress used video clipping services themselves and were sympathetic, key Congressional leaders did what they often do when someone asks Congress to intervene in a dispute between two industries: they urged broadcasters and video clipping services to try to resolve their differences privately. The major networks and local stations eventually authorized the clipping services to use their newscasts in return for relatively modest license fees.

A related controversy has arisen from the wholesale use of video news footage by competing news organizations. Whenever one station or network comes up with a particularly powerful video segment, everyone else rushes to get it on the air—and worries about copyright permissions later. The celebrated amateur video of the Rodney King assault by Los Angeles police officers is a prime example. George Holliday, the man who made the King video, granted one Los Angeles station (KTLA) permission to use the video—under terms later hotly disputed—but the video quickly appeared on stations and networks around the world. Holliday filed a copyright infringement lawsuit. A federal judge dismissed Holliday's lawsuit in 1993, saying that Holliday gave KTLA permission to use the tape and release it to other media outlets, and the consent precluded later infringement claims. Moreover, the use of his tape fell within the fair use doctrine, and the First Amendment permits public airing of certain works "of great importance to democratic debate."

However, the Ninth Circuit alarmed many broadcast journalists by ruling in 1997 that the fair use doctrine may *not* necessarily cover the use of another highly newsworthy video that was taken from a helicopter during the riots that occurred in Los Angeles after the first trial and acquittal of the officers who beat King. In *Los Angeles News Service v. KCAL-TV Channel 9* (108 F.3d 1119), the appellate court overturned a trial court's dismissal of a lawsuit stemming from the unauthorized use of video of the beating of Reginald Denny, a white truck driver, by Black youths at the beginning of the riots.

The video was taken by Los Angeles News Service (LANS) and provided to several stations, but LANS refused to authorize KCAL-TV to broadcast the tape. KCAL obtained the tape from another station and aired it without LANS' consent. When LANS sued for copyright infringement, KCAL argued that the riots were so newsworthy that the fair use doctrine would permit the use of the tape. However, the appellate court held that other fair use factors besides newsworthiness had to be considered, including the economic effect of KCAL's use of the tape. To weigh all of these factors, a full trial would be needed, the court ruled. Under the *KCAL* decision, broadcast journalists who use even highly newsworthy video footage on the air without first obtaining a copyright clearance may risk a lawsuit.

In a related decision a year later, the Ninth Circuit held that LANS could recover damages from overseas use of the Denny video because it was copied illegally in the United States (*Los Angeles News Service v. Reuters Television*, 149 F.3d 987). However, in 2002 the same court held that use of a few seconds of the Denny video by Court TV *was* a fair use, noting the brevity of the segment used as well as the fact that Court TV used it not as news coverage of the beating in competition with the copyright owner but rather to promote its coverage of the later trial of the accused (*Los Angeles News Service v. CBS Broadcasting*, 305 F.3d 924).

Online "scraping." Is an online news "scraping" service like a search engine or a traditional clipping service—and is it fair use or a copyright infringement? A federal judge rejected scraper Meltwater's claims that it was a search engine, searching the internet for articles of interests to its clients. Meltwater claimed that this use was transformative and made its use of AP's and other news articles a fair use. The judge performed a very thorough fair use analysis and concluded that "Meltwater News is an expensive subscription service that markets itself as a news clipping service, not as a publicly available tool to improve access to content across the Internet." It is not public, thus not like Google or other search engines that are available to anyone (*Assoc. Press v. Meltwater U.S. Holdings* (931 F. Supp. 2d 537, 2013).

But what about scraping of public data? Two circuits have weighed in. The Ninth Circuit found in favor of scraper hiQ Labs in 2019 (*hiQ Labs, Inc. v. LinkedIn Corp.*, 938 F. 3d 985). LinkedIn authorized hiQ to gather data but then withdrew the permission, citing privacy concerns and the Computer Fraud and Abuse Act (CFAA, discussed in Chapter Eleven), and hiQ sought to enjoin LinkedIn from stopping it. A district court granted the injunction; the Ninth Circuit affirmed. The court noted not only that LinkedIn's perspectives about user privacy were inconsistent—it had expressed its own intent to leverage user data—but that LinkedIn doesn't own its users' data: "LinkedIn has no protected property interest in the data contributed by its users, as the users retain ownership over their profiles. And as to the publicly available profiles, the users quite evidently intend them to be accessed by others, including for commercial purposes."

However, the Eleventh Circuit in 2020 said that similar scraping may be a *trade secret* violation (*Compulife Software, Inc. v. Newman*, 959 F.3d 1288). Newman used an automated technique to scrape data from Compulife's public database (a trade secret), and that, said the court, might violate Florida law forbidding acquisition of trade secrets by "improper means." As the case wasn't brought using the CFAA, the usual law invoked to challenge scraping, it may be an important precedent for future cases.

Fair use and advertising. May a company show a competitor's copyrighted material to do comparison advertising? Is that a fair use or a copyright infringement? By 2000, two different federal appellate courts had addressed this issue, and both held that a competitor's material may indeed be used in comparison advertising. In *Sony Computer Entm't v. Bleem* (214 F.3d 1022), the Ninth Circuit held that Bleem, a videogame producer, could display screenshots from games played on the Sony PlayStation video console in an attempt to show that its software is superior to Sony's.

In the *Bleem* case, the court ruled that a competitor may use single-frame screenshots for comparative advertising. The court did not grant Bleem a free hand to use computer-generated simulations of the TV screen; the holding was limited to actual single-frame photographs of Sony's games taken from a TV screen. In weighing the four factors that determine whether a particular use of a copyrighted work is a fair use or an infringement, the court concluded that all four factors favored Bleem's use of Sony's screen images. The Fifth Circuit ruled similarly in *Triangle Publications v. Knight-Ridder Newspapers* (626 F.2d 1171, 1980), allowing a newspaper to display the cover of *TV Guide* to compare its own TV program magazine with the national publication.

◼ COPYRIGHTS AND MUSIC LICENSING

Mass communicators are finding themselves increasingly involved in the copyright problems of the music industry, whether they want to be or not. As indicated earlier, there is *compulsory licensing* in the music field, which means anyone can record copyrighted music by merely paying a specified royalty for each CD or tape sold. Also, once a song is recorded, anyone can play the recording without paying the recording artist for *performance rights*: the Copyright Act does not give recording artists the right to collect royalties for "performances" that consist of merely playing their *sound recordings* privately (with a notable exception, explained later). However, the law does recognize performance rights in the underlying music and lyrics that are used in a sound recording. So broadcasters have to pay for the right to play copyrighted music on the air, but the money goes only to composers and music publishers, not to recording artists and record companies (unless they also hold the copyrights to the underlying music and lyrics). Business establishments that play music often pay royalties to composers and music publishers but not to recording artists for the same reason.

How can a composer or music publisher ever keep track of all the different radio stations and nightclubs, for instance, that are using his or her copyrighted material? Wouldn't it be impossible to monitor every single radio station, let alone visit every club?

Performing rights organizations. To solve that practical problem, several music licensing organizations have been established to represent composers, lyricists, and music publishers. The most important ones in the United States are the American Society of Composers, Authors and Publishers (ASCAP) and Broadcast Music Inc. (BMI). Using sampling techniques, both organizations keep track of whose music is being played on the air—and collect money for the copyright owners that they represent. Both ASCAP and BMI sell most broadcasters (and other users of copyrighted music) *blanket licenses* that allow them to use all of the music whose copyright owners are represented by ASCAP or BMI. (As noted earlier, some stations find it less expensive to purchase *per-program licenses* instead.) Altogether, ASCAP and BMI control the copyrights to some 10 million songs and collect more than $300 million a year from broadcasters for the right to *perform* these songs by playing them over the air. They collect millions more for non-broadcast uses of copyrighted music. While ASCAP and BMI dominate the U.S. music licensing business, a third licensing organization, the Society of European Stage Authors and Composers (SESAC), has been seeking to increase its share of the American licensing business—and signed up several well-known copyright owners as clients. The International Confederation of Societies of Authors and Composers, in France, coordinates international music licensing by members in about 100 countries.

ASCAP, BMI, and SESAC grant licenses only for the *performance* of copyrighted music, including live performances and playing recorded music. Those who wish to make their own recordings or include copyrighted music in a video production must obtain separate *synchronization* or *mechanical licenses* from the Harry Fox Agency, established by the National Music Publishers Association to coordinate this licensing; Harry Fox also works with the Mechanical Licensing Collective (discussed below). All these organizations have websites that explain which uses of copyrighted music fall within the jurisdiction of each.

Given the large amount of money involved, there are recurring disputes (and lawsuits) over the collection and distribution of royalties for copyrighted music. But in the end, most broadcasters and other users of copyrighted music have little choice but to pay up: music is essential to their programming, and ASCAP and BMI between them control the performance rights to the vast majority of copyrighted music.

Blanket licenses. ASCAP and BMI send representatives out to collect royalties from the owners of nightclubs and other business establishments where copyrighted music is played or performed. The performing rights organizations have formulas based on such things as the size of the establishment and its business volume to determine the amount that each business has to pay for its blanket license. Even non-profit organizations such as schools and churches are required to pay royalties for certain uses of copyrighted music, although some uses of music in classrooms and at "services at a place of worship" are exempt under Section 110 of the Copyright Act. The National Association for Music Education maintains a website (nafme.org) with more information about classroom uses of copyrighted music.

ASCAP and BMI both charge radio stations flat fees for blanket licenses. Music licensing costs most stations about 3% of their net revenues after deductions. Stations buying only per-program licenses pay a higher rate, but only for the times when music is played. There are separate fee schedules for bars and concert halls, among other venues.

SoundExchange. Created as part of the Recording Industry Association of America in 2000 and then spun off as a nonprofit organization of the Copyright Royalty Board in 2003, SoundExchange collects and distributes royalties on behalf of recording artists, independent artists, and owners of master rights from webcasters, satellite and digital cable television, and satellite radio services. It also has agreements rights with international rights-management organizations, enabling it to gather royalties from 80% of the world's music markets; as of 2020, it had paid out $7 billion in royalty distributions.

SoundExchange also engages in royalty rate-setting activities and negotiations. Every five years, the Copyright Royalty Board sets standard royalties that *non-interactive services* (where listeners just listen, as opposed to *interactive services* that allow user interaction, like Pandora and Spotify, also discussed elsewhere) must pay to play recordings online, and lawsuits are sometimes filed by SoundExchange and others challenging that standard royalty.

Sampling. In this era of digital technology, it has become increasingly commonplace for artists to sample the work of others in their new recordings. In a 2003 decision involving the punk-rap group the Beastie Boys, the Ninth Circuit held that the group's use of a six-second, four-note excerpt did not infringe the copyright on a musical composition. The group paid a license fee to sample the six seconds of a *recording* by jazz flutist James Newton, but didn't pay to use the *underlying composition* (*Newton v. Diamond*, 388 F.3d 1189). The Supreme Court declined to hear an appeal of this decision, although many in the music industry think the high court needs to clarify when it's okay to sample someone else's copyrighted work. See a discussion of a famous drumbeat sample, the Amen Break, elsewhere in this chapter.

Music Modernization Act. An attempt by Congress to smooth the process of handling licenses and royalties for covers and sampled work, the Music Modernization Act was signed by President Trump in 2018 to create a new system for royalty distribution for music and audio creators; this new approach was necessary due to new technologies and digital streaming services. Under the act, the Mechanical Licensing Collective (The MLC), a nonprofit agency, will establish a database of owners of the mechanical licenses of sound recordings (composition and lyrics copyrights), set blanket royalty rates under a compulsory license for various copyright holders as well as collect and distribute these royalties, and manage disputes. It was supported by digital streaming services and leaders of the recording industry.

As of Jan. 1, 2021, songwriters and music publishers must register online with The MLC to receive royalties. The MMA also creates a public performance right for works recorded prior to 1972 which were not previously protected under federal copyright law (the Compensating Legacy Artists for their Songs, Service, and Important Contributions to Society Act, or CLASSICS Act), protecting them until 2067, and permits SoundExchange to directly pay record producers. In Feb. 2021, 20 digital service providers paid a total of $424.38 million to The MLC for *unmatched royalties* (royalties for which a copyright holder cannot be identified) along with a massive number of records. The MLC will examine those records to determine who should be paid and how much. The biggest checks came from Apple Music ($163.34 million) and Spotify ($153.23 million).

Why is sampling (or parodies, for that matter) not permitted automatically under the compulsory licensing provision of the Copyright Act? That provision allows anyone who pays the prescribed royalties to record a copyrighted song; it does *not* permit major revisions and adaptations without the consent of the copyright owner.

Music in retail stores. Should store or restaurant owners have to pay royalties for merely playing a radio in their establishments? For many years, the legal rule was that all but the smallest stores had to pay royalties if a radio was turned on. The Supreme Court ruled that very small stores that played a "homestyle" radio were exempt from royalties (*Twentieth Century Music Corp. v. Aiken*, 422 U.S. 151, 1975, involving a fast-food chicken shop with 1,055 square feet of total floor space). But the Second Circuit said this exemption did *not* apply to a chain of large clothing stores with radios hooked up to commercial-quality sound systems (*Sailor Music v. The Gap Stores*, 668 F.2d 84, 1981). Based on that case, ASCAP and BMI demanded royalties from virtually all retail chains and from individual stores larger than 1,055 square feet of floor space.

In 1991, however, two federal appellate courts ruled that large chains of retail stores are exempt from royalties if each store has no more than one homestyle radio playing, with small home speakers placed nearby. *BMI v. Claire's Boutiques* (949 F.2d 1482) involved a chain of 749 stores, mostly smaller than 1,000 square feet. Each store had a small radio and two speakers from Radio Shack. BMI contended that all stores in the chain had to be counted together, so Claire's was really playing 700 radios, not one radio as permitted by copyright law. The Seventh Circuit didn't buy that argument and ruled that each store should be counted separately. Even the larger stores in the Claire's Boutiques chain were ruled to be exempt from paying royalties as long as they had only one radio and two speakers.

In 1992, the Eighth Circuit went even further. In *Edison Brothers Stores v. BMI* (954 F.2d 1419), the court ruled that the size of the store isn't a crucial factor. The court held that this major retail chain, whose stores average 2,000 square feet, is exempt from paying royalties as long as each store plays a homestyle radio with speakers in or near the radio (as opposed to a commercial sound system with many speakers in the ceiling).

BMI appealed both cases to the Supreme Court. But the Court declined to take up either case. The result: it was perfectly legal for a store owner to play a homestyle radio with a couple of speakers without paying royalties. That is still often true, but not always.

A compromise: Fairness in Music Licensing Act. After years of debate about this issue, Congress passed the Fairness in Music Licensing Act in 1998. Expanding on the two *BMI* court decisions, this law exempted small retail establishments, restaurants, and bars from paying royalties for playing copyrighted music on radio or TV sets in their establishments. As a compromise between the business community and copyright owners, retail businesses smaller than 2,000 square feet and restaurants and bars smaller than 3,750 square feet were exempted from paying royalties if all they do is play homestyle radio or TV sets. Larger businesses qualify for the exemption if they have no more than four TV sets or six speakers.

However, these rules apply only to the reception of *broadcast music*. Business owners are not exempt from paying copyright royalties for the use of recorded or live music. To collect the royalties, ASCAP and BMI filed numerous lawsuits against retail stores and club owners who are using copyrighted music but refuse to obtain licenses. Rather than pay royalties directly, many business establishments instead buy a canned music service, which provides music for a flat fee that includes the cost of royalty payments.

Once ASCAP, BMI, and other licensing agencies have collected the royalties from broadcasters, owners of business establishments, and others, the money is distributed to copyright owners on the basis of formulas that account for the amount of air time each owner's material has been receiving. It is assumed that each song's popularity in nightclubs and other businesses like retail stores parallels the song's popularity on the nation's radio stations.

■ CABLE TELEVISION COPYRIGHT PROBLEMS

Another major feature of the 1976 Copyright Act is a section dealing with the special problems created by cable television systems. In fact, one of the major reasons Congress finally passed the 1976 Copyright Act after years of stalemated deliberations was a pair of U.S. Supreme Court decisions on cable television and copyright law.

In the 1968 case of *Fortnightly v. United Artists* (392 U.S. 390), the Supreme Court had ruled that a cable television system is really nothing more than a sophisticated receiving antenna. Thus, cable systems—or community antenna television (CATV) systems, as they were then called—were not "performing" the copyrighted programming they picked up off the air, amplified, and delivered to their subscribers' homes for a fee. In so ruling, the Court exempted CATV systems from any obligation to pay royalties.

Then in a 1974 decision, *Teleprompter v. CBS* (415 U.S. 394), the Court went even further. It held that CATV systems were still not performing the programming even if they retransmitted it over great distances via microwave relay. Only if they copied and replayed the material rather than delivering it "live" would they be liable to pay royalties, the Court ruled.

Alarmed by these two Supreme Court decisions, motion picture and television producers, broadcasters, and others with a stake in the protection of copyrighted works banded together and began lobbying Congress for legislation to establish copyright royalties for cable television systems. They prevailed, and the 1976 Copyright Act was written to require cable systems to pay royalties for all distant television stations they import. The 1976 law did not require cable systems to pay royalties for picking up local television and radio signals and delivering them to their subscribers' homes. However, as Chapter Eleven explains, the 1992 Cable Television Consumer Protection and Competition Act allows broadcasters to demand compensation from local cable operators for the use of their copyrighted programming.

The royalties that cable and satellite systems, and now internet broadcasters, pay to copyright owners are determined by an entity within the Copyright Office, the Copyright Royalty Board (the same one that works with SoundExchange in music). This board replaced the Copyright Arbitration Royalty Panels that were used to set royalty rates for many years.

Another broadcast copyright issue became controversial in the late 1990s—"white areas" where TV signals cannot be received over the air. The major TV networks and local stations filed infringement lawsuits against satellite providers for signing up customers for network programming in communities that weren't "white areas" but easily within range of local stations. For a time, satellite subscribers had to get permission from their local stations to receive network TV via satellite—a request that was not often granted: most local stations didn't want to lose viewers.

Finally Congress intervened in 1999, passing the Satellite Television Home Viewers Act. This law authorized satellite providers to deliver local TV stations to subscribers in each station's service area if they paid royalties to the stations, enabling satellite services to compete on an equal basis with cable for the first time. Their inability to carry local TV stations had handicapped them in their competition with cable. But this law created another kind of unfairness, broadcasters said. Most had not been able to negotiate cash payments from cable systems under retransmission consent (see Chapter Eleven). Armed with the new rules giving them royalties from satellite TV services, they attempted to win payments for the use of their signals from cable systems as well—with mixed success. See also discussions in Chapter Eleven on the government's attempts to define a cable company, as well as *Cartoon Network and CNN v. CSC Holdings (Cablevision)*, a case on copyrights and cable on-demand service and the *ivi*, *Aereo*, and Aereokiller cases that depend on *Cablevision*.

■ RECORDING TECHNOLOGIES AND COPYRIGHT LAW

While cable and satellite interests, broadcasters, and program producers were battling in Congress, another equally intense battle over copyright protection was waged on Capitol Hill: the fight over copyrights and new technologies, such as home video and audio tape (and now DVR) recording and the exchange of copyrighted materials online. And like the cable copyright dilemma, some of these battles over copyright protection were triggered by a controversial Supreme Court decision.

When video cassette recorders (VCRs) began to gain popularity in the late 1970s, movie and TV producers became alarmed by the ease with which the public could tape programs off the air for later viewing. The producers saw the sale of home videotapes as a lucrative new market, and they felt that market would be jeopardized if consumers could simply tape movies and TV shows off the air for free.

In a landmark Supreme Court decision, the justices ruled in 1984 that home videotaping is *not* necessarily a copyright infringement. In *Sony Corp. of Am. v. Universal City Studios* (464 U.S. 417), sometimes called the "Betamax case," the Court split 5-4 in ruling in favor of the estimated 20 million Americans who had VCRs in their homes by then.

Time shifting. Writing for the majority, Justice John Paul Stevens pointed out that nothing in the Copyright Act specifically prohibits consumers from taping TV shows for later viewing, a practice commonly called "time shifting." Instead, such noncommercial videotaping is a fair use of copyrighted programming, Stevens wrote in his majority opinion:

> One may search the Copyright Act in vain for any sign that the elected representatives of millions of people who watch television every day have made it unlawful to copy a program for later viewing at home, or have enacted a flat prohibition against the sale of machines that make such copying possible.

Forecasting the legislative battle he knew would follow the decision, Stevens conceded that Congress could "take a fresh look at this new technology just as it so often has examined other innovations in the past. But it is not our job to apply laws that have not yet been written," he added. In so ruling, the justices reversed a federal appellate court decision that held private at-home videotaping to be a copyright infringement. The lower court suggested that a flat royalty fee could be added to the price of each blank tape and each video recorder to compensate the entertainment industry for the copying that consumers would do. Critics of the lower court decision pointed out that not all VCRs and blank tapes were used to tape copyrighted TV shows, so a blanket royalty would force many VCR owners to pay for copyright infringements they didn't commit.

The Supreme Court's majority was clearly influenced by the fact that some uses of VCRs are clearly *not* copyright infringements. In fact, Justice Stevens noted that the television production community itself was divided on home videotaping: children's television host Fred Rogers had made it clear that he *wanted* those who could not view *Mr. Rogers' Neighborhood* at its scheduled time to tape it for later viewing. So noncommercial use of VCRs and other technology for time shifting is still a legal fair use. However, copying rented movies and keeping them indefinitely isn't a fair use under *Sony*, nor was any non-home use of off-air videotapes. Eventually the Supreme Court ruled that the *Sony* precedent does not protect some new digital technologies. That decision, *MGM v. Grokster*, is discussed later.

■ COMPUTERS, THE INTERNET, AND COPYRIGHT LAWS

The mushrooming growth of the personal computer business created many copyright dilemmas—problems involving both computer software and the internet. When Congress enacted the 1976 Copyright Act, personal computers were primitive gadgets being built by a handful of hobbyists. Only a few years later, millions of personal computers had been sold to the general public, and copyrighted computer software, music, and movies were being traded openly at almost every high school in America.

Several legal questions have become controversial, including the protection of software copyrights, problems of digital copying and copy-protection, and questions of sharing copyrighted files over the internet (particularly music and movies). There are also legal issues regarding internet broadcasting, streaming, and podcasting, and problems that arise when publishers began placing their printed materials online.

Copyright Law and Computer Software

Like movies, music, and TV shows, computer software has been copied by consumers on an enormous scale, prompting copyright owners to look for new ways to control what they see as a flagrant copyright infringement by the public. Moreover, several leading computer hardware and software companies waged a long—and ultimately unsuccessful—legal battle to keep competitors from making products that had a "look and feel" similar to theirs.

At first, it was not clear that certain types of computer software could even be copyrighted. Software is a complex pattern of binary numbers (ones and zeros) stored inside an electronic component known as a "read-only memory" (ROM) chip. Because these operating instructions for computers are readable only by the machines themselves and not by humans, some copyright experts questioned whether they could even be covered by copyright law (as opposed to patent law, which is normally what protects the designs of electronic and mechanical devices from infringement). But, since securing a patent is a difficult and time-consuming process, while registering a copyright is easy, computer manufacturers wanted to copyright rather than patent their software.

What brought this esoteric legal dilemma into focus was the appearance of the Apple II computer in the late 1970s for which thousands of programs were written. Few people questioned the rightness of extending copyright protection to these "application programs" that made it possible to play video games, do word processing, or solve complex math problems on a personal computer. However, the Franklin Computer Company began making "Apple-compatible" computers that used a basic operating system so similar to the Apple II operating system that the Franklin Ace computers would run programs written for the Apple.

Franklin was followed by other companies manufacturing compatible computers. Since some of these competing computers sold for less than half the price of an Apple, Apple began an aggressive legal campaign to halt the sale of Apple-compatible computers.

Are operating systems copyrightable? The legal rationale for Apple's campaign was that its operating system (OS) was a legitimately copyrighted product that no one else could duplicate without permission. Franklin and others pointed out that copyright law had not previously covered "useful devices" like a ROM chip containing computer code. To apply the Copyright Act to such things would be like letting General Motors copyright the designs of the parts in its cars so no one else could make tires or carburetors that would fit on GM cars. Such things should be patented if they are really novel inventions, but if they are not novel enough to be patented, competitors should be free to copy the designs without fear of a lawsuit, Franklin and other Apple-compatible computer makers argued.

Two federal appellate court decisions gave decisive copyright victories to Apple. In *Apple Computer Inc. v. Franklin Computer Corp.* (714 F.2d. 1240), the Third Circuit in 1983 upheld the validity of Apple's OS copyright. The judge rejected the argument that a pattern of ones and zeros in a computer chip was not copyrightable, adding that copyright protection "is not confined to literature in the nature of Hemingway's *For Whom the Bell Tolls.*" The Ninth Circuit agreed in a 1984 case, *Apple Computer Inc. v. Formula Internat'l* (725 F.2d 521).

"Look and feel." Later, Apple took aggressive steps to keep others from making software that looked and operated like the software used on the Macintosh line of personal computers.

In 1988, Apple sued Microsoft Corp. and Hewlett-Packard Co.—two major producers of competing computer software—for software using pull-down menus, icons, and a "mouse" as a pointing device, all key features of the Macintosh system. Apple contended that these features are too close to the "look and feel" of the Macintosh—even though the company hadn't originated the "look and feel" it was trying to prevent others from using, having "borrowed" pull-down menus with a pointing device and icons from Xerox and others.

Many critics felt Apple's desire to keep the Macintosh "look and feel" unique was like General Motors saying that other brands of cars could not have steering wheels or a brake pedal to the left of the accelerator. If users are to be able to freely move back and forth among different brands of computers, all should operate in essentially the same way, just as cars do, they argued. In 1992, a federal judge dismissed most of Apple's copyright infringement lawsuit against Microsoft and Hewlett-Packard, largely rejecting the idea that the "look and feel" of a computer program can be protected under copyright law. The rest of Apple's lawsuit was dismissed in 1993—and Apple's appeals were not successful (*Apple Computer Inc. v. Microsoft Corp.*, 35 F.3d 1435). In 1995, the Supreme Court refused to review the lower court decisions against Apple. By then it was clear that Microsoft could continue to produce its popular Mac-like Windows software, with or without Apple's blessing—and the Justice Department was investigating Microsoft rather than Apple for engaging in monopolistic business practices in the computer industry (see Chapter Twelve).

Enter 2021: Copyright in APIs. In a highly anticipated 2021 decision—with potentially significant repercussions for fair use—between two tech giants, the Supreme Court said that Google's use in its Android smartphone system of 11,500 lines of code from the Java SE platform developed by Sun Microsystems (now owned by Oracle) was a transformative fair use (*Google LLC v. Oracle Am., Inc.*, No. 18-956). The code was copied from Java's *application programming interface* (API), which lets programmers call other tasks for use in their own programs—or, as a Sun marketing slogan put it, "write once, run anywhere." At issue before the justices was the question of whether software interfaces like API could be copyrighted, and, if so, whether Google's use of Oracle's code was a fair use.

Earlier in the case, Oracle got a ruling establishing the copyrightability of APIs but failed to secure wins on its claims of patent infringement. The questions before the high court dealt solely with copyright. The case was delayed at the Court for a year because of the COVID-19 pandemic.

Writing for a 6-2 majority, Justice Stephen Breyer dodged the question of whether APIs could be copyrighted: "Given the rapidly changing technological, economic, and business-related circumstances, we believe we should not answer more than is necessary to resolve the parties' dispute." Assuming "purely for argument's sake" that the API could be copyrighted, he then turned to whether Google's use of the Oracle code was a fair use. Noting that such a fair use analysis is a "mixed question of fact and law," Breyer evaluated the four elements of the doctrine, and he found that each supported a determination of fair use.

The nature of the work, software code, Breyer said, is functional rather than expressive and should receive "thin" protection, adding, "Unlike many other programs, its value in significant part derives from the value that those who do not hold copyrights, namely, computer programmers, invest of their own time and effort to learn the API's system." The nature of Google's use of the API code, he went on, "to create new products" and "to expand the use and usefulness of Android-based smartphones," is sufficiently transformative, and besides, Java was originally written for desktop and laptop computers, not for phones. As for the amount and substantiality of the use, the 11,500 lines comprised only 0.4% of the entire Java code set. And Google took Java's code "only insofar as needed to include tasks that would be useful in smartphone programs" and "to allow programmers to call upon those tasks without discarding a portion of a familiar programming language and learning a new one." Finally, Breyer said, "Sun's mobile phone business was declining, while the market increasingly demanded a new form of smartphone technology that Sun was never able to offer," and that failure was not due to the successful development of the Android system. Moreover, Java and Android were not competing in the same markets, and enforcing Oracle's copyright in the Java API would risk public harm, given the expense and challenges of developing alternative API systems. Thus Google's use of the Java code was a fair use.

Justice Clarence Thomas, joined by Justice Samuel Alito, dissented on two grounds. First, he said, the majority's dodge of the copyrightability question was problematic, as it left out a lot of important legal analysis. He would have declared that the API code was indeed copyrightable and copyrighted by Oracle. Second, he scorned the majority's fair use finding: Google's copying of the Java code, he said, "erased 97.5% of the value of Oracle's partnership with Amazon, made tens of billions of dollars, and established its position as the owner of the largest mobile operating system in the world"—and still, he marveled, the Court called it a fair use. He would not have.

The decision ended more than a decade of litigation between the parties over both patent and copyright issues, called by one trial court "The World Series of IP cases." As with any high-profile case, opinions varied on its current and future usefulness. Some commentators mourned that Breyer didn't address the question of whether software like APIs can qualify for copyright protection, hoping for a decisive (or at least clearer) holding. A common take among legal scholars was that Breyer's opinion offers an expansive reading of what counts as a "transformative" use. As mentioned earlier, the Andy Warhol Foundation used this interpretation to challenge a finding of infringement against Warhol in the *Goldsmith* case discussed elsewhere in this chapter. Stay tuned.

In general, as *Google v. Oracle* suggests, the trend today appears to be for the courts to take a narrow view of software copyrights, or at least apply a generous fair use analysis, allowing new competitors to enter the field with products similar to or compatible with industry leaders' products. This is true in the video game field as well as the software market.

Reverse engineering. A 1992 federal appellate court decision involving rival video game manufacturers further limited the right of any software producer to use the Copyright Act to avoid competition. In *Sega Enter. v. Accolade Inc.* (977 F.2d 1510), the Ninth Circuit held that computer software companies may disassemble a competitor's code to determine how to make compatible products. The *Sega* case, which is widely regarded as a landmark case in the software industry, extended the fair use doctrine to cover this kind of "reverse engineering." If the court had ruled that it is a copyright infringement to dismantle a competitor's software and examine its inner workings to make a compatible product, competition in the software industry would have been severely curtailed.

In 2000, the Ninth Circuit again held that reverse engineering is a fair use and not a copyright infringement, allowing a company whose software emulates the functions of Sony's PlayStation game machines to disassemble Sony's copyrighted software in order to determine how to make compatible products (*Sony Computer Entm't v. Connectix Corp.*, 203 F.3d 596). The court suggested that Sony could file for a patent to protect its PlayStation game machine, saying, "If Sony wishes to obtain a lawful monopoly on the functional concepts in its software, it must satisfy the more stringent standards of the patent laws." So Sony quickly did just that.

"Shrinkwrap" and "clickwrap" licenses. In recent years, another software copyright-related controversy arose. Many software providers include "shrinkwrap" contracts in their packaging. By breaking the seal, the user agrees to the terms of a contract that may carry far greater restrictions than copyright law would allow, often completely overriding the fair use doctrine and also the *first sale doctrine*, a rule under which the original purchaser of a copyrighted work (such as a book) is free to resell it used without paying additional royalties. Many shrinkwrap contracts simply nullify fair use and first sale concepts. Are these shrinkwrap contracts valid? Generally, copyright owners and those they authorize to use a copyrighted work may enter into contracts that override copyright law.

Some courts have upheld the restrictions imposed by shrinkwrap contracts (e.g., *ProCD v. Zeidenberg*, 86 F.3d 1447, 1996). Some advocates of consumer rights see the *copyright misuse doctrine* as a possible remedy. Under that doctrine, it is a copyright misuse to secure an exclusive right or limited monopoly not granted by copyright law that is contrary to public policy. Some also say shrinkwrap contracts are not valid when they conflict with federal copyright law because of the federal preemption provision of the Copyright Act.

First sale doctrine. The first sale doctrine appears in Section 109(a) of the Copyright Act. It reads: "Notwithstanding the provisions of section 106(3) [which grants exclusive distribution rights], the owner of a particular copy or phonorecord lawfully made under this title... is entitled, without the authority of the copyright owner, to sell or otherwise dispose of the possession of that copy or phonorecord."

In 2010, the Supreme Court affirmed a Ninth Circuit decision on the first sale doctrine, denying a discount store's right to buy items overseas and bring them back for resale without the copyright holder's consent. Costco got Omega Swiss watches by buying them from a New York company who had bought them on the "gray market" overseas from authorized distributors. Omega had not given permission for the watches to be imported to the United States or sold by Costco. The Ninth Circuit said that the first sale doctrine does not apply to foreign imports that are manufactured and first sold abroad. Why? The court said that to interpret the doctrine otherwise "would be to ascribe legality under the Copyright Act to conduct that occurs entirely outside the United States, notwithstanding the absence of a clear expression of congressional intent in favor of extraterritoriality." Thus foreign companies would get more protection than those in the United States. The Supreme Court affirmed that decision by a split vote in *Costco Wholesale Corp. v. OMEGA, S.A.* (562 U.S. 40, 2010). This decision by the Court does not create national precedent.

The high court revisited the first-sale doctrine in 2013. The Second Circuit had found that Supap Kirtsaeng, a Thailand native, violated copyright law by importing foreign-made editions of U.S. textbooks into the United States to sell on eBay. The first-sale doctrine, said the court, does not apply to goods manufactured in a foreign country. In *Kirtsaeng v. John Wiley & Sons* (568 U.S. 519), the Court disagreed with the Second Circuit and said that the first sale doctrine protects the right to import and sell these "gray market" goods. Justice Stephen Breyer, writing for a 6-3 majority, said that the language of the doctrine, as well as "its context, and the common-law history of the 'first sale' doctrine, taken together, favor a non-geographical interpretation." Thus, contrary to what the publisher said, the first sale doctrine does not leave out works lawfully made abroad and imported to the United States.

Justice Ruth Bader Ginsburg dissented, saying that the majority "adopts an interpretation of the Copyright Act at odds with Congress' aim to protect copyright owners against the unauthorized importation of low-priced, foreign made copies of their copyrighted works."

First sale and "used music." ReDigi was a company that marketed "used music." It created a website that allowed users to sell copies of digital music files that they'd legally acquired and buy "used" music from others at lower prices than on iTunes and other sources. ReDigi also had a "Media Manager" to ensure that users did not keep copies of the songs they sold. The company claimed the first sale doctrine protected this business. However, a federal district court disagreed in 2013, saying that when a work goes from a user's computer to ReDigi's server, that is an unauthorized infringement. Because of this, then, the first sale doctrine does not protect the digital sale.

ReDigi lost again in 2018 at the Second Circuit (*Capitol Records, LLC v. ReDigi Inc.*, 910 F.3d 649). Judge Pierre Leval, the same highly influential copyright judge who created the concept of transformation adopted by the Supreme Court, wrote the opinion. He said that while ReDigi was acting in good faith in its resale efforts, the first sale doctrine didn't protect them. The ways in which the digital music files were handled, he said, created a reproduction of that file for longer than "a transitory time." This reproduction "creates a new phonorecord," and "the creation of such new phonorecords involves unauthorized reproduction." Nor is this creation a fair use, Judge Leval added. The Supreme Court denied *cert.*

Moving away from transformation? The Second Circuit in *ReDigi* also relied on a 2018 case (*Fox News Network, LLC v. TVEyes, Inc.*, 883 F.3d 169) in which it had emphasized the effect of the use on the market over the transformation element. TVEyes compiled a searchable database all national TV programming and sold subscriptions which would display 10-minute segments of video. The court said this wasn't a fair use; while there was some transformative value in the scheme, the court said that by using content without paying for it, TVEyes was "depriving Fox of licensing revenues from TVEyes or from similar entities." Judge Leval was explicit about the *TVEyes* case's importance to *ReDigi*, calling *TVEyes* "a substantial precedent for our holding here"—and this from the judge who created the notion of transformation. Could these holdings signal a movement away from the trend toward significant focus on transformation in copyright infringement cases? The Second and Ninth Circuits are key players in copyright issues, as they contain New York and California, the homes of many publishing and entertainment companies.

Own versus license. If you buy software, do you own, or just license, the copy of the software you bought? That question was addressed before the Ninth Circuit in three cases, one having to do with the hugely popular video game *World of Warcraft* (WoW).

In the first of these cases, the Ninth Circuit heard an appeal of a case in which Timothy Vernor sold used but legitimate versions of Autodesk computer-assisted design software on eBay; the software company said he was infringing copyright in doing so because the license was not a transfer of ownership. The district court pointed out that the Ninth Circuit had two views on who owns the software, and found in Vernor's favor using the older of the two precedents. The Ninth Circuit reversed, saying that "Autodesk retained title to the software and imposed significant transfer restrictions: it stated that the license is nontransferable, the software could not be transferred or leased without Autodesk's written consent, and the software could not be transferred outside the Western Hemisphere." Thus, because Vernor never actually owned the software, he could not sell it without permission, as he could under the first sale doctrine as an owner (*Vernor v. Autodesk*, 621 F.3d 1102, 2010).

In the second case, the makers of World of Warcraft, Blizzard Entertainment, won at the district court level against MDY Industries, maker of a program called a "bot," named Glider, that lets users play WoW unattended. The court said that WoW players do not own the physical copy of the game software but can only load a copy into their computers' memories, subject to Blizzard's license. The Ninth Circuit sided with the "bot" makers—but not completely (*MDY Industries v. Blizzard Entertainment*, 629 F.3d 928, 2010). "A Glider user violates the covenants with Blizzard, but does not thereby commit copyright infringement because Glider does not infringe any of Blizzard's exclusive rights. For instance, the use does not alter or copy WoW software," said the court. However, Blizzard's license for WoW did the same thing it did for Autodesk in the *Vernor* case: "a software user is a licensee rather than an owner of a copy where the copyright owner (1) specifies that the user is granted a license; (2) significantly restricts the user's ability to transfer the software; and (3) imposes notable use restrictions." Blizzard did all this, so it owns the copyright and licenses it to WoW players.

Finally, the Ninth Circuit said the first sale doctrine protects the sale of promotional CDs, even though the CDs contained licenses that attempted to limit resale and transfer. In *UMG Records, Inc. v. Augusto* (628 F.3d 1175, 2011), the court said that Troy Augusto could lawfully sell promo CDs on eBay, supporting the first sale doctrine, even if the CDs had "Promotion—Not for Sale" labels on them. The court said, "UMG's distribution of the promotional CDs under the circumstances effected a sale (transfer of title) of the CDs to the recipients. Further sale of those copies was therefore permissible without UMG's authorization."

Thus, the first sale doctrine is a decidedly mixed bag of results for both copyright holders and the purchasers of their products. Given the complexity of the copyright and patent issues involved in these cases—and the enormous amount of money at stake—it is certain that these legal battles will continue, with unpredictable results.

Online Copyright: The Digital Millennium Copyright Act of 1998

Inevitably, questions of copyright ownership in cyberspace have become controversial as millions of people began accessing the internet. The problems became even more complex and controversial when millions of people also began exchanging music and digital video—and posting their own content that includes copyrighted material—on the internet, to the horror of copyright owners. Although there is much uncertainty in this newly developing area of the law, a few principles are clear.

The basic principle is that *a copyright is still a copyright*, regardless of the means by which a copyrighted work is published, performed or distributed (although those three legal terms are being redefined in the cyberspace age). Also, the fact that a document is posted online somewhere without a copyright notice does not prove that the document is in the public domain. Under current law, no recently created work falls into the public domain unless the creator or other copyright owner expressly places it in the public domain.

One of the fundamental issues is the question of holding internet service providers liable for what their subscribers do (not unlike the concerns that gave rise to Section 230). Congress included provisions in the 1996 Telecommunications Act under which internet service providers (ISPs) and websites can escape liability for both libel and copyright infringements committed by their millions of customers and contributors if they act promptly to remove allegedly unlawful materials.

DMCA details. In 1998, Congress passed the Digital Millennium Copyright Act (DMCA), a far-reaching new law that expanded on the Telecommunications Act, giving both copyright owners and ISPs extensive legal protection—but at the expense of those who post and use material on the internet, including librarians, educators, website owners, the internet-surfing public, and even broadcasters. In passing this law, Congress recognized that it is impossible for ISPs to monitor everything that every user does online.

The DMCA has many provisions. Among other things, it brought the United States into compliance with the provisions of two World Intellectual Property Organization (WIPO) treaties. Perhaps the most noteworthy of these provisions is a requirement that VCR manufacturers start adding circuitry that will make it impossible for consumers to copy rental videos and pay-per-view television programming. Another little-noticed provision gives copyright protection to "cookies," the small files that are quietly placed on computers when they are used to surf the internet, enabling some internet hosts to ascertain what sites a computer user has visited. Some attorneys said this provision makes it a copyright infringement for computer users to delete these cookies from their own computers, even though the cookies may have been placed there without the users' knowledge or consent.

The DMCA also established new rules governing digital copyrights, giving additional copyright protection to digital renderings of motion pictures, videos, sound recordings, photography, and

webcast:
media content delivered over the internet, either on demand or live, including podcasts and music streaming services like Spotify.

CSS:
Content Scramble System, a digital rights management (copy protection) scheme licensed by the DVD Copy Control Association.

Focus on...
The infamous monkey selfies

A monkey took selfies that went viral. Who owns the copyrights—and the resulting royalties? The owner of the camera? The monkey? Turns out that it's no one.

In 2011, photographer David Slater sold photos of a crested macaque monkey named Naruto to several news outlets with an adorable story: He went to Indonesia to photograph the crested macaques, and after he'd gained the monkeys' trust, he'd set the camera down, and a macaque picked it up to play, snapping several amazing selfies. Her toothy grin and the sweet tale captured hearts, and the photos were suddenly everywhere. The People for the Ethical Treatment of Animals (PETA) thought Naruto should benefit, so they as Naruto's "next friend" sued Slater for damages, saying that Naruto owned the copyright (*Naruto v. Slater*, 888 F.3d 418, 2018).

FIG. 60. *Macaca nigra* self-portrait.

Public domain, via Wikimedia Commons.

The Ninth Circuit ruled against Naruto on two grounds. First, a monkey has no statutory standing under the Copyright Act to bring an infringement case. Second, PETA cannot be Naruto's "next friend"—in an earlier case about dolphins, porpoises, and whales, the court held that "if animals are to be accorded rights to sue, the provisions involved therefore should state such rights expressly." There is no right for "next friend" for animals, and the court declined to create one.

So the selfies are in the public domain; no one owns the copyright. The U.S. Copyright Office "will not register works produced by nature, animals, or plants" (providing "A photograph taken by a monkey" as an example). In 2018, the Ninth Circuit declined to rehear the case *en banc*.

graphics. The act also banned many technologies that could circumvent encryption and copy-prevention schemes.

DMCA's "notice and takedown." One of the DMCA's most controversial features concerns the handling of alleged copyright infringements on the internet. The law exempted internet service providers and services like YouTube from liability for what their subscribers or users may post if they act quickly to deny access to content containing alleged infringements. A copyright owner merely notifies the host that the material infringes a copyright, providing a statement of a "good faith belief" that the use of the disputed material is an infringement. The internet provider must then notify the poster of the material and promptly shut down access to it. The poster, in turn, can oppose the shutdown only by stating *under penalty of perjury* that the challenged material is being removed by mistake or was wrongly identified. In contrast, the copyright owner is *not* obligated to declare anything under penalty of perjury. Nor is the poster of the material allowed to make a fair use defense of the use of the challenged material.

In effect, this allows copyright owners to shut down websites or internet postings without ever going to court to prove that an infringement has in fact occurred. Internet providers and hosts are exempt from copyright liability—if they act as copyright enforcers by responding quickly to "take-down" requests (valid or not). If they fail to play that role, they can be held liable for any infringement that may occur.

Critics of these provisions of the DMCA have pointed out that the act was the result of a compromise between copyright owners and ISPs. Website owners, educators, librarians, and others who advocate a broad fair use doctrine were not at the bargaining table when this law was negotiated. Another criticism of the act is that it made it easier for companies to use copyright law to seek a monopoly over products like garage door controls and ink cartridges for printers, to the detriment of consumers. In 2004, federal appeals courts ruled against a manufacturer who wanted to prevent a competitor from making compatible garage door remote controls (*Chamberlain Group v. Skylink Technologies*, 381 F.3d 1178) and a printer maker who wanted to prevent others from making ink cartridges that would work on its printers (*Lexmark Int'l v. Static Control Components*, 387 F.3d 522). The Lanham Act issues in *Lexmark* will be discussed in Chapter Thirteen.

DMCA and social media. In June 2021, Twitter users reported that they received notices of DMCA violations from tweets posted years earlier. Not only was the allegedly infringing material taken down, but the users' accounts were "sent to Twitter jail" (locked). In some cases, the copyrighted material was incidental to the tweet, such as music playing in the background of a video of a puppy's antics. As expected, these actions drew users' ire; the puppy's infuriated owner tweeted upon her release from Twitter jail: "dont y'all have better shit to do than lock my account over a 3 year old tweet that had 2 likes?" There have also been instances of police departments using the DMCA to block citizen recordings of their officers; if copyrighted music could be heard on the recording, the department sent DMCA takedown notices to the video host. In fact, as legal blog Techdirt noted in Feb. 2021, some officers have adopted the practice of starting to play music on their own cellphones as soon as they see themselves being recorded so they can file DMCA takedown notices.

Contributory infringement under DMCA. Under what grounds do ISPs give up DMCA safe harbor protections? At issue in an important 2018 Fourth Circuit case, *BMG Rights Mgmt. (US) LLC v. Cox Commc'ns., Inc.* (881 F.3d 293), was a DMCA obligation to create and implement a policy to eliminate accounts of "repeat infringers." Music publisher BMG hired copyright enforcer Rightscorp to look for infringing activity by Cox internet subscribers. Rightscorp then sent notices to Cox identifying allegedly infringing subscribers and asking Cox to forward its notices to those subscribers (which included a settlement option for subscribers to avoid litigation by paying $30, causing some to label Rightscorp a "copyright troll"—discussed later). Cox refused to process those settlement notices, so BMG sued. Cox argued that it met DMCA's repeat-infringer requirement because "repeat infringers" meant only those who had been actually judged to be infringers, not just those alleged to be.

A district court said that "Cox knew accounts were being used repeatedly for infringing activity yet failed to terminate" them and thus hadn't met the repeat-infringer requirement. The Fourth Circuit agreed. Cox's policy consisted of "only a very limited automated system to process notifications of alleged infringement" that heavily favored its subscribers. And the language of the DMCA, the court said, distinguished between alleged and adjudged infringement in other sections, so there was no reason to believe it should be otherwise for repeat infringers. Cox, the court added, "does not cite a single case adopting its contrary view that only adjudicated infringers can be 'repeat infringers' for purposes of the DMCA." This decision may well have prompted a breathtaking 2019 jury judgment for *$1 billion* against Cox ($99,830.29 each for 10,017 infringements alleged by 53 music publishers) that was upheld by a federal district court in 2020 (*Sony Music Entm't. v. Cox Commc'ns, Inc.*, 464 F. Supp. 3d 795). That court upheld the verdict again in 2021 after allowing Cox to argue (unsuccessfully) that some of the 10,017 works were derivative, a move that would have saved it a quarter-billion dollars. Cox appealed to the Fourth Circuit in May 2021. Stay tuned.

And also in May 2021, Cox was back in California federal court. The company said that, despite public notice and multiple notifications of a new email address tied to its updated automated copyright-management system (and the fact that "virtually every notice sender *except for Rightscorp*" used the new address), BMG and Rightscorp flooded the old (but still active) address with infringement notices to "fabricat[e] massive claims for secondary infringement." These notices were invalid under DMCA, said Cox, because they were sent to the wrong address, outside Cox's automated system. Stay tuned here, too.

Filesharing

Filesharing became the major copyright issue in cyberspace in the 2000s. One internet start-up company particularly incurred the wrath of the recording industry: Napster, an internet-based peer-to-peer music sharing service. Napster enabled millions of users to share music—most of it copyrighted. The larger problem of filesharing—"piracy" according to copyright owners—produced numerous lawsuits, countersuits, proposals for legislation, and technical "solutions" intended to make various kinds of copying more difficult. After the recording industry won a series of legal victories over Napster, it eventually went bankrupt (the name was later taken over by a for-pay music downloading service). The original Napster service was replaced by several others after it was shut down, and the recording industry responded with lawsuits against them and their users, too.

Filesharing not a fair use. The recording industry's legal attack on Napster began with a request for an injunction to halt the filesharing. A federal judge granted an injunction in 2000, but the Ninth Circuit issued a stay, allowing Napster to continue for a few more months while an appeal was heard. In 2001, the court upheld much of the recording industry's case. In *A&M Records et al. v. Napster* (239 F.3d 1004), the appellate court held that when computer music enthusiasts exchange digital music files via Napster, that is often a copyright infringement. The court rejected Napster's contention that music sharing should be a fair use, just as home videotaping television programs for later viewing is a fair use.

At one time about 10% of the music being exchanged via Napster either was not covered by a current copyright or was exchanged with the copyright owner's permission. So Napster was allowed to continue operating for a time, but the copyrighted music had to be removed. In ruling that the non-infringing uses of Napster precluded a judicial decree to shut it down altogether, the appellate court was echoing its own earlier ruling when the recording industry tried to ban the sale of the Diamond Rio portable MP3 player (*RIAA v. Diamond Multimedia Systems*, 180 F.3d 1072). In that 1999 decision, the appellate court said it was inappropriate to ban the sale of a product that has *substantial non-infringing uses*.

Meanwhile, several record labels announced their own internet music distribution systems, most of which charge subscribers a monthly fee for the privilege of downloading music. In 2003, Apple Computer Inc. launched iTunes, a fee-based music service, with the blessing of the recording industry, and introduced the iPod portable music player. By 2007, iTunes and the iPod were so popular that when Apple CEO Steve Jobs said he would drop all copying restrictions from music sold by iTunes "in a heartbeat" if he could, some industry analysts thought it might happen. That would be a fundamental change in industry thinking about "digital rights management" (i.e., copy prevention).

Encouraging infringement. In 2005, the recording and motion picture industries won a major victory when the U.S. Supreme Court ruled in *MGM v. Grokster* (545 U.S. 913) that copyright owners can sue technology companies who encourage consumers to share copyrighted files. The unanimous decision held that modern filesharing is different from what was happening at the time of the *Sony* Betamax decision in 1984. Not only is copying of digital files easier and more widespread than home video copying was then, but companies like Grokster and StreamCast Networks (another defendant in this case) actively facilitate the process. These companies make no effort to prevent illegal filesharing, the Court said.

"We hold that one who distributes a device with the object of promoting its use to infringe copyright, as shown by the clear expression or other affirmative steps taken to foster infringement, is liable for the resulting acts of infringement by third parties," Justice David Souter wrote for the Court. However, the *Grokster* decision also set up a balancing test to provide some protection to scientific innovators. The Court said it was unrealistic to force a company developing a new product to predict how consumers might use its product months or years later. If a company merely learns that consumers are using its product for an illegal purpose, that is not sufficient to make the company liable for the acts of others. This balancing is needed so as not to "compromise legitimate commerce or discourage innovation having a lawful purpose," the Court said.

Grokster cleared the way for the recording and motion picture industries to go after companies that encourage filesharing as well as cracking down on individual users of filesharing networks like Grokster, as the industries did starting in 2003. Industry lawyers filed lawsuits against thousands of individuals who allegedly shared music or movies online. After rulings from federal appeals courts that internet providers need not reveal their subscribers' names to recording industry attorneys without a judge's subpoena, the industry then began seeking individual subpoenas to identify targeted filesharers. Armed with the *Grokster* decision, the industry went after software and hardware creators who facilitate copying within the jurisdiction of U.S. courts. The industries won a large settlement from the Australia-based KaZaA network and then won a court judgment against the makers of the Morpheus software. In 2008, the six leading Hollywood studios won a verdict of $111 million from the TorrentSpy.com filesharing website. Its parent company filed for bankruptcy protection in the United Kingdom.

Peer-to-peer sharing. Peer-to-peer services haven't fared well in the courts. As discussed in Chapter Three, the Second Circuit in 2010 refused to overturn a district court's order to an ISP to disclose the identities of individuals alleged to be involved in filesharing (*Arista Records LLC v. Doe 3*). A federal district court also found in 2010 that LimeWire had induced its users to engage in infringing actions in *Arista Records LLC v. Lime Group* (715 F. Supp. 2d 481). The judge said that LimeWire was aware of infringing activity, attempted to attract infringing users and enable them to commit infringements, depended on infringements for business success, and didn't try to reduce these activities. The RIAA got a permanent injunction against LimeWire, and LimeWire settled for $105 million in 2011.

As part of their ongoing battles with peer-to-peer piracy, the Center for Copyright Information (CCI), a consortium of several large copyright owners and five major internet service providers, piloted the Copyright Alert System (CAS) in 2013. Also called the "Six Strikes" program, CAS monitored illegal downloading sites and torrents and sent notices to those allegedly participating in infringement with escalating censures, up to and including throttling (slowing down) the user's internet connection. Critics said that rather than being about educating those who may not be aware they're infringing, CAS was about intimidation, while others suggested that this is really no different than what ISPs and copyright holders have been doing for a long time. Did CAS work? Not according to a group who ran an orchestrated attempt at infringement in 2013, downloading big-name titles like *Game of Thrones* and *The Avengers* from major torrent sites—and not getting a single peep from CAS. CCI shut the CAS program down in Jan. 2017.

The RIAA beats Jammie and Joel. The most controversial thing the record industry did was filing lawsuits against individuals who allegedly shared copyrighted music. By 2008, at least 30,000 such suits had been filed—and some went to trial when defendants refused to settle. Two high-profile defendants made the news in the late 2000s: Jammie Thomas-Rasset and Joel Tenenbaum. But these cases ended with a whimper rather than a bang.

In the largest verdict at the time, a federal jury in October 2007 ordered a Minnesota woman to pay a $222,000 fine ($9,250 for each of 24 copyrighted songs shared online). Jammie Thomas (now Thomas-Rasset), a 30-year-old single mother of two who earned $36,000 a year as an employee of an Native American reservation, was found by the jury to have shared songs via the KaZaA filesharing site, although she denied it. After a series of decisions and appeals, the Eighth Circuit in 2012 reinstated that judgment (*Capitol Records Inc. v. Thomas-Rasset*, 692 F.3d 899), which was confirmed by the Supreme Court denying *cert*.

In the second of these cases, Boston University graduate student Joel Tenenbaum faced the RIAA in federal court for sharing 30 songs over KaZaA. His motion for dismissal was denied and the case went to a jury (*Capitol Records Inc. v. Alaujan*, 626 F. Supp. 2d 152, 2009). The judge allowed the hearing to be webcast but the RIAA objected and the decision overturned by the First Circuit; that issue is discussed in Chapter Seven.

After Tenenbaum admitted on the stand that he did indeed download the files in question, the judge told the jury that they could no longer decide the issue of infringement, and instead would only be addressing willfulness and damages. The jury returned a verdict of $675,000—$22,500 per song. The judge reduced the damages to $67,500, calling that award "significant and harsh." However, on appeal, a district judge put back the original

$675,000 fine, saying that it did not offend due process. The Second Circuit in 2013 upheld the $675,000 fine against Tenenbaum (*Sony BMG Music Entm't v. Tenenbaum*, 719 F.3d 67), and the Supreme Court again denied *cert.*

At the end of 2008, after a spate of bad publicity for these legal actions, the RIAA announced that it would no longer pursue lawsuits against filesharers but would form partnerships with ISP to restrict online access of those sharing files.

BitTorrent. One of the most popular filesharing protocols is called BitTorrent, which distributes the download burden among many users. Torrent-tracking websites facilitate communication among "peers" sharing files. In Stockholm in 2009, the Swedish owners of the popular torrent-tracking website The Pirate Bay were found guilty of promoting copyright infringement and sentenced to serve one year in prison and pay a fine of 30 million Swedish kroner (about $3.5 million). A Swedish court denied the request for a retrial. After the Swedish Supreme Court refused to hear their appeal, two of the Pirate Bay's founders, in a last-ditch effort to avoid jail time, appealed to the European Court of Human Rights in June 2012—probably postponing the final outcome for several years.

YouTube, Veoh, and Vimeo suits. Social networking and video sharing sites became so popular that they attracted a series of high-profile lawsuits by copyright owners. Media conglomerate Viacom sued YouTube for more than $1 billion because YouTube users posted thousands of videos containing copyrighted material. While Viacom and YouTube privately negotiated, YouTube said in court that it should not be liable because it promptly takes down all infringing material and therefore falls within the copyright safe harbor of the Digital Millennium Copyright Act. YouTube installed its own internal filters in an attempt to prevent the posting of copyrighted content. Critics of these lawsuits argued that they ignore the fair use doctrine, under which many postings are perfectly legal even if they make some use of copyrighted material.

A federal district court in 2010 initally dismissed the billion-dollar claim, saying that YouTube fully qualifies for DMCA "safe harbor" protection, and YouTube promptly responded to Viacom's requests under DMCA to take down infringing material. However, the Second Circuit in *Viacom Int'l, Inc. v. YouTube, Inc.* (676 F.3d 19, 2012) supported YouTube, reversing the lower court's decision to toss out the $1 billion award and reviving the lawsuit. "[A] reasonable jury could find that YouTube had actual knowledge or awareness of specific infringing activity on its website," said the court. The parties settled in 2014.

Veoh, another video-hosting site, had won a summary judgment claim in 2009 against Universal Music Group under the DMCA's safe harbor. Veoh claimed that it had no actual knowledge of infringing materials being posted by their users, and the district court agreed. UMG appealed. In 2011, the Ninth Circuit said that Veoh *was* protected under the DMCA's safe harbor, and UMG appealed. The Ninth Circuit, in response to UMG's appeal, asked for more information on actual knowledge of infringement and on whether "a service provider [has] to be aware of the specific infringing material to have the 'right and ability to control' the infringing activity." In 2013, the court again held that Veoh was protected under the DMCA safe harbor, as that no jury could find that Veoh exercised enough control over user submissions to lose safe-harbor protections (*UMG Recs. v. Veoh Networks*, 718 F.3d 1006).

In yet another video-hosting site case, *Capitol Records, LLC v. Vimeo, LLC* (2016 U.S. App. LEXIS 10884), the Second Circuit said that the DMCA's safe harbor, Section 512(c), applies to pre-1972 sound recordings, and Vimeo could not be held to be ignoring red-flag copyright issues (and is under no legal obligation to go actively searching for copyright infringement on its site). Noting that to lose safe-harbor protections, "the service provider must have actually known facts that would make the specific infringement claimed objectively obvious to a reasonable person," the court said that Capitol had not demonstrated this was true, and further, pointed out that a "reasonable person" in this case would not be one with an extensive understanding of the nuances of copyright law.

YouTube's Content ID system: the "dancing baby" case. Despite the fact that YouTube flashes a warning before allowing users to upload their videos that tells them not to post copyrighted material, plenty of unauthorized content reaches YouTube. Under the DMCA's rules, when copyright holders notify YouTube of infringing material, YouTube will take the content down. Still, several media companies sued YouTube for infringement. In the wake of these lawsuits, YouTube instituted a "Content ID" system that it says lets copyright owners "identify user-uploaded videos comprised entirely OR partially of their content, and choose, in advance, what they want to happen when those videos are found." Critics of this system say that it flags more than it should without regard to whether a use is a fair use. No case has illustrated this better than what's been called "the dancing baby case."

In 2008, a federal district court ruled in favor of Stephanie Lenz, a Pennsylvania mom who videotaped 29 seconds of her toddler dancing to Prince's hit "Let's Go Crazy" and posted it on YouTube. Universal Music Corp. informed YouTube that the video was infringing and ordered it to be removed. YouTube did so and informed Lenz. Claiming that Universal removed the video just to satisfy Prince, who was not shy about asserting his rights, Lenz said Universal had no right to remove her video without considering that it might be a fair use. The court agreed with Lenz: "[T]he unnecessary removal of non-infringing material causes significant injury to the public where time-sensitive or controversial subjects are involved and the counter-notification remedy does not sufficiently address these harms. A good faith consideration of whether a particular use is fair use is consistent with the purpose of the statute." The court also cleared the way for Lenz to bring suit against Universal for bad faith.

Lenz won again at the district court in 2010 when it granted her partial summary judgment against Universal's defenses in a counterclaim. The DMCA says that a copyright owner who makes false statements in a takedown notice will be liable for damages for "relying upon such misrepresentation in removing or disabling access to the material or activity claimed to be infringing." In other words, a company who falsely claims a use is copyrighted must pay damages if the ISP uses that false claim to take down the use.

Focus on...
Dr. Seuss vs. Star Trek

You may have gotten a copy of Dr. Seuss' famous book *Oh, the Places You'll Go!* as a graduation or birthday gift. The book inspired a "Star Trek" mashup called *Oh, the Places You'll Boldly Go!* with Captain James Kirk from the original series as the narrator.

As discussed in this chapter, *The Cat NOT in the Hat*, a 1997 summary of the O.J. Simpson murder trial based on Seuss, was not a fair use. The *Boldly* creators fared no better, illustrating the challenge of fair use analysis.

In *Dr. Seuss Enter. v. ComicMix LLC* (983 F. 3d 443, 2020), the Ninth Circuit overturned the district court's fair use finding and said that *Boldly* was not a parody; like *Cat*, it merely mimicked Seuss' language and imagery without commenting on or critiquing it. And, the judge noted, "the addition of new expression to an existing work is not a get-out-of-jail-free card that renders the use of the original transformative."

The Ninth Circuit in 2015 upheld Lenz's position against Universal's arguments that having to proactively consider fair use would slow down the whole infringement combat process (*Lenz v. Universal Music Corp.*, 801 F.3d 1126). Universal said that fair use is not "'authorized by the law' because it is an affirmative defense that excuses otherwise infringing conduct." But the court was having none of it: "Universal's interpretation is incorrect as it conflates two different concepts: an affirmative defense that is labeled as such due to the procedural posture of the case, and an affirmative defense that excuses impermissible conduct." Someone who makes a fair use of something is *not* an infringer, the court said, adding, "Fair use is not just excused by the law, it is wholly authorized by the law."

But it wasn't a total win for Lenz, either, since the court did say that human review wasn't necessary for a fair use evaluation. The judges offered an example of a computer algorithm that could accomplish the same thing, and Universal must only offer evidence that it acted in good faith in evaluating whether a use was a fair use. In 2017, the Supreme Court declined to hear an appeal of the case, ending more than a decade of litigation.

Google's digital book project and the Authors Guild. The digital environment has created new issues in book publishing and access. In 2008, book authors and Google reached a settlement agreement for Google's "Library Project" or Google Books. Google had contracted with public and university libraries, including the University of Michigan, to create a digital archive of their holdings—many of which were still under copyright—for users to search for text online. The Authors Guild filed a class-action suit against Google. In the settlement, *Authors Guild v. Google* (No. 05 CV 8136, S.D.N.Y. 2008), the authors would receive $125 million in damages for those books scanned without permission, and a new not-for-profit organization controlled by authors and publishers would be created. Profits would be shared between Google and authors according to the terms of the settlement. Out-of-print books will be scanned and included by default, but books in print must be actively included. Google argued that providing small samples of the material in larger works is a fair use, not an infringement. Google and the Authors Guild thought they settled this case in 2008 and again in 2009 with an amended settlement, with Google agreeing to compensate authors, but the settlement agreement is still up in the air: a judge said in 2011 that the settlement is not "fair, adequate, and reasonable" (*Authors Guild v. Google*, 770 F. Supp. 2d 666).

In 2012, Judge Denny Chin, who moved to the Second Circuit but still presided over this case, granted the authors class status to sue. Judge Chin wrote, "Class action is ... more efficient and effective than requiring thousands of authors to sue individually" (*Authors Guild v. Google*, 282 F.R.D. 384). The Second Circuit, however, thought the class certification was premature and remanded the case for a consideration of Google's fair use defense (*Authors Guild v. Google*, 721 F.3d 132, 2013).

Judge Chin then granted summary judgment to Google in 2013, saying that the scanning was a fair use (*Authors Guild v. Google*, 954 F. Supp. 2d 282). He based that finding on a fair use analysis, key to which was his assertion that Google's use was transformative under the "purpose of the use" prong. He also found for Google on the other three parts of the fair use test: published books deserve less deference than unpublished; even though entire books are copied, that's critical to the search function; and Google Books is not a replacement for the books themselves.

The Authors Guild took the case to the Second Circuit, which affirmed the lower court's holding in 2015 (*Authors Guild v. Google*, 804 F.3d 202). The Supreme Court denied *cert* in 2016. The Guild's website left no question about how it felt about the Second Circuit's decision, calling it an "unprecedented expansion of the fair use doctrine—holding that Google's copying and providing access to some four million copyrighted books for profit-making purposes was a fair use." Indeed, the Second Circuit did say that Google's uses of the copyrighted works were non-infringing fair uses—the uses were transformative, the display of the text to the public was limited, and those displays were not a market substitute for the originals. Moreover, Google's profit motivation didn't stop the uses from being fair uses. To the Guild's claim that libraries might misuse Google offerings, the court agreed, but then added, "If they do, such libraries may be liable to Plaintiffs for their infringement."

While the Court's denial of *cert* might mean the end of this lengthy suit, the Guild is still optimistic about the law's ultimate resettling of fair use: "We trust that the Supreme Court will soon address the underlying legal issue in this case—the expansion of the fair use doctrine in the digital age—and reset the balance in fair use law."

The Authors Guild also (unsuccessfully) sued libraries that were cooperating with Google in this endeavor. In *Authors Guild v. HathiTrust* (755 F.3d 87, 2014), the Second Circuit found that the libraries were not guilty of infringing the copyrights of authors whose books they provided for scanning. Agreeing with Judge Chin, the three-judge panel unanimously said that the scanning was transformative. "There is no evidence that the Authors write with the purpose of enabling text searches of their books. Consequently, the full-text search function does not 'supersede[] the objects [or purposes] of the original creation," wrote the court. And, it added, "by enabling full-text search, the [HathiTrust Digital Library] adds to the original something new with a different purpose and a different character."

DVD copy-protection and contributory infringement. The international issues involved in internet filesharing were central to the movie industry's fight against the DeCSS software, which defeats the CSS (Content Scramble System, licensed by the DVD Copy Control Association) encryption system used on DVD movies. The DeCSS software was written primarily by Jon Lech Johansen, a Norwegian youth, so he could view DVD movies on a Linux-based computer. In 2003, a court in Oslo, Norway, acquitted Johansen of violating Norway's anti-piracy laws because he owned the DVDs he wanted to copy. The court said a person has the right to copy his own DVDs in Norway. Many European countries have similar laws, allowing consumers to make copies of their DVDs and audio CDs for private use.

DeCSS overrides the copy-prevention features of DVDs, allowing them to be viewed and copied on Linux computers. A federal judge initially ruled that even linking to sites hosting DeCSS software is a *contributory copyright infringement* in violation of the DMCA. The defendants raised First Amendment questions and appealed the ruling—with the support of civil liberties and advocacy groups such as the Electronic Frontier Foundation.

But in 2001, the Second Circuit rejected the First Amendment claims and upheld most of the judge's order. Ruling in *Universal City Studios v. Corley* (273 F.3d 429), the court concluded that the DMCA does not violate the First Amendment by banning not only software that defeats copy-protection schemes but also information about such software. In essence, the appellate court said it is up to Congress to weigh the First Amendment against the claims of copyright owners.

In 2005, however, the DeCSS code was so widely circulated that a court said it could no longer be considered a trade secret, refusing to enjoin its posting online (*DVD Copy Control Association v. Bunner*, 116 C.A.4th 241). Copyright owners continued to press their case against DVD copying software under the DMCA and other legal grounds. By then, millions of computer owners were copying DVD movies with little regard for its alleged illegality.

The DVD Copy Control Association litigated two other cases in 2009 involving the CSS technology. In *RealNetworks Inc. v. DVD Copy Control Assn.* (641 F. Supp. 2d 913), a federal district court ruled that RealNetwork's product RealDVD can no longer be sold; the judge wrote, "RealDVD makes a permanent copy of copyrighted DVD content and by doing so breaches its CSS license agreement... and circumvents a technological measure that effectively controls access to or copying of [defendants'] copyrighted content on DVDs." In *DVD Copy Control Assn. v. Kaleidescape* (176 Cal. App. 4th 697), the association alleged that Kaleidescape's system, which stores copies of DVDs and would allow a user to create a large library of DVDs without buying a single one, was a violation of the CSS license. A California appellate court said that it was unclear whether Kaleidescape had actually breached the license. The case was remanded to the trial court for that determination.

A new law. In 2005, Congress enacted the Family Entertainment and Copyright Act, making it a federal crime to record a movie in a theater or to offer online even one movie, song, or software program before its official release date. The bill also legalized products that enable consumers to filter out portions of DVDs that they may find offensive. Those provisions were backed by both conservatives and advocates of high-tech civil liberties such as the Electronic Frontier Foundation.

CD copy-protection. Meanwhile, record companies began marketing CDs in a copy-protected format without labeling them. Those CDs often would not play on computers. That led consumer advocates to sue the industry, seeking an order requiring that the copy-protected CDs at least be labeled and seeking compensation to consumers for alleged damage to their equipment by the new CDs. And technology buffs in England reported that Sony's proprietary CD copy-protection system could be defeated by scribbling around the rim of the disk with a felt-tip marker. Sony and other record labels abandoned their CD copy-protection systems, at least temporarily. The industry also began aggressively lobbying for state anti-piracy laws. About 20 states had enacted or were considering such laws by 2006.

The Electronic Frontier Foundation sued the major studios and TV networks in 2002 in an attempt to define consumers' TV-recording rights in the digital age. The online civil liberties group asked a federal judge to declare that consumers can use digital recorders to watch shows after they are broadcast, skip all commercials, transmit recordings to members of their households, and send copies of free TV broadcasts to anyone on the internet provided they receive no compensation. This was a countersuit filed in response to an industry lawsuit intended to halt the sale of digital video recorders (DVRs) that allow commercial-skipping. Eventually the lawsuits were dropped and the broadcast networks agreed on a new rating system that takes into account commercial-skipping with DVRs. Most TV advertising prices are based on measurements of the actual viewership of advertising, including DVR replays after the scheduled viewing time.

In 2004, the European Parliament approved new copyright rules for the European Union that are similar to the Digital Millennium Copyright Act, to the alarm of civil liberties and consumer groups in Europe. As a compromise, European regulators deleted a ban on devices that circumvent copy-protection measures and added protections for consumers "acting in good faith" who make copies for their own use. Each individual EU member country must approve the rules. In 2008, President George W. Bush signed the *Prioritizing Resources and Organization for Intellectual Property (PRO-IP) Act of 2008*, legislation toughening piracy penalties, and creating an "intellectual property czar" who advises the president on strengthening copyrights domestically and internationally.

Webcasting, Streaming, Podcasting, and Copyrights

With little controversy, Congress quietly passed the Digital Performance Right in Sound Recordings Act of 1995, a law that forced many broadcasters to think twice about streaming their regular programming online. For the first time, this law gave record companies the right to receive royalties when their recordings are played over the air—but only on digital audio broadcast services, not ordinary AM and FM radio stations. As noted earlier, free over-the-air broadcasters pay performance royalties only to the owners of music copyrights (via agencies such as ASCAP and BMI), not to record companies and recording artists.

At first most broadcasters weren't alarmed by the 1995 law because it didn't seem to affect them, but it made music more costly for one of their competitors: satellite-based for-pay digital audio broadcasters. However, the law quickly became a huge problem once they started doing webcasting, streaming their over-the-air programming on the internet.

In 2000, the U.S. Copyright Office issued rules explaining how the 1998 Digital Millennium Copyright Act and the 1995 Digital Performance Right law would apply to broadcasters. The new rules decreed that broadcasters, like other digital programmers, would pay separate royalties for streaming copyrighted music on their websites, and that for the first time they would pay royalties not only to music licensing agencies such as ASCAP and BMI but also to record companies for the use of sound recordings. But a variety of rules on identification of music and limits on song repetition meant that many broadcasters could not put their over-the-air programming on the internet.

In 2002, matters only got worse. A Copyright Arbitration Royalty Panel that had been established to set royalty rates proposed rates so high that most webcasters said they could not afford to pay them. The panel also said the rates would be *retroactive* to 1998. Many webcasters protested that the rates exceeded their total income. Eventually the Copyright Office modified the rates set by the panel but still left the rates prohibitively high for many webcasters. Then, in 2007 the newly established Copyright Royalty Board adopted *still higher* webcasting rates with no discount for small webcasters, prompting Congress to again consider reducing the rates. In response, SoundExchange (as mentioned earlier, the entity that collects digital royalties for the recording industry) said it would negotiate with webcasters for possible temporary royalty rate reductions. The Copyright Royalty Board also established a $500-a-year "administrative" fee that each webcaster would have to pay, regardless of its audience size or revenue. These fees would force many webcasters, who made no money or were hobbyists, to shut down. As an example, Live365, a company with an annual profit of $7,000, would owe $5 million a year in royalties and other fees.

In 2007, a group representing online audio broadcasters reached a royalty agreement with SoundExchange. The deal temporarily reduced rates sufficiently that many internet broadcasters could continue their programming. Online broadcasters were also negotiating separately with ASCAP and BMI to reduce the royalties they have to pay to the copyright owners of the underlying music as opposed to the recorded performances. In 2009, SoundExchange and radio broadcasters also came to an agreement where SoundExchange would discount royalty rates for radio broadcasters who also simulcast online; this agreement does not extend to internet-only radio stations, some of which were facing bankruptcy.

Podcasting, which exploded on the scene in the 2000s, is subject to royalty payments if copyrighted material is used. Podcasting is designed to be downloaded for later playing on a portable player, although it can also be streamed.

Interactive services. What is an *interactive service?* The Digital Millennium Copyright Act requires websites that stream music pay copyright owners individually if they are considered "interactive services"—meaning that they allow users to customize their experiences (such as Pandora and Spotify). At issue in the 2009 case of *Arista Records, LLC v. LAUNCHcast* (578 F.3d 148), was whether webcaster LAUNCHcast was an interactive service. If it was, then the company must pay individual licensing fees to copyright holders; if not, it would only have to pay a lower statutory licensing fee. LAUNCHcast allows users to create "stations" that play songs within a genre or similar to artists that users select. The Second Circuit said that this was not sufficiently interactive to qualify LAUNCHcast as an interactive service. Users cannot request a particular song, and the webcaster "does not provide sufficient control to users such that playlists are so predictable that users will choose to listen to the webcast in lieu of purchasing music, thereby—in the aggregate—diminishing record sales."

Freelancers and Electronic Publishing

Until about 1995, most major publishers did not include a provision in the contracts signed by freelancers to cover electronic rights. The National Writers Union, an organization that represents about 3,000 freelance writers, sued the New York Times Co., other major publishers, and the Lexis-Nexis computer database for using the writers' work electronically without specific permission. The publishers contended that these electronic databases were merely reproductions of the printed versions—and no separate permission was required.

A win for freelancers. In 2001, the Supreme Court sided with the writers in *New York Times v. Tasini* (533 U.S. 483). In this case, the Court ruled that Jonathan Tasini, former president of the National Writers Union, and other freelancers own the electronic rights to their works unless they specifically assign those rights to a publisher.

The case involved only material produced by *freelancers* as opposed to staff writers. Under the "works made for hire" provision of the Copyright Act, employers automatically own the copyrights to works created by employees within the scope of their employment. It also does not involve most freelance works published since 1995, when major publishers began including specific provisions to authorize electronic republication in their standard contracts.

Responding to the decision, the *New York Times* pointed out that between 1980 and 1995, the years covered by *Tasini*, the *Times* had published about 115,000 articles written by 27,000 different freelancers. Because of the difficulty of tracking down all these authors and securing permission, *Times* publisher Arthur Sulzberger, Jr. said the *Times* "will now undertake the difficult and sad process of removing significant portions from its electronic historical archive." Some historians, including filmmaker Ken Burns and historian Doris Kearns Goodwin, who filed an *amicus curiae* ("friend of the court") brief supporting the publishers, also lamented the gaps in the historical record that would result from the *Tasini* decision because publishers eventually removed so much freelance work from their databases.

Tasini said his union would be happy to work out a licensing system for freelancers similar to that used by ASCAP and BMI to compensate music copyright owners, with freelancers compensated each time someone accesses the electronic version of a story or other material that appeared in the major media. But by 2002, it was clear that the historians' worst fears were coming true. The *New York Times* removed more than 100,000 articles from its online archive and only restored about 15,000 of them after coming to terms with authors. Many of the other authors either could not be located or had not reached an agreement with the newspaper. And other newspapers that were not as concerned about being a newspaper of record as the *Times* simply deleted all pre-1995 freelance materials from their online archives and made no attempt to strike deals with freelance authors.

In joining Justice John Paul Stevens' dissenting opinion in the *Tasini* case, Justice Stephen Breyer said, "We may wipe out much of the history of the 20th century." The history isn't really gone. For those with the time and money to do research page by page, the full text of many newspapers remains intact on microfilm in some libraries. But for those who need the speed and global reach of online research, Justice Breyer's concern seems well founded.

A New York federal district court approved an $18 million settlement in a class action suit brought by freelance writers whose publishers reproduced the works for electronic distribution without authorization in the wake of *Tasini.* Freelancer Irvin Muchnick and others brought suit in the Second Circuit, claiming the settlement was inadequate and problematic because of its division of works into categories based on their times and statuses of copyright registration. The Second Circuit overturned the settlement in 2007, saying the trial court could not rule on claims relating to unregistered works, as the Copyright Act grants federal district courts jurisdiction only over claims on registered works. Thus, the federal district court could not certify a class in the litigation.

But the Supreme Court in 2010 said the Second Circuit had erred. Writing for an 8-0 Court (Justice Sonia Sotomayor did not participate), Justice Clarence Thomas said that a copyright holder's failure to register a work does not restrict a federal court's jurisdiction over claims related to unregistered works. While most copyright holders are required by the Copyright Act to register their works prior to filing a federal lawsuit, the registration requirement "is a precondition to filing a claim that does not restrict a federal court's subject-matter jurisdiction," Thomas wrote (*Reed Elsevier, Inc. v. Muchnick*, 559 U.S. 154).

In 2011, the Second Circuit said that the settlement did not represent the interests of most of the class. There was differential payment based on whether an article had been registered with the Copyright Office (registered articles were entitled to more money). Thus, the court concluded, "the district court abused its discretion in certifying the class and approving the settlement, because the named plaintiffs failed to adequately represent the interests of all class members"—one of the main requirements to certify a class (*In re Literary Works in Elect. Databases Copyright Litig.*, 654 F.3d 242).

Copyright Trolls

A new type of plaintiff made the news in the early 2010s, pejoratively labeled "copyright trolls." These companies approach copyright owners to purchase their rights and then aggressively sue multiple defendants who allegedly infringe those works. Many users will settle, paying statutory damages rather than going to court—an outcome that these companies count on. One judge disparaged the "business model" of these groups:

> Digiprotect acquires such rights from various copyright holders in order to—as Digiprotect's counsel described it—"educate consumers." This "education" of consumers consists primarily of bringing suit against such consumers and seeking "modest settlements" (*Digiprotect USA Corp. v. Does 1-266*, 2011 U.S. Dist. LEXIS 40679, 2011).

There are a number of such groups in action. For example, a group of attorneys calling themselves the U.S. Copyright Group (USCG) made the news in 2010 by including nearly 5,000 anonymous defendants who downloaded the movie *The Hurt Locker* in one suit for one filing fee—what the EFF calls "spamigation." Such a move could be a money-maker for the USCG and copyright holders, as most defendants will likely pay $1,500–2,500 to escape the potential to have to shell out $150,000 or more. The judge in the case asked the USCG to explain why she should not remove 4,576 of the 4,577 anonymous defendants. The USCG said that all infringers "are both uploading and downloading portions of the file simultaneously." In 2011, USCG and Voltage Pictures, the studio behind *The Hurt Locker*, added 25,000 anonymous defendants to the list—making the case the largest one to date against filesharers, but the case was dropped without explanation in 2013.

One of the more notorious trolls, Righthaven LLC, bought rights for old news stories from the *Las Vegas Review-Journal* and brought over a hundred infringement suits in Nevada federal court. In one case against Democratic Underground, an online community for Democrats and progressives, the website (represented by Electronic Frontier Foundation [EFF]) claimed that the quote targeted by Righthaven (five sentences out of a 54-sentence article) was a fair use—and filed a counterclaim against Righthaven.

A Nevada federal district court ruled for Democratic Underground. The judge said Righthaven had never owned the copyright, and the actual owner was not named in the suit. Moreover, the judge called the claims of ownership "disingenuous, if not outright deceitful," and gave Righthaven two weeks to explain to him in writing "why it should not be sanctioned for this flagrant misrepresentation to the Court" (*Righthaven LLC v. Democratic Underground LLC*, 791 F. Supp. 2d 968, 2011). Righthaven fared no better at the Ninth Circuit in 2013, where the court said that the company did not have standing to sue for copyright infringement under the rights it had obtained (*Righthaven LLC v. Hoehn*, 716 F.3d 1166).

Star Trek ftw. In perhaps the most quotable slapdown of a copyright troll (a troll of a troll?), in 2013 a district judge ruled (in an opinion filled with *Star Trek* references) that Prenda Law's filing of dozens of copyright infringement suits using the same boilerplate language "raised the Court's alert. It was when the Court realized Plaintiffs engaged their cloak of shell companies and fraud that the Court went to battlestations" (*Ingenuity 13 LLC v. Doe*, Copy. L. Rep. (CCH) P30,423). Most damaging to Prenda, however, was the judge's referral of the egregious case to state and federal agencies: "[T]hough Plaintiffs boldly probe the outskirts of law, the only enterprise they resemble is RICO. The federal agency [the IRS] eleven decks up is familiar with their prime directive and will gladly refit them for their next voyage. The Court will refer this matter to the United States Attorney for the Central District of California."

All levity aside: does this spell the end of copyright trolling? Nope. Given the amount of money at stake in these kinds of cases, groups like Prenda, Digiprotect, Righthaven, and USCG will try other legal techniques before the courts before they throw in the towel. Many such cases are dismissed, with the plaintiffs ordered to pay attorneys' fees. And even big companies sometimes hire these types of companies, as *BMG v. Cox* demonstrated earlier.

Other Internet Copyright Issues

Still other copyright problems have been created by cyberspace. A number of individual website owners have faced lawsuits because copyrighted materials were posted on their sites that could be downloaded. Several cases involved copyrighted software or digitized images.

Playboy Enterprises has aggressively pursued the owners of internet sites containing images owned by Playboy. In 1998, Playboy won what was then the largest statutory damage award in the history of American copyright law, a $3.74 million judgment against the owner of a site that allegedly distributed 7,475 Playboy-owned photographs over the internet (*Playboy Enter. v. Sanfilippo*, 1998 U.S. Dist. LEXIS 4773). In the 1990s Playboy also won six- and seven-figure statutory damage awards against other website operators.

Playboy also sued Terri Welles, the 1981 *Playboy* magazine "Playmate of the Year," in an attempt to keep her from identifying herself by that title on her website. However, a federal judge refused to grant a preliminary injunction in that case, holding that Playboy was unlikely to prevail in court even though "Playmate of the Year" is a registered trademark of Playboy. The judge said that a title like "Playmate of the Year" becomes a part of a person's identity, like being an Academy Award winner, a former Miss America, or a Heisman Trophy winner. To indicate this status on a website is a fair use under trademark law. Playboy appealed and the Ninth Circuit affirmed the judge's ruling. In a later decision, the appellate court also held that Welles not only could identify herself as Playmate of the Year but that she could use words such as "playboy" and "playmate" in *metatags*—hidden keywords used by search engines. The court concluded that there were no suitable alternate words she could use in her metatags (*Playboy Enter. v. Welles*, 162 F.3d 1169, 1998; 279 F.3d 796, 2002).

Search engines have also encountered other copyright and trademark problems. For one, Google.com and Yahoo.com have been sued by trademark owners for their lucrative practice of selling *sponsored links*—advertising tied to keyword searches. For example, if someone types the name of an insurance company or even a generic term like "car insurance," an ad for particular insurance company may appear along with the non-paid search results. Both Yahoo and Google now identify sponsored links, but they still sell ads that pop up when a user types certain keywords, including brand names of competing products.

AdWords (Google Ads). The Google AdWords program (now called Google Ads) allows businesses to pay for certain keywords that will get their ads displayed on Google search results pages for those words. Advertisers pay Google every time a user clicks on one of their ads and can also buy their competitors' names as keywords.

In 2009, Rescuecom, a computer-service franchising company, brought suit, saying that because Google recommended that Rescuecom's competitors buy its trademark as a keyword, users may be confused by Google's labeling of "sponsored link" into thinking that Rescuecom was affiliated with or supported its competition. The Second Circuit agreed: Google's keyword ad sales may be a use in commerce under the Lanham Act (*Rescuecom v. Google*, 562 F.3d 123), adding that "Google's recommendation and sale of Rescuecom's mark to Google's advertisers, so as to trigger the appearance of their advertisements and links in a manner likely to cause consumer confusion when a Google user launches a search of

Rescuecom's trademark" is an appropriate claim. The court remanded the case for a decision on whether Google's use of Rescuecom's trademark in the AdWords program causes consumer confusion, but in 2010 Rescuecom dropped all proceedings.

The question was answered in 2012. In the last serious challenge to the Google AdWords/Ads program, the Fourth Circuit said in *Rosetta Stone v. Google* (676 F.3d 144) that a district court improperly dismissed Rosetta Stone's trademark infringement case against Google AdWords, the first time an appellate court allowed a company to bring a trademark infringement suit on allegations that Google's sponsored links confuse consumers. The court asked "whether there is sufficient evidence for a finder of fact to conclude that Google's 'use' of the mark in its AdWords program is 'likely to produce confusion in the minds of consumers about the origin of the goods or services in question.'" In answering yes, the court noted that it was possible to find that "Google intended to cause confusion in that it acted with the knowledge that confusion was very likely to result from its use of the marks." In 2012, Rosetta Stone and Google settled for an unspecified amount.

Copyright management information. Federal law regulates "false copyright management information," punishing the publication or distribution of knowingly false copyright management information (17 U.S.C. §1202). But what information is covered in copyright management information (CMI)? The Third Circuit reversed a DMCA claim based on CMI in *Murphy v. Millennium Radio Group LLC* (650 F.3d 295). Peter Murphy, a photographer, was hired by *New Jersey Monthly* magazine to photograph two New Jersey radio hosts for WKXW, owned by Millennium Radio Group; the image made it look like the hosts were nude, standing behind a WKXW sign. The radio station uploaded the image on its website without Murphy's permission and removed the identifying information, including the "gutter credit" identifying Murphy as the photographer. Moreover, visitors to the WKXW website were encouraged to manipulate the photo. The hosts made Murphy a subject of one of their shows, calling him "gay" (that part of the case is discussed in Chapter Four).

Murphy sued, saying that the CMI statute was violated when his credits were removed and the use was not a fair use. The district court dismissed both claims, but the Third Circuit reversed: "the mere fact that Murphy's name appeared in a printed gutter credit near the Image rather than as data in an 'automated copyright protection or management system' does not prevent it from qualifying as CMI or remove it from the protection of §1202." The photo on WKXW's website was not a fair use. The Third was among the first circuits to address what kind of information is included in CMI.

■ INTERNATIONAL COPYRIGHTS

So far, this discussion has concerned mostly domestic copyrights in the United States. But copyrights are becoming more and more an international matter. For more than 100 years the United States refused to participate in the *Berne Convention,* a major international copyright agreement. When the Berne Convention for the Protection of Literary and Artistic Works was established in 1886, the United States was probably the world's leading copyright pirate. American publishers freely republished European books without paying any royalties to the copyright owners. While most nations agreed on a system of international copyright control, the United States simply refused to sign up.

UCC. How, then, have American works gained international copyright protection over the years? The United States has participated in another international copyright agreement called the *Universal Copyright Convention* (UCC) since 1954 and also entered into reciprocal copyright agreements with individual countries. But perhaps more important, major U.S. publishers often arranged for the simultaneous publication of major works in Berne Convention member countries such as Canada to obtain full international copyright protection.

Finally, the Berne Convention. During the twentieth century, the United States ceased to be a major copyright pirate and has instead become the world's leading *victim* of international copyright infringement. The result: U.S. copyright owners, including authors, filmmakers, and software creators, began pressing Congress to join the Berne Convention. After 102 years of U.S. non-participation in Berne, Congress finally acted to allow this country to join—by approving the Berne Convention Implementation Act of 1988. On March 1, 1989, the United States officially joined the Berne Convention, becoming the 79th nation to do so; there are currently nearly 180 participants. That gave American copyright owners protection in 24 countries with which the United States had no other copyright arrangement.

The Berne Convention offers far more copyright protection than the Universal Copyright Convention, of which the United States has long been a member. In essence, the UCC merely says copyright owners in any member country have whatever rights local citizens have in other member countries. If a country has little copyright protection, foreigners as well as that country's own citizens have little protection from piracy there. The Berne Convention, on the other hand, sets *minimum standards* for copyright protection, requiring each member country to provide at least that much protection. One of the biggest stumbling blocks for U.S. participation in Berne results from a moral rights requirement, discussed below.

The 1988 legislation made a number of revisions in U.S. copyright law to bring it into compliance with the requirements of the Berne Convention. For example, international copyrights are now protected under U.S. law *without registration*. But works published in the United States still must be registered before the owner can sue an infringer in U.S. courts.

Foreign copyright owners may sue for *actual damages* and other remedies (as opposed to statutory damages) without ever registering, although actual damages are often nonexistent in copyright cases (because the infringer often makes no profit). Domestic copyright owners may also sue for actual damages even if the copyright is unregistered when the infringement occurs—but they must still register before filing an infringement lawsuit, as explained earlier. Foreign holders don't have to do that.

URAA and the public domain. The complete elimination of copyright notice requirements was also required by the Berne Convention. Berne member countries must provide copyright protection *without any formalities*. However, compliance with the Berne Convention must comply with the First Amendment. A federal district court held a part of the Copyright Act violates the First Amendment in 2009. The case was remanded from the Tenth Circuit to reevaluate part of the Copyright Act, the Uruguay Round Agreement Act (URAA), which restores the U.S. copyrights of "foreign authors who lost those rights to the public domain for any reason other than the expiration of a copyright term." The plaintiffs, American performing artists who used works by foreign artists that were in the public domain, such as Sergei Prokofiev's "Peter and the Wolf," claimed they were harmed by higher licensing costs on the renewed copyrighted work. On remand, the judge said that although the Berne Convention does require some copyright restoration, URAA violates the First Amendment.

In 2011, the Supreme Court said that Section 514 of URAA did *not* exceed Congress' authority under the Copyright Act (*Golan v. Holder*, 565 U.S. 302). Justice Ruth Bader Ginsburg, writing for a 6-2 majority, said that no one gets personal benefit to copy a work in the public domain, so returning works to copyright protection doesn't abridge anyone's rights.

trade dress:

packaging or design of a product that promotes the product and distinguishes it from similar products; e.g., the shape of a Coca-Cola bottle.

secondary meaning:

a meaning that develops when the public associates a trademark with a particular producer, rather than the underlying product.

Berne convention:

an international copyright agreement that requires all signatory countries to recognize the same rights for foreign creators as they do for their own citizens as well as adhere to certain minimum standards of protection.

moral rights:

from the French *droit moral*, a legal right owned by creators to control the fate of their works based on the idea that there is a connection between creators and their creations.

Moreover, she added, there is historical precedent that there is nothing sacred about the public domain: "The First Congress, it thus appears, did not view the public domain as inviolate." The implications are clear; the Court supported Congress' desire to have all works governed by the same legal policies, regardless of their circumstances of publication. The law, Ginsburg said, "continued the trend toward a harmonized copyright regime by placing foreign works in the position they would have occupied if the current regime had been in effect when those works were created and first published."

Justice Stephen Breyer, joined by Justice Samuel Alito, dissented. Breyer said that Congress did not, under the Copyright Act, have the authority to enact Section 514. Moreover, he said, since the Copyright Act is intended to encourage production of new works, this law should fail because it "provides no monetary incentive to produce anything new" as it affects only works already created.

GATT and WIPO. American copyright owners gained even more international protection under the intellectual property provisions of the General Agreement on Tariffs and Trade (GATT), which was signed by 117 countries in 1994. GATT is a worldwide agreement covering many aspects of international business; its intellectual property provisions cover patents and trademarks as well as copyrights. In general, the GATT copyright provisions closely parallel the Berne Convention rules, setting minimum standards for international copyright protection. Perhaps the most important change is that the GATT provisions, once ratified by the signing countries, will apply in many countries that never joined the Berne Convention. The GATT provisions are administered by the World Trade Organization through the World Intellectual Property Organization (WIPO). Over time, GATT will have a major impact on U.S. copyrights, patents, and trademarks. Perhaps GATT's major weakness is that, like many global agreements, it may be difficult to enforce in some signing countries.

Because the GATT agreement is so far-reaching, copyright lawyers spent years trying to sort out how it affects U.S. law. One of the first issues to arise was the question of *copyright restoration*. Under GATT, a large number of foreign works that had fallen into the public domain under U.S. law had their copyright protection restored. This is true because the copyrights of many pre-1978 works that had expired under U.S. law were restored under the longer copyright terms provided by other countries and recognized by the U.S. legislation to implement GATT. (See *Golan v. Holder*, in this chapter.) This particularly affects those who use footage from old movies that were once in the public domain but may now be protected by copyright law again. A major concern is so-called "*orphan works*": works whose copyright owners have vanished.

Under the new rules, some of these old, formerly public-domain works again have valid copyrights—but there is no one available to grant permission for anyone to use these works. Companies that provide stock movie footage have been concerned that if they continue to use these ex-public-domain works without obtaining copyright clearances, owners of some of the reinstated copyrights may suddenly appear out of the blue and sue for copyright infringement. Because of extended copyright terms, millions of copyrighted works have also become orphan works.

The U.S. Copyright Office issued a lengthy report on the problem of orphan works in 2006, recommending new rules under which those who make a good-faith effort to find a work's owner would be liable only for modest fees and not the normal copyright infringement penalties if the owner turns up.

ACTA: pretty much dead. In 2011, the United States signed a new international initiative called the Anti-Counterfeiting Trade Agreement (ACTA) to fight piracy. Critics point out that it contains fewer protections for online service providers, leaves out key definitions for "piracy" and "counterfeiting," and lacks many of the balancing elements that are currently part of U.S. intellectual property law. So far, only Japan has formally ratified it; it isn't active in the United States or anywhere else, as the act requires six countries to ratify it before it activates.

Despite the international agreements, Congress still has not fully addressed one major difference between U.S. law and the seemingly mandatory requirements of international copyright law: the recognition of moral rights.

Moral Rights

In essence, *moral rights* give the creator of a copyrighted work some say over what happens to it later, even if the copyright is sold to someone else (such as a publishing house or a motion picture distributor). Under American law, the copyright owner (who is often not the creator of the work) has the absolute right to change a literary or artistic work without the consent of the original author or artist. But under Article 6 of the Berne Convention, each member country must recognize moral rights, thereby giving the original artist the right to prevent the work from being changed without his or her consent. The debate over moral rights became heated when Congress voted to change U.S. copyright law to make it (more or less) compatible with the requirements of the Berne Convention.

The moral rights question has always been a major obstacle to American participation in the Berne Convention: U.S. copyright owners strongly oppose any recognition of moral rights, while groups of authors and artists want such rights.

Colorization. The moral rights issue received considerable publicity in connection with the colorization of older black-and-white motion pictures. Many of the actors and directors who made these movies view colorization as a sacrilege—like mutilating a classic painting. But copyright owners see colorization as a way to make the films more appealing to a new generation of viewers. Cable entrepreneur Ted Turner was at the center of this controversy because his company colorized almost the entire MGM library of classic films. He purchased their copyrights in the mid-1980s and then had them colorized, something he had every right to do, despite the bitter objections of many actors and directors.

For the most part, Congress sided with Turner and other copyright owners, refusing to recognize moral rights. When the United States joined the Berne Convention—still without recognizing moral rights—that action stirred a controversy among copyright lawyers. Some contended that signing the Berne Convention automatically gave legal recognition to moral rights in the United States. Others pointed out that Berne specifically said joining the Berne Convention did not change American law on this point.

To address the issue of colorization, in 1988 Congress enacted a compromise law that pleased almost no one: the National Film Preservation Act. It created a National Film Preservation Board with representatives from 13 industry groups, including both the creative community and copyright owners. The board may nominate up to 25 films per year for inclusion in a National Film Registry. Each nominated film must be at least 10 years old, and only films released in theaters are eligible. The Librarian of Congress chooses some or all of the nominated films for inclusion in the registry. If a film is included, it can still be altered (or colorized) by the copyright owner, but there must be a conspicuous statement included in the altered version saying that the original film has been altered.

Trademark in moral rights. Some copyright owners argued that U.S. trademark laws give adequate protection to moral rights, and that the United States could comply with the Berne Convention's moral rights provisions without changing American copyright law. To support that claim, they pointed to cases such as *Lamothe v. Atlantic Recording Corp.* (847 F.2d 1403), a 1988 decision of the Ninth Circuit. That case held that two rock musicians could use the Lanham Act, the federal trademark law, to sue a third musician who falsely claimed that he was the sole author of songs they co-authored. They claimed that the third musician, Robinson Crosby of Ratt, falsely claimed sole credit for two songs on the album *Out of the Cellar.*

On the other hand, many in the creative community scoffed at the idea that U.S. trademark law provides adequate protection for moral rights. Trademark law only requires accurate labeling, not keeping the works true to the original artistic intent, they pointed out. For example, U.S. trademark law would allow a Picasso painting to be cut into pieces and sold as long as each piece is truthfully labeled as a Picasso. Under *Lamothe*, the copyright owner is still free to change a creative work without the creator's permission—as long as authorship credit is given. To creators of copyrighted works, changing their artistic intent and leaving their names on the work may be worse than changing the work and dropping their names.

VARA. In 1990, Congress went a step further in protecting the rights of visual artists but still stopped far short of giving full recognition to moral rights. The Visual Artists Rights Act (VARA) of 1990 gives sculptors, painters, and other visual artists the final say over whether their names are used on their works. Thus, artists can require that their names be kept on their works, and they can prevent their names from being used on works that have been altered without permission. VARA also gives visual artists the right to sue those who mutilate or destroy their art—even if they no longer own the copyright. However, it does not apply to many works created before this law went into effect, nor does it apply to "works made for hire": if the owner of a building commissions an artist to do a sculpture for the lobby, for example, the building's future owner can remove the sculpture without violating the law.

The act also gives artists the right to "salvage" their works when they are about to be demolished—when a building with a mural on a wall is to be torn down, for example. But the law says the artist has to pay for the removal process, which can be expensive. VARA does not change the law concerning the colorization of motion pictures.

Moral rights today. If you're hoping for a strengthening of moral rights recognition in the United States, the Copyright Office's most recent report (*Authors, Attribution, and Integrity: Examining Moral Rights in the United States*, April 2019) is no cause for celebration. That report said that no changes need to be made to how moral rights function in the United States: "many diverse aspects of the current moral rights patchwork—including copyright law's derivative work right, state moral rights statutes, and contract law—are generally working well and should not be changed," concluding that "there is no need for the creation of a blanket moral rights statute at this time."

However, the Copyright Office did propose legislative changes that Congress could enact to improve the operation of moral rights in American works, including amendments to VARA and the Lanham Act, and "suggestions to expand authors' recourse for removal or alteration of copyright management information." The report also suggested that Congress consider a federal right of publicity law to resolve issues created by the many state right-of-publicity laws.

A side note: Predicate Acts Doctrine. The Copyright Act does not usually reach outside the United States. If someone infringes your rights outside the United States, you can't use the Copyright Act to go after the infringer. But what if the infringement happens inside the United States, and then the infringer distributes illegal copies *outside* the United States? You may have some recourse under what's known as the *predicate acts doctrine.* The Fourth Circuit became the third circuit (after the Ninth and the Second) to address this doctrine in 2012 in *Tire Eng'g & Distrib. v. Shandong Linglong Rubber Co.* (682 F.3d 292), a non-media case involving specialized tires for underground mining. The Fourth Circuit was explicit, saying "We adopt the predicate-act doctrine, which posits that a plaintiff may collect damages from foreign violations of the Copyright Act so long as the foreign conduct stems from a domestic infringement," adding that plaintiffs who prove infringement in the United States that results in damages outside may collect on those "foreign violations that are directly linked to the U.S. infringement."

Unfair Competition: A State Supplement to Copyright

Earlier in this chapter we pointed out that news, factual information, and ideas cannot be copyrighted. However, there is another type of law that may prevent one news medium from systematically pirating its news from another. That legal action is called *unfair competition* or *misappropriation.* As a Second Circuit judge put it, "The essence of unfair competition under New York common law is the bad faith misappropriation of the labors and expenditures of another, likely to cause confusion or to deceive purchasers as to the origin of the goods" (*Jeffrey Milstein, Inc. v. Greger, Lawlor, Roth, Inc.,* 58 F.3d 27, 1995). Unlike copyright, which is now exclusively governed by a federal statutory law, unfair competition is a common-law tort action that developed primarily through state court decisions. There is no federal unfair competition statute.

Unfair competition was recognized as a separate legal action largely as a result of a 1918 Supreme Court decision that came to be regarded as a classic ruling: *Int'l News Serv. v. Assoc. Press* (248 U.S. 215). The case arose because INS, owned by the Hearst newspaper chain, consistently "borrowed" AP stories (this was possible because some Hearst papers were also AP members) and distributed them to INS customers as if they were INS stories. The Supreme Court acknowledged that the news cannot be copyrighted, but it ruled that no business may purloin its basic commodity from a competitor, "reaping where it has not sown," a paraphrase from the Bible.

Following this precedent, other courts have ruled similarly in similar situations, creating a new common law legal action for such misappropriation. A 1973 U.S. Supreme Court decision also offered unfair competition as a viable legal action. In *Goldstein v. California* (412 U.S. 546), the Court upheld a California law against record piracy at a time when copyright law did not cover sound recordings, despite the defendant's contention that the federal government had preempted the field. There have been numerous unfair competition lawsuits in various states—and the courts have held that unfair competition still exists as a valid basis for a lawsuit, although it only covers a few activities that fall very close to the news piracy that led to the original *INS v. AP* case.

In recent years, courts have sometimes said that state unfair competition actions are preempted by federal law. For example, in 2016 a Texas federal court held that a state unfair competition claim by a medical device company against its rival was preempted by federal copyright law. "[E]ven if works are not actually protected by copyright, if they are the types of works contemplated by copyright, state law cannot extend those works additional protection," the court explained (*ThermoTek, Inc. v. Orthoflex, Inc.*, Civil Action 3:11-CV-0870-D).

"Hot news." A New York federal judge allowed a lawsuit to go forward by the Associated Press against a competitor for copyright infringement and violation of the "hot news" tort. The "hot news" tort comes from *INS v. AP*, where the Court said that breaking news could be considered the "quasi property" of a news service. In *Assoc. Press v. All Headline News Corp.* (37 Media L. Rep. 1403, 2009), the AP alleged that AHN rewrote and repackaged breaking news stories and infringed its copyright; AHN said that "hot news" is protected from infringement. The judge disagreed with AHN, using the NBA pager case below as precedent, and allowed the infringement case to stand. The five elements to bring a "hot news" tort in New York were met, the judge said:

> (i) a plaintiff generates or gathers information at a cost; (ii) the information is time-sensitive; (iii) a defendant's use of the information constitutes free riding on the plaintiff's efforts; (iv) the defendant is in direct competition with a product or service offered by the plaintiffs; and (v) the ability of other parties to free-ride on the efforts of the plaintiff or others would so reduce the incentive to produce the product or service that its existence or quality would be substantially threatened.

The case settled in 2009 for an unspecified sum, although a joint press release acknowledged that AHN had often "improperly used AP's content without AP's consent."

But "hot news" is still in the news: In *Barclays Capital Inc. v. TheFlyOnTheWall.com Inc.*, the Second Circuit overturned a New York federal court ruling against a financial news website for publishing stock recommendations of Wall Street banking firms, calling it a "hot news" misappropriation. But the appellate court reversed: "A firm's ability to make news—by issuing a recommendation that is likely to affect the market price of a security—does not give rise to a right for it to control who breaks that news and how" (650 F.3d 876, 2011). In addition, the court said, Fly's website, "which collects, summarizes, and disseminates the news of the firms' recommendations—is not the 'INS-like' product that could support a non-preempted cause of action for misappropriation"—rejecting *INS* as a precedent here.

Unfair competition in sports reporting. A controversy over the concept of unfair competition arose in the 1990s when companies began providing sports scores and statistics *during actual sporting events*. For a fee, both computer and pager users could receive information in real time. The National Basketball Association (NBA)—backed by other sports leagues—sued over this practice, alleging misappropriation under New York's unfair competition laws. In *NBA v. Motorola* (105 F.3d 841), a significant 1997 decision, the Second Circuit held that providing sports information this way is neither a copyright infringement nor unfair competition.

Focus on...
A presidential patent

The only president to have held a patent is Abraham Lincoln. On May 22, 1849, Lincoln was awarded Patent #6,469, "A Device for Buoying Vessels Over Shoals."

Lincoln's patent reads: "Be it known that I, Abraham Lincoln, of Springfield, in the County of Sangamon, in the State of Illinois, have invented a new and improved manner of combining adjustable buoyant air chambers with a steamboat or other vessel for the purpose of enabling their draught of water to be readily lessened to enable them to pass over bars, or through shallow water, without discharging their cargoes."

The U.S. Patent and Trademark Office reports that Lincoln whittled the model for his invention by hand, and the model is on display at the Smithsonian Institution National Museum of American History.

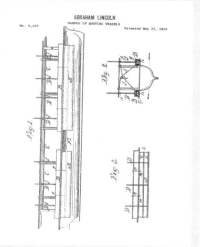

FIG. 61. Patent #6,469.

U.S. Patent and Trademark Office.

The court noted that only the broadcast descriptions of the games (not the games themselves) can be copyrighted. And these services were not even copying the broadcast descriptions, the court held. Instead, they monitored the broadcasts and compiled their own statistics—using factual information that is available to all. In essence, the court said this was different from systematically taking someone else's news stories, rewriting them, and then selling them via a competing wire service. Even if the NBA develops its own real-time sports information service, others may monitor broadcasts to provide factual information to competing services, the court said.

A related controversy arose in 2007 when the National Collegiate Athletic Association (NCAA) ordered the University of Louisville to expel a *Louisville Courier-Journal* reporter from a baseball playoff game for blogging about the game while it was taking place. In essence, the NCAA claimed that it has an exclusive right to forbid the dissemination of factual information about a game in progress. The newspaper's lawyers, among others, said the NCAA has the right to control television coverage of the game, but not the use of uncopyrightable factual information.

Fantasy sports and copyright. An estimated 45.9 million Americans were playing fantasy sports by 2019, often in arrangements licensed by sports leagues. But in 2005 an outside company was sued by Major League Baseball (MLB) in a contractual dispute. MLB contended that C.B.C. Distribution and Marketing's fantasy games violated its copyrights and the rights of publicity of the players. C.B.C. contended that it has a First Amendment right to use the names and statistics of players whose names are in the news media daily—and without paying licensing fees. The Eighth Circuit ruled that C.B.C.'s use of players' names and statistics is protected by the First Amendment, raising doubts about the validity of other fantasy sports license agreements that involve paying sports leagues for the use of players' names and stats (*C.B.C. Distrib. & Mktg. v. Major League Baseball*, 505 F.3d 818, 2007).

Fantasy sports league players won again in 2009. Relying on *C.B.C. Distrib.*, a federal district court in Minnesota said that a fantasy football game provider didn't need a license from the National Football League (NFL) to use player names, statistics, and other information for its game (*CBS Interactive Inc. v. Nat'l Football League Players Inc.*, 259 F.R.D. 398, 2009). In trying to differentiate the two cases, the NFL argued that perhaps the First Amendment implications of fantasy football may be less than those of fantasy baseball because there was no evidence presented about which sport had more public interest. The judge wisely avoided getting into that debate: "[T]he Court declines to indulge in a philosophical debate about whether the public is more fascinated with baseball or football or the statistics generated by each. Suffice it to say that there is no dispute that both professional baseball and professional football and the statistics generated by both sports are closely followed by a large segment of the public."

■ TRADEMARKS

Another area of intellectual property law that fills a gap in copyright protection is trademark, tradename, and service mark law. The basic purpose of trademark laws is to prevent customer confusion. A new company that adopts a logo or name that looks like or sounds like a famous trademark for a similar product is likely to run afoul of the law, even if the logo or name is slightly different.

States can regulate trademarks. There is a federal trademark law, the Lanham Act (officially, the Trademark Act of 1946). But unlike the Copyright Act, it is nonexclusive; it does *not* preempt state trademark laws. In fact, many states have their own trademark statutes, and all states recognize at least some kind of inherent right of a business to adopt a name and prevent imitators from using it under the common law. A person who infringes someone else's trademark may be sued in federal court, in state court, or both. About 30 states have adopted all or most of the provisions of a Model State Trademark Bill. These laws govern the slogans or other short phrases, logos and designs, symbols and names under which businesses operate and market their products and services. An understanding of this area of law is especially important for those planning a career in advertising or public relations.

Federal law: Lanham Act. The Lanham Act established a nationwide registration system for trademarks and service marks (a subcategory of trademarks for service companies, like insurance or banking). When a business wants to adopt a mark, the first step is to conduct a search to see if any competitor is using a similar name. Most businesses pay a commercial research firm to find out whether their chosen name is available by searching the voluminous files of past trademark registrations and other sources of information on trademark usage. If no one else has registered the name, the business follows a registration and filing procedure with the U.S. Patent and Trademark Office (USPTO) not unlike that set up by the Copyright Act. As part of the process, proposed trademarks are published, and rival businesses may challenge the registration of a new trademark if they wish.

What sort of names may and may not be registered under the Lanham Act? Generally, any name, phrase, or symbol that distinguishes a firm's goods or services may be registered, but there are some exceptions. Flags and symbols for cities, states, and countries cannot be registered. Nor may the name, portrait, or signature of a living person be registered as a company's trademark—except under circumstances where the name or likeness has already become distinctively associated with a firm. However, well-known individual celebrities can register their names as trademarks for their own marketing purposes. A number of celebrities have done that since it became legally possible. (As Chapter Five explains, celebrities can also protect their names under right of publicity laws in many states.)

In addition, purely geographic names and descriptive terms (for instance "first rate," "high quality," "blue ribbon," and "A-1") are usually unregisterable. One reason for this rule is that most popular names, descriptive terms, and geographic names are so widely used that no one may gain a monopoly on their use nationally in connection with trade. This is not to say you can't open a business and call it "A-1 Auto Repair" or "Blue Ribbon Burgers," but you'll have a tough time getting it registered nationally as your exclusive trademark. Even if a name is so widely used that no one can register it as a national trademark, someone may gain the exclusive right to use it locally. For instance, if you start a business called "A-1 Auto Repair" when there is already a business in the area called "A-1 Car Repair Company," you may be sued in a state court.

Because there have been many businesses seeking distinctive trademarks for many years, the surest way to get a new trademark registered nationally is to come up with a *new* word. Many trademarks have been created this way: Exxon, Kodak, and Lexus, for example.

Registration and renewal. Assuming a business gets its proposed trademark past the hurdles of USPTO registration, the firm may use the trademark in various ways. The name may appear on products, in advertising, and on the corporate letterhead. The fact that the trademark is registered under the Lanham Act is indicated by the ® symbol after the word or phrase. However, trademarks may also be indicated in other ways. For instance, when registration has not yet been secured, a firm may indicate that it claims a word or phrase as a trademark by placing "TM" after the name (or "SM" for a service mark).

Once registered under the Lanham Act, a trademark is valid for 10 years but must be reaffirmed after the first five years. Thereafter, a renewal every 10 years is required. There is no limit to the number of times a trademark may be renewed, as long as the trademark owner can show that it is still being "used in commerce." Unlike a copyright, a trademark can be maintained as private property indefinitely.

Abandonment and genericide. However, a trademark may also be abandoned or lost. Under the Lanham Act, failure to use a trademark for two years creates a presumption that it has been abandoned. Acquiescence in allowing others to use your trademark in a generic way can also result in its loss, which explains why trademarks such as "Xerox" and "Coca-Cola" are so vigorously defended by their owners. Should those words be allowed to become generally descriptive of all photocopying or all cola-type beverages, the owners could lose their exclusive rights to these names, as did the owners of ex-trademarks such as "aspirin," "cellophane," "cornflakes," "yo-yo," and "linoleum."

Anti-genericide tactics. Companies do various things to avoid losing their trademarks through widespread usage as generic words. Some companies advertise in magazines read by journalists to admonish writers and editors about the correct usage of their trademarks. The Xerox Corporation, for example, reminds journalists to capitalize "Xerox" and use it as an adjective referring to a Xerox-brand product. Never use the word as a verb, the company insists, expressing outrage at statements such as "Go xerox this for me." Some companies have made funny videos to remind consumers: check out Velcro's videos on YouTube.

Ideally, trademark owners want the news media to use their names as adjectives followed by a generic name for the product, such as "Dolby noise reduction system" or "Plexiglas acrylic sheeting." What happens to writers who misuse a trademark? Journalists who break the rules may receive pointed letters from a trademark owner's lawyers—all as part of the company's effort to demonstrate that it is not acquiescing to the generic use of its trade-mark. However, a company's lawyers can do little more than write angry letters when the

FIG. 62.
The Slants, live at Flying Dog Brewery in Frederick, Maryland, Apr. 16, 2017. Lead singer Simon Tam (center) won the right at the high court to trademark his band name in *Matal v. Tam,* overturning part of the Lanham Act.

Grudnick, "DSC_0051," via Flickr, public domain.

news media use trademarks as if they were generic terms. In fact, courts sometimes regard the widespread generic use of a trademark in the news media as one form of proof that the word or phrase has lost its special meaning. However, *non-journalistic* abuses of trademarks are another matter. News writers may get away with misusing trademarks, but when one company misuses another's trademark in its advertising or on a product, a lawsuit is likely to result. Even book authors must be careful to use trademarks correctly. It would be quite legal for someone not associated with Ford Motor Company to publish a book called, "How to Repair Fords," as long as it is made clear that Ford is a trademark, and that the author is not claiming it as his or her own trademark.

Although federal registration of a trademark is obviously desirable if it can be secured, a person or business that has used a name over a period of time acquires some special rights with or without federal registration. In fact, Lanham Act registration is unavailable to purely local businesses, although most states have their own registration systems under which local trademarks may be protected. State trademark protection varies widely. But whatever the specific rules are in a given state, the courts will step in to prevent a new business from creating public confusion by imitating the name or trademark of an old, established one.

"Secondary meanings." Under the principles of common law and equity trademark protection (which protect trademarks regardless of whether they are registered at the state or federal level or unregistered), the key issue in a lawsuit is whether a word or phrase has acquired a *secondary meaning* in connection with a certain product or service. There is a secondary meaning if the words connote something more than their dictionary definition because of the commercial usage. For instance, the word "playboy" has one meaning in the dictionary, but when applied to a magazine, it has a special meaning beyond that.

If a word or phrase is found to have a secondary meaning to a substantial number of people, no one else may use the name for a similar kind of business in that locality without creating confusion and misleading the public. With or without a trademark registration under federal or state law, the mere use of a tradename over time gives the user certain ownership rights: no business is entitled to pass off its product or service as someone else's. Even if a newcomer registers the name as a trademark first, the original user of the name

FIG. 63.
"FUCT" t-shirt.
This trademark
was rejected for
registration by
the U.S. Patent &
Trademark Office,
resulting in a lawsuit
(*Ianci v. Brunetti*)
that invalidated
another content-
based element of
the Lanham Act.

Author's collection.

will often prevail in court. The goal is to prevent a newcomer from fraudulently trading on the goodwill of an established business. This is the overriding objective of the common law of trademarks, of state trademark laws, and of the federal Lanham Act.

What sort of words can acquire a secondary meaning? A good illustration of how trademark law works was provided by two federal appellate court decisions handed down on the same day in 1993: *Pacific Telesis Group v. Int'l Telesis Commnc'ns* (994 F.2d 1364) and *Fruit of the Loom v. Girouard* (994 F.2d 1359). Pacific Telesis, at one time a large regional telephone company, began using "Telesis" as part of its name in 1983. Two years later, a new firm adopted "International Telesis" as its name and entered the telecommunications consulting business. Pacific Telesis sued, and the Ninth Circuit ruled that "telesis" (a Greek word meaning "event" or "fulfillment") is such a unique word when applied to the telephone industry that no one else in that line of business may use it without Pacific Telesis' permission.

On the other hand, the Ninth Circuit refused to give Fruit of the Loom, a large clothing manufacturer, the exclusive right to use the word "fruit" in the apparel industry. Ken Girouard created a company called "Two Left Feet" and began making flip-flops called "Fruit Flops" and bustiers called "Fruit Cups." The court agreed that "Fruit of the Loom" has a secondary meaning; in fact, it's one of the oldest trademarks still in use, first registered in 1871. However, the court ruled that the use of the word "fruit" by itself is not enough to constitute a trademark infringement, even when used by another clothing manufacturer. There was little likelihood that consumers would confuse the two names or product lines.

Damages. The Lanham Act offers a host of options for damage awards, including profits, damages, and costs. At issue before the Supreme Court in 2020 was the question of whether, as one circuit required, the repayment of profits could only occur on a finding of willful (knowing, rather than innocent) infringement. In *Romag Fasteners, Inc. v. Fossil, Inc.* (140 S. Ct. 1492), the justices unanimously said no. Romag, a manufacturer of handbag fasteners, sued Fossil for using fake Romag products and falsely representing that the fasteners were actually Romag's, and it won $6.8 million from Fossil's profits. But Romag could not collect because it couldn't prove that Fossil had acted willfully, as required by the Second Circuit. Justice Neil Gorsuch turned to the language of the law and, noting that the justices will not "read into statutes words that aren't there," found no support for Fossil's claims of a requirement of willfulness, particularly when such requirements do appear elsewhere in the Lanham Act's language. Gorsuch made the rule clear: To recover profits from a defendant in a trademark infringement suit, a plaintiff is not required to show that the defendant's infringement was willful.

Litigating Lanham

There are dozens of cases each year in which courts interpret the Lanham Act or state trademark laws. What follows here is a selection of recent and past cases of note.

"Disparaging" or "scandalous" marks. A controversial trademark decision by the Trademark Trial and Appeal Board (TTAB), a board that addresses trademark registration disputes, made news in 2014 when the board revoked the Washington football team's "R*******" trademark after complaints that the mark was disparaging. In a 177-page report, the TTAB reviewed decades of these trademarks and images, concluding that "*at a minimum,* approximately 30% of Native Americans found the term R******* used in connection with respondent's services to be disparaging at all times including 1967, 1972, 1974, 1978 and 1990." The team appealed, but a federal district court in 2015 upheld the TTAB decision, saying that the trademark registration program is government speech and thus exempt from the First Amendment. Moreover, the court added, the team could still use unregistered trademarks (*Pro-Football, Inc. v. Blackhorse,* 112 F. Supp. 3d 439).

But the Supreme Court made all this moot. Two cases announced a year apart in 2018 and 2019 instituted significant changes to Section 2(a) of the Lanham Act, eliminating clauses that regulated the content of potential trademarks. Prior to the decisions in *Matal v. Tam* and *Iancu v. Brunetti,* the act forbade the registration of any trademark which "[c]onsists of or comprises immoral, deceptive, or scandalous matter; or matter which may disparage or falsely suggest a connection with persons, living or dead, institutions, beliefs, or national symbols, or bring them into contempt, or disrepute," known as the "Immoral/Scandalous" and "Disparagement" Clauses. Both clauses were ultimately held unconstitutional.

Goodbye, "disparagement." In 2017, the Court first handed a win to Simon Shaio Tam, founder of San Francisco-based Asian-American rock group "The Slants," on an appeal of a TTAB decision against his trademark registration of the band's name. The Federal Circuit had said that the "Disparagement Clause" of Section 2(a) of the Lanham Act violated the First Amendment because it "discriminates on the basis of the content of the message conveyed by the speech." The Court agreed, in a case that one Court watcher called "one of the most important First Amendment free speech cases to come along in many years," *Matal v. Tam* (137 S. Ct. 1744).

In the majority opinion, Justice Samuel Alito disposed of three arguments under which the TTAB tried to justify Section 2(a). First, he said, trademarks are *not* government speech, and registration of a mark does not mean that the government approves of it. Second, *Rust v. Sullivan* and *NEA v. Finley* (discussed in Chapter Three and elsewhere), where the government grants money for certain things, do not apply, as they involved subsidies *given by* the government, not *paid to* it; trademark registration requires payment of fees.

Finally, Alito rejected the government's attempt to create a new doctrine. Agreeing that in past cases the Court has held viewpoint discrimination unlawful (as in *Rosenberger,* discussed in Chapter Fourteen), Alito said that this case proves his point: Section 2(a), the Disparagement Clause, "denies registration to any mark that is offensive to a substantial percentage of the members of any group. But in the sense relevant here, that is viewpoint discrimination: Giving offense is a viewpoint."

Justice Anthony Kennedy, joined by Justices Ruth Bader Ginsburg, Sonia Sotomayor, and Elena Kagan, wrote to note that the Court's finding of viewpoint discrimination should have ended its inquiry. Justice Clarence Thomas also joined in the judgment, but added a brief statement in his concurring opinion that has become a common refrain since he first articulated the idea in 1996 (in a case discussed in Chapter Thirteen, *44 Liquormart v. Rhode Island*): "I continue to believe that when the government seeks to restrict truthful speech in order to suppress the ideas it conveys, strict scrutiny is appropriate, whether or not the speech in question may be characterized as 'commercial.'"

See ya, "scandalous." In 2019, on the heels of the *Tam* case, came the challenge to the "Immoral/Scandalous Clause." Erik Brunetti, an apparel manufacturer, sought to register the trademark "FUCT," which Justice Elena Kagan, writing for the Court, noted was supposed to be "pronounced as four letters, one after the other: F-U-C-T." But, she added, "you might read it differently and, if so, you would hardly be alone." That pronunciation was what triggered the USPTO to deny the registration.

Based on *Tam*, the Supreme Court overturned the immoral/scandalous clause of the Lanham Act (*Iancu v. Brunetti*, 139 S. Ct. 2294). Calling the clause viewpoint-based, Justice Kagan gave examples: the USPTO said no to "YOU CAN'T SPELL 'HEALTHCARE' WITHOUT THC" (glamorizing drug abuse), but yes to "D.A.R.E. TO RESIST DRUGS AND VIOLENCE" (condemning drug abuse). And: No to "trademarks associating religious references with products (AGNUS DEI for safes and MADONNA for wine) because they would be 'offensive to most individuals of the Christian faith' and 'shocking to the sense of propriety'" but yes to "PRAISE THE LORD for a game and JESUS DIED FOR YOU on clothing—whose message suggested religious faith rather than blasphemy or irreverence." These distinctions, she concluded, were viewpoint-based and thus ran afoul of the First Amendment. "There are a great many immoral and scandalous ideas in the world (even more than there are swearwords), and the Lanham Act covers them all. It therefore violates the First Amendment," she added.

This decision, however, wasn't wholly unanimous. While all justices agreed that the "immoral" part of the clause clearly discriminated based on viewpoint and must be overturned, Chief Justice John Roberts and Justices Stephen Breyer and Sonia Sotomayor suggested that the "scandalous" ban could be left in place if the definition was narrowed to include only obscene, vulgar, and profane marks. Fearing an onslaught of trademark applications containing "the most vulgar, profane, or obscene words and images imaginable," Justice Sotomayor said that restricting the clause would be "a reasonable, viewpoint-neutral restriction on speech that is permissible in the context of a beneficial governmental initiative like the trademark-registration system." Chief Justice Roberts agreed with her, saying that he didn't think refusing to register profane or vulgar marks violated the First Amendment.

Justice Breyer also agreed, but he took a different tactic, questioning the Court's oft-employed categorical approach to freedom of expression. He would avoid that: "I believe we should focus on the interests the First Amendment protects and ask a more basic proportionality question: Does 'the regulation at issue wor[k] harm to First Amendment interests that is disproportionate in light of the relevant regulatory objectives?'"

It is also worth noting that Justice Samuel Alito, in his concurrence, suggested that Congress is free to step in to provide more clarity. The *Brunetti* decision, he said, "does not prevent Congress from adopting a more carefully focused statute that precludes the registration of marks containing vulgar terms that play no real part in the expression of ideas." Will Congress do so? Time will tell.

Domain names. Although domain names will be discussed more later in this chapter, it's worth noting here that with the surging growth of the internet in the late 1990s, new legal dilemmas arose for trademark owners and others who wanted to register names for websites and email addresses. For example, xerox.com is Xerox Corporation's domain name, just as harvard.edu is Harvard University's. Likewise, fcc.gov is the Federal Communications Commission's domain name. These domain names will take you to the organization's website. The "Xerox" or "Harvard" or "FCC" is the specific entity's (second-level) domain name; the ".com" or ".edu" or ".gov" is a generic *top-level domain name (TLD)* shared by many organizations. Other currently recognized top-level domain names include ".mil" for military organizations, ".org" for noncommercial organizations, and ".net" for entities loosely defined as computer networks. Nations also have top-level domain names, such as ".us" for the United States and ".eu" for the European Union.

Online shopping is kind of a big deal, particularly during a pandemic; one 2021 estimate suggests a range of between 12 and 24 million shops worldwide (2.1 million in the United States alone) used by 2.14 billion online customers, over a quarter of the global population. Given those numbers, and even though there are millions of potential domain names available as combinations of a word and a top-level domain (like .com or one of the 1,500 other "dot" options currently recognized), it's become increasingly difficult to find domain names that accurately reflect the site's purpose or product and increasingly inevitable that trademark challenges will arise. One case arose in 2020, when the USPTO declined to allow online travel company Booking.com to register its domain name as a service mark. The office followed its policy that the combination of a generic term (like "booking" for hotel and airline arrangements) with ".com" was too generic to be eligible for trademark protection.

Both a district and an appellate court said that the USPTO policy was wrong; the term "Booking.com," unlike "booking" by itself, wasn't generic. The Court agreed on an 8-1 vote. In *U.S. Patent & Trademark Office v. Booking.com B.V.* (140 S. Ct. 2298)—the first case argued over telephone due to the COVID-19 pandemic—Justice Ruth Bader Ginsburg said that consumers' interpretations of a term should determine whether a term was generic or not, as well as whether that term had acquired "secondary meaning" necessary to qualify for trademark protection. "Because 'Booking.com' is not a generic name to consumers, it is not generic," she said.

Justice Stephen Breyer, dissenting, claimed that Booking.com "informs the consumer of the basic nature of its business and nothing more," so it is too generic for trademark protection. In addition, he discounted the importance of consumer survey data in determining whether a mark is generic, noting that it "may be an unreliable indicator of genericness."

Colors and sounds. Under certain circumstances not only a name or symbol but also a *color* may be protected as a trademark, according to a 1995 U.S. Supreme Court decision, *Qualitex Co. v. Jacobson Products Inc.* (514 U.S. 159). The Court said that if a company uses a distinctive color for its products for a long enough time, the color may become sufficiently associated with the product in consumers' minds that it has a secondary meaning.

Sometimes even a distinctive *sound* can qualify for trademark protection. For example, the roar of MGM's lion, the phrase "AT&T" spoken over a musical sound, and NBC's three-note chime—famous since radio days—have trademark protection.

Focus on...

Trademark dilution, parody, and squeaky pet toys

As we've learned, parody is highly protected. While early attempts by companies to leverage parody in their advertising were rebuffed by the courts (see wins by Vanna White and Bette Midler in Chapter Five), products that riff on popular brands in parodies that obviously aren't extensions of that brand are getting protection from trademark dilution claims. And oddly, pet products seem to be common defendants.

Take a 2002 case that featured parody perfume for pets. Nature Labs' perfumes are based on and named for famous scents, like "White Dalmatians" (Elizabeth Taylor's White Diamonds). But Tommy Hilfiger was not amused at "Timmy Holedigger" perfume and sued for dilution. A federal district court found for Nature Labs (*Tommy Hilfiger Licensing, Inc. v. Nature Labs, LLC*, 221 F. Supp. 2d 410), saying that although the marks resembled each other, it was clear that the Holedigger pet

FIG. 64. "Bad Spaniel," "White Paw," and "Chewy Vuiton" toys.

Author's collection.

perfume was a parody and wouldn't be confused with the Hilfiger scent for humans. Following this trend, in 2007 the Fourth Circuit protected a small company's line of "Chewy Vuiton" pet toys against Louis Vuitton's charges of dilution under the Trademark Dilution Revision Act (*Louis Vuitton Malletier S.A. v. Haute Diggity Dog, LLC*, 507 F.3d 252). The court held that not only would consumers know that the high-end fashion designer was not the source of cheap dog toys, Vuitton had "an increased burden" to demonstrate that its marks were harmed because a successful parody, like Chewy, communicates that "it is not the famous mark, but is only satirizing it."

The trend continues: in 2021 the Supreme Court denied *cert* to Jack Daniels' appeal from its 2020 dilution claim loss at the Ninth Circuit against a "Bad Spaniels" chew toy (*VIP Prods. LLC v. Jack Daniel's Props., Inc.*, 953 F.3d 1170). The appeals court said that the toy's humor element offered additional protection, and that humor also makes the use "noncommercial," so dilution doesn't apply. And, the court said, the work is a well-targeted parody: "Bad Spaniels comments humorously on precisely those elements that Jack Daniels seeks to enforce."

What does this suggest for companies whose products are parodied? These plaintiffs, as the judge said in *Nature Labs* (quoting former Ninth Circuit judge Alex Kozinski), are "advised to chill."

Standard character marks in trademark. In one of many POM Wonderful legal actions, POM's makers alleged that Pur Beverages, in using the word "pŏm" on a pomegranate-flavored energy drink, infringed POM's trademark under the Lanham Act. The district court found for Pur, saying that it was unlikely that POM could demonstrate consumer confusion. However, in *POM Wonderful, LLC v. Hubbard* (775 F.3d 1118), the Ninth Circuit reversed. "Standard character registrations 'are federal mark registrations that make no claim to any particular font style, color, or size of display,'" the court said. So the fact that "POM" and "pŏm" were comprised of the same letters in the same order and meant basically the same thing meant that POM's mark was protected.

Trade dress. Another aspect of trademark law has provoked enough controversy to produce two Supreme Court decisions: the question of whether a business can keep a competitor from imitating its *trade dress*—the look and feel of a product that identifies its source (think the familiar curvy Coca-Cola bottle, as compared to Pepsi). In *Two Pesos v. Taco*

Cabana (505 U.S. 763, 1992), the Court upheld a federal court judgment in favor of Taco Cabana, a Mexican fast-food restaurant chain that claimed Two Pesos imitated the appearance and decor of its restaurants. The justices unanimously ruled that a store's trade dress can have "inherent distinctiveness," and if it does, that "look" can be protected under the Lanham Act. That may be true even if the trade dress has not acquired a *secondary meaning*, the Court ruled. But the Court didn't define "inherent distinctiveness," creating uncertainty about what is and is not protected as a part of a company's trade dress.

In 2000, the Supreme Court revisited the trade dress question, ruling unanimously that clothing designers may not ordinarily use federal trademark law to prevent others from making similar-looking apparel. Ruling in *Wal-Mart Stores v. Samara Brothers* (529 U.S. 205), the Court held that designers may not gain trademark protection for their designs merely by claiming that the product is inherently distinctive. Instead, they must prove that the public so strongly associates the design with a designer that there is a secondary meaning. This is generally very difficult to prove. The Court said a product has a secondary meaning only when, "in the minds of the public, the primary significance of a (trademark) is to identify the source of the product rather than the product itself."

This decision leaves discounters such as Wal-Mart free to sell merchandise similar to high-end brand-name products as long as there is no actual counterfeiting or other deceptive marketing. Only if the public is deceived into believing they are buying the brand-name item is there likely to be a trademark infringement, the Court indicated. A product can resemble a brand-name item such as the children's clothing decorated with hearts and flowers that Samara designed and Wal-Mart's supplier imitated.

The *Wal-Mart* case limits the impact of the high court's earlier *Two Pesos* case. In *Two Pesos*, the Court *upheld* a restaurant chain's right to protect the trade dress of its restaurants from imitators *without* proving the existence of a secondary meaning. But now the Court has refused to protect the trade dress of products unless there is a secondary meaning.

Contributory infringement in trademark. In an important development in trademark infringement, Gucci was permitted to bring suit against credit card processors for contributory infringement for processing payments for fake Gucci products (*Gucci America v. Frontline Processing Corp.*, 721 F. Supp. 2d 228, 2010). Gucci could proceed with the suit if it could show that the credit card processors "(1) intentionally induced the website to infringe through the sale of counterfeit goods or (2) knowingly supplied services to websites and had sufficient control over infringing activity to merit liability." In allowing the case to go forward, the court said that a defendant may be liable for infringement "if it supplied services with knowledge or by willfully shutting its eyes to the infringing conduct, while it had sufficient control over the instrumentality used to infringe."

Online auction site eBay avoided liability for contributory infringement because it apparently didn't just "shut its eyes" to alleged violations. In 2010, the Second Circuit said that eBay was not liable for contributory infringement of Tiffany trademarks by allowing sales of alleged counterfeit Tiffany goods by others on its site (*Tiffany (NJ) Inc. v. eBay Inc.*, 600 F.3d 93). The court found that eBay used Tiffany's marks lawfully, "to describe accurately the genuine Tiffany goods offered for sale on its website." Moreover, the court pointed out that Tiffany's page on eBay notified consumers that most of the goods offered on eBay identified as Tiffany were fakes, and eBay removed allegedly counterfeit listings and engaged in affirmative actions to seek out forgeries. The court concluded, "To impose liability because eBay cannot guarantee the genuineness of all of the purported Tiffany products offered on its website would unduly inhibit the lawful resale of genuine Tiffany goods."

And taking action matters. The Eleventh Circuit said in 2019 that a trademark owner can sue a landlord for contributory infringement if the landlord knows or should have known that a tenant is engaging in counterfeiting but does nothing (*Luxottica Group, S.p.A. v. Airport Mini Mall, LLC*, 932 F.3d 1303). Luxottica, owner of high-end sunglass brands Oakley and Ray-Ban, alleged that the owners of a Georgia mall contributed to trademark infringement after law enforcement raids on the mall—one that took 14 hours and required a trailer to haul away seized goods—turned up counterfeit sunglasses being sold. Luxottica sent letters notifying the owners about the allegedly infringing tenants, and a company investigator was able to buy counterfeit Ray-Bans for $15–$20 at several booths (authentic Ray-Bans sell for $140–$220). When the landlords took no action to evict the infringing tenants, Luxottica sued. The Eleventh Circuit upheld both a jury verdict and the district court's findings in favor of Luxottica, saying that even if the landlords did not personally see the fake sunglasses, they should have known that infringement was occurring based on the raids and the letters, and they should have acted to stop it. "We agree with the other circuits that willful blindness [knowing about potential wrongdoing and failing to investigate] is a form of constructive knowledge for contributory trademark infringement," said the court.

Barbie goes to court. The iconic Barbie doll, a mainstay of Mattel's toy line, has been the subject of several trademark (and copyright) lawsuits. A 2002 Ninth Circuit decision held that the song "Barbie Girl" on a 1997 album by the Danish band Aqua did not infringe Mattel's trademark rights in the name "Barbie" for dolls. The court cited the First Amendment in allowing this parody of a toy line that has become a cultural icon and said there was no danger of consumer confusion here (*Mattel Inc. v. MCA Records*, 296 F.3d 894). And in *Mattel Inc. v. Walking Mountain Prods.* (353 F.3d 792, 2003), the Ninth Circuit also upheld Utah artist Tom Forsythe's right to make satirical use of naked Barbie dolls posed with kitchen appliances in a series of photographs called "Food Chain Barbie." A judge later ordered Mattel to pay $1.8 million to the artist to cover attorney's fees.

In *Mattel Inc. v. Goldberger* (365 F.3d 133, 2004), an appellate court held that facial features of the Barbie doll such as the eyes, nose, and mouth are protectible under copyright law. But Mattel was soon back in court fighting MGA Entertainment, the company that makes Bratz dolls. In a hotly contested series of cases, Mattel in 2008 initially won a $100 million judgment, successfully arguing that Carter Bryant, designer of the pouty Bratz, invented them while he worked for Mattel. But the Ninth Circuit in 2010 ruled for MGA (*Mattel, Inc. v. MGA Entm't, Inc.*, 616 F.3d 904). "It is not equitable to transfer this billion dollar brand—the value of which is overwhelmingly the result of MGA's legitimate efforts—because it may have started with two misappropriated names," said the court. In a 2011 remand, a jury awarded Bryant $88.4 million, saying that Mattel may have misappropriated trade secrets from MGA. Both parties could claim a Ninth Circuit win in 2013 (*Mattel, Inc. v. MGA Entm't, Inc.*, 705 F.3d 1108), in which the court threw out a $172.5 million award against Mattel for theft of trade secrets but upheld a trial court's award of $137.2 million to MGA on the copyright elements—ending the long-running dispute. The case gave the quotable former chief judge Alex Kozinski a chance to admonish the parties, suggesting that "perhaps Mattel and MGA can take a lesson from their target demographic: Play nice."

Other trademark issues. The Supreme Court decided less common issues in two trademark cases in 2015: *B&B Hardware, Inc. v. Hargis Indus., Inc.* (135 S. Ct. 1293) and *Hana Fin., Inc. v. Hana Bank* (135 S. Ct. 907). In the first, B&B produced hardware under the mark SEALTIGHT since 1990, and the mark was registered in 1993. Since then, Hargis used the mark SEALTITE for self-drilling and self-taping screws and tried to register that mark in 1996, but the Patent and Trademark Office refused because of the B&B registration. The Trademark Trial and Appeal Board (TTAB) eventually found that Hargis' SEALTITE mark was likely to be confused with B&B's SEALTIGHT mark. But the Eighth Circuit reversed, saying that a jury's opposite conclusion (no confusion) should rule.

The Supreme Court, in a 7-2 decision, focused on *issue preclusion,* also known as *collateral estoppel.* Issue preclusion means that once an issue of fact has been determined in a proceeding between two parties, the parties may not re-litigate it, even in a different cause of action. Thus, wrote Justice Samuel Alito, "So long as the other ordinary elements of issue preclusion are met, when the usages adjudicated by the TTAB are materially the same as those before the district court, issue preclusion should apply." What does this mean? Ronald Mann, writing for the Supreme Court watch blog SCOTUSblog, provided the "plain English" meaning: "The question in this case is whether a TTAB decision deciding that two trademarks are (or are not) similar can ever bind a later court in a routine infringement proceeding. The court of appeals said the TTAB ruling never can bind the later court. The Supreme Court disagrees; it says that the TTAB ruling can bind the later court, at least some of the time."

Justice Clarence Thomas, joined by Justice Antonin Scalia, dissented. Thomas said that the majority wrongly assumes "that when Congress enacts statutes authorizing administrative agencies to resolve disputes in an adjudicatory setting, it intends those agency decisions to have preclusive effect in Article III courts." He believed that courts should not presume, as the majority seemed to do here, that agency proceedings are preclusive.

In the second case, the justices took on a trademark doctrine called "tacking." As the Ninth Circuit explained it in *Hana Fin., Inc. v. Hana Bank* (735 F.3d 1158), "Tacking allows a party to 'tack' the date of the user's first use of a mark onto a subsequent mark to establish priority where the two marks are so similar that consumers would generally regard them as being the same." The Court faced the question of whether a jury or a court determines whether the use of an older trademark may be tacked to a newer one.

Writing for a unanimous Court, Justice Sonia Sotomayor agreed with the Ninth Circuit's call, saying that a tacking determination is "a question for the jury." She added, "Application of a test that relies upon an ordinary consumer's understanding of the impression that a mark conveys falls comfortably within the ken of a jury."

Trademark isn't copyright. Finally, it bears repeating that trademarks remain separate and distinct from copyrights. A 2003 Supreme Court decision underscored that principle in a case involving a release on videotape of an old TV series after its copyright expired. An Oregon company, Dastar Corp., released a video version of Twentieth Century Fox Film Corp.'s 1949 series, "Crusade in Europe" about World War II. Fox tried to stop this by claiming a trademark infringement and false designation of origin of the new videotape series, named "Campaigns in Europe." The Court ruled unanimously that this was an improper use of trademark law to prevent the re-release of a television series that is now in the public domain under copyright law (*Dastar Corp. v. Twentieth Century Fox Film Corp.,* 539 U.S. 23).

Other Changes in Trademark Law: Revision, Dilution, and Tarnishment

As we've discussed, the Court ruled two content clauses (disparagement and scandalous) of the Lanham Act unconstitutional in 2018 and 2019. The act was also extensively revised by Congress in the *Trademark Law Revision Act of 1988.* Although many of the changes are technical, several have had an important effect on the media—particularly advertising.

False comparative ads will cost 3x damages. It's fine to engage in comparative advertising, but not using false claims. Under the 1988 law, trademark owners may sue competitors who falsely malign their products or services for *treble damages* (three times the actual damages). But in an effort to avoid undue restrictions on First Amendment freedoms, Congress limited this right to comparative brand name advertising by businesses, not to political advertising or editorial commentary. As noted in Chapter Four, some states have long recognized a right to sue for "trade libel" or "product disparagement." This law adds a *federal* legal right with a treble damage provision, making it easier for companies to deter false comparative advertising by competitors. Significantly, Congress rejected a proposed amendment to the new law that would have allowed *consumers* to sue for false advertising under the same provision of the law. Most states already allow consumers to sue false advertisers.

The revised Lanham Act also has a provision allowing businesses to apply for trademark protection as much as three years before they actually put a product or service on the market by filing an "intent-to-use" application. A company may reserve a name before launching the product or service. Under the old law, a product had to be in the marketplace before the application could be filed ("no trade, no trademark"), forcing companies to make a token distribution of their new products and services in interstate commerce, but to do so quietly to avoid alerting potential competitors before the name or logo could be fully protected.

Dilution and tarnishment. The *Federal Trademark Dilution Act of 1995* made additional changes in the Lanham Act. Under this law, a trademark owner can sue an infringer for "lessening of the capacity of a famous mark to identify and distinguish goods or services, regardless of the presence or absence of competition between the parties or likelihood of confusion." Many trademark lawyers saw this as a major expansion of trademark law, allowing lawsuits for "blurring" or "tarnishing" a trademark by someone who is not a competitor of the trademark owner. *Blurring* might occur when someone makes an unrelated product and uses a famous name, as Toyota did when it launched the Lexus, a car with virtually the same name as the pre-existing Lexis-Nexis computer data service (Toyota won the right to use the Lexus name after defending a lawsuit against Lexis-Nexis). *Tarnishment* involves the use of a word or phrase that creates a negative association with an established trademark. Under the concept, courts have halted practices like the sale of "Enjoy Cocaine" posters using typefaces and colors similar to those in Coca-Cola's posters.

Many states already had anti-dilution laws; this law creates stronger *federal* protection from trademark dilution. Again, critics of the continuing growth of trademark and copyright law saw this as an example of the public domain shrinking. As intellectual property law grows, there are fewer and fewer words, phrases, and creative materials left that the general public may use without risking a lawsuit—one of the major dilemmas in this area of law.

The question of trademark dilution led to a Supreme Court decision in 2003, followed by new federal legislation in 2006 and additional cases in the late 2000s. In *Moseley v. V Secret Catalogue Inc.* (537 U.S. 418), the Supreme Court made it more difficult for the owners of famous trademarks to prevent others from using similar names for their businesses. Interpreting the Federal Trademark Dilution Act, the Court unanimously overturned a lower court decision in favor of apparel brand Victoria's Secret, which was trying to stop a Kentucky sex shop owned by Victor and Cathy Moseley from using "Victor's Little Secret" as its name.

Writing for the Court, Justice John Paul Stevens said trademark owners must show *actual* blurring or tarnishing of the trademark, not just the likelihood of dilution, to enjoin a business from using a similar name. He said it is not necessary to show an "actual loss of sales or profits," but a trademark owner must show "a lessening of the capacity of a famous mark to identify and distinguish goods or services." Stevens added that Victoria's Secret had not shown that the Kentucky store's name resulted in any real dilution of its trademark.

Revising dilution law. In 2006, Congress responded to the Victoria's Secret case by passing the *Trademark Dilution Revision Act* (TDRA). Written primarily by trademark lawyers, the act eliminated the Supreme Court's requirement that a trademark owner who sues for dilution must show that actual dilution. Rather, under the TDRA, a trademark owner has to prove only that a *likelihood* of harm exists. It also revised the definition of dilution and tarnishment to make it easier for trademark owners to sue without proving consumer confusion. The law retains protections to allow parodies, news commentary, and comparison advertising that may use a famous trademark. But it also allows lawsuits for damages against those who "willfully intend to harm the reputation of a famous mark."

The 2006 TDRA was widely criticized by legal scholars and consumer advocates, who predicted that trademark owners could use it to stifle First Amendment freedoms. The Sixth Circuit interpreted the TDRA in 2010 to affirm a permanent injunction against the Moseleys (who had been operating their shop as "Cathy's Little Secret") from using "Victor's Little Secret." The court said that Victoria's Secret did have a valid dilution-by-tarnishment claim under the revised act and added that "the creation of an 'association' between a famous mark and lewd or bawdy sexual activity disparages and defiles the famous mark and reduces the commercial value of its selling power" (*V Secret Catalogue v. Moseley*, 605 F.3d 382).

The TDRA does not require that a plaintiff prove "substantial similarity" between trademarks for a trademark owner to establish dilution by blurring, said the Second Circuit in 2009 (*Starbucks Corp. v. Wolfe's Borough Coffee, Inc.*, 588 F.3d 97). A family-owned coffee shop, Black Bear Micro Roastery, began selling dark-roasted coffee in 1997 under the name "Charbucks Blend" (later "Mister Charbucks"). National coffee company Starbucks brought suit and lost in the district court; as the appeal was pending, Congress passed the TDRA. The Second Circuit sent the case back to be determined under the new law, and Starbucks lost again. On appeal, the Second Circuit said that Black Bear's logo was significantly different from Starbucks' logo, and their coffee products displayed the logo and name prominently. And Black Bear did not tarnish Starbucks' mark, the court said, because it was marketing the "Charbucks" brand in a positive way rather than using it to disparage Starbucks.

In 2013, the Second Circuit upheld a district court's finding that the Charbucks mark did not dilute Starbuck's marks (*Starbucks Corp. v. Wolfe's Borough Coffee, Inc.*, 736 F.3d 198). The district court said that an association between Starbucks and Charbucks had not "impair[ed] the distinctiveness of the famous mark," and the Second Circuit agreed, saying that "the distinctiveness, recognition, and exclusive use of the Starbucks Marks do not overcome the weak evidence of actual association between the Charbucks and Starbucks marks." Nor had Starbucks demonstrated that its marks were blurred by the Charbucks marks.

Trademarks, Domain Names, Linking, and Embedding

Almost every large government agency, educational institution, and corporation has a website—and wants it identified by the organization's popular name or trademark. Hundreds of lawsuits have been filed by trademark owners and others to contest the ownership of domain names (an important 2020 Supreme Court decision, the *Booking.com* case, is discussed above). For many years Network Solutions Inc. (NSI), a Virginia-based company, had a government-sanctioned monopoly on registering domain names. By 2001 NSI had registered about 15 million domain names, receiving an annual fee directly or indirectly from each name registrant for maintaining the domain name database. NSI's contract expired in 1998, but it won a two-year extension by promising to share its registration authority.

ICANN and IANA. The Internet Corp. for Assigned Names and Numbers (ICANN) was established in 1998 with the backing of the U.S. government and the World Intellectual Property Organization and given the authority to designate new name registrars who would share that task with NSI. An organization called the Internet Assigned Numbers Authority (IANA), established in 1988, allocates the unique names and numbers for use in internet protocols like email and web browsing; ICANN is its oversight organization.

In 1999, NSI's monopoly ended when ICANN began accrediting private companies to handle registrations for the .com, .org, and .net domains. There are now thousands of ICANN-accredited registrars from which to choose; the largest is GoDaddy, which in 2020 served 76.2 million domains. In 2000, ICANN approved seven new domain names (.aero, .biz, .coop, .info, .museum, .name, and .pro) and announced plans to approve many more. As of 2021, there are more than 1,500 top-level domains, from .aaa, owned by the American Automobile Association, to .zw, the country domain for Zimbabwe. ICANN also set up a global arbitration system so that disputes over domain names could be resolved quickly without lawsuits. That system is widely used as an alternative to taking these disputes to court.

Disparaging websites. Another domain name and trademark dispute is the use of a company's trademark on a website designed to *criticize* the company. Disenchanted former customers and former employees often set up websites to express their displeasure with companies. In one case, a website critical of the Bally Total Fitness Holdings Corp. was set up under the title "Bally Sucks." It displayed Bally's logo with the word "sucks" printed across it. When Bally sued for trademark infringement and dilution, a federal court held that sites such as this one are protected by the First Amendment. The court rejected Bally's attempt to use trademark law to shut down the site (*Bally Total Fitness v. Faber*, 29 F.Supp.2d 1161, 1998).

Domain renewals. Another domain name problem involves renewals. Several domain name registrars immediately hand names over to domain name auction houses as soon as they expire, deriving a handsome profit from the resale of the name. There is little incentive for the registrar to make sure the name-holder renews on time, because the name may bring in far more than the renewal fee if it is re-sold at auction. Reputable registrars send out renewal notices, but if the name-holder misses the renewal deadline the name may be gone—short of litigation. Domain names are big business: by 2008, large companies were bidding huge sums for names that could be valuable. The name "porn.com" reportedly sold for $9.5 million—just for the name. Speaking of sex, in 2010 ICANN approved the .xxx generic top-level domain for pornography, ten years after it had first been suggested. No one seemed happy with that decision; some religious groups fear that the domain will lend legitimacy to pornography, while purveyors of sexual materials express concern that it would be easy to censor the entire top-level domain in one sweep.

Cybersquatting, domain tasting, and domain kiting. As NSI demonstrated when it had a monopoly, registering internet names can be a lucrative business, but it also invites lawsuits: the company has been sued hundreds of times in disputes over domain names, which it has generally issued on a first-come, first-served system. In some cases, individuals have registered hundreds of names with hopes of selling the names to trademark owners at a large profit. These people accused of domain name hijacking have been called "cybersquatters."

Instead of paying, many companies have sued—and usually prevailed based on proof that they hold a valid trademark in the name.

Cybersquatting is the practice of registering someone else's trademark or a famous person's name as an internet domain name in bad faith, hoping to make a profit by selling the name to its rightful owner. Perhaps the best known cybersquatter was Dennis Toeppen, who registered at least 240 different domain names and demanded payment for turning over those names to trademark owners. Among others, he had registered Delta Airlines, Panavision, Neiman Marcus, Lufthansa, and Eddie Bauer. When he demanded $13,000 from Panavision, that company sued and a federal court ordered Toeppen to hand over the names "Panavision" and "Panaflex" (*Panavision Int'l v. Toeppen*, 141 F.3d 1316).

In 1999, Congress stepped into the ongoing disputes over domain names by enacting the Anticybersquatting Consumer Protection Act (ACPA), a law intended to ban (and criminalize) the practice. The law allows fines of up to $100,000 for cybersquatting. The law also authorizes courts to order the cancellation of internet names registered in bad faith, and it applies to names already registered as well as new registrations. In short, ACPA establishes civil and criminal remedies for cybersquatting, allowing those who choose to go to court with domain name disputes (as opposed to using ICANN's arbitration procedure) to do so under ground rules favoring trademark owners.

In an attempt to reduce "typosquatting" through the processes of *domain tasting* and *domain kiting*, ICANN revised its domain name registration policy in 2008. Domain tasting is the act of buying up domain names that are variations or spelling errors of trademarked corporate names and making money when users go there and click on ads; the holder can also try to sell the name during that time. Because ICANN had a five-day grace period after which a domain name can be dropped (and a refund given), many squatters registered names and made ad money until the grace period was up, then dropped them and got the refund. Domain kiting gives a taster a bit longer to sample the goods; it is the practice of returning a name just before the grace period expires and then immediately re-registering it—thus extending the grace period. An ICANN study demonstrated the problem: in January 2007, 51 million domains were registered, but 48 million, or 94%, of those were dropped. ICANN kept the grace period but no longer makes those refunds, which were about 20 cents per name, and it saw an 84% drop in domain name drops.

Linking. A separate trademark controversy arose over *links*, which allow surfers to click on a highlighted word or phrase and move quickly to a different site. Several companies objected to the use of their trademarks by others in links—and filed lawsuits. Ticketmaster, the electronic ticketing agency, sued Microsoft in 1997 for its inclusion of links to Ticketmaster in its web pages. Ticketmaster's main objection was that Microsoft routed users to Ticketmaster by way of other Microsoft-controlled sites that carried advertising (for Microsoft's profit, not Ticketmaster's). The case settled in 1999 when Microsoft agreed not to link its Sidewalk city guides to pages within Ticketmaster's site. In several other cases, web businesses objected when someone else linked to a page deep inside their sites (*"deep linking"*), preventing customers from seeing their advertising. This issue is not resolved, although linking itself is perfectly legal.

However, linking can result in lawsuits. In *Kelly v. Arriba Soft Corp.* (336 F.3d 811), a federal appellate court ruled in 2003 that the fair use doctrine permits a search engine to reproduce small "thumbnail" copies of images from a website, but not full-size images. And the Ninth Circuit agreed, ruling against Perfect 10, an online purveyor of nude photographs, in a 2007 decision reaffirming an earlier ruling that Google could continue to use thumbnails of Perfect 10 images pending a full trial on the merits of a lawsuit by Perfect 10 against Google, Amazon.com, and others.

The court said in *Perfect 10* that the burden of establishing that use of the thumbnails is a fair use and not a copyright infringement should be on Google, even at this preliminary stage of a lawsuit. Google met this legal requirement, said the court; however, Google's links to other sites that display unauthorized full-size copies of Perfect 10's images may not be a fair use (*Perfect 10 v. Amazon.com*, 508 F.3d 1146, 2007). Perfect 10 sought to force Google to remove the links to other websites and also to remove the thumbnails—before a full trial.

Google could face *secondary liability* for helping web surfers find other websites that display Perfect 10's full-size images in violation of Perfect 10's copyrights. That, like deep linking in which full-size images appear to be part of a website other the one where they are posted, may constitute copyright infringement. Deep linking is akin to *framing*, in which pages of one website appear to be part of another website.

Embedding videos. But what about *embedding* a video? Is that direct copyright infringement? No, said the Seventh Circuit in *Flava Works v. Gunter* (689 F.3d 754, 2012). Pornography company Flava Works found that Marques Gunter's company, myVidster, a video bookmarking site, had many embedded videos (but not hosted—the videos were hosted elsewhere) that belonged to Flava. Flava demanded that myVidster remove those embeds, and myVidster complied, but Flava still sued for infringement.

The district court found for Flava, but the Seventh Circuit reversed. The judge said that "the infringers are the uploaders of copyrighted work," not Gunter, and, he added, unless myVidster visitors "copy the videos they are viewing on the infringers' websites, myVidster isn't increasing the amount of infringement." Nor did myVidster encourage infringement by inviting the posting of copyrighted videos, the judge said.

Embedding tweets. However, things may be changing. A photo of New England Patriots quarterback Tom Brady and Boston Celtics president Danny Ainge went viral and resulted in what could be a dangerous case for Twitter and other sites that allow linking and embedding of content. In *Goldman v. Breitbart* (302 F. Supp. 3d 585, 2018), a New York federal district judge said that such linking and embedding *could* be in violation of copyright. Justin Goldman's copyrighted photo of Brady and Ainge was newsworthy because at the time the Celtics were trying to recruit Kevin Durant, and speculation was rampant that Brady might be assisting. The photo made its way around, and Goldman, backed by Getty Images, sued.

The judge relied on two cases: *Perfect 10*, discussed above, and *ABC v. Aereo*, discussed in Chapter Eleven. She noted that *Perfect 10* dealt with search engines and a "server test"— a test she didn't think applied because users using a search engine make a choice to click on an image, whereas sites like Twitter display the image regardless of a user's choice in the matter. Then the judge invoked *Aereo*, a case dealing with copyright in over-the-air TV broadcasts, to say that users don't see how an image is delivered when they click on it: "mere technical distinctions invisible to the user should not be the lynchpin on which copyright liability lies." This area of law is not yet settled, she noted, and there is a question whether Goldman "effectively released his image into the public domain when he posted it to his Snapchat account"—which would be another huge finding if it were held to be the case. In 2019, more media companies settled with Goldman, thus leaving the law in the Second Circuit (and elsewhere) uncertain in this area.

■ PATENTS

Patent law, also addressed in the Constitution, provides protection for inventions. The U.S. Patent and Trademark Office is the government organization in charge of registration of patents. A patent gives the holder "the right to exclude others from making, using or selling the invention throughout the United States" for a certain amount of time in exchange for making information about the invention public by registering the patent. There are three types of patents: *utility patents*, for new and useful processes or machines (or improvements to them); *design patents*, for new, original, and ornamental designs; and *plant patents*, for new varieties of plants.

As mentioned earlier, patent law usually is not of much concern to mass communicators, but in 2010 a high-profile Supreme Court case brought the issue to national attention. The Supreme Court in *Bilski v. Kappos* (561 U.S. 593) took up a question regarding the patenting of methods claims, particularly business methods. The question before the Court was whether a "process" must be tied to a particular machine or transform a particular article into a different state or thing (called the "machine-or-transformation" test), to be eligible for patenting. The patent under consideration was a "procedure for instructing buyers and sellers how to protect against the risk of price fluctuations in a discrete section of the economy."

The Court rejected the patent on the financial method, and in so doing also rejected the "machine-or-transformation" test as the exclusive means of defining a patentable process. However, patents cannot be approved for abstract ideas. The Court declined to refine a definition of what would constitute a patentable process.

The Supreme Court handed down a high-profile patent case in 2013, *Assoc. for Molecular Pathology v. Myriad Genetics, Inc.* (569 U.S. 576). Myriad Genetics had patented the BRCA1 and BRCA2 genes; if these genes mutate, they can dramatically increase occurrences of breast and ovarian cancer. Justice Clarence Thomas wrote for a unanimous Court that human DNA is not patentable because it is naturally occurring (and not invented or created). However, another type of DNA, cDNA (complementary DNA), is created synthetically, so it can be patented; Thomas said that "the lab technician unquestionably creates something new when cDNA is made."

■ AN OVERVIEW OF MAJOR ISSUES

Intellectual property law is full of unresolved questions, many of them created by digital technologies. When copyright and patent were protected in the Constitution, communication technology was largely limited to print—books, some magazines, and newspapers. Some wonder whether *any* copyright can (or should) ever again be protected, given the ease with which digital images, music, and movies can be exchanged worldwide—and the seeming ease with which copy protection schemes can be circumvented.

How can the movie and recording industries deal with the sharing of copyrighted materials when new laws, court decisions, and technical "solutions" so often fail? Is it right for major corporations to sue millions of individual computer owners? Should the industry even try to catch every computer user who shares songs or movies with others? Don't some of the industry's anti-copying tactics violate the fair use doctrine, if not the First Amendment?

Shouldn't American consumers have the right at least to make backup copies of CDs and DVDs for their own use and to convert movies or music from one format to another? Consumers have that right in many European countries. Recent industry proposals would curtail even the right to copy free, over-the-air TV shows, long protected by the *Sony* Supreme Court decision, when broadcasts are digital. (Does that right even matter in the age of digital downloads?) And in 2005, the high court ruled in *MGM v. Grokster* that technology manufacturers can be sued for products they know will facilitate illegal copying.

The digital environment raises many more issues. What about embedding of photos and videos in tweets and social media posts? It's commonplace, and yet at least one court suggests that it's an infringement. Still another court suggests that when someone posts work to a social media account, that might be releasing it into the public domain. What about questions of linking? How about sampling? Mixups and mashups? Parodies?

Underlying all of this is a basic question. Corporate copyright owners are winning more and more rights at the expense of consumers with the passage of each new law that extends copyright terms or restricts what can be copied. The copyright lobby has won many battles over consumer advocates in Congress, but have copyright owners forfeited their chance to win the battle of public opinion? If the Copyright Office and industry-backed groups sponsor Copyright Awareness Weeks to educate the public (and especially students) about the importance of obeying the latest copyright restrictions, hasn't the battle already been lost?

The internet has given us an entirely different kind of world where the old definitions of publishing, distribution, and performance don't fit modern realities. It took nearly a year to circulate a book around the United States in 1790, and the duration of a copyright was just 14 years. Now a book, movie, or just about any other form of intellectual property can be circulated around the world in seconds—and corporate copyrights remain in effect for 95 years. Does that make sense? Apparently, the Supreme Court thinks so. When the latest copyright term extension was challenged by legal scholars and others, the Court ruled in the *Eldred* case that even copyrights lasting 120 years comply with the constitutional requirement that copyrights be for "limited times." Jack Valenti, longtime president of the Motion Picture Association of America, was quoted—in Congress and elsewhere—as saying copyrights should last "forever less one day." That would comply with the U.S. Constitution by being a "limited time," right? Is there *ever* a time when creative works—let's take music and movies as an example—become part of the culture that should belong to *everyone* and not just to the corporations that bought the copyrights so long ago?

One final thought: As copyright law becomes more unconscionable in many minds, and damage awards rise to impossibly high totals that the average person couldn't pay, isn't it inevitable that illegal copying will come to be seen as a legitimate form of civil disobedience?

**WHAT
SHOULD
I KNOW
ABOUT
MY STATE?**

- Both copyright and patent law are *federally preempted* (they may be regulated only by the federal government), so there is little intellectual property state law, other than state trademark litigation, registration, and common law.

A SUMMARY OF COPYRIGHT LAW

What May (and May Not) Be Copyrighted?

Many types of literary and artistic works may be copyrighted, including prose (fiction and non-fiction), poetry, scripts, musical scores and lyrics, photographs, films, videos, sound recordings, software, maps, paintings, sculptures, and advertising layouts Facts and historical information (including news) may *not* be copyrighted, although a *description* of a news event or production may. Ideas, processes, inventions, and trademarks may *not* be copyrighted (inventions and processes may be patented and trademarks protected under state and federal trademark laws).

How Does One Secure a Copyright?

Copyright protection is automatic under U.S. law and international treaties. While it's advisable to include a *copyright notice* (©) to notify any would-be infringer of your ownership, the copyright is valid without it. If you register *before* an infringement occurs, you have more legal rights than if you didn't, including the right to win statutory damages and lawyer's fees if a suit is filed. And you *must* register before filing a lawsuit. To do so, go to copyright.gov and follow the directions for online or traditional filing.

What Does a Copyright Give You?

The copyright owner has the right to reproduce, perform, revise, or display the work for the duration of the copyright, which normally runs for the author's life plus 70 years (95 years for corporate works). The owner may sell any or all of these rights. Under certain conditions copyrighted music may be recorded by anyone who pays the prescribed royalties (*compulsory licensing*).

What Is the Fair Use Doctrine?

The Fair Use Doctrine allows limited use of copyrighted works (like quoting or copying a small portion). Whether a use is fair is determined by weighing whether the use is commercial or educational in character, if/how the original work was transformed by the use, the nature of the original work, the percentage that is copied, and the effect of the use on the owner's profits.

What Is "Transformation" under the Fair Use Doctrine?

Transformation is an addition to the doctrine by the U.S. Supreme Court in 1994. A work is "transformed" if it is changed to such a degree that it no longer resembles the original copyrighted work and/or adds new interpretations or value to that work.

What Is Creative Commons?

Creative Commons is an alternative to traditional copyright law. A creator may choose to license work under a CC license which grants more rights for others to lawfully use the work for remixing, mash-ups, and other creative works.

7 | *Fair Trial-Free Press Conflicts*

One of the most troublesome conflicts inherent in the U.S. Constitution is a problem called *fair trial-free press*. The Sixth Amendment guarantees a person accused of a crime "the right to a speedy and public trial *before an impartial jury*." On the other hand, the First Amendment gives the media the right to report crime news, including information and visual images that could prejudice an entire community against someone who has not yet stood trial and is still presumed innocent by the law.

In recent years there have been many confrontations between the nation's courts and the media over this problem. In recent years, fair trial-free press issues were raised by the trials of celebrities (or people whose trials made them celebrities) like Robert Blake, Kobe Bryant, Michael Jackson, Scott Peterson, Martha Stewart, Casey Anthony, and Jodi Arias. As illustrated by the celebrated O.J. Simpson murder trial in 1995, live coverage of a trial may leave a large segment of the population convinced that the defendant is guilty after a jury rules otherwise.

In 2021, the highest profile murder trial in America was that of Derek Chauvin, the Minneapolis police officer convicted of killing George Floyd, whose death by a police officer, recorded by bystanders on cell phone video, set off waves of protests around country about racism against Black Americans. Following Chauvin's conviction by a jury, his attorney unsuccessfully sought dismissal of the verdict because he claimed pretrial publicity had prejudiced the jury against his client.

In attempting to control prejudicial publicity and ensure fair trials for defendants in sensational cases like these, the courts have taken steps to limit publicity and thereby protect the Sixth Amendment rights of defendants. However, some of these steps limit the media's First Amendment freedoms. There is no easy solution to this conflict between two constitutional rights: both freedom of the press and the right to trial before an impartial jury are central to the American ideal of a free society.

Related issues include public and media access to video and audio from courtrooms. The COVID-19 pandemic caused most courts to operate virtually, and the Supreme Court granted access to a live stream of its oral arguments (audio only) for the first time in its history,

▮ PREJUDICIAL PUBLICITY AND FAIR TRIALS

Many judges and attorneys contend there is an overabundance of crime news in the media. Many believe such news is so sensationalized that some celebrity defendants may be denied a fair trial by

Chapter Objectives:

- Discuss the effects of prejudicial publicity on fair trials.
- Identify ways judges can mitigate effects of prejudicial publicity.
- Evaluate when cameras can be allowed in courtrooms.

Essential Questions:

- What role does the First Amendment play in granting media access to the court system?
- What must judges do in order to address the potentially damaging effects of prejudicial publicity before they consider closing a courtroom or issuing a gag order against the press?
- Under what circumstances might a judge be able to close court proceedings to the public or issue a valid gag order against the press for media coverage of the courts?
- When are cameras allowed in courtrooms?

FIG. 65.
Oneida County
courthouse in
Rhinelander,
Wisconsin.

Author's collection.

an impartial jury. Some believe the media can make it impossible for the prosecution (*the people*, if you will) to get a fair trial. The jury is supposed to consider only the defendant's guilt or innocence in the case before the court, not whether the person has high moral character. A defendant's past record is not considered relevant evidence, although there are notable exceptions. But sometimes the media report inflammatory information about a person's past that may not be admitted as evidence when the trial occurs. Moreover, the media may report unsubstantiated details of an arrest or unverified test results. Or they may reveal the existence of a "confession" that may not be admitted into evidence if it was given under duress. The media may also reveal details about the prosecution's case that the jury is not supposed to consider. Thus it may be difficult to find unprejudiced jurors. Lawyers and judges may feel that drastic measures are necessary to control what they see as irresponsible journalism that interferes with criminal defendants' constitutional rights.

However, defenders of the press often cite the important role of the media in keeping the public informed about modern society—a society with a high crime rate. They point out that the press performs an important watchdog role in monitoring the administration of justice. Even most judges will concede that covering the criminal justice system is an important function of the media. And, of course, judges cannot ignore the fact that the media's right to cover the news is constitutionally protected.

The O.J. Simpson Case and its Consequences

Perhaps no courtroom drama in American history better illustrates the problems of fair trial-free press than the criminal and civil trials of O.J. Simpson, the football legend and media celebrity. A criminal jury acquitted Simpson of killing his ex-wife and her friend Ronald Goldman in a brutal knife attack, while a jury in a later civil trial found him to be liable for the two deaths. The civil jury verdict, including a large punitive damage award, was later upheld on appeal (*Rufo v. Simpson*, 86 C.A.4th 573, 2001).

O.J.'s criminal case. From the moment Simpson failed to surrender to police under a pre-arranged plan and was declared a fugitive, there was a worldwide media bonanza. At least 95 million viewers in the United States alone watched the two-hour pursuit leading to

Simpson's arrest on live television. Within days, hundreds if not thousands of journalists were covering the story, and numerous incriminating details of the case were widely publicized. Almost all major American media outlets carried the tape or transcript of a 911 emergency call that Nicole Brown, Simpson's ex-wife, made a few months before she was killed, in which she said Simpson had broken down her door. Almost everyone knew that Simpson had entered a no-contest plea to misdemeanor wife-beating charges in 1989, and that Nicole had repeatedly called the police about earlier incidents in which Simpson allegedly beat her. The world learned that in 1985 Simpson allegedly broke Nicole's windshield with a baseball bat.

The publicity frenzy became so intense that a judge took the extraordinary step of disqualifying the Los Angeles County Grand Jury from hearing evidence and deciding whether to indict—on the ground that the grand jurors might be prejudiced by media publicity. Instead, the case proceeded to a preliminary hearing (which would have been unneeded if there had been a grand jury indictment), with the major networks providing gavel-to-gavel live coverage of the courtroom proceedings. And in another Los Angeles County courthouse a few miles away, a judge took the unheard-of step of postponing an *unrelated* murder trial, ruling that the Simpson publicity made it impossible for this defendant to get a fair trial because the two cases were similar (like the Simpson case, this case involved a middle-aged African-American man accused of killing his younger, Caucasian ex-wife in a brutal knife attack that followed earlier incidents of domestic violence).

Once the Simpson trial began in 1995, the live television coverage repeatedly forced Judge Lance Ito to alter normal courtroom procedures. Time and again, millions of viewers got to see courtroom scenes on television that the jurors were not permitted to observe. As the trial increasingly focused on issues of race, police detective Mark Fuhrman was accused of using America's most inflammatory racial epithet more than 40 times. The jurors were not allowed to hear testimony about most of those times; Judge Ito ruled that its prejudicial effect would greatly outweigh its probative value as evidence. But Fuhrman's choice of words was a major story in the media for weeks. The jurors were sequestered—confined in a hotel and supervised to insulate them from the pervasive media publicity. However, they were allowed to have private conjugal visits. Can we ever know for sure that no visitor ever told any of the jurors the details of the Fuhrman controversy or other sensational developments in the case that occurred outside their presence but were shown on television?

Despite Judge Ito's efforts to assure that an impartial jury was selected, the news media carried many stories suggesting that some of the jurors were not impartial. When the jury rendered its not-guilty verdict, the event was viewed by the largest television audience in American history. Then the real controversy began—in the media and around the world.

Perhaps the one thing about Simpson's criminal trial that everyone on all sides agreed upon was that the media scrutiny was so intense that the American justice system may never be the same. Many believed that Simpson's real trial was in the media, and that the fair-trial, free-press issue was a more serious problem than it had ever been before. The case prompted California and many other states to adopt new rules restricting what lawyers can say to the media before and during a trial. Another response was that judges had second thoughts about permitting TV coverage of celebrated trials. Exercising powers they have in almost every state that allows cameras in trial courtrooms, judges have barred coverage of many sensational trials since Simpson's criminal trial attracted an international TV audience.

O.J.'s civil case. When the families of Ron Goldman and Nicole Brown Simpson sought monetary damages from Simpson in a civil lawsuit, cameras were barred from the trial.

Of course, the civil trial was very different from the criminal trial for many reasons. In civil cases, courtroom procedures, the rules of evidence, and the standard of proof are all different than in criminal cases. For instance, a civil jury may rule based on *the preponderance of the evidence* without being convinced *beyond a reasonable doubt* as is required for a conviction in a criminal case. And many trial lawyers saw the very different composition of the jury as a crucial difference between the criminal trial that led to Simpson's acquittal and the civil trial in which he was held liable for the deaths. Nonetheless, many observers also saw the absence of cameras as a significant factor in the dramatic reversal in the outcome of the case.

Alan Dershowitz, a prominent law professor who was a member of Simpson's "dream team" of defense attorneys, defended its role in his book *Reasonable Doubts*, saying, "A criminal trial is anything but a pure search for truth. When defense attorneys represent guilty clients—as most do, most of the time—their responsibility is to try, by all fair and ethical means, to *prevent* the truth about their client's guilt from emerging. Failure to do so...is malpractice." In 2004, a decade after the murders, Simpson discussed his case in retrospect during a rare interview with the Associated Press. He blamed the media for the fact that so many still consider him guilty long after he was acquitted. He eventually moved from California to Florida, but that did little to reduce media scrutiny of his case—and his still-newsworthy life, which became even more newsworthy after his arrest and conviction in a Las Vegas robbery scheme in 2008. He served nine years in prison and was paroled in 2017.

Lessons from Recent High-Profile Cases

The 2005 child molesting trial of singer Michael Jackson, the prosecution of basketball star Kobe Bryant in 2003 and 2004, and several other recent celebrity cases have again illustrated the fair trial-free press problem. Unfortunately for the news media, both the Jackson and Bryant trials had an effect that the Simpson case did not have: they led to precedent-setting appellate court decisions that could limit public access in future cases.

Michael Jackson. In the Jackson case, Judge Rodney S. Melville took many steps to reduce the possibility of prejudicial publicity. He not only barred cameras from his courtroom and the courthouse but also ordered attorneys and others not to discuss many topics with the media. The judge also sealed such a normally public record as an affidavit used to obtain a warrant to search Jackson's Neverland Ranch, in addition to the transcript of grand jury proceedings. When the media appealed Judge Melville's sealing of documents, a California appellate court upheld most of his order. The court held that the danger of "public outrage" from prejudicial publicity was so great that these records had to be kept confidential until after the trial (*People v. Jackson (NBC Universal Inc.)*, 128 C.A.4th 1009, 2005). The appeals court noted that the most sensational portions of these documents had been leaked to the media and widely publicized—but upheld the secrecy order even though it seemed moot by then. When the Jackson case ended with an acquittal on all charges, several jurors said in interviews that they made it a point to decide the case *only* on evidence presented in the courtroom. At least two said they thought Jackson probably was a child molester—but the evidence presented was insufficient for them to find him *guilty beyond a reasonable doubt.*

Kobe Bryant. In the Bryant case, a more fundamental First Amendment issue arose. In 2003, Bryant was accused of sexually assaulting a woman who went to his hotel room in Colorado. The case was eventually dropped at the request of the alleged victim after she saw her name and details of her sexual history publicized in apparent violation of Colorado law.

The judge held a closed pretrial hearing at which the alleged victim's sexual history was discussed. A court clerk erroneously emailed the transcript of the hearing to seven news organizations. The trial judge quickly ordered the media not to publish information from the transcript, an order that was clearly a prior restraint. The Colorado Supreme Court heard an appeal and upheld much of the judge's order, ruling that protecting the privacy of an alleged rape victim is "a state interest of the highest order," and "sufficiently weighty to overcome the presumption in favor" of the media's right to publish (*People v. Bryant*, 94 P.3d 624, 2004). The media asked U.S. Supreme Court Justice Stephen Breyer to intervene, but he declined to act immediately. Instead, he said in a short opinion, "I recognize the importance of the constitutional issues at issue, but a brief delay will permit the state courts to clarify, perhaps avoid, the controversy at issue." The trial judge then released an edited version of the transcript, rendering the media's challenge moot. However, the Colorado Supreme Court decision upholding a gag order against the press remains a legal precedent that could limit the media's right to publish court documents in future cases.

Jeffrey Skilling. A defendant's fame (or infamy) does not automatically mean that jurors will be biased against him/her, the Supreme Court ruled in 2010. *Skilling v. U.S.* (561 U.S. 358) primarily addressed whether a fraud law was unconstitutional as applied to former Enron executive Jeffrey Skilling (it was), but a secondary question dealt with the impact of prejudicial publicity on Skilling's trial. The Fifth Circuit had ruled that prejudice could arise simply from the fame of the defendant. Justice Ruth Bader Ginsburg, writing for the Court, disagreed, saying that Skilling had not shown that the *voir dire* process was insufficient to weed out biased jurors. She added, "Prominence does not necessarily produce prejudice, and juror *impartiality*, we have reiterated, does not require *ignorance*." Justice Sonia Sotomayor dissented from this part of the opinion, saying that she believed that the *voir dire* was not sufficient to eliminate bias. "Under our relevant precedents, the more intense the public's antipathy toward a defendant, the more careful a court must be to prevent that sentiment from tainting the jury," she wrote.

Long before these cases forced this problem into the limelight, the Supreme Court had already dealt with fair trial-free press issues, and ruled that all defendants must be assured of a fair trial, media publicity notwithstanding. Although events of recent years may have dramatized the fair trial-free press problem as never before, the issues are by no means new.

Early Fair Trial-Free Press Cases

The Supreme Court has struggled with fair trial-free press questions for more than 50 years. The court first took the drastic step of reversing a state court's murder conviction on the grounds of prejudicial publicity in the 1961 case of *Irvin v. Dowd* (366 U.S. 717). Even before that, the Court had expressed concern about the effect of publicity on trials, and it had reversed a federal conviction due to prejudicial publicity in the 1959 case of *Marshall v. U.S.* (360 U.S. 310), but *Irvin* is especially noteworthy because it was a murder case and because it was the first state conviction to be reversed mainly due to prejudicial publicity.

"Mad Dog" Irvin. The case involved Leslie Irvin, who was convicted of murdering six people near Evansville, Indiana, and Kentucky. Irvin had been arrested on suspicion of burglary and writing bad checks a month after the murders. However, the county prosecutor—under political pressure to come up with a suspect—issued press releases calling him a "mad dog" and saying he had confessed to the murders. Since the murders had received extensive news media coverage, the "confession" (which Irvin denied) led to a barrage of publicity in which he was branded "the mad dog killer." Other stories focused on Irvin's criminal past, revealing information that would never be admitted into evidence at his trial.

The defense was granted a *change of venue* (a change in the location of the trial), but only to a nearby county where there had also been extensive publicity about the crimes and "confession." A second request for a change of venue was denied because Indiana law allowed only one change of venue. Subsequently, of 430 prospective jurors examined by the prosecution and defense attorneys, 370 admitted they had formed some opinion about Irvin's guilt. And of the 12 jurors finally seated to hear the case, eight admitted they believed Irvin was guilty before hearing any evidence in court but said they could be impartial anyway. Because they claimed they would be impartial, the defense could not show cause to have them discharged as jurors, and Irvin's lawyer had used up all *peremptory challenges* (requests to discharge prospective jurors without having to prove they would not be impartial).

The U.S. Supreme Court reviewed the case more than five years after Irvin was originally convicted and sentenced to death. (In the meantime he had escaped from Indiana's death row and been recaptured in San Francisco.) The Court found that Irvin had not received a fair trial and set aside his conviction. In 1962 Irvin was retried, convicted of one murder, and sentenced to life in prison, where he died in 1983.

Wilbert Rideau. "Trial by television" resulted in a U.S. Supreme Court reversing a murder conviction in 1963. Wilbert Rideau was arrested and charged with robbing a bank, kidnapping three bank employees, and killing one of them in 1961 in Louisiana. During jail-house interrogation by the local sheriff, he confessed. The session was filmed and the film was shown on local TV three times. The Supreme Court held that it was a denial of Rideau's right to a fair trial not to grant him a change of venue after the people "had been exposed repeatedly and in depth to the spectacle of Rideau personally confessing in detail to the crimes...." The Court said his real trial occurred on television, not in the courtroom (*Rideau v. Louisiana*, 373 U.S. 723). Rideau was retried, convicted, and sentenced to life in prison. Later he was retried again for other legal reasons and again convicted of murder. He was eventually given a fourth trial on the grounds that African-American jurors were excluded from his earlier trials. At that trial, he was convicted only of manslaughter. He was released in 2005 after 44 years in prison, during which he had become famous as a writer and speaker.

Contempt by Publication (Indirect Contempt)

Courts have broad power to hold others in contempt of court. In addition to *direct contempt* (an act that violates the decorum of the court or shows disrespect for the legal process) there is *indirect contempt* (sometimes called *constructive contempt* or *contempt by publication*), which involves a disrespectful act outside the courtroom. From the early 1800s until the 1940s, one of the major legal threats to journalists was indirect contempt. Journalists were frequently cited for contempt because of what they wrote about a judge or the justice system. Unlike other public officials, judges had the power to punish journalists—directly and immediately—for publishing things they did not like, and some judges used that power freely. Surprisingly, the First Amendment was not a constraint upon contempt powers until the 1941 Supreme Court decision *Bridges v. California* (314 U.S. 252), a landmark decision on contempt of court that stripped judges of their vast power to use indirect contempt against the media. The case resulted from two unrelated contempt citations, one against Long-shoremen's Union leader Harry Bridges and another against the *Los Angeles Times*. Bridges sent a telegram to the secretary of labor threatening to call a massive West Coast dock strike if a court ruling unfavorable to him was enforced. Meanwhile, the *Times* published several editorials that judges disliked, including one entitled "Probation for Gorillas?" that admonished a judge to impose tough sentences on a group of Teamsters Union organizers.

Both Bridges and the *Times* were cited for indirect contempt, or contempt by publication. Deciding the two cases together, the Supreme Court ruled that these contempt citations violated the First Amendment. The Court prohibited contempt citations for public statements about pending cases in the future, unless it could be shown that the publication created a clear and present danger to the administration of justice. As a result, it became much harder for a judge to justify citing a journalist for indirect contempt of court.

A few years later, the Supreme Court overturned two more indirect contempt citations against newspapers, in *Pennekamp v. Florida* (328 U.S. 331, 1946) and *Craig v. Harney* (331 U.S. 367, 1947). In *Pennekamp*, the Florida Supreme Court had upheld a contempt citation against the *Miami Herald* for publishing editorials accusing local judges of being soft on criminals. The *Craig* case arose when a Corpus Christi, Texas, newspaper criticized a judge for his handling of a minor landlord-tenant dispute. In both cases, the Court reversed, reiterating that the clear and present danger test applies to indirect contempt citations.

After those decisions, the use of indirect contempt against the media almost disappeared. For a time, about the only sort of contempt threat journalists faced was the kind that arises when a photographer is caught taking illicit courthouse pictures. To be cited for contempt, one almost had to advocate marching on the courthouse (*Cox v. Louisiana*, 379 U.S. 559, 1965). In short, contempt of court citations stemming from what was published ceased to be a major legal problem for the media.

The Sheppard v. Maxwell Decision

In 1966, the U.S. Supreme Court handed down the ruling on prejudicial media publicity that has come to be regarded as the landmark decision in this area, *Sheppard v. Maxwell* (384 U.S. 333). Dr. Sam Sheppard, a socially prominent Cleveland, Ohio, osteopath, was involved in one of the most famous criminal trials of his generation, a case that was the subject of a television documentary, a long-running fictionalized television series, and a motion picture (*The Fugitive*). At the time, many called it "the trial of the century."

Sheppard's pregnant wife, Marilyn Sheppard, was murdered at their home overlooking Lake Erie in 1954. "Dr. Sam" said he was asleep on a downstairs sofa when he was awakened by his wife screaming upstairs. On the way upstairs to investigate, he was accosted from behind by a "bushy-haired" intruder who knocked him unconscious and fled.

Within a few weeks, the local papers were editorially demanding Dr. Sam's trial and conviction. The media literally took over the courtroom during his trial, and at one point the jurors' home telephone numbers were published in a gesture certain to build pressure on them for a guilty verdict. The press reported all sorts of "evidence" that was not admitted at the trial. Some of the evidence that came out didn't help Dr. Sam. Although he initially denied it, at least one woman said she had an extramarital affair with him. And his account of what happened on the night of Marilyn Sheppard's murder was vague and confusing.

Sheppard was convicted and his conviction was affirmed by the Ohio courts. The U.S. Supreme Court declined to review the case at that point. However, when the high court took a new interest in the free press-fair trial problem in the 1960s, Sheppard's lawyers again asked the Supreme Court to review the case. This time the court did so, and in 1966—12 years after his original trial—Dr. Sam had his conviction reversed and was granted a new trial at which he was acquitted. (Sheppard's defense attorney at the second trial was a young F. Lee Bailey, who, almost 30 years later, would be on the "dream team" of defense attorneys who helped get O.J. Simpson acquitted at the next

protective order (gag order):
a court order preventing the media from publishing information about a case.

continuance:
a delay in a trial to allow publicity to die down.

sequester the jury:
to confine a jury in a way that the members will be unable to consume any media content about the case.

change of venue:
moving a court proceeding from one location to another to avoid prejudicial publicity.

"trial of the century.") But the Sam Sheppard story does not have a happy ending: four years after his acquittal, he died at age 46, after spending more than 10 prime years of his short life in prison.

In the mid-1990s, Cuyahoga County authorities reopened the case as new evidence emerged pointing to Richard Eberling, who said he had done handyman work at the Sheppard home just before the murder, as the real killer. Eberling, who was later convicted and sentenced to life in prison for the murder of another woman, publicly denied killing Marilyn Sheppard. When forced to submit new blood samples for comparison to blood stains found in the Sheppard home, Eberling volunteered that his blood might have been there because he suffered cuts while replacing a storm window at the home. Meanwhile, a supervisor at a home health care agency where Eberling once worked was widely quoted as saying Eberling told her in 1983 that he killed Marilyn Sheppard. She said she went to the police soon after Eberling confessed to her, but they showed no interest in reopening the case then.

Later, other evidence surfaced that might have helped to acquit Dr. Sam. Although the police knew there was evidence of forced entry into the home, they did not reveal it at the time of the trial. Nor did they initially reveal that there was a trail of blood from the bedroom where Marilyn Sheppard died down to the cellar, and that two of her teeth were broken outward, suggesting that she bit her assailant, and he left the blood trail while fleeing. Dr. Sam had no cuts when police arrived to investigate the crime, but Eberling was later observed with a prominent scar on his left wrist. In 1959, Eberling was arrested for unrelated crimes, and a ring belonging to Marilyn Sheppard was found in his home. In later years, Eberling dropped tantalizing hints while still denying that he murdered Marilyn Sheppard. In one letter, he wrote, "Sam, yes, I do know the entire story." Another time he wrote, "The Sheppard answer is in front of the entire world. Nobody bothered to look."

In 1997, DNA testing of 43-year-old blood samples from the Sheppard home and tissue samples from Dr. Sam's body provided more evidence that Dr. Sam's account was accurate and Eberling was the real killer. The DNA tests indicated that blood stains found around the home, including a stain on a wardrobe door two feet from Marilyn Sheppard's body, did not match Dr. Sam's blood, but did match Eberling's. In December 1998, the Ohio Supreme Court allowed Sam Reese Sheppard, the Sheppards' son who has worked for many years to clear his father's name, to go to trial with a lawsuit alleging that Dr. Sam was wrongfully convicted and imprisoned.

In 1954, the Cleveland media had been anything but sympathetic to Dr. Sam's cause. By 1999, however, the media were taking a very different view of Sam Reese Sheppard's cause. Although the media may have sympathized with Sam Reese Sheppard, the same cannot be said of the jury that heard his civil lawsuit in 2000. The jury rejected Sam Reese Sheppard's attempt to clear his father's name and win damages for his alleged wrongful imprisonment. The eight-person jury declined to rule that Sheppard had proven his father's innocence by the preponderance of the evidence, as required in a civil case. But this verdict failed to end the controversy: the public debate about the original Sheppard trials continued.

The landmark case's results. Whatever the ultimate verdict of history may be about Dr. Sam Sheppard, his case prompted a landmark Supreme Court decision on fair trial-free press. In an 8-1 opinion written by Justice Tom Clark, the Court ruled that "the state trial judge had not fulfilled his duty to protect Sheppard from the inherently prejudicial publicity which saturated the community." The Supreme Court went on to instruct trial judges as to what they must do to ensure a fair trial. The Court warned that failure to follow these safeguards would result in more reversals of convictions.

The Supreme Court's *Sheppard* decision suggested a number of specific things the nation's trial judges could do to protect defendants from sensational media publicity. The court said judges should do some or all of the following things to control publicity and protect defendants' rights:

1. Adopt rules to *curtail in-court misconduct by reporters*;
2. Issue *protective orders* (sometimes called *gag orders*) to control out-of-court statements by trial participants such as lawyers;
3. Grant a *continuance* to postpone the trial until community prejudice has had time to subside;
4. Grant a *change of venue* to a place with less prejudicial publicity;
5. *Admonish the jury* to disregard the media publicity about the case; or
6. *Sequester the jury* (confine them in a place where they will not be able to read about the trial in newspapers or hear about it on radio or television).

Basically, Justice Clark was suggesting two different kinds of remedies: remedies that *compensate for* potentially prejudicial media publicity and remedies intended to *eliminate* such publicity—but at the expense of First Amendment freedoms. In the years following *Sheppard*, judges tried all of these things to control publicity. Some also began to do things the Supreme Court didn't recommend in the *Sheppard* case, such as closing their courtrooms to the press and public and holding preliminary proceedings—or entire trials—in secret. These judicial actions raised new constitutional issues.

"Gag" Orders and the News Media

Of all these remedies for prejudicial publicity, the one that generated the most controversy involved the suppression of information about the trial. In the *Sheppard* decision Justice Clark wrote, "Neither prosecutors, counsel for defense, the accused, witnesses, court staff nor enforcement officers coming under the jurisdiction of the court should be permitted to frustrate its function." Responding to this mandate, jurists all over the country began issuing orders that they call *protective orders* or *restrictive orders*; journalists tend to call them *gag orders*. Originally, these orders fell into two categories: those directed against only the participants in the trial, ordering them not to reveal prejudicial information to the media, and those directed against the media, ordering them not to publish prejudicial information even if they lawfully obtain it. The first category (orders intended to dry up the media's sources of prejudicial information) usually has been upheld when challenged on First Amendment grounds. But the second kind (those exercising prior restraint of the media) has not fared as well and they are rarely issued today—the Kobe Bryant case in 2004 being a rare exception.

In fact, in a television interview nine years after the *Sheppard* decision, Justice Clark said he did not mean that the media should be prohibited by judges from publishing information in their possession. Instead, gag orders were to be imposed only on those who might give prejudicial information to the press. More will be said of these orders shortly.

Other Remedies Proposed by Sheppard

The protective or gag order is just one of the remedies for prejudicial publicity recommended in the *Sheppard* decision, but it has surely been the most viable and controversial one. All of the others—which are really intended to compensate for prejudicial publicity instead of eliminating it—have limitations that sometimes render them impractical.

For example, a change of venue is expensive: it means all parties to the case, including witnesses, must travel a long distance for the trial, and it abridges the defendant's right to be tried in the place where the crime was committed, another constitutional right. Moreover, with today's pervasive media, the new community may be just as aroused about the case as was the community where the trial was originally scheduled.

Ordering a postponement of the trial also has major disadvantages. For one thing, it denies defendants their constitutional right to a speedy trial. For another, witnesses tend to become unavailable after a period of time. And finally, there is no assurance that the prejudicial publicity will not resume as the date of the long-delayed trial finally approaches.

Likewise, sequestering the jury has its drawbacks, although some states do sequester juries routinely in cases where the death sentence may be imposed. Nevertheless, many prospective jurors are unwilling to serve in a case where they will be isolated from the modern world for weeks or months. Moreover, sequestering a jury is expensive—the jurors must be provided food, lodging, and entertainment.

And finally, it has become almost impossible to completely insulate jurors from the media. The celebrated trial of Charles Manson and his followers for the murder of actress Sharon Tate and her friends provides a good illustration of the problems involved with sequestration. In the Manson trial the jury was sequestered, but on various occasions newspapers containing prejudicial stories appeared in the courtroom, in the restrooms used by the jurors, and on newsracks the jurors saw during the bus ride from their hotel to the court. At one point, Manson himself held up a newspaper in court so that the jurors could see the main headline, which proclaimed, "Manson Guilty, Nixon Says." The judge immediately stopped the proceedings and asked the jurors if seeing that headline would influence their verdict and they all said it would not, but no one will ever know for sure if that was true.

Other ways to protect the defendant from prejudicial publicity are closing the trial or pretrial proceedings and directly questioning the jurors about their potential prejudices. The problems of closing the trial or pretrial hearings will be treated later in this chapter.

The difficulties of questioning the jurors about their prejudices (a procedure called *voir dire*) were already cited in connection with the *Irvin* case. Jurors may say they can be impartial when in fact they harbor strong prejudices based on the media publicity. Each side in a criminal trial is allowed to dismiss only a few jurors on peremptory challenges (i.e., without having to prove they are prejudiced). As the *Irvin* case illustrated, in a sensational case the defense may use all of its peremptory challenges and still be stuck with jurors who cannot be shown to be prejudiced but who are *not* impartial.

Furthermore, admonitions to the jury to disregard publicity they may see or read—another of the means of protecting the defendant's rights suggested in *Sheppard*—can hardly be expected to ensure that the jurors will not base their "guilty" or "not guilty" verdict on what they learn from the media as well as what they hear in court. Jurors being human, they will usually consider everything they know about the case in reaching a verdict, regardless of the source of that information. But the Supreme Court has said that *voir dire* proceedings should under most circumstances be open to the public.

This brings us back to protective (or "gag") orders, the most controversial but perhaps also the most practical means of protecting defendants from prejudicial publicity—these orders may actually eliminate the prejudicial publicity rather than merely compensate for it.

"Gag" Orders as Prior Restraints: The Nebraska Press Association *Case*

Protective (or "gag") orders were in the center of a bitter debate between the media and the judiciary from the time of the *Sheppard* decision until the U.S. Supreme Court finally clarified the constitutional issues involved a decade later in *Nebraska Press Association v. Stuart* (427 U.S. 53, 1976). Gag orders were widely used all over the country in the early 1970s. A judge who believed an upcoming case might generate extensive publicity would almost routinely issue an order forbidding all parties in the case to make statements to the media. Such orders usually prohibited disclosing a defendant's prior criminal record, discussing the merits of the evidence in the case, and revealing the presence or absence of any confession. In many instances, this kind of information would be excluded as evidence at the trial, which would do little good if the jurors already know about it from watching TV or reading the newspapers. But some judges went beyond these restrictions and actually attempted to censor the media by ordering journalists not to disseminate information they already had.

After a number of state and lower federal court decisions on the validity of gag orders, the Supreme Court finally ruled on the issue in *Nebraska Press Association*. That ruling all but eliminated gag orders that directly restrained the press (as opposed to orders that prohibited trial participants from giving prejudicial information to reporters).

The case involved Erwin Charles Simants, an unemployed handyman with a purported IQ of 75. Simants borrowed his brother-in-law's rifle, walked to the house next door, and murdered six members of the James Henry Kellie family. Simants turned himself in the day after the murders and confessed. However, there were legal questions about whether he had sufficient mental capacity to understand his rights; his confession was quickly challenged.

At the preliminary hearing, a county judge ordered the media not to report any of the testimony. This gag order was appealed to District Court Judge Hugh Stuart by Nebraska news organizations. Stuart replaced that order with his own. The order prohibited the publication of prejudicial information. Later, the Nebraska Supreme Court modified the order to prohibit publishing only Simants' confession and any other facts "strongly implicative" of the suspect. The press was ordered not to even mention the existence of a confession.

The news organizations appealed the order to the Supreme Court. The high court ruled unanimously that this order was a violation of the First Amendment in that it imposed a prior restraint on publication. In striking down the order, Chief Justice Warren Burger referred to previous prior restraint cases and wrote, "If it can be said that a threat of criminal or civil sanctions after publication 'chills' speech, prior restraint 'freezes' it at least for the time." But the Court did not totally rule out the possibility of such orders being directed against the media in future cases. It said that in "extraordinary circumstances" such an order might be imposed. However, there must be sufficient evidence to reasonably conclude that:

1. There will be *intense and pervasive publicity* concerning the case;
2. *No other alternative measure*—such as a change of venue or continuance or extensive *voir dire* process— is likely to mitigate the effects of the pretrial publicity; and
3. The restrictive order *will in fact effectively prevent prejudicial material* from reaching potential jurors.

Post-script on Simants. A jury found Simants guilty of the murders, but a new trial was ordered, in which he was found not guilty by reason of mental insanity. As of 2020, Simants remained alive in a psychiatric hospital in Lincoln, Nebraska. Local newspapers reported his 45th petition for release to another facility was denied in 2020.

CNN fined for violating gag order. These guidelines from the *Nebraska Press Association* case were widely discussed again when a federal judge ordered CNN not to broadcast tape recordings of conversations between former Panamanian dictator Manuel Noriega and his lawyers. Noriega was in jail awaiting trial on drug trafficking charges at the time. The judge's order, a direct prior restraint, was quickly appealed by CNN, but the Supreme Court refused either to set aside the gag order or to take up the case at that point. The judge who had issued the order later reviewed the controversial tapes and concluded that their broadcast would not interfere with Noriega's right to a fair trial, so he decided not to make the order permanent. However, in 1994 the U.S. Attorney's office in Miami filed criminal contempt of court charges against CNN for broadcasting excerpts from the tapes while the order was in effect, and a federal judge fined CNN for the broadcast (*U.S. v. Cable News Network*, 865 F.Supp. 1549). The Noriega case was unusual: in most instances gag orders targeting the media are overturned on appeal. Within weeks of CNN's contempt of court conviction, three state appellate courts overruled gag orders targeting the news media.

Upheld gag orders. But not all gag orders are overturned on appeal. The Fifth Circuit in 2012 *upheld* a gag order that restricted access to individuals involved with the proceedings of a trial (e.g., attorneys) against Khalid Ali-M Aldawsari, a Saudi Arabian student accused of planning to create weapons of mass destruction. In denying the reporter's request to have the gag overturned, the court noted that it was a narrow order and that news media had successfully been relying on information in the public record and public hearings to cover the case (*U.S. v. Aldawsari v. Clark*, 683 F.3d 660).

Gagging Lawyers and Judges

Although the *Nebraska Press Association* case limited the power of judges to restrain the press, it had little effect on their power to impose gag orders on trial *participants*. By the 2000s, at least 40 states had rules regulating what lawyers may say publicly while they are handling a newsworthy case.

The American Bar Association has guidelines for professional conduct by lawyers. Among other things, these ABA "Model Rules" cover extrajudicial (out of court) statements. Although these rules are voluntary, many states' mandatory rules are based on them. The ABA rules were extensively revised in 1994. The ABA felt obliged to rewrite and in some ways liberalize its Model Rules because a Nevada state rule based on an earlier version of the ABA rules was declared unconstitutional in *Gentile v. State Bar of Nevada* (501 U.S. 1030, 1991). In that case, Nevada disciplined Dominic P. Gentile, a criminal defense lawyer, for making allegedly improper public comments after a client was indicted. Like the earlier ABA rule, the Nevada rule permitted attorneys to publicly describe the "general nature of the claim or defense," but only if it is done "without elaboration." Nevada Bar authorities punished Gentile for saying too much to the media. He appealed, and the Supreme Court held that Nevada's rules were too vague and therefore violated Gentile's First Amendment rights.

The *Gentile* case triggered a divisive controversy within the ABA. In the end, the ABA adopted new limits on what trial lawyers may say to the media about a pending case, but with the right-of-reply provision. After much debate, the ABA decided to retain a *substantial likelihood* test for public statements by lawyers: this forbids lawyers to say anything that would have a substantial likelihood of prejudicing a pending case.

Judicial candidates' speech. Many of the same issues have been raised concerning ethical rules and state laws forbidding candidates in judicial elections to announce their views on political and legal issues—issues that might come before them as judges. In *Republican Party of Minnesota v. White* (536 U.S. 765), the U.S. Supreme Court ruled in 2002 that Minnesota's restrictions on judicial candidates violated the First Amendment. The 5-4 majority rejected the argument that judges and prospective judges should always present the appearance of impartiality and instead ruled that judicial candidates, like other candidates for public office, have a right to speak about controversial issues, even if they might have to rule on some of those issues later. However, the Court did *not* decide whether judicial candidates have a right to pledge or promise that they will decide any particular case or issue a certain way. Many states have rules prohibiting such promises, and those rules may be challenged on First Amendment grounds in future cases.

It has become routine for judges to order lawyers and other participants not to talk to the news media in sensational cases. Gag orders were imposed on lawyers in the Robert Blake, Kobe Bryant, and Michael Jackson criminal cases, among others. That did not prevent the media from covering these and other sensational cases in ways that many judges considered improper and prejudicial. For example, a cable network aired a made-for-television movie about the Scott Peterson case before he could be put on trial for murdering his wife Laci (he was later convicted).

■ CLOSED COURTROOMS

Soon after the Supreme Court's *Nebraska Press Association* decision, a new conflict between judges and journalists assumed even greater proportions. Judges began to bar the press and the public from preliminary hearings, hearings on motions to suppress evidence, and sometimes even from trials.

Although it has been customary for courtrooms to be open to the public throughout American history, there are a number of circumstances that may lead to a courtroom closure. Courtroom closures to protect a defendant's right to a fair trial are the primary subject of this chapter. However, courtrooms are also closed at times to protect an individual's privacy, to ensure the secrecy of information affecting national security, or to keep the details of a police investigation confidential—to cite just three examples.

In the late 1970s there were increasingly frequent instances of preliminary criminal proceedings—and even trials—being closed to the press and the public in an effort to curtail prejudicial publicity. Gag orders directed against trial participants do not always stop the flow of prejudicial information to the press, and *Nebraska Press Association* imposed limits on judges' power to gag the press directly. Therefore, judges increasingly saw closed pretrial hearings as the best way to limit prejudicial publicity in sensational cases.

Pretrial hearings. To understand the judges' viewpoint, we should explain why pretrial hearings occur and what happens at these proceedings. A *preliminary hearing* is a check on law enforcement officers and prosecutors. It is a hearing where the case against the accused is reviewed by a judge, not to determine guilt or innocence but merely to decide whether there is enough evidence to justify a full trial. This is supposed to be a shortcut out of the criminal justice system for defendants who should never have been charged in the first place. The purpose is *not* to decide if the accused is guilty beyond a reasonable doubt (the standard of proof required in a criminal trial) but to see if there is enough evidence to justify a trial.

As a result, only the prosecution presents evidence at most preliminary hearings. If there is enough evidence, a trial is scheduled, almost without regard to the strength of the defense's case. Thus, as a matter of strategy, the defense often waits until the full trial before presenting its side of the case. As a result, news coverage of a preliminary hearing is necessarily imbalanced in most instances since only one side has been heard. The defense does have the right to cross-examine prosecution witnesses, but even so, if the hearing is covered by the media, most of the news generated there is going to be unfavorable to the defendant, who may have to stand trial before jurors who read about the preliminary hearing in the papers.

Pretrial hearings on motions to suppress evidence are even more likely to produce prejudicial publicity. At these hearings, the defense asks a judge to throw out damaging evidence, often because it was obtained by an unlawful search or seizure. Or perhaps the challenged evidence is a confession that was secured through coercion. In any event, what good does it do to have the tainted evidence *suppressed* (i.e., ruled inadmissible at the trial) if prospective jurors learn about it on the evening news? For these reasons, many judges and lawyers feel that hearings on motions to suppress evidence should be closed to the press and public.

In addition to preventing jury prejudice, closing preliminary court proceedings protects the reputations of defendants who have been charged with a crime but are not held for trial because the hearing reveals that the prosecutor has little evidence.

Few journalists would deny that there are powerful arguments for secrecy at the pretrial stage in criminal proceedings, except for one thing: more than 80% of all criminal prosecutions in America are resolved without the case reaching a full trial. Because the judge's ruling on a motion to suppress crucial evidence is the decisive step in many criminal cases, serious plea bargaining usually occurs after these pretrial proceedings. If key evidence is barred, the prosecutor may accept a guilty plea to a lesser charge or even drop the charges. If the evidence is ruled admissible, on the other hand, the defendant may plead guilty as charged, perhaps in return for a promise of a light sentence. In the vast majority of criminal proceedings, the last chance the public will have to monitor the justice system is at the pretrial hearing stage.

Closed courtrooms as defendants' rights. As a trend toward closed pretrial hearings developed, a constitutional challenge to this practice reached the Supreme Court in the 1979 case of *Gannett v. DePasquale* (443 U.S. 368). The Court upheld a judge's order barring a newspaper reporter from a pretrial evidentiary hearing in upstate New York. The case arose when two young men were charged with murdering a former New York policeman. They reportedly confessed to the crime and were later indicted by a grand jury. Because of the intense publicity surrounding the incident and the arrest, the defense and prosecution concurred in closing the pretrial hearing. When Judge Daniel DePasquale barred the press and public, the Gannett newspapers appealed the ruling. The state's highest court affirmed the order and Gannett asked the Supreme Court to hear the case.

In affirming the closure, Justice Potter Stewart, writing for a 5-4 majority, acknowledged that "there is a strong societal interest in public trials." His opinion also noted that "there is no question that the Sixth Amendment permits and even presumes open trials as a norm." However, Stewart continued, the Sixth Amendment right to a public trial belongs to the defendant and not the public, and it is a right the defendant may waive.

Justice Stewart agreed with the trial judge's decision that the press' right of access to this particular hearing "was outweighed by the defendant's right to a fair trial ...because an open proceeding would pose a reasonable probability of prejudice to these defendants." Justice Stewart's opinion was joined by Justices John Paul Stevens, Lewis Powell, William Rehnquist, and Chief Justice Burger. The latter three also wrote separate concurring opinions. Justice Blackmun wrote a concurrence and dissent, joined by Justices Marshall, Brennan, and White. He wrote, "Secret hearings ...are suspect by nature. Unlike any other provision of the Sixth Amendment, the public trial interest cannot adequately be protected by the prosecutor and judge in conjunction or connivance with the defendant."

Justice Powell's concurring opinion was noteworthy in that it said the press and public should have a right to challenge courtroom closures. In the years since *Gannett,* many journalists have done precisely that, sometimes successfully. Many reporters who regularly cover the courts carry a card with them containing the correct legal phrasing of a motion to object to a courtroom closure.

Nevertheless, the *Gannett* decision stood as a precedent permitting judges to close at least pretrial hearings when they felt the danger of prejudicial publicity would outweigh the public's right to observe the proceedings.

As a result, there was an avalanche of closed hearings—and even trials—in 1979 and 1980. The Reporters Committee for Freedom of the Press counted 21 courtroom closures ordered or upheld on appeal in the first 30 days after the *Gannett* ruling was announced. Within the year, there were at least 100 more such courtroom closures around the nation.

Open Trials: **Richmond Newspapers v. Virginia**

Apparently alarmed at the reaction to *Gannett* by trial judges, several Supreme Court justices made public statements condemning the trend toward courtroom closures. And the high court quickly agreed to review another related case, this one involving a closure of a full trial in Virginia. In this case (*Richmond Newspapers v. Virginia*, 448 U.S. 555, 1980), a county judge had cleared his courtroom of reporters and spectators before the fourth trial of a man who was charged with murdering a hotel manager. His first trial had been invalidated on a technicality, and the next two resulted in mistrials. Relying on a Virginia statute that allowed "the removal of any persons whose presence would impair the conduct of a fair trial," the judge simply closed the trial. The defendant was acquitted after a two-day closed trial because there were "too many holes" in the prosecution's case, the judge said.

Two jointly owned Richmond, Virginia, newspapers challenged the courtroom closure. Just a week after the *Gannett* ruling of the U.S. Supreme Court, the Virginia Supreme Court upheld the ruling closing this trial. Ruling in 1980—a year to the day after its controversial *Gannett* decision—the Court voted 7-1 to overrule this trial closing, a decision that was widely seen as a major victory for the media. Not only did the high court invalidate the closing of this particular trial, but Chief Justice Burger's opinion for the court recognized for the first time that there is a constitutional right of access to information inherent in the free press guarantees of the First Amendment:

> We hold that the right to attend criminal trials is implicit in the guarantees of the First Amendment; without the freedom to attend such trials, which people have exercised for centuries, important aspects of freedom of speech and of the press could be eviscerated.

Moreover, Burger's opinion went to some trouble to make it clear that this public right to attend trials, although only an implied right and not one specifically stated in the Constitution, was nonetheless legitimate. He pointed to a variety of other constitutional rights the Supreme Court has recognized over the years, although those rights too were only implied in the Constitution. Burger noted that the rights of association and privacy, the right to

FIG. 66.
Chief Justice Warren E. Burger, official Supreme Court portrait, 1976.

Library of Congress, Prints & Photographs Division, Reproduction number[LC-USZ62-60136 (b&w film copy neg.)]

travel, and the right to be judged by the "beyond-a-reasonable-doubt" standard of proof in criminal cases were only implied and not stated in the Constitution.

Although this opinion was joined by only two other justices, at least two additional justices recognized a right of the public to attend trials in a separate opinion in the *Richmond* case. However, Justice Rehnquist (the only dissenter) said the states should be free to set their own standards on the administration of justice and found no provision in the federal Constitution that prohibited the Virginia judge from doing what he did.

In overturning the closure of a trial in the *Richmond Newspapers* decision, the Supreme Court avoided reversing its year-old *Gannett* ruling, leaving judges free to close pretrial hearings in some instances where a closed trial might not be permitted. In fact, on the same day the Supreme Court handed down that decision, it declined to review a lower court decision authorizing another closed pretrial hearing in New York. Moreover, the Court didn't even flatly forbid closed trials in *Richmond Newspapers*. Instead, the high court said trials could still be closed under extraordinary circumstances. "Absent an overriding interest (in closing the trial) articulated in the (judge's) findings, the trial of a criminal case must be open to the public," Burger wrote. The Court didn't give any guidelines for determining when a trial should be closed, but it did make clear that a judge must pursue alternative means of ensuring a trial's fairness before barring the press and public.

In short, *Richmond Newspapers* limits a judge's discretion in barring the press and public from a trial, while permitting trial closures in extreme circumstances if the judge can set forth valid reasons for his action. This decision may not have gone quite as far as many journalists hoped it would, but it nonetheless sharply curtailed the nationwide trend toward closed courtrooms that had developed in the year between the *Gannett* and *Richmond* decisions.

Open Courtroom Cases After Richmond Newspapers

The *Richmond Newspapers* decision was a vindication of the principle of open courtrooms in the United States. While there have been a number of controversial courtroom closures since that bellwether 1980 Supreme Court decision, the trend toward closed trials has been reversed. In fact, the Court has since handed down several more decisions overruling courtroom closures. In 1982, the Court invalidated a Massachusetts law that automatically closed the courtroom whenever a juvenile victim of a sex crime was to testify.

In *Globe Newspaper Co. v. Superior Court* (457 U.S. 596), the Court said judges must evaluate each trial closure on a case-by-case basis rather than automatically closing a trial whenever a young victim is testifying. The high court found the Massachusetts law unconstitutional because it made the closure mandatory. The case arose when a judge closed a rape trial in which the victims were three girls under age 18. The *Boston Globe* challenged the closure, and the state high court upheld the mandatory closure provision. The *Globe* appealed.

Writing for the majority, Justice William Brennan took note of the Court's ruling in *Richmond Newspapers* that the public has a constitutional right of access to criminal trials. However, Brennan pointed out that this right is not absolute: a trial may be closed if a state can show two things: (1) a "compelling governmental interest" that requires the closure and (2) that the law requiring closure is "narrowly tailored to serve that interest." Weighing the Massachusetts statute—as interpreted by that state's highest court—the Supreme Court concluded that it failed this two-part test because a case-by-case determination of whether a criminal trial should be closed would be sufficient to protect young victims. The justices took pains to point out that judges could exclude the press and public in cases where

preliminary hearing:
a hearing where
the case against the
accused is reviewed
by a judge to decide
whether there is
enough evidence to
justify a full trial.

voir dire:
the process of select-
ing a jury for trial.

they found that a minor's well-being would be in jeopardy if the trial were open. The gist of the *Globe Newspaper* decision is nicely summarized by a footnote in the majority opinion:

> We emphasize that our holding is a narrow one: that a rule of mandatory closure respecting the testimony of minor sex victims is constitutionally infirm. In individual cases, and under appropriate circumstances, the First Amendment does not necessarily stand as a bar to the exclusion from the courtroom of the press and general public during the testimony of minor sex-offense victims. But a mandatory rule, requiring no particularized determinations in individual cases, is unconstitutional.

The ruling produced dissents from Chief Justice Warren Burger and Justice William Rehnquist, who felt the mandatory closure rule was not unconstitutional, and from Justice John Paul Stevens, who felt the case should not have been heard.

Press-Enterprise I. In 1984, the Supreme Court took another step to ensure public access to the criminal justice system when it ruled that the jury selection process must also normally be open to the public. In the case of *Press-Enterprise Co. v. Superior Court (P-E I)* (464 U.S. 501), the court unanimously overturned a Riverside, California, judge's decision to close almost six weeks of jury selection procedures during a 1981 murder trial. The *Riverside* (Calif.) *Press-Enterprise* challenged the judge's actions.

The judge not only closed the *voir dire* process but also refused to make a transcript of the proceeding public after the defendant was tried, convicted, and sentenced to death for raping and killing a 13-year-old girl. The effect of the judge's decision was to ensure that the public would never know how the jury was selected for a trial that ended with a death sentence.

Writing for the Supreme Court, Chief Justice Warren Burger emphasized that the jury selection, like other aspects of criminal trials, has traditionally been open to the public—and should continue to be open in all but very unusual circumstances. He wrote, "Proceedings held in secret would ...frustrate the broad public interest; by contrast public proceedings vindicate the concerns of the victims and the community in knowing that offenders are being brought to account for their criminal conduct by jurors fairly and openly selected." However, Burger said there might be rare occasions when prospective jurors could be questioned in private in the judge's chambers to protect their privacy during discussions of "deeply personal matters." However, a transcript of the proceedings should be made available within a reasonable time unless that would further invade a juror's privacy. But to close the entire process for "an incredible six weeks" (as Burger put it) was going much too far.

Although the decision that the judge should not have closed the jury selection in this case was unanimous, three justices wrote separate opinions. Justice Thurgood Marshall said the jury selection and "all aspects of criminal trials" should be open, regardless of whether open jury selection might embarrass a prospective juror. Justices Harry Blackmun and John Paul Stevens wrote a separate opinion emphasizing the importance of jurors' privacy rights.

Open *voir dire.* The importance of the 1984 *Press-Enterprise* decision was underscored 20 years later when a New York federal judge closed much of the jury selection process during the trial of home-lifestyle doyenne Martha Stewart. In a strong reaffirmation that jury selection must normally be open, the Second Circuit reversed the judge's order and said most of the jury selection process should have been open (*ABC Inc. v. Stewart*, 360 F.3d 90, 2004). Stewart was later convicted of lying to federal investigators during an inquiry into possible insider trading. She had sold nearly 4,000 shares of stock in a biotech company just before a public announcement of business reverses caused the stock price to plummet.

The Supreme Court may have settled the issue when it announced a constitutional right to an open *voir dire* in 2010. Eric Presley claimed that the exclusion of his uncle from *voir dire* proceedings in his drug trafficking trial abridged his Sixth Amendment right to a public trial. The Court agreed in a *per curiam* (unsigned) opinion in *Presley v. Georgia* (558 U.S. 209), saying, "Trial courts are obligated to take every reasonable measure to accommodate public attendance at criminal trials." Justices Clarence Thomas and Antonin Scalia dissented, noting that a public *voir dire* had never before been considered part of the Sixth Amendment's guarantee of a public trial and should not be simply assumed.

Also in 2010, the highest court in Massachusetts followed suit, saying that even a partial closure of jury selection proceedings could violate both the First and Sixth Amendments: "The public trial right applies to jury selection proceedings ... which are 'a crucial part of any criminal case'" (*Commonwealth v. Cohen*, 921 N.E.2d 906).

The media were successful in 2010 and 2011 in ultimately gaining access to various court proceedings after they had initially been denied. The Kentucky Supreme Court said that reporter Jason Riley and the *Louisville Courier-Journal* should have been granted access to a juror contempt hearing (the court decided the case even though it was moot because the situation is "capable of repetition, yet evading review"—thus appropriate for decision). The court said that "if it can be established that all defendants, or the public at large, have a stake in the process and outcome of such proceedings, then public access must be allowed" (*Riley v. Gibson*, 338 S.W.3d 230, 2011).

The Second Circuit said that a lower court's closing of the *voir dire* proceedings in an immigration case was incorrect but did not result in the vacating of the defendant's sentence (*U.S. v. Gupta*, 650 F.3d 863, 2011).

See but not hear? An interesting case arose in 2019 over whether public voir dire proceedings can be seen but not heard. In the District of Columbia, trial judges regularly conduct individual juror questioning at the bench, using a white noise machine or "husher" to obscure answers from being heard by others in the courtroom. In a criminal case involving a shooting incident, a defense attorney objected to the practice as a violation of the defendant's Sixth Amendment right to a public trial. The District of Columbia Court of Appeals upheld the practice. The court ruled that the public's ability to see, but not hear, individual prospective juror's questioning fulfilled the "in public" requirement. The use of hushers protected the individual privacy of prospective jurors and encouraged their truthfulness to be able to answer sensitive questions out of earshot of the public and other prospective jurors, the court ruled. (*Blades v. U.S.*, No. 15-CF-663, 2019). In an *amicus curiae* brief to the U.S. Supreme Court, the Reporters Committee for Freedom of the Press argued the broad practices amount to a partial closure of voir dire in violation of the Sixth and First Amendments. "The very purposes of the First Amendment right of access — to allow the public to oversee and understand what is transpiring in the courtroom, and to monitor judges and participants — cannot be achieved if the public cannot hear what is being said," the media coalition wrote in the brief. "The First Amendment creates a strong presumption of public access to all aspects of criminal trials, including voir dire." The RCFP cited several precedents discussed in this chapter supporting the principle of open and public access to trials. In 2020, the U.S. Supreme Court denied *cert*, and the practice in D.C. continues.

Pre-trial hearings. A few months after the 1984 *Press-Enterprise* decision, the Supreme Court again reiterated that criminal proceedings *other than* the trial itself must normally be open. In *Waller v. Georgia* (467 U.S. 39, 1984), the high court overturned a judge's decision to close a pretrial evidence suppression hearing in a case where the police had searched numerous homes and conducted wiretaps to gather evidence of gambling. The defendants claimed much of the evidence was unlawfully obtained, and they wanted it suppressed. Moreover, they demanded that the evidence suppression hearing be open to the public, but the judge refused. Then he admitted most of the evidence and convicted several defendants of various crimes.

The Court ruled that most of this evidence-suppression hearing, like the jury selection in the 1984 *Press-Enterprise* case, should have been open to the public. Only a little of the seven-day hearing involved material that might invade anyone's privacy, the Court noted. In *Waller*, the Court again emphasized the right of the public—as well as defendants—to have criminal trials and pretrial proceedings held in open court under most circumstances.

Two years after the original *Press-Enterprise* decision, the Supreme Court handed down another important decision with exactly the same name—and on a closely related aspect of the open-courtroom issue. In this 1986 case, *Press-Enterprise Co. v. Superior Court (P-E II)* (478 U.S. 1), the Court ruled that preliminary hearings and similar pretrial proceedings must be open unless there is a *substantial probability* that an open hearing will prejudice the defendant's right to a fair trial.

Press-Enterprise II. The 1986 case, commonly identified as *Press-Enterprise II* to distinguish it from the 1984 case, involved exactly the same two parties: the *Riverside* (Calif.) *Press-Enterprise* and the Riverside County Superior Court. This time, the newspaper protested the closing of a 41-day preliminary hearing for a male nurse accused of killing a dozen hospital patients with massive drug overdoses. In California and many other states, a preliminary hearing is held in most major criminal cases. As explained earlier, these hearings are conducted by a judge to determine if there is sufficient evidence to hold the defendant for a full trial. The preliminary hearing is the only significant court proceeding in the great majority of criminal cases: less then 20% of major criminal cases actually go to trial. Therefore, the preliminary hearing is often the only opportunity the public will ever have to learn of the evidence against the accused. California law permitted the closing of a preliminary hearing whenever there was a *reasonable likelihood* that prejudicial publicity would result from an open hearing.

Writing for a 7-2 majority, Chief Justice Warren Burger objected to the almost-routine closing of preliminary hearings in California. Noting that they are often lengthy proceedings, he said they should be open to the public unless "there is a substantial probability that the defendant's right to a fair trial will be prejudiced by publicity that closure would prevent and ...(that) reasonable alternatives to closure cannot adequately protect the defendant's free trial rights." Burger also declared that if the courtroom is closed during a preliminary hearing, it must be for as short a period of time as possible. He cautioned against closing a lengthy preliminary hearing: "Closure of an entire 41-day proceeding would rarely be warranted. The First Amendment right of access cannot be overcome by the conclusory assertion that publicity might deprive the defendant of (the right to a fair trial)."

In the aftermath of the Court's *Press-Enterprise II* decision, closed preliminary hearings have become rare—and judges are more reluctant to close other pretrial proceedings now. This ruling strengthens the growing body of constitutional law saying that the criminal justice system must be conducted openly, with the press and public invited to view the process.

In 1993, the Supreme Court reaffirmed the *Press-Enterprise II* decision, overturning a Puerto Rican law allowing closed preliminary hearings there. Puerto Rico, which has considerable local autonomy but must obey the U.S. Constitution, continued to hold closed preliminary hearings in felony cases whenever a defendant requested it, in spite of the *Press-Enterprise II* decision. Ultimately, a journalist asked to be allowed to attend a closed preliminary hearing and was turned down. He then challenged the constitutionality of the Puerto Rican court rules and prevailed when the Supreme Court held that Puerto Rico, too, must allow public access to these proceedings (*El Vocero de Puerto Rico v. Puerto Rico*, 508 U.S. 147).

Access to sentencing hearings. Most federal circuits have extended the access principles to sentencing hearings. The Fifth Circuit said that "the press and public have a First Amendment right of access to sentencing hearings, and that the district court should have given the press and public notice and an opportunity to be heard before closing the sentencing proceeding" in the conviction of a drug cartel leader (*Hearst Newspapers, LLC v. Cardenas-Guillen*, 641 F.3d 168, 2011).

The Eighth Circuit in 2013 joined the Second, Fourth, Fifth, Seventh, and Ninth Circuits in holding that the First Amendment public trial right applies to sentencing (*U.S. v. Thompson*, 714 F.3d 946). The court noted that "sentencing hearings are 'trial like' in that witnesses are sworn and testify, factual determinations are made, and counsel argue their positions," and the support the U.S. Supreme Court has given to sentencing as an open proceeding.

Civil proceedings. All of the cases summarized up to now involved *criminal* court proceedings. In 1999, the California Supreme Court ruled that *civil* courtrooms should usually be open to the public. In *NBC Subsidiary v. Superior Court* (20 C.4th 1178), the court overturned a number of restrictions that a judge had imposed on the press and public during a trial pitting actor Clint Eastwood against his former lover, actress Sondra Locke. The California Supreme Court recognized a broad constitutional right of the press and public to attend civil court proceedings as well as criminal proceedings. In a sweeping decision, the state supreme court unanimously ruled that the First Amendment protects the right to attend civil trials. The judge traced the tradition of open courtrooms through history and relied heavily on the U.S. Supreme Court's landmark *Richmond Newspapers v. Virginia* decision in concluding that there is a constitutional right to attend civil court proceedings. Although *Richmond Newspapers* specifically affirmed the public's right to attend only criminal trials, he noted that there are strong public policy reasons to recognize a similar right in civil cases, marking the first time that any state's highest court had clearly recognized a constitutional right to attend civil court proceedings.

■ ACCESS TO COURTROOM DOCUMENTS

If the nation's courtrooms are supposed to be open to the public under most circumstances, what about public access to *court documents*? In the aftermath of the Supreme Court's *Richmond Newspapers* decision and the cases that followed it, a number of lower courts have ruled that the press and public have a right to see and copy court documents even in sensational cases. Actually, court documents have normally been open for public inspection ever since colonial times: both the common law and many state constitutions require that court records generally be open.

Recent decisions have reinforced that principle—and established that there is a First Amendment right of access to many court documents. No longer may a judge freely seal court records without considering the public's right to know.

A qualified right of access. A good example of a court decision affirming the right of access to court documents as well as the right to attend courtroom proceedings is *Associated Press v. District Court* (705 F.2d 114, 1983), a decision of the Ninth Circuit. This case arose when a federal judge closed some of the pretrial proceedings and also sealed many court documents in the celebrated federal drug case against automaker John DeLorean, who was accused of arranging a multimillion dollar cocaine deal to save his failing auto company.

The appellate court ruled that the judge's secrecy orders violated the public's First Amendment right of access to court documents and proceedings that have traditionally been open. The decision is noteworthy because of the court's specific recognition that the First Amendment includes a right of access to court documents.

However, the court said this right must be balanced against other rights, notably the defendant's right to a fair trial. Reiterating earlier decisions, the court said a three-part test should be used in deciding whether pretrial secrecy is justified. Before sealing documents or barring the public from the courtroom, the judge must determine that:

1. Allowing public access would cause "a substantial probability that irreparable damage to (a defendant's) fair trial right will result;"
2. There are no alternative ways to protect the defendant's right to a fair trial;
3. There is "a substantial probability" that the secrecy would actually prevent the defendant's rights from being violated.

In ordering the DeLorean records opened, the appellate court noted that there had been extensive publicity about the case in spite of the court records being sealed. The secrecy was not working and therefore could not be justified.

Also, in recent years the media have increasingly sought—and been granted—access to pretrial *discovery* materials and proceedings. As Chapter One explains, during the discovery process each side is permitted to obtain information from the other through a variety of techniques including depositions (in which witnesses answer questions under oath, with the responses recorded by a court reporter) and written statements of various types. Often these discovery materials are newsworthy—and crucial to the success or failure of a lawsuit. These materials often become a part of the public record, available for anyone to read or copy.

There has also been debate about the circumstances under which courts should allow broadcasters to copy and air audio and videotapes submitted as evidence. For example, in

1986 the Ninth Circuit held that broadcasters have a limited right of access to taped evidence in *Valley Broad. v. U.S. District Court* (798 F.2d 1289). The appellate court said there is a "strong presumption" that broadcasters are entitled to copy taped evidence unless a judge has "articulated facts" to show that the copying would jeopardize a defendant's right to a fair trial. The court said there was no risk of the evidence being destroyed during the copying because the court's tapes were only copies of the FBI's masters. Also, the court saw no more risk of jurors being prejudiced by seeing the taped evidence on television than by watching the normal news coverage of the trial.

Access to sealed records. Several state supreme courts and federal appellate courts have ruled on the extent to which there is a right of public access to court records under common law principles. The results have been mixed.

The Ninth Circuit held in 1998 that federal courts in that circuit must follow specific guidelines to determine when the press and public are entitled to see sealed transcripts of closed court hearings and similar court records. In a case involving alleged criminal wrongdoing by former Arizona Governor Fife Symington, the media objected to the sealing of transcripts of two hearings concerning alleged jury tampering during the trial. The court said judges must provide some safeguards before sealing records in newsworthy cases: "If a court contemplates sealing a document or transcript, it must provide sufficient notice to the public and press to afford them the opportunity to object or offer alternatives," the court wrote in *Phoenix Newspapers v. U.S. District Court* (156 F.3d 940). "If objections are made, a hearing on the objections must be held as soon as possible," it added.

In another 1998 decision, the Ninth Circuit held that the public also had a right to see the psychiatric evaluation of the "Unabomber," Theodore Kaczynski. In *U.S. v. Kaczynski* (154 F.3d 930), the court held that the public's right to know outweighed Kaczynski's right of privacy. This decision was again based on common law principles, which require this balancing test to determine when court records should be open to the public. The court did not address another argument made by news organizations: that the press and public have a First Amendment right of access to documents as significant as Kaczynski's psychiatric evaluation. (Kaczynski eventually pleaded guilty to charges of making and mailing letter bombs that killed several people over a period of years.)

An error in court records sealing resulted in a rare prior restraint on the media (similar to the issue in the Kobe Bryant case discussed earlier in this chapter). In 2010, juice maker POM Wonderful was engaged in a bitter court battle with its former law firm in which the firm alleged that POM owed over $500,000

Focus on...
Court documents

In the online age, finding and obtaining court documents has become much easier. Although one can still go to the courthouse (and that may sometimes be easiest), most jurisdictions have electronic versions.

The PACER (Public Access to Court Electronic Records) system at pacer.gov) "allows users to obtain case and docket information from federal appellate, district and bankruptcy courts." Cost: eight cents a page. In 2009, a free browser extension called RECAP posts documents downloaded via PACER on a public website and suggests where free documents can be found.

Want decisions on your desktop right away? Many courts have free RSS (Real Simple Syndication) feeds to which you can subscribe that will send breaking decisions to your computer or cell phone. For a list of law-based RSS feeds, see www.findlaw.com/rss-index.

in legal fees generated during a standoff with a federal regulatory agency investigation. POM won a judge's order to seal court records; District of Columbia Superior Court Judge Judith Bartnoff sealed the records but they remained open by mistake, and a reporter for the *National Law Journal*, a legal newspaper, obtained them and prepared a story. The judge, on POM's request, issued a restraining order on July 23. ALM Media Properties, the owner of the *National Law Journal*, appealed the order to the D.C. Circuit on July 28, and major media companies joined together in an *amicus curiae* ("friend of the court") brief in support of ALM.

Shortly after the brief was filed on July 30, POM's lawyers reversed themselves and asked the judge to lift the order, which she did—and media organizations could publish that it was the Federal Trade Commission investigating POM. The media breathed a sigh of relief. However, Judge Bartnoff seemed not to have minded issuing the gag order; the *Washington Post* quoted her as saying at the July 23 hearing, "If I am throwing 80 years of First Amendment jurisprudence on its head, so be it. None of that First Amendment jurisprudence, to my knowledge, is dealing with this issue." The FTC's investigation of POM Wonderful's assertions of health benefits in pomegranate juice is discussed in Chapter Thirteen.

The Oregon Supreme Court in 2012 allowed public access to 20,000 pages of "perversion files" kept by the Boy Scouts of America to keep sex offenders out of leadership roles. The Scouts had argued to keep the records sealed after they were used in a court case against a Scout leader accused of molesting a child. The state high court agreed that names of victims and those who made the accusations should be redacted (removed), but said that "the constitutional requirement of visibility in the administration of justice was important in the context of both civil and criminal justice" (*Doe v. Corporation of the Presiding Bishop of the Church of Jesus Christ of Latter-Day Saints*, 352 Ore. 77).

How about access to records filed in support of requests for search warrants after the investigation is over? The Ninth Circuit said a qualified common law right of access applies, noting that access is "important to the public's understanding of the function and operation of the judicial process and the criminal justice system and may operate as a curb on prosecutorial or judicial misconduct" (*U.S. v. Business of Custer Battlefield Museum & Store*, 658 F.3d 1188, 2011).

However, courts have found reasons to seal court records to which even some media organizations might not object. For example, in *U.S. v. Brice* (649 F.3d 793), the D.C. Circuit said that the records of two juvenile victims of Jaron Brice's underage prostitution scheme who were material witnesses in his conviction could be sealed. Brice requested that the records be unsealed, and the district court denied. In affirming the lower court, the appellate court assumed that material witness proceedings were generally considered to be public; however, in this case, "the public was not entitled to the records here, which contained 'substantial amounts of material of an especially personal and private nature relating to the medical, educational, and mental health progress' of the victims."

No First Amendment right in Colorado. In a recent case, *In re People v. Owens* (420 P.3d 257, 2018), the Colorado Supreme Court ruled there is no First Amendment qualified right of access to court documents in criminal cases. "We find no support in United States Supreme Court jurisprudence for Petitioner's contention that the First Amendment provides the public with a constitutional right of access to any and all court records in cases involving matters of public concern," the Court wrote. The case involved a petition from *The Colorado Independent* newspaper to unseal court records in a long-running capital murder case. In 2017, a judge upheld the death sentence of the defendant but found a pattern of misconduct by state prosecutors. The newspaper wanted to review specific documents the judge relied on, but the judge denied the request. The newspaper appealed, but the Colorado Supreme Court said the law does not require "unfettered access" to court records. "Not only is (the state supreme court) sealing court records with no legal justification, but it has given Colorado the dangerous distinction of being the only state in the nation without a presumed First Amendment right for the public and news media to keep tabs on our criminal justice system and elected officials," Susan Greene, the editor of the *Independent*, was quoted as saying after the decision. The Reporters Committee for Freedom of the Press and 47 media organizations filed an *amicus curiae* brief urging the U.S. Supreme Court to overturn the decision, but the court denied *cert* in 2019, leaving the Colorado Supreme Court decision to stand.

Other access denials. Several cases have addressed the definition of "judicial records" and the rules to access them, with markedly mixed results for journalists. For example, the Massachusetts Supreme Judicial Court (the state's high court) in 2013 declined a filmmaker's request for an audio "room recording," saying that "where the court reporter's room recording is not the official record of the trial and is not filed with the court or referenced in the court file, the film maker is not entitled to a copy under the public's right of access to criminal proceedings guaranteed by the First Amendment" (*Commonwealth of Massachusetts v. Winfield*, 464 Mass. 672).

The D.C. Circuit refused to grant a journalist access to reports compiled by an independent consultant by American International Group, Inc. (AIG) as part of its consent decree (*SEC v. Am. Int'l Group, Inc.*, 712 F.3d 1, 2013). The court said that the reports "are not judicial records subject to the right of access because the district court made no decisions about them or that otherwise relied on them."

And the Washington Supreme Court found no constitutional right of access to any case record until and unless the record becomes "relevant to a decision actually made by the court" (*Bennett v. Smith Bunday Berman Britton, PS*, 291 P.3d 886, 2013), adding, "Simply put, information that does not become part of the judicial process is not governed by the open courts provision in our constitution."

Not all bad news. But there are bright spots. The Ohio Supreme Court ordered the unsealing of records in a dismissed but high-profile criminal case (*Vindicator Printing Co. v. Wolff*, 132 Ohio St. 3d 481, 2012), saying that according to the rules in Ohio that govern court documents, "to qualify as a case document that is afforded the presumption of openness for court records, the document or information contained in a document must merely be 'submitted to a court or filed with a clerk of court in a judicial action or proceeding' and not be subject to the specified exclusions." Finding the requested records to meet these requirements, the court ordered them unsealed.

And, in a rare holding, the Virginia Supreme Court held in 2013 that a judge erred by withholding access to trial exhibits in a 2011 child murder case, saying the case was not moot even though the records that were requested by the Newport News Daily Press were released two years ago. In *The Daily Press, Inc. v. Commonwealth of Virginia* (285 Va. 447), the court said that "the mootness doctrine may be inapplicable when a proceeding is short-lived by nature," which these kinds of sealings often are. Moreover, the court added, "To delay or postpone disclosure undermines the benefits of public scrutiny and may have the same result as complete suppression."

In a win for news organizations, the Second Circuit allowed access to a sealed court-room proceeding and investigative report of the Nassau County Police Department in a high-profile civil federal case against the department (*Newsday LLC v. County of Nassau*, 730 F.3d 156). A district court had released only a redacted (edited) transcript of civil contempt hearings, and the news organizations wanted more. They appealed under both the First Amendment and the common law right of access, and the Second Circuit agreed. The court pointed out that "the First Amendment "'does not distinguish between criminal and civil proceedings,' but rather 'protects the public against the government's arbitrary interference with access to important information.'" The full, unredacted transcript, said the court, did not pose significant confidentiality concerns and was therefore released.

The Fourth Circuit in 2014 ordered the unsealing of an *entire* court record from a trial that had taken place entirely behind closed doors. The U.S. Consumer Product Safety Commission created a new online database to publish news of harms from products, and this was the first challenge to that database. The company, known as Company Doe, asked for that record to be sealed and the information about its trial to be kept out of the database. Three consumer groups (Public Citizen, Consumer Federation of America, and Consumers' Union) filed suit after the court released heavily-redacted versions of some of the proceedings. Because the groups were not appealing the findings of the trial but only the sealed transcripts and records, the court ruled they had standing. "The public has an interest in learning not only the evidence and records filed in connection with summary judgment proceedings but also the district court's decision ruling on a summary judgment motion and the grounds supporting its decision. Without access to judicial opinions, public oversight of the courts, including the processes and the outcomes they produce, would be impossible," the court wrote in opening the records (*Company Doe v. Public Citizen*, 749 F.3d 246).

Bottom line. In short, the right of the press and the public to inspect court documents, obtain copies of videotaped evidence, and to attend courtroom proceedings has been often upheld since the Supreme Court put those rights in question with its *Gannett v. DePasquale* decision in 1979. Today, in most jurisdictions and with important exceptions, a judge can deny public access to court documents and close courtroom proceedings only if it is necessary to protect a defendant's right to a fair trial. However, this trend may be changing. One example: Courts and legislatures are increasingly concerned with the prejudicial impact of court records on individuals' reputations and privacy. In 2014, the highest court in Massachusetts articulated a new balancing test for when it should seal past court records in *Commonwealth v. Peter Pon* (469 Mass. 296). The privacy interests in sealing court records include "the compelling governmental interests in reducing recidivism, facilitating reintegration, and ensuring self-sufficiency by promoting employment and housing opportunities for former criminal defendants," the court wrote.

■ CAMERAS IN COURT

To the surprise of many Americans today, the kind of televised spectacle that unfolded in the O.J. Simpson murder trial could not have happened until recently: both television cameras and still photography were prohibited in almost all American courtrooms for many years, and those restrictions were not abolished until the 1980s.

Long before the Supreme Court addressed the fair trial-free press problem in the 1960s, there were controversies about the effect the media had on the decorum of a courtroom.

This debate centered on the presence of cameras and broadcast equipment in court. An early case that dramatized the problem was the 1935 trial of Bruno Hauptmann, the alleged kidnapper and murderer of celebrated aviator Charles Lindbergh's young son. Although Hauptmann's trial did not take place until nearly two and a half years after the kidnapping, the courtroom was so jammed with reporters and photographers that it was often impossible to conduct orderly proceedings. There was a great deal of inflammatory publicity.

After Hauptmann was convicted and executed for the crime, a Special Committee on Cooperation between Press, Radio and Bar was established to recommend standards of publicity in judicial proceedings. In its final report, the committee said the Hauptmann trial was "the most spectacular and depressing example of improper publicity and professional misconduct ever presented to the people of the United States in a criminal trial."

At least partly in response to the Hauptmann trial, the American Bar Association in 1937 added new rules to its recommended Canons of Judicial Ethics, prohibiting broadcasting and taking photographs in a courtroom. These rules were eventually rewritten to allow much more extensive television coverage, but before that happened, journalists fought a long battle for access to the nation's trial courtrooms. These ABA rules, of course, were merely recommendations to the state and federal court systems; they were not mandatory. However, by the 1960s every state except Colorado and Texas had adopted rules forbidding most camera and broadcast coverage of court proceedings. And in 1946, radio broadcasts and photography were prohibited in federal courts by Rule 53 of the Federal Rules of Criminal Procedure. That rule was also later expanded to forbid television broadcasting and to prohibit photography or broadcasting in the "environs of the (federal) courtroom."

Estes sets the negative tone. Stunned by these restrictions, broadcast journalists and photographers wondered why the First Amendment didn't protect their right to cover trials. The Supreme Court eventually ruled on these questions in a 1965 case, *Estes v. Texas* (381 U.S. 532). The case involved a Texas grain dealer with political connections, Billie Sol Estes. He was convicted of swindling a group of investors, but his conviction was reversed by the U.S. Supreme Court because two days of the preliminary hearing and part of the trial were televised under Texas' highly unusual court rules permitting it.

The television coverage of the pretrial hearing was obtrusive: there were bright lights, bulky cameras, and cables trailing around the courtroom. Before the actual trial, the judge imposed some restrictions on the media, and the TV cameras were confined to a booth in the back of the room. However, it was still obvious to everyone in the courtroom that the cameras were there. In reversing Estes' conviction, five justices said the television coverage had denied him a fair trial. Four justices agreed that the presence of television cameras inherently denied a defendant the right to a fair trial. The fifth member of the majority, Justice John Marshall Harlan, said it might be possible to televise ordinary trials—but not celebrated ones such as Estes'. However, the Court also predicted that future technical advances might make television cameras unobtrusive enough for use in courtrooms.

Admitting Cameras: **Chandler v. Florida**

By 1980, broadcast technology had advanced. Thanks to solid-state electronics, cameras became much smaller and usable with far less lighting than was required in 1965. As a result, the rules began to change. A few more states began admitting still photographers and video crews into their courts. By 1980, about 10 states allowed broadcast coverage *even without the consent of the defendant*, something the *Estes* decision would not have permitted in major cases. Clearly, it was time for a new Supreme Court decision.

In 1981, the Supreme Court responded to the changing technology by changing the rules on courtroom television coverage. That happened in *Chandler v. Florida* (449 U.S. 560), a case in which two police officers were convicted of using their squad car and police radios in a burglary of a restaurant. At the time of their trial, Florida allowed television coverage of criminal trials on an experimental basis. Although the two officers objected, much of their trial was videotaped, and portions were shown on television. The two officers, Noel Chandler and Robert Granger, appealed their convictions, contending that the television coverage denied them a fair trial.

The Court ruled against Chandler and Granger. Voting 8-0, the justices held that the presence of television cameras does not inherently violate a defendant's constitutional right to a fair trial, although they left open the possibility that defendants could show that their rights were violated in a specific case. Thus, the Court refused to overturn Florida's rules allowing television coverage of trials even without the defendant's consent. The Court said that the states were free to adopt such rules if they wished. Chief Justice Warren Burger wrote, "An absolute constitutional ban on broadcast coverage of trials cannot be justified simply because there is a danger that, in some cases, prejudicial broadcast accounts of pretrial and trial events may impair the ability of jurors to decide the issue of guilt or innocence uninfluenced by extraneous matter." But Burger's opinion made it clear that criminal defendants are entitled to protest their convictions if they can show that media coverage actually prejudiced the jury. Chief Justice Burger cited the dramatic changes in broadcast technology between the 1960s and the 1980s. Burger made it clear that *Estes* had not prohibited all experimentation with cameras in the courtroom. He noted that Chandler and Granger had not shown that their right to a fair trial was actually jeopardized by the broadcast coverage.

After *Chandler*. Obviously, the *Chandler* decision was a victory for the media, but it is important to remember what it did and did not say. It simply said there is no constitutional prohibition on cameras in the courtroom. It did *not* say the broadcast media have any special right of access to the nation's courts. Rather, *Chandler* said that the states are free to allow cameras in court if they choose to do so. Even then, when a particular defendant can show that media coverage denied him/her a fair trial, that person is entitled to a new trial.

The response to the *Chandler* decision came quickly. In 1982, the American Bar Association recognized the new trend and revised its rule which previously urged the states to impose severe restrictions on broadcast and photographic coverage of criminal trials. As rewritten, the rule says the states may allow judges to permit photographic coverage if certain safeguards are met. It specifies that the coverage must be "consistent with the right of the parties to a fair trial" and must be handled so that cameras "will be unobtrusive, will not distract trial participants, and will not otherwise interfere with the administration of justice." However, this rule is still voluntary and not all states adhere to it.

As a result of the *Chandler* decision, the states that already allowed television coverage or still photography in their courtrooms were free to continue doing so, and a number of additional states authorized electronic and photographic courtroom coverage after that. Some states that previously permitted cameras in their courtrooms only with the consent of defendants dropped that requirement after the *Chandler* ruling was announced.

Cameras in State Courts

States have taken different approaches to cameras in courtrooms. Following the O.J. Simpson trial, measures to ban cameras were defeated in both Virginia and Georgia. But the Simpson case clearly had an effect, especially in New York.

New York allowed cameras in its trial courts on an experimental basis in 1987, and the experiment was renewed several times. In 1995, the state legislature seemed ready to make it permanent until the Simpson murder trial captured the nation's attention. Amid that spectacle, the legislature balked and almost barred cameras altogether. But on the day before the third extension of the camera experiment was to expire in 1995, the legislature relented and extended the experiment again. But in mid-1997, the legislature allowed it to end, thereby closing the state's trial courts to cameras. In 2005, New York's highest court ruled that the ban on cameras does not violate either the First Amendment or the state constitution (*Courtroom TV Network v. State of New York*, 5 N.Y.3d 222).

If televising the Simpson murder trial had a major impact in New York, it also had impact in California itself, where the state Judicial Council set up a task force to reconsider cameras in the courtroom. The task force urged severe restrictions on cameras in California trial courts, including a ban on camera coverage of almost all pretrial proceedings. The Judicial Council rejected that proposal and retained a system in which it is up to the judge in each case to decide whether to admit cameras. However, judges were given strict new guidelines to follow in making this decision, and media lawyers predicted that the new guidelines would lead to cameras being barred more often. Among other things, the new rules forbid camera coverage of jury selection and proceedings that are closed to the public.

By the 2000s, all 50 states were allowing television or still photographic coverage of some court proceedings. South Dakota became the 50th state to admit cameras when the state supreme court announced in 2001 that it would allow video and audio coverage of oral arguments. However, only 41 states allow camera coverage of criminal trials as opposed to appellate court proceedings, and a few of those permit cameras *only with the consent of the defendant*, something that is rarely granted. Several other states have other rules so restrictive that they effectively bar cameras from most trial courts. On the other hand, at least 35 states allow trial judges to admit cameras to their courts even if a defendant objects.

In 2018, the Florida Supreme Court allowed its proceedings to be broadcast on Facebook Live, the first known high court to allow live social media streaming. In a statement, Chief Justice Jorge Labarga said, "In the 1970s, Florida became the first state to allow broadcasts of its court cases at a time when every other court in the nation refused it. This court's experiment with transparency showed everyone a better way to balance First Amendment rights against the rights of people involved in a trial or appeal. Social media will be our next step in moving this highly successful model of openness into the twenty-first century."

Cameras in Federal Courts

The last major holdout in admitting cameras has been the federal court system. However, the federal courts have been under increasing pressure from members of Congress as well as media representatives to open their doors to the electronic media.

Cameras in the lower courts. The federal judiciary in 1991 began a three-year experiment allowing cameras in two U.S. (circuit) Courts of Appeals and six federal trial courts, but only civil trials and appellate proceedings, not criminal. The federal experiment was extended through 1994 by the U.S. Judicial Conference. However, the conference declined to extend the experiment beyond that date or to make it permanent. For a time, cameras were again barred from almost all federal court proceedings. The Judicial Conference backpedaled a little in 1996, adopting rules under which each federal appellate court may decide for itself whether to admit cameras to *appellate proceedings*. The 1996 rules discouraged federal *trial courts* from admitting cameras even during civil cases, but they did not flatly forbid cameras except during criminal cases. By 1999 the Second Circuit in New York and the Ninth Circuit on the West Coast voted to admit cameras in some cases, while other federal circuits declined to do so.

In recent years Congress has considered—but never approved—legislation to open various federal courts to cameras. One bill to allow cameras in federal courts gained support when the American Bar Association endorsed the idea of having television cameras in courts to provide gavel-to-gavel coverage from the U.S. Supreme Court down to the local level. Advocates of greater electronic media access to federal courts were encouraged by the fact that the Supreme Court released audio tapes of oral arguments in *Bush v. Gore*—the case that ultimately determined the outcome of the 2000 presidential election. No one seriously suggested that the airing of those tapes caused any problem for the court. But it did allow millions of people to hear for themselves the arguments in this crucial Supreme Court case.

In 2007, the Judicial Conference approved a voluntary pilot program to allow federal courts to place audio recordings of proceedings online. Judge Thomas F. Hogan, the executive committee chair, said he expected many federal courts to participate.

The Judicial Conference of the United States, the administrative body of the federal courts, conducted a four-year pilot project to evaluate the effect of cameras in district courtrooms, as well as video recordings of civil proceedings and their publication. From July 2011 to July 2015, 158 proceedings were recorded and published in 14 of the 94 U.S. district courts. Three-fourths of participating judges and lawyers responded favorably to the project, however in 2016 the Judicial Conference decided to keep the camera ban in place. Officials said there was not enough evidence of benefits to the judiciary to justify the negative effect on witnesses and the equipment and personnel costs with the recordings.

In 2019, the House Subcommittee on Courts, Intellectual Property, and the Internet held a hearing titled "The Federal Judiciary in the 21st Century: Ensuring the Public's Right of Access to the Courts." It was clear that while some in Congress, and many in the media and advocacy groups, want more audio and video access to court proceedings, others continue to worry about the negative effects of cameras in courtrooms.

Today, most federal trial courts prohibit audio and video coverage of their proceedings, based largely on concerns about a defendant's right to a fair and impartial trial. Judge Audrey Fleissig, U.S. District Judge of the Eastern District of Missouri, testified before Congress in 2019 on behalf of the Judicial Conference of the United States, and said:

> After careful consideration and two multi-year studies, the Judicial Conference
> has consistently expressed the view that camera coverage can cause irreparable
> harm to a citizen's right to a fair and impartial trial. The Conference believes
> that the effect of cameras on litigants, witnesses, and jurors can have a profound-
> ly negative impact on the trial process. In civil and criminal cases, cameras can
> intimidate defendants who, regardless of the merits of the case, might prefer to
> settle or plead guilty rather than risk airing damaging accusations in a televised
> trial. Cameras also create security and privacy concerns for individuals, many of
> whom are not even parties to the case, but about whom personal information
> may be revealed at trial.

As one example of the lack of support for cameras in federal trial courts, the Supreme Court in 2010 then declined to allow the Proposition 8 trial proceedings in a federal court in California, discussed in Chapter Five, to be broadcast or streamed in real time to other courthouses. In *Hollingsworth v. Perry* (558 U.S. 183), the Court in a *per curiam* (unsigned) opinion dodged the general question about whether trials should or should not be broadcast. In this case, the Court said, the lower court failed to follow proper procedures; it "attempted to change its rules at the eleventh hour to treat this case differently than other trials in the district." Justice Stephen Breyer, joined by three others, dissented, saying that the Court should have no standing to make such a determination: "This Court has no legal authority to address that larger policy question *except insofar as it implicates a question of law.*"

Appellate courts allow some audio and video recordings. Things are different at the appellate level. According to the advocacy group Fix the Group, by 2019, almost all federal appellate circuit courts disseminate audio of their proceedings, although only a minority of them provide live audio.

Only the Ninth Circuit regularly allows live video of their proceedings. Seven federal appellate circuits do not allow any video, live or recorded, of their proceedings.

Cameras at the Supreme Court. Cameras are not allowed in the nation's highest court, nor is there any likelihood of that happening anytime soon.

In 1990, U.S. Chief Justice William Rehnquist went on the record as "by no means averse to the idea" of allowing cameras in federal courts. Writing a letter to a member of Congress who was concerned about this question, Rehnquist took a position opposite to that of former Chief Justice Warren Burger, who once said cameras would be allowed in federal courts "over my dead body." At a 2006 Senate hearing, Justice David Souter used those same words in testimony opposing the use of cameras at the Supreme Court. Justice Anthony Kennedy said basically the same thing, but not in those words, in 2007 Congressional testimony.

On the other hand, Supreme Court justices have begun appearing in televised interviews much more frequently since John G. Roberts became chief justice. Even Antonin Scalia, who refused to allow media coverage of an event where he received an award for protecting freedom of speech in 2003, granted several media interviews in 2007 and 2008. Roberts has also discussed possible camera access to the Supreme Court with representatives of the Radio Television News Directors Association.

FIG. 67.
U.S. Supreme
Court building,
Washington, D.C.

Author's collection.

A C-SPAN poll in 2012 found that 95% of Americans believe the Court should be "more open and transparent"—but don't expect to see cameras rolling into the Supreme Court anytime soon. In 2013, four justices spoke against the idea. Both Justices Sonia Sotomayor and Elena Kagan, who had expressed some support for the idea in their confirmation hearings, have changed their minds. Justice Sotomayor told interviewer Charlie Rose, "I don't think most viewers take the time to actually delve into either the briefs or the legal arguments to appreciate what the court is doing."

And Justices Stephen Breyer and Anthony Kennedy were no more supportive in a hearing of a House Appropriations Committee subpanel. Justice Breyer said, "[T]he first time you see on prime time television somebody taking a picture of you and really using it in a way that you think is completely unfair... to caricature [your position]... you will watch a lot more carefully what you say."

Nonetheless, the COVID-19 pandemic had one positive effect: the U.S. Supreme Court began live streaming its oral arguments during the 2020 term. For the first time in history, citizens could listen in real time to lawyers presenting their arguments—and justices asking questions.

Beyond Cameras: New Technologies in the Courtroom

Most judges focus their attention on print and broadcast access to courtrooms, but what about new technologies, like Twitter, commenting and blogging, and webcasting? Clearly, jurors should not use these technologies inappropriately; in 2010, the Judicial Conference endorsed model jury instructions for district courts to tell jurors that they may not use cell phones, computers, or other such technologies in the court, during jury deliberations, or outside the courthouse to discuss or research cases on which they are serving. But what about reporters or others using these technologies? The record is mixed.

A Colorado judge in 2009 allowed the use of Twitter, a micro-blogging tool where users can "tweet" short blurbs about their lives, and blogs in an infant-abuse trial. A *Wichita Eagle* reporter had already "tweeted" coverage of a capital murder trial in 2008. At least some judges view the new technology as similar to traditional reporting techniques, only faster.

But Twitter is still a sticky subject for many courts. The judge in the 2012 Chicago case of the murder of singer Jennifer Hudson's family banned Twitter from the courtroom (although there was a room just outside where reporters could tweet, it did not have an audio/video feed, just a rolling transcript) and reversed his ruling on allowing journalists to have cell phones after they kept ringing during testimony.

The Supreme Court has never been welcoming to technology; in 2012 the Marshal's Office shut down an attorney who was doing live tweets from the overflow room during the Patient Protection and Affordable Care Act ("Obamacare") oral arguments. The high court prohibits all outside technology to maintain judicial decorum.

Things are different at the state level. Kansas and Utah, for example, permit journalists to tweet, livestream, and blog from their states' courtrooms. In Kansas, journalists need judges' permission to take laptops and cell phones into the courtroom, and they cannot photograph jurors, juveniles, or undercover agents. In Utah, journalists will have to complete applications, and they are also prohibited from taking pictures of minors, jurors, or documents.

■ AN OVERVIEW OF MAJOR ISSUES

Despite several Supreme Court cases holding that the First Amendment rights of the press and public cannot be ignored in an attempt to protect a defendant's Sixth Amendment rights, the fair trial-free press problem is still with us. Many high-profile trials, such as those involving O.J. Simpson and Michael Jackson, for example, have underscored this problem.

The trend toward closed courtrooms was slowed considerably by the Supreme Court's *Richmond Newspapers v. Virginia, Globe Newspaper Co. v. Superior Court* and *Press-Enterprise v. Superior Court* decisions. However, courtroom closures remain a problem for the media in some states. Judges cite the threat of prejudicial publicity to justify closing the doors. But are they right? Do the media still tend to inflame public opinion in celebrated cases? Do the media have a right to cover crime news aggressively? Are the media sometimes *too* aggressive?

For years, journalists have also been fighting for camera and video access to the nation's courtrooms—with some success. All states now permit cameras and broadcast equipment in some courts, although not necessarily in trial courts. That trend was encouraged by the Supreme Court's *Chandler v. Florida* decision, which said broadcast coverage of court proceedings is not inherently prejudicial to defendants. The Court left it up to the *states* to decide when (and if) cameras will be admitted to their courtrooms, leading to policies that vary from state to state. Meanwhile, the battle for camera access to *federal* courts has been difficult for journalists and their supporters. Will Chief Justice John Roberts allow cameras in the Supreme Court? (Admittedly, that's unlikely given the current justices' opinions.)

Fortunately for the media, another major fair trial-free press problem of an earlier era has largely disappeared. Thanks to *Nebraska Press Association v. Stuart*, "gag" orders have been imposed on the media only rarely in recent years. But those problems have been replaced by issues of new technology. How will the legal and judicial communities deal with situations rising from webcasting, social networking sites, public comments, and Twitter?

Nevertheless, conflicts between the rights of a free press and the rights of those accused of crimes will surely continue as long as both the First and Sixth Amendments remain in effect. This is not a legal problem that is likely to be resolved soon—if ever. Moreover, the fair trial-free press controversy has generated related legal problems, including the threat of contempt of court that arises when a judge demands—and a journalist declines to reveal—the source of information leaked to the press in violation of a gag order. The next chapter addresses these issues, detailing the growth of shield laws and the increasing use of contempt citations against reporters who refuse to reveal their sources.

WHAT SHOULD I KNOW ABOUT MY STATE?

- What is my state's position on cameras in the courtroom: what kind of cases, what levels of court, what regulations must be followed?
- What is my state's court records policy and procedure? (See the Reporters Committee for Freedom of the Press' excellent "Open Government Guide" for a state-by-state comparison: http://www.rcfp.org/open-government-guide.)

**A SUMMARY
OF FAIR
TRIAL-FREE
PRESS
ISSUES**

What Is the Problem?

The First Amendment guarantees freedom of the press—and that includes the right to cover crime news. However, a person charged with a crime has a Sixth Amendment right to a trial before an impartial jury—a jury made up of impartial persons who will base their decision solely on what they learn in court.

Why Shouldn't Jurors Learn About a Case in the Media?

Much information that may be published in the media will never be admitted into evidence in court and is not supposed to be considered by a jury.

Why Do the Courts Ignore Some of the Evidence?

A court may only hear evidence gathered by lawful means, not secured in violation of constitutional ban on illegal coerced confessions and illegal searches. And a jury is only supposed to decide whether a defendant is guilty as charged; information about a person's past is often irrelevant (but newsworthy).

What Has Been Done About This Problem?

The Supreme Court has urged trial judges to take steps to control inflammatory publicity, such as "gagging" participants in trials so they will not reveal prejudicial (and inadmissible) evidence to the media. However, the Court has also ruled that closing the courtroom is not usually the solution, saying that trials and pretrial proceedings should be open to the press and public unless the trial judge determines that a closed session is absolutely necessary to protect the defendant's rights. Many journalists oppose the judiciary's attempts to control publicity; they believe that these efforts interfere with the public's right to know about the administration of justice.

Are Cameras and Video Equipment Allowed in Court?

Many lawyers and judges question photographic and television coverage of the courts. They feel this may turn a dignified proceeding into a circus. However, the Supreme Court has ruled that the presence of cameras in court does not necessarily violate the right to a fair trial. All states allow cameras in some of their courtrooms, but not necessarily during criminal trials. Cameras have not generally been permitted in federal criminal courts.

What About New Technologies in the Courtroom?

There is inconsistency among courts and judges in allowing the use of technologies like webcasting and live posting on social media during trials.

8   *Newsgatherer's Privilege*

Sometimes journalists become participants instead of observers of the legal system. Journalists can be jailed and sued for refusing to identify confidential news sources—and they have also been sued for identifying confidential sources. Journalists have seen their newsrooms ransacked by law enforcement officials in search of evidence, and contempt of court—a legal threat that seemed to be disappearing at one time—has reappeared as a major problem for the news media.

In recent years, journalists have faced subpoenas for newsgathering and confidential source information like never before. More aggressive attempts to compel journalists to turn over information to prosecutors and courts have resulted in unprecedented jailings and legal fines against journalists and news organizations. The three longest jail terms in American history for journalists refusing to turn over newsgathering material have all occurred since 2001: freelance writer Vanessa Leggett served 168 days in jail after being held in contempt for refusing to turn over notes about a murder investigation; *New York Times* reporter Judith Miller served 85 days until she decided to reveal the identity of a source who leaked the name of a CIA agent; and video blogger Josh Wolf spent 226 days in prison after he refused to turn over to the FBI videotapes of a street protest in San Francisco.

Following the Sept. 11 terrorist attacks, the government significantly cracked down on journalists using confidential sources to report on national security. The George W. Bush and Barack Obama administrations approved subpoenas for several journalists in cases where government officials were accused of leaking information to reporters. Under President Obama, more government officials were prosecuted under the Espionage Act for providing information to journalists than during all previous presidencies combined. President Donald J. Trump launched many leak investigations as well (even though he himself was a prolific leaker during his career as a businessman and reality TV star). Within his first year as president, Trump's Justice Department had launched 27 criminal investigations into who leaked information to the press.

Technology has also played a role in the changing nature of leak investigations. Today, rather than hauling a reporter into court and asking them to name a source, the government has many tools at its disposal to trace the digital communications of journalists and sources, including subpoenas for phone and email records.

Following disclosures in 2021 of several secret subpoenas by the Trump administration for electronic records of journalists, President Joe Biden promised no such actions would happen on his watch. Stay tuned.

Chapter Objectives:

- Describe the rationales for a journalist's privilege to protect confidential sources.
- Explain challenges journalists have in protecting confidential sources and newsgathering information.
- Evaluate the strength of the journalist's privilege under federal and state law.

Essential Questions:

- Why do journalists argue that "freedom of the press" requires that they protect confidential sources from compelled disclosure?
- What are the essential differences between journalist privilege protection at the federal and state level?
- Who is a journalist under privilege law?
- Under what circumstances might journalists be sued for violating promises of confidentiality?
- Can newsrooms be physically searched by police like other places?

Why protect sources? Since colonial times, newspaper editors and journalists have advanced several arguments for why confidential sources are necessary to their role in informing the public about news. First, they argue that without the right to protect confidential sources, freedom of the press could be eviscerated, and thus they believe the First Amendment gives them a legal right to protect sources. Second, journalists contend that without confidential sources, many news stories could never be reported. It is commonplace for "whistleblowers" (people with inside information about wrongdoing in government or business) to come forward and talk to a reporter in secret, something they could not do without a pledge of confidentiality. If reporters had to reveal their sources, many people with important information would not talk to them out of fear of the recriminations that might result. Therefore, many journalists believe their moral and ethical responsibilities to protect sources are so compelling that they would rather go to jail than break a promise of confidentiality.

On the other hand, prosecutors, lawyers, and judges want all relevant information available to the court, and they are increasingly using their contempt of court power to enforce orders requiring journalists to supply confidential information. Judges often feel that journalists are no different from other citizens and should comply with subpoenas. And if journalists choose to break a valid court order, many judges believe that they should face the consequences—jail and/or fines—just like any other lawbreaker.

The law for journalists is complex, as this chapter shows. First, there exists a limited constitutional and common law privilege in the federal courts, or at least in most appellate circuits. This *qualified federal reporter's privilege* is rooted in constitutional law, common law, and judicial rules. Additionally, federal administrative rules place limitations on subpoenas to journalists. Second, almost all states have some type of reporter's privilege that applies to actions by state and local officials and state courts. While some of these laws are rooted in constitutional and common law, many are based in statutory law, known as *shield laws* (laws that sometimes excuse journalists from disclosing confidential information).

Because of the patchwork of legal protections, it's possible for a journalist to be legally entitled to protect a source in state, but not federal, courts. Thus, it's important for journalists to know their legal rights and vulnerabilities when making promises of confidentiality.

■ TOOLS OF THE COURT

Judges, grand juries, lawyers, and legislative committees have the power to issue *subpoenas* in the legal system. As a general principle, the courts operate under the notion that *anyone* with relevant information to legal proceedings has a citizen's duty to cooperate. When individuals do not comply with valid subpoenas and court orders, they may be held in *contempt of court*. Journalists have often chosen to be held in contempt rather that reveal their sources as a matter of ethical principle. For much of American history, journalists held in contempt generally avoided harsh consequences in part because of the professional support they received for upholding journalism ethical principles. However, in recent years the consequences for journalists have become more severe.

"Privilege." Whether journalists have a privilege against testifying depends on the context and jurisdiction. The term *privilege*, as used here, means an exemption from a citizen's normal duty to testify when ordered to do so in court or in another official information-gathering proceeding. In earlier chapters, "privilege" has been used in a different sense.

Focus on...
Protecting "Deep Throat"

The most famous, and perhaps most consequential, confidential source in modern American journalism was "Deep Throat." For more than 30 years, *Washington Post* reporters Bob Woodward and Carl Bernstein protected the identity of the notorious man who leaked damaging information about President Nixon and his administration during the Watergate investigation in the 1970s.

Coined "Deep Throat" by a managing editor of the *Post* in reference to a pornographic movie because the source spoke to the journalists clandestinely and only on "deep background," the source was pivotal in pointing the two rookie reporters in the right direction as they investigated a web of illegal and unethical activity by Nixon and his top aides. The reporters won a Pulitzer Prize for their reporting.

FIG. 68. President Nixon leaving the White House after his resignation, August 9, 1974.

Oliver F. Atkins, White House photographer.

In 2005, W. Mark Felt was identified as "Deep Throat" by his family near the end of his life as he was suffering from dementia. Felt had been the No. 2 man in the FBI during the Nixon years. In his book *The Secret Man: The Story of Watergate's Deep Throat*, published after Felt identified himself, Woodward wrote that he believed Deep Throat was motivated by a desire to make sure journalists continued to dig into conduct of the administration, which had been successful in a number of cover-ups. In the end, more than 30 administration officials had committed major crimes.

In libel law, for example, privilege is a defense, a concept that allows public officials to make defamatory statements while performing their duties without fear of a lawsuit—and allows the media to accurately report those statements without the risk of a libel judgment.

In this chapter, however, "privilege" means an exemption from having to testify about confidential matters. The privilege concept is an old one that developed under English common law. Several kinds were recognized under the common law, including the husband-wife, doctor-patient, lawyer-client, and priest-penitent privileges. Each of these was established to protect a relationship that needed to be kept confidential for socially important reasons. These privileges have numerous exceptions, but all still remain viable today, at least under some circumstances. A doctor or lawyer, for instance, cannot be compelled to testify in court about many of the confidential things a patient or client may reveal.

Quashing Subpoenas

Journalists and news organizations routinely get subpoenas for all sorts of information. Police agencies or lawyers may seek outtakes from broadcasters as part of an investigation or during the discovery process. Grand juries may subpoena journalists for eyewitness testimony or to verify the contents of a news story. And sometimes, subpoenas seek the identity of a confidential source. According to one study in 2006, 7,000 subpoenas were issued to newspapers and broadcasters in the United States.

If a journalist is served with a subpoena for newsgathering information, that person will often fight the subpoena in court by filing a *motion to quash*. A motion to quash is a request for a judge to vacate the order and dispose of the subpoena. If the action occurs in a state

reporter's or newsgatherer's privilege:
a limited right for reporters to keep sources and/or unpublished information confidential against subpoenas.

subpoena:
Latin for "under penalty"; an order to an individual to appear before a body at a particular time to give testimony.

contempt:
judges' tool to keep order in the courtroom and to enforce their orders.

types of contempt:
direct contempt: an act that violates the decorum of the courtroom.

indirect contempt: an act outside the courtroom that disrespects the court.

criminal contempt: punishment for an act of disrespect to the court.

civil contempt: a coercive technique to encourage compliance with the court's order.

motion to quash:
request for a judge to dispose of a subpoena.

court where a shield law provides protections in the case, judges will regularly grant a motion to quash. In the federal courts, judges apply a complex balancing test to determine whether to quash the subpoena. According to one study by the Reporters Committee for Freedom of the Press, a state shield law was cited as the most common reason for the successful quashing of a subpoena. In other cases, subpoenas were regularly quashed because judges deemed they were overbroad, the information sought was not necessary to the case, and there were other ways to obtain the information that were less intrusive to the First Amendment.

Contempt of Court

Contempt of court is a very old—and very new—legal problem for journalists. Basically, it originated with the idea that a judge should be able to control the decorum of the courtroom and should have the authority to summarily punish those who violate that decorum. American judges have had contempt powers ever since the founding of the republic, and English and colonial judges exercised the power considerably before that.

Direct versus indirect contempt. There are several different kinds of contempt of court, and the distinctions among them are sometimes crucial in cases involving the media. First, there is *direct contempt*, which involves an act that violates the decorum of the court or shows disrespect for the legal process. A citation for direct contempt usually results from either misconduct in or near the courtroom or from the refusal to obey a judge's order. A photographer who surreptitiously takes a picture in a courtroom where cameras are not permitted risks a citation for direct contempt of court. Similarly, a reporter who refuses to reveal a source of information when ordered to do so by a judge may be cited for direct contempt.

Contempt may be either criminal or civil in nature. *Criminal contempt*, as the name suggests, is a punishment for an act of disrespect for a court. That disrespect might be in the form of a photographer taking unauthorized pictures in court or a lawyer violating court rules in her zeal to win her case. In either instance, the offense would be an example of direct contempt of court and would lead to a criminal sanction. The punishment might be a fine or a jail sentence, or both.

Civil contempt, on the other hand, is not a punishment at all, although it may lead to a stay in jail. Civil contempt is a form of coercion: a person who is disobeying a court order is locked up until he or she decides it would be better to obey the court order. Thus, it can result in an indefinite sentence. The *contemnor* (the person cited for contempt of court) is free to leave any time—if he or she obeys the court order. But if this person stands on principle and steadfastly refuses to obey the order, the jail term could theoretically last for a lifetime in some states. Reporters who refuse to reveal their sources are often cited for civil contempt, and thus run the risk of an extended stay in jail if no compromise can be reached.

One thing particularly troubles many journalists about contempt of court: often the judge unilaterally defines the offense, determines that there has been a violation, tries and convicts the guilty party, and sets the sentence—all within a few minutes. Contempt citations may be appealed, and many involving journalists are, but the fact remains that judges have enormous power in this area. Unfortunately, that power is sometimes abused.

Nevertheless, a judge's contempt power has limits other than the recourse to a higher court. For example, if a criminal contempt sentence exceeds six months, the judge is not permitted to decide the case unilaterally—without a jury. The U.S. Supreme Court has ruled that there is a constitutional right to a jury trial in cases of "serious" criminal contempt, but not in "petty" cases—which the court has defined as cases involving jail sentences of six months or less (*Baldwin v. New York*, 399 U.S. 66, 1970). This constitutional limit doesn't necessarily affect civil contempt, which has no fixed term in many instances.

◼ THE FIRST AMENDMENT AND REPORTER'S PRIVILEGE

While privileges have been recognized for hundreds of years, the idea of a journalist's privilege developed mostly in the twentieth century. The common law traditionally did not recognize journalists as among the people who could invoke privilege. Maryland adopted a *shield law* (a statutory law shielding a reporter from the duty to reveal sources of information) in 1896, but it was some 30 years before the next such law was enacted anywhere in the United States. By 2011, statutory shield laws had been enacted in 40 states and the District of Columbia. A number of other states have recognized a reporter's shield either by formal court rules or by precedent-setting court decisions. However, many journalists have argued that, even in the absence of a shield law, the First Amendment protects their right to keep their sources confidential.

The first time an appellate court ruled on the argument that the First Amendment constitutes a shield law was in a 1958 libel decision, *Garland v. Torre* (259 F.2d 545). Columnist Marie Torre made some unflattering statements about actress Judy Garland and attributed them to an unnamed CBS executive. Garland sued for libel and demanded the identity of the source during pretrial discovery. Torre refused to name her source, and a federal trial court cited her for contempt. She appealed, and the Second Circuit upheld; Torre was sentenced to 10 days in jail. In an opinion by Potter Stewart (later a Supreme Court justice) the court said this case required a balancing of two rights, but the information sought went to the heart of Garland's claim. Thus, the reporter's right to keep a source confidential had to yield to the right of a court to require the disclosure of relevant information.

After that decision, the idea of a constitutional privilege for journalists remained in limbo for a decade. But a flood of contempt citations of journalists forced them to try again. In 1970 and 1971, three rulings on the issue were appealed to the Supreme Court. In one of these cases a court recognized a constitutional privilege, while in the other two the lower courts did not. To resolve this conflict, the Court agreed to hear the three cases together.

Branzburg v. Hayes

As a result of the split between appellate circuits, the Supreme Court consolidated the cases under *Branzburg v. Hayes* (408 U.S. 665), an important 1972 decision that denied the

FIG. 69.
Black Panther
Convention, Lincoln
Memorial, June
1970.

*Library of
Congress, Prints &
Photographs Division,
[LC-DIG-ppmsca-04303]*

existence of a journalist's constitutional privilege in cases such as the ones before the Court. However, the ruling was confusing because the vote was 5-4, with only four justices rejecting a constitutional shield outright while another four (the dissenters) said there should be a qualified constitutional shield. A few years later, Justice Potter Stewart gave a speech in which he called the vote "four and a half to four and a half." The swing vote was provided by Justice Lewis Powell, who said the First Amendment should not excuse journalists from revealing their sources in these cases. However, Powell also suggested that the First Amendment might protect journalists' sources under some other circumstances.

Three plaintiffs. The three cases that were consolidated in *Branzburg* involved widely varying circumstances, but all had one thing in common: reporters had refused to answer grand juries' questions about possible criminal activity they witnessed. The case where a court recognized a constitutional shield, *U.S. v. Caldwell*, involved Earl Caldwell, an African-American reporter for the *New York Times*. Caldwell interviewed leaders of the militant Black Panther movement. In California, a federal grand jury investigating militant groups subpoenaed Caldwell to testify and to bring along his notes. Caldwell refused even to appear. Not only would testifying breach his confidential relationships with his news sources, he said, but merely *appearing* would undermine that confidential relationship. Since federal grand jury proceedings are secret, the Panthers might never know for sure whether he kept his promises of confidentiality if he appeared.

Caldwell and the *Times* asked a federal district court to *quash* (set aside) the grand jury subpoena. The court granted the request only in part, and Caldwell appealed. The Ninth Circuit ordered the subpoena quashed, ruling that Caldwell had a First Amendment right to keep his sources confidential. The U.S. government appealed to the Supreme Court.

In the second case of the *Branzburg* trilogy, *In re Pappas,* television journalist Paul Pappas was invited to a Black Panther headquarters in Massachusetts. He also promised not to disclose any information he was given in confidence. A county grand jury summoned him and asked what he had seen at Panther headquarters. He refused to answer many of the grand jury's questions, citing the First Amendment. The state supreme court rejected his argument and he appealed to the U.S. Supreme Court.

In the *Branzburg* case itself, *Louisville Courier-Journal* reporter Paul Branzburg observed two young men processing hashish and wrote a bylined story about it. The article included a tightly cropped photo of a pair of hands working with what the caption said was hashish.

Later, Branzburg wrote an article about drug use in Frankfort, Kentucky. The article said he spent two weeks interviewing drug users. Branzburg was twice subpoenaed by grand juries, but he refused to testify, citing both a Kentucky shield law and the First Amendment. He challenged both subpoenas, but the Kentucky Court of Appeals ruled against him. The Kentucky shield law, the court said, only applied to the identities of informants; it did not excuse a reporter from testifying about events he personally witnessed, and the First Amendment did not protect him. Branzburg also appealed to the U.S. Supreme Court.

Consolidating the three cases, the majority said all three reporters had to comply with the grand jury subpoenas. Thus, the high court affirmed the lower court rulings in *Branzburg* and in *In re Pappas* while reversing the *Caldwell* decision. Four justices said flatly that a journalist has the same duty as any other citizen to testify when called upon to do so.

Majority opinion: No privilege. The majority's decision, written by Justice Byron White, framed the issue as this: "The sole issue before us is the obligation of reporters to respond to grand jury subpoenas as other citizens do and to answer questions relevant to an investigation into the commission of crime." Grand juries, Justice White wrote, have two primary functions in our society: to determine if probable cause exists to believe a crime has been committed and to protect citizens from unfounded criminal prosecutions. Its investigative powers are necessarily broad, and the grand jury plays an important, constitutional role that outweighs any burden on newsgathering that might come from the occasional subpoena to reporters. He said a rare subpoena to a journalist would only have an *incidental burden* on newsgathering. Interestingly, he concluded the decision by writing, "We do not question the significance of free speech, press or assembly to the country's welfare. Nor is it suggested that news gathering does not qualify for First Amendment protection; without some protection for seeking out the news, freedom of the press could be eviscerated."

Justice Lewis Powell, who provided the crucial fifth vote to reject a reporter's privilege in these cases, wrote an important concurrence that left open the possibility that the First Amendment might excuse a reporter from revealing confidential information under other circumstances. Powell said, "The asserted claim to privilege should be judged on its facts by striking of a proper balance between freedom of the press and the obligation of all citizens to give relevant testimony with respect to criminal conduct. The balance of these vital constitutional and societal interests on a case-by-case basis accords with the tried and traditional way of adjudicating such questions." Thus, Powell felt a balancing process was necessary, with a constitutional shield for journalists available in some cases.

Stewart's test. One dissenter (Justice Douglas) took the absolute position that no restriction on freedom of the press was constitutional, not even the requirement that reporters testify in a court. Justice Potter Stewart (joined by Brennan and Marshall) believed the First Amendment requires a qualified journalist's privilege. These justices said that, to justify requiring a journalist to reveal his sources, the government should have to show:

1. That there is probable cause to believe the journalist has *clearly relevant information* regarding a specific probable violation of law;
2. That the *information cannot be obtained in some other way* that doesn't so heavily infringe on the First Amendment;
3. That there is a *compelling and overriding interest* in the information.

Even though Justice Stewart's three-part test appeared in a dissenting opinion, it has been used by many lower federal and state courts in deciding journalist's privilege cases. The *Branzburg* decision, it turns out, was not quite the defeat for the media that it first appeared to be. The high court refused to create a constitutional shield law, but five of the nine justices (the four dissenters plus Powell) did say that the Constitution gives journalists at least a *limited* right to withhold confidential information. Since then, a number of lower courts have undertaken the balancing process suggested by Powell, often ruling that journalists' confidential information is privileged in situations different from the ones that led to the *Branzburg* ruling (grand jury investigations). In so ruling, courts have often looked to the guidelines in Stewart's *Branzburg* dissent.

After Branzburg: *A Qualified Privilege Develops*

Immediately after *Branzburg*, news organizations feared that confidential sources would dry up. They first turned to Congress for help, lobbying for the passage of a federal shield law. Between 1972 and 1975, Congress debated dozens of qualified and absolutist proposals but failed to pass a law. But journalists began to see that the lower courts were beginning to interpret *Branzburg* in ways favorable to them. Perhaps foreshadowing things to come, only a few months after *Branzburg* a federal appellate court looked to the dissenting and concurring opinions rather than the opinion of the court to find a precedent. It would be the first of hundreds of lower court decisions to do so, in what makes *Branzburg* just a peculiar Supreme Court decision. The majority of federal appellate circuits now recognize a limited, or qualified, journalist's privilege and apply some version of Justice Stewart's three-part test to determine whether journalists can be compelled to testify. The circuits split on several key issues, including how strong the privilege is in criminal cases, whether it applies to both criminal and civil cases, and to both confidential and non-confidential information.

The first case to interpret *Branzburg* beyond its majority decision came just months after the Court's decision. In 1972, the Second Circuit ruled that a case was sufficiently different from *Branzburg* to justify a different result. In *Baker v. F&F Investment* (470 F.2d 778), the court said a journalist has a constitutional right not to reveal his sources, at least under certain circumstances. In *Baker*, the author of an article exposing the "blockbusting" practices of real estate agents (tactics calculated to panic white homeowners into selling out at low prices) was asked to reveal his source in a civil lawsuit between Black home buyers and real estate firms. Since the source was in the real estate business, he could be subjected to harassment and economic harm if identified. The court allowed this writer to keep his source confidential, noting that unlike *Branzburg* (which involved grand jury investigations) this was a civil lawsuit to which the journalist was not a party. In this instance, the court said the First Amendment protected the author's right to keep his source confidential.

In the decades since *Branzburg* and *Baker*, courts have cited several rationales in addition to the constitutional argument for a reporter's privilege. Some federal courts have recognized a limited federal common law journalist's privilege within the Federal Rules of Criminal Procedure, the Federal Rules of Civil Procedure and the Federal Rules of Evidence. None of these rules actually mentions a reporter's privilege, but several federal courts have held that a qualified reporter's privilege is inherent in them. For instance, Rule 17(c) of the Federal Rules of Criminal Procedure authorizes courts to set aside subpoenas that are "unreasonable or oppressive." Rule 501 of the Federal Rules of Evidence recognizes the concept of evidentiary privileges. It doesn't specifically cite a reporter's privilege, but the congressperson most responsible for drafting Rule 501 said: "The language of Rule 501 permits the courts to develop a privilege for newspaper people on a case-by-case basis."

Throughout the 1980s and 1990s, a number of federal appellate courts recognized a limited reporter's privilege on various grounds, including the First Amendment, the federal rules of procedure, federal common law, or a combination of these. However, none of the federal courts recognized the sort of absolute privilege journalists wanted. Instead, the courts have weighed reporter's privilege claims against other considerations, often ruling that the privilege must give way—or at least that the media must let a judge examine the purportedly confidential information to determine whether it should be disclosed. In such cases, difficult confrontations between the press and the judiciary often result.

Civil versus Criminal Proceedings: The Federal Circuits Weigh In

As a general rule, federal courts are more likely to recognize a privilege for journalists in the context of civil proceedings. In criminal cases, the privilege is balanced against a defendant's Sixth Amendment rights to a fair trial or law enforcement requirements to conduct a full investigation. And the privilege has rarely, if ever, been upheld in grand jury investigations.

Civil case examples. In 1981, for example, the D.C. Circuit in 1981 endorsed a strong reporter's privilege in civil litigation. In *Zerilli v. Smith* (656 F.2d 705), U.S. Justice Department officials allegedly leaked wiretapped telephone conversations of Detroit underworld leaders to the *Detroit News*. Two reputed underworld figures sued the Justice Department and sought a court order requiring a reporter to reveal his sources. The judge refused to issue the order, and his decision was appealed. The appellate court affirmed the refusal, noting that the plaintiffs had not exhausted alternative means of securing the information. They had not queried Justice Department employees who had access to the tapes, for instance. In civil cases to which the reporter is not a party, a reporter is exempt from revealing his or her sources "in all but the most exceptional cases," the appellate court held.

Similarly, the Third Circuit affirmed a reporter's right to keep her sources confidential in a civil case, *Riley v. Chester* (612 F.2d 708, 1979). A police officer who was involved in a dispute with the local police chief made news by suing the chief. Then he subpoenaed a reporter to learn the source of a news story he considered unfavorable. However, the reporter refused to identify the source at a court hearing. Reporter Oliver was cited for contempt, but the appellate court overturned the citation because the identity of the source was not relevant enough to the case to override the qualified reporter's privilege, relying on a test similar to that in *Branzburg*.

In a civil libel case, the First Circuit handed down yet another decision recognizing the existence of a journalist's privilege. In *Bruno & Stillman v. Globe Newspaper Co.* (633 F.2d 583, 1980), the court ruled on a dispute over pretrial discovery of a reporter's confidential sources by emphasizing the balancing of rights necessary in such cases. The court reaffirmed the privilege, but said the trial court had to balance First Amendment interests against the plaintiff's need for the information. The case was remanded, with instructions for the trial judge to follow in deciding whether to order the newspaper involved (the *Boston Globe*) to disclose its sources for a series of stories criticizing the plaintiff's products (fishing boats).

Criminal case examples. In criminal cases, federal courts have sometimes recognized a qualified privilege, but in some cases rules that journalists must nonetheless testify. For example, the Third Circuit refused to uphold the reporter's privilege in a 1980 decision, *U.S. v. Criden* (633 F.2d 346). In that case, Jan Schaffer, a *Philadelphia Inquirer* reporter, refused to testify about her conversations with a U.S. attorney during the "Abscam" case, in which public officials were charged with bribery. The U.S. attorney admitted the conversations had occurred, and Schaffer was cited for contempt. The Third Circuit affirmed a contempt citation, noting that the issue was not confidentiality (the source had already waived his right to confidentiality) but the conduct of the U.S. attorney in allegedly "leaking" word of the investigation to the press. The appellate court ruled that the reporter's testimony was crucial to investigating prosecutor misconduct and thus affirmed the civil contempt citation. In so ruling, the court noted, "When no countervailing constitutional concerns are at stake ... the privilege is absolute; when constitutional precepts collide, the absolute gives way to the qualified and a balancing process comes into play to determine its limits." The Third Circuit then applied the three-part test it enunciated in *Riley* and found it satisfied. Thus, the court said the reporter's privilege had to yield to the defendants' Sixth Amendment right to a fair trial in this particular case.

Grand juries. Grand jury subpoenas remain the most difficult type of subpoena for journalists. Because *Branzburg* focused entirely on these types of subpoenas—and rejected them—the federal courts have been hesitant to extended the qualified privilege to these types of subpoenas. Perhaps no journalist who ever faced a subpoena for refusing to reveal confidential information started with less backing and ended up with more national recognition than Vanessa Leggett, who was jailed for 168 days in 2001 and 2002 for refusing to reveal her notes, tapes, and confidential sources to a federal grand jury investigating a murder in Houston. Leggett, who spent several years investigating the murder of Houston socialite Doris Angleton, was not initially recognized as a journalist by some. Although she was writing a book about the murder, she had not yet signed a contract when she was subpoenaed. Leggett spent many hours interviewing Roger Angleton, who was accused of murdering Doris Angleton, the estranged wife of his wealthy brother, Robert Angleton. Roger apparently confessed during his interviews with Leggett—and then committed suicide shortly before his trial. Prosecutors brought charges against Robert for allegedly arranging the murder but he was acquitted in state court.

When a federal grand jury began investigating the case, Leggett was served with a subpoena. She refused to comply, citing her need for confidentiality. She was cited for contempt and jailed in a federal detention center. When it became clear that she was prepared to stay in jail indefinitely to protect her notes, tapes, and confidential sources, the local and national media rallied to her cause. A prominent Houston attorney for whom Leggett had worked as an investigator defended her, with support from attorneys representing news organizations, but both a federal judge and the Fifth Circuit rejected Leggett's First Amendment claims.

In an unpublished opinion that set no legal precedent, the Fifth Circuit refused to set aside her contempt citation, declaring that reporter's privilege does not apply to federal grand jury investigations—or even to criminal proceedings. The Supreme Court later declined to hear an appeal of this questionable decision; federal prosecutors argued that the case was moot because Leggett was out of jail by then. She was only released from jail because the grand jury adjourned in early 2002 without issuing any indictments. A second federal grand jury was convened later and did indict Robert Angleton, but without issuing a subpoena to Leggett.

Confidential vs. non-confidential information. Many times, journalists are subpoenaed for *non-confidential* information rather than the identity of a confidential source. For example, broadcasters are particularly vulnerable to subpoenas for outtakes or unaired video. As a general rule, the federal courts have been less likely to protect this kind of information under the federal qualified privilege.

In the Second Circuit, for example, the appeals court has ruled that a privilege exists, but the interests in non-confidential information are less important than confidential sources. In 1999, the Second Circuit reaffirmed that reporter's privilege exists in that circuit, which is important for journalists because that circuit includes New York, the home of many major print and broadcast news organizations. Ruling in *Gonzales v. NBC* (194 F.3d 29), the court upheld the privilege after initially denying its existence—but then held that NBC did not qualify for it in this instance. The case resulted from a 1997 NBC *Dateline* story about alleged police misconduct against minorities in Louisiana. The story led to a lawsuit against the police by a Hispanic couple, and they sought outtakes from NBC. The appellate court eventually ruled that the outtakes were relevant to a significant issue in the case and were unavailable elsewhere—and ordered NBC to comply with a subpoena for the outtakes.

A New Era of Jail Threats

By the mid-2000s, the federal government was issuing subpoenas to journalists in record numbers, and many federal courts were backing away from the concept of reporter's privilege.

McKevitt v. Pallasch. One influential federal appeals court refused to recognize the privilege in a widely noted 2003 decision, *McKevitt v. Pallasch* (339 F.3d 530). Richard A. Posner, a nationally known judge who has backed the news media in privacy cases, issued a ruling in *McKevitt* that shocked journalists. He rejected the idea of a reporter's privilege, saying, "We do not see why there need to be special criteria merely because the possessor of the documents or other evidence sought is a journalist." Writing for a unanimous Seventh Circuit panel, Posner issued his ruling *after* three journalists had already handed over tapes of interviews with an American who infiltrated the "Real IRA," a militant Irish organization. Michael McKevitt, who allegedly planned terrorist acts as head of the Real IRA, was on trial in Dublin. His lawyers wanted tapes of interviews with David Rupert, the American informant, to determine if they contradicted Rupert's testimony against McKevitt in an Irish court. When Abdon Pallasch and other reporters were ordered to produce the tapes by a federal judge, they sought an emergency stay from the appellate court. After it was denied, they relinquished the tapes to avoid what their lawyers feared would be a bad legal precedent. But Posner's court issued an opinion anyway, without requesting briefs or oral arguments.

Jim Taricani. Another federal appeals court reaffirmed the principle that reporter's privilege does not apply to federal grand jury investigations in a 2004 case that led to four month's home

---

Focus on...
Digital security

In many recent cases, digital footprints have helped the government identify journalists' confidential sources.

Experts say journalists should consider digital security strategies to protect source confidentiality.

Some tips from the Harvard Kennedy School's Shorenstein Center on Media, Politics and Public Policy include:

1. Don't bring cell phones or laptops with GPS tracking tools to meetings with sources.

2. Use encrypted instant messaging apps like Signal or WhatsApp.

3. Use data encryption on all phones, laptops and computers.

4. Have strong password and two-factor authentication habits.

5. Protect your web search data with a browser like Tor.

confinement for a television reporter. The First Circuit upheld a $1,000-a-day civil contempt penalty against Jim Taricani, a reporter for WJAR-TV in Providence, Rhode Island. Taricani obtained and WJAR aired a videotape of an undercover FBI investigation of alleged corruption by Providence city officials. Both federal prosecutors and defense lawyers in the corruption case were under a gag order forbidding them to reveal the tape. A federal judge ordered Taricani to identify his source. When he refused, the judge imposed the $1,000 daily fine. Applying the *Branzburg* precedent, the federal appeals court ruled that reporter's privilege does not protect Taricani because the corruption case involved a federal grand jury proceeding (*In re Special Proceedings*, 373 F.3d 37). Taricani's source, a defense attorney, later identified himself and was convicted of perjury for denying under oath he was the source.

Judith Miller. Another federal appeals court issued a ruling that eventually sent Judith Miller of the *New York Times* to jail for 85 days for refusing to reveal her sources during a federal investigation of a leak to the media of the name of an undercover CIA officer. In the same case, Matthew Cooper of *Time* magazine also faced jail until his source released him from his promise of confidentiality, leaving him free to testify.

Syndicated columnist Robert Novak identified a woman named Valerie Plame as an undercover CIA operative. There was speculation that someone in the Bush administration had revealed her name as retribution for a newspaper article by her husband, retired diplomat Joseph C. Wilson, contradicting President George W. Bush's claim that Iraq had attempted to obtain materials for nuclear weapons in Africa. Miller, a Pulitzer Prize winner for her reporting about international terrorism, gathered information about the Plame incident, but she never published anything about it. She and Cooper received subpoenas from a special prosecutor investigating the possible leak of Plame's identity. When they refused to reveal their sources, they were cited for contempt of court.

In 2005, the D.C. Circuit rejected Miller's and Cooper's claims of reporter's privilege under the First Amendment (*In re Grand Jury Subpoena - Miller*, 397 F.3d 964). The court relied on the *Branzburg* decision in ruling that federal investigations such as these are beyond the scope of any journalistic privilege. Miller went to jail to protect the identity of her source. She was released when she agreed to testify before the grand jury investigating the leak of Plame's identity. Miller said her source released her from her promise not to name him, both in a letter and a phone call to her in jail. She then testified before the grand jury and identified the source as I. Lewis "Scooter" Libby, onetime top aide to Vice President Dick Cheney. Libby was indicted on several criminal charges by the grand jury and resigned from his White House post. In 2007, he was convicted of perjury and obstruction of justice and ordered to prison, but his prison sentence was commuted by President Bush. The basic charge against him was trying to cover up his role in identifying Plame as a CIA operative.

However, Miller became part of the story herself. Amid a growing controversy about her reporting methods, both among *New York Times* staffers and among media watchers elsewhere, Miller resigned from the *Times*. Among other things, the *Times'* senior editors questioned whether she misled them or at least failed to fully inform the *Times'* Washington Bureau chief about her dealings with Bush administration officials.

Other cases. In 2005, the D.C. Circuit also upheld contempt citations against four other journalists in *Wen Ho Lee v. Dept. of Justice* (413 F.3d 53). The court again held that reporter's privilege did not apply, ruling that the sources' names were central to the case and could not be obtained elsewhere. The four included reporters for the Associated Press, CNN, the *Los Angeles Times*, and the *New York Times*. They reported on the prosecution of nuclear scientist

FIG. 70.
Mike Pence, as an
Indiana congressman who
supported a federal shield
law, meeting in 2005 with
New York Times reporter
Judith Miller, who spent 85
days in prison for failing
to reveal the identity of a
confidential source.

*Office of Congressman Mike
Pence.*

Wen Ho Lee. After 58 of 59 charges against him were dropped, he sued the federal govern-ment for invasion of privacy because information about his case was leaked to the press. Fearing that four more reporters would be jailed, the news organizations in 2006 agreed to settle the case by paying Lee a total of $750,000. The federal government gave Lee another $895,000 to drop the case. By then the news organizations had also run up legal expenses of about $5 million to defend their reporters.

While these cases were unfolding, several other journalists faced—or served—jail time for refusing to reveal their sources or confidential information.

The *New York Times* was forced to give reporters' telephone records to federal authorities in another 2006 case, *New York Times v. Gonzales* (459 F.3d 160). The case involved two report-ers who didn't want to turn over their telephone records so as to avoid identifying their sources. The Second Circuit voted 2-1 to reject the reporters' arguments, and the Supreme Court denied the *Times'* request for an emergency stay of the order. As part of a federal grand jury investigation, prosecutors sought the records to identify their sources for stories about two U.S.-based Islamic charities that were under investigation for allegedly funding terrorist activities. Investigators said calls by the reporters to the charities seeking comments alerted the charities about the government's plans to raid their facilities and freeze assets. The court said the telephone records were vital to the grand jury investigation, but they also said that under some other circumstances, such as reporting about government misconduct, report-ers would have a greater right to protect phone records that might identify their sources.

Also in 2006, two *San Francisco Chronicle* reporters were ordered to serve 18 months in jail unless they identified their sources for stories about alleged steroid use by Barry Bonds and other athletes. The two reporters, Mark Fainaru-Wada and Lance Williams, wrote *Game of Shadows*, the book that revealed the activities of the Bay Area Laboratory Co-Operative (BALCO) steroid network. They also wrote about steroid use by athletes in a series of *Chroni-cle* stories. They were released from their pending sentences in 2007 when a BALCO defense attorney admitted revealing secret grand jury testimony to them. In a plea bargain, the lawyer was convicted of contempt of court and other charges; the Justice Department then dropped its attempt to force the reporters to testify.

(L) FIG. 71.
Former President
Barack Obama.

*Official portrait,
White House.*

(R) FIG. 72.
President Obama's
first attorney
general, Eric
Holder.

*Official portrait, U.S.
Department of Justice.*

Obama leak investigations. While President Barack Obama was elected on a campaign of unprecedented government transparency, his administration prosecuted more government employees and contractors for leaking information to journalists than all previous presidential administrations combined. The Obama Justice Department accused journalists of taking part in criminal conspiracies for receiving classified documents, and journalists' phone records and emails were secretly seized by the government. Government employees and contractors went to jail, and one fled the country.

The most notable cases involved the highly publicized leaks by Chelsea (formerly Bradley) Manning to the Wikileaks website, as well as Edward Snowden's leaks to the *Guardian* and the *Washington Post* (discussed in Chapter Two). Other cases include the successful prosecutions of Shamai Leibowitz, sentenced to 20 months in prison for leaking information to a blogger; John Kiriakou, sentenced to 30 months in prison for leaks to the *New York Times* and a freelance journalist; Donald Sachtleben, sentenced to 43 months in prison for leaks to the Associated Press; and Stephen Jin-Woo Kim, sentenced to 13 months in prison for leaks to Fox News. Thomas Drake's prosecution fell apart in court proceedings and he was sentenced to time served for his leaks to the *Baltimore Sun*.

James Risen. Another journalist, James Risen of the *New York Times*, spent seven years fighting a subpoena for information about who leaked to him details of the Iranian nuclear program for his book, *State of War: The Secret History of the CIA and the Bush Administration*. In 2011, Risen won the right not to testify during the trial of former CIA officer Jeffrey Sterling, who was indicted under the Espionage Act on charges that he disclosed top-secret information to Risen about a CIA effort to combat Iran's nuclear weapons program with erroneous weapon designs. But in 2013 the Fourth Circuit on a split vote overturned (*U.S. v. Sterling,* 724 F.3d 482). Saying that Risen's testimony was critical in the government's prosecution of Sterling, the court stated that Risen's status as a journalist provided him no additional protection. The court wrote, "Indeed, [Risen] can provide the *only* first-hand account of the commission of a most serious crime indicted by the grand jury—the illegal disclosure of classified, national security information by one who was entrusted by our government to protect national security, but who is charged with having endangered it instead." The Supreme Court declined to take the appeal. However, in 2015, after seven years of court battles, the Justice Department finally dropped their attempt to coerce Risen after he refused to reveal his sources at yet another court hearing just before the trial of Sterling. The fact that Risen did not testify about his sources did not ruin the government's case. Sterling was convicted of espionage charges and sentenced to three and a half years in prison.

Right against self-incrimination. Journalists are regularly called to testify or be deposed in federal lawsuits, from which state shield laws cannot protect them. For example, David Ashenfelter, a *Detroit Free Press* reporter, was called in 2009 to be deposed in a Privacy Act lawsuit against the Department of Justice (DOJ) brought by former federal prosecutor Richard Convertino. Convertino sought information about confidential sources used by Ashenfelter in his reporting on an investigation into alleged misconduct by Convertino in a federal terrorism trial. The Sixth Circuit (*In re Ashenfelter*, 2009 U.S. App. LEXIS 29512) said that Ashenfelter had to testify; he had not made the case for an "extraordinary" situation that would warrant the court stepping in before the testimony.

When put on the stand in 2009, Ashenfelter invoked his Fifth Amendment right against self-incrimination, saying that he could be liable if he revealed his sources. A federal judge accepted that argument, so Ashenfelter was able to keep his sources confidential. As this was a federal case, the Michigan shield law was of no help to Ashenfelder. In 2013, the *Free Press* was ordered by a Michigan court to hand over documents and provide a witness in the case (*Convertino v. Dept. of Justice*, 2013 U.S. Dist. LEXIS 5716). Because Ashenfelter invoked the Fifth Amendment, Convertino could not depose him, and as a result, the court said, "The *Free Press* is now Convertino's best, and perhaps only, opportunity to learn the identity of Ashenfelter's sources." Ashenfelter retired from the *Free Press* in 2013. That same year, Convertino's request for reconsideration failed, with the court saying that Ashenfelter could claim Fifth Amendment protection against divulging his source's name (*Convertino v. Dep't of Justice*, 42 Media L. Rep. 1030).

Jana Winter. Journalists are subpoenaed to testify in all kinds of proceedings. Probably the most dramatic privilege story of 2013 arose after James Holmes opened fire in an Aurora, Colorado, theatre in July 2012, killing 12 people and injuring many more. FoxNews.com reporter Jana Winter received information from a confidential source about a notebook Holmes had mailed to his psychiatrist and published it online, in violation of a gag order

FIG. 73.
Journalist James Risen spent seven years fighting a subpoena from the federal government over a source for his book on the history of the CIA and the Bush administration.

Miller Center, November 12, 2014, via Flickr, Creative Commons attribution license.

on the case. She alleged that the notebook contained disturbing images and writings about Holmes' desire to kill people and claimed she got the information from law enforcement sources. A Colorado judge ordered Winter to appear in court to testify about her sources. Winter refused, relying on the New York shield law that applies to Fox News, and asked a judicial panel in New York to apply the New York law protections to her. The state appeals court sided with Winter (*In the Matter of James Holmes v. Winter*, 3 N.E.3d 694). Emphasizing New York's powerful shield law, its history of extending strong protections to its reporters, and the current international media market, the court wrote, "New York journalists should not have to consult the law in the jurisdiction where a source is located or where a story 'breaks' (assuming either is ascertainable) in order to determine whether they can issue a binding promise of confidentiality."

Federal shield law fails to pass. After the string of negative precedents between 2001 and 2007, the media once again turned to Congress. In 2007, the House of Representatives overwhelmingly approved a federal shield law. At about the same time, a similar proposal was approved by the Senate Judiciary Committee. The bill would have covered professional journalists but *not* bloggers or others who do not earn substantial money by their journalistic work. It would have protected journalists from being required to reveal confidential information or the names of their sources under many circumstances. Courts would be able to set aside the shield and force journalists to provide certain information that might assist in solving crimes, prevent an act of terrorism, or track down leaks of information that would endanger national security. However, the bill did not get a Senate vote and died when Congress adjourned in 2008.

After the election of Barack Obama as president, the House in 2009 again passed a federal shield law by voice vote and again the bill passed the Senate Judiciary Committee. The bill appeared poised for passage—more than 80 years after the first shield bill was introduced in Congress. The Department of Justice was not standing in the way: Obama's Attorney General Eric Holder said that DOJ can support a federal shield law if it does not interfere with efforts to protect national security or to discover the identities of those who leak classified information. And for the first time, the bill had the support of a president. But failure by the full Senate to pass the bill before the congressional session adjourned in late 2010 meant yet another failure. Since then, no bills have advanced as far in Congress.

AP phone numbers subpoenaed. There was momentary renewed interest in a federal shield law after it was revealed in 2013 that the DOJ subpoenaed phone records for numbers connected with the Associated Press. These records included outgoing calls for work and personal numbers for AP reporters and AP office numbers in New York, Washington, and Hartford, Connecticut, and the main AP number for the House of Representatives press gallery. Although the DOJ would not confirm why it chose those numbers, the AP ran a story in May 2012 about an al-Qaeda terror plot foiled by the Central Intelligence Agency in Yemen, and several of the numbers belonged to reporters and an editor who had worked on that story. The DOJ defended its actions in a letter to the AP, saying that the subpoenas were narrowly drawn to be limited in time and scope, and were necessary to investigating "cases in which government employees and contractors trusted with our nation's secrets are suspected of willfully disclosing that information to individuals not entitled to them."

DOJ Guidelines. As a result of the AP phone subpoenas, in July 2013 the Department of Justice announced new rules on investigations involving journalists. According to a report on the new policies, news organizations would be notified in advance of Justice Department

(L) FIG. 74.
Former President
Donald J. Trump.

Official portrait,
White House.

(R) FIG. 75.
President Trump's
first attorney
general, Jeff
Sessions.

Official portrait, U.S.
Department of Justice.

interest in their information, the standards for search warrants, and Privacy Act orders would be heightened, a News Media Review Committee would be established to advise the attorney general and others, among other changes. Attorney General Eric Holder said in a press release, "These revised guidelines will help ensure the proper balance is struck when pursuing investigations into unauthorized disclosures."

Trump leak investigations. During Donald J. Trump's presidency, leaks to journalists proliferated. One study of news stories during Trump's first four months in office found 125 news stories that included leaked information potentially damaging to national security. Some leaks clearly came from Trump's inner circle, and some of them were particularly damning, including details of President Trump's phone calls and meetings with world leaders. President Trump demanded his attorney general investigate the leaks, and in late 2017 Attorney General Jeff Sessions told Congress his agency was overseeing 27 criminal investigations into leaking, a big spike from the Obama and Bush administrations.

The Trump administration charged at least eight individuals with crimes associated with leaking to journalists. In many of the cases, it was clear prosecutors used electronic surveillance tools and subpoenas for phone and email records to make their cases, suggesting that subpoenas to journalists to reveal their confidential sources were no longer necessary in the majority of leak investigations.

The first leak prosecution in the Trump administration had to do with allegations of Russian interference in the 2016 elections. Reality Winner, a government contractor and Air Force veteran, was charged with violating the Espionage Act for leaking a top-secret report to *The Intercept* website in June 2017 that detailed evidence of Russian attempts to hack into state voting systems in the 2016 elections. The leak came at a time when officials were denying there were serious efforts to hack into election voting systems, and the leak provided some of the first public evidence of the efforts. The FBI identified Winner as the source by tracing her digital footprints, aided in part by *The Intercept's* sloppy handling of the primary documents that allowed the government to quickly identify Winner as the suspect. In 2018, she pled guilty and was sentenced to more than five years in prison.

Issues related to the 2016 election played a role in other leak prosecutions. John Fry, a San Francisco–based employee of the Internal Revenue Service, pleaded guilty to leaking confidential banking information about former Trump lawyer Michael Cohen to Michael

Avenatti, the lawyer for porn star Stormy Daniels (real name Stephanie Clifford), that later appeared in the *Washington Post* and *New Yorker*. The documents revealed suspicious money transfers Cohen made with his shell company, Essential Consultants LLC, that Cohen used to pay Daniels to keep quiet about her affair with Donald Trump. Fry was sentenced to five years probation and a $5,000 fine. In another case, Natalie Edwards, a former senior U.S. Treasury Department official, pleaded guilty in 2020 for leaking financial "Suspicious Activity Reports" to *BuzzFeed News* reporter Jason Leopold. The leaked documents revealed suspicious money transfers among several Trump associates under investigation for their connections to Russia before the 2016 presidential election. Edwards claimed she was acting as a whistleblower and was not acting with malicious intent. In 2021, she was sentenced to six months in prison and three years of supervised release.

Similar whistle-blowing motives were advanced by Terry J. Albury, who in 2018 was sentenced to four years in prison for sending confidential documents about FBI practices in recruiting confidential informants. Albury had been the only African American agent assigned to a counterterrorism unit focusing on Minnesota's Somali-American community, and he had grown disenchanted with what he viewed as "widespread racist and xenophobic sentiments" in the FBI. He took photos of documents and sent them to *The Intercept*, which published a series of stories titled "The FBI's Secret Rules."

National security leaks were the focus of other leak investigations. Joshua Shulte, a former CIA employee, was accused of leaking to Wikileaks documents from 2013 to 2016 about the CIA's ability to hack phones, cars, computers, and smart TVs and turn them into listening devices. In 2020, a jury convicted him on two lesser counts of contempt of court and making false statements to the FBI but deadlocked on eight other counts, including illegally gathering and transmitting national defense information. In another case, Daniel Hale, a former Air Force intelligence analyst and government contractor, was charged in 2019 with violating the Espionage Act for allegedly leaking information to *The Intercept's* Jeremy Scahill about the U.S. military's expanding use of drones to kill combatants and innocent civilians in Afghanistan, Yemen, and Somalia that served as the basis for the website's "The Drone Papers" series and a book titled *The Assassination Complex: Inside the Government's Secret Drone Warfare Program.* In 2021, Hale pled guilty to one count of violating the Espionage Act and faced up to 10 years in prison.

Two leak cases seemed to involve government employees providing information to romantic partners. Henry Kyle Frese, a former contract employee of the Defense Intelligence Agency, was sentenced in 2020 to 30 months in prison for leaking information to two unnamed reporters, one of whom appeared to be a woman he was living with, about foreign military capabilities, including China's installation of missile systems in the South China Sea. News reports identified the reporters as Amanda Macias of CNBC and Courtney Kube of NBC News. Another case involved the arrest of James A. Wolfe, a top aide to the Senate Intelligence Committee for three decades. Wolfe was arrested in June 2018 as part of a leak investigation. He was not accused of leaking classified information but for lying to FBI investigators about contacts with journalists. As part of its investigation, the DOJ secretly obtained a warrant for email accounts and cell phone records of Ali Watkins, a reporter for the *New York Times* who worked at *BuzzFeed News* and *Politico* during the time she allegedly had both a personal and professional relationship with Wolfe. He was sentenced to two months in prison after pleading guilty to lying to investigators.

(L) FIG. 76. President Joe Biden.

Official portrait, White House.

(R) FIG. 77. President Biden's attorney general, Merrick Garland.

Official portrait, D.C. Circuit Court of Appeals.

The secret seizure of Watkin's emails and phone records raised the same questions as the Obama administration's seizures in the AP case. While the DOJ guidelines ostensibly preclude secret seizures in these kinds of cases, new questions were being asked about the Trump administration's adherence to the rules. It seemed clear they were ignored, after revelations of other leak investigations surfaced after Trump left office.

In mid-2021, it was revealed that journalists at the *New York Times*, the *Washington Post*, and the Cable News Network (CNN) had their phone and email records secretly subpoenaed from service providers as part of investigations into leaks. Some of the subpoenas came with gag orders against the service providers from informing the subjects about the subpoenas, and lawyers representing the news organizations were also prohibited from discussing the subpoenas with their clients, some of them said. "Secret proceedings, gag orders so CNN attorneys can't speak to me, and eight reporters being swept up in investigations with no explanation—these are not part of a free press in the United States. I am genuinely horrified by what happened," wrote CNN's Barbara Starr, one of the reporters whose records were subpoenaed.

Leak investigations under the Biden administration. In his first months in office, President Joe Biden called the subpoenas for journalists' email and phone records by the DOJ under Trump "simply, simply wrong." Biden's Attorney General Merrick Garland, the man who was nominated to the U.S. Supreme Court by President Obama in 2016 but who the Republican-controlled Senate refused to confirm, announced changes to prohibit subpoenas of journalists' phone and email records in the future. Media groups welcomed the news but called on the DOJ to codify the changes in formal regulations. Garland also voiced support for a federal shield law.

State Rulings on the Constitutional Reporter's Privilege

In addition to the rulings by federal courts, a number of state supreme courts have recognized a journalist's privilege, based on First Amendment principles, even in the absence of a statutory shield law. For instance, in 1977 the Iowa Supreme Court recognized a qualified First Amendment privilege for reporters. In a libel case, *Winegard v. Oxberger* (258 N.W.2d 847), the court roughly followed Justice Stewart's three-part test in the *Branzburg* dissent, indicating that a reporter could refuse to reveal confidential information, at least in a civil proceeding, unless: (1) the information sought "goes to the heart of the matter" before the court; (2) other reasonable means of obtaining the information have been exhausted; and

(3) the lawsuit in which the information is sought does not appear to be "patently frivolous." However, the Iowa Supreme Court weighed the case and decided that three-part test was met, so the reporter was not excused from revealing her sources for stories about a protracted divorce case that led to a libel suit.

A number of other state courts have also found a constitutional basis for a journalist's privilege, sometimes even in criminal proceedings when a defendant contended the information was needed for his or her defense. In so doing, some state courts have ruled that a qualified reporter's privilege is inherent in their own state constitutions as well as the federal Constitution. The Wisconsin Supreme Court so ruled in a murder case (*Zelenka v. Wisconsin*, 266 N.W.2d 279, 1978), although the court emphasized that the journalist's right to withhold confidential information had to be balanced against the defendant's need for the information. The case stemmed from a drug-related murder, and the defendant sought the identity of the source for an underground newspaper story that claimed the victim had been cooperating with narcotics officers. The state supreme court said the defendant had not shown that the privileged information would have helped him in his defense. Thus, the court upheld the reporter's right to keep a source confidential.

In 1982, the New Hampshire Supreme Court ruled in much the same way in another murder case: *New Hampshire v. Siel* (8 Media L. Rep. 1265). In that case, two student journalists at the University of New Hampshire refused to release documents that would have revealed their sources for a story about the murder victim's alleged drug dealings. The state supreme court affirmed a judge's ruling that the materials sought from the student journalists would not have affected the outcome of the case. Similarly, courts in many other states have recognized at least a limited reporter's privilege in the absence of a state shield law.

Although California has a strong shield law, the California Supreme Court has also ruled that the concept of reporter's privilege sometimes protects journalists in situations not covered by the shield law. In *Mitchell v. Superior Court* (37 C.3d 268, 1984), the court ordered a trial judge to reconsider an order requiring a small newspaper to reveal its sources during a libel lawsuit. The Court conceded that the shield law did not protect journalists from having to reveal their sources when defending a libel case. But the plaintiff had a very weak libel case. The court said reporter's privilege should excuse journalists from revealing their sources when a libel case appears to be without merit or when the social importance of protecting the identities of sources outweighs a libel plaintiff's need for the information.

On the other hand, some state supreme courts have flatly refused to recognize any reporter's privilege, even a qualified one. The Idaho Supreme Court, for instance, once refused to recognize any sort of First Amendment privilege for journalists, even in a civil libel suit (*Caldero v. Tribune Publishing*, 562 P.2d 791, 1977), although that court later moderated its stand on this issue in *Sierra Life v. Magic Valley Newspapers* (6 Media L. Rep. 1769, 1980), another libel case in which the plaintiff demanded the identity of confidential sources during pretrial discovery proceedings. The court acknowledged that a journalist's confidential information has to be shown to be *relevant* before it can be discovered and said the plaintiff had not shown that knowing the identity of the sources would help prove its libel case. Thus, while the Idaho Supreme Court afforded limited protection to sources in *Sierra Life*, Idaho journalists enjoy far less protection from indiscriminate discovery or subpoenas than do journalists in some states. In states like Idaho, journalists need a statutory shield law far more than they do in states where courts have given them more constitutional protection.

■ STATE SHIELD LAWS

Most states have now enacted statutory shield laws, but these laws vary widely in philosophy and approach.

The following states adopted shield laws in the years shown here (listed in the order of adoption): Maryland (1896), New Jersey (1933), Alabama (1935), California (1935), Arkansas (1936), Kentucky (1936), Arizona (1937), Pennsylvania (1937), Indiana (1941), Montana (1943), Michigan (1949), Ohio (1953), Louisiana (1964), Alaska (1967), New Mexico (1967), Nevada (1967), New York (1970), Illinois (1971), Rhode Island (1971), Delaware (1973), Nebraska (1973), North Dakota (1973), Minnesota (1973), Oregon (1973), Tennessee (1973), Oklahoma (1974), Colorado (1990), Georgia (1990), South Carolina (1993), Florida (1998), North Carolina (1999), Connecticut (2006), Washington (2007), Maine (2008), Texas (2009), Kansas (2010), Wisconsin (2010), and West Virginia (2011). (The number dropped back to 39 when Hawaii's shield law, enacted in 2008, expired in 2013. Lawmakers could not agree on revisions, so a new bill was not passed.)

Many of these statutes have been extensively revised since their original enactment and many have been heavily modified by judicial interpretation. Some state shield laws appear to be strong but have been weakened by court decisions. Others have been upheld and even strengthened by court decisions. California, for example, placed its shield law in the state constitution to make it safer from attacks on its constitutionality in the courts. In several states, the highest court has recognized a reporter's privilege that is about as strong as most statutes. For example, in 2008 the Utah Supreme Court adopted Rule 509 of the Utah Rules of Evidence, requiring all Utah courts to respect the right of journalists to keep unpublished information and the identity of their sources confidential in most circumstances.

Generally, shield laws fall into three groups: (1) absolute privilege laws, which seemingly excuse a reporter from ever revealing a news source or other confidential information in a governmental inquiry; (2) laws that only apply the privilege if information derived from the source is actually published or broadcast; and (3) qualified or limited privilege laws, which may have one or many exceptions, often allowing the courts to disregard them under certain circumstances.

The Courts and State Shield Laws

Sadly, the reality about shield laws is that many lawyers and judges don't like them. Judges sometimes find themselves dealing with reporters who possess important information—information that might well affect the outcome of a case—but who simply refuse to fulfill what judges see as a civic responsibility by disclosing it. Some judges wonder how a court can seek the truth under those circumstances, and they view shield laws as obstacles to justice, laws made by people who are, after all, politicians. Shield laws, they feel, strip the courts of some of their authority to do an important job. Many judges seem perfectly willing to weigh a journalist's privilege against other interests; some are willing to create such a privilege judicially in the absence of a statutory law, as already explained. However, when a legislature makes the decision for them—and makes the privilege absolute under all circumstances—judges tend to look for loopholes.

Overturning a shield law. Probably the most notable example of a court decision overturning a shield law is *Ammerman v. Hubbard Broadcasting* (89 N.M. 307, 1976). In that decision the New Mexico Supreme Court said the legislature doesn't have the power, under the state constitution, to restrict a judge's authority in this way. Thus, the court simply invalidated the whole shield law by declaring it to be a *procedural* rule. The legislature has no authority to dictate procedural court rules to the judiciary, the court said. However, amid outcries from journalists and their supporters, the New Mexico Supreme Court added a provision to the state's Rules of Court to replace the invalidated shield law. This court rule is similar to many newer state shield laws in its scope. It excuses journalists from disclosing their sources' names and other confidential information unless the information is (1) "material and relevant" to a pending case, (2) not available elsewhere, (3) crucial to the party seeking its disclosure, and (4) so important that the need for it outweighs the "public interest in protecting the news media's confidential information and sources."

No other state's highest court has gone quite as far as New Mexico's did in overturning a statutory shield law, but several other courts have handed down decisions narrowing the scope of state shield laws or broadening their exceptions.

Narrowing shield laws. Responding to that trend, in 1990 the New York legislature effectively overruled many of these court decisions by strengthening the state shield law. As revised, the shield law protects not only the names of sources but also virtually all other unpublished information, including reporters' notes, film and video outtakes, and information that came to a reporter unsolicited. Such information need not be revealed by a journalist except if it is proven necessary in a criminal case and is unavailable elsewhere.

Across the Hudson River in New Jersey, a large loophole was created in the state shield law by a state supreme court decision—but then the law was significantly strengthened. In the celebrated Myron Farber case, the court said the shield law must give way when a criminal defendant seeks evidence held by a journalist. At the very least, the journalist must submit the material to a judge, who is to make an in-chambers evaluation and decide whether to release the information (*In re Farber*, 394 A.2d 330, 1978).

Myron Farber's troubles were short-lived but still painful, both for Farber (who eventually spent 40 days in jail) and the *New York Times* (which was assessed $285,000 in fines). The case arose from stories Farber wrote in 1976, investigating a series of mysterious deaths at a New Jersey hospital 10 years earlier; the stories were largely responsible for the indictment of Dr. Mario Jascalevich for murder. About halfway through the eight-month trial in 1978, Farber and the *Times* were subpoenaed to release information from interviews with witnesses at the trial. Farber and the *Times* refused and were cited for criminal and civil contempt. Farber was fined $1,000 and ordered jailed until he chose to provide the subpoenaed information. The *Times* was fined $100,000 plus $5,000 a day until the court order was obeyed.

Farber and the *Times* appealed the orders to the New Jersey Supreme Court, contending that both the First Amendment and the New Jersey shield law, a seemingly absolute one, protected them. The state supreme court denied their appeal, ruling that the shield law does not apply when a criminal defendant needs information from a journalist for his defense. The court ordered Farber and the *Times* to submit the requested material to the trial judge to examine in his chambers so the judge could decide whether the material was necessary to the defense or if it should be kept confidential.

Both Farber and the *Times* refused to comply. Farber went to jail and the *Times* paid $5,000 a day until the trial was concluded and the case went to the jury, which quickly acquitted Dr. Jascalevich. After that, all contempt citations were dropped. Eventually the New Jersey shield law was strengthened and the governor pardoned both Farber and the *Times*, refunding the fines. In the aftermath of the *Farber* decision, both the New Jersey Legislature and the state supreme court acted to *strengthen* that state's shield law. In *Maressa v. New Jersey*

Monthly (445 A.2d 376, 1982) and *Resorts International v. New Jersey Monthly* (445 A.2d 395, 1982), the New Jersey Supreme Court ruled the shield law is virtually absolute in libel cases.

Across the continent in California, the pattern was much the same. State courts repeatedly narrowed the scope of a seemingly absolute shield law, even though the law itself was strengthened. First, an appellate court said the law didn't apply when a judge was trying to find out who violated a judicial "gag" order; the legislature doesn't have the authority to pass a law that makes it impossible for courts to investigate violations of their orders (*Farr v. Superior Court*, 22 C.A. 3d 60, 1971). Later, another California appellate court said the shield law didn't apply when the information might help exonerate someone charged with a crime, because the defendant's constitutional right to a fair trial was paramount (*CBS v. Superior Court*, 85 C.A.3d 241, 1978). In 1980 the people of California voted to place the shield law in the state Constitution, where it was somewhat safer from judicial modification.

In Minnesota, the state shield law was severely narrowed by a 1996 Minnesota Supreme Court decision, *Minnesota v. Turner* (550 N.W.2d 622). In that case, the court held that the shield law protected only the names of news sources and not other confidential information such as reporters' unpublished notes. In response, the Minnesota media launched a coordinated campaign to persuade the legislature to strengthen the shield law—and the legislature did so in 1998. The amended version of the Minnesota shield law specifically protects confidential information as well as the names of sources. Like many shield laws in effect today, the revised Minnesota shield law requires journalists to disclose otherwise-confidential information if it is clearly relevant to a court case, cannot be obtained elsewhere, and is so important that there is a compelling and overriding interest requiring disclosure.

Some states have expanded their privilege protections in recent years. In 2015, Montana amended its shield law to prohibit subpoenas to third-party communications service providers. While the old law protected journalists from subpoenas, it did not address subpoenas to internet or phone companies seeking information about journalists. Many states have not updated their protections to address the realities of a digital trail of communications.

■ WHO IS A JOURNALIST?

Among the most controversial aspects of the reporter's privilege today is whether, and under what circumstances, bloggers are considered journalists. But the question of "non-traditional" journalists has been around for decades. Even in *Branzburg*, the majority said defining who is a journalist for legal protections "would present practical and conceptual difficulties of a higher order. Sooner or later, it would be necessary to define those categories of newsmen who qualified for the privilege, a questionable procedure in light of the doctrine that liberty of the press is the right of the lonely pamphleteer who uses carbon paper or a mimeograph just as much as of the large metropolitan publisher who utilizes the latest photocomposition methods." Since 1972, many "non-traditional" and "self-described" journalists have sought protection. Under the federal qualified privilege, courts have examined how closely the individuals resemble traditional journalists. Under state laws, courts look to the definitional clauses of state statutes to determine whether someone qualifies.

Under the Federal Qualified Privilege
Several federal cases established that investigative book authors and documentary filmmakers are sufficiently like traditional journalists to invoke the reporter's privilege.

Filmmakers. For example, in *Silkwood v. Kerr-McGee* (563 F.2d 433, 1977), the Tenth Circuit recognized the reporter's privilege and said it applied to a documentary filmmaker. The court overturned a trial judge's order requiring the filmmaker to reveal his confidential information because the party seeking it (the Kerr-McGee Corporation) had not tried to secure it elsewhere first. In any future request for the filmmaker's (or any other journalist's) confidential information, the trial court was ordered to weigh: (1) the relevance and necessity of the information; (2) whether it went "to the heart of the matter"; (3) its possible availability elsewhere; and (4) the type of case involved. The *Silkwood* case attracted wide attention because Karen Silkwood was killed in an auto accident *en route* to testify to the Atomic Energy Commission about allegedly dangerous practices of Kerr-McGee. In this civil lawsuit, her heirs and others charged the company with violating her civil rights.

Book authors. An investigative book author was also granted protection in the case of *Shoen v. Shoen* (5 F.3d 1289, 1993). The case began after author Ronald Watkins began doing research for *Birthright*, a book about the battle between Leonard Shoen, the U-Haul founder, and his sons Mark and Edward. During the feud, Eva Berg Shoen, the wife of a third son, was brutally murdered at the family's vacation home in Colorado. Before Watkins interviewed him for the book, Leonard was widely quoted in the media as saying the two sons with whom he was feuding were responsible for Eva's death. The sons sued their father for libel and subpoenaed Watkins, demanding the notes and tapes from his interviews with their father.

Watkins appealed the subpoena, and the Ninth Circuit ruled that an investigative book author could be protected by reporter's privilege. The court held that Watkins could not be forced to reveal his journalistic work product because the sons had not exhausted all other possible sources of the information they wanted. They had not even taken a deposition to obtain the information directly from their father before seeking it from Watkins. Like conventional news reporters, book authors have historically played an important role in bringing newsworthy events to light, the court noted.

The sons then obtained a court-ordered deposition from their father and went after Watkins' notes and tapes again. Watkins again refused to cooperate and was cited for contempt of court. Just before Watkins was to be jailed for contempt, the Ninth Circuit intervened again. In *Shoen II* (*Shoen v. Shoen*, 48 F.3d 412, 1995), the court delivered another strong affirmation of the reporters' privilege concept. Here was a book author whose source was not confidential (everyone knew it was the elder Shoen). Nor did the source object to Watkins turning over his notes and tapes. Nonetheless, the court said a journalist could not be forced to turn over his research materials except as a last resort.

The court adopted a new three-part test for cases like this (i.e., involving a reporter who is not a party to a civil lawsuit, has no confidential sources, and whose sources do not object to the disclosure of the information sought). The judge said that in this kind of case the party seeking to overcome the journalistic privilege must show that the information is "unavailable despite exhaustion of all reasonable alternative sources," is not cumulative (i.e., repetitive), and is "clearly relevant to an important issue in the case."

Who is *not* a journalist? Two federal appellate decisions provide some guidance for when someone *does not* qualify for protection. In 1987, the Second Circuit in *von Bulow v. von Bulow* (811 F.2d 836) ruled that Andrea Reynolds could not invoke the privilege after she received a subpoena for information she collected during the trial of Claus von Bulow, who was accused of poisoning his wife. Reynolds, who the court described as an "intimate friend" of Claus von Bulow, had collected investigative reports on von Bulow's children and had

Focus on...
Was Josh Wolf a journalist?

Josh Wolf claims to be the longest jailed journalist in American history for committing journalism. But is he? In 2005, the 22-year-old Wolf headed out to the streets of San Francisco to record an "anarchist" protest. The protest turned violent when a police officer was struck by a pipe and seriously injured. Demonstrators also attempted to set a police car afire. Wolf sold some of his footage to local television stations and posted some of it on his blog.

When Wolf refused to hand over all of his video to authorities or to testify before a federal grand jury, a judge found him in contempt and jailed him. The Ninth Circuit declined to decide whether or not Wolf was a journalist for purposes of privilege protection, but said that all citizens have a duty to comply with grand jury subpoenas—journalist or not.

In early 2007, Wolf was released from prison after 226 days when he agreed to post the video sought by authorities on his website and to answer two questions under oath: did he see the officer being struck, and did he see the attempted burning of the police car. He answered no to both questions. It turned out his video didn't show either incident.

Wolf claimed that he was a citizen journalist who regularly blogged about local anarchists and thus was a journalist under the law. The Reporters Committee for Freedom of the Press agreed and helped pay his legal bills.

FIG. 78. Josh Wolf, April 2006.

Flickr with a CC-BY license (https://www. flickr.com/photos/diversey/2556824561/

taken notes for a potential autobiography. In rejecting Reynolds' claim to be a journalist, the Court ruled that an individual needed to have an intent at the beginning of a newsgathering process to disseminate news publicly in order to qualify for privilege protection.

Similarly, in 1998 the Third Circuit rejected the privilege for a professional wrestling commentator. In *In re Madden (Titan Sports v. Turner Broadcasting)* (151 F3d. 125), Mark Madden, a professional wrestling commentator for World Championship Wrestling (WCW), was subpoenaed by a competing professional wrestling company, the World Wrestling Federation (WWF), in a lawsuit about unfair competition. Madden claimed that because he recorded a commentary for a 1-900 line for fans to call, he was a journalist and could avoid complying with a subpoena. The Third Circuit ruled that Madden was not a journalist because he was not engaged in investigative reporting, not gathering news, and did not possess an intent at the start of a newsgathering process to disseminate news to the public.

Independence. One case suggests that courts might take into account an individual's adherence to basic journalistic standards. If individuals get too close to their sources or give up their editorial independence, they may be less likely to invoke the privilege. For example, in 2011 the Second Circuit ruled that a documentary filmmaker was *not* entitled to privilege protection because he had not established that he was an independent journalist while working on a film about alleged environmental damage in Ecuador caused by the Texaco Petroleum Company. At issue in *Chevron v. Berlinger* (629 F.3d 297) was whether award-winning documentary filmmaker Joseph Berlinger was essentially acting as a public relations tool to tell the story from the plaintiff's perspective and under their control or if he was collecting information for the "purpose of independent reporting and commentary."

For three years, Berlinger followed the plaintiffs and their attorneys, accumulating more than 600 hours of video for his 2009 film *Crude*, which detailed environmental damage and health effects allegedly caused by Texaco. Berlinger's outtakes were subpoenaed as part of litigation in Ecuador, and American courts were asked to compel the production of that evidence. Texaco believed the "outtakes" could show improper conduct by the plaintiffs' attorneys. While one issue in the case was the lower protection afforded to "outtakes" than confidential source information, another was whether the filmmaker was acting as an independent journalist. The district court emphasized the fact that Berlinger got the idea for the film after he was approached by the plaintiff's lawyers, and that Berlinger removed a scene from a first cut of the film because the plaintiffs' lawyers objected, as evidence that he lacked sufficient independence as a journalist. The Second Circuit focused on the supposed lack of *independence of the journalistic process* to uphold the district court's order.

But the *Berlinger* case prevented filmmaker Ken Burns, his daughter Sarah, and their film company from having to turn over materials used in the documentary *The Central Park Five*. The judge quashed the subpoena from the city of New York in the five men's civil lawsuits against the city after they had been wrongfully imprisoned. The city didn't help its case; it had taken a Ken Burns quote out of context in its brief, suggesting that Burns' major goal in making the film was to settle the civil suit. The judge focused on the independence of the filmmakers in the creation of the film, saying, "A journalist seeking to invoke the privilege must also demonstrate that her intention *at the time the information in question is gathered* was for the purpose of disseminating the information to the public, and not for different reasons" (*In re McCray et al.*, 41 Media L. Rep. 1313, 2013).

International law. Internationally, journalist's privilege laws vary in different jurisdictions. The United Nations Human Rights Committee endorsed a journalist's privilege in international law in 2011, following the European Court of Human Rights' recognition of a journalist's privilege first in 1996. Many countries provide a journalist's privilege in their country's laws, including Canada, New Zealand, Norway, Sweden, Finland, and Portugal.

State Statutory Construction

Under state law in the United States, the question of who is a journalist often requires courts use statutory construction approaches to determine applicability of the law. Some statutes have very broad definitions, such as the District of Columbia, which defines "news media" as "newspapers, magazines, journals, press associations, news agencies, wire services, radio, television, or any printed, photographic, mechanical, or electronic means of disseminating news and information to the public." Others are quite narrow, such as Georgia, which provides protection to individuals who disseminate "through a newspaper, book, magazine, or radio or television broadcast." The statutory definitions can be very important. For example, in 2005 in *Price v. Time* (416 F. 3d 1327), the Eleventh Circuit ruled that a reporter for *Sports Illustrated* could not invoke the privilege in a libel lawsuit because the Alabama statute only applied to "any newspaper, radio broadcasting station or television station"—not a magazine. And, as noted earlier, at least one New York court has interpreted that state's shield law to extend to New York–based reporters working on stories in other states.

Bloggers. In recent years, bloggers have increasingly sought privilege protection. In one case, a California appellate court ruled that bloggers for the "O'Grady's Powerpage" website qualified as journalists under California's shield law. A district court had upheld a subpoena against the bloggers, requiring them to reveal who leaked to them information about yet-to-be-released Apple Computer products. But the California Court of Appeals in *O'Grady v. Superior Court* (44 Cal. Rptr. 3d 72, 2006) said the bloggers and their website were sufficiently like traditional journalism to qualify them for protection. Because the bloggers regularly reported about Apple and were in the habit of "gathering and disseminating of news," the court said they met the statutory language that protects a person "connected with or employed" by a "newspaper, magazine or other periodical publication." The bloggers were more like online newspapers because their website posts "reflect a kind and degree of editorial control that makes them resemble a newspaper or magazine far more closely" than other online websites. "In no relevant respect do they appear to differ from a reporter or editor for a traditional business-oriented periodical," the court wrote. The court emphasized that the bloggers employed traditional journalistic methods and values in their work, and the decision was the first decisive victory for bloggers invoking the reporter's privilege.

Not all bloggers or online writers will qualify for protection. While the New Hampshire Supreme Court allowed the state reporter's privilege law to apply to an online website's attempts to protect an anonymous poster (*Mortgage Specialists Inc. v. Implode-Explode Heavy Industries Inc.*, discussed in Chapter Three), the New Jersey Supreme Court ruled otherwise. In the 2011 case of *Too Much Media LLC v. Hale* (206 N.J. 209), the New Jersey Supreme Court ruled that Shellee Hale must reveal the sources of information she posted on various website forums. Hale posted allegedly defamatory content about the owners of a web company that provides financial transaction software to online adult websites. She claimed she would be protected as a journalist under New Jersey's broad shield law. However, the court said that people who post on unmoderated web forums are not connected with the "news media."

Freelancer's home raided. In a highly unusual case, a freelance reporter had his home raided by police who were searching for the identity of the reporter's sources. In May 2019, San Francisco city police and FBI agents used a sledgehammer to break into the front gate of the home of Bryan Carmody, who works as a stringer for San Francisco broadcast stations. The police had obtained search warrants for Carmody's home looking for evidence of who leaked an autopsy report to Carmody about the death of a public defender. Carmody said he spent six hours in handcuffs while police searched his home and confiscated computers, tablets, and cell phones. Five different judges approved the search warrants, which were later quashed after lawyers went to court to get them unsealed. A judge ruled at least one warrant violated California's shield law, and the police were ordered not to use any evidence seized in the raid. San Francisco's police chief apologized for the raid, admitting his department failed to appropriately consider Carmody's status as a journalist in its investigation. Ultimately, the San Francisco Board of Supervisors paid $369,000 to settle legal claims filed by the journalist.

◼ LAWSUITS BY NEWS SOURCES

Ordinarily, when journalists promise confidentiality to a news source, they will go to great lengths to keep that promise. But on rare occasions a reporter—or perhaps an editor—will decide that a source's name is so important to a story that the name must be used, despite the fact that the source was promised anonymity.

Such a situation led to a landmark Supreme Court decision in the 1991 case of *Cohen v. Cowles Media Co.* (501 U.S. 663). By a 5-4 vote, the Court ruled that the First Amendment does *not* protect the media from being sued by a news source if a promise of confidentiality is broken, regardless of the newsworthiness and relevance of the name to an important story.

The case began in 1982 when Dan Cohen, a public relations aide to the Republican candidate for the governor of Minnesota, gave several reporters documents that revealed petty misdeeds many years earlier by the Democratic candidate for lieutenant governor (an arrest at a protest rally during the 1960s and a $6 shoplifting conviction that was later set aside). Cohen leaked the information to the press just before the election.

Although the reporters promised not to identify Cohen, the editors of the *Minneapolis Star Tribune* and *St. Paul Pioneer Press* decided to use his name. If they were to run the story anonymously, they would be dealing an unfair last-minute blow to the Democrats. If they did not publish the story, they could be accused of a cover-up to *aid* the Democrats. Thus, they felt the fairest way to handle the story was to run it and identify the Republican source. When Cohen's name was used, he was immediately fired and sued for breach of contract, arguing that the promise of confidentiality was an enforceable contract under Minnesota law. A jury awarded him $200,000 in actual damages and $500,000 in punitive damages.

The two newspapers appealed, arguing that they should have a First Amendment right to publish truthful information about an event as newsworthy as an election—without risking a lawsuit afterward. The Minnesota Supreme Court agreed and overturned the jury verdict, ruling that the First Amendment does protect the media from liability for publishing the name of the source for a clearly newsworthy story. The state court also ruled that Cohen could not sue for breach of contract under Minnesota law. However, the court said that a legal doctrine called *promissory estoppel* might allow Cohen to sue if the case were not barred by the First Amendment. In essence, *promissory estoppel* is a remedy for a person who does something in reliance on someone else's promise and is injured when that promise is broken, but who does not have a valid contract for some reason.

Promissory estoppel. The U.S. Supreme Court overturned the Minnesota court's ruling. The high court said that *promissory estoppel* is a "generally applicable law" (i.e., a law that applies to everyone, not just the media). Generally applicable laws, the five-member majority said, apply to the media—despite the First Amendment. The First Amendment protects the media's right to publish truthful information, but only if it is lawfully obtained. Writing for the majority, Justice Byron White said Cohen's information was not lawfully obtained because of the broken promise of confidentiality:

> The press may not with impunity break and enter an office or dwelling to gather news. Neither does the First Amendment relieve a newspaper reporter of the obligation shared by all citizens to respond to a grand jury subpoena and answer questions, even though the reporter might be required to reveal a confidential source.... (T)he First Amendment does not confer on the press a constitutional right to disregard promises that could otherwise be enforced under state law....

The four dissenting justices disagreed with that reasoning, arguing that the story was so newsworthy that the use of Cohen's name was justified: voters had the right to know that the Republican gubernatorial candidate's public relations person was leaking stories to the press about a Democratic candidate. In his first major dissent as a Supreme Court justice, David

Souter argued for more First Amendment protection than the majority was affording to the media. Souter wrote: "There can be no doubt that the fact of Cohen's identity expanded the universe of information relevant to the choice faced by Minnesota voters ...(and) the publication ...was thus of the sort quintessentially subject to strict First Amendment protection."

The *Cohen* decision produced a variety of reactions among journalists. Many noted the irony of the press having to defend a lawsuit for *revealing* a source when reporters are much more likely to get into legal trouble for *not revealing* a source. And several media attorneys warned that the *Cohen* decision could encourage news sources who are unhappy with the way they appear in print or on television to sue the media, contending that they were promised confidentiality. Since most interviews between a reporter and a news source are private meetings between two people (with no witnesses available to corroborate either party's claims), such a lawsuit would end up being a credibility contest between the source and the journalist on the witness stand—with a jury acting as referees.

In the end, it will be up to each state to determine when news sources may sue the media for naming them. Some states may not allow such lawsuits except if there is a written contract promising confidentiality and it is breached (a remote possibility). Others may allow cases like this one to go to court on a *promissory estoppel* theory.

For Cohen, the lawsuit ended in 1992—10 years later—when the Minnesota Supreme Court held that he was entitled to collect $200,000 in actual damages but no punitive damages. The state court said the *promissory estoppel* doctrine did apply in his situation.

■ NEWSROOM SEARCHES

For a time, a related legal problem produced some alarm among journalists: law enforcement searches of print and broadcast newsrooms. In a disturbing 1978 decision, the U.S. Supreme Court ruled that the First Amendment does not create any privilege that would protect the media from newsroom searches even if no journalist is suspected of a crime (*Zurcher v. Stanford Daily*, 436 U.S. 547).

The case began in 1971 when a large group of demonstrators occupied the Stanford University Hospital and were forcibly ejected by Santa Clara County (California) sheriff's deputies and Palo Alto police. The *Stanford Daily*, the student newspaper at Stanford University, covered the incident, which was marked by considerable violence. A number of persons, including several law enforcement officers, were injured. Two days later, the *Daily* ran a special edition with a number of photographs of the disturbance. The Santa Clara County district attorney's office got a search warrant and four police officers searched the *Daily's* office in the presence of several staff members. No member of the staff was suspected of any involvement in the violence, but the police searched the offices for additional photographs or relevant information. They found none. The *Daily* staff sued the local officials in a federal civil action, alleging violations of the First, Fourth, and Fourteenth Amendments. Both the federal district court and the Ninth Circuit ruled in the student journalists' favor, but the Supreme Court reversed those rulings.

In a 5-3 decision, the Supreme Court said the Constitution does not prevent an unannounced search of a newspaper, even when no member of the staff is suspected of any crime. The Court said that such a search is constitutional as long as the normal requirements of specificity and reasonableness are satisfied by the search warrant. Police would not be permitted to go rummaging through a newspaper's files indiscriminately, but if a warrant described specific evidence, the police could conduct a newsroom search in an attempt to obtain that evidence, the Court ruled.

However, the Supreme Court made it clear that Congress or state legislatures could act to forbid newsroom searches; the high court merely said it wasn't going to forbid them judicially. Within days of the *Zurcher* decision, anti-newsroom search bills were introduced in a number of state legislatures and in Congress. Eventually, at least eight states passed such laws: California, Connecticut, Illinois, Nebraska, New Jersey, Oregon, Texas, and Washington.

The Privacy Protection Act of 1980

Congress also passed a comprehensive federal law limiting newsroom searches, the Privacy Protection Act of 1980. This far-reaching federal law effectively overruled *Zurcher*, outlawing most newsroom searches by federal, state, and local law enforcement officials.

Under the Privacy Protection Act, law enforcement officials are prohibited from conducting searches and seizures involving "documentary materials" (photographs, tapes, films, etc.) held by newsgatherers except under very limited circumstances. The law allows searches and seizures only when: (1) the person holding the information is suspected of a crime; (2) there is reason to believe the materials must be seized immediately to prevent someone's death or serious injury; (3) there is reason to believe giving notice and seeking a subpoena would result in the materials being destroyed, changed, or hidden; or (4) the materials were not produced as a result of a court order that has been affirmed on appeal.

The rules regarding a journalist's *work product* (e.g., notes and rough drafts) are even tougher. These materials cannot be seized except when the journalist is suspected of a crime or when necessary to prevent someone's death or bodily injury.

Anyone who is searched in violation of the Privacy Protection Act may sue the federal government and most state and local governments, but evidence secured in violation of the bill may nonetheless be used in court. The law also directed the U.S. Justice Department to prepare guidelines for searches by federal officers involving evidence held by someone not suspected of a crime but also not working in a First Amendment–related area such as a newsroom. Perhaps the major virtue of the Privacy Protection Act is that it usually requires law enforcement officials to get subpoenas instead of search warrants if they wish to obtain information from journalists. Why is this distinction important? Search warrants are ordinarily authorized by judges unilaterally; the person who is the object of the search has no chance to argue against the issuance of the warrant. He or she first learns of the warrant's existence when law enforcement officers show up and enter the premises (by force, if necessary).

Subpoenas, on the other hand, are merely court orders directing someone to produce information. They can be challenged on legal grounds, and their issuance can be appealed. Granted, subpoenas are a major problem for journalists; some large newspapers and television stations have attorneys working nearly full time on the job of resisting subpoenas. Nevertheless, most journalists would much rather face a subpoena than have their offices raided by law enforcement officers armed with a search warrant.

The Privacy Protection Act is an improvement over the situation in which journalists found themselves after the *Zurcher* decision. However, many journalists wish the law had been made even tougher: evidence secured during illegal newsroom searches should not be admissible in court, they contend. In the area of newsroom searches, as in the broader area of reporter's privilege, the major legal problems are not completely resolved.

■ AN OVERVIEW OF MAJOR ISSUES

There is an inherent conflict between the need of journalists to protect their sources and other confidential information, on the one hand, and the need of the courts to obtain all relevant facts on the other. Judges believe they cannot mete out justice if they are denied access to crucial information. But journalists believe they must protect confidential information—for a number of socially important reasons.

Although a significant majority of states have shield laws, the courts have repeatedly carved out judicial exceptions to these laws, requiring reporters to disclose confidential information despite the seeming applicability of a shield law. In a number of states, the appellate courts have significantly weakened state shield laws by judicial interpretation. In response to that trend, the voters in one state (California) placed their shield law in the state constitution. But almost as soon as that happened, the courts began whittling away at this new constitutional shield law just as if it were still merely an act of the state legislature.

However, there is a countervailing trend in the development of the reporter's privilege: a surprising number of both federal and state courts have recognized the privilege judicially, even in the absence of a statutory shield law. In no fewer than seven states lacking shield laws, the state's highest court has taken this step.

Moreover, many federal courts have recognized a reporter's privilege as a matter of federal common law if not constitutional law. This judicially created reporter's privilege is by no means absolute: the courts are reserving the right to weigh the privilege against other factors, such as the relevance of the requested information and the court's need for it.

However, by the mid-2000s some federal courts were refusing to recognize any right of journalists to protect confidential information, and a number of journalists faced jail sentences. Record numbers of journalists were being issued federal subpoenas—65 between 2001 and 2007, by one count. A federal shield law having failed several times, the protections for reporters called to testify in federal cases are not as robust as they might be. Aggressive leak investigations in the Obama and Trump administration saw the convictions of several government employees for providing information to journalists. President Biden promises more deference to journalists protecting confidential sources, and we shall see what happens.

Reporters and judges both feel there are important ethical principles at stake in this area. Like fair trial-free press, this issue represents an inherent conflict between two important rights, both of which must be respected in a democratic society. And like fair trial-free press, this dilemma is not likely to be resolved soon.

WHAT SHOULD I KNOW ABOUT MY STATE?	• Does my state have a shield law? What does it cover? What does it NOT cover? • What does my state's common law say about reporter's privilege? • What are the relevant precedents in my federal district court and circuit court? • An excellent resource for all these questions: Reporters Committee for Freedom of the Press' "Privilege Compendium" at http://www.rcfp.org/privilege.

SUMMARY

A SUMMARY
OF NEWS-
GATHERER'S
PRIVILEGE

What Is Contempt of Court?

Judges may punish persons who show disrespect for a court or disobey a court order by citing them for contempt. When a journalist promises to keep information (like the identity of a news source) confidential, that journalist has an ethical obligation to keep that promise, even if a court asks. Thus, an ethical journalist may risk a contempt citation—and perhaps a jail sentence. The Supreme Court has said that *promissory estoppel* applies to journalists, so if a journalist makes a promise, the promise must be kept.

What Is Reporter's Privilege?

Because many important stories could not be researched without promising confidentiality to key news sources, journalists believe they should have a right to keep their film outtakes, unpublished notes, and sources' names confidential. Reporter's privilege is the concept that a newsgatherer has at least a limited right to withhold this information, even when asked to reveal it by a judge.

What Is a Shield Law?

A *shield law* is a statutory law that excuses journalists from revealing confidential information when asked to do so in court. About 37 states have such laws, but some of them have so many exceptions that they provide a reporter little protection from a contempt of court citation. Also, courts have sometimes declined to accept shield laws, ruling that they improperly abridge the judiciary's authority. There is currently no federal shield law.

Without a Shield Law, Does Reporter's Privilege Exist?

In *Branzburg v. Hayes*, a majority of the Supreme Court justices said a limited constitutional reporter's privilege exists under certain circumstances, but not under the circumstances that led to the *Branzburg* case (grand jury investigations where reporters allegedly knew of or witnessed unlawful activity). A number of federal and state courts have recognized a qualified privilege for reporters to withhold confidential information. This privilege usually does not apply if the information is clearly relevant and necessary to the case and is unavailable from other sources.

9 *Freedom of Information*

Without the freedom to gather the news, the freedom to publish is little more than a right to circulate undocumented opinions—a right to editorialize without any right to report the facts. Among the cornerstones of modern law and policy governing the public's right to access government information are public records and open meetings.

The federal Freedom of Information Act (FOIA) celebrated its 55th anniversary in 2021. The law has been a beacon for modern media organizations who often must fight difficult legal battles to gain access to government information. In the last 55 years, the media have made significant gains in the battle for access to government meetings and records, but there have been defeats. As governments have expanded in size, their sheer vastness has made it easy for them to conceal important information from public scrutiny. Moreover, the tendency of the federal government to keep secrets in the name of national security has grown drastically. To be sure, almost no one would argue that governments should release information that could assist potential terrorists, but if democracy itself is to work, the public still must be well informed about the activities and policies of government.

Clearly, the need for national security must be balanced against the need for openness in government. The threat of terrorism might justify secrecy about the intricacies of a nuclear power plant. But how can voters know if the city budget or school policies are reasonable unless they know what the budgets and policies actually are and how they were determined? Recognizing these needs, journalists and public interest groups have campaigned for openness in local, state, and national government for years. That fight has produced significant improvements in public access to official records and proceedings.

The federal FOIA is just one law among many intended to open closed doors and unlock secret files. Today, all 50 states have laws requiring most agencies of state and local government to hold open meetings as well as laws guaranteeing public access to many government records. When World War II ended, only a few states had such laws.

In this chapter, we will review the major principles of access laws found in the federal FOIA and in state open meetings and public records law. This chapter summarizes these freedom of information laws and then surveys other problems media organizations and the public encounter in their quests for information. We'll also look at the outcomes from the courts, as judges have heard increasing numbers of cases on FOIA and open meetings and public records issues at the state level.

Chapter Objectives:

- Explain the purpose and history of public records and open meetings laws at the federal and state levels.
- Describe the process of requesting government records at the federal and state levels.
- Evaluate exemptions to access laws and court challenges over them.

Essential Questions:

- What are the underlying theories/rationales for public records and open meetings laws?
- Generally speaking, what is the process for obtaining public government records at the federal and state levels?
- What options exist when the government denies records requests or closes access to meetings of governmental bodies?

■ THE FEDERAL FREEDOM OF INFORMATION ACT

When Congress enacted the federal FOIA in 1966, its primary users were expected to be journalists. Certainly, journalists who were alarmed at the growing trend toward government secrecy took the lead in lobbying for its passage. But ever since the FOIA was approved, its main users have been corporations, academic researchers, and private individuals with a special interest in a particular topic. Most of those actually filing formal requests for information are lawyers representing private clients, not journalists representing the public interest. In fact, historians and other academicians file far more requests under the FOIA than journalists. FOIA requests take time, and journalists tend to need information too quickly to wait for a formal request to be honored by a slow-moving bureaucracy. Perhaps the authors of the FOIA were a little naive when they ordered government agencies to respond to FoI requests in 10 working days; critics have said that no government agency moves that quickly. Recognizing this fact, in 1996 Congress extended the time limit to 20 working days as part of a major FoI reform, which is discussed later.

The Basics of FOIA

What are the basic provisions of the FOIA? It declares that a vast number of records kept by administrative agencies of the federal government shall be open for public inspection, and that copies are to be provided at a reasonable cost. Unless these "agency records," as they are called, fall within one or more of nine specific exemptions, they must be opened to the public on request.

To facilitate this process, a 1974 amendment to the FOIA requires agencies to publish lists of their records and their fee schedules for making copies in response to FoI requests. Fees may be waived or reduced when an agency feels that releasing a document would benefit the general public and not just one individual or company. That provision has caused some controversy, since it allows agencies to charge one requester more than another for the same information. The FBI once charged the major wire services $9,000 for material that it provided free to one writer whose work was a public service (in the FBI's opinion).

A requester need not justify a FOIA request, but those who convince an agency that they are serving the public interest have a big advantage at the agency's cash register. In 1986, Congress amended the FOIA to reduce the fees government agencies may charge news organizations and nonprofit educational or scientific institutions while increasing the fees that commercial businesses must pay. Businesses must usually pay for the time government agencies spend searching for requested documents and reviewing them prior to their release. Journalists and nonprofit groups are usually excused from those charges altogether. Other noncommercial requesters may encounter different rules, depending on the agency they are dealing with. The Federal Communications Commission, for example, does not charge noncommercial requesters for the first two hours of search and review time or the first 100 pages released in response to a request. But after that, the meter starts running.

Although federal agencies may give a price break to journalists and nonprofit groups, they are not supposed to consider the identity or purpose of a requester in deciding whether to release a particular document. For FOIA purposes, the term "agency" is defined to include executive departments, military departments, government corporations, government-controlled corporations, other executive agencies, and independent regulatory agencies.

FIG. 79. Lyndon B. Johnson.

Yoichi R. Okamoto, White House Press Office, January 9, 1969 via Wikimedia Commons.

Focus on...
LBJ and the FOIA

Lyndon Baines Johnson, the 36th president, signed the Freedom of Information Act on July 4, 1966. Johnson was no fan of the FOIA; he did not hold a signing ceremony and edited the signing speech written by his aide, Bill Moyers, to be more cautious.

Moyers had originally written: "This legislation springs from one of our most essential principles: a democracy works best when the people know what their government is doing. They must have access to the policies and rules by which department and agencies operate. Government officials should not be able to pull curtains of secrecy around decisions which can be revealed without injury to the public interest. Good government functions best in the full light of day."

LBJ's edits: "This legislation springs from one of our most essential principles: a democracy works best when the people have all the information that the security of the nation will permit." (The rest of the paragraph was cut.)

Moyers later said that LBJ "hated the thought of journalists rummaging in government closets and opening government files; hated them challenging the official view of reality."

In short, it covers just about the entire federal government except for Congress and the courts. In an effort to avoid complying, federal agencies have sometimes claimed that honoring a certain FOIA request would be prohibitively expensive. The courts have generally not heeded that argument, instead compelling agencies to comply despite the cost.

Once an agency receives a formal request for a record, it is supposed to respond by either providing the record or denying the request (and explaining why it did so) within 20 working days. However, the courts have repeatedly excused government agencies from this time limit, ruling that the deadline is "directory" rather than "mandatory." The OPEN Government Act of 2007, however, ordered federal agencies that fail to meet the 20-day deadline to refund search and copying fees to noncommercial requesters. If a request is denied, the requester has a right to appeal the denial, first through the agency's appeals procedures and then to the federal courts.

Exemptions from disclosure. The judge must decide if the documents properly fall within one of the exemptions, thus justifying government secrecy. Briefly, the nine exemptions are:

1. Documents that have been properly classified as confidential or secret in the interest of national security or U.S. foreign policy;
2. Documents relating to "internal personnel rules and practices" of federal agencies;
3. Matters that are specifically exempted from public disclosure by some other statutory law;
4. Trade secrets and certain other financial and commercial information gathered by government agencies;

5. Interagency and intra-agency memoranda that involve the internal decision-making process (e.g., working papers and tentative drafts);

6. Personnel and medical files and similar documents that should be kept confidential to protect individual privacy;

7. Investigatory files compiled for law enforcement purposes, but only when the disclosure of such files would: (a) interfere with law enforcement; (b) deprive a person of a fair trial; (c) constitute an unwarranted invasion of personal privacy; (d) disclose a confidential source; (e) disclose investigative techniques and thereby permit someone to circumvent the law; or (f) endanger the life or safety of any individual;

8. Documents prepared by or used by agencies regulating banks and other financial institutions;

9. Oil and gas exploration data, including maps.

Obviously, many of these exemptions are so broad and all-encompassing that they can be used to justify massive government secrecy. In addition to millions of government documents that are classified for national security reasons, millions more are confidential for other reasons. The exemptions for law enforcement files and internal memoranda, for example, have been widely used to withhold information from the public.

Using the FOIA. Anyone seeking information under the FOIA should make it clear in writing that he or she is making a FOIA request, perhaps mentioning the act by its official citation: Title 5 of the United States Code, Section 552 (or simply 5 U.S.C. 552). The request should be as specific as possible, identifying the desired record exactly as the agency identifies it, and how much the requester is willing to pay. Each agency publishes information about its record-keeping scheme in the *Federal Register,* available online and in many large libraries, to assist FOIA users in identifying the records they seek. Many agencies allow FOIA requests to be submitted online. A FOIA request should first be directed to the official designated to handle FoI requests within a particular agency. If that fails, the request should next go to the agency head, unless the agency has specified a different appeals procedure. If that too fails, the requester has little recourse except to go to court—or perhaps cultivate "sources" within the agency who may be willing to "leak" the material surreptitiously.

If a request for information under the FOIA is denied, the person who made the request is supposed to receive a list of the documents withheld with an explanation of the legal justification for withholding each document. This list is called a *Vaughn Index,* because a federal appellate court ruled that such an accounting is necessary in *Vaughn v. Rosen* (484 F.2d 820, 1973).

How significant is FOIA? It would take a book as long as this one just to summarize all of the FOIA lawsuits that have been filed. But is the information that is ferreted out of once-locked government files under FOIA really important?

Using the FOIA, researchers learned that the Central Intelligence Agency (CIA) spied on Martin Luther King, Jr. and other pioneer civil rights leaders, and that longtime FBI Director J. Edgar Hoover used the FBI in efforts to discredit King. Other FOIA inquiries revealed government experiments with mind-controlling drugs that killed at least two persons in the 1950s. Meanwhile, still other researchers using the FOIA learned of CIA efforts to overthrow the government in Chile and to use journalists as foreign agents. The FOIA also forced the FBI to acknowledge—after waging a 20-year legal battle with a historian to keep the information secret—that it had spied on singer John Lennon.

Journalists also used the FOIA to expose the safety hazards posed by the Ford Pinto's gas tank, to help find out why the Hubble Space Telescope's mirror failed to work properly, and to alert citizens to the environmental hazards posed by the Department of Energy's nuclear weapons plants in several states. Many socially important and newsworthy government secrets have been uncovered because of the FOIA. The act was used to discover long-concealed health hazards caused by radiation and the dangers of Agent Orange to Vietnam War veterans. It was also used to unearth important details of America's unsavory role in the Bay of Pigs invasion of Cuba and President Nixon's plans for military action in Cambodia.

FOIA Amendments

The FOIA statute has undergone several changes in the last generation. Here, we'll briefly summarize FOIA developments initiated during the presidencies of Bill Clinton, George W. Bush, Barack Obama, and Donald J. Trump.

Clinton administration. Responding to some of the new FOIA problems and opportunities created by the internet and the rapid growth of computer usage in and out of government, Congress extensively amended the FOIA in the Electronic Freedom of Information Act Amendments of 1996.

The Electronic FOIA changed the way federal agencies respond to FoI requests in three basic ways: (1) it required agencies to make it easier for the public to identify and access government records, (2) it facilitated the computerization of the FoI compliance process, and (3) it completely reformed the timetable and procedures that agencies must follow in responding to FOIA requests. To assist the public in accessing federal records, the 1996 law required agencies to provide detailed indexes and guides to explain what records are available and where they may be found. Also, the law divided government records that fall under the FOIA into three categories: those that must be published, those that must be made available in agency reading rooms or placed online even if no one makes a request, and those that must be made available when there is a request.

To computerize compliance, the 1996 law required many agencies to set up "electronic reading rooms." Whereas those seeking government information previously had to go to an agency's headquarters in Washington and camp out in a "public reading room," in many instances the documents kept in those rooms are now online. This one provision of the 1996 act alone vastly increased public access to federal records. In fact, it may have increased public access as much as the FOIA itself did 30 years earlier.

The Electronic FOIA Amendments also provided for other enhancements of the FoI process. In addition to flatly declaring that records kept in electronic form are fully covered by the FOIA, the law required agencies to provide materials in a variety of computer formats.

The 1996 act also seriously addressed the problem of redactions for the first time. When electronic records are *redacted* (i.e., blacked out), it is often impossible even to tell that this has happened. Entire sections can be deleted—with no paper trail to show where the deletions occurred. The 1996 law said that agencies must indicate where there have been redactions and how much was redacted where it is feasible to do so and where disclosing that information will not in itself reveal confidential information.

Finally, the 1996 act addressed the chronic problem of interminable delays. It gave agencies 20 working days instead of 10 to respond to requests, but it also made major changes in what agencies must do if they will miss this deadline. For one, journalists and a few others were authorized to have their requests expedited in some instances. In addition, those whose requests are complex and may require considerable agency time are given an opportunity to scale back or simplify their requests in return for faster processing. And requesters who face delays are supposed to be notified and given an estimated compliance time.

One of the most important innovations in this law was the requirement that agencies identify repeatedly requested information and avoid wasting time processing duplicative requests. When an agency determines that particular information must be released under the FOIA—and is likely to be requested again—the agency must put that information where the public can access it routinely (usually without even filing a formal FoI request).

Bush administration. Under a policy adopted by the George W. Bush administration after the Sept. 11, 2001 terrorist attacks, federal agencies were directed to abandon a Clinton administration policy adopted in 1993 that required the release of information unless it is "reasonably foreseeable that disclosure would be harmful." Under this policy, announced by Attorney General John Ashcroft on Oct. 12, 2001 (sometimes called the Ashcroft memo), agencies were encouraged to keep information secret whenever there is a "sound legal basis" for doing so. This new directive cited the importance of "safeguarding national security, enhancing the effectiveness of law enforcement agencies, protecting sensitive business information and, not least, preserving personal privacy." When requested information fell into a gray area where either openness or secrecy might be legally defensible, the policy encouraged officials to opt for secrecy. (The OPEN Government Act of 2007 reversed this presumption, directing government agencies to favor disclosure in gray areas, setting aside the Ashcroft memo.)

In 2005, President Bush issued another FOIA-related executive order, directing federal agencies to create FOIA Service Centers and to designate executives to hear complaints about the performance of these service centers. Agencies were directed to post information about this on their websites. The order also directed agencies to reduce their backlogs of FOIA requests.

The Bush administration's FOIA directives did not rescind a second Clinton administration policy, an executive order signed by President Clinton in 1995 that changed the way federal agencies handle secret information. The executive order revised the rules under which agencies classify documents as secret for national security reasons. Among other things, the 1995 executive order requires agencies to declassify most documents after 25 years and make them available for public inspection. Agency heads such as the director of the CIA are permitted to make exceptions to the 25-year disclosure rule, but only with the approval of a committee set up to review these exceptions. The 1995 rule exempts CIA documents that would reveal the names of its "intelligence sources" as well as Defense Department documents relating to such things as war plans.

In 2007, Congress approved and President George W. Bush signed a new law to make various changes in the FOIA, the OPEN Government Act of 2007. The new law reversed many Bush administration efforts to increase government secrecy after the 2001 terrorist attacks. Among other things, the 2007 law brought nonproprietary information held by government contractors within the scope of FOIA. It required agencies to meet the 20-day deadline for responding to requests or else refund search and duplication fees paid by noncommercial requesters. Also, agencies now must explain instances where part of a document is redacted before it is released. In addition, the 2007 legislation set up a system for requesters to track the status of their queries and created an ombudsman in each agency to deal with disputes over information requests without litigation.

Obama administration. Issues of open government and freedom of information were high on President Barack Obama's agenda. On his first full day in office, Obama issued a memorandum on the FOIA that called on agencies to "usher in a new era of open government." In 2009, Attorney General Eric Holder issued new guidelines that direct all executive branch departments and agencies to apply a presumption of openness when dealing with FOIA requests. Holder's memo said that agencies should not withhold information simply because it would be legal to do so and should always consider whether they could make partial disclosures rather than withholding documents completely. And in 2009, the director of the Open Government Directive ordered departments "to take specific actions to implement the principles of transparency, participation, and collaboration" President Obama had announced his first day, and set deadlines for those actions.

But the administration dragged its feet in releasing White House visitor logs. A federal district court said the logs are properly considered agency records held by the Secret Service, not the White House itself, and subject to FOIA. On appeal, the D.C. Circuit reversed in part and affirmed in part (*Judicial Watch, Inc. v. U.S. Secret Serv.*, 726 F.3d 208, 2013). Saying that on several occasions "Congress made clear that it did not want documents like the appointment calendars of the President and his close advisors to be subject to disclosure under FOIA," the court determined those records are not "agency records" subject to disclosure.

And in 2009 the administration exercised secrecy regarding the release of photos allegedly showing U.S. troops abusing Iraqi and Afghan prisoners during the Bush administration. The Second Circuit had ruled that the photos must be publicly disclosed under the Freedom of Information Act (*ACLU v. Dep't of Defense*, 543 F.3d 59). President Obama initially said that the photos would be released after the decision but then asked government attorneys to object to the court's order, saying that the release of the photos would "further inflame anti-American opinion" and "put our troops in greater danger," reversing himself. The court complied, saying that the government did not immediately have to turn over photos but can have more time for other legal options. Then Congress passed a bill to prevent the release of controversial photos of alleged U.S. abuse of prisoners and detainees. Called the Detainee Photographic Records Protection Act of 2009, the act amended FOIA to bar from release any photograph "taken between September 11, 2001 and January 22, 2009 relating to the treatment of individuals engaged, captured, or detained after September 11, 2001, by the Armed Forces of the United States in operations outside of the United States." It was included in a Homeland Security appropriations bill and signed into law in 2009.

In 2009, the Supreme Court vacated the Second Circuit opinion and sent the case back to the lower court for review under this law.

But there were some bright spots. In May 2009, the administration revealed Data.gov, whose purpose is "to increase public access to high value, machine readable data sets generated by the Executive Branch of the Federal Government." Departments are instructed to post "high-value" data sets. And, as part as the Open Government initiative, the website FOIA.gov contains all the annual reports made to the Department of Justice as part of agencies' FOIA compliance. Other attempts to provide information like this are government websites such as USAspending.gov and Recovery.gov.

Happy 50th birthday, FOIA! On June 30, 2016, President Obama signed into law the FOIA Improvement Act of 2016, what some commentators called the most significant overhaul of the act since 2007. Among other things, the FOIA Improvement Act:

- required federal agencies to make their disclosable records and documents available for public inspection electronically;
- required agencies to make available for inspection electronically records that have been requested three or more times (frequently requested records);
- prohibited an agency from charging a fee for providing records if the agency misses a deadline for complying with an FOIA request unless unusual circumstances apply and more than 5,000 pages are necessary to respond to the request;
- prohibited an agency from withholding information requested under FOIA unless the agency reasonably foresees that disclosure would harm an interest protected by a FOIA exemption or disclosure is prohibited by law (presumption of openness);
- limited the FOIA exemption for agency communications to allow the disclosure of agency records created 25 years or more before the date of a FOIA request;
- established a Chief FOIA Officers Council to develop recommendations for increasing compliance and efficiency in responding to FOIA requests; disseminating information about agency experiences, identifying, developing, and coordinating initiatives to increase transparency and compliance; and promoting performance measures to ensure agency compliance with FOIA requirements; and
- required the Office of Management and Budget to ensure the operation of a consolidated online request portal that allows a member of the public to submit a request for records to any agency from a single website.

FOIA under President Trump. Challenges to access continued during President Donald J. Trump's first year in office. Data analyzed by the Associated Press found that the government "censored, withheld or said it couldn't find records" more during President Trump's first eight months in office than at any point in the prior decade. The AP analysis found that only one in five FOIA requests were fulfilled in their entirety. Another analysis found that the average responder waited 169 days for a response (remember, the allowed time is 20 days!). Lawsuits challenging FOIA denials or non-responses also spiked, with 651 lawsuits filed, up 26% in 2017 from the year before, according to The FOIA Project.

FIG. 80.
President Donald
J. Trump on Twitter
praising the release
of some records from
John F. Kennedy's
administration.

Source: Twitter, Inc

In one notable FoI-related decision, President Trump ordered the long-awaited release of some records related to the 1963 assassination of President John F. Kennedy. In 1992, Congress passed the President John F. Kennedy Assassination Records Collection Act, requiring the release of government documents related to the assassination investigation after 25 years. When that deadline arrived in October 2017, the government began releasing records in batches. However, President Trump granted a three-year extension for some sensitive records due to "identifiable national security, law enforcement and foreign affairs concerns." Those were expected to be released in late 2021, unless President Joe Biden decides to withhold them.

FOIA today. The federal government received 790,688 FOIA requests in fiscal year 2020, according to the Department of Justice. Of the 772,869 requests processed in 2020, 63% were fully or partially granted, according to the DOJ. The total number of backlog requests in 2020 was 141,762, an increase of nearly 18% from the prior year. The government took an average of 30 days to process "simple requests," the DOJ reported. Complex requests range widely, while the majority of them were processed within 60 days.

In 2019, a bipartisan group of lawmakers called on the Government Accountability Office to conduct a review of government compliance with FOIA. The GAO found that the backlog of FOIA requests had grown by more than 80% between 2012 and 2018, while only 27% of requests in 2018 were fully granted.

Media organizations filed 122 lawsuits in 2020 over FOIA denials, more than any previous year, according to the FOIA Project. The majority of those lawsuits were filed in the District of Columbia and the Southern District of New York.

■ LAWSUITS OVER FOIA EXEMPTIONS

If the time comes when an FOIA lawsuit is necessary, the act includes a provision allowing a court to require the government to pay the requester's attorney's fees and court costs if the lawsuit is successful. And if the court finds that agency personnel acted capriciously in denying the original request, the Civil Service Commission is required to hold a proceeding to decide if the government employees who denied the request should be disciplined.

Focus on...
Exception 3 statutes

Exception 3 of the FOIA says that certain statutes may exempt information from release under FOIA. To qualify, a statute must either leave no discretion for release to the agency or must establish criteria for withholding, or refer to particular information to be withheld.

In 2010, the Department of Justice released a list of statutes that courts have over the years found to qualify as Exception 3 statutes. Some examples:

FIG. 81. Gavel and law book.

Author's collection.

- Immigration and Nationality Act: exempts "certain records pertaining to the issuance or refusal of visas to enter the United States";
- Espionage Act: exempts "certain classified information pertaining to the communication intelligence and cryptographic devices of the United States or any foreign government";
- Federal Victims' Protection and Rights Act: exempts "certain records containing identifying information pertaining to children involved in criminal proceedings"; and
- Social Security Act: exempts "death certificates and records pertaining to deaths provided to the Commissioner of Social Security."

Thousands of lawsuits have been filed in federal courts under the FOIA. As a result of amendments to the FOIA in 1974 and 1976, federal judges are empowered to review the requested documents in private in their chambers and then rule on the validity of an agency's decision to deny the request. Of the numerous lawsuits filed under the FOIA, a few should be summarized to illustrate the typical workings of the act and the role of the courts in interpreting it.

Records Related to National Security

The first exemption (for national security) is a broad one that courts have tended to uphold. In fact, judges have sometimes declined to even look at classified material in chambers if an agency submits a convincing *affidavit* (a statement made under oath) to justify the need for keeping the document secret. However, other courts have ruled that documents must have been properly classified for the national security exemption to apply. The national security exemption remains a gigantic and very troublesome loophole in the FOIA. Numerous abuses of the classification system have been revealed, among them instances where it was used to conceal corruption, government waste, and bureaucratic bungling.

The Assassination Records Review Board, created by Congress in 1992 after years of protests about the federal government's insistence on keeping so many records about the assassination of John F. Kennedy secret, completed a lengthy review of classified records in 1998. The board concluded that the government had "needlessly and wastefully" withheld millions of records that did not need to be secret, and this secrecy "led the American public to believe that the government had something to hide" about the Kennedy assassination.

Another noteworthy illustration of the same point was the government's attempt to censor *The Progressive* magazine when it planned to publish an article on the hydrogen bomb, an article prepared from readily available public information. (That case is also discussed in Chapter Three.) It has been suggested more than once that foreign spies in America should spend their time reading popular newspapers and magazines, doing Google searches, and browsing in public libraries rather than snooping around the Pentagon.

Nevertheless, the national security exemption to the FOIA must be taken seriously because it allows the government to withhold many important documents from public inspection, thus concealing not only legitimate military and diplomatic secrets but also much information that should be public in a democracy. Since Sept. 11, the national security exemption has evolved into a more generic homeland security exemption that has been used to justify unprecedented secrecy, some critics have charged.

In 2012, the Second Circuit found that the government may withhold certain redactions dealing with the Central Intelligence Agency's use of waterboarding as an interrogation method because the information pertained to "a highly classified, active intelligence method" (*ACLU v. Dep't of Justice*, 681 F.3d 61).

Even non-binding documents can be withheld under Exemption 1. The D.C. Circuit said in 2013 that it was appropriate for the Office of the U.S. Trade Representative to decline to release under Exemption 1 a document used in failed trade negotiations with several countries (*Ctr. for Int'l Envtl. Law v. Office of the U.S. Trade Representative*, 718 F.3d 899). The question turned on a non-binding white paper discussing the meaning of "in like circumstances," a phrase that the office said "is a key element of two nondiscrimination provisions integral to trade and investment agreements entered into by the United States—the "most-favored-nation treatment" and the "national treatment" provisions. The appellate court said that the white paper could still have impact on foreign relations: "We do not see why... it is so implausible that an arbitrator would look to the white paper as evidence of the United States' interpretation of the phrase ["in like circumstances"]—even if that document is not binding on the United States."

bin Laden images. After President Obama announced that Osama bin Laden had been killed in a military action at his compound in Abbottabad, Pakistan in May 2011, several media organizations filed FOIA requests for information on the raid. A district judge in 2012 said that the Department of Defense didn't have video or photographs taken during or after the raid that ended with the death of bin Laden requested by conservative government watchdog group Judicial Watch, but the Central Intelligence Agency did—and claimed exemptions against releasing any of them. Citing concerns that "extremist groups will seize upon these images as grist for their propaganda mill," the court said that it would not compel the release of the documents. The D.C. Circuit in 2013 upheld the CIA's classification of the documents (*Judicial Watch, Inc. v. Dep't of Defense*, 715 F.3d 937). Noting CIA concerns that these images would inflame U.S. enemies, the court said the agency was correctly "predicting the consequences of releasing an extraordinary set of images, ones that depict American military personnel burying the founder and leader of al Qaeda." However, Judicial Watch was successful in obtaining documents in 2012 that included meetings between government agencies and Kathryn Bigelow, Academy Award–winning director of *The Hurt Locker*, and a screenwriter to provide information for a feature film.

Reverse FOIA suits. Among the other exemptions, several have stirred considerable controversy. The trade secrets and private business information exemption, for instance, has prompted a number of double lawsuits with federal agencies caught in the middle. On one side, someone (often a competitor) is seeking information that may be covered by the trade secrets exemption. On the other, the private company that originally submitted the information is suing to compel the government to keep the material confidential. The latter kind of lawsuit is called a *"reverse FOIA"* suit.

Here's an example of a reverse FOIA suit: A district court in Washington, D.C., granted summary judgment to the Federal Aviation Administration (FAA) in a case filed by the National Business Aviation Association to prevent the FAA from releasing a list of aircraft registration numbers to ProPublica, an investigative journalism website. The association argued that the records should be withheld under Exemption 4, covering trade secrets. The FAA said that the information must be released, and the court agreed (*National Business Aviation Association v. FAA and ProPublica*, 686 F. Supp. 2d 80, 2010). The list requested by ProPublica contained those aircraft that had elected to be on the FAA's "Block List" managed by the association; flights by aircraft on that list were kept secret from the public.

The Privacy Exemptions

Federal agencies often cite personal privacy to justify secrecy, sometimes in absurd ways. The National Highway Traffic Safety Administration (NHTSA) was widely criticized by journalists and safety advocates in the mid-2000s when it removed from its website the entire database of the exact locations of auto fatalities. When a safety advocate filed a FOIA request for the data, the request was denied on the ground that revealing where accidents occurred would invade victims' privacy. Safety advocates pointed out that police agencies routinely disclose not only locations of accidents but also names of victims. NHTSA has accident location data nationwide, and it would be useful for studying traffic safety to know which highways and intersections are most hazardous, but the database is a secret.

Many other practical problems have become evident as federal agencies, information seekers, and the courts have attempted to live under the FOIA. One of the most important of these problems is the fact that agencies can escape the law by either destroying or concealing sensitive records, and public officials can sometimes circumvent it by simply taking their records home with them. There may be no way for anyone outside an agency to prove that a given document ever existed, if the agency steadfastly maintains that it didn't.

Moreover, in a 1980 decision (*Kissinger v. Reporters Committee for Freedom of the Press*, 445 U.S. 136), the Supreme Court ruled that former Secretary of State Henry Kissinger could keep his diary of official telephone calls secret because he took the diary home with him, unless the government compelled him to return it. The dissenters warned that this ruling would give government officials freedom to completely escape FOIA's reach by simply taking their important papers home.

In another major 1980 decision (*Forsham v. Harris*, 445 U.S. 169), the Supreme Court made it clear that private organizations doing research under government grants need not make their data public. The Court ruled that such research data simply doesn't fall within the definition of "agency records" and is thus not covered by the FOIA.

In 1982, the Supreme Court continued the trend toward a narrow interpretation of the FOIA, handing down two more decisions that restricted public access to government information under the act: *FBI v. Abramson* (456 U.S. 615) and *Dept. of State v. Washington Post* (456 U.S. 595). In *Abramson*, the high court ruled that some of the information compiled by the Nixon administration about its critics was exempt from disclosure under the FOIA. The FBI had originally gathered the information for investigatory purposes, and the Court said the information was covered by the law enforcement investigatory exemption even though it was eventually recompiled and put to partisan political uses.

The *Washington Post* case expanded the scope of the exemption for "personnel, medical and similar files." The Court held that records indicating whether an individual holds a

U.S. passport are a "similar file" that falls within the exemption if the individual's interest in privacy outweighs the public interest in disclosure. A virtually unanimous Court said, "Although Exemption 6's language sheds little light on what Congress meant by "similar files," the legislative history indicates that Congress did not mean to limit Exemption 6 to a narrow class of files containing only a discrete kind of personal information, but that "similar files" was to have a broad rather than a narrow meaning."

Again considering privacy issues, the Supreme Court ruled in 1997 that a government agency's mailing list should not be disclosed under the FOIA (*Bibles v. Oregon Natural Desert Assn.*, 519 U.S. 355). The court balanced the public's right to know against the privacy rights of those on the list, and ruled that names on such a list should only be released when their disclosure would "shed light on an agency's performance of its statutory duties or otherwise let citizens know what their government is up to."

A 2004 Supreme Court decision expanded the privacy exemption to the FOIA further, holding for the first time that a deceased person's relatives may invoke it. In *Nat'l Archives and Records Admin. v. Favish* (541 U.S. 157), the high court upheld a decision by the federal government to deny public access to photographs of the body of Vincent Foster, Jr., a Clinton administration official who committed suicide in 1993. His body was found in an area managed by the National Park Service. Attorney Allan Favish, who disputed the verdict of several investigative bodies that Foster's death was a suicide, sued under the FOIA for access to photos taken by the U.S. Park Police. The Supreme Court said the privacy rights of Foster's family outweighed the public interest in disclosure.

But the Supreme Court in 2011 *declined* to extend the privacy element in Exemption 7 to corporations. The Court reversed a Third Circuit decision extending personal privacy exemptions in FOIA to corporations. In *FCC v. AT&T, Inc.* (562 U.S. 397), the Court said that Exemption 7(C), exempting "records or information compiled for law enforcement purposes" that "could reasonably be expected to constitute an unwarranted invasion of personal privacy," did not apply to AT&T's records that were handed over to the Federal Communications Commission as part of an agency investigation on alleged overcharging. CompTel, a trade association of competitors, used the FOIA to request those records.

The Court unanimously said that the exemption did not extend to corporations. The term "personal," Chief Justice John Roberts said, was intended to apply to people only. "In fact, we often use the word 'personal' to mean precisely the opposite of business-related: We speak of personal expenses and business expenses, personal life and work life, personal opinion and a company's view," wrote Roberts, adding with a judicial wink, "We trust that AT&T will not take it personally."

Privacy concerns still cover even 40-year-old documents. A federal D.C. court released a number of Watergate documents in response to a request from a university professor in 2012, although not everything the professor requested due to privacy issues. Texas A&M history professor Luke Nichter requested records about the wiretapping at the Watergate and the trials of the conspirators, among other things, and the court agreed that all documents that the government did not object to releasing should be released, and the others reviewed. The government complied, and in a second 2013 case, the judge, after reviewing the documents *in camera* (in his chambers), said that some records would be withheld because "at least one of the subjects of grand jury testimony ... is still living and these documents should remain sealed to protect his privacy. It is also possible that other individuals—grand jurors and witnesses—named in the materials are still living. Revealing the names of Watergate grand jurors and grand jury witnesses could bring these individuals or their families unwanted media attention" (*In re Petition of Luke Nichter*, 949 F. Supp. 2d 205).

FBI records. The Supreme Court drastically restricted public access to FBI records in a 1989 case, *Dep't of Justice v. Reporters Cmte. for Freedom of the Press* (489 U.S. 749). In one sweeping decision, the Court ruled out public access under the FOIA to the FBI's criminal histories on at least 24 million people. These criminal histories—often called "rap sheets"—are computerized compilations of personal information from various sources, including state and local law enforcement agencies. The Court's unanimous ruling created a vast across-the-board exception to the FOIA for records that might in any way affect personal privacy. Moreover, the Court's language is so broad that it may apply to other government agencies and not just the FBI, severely limiting the FOIA's applicability to records about individual people. Explaining the Court's decision, Justice John Paul Stevens wrote:

> [W]e hold as a categorical matter that a third party's request for law enforcement records or information about a private citizen can reasonably be expected to invade that citizen's privacy, and that when the request seeks no "official information" about a government agency, but merely records that the government happens to be storing, the invasion of privacy is "unwarranted."

The Supreme Court said in this far-reaching decision that there is a difference between records about the activities of a federal agency itself and records maintained by the agency about individuals, with individual records broadly exempted from the FOIA.

This ruling was widely assailed by journalists and others who pointed out that many of the most telling revelations about past government wrongdoing have come from records about individuals. The mere fact that the FBI is keeping records on some individuals not suspected of a crime may raise serious questions.

A few months later, the Court went still further, ruling that many documents obtained by the FBI from other government agencies are also exempt from disclosure. In *John Doe Agency v. John Doe Corp.* (493 U.S. 146, 1989), the high court said the government could not be compelled to release certain documents concerning the Grumman Corp. because they were "compiled for law enforcement purposes." Grumman requested the documents from the Defense Contract Auditing Agency during a federal grand jury investigation of aerospace industry accounting practices. The auditing agency responded by turning the documents over to the FBI, which then refused to release copies under the FOIA exemption for documents compiled for law enforcement purposes. The Court agreed that such documents should be exempt from disclosure.

Taken together, these 1989 rulings and several earlier Supreme Court decisions seem to be sending a message to the federal bureaucracy, and especially to the FBI: when in doubt, withhold information requested under FOIA. The Court has repeatedly declared that FOIA exemptions "must be narrowly construed." But when faced with a specific request for information, the Court continues to rule that the exemptions allow broad government secrecy.

However, the Supreme Court backpedaled a little in a 1993 decision, *Dep't of Justice v. Landano* (508 U.S. 165). In that case, the Court held that the exemption for law enforcement records does not give the FBI an automatic right to refuse to release information that might identify a source. The Court acknowledged that ordinarily FBI informants' names should be kept confidential, but the justices said the FBI is not entitled to a legal presumption

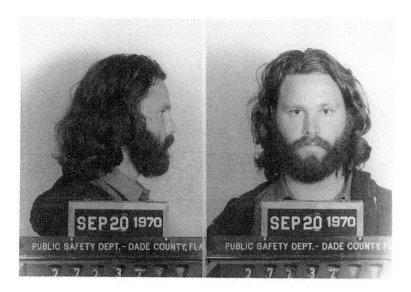

FIG. 82.
A mug shot of the singer Jim Morrison, after he was arrested for indecent exposure and profanity at a 1969 concert in Miami. Mug shots may be withheld from public disclosure under FOIA, courts have ruled.

Dade County Public Safety Department.

that this kind of information is *always* confidential. Instead, the FBI must consider such requests for information on a case-by-case basis.

Mug shots. Since photographic technology has existed, journalists have published mug shots of individuals arrested for crimes. Are mug shots exempt from public disclosure under FOIA's law enforcement exemption? Exemption 7(C) permits agencies to withhold "records or information compiled for law enforcement purposes" if the disclosure "could reasonably be extended to constitute an unwarranted invasion of personal privacy." An appellate court ruling in 2016 elevated privacy rights over the rights of the public to obtain mug shots.

After four police Michigan police officers were charged with bribery and drug conspiracy, the *Detroit Free Press* filed a FOIA request for their mug shots. The US Marshals Service denied the request, and the newspaper sued. The newspaper had strong grounds given a 1996 ruling by the Sixth Circuit Court of Appeals that found criminal defendants lacked a personal privacy interest in mug shots (*Detroit Free Press, Inc. v. Dep't of Justice* ("*Free Press I*"), 73 F.3d 93). In 2016, the full Sixth Circuit reversed its 1996 ruling, finding that new technologies made mug shot disclosure more detrimental to individuals' privacy rights (*Detroit Free Press, Inc. v. Dep't of Justice* ("*Free Press II*"), 829 F.3d 478). "A disclosed booking photo casts a long, damaging shadow over the depicted individual. In 1996, when we decided *Free Press I*, booking photos appeared on television or in the newspaper and then, for all practical purposes, disappeared," the appellate court wrote. "Today, an idle internet search reveals the same booking photo that once would have required a trip to the local library's microfiche collection." As a result, the court found a privacy interest in the mug shots and ruled that disclosure could be prevented on a case-by-case basis.

Other Exemptions, Provisions, and Precedents

Although many Supreme Court decisions interpreting the FOIA have involved the national security and law enforcement exemptions, the high court and the appellate courts have interpreted a number of other provisions of the law.

CIA records. In 1985, the Supreme Court restricted the scope of the FOIA in another way, this time by excluding many Central Intelligence Agency (CIA) records from disclosure under the FOIA. In the case of *CIA v. Sims* (471 U.S. 159), the Court ruled that the CIA may keep the identities of its sources of intelligence data secret even when national security is not involved. The case arose when the Ralph Nader Public Citizen Health Research Group sought the names of researchers and institutions that participated in a CIA project involving mind-altering drugs during the 1950s. The project required researchers to administer drugs that are now illegal to unwitting subjects. Some of the researchers and institutions agreed to have their names released, but many others refused—and the CIA withheld their names. The Nader organization then sued to obtain the names.

The FOIA has no specific exemption to protect the identities of the CIA's sources. However, the blanket exemption for information exempted from disclosure by another law (Exemption 3) has been used by the CIA to keep its sources secret. The law that established the CIA authorized it to keep its sources of information secret. In ruling in favor of the CIA, the high court emphasized that intelligence work requires secrecy, and that the fear of being identified may lead intelligence sources to refuse to cooperate with the CIA. Thus, the Court chose to liberally interpret the law allowing the CIA to keep its sources secret.

Interagency records. Exemption 5 allows the government to withhold interagency and intra-agency memoranda that involve the internal decision-making process. This is sometimes called the "deliberative process" privilege.

In 2001, for example, the Supreme Court unanimously ruled that the Bureau of Indian Affairs (BIA) cannot keep its correspondence with Indian tribes confidential under this exemption. In *Dep't of the Interior v. Klamath Water Users Protective Ass'n* (532 U.S. 1), the Court said communications between the BIA and Indian tribes are not comparable to communications between government agencies and their paid private consultants, which were previously ruled confidential under this FoI exemption.

And in *U.S. Fish and Wildlife Serv. v. Sierra Club* (No. 19-547, 2021) the Supreme Court ruled 7-2 that FOIA exemption 5 broadly covers internal reports of government agencies. The case involved a request for so-called "biological reports" prepared by the U.S. Fish and Wildlife Service and the National Marine Fisheries Service for the Environmental Protection Agency regarding the environmental impact of construction projects on aquatic wildlife. The Ninth Circuit Court of Appeals ordered disclosure of the records because even though they were labeled as drafts, they reflected the "final opinion" of the agencies that wrote them. The Supreme Court disagreed, finding the documents in question to be "predecisional" and "deliberative" records covered by the exemption rather than a final report of a settled decision.

Trade secrets. In *Food Mktg. Institute v. Argus Leader Media* (139 S.Ct. 2356, 2019), the Supreme Court issued a decision expanding the scope of documents that can be withheld from public disclosure under FOIA. The case involved a FOIA request from the Sioux Falls *Argus Leader* for records showing how much money businesses received in food stamp reimbursements. The government denied the request, saying the data was exempt from disclosure under exemption 4 of FOIA, which allows the government to withhold "trade secrets and commercial or financial information obtained from a person and privileged or confidential." Federal appellate circuits have split on the meaning of "confidential" and the scope of exemption 4. In a 6-3 ruling, the Supreme Court said that information is confidential for purposes of the statute when the information is "both customarily and actually treated as private" by its owner and provided to the government under an assurance of privacy. The *Argus Leader* called the decision a "shattering blow to government transparency."

Internal personnel rules and procedures. Exemption 2 should not be divided into "high" and "low" standards, said the Supreme Court in 2011 in *Milner v. Dep't of the Navy* (562 U.S. 562). Some circuits had divided internal information into two categories, "Low 2" and "High 2." Routine or trivial information was "Low 2," of low societal value, such as agency management or "housekeeping" information; the Court had already held that there is no substantial public interest in its disclosure in *Dept. of the Air Force v. Rose* (discussed earlier). But it had not ruled on the "High 2" category, which includes more substantial matters, and the circuits were split in their decisions. At issue in *Milner* was the Ninth Circuit's decision that the Navy could keep secret documents that record locations of explosives stored near Port Townsend, Washington. Plaintiff Glen Scott Milner lived nearby. The Navy denied Milner's request under Exemption 2; the district court agreed, and a divided Ninth Circuit affirmed.

The Supreme Court reversed on an 8-1 vote, saying that Exemption 2 pertains only to "records relating to employee relations and human resources issues." Justice Elena Kagan made the holding clear: "Our construction of the statutory language simply makes clear that Low 2 is all of 2 (and that High 2 is not 2 at all)." She did not want the government to be able to use Exemption 2 as a fallback reason for record denial. There are other alternatives for the Department of Defense to keep the information confidential if it truly believes that is necessary, including Congressional action, she said. Justice Stephen Breyer dissented, saying that because the High 2/Low 2 distinction had been applied consistently for 30 years and seemed to be working for all involved, he would "let sleeping dogs lie."

■ OTHER FOIA LIMITATIONS

Users of the FOIA also encounter other practical problems. One of them, as already noted, is the problem of delays in compliance. Many federal agencies have large backlogs of FoI requests. This poses a particular problem for journalists. While a historian or a business enterprise may be prepared to wait a year or two for information, that kind of a delay is often fatal for a journalist working on a timely news story.

Delays. In 2010, the National Security Archive and George Washington University conducted a FOIA audit. They found that "the Obama Administration ... has clearly stated a new policy direction for open government but has not conquered the challenge of communicating and enforcing that message throughout the Executive Branch." FOIA requests as old as 18 years linger in some agencies, few agencies made concrete changes in their policies to comply, and only four agencies showed both increases in information releases and decreases in denials. A new NSA audit in December 2012 showed some agencies have been slow to respond to many FOIA legislative improvements. The audit revealed that 56 agencies out of 99 audited have not updated their FOIA guidelines in accordance with the OPEN Government Act. Moreover, 17 agencies have not posted FOIA guidelines online as required by the e-FOIA Amendments. The audit identified the Department of Justice as the worst offender, "for attempting to sneak through regulations that would allow lying to FOIA requesters, exempting online publications from being considered news media, and disqualifying most students from receiving FOIA fee waivers."

A judge even slapped the hand of one agency for sloppiness in its FOIA process, saying that the U.S. Citizenship and Immigration Services (part of the Department of Homeland Security) gave American Immigration Council a FOIA report "riddled with errors" after a

reverse FOIA suit:
a suit filed by a company against a government agency to try to prevent the agency from revealing information.

Glomar response (or Glomarization):
when an agency says it can neither confirm nor deny the existence of records requested under the FOIA.

Vaughn index:
in denials of FOIA requests, a list that must identify each document the agency withheld; the statutory exemption(s) under which it was withheld; and how disclosure would harm the interests of the exemption(s).

year's delay. The judge wrote, "After in camera review, the Court concludes that two-thirds of the withheld records contested by the Council should have been largely or wholly released. FOIA cases count on agencies to do their jobs with reasonable diligence. USCIS must do better" (*Am. Immigration Council v. Dept. of Homeland Sec.*, 905 F. Supp. 2d 206, 2012).

But requesters can immediately sue if statutory deadlines are missed, the D.C. Circuit said in 2013 (*Citizens for Responsibility and Ethics in Washington v. FEC*, 711 F.3d 180). CREW said that to meet the 20-day requirement for a "determination," the FEC "must at least inform the requester of the scope of the documents it will produce and the exemptions it will claim with respect to any withheld documents," while the FEC argued that it merely needed "to express a future intention to produce non-exempt documents and claim exemptions." Siding with CREW, the court said that for an agency to make a "determination" under FOIA, it must at least "(i) gather and review the documents; (ii) determine and communicate the scope of the documents it intends to produce and withhold, and the reasons for withholding any documents; and (iii) inform the requester that it can appeal whatever portion of the 'determination' is adverse."

Costs. Another problem with the FOIA can be high court costs and attorney's fees. Those who sue the government for the release of documents and "substantially prevail" in court are entitled to have the government pay their costs and attorney's fees. However, if the lawsuit is not successful, the document requester is likely to have a large legal bill to pay. The FOIA doesn't say anything about those who seek documents having to pay the government's expenses if they lose. However, the general rules governing federal appellate court proceedings say that the winner is entitled to recover court costs (not lawyers' fees) from the loser in any lawsuit that reaches a federal appellate court.

On the basis of these rules, the Justice Department sought—and eventually won—an order from a federal appellate court requiring singer Joan Baez to pay $365 of the government's court costs in an FOIA appeal. Baez got about 1,500 pages of FBI records about her, but she sued to obtain additional files the government had kept secret. Although she lost, at first the appellate court refused to order her to pay the government's court costs. Then the court reconsidered and ruled that she had to pay (*Baez v. U.S. Justice Department*, 684 F.2d 999, 1982). This case was troubling to many civil libertarians, not because of the amount of money Baez was ordered to pay but because of the precedent it established.

Redactions. Still another problem encountered by those who use the FOIA is the legally sanctioned censoring of documents. The act permits agencies to delete portions of documents that fall within an exemption while releasing the remainder of the document. The result is sometimes a document with page after page of *"redactions"*—black or blank space, interrupted only by conjunctions and prepositions.

Perhaps the most serious FOIA problem of all is that the federal bureaucracy has made concerted efforts to weaken the FOIA time and again. Both the FBI and the CIA have lobbied Congress for a blanket exemption from the act. Citing the cost of complying with FOIA requests and alleged breaches of national security, some officials argued that public access rights should be sharply curtailed. In 1982 Congress restricted access to information involving the CIA by passing the Intelligence Identities Protection Act. That law made it a crime to engage in a "pattern of activities" with the "intent to identify and expose covert agents." The law was apparently aimed at former CIA agents who reveal agency secrets—a troubling instance of prior censorship in and of itself.

Glomarization. Congress never gave the FBI and CIA the blanket exemptions they wanted. However, in 1986 Congress authorized the FBI and other federal law enforcement agencies to reject FOIA requests without confirming or denying the existence of the requested documents. Previously, the FBI often had to disclose the existence of a document to justify not releasing it. That gave useful information to people who wanted to know if they were under FBI scrutiny. A *Glomar response* (or "Glomarization") is when an agency says it can neither confirm nor deny the existence of requested records. The name comes from a case in which the Central Intelligence Agency refused to confirm or deny ties to a submarine retrieval vessel named the Glomar Explorer, owned by Howard Hughes (*Phillippi v. CIA*, 546 F.2d 1009, 1976).

The Second Circuit allowed the National Security Agency to Glomarize seven requests from attorneys who were trying to determine whether their phone calls with clients in Guantánamo Bay detention had been intercepted. After establishing that the *Glomar* response has been adopted in other circuits (precedents in the First, Seventh, Ninth, and D.C. Circuits), the Second Circuit said that it was also acceptable in its jurisdiction and moreover, could be applied to the requests in the case (*Wilner v. Nat'l Security Agency*, 592 F.3d 60, 2009).

However, the FBI was *not* permitted to Glomarize in response to a death-row inmate's request for information that he claimed might exonerate him in four murders for which he was convicted (*Roth v. Dep't of Justice*, 642 F.3d 1161, 2011). In denying the agency's response, the D.C. Circuit said that the public had an interest in knowing if the FBI held information that could substantiate the inmate's claims and that any privacy issues that the men that the inmate claimed were responsible for the deaths were outweighed by that interest.

redact:
to edit or black out sensitive parts of a document before its release; for examples of redacted documents, visit The John Lennon FBI Files website at www. lennonfbifiles.com.

"High 2" and "Low 2" categories:
categories that were used by some appeals courts to determine the importance of information under Exception 2 of the FOIA, eliminated by the Supreme Court in 2011.

virtual representation:
a doctrine where a non-party may be bound to the judgment in a previous case if certain factors are met.

qui tam actions:
from the Latin phrase *qui tam pro domino rege quam pro se ipso in hac parte sequitur*, meaning "[he] who sues in this matter for the king as for himself"; an action brought by a private person on behalf of the government, and the person may be awarded some of the damages if they are found.

The D.C. Circuit also said that the CIA could *not* Glomarize records on unmanned aerial vehicles (drones) in *ACLU v. CIA* (710 F.3d 422, 2013). The court said that it was illogical to assume that drones did not exist because they had been discussed in the news by government officials: "[I]t is neither logical nor plausible for the CIA to maintain that it would reveal anything not already in the public domain to say that the agency 'at least has an intelligence interest' in such strikes." (See another decision on drones earlier in this chapter.)

False Claims Act. The Supreme Court also limited the use of FOIA in actions under the False Claims Act (FCA). The FCA is a federal law, similar to whistleblowing statutes, that allows non-government workers to file *qui tam* (on behalf of the government) actions against federal contractors, alleging wrongdoing by those contractors, with the possibility of recovering a percentage of any damages. The act bars claims "based upon the public disclosure of allegations or transactions in a criminal, civil, or administrative hearing, in a congressional, administrative, or Government Accounting Office report, hearing, audit, or investigation, or from the news media." The question before the Court in a 2011 case, *Schindler Elevator Corp. v. U.S. ex rel. Kirk* (563 U.S. 401), was this: "whether a federal agency's written response to a request for records under [FOIA] constitutes a 'report' within the meaning of the public disclosure bar." The Second Circuit said it didn't, but the Court said it does—thus saying that FOIA requests could not be used to support *qui tam* cases under the FCA.

Justice Clarence Thomas wrote for a 5-3 majority that the government provided "no principled way to define 'report' to exclude FOIA responses without excluding other documents that are indisputably reports." In dissent, Justice Ruth Bader Ginsburg, joined by Justices Sonia Sotomayor and Stephen Breyer, expressed concern about the effect on whistleblowers. She wrote that the Court's opinion "severely limits whistleblowers' ability to substantiate their allegations before commencing suit" and called on Congress to remedy that.

Records in databases. In today's digital information era, many FOIA requests seek information that is stored in electronic databases. Importantly, FOIA provides access to existing records only and does not require the government to create new records. How far can requesters go in asking the government to generate specific reports from those databases?

The Ninth Circuit Court of Appeals ruled in 2020 that a request for information from a government database did not necessarily create a "new record." The case, *Center for Investigative Reporting v. Dep't of Justice* (No. 18-17356, 9th Cir. 2020), involved a FOIA request for aggregate data about weapons used in crimes that were originally purchased by law enforcement. The government denied the request on two grounds: first, that another law prohibited disclosure of the information, and two, that the request required the government to generate a new record by running database queries. A district court ruled for the government, but the Ninth Circuit overturned. "(W)hether a search query of an existing database entails the creation of a 'new record' is a question of great importance in the digital age," the court wrote. "[I]f running a search across these databases necessarily amounts to the creation of a new record, much government information will become forever inaccessible under FOIA, a result plainly contrary to Congress's purpose in enacting FOIA." The court remanded the case to consider the technical details of the database searches necessary to respond to the request. "By recognizing that FOIA allows requesters to seek aggregate data from federal agencies, the court ensured that the transparency law remains an important tool for people to learn about government use and abuse of the data it collects," the Electronic Frontier Foundation said.

Despite all of these difficulties, the FOIA remains a valuable tool for information gathering. This law has opened millions of files to public scrutiny, files that otherwise would have remained secret indefinitely.

Executive Privilege

Ever since the days of George Washington and Thomas Jefferson, American presidents and others in the executive branch have asserted a right to withhold information from Congress and the courts under a concept called *executive privilege.* The legal foundation for executive privilege is vague; chief executives won the right to keep many of their working papers confidential because no one was really in a position to challenge that kind of secrecy.

Executive privilege has also been claimed by some executive officers of state and local governments. As it developed, the privilege generally covered not only military and diplomatic secrets but also many of the internal documents generated within the executive branch of government.

The executive orders issued by Presidents Harry Truman and Dwight D. Eisenhower in the 1950s to govern the rapidly growing national security classification system were justified by the concept of executive privilege. Those orders allowed military and diplomatic secrets to be classified on three levels: confidential, secret, and top secret. Only those who had been granted an appropriate security clearance were to be given access to this information.

As the national security classification system grew, it became a complicated bureaucratic operation that annually locked up millions of documents, as mentioned earlier. The Pentagon Papers case (discussed in Chapter Three) illustrates the problems in this area. The newspapers' editors felt the public should know about the conclusions reached in the Pentagon Papers. They believed these papers were classified not so much to protect national security as to conceal the diplomatic errors of several presidents and their administrations.

In resolving the case, the Supreme Court allowed the papers to be published but did not rule on the concept of executive privilege itself. The FOIA in effect recognized executive privilege by exempting two kinds of information that executive privilege had covered: matters affecting national security and the internal working documents of federal agencies.

Watergate. However, executive privilege was carried a step too far by the Nixon administration during the Watergate scandal, and the result was a U.S. Supreme Court decision that severely restricted its scope. As the scandal drifted nearer to the president himself, Nixon sought to invoke executive privilege to avoid releasing some incriminating tape recordings to a court. The tapes included a number of conversations between Nixon and his aides, and Nixon realized how damaging some of them would be if made public. The Watergate special prosecutor contended that the tapes were needed in the prosecution of several Nixon aides.

Nixon's refusal to release the tapes, which he justified by citing executive privilege, was challenged by the special prosecutor, and the case reached the Supreme Court. In the resulting 1974 decision (*U.S. v. Nixon*, 418 U.S. 683), the scope of executive privilege was drastically curtailed. In a unanimous decision, the Supreme Court ruled that executive privilege is absolute only in connection with military and diplomatic information that must be kept secret to protect national security. In other areas, the high court said, the privilege has to be balanced against other interests, such as the obligation of every citizen (including the president) to step forward with evidence of a crime that may be in his possession. Like the reporter's privilege, executive privilege has its limits.

The Supreme Court ordered the president to release the Watergate tapes. That, of course, accelerated the chain of events that led to Nixon's resignation from the presidency later in 1974. The tapes revealed ever more incriminating evidence that Nixon and his top aides had conspired to cover up crimes that were planned in the White House.

Thus, executive privilege is a less formidable justification for government secrecy today than it once was. However, these new limitations on executive privilege are of little help to the press and public, since the FOIA still exempts so much of the information that was once kept secret under the justification of executive privilege.

Nevertheless, some of the internal government information that was once hidden by executive privilege is now available at least to the courts. And when such information is presented as evidence in court, it may become a part of the public record. The problem of public access to court records is discussed later in this chapter; Chapter Seven discusses courtroom closures to protect confidentiality.

The 1974 Privacy Act

Journalists and civil libertarians—normally allies on First Amendment issues—are often on opposite sides of one of the most troubling problems in the freedom of information area. When the public's right to know and the individual's right to personal privacy conflict, the two groups often sharply disagree. Organizations such as the American Civil Liberties Union (ACLU) argue strongly for laws ensuring the secrecy of personal information collected by government agencies, even at the expense of journalists' access to information.

Congress attempted to deal with this problem by enacting the 1974 Privacy Act, the first comprehensive federal law intended to protect individuals from improper disclosure of personal information by government agencies. The Privacy Act was a response to the growing public alarm over the massive amount of personal information government agencies were placing in computerized data banks. Groups such as the ACLU argued that these data banks constituted a major threat to individual freedom. If the private information kept in these data banks were to fall into the wrong hands, flagrant abuses could occur. Journalists, on the other hand, feared that a strong privacy protection law would be misused by government officials as an excuse for needless secrecy. Bureaucrats could avoid public scrutiny of their own deeds (and misdeeds) in the name of protecting individual privacy.

As it was finally enacted, the 1974 Privacy Act (5 U.S.C. § 552a) represents something of a compromise. The act applies to all information contained in government record-keeping systems, placing strict limits on the manner in which the records are used. The act forbids federal agencies to release personal data from these record-keeping systems, or even transfer it to another federal agency without the permission of the person the information concerns.

The Privacy Act grants private individuals certain rights to inspect their own records in government data banks, with provisions allowing them to correct errors they discover. In addition, federal officials who improperly release personal records may be sued for damages, attorney's fees and court costs. The act includes a number of exemptions, allowing government agencies to release personal information without the affected person's permission for law enforcement purposes, for use by the Census Bureau and Congress itself, and for similar purposes. Significantly, the Privacy Act also allows the release of personal data that is defined as public information under the FOIA. The Privacy Act was written this way to minimize its effect on the FOIA.

Privacy Act versus FOIA. As it turned out, the Privacy Act generally created only minor problems for most journalists, but problems nonetheless. One of the exemptions to the FOIA excludes "personnel and medical files and similar files the disclosure of which would constitute a clearly unwarranted invasion of personal privacy." That language is broad enough to give federal officials considerable leeway in deciding what personal information they must release under the FOIA, and what they may withhold. Furthermore, the Privacy Act tends to discourage officials from releasing information in borderline cases because of the disparity between the consequences of violating the two laws. The FOIA allows those seeking information to sue officials who balk at releasing information, but only for attorney's fees and court costs. The Privacy Act, on the other hand, provides penalties for violations as well.

Thus, although the Privacy Act was written in such a way as to minimize restrictions on the release of information that would otherwise be accessible under the FOIA, it does discourage openness in some cases. An official who errs in the direction of disclosing too little information faces no monetary penalty and only a vague threat of disciplinary action under the FOIA; the official who errs in the direction of disclosing too much information faces monetary penalties under the Privacy Act.

Perhaps the most controversial data to which the Privacy Act provided personal access is the one maintained by the Federal Bureau of Investigation. One problem is that the FBI is often slow in releasing individual files, and when files are released they are often censored. (File censoring is permitted by the Privacy Act because these are, after all, law enforcement investigatory files.) Moreover, there are several exceptions that sometimes permit the FBI to refuse to disclose even the existence of personal records. But nonetheless, the act gives private persons their first opportunity to learn something about the records the FBI may be keeping on them. Note that the Privacy Act gives individuals a limited right to inspect *their own files*. The Supreme Court's 1989 decision in the *Reporters Cmte.* case held that the FBI has an across-the-board right to refuse to release files about individuals to *other persons*. That decision doesn't affect the right of an individual to seek access to a file that person owns.

In 1988, Congress strengthened the Privacy Act by passing the Computer Matching and Privacy Protection Act. This law governs the transfer of information between government agencies' computer databases. A great deal of this information is transferred from one agency to another to cross-check whether individuals are entitled to government assistance they may be receiving. This law added a verification requirement to prevent individuals from losing their benefits through misidentification and other data-handling errors. It also established Data Integrity Boards in many federal agencies to oversee the use of computerized data-matching programs.

The "Buckley Amendment" and the Clery Act

At the same time as the enactment of the 1974 Privacy Act and the 1974 amendments to the FOIA, Congress also approved the "Buckley Amendment," more formally known as the Family Education Rights and Privacy Act (20 U.S.C. 1232g). That federal law, which is sometimes identified by its initials (FERPA), is often confused with the more general 1974 Privacy Act, and in fact the two have similar provisions. The Buckley Amendment was so named because Sen. James Buckley of New York led the effort to add it to the 1974 Elementary and Secondary Education Act amendments, a major federal-aid-to-education bill.

The Buckley Amendment gives parents the right to see their children's school records and forbids the release of these school records to outside parties without the parents' consent. Similarly, it allows students over age 18 to see their own school records, and requires their consent before these records may be released to outside parties. School systems that fail to obey the Buckley Amendment may be denied federal funds. In 2002 the U.S. Supreme Court made it clear that the denial of federal funds is usually the sole remedy for non-compliance: students cannot use the Buckley Amendment to sue schools that divulge their personal information (*Gonzaga University v. Doe*, 536 U.S. 273). The Supreme Court also clarified another aspect of the Buckley Amendment in 2002, ruling that it does not preclude such everyday classroom practices as having students grade each others' quizzes (*Owasso Independent School District v. Falvo*, 534 U.S. 426). The court said the law was intended by Congress only to cover permanent records maintained by teachers and other school employees.

The Buckley Amendment has had some impact on the newsgathering activities of the media, at times in absurd ways. Overzealous school officials have sometimes used it as an excuse to withhold newsworthy and non-sensitive information about students involved in athletics or other newsworthy extracurricular activities. But perhaps the Buckley Amendment's most serious effect on newsgathering has been to increase the secrecy of school disciplinary records. That has sometimes made it difficult to report on newsworthy disciplinary actions, such as those involving student athletes or political activists. Fearful of losing federal money, school officials have tended to avoid risking any appearance of non-compliance with the Buckley Amendment.

Buckley and Clery on campus. Campus newspapers are sometimes accused of violating the Buckley Amendment by reporting on the academic eligibility of student athletes and government officers, who are usually required to maintain certain grades to be eligible for their positions. College administrators responsible for making sure that student officers and athletes are eligible are not always diligent in checking grade records. Investigative journalists may learn that a particular student leader is academically ineligible—and publish that newsworthy fact. That inevitably brings charges that the campus newspaper has violated the Buckley Amendment by revealing student grades, which are supposed to be confidential.

Controversies of this type have occurred at many colleges—almost invariably because college officials do not understand what the Buckley Amendment really does and doesn't say. The Buckley Amendment says schools that have *ongoing policies* of not keeping grades confidential *are ineligible for federal funds*. It does *not* forbid student newspapers to publish student leaders' grades to prove that they are academically ineligible. Nor does it say that a college could lose its federal funds just because the campus newspaper reveals a few student leaders' grades in a clearly newsworthy story about their fitness to serve.

Campus officials often cite the Buckley Amendment as a basis for keeping reports of campus crimes secret. However, there has been a national movement in recent years to force officials to reveal campus crime rates and in some cases information about specific crimes.

In 1990, Congress enacted the Crime Awareness and Campus Security Act, requiring all colleges and universities receiving federal funds to issue annual reports of crime statistics as well as descriptions of security arrangements. The law requires the use of uniform crime reporting procedures so that students and their families can compare the crime rates at different institutions as a factor in choosing a college. It does not require campuses to open their police records to the press, however. This campus crime law is now officially known as the Jeanne Clery Disclosure of Campus Security Policy and Campus Crime Statistics Act. It is named in memory of a Lehigh University student who was unaware of recent crimes on her campus and who left her security door propped open, enabling an intruder to enter her room and murder her. Reports of campus crime that are filed as required by this law are sometimes called Clery Act reports.

Congress also revised the Buckley Amendment to declare that "law enforcement unit" records on college campuses are not "educational records" that must be kept confidential. However, this revision of the Buckley Amendment stopped short of requiring campus officials to make information about specific crimes public. It merely declared that the Buckley Amendment does not require such information to be kept secret.

The 1990 Congressional action did not settle the matter, however. On many campuses, administrators continued to cite the Buckley Amendment as a basis for keeping campus records concerning specific crimes and court proceedings confidential.

Initially, several courts responded by ruling that the Buckley Amendment cannot be used to justify keeping campus crime records secret if they are supposed to be open under state law. For example, a federal judge so ruled in a pioneering lawsuit filed by Traci Bauer, editor of the Southwest Missouri University *Standard*, to compel the administration to open these records (*Bauer v. Kincaid*, 759 F. Supp. 575, 1991).

Soon other student editors filed similar lawsuits to force administrators to disclose campus crime or court information under state freedom of information laws. By 1997, both the Ohio and Georgia Supreme Courts had ruled that campus officials had to release information about campus crimes or court proceedings in spite of the Buckley Amendment (see *The Miami Student v. Miami University*, 680 N.E.2d 956, 1997; and *Red & Black Publishing Co. v. Board of Regents of the University of Georgia*, 427 S.E.2d 257, 1993). Both courts concluded that the Buckley Amendment does not apply to campus crime and court records. Note that these cases did not create any new legal right of access to university crime and court records; that is governed by state FoI laws. But if such records would otherwise be public under the applicable state law, these courts held that the Buckley Amendment does not override state laws and transform crime records into "educational records."

Congress entered this controversy by adding language to the 1998 reauthorization of the Higher Education Act declaring more emphatically that the Buckley Amendment cannot be used to justify secrecy about violent crimes and certain other crimes committed on campus. If this information would otherwise be made public (under a state open record law, for example), Congress declared that the Buckley Amendment does not change that.

Perhaps more important, the 1998 version of the Higher Education Act also included language requiring all colleges and universities receiving federal funds (including private schools with federally insured student loans) to create and maintain a log of criminal incidents reported to campus police or security departments—and make this log public. This log must include the nature, date, time,

Focus on...
FERPA

In June 2009 the *Columbus Dispatch* ran a story that began: "Across the country, many major-college athletic departments keep their NCAA troubles secret behind a thick veil of black ink or Wite-Out."

The *Dispatch* undertook a six-month investigation of public records requests to college athletic departments all over the nation. Their findings suggested that schools use FERPA to keep much more information private than just transcripts. Among the findings:

* Florida blacked out "nearly every word" of NCAA violations involving its football and basketball teams, but not those about other sports.

* Kentucky did not identify any of the men's basketball players who ate free at a booster's restaurant.

* Nebraska, Nevada and West Virginia refused to release any documents on NCAA violations.

general location and disposition of each complaint. The log must be made public within two business days, and new information that is later discovered about an incident must be added to the log and made public within two business days. There is an exception for information that would identify a victim or jeopardize an ongoing investigation. The 1998 law also strengthened the requirements in the legislation that colleges and universities must publish an annual report of campus crime statistics.

Unfortunately for the student press, that's not the end of the story. In 1998, the U.S. Department of Education filed a lawsuit in federal court to override the Ohio Supreme Court decision and force university officials in Ohio to keep campus crime information secret when an offense is handled through campus disciplinary proceedings. In 2002, the Sixth Circuit upheld an injunction, ruling that the Buckley Amendment requires campus disciplinary records and proceedings to be confidential (*U.S. v. Miami University*, 294 F.3d 797). This decision did not affect the requirement that *all* colleges and universities disclose general information about campus crimes as well as the police log, but it did uphold the rule that campus disciplinary proceedings are confidential under the Buckley Amendment. Inasmuch as they are confidential under the Buckley Amendment, that also makes them confidential under the Ohio Public Records Act because that law exempts from disclosure anything that is secret under another state or federal law, the court concluded.

The Student Press Law Center has a detailed report for journalists about covering campus crime available on its website (www.splc.org).

The Federal Advisory Committee Act

Congress enacted the Federal Advisory Committee Act (FACA) in 1972 to try to control the growing use of secret advisory committees by the executive branch of government. It requires various non-government organizations that give advice to the government to hold open meetings and maintain public records. It covers a variety of advisory bodies—entities that include one or more persons who are *not* federal "officers" or "employees" and that give advice to the president or an agency in the executive branch of the federal government.

However, FACA's usefulness was limited by a 1989 Supreme Court decision, *Public Citizen v. Dept. of Justice* (491 U.S. 440). The Court ruled that Congress did not intend for the act to cover privately funded bodies such as the American Bar Association committee that reviews the qualifications of prospective federal judges. Thus, the ABA panel can continue to meet in secret and maintain secret records when it evaluates potential judges (including possible Supreme Court justices). The decision also means that many other private groups may meet secretly and make recommendations to government officials. The Court did not overturn the act itself, but by ruling that the act does not apply to the ABA panel it opened the way for other groups to claim that they are exempt from the act's open-meeting and open-record provisions. This could curtail the public's right to know about many advisory group recommendations that shape federal government policy.

A highly publicized FACA case arose in 1993, when President Bill Clinton established a President's Task Force on National Health Care Reform and named his wife, Hillary Rodham Clinton, to head it. The Task Force, which almost always met in secret, consisted entirely of senior government officials—except for the First Lady, who held no official government position (nor could she, under the Anti-Nepotism Act, the law forbidding federal officials to appoint close relatives to government positions). In *Assoc. of American Physicians & Surgeons v. Hillary Rodham Clinton* (997 F.2d 898), a federal appellate court said that the task force

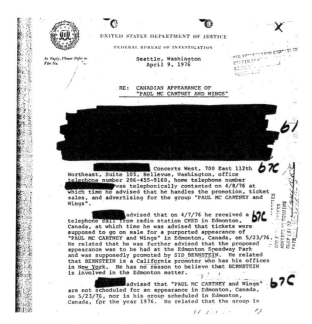

FIG. 83.
Partial page from the FBI FOIA online reading room, showing redaction of information about a Paul McCartney and Wings concert in Edmonton, Canada in May 1976.

Federal Bureau of Investigation FOIA Reading Room, full file available at http://vault.fbi. gov/The%20Beatles/The%20 Beatles%20Part%204%20 of%209/view (it's page 5).

was not subject to FACA—and thus not required to hold open meetings. The key issue was Hillary Rodham Clinton's status. If she did not qualify as a full-time federal "officer" or "employee," then FACA would apply to the task force (because one of its members would have been a private citizen, not a government official). But the court traced the history and status of "first ladies" and concluded that the first lady was the equivalent of a federal "officer" or "employee" even though she could not be paid or hold any official position while married to the president. As a result, her task force was not a private advisory body subject to FACA, the court held. Therefore, it could meet in secret.

President Barack Obama has also had at least one FACA case against him: *Freedom Watch, Inc. v. Obama* (859 F. Supp. 2d 169, 2012). Freedom Watch had alleged that the president violated FACA by failing to make available documents from the Health Reform De Facto Advisory Committee, a committee that Freedom Watch said was governed by FACA. While an earlier case found that the committee did qualify under FACA as an advisory committee, a federal judge said the fact that the committee no longer meets means that the case is moot.

Criminal History Information

For many working journalists, another serious obstacle in gathering information has been the effect of state and federal privacy laws on access to information about persons accused of crimes. In 1976, the federal Law Enforcement Assistance Administration (LEAA, which was abolished in 1982) issued a controversial set of guidelines intended to restrict the release of personal information by law enforcement agencies. The guidelines required state and local police agencies receiving federal aid to develop policies governing the release of information about persons arrested or charged with crimes. In their final form, the guidelines did not specifically tell local police agencies what their information policies had to be, but they did require them to develop consistent policies.

As a result of the LEAA recommendations, some law enforcement agencies stopped releasing criminal history information to the press. Even current police blotter information that had traditionally been available was sometimes denied to the press. In many states, all records of arrests that do not lead to convictions—and even some records of arrests that do lead to convictions—are now sealed or simply destroyed. At least 47 states restrict access to criminal history "rap sheets" under some circumstances. (FBI rap sheets were addressed by the *Reporters Committee* case discussed earlier.)

Information-seeking journalists and open government advocates often disagree with civil liberties groups about this issue. Civil libertarians argue that a person should not be permanently stigmatized by public access to his or her police arrest record, particularly if the arrest does not lead to a conviction. When a record of an arrest has been legally *expunged* (erased), ACLU leaders are particularly emphatic in their contention that making information about it public is an injustice. Many journalists, meanwhile, feel that while closing these records does protect individual privacy, it also allows abuses by law enforcement agencies. To support that assertion, they cite the dangers to civil liberties inherent in secret arrests and police activities. Also, they argue that society needs protection from persons with criminal records, citing instances when privacy laws prevented employers from discovering employees' criminal records, so that ex-convicts were placed where they could commit similar crimes again.

This ongoing conflict will not soon be resolved. As Chapter Seven points out, there has been a long-term trend away from easy access to information about criminal suspects' past deeds, a trend prompted by the fair trial-free press dilemma at least as much as by the concern for personal privacy.

Federal Driver's Privacy Protection Act

With little debate or even publicity in the news media, Congress passed a law in 1994 that significantly curtailed access to motor vehicle registration records and driving records. The federal Driver's Privacy Protection Act (DPPA) was enacted as a part of the omnibus 1994 anti-crime bill. This law requires every state to close its motor vehicle registration and driving records to the press and public, although there is an exception allowing insurance companies and private investigators, among others, to retain access to these records. Any state may pass legislation to opt out of the across-the-board federal secrecy requirements as long as individuals may arrange to have their own records kept confidential.

The DPPA was enacted as a public safety measure. To justify the bill, Congress cited the 1989 murder of actress Rebecca Shaeffer by a fan. The fan obtained her address from a private investigator who had access to California Dept. of Motor Vehicles records. However, journalists who opposed the bill pointed out that this rationale makes no sense: private investigators are exempt from the new secrecy requirements.

To journalists, the DPPA represents the loss of a powerful investigative tool. Columnist Dan Lynch of the *Albany Times Union* pointed to numerous important stories developed by reporters using motor vehicle and driving records. For example, the media have checked driving records to learn that some airline pilots and the captain of the Exxon Valdez (the tanker that ran aground, causing a disastrous Alaskan oil spill), among others, had drunk driving convictions and should not have been placed in jobs where they could endanger public safety. Several states challenged Congress' authority to tell them how to handle driving records, but in 2000 the U.S. Supreme Court upheld this controversial law.

Ruling in *Reno v. Condon* (528 U.S. 141), the Court upheld the right of Congress to use the Commerce Clause of the U.S. Constitution as a basis for requiring the states to keep these records secret. The Court unanimously deviated from a recent pattern of overturning federal laws regulating conduct by the states. This time, the Court held that the principles of federalism were not violated by an act of Congress. The justice concluded that selling driver's license information to advertisers and insurers, which a number of states did, was commercial activity that could be regulated under the Commerce Clause, reversing a decision by the Fourth Circuit, which upheld a challenge to the DPPA by South Carolina.

Even companies "stockpiling" driver data for future use is acceptable under DPPA, said the Eighth Circuit in 2011 in *Cook v. ACS State & Local Solutions, Inc.* (663 F.3d 989). Janice Cook, a Missouri driver, brought suit against several businesses who had obtained information under DPPA, and Cook alleged that the lack of immediate use of the data by these companies violated the DPPA. In denying the claim, the court said that DPPA "only requires that the information be obtained for a permissible purpose" and no mention was made in the law about when the information must be used.

The Supreme Court heard a challenge to an exception in the act in 2013. Ruling in *Maracich v. Spears* (570 U.S. 48), the justices said that the DPPA prohibits the use of certain data from state drivers' databases to solicit clients; the "litigation exception" does not apply to these uses. Justice Anthony Kennedy, writing for a 5-4 majority, said that if the exception "were read to permit disclosure of personal information whenever any connection between the protected information and a potential legal dispute could be shown, it would undermine in a substantial way the DPPA's purpose of protecting an individual's right to privacy in his or her motor vehicle records."

■ FEDERAL OPEN MEETING LEGISLATION

Another aspect of the struggle for freedom of information involves access to the meetings of government agencies. This is one of the oldest and most difficult information-gathering problems encountered by journalists. In theory, all public agencies should conduct the public's business openly, with citizens invited to listen in. But in practice many public officials find it tempting to make their decisions behind closed doors, announcing them in carefully worded press releases afterward. Obviously, if the press is to serve as a watchdog on behalf of the public, reporters must have a right to attend the meetings where public officials make their important decisions. To ensure this right, journalists have campaigned for open-meeting laws for many years—with some success.

Government in the Sunshine Act. In fact, at least 46 states already had open-meeting laws before Congress finally enacted such a law in 1976. That 1976 federal law, the Government in the Sunshine Act (5 U.S.C. 552b), requires about 50 administrative agencies to conduct some of their meetings in public. The policy-making boards and commissions of these agencies must meet at announced times and places, with the public generally invited to attend. However, closed sessions are still permitted for 10 different reasons; the legal officer of the agency must specify the basis for each closed meeting.

The first nine grounds for secret meetings closely parallel the nine FOIA exemptions, listed earlier in this chapter. They include such things as matters affecting national security, personnel matters, law enforcement investigations, discussions of trade secrets, and the like. The tenth subject that may be discussed in a closed meeting is pending litigation and similar adjudicatory matters. Whatever the reason for a closed meeting, the board or commission must vote to close a meeting before the public may be excluded, and the vote must be recorded. The agency must then keep accurate and complete records of what goes on during the closed meeting. That record must be either a verbatim transcript or a tape recording of all proceedings. In some instances, detailed minutes are permitted instead.

When an agency holds a closed meeting, it must quickly publish the results of any votes, including a record of how each commissioner or board member voted.

Any person may initiate a lawsuit against an agency that appears to be violating the Government in the Sunshine Act, and federal district courts are authorized to issue injunctions ordering federal agencies to comply with the law. When a complaining party wins such a lawsuit, the federal court is authorized to require the federal government to pay his or her attorney's fees and court costs. However, the act contains no civil or criminal penalties for government officials who violate its provisions. In addition, the law specifically orders federal courts not to invalidate actions taken by agencies during illegal secret meetings. Thus, the federal open meeting law has virtually no "teeth" in it. As we shall see shortly, it is much weaker than many state open meeting laws in this respect.

Another major loophole in the Government in the Sunshine Act is that it does *not* prohibit government agencies from making major decisions by circulating private policy memoranda among commissioners. Some federal agencies decide many important matters by circulating memos and then merely announce their decisions at open meetings, which may occur only once a month or, in some instances, even less frequently. The Nuclear Regulatory Commission (NRC) and the Equal Employment Opportunity Commission (EEOC) have both been accused of using such tactics to evade the spirit of the Sunshine Act.

The act covers a number of well-known agencies in addition to the NRC and EEOC, including the Federal Communications Commission, Federal Trade Commission, Interstate Commerce Commission, Consumer Product Safety Commission, National Transportation Safety Board, Civil Service Commission, Securities and Exchange Commission, U.S. Postal Service board of governors, and Federal Reserve Board. The act applies to the central policy-making board of these agencies but not to local or national staff meetings, even if those meetings involve important policy matters. Nor does it apply to cabinet-level departments or to some advisory bodies closest to the presidency, such as the National Security Council.

Limitations. The Government in the Sunshine Act excludes most informal gatherings and unofficial meetings held by members of federal boards and commissions. In a 1984 decision, the U.S. Supreme Court ruled that it was proper for a majority of the members of the Federal Communications Commission to meet in private with communications leaders from other countries at an international conference. The Court said the gathering in question was not a "meeting" and the international body itself was not an "agency" within the meaning of the law (*FCC v. ITT World Communications*, 466 U.S. 463).

In short, the federal open meeting law leaves much to be desired. It allows closed meetings for a wide variety of dubious reasons. Moreover, its enforcement provisions are notably weak, and it fails to cover many of the federal bodies that make the most important decisions. Nevertheless, it is a first step toward openness in the gigantic federal bureaucracy, a bureaucracy that once felt it had an absolute right to do the public's business in private without interference from meddlesome reporters or private citizens.

■ STATE OPEN MEETING AND PUBLIC RECORD LAWS

Although the federal FOIA and Government in the Sunshine Act are important, most journalists find their own state FoI laws even more relevant than the federal laws. On a daily basis, thousands of journalists rely on state open meeting and public record laws to provide access to many of their most important news sources.

But while state public record and open meeting laws are of paramount importance to many journalists, they vary enough that summarizing all of them in a national textbook isn't feasible. There are dozens of such cases annually. An online search will often lead to a website that summarizes the open meeting and public record laws of a particular state. The website of the Reporters Committee for Freedom of the Press (www.rcfp.org) is a good place to start. Its "Open Government Guide," available online, is searchable by state. Most state open meeting and public record laws resemble the federal laws in some respects.

State Open Meeting Laws

Many state open meeting laws were extensively revised in the late 1960s and 1970s—the era when the federal laws were enacted—and many new state laws were approved then, too. State open meeting laws typically apply to the agencies of both state and local government. Most require state boards and commissions, city councils, school boards and county governing boards to hold open meetings at regularly announced times and places. Any person is permitted to attend most of these open meetings, although some state laws have provisions authorizing public officials to remove anyone who creates a disturbance.

Virtually all state open meeting laws provide for closed or "executive" sessions. Most state laws spell out the circumstances under which these closed sessions are permitted, authorizing private meetings for matters affecting national security, personnel matters, discussions of pending lawsuits and usually various other subjects. Some states allow closed meetings for only a few reasons, while others allow them for many more.

An increasing number of state open meeting laws provide legal remedies for violations, allowing any citizen to sue the offending government body for an injunction to halt further illegal secret meetings. In addition, many state open meeting laws authorize the courts to invalidate actions taken at unlawful closed meetings, a provision the federal Government in the Sunshine Act lacks. Such provisions are important, because the possibility of having a major action overturned in court is a strong deterrent to holding secret meetings.

Another provision missing in the federal law—but present in many state open meeting laws—is criminal sanctions for knowing violations. In many states it is a misdemeanor for government officials to participate in a closed meeting if they know the subject at hand should be discussed only during an open meeting. However, criminal prosecutions remain rare because it is difficult to prove that a government body actually discussed an illegal subject behind closed doors and that the officials involved knew they were violating the law.

In some states, there is a state-level freedom of information commission that serves as a watchdog agency, enforcing the open meeting and public record laws. Other states have similar commissions, but without enforcement powers. And in others, enforcement is in the hands of the attorney general or local prosecuting attorneys. In some states—Ohio, for example—the courts can remove officials from office for violating the open meeting laws.

State Public Record Laws

All 50 states have public record laws, but they vary greatly. Most states define the term "public records" broadly to encompass many documents maintained by agencies of state and local government. And most such laws allow general public access without requiring that the person inquiring demonstrate any special interest or "need to know."

State public record laws consistently exempt certain kinds of records from public disclosure, most often personnel records, law enforcement investigatory records, and records of juvenile courts, adoptions, parole matters, etc.

Most state public record laws specifically provide for judicial review in instances where public access is denied, and about two-thirds of the states provide criminal sanctions for officials who improperly deny public access. About one-third of the states require government agencies to pay the attorneys' fees of those who successfully sue for access to public records.

In all 50 states the comprehensive public record laws supplement other provisions for public access to government records. Long before it was fashionable to enact comprehensive open records legislation, various records were open to the public under the common law, and many of these miscellaneous common law provisions for public access have also been codified. Records that were traditionally open under the common law include records of the ownership of private land, birth, marriage and death records, and various court records.

In some instances, lawmaking in this area has occurred by vote of the people. For example, the people of Washington State enacted a public record law by popular vote in 1972. In 1992, Florida voters approved a constitutional amendment creating a constitutional right of access to public records and meetings in the Florida Constitution. In 2002, Floridians voted three-to-one in favor of a constitutional amendment to strengthen this provision, requiring a two-thirds vote of the state legislature to create new exceptions to the Florida FoI laws. This came just after the state legislature created a new exception to the state's Public Records Act, exempting autopsy photographs from public disclosure.

In 2004, California voters approved a constitutional amendment that reaffirmed the state's open meeting and public records laws and wrote the right of public access into the state constitution. The amendment, approved by 83% of the voters, declared that the state's sunshine laws "shall be broadly construed" when they further "the people's right of access" and "narrowly construed" when they limit access. Almost immediately Gov. Arnold Schwarzenegger and 10 other state officials made their appointment calendars public.

As on the federal level, state public record laws have had to be reconciled with privacy laws. Most states have privacy statutes that limit public access to personal information in state databases. These laws, sometimes given euphemistic titles such as "Information Practices Act," usually forbid state officials to release personal information without the individual's permission. Some of them go much further than the federal Privacy Act in sealing records that would otherwise be open under public records laws.

Court Cases on State Laws

Commercial uses. In 1999, the U.S. Supreme Court ruled on a case concerning access to public records under state law. In *Los Angeles Police Dept. v. United Reporting Publ'g Co.* (528 U.S. 32), the Court upheld a provision of the California Public Records Act forbidding the release of addresses of crime victims and persons arrested for a crime for commercial use. The Court upheld California's right to release these addresses to noncommercial users while denying them to lawyers, insurance companies, drug counselors, driving schools, and others who might use the information commercially. A provision of the California law requires law enforcement agencies to release such information to journalists, scholars, and politicians, among others, while denying it to commercial users. The Court pointed out that a state is under no obligation to release such information to *anyone*, much less to *everyone*. The Court seemed deeply divided over the rationale for this decision, although the 7-2 majority said the state law was not invalid on its face. However, it seemed to be inviting a future legal challenge based on the argument that the law is invalid as applied to companies such as United Reporting by denying them equal protection of the law.

Petition signers. The Supreme Court ruled on another state open records law in 2010, holding that petition signers don't have a constitutional right to keep their identities private, and state open record laws treating those signatures as public records are valid. In *Doe v. Reed* (561 U.S. 186), the Court said, "Disclosure of referendum petitions does not as a general matter violate the First Amendment." Washington passed a law that expanded the rights of registered domestic partners, include same-sex partners. A political committee, Protect Marriage Washington, gathered petition signatures to place a referendum on the ballot challenging the domestic partnership law. Another group invoked the Washington Public Records Act (PRA) to obtain copies of the petition, which contained signers' personal information. Chief Justice John Roberts wrote for an 8-1 Court. He applied "exacting scrutiny" to the PRA challenge, which "requires a 'substantial relation' between the disclosure requirement and a 'sufficiently important' governmental interest." The state has an interest in combating election fraud and providing information to the electorate, and Roberts said that citizen participation in the verification process was related to the interest. He also said that Protect Marriage Washington had not offered sufficient evidence that they would suffer harm if the information was disclosed; the organization had only offered concerns about what *might* happen. Roberts also noted that "the PRA is not a prohibition on speech, but instead a *disclosure* requirement." No one is being forced not to speak by the PRA. The Supreme Court left open the option for Protect Marriage Washington to file an "as-applied" challenge, which it did, on First Amendment grounds, and lost. A district court dissolved the injunction keeping the names private, and they were made available and are searchable online. The Ninth Circuit dismissed as moot the appeal in 2012 because the records were already public (*Doe v. Reed*, 697 F.3d 1235).

Limitations to state residents. In 2013, the Court also unanimously held that a provision in the Virginia freedom of information law making state records only open to residents was constitutional (*McBurney v. Young*, 569 U.S. 221). Justice Samuel Alito wrote that the Virginia law "provides a service that is related to state citizenship," and that the petitioners, residents of California and Rhode Island, did not have their rights violated when the state declined their request. Moreover, there was no Commerce Clause violation because the law "does not regulate commerce in any meaningful sense."

Private email accounts. Lawsuits are filed in many states seeking public access to government officials' emails and text messages under state freedom of information laws. Some government officials claim they do not use email in their official capacities. Others say they delete all emails daily or weekly and insist that there are no archived backup copies on their government-sponsored servers. In many states government officials' email messages, like their "snail-mail" correspondence, are public records unless the subject matter falls within a specific exemption.

Following similar rulings in 11 other states, the California Supreme Court unanimously ruled in March 2017 that the state public records laws apply to public business conducted on private accounts of public officials. In *City of San Jose v. Superior Court* (2 Cal. 5th 608, 2017), the state court ruled that communications of public officials on private devices are public records if "relate in some substantive way to the conduct of the public's business." The case involved a public records request filed by a lawyer and community activist about a redevelopment project in San Jose, which argued that communications on private devices were not government records under the law. But given the ways in which people use different devices to conduct business, a ruling in the city's favor would have only encouraged public officials and employees to use private devices and accounts to avoid having to respond to public records requests. "A city employee's communications related to the conduct of public business do not cease to be public records just because they were sent or received using a personal account," wrote Justice Carol A. Corrigan.

■ ACCESS TO OTHER PLACES AND PROCEEDINGS

Having a strong public records or open meeting statute solves some of a journalist's information-gathering problems, but in a number of circumstances these laws are of little help. For instance, public records laws rarely govern the release of court records, and open meeting laws do not guarantee access to either the courts or the scene of a news event. These laws are of little value when a journalist needs to cross police lines to reach the scene of a disaster. Nor are they of any assistance when a journalist wishes to cover a controversial criminal trial or visit a prison where inmates are allegedly mistreated.

Access to prisons. In the absence of a statutory law assuring journalists access to these places and proceedings, is there any constitutional right of access to the news? In several cases involving access to prisons, the U.S. Supreme Court has said there is no such right.

The high court decided two such cases, *Saxbe v. Washington Post* (417 U.S. 843) and *Pell v. Procunier* (417 U.S. 817), the same day in 1974. The Court said prison rules against interviewing individual prison inmates were not a violation of the First Amendment. The *Pell* case arose in California when a policy that gave journalists freedom to interview specific prisoners was eliminated. That happened after an escape attempt in which several persons were killed. Thereafter, the media were only allowed to interview inmates selected more or less at random, not the inmates they wished to interview. Prison officials contended that media interviews had made celebrities of certain prisoners and helped provoke the escape attempt. The *Saxbe* case challenged federal rules that prohibited media interviews with inmates. The Court said these rules do not violate the constitutional rights of journalists since journalists have no special right of access to prisons. The justices said neither journalists nor ordinary citizens have a right to freely visit prisons and interview inmates.

However, lower federal courts in California tried to avoid following this precedent, and the result was another Supreme Court ruling on prison access in 1978, *Houchins v. KQED* (438 U.S. 1). In that case, TV journalists wanted to visit a portion of a jail where an inmate had committed suicide, a place where a psychiatrist said conditions were so bad that inmates could suffer psychological damage. Jail authorities denied access to the reporters, and the reporters sued, contending that prison conditions were a matter of legitimate public concern. A federal district court agreed, ordering authorities to let journalists see and photograph the controversial area of the jail.

The Ninth Circuit affirmed the decision, but the Court reversed. Writing for the majority, Chief Justice Warren Burger reiterated the Court's view that journalists have no constitutional right of access to prisons. He acknowledged that prison conditions are a matter of public concern, but he said, in effect, that the subject is none of the media's business: "The media are not a substitute for or an adjunct of government, and like the courts, they are ill-equipped to deal with the problems of prison administration." Burger said that if journalists wanted to find out about prison conditions, they should interview former inmates, prisoners' lawyers, prison visitors, and public officials.

The *Houchins* decision was alarming enough, but a year later the Supreme Court handed down *Gannett v. DePasquale* (discussed in Chapter Seven), allowing even pretrial courtroom proceedings to be closed to the press and public. But during the 1980s the Court backed away from these denials of First Amendment protection for newsgathering activities. As noted in Chapter Seven, in *Richmond Newspapers v. Virginia* (the landmark 1980 decision holding that closed trials are not ordinarily permitted by the Constitution), the majority opinion included language suggesting that the Court recognized a First Amendment right to gather news. In a concurring opinion in the *Richmond Newspapers* case, Justice John Paul Stevens put it strongly: "Until today the court has accorded virtually absolute protection to the dissemination of ideas, but never before has it squarely held that the acquisition of news-worthy matter is entitled to any constitutional protection whatsoever." However, the majority opinion was somewhat less enthusiastic here than Justice Stevens, and subsequent decisions have not extended the concept far beyond its original application (access to courtrooms).

The *en banc* Seventh Circuit upheld a ban on death row interviews requested by prison-ers in *Hammer v. Ashcroft* (570 F.3d 798, 2009). Based on *Pell,* Judge Frank Easterbrook said that "the Bureau of Prisons could enforce a system-wide rule against personal or video inter-views between prisoners and reporters"—even when, as here, it is the *prisoner* requesting the interview, not a member of the media. Dissenters claimed that the majority "concludes with the astonishing proposition that the government may limit a prisoner's access to the media based on its distaste for the anticipated content of the prisoner's speech."

Covering executions. As more and more states resumed capital punishment, this contro-versy grew—and ended up in court. In the late 1990s and 2000s, the Ninth Circuit upheld, and then overturned, a prison warden's restrictions on the viewing of executions in Califor-nia. The court initially ruled that journalists have no special right to view an execution, and these restrictions were reasonable (*California First Amendment Coalition v. Calderon*, 138 F.3d 1298, 1998). Then, in *California First Amendment Coalition v. Woodford* (299 F.3d 868, 2002), the court rejected the contention of prison officials that witnesses should not be allowed to see guards or medical technicians prepare the inmate for the lethal injection to protect them from threats or acts of violence.

The Ninth Circuit in 2012 scolded Idaho for failing to bring its execution rules into line in *Assoc. Press v. Otter* (682 F.3d 821). Saying that the state "has had ample opportunity for the past decade to adopt an execution procedure that reflects this settled law," the court rejected all arguments the state offered to override the First Amendment presumption for the media to view executions in their entirety.

Journalists in Pennsylvania now have a greater right to see executions, after the *Phila-delphia Inquirer* and the (Harrisburg) *Patriot-News* won their 2012 suit (*Philadelphia Inquirer v. Wetzel*, 906 F. Supp. 2d 362) arguing to see two entire lethal-injection executions. The news-papers claimed the need to be able to observe and verify the process. Echoing the decision in the Ninth Circuit, the judge said, "[H]istorical practice in Pennsylvania indicates that the public and press have traditionally enjoyed a right of access to executions. Even after Penn-sylvania abolished public hangings [on April 10, 1834], witnesses were still invited to view the entirety of the hanging."

Access to press credentials. May authorities play favorites among journalists without violating the First Amendment? A federal appellate court ruled on this question involving the granting of White House press credentials. In that case (*Sherrill v. Knight*, 569 F.2d 124, 1978), the Secret Service had denied press credentials to two "underground" newspaper reporters on the grounds that they had been convicted of crimes. The court refused to accept the Secret Service's argument that it had complete discretion in granting or denying White House press credentials; the agency had to establish procedures for granting press passes. Reporters must be told the reason for any denial and given an opportunity to reply.

Courts overturn Trump ban of White House reporters. The *Sherrill* decision served as an important precedent in two cases in which President Donald Trump restricted the press credentials of White House correspondents. The reporters had their access restored only after filing federal lawsuits.

In 2018, the White House denied CNN reporter Jim Acosta access to White House grounds after he asked questions at a press conference the president did not like. CNN quickly filed a lawsuit in federal court claiming the actions violated the First Amendment. In *CNN v. Trump* (No. 1:18-cv-02610-TJK), U.S. District Court Judge Timothy J. Kelly issued a preliminary ruling, ordering the Trump administration to restore Acosta's credentials, ruling that the denial was likely a violation of Acosta's due process rights. CNN dropped its lawsuit after the White House restored Acosta's access rights and issued new guidelines for reporters actions during press conferences.

In 2019, the Trump administration lost another legal battle over its suspension of a White House press pass. The Trump administration suspended the credentials of Brian Karem, who worked as a correspondent for *Playboy* magazine, after he got into a dispute with former Trump aide Sebastian Gorka at an event outside the White House. Karem sued, and a federal district court in Washington D.C., in *Karem v. Trump* (404 F. Supp. 3d 203, 2019) granted Karem's motion for a preliminary injunction ordering Karem's press pass be restored. The judge said the ban was not based on a fair notice of standards of professional behavior and therefore violated Karem's due process rights as a journalist. The Trump administration appealed the preliminary injunction. The Reporters Committee for Freedom of the Press and 44 media organizations filed an *amicus curiae* ("friend of the court") brief with the Court of Appeals for the District of Columbia Circuit in support of Karem. In June 2020, the appeals court upheld the district court's decision granting the preliminary injunction in Karem's favor (*Karem v. Trump*, 960 F.3d 656, 2020). The appeals court embraced the *Sherrill* decision, ruling that credentialed journalists have a First Amendment interest in their press pass, which the government cannot restrict without due process. Due process in this case includes, at a minimum, providing journalists with a notice that provides the reasons for revocation and an appeal process, the court said.

Cases like this suggest that the government may grant information-gathering privileges to some journalists and not to others, but only if there are defensible guidelines to govern the awarding of these privileges. The decision cannot be arbitrary. However, the issue becomes foggy when one considers whether bloggers are to be considered "journalists."

Access to public officials' social media feeds. Can government officials block critics and others from accessing their social media feeds? In three recent cases, federal judges have said no. The decisions could have ramifications across the country for how citizens interact with their elected officials. The cases pit competing First Amendment principles against each other: the rights of speakers to control their messages and the rights of citizens to be free from viewpoint discrimination in being shut out of virtual designated public forums. The decisions are victories for important democratic values, including unfettered access to politicians' communications. But they also may make it more difficult for individuals, including politicians, to moderate reasoned, civil discussion on their social media feeds.

One of the first legal cases filed involved President Donald Trump's Twitter account. The Knight First Amendment Institute at Columbia University filed a lawsuit on behalf of several plaintiffs who Trump blocked from his Twitter account. In May 2018, a U.S. district court judge ruled that Trump's actions violated the First Amendment, and the Second Circuit Court of Appeals upheld the decision in 2019 (*Knight First Amendment Inst. at Columbia Univ. v. Trump*, 928 F.3d 226). The court said the First Amendment prohibits government officials from excluding people from public forums based on their viewpoints, and public officials who have social media accounts for official business have created interactive public forums.

Other decisions suggested similar legal approaches. In 2019, the Fourth Circuit Court of Appeals ruled that a county school board official in Virginia violated the First Amendment when she briefly blocked constituents on her Facebook page (*Davison v. Randall*, 912 F.3d 666). And in Wisconsin, a federal judge in 2019 ruled that the First Amendment prohibited several state legislators from blocking constituents on their Twitter accounts (*One Wisconsin Now v. Kremer et al.*, 354 F. Supp.3d 940, 2019).

However, citizens do not have a First Amendment right to access *all* accounts from public officials, at least according to one federal appeals circuit. In 2021, the Eighth Circuit Court of Appeals ruled in *Campbell v. Reisch* (986 F.3d 822) that a Twitter account created by Missouri state representative Cheri Toalson Reisch when she first ran for office was not an "official" government account. While Reisch appeared to blend official and nonofficial business on her Twitter page, the page was created long before she ran for office and was used largely for a campaign purpose, rather than official government business, the court ruled. "[W]e think Reisch's Twitter account is more akin to a campaign newsletter than to anything else, and so it's Reisch's prerogative to select her audience and present her page as she sees fit," the court wrote.

The cases suggest a murky line to be drawn between social media feeds of public officials that are for "official" government business and those that are used for campaigning or advocacy purposes. But generally, if individuals are using their pages as designated public forums "under color of law" in their capacity as government officials, they cannot engage in content-based discrimination in blocking citizens without raising First Amendment problems.

Access to Judicial Proceedings and Documents

Another problem of access to information has involved the nation's judiciary. As Chapter Seven indicates, there was a nationwide trend toward closed preliminary courtroom proceedings immediately after the Supreme Court's *Gannett v. DePasquale* decision.

For a time, preliminary hearings were routinely closed in many states when a judge felt that prejudicial publicity would result from an open hearing. Similarly, pretrial hearings on motions to suppress evidence were often closed, again to prevent publicity about evidence that may never be presented to a jury. However, since the Supreme Court's decision in the *Richmond Newspapers v. Virginia* case and several others that followed it, courtroom closures have become much less common—and less of a problem for journalists. The problems of closed courtrooms and sealed documents are discussed in detail in Chapter Seven.

Another problem for journalists is access to *grand jury* proceedings. Grand juries are bodies that hear evidence and decide whether to charge persons with a crime. All major federal criminal prosecutions begin with a grand jury indictment, and many politically sensitive—and newsworthy—state cases are initiated this way. The Fifth Amendment to the U.S. Constitution requires grand jury indictments in major federal cases but not state cases.

Grand jury proceedings are almost always closed, in part to keep suspects from learning what is happening and fleeing before they can be charged and arrested. Grand jury transcripts (i.e., the official record of the grand jury proceeding) are also closed in most states, although some states make transcripts public after all of those charged with crimes are actually arrested. If no one is charged with a crime, the grand jury transcript remains sealed in most cases. And even in states that normally allow public access to the transcripts after all of those charged are arrested, courts may order the transcript sealed in newsworthy cases, such as those involving wrongdoing by public officials or celebrities.

If a grand jury transcript is sealed, there is little a journalist can do to learn its contents, aside from engaging in such investigative reporting techniques as inquiring of persons who were present at the closed proceedings. Judges sometimes object to that kind of newsgathering, but what grand juries do is often newsworthy.

Other records kept by the judiciary are usually open under an old common law tradition, but there are important exceptions. Much news can be gleaned from the filings that occur in both civil and criminal lawsuits. The complaints and responses filed by those involved in lawsuits are usually public, and they may reveal newsworthy details about individuals' and businesses' plans, finances, and past deeds (or misdeeds). One thing to remember about these documents is that they may not be protected by the qualified privilege libel defense until they are acted upon by a judge; reporters must be especially careful about reporting potentially libelous information contained in newly filed court records.

Some court records involving personal matters are sealed in many states. Probation department reports that recommend jail terms or probation for those convicted of crimes may be kept secret because they contain very personal information. In addition, entire categories of court information may be off-limits to reporters. For example, juvenile proceedings are almost always closed and the records kept confidential. Some states have laws requiring confidentiality of proceedings and records involving rape victims.

Access to Private Organizations and Property

Everything we have discussed so far in this chapter involves access to government information. However, many newsworthy things happen in private business enterprises. For instance, when a corporation decides to open or close a plant, the economy of an entire city can be drastically altered. What right of access, if any, does a reporter have to investigate?

Unfortunately, the answer is often "none." Private businesses need not admit reporters to their policy-making board meetings, and private business records are rarely open for public inspection. However, there are ways private corporate information can be researched.

The SEC. Perhaps most important, almost all corporations whose stock is publicly traded are subject to very specific disclosure requirements under federal securities laws. The federal Securities and Exchange Commission is responsible for enforcing two important Depression-era laws that require honesty and openness in the release of corporate information. These laws, the Securities Act of 1933 and the Securities Exchange Act of 1934, were passed to correct some of the abuses that led to the stock market collapse in 1929. The corporate takeover battles of the 1980s led to demands that these laws be made even stronger.

The Securities Act requires most corporations to file detailed reports on their management and business prospects with the SEC before they may offer their stock for public sale.

Focus on...
A right to record police?

Do you have a right to record the activities of police in public places? Six appellate circuits say yes, based on the First Amendment.

As cell phone cameras become ever present, and police themselves are increasingly wearing body cameras, legal disputes over police recordings have been common, raising questions about balancing access and privacy rights.

FIG. 84. Police officers with body cameras look at a cell phone.

Utility_Inc, June 2, 2015, via Pixabay.

The Third Circuit of Appeals in July 2017 joined five other appellate circuits (First, Fifth, Seventh, Ninth, and Eleventh) in ruling that citizens have a First Amendment right to record the police in public places.

In *Fields v. City of Philadelphia* (862 F.3d 353, 2017), the Sixth Circuit overturned a district court ruling that sided against citizens, writing, "Simply put, the First Amendment protects the act of photographing, filming, or otherwise recording police officers conducting their official duties in public." The right to record police is based on the First Amendment's protection "of access to information about their officials' public activities" and is an important part of keeping police accountable to the public, the appellate judges said.

In *Glik v. Cunniffe* (655 F.3d 78, 2011), the First Circuit ruled that individuals have a First Amendment right to record police officers in public. Simon Glik openly recorded three police arresting someone in Boston in 2007 with his cell phone, and he was charged with violating the Massachusetts wiretapping law, disturbing the peace, and aiding the escape of a prisoner. "[A] citizen's right to film government officials, including law enforcement officers, in the discharge of their duties in a public space is a basic, vital, and well-established liberty safeguarded by the First Amendment," the court wrote.

And in 2012, the Seventh Circuit ruled similarly in *ACLU v. Alvarez* (679 F.3d 583). The ACLU sought to enjoin the enforcement of an Illinois wiretapping law that would make public recording "a class 1 felony—with a possible prison term of four to fifteen years—if one of the recorded individuals is performing duties as a law-enforcement officer." The Seventh Circuit established that "[a]udio recording is entitled to First Amendment protection" and then evaluated the law under intermediate scrutiny. In finding the law too broad, the majority said, "The ACLU wants to openly audio record police officers performing their duties in public places and speaking at a volume audible to bystanders. Communications of this sort lack any 'reasonable expectation of privacy' for purposes of the Fourth Amendment." The court allowed the preliminary injunction.

The Securities Exchange Act requires publicly traded corporations to continue providing current information on their business and financial conditions even when they are not issuing new stock. A publicly held company cannot conceal either good news or bad news to defraud the investing public. Nor may a corporation's officers use what the securities laws call "insider information" to profit at the expense of unwary investors. For instance, when an oil company discovers a promising new field, its executives cannot quietly buy up a lot of stock at low prices before they publicly announce the discovery. And when a company is the target of a takeover bid, that fact must be disclosed in a timely manner.

As a result of these laws and the SEC's traditionally vigorous enforcement, major corporations must disclose a great deal of corporate information to the public. The 1934 Securities Exchange Act is no freedom of information law, but at least it does provide the press and public with more information about corporate doings than might otherwise be available. In compliance with these laws, major corporations provide a steady stream of news releases that are supposed to be frank and forthright in describing the company's business prospects.

When it comes to businesses that are operated as purely private entities (such as sole proprietorships, partnerships, and non-publicly traded corporations), there are few legal requirements for the public release of information. However, even the smallest and most secrecy-prone private firm has to deal with federal, state, and local governments, and its government filings can provide valuable information. The federal FOIA and virtually all state public records laws exempt trade secrets from disclosure, but private businesses must file a variety of other documents that an inquiring reporter may be able to see and copy. For instance, often a private land developer will file detailed reports and plans to win local approval for a new construction project, generating public records that an alert reporter can use to learn many details about what would otherwise be a hush-hush deal. In addition, when a private company is involved in litigation, it must often disclose information in court records that it would never otherwise release.

■ PRACTICAL SUGGESTIONS FOR MEDIA PROFESSIONALS

The procedures for using the federal FOIA were discussed earlier, and the procedures under state public records laws are generally similar, but how does one gain access to a government meeting that is closed when it shouldn't be? In fact, how do you know for sure what is really happening behind closed doors? The first step is to be absolutely sure what your rights are under the applicable open meeting law. Many journalists carry a copy of their state's open meeting and public records laws with them whenever they are on an assignment. When an agency you are covering goes into a closed session, insist on learning the specific legal basis for the closure. Make it clear that you understand the open meeting law too—and are prepared to assert your rights.

If a public agency still insists on going into a closed session when you doubt its legality, you have a dilemma. You should make it known that your employer is prepared to challenge any unlawful closed meeting in court, if in fact your employer will back you. If not, you have to decide if you are prepared to go it alone. Many state laws (and the federal Government in the Sunshine Act) provide for the government to pay your attorney's fees if you win, but if you lose, you may be out a lot of money.

There is, of course, a second problem: reporting what happens in a closed meeting. In many states and under the federal law, government bodies are required to keep either minutes or a transcript of closed proceedings. Find out what the requirements are in your state, and make it clear you want to see minutes at the earliest possible time. Failing that, many journalists simply wait out the closed meeting and interview some of the participants.

And there are always whistleblowers, often with their own private agendas—but they can nevertheless provide useful information. Individuals may provide journalists with background and information that sometimes is not available through official channels, despite laws like the Freedom of Information Act and state open meeting and public record laws.

■ AN OVERVIEW OF MAJOR ISSUES

Secrecy is an inherent part of the management style of so many government officials that no experienced journalist really expects the battle for freedom of information to end—ever. Although America has had federal and state FoI laws in effect for several decades, governments show no great enthusiasm for open meetings and records. Given the slightest excuse, many government agencies will close their files and lock their meeting-room doors. After Sept. 11, 2001, there was a major effort by federal officials to narrow FOIA's scope in the name of homeland security. Where should the line be drawn between national security and government openness? Should it be different due to the threat of international terrorism?

Raising even more concerns from open government advocates, the Department of Justice in 2011 had considered a revision to FOIA that would permit agencies to say records did not exist, even if they do, in response to FOIA requests that the agency wished to deny (the actual language said that the agency "will respond to the request as if the excluded records did not exist"). Bowing to public pressure and outrage from all sides of the political spectrum, the department dropped the proposed rule.

The growth of the internet has triggered another challenge for the advocates of open government. Americans are demanding more protection for their personal information from government and corporate intrusion, but the public interest in WikiLeaks is undeniable. Is there a way to reconcile this with the need of journalists for access to information, even personal information? Should it be different when information is *online*? While Congress recommitted to "electronic" openness with the FOIA Improvement Act of 2016, is this enough to ensure true openness to electronically held records?

A major goal of FOI advocates may be to reduce the number of exceptions to FOI laws while adding effective legal remedies for unlawful government secrecy—warding off bureaucrats' attempts to rid themselves of the onerous task of doing the public's business in public.

Like many other issues that are both legal and ethical, freedom of information is not a simple problem with simple solutions. In a democracy, the public has a right to know what government officials are doing and how they are spending taxpayers' money. The public watchdog function is one of the key roles of the press—and now of online media. All too often government misconduct is hidden in the guise of protecting national security or individual privacy—or any of a dozen other high-sounding excuses for secrecy. Nevertheless, there are times when public access to information creates troubling ethical questions.

Perhaps the media can best safeguard the public's right to know by aggressively fighting government secrecy, while at the same time exercising restraint in publishing information when the potential for private harm outweighs the potential for public good.

> **WHAT SHOULD I KNOW ABOUT MY STATE?**

- What are my state's open meetings and records laws?
- What do those laws protect, and what do they limit?
- How have my state's open meetings and records laws been interpreted in state or federal courts? A great resource, noted in Chapter Seven: the Reporters Committee for Freedom of the Press' "Open Government Guide" found at www.rcfp.org/open-government-guide.

A SUMMARY OF FOI LAWS

What Are Freedom of Information (FoI) Laws?

Taken as a group, FoI laws are state and federal statutory laws that permit public access to the documents generated by government agencies and to the meetings of government bodies. While granting general public access, virtually all such laws also contain numerous exceptions, limiting public access to meetings and records that deal with certain subjects.

What Is the Federal FOIA?

The federal FOIA is an act of Congress requiring many federal agencies to open their records for public inspection and copying. Government agencies must publish lists of their records to assist FOIA users in identifying the records they wish to see. Agencies now have 20 working days to respond to most FoI requests, but that deadline is often ignored. Information falling into any of nine specified categories is exempt from public disclosure.

How Does the Privacy Act Affect the FOIA?

Theoretically, the 1974 federal Privacy Act does not limit public access to government records. Instead, it allows an individual to inspect many personal records in government data banks, and it protects those personal records from misuse. However, its practical effect is to restrict access to much information about individuals that might otherwise be accessible to journalists.

What Is the Government in the Sunshine Act?

The Sunshine Act is a law requiring the governing boards of about 50 federal agencies to hold open meetings. These boards must announce their meetings in advance and must allow the public to attend unless certain confidential subject matter is being discussed.

Do the States Have FoI Laws?

All 50 states have laws requiring government agencies to hold open meetings and permitting some public access to government records. These laws generally apply to both state and local government agencies, but they usually limit or deny public access to meetings and records dealing with certain subjects, most commonly personnel matters (the hiring and firing of employees).

What Can a Citizen Do If an FoI Law Is Violated?

The federal FOIA and Sunshine Act both authorize private citizens to sue offending government agencies, with the agency required to pay attorney fees and court costs if the plaintiff wins the lawsuit. Many state laws have similar provisions.

10 *Obscenity and Pornography*

here may be no more controversial problem in First Amendment law than the conflict between free expression principles and the right of those who make or enforce the laws to set limits on sexual communications.

The Supreme Court has made it clear that *legally obscene materials* are not protected by the First Amendment and may be suppressed by local, state, or federal authorities. But if, on the other hand, a work is *not* obscene, it is constitutionally protected and may not be completely banned. Thus, it is essential to define obscenity—and yet that task has stymied the courts over the years. The nation's highest court has had to intervene in this field repeatedly, sometimes reviewing specific works to decide if they are obscene on a case-by-case basis. In a moment of utter frustration, former Supreme Court Justice Potter Stewart once famously admitted he couldn't define obscenity, but added: "I know it when I see it."

Even if the Supreme Court has had trouble defining it, many people besides judges and professional pornographers need to know what is and isn't legally obscene. Cinematographers, photographers and website hosts, for instance, need to know the ground rules. And anyone with a smart phone and internet connection can run afoul of obscenity laws in the digital era.

All 50 states have laws to control obscenity, and federal law prohibits both the importation and distribution of obscene works. In addition, federal law bans the use of minors—or adults appearing to be minors—in sexually explicit media of all types. Federal law allows heavy fines and prison terms for violators of these laws. Also, the federal Racketeer Influenced and Corrupt Organizations Act (RICO) allows seizure of the assets of businesses that deal in obscenity. Separate laws allow customs agents, among other federal officials, to seize and destroy obscene materials. Many state laws make producing, performing, or selling obscene works a crime and also allow their seizure.

As the ultimate interpreter of the meaning of the First Amendment, the Supreme Court often must resolve these controversies over obscenity. But in the years since the Court first tried to define obscenity in 1957, its attempts to define what is—and isn't—legally obscene have sometimes caused more confusion than enlightenment. Given the difficulty of coming up with a legally sound definition of obscenity, many states and cities have looked for alternate ways to control the sale or exhibition of sexually oriented books, magazines, and films. For example, many cities have attempted to zone adult businesses out of residential neighborhoods. And some communities have used nuisance laws against these businesses—with varying degrees of success.

Chapter Objectives:

- Summarize the evolution of government attempts to regulate sexual expression.
- Apply the *Miller* test to determine whether a work is legally obscene.
- Explain different legal standards for child pornography and municipal regulations of adult businesses.

Essential Questions:

- What are the government interests in regulating sexual expression?
- What First Amendment values are infringed on by attempts to regulate sexual expression?
- Where is the line between legally protected pornography and unprotected obscenity?
- How does government regulate adult businesses based on their "secondary effects"?

obscenity:

sexual material that gets no First Amendment protection.

Hicklin rule:

an early rule for determining obscenity in which isolated passages taken out of context were evaluated for their effect on the most susceptible members of society.

variable obscenity:

sexual material that is considered to be obscene on the basis of its appeal to minors, whether or not it would be obscene to adults.

■ EARLY PORNOGRAPHY BATTLES

In colonial America and Victorian England there were fervent but inconsistent efforts to eradicate literature that those in power considered obscene. As early as 1712, the Massachusetts colonial legislature passed a law that made it a crime to publish "any filthy, obscene, or profane song, pamphlet, libel or mock sermon."

Meanwhile, the English common law on obscenity was evolving through court decisions, and colonial courts and legislatures looked to the common law for guidance. The common law foreshadowed things to come by failing to define obscenity and instead focusing on the alleged corruption of youth and threats to order. By the mid-1800s, however, England and America were moving toward specific statutory laws aimed at obscene works. The Tariff Act of 1842 was the first federal law in America designed to restrict the flow of obscenity. It prohibited the "importation of all indecent and obscene prints, paintings, lithographs, engravings and transparencies." In 1857, it was expanded to include printed matter. The U.S. Post Office entered the field in 1865, when Congress enacted a law that made mailing obscene materials a crime.

Meanwhile, what was happening in England continued to shape American law. Lord Campbell's Act of 1857 and the first case tried under it produced a standard for obscenity that was followed in America as well as England for many years. Adopted as the Victorian period was beginning, the act prohibited obscene books and prints. It was tested in 1868 when a judge seized copies of an anti-Catholic pamphlet by a man named Henry Scott. Scott appealed to Benjamin Hicklin, recorder of London, and Hicklin ruled in Scott's favor. However, Britain's chief justice, Alexander Cockburn, reversed Hicklin's decision and ruled:

> The test of obscenity is whether the tendency of the
> matter charged as obscenity is to deprave and corrupt
> those whose minds are open to such immoral influences
> and into whose hands a publication of this sort may fall.

In short, Scott's work was held obscene because of how certain passages in the work might affect the most susceptible readers. And that concept came to be known as the "*Hicklin* Rule" because the case was named *Regina v. Hicklin* (L.R. 3 Q.B. 360, 1868).

The *Hicklin* Rule was enthusiastically adopted by American courts in the late 1800s and early 1900s. The *Hicklin* Rule allowed a work to be ruled obscene based on isolated passages taken out of context, and it defined obscenity in terms of its effect on the *most susceptible* members of society. As a result, all sorts of once-respected classical literature became suspect. The country was in the mood for a moral crusade.

Focus on...
Anthony Comstock

In the 1870s, Anthony Comstock began an anti-indecency crusade that encompassed not only sexual content but also birth control and abortion issues. In the early 1870s he raided Manhattan bookstores for their erotica, and in 1873 he joined the the New York Society for the Suppression of Vice.

Comstock used that position to lobby for the passage of the 1873 act for the "Suppression of Trade in, and Circulation of, Obscene Literature and Articles of Immoral Use," or the Comstock Act, which allowed for federal marshals to seize obscene materials from the mails, as well as any information about birth control. George Bernard Shaw coined the term "comstockery" to mean "moralistic censorship;" Comstock had targeted Shaw's play *Mrs. Warren's Profession* about prostitution.

In his 1883 book, *Traps for the Young,* Comstock instructed parents or anyone who has "the welfare of the rising generation at heart," to refuse to "patronize any person who exposes to public view or keeps for sale the vile and crime full illustrated papers of the day."

FIG. 85. The arrest of abortionist Ann Lohman (a.k.a. Madame Restell) by Anthony Comstock.

From the 23 February 1878 edition of the New York Illustrated Times, via Wikimedia Commons.

Anthony Comstock. It wasn't long until a crusader came along to meet the need. His name was Anthony Comstock, and he developed a following as he campaigned for morality. He and his supporters spent four months in 1873 lobbying Congress; the result was what came to be known as the Comstock Law, or more officially the federal Anti-Obscenity Act of 1873. This act went far beyond the 1865 law, giving the U.S. Post Office the power to banish from the mails any "obscene, lewd, lascivious, or filthy book, pamphlet, picture, paper, letter, writing, print, or other publication of an indecent character."

Conspicuously absent was any definition of obscenity; that would be left up to the people at the post office who would enforce the law. And who would that be? None other than Anthony Comstock, who became the post office's special agent to ferret out obscenity and banish it from the mails. He pursued his new duties with a passion, and once boasted that he had "destroyed 160 tons of obscene literature." Not content to bar dirty books from the mails, Comstock organized citizens groups to suppress "immoral" books even if they weren't mailed anywhere. Two of the most famous of these groups were the New York Society for the Suppression of Vice and the New England Watch and Ward Society.

These organizations cared little about the distinctions between great literature and pure pornography; anything "immoral" was fair game. Anthony Comstock and his followers made the word "Victorian" mean prudish. For 70 years, almost any sort of material depicting or referring to any kind of sex was likely to be censored.

What about the First Amendment? Apparently it never even occurred to the Victorians that freedom of the press included any protection at all for erotic expression. But somehow, both literature and human life survived—and the *Hicklin* Rule drifted out of style in the twentieth century.

■ CHANGING STANDARDS AFTER 1900

By 1920 times were changing, and so was the law. In that year a New York appellate judge ruled that a book must be evaluated as a whole rather than being banished because of isolated passages. Further, the judge said the opinions of qualified critics should be considered before a book is ruled obscene. That happened in *Halsey v. New York Society for the Suppression of Vice* (180 N.Y.S. 836).

Finally, in 1933 federal Judge John Woolsey refused to follow the most basic part of the *Hicklin* Rule, the idea that a work was to be judged by its effect on the most susceptible members of society. In reviewing James Joyce's classic work, *Ulysses*, he refused to follow the *Hicklin* Rule, under which he would have had to rule it obscene. He said a work must be judged by its effect "on a person with average sex instincts" rather than by its influence on the most corruptible members of society. Moreover, he said the work had to be judged as a whole, not by looking at isolated parts. In 1934 the Second Circuit upheld that decision (*One Book Entitled 'Ulysses' v. U.S.*, 72 F.2d 705). The appellate court—with Augustus and Learned Hand, two famous jurists who were cousins, in the majority—handed down a ruling that all but abolished the *Hicklin* Rule. The appellate court affirmed Judge Woolsey's view that the work should be judged as a whole and weighed by its effect on the average person.

Motion picture censorship. Motion pictures have created censorship problems ever since the cinema emerged as a form of entertainment and art. From the early days of magic lantern shows to the modern era of adult films, citizens' groups have demanded censorship to protect public morals. For years the movies were criticized for offering irrelevant escapism—and for being too relevant. From the 1920s until the 1960s, it was common for cities and states to operate film censorship boards that engaged in prior restraint of motion pictures, something that would have been unconstitutional if applied to almost any other communications medium. That practice ended gradually, as the Supreme Court extended more First Amendment protection to motion pictures.

Amidst a furor, Ohio authorities censored a film and then won the Supreme Court's blessing in 1915. That case (*Mutual Film Corp. v. Industrial Comm'n of Ohio*, 236 U.S. 230) set a precedent that stood for 37 years: movies were *not* protected by the First Amendment, the Court said. Justice Joseph McKenna, writing for a unanimous Supreme Court, said, "The exhibition of motion pictures is a business pure and simple." Thus, movies should not be regarded as part of the press. Instead, they were mere entertainment and did not purvey ideas or public opinion. Moreover, movies had a special capacity for evil, the Court said.

The *Mutual Film* decision was both a cause and the result of mediocrity in the film industry. Because early films were often unsophisticated and lacking in artistic quality, the Supreme Court had no problem dismissing them as frivolous entertainment and not a vehicle for significant ideas. But at least in part because of the Supreme Court's ruling, American films remained a frivolous form of entertainment for many years.

Movies get First Amendment coverage. It was not until 1952 that the Supreme Court finally said films were a vehicle for important ideas, and it took an Italian film to make the high court change its mind. New York authorities banned a Roberto Rossellini film called *The Miracle*, in which a peasant girl encounters a stranger she believes to be the Biblical Joseph and gives birth to a child she imagines to be the Christ child. The film was initially licensed for showing in New York, but religious leaders launched a major protest. In the face of this pressure, the film board reversed itself and prohibited further showings, declaring the film to be "sacrilegious." That decision was appealed, and in *Burstyn v. Wilson* (343 U.S. 495), the Supreme Court said for the first time that films are "a significant medium for the communication of ideas," and afforded them First Amendment protection.

The Court said *The Miracle* could not be banned, but the ruling did not preclude later censorship of other films. Unfortunately, no guidelines for review boards were provided, and the licensing of films continued for another two decades in many states and cities.

But: ongoing film censorship. Thus, several more film censorship cases followed. In *Times Film Corp. v. Chicago* (365 U.S. 43, 1961) the Supreme Court upheld the constitutionality of a film prior censorship system, but in 1965 in *Freedman v. Maryland* (380 U.S. 51) the high court required film censors to observe procedural safeguards in reviewing films. In the meantime, however, both the Supreme Court and lower courts considered a number of other film censorship cases, often overruling specific instances of prior restraint. *Times Film* involved a challenge to Chicago's licensing system by the producer of a movie that obviously would have been granted a license: a movie version of a Mozart opera. But Times Film refused to submit the film to the licensing board and instead challenged the system. The Supreme Court upheld the city's power to license films, finding films beyond the scope of the *Near v. Minnesota* ruling on prior censorship (see Chapter Three).

However, four years later in *Freedman v. Maryland*, the Supreme Court backed away from giving *carte blanche* to film censors. The case arose from a challenge to Baltimore's censorship system, which was much like Chicago's. As in the Chicago case, the film in question (*Revenge at Daybreak*) was not sexually explicit, but it still had to be licensed.

The Landmark Roth *Case*

By the 1950s, many state and federal courts had abandoned the *Hicklin* Rule in favor of the more liberal one suggested in the *Ulysses* decision, but the U.S. Supreme Court had not attempted to write a definition of obscenity that would square with the First Amendment.

Children versus adults. In 1957, the Supreme Court reviewed a series of obscenity prosecutions and finally dealt with this issue. In *Butler v. Michigan* (352 U.S. 380), the Court overturned a Michigan law that prohibited the sale of any book that might incite minors to commit depraved acts or corrupt their morals. The justices said that states cannot quarantine "the general reading public against books not too rugged for grown men and women in order to shield juvenile innocence." If that were allowed, the Court said, the result would be "to reduce the adult population of Michigan to reading what is only fit for children."

Thus, the Supreme Court had taken its first step toward the ultimate elimination of the *Hicklin* Rule: it said material cannot be forbidden to adults just because it may be considered bad for children. Four months later, the Court handed down another obscenity decision, and this one has been viewed as a landmark ruling in the field. The case was *Roth v. U.S.* (354 U.S. 476, 1957). Samuel Roth was convicted under federal law for mailing erotic materials and nude images that federal prosecutors alleged to be obscene. It was decided with another case, *Alberts v. California*, in which David Alberts had been convicted of violating a California law against possessing obscene materials for sale. The Supreme Court upheld both convictions, deciding that the laws under which they were convicted did not violate the Constitution. The Court specifically ruled that *obscene materials are not protected by the First Amendment*.

Prurient interest. However, Justice William Brennan's majority opinion also adopted a definition of obscenity that some lower courts had been following in lieu of the *Hicklin* Rule. The court said that henceforth no state could ban sexually oriented materials as obscene unless they were legally obscene under this new definition. Using the new definition, a court determines whether a work is obscene by asking "whether to the average person, applying contemporary community standards, the dominant theme of the material taken as a whole appeals to prurient interest." Thus, the Supreme Court specifically disavowed the *Hicklin* test, partly because it permitted judging obscenity "by the effect of isolated passages upon the most susceptible persons." The *Hicklin* test violates the First Amendment, the high court ruled. However, the courts that tried Roth and Alberts both used proper definitions of obscenity, so their convictions were affirmed. Still, *Roth* is a very important case because it officially adopted a new definition of obscenity and made it binding everywhere in America.

The *Roth* case produced the first of a series of dissenting opinions on obscenity law by Justices Hugo Black and William O. Douglas. These two jurists took an absolutist position about the First Amendment. They said the First Amendment protects even obscenity. Thus, they argued that criminal prosecutions based on the content of the materials—or the bad thoughts they allegedly inspire—should be unconstitutional. However, on several occasions this stance created problems: it enabled the Court to reverse obscenity convictions but made it impossible for a majority of the justices to agree on the reason for the reversal. The result was a series of plurality decisions that left the nation unsure what the law really was.

Shortly after the *Roth* decision, the Supreme Court was called on to review a number of other cases involving sexually explicit material. Soon a trend began: the Court repeatedly overturned lower courts' determinations that various works were obscene. In 1958 and 1959 alone, the high court reversed obscenity rulings involving a collection of nudist and art student publications, a gay magazine, and another magazine that included nudity. The Court also overturned a state statute prohibiting movies depicting adultery and reversed a ruling that held bookstore owners responsible for the content of all the books they offered for sale.

Expanding the Roth *Test*

The *Roth* case was a landmark decision, and like many landmark decisions it left some questions unanswered. For instance, what is the definition of a community for "community standards"? Does it encompass a local area, or is it something larger than that? And what does it take to violate those community standards?

The Supreme Court addressed the latter issue in a 1962 decision, *Manual Enterprises v. Day* (370 U.S. 478). The case involved the Post Office's attempts to ban from the mail several magazines intended mainly for a gay audience. Although the majority opinion branded the magazines "dismally unpleasant, uncouth and tawdry," the Court said they were not obscene and thus upheld their right to use the U.S. mail. Under the federal obscenity law in force at the time, a work had to appeal to "prurient interest" and be "patently offensive" before it could be banned. The Court said these publications were not patently offensive and also affirmed a position it had previously taken that mere nudity is not obscene.

"I know it when I see it." That case left "community standards" undefined, but a 1964 Supreme Court decision, *Jacobellis v. Ohio* (378 U.S. 184), addressed that problem. Nico Jacobellis, a theater manager, was convicted of violating an Ohio law by showing an allegedly obscene French film, *Les Amants*. The Court reversed Jacobellis' conviction, ruling the film non-obscene. It had been shown in about 100 cities, including at least two others in Ohio. Justice Brennan, writing for the Court's plurality, said the Constitution requires *national* standards on obscenity. "The federal Constitution would not permit the concept of obscenity to have a varying meaning from county to county or town to town," he said.

However, Brennan's reference to national standards attracted strong protest from Chief Justice Earl Warren, who argued that *local* standards are precisely what was intended in *Roth.* "[C]ommunities throughout the nation are in fact diverse, and it must be remembered that, in cases such as this one, the Court is confronted with the task of reconciling conflicting rights of the diverse communities within our society and of individuals," Warren said. And it was in this case that Justice Potter Stewart made his famous quote: "I shall not today attempt further to define the kinds of material I understand to be [hard-core pornography]; and perhaps I could never succeed in intelligibly doing so. But I know it when I see it, and the motion picture involved in this case is not that."

As we shall see, Warren's view rather than Brennan's eventually prevailed, but for a decade judges assumed there should be *national* obscenity standards, with local juries obliged to follow them, no matter how much those standards differed from local sentiment.

"Fanny Hill" and "Social Value"

The constitutional law of obscenity was further expanded in 1966, when the Supreme Court ruled that a 200-year-old erotic work, *Memoirs of a Woman of Pleasure* (often called "Fanny Hill"), was not obscene. In *Memoirs v. Massachusetts* (383 U.S. 413), the Supreme Court was again unable to reach enough of a consensus for a majority opinion, but the plurality opinion authored by Justice Brennan suggested a three-part test for obscenity: the original *Roth* test, plus "patent offensiveness," and a requirement that the work be "utterly without redeeming social value."

Social value. The *Memoirs* case involved what some might consider a classic bit of erotica. Written about 1749 by an Englishman named John Cleland (1709–1789), it is a first-person account of the activities of a high-class prostitute in London. The book attracted the censors of Massachusetts as early as 1821. In *Roth,* Brennan had said works that are obscene lack any "redeeming social importance," but the *Roth* decision did not specifically make the absence of "social importance" a part of the test for obscenity. However, lower courts began to consider that factor, and Brennan referred to it again in *Jacobellis.*

In *Memoirs,* Brennan said a liberalized version of the "redeeming social importance" concept was a constitutionally required part of the obscenity test. He said a work could not be considered obscene if it had "social value." But Brennan's opinion in *Memoirs* was only a plurality opinion. Justices Black and Douglas continued to vote to overturn obscenity convictions—but on the rationale that the First Amendment protects even obscene materials.

But despite its lack of majority support on the Supreme Court, the "social value" test was very widely accepted after 1966. Like Brennan's concept of national standards, the "social value" test would eventually be abandoned by the Supreme Court, but for a time it made obscenity prosecutions extremely difficult. Proving that a work is "utterly without redeeming social value" is by no means easy. Almost any obscenity defendant could find an expert witness somewhere who would testify that the work in question has some sort of social value.

By the 1960s, "Fanny Hill" had been translated into Braille, placed in the Library of Congress, and purchased by hundreds of other libraries. And yet, the Massachusetts attorney general tried to have it banned in Boston again, nearly 150 years after the first such effort. This final attempt to ban "Fanny Hill" in Boston failed, of course, when the nation's highest court ruled that the book was not legally obscene.

Alternatives to Proving Obscenity

After the *Memoirs* decision, the Supreme Court moved away from attempting to define obscenity and looked to other factors in deciding three important obscenity cases.

In *Ginzburg v. U.S.* (383 U.S. 463), the Court upheld the federal obscenity conviction of a well-known pornographer, Ralph Ginzburg. In so ruling, the justices avoided dealing with the question of whether the publications he was convicted of marketing were inherently obscene and instead took note of the way he promoted his works. The Court said there was abundant evidence of pandering, "the business of purveying textual or graphic matter openly advertised to appeal to the erotic interest of their customers."

Ginzburg originally tried to mail his publications from Intercourse and Blue Ball, Pennsylvania, but the post offices in those small towns couldn't handle the volume, so he settled for Middlesex, New Jersey. The Court concluded that those mailing points were selected only for the effect their names would have on his sales. Thus, the Court affirmed an obscenity conviction based on the conduct of the seller rather than the content of the works.

The next year, in *Redrup v. New York* (386 U.S. 767, 1967), the Supreme Court reversed three state obscenity convictions. In all three cases, a state court had assumed the material was "obscene in the constitutional sense," but the Court said those decisions were wrong. However, the justices could not agree on any one standard by which to judge obscenity.

"Reverse on *Redrup*." As a result, the Court backed away from defining obscenity and simply listed three categories of marketing that might justify state prosecutions without any finding that the works themselves are obscene. The three were: (1) the sale of sexually titillating material to juveniles; (2) the distribution of such materials in a manner that is an assault on individual privacy because it is impossible for unwilling persons to avoid exposure to it; and (3) sales made in a "pandering" fashion. The result of *Redrup*, apparently, was that only hard-core pornography could be banned. The Court seemed to be extending constitutional protection to materials that, though possibly obscene, were neither pandered nor forced upon unwilling recipients. The impact of the *Redrup* decision is shown by the fact that it was cited as a basis for the *reversal* of 35 reported obscenity convictions in the next year and a half. Some of these reversals came in additional Supreme Court rulings that were decided without formal opinions, with others in decisions of lower state and federal courts.

The Supreme Court affirmed its suggestion in *Redrup* about obscenity and minors a year later in *Ginsberg v. New York* (390 U.S. 629, 1968). There, the Court upheld the conviction of Sam Ginsberg (not to be confused with Ralph Ginzburg) for violating a state law against selling to minors material defined to be obscene on the basis of its presumed effect on them. In affirming Ginsberg's conviction, the Court accepted the concept of *"variable obscenity"*—that is, "material defined to be obscene on the basis of its appeal to [minors] whether or not it would be obscene to adults." This concept is important in understanding the violent video-game law struck down by the Court in 2011 to be discussed in Chapter Eleven.

But things were changing in the obscenity law field.

The Warren Court's Finale

In 1969, the Supreme Court handed down the last major obscenity decision of the liberal Warren era (Chief Justice Warren retired later that year). But that last decision went a long way toward protecting the private possession of obscene matter from government scrutiny.

In *Stanley v. Georgia* (394 U.S. 557), the high court overturned an obscenity conviction that resulted from a law enforcement "fishing expedition." Police searched Robert Eli Stanley's home in quest of bookmaking materials, but instead they found some possibly interesting films in a dresser drawer in his bedroom. They set up his movie projector, watched the films, and then arrested him for possessing obscene matter in violation of a Georgia law.

In the Court's majority opinion, Justice Thurgood Marshall said, "Whatever may be the justification for other statutes regulating obscenity, we do not think they reach into the privacy of one's home. If the First Amendment means anything, it means that a state has no business telling a man, sitting alone in his own house, what books he may read or what films he may watch." Also, Marshall wrote, the First Amendment protects the "right to receive information and ideas, regardless of their social worth."

However, the Court warned that this ruling was not intended to abolish "*Roth* and the cases following that decision." This was a unique set of facts, and two years later the Supreme Court refused to extend *Stanley* to other situations. In the meantime, Chief Justice Earl Warren had retired and the makeup of the nation's highest court was shifting.

In two cases decided the same day in 1971, *U.S. v. Reidel* (402 U.S. 351) and *U.S. v. Thirty-Seven Photographs* (402 U.S. 363), the Court backed away from the *Stanley* principle. In *Reidel*, the Court upheld the constitutionality of the federal obscenity law's ban on mailing obscene matter even to consenting adults, avoiding the "right to receive" concept from *Stanley*. In *Thirty-Seven Photographs*, the Court said customs officials could still seize obscene materials from a returning traveler's luggage, even if they were intended for private use.

Two years later, in *U.S. v. Twelve 200-foot Reels of Super 8mm Film* (413 U.S. 123, 1973), the Court was even more emphatic in saying the First Amendment does not give a private individual any right to bring allegedly obscene materials back from abroad. Once a person makes it home with his obscene materials he is safe, but if officials catch him en route...

These decisions were widely criticized as inconsistent with the language of *Stanley*. The *Stanley* decision was only *distinguished* and not reversed, but it was obvious by 1973 that the Supreme Court's view of obscenity was changing. Richard Nixon had by then appointed four new justices to the Supreme Court, and he made it clear that one of the things he was looking for was justices who would crack down on pornography. A new and more conservative majority on obscenity matters was coalescing.

■ SETTING A NEW STANDARD

The new U.S. Supreme Court majority had an opportunity to make its own statement on obscenity law in 1973, and the result was a new landmark decision that revised much of what the Warren court had done, *Miller v. California* (413 U.S. 15). The four Nixon appointees and Justice Byron White made a five-justice majority, and Justice Brennan, long the author of important majority and plurality opinions on obscenity, began writing dissents.

In *Miller* and four other cases decided at the same time, the Court revised the *Roth-Memoirs* test, abandoning the "redeeming social value" concept. The new majority also disavowed the idea of requiring nationally uniform "community standards," freeing each state to adopt standards that might differ from those in other states—or even from one community to the next within a state. The *Miller* case arose when Marvin Miller conducted a mass mail campaign to sell "adult" material. Five of his brochures were sent to a Newport Beach, California, restaurant, and the recipients complained to police. Miller was convicted of violating California obscenity law and appealed to the U.S. Supreme Court.

The *Miller* test. The Court took the occasion to write a specific new test for obscenity. The new test said a work is obscene if:

1. An average person, applying contemporary community standards, would find that the work, taken as a whole, appeals to the *prurient interest;*
2. The work depicts or describes, in a *patently offensive* way, sexual conduct, and the applicable state law specifically defines what depictions or descriptions are prohibited; and
3. The work, taken as a whole, lacks *serious literary, artistic, political, or scientific value.*

Thus, the Court reaffirmed the first two parts of the test set forth in *Memoirs,* although the community standards could now be local. Also, the term "patently offensive" would have to be defined in statutory law. However, the third part of the *Memoirs* test, the "redeeming social value" concept, was abandoned in favor of "serious literary, artistic, political or scientific value," something slightly easier to prove in a criminal proceeding. This was still only a 5-4 decision, but the *Miller* decision marked the first time since 1957 that a majority of the Supreme Court had been able to agree on "concrete guidelines to isolate 'hard core' pornography from expression protected by the First Amendment."

In abandoning national standards, Chief Justice Warren Burger emphasized the diversity of the communities of America. "It is neither realistic nor constitutionally necessary to read the First Amendment as requiring that the people of Maine or Mississippi accept public depiction of conduct found tolerable in Las Vegas, or New York City," Burger said. One of the Court's goals in allowing the states to adopt local standards, certainly, was to reduce the workload of the federal courts. But if the Court was seeking to get out of the obscenity business, it failed. In the years after *Miller,* the justices had to accept additional obscenity cases.

Objective Standards and Forum Shopping

The Supreme Court answered another important question about the *Miller* decision some years later in *Pope v. Illinois* (481 U.S. 497, 1987). In this case the high court clarified the way the three-part *Miller* test must be applied in state obscenity prosecutions.

The *Pope* case involved a challenge to the validity of an Illinois obscenity conviction in which all three parts of the *Miller* test were measured against prevailing community standards. Although *Miller* had said either statewide or local community standards could be used to determine whether a given work was obscene, that was only one part of the test. An Illinois court used subjective community standards to determine all three parts, including the question of whether the work had serious value.

Objective standards. The Supreme Court held that the measurement of "serious ...value" was to be based on *objective standards.* The court said a *"reasonable man"* test should be used to determine whether a literary work has serious value. Expert witnesses could be summoned to testify as to the serious literary, artistic, political, or scientific value, if any, of a work.

Writing for the Court, Justice Byron White said, "The proper inquiry is not whether an ordinary member of any given community would find literary, artistic, political, or scientific value in allegedly obscene material, but whether a reasonable person would find such value in the material taken as a whole." This hardly represented a major change in obscenity law: an objective standard is usually employed to determine whether questionable works have serious value. However, in this case the Court made it clear that the use of such a standard is required by the First Amendment. Without it, local communities could declare important literary works to be obscene by citing their own standards for seriousness.

In so ruling, the Supreme Court was responding to its own experience with situations in which local juries did apply parochial standards in obscenity cases and rule a serious literary work to be obscene, forcing the appellate courts to intervene. That is precisely what happened in *Jenkins v. Georgia* (418 U.S. 153, 1974). A jury convicted Billy Jenkins, a theater manager, of violating the Georgia obscenity statute by showing an Academy Award-nominated R-rated film, *Carnal Knowledge.* The film had occasional scenes of nudity and non-explicit scenes suggesting that sexual intercourse occurred. The case reached the Supreme Court, which said the film did not depict sex in a patently offensive way and was thus not outside the protection of the First Amendment. Local juries must consider all parts of the *Miller* test, including the "patent offensiveness" factor, in determining obscenity, the Court said.

What are community standards? But more to the point, perhaps, was the fact that this case forced the Court to hedge on its commitment to local standards. If a jury in an isolated community somewhere decides a work that is considered a serious one everywhere else violates the local standards there, isn't that exactly what the justices invited in *Miller*?

Aside from the problem of varying "community standards," doesn't this sort of thing also raise issues of fundamental fairness? Is a publisher or actor afforded "due process of law" when forced to defend a lawsuit hundreds or thousands of miles from where he or she lives and works, just because a copy of the allegedly obscene material made its way there? These questions were raised repeatedly as the Justice Department launched wave after wave of criminal actions against Los Angeles–based adult video producers by obtaining grand jury indictments in Florida, Oklahoma, Pennsylvania, and Texas, not in Los Angeles.

In 2006, this issue was again controversial when the Supreme Court refused to review a federal appeals court decision allowing criminal prosecution in western Pennsylvania of a Los Angeles–based adult video producer. In *U.S. v. Extreme Associates* (431 F.3d 150), the circuit court rejected the company's argument that its customers had a privacy right to download videos from its website or receive them in the mail. This continued the Bush administration's promised return to aggressive obscenity enforcement after a 10-year hiatus. The Clinton administration generally did not make obscenity enforcement a priority. But here, a Los Angeles company faced a criminal trial in Pennsylvania because some of its adult videos were received by customers there.

**Focus on...
Definitions for porn**

While it's common to use the word "pornography" for any kind of sexual content, the legal system recognizes several levels of sexual materials with different levels of protection.

Obscenity gets no protection. Obscene material is material that a jury believes appeals to the prurient interest, contains patently offensive portrayals of sex, and has no serious literary, artistic, political, or scientific value.

Indecency, discussed in Chapter Eleven, is a standard only for broadcast.

Child pornography need not meet the legal test for obscenity; as long as there are minors involved, it can generally be banned.

Finally, *pornography* is a generic term for sexual content that gets First Amendment protection. Some use the term *erotica* to describe artistic sexual material as opposed to the commercialized variety.

Forum shopping. Even the Clinton administration was inconsistent about prosecuting obscenity cases in faraway venues. In 1993 it said that policy was being reconsidered. However, a year later the Justice Department filed criminal charges in Memphis against a couple who lived near San Francisco because they maintained pornographic computer images on a private bulletin board system at their home in California. An undercover federal agent in Tennessee signed up for access and paid a fee to obtain a password—and then downloaded enough images to persuade a jury in Memphis to convict them on federal obscenity charges. Their convictions were upheld on appeal in *U.S. v. Thomas* (74 F.3d 701, 1996).

Although federal prosecutors still engage in forum shopping at times, the lower courts everywhere must follow the Supreme Court's instructions in *Pope v. Illinois*: they must decide the "serious... value" part of the *Miller* test on the basis of an *objective* analysis of what is and isn't serious value. That cannot be determined by local community standards alone. This is why the Eleventh Circuit overturned a federal judge's determination that 2 Live Crew's album, "As Nasty As They Wanna Be," was obscene. In *Luke Records v. Navarro* (960 F.2d 134, 2002), the federal appellate court noted that the judge based his determination of community standards in South Florida on his own experience in the community, without expert testimony. But the defense produced several experts on music, literature, and African-American culture who testified that the album did indeed have serious value. In view of that, the court ruled that the sheriff failed to prove that the 2 Live Crew album was legally obscene.

■ PORNOGRAPHY AND MINORS

While the courts were wrestling with the problems of community standards, another trend has been developing in obscenity law: a nationwide crackdown on the production and distribution of films and other works depicting minors in sexually explicit roles. By the early 1980s the federal government and at least 20 states had passed laws to ban the use of minors in such roles even if the work was not legally obscene.

Child pornography. In 1982, the Supreme Court ruled on the constitutionality of these laws in *New York v. Ferber* (458 U.S. 747). The Court carved out an exception to the normal rules on obscenity, upholding a New York law that permitted criminal prosecutions for those who produce or sell printed matter or movies in which minors perform sex acts, *without* proof of obscenity. The Court ruled that states have the right to prohibit children from appearing in sexually explicit scenes regardless of the literary merit or non-obscene nature of the work. Where such a scene is needed for literary or artistic reasons, the justices said that "a person over the statutory age who looked younger could be utilized." The Court gave the states a relatively free hand to regulate the use of minors in sexually explicit roles.

In 1990, the Supreme Court again allowed the states to adopt *more* restrictive rules for minors than for adults. In *Osborne v. Ohio* (495 U.S. 103), the court carved out an exception to the *Stanley v. Georgia* ruling (discussed earlier). *Stanley* had created a right to possess even obscene books or movies in the privacy of one's own home without government interference. In *Osborne*, the Court said Ohio could prosecute a person for the mere private possession of sexually oriented materials in his own home *if the materials involved children.*

In a controversial 6-3 ruling, the Court rejected arguments that upholding the Ohio law could open the way for laws to punish parents who possessed nude photographs of their own children. The majority held that the Ohio law was not unconstitutionally broad or vague. (The Ohio law contained an exemption allowing parents to possess photographs of their own children.) Writing for the Court, Justice Byron White said the need to control child pornography was so "compelling" that the states were free to enact laws that might be unconstitutional under other circumstances.

Lying about age. What about sexually explicit videos starring an actor or actress who claimed to be an adult at the time the videos were made, but who turns out to have been under age? The 1977 Protection of Children Against Sexual Exploitation Act seemingly made it a federal crime to produce or distribute sexually explicit materials involving minors, regardless of whether the producer or distributor knows that a performer is under 18. In 1994, the Supreme Court interpreted the 1977 law and ruled that it does not permit the criminal prosecution of anyone who does not know that a person appearing in an adult video is under age (*U.S. v. X-Citement Video Inc.*, 513 U.S. 64).

In 2016, the Third Circuit determined that federal recordkeeping statutes (18 U.S.C. Sections 2257 and 2257A), in light of the Supreme Court's decision in *Reed v. Town of Gilbert* (discussed in Chapter Three), were content-based and thus needed to survive strict scrutiny. These laws require producers of visual depictions of "actual sexually explicit conduct" to keep "individually identifiable records" documenting the identity and age of every performer appearing in those productions. In earlier cases prior to *Reed*, the Third Circuit had agreed with other circuits that the laws were content neutral and in keeping with Congressional desires to protect underage actors from participating in pornography production. However, a divided panel said that Reed requires the laws to undergo a strict scrutiny analysis because their "restrictions 'depend entirely on the communicative content' of the speech" (*Free Speech Coalition v. Att'y Gen'l*, 2016 U.S. App. LEXIS 10356). The court remanded the case for an evaluation of the laws under strict scrutiny. One judge disagreed with the application of *Reed* as the ruling precedent; she would have used the Supreme Court's secondary effects jurisprudential line (discussed later) to find the laws constitutional.

Computer-generated children. Congress offered prosecutors a way around the safeguards for film producers in the *X-Citement Video* decision by passing the Child Pornography Prevention Act of 1996. In sweeping terms, this law banned not only the use of minors in sexually explicit roles (even non-obscene ones) but also images that "*appear to depict* a minor engaged in sexually explicit conduct." The law established fines and prison sentences for producers of films, videos, photographs, or computer-generated images that appear to depict a minor engaged in sexual activity and for those who merely possess such materials.

The Child Pornography Prevention Act was immediately challenged by civil libertarians, booksellers, photographers, adult film producers, and others who said it could be used to prosecute anyone who possessed a copy of many mainstream movies, including *Taxi Driver*, *The Exorcist*, *Dirty Dancing*, *Animal House*, or *The Last Picture Show*, among many others.

Explaining the intent of the 1996 law, Sen. Orrin Hatch, R-Utah, its primary sponsor, said that computer-generated images are virtually impossible to distinguish from photographs, making it difficult for law enforcement authorities to act against child pornography because no minor's face is identifiable. But in 2002 the U.S. Supreme Court overturned the provision of the Child Pornography Prevention Act that banned computer-generated images and other images that only "appear to" depict a minor engaged in a sex act. Ruling in *Ashcroft v. Free Speech Coalition* (535 U.S. 234), the Court voted 6-3 to overturn that part of the law.

Justice Anthony Kennedy agreed that the Child Pornography Prevention Act was overly broad and vague. Congress had tried to justify the ban on computer simulations on the ground that while no actual children were exploited in the creation of such images, real children could be harmed because the images could feed the prurient appetites of pedophiles. But Kennedy's majority opinion said that the government had failed to show a link between computer-generated images and exploitation of children.

This decision does not affect provisions of the Child Pornography Prevention Act and state laws banning the creation, sale, or mere possession of images of real children engaging in sex acts—those laws remain intact and have been upheld by numerous state and federal courts. It doesn't affect provisions of the law that ban computer-morphing techniques to alter images of real children to make it appear that they are engaged in sex acts. The issue here was prosecutions based on images that are not legally obscene and do not involve the use of real children as models.

PROTECT Act. In 2003, Congress approved a law designed to get around the *Free Speech Coalition* decision and again ban computer-generated child pornography. This law prohibited the sale of materials represented to be child pornography, allowing prosecution of those who intend others to believe that the material offered is child pornography—whether it is or not. Among other provisions, it also criminalized the use of child pornography by sexual predators to entice minors to engage in sexual activity or to appear in pornographic materials. Congress, which has come to love acronyms, called the law the PROTECT Act ("Prosecutorial Remedies & Other Tools to end the Exploitation of Children Today" Act).

In 2008, the Supreme Court upheld the major feature of the PROTECT Act—the ban on offering material purported to be child pornography. In *U.S. v. Williams* (553 U.S. 285), the 7-2 majority put dealing in child pornography beyond the protection of the First Amendment. Justice Antonin Scalia said, "Child pornography harms and debases the most defenseless of our citizens.... We hold that offers to provide or requests to obtain child pornography are categorically excluded from the First Amendment."

The case restored the conviction of a man who told an FBI agent posing as a customer that he had photos of his own four-year-old daughter engaged in sex. Agents raided his home and found child pornography—but not the photos he had described. He was convicted but a federal appeals court overturned the conviction.

Justices David Souter and Ruth Bader Ginsburg dissented. Noting that the Justice Department prosecuted over 1,200 child pornography cases in 2006, Souter said, "Perhaps I am wrong, but without some demonstration that juries have been rendering exploitation of children unpunishable, there is no excuse for cutting back on the First Amendment."

Defendants can't always hide behind their own digital creations. In *U.S. v. Schales* (546 F.3d 965, 2008), the Ninth Circuit said that images created by taking non-pornographic pictures of local minors and using photoediting software to paste those minors' faces onto images of child pornography that he downloaded from the internet were included in PROTECT's prohibitions, saying that "the existence of an actual minor is unnecessary."

However, some were shocked when a California appeals court found that a man did *not* engage in child pornography when he used photo-editing software "to alter pornographic pictures of women he had collected from the internet by replacing a woman's head with [his girlfriend's 13-year-old daughter's] head." The court said that the California penal code's language ("a person under the age of 18 years *personally* engaging in or simulating sexual conduct") "requires a real child to have actually engaged in or simulated the sexual conduct depicted."

FIG. 86.
"Pinky St." dolls
based on Japanese
anime.

Author's collection.

The decision turned on the word "personally"—the court said that because the daughter did not personally engage in the conduct, but an image of her head was pasted onto another body, the man's conviction was overturned (*People v. Gerber*, 196 Cal. App. 4th 368, 2011).

Searching for child porn online. In *Commonwealth of Pennsylvania v. Diodoro* (970 A.2d 1100, 2009), the fact that someone had just *searched* for child pornography was sufficient for a conviction. The Pennsylvania Supreme Court said that searching for child pornography, following links to that pornography, and having child pornography images in the computer *cache* (a temporary storage area where data is stored for fast access) counts as "knowing possession or control" of child pornography under Pennsylvania law. The court said that to interpret the law in the way Diodoro suggested (cached images don't count) would be to open up a loophole in the state child pornography law that the legislature did not intend.

But another state supreme court disagreed. The Oregon Supreme Court said that searching did *not* count as possession in a 2011 case, *Oregon v. Barger* (247 P.3d 309). The defendant, Barry Barger, was convicted for possession of child pornography when investigators found eight child porn images in the cache of Barger's computer. Barger argued that the Oregon law required him to "possess" and "control" the images, and a finding that they were just in a temporary cache was not enough. The state high court agreed. Saying that Barger's acts of "obtaining" and "viewing" the images did not constitute "possession" and "control" of them, the court overturned the conviction. Cases like this, turning on the meaning of words like "possess" and "view," demonstrate the difficulty courts have in determining what statutes mean when applied, or what legislatures intended them to mean when they passed them.

Anime and manga. *Anime* or *manga* (Japanese video and still comics) works that portray children engaged in sexual activities have been included in the PROTECT Act's prohibitions in several jurisdictions in the late 2000s. In *U.S. v. Whorley* (550 F.3d 326, 2008), the Fourth Circuit said that the PROTECT Act applies to cartoon depictions of child pornography that are deemed to be obscene. Dwight Whorley was arrested for using a state computer to download Japanese anime cartoons depicting children in sexual situations. The court said, "It is not a required element of any offense under this section that the minor depicted actually exist" and said that PROTECT "criminalizes receipt of '*a visual depiction of any kind,* including *a drawing, cartoon,* sculpture, or painting,' that 'depicts a minor engaging in sexually explicit conduct' and is obscene." The court declined to rehear the case *en banc.*

Manga collector Christopher Handley pled guilty in 2009 under the PROTECT Act to "possessing obscene visual representations of the sexual abuse of children" when he received sexually explicit comic books containing illustrations of child sex abuse and bestiality in the mail. None of Handley's collection portrayed real children or adults; it was all cartoon depictions. A federal district court in Iowa struck down parts of PROTECT in 2008 (*U.S. v. Handley*, 564 F.Supp.2d 996), saying that the sections of the Act that substitute Congressional standards for obscenity for jury findings were unconstitutional.

Possessing child porn for other reasons. But what about attorneys creating or viewing child pornography for their defendants' cases, or law enforcement hosting such services to nab those who buy and sell it for real? Federal cases are bound by the Adam Walsh Child Protection and Safety Act of 2006, which holds that as long as government, who holds the evidence, makes it reasonably available to the defense, courts must deny defense attorneys the ability to copy or reproduce child pornography. But states may choose their own approaches. In *State v. Scoles* (214 N.J. 236), the Supreme Court of New Jersey said in 2013 that because these prosecutions are becoming more numerous and there should be consistency in how they're handled, defense lawyers may view the images in their offices, subject to certain strict restrictions. There is a need to balance the harms of revictimization of the children with the need for defense counsel to competently do their jobs. Thus, the court said, "when counsel requests access to discovery in their office, through copies of the images released to their custody, they must demonstrate their ability and willingness to abide by stringent conditions of control before their request will be granted."

However, a defense attorney who created child pornography by digitally altering images of two children to demonstrate how hard it could be to identify actual children was sued by their parents under federal child pornography statutes, and the Sixth Circuit upheld this fine (*Doe v. Boland*, 630 F.3d 491, 2011). The court put it bluntly: "Even when federal law allows participants in the criminal justice system to possess contraband, it does not allow the creation and possession of *new* contraband." And the Federal Bureau of Investigation made news when it seized, and then ran for several weeks, a Nebraska-based child pornography service in 2012. This seizure, intending to identify the 5,600 customers of the website (called "Website A), resulted in the distribution of many images, although the FBI did not say how many, nor how its investigation is proceeding.

Compensating child porn victims. In 2014, the U.S. Supreme Court handed down *Paroline v. U.S.* (572 U.S. 434), a case that addressed how victims of child pornography should be compensated for the harms done to them. The victim, "Amy," whose images of her exploitation by her uncle were among the most widely circulated child pornography on the internet, sought compensation from Doyle Randall Paroline, who admitted to possessing those images. The Court was faced with the question of how to determine damages under 18 U. S. C. §2259, part of the Violence Against Women Act of 1994. In a 5-4 decision, the Court said that all the individuals who possessed "Amy's" images owed her a non-trivial sum, but no single owner would be forced to pay all $3.4 million that "Amy" alleged she was owed for lost wages and future counseling. The Court did not provide a formula, but suggested that lower court judges might try to "determine the amount of the victim's losses caused by the continuing traffic in the victim's images… then set an award of restitution in consideration of factors that bear on the relative causal significance of the defendant's conduct in producing those losses."

Sentencing issues. Those convicted of child pornography distribution or possession have argued in recent years that their sentences were unreasonable—particularly those requiring computer or internet bans—with mixed results. A sampling of the dozens of such cases each year: The Third Circuit upheld one ban on internet access for a man convicted of child pornography and of enticing the molestation of a child (*U.S. v. Thielemann*, 575 F.3d 265, 2009) but overturned a lifetime ban on internet usage as "plain error" (*U.S. v. Heckman*, 592 F.3d 400, 2010). The D.C. Circuit upheld a sentencing enhancement, saying that it was correctly applied when the defendant transferred child pornography with the knowledge that it will be viewed by a minor (*U.S. v. Love*, 593 F.3d 1, 2010), but the same court overturned a 30-year ban on computer use for another defendant, sending the case back to allow for the use of computers for work (*U.S. v. Russell*, 600 F.3d 631, 2010). In *Doe v. City of Albuquerque* (667 F.3d 1111, 2012), the Tenth Circuit rejected a ban placed on a sex offender from entering a public library, saying that the First Amendment right to receive information was denied to the man, and the total ban on entry was overbroad.

In 2017, the Supreme Court struck down a state law that prohibited registered sex offenders from using social media sites such as Facebook. In *Packingham v. North Carolina* (137 S. Ct. 1730), a unanimous Court ruled the state law was not narrowly tailored because it burdened substantially more speech than is necessary to further the government's legitimate interests. "By prohibiting sex offenders from using those websites, North Carolina with one broad stroke bars access to what for many are the principal sources for knowing current events, checking ads for employment, speaking and listening in the modern public square, and otherwise exploring the vast realms of human thought and knowledge," Justice Anthony Kennedy wrote.

Perhaps more importantly, though, Kennedy waxed rhapsodic about the importance of social media in American lives. "[T]he statute here enacts a prohibition unprecedented in the scope of First Amendment speech it burdens," he wrote. Social media users can "gain access to information and communicate with one another on any subject that might come to mind," he went on, adding, "Foreclosing access to social media altogether thus prevents users from engaging in the legitimate exercise of First Amendment rights."

Self-regulation: the MPAA. Given concerns about parental rights to control their children's access to sexual content in movies, the motion picture industry attempted to ward off government control with vigorous self-regulation. Beginning in the 1920s, the Motion Picture Association of America (MPAA) maintained a tough code governing movie content, and a code committee exercised censorship powers. Critics attributed the irrelevance and frivolity of early American movies more to the influence of the MPAA than to direct government controls.

In 1968, the MPAA shifted to a more permissive approach. Rather than attempting to censor movies, the MPAA introduced a rating system that would simply advise theatergoers about the content of each movie in advance. The rating system, with its ubiquitous G, PG, PG-13, R, and NC-17 ratings, has largely accomplished its objective of protecting unwilling persons from offensive material while allowing others to see more explicit movies.

This rating system, however, has raised new questions. For example, participation in the rating system is voluntary, but the ratings are sometimes used as the basis for laws regulating the video business. Some states have considered laws that would forbid renting R or NC-17 rated videos to minors, and Utah banned the showing of such movies on cable television. As Chapter Eleven explains, the Utah law was eventually overturned by the Supreme Court.

If laws are to be enacted that base censorship decisions on these ratings, that means the MPAA—a private entity dominated by a few large film companies—is engaging in prior restraint without any constitutional safeguards for movie producers and exhibitors, much less for the general public.

This is particularly true because an unfavorable rating (or having to release a film with no rating at all) can be a financial disaster for a movie distributor. In fact, the rating system itself was revised in 1990 to eliminate the old X rating after several high-budget movies received the X rating. In the minds of many theater-goers, an X rating meant that the film was basically an adult film with hard-core pornographic scenes. Few newspapers would even accept advertising for X-rated films.

The MPAA revised the system after such movies as *Wild Orchid* and *Henry & June* were given X ratings. The association simply eliminated the X rating altogether and replaced it with NC-17 (no children under 17 admitted). Although critics of the movie industry contended that this was nothing more than a cosmetic change, the NC-17 designation lacked the stigma of the old X rating—and most newspapers began accepting ads for some NC-17 movies. Ironically, *Wild Orchid* and several other movies of that period that had initially been given X ratings were edited to qualify for R ratings before their release in mainstream theaters. (*Henry & June* was released with an NC-17 rating and was shown in many theaters that did not normally carry X-rated fare.)

The rating system continued to draw criticism for its arbitrariness in the 2000s. In 2007, the MPAA said it would allow movie makers appealing a rating to cite examples from other movies that were given a less restrictive rating. The MPAA also said it would post the rating standards and appeal procedures on its website.

■ MUNICIPAL PORNOGRAPHY REGULATION

Given the difficulty of defining obscenity and winning criminal convictions, many local governments have attempted to control adult-oriented businesses in other ways.

Nuisance laws. One method used by local governments is to ask a court to declare an adult-oriented business a *public nuisance*. In this civil action, a city may be able to win a court-ordered closure by meeting a lower standard of proof than is required in criminal cases.

However, the Supreme Court placed constitutional limits on this approach in a 1980 decision, *Vance v. Universal Amusement* (445 U.S. 308). The case involved a Texas nuisance law that was construed to authorize closing down adult movie theaters merely because they had shown obscene films in the past. It was not necessary to prove that any film currently showing was obscene. The Court said the Texas law lacked adequate procedural safeguards to protect the movie exhibitor's rights and that it posed an unconstitutional prior restraint.

But the Court ruled in 1993 that federal officials have the legal authority to shut down a chain of adult businesses and seize its assets after a few items are ruled legally obscene. The 5-4 majority held that this is a *subsequent punishment* for the crime of selling obscene matter, not an unlawful *prior restraint* in violation of the First Amendment (*Alexander v. U.S.*, 509 U.S. 544). In this case, the Court majority upheld the right of federal agents to use the Racketeer Influenced and Corrupt Organizations (RICO) Act to seize the assets of adult book and video stores once some materials are ruled legally obscene. However, in a companion case on the same day, the justices ruled that such a forfeiture of assets could be so excessive as to violate the Eighth Amendment, which forbids cruel and unusual punishments and "excessive fines" (*Austin v. U.S.*, 509 U.S. 602). Based on that ruling, the high court sent *Alexander* back to a lower court to decide whether seizing 100,000 books and videos after only seven items were ruled obscene might constitute an excessive fine.

Women's rights and pornography. In the 1980s several cities had laws that would control pornography in another way—by declaring that its existence violates the civil rights of women. Such a law was adopted in Indianapolis and later ruled unconstitutional. In effect, this law gave women the right to complain of civil rights violations when material that they found offensive was offered for sale at local stores or shown in local theaters. However, the ACLU and other groups protested that these laws flagrantly violated the First Amendment. If material not legally obscene under the *Miller* test is censored due to civil rights complaints, the result would be an unconstitutional denial of free expression, they contended.

In 1986, the Indianapolis law was ruled unconstitutional by the Supreme Court. In *Hudnut v. American Booksellers Assoc.* (475 U.S. 1001), the high court affirmed a Seventh Circuit decision without issuing an opinion. In overturning the law, the appellate court had pointed out that the law could be used to outlaw classic literary works such as Homer's *Iliad* because they depict women as "submissive objects for conquest and domination." Such works could be banned under the law regardless of their literary, artistic, or political value. "The state may not ordain preferred viewpoints in this way," the justices concluded.

Zoning, Decency Laws, and Adult Businesses

Communities have also attempted to control adult-oriented businesses through zoning powers and public decency laws, and they have enjoyed some success.

Zoning. The use of zoning to control adult businesses has been encouraged by several Supreme Court decisions, starting with a 1976 case, *Young v. American Mini-Theatres* (427 U.S. 50). That case arose in Detroit, where city officials attempted to limit the number of adult-oriented businesses that could exist in a given neighborhood. The Court said this was constitutionally permissible, even if the city didn't define obscenity with great precision, since the city wasn't *forbidding* adult materials altogether but simply controlling the time, place, and manner of their distribution. Encouraged, hundreds of other American cities adopted zoning restrictions on adult businesses, sometimes zoning them out of town altogether.

However, in 1981 the Supreme Court made it clear that communities could not use zoning to banish adult entertainment entirely without violating the First Amendment. That ruling came in *Schad v. Mt. Ephraim* (452 U.S. 61). In that case, the Supreme Court overturned a New Jersey community's ban on live entertainment as a violation of the First Amendment. Under its zoning powers, the city attempted to outlaw nude dancing and other forms of live entertainment. Overruling the local ordinance, the Court said that mere nudity does not make entertainment obscene. The majority said the city could ban all forms of entertainment (including motion picture theaters), but that local officials could not use their zoning powers to forbid nude dancing while allowing other forms of entertainment. The Court pointed out that this case was different from the Detroit case, in which adult-oriented businesses were dispersed around town and not banned altogether.

While the *Schad* decision held that nude dancing is not necessarily obscene, and therefore does have some First Amendment protection, a decade later the Supreme Court hedged a little in another case involving nude dancing, *Barnes v. Glen Theatre* (501 U.S. 560, 1991). The *Barnes* case was a challenge to Indiana's public decency law which, like similar laws in many cities and states, prohibits nudity in public places, including private business establishments such as bars. Based on *Schad* and other court decisions, authorities in most states assumed that these laws against public nudity did not apply to performances onstage or other activities in the performing arts. However, in *Barnes*, a divided Supreme Court upheld the application of a public decency law to nude dancing in a bar, although only three justices could agree on a legal rationale for doing so.

In essence, the three justices in the Court's main opinion in the *Barnes* case said that nude dancing, while marginally an expressive activity protected by the First Amendment, could be banned in a bar or other private establishment because the limitation on expressive activity was "incidental" to the state's larger goal of banning public nudity to prevent crime and protect public morals. They seemed to feel that First Amendment freedoms were not seriously impaired here because all an erotic dancer had to do to avoid violating the law was to wear "pasties" and a "G-string," as Chief Justice William Rehnquist put it.

Justice Antonin Scalia concurred but said he thought nude dancing should be completely beyond the protection of the First Amendment. Justice David Souter, on the other hand, concurred in the Court's decision to uphold the Indiana law, but on narrower grounds. Unlike the other justices voting to uphold the anti-nudity law, Souter seemed to be saying he would not support a broader ban on nudity in the visual or performing arts but was concerned about "combating the secondary effects of adult entertainment establishments." The four dissenters (Byron White, Thurgood Marshall, Harry Blackmun, and John Paul Stevens) would have overturned the public decency law as a First Amendment violation.

The *Barnes* ruling was widely assailed by advocates of full First Amendment protection for the performing arts, but praised by groups that favor restrictions on what they view as obscenity or indecency in the arts. However, the case did not signal any immediate change in broader applications of obscenity law to the performing arts because five justices (Souter plus four dissenters) were unwilling to support an across-the-board ban on nudity in the arts.

The Supreme Court ruled on nude dancing in private clubs again in 2000, again upholding a government's right to ban nude dancing in private clubs. In *City of Erie v. Pap's A.M.* (529 U.S. 277), the Court overturned a Pennsylvania Supreme Court decision that an Erie, Pennsylvania, ordinance violated the First Amendment. In a 6-3 decision, the Court said that Erie did not violate the First Amendment when it banned nude dancing at a club called

FIG. 87.
Local muncipalities can regulate adult businesses under the "secondary effects" doctrine.

Klugzy Wugzy, Apr. 7, 2021, via Unsplash.

"Kandyland" and required performers to wear at least "pasties" and a "G-string."

Secondary effects. Of the six justices in the majority, four (including Souter) said nude dancing is expressive activity that is entitled to some First Amendment protection. However, they concluded that *"secondary effects"*—neighborhood problems associated with nude dancing establishments such as crime and illegal drug use—justified the city's requirement that performers wear minimal clothing. This concept was first introduced in *Renton v. Playtime Theatres* (discussed below). As in the *Barnes* decision, the plurality stopped short of ruling that all nudity in the performing arts could be banned. Instead, they said only that Erie officials had adequately justified their ban on nude dancing in private clubs by showing its ill effects on the community.

Writing for the plurality, Justice Sandra Day O'Connor said that although "few of us would march our sons or daughters off to war to preserve the citizens' right to see specific anatomical areas exhibited at establishments like Kandyland," nude dancing is nonetheless entitled to some First Amendment protection.

The Fourth Circuit upheld Virginia's alcohol licensing scheme against an overbreadth challenge by a nightclub where the dancers wear only "pasties" and "G-strings" using intermediate scrutiny. In *Imaginary Images, Inc. v. Evans* (612 F. 3d 736, 2010), the appellate court said that "Virginia's policy regarding alcohol at erotic dancing locales is about as tame as one could imagine," allowing a lot of freedom in regards to the consumption of alcohol around erotic performances. Given this existing restraint, the court said, the law was constitutional.

In short, it is constitutionally permissible for a city to ban nude dancing in private clubs based on a "secondary effects" rationale, and to ban all adult businesses in residential areas or near churches and schools. However, many courts have now ruled that a city cannot use its zoning powers to force all adult-oriented businesses to get out of town. To completely banish adult businesses, local officials must prove that each one is engaged in producing, exhibiting, or selling legally obscene works. In some states, even that isn't enough: the most local authorities can do is to have each legally obscene work banned on a case-by-case basis—a very costly and cumbersome process.

Full exclusion. On the other hand, in 1986 the Supreme Court had reaffirmed the right of local governments to use zoning ordinances to exclude adult theaters in all but remote areas, even if the practical result is to make it impossible for any adult business to make a profit. In *Renton v. Playtime Theatres* (475 U.S. 41), the Court ruled 7-2 that the city of Renton, Washington, could prohibit adult businesses within 1,000 feet of any park, school, church, or

community standards:
local customs or norms that govern what is acceptable in sexual material.

zoning laws:
laws that regulate how land can be used.

secondary effects:
harmful side effects allegedly associated with adult businesses, such as increased crime, drugs, prostitution, and lower property values.

private residence. This meant that adult businesses could only operate in one isolated and largely vacant area of the city. The Court rejected arguments by adult business owners that this zoning policy would force them to locate only in an unprofitable "industrial wasteland." The Court said that as long as some sites are available for adult businesses, cities may prevent them from locating in most neighborhoods.

Writing for the Court, Justice William Rehnquist said that sexually explicit speech does not deserve as much constitutional protection as political speech. Therefore, stringent time, place, and manner restrictions on adult businesses are constitutional even when similar restrictions on other speech might be unconstitutional. In essence, the Court was recognizing a "hierarchy-of-speech" theory in which sexually explicit communications are near the bottom. The Court also accepted Renton officials' argument that their zoning policy was needed to prevent urban decay, despite the fact that fear of blight was based on the experiences of other cities and not on local experience. The chief justice added that "the Renton ordinance is aimed not at the content of the films shown at 'adult motion picture theatres,' but rather at the secondary effects of such theaters on the surrounding community."

Vague and unjustified zoning. In 2002, the Supreme Court once again addressed the use of zoning to curb adult businesses without proving that the materials they offer are obscene. Ruling in *City of Los Angeles v. Alameda Books* (535 U.S. 425), the Court upheld key portions of a Los Angeles ordinance that prohibits adult stores from providing video viewing booths as well as selling books and videotapes if the combined business (an "adult superstore") causes more problems for the neighborhood than a video store or video viewing parlor would by itself. The Court voted 5-4 to allow cities to ban the combination of the two types of business at a single location. In 2011, the Ninth Circuit reversed a summary judgment by a district court in favor of Alameda Books, saying that the plaintiffs had not presented "actual and convincing" evidence "casting doubt" on the city's rationale for its rule (*Alameda Books v. City of Los Angeles*, 631 F.3d 1031).

Zoning ordinances have come under attack for vagueness and lacking justification. Indiana passed an ordinance in 2003 that said that any business that derives 25% or more of its revenue from adult products or devotes 25% or more of its space or inventory to such products would be considered an adult entertainment business, subject to additional licensing and restrictions on business hours. The ordinance was overturned in 2009 in *Annex Books v. City of Indianapolis* (581 F.3d 460). Judge Frank Easterbrook, writing for the Seventh Circuit, said that the city had provided no evidence to justify the ordinance.

But courts differ on issues of vagueness. Berlin, Connecticut, passed a zoning ordinance saying that adult-oriented stores, defined as having "a substantial or significant portion of its stock in trade in Adult Books, Adult Videos or Adult Novelties or any combination thereof," could not operate within 250 yards of residential areas. The Connecticut Supreme Court upheld the ordinance in 2008. A company alleged that the "substantial or significant portion" part of the ordinance was unconstitutionally vague, and a district court agreed. The Second Circuit reversed; even though only 12% of the company's stock consisted of adult materials, that was "substantial" enough (*VIP of Berlin v. Town of Berlin*, 593 F.3d 179, 2010).

The Second Circuit ruled in 2010 that when courts evaluate the constitutionality of zoning ordinances regarding adult businesses, alternative sites must be evaluated both at the time the ordinance is passed and at the time it is challenged. The town of Smithtown, New York, created a zoning ordinance for adult businesses, and at the time it was passed, there were plenty of places for adult businesses to relocate. However, by the time of the challenge, the rules had been changed—to the dismay of TJS, operating the Oasis Gentleman's Club. The court, holding for TJS, said that "the First Amendment does not allow courts to ignore post-enactment, extralegal changes and the impact they have on the sufficiency of alternative avenues of communication" (*TJS of New York, Inc. v. Town of Smithtown*, 598 F.3d 17).

Mandatory condom laws. Laws requiring condoms to be used in professional pornography productions have recently caused major headaches for the pornography industry in greater Los Angeles.

Los Angeles had long been called the "porn capital" of the world, and one 2005 study estimated that 80% of all heterosexual commercial pornography was filmed in L.A.'s San Fernando Valley. One of the reasons California became home to the pornography industry was a California Supreme Court decision in 1988 that found a First Amendment right to engage in pornography production. In *People v. Freeman* (46 Cal. 3d. 419), the state court overturned the conviction of a pornographer who had been convicted on prostitution charges. Local police reasoned that if it was illegal to pay someone for sex, under the same logic it is illegal to pay people to have sex on camera. The state court rejected this argument, ruling that if the U.S. Supreme Court says non-obscene pornography is protected by the First Amendment, individuals must have First Amendment rights to produce it.

Beginning in the late 1990s, safe-sex advocates led by the AIDS Healthcare Foundation tried to pass laws in California requiring all adult-film actors to use condoms during sex scenes. While the state legislature declined to enact a law, voters in Los Angeles County in 2013 approved a ballot measure, Measure B, the "County of Los Angeles Safer Sex in the Adult Film Industry Act." The law requires condoms to be used in sex scenes and also requires additional film permitting fees and other requirements. Within months of passage, established porn companies began moving their filming elsewhere.

Porn companies sued to block Measure B from enforcement, arguing that the law was a violation of the First Amendment. They said the law was essentially a prior restraint against some kinds of expression—i.e., "condomless sex"— and therefore was a violation of their creative and political expressive rights. In 2014, after oral arguments before a three-judge panel, the Ninth Circuit Court of Appeals in *Vivid Entertainment v. Fielding* (774 F.3d 566) struck down parts of the law but upheld Measure B's mandatory condom requirement. The court applied intermediate scrutiny in the case, based on past precedents that gave greater deference to government actions aimed at regulating sexual content based on secondary effects. "The condom mandate survives intermediate scrutiny because it has only a de minimis effect on expression, is narrowly tailored to achieve the substantial governmental interest of reducing the rate of sexually transmitted infections, and leaves open adequate alternative means of expression," the court wrote.

In 2016, public-health advocates pushed for a statewide ballot measure in California. Proposition 60, titled the "Condoms in Pornographic Films Initiative," would have required condoms to be used in all commercial pornography produced in the state. In November 2016, voters rejected the ballot measure by a vote of 54% to 46%. While Measure B remained mostly intact, the defeat of Proposition 60 saw at least some commercial pornography return to California.

■ SEXUAL CONTENT IN THE DIGITAL ERA

Starting in the late 1990s, a new issue concerning censorship and pornography gained worldwide attention: the question of censoring pornographic or indecent messages and discussions on the internet. As noted earlier, Title V of the Telecommunications Act of 1996 (known as the *Communications Decency Act of 1996*, or CDA) prohibited not only obscenity but also "indecent" or "patently offensive" material on any part of the internet that is accessible to minors. Transmitting such material to a site on the internet accessible to minors was declared to be a crime punishable by a $250,000 fine and two years in prison.

Amidst a worldwide online protest of government censorship of the internet, several lawsuits were quickly filed to challenge this law, and two federal courts barred its enforcement in mid-1996. The Supreme Court heard an immediate appeal, and in 1997 the high court ruled that the key provisions of the Communications Decency Act were unconstitutional (*Reno v. ACLU*, 521 U.S. 844).

Full internet protection. In the *Reno v. ACLU* decision that was unanimous in most respects, the high court declared for the first time that the internet is entitled to the *highest* level of First Amendment protection, like newspapers and books. The extension of full First Amendment protection to the internet—in contrast to the more limited protection available to most of the electronic media—is perhaps the greatest victory the Supreme Court has given to free expression advocates in many years. Those who challenged the CDA included a diverse list of organizations: the American Library Association, the American Civil Liberties Union, the Electronic Frontier Foundation, newspaper publishers, book publishers, writers' groups, and large corporations such as Apple and Microsoft. They had expressed concern that the law was so broad and vague that it could be used to criminalize many internet sites and prevent the discussion of topics such as abortion, breast cancer, and AIDS prevention.

The Court agreed. All nine justices voted to overturn the act's provision banning the display of patently offensive material at any site where minors could see it. Seven of the nine also voted to overturn a section prohibiting the transmission of indecent material if minors could receive it. Justice John Paul Stevens wrote for the majority, "The interest in encouraging freedom of expression in a democratic society outweighs any theoretical but unproven benefit of censorship." Stevens also noted that on the internet "any person with a phone line can become a town crier with a voice that resonates farther than it could from any soapbox" and that "the same individual can become a pamphleteer." Therefore, there is "no basis for qualifying the level of First Amendment scrutiny that should be applied to this medium."

Concurring in part and dissenting in part, Justice Sandra Day O'Connor, joined by Chief Justice William Rehnquist, said she too found much of the law to be unconstitutionally broad and vague. But she said she would uphold the part of the law that forbids the deliberate transmission of indecent material from an adult to minors—provided all of the recipients are minors. She likened the CDA to a law requiring a bookstore owner to stop selling sexually oriented magazines to adults if a minor walks into the store.

The Court did not comment on the provisions of the Communications Decency Act banning obscene materials. In fact, those provisions were not even challenged in the *Reno v. ACLU* case. As explained earlier, if something is legally obscene, it is not protected by the First Amendment and may be barred from all media including books, magazines, and newspapers. But many things that are offensive to many people are *not* obscene in a legal sense.

What is historic about this case is that it rejected the federal government's attempt to ban *non-obscene material* from the internet if it is indecent or patently offensive and thereby make the internet legally equivalent to the broadcast media, not the print media.

In 1999, the Supreme Court upheld a section of the CDA banning obscene email (*ApolloMedia Corp. v. Reno*, 526 U.S. 1061). In a one-sentence order, the Court affirmed a lower court ruling that interpreted the email ban to apply *only* to obscenity and not to indecency.

Internet filtering. In *Reno v. ACLU,* the Court also noted that there are other less intrusive means of protecting children from adult material on the internet, including filtering software that can be installed on a computer to keep children from accessing adult sites. Internet filtering software soon became the focus of a new round of legislation and lawsuits. In 2000, Congress enacted a law called the *Children's Internet Protection Act.* It directed the Federal Communications Commission to adopt new rules under which libraries and schools must install internet filtering software to be eligible for federal aid for online access. After the FCC complied with Congress' mandate, the American Library Association and civil liberties groups joined in a lawsuit challenging this new law. They contended that it violates the First Amendment by denying students and library patrons access to many non-obscene websites, including some that aren't even adult-oriented in their content.

In a 2003 decision, the U.S. Supreme Court *upheld* the Children's Internet Protection Act, ruling that it does not violate the First Amendment for Congress to impose conditions such as internet filtering on grants awarded to libraries and schools (*U.S. v. American Library Association,* 539 U.S. 194). Writing for the 6-3 majority, Chief Justice William Rehnquist called the filtering requirement "a valid exercise of Congress' spending power." He said, "Congress has wide latitude to attach conditions to the receipt of federal assistance to further its policy objectives." One key to that conclusion was the fact that the law does not prevent librarians from disabling the filtering at the request of any adult. Libraries are also free to maintain separate, non-federally funded computers that don't have the software installed. Dissenting, Justice John Paul Stevens, joined by Ruth Bader Ginsburg and David Souter, said the law amounts to legislative overkill—"a statutory blunderbuss that mandates this vast amount of overblocking" of protected material on the internet.

But the Washington Supreme Court in 2010 said that libraries could, in accordance with the First Amendment and the state constitution, *refuse* to disable their filters or unblock sites on an adult's request. Several patrons complained that some sites they thought were protected were blocked by the library's filters, and the library decided that it would not unblock the sites except when they were erroneously blocked because they did not fall into prohibited categories (like pornography or spyware). In *Bradburn v. North Central Reg'l Library Dist.* (231 P.3d 166), the state high court said the library's policy "is a standard for making determinations about what will be included in the collection available to [library] patrons." Thus, the policy is just a part of regular library decisions about what it will offer as part of its collection.

The long COPA saga. Even before the Children's Internet Protection Act was passed in an attempt to mandate library filtering, Congress attempted to get around the *Reno v. ACLU* Supreme Court decision in other ways. In 1998, Congress banned sexually explicit materials at internet sites accessible to minors by passing the Child Online Protection Act (COPA). In this law, Congress avoided the indecency concept and attempted to ban material "harmful to minors"—and only from commercial websites that are accessible to minors.

Ten years of litigation resulted in the law never taking effect. Immediately after COPA was enacted in 1998, a coalition of civil libertarians and others made essentially the same argument as in the challenge to the Communications Decency Act: because it is so difficult to keep minors away from any internet site, this would force sites to engage in self-censorship, denying adults access to constitutionally protected material. A federal judge issued an injunction to prevent it from going into effect until a trial could be held on the constitutional arguments raised by those challenging the law. Then in 2001, a federal appellate court in Philadelphia upheld the injunction, declaring that with today's technology there may be no constitutional way to deny minors access to objectionable websites.

Focus on...
A national obscenity standard for online content?

It's the Brennan/Warren argument brought online: should obscenity standards be national or local? In 2009, the Ninth Circuit in *U.S. v. Kilbride* (584 F.3d 1240) advocated a national obscenity standard. The defendants' bulk email business contained some sexual ads, leading to a federal obscenity conviction. The court affirmed the convictions but, more importantly, said that a national standard "must be applied in regulating obscene speech on the Internet, including obscenity disseminated via email," agreeing with five justices in *Ashcroft v. ACLU*, the Supreme Court's 2002 case dealing with the constitutionality of the Child Online Protection Act (COPA).

FIG. 88. "Rice and Barton's Big Gaiety Spectacular Extravaganza Co.," an 1890s burlesque show.

Library of Congress Prints and Photographs Division, [LC-USZC2-1386]

However, the Eleventh Circuit, in an unpublished (non-precedential) opinion, disagreed. In *U.S. v. Little* (38 Media L. Rep. 1289), the court said that the traditional *Miller* test was appropriate for judging the obscenity of online trailers for explicit videos—explicitly declining to follow the Ninth Circuit's lead. That court said that to the extent that *Ashcroft* advocated a national obscenity standard, those statements were *dicta* (not the official ruling of the Court). Even though the Eleventh Circuit's decision was non-precedential, some believe that this split in the circuits makes it possible that the Supreme Court will take up the question.

In 2002, the Supreme Court reversed the appellate court and suggested that the use of community standards on the internet does *not* violate the First Amendment. However, the Court left the injunction against enforcing the law intact until the lower court could reconsider First Amendment questions raised by those challenging the law. In its decision, *Ashcroft v. ACLU* ("*Ashcroft I*," 535 U.S. 564), the Court voted 8-1 to allow community standards to be used to judge websites, although several justices issued opinions expressing concern about the potential for conservative communities to censor what online surfers may view elsewhere.

In 2003, the federal appeals court in Philadelphia again ruled that COPA is unconstitutional because it makes it too difficult for adults to view materials protected by the First Amendment, including nonpornographic materials. The court said the law is invalid for several reasons, including its lack of a distinction between materials inappropriate for young children and for teenagers (*ACLU v. Ashcroft*, 322 F.3d 240).The Supreme Court ruled on COPA again in 2004 (*Ashcroft v. ACLU*, "*Ashcroft II*," 542 U.S. 656). The Court voted 5-4 to sustain the injunction until a lower court could again reconsider and perhaps hold a trial on the constitutional issues raised. Justice Anthony Kennedy emphasized that the use of filtering software may be a less restrictive way to achieve Congress' objective of keeping harmful materials away from minors than censoring material at its source. "There is a potential (in COPA) for extraordinary harm and a serious chill upon protected speech," he wrote.

In 2007, Judge Lowell Reed Jr. in Philadelphia ruled that COPA is unconstitutional after conducting a month-long trial. He issued a permanent injunction barring the law's enforcement. Reed said filtering software is a more effective means of keeping pornography away from children, imposing less of a burden on First Amendment freedoms. Reed also noted that since the law was enacted in 1998, new issues have arisen that are not covered by COPA, including the presence of online predators on social networking sites that are exempt because COPA targets only commercial internet publishers.

In *ACLU v. Mukasey* (534 F.3d 181), the Third Circuit affirmed the district court's injunction against COPA, saying that the district court had correctly found that filtering software was a less restrictive means of achieving the government's goals, and in January 2009 the Supreme Court declined to hear an appeal, ending COPA's 10-year saga of litigation.

Sexting. Sexting ("sex" plus "texting"), the practice of sending and receiving sexually explicit pictures electronically, often between cell phones, has come under legal scrutiny, raising questions of whether teens who sext are engaging in illicit child pornography. Studies on the phenomenon have put the number of teens who have sexted nude or partially nude pictures of themselves as high as one in five.

In one controversial case, a county district attorney threatened to bring felony child pornography charges against three Pennsylvania teens who appeared partially nude in cell phone pictures unless the girls went on probation and completed an education and counseling program—an option several other teens had accepted. One picture at issue showed two girls from the waist up, wearing white bras, and the other showed a girl with a towel around her waist, her breasts exposed. The girls and their parents alleged that these images were not child pornography and were protected by the First Amendment. The Third Circuit did not address all the First Amendment implications of sexting, but it did order the district attorney not to initiate criminal charges. It added that requiring the girls to participate in an education program where they would be forced to write about why sexting was wrong and address questions about "[w]hat it means to be a girl; sexual self-respect, [and] sexual identity" would be a violation of their First Amendment rights against compelled speech (*Miller v. Mitchell*, 598 F.3d 139).

Some states have passed legislation that would reduce the penalty for minors caught sexting, either sending or receiving, to avoid having teenagers labeled sex offenders. Utah did so in 2009, reducing the penalty to a misdemeanor for minors (it remains a felony for those over the age of 18). Also in 2009, child pornography charges were dropped against a 14-year-old New Jersey girl for posting nude pictures of herself on MySpace. The teenager agreed to probation and an education and counseling program.

But, in 2011, a federal judge in Kentucky applied the law regarding sexual exploitation against minor children to 14-year-olds. In a scenario that is probably all too common in junior highs and high schools, an eighth-grade girl recorded a video of herself masturbating and sent it to the cell phone of a boy she liked because he told her he would not be her friend if she didn't. Despite promises to keep it to himself, he uploaded it to a computer, and it was posted online—causing her mental anguish. The girl sued under the federal law against sexual exploitation of children, which applies to "any person who employs, uses, persuades, induces, entices, or coerces any minor to engage in...sexually explicit conduct for the purpose of producing any visual depiction of such conduct" if it crosses state lines (which makes it a federal case). The boy moved for dismissal. The judge, denying the motion to dismiss, said the federal law applied even to minors, as there was nothing in the text of the law to say it didn't. The judge added that it was "not surprising that no federal precedent exists for a suit against a minor under these statutes, given the relatively recent rapid emergence of 'sexting' by minors. However, prosecutors have begun to charge minors under child pornography statutes." So the girl's action could proceed against the boy. Why wasn't she charged? She claimed she was "induced" to make and send the video, and if she was successful in that claim, she would be a victim of child pornography, not a perpetrator (*Clark v. Roccanova*, 772 F. Supp. 2d 844).

Sex trafficking and FOSTA/SESTA. Websites that facilitate sex trafficking and prostitution have come under scrutiny as law enforcement runs into hurdles in tracing the digital footprints of individuals who use the Web to engage in illegal sexual activity. One of the primary targets has been Backpage.com. Although Backpage had survived several legal attempts, rebuffed by CDA Section 230, to impose liability on it for allegedly hosting ads for sex trafficking, in April 2018 the FBI seized the site and raided its founder's home.

Meanwhile, lawmakers worked to combat the immunity that Backpage.com insisted it had. In 2018, under criticism from some free speech and privacy groups, Congress passed the *Fight Online Sex Trafficking Act of 2017 (FOSTA)*, which incorporated a Senate version known as the *Stop Enabling Sex Trafficking Act (SESTA)*. The law made it easier to target sex-related websites by eliminating Section 230 immunity for websites that facilitate sex trafficking. It was pushed by lawmakers who said Backpage's use of the CDA hindered legitimate law enforcement investigations into sex trafficking. President Donald J. Trump signed the FOSTA/SESTA package into law after the House approved the bill by a 388-25 vote and the Senate by a 97-2 vote. "Human trafficking is a modern form of the oldest and most barbaric type of exploitation," President Trump said in his bill signing. "It has no place in our world."

But the law's provisions included broad language beyond sex trafficking, extending to online prostitution and consensual sex work. Critics worried the bill would encourage internet censorship by weakening Section 230 protections for websites used by sexual minorities and sex workers, creating more causes of action to sue websites for content on their sites, and enhancing penalties for hosting content that facilities sex trafficking.

After the bill became law, several websites shut down their personals sections and other content, including the popular websites Craigslist and Reddit.

Legal challenges to FOSTA/SESTA. At least two lawsuits have been filed challenging the constitutionality of FOSTA/SESTA. As discussed in Chapter Four, in *Woodhull Freedom Found. v. U.S.* (948 F.3d 363, 2020), the District of Columbia Circuit Court of Appeals overturned a lower court's ruling that the plaintiffs lacked standing. Woodhull Freedom Foundation, a nonprofit organization devoted to sexual freedom, and other sex-worker advocacy groups

FIG. 89.
Backpage.com
homepage after the
FBI seizure.

Author's collection.

represented by the Electronic Frontier Foundation, filed suit claiming the law was an overbroad and vague content-based restriction on speech that failed to survive strict scrutiny. The EFF called the law "unconstitutional, muzzling online speech that protects and advocates for sex workers and forces well-established, general interest community forums offline for fear of criminal charges and heavy civil liability for things their users might share." The case continues.

And in Texas, a federal judge in 2021 ruled that FOSTA/SESTA was constitutional, in a case involving the prosecution of a man who was accused of creating websites such as CityXGuide that advertised prostitution and sex trafficking services following the closure of Backpage. The defendant challenged his prosecution in part by arguing that FOSTA/SESTA was unconstitutional. District Judge David C. Godbey found the law neither overbroad or vague and upheld the indictment (*U.S. v. Martono*, 2021 WL 39584, 2021).

Revenge porn. So-called "revenge porn," also referred to as nonconsenual pornography, refers to the dissemination of nude photos without permission of the person depicted. In recent years, many people have found themselves having sent a nude selfie to a lover only to find it posted on the internet later. The Cyber Civil Rights Initiative said in a 2017 study that one in eight adults have been victims of, or threatened with, revenge porn.

Individuals have sued after discovering nude photos of themselves on the internet, published without their permission and bringing them terrible embarrassment, and worse. In a 2011 federal court case, *Taylor v. Franko* (D. Haw. No. 09-00002), a woman sued an ex-boyfriend after discovering he had posted nude photos of her on at least 23 websites with her name and contact information. She had taken the photos and shared them with her boyfriend, but she never gave consent for them to be posted online. Some of the websites depicted her falsely as being interested in sexual fetishes, including bondage and bestiality. The woman said she received an average of three calls a day for months from strangers as a result. A district court awarded the woman $425,000 in damages for invasion of privacy, intentional infliction of emotional distress and defamation.

Some websites have also been the subject of lawsuits, including some that charged victims a fee to remove the photos. In 2013, the owners of You Got Posted, a website that hosted pornographic images of individuals and demanded money to remove the images, were slapped with a $385,000 award by a woman who found underage sexually explicit images of herself on the site (*Doe v. Bollaert*, Case No. C2-13-486, SD-Ohio). In 2015, Kevin Bollaert was convicted by a San Diego jury of extortion and identity theft as a result of the website's practices. Multiple victims testified about the harms they incurred due to the sexual images of them on the internet, including some who said they contemplated suicide after family and co-workers learned of the photographs. Bollaert was sentenced to 18 years in prison.

Revenge porn has also prompted legislatures to pass laws specifically criminalizing the publication of nude photos without the subject's permission. By 2021, 46 states and the District of Columbia had passed revenge porn laws. Congress has also begun to consider federal revenge porn legislation. Because websites generally are not responsible for liability for user-posted content based on Section 230 of the Communications Decency Act, some federal lawmakers say additional protections may be necessary to combat revenge porn.

In what was believed to be the first conviction under California's revenge porn law, in December 2014 a Los Angeles man was sentenced to one year in jail after a jury found him guilty of posting nude photos of his ex-girlfriend on her employer's Facebook page.

Courts uphold revenge porn laws. Could revenge porn laws be used to suppress protected speech? Some free-speech advocates argue that laws punishing publication of images will be overbroad and constitutionally suspect. So far, most courts disagree. At least four states have had their highest courts uphold their states' revenge porn laws in recent years.

The Minnesota Supreme Court in 2021 upheld its state revenge porn law, ruling that the law met strict scrutiny standards and overturning a court of appeals decision that found otherwise (*Minnesota v. Casillas*, A19-0576). The case involved a man who accessed his ex-girlfriend's password-protected cloud files and after finding a photograph and video of the woman having sex with another man, shared it with 44 individuals and posted it online. He was convicted under Minnesota's revenge porn law and sentenced to 23 months in prison.

In finding the law served a compelling government interest, the Minnesota high court said that protecting people from revenge porn is a problem of "paramount importance," as victims "suffer from post-traumatic stress disorder, anxiety, depression, despair, loneliness, alcoholism, drug abuse, and significant losses in self-esteem, confidence, and trust." Victims also "may have their reputations permanently tarnished," and some commit suicide. "Based on this broad and direct threat to its citizens' health and safety, we find that the State has carried its burden of showing a compelling governmental interest in criminalizing the nonconsensual dissemination of private sexual images." The court also found the law was narrowly tailored and the least restrictive means to address the problem. The court identified five elements of the law to conclude it was narrowly tailored: 1) the law was limited to depictions of sexual activity where in individuals had a reasonable expectation of privacy; 2) the defendant must "intentionally" disseminate the image; 3) the law has seven exemptions including images shared for medical, scientific, or educational purposes, and images in public interest; 4) the law requires a lack of consent; 5) the law applies to purely private expression.

In Texas in 2021, the Court of Criminal Appeals, the state's highest court for criminal cases, similarly ruled that Texas' revenge porn law did not violate the First Amendment, finding it was narrowly tailored to serve a compelling government interest (*Ex parte Jones*, No. PD-0552-18). The high court overturned a Texas appeals court that ruled otherwise. In *Ex parte Jones* (2018 Tex. App. LEXIS 3439), the appeals court said that because the law potentially covered individuals who shared nude photographs of others not knowing who the individuals were or the circumstances under which the photographs were taken, the law did not use the least restrictive means to protect the substantial privacy interests asserted by the government.

The Minnesota and Texas rulings followed similar rulings in Vermont and Illinois. In Vermont in 2018, the state supreme court upheld its state law under strict scrutiny analysis as being narrowly tailored to serve a compelling government, overturning a lower court decision that had found the law to violate the First Amendment (*Vermont v. Van Buren*, 2018 VT 95). However, the Court also applied the law strictly in ruling that the woman in the case did not have a reasonable expectation of privacy, one of the elements of the state statute, when she sent nude photos via Facebook Messenger to an ex-boyfriend. The ex's current girlfriend saw the pictures and posted them publicly to the sender's Facebook page.

In 2019, the Illinois Supreme Court overturned a lower court ruling that found its revenge porn law unconstitutional, in a case involving a woman who shared photos and texts of her ex-finance and another woman (*People v. Austin*, 155 N.E.3d 439). The Court used intermediate scrutiny to analyze the statute, arguing that because the law focused only on speech of a "purely private matter," a lower standard than strict scrutiny was appropriate.

Key takeaway. The four supreme court rulings suggest there is a growing view that narrowly drafted laws to protect people against the posting of sexual photos and videos of them without their consent will be upheld by courts applying strict scrutiny analysis.

■ AN OVERVIEW OF MAJOR ISSUES

The overriding issue about obscenity and the First Amendment today is a very old one: who should have the right to decide what is obscene in a diverse, democratic society? The rules governing allegedly obscene matter have undergone rapid change in the last few decades, but the underlying issue is not new. We have seen the spectacle of book burnings throughout American history. We have even seen the *same book* banned in three centuries.

Is there a movement away from tolerance for erotic expression that marked the recent past? Criminal prosecution again awaits some of those who produce, sell, or display sexually oriented books, movies, music, and visual images, materials that some see as art and others regard as filth.

In trying to strike a balance between First Amendment freedoms and moral standards, aren't we debating the same issues today that have been debated for centuries? Has anything really changed except the technology we use for the explicit depiction of sex?

Is Congress right to see new threats to morality in the new technologies? Should the global reach of the internet make a difference? Should freedom in all countries be limited to what is acceptable in the most morally conservative countries? Can we really have *community standards* on the internet, as the Supreme Court has suggested?

The digital era has made sexually explicit materials widely available on the internet. But it has also created new problems for keeping sexually explicit materials out of the hands of children. It has also allowed new platforms for sex trafficking and for people to seek revenge by making public nude photos taken under the guise of an expectation of privacy. The actions by several state high courts suggest a consensus that the government can protect citizens from the harms of nonconsensual pornography without running afoul of the First Amendment.

Although the issues of censorship and freedom are not new, the explosion of digital communications technology has given them a new currency. Will we ever reach a consensus about the appropriate limits of erotic expression, if in fact there should be limits?

WHAT SHOULD I KNOW ABOUT MY STATE?

- What are my state's obscenity laws, and how have those laws been interpreted in the courts?
- How is my community zoned? Where, if they exist, are adult businesses permitted?
- What are my state's child pornography laws, and how have they been interpreted?
- What are my state's and community's public nuisance laws?
- Does my state have any laws that attempt to regulate what children see online?

A SUMMARY OF OBSCENITY AND THE LAW

Does the First Amendment Protect Obscenity?

The Supreme Court has consistently held that the First Amendment does *not* protect materials that are legally obscene, but it does protect materials that may be indecent or offensive but not legally obscene. If a work is legally obscene, it may be censored and its producer may be punished. If not, it is protected by the First Amendment and cannot be censored.

What Was the *Hicklin* Rule?

For many years, obscenity in both England and the United States was defined by the *Hicklin* Rule, which looked to *a work's effect on the most susceptible members of society* to determine if it was obscene. The *Hicklin* Rule classified a work as obscene even if only isolated passages were obscene, regardless of the merit of the work as a whole. This rule was abandoned after the *Ulysses* decision, in which a federal court ruled that James Joyce's classic work, taken as a whole, was not obscene to average persons.

What Was the *Roth* Test?

Handed down by the Supreme Court in 1957, the *Roth* test defined obscenity as "whether to the average person, applying contemporary community standards, the dominant theme of the material taken as a whole appeals to prurient interest." First Amendment protection was thus extended to works that might have been classified as obscene in an earlier era. During the 1960s, the Court expanded on *Roth*. For a time, it appeared "community standards" were national standards (which could happen again), and a work could not be censored unless it was "patently offensive" and "*utterly* without redeeming social value."

What Was the *Miller v. California* Decision?

In 1973, a new conservative majority on the Supreme Court redefined obscenity, abandoning both national standards and the "social value" test. Instead, the Supreme Court said a work is legally obscene if: (1) it meets the original *Roth* test; (2) it describes sexual conduct in a "patently offensive" way; and (3) taken as a whole, it lacks serious literary, artistic, political, or scientific value. The court said that local community standards could vary, although works with serious value determined by objective standards cannot be censored anywhere.

May the Distribution of Non-Obscene Erotic Works Be Restricted?

Cities may use zoning laws to restrict adult businesses to certain areas. Also, minors may be forbidden to appear in or purchase non-obscene erotic works.

11 *Regulation of Electronic Media*

The legal status of the electronic media is unique. In addition to other legal problems that confront all media, broadcasters, cable systems, cell phones, and satellite television providers must deal with a federal agency—the Federal Communications Commission—whose specific task is to supervise and regulate them. Like publishers, these companies may be sued for libel, invasion of privacy, or copyright infringement. Likewise, they share with other media the problems of advertising regulation, antitrust law, and restrictions on their access to information. However, the electronic media must also contend with direct FCC regulation. An over-the-air broadcaster must also get a license from the FCC before going on the air and must renew it periodically. Cable systems are not formally licensed by the FCC, but they are subject to various federal laws, FCC regulations, and rules imposed by the local governments that grant their franchises. In between license or franchise renewals, broadcasters and cable and satellite operators must comply with hundreds of government regulations covering everything from the content of their programming to the technical quality of their signals. The print and internet media face no comparable rules.

This chapter doesn't only deal with traditional over-the-air broadcast media, like terrestrial radio and formerly "antenna" or "free" TV. The reach of electronic communications has grown exponentially as technology has developed and dispersed. The widespread adoption of the internet, cell phones, and other wireless technologies has engaged not only tech companies all over the world but also government. How should these communication tools be regulated? Who has the right to do so, and how?

This chapter will take a more or less historical approach to these questions in an attempt to trace the development of regulations in media products that are, for lack of a better distinction, not print—that is, that can be reasonably called "electronic media." That term includes broadcast television and radio, but it also includes cable, satellite, the internet, wireless communication, telephony (landlines and cell phones), and other media forms.

A two-tiered system—why? Before we turn to the "how," we should address the "why"—why is the electronic media regulated more strenuously than the print media? The answer is historical, and scholars have long argued whether it's a valid argument in today's media environment. It lies in the nature of the *radio spectrum and its scarcity*. Only a limited number of frequencies are available, and the number of stations that may transmit at one time without causing interference is also limited. The idea that this justifies government regulation of broadcasting is called the *scarcity rationale*. Early in the twentieth century, Congress relied on this

Chapter Objectives:

- Summarize the development of U.S. electronic media law, from the early Radio Acts to the Telecom Act, net neutrality, and beyond.
- Explain how and why electronic media regulation differs from that for the print media.
- Identify past and potential trends in the regulation of online media.

Essential Questions:

- The foundation of electronic media regulation rests on historic ideas of scarcity and access. To what extent do these limitations still exist? Should they continue to serve as rationales for treatment that differs from print?
- How has the internet changed how courts and legislatures create and apply laws in this area?
- If you could change how online media companies (including social and streaming media) are regulated, how would you do it? Why is that way better?

rationale when it decreed that the entire radio spectrum would be used to serve *the public interest, convenience, and necessity.* Congress said those chosen to use the limited space available in the radio spectrum had a special obligation to the public.

As a result, the Federal Communications Commission was established to regulate broadcasting and other non-governmental uses of the radio spectrum. Over the years, the FCC assumed broad authority over the electronic media under the scarcity rationale. However, today there are many new technologies of mass communication, and the entire philosophy of broadcast regulation—including the scarcity rationale itself—has been reexamined by the FCC, Congress, and the courts. In 2006, Congress passed legislation requiring broadcasters to go all-digital in 2009 as well as relinquish channels 52 through 69 for public safety communications and additional wireless broadband services. Moreover, while the broadcast spectrum is a limited resource, sophisticated engineering can coax more space out of that resource. In 2008, the FCC unanimously approved rules for devices using spectrum that sits *between* broadcast TV channels. This unused space, about 300 mHz to 400 mHz, is known as "white space." Because it can travel long distances and penetrate walls, it is best for wireless services. And there is also potential to develop high-frequency spectrum, above 3,000 mHz. While costs for using this spectrum are steep, because those frequencies are good for cell phones, that resource won't go untapped.

Although cable television systems use wires rather than the airwaves to deliver programming to their subscribers, the FCC has broad jurisdiction over cable systems too. Satellite radio and TV systems use the airwaves to deliver programming to their subscribers, and cable systems use the airwaves to receive the content that they send on to subscribers. And yet cable and satellite broadcasters, as well as online streamers, are exempt from some of the rules that over-the-air broadcasters find most objectionable, such as the ban on "indecency" except late at night. One of the basic questions in broadcast regulation is why the scarcity rationale justifies heavier government regulation of broadcasters than its fee-based competitors. How the FCC acquired its regulatory powers and how it exercises them are among the major topics of this chapter.

In 1996, Congress approved the Telecommunications Act, the most comprehensive communications legislation enacted since 1934 when the first Communications Act was passed. Congress at the time took major steps to foster new competition among broadcasters, cable systems, telephone companies, and others who offer communications services. Many provisions of this law freed the communications industries from long-standing government rules and regulations. But Congress also endorsed new government controls on broadcast content, including the widely debated (but widely ignored and perhaps problematic) V-chip system to allow viewers to exclude sexually oriented or violent programming. And now, over 20 years later, is the Telecom Act doing what its authors intended?

But for now, let's leave the world of broadband and cell phones and return to radio.

■ THE BIRTH OF BROADCAST REGULATION

When the pioneers of radio were conducting their experiments at the start of the twentieth century, they had no idea they were developing a new mass communication medium. They were looking for a way to send Morse code messages from one point to another without telegraph wires. The first serious users for radio communication (it was called "wireless" then) were the world's navies and commercial shipping lines. By the early 1900s, Europe and

FIG. 90.
National
Broadcasting Co.,
30 Rockefeller
Plaza, New York City.
Radio broadcast in
studio, 1945.

*Library of Congress
Prints and
Photographs Division
[LCG613- T-48380]*

North America were criss-crossed with telegraph wires, so the early inventors saw only one obvious need for wireless communication: at sea.

Radio Act of 1912. The first major legislation governing radio in the United States, the Radio Act of 1912, recognized this reality. It did not anticipate the development of commercial radio broadcasting, but it did provide for the licensing of shipboard and shore stations, among other things. The 1912 act was prompted in part by the sinking of the luxury liner *Titanic.* The fact that the *Titanic* had a wireless station was credited with saving hundreds of lives, but many more might have been saved had the wireless stations of that era been better organized. There was a ship much closer to the *Titanic* than the one that came to its rescue, but that ship's wireless operator was off duty when the disaster struck, so no one aboard knew what was happening. Consequently, the 1912 Act required all large ships to be equipped with wireless and to have operators on duty full time. Also, the act established qualifications for wireless operators, set technical standards for wireless stations, and reserved certain wavelengths for government use and for distress signals.

After World War I, radio broadcasting developed almost overnight and almost by accident. Westinghouse and other equipment manufacturers supported stations such as Dr. Frank Conrad's widely noted Pittsburgh station, KDKA, mainly to promote the sale of more equipment, not to establish a new mass medium of communications.

However, in 1921 and 1922, radio broadcasting suddenly caught on much as the internet caught on in the 1990s. Hundreds of stations rushed in to fill the available space in what is now the AM broadcast band. By the mid-1920s, there were so many stations that conditions were, at best, chaotic. Interference, not all of it accidental, reached intolerable levels.

Although the 1912 Radio Act had authorized the Department of Commerce to license radio operators and stations, federal courts ruled that Secretary of Commerce Herbert Hoover had no authority to stop issuing licenses when the entire AM radio band was occupied. Nor did Hoover have the authority to tell broadcasters which frequencies to use. Some stations jumped from frequency to frequency in a frantic effort to avoid interference.

Radio Act of 1927. The AM broadcast band by 1926 or 1927 had layer upon layer of signals, with louder ones covering up weaker ones and signals suddenly disappearing and

Focus on...
Technical jargon

There's a lot of terminology in the broadcast industry, and chances are that you know at least some of it from your own experiences with the radio in your car. Here are a few key terms.

AM: *amplitude modulation;* the original means by which sound was superimposed on a radio signal. Travels longer distances during nighttime than FM.

FM: *frequency modulation;* a newer method of putting sound on a radio signal. Provides better sound quality and greater immunity to static than AM.

Hertz (Hz): unit of measurement of frequency in the radio spectrum. Honors Heinrich Hertz, a German scientist whose research proved the existence of radio waves. Every station is assigned to transmit on a certain frequency or "channel" measured in Hertz. One Hertz equals one electrical cycle per second. One *kiloHertz* (kHz) is 1,000 Hertz; one *megaHertz* (mHz) is 1,000 kiloHertz, or one million Hertz. A station's frequency, in kiloHertz or megaHertz, is its home address in the radio spectrum (an AM radio station might operate on 1070 kHz, or 1.07 mHz, while an FM station might operate on 94.7 mHz). Only one station can transmit on each frequency in a geographic area; if two or more stations try to, interference will result and neither station can be heard. So each radio and TV station has a unique frequency on which no one else may transmit in that station's service area.

FIG. 91. Heinrich Hertz, ca. 1890.

Wikimedia Commons, public domain.

VHF: "very high frequency," from 30 MHz to 300 mHz, used for FM radio and TV broadcast.

UHF: "ultra high frequency," between 300 mHz and 3 gHz (3,000 mHz), used for two-way radio systems and cordless telephones. If you have a 4G wireless plan for your cell phone, you're probably working with 700 mHz, 1700–2100 mHz, 1900mHz, and 2500–2700 MHz.

Propagation: the method by which signals travel from their transmission points to listeners' receivers. AM radio signals propagate differently than FM radio or TV signals. VHF television signals propagate differently than UHF signals.

Further complicating matters for radio, an AM radio broadcaster's service area may be different at night than it is in the daytime. AM radio signals propagate mainly by *groundwave* during the day. That means signals literally travel along the surface of the earth. AM stations with high-power transmitters have a reliable groundwave range of roughly 100 miles, depending on the terrain. At night, local groundwave propagation still occurs, but AM radio signals also travel by *skywave* propagation: some of the transmitted energy travels out toward space and is reflected back to distant points on the earth by the ionosphere (Earth's upper atmosphere).

showing up elsewhere on the dial. In a move that some in the industry have regretted ever since, the nation's broadcasters demanded government action to bring order out of chaos. For five consecutive years in the 1920s, national radio conferences were held to make these demands. Most industries dread government regulation; here was an industry *asking* for it.

Congress responded with the Radio Act of 1927, which set up a separate regulatory body for radio communications, the Federal Radio Commission. The FRC was composed of five commissioners, appointed by the president. Significantly, the FRC was given the authority to assign broadcasters to specific frequencies and to deny licenses when there was no room for additional stations. The FRC's staff was still housed within the Department of Commerce, but the commission had wide authority. The FRC quickly went to work creating order on the AM broadcast band. There were simply too many stations on the air, so the commission began gradually reducing the number. In deciding who should get a license, the FRC had several goals, including assuring that everyone in America could receive at least one radio station; providing service to as many persons as possible from as many diversified sources as possible; and providing outlets for local self-expression.

The FRC's authority was based on the Interstate Commerce Clause in the U.S. Constitution. For a time after the 1927 Radio Act was passed, some broadcasters contended that they were exempt from Federal Radio Commission regulation because their signals did not cross state lines. However, the FRC claimed jurisdiction over all broadcasters as *ancillary* to the regulation of interstate broadcasting: even purely local broadcasting could interfere with stations whose signals did cross state lines, the FRC said.

Within a few years, the AM band was an orderly place, with each station assured an interference-free frequency, at least in its local area. The commission created several classes of stations to serve different purposes. First, certain powerful stations were designated as "clear channel" stations—stations that shared their frequencies with no one else anywhere in the country at night. These assignments went to stations that already had wide listening audiences and high-power transmitters. Their mission was to serve their metropolitan areas in the daytime and vast regions of the country at night.

Other stations were restricted to lower transmitter power and forced to share their frequencies with other broadcasters. At the bottom of the pecking order were daytime-only stations that had to leave the air at nightfall to make way for the clear channel giants.

Communications Act of 1934. Although the FRC was effective in achieving its major goals, it was replaced during President Franklin D. Roosevelt's "New Deal" administration. Roosevelt set out to systematically reorganize the federal government, and he felt the FRC should have both broader authority and a separate administrative staff. To effect those changes, the Communications Act of 1934 was passed, establishing the basic regulatory structure that exists today. The FRC was replaced by the Federal Communications Commission. The FCC was given a separate staff, making it a fully independent regulatory agency. In addition to radio broadcasting, its jurisdiction was extended to include long-distance telephone service as well as virtually all non-governmental uses of the radio spectrum.

The FCC was specifically forbidden to "censor" broadcasting, but it was given extensive authority to regulate broadcasters in other ways. The most important power given the FCC, of course, was the power to grant or deny licenses. Broadcasters were required to renew their licenses periodically, as they still must today. The FCC was authorized to ensure that broadcasters served *"the public interest, convenience and necessity,"* a mandate the FCC used as a basis for imposing various programming requirements on broadcasters.

FCC authority expands. Within a few years, the FCC moved far beyond its original role as traffic cop of the airwaves. The commission began not only saying who could use what frequency but also issuing detailed rules to govern broadcasters' content and business practices. When the FCC adopted a package of "Chain Broadcast Regulations," the major radio networks said the FCC had gone too far. The networks went to court to test the commission's right to make such rules. In a landmark 1943 decision, the Supreme Court relied on the scarcity rationale to uphold the FCC's authority. The Court said the agency *was* entitled to regulate broadcasting comprehensively, going far beyond its role as a traffic cop (*NBC v.*

FIG. 92.
U.S. Frequency
Allocations, National
Telecommunications
& Information
Admin., U.S. Dep't
of Commerce, Jan.
2016 (most current).

*See it in full-color and
much larger at https://
www.ntia.doc.gov/
files/ntia/publications/
january_2016_
spectrum_wall_chart.pdf.*

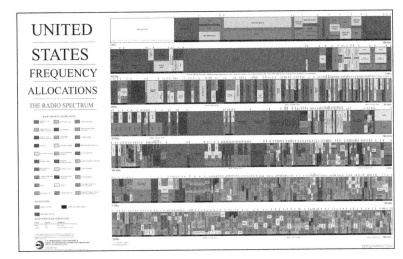

U.S., 319 U.S. 190). That case (and other early decisions) gave the FCC broad authority over all radio and television broadcasting as well as many other telecommunications services.

The FCC's authority is limited in certain respects. For example, the commission has little authority over government and military uses of the radio spectrum. A large part of the useful radio spectrum is reserved for federal government and military uses, including an enormous chunk of the VHF, UHF, and microwave regions. Government uses of the spectrum are coordinated by the National Telecommunications and Information Administration (see the chart above). Earlier, the authority now exercised by the NTIA was exercised by various executive offices. Although the FCC consults with the NTIA on many spectrum use matters, the NTIA has the final say over most federal government telecommunications.

■ AN OVERVIEW OF THE FCC

The Federal Communications Commission's basic mandate has remained much the same ever since 1934, although the commission itself was reduced from seven members to five in 1982. The five commissioners serve as the agency's policy makers. They are appointed by the president with the consent of the Senate for five-year terms. Only three of the five may come from one political party. President Donald Trump chose commissioner Ajit Pai to be chair, who then stepped down when President Joe Biden took office. Soon after his inauguration, Biden tapped commissioner Jessica Rosenworcel to serve as acting chair, and as of this writing, there has been no nomination for a permanent chair.

The FCC has the power to adopt administrative regulations that have the force of law, so it is a lawmaking body. But it is a law enforcement and executive body as well. It makes judgmental decisions—often crucially important ones to broadcasters—in selecting among competing applicants for an available frequency. Moreover, it functions somewhat as a court would in weighing evidence in proceedings to penalize those who violate its rules. In short, the agency makes the rules, it enforces them, and it judges alleged violators.

However, the FCC's powers are limited. It must afford all parties who appear before it "due process of law" as required by the Fifth Amendment, and it must not violate the First Amendment—or any other part of the Constitution. Also, its jurisdiction is limited by the Communications Act of 1934, and its decisions may be appealed to the U.S. Courts of Appeals, and from there to the Supreme Court. On numerous occasions the federal courts have overturned decisions of the FCC. When an FCC decision is appealed, the court must determine if the FCC exceeded its statutory authority or violated the Constitution, or if the agency "abused its discretion" by reaching a decision that was not justified by the facts.

FCC Procedures

As a rule-making body, the FCC must follow specific procedures, as must other federal administrative agencies such as the Federal Trade Commission (see Chapter Thirteen). When the commissioners need information on a particular subject, they may issue a *Notice of Inquiry*. Then they will await responses from interested parties. Or they may propose new regulations by issuing a *Notice of Proposed Rulemaking*. These notices are published online on the FCC's website (located at www.fcc.gov) and in the *Federal Register*, a daily publication of the federal government that announces actions by many federal agencies. After a rulemaking proposal is announced, interested parties are invited to respond with comments. Then anyone who wishes may react to the comments by submitting "reply comments."

After receiving written comments, the commissioners may also conduct a hearing at which oral arguments are presented. Finally, the commissioners vote on the proposed rule. If it is approved, the new rule becomes a part of the agency's official regulations, which appear in Title 47 of the *Code of Federal Regulations*. If you have a special interest in a particular FCC rule, you can look up both the rule and the commission's detailed statement about the rule on the FCC's website or in the *Federal Register*, which you will find in any well-equipped law library and many large city libraries. The website also includes other information about the agency and the issues it is considering.

Although major policy decisions are made by the five commissioners, the bulk of the FCC's work is carried out by the agency's administrative staff. The agency does most of its work through "bureaus," currently seven, each of which has a separate area of responsibility.

The *Media Bureau* is of primary concern to broadcasters and cable systems. It is responsible for licensing and supervising radio and television stations and cable television systems. It also handles many post-licensing matters concerning direct broadcast satellite systems. The bureau handles the paperwork of licensing and other administrative matters, referring only the most controversial questions to the commission itself. However, the commissioners and ultimately the federal courts often review the bureau's decisions.

The *Wireline Competition Bureau* regulates landline telephone and other common carrier communications. A *common carrier* is a utility-like operation that must serve everyone who seeks service and is prepared to pay for it—and without discrimination, by content or otherwise. The states regulate these services within their boundaries through their public utilities commissions; the FCC regulates services and rates. The bureau's stated goals include fostering competition and promoting fairness in these industries. It's also responsible for encouraging and monitoring *universal service*, a concept related to but distinct from common carriage. Common carriers are required to treat all users the same in the offering and delivery of their services; universal service is intended to expand the reach of vital technologies to everyone at costs that all can afford. Another way to think about it: common carriage works toward fairness, while universal service fosters expansion, in providing critical services such as heat, electricity, and water—and, important for our purposes, telecommunications.

The *Wireless Telecommunications Bureau* handles most domestic wireless and two-way communications services, including cellular telephone and similar services, paging, public safety communications, and amateur radio. It licenses and regulates most kinds of private, non-broadcast radio operations.

The *International Bureau* licenses shortwave stations whose signals routinely cross international borders. In addition, it licenses satellite communications systems (which also transmit signals that often cross international boundaries), and handles much of the work required for U.S. participation in World Radio Conferences and other international activities.

The *Enforcement Bureau* enforces the FCC's regulations, supervising everything from broadcasters' compliance with technical standards to the enforcement of local telephone companies' compliance with regulations designed to foster competition.

The *Consumer & Governmental Affairs Bureau* handles all kinds of consumer-related matters, responding to inquiries from individual consumers as well as maintaining contacts with state and local governments and industry groups.

The *Public Safety and Homeland Security Bureau* was established in 2006. Its mandate is to improve communications during national emergencies such as Sept. 11, 2001, and natural disasters such as hurricanes and earthquakes.

In addition to these specialized bureaus, the FCC has a central administrative staff, a science and technology office, a large legal staff, and a plans and policies office, among other offices and divisions. Obviously, the FCC has vast responsibilities beyond the regulation of broadcasting. Only a small part of the FCC's regulatory energy is directed toward such high-profile activities as regulating the nation's television and radio stations.

Agency practices: fines. It's worth mentioning a few Supreme Court decisions that address agency workings. The Court, in a non-media case, suggested in 2013 that the usual way to handle an appeal of an agency's fine (paying the fine and then going to court) was problematic (*Horne v. Dept. of Agriculture*, 569 U.S. 513). Raisin growers Marvin and Laura Horne were fined when they failed to turn over a portion of their crop to the government under a Depression-era law. They argued that having to give the government their raisins was an unauthorized "taking," and they should be able to sue without paying the fine first. A unanimous Court agreed. Justice Clarence Thomas wrote, "In the case of an administrative enforcement proceeding, when a party raises a constitutional defense to an assessed fine, it would make little sense to require the party to pay the fine in one proceeding and then turn around and sue for recovery of that same money in another proceeding." This has implications for FCC (and other agency) fines: it may make appeals more numerous, since it's possible that plaintiffs may not have to pay fines up front if they raise constitutional issues.

What about the relationships between administrative agencies and other governmental bodies? When organizations disagree, whose interpretations of the law should reign supreme, and how must agencies go about revising their own rules?

Agency interpretations and judicial deference. As we've seen by now, administrative agencies are often challenged in court, and judges must decide how much deference to give an agency's interpretation of a statute. In a 2013 case that may have important implications for FCC and FTC issues, the Supreme Court decided *City of Arlington v. FCC* (569 U.S. 290). The Court said that a test developed in an earlier case to determine the appropriateness of an agency's interpretation of a statute (*Chevron U.S.A. Inc. v. Nat. Res. Def. Council*, 467 U.S. 837, 1984) would also apply to agencies' interpretations of their own jurisdictions.

In the *Chevron* test, a court looks at what Congress said about the statute, and if that's clear, the inquiry is over, as Congress' intent governs. If it's not clear or not addressed, then

FIG. 93.
FCC commissioners,
June 2021.

Top, left to right:
Acting chair Jessica
Rosenworcel,
Commissioner
Brendan Carr.
Bottom, left to right:
Commissioner
Geoffrey Starks,
Commissioner Nathan
Simington.

*Official portraits,
Federal Communications
Commission.*

the court, regardless of what it thinks of the agency's interpretation of the statute, defers to that interpretation. *Arlington* extends that deference to an agency's interpretation of its own jurisdiction. Both *Arlington* and *Chevron* will likely continue to undergo close scrutiny.

And, as will be discussed later in this chapter, the Supreme Court in 2020 may have added another wrinkle: it asked an appellate court to interpret how yet *another* act dealing with agency deference, the Administrative Orders Review Act, commonly known as the Hobbs Act, interacts with FCC orders interpreting Congressional rules. It's kind of a mess, and it's likely this area of administrative law will heat up in coming years.

Agency rule revisions. In the same vein, the high court in 2015 examined an agency's rule revision capacity (*Perez v. Mortg. Bankers Ass'n*, 135 S. Ct. 1199). The justices overturned an appellate court's doctrine for the Administrative Procedure Act mandating agencies use a notice-and-comment process before they significantly revise their rules as counter to the clear text of the act's rulemaking provisions. Justice Sonia Sotomayor wrote for the Court a summary of the relevant part of the act: the agency must offer a notice of rulemaking, followed by acceptance of comments from interested persons, and then in its final rule include "a concise general statement of [its] basis and purpose." She added, "Because an agency is not required to use notice-and-comment procedures to issue an initial interpretive rule, it is also not required to use those procedures when it amends or repeals that interpretive rule."

◼ BROADCAST CONTENT REGULATION

One of the FCC's main jobs is to supervise the ongoing operations of its licensees. While a certain amount of that supervision involves technical matters—frequency stability, modulation percentage, power level, and such—a far greater concern to the public (and to most broadcasters themselves) is the FCC's rules governing *content.*

Although Section 326 of the 1934 Communications Act specifically forbids the FCC to "censor" broadcasters, over the years the commission has adopted a number of rules to regulate broadcast content. Also, both the 1934 Communications Act and the 1996 Telecommunications Act, among other federal laws, have provisions governing broadcast content.

One of the FCC's major goals for many years was to disentangle itself from content regulation. FCC regulators in the 1980s pointed out that no government agency has the authority to tell the print media how much of a specific kind of material to publish (a view endorsed by the Supreme Court in the *Tornillo* case, discussed elsewhere). Nor does any government agency have that kind of control over cable and satellite television or the internet media. Why, the FCC asked, should broadcasters be second-class citizens when it comes to First Amendment freedoms? Some citizen groups responded to that question by arguing that broadcasters are given a government-sanctioned monopoly and should have to provide some mandatory public service in return. After all, the FCC does select just one broadcaster to operate on a given frequency in each community, denying that privilege to all others.

Whatever the pros and cons of deregulation, during the 1980s the FCC eliminated many of its rules governing broadcast content on the grounds that they were inappropriate if not unconstitutional. By 2000, though, the FCC reversed its philosophy and started imposing new controls on broadcast content.

This section is about regulation and deregulation. A number of important restrictions on broadcast content are still in force or have recently been added—restrictions that do not apply to most other communications media. Other restrictions, including the Fairness Doctrine, perhaps the most controversial content regulation of all, have been abolished. First, though, let's look at the still-good rules governing the broadcast of political advertising.

Broadcasting Political Advertising

Probably the most important aspects of broadcast content regulation are the laws and rules concerning political broadcasting. The key provision is Section 315 of the Communications Act, often called the *Equal Time Rule* or "equal opportunity provision." It has been a part of the Communications Act ever since it was enacted in 1934. In addition to Section 315—which is an act of Congress and cannot be unilaterally rewritten by the FCC—there are many FCC rules that spell out the details of broadcasters' obligations during election campaigns. The FCC adopted a major revision of these rules in 1991.

Section 315: state and local offices. Section 315 requires broadcasters to provide equal access to all legally qualified candidates for a public office during election campaigns. It reads in part:

> If any licensee shall permit any person who is a legally qualified candidate
> for any public office to use a broadcasting station, he [sic] shall afford equal
> opportunities to all other such candidates for that office in the use of such
> broadcasting station....

The Equal Time Rule has a number of provisions, some of them troublesome for broadcasters. Section 315 specifically exempts *bona fide* (good faith) newscasts, news interviews, news documentaries, and, significantly, coverage of news events such as political conventions and debates between candidates. That means a broadcaster can cover news stories involving one candidate without having to include all other candidates.

Section 315 doesn't require broadcasters to *give* politicians free time for campaign advertising. Rather, it says that all candidates must be treated equally. If one is sold airtime for a certain fee, the Equal Time Rule merely requires that others be allowed to purchase equal time in the same part of the broadcast day for the same price. If other candidates can't afford to buy the airtime, the station has no obligation to give them free time. But if one candidate is given free airtime, all other candidates for the same office must also be given free airtime.

In 1984, the FCC extended the exemption for news and public affairs programs to many talk shows, thus allowing them to host political candidates during election campaigns without having to give equal time to all other candidates for the same office. In its 1991 rewrite of the rules, the FCC expanded this provision by saying that Section 315 really only applies to "uses" of a station that are controlled, approved, or sponsored by a candidate, such as political and campaign advertising.

Because the Equal Time Rule only requires equal treatment for candidates running in the *same election*, stations may sell advertising during a non-federal *primary election* only to those running for the Democratic and Republican nominations and not to those seeking minor party nominations. In the primary, the minor party candidates aren't running against the Democratic and Republican candidates. However, during the general election campaign all candidates for the same office must be allowed to buy comparable airtime at the same rates, said the D.C. Circuit interpreting Section 315 in 1970 (*Kay v. FCC*, 443 F.2d 638). But remember, in federal elections, all candidates must be offered "reasonable access" to broadcast airtime if they can pay for it. And once a broadcaster sells (or gives) airtime to *any* candidate, federal, state, or local, other candidates in the same election must be treated equally. Under these rules, it has become commonplace for broadcasters to accept advertising from federal candidates and candidates for the most prominent state and local offices, while rejecting advertising from all candidates for less important state and local offices.

Section 312(a)(7): federal offices. If Section 315 were the only applicable provision of the Communications Act, a station could comply with the Equal Time Rule by simply excluding *all* political advertising. That would, after all, be providing all candidates *equal* time—none. However, another provision of the Communications Act places an additional requirement on broadcasters. Section 312(a)(7)—or just Section 312—says broadcasters may have their licenses revoked if they fail to provide *reasonable access* to candidates *in federal elections*. ("Federal" means elections for the House and Senate as well as the presidency and vice presidency.) So a broadcaster cannot avoid the Equal Time provision by simply turning away all federal candidates; these candidates must be allowed to purchase airtime for

FIG. 94.
Robert M. ("Fighting Bob") La Follette, Sr. from Wisconsin, giving first radio campaign speech, Sept. 1, 1924.

Library of Congress Prints and Photographs Division, [LC-USZ62-42073] political advertising. But the 1991 revision of the rules makes it clear that broadcasters are not obligated to provide "reasonable access"—or any access at all—to candidates for state and local offices. Section 315 does require broadcasters to "afford reasonable opportunity for the discussion of conflicting views on issues of public importance," but the FCC has interpreted that to mean only that each station must cover the issues, not provide access to candidates for any particular non-federal office. However, if a station sells airtime to a non-federal candidate, it must offer to sell equal time to other candidates for the same office.

Jimmy Carter's case. During the 1980 presidential election campaign, the constitutionality of Section 312 was tested in court. The Carter-Mondale presidential campaign asked to purchase 30 minutes of airtime on each network in late 1979, about a year before the election. All three networks refused to honor the request, despite the provisions of Section 312. CBS offered only five minutes during prime time, while NBC and ABC flatly rejected the request. The FCC ruled that the networks had failed to meet their obligation to provide federal candidates "reasonable access" under Section 312. The networks challenged the ruling in court, leading to an important 1981 Supreme Court decision upholding the commission, *CBS v. FCC* (453 U.S. 367).

Voting 6-3, the high court affirmed the FCC's authority under Section 312 to order broadcasters to air federal candidates' political statements. The Court agreed with the FCC that the campaign had begun, even though the general election was nearly a year away at the time. The decision came too late to help the Carter-Mondale campaign, but it was a major victory for future candidates and a defeat for broadcasters. The majority ruled that the First Amendment rights of candidates and the public outweighed the First Amendment rights of broadcasters in this particular context. Writing for the Court, Chief Justice Warren Burger pointed out that the FCC need not (and does not) honor all requests for airtime by federal office seekers, but the FCC was well within its statutory authority in ordering the networks to air the Carter-Mondale campaign statements in late 1979. In fact, Burger noted that the FCC had set forth specific guidelines for broadcasters to follow in determining when candidates would have a right of access to the airwaves under Section 312. In this case, the FCC was justified in concluding that the three major networks had violated those guidelines.

Public TV political ads. In 2012, a divided Ninth Circuit panel said that provisions of the Communications Act that ban political and issue ads on public broadcasting stations violate the First Amendment out of fear of the "corrosive impact" of commercial ads. The Ninth Circuit heard the case *en banc* and *reversed* the panel's decision in 2013 (*Minority Television Project, Inc. v. FCC*, 736 F.3d 1192), restoring the prohibitions on political and issue advertising in the law governing advertising on public television, 47 U.S.C. § 399b.

The majority used an intermediate scrutiny test (rather than strict, as Minority Television recommended) to conclude "that substantial evidence before Congress supported the conclusion that the advertising prohibited by §399b posed a threat to the noncommercial, educational nature of NCE [non-commercial educational] programming." Then-chief judge Alex Kozinski, in typical language, dissented against the use of intermediate scrutiny:

> The very indeterminacy of the [intermediate scrutiny] standard enables—nay, encourages—judges to apply their own values. Speech that judges like gets protected, and speech that judges don't like gets the back of the hand. And judges like public radio and television, while pretty much nobody likes commercials.

Politicians and Lowest Unit Charges

Still another aspect of the political broadcasting rules has become a bookkeeping nightmare for both broadcasters and candidates: the *lowest unit charge* provision in Section 315(b). This provision requires broadcasters to charge candidates the lowest rate that they charge their most favored commercial advertisers for advertising within the 45 days of a primary election and 60 days of a general election. Note that this provision applies to *all* candidates, not just federal candidates.

The lowest unit charge rule means the candidates get the rate charged the largest volume advertisers, even if that discounted rate isn't normally offered to one-time or short-term advertisers. Prior to the 45- and 60-day periods, candidates may be charged rates "comparable" to those charged other advertisers, which means that a candidate doesn't get the quantity discount then without buying enough advertising to qualify for it.

In its 1991 rewrite of the political broadcasting rules, the FCC went to great lengths to clarify the lowest unit charge rule. In addition to volume discounts, most stations offer lower rates for *preemptible* airtime (that is, an ad that can be dropped if someone else comes along later and offers to pay more for the same airtime). On the other hand, someone who purchases *non-preemptible fixed* airtime is guaranteed that the ad will air at a specific time—but that kind of advertising costs more. Many stations have found that they can maximize their advertising revenue by using this system.

The FCC conducted an audit of stations' political advertising sales practices in 1990 and learned that many politicians were actually paying more than commercial advertisers because they were compelled to buy non-preemptible fixed airtime instead of preemptible airtime. That was defeating the purpose of the lowest unit charge provision in Section 315(b). In fact, the FCC found that candidates often weren't even told that preemptible time was available at a lower cost.

To remedy these problems, the FCC's 1991 rewrite of the rules requires broadcasters to tell candidates about all of the rates and classes of airtime available, and to allow candidates to purchase the least expensive airtime offered to anyone. And if a candidate's ads are preempted (i.e., taken off the air to make time for an advertiser willing to pay a higher rate), the station must provide a "make good" (i.e., get the candidates' ads on the air at another time) before the election if it has provided "time-sensitive" make goods to any commercial advertiser in the previous year. Also, the FCC ordered broadcasters to apply the same rules to candidates as to their most favored commercial advertisers in establishing priorities for protection against preemption.

And in the wake of the 2020 election, where there was both a delay in calling the presidential election for Joe Biden and a run-off election planned in Georgia for both Senate seats (no candidate got the necessary majority), questions arose of whether lowest unit charge rates would apply to political ads running after Nov. 2. The FCC issued guidance that said no; "even where the results of an election remain pending, broadcast stations are under no obligation to provide lowest unit charge after November 3, 2020," the agency ruled.

Lawsuits over lowest unit charge. Given the complexity of the lowest unit charge rule, there have been numerous disputes—and lawsuits—between broadcasters and candidates over political advertising rates. Candidates have sued broadcasters in state courts, alleging that they were overcharged for advertising in violation of the lowest unit charge rule.

In response to these suits, the FCC issued a declaration that the FCC itself, not the courts, has exclusive jurisdiction over lowest unit charge disputes. Then the Eleventh Circuit dismissed the FCC ruling as an "agency opinion" that does not prevent the courts from hearing

Section 315:
also called the Equal Time Rule, the rule that requires broadcasters to provide equal access to the airwaves to all legally qualified candidates for a given public office during election campaigns; broadcasters cannot censor political messages.

Section 312(a)(7):
often called just Section 312, the rule that requires broadcasters to provide reasonable access to candidates in federal elections.

lowest unit charge:
the requirement that broadcasters must charge candidates the lowest rate they charge their best advertisers for 45 days before a primary and 60 days before a general election.

safe harbor:
in broadcast law, the time (10:00 p.m. to 6:00 a.m.) during which over-the-air TV and radio stations may broadcast material that may be indecent. The FCC defines indecency as material that "portrays sexual or excretory organs or activities in a way that is patently offensive" but doesn't meet the *Miller* test (from Chapter Ten) for obscenity.

lowest unit charge lawsuits (*Miller v. FCC*, 66 F.3d 1140, 1995). But a few months later the Ninth Circuit said the Eleventh Circuit was wrong: the FCC's declaration is valid and deprives the courts of jurisdiction over these cases (*Wilson v. A.H. Belo Corp.*, 87 F.3d 393). While the courts quarrel among themselves, political candidates who think they were overcharged can take their complaints to the FCC for certain, and maybe in some parts of the country the courts will hear their cases, too.

Because the lowest unit charge rule applies only to candidates and not *ballot propositions*, some broadcasters who reject advertising from all candidates for minor state and local offices are perfectly willing to accept advertising for state and local ballot propositions—but at higher ad rates than candidates pay.

Political Debates and Other Problem Areas

Another messy area under the Equal Time Rule has been candidates' debates. For many years, the rule was interpreted to require broadcasters who aired debates between the major candidates to give equal time to all minor candidates as well. The major networks said they could never afford the airtime to do that. In 1960, when John F. Kennedy and Richard Nixon held the first nationally televised presidential debates, Congress passed a law temporarily setting aside Section 315 so equal time would not have to be given to minor candidates.

In several subsequent presidential elections, no nationally televised debates occurred because Congress chose not to set aside Section 315 again. In 1964, for instance, the polls indicated that Lyndon Johnson was far ahead of his Republican challenger, Barry Goldwater. Johnson's strategists felt he had nothing to gain and a lot to lose if he debated Goldwater, so the Democratic majority in Congress refused to set aside Section 315. For various reasons there were no nationally televised debates during the 1968 and 1972 campaigns, either.

However, in 1975 the FCC reinterpreted Section 315 to mean that a debate sponsored by a non-broadcast organization would be considered a *bona fide* news event, and hence exempt from the requirements of Section 315 (see *In re Aspen Institute and CBS*, 55 F.C.C.2d 697). That new interpretation, which came to be known as the *Aspen Rule*, was quickly challenged by Shirley Chisholm, a candidate in the 1976 presidential election, but a federal appellate court upheld the rule (*Chisholm v. FCC*, 538 F.2d 349, 1976).

Thus, in both 1976 and 1980, presidential debates were sponsored by the League of Women Voters and dutifully covered as *bona fide* news events by the networks. Had the debates been staged by a broadcaster or network, it would have been necessary to include (or give equal time to) perhaps 30 lesser-known candidates for president.

The FCC ruled in 1983 that broadcasters could sponsor debates directly instead of having them sponsored by third parties such as the League of Women Voters. At the same time, the FCC dropped rules that restricted the use of debates or segments of debates in news programs. The League of Women Voters challenged that reinterpretation of the rule, but lost in the U.S. Court of Appeals (*League of Women Voters v. FCC*, 731 F.2d 995, 1984).

Nevertheless, whether candidates' debates are sponsored by broadcasters or outside organizations, ethical questions arise when only certain candidates are invited to take part. Because of television's great influence, some would argue that any debate that excludes some candidates for an office violates the spirit if not the letter of the Equal Time provision. A particularly strong argument for this position can be made in state and local elections, where there may be only three or four candidates running (as opposed to the 30 or so who usually become legally qualified candidates for president).

The Supreme Court ruled on this aspect of the Equal Time Rule in a 1998 decision: *Ark. Educ. Television Comm'n v. Forbes* (523 U.S. 666). At issue was whether public television stations licensed to a government entity such as a state have a First Amendment obligation to include *all* candidates in a political debate—even the ones who have no realistic chance of winning. By a 6-3 vote, the Court ruled that even government-owned television stations have *no* obligation to include all candidates in a debate. The majority held that government-run stations, like private ones, have the right to make news judgments about which candidates are viable enough to be included in a debate sponsored by the station.

Justice Anthony Kennedy, writing for the Court, said that forcing public broadcasters to include all candidates "would result in less speech, not more" because debates simply could not be held if 20 or 30 different candidates for president had to be included in each debate.

However, Kennedy added that government-controlled stations have a special obligation to be "viewpoint neutral" in their standards for deciding which candidates to include in a debate, never excluding a prominent candidate because he or she might oppose abortion or affirmative action, for example. Justices John Paul Stevens, David Souter, and Ruth Bader Ginsburg dissented, arguing that for a government entity to exclude some candidates from a debate while including others "implicates constitutional concerns of the highest order." They were particularly troubled because the five Arkansas state-owned stations involved in this case did not have clear, objective criteria to be used in determining which candidates

FIG. 95.
President Gerald Ford and Jimmy Carter on television during presidential debate in Philadelphia, Sept. 23, 1976.

National Archives and Records Administration.

are viable enough to be included in debates. This case was seen as particularly important for public broadcasters because about two-thirds of the nation's 350 public television stations are licensed to a state (similarly, about two-thirds of NPR public radio stations are licensed to or affiliated with colleges or universities; the rest are governed by community-based boards).

There are other ethical and legal problems in political broadcasting. For example, the fact that news events are excluded from the Equal Time Rule allows incumbents to get extensive media coverage without other candidates having similar opportunity. When Senator Edward Kennedy was challenging Jimmy Carter for the 1980 Democratic presidential nomination, he asked the FCC to require the networks to give him equal time to reply to one of Carter's nationally televised news conferences. The FCC turned Kennedy down, and the D.C. Circuit upheld that decision (*Kennedy for President Comm. v. FCC*, 636 F.2d 432, 1980).

Showing the old movies of actors who become politicians (such as Arnold Schwarzenegger) poses a problem for broadcasters: the Equal Time Rule requires stations that air movies in which a candidate appears (even in a non-political dramatic role) to give equal time to other candidates for the same office if the movie is aired during the campaign period. A federal appellate court once upheld this interpretation of the rules (*In re Paulsen v. FCC*, 491 F.2d 887, 1974). The FCC's 1991 rewrite of the rules temporarily eliminated this problem, but the FCC later reinstated its earlier interpretation of Section 315.

Section 315 does not allow broadcasters to "censor" a political broadcast. If a candidate libels someone on the air, there is nothing the broadcaster can do to stop it. However, the Supreme Court has exempted broadcasters from any liability for defamatory remarks on such occasions (see *Farmers Educ. & Coop. Union v. WDAY*, discussed in Chapter Four).

This ban on censorship of political broadcasts also poses other dilemmas for broadcasters. For example, what happens if a candidate chooses to include language the broadcaster considers distasteful? Occasionally, a candidate insists on including vulgar or offensive language in a political statement—language that a broadcaster could not ordinarily air without incurring the wrath of the FCC. In 1984, the FCC issued a statement declaring that despite Section 315 broadcasters can prevent a candidate from using language that is not normally permitted on the airwaves.

However, broadcasters sometimes must allow candidates to include material that offends some (or many) viewers. For example, in recent years a number of candidates who opposed abortions have included photographs of aborted fetuses in their advertising. Acting on the advice of the FCC, a number of stations refused to air these ads in prime time—even if an opposing candidate had advertised in prime time. In 1996, a federal appellate court held that this "channeling" of anti-abortion campaign ads to times when the audience is small violates the Equal Time Rule. The court said that political candidates have a special right of access, even if their ads are offensive (*Becker v. FCC*, 95 F.3d 75).

Other problems have arisen as broadcasters tried to apply the Equal Time Rule. For example, what happens when on-air broadcast employees run for public office? Suppose a deejay with a four-hour show runs for the city council. If he or she doesn't take a leave of absence, must all other candidates be given similar deejay shows? The FCC's traditional answer to that question has been yes: the station must either take the broadcaster-candidate off the air during the campaign period or give all other candidates equal time—for free. In *Branch v. FCC* (824 F.2d 37), the D.C. Circuit in 1987 upheld the FCC's interpretation of the rules. The Equal Time Rule means what it says, even if a candidate is also a broadcaster, the court held. The Supreme Court refused to review the decision.

The Fairness Doctrine and Similar Rules: No More, But Still Controversial

Arguably, no rule that the FCC ever adopted has been as controversial as the Fairness Doctrine, established in 1949, abolished in 1987, and finally formally taken off the books in 2011. The Fairness Doctrine is relevant today because there have been repeated proposals in Congress to reinstate it. President Barack Obama did not support its return, but as recently as October 2017 President Donald J. Trump tweeted his displeasure with what he perceived as a lack of equal time for Republicans on "late night" television, calling for "Equal Time." Some commentators suggested these tweets signaled support for a return to the Fairness Doctrine, an allegation that the White House would neither confirm nor deny.

What did the doctrine do? The Fairness Doctrine required commercial broadcasters to keep their public affairs programming reasonably balanced: when they covered one side of a controversial issue, they had to balance that presentation by seeking out and airing opposing viewpoints—even if they had to give representatives of opposing views free airtime. Many members of Congress, some public interest groups, and many others advocate restoring the Fairness Doctrine. On the other hand, most broadcasters (especially broadcast journalists) have vehemently opposed it as a violation of their First Amendment rights because it allowed government bureaucrats to second-guess their news judgments.

When the FCC abolished the Fairness Doctrine in 1987, that may have been the FCC's most controversial decision ever: the Democratic majority in Congress voted to overrule the FCC and put the Fairness Doctrine into statutory law, only to have President Reagan veto that legislation. In 1989, Congress again considered legislation to reinstate the Fairness Doctrine—and President George H.W. Bush made it clear that he, too, would veto it. When Bill Clinton's victory in the 1992 presidential election gave the Democrats control of the White House as well as both houses of Congress, legislation to reinstate the Fairness Doctrine was again introduced. All attempts went nowhere.

The Fairness Doctrine was always a vague, general policy that led to relatively few disciplinary actions against broadcasters and almost no license non-renewals. The FCC didn't even forward most complaints of Fairness Doctrine violations to broadcasters. The agency received thousands of these complaints each year, and only a few resulted in an inquiry, let alone a formal action against the broadcaster. Unlike the Equal Time Rule, which requires broadcasters to sell/give *equal* time to opposing candidates, the doctrine never required minute-for-minute equality. Instead, it merely said broadcasters had to provide overall balance in their programming.

Why abolished? Several rationales for abolishing the Fairness Doctrine were offered. It gave government bureaucrats the right to second-guess the news judgments of broadcast journalists, opening the door for potentially dangerous violations of the First Amendment. It also deterred instead of encouraging full news coverage: the fear of having to provide free airtime to a variety of dissenting groups led many broadcasters to avoid controversial stories, or at least to tone them down to avoid offending anyone. These tendencies were evidence of the "chilling effect" the Fairness Doctrine had on the First Amendment rights of broadcasters. And finally, the scarcity rationale traditionally given to justify broadcast regulation simply didn't make sense anymore because of the many news sources available to the public (an even stronger argument today with the proliferation of online news).

The *Red Lion* and *Tornillo* cases: a clash of media. But the Fairness Doctrine was always constitutional. In 1969, the high court upheld the Fairness Doctrine in *Red Lion Broad. v. FCC* (395 U.S. 367). That case arose at the end of the 1964 presidential election when radio evangelist Billy James Hargis attacked Fred Cook, the author of a book that criticized Republican candidate Barry Goldwater. The attack was aired over Red Lion's radio station in Pennsylvania, and Cook demanded reply time under the Personal Attack Rule (discussed below).

Red Lion replied by telling Cook, in effect, to buy an ad. Instead, Cook complained to the FCC, which ordered the station to give Cook reply time. Red Lion appealed, charging that it violated a broadcaster's First Amendment rights to be forced to provide free airtime to someone like Cook. The Court agreed with Red Lion that the case involved First Amendment rights. However, the justices were clear about whose rights those were: "It is the right of the viewers and listeners, not the right of the broadcasters, which is paramount." Red Lion was ordered to give Cook time to reply to the personal attack.

In contrast, a few years later the Supreme Court said that the print media have no obligation whatever to give space to those with whom they disagree. In the landmark case of *Miami Herald v. Tornillo* (418 U.S. 241, 1974), the justices overturned a Florida law requiring newspapers to publish replies from political candidates who are personally attacked in print. The Court said the print media have a First Amendment right to publish only one side of controversial issues and to attack people without granting them space for a reply, if they so choose. Thus, there cannot be a Fairness Doctrine or Personal Attack Rule for the print media under the First Amendment. Many broadcasters felt this disparity in editorial freedom made them second-class citizens under the First Amendment.

In 1984, the Supreme Court addressed the First Amendment rights of public noncommercial radio and television stations—and suggested that it might be time to reconsider the constitutionality of the Fairness Doctrine. That happened in the case of *FCC v. League of Women Voters of California* (468 U.S. 364). This case was a challenge to a Congressional ban on editorializing by public broadcasters, and the Court said it violated the First Amendment. It was the first time the high court had ever overturned a federal content restriction on broadcasters on First Amendment grounds, and the justices seemed to invite a review of the validity of many other broadcast content restrictions, including the Fairness Doctrine.

Justice William J. Brennan, writing for the majority, rejected the arguments of those who felt public broadcasters should not carry editorials expressing their own views because they receive government funds. Congress had banned editorializing by stations receiving federal funds on the theory that if they editorialized, these stations would feel obligated to support the government's policies. Justice Brennan said there were many ways public broadcasters could be insulated from political pressures that might influence their editorial policies without simply forbidding them to speak out on the issues.

Although the decision came on a narrow 5-4 vote, the majority opinion was so sweeping that it raised doubts about the continuing validity of the entire range of broadcast content controls. Justice Brennan included a footnote that said the Court might be prepared to reexamine the scarcity rationale that justified the restrictions on broadcast content: "We are not prepared, however, to reconsider our long-standing approach without some signal from Congress or the FCC that technological developments have advanced so far that revision of the system of broadcast regulation may be required." That signal came within the next few years, of course, when the FCC abolished the Fairness Doctrine. Today, broadcasters have no obligation even to carry opposing viewpoints under most circumstances. Putting the final nail in the coffin, in August 2011, the FCC finally officially axed the Fairness Doctrine, along with 83 other rules that the agency believed were no longer necessary

Personal Attack and Political Editorializing Rules: also no more. Shortly after the FCC eliminated the Fairness Doctrine in 1987, a coalition of media organizations asked the commission to clarify whether some related rules had also been abolished. The FCC eventually declared, to the surprise of many, that the *Personal Attack Rule* remained in force, requiring broadcasters to continue notifying the victims of personal attacks (and in some instances, to give these persons free airtime for a reply). The FCC also reaffirmed its *Political Editorializing Rule*, which required broadcasters who endorse candidates to offer opponents free time to reply on the air. But in 2000 the D.C. Circuit overturned both rules. In *Radio-Television News Directors Association v. FCC* (229 F.3d 269), the court, saying that the rules "interfere with the editorial judgment of professional journalists and entangle the government in day-to-day operations of the media," ordered the FCC to eliminate them permanently because it had failed to justify their continued existence. Broadcast journalists praised the decision; they had argued from the beginning that these rules forced them to avoid covering certain issues and therefore had a chilling effect on freedom of expression.

Of course, nothing in the decision to abolish the Fairness Doctrine or the related rules affects the Equal Time provisions of the Communications Act (Section 315). Section 315 still requires broadcasters to offer all candidates for a given office equal opportunities to purchase airtime, as it has ever since the Communications Act was enacted in 1934.

Banning Indecency on the Airwaves

The FCC's *Indecency Rule*, a controversial topic for more than 40 years, is a major issue again in the 2000s. Indecency, never defined in a way that most broadcasters considered clear, involves the use of offensive language or images by broadcasters. The rule does *not* apply to cable and satellite television networks, nor to internet webcasting and podcasting—all of which have greater First Amendment protection than over-the-air broadcasting.

Incidentally, the FCC does not just fine stations for indecency; it can also levy fines for a station's refusal to respond to its requests for information. In 2010 it proposed a $25,000 fine against Fox TV Stations. This was not because of its broadcast of a controversial episode of *American Dad*, but because the FCC said Fox didn't answer questions about which stations actually broadcast that episode, which allegedly drew 100,000 indecency complaints.

Indecency has recently returned in full force to the public radar. The latest controversies were triggered by several incidents where celebrities were accused of violating the rules on national television. Perhaps most notably, singer Janet Jackson's halftime performance with Justin Timberlake during the 2004 Super Bowl included a brief breast-baring scene that sparked outrage in Washington and across the country.

Focus on...
Types of regulation

There are several kinds of regulations that affect media organizations. All of them have the potential to alter what those media organizations can publish and what the public can consume.

Structural regulations deal with relationships between media companies and with issues of ownership. Antitrust law is about managing structural regulations, and that will be covered in Chapter Twelve.

Content regulations regulate what is being said, whether to prevent, encourage, or demand certain kinds of speech. Much of what we've discussed in this book has dealt with content regulation.

Technical regulations, which don't often implicate First Amendment concerns, regulate how technology works; for example, regulations on radio transmitters that control radio frequency interference.

But before we turn to the more recent cases, it is important to understand some of the history behind the concern with sexual content on the airwaves.

The foundations in *Pacifica*. Long before current controversies over broadcast indecency began, the Supreme Court declared that indecent but non-obscene material could be banned from the airwaves during daytime hours, even if the same material was legal in other media. In the 1978 *FCC v. Pacifica Found.* case (438 U.S. 726), the Court voted 5-4 to uphold a mild FCC sanction against Pacifica, a foundation that operates several noncommercial radio stations, including WBAI in New York City. WBAI aired a program on contemporary attitudes toward language, and it included a 12-minute monologue by comedian

Focus on...

Social media as ... telephone companies ... or restaurants?

FIG. 96. Telephone and directory, Dubuque, Iowa, 1940, by John Vachon.

Library of Congress.

As we saw in Chapter Nine, the Second Circuit said in the 2019 *Knight First Amendment Inst.* case that former president Donald Trump couldn't block users from his personal Twitter account, since his use of the account made it a public forum. Trump appealed to the Supreme Court. But before the justices could act, two things happened: Joe Biden was elected in 2020, and Trump's Twitter account was suspended and then permanently banned in the wake of the Jan. 6, 2021 U.S. Capitol insurrection.

This case is a classic example of mootness: not only would Trump be a private citizen as of Jan. 20, 2021, but he no longer even had a Twitter account from which to block anyone. In April 2021, the Supreme Court granted *cert*, vacated the judgment, and remanded to the Second Circuit to declare moot (*Biden v. Knight First Amendment Inst.*, No. 20–197). More interesting, though, was Justice Clarence Thomas' concurrence in which he mused about how the power of huge social media companies could be curbed. While he agreed that this case should be moot, he did offer two suggestions for regulation: common carriage and public accommodations laws.

"A traditional telephone company laid physical wires to create a network connecting people. Digital platforms lay information infrastructure that can be controlled in much the same way," Thomas noted. Moreover, very few people own these giant companies, thus concentrating their power. Why is this important? As the justice tells us: "If part of the problem is private, concentrated control over online content and platforms available to the public, then part of the solution may be found in doctrines that limit the right of a private company to exclude."

Enter common carriage, mandating equal treatment by companies like freight haulers—and telephone services. The government gives common carriers some legal benefits but says that in exchange, they can't discriminate against potential users. If that analogy doesn't work, Thomas thought that instead social media might be regulated under public accommodations laws, which apply to companies like restaurants and theatres "that hold themselves out to the public but do not 'carry' freight, passengers, or communications." No other justices signed onto this opinion, but it does strongly suggest that Thomas is looking for new ways to regulate social media.

And just as this book was going to press, in July 2021, Trump announced that he was suing Facebook, Twitter, and Google for blocking him. Alleging that the bans violated his First Amendment rights, the former president called for Section 230 to be overturned, saying at a press conference, "Our case will prove this censorship is unlawful, it's unconstitutional and it's completely un-American." Most legal commentators (unsurprisingly) called the suit DOA. Stay tuned.

George Carlin entitled "Filthy Words." In it, Carlin named "the original seven words" that "you couldn't say on the public...airwaves" and ridiculed society's taboos about the words ("shit, piss, fuck, cunt, cocksucker, motherfucker and tits"). The program was broadcast at 2:00 p.m., preceded by a warning that some of the content might be offensive. Those words, by the way, appeared in the official Supreme Court decision (unlike in some later decisions). A man who said he and his son inadvertently stumbled on the monologue while listening to their car radio complained to the FCC, and the FCC eventually placed a warning notice in the station's license renewal file. The FCC did not find the language obscene but said it was "patently offensive" and indecent—and therefore inappropriate for the airwaves. Further such incidents could lead to a license nonrenewal, the FCC said.

Pacifica Foundation appealed to the courts. The Supreme Court ruled that the language, though not legally obscene, was inappropriate for broadcasting, at least during the daytime. The Court said the words were indecent even if they might be constitutionally protected under other circumstances. Explaining his decision, Justice John Paul Stevens made an analogy to nuisance law and quoted an earlier decision defining a nuisance as "merely a right thing in the wrong place—like a pig in the parlor instead of the barnyard." He then concluded: "We simply hold that when the commission finds that a pig has entered the parlor, the exercise of its regulatory power does not depend on proof that the pig is obscene."

Indecency defined. So what is indecency? For many years the FCC used a definition of indecency that the Supreme Court employed in *Pacifica Found.*:

> [Indecency is] language or material that, in context, depicts or describes, in terms patently offensive as measured by contemporary community standards for the broadcast medium, sexual or excretory activities or organs.

Under that definition, which has been given a variety of different interpretations over the years, frontal nudity and certain offensive words have been banned except during a *"safe harbor"* overnight between 10 p.m. and 6 a.m. Separate laws also ban profanity and legally obscene material on the air.

Safe harbors. By the mid-1990s, the D.C. Circuit handed down four separate decisions on the FCC's post-*Pacifica* indecency enforcement. In the end, the court issued an *en banc* decision holding that the FCC, acting on orders from Congress, could ban indecency from the airwaves at all times except during a "safe harbor" period between 10 p.m. and 6 a.m.—hours when relatively few children are in the broadcast audience (*Action for Children's Television v. FCC*, 58 F.3d 654, 1995). The 7-4 majority held that there is a compelling government interest in protecting children from indecent material that justifies banning broadcast indecency from over-the-air stations during the daytime when many children are in the audience. Armed with that ruling, the FCC began its recent crackdown in 2004.

Stern gets burned. The longest-running target of the FCC's crackdown on alleged broadcast indecency has been Howard Stern's syndicated radio program. Stations that carried Stern's controversial show were hit with fines of about $2 million by the mid-1990s. Stations owned by Infinity Broadcasting alone were fined $1.7 million for indecency violations on Stern's show. In 2004, the nation's largest radio group, Clear Channel Communications, paid a fine of $1.75 million on top of an earlier $755,000 fine for alleged indecency in its programming, including Stern's show. Stern was then dropped by the six Clear Channel stations that carried him, and the giant radio group launched a broad effort to curb the language and visual images used on its radio and TV stations.

Meanwhile, other broadcasters felt the FCC's new wrath over indecency. NBC was condemned but not fined by the FCC for rock star Bono's use of the phrase "fucking brilliant" during a live telecast of the 2003 Golden Globe awards. The FCC overruled its own staff, which had ruled Bono's words non-indecent because they were not used in a sexual context. In so ruling, FCC chair Michael Powell acknowledged that the FCC's enforcement policies were being changed in 2004. NBC apologized for the incident but emphasized that the rules in place in 2003 "did not subject broadcasters to strict liability for fleeting utterances in live broadcasts."

Janet's Super Bowl "wardrobe malfunction." The FCC voted in September 2004 to impose a $550,000 penalty on CBS for the breast-baring incident involving singer Janet Jackson during the 2004 Super Bowl halftime show. The fine was aimed at 20 CBS-owned stations, each facing what was then the maximum penalty, $27,500. At the time it was the largest fine ever imposed on TV stations as opposed to often-fined radio stations. Viacom, then the parent company of CBS, eventually paid the fine—and then challenged the FCC in federal court, seeking a refund. Although CBS apologized to viewers, Viacom officials said the incident did not meet the legal standard for a finding of broadcast indecency, which must include a determination that the broadcast was patently offensive.

In 2009, the Third Circuit threw out the $550,000 fine against CBS for the Jackson "wardrobe malfunction" in *CBS v. FCC* (535 F.3d 167), saying that the FCC had "strayed from its long-held approach of applying identical standards to words and images when reviewing complaints of indecency." The FCC appealed to the Supreme Court. After the Court ruled narrowly in favor of the FCC in the "fleeting expletive" indecency case, *FCC v. Fox Television*, it remanded the case back to the Third Circuit to evaluate in light of that decision (*FCC v. CBS Corp.*, 556 U.S. 1218, 2009). In 2011, the Third Circuit again vacated the FCC's fine

FIG. 97.
Artist's portrait of George Carlin (1937–2008) in acrylics. When a New York City radio station played Carlin's monologue about "filthy words" during the day, a listener complained, resulting in *FCC v. Pacifica* and the rise of indecency policies, laws, and fines.

katherine Bingley, "george carlin," Feb. 26, 2011, via Flickr, Creative Commons attribution license.

against CBS for the "wardrobe malfunction," saying that the agency "failed to acknowledge that its order in this case reflected a policy change and improperly imposed a penalty on CBS for violating a previously unannounced policy" (*CBS Corp. v. FCC*, 663 F.3d 122). The court said that the FCC did not tighten its policies until *after* the Super Bowl broadcast.

The Supreme Court denied *cert* to hear an appeal, but Chief Justice John Roberts took the unusual step of issuing a two-page concurring opinion of the denial of *cert*, saying that he wasn't sure the Third Circuit had it right: the "fleeting expletive" policy was for words, and the FCC "never stated that the exception applied to fleeting *images* as well, and there was good reason to believe that it did not" (*FCC v. CBS Corp.*, 567 U.S. 953). Justice Ruth Bader Ginsburg also added a brief concurrence urging the FCC to revisit its indecency policy.

Other FCC actions. In 2004, Viacom had agreed to pay $3.5 million to settle a series of other indecency charges unrelated to the Janet Jackson case. Although many involved Howard Stern's show on Viacom's Infinity Broadcasting radio stations, the settlement also resolved indecency complaints that had been filed against such TV programs as *CSI* and *Big Brother*. In the settlement, Viacom also agreed to put a time delay on all live programming, discipline employees who violate FCC rules, and hold classes on indecency compliance.

The FCC also announced fines totaling $1.18 million against Fox television stations for a sexually explicit episode of *Married by America*. Unlike the fines Viacom faced for the Janet Jackson incident, this sanction applied to all stations that carried the Fox feed, not just network-owned stations. Many Fox stations were challenging the fines, contending that they had no way to know in advance what the content of this unscripted reality show would be and that they merely passed through network programming.

Congress raises the financial stakes. Congress responded to public outrage after the 2004 Super Bowl incident in 2006 by passing the *Broadcast Decency Enforcement Act*, a law that increased the maximum fines the FCC may impose on broadcasters by a factor of 10. Now a single station can be fined $325,000 for one profane or indecent word or image, up to a maximum of $3 million for one program. If 100 stations carry the same network feed, they could be fined a total of $32.5 million for one word or $300 million for one program.

In 2006, the FCC imposed more large indecency fines, including $3.6 million in fines of CBS stations for airing a partially obscured teen sex scene on "Without a Trace." The penalty was later reduced to $3.35 million when the FCC learned that some of the 100-plus stations that had been fined actually aired the show during the safe harbor after 10 p.m.

At the same time, the FCC fined broadcasters for a number of other programs. One college-owned station was fined for airing *Godfathers and Sons*, a widely acclaimed PBS documentary on the blues as a musical genre. That prompted PBS to urge its stations to bleep all potentially offensive words in PBS programming, and even to obscure the faces of people who uttered bleeped-out words.

In 2008, the FCC fined ABC $1.4 million for an episode of *NYPD Blue* that showed a woman's nude buttocks. ABC was fined because the scene was aired before the 10 p.m.-6 a.m. safe harbor in the Central and Mountain time zones. The FCC did not fine ABC for airing the show on the east and west coasts, where it was broadcast after 10 p.m. ABC said it would appeal the fines.

In 2007, the Second Circuit overturned many of the FCC's recent indecency enforcement actions and ordered the agency to reconsider (*Fox Television v. FCC*, 489 F.3d 444). Specifically, the court overturned the FCC's sanctions of the fleeting use of four-letter words during live broadcasts. This case did not involve the Janet Jackson/Justin Timberlake Super Bowl performance, although that episode was on everyone's mind as this litigation unfolded. A separate legal challenge to the FCC's $550,000 fine in that case was thrown out by the Third Circuit in 2009, and the Supreme Court finally closed the case in 2012, erasing the fine against CBS.

In a strongly worded opinion in the *Fox* case, the appellate court condemned the FCC for changing its rules concerning spontaneous utterances without justifying the change. Tracing the history of indecency enforcement, the court noted that the FCC had not considered fleeting utterances to be indecent until recently—and still didn't seem to mind if they occurred during news broadcasts. The court was particularly troubled that the FCC allowed the airing of some movies with four-letter words, including *Saving Private Ryan*, while punishing broadcasters when a celebrity used the same words during a live awards show. The court didn't mention the fact that President Bush used one of the forbidden words during a major international conference in 2006. Fearing the FCC's wrath, most networks bleeped the President's word from their news coverage—an action with huge First Amendment implications.

The decision was actually a narrow one, not addressing the basic First Amendment issues raised by Fox and other television networks. All the court really said was that the FCC had to reconsider cases where it penalized broadcasters for airing fleeting offensive utterances.

The other issue that the appellate court didn't decide was the reasonableness of punishing over-the-air broadcasters for the use of four-letter words when the same words are perfectly legal at all hours of the day and night on cable and satellite networks. At least 85% of U.S. households received cable or satellite television at the time (although those numbers are dropping as streaming video services take hold; only 45% of those surveyed said they subscribed to a cable service by December 2020). The FCC appealed.

The high court steps in. The FCC won a narrow victory on appeal in the Supreme Court (*FCC v. Fox Television*, 556 U.S. 502, 2009). In one of the most highly anticipated decisions of the year, the Court reversed the Second Circuit's decision in favor of Fox and said that the FCC's "fleeting expletives" policy did not violate the Administrative Procedure Act (APA).

Justice Antonin Scalia wrote the opinion for the Court. He did not use any of the expletives at issue in the opinion, referring to them as the "F-word" and "S-word" or using asterisks in place of some of the letters (e.g., quoting Cher as saying "So f 'em"). He traced the development of FCC indecency policy and said that the FCC's changes in how it dealt with "fleeting expletives" were not arbitrary and capricious under the APA. The agency, said Scalia, "need not demonstrate to a court's satisfaction that the reasons for the new policy are *better* than the reasons for the old one; it suffices that the new policy is permissible under the statute, that there are good reasons for it, and that the agency *believes* it to be better." Moreover, he added, the Court would not apply a more stringent definition of the "arbitrary and capricious" standard to an agency whose actions implicated constitutional liberties.

In responding to a concern raised in Justice Stephen Breyer's dissent that the Court's decision would require small broadcasters to invest in expensive screening technology, and some of those broadcasters would be unable to afford such technology, Scalia took a swipe at Hollywood celebrities:

> We doubt, to begin with, that small-town broadcasters run a heightened risk of liability for indecent utterances. In programming that they originate, their down-home local guests probably employ vulgarity less than big-city folks; and

small-town stations generally cannot afford or cannot attract foul-mouthed glitteratae from Hollywood.

Justices John Paul Stevens, David Souter, Stephen Breyer, and Ruth Bader Ginsburg dissented. Stevens said that the FCC's initial views, formed in close proximity to Congressional mandates delegating the agency's actions, had worked fine for decades and should be presumed to be closest to what Congress wanted when it gave the agency authority to act. Ginsburg said that in her view, the change in policy exemplified arbitrary and capricious decision-making, and moreover, "there is no way to hide the long shadow the First Amendment casts over what the Commission has done."

Justice Anthony Kennedy concurred in part and dissented in part. While he agreed that the judgment against the FCC should be reversed, he also agreed with Breyer that under the APA the agency must explain its rejection of "the considerations that led it to adopt that initial policy." Justice Clarence Thomas concurred in the outcome but, in an opinion that gives hope to those who dislike the two-tired regulatory regime, he said that he has grave concerns about the cases on which that regime rests: *Red Lion Broad. v. FCC* and *FCC v. Pacifica Found.* He pointed to changes in technology that have taken place since those decisions were handed down and explicitly invited a case where those precedents could be evaluated: "I am open to reconsideration of *Red Lion* and *Pacifica* in the proper case."

The Second Circuit heard oral arguments for the second time in January 2010 on the remand of the indecency case. The oral argument did not go smoothly for the FCC; thus, it was not much of a surprise when the Second Circuit in *Fox Television v. FCC* (613 F.3d 317) dropped its bombshell: the entire FCC indecency regime was unconstitutional, and it "violates the First Amendment because it is unconstitutionally vague, creating a chilling effect that goes far beyond the fleeting expletives at issue here."

The media environment, the Second Circuit said, has changed since the rules were enacted in 1978, and technology like the V-chip enables parents to exercise more control over children's television viewing. Moreover, the FCC's policy is vague: "For instance, while the FCC concluded that 'bullshit' in a 'NYPD Blue' episode was patently offensive, it concluded that 'dick' and 'dickhead' were not." Networks thus do not know what exactly will be deemed indecent under the standard.

The FCC appealed to the Supreme Court, but the justices dodged First Amendment questions about indecency in the 2012 decision (*FCC v. Fox Television*, 567 U.S. 239). Instead, the Court relied on Fifth Amendment due process grounds to find the FCC's policies on fleeting expletives to be unconstitutionally vague. Justice Anthony Kennedy wrote for the majority invalidating the order, saying, "The Commission failed to give Fox or ABC fair notice prior to the broadcasts in question that fleeting expletives and momentary nudity could be found actionably indecent." Justice Ruth Bader Ginsburg, concurring, urged the reconsideration of *Pacifica*, agreeing with Justice Thomas in the 2009 *Fox* case.

The Court's 2012 *Fox* case is perhaps more notable for what it did *not* do. The justices, in addition to declining to review the First Amendment implications of the FCC's overall regulation of indecent speech, also did not review the FCC's current indecency policies. Nor did the justices close the door on a revised indecency policy or on judicial review of the current or revised policies, instead saying the FCC could "modify its current indecency policy in light of its determination of the public interest and applicable legal requirements."

Aftermath of the Court's rulings. The FCC levied the largest indecency fine for a single incident in 2015 against a Roanoke, Virginia, TV station that ran a three-second visual image of a "naked, erect penis and sexual manipulation thereof" in the corner of the screen one time on a 6:00 p.m. news broadcast: $325,000 (*In the Matter of WDBJ Television, Inc.*, NAL/Acct. No. 201532080010). The station argued that the image was fleeting and not visible to many of those responsible for editing the story (one of local public interest about an ex-porn star), and that it did not have an appropriate basis on which to judge potential indecency, "especially in the context of a news broadcast of a story of interest to the community" and the fact that the agency is reviewing its own rules. The FCC disagreed, claiming that there is no exception for indecency of news broadcasts and that its indecency rules, contrary to the station's claim that they are unconstitutional and also under review, derive from the *Pacifica* case and are still good law.

Indecency is still very much on the agendas of both the government and the public. In 2008, Congress passed, and President George W. Bush signed, the *Child Safe Viewing Act*. The act requires the FCC to study advanced blocking technologies (as well as their availability and encouragement) that would help parents keep "indecent or objectionable" content from their children. These technologies could apply to a variety of electronic communication, including the internet. The FCC called for comments and in 2009 reported that the consensus seemed to be that there was no one technology that would work across all platforms. Moreover, the FCC acknowledged "the need for greater education and media literacy for parents and more effective diffusion of information about the tools available to them."

Egregiousness? In a move that had policy watchers scratching their heads, the FCC announced on April 1, 2013, that it had cleared a number of old indecency cases off its docket (more than 70% of the backlog was cleared) and would be focusing on those that were most "egregious." The agency didn't provide any definitions or information on what would be considered "egregious" (causing some commentators to wonder if this was an FCC April Fool's joke). At the same time, the agency called for "comment on whether the full Commission should make changes to its current broadcast indecency policies or maintain them as they are." As of 2021, nothing suggests that the agency's policy on pursuing indecency violations has changed from its focus on "egregious" cases.

Regulating Children's Programming ("KidVid" rules)

In addition to its rules on political broadcasting and indecency, the FCC has at various times enforced a number of other broadcast content regulations. Agency rules on how broadcasters serve the public interest through children's programming, or what the industry calls "KidVid," have long been both controversial and subject to regular updates.

Children's Television Act of 1990. Congress passed a law to regulate children's programming in 1990, the Children's Television Act. It limits advertising on children's shows to 12 minutes per hour on weekdays and 10.5 minutes per hour on weekends. This provision applies only to shows intended for children age 12 and younger. The law requires broadcasters to prove at license renewal time that they have met the "educational and informational needs" of children age 16 and younger by airing programs *specifically designed for that purpose*. This law has been amended several times.

Ad rules for cable and satellite, too. The limits on commercials also apply to cable and satellite TV, including both cable network shows and locally produced programming, and have been enforced aggressively. The FCC conducts audits of station compliance, and stations carrying excessive advertising have often been fined. For example, in 2004, the FCC hit two cable networks with large fines for carrying too many commercials during children's television programs: Nickelodeon got a $1 million fine and ABC Family a $500,000 fine. These fines seemed small in comparison to a record $24 million fine that Univision Communications agreed to pay in 2007. Univision, the United States' largest Spanish-language broadcaster, incurred the FCC's wrath by airing telenovelas to fulfill its obligation to carry three hours of children's educational programs a week. It apparently agreed to pay the fine to win FCC approval of the network's sale to an investor group in Los Angeles.

Most recently, in Nov. 2020, the FCC fined Baltimore station WUTB-TV for eight KidVid ad violations. During eight showings of "Team Hot Wheels" between Nov. and Dec. 2018, WUTB aired 11 commercials for a "Hot Wheels Super Ultimate Garage" play set. The station admitted its mistake but claimed that it wasn't entirely responsible: the ads were placed by the company from which the station licensed the show (which removed them as soon as it was notified). The FCC responded that the 11 inappropriate ads constituted "a substantial number of violations," and it didn't matter if the source of those ads was a third party—WUTB was still liable for a $20,000 fine (more than the $8,000 base fine because of the station's "willful and repeated violation" of the rules).

Children's TV Act 1991 and 1996 amendments. The Children's Television Act also established a National Endowment for Children's Television to support educational programs. In addition, Congress directed the FCC to address the problem of toy-based shows and determine if they were improper *program-length commercials* because they promoted toys based on the shows' characters (e.g., Smurfs or Power Rangers)—a concern voiced again a decade later. Acting in 1991, the FCC adopted new rules concerning toy-based shows in response to the Congressional mandate. The rules forbid commercials within a show (or within one minute on either side of the show) for toys based on characters in that show. And the rules also forbid hosts of children's shows from doing commercials, on the premise that young children cannot distinguish commercials from the show. Any commercials must be separated from noncommercial segments of children's shows. But the FCC declined to ban toy-based shows altogether, a decision that was widely criticized by groups advocating quality children's programming.

Then in 1996 the FCC adopted new rules requiring all commercial TV stations to offer at least three hours a week of regularly scheduled programming to meet the *educational and informational* needs of children. When a digital TV station airs multiple program streams, each stream must include three hours of children's programming per week.

The adoption of these rules followed an extended controversy in which advocacy groups argued that all TV stations have a duty to provide educational programming for children. The networks and major station groups responded by pointing to the various programming and community services they were already providing that had educational value for children. Some pointed out that despite its widely praised quality, PBS educational programming has had low ratings. Given a choice, most viewers have voted with their remote controls for other kinds of programming.

The trade press and other First Amendment advocates expressed concerns about the implications of the mandatory children's programming requirements for other reasons. Here, they noted, is a government agency dictating program content, telling commercial broadcasters to provide the kind of children's programming that *the government thinks children should be watching*—and then to promote it to persuade viewers to watch what's good for them instead of the programming they might prefer to watch.

2019 update. The FCC announced it would be closely examining its current KidVid rules in 2018. In 2019, the agency issued those rules. Among key requirements, some of them new: Stations must air at least 156 hours per year of core children's programs (still three hours a week), including at least 26 hours per quarter of regularly scheduled weekly programs. Most of that programming must be regularly scheduled and at least 30 minutes long, but stations can air occasional programs that aren't regularly scheduled (like educational specials) and short-form programs (like public service announcements) as part of core programming.

Some regulations were eased: broadcasters could start children's programming an hour earlier, at 6 a.m., so core programming hours run from 6 a.m. to 10 p.m. Stations were also allowed up to 13 hours per quarter of regularly scheduled weekly programming on a multi-cast (online) stream (52 hours online and 104 hours over-the-air per year). The commission also made changes to its preemption policy: a station that preempts its regular programming (for example, to broadcast Super Bowl programming) can broadcast the preempted episode anytime during core programming hours within a seven-day span before or after the original airdate. Breaking-news coverage, including local coverage of non-breaking live news like local officials' swearings-in, doesn't require rescheduling of preempted programming. The FCC also called for another rulemaking.

Support for the rules wasn't unanimous: both Democratic commissioners dissented. Jessica Rosenworcel expressed disappointment that the new rule "slashes so much of our children's television policies." She went on, "We make it harder for parents to find content by reducing regularly scheduled programming. We shuttle off programming to multicast streams that most people don't watch and few parents are ever likely to locate." Geoffrey Starks echoed some of her concerns, adding that the new rules "will significantly reduce the amount of free, over-the-air children's programming aired by broadcasters"—free programming he deemed essential for many families who don't subscribe to any outside services.

Regulating Violent Programming

Another controversy about government regulation of broadcast content involved television violence. The Telecommunications Act of 1996 required all television set manufacturers to include a so-called *V-chip* in all but the smallest television sets so parents could program their TV sets to block programming they didn't want their children to watch. The act also required the industry to come up with a "voluntary" rating system so programs with ratings for excessive violence or sexual content can be blocked by parents. Programs not rated as suitable for children were to carry an encoded signal to prevent television sets with the V-chip from receiving them unless parents (or whoever controls the TV set) enter the correct code to receive these shows. In 1998, the FCC adopted rules requiring manufacturers to include the V-chip in all new TV sets with screens larger than 13 inches by January 2000.

V-chip. In mandating the V-chip system, Congress and the FCC were responding to a public outcry about the high rate of violent crime and pregnancy among teenagers in America. Congress apparently accepted the argument of many parents and others that at least part of the blame lies with violent and sexually oriented programming on television. The 1996 law gave the industry one year to come up with a "voluntary" rating system—or else the FCC would convene an advisory committee to set up the ratings.

Ratings system. Soon after the Telecommunications Act became law, the industry set up its own task force to develop a rating system for television shows, drawing on the experience of the Motion Picture Association of America with its rating system for movies. However, the original TV rating system did not provide the one thing that many groups critical of television programming wanted the most: program ratings specifically indicating violent or sexually oriented content or offensive language with letter ratings. Industry critics, backed by key members of Congress and the Clinton administration, demanded changes. In mid-1997, the industry agreed to modify the system, adding letters to designate violence, sexual content, suggestive dialogue, offensive language or fantasy violence. The rating is displayed in a corner of the screen at the beginning of each rated show.

Perhaps the most basic concern about the ratings and the V-chip system is whether it really works. "Unless a new V-chip television is going to come equipped with a pair of hand-cuffs, it won't stop kids from finding ways to watch forbidden shows," one network executive told the trade press after the 1996 law was passed.

In fact, one thing that delayed progress in developing V-chip technology was the difficulty of designing a programming system too complex for adolescents to figure out but simple enough for most adults. Leaders of the Consumer Electronics Manufacturers Association predicted that many children, especially teens, would devise ways to get around the program blocking. When V-chip-equipped TV sets began appearing in stores in early 2000, merchants reported widespread consumer indifference to the system. In 2005, the broadcast industry began a campaign to make parents more familiar with the V-chip system, hoping to ward off additional government regulation of content. Despite that campaign, a nationwide survey by the nonpartisan Kaiser Family Foundation said in 2007 only 16% of parents said they ever used the V-chip, although 71% of those who had used it found it to be "very useful."

For the first time since it was adopted 22 years ago, the content rating system was reviewed and evaluated. In 2019, as part of an omnibus spending bill, the FCC was ordered to report to Congress about the accuracy of the ratings system and the efficiency of the TV Parental Guidelines Oversight Monitoring Board (TVOMB) "to address public concerns." The agency undertook the review and called for public comments, and the results, issued three months later, surprised no one. The FCC heard from many advocacy groups how flawed the ratings system was: instances of different ratings for original and syndicated showings, inappropriate ratings, and "ratings creep" toward more permissive ratings over time. Causes suggested for these problems included self-rating by program creators and a rating system that is difficult to understand and apply. The agency also heard from industry groups whose perspectives directly conflicted with advocacy groups' views: parents were happy with the system and didn't think that shows were inaccurately or inconsistently rated. Opinions on the TVOMB were similarly split, but the FCC itself felt that the board was not sufficiently transparent or accessible and recommended that this be addressed.

So what happened? Not enough to please advocacy groups like the Parents Television Council, who complained to the TVOMB in 2020 that the board's 2019 annual report demonstrated "woefully inadequate output"—for example, making few media appearances and repeating the "same hollow talking points" it made in the FCC's 2019 report. The TVOMB's 2020 report issued in January 2021, however, claimed that the board responded to over 600 public complaints, created a streaming media task force, and completed a biennial (every two years) survey of over 1,000 parents with kids aged 2–17 in which 80% of parents approved of the ratings system and 95% were happy with the accuracy of ratings.

Other Content Regulations

For almost 25 years, broadcasters were subject to another content control that was always controversial and, some said, never successful: the *Prime Time Access Rule*. It was adopted by the FCC in 1971 and abolished in 1995. Under this rule, the ABC, NBC, and CBS networks were generally limited to three hours of evening programming during the four-hour period from 7 to 11 p.m. Monday through Saturday (6 to 10 p.m. in the central and mountain time zones), with exceptions for news events and special occasions. The rule only applied in the 50 largest metropolitan areas. But other rules regarding content still exist.

VNRs and other sponsored programming. Among other FCC regulations governing content are rules governing sponsorship identification. Broadcasters must identify the sponsors of ads and disclose if someone has paid for the airing of non-advertising material. The sponsor identification regulations were at the center of a controversy in the mid-2000s. Broadcasters sometimes use *video news releases* (VNRs) that appear to be news stories but are actually produced by corporations or government agencies. There was widespread criticism when the White House Office of National Drug Control Policy distributed VNRs that looked like news stories with a narrator who identified herself as "Karen Ryan" and said she was "reporting." Some stations aired these releases without identifying their government origin.

The FCC issued a public notice in 2005 warning that such practices violate the sponsor ID rules. Calling VNRs "prepackaged news stories," the notice went on, "Listeners and viewers are entitled to know who seeks to persuade them." The FCC was clear: "Whenever broadcast stations and cable operators air VNRs, licensees and operators generally must clearly disclose to members of their audiences the nature, source and sponsorship of the material."

The FCC also asked for assistance from the public in identifying "covert commercial pitches" (as Commissioner Jonathan S. Adelstein put it) in which a company pays for product placement in a TV show. The FCC reiterated that under the rules paid endorsements and product placements must be identified as such, something that often doesn't happen. In 2006, the FCC sent inquiries to 77 television stations that were accused by a watchdog group of airing VNRs without identifying their source.

The Government Accountability Office (GAO) issued a 2013 report with the telling title "Requirements for Identifying Sponsored Programming Should Be Clarified." For example, the GAO pointed out that there was some confusion as to whether there needs to be a sponsorship announcement as part of a VNR when no payment is made for the broadcast—a requirement for sponsorship identification. Moreover, the GAO said, "While most complaints do not end with an enforcement action, FCC generally does not communicate with the broadcaster named in the complaint when it closes sponsorship identification investigations." The FCC said it would review the recommendations in the report and consider how to implement changes.

Hoaxes. The FCC also has another rule governing broadcast content: a restriction on over-the-air hoaxes. The rule was enacted in response to several widely publicized incidents in which radio stations reported fake events in the early 1990s. For example, a Los Angeles station aired a phony murder confession, a station in St. Louis reported during the Persian Gulf war that the United States was under nuclear attack, and a Virginia station reported that a large waste dump was about to explode. The potential dump explosion created a panic reminiscent of the one caused by Orson Welles' classic "War of the Worlds" broadcast in 1938. (In a special Halloween broadcast on network radio, Orson Welles dramatized H.G. Wells' tale about an invasion of Earth by Martians. In Welles' program, music was interrupted by authentic-sounding news bulletins that terrified millions of people, especially near the Martians' purported landing site in New Jersey.)

The FCC responded to the more recent hoaxes by banning broadcast fabrications about crimes and catastrophes that "divert substantial public safety resources" or "cause substantial harm to public health and welfare." Hoaxes raise troubling ethical questions, of course, but the FCC's response to these hoaxes again illustrates the limited First Amendment rights of broadcasters. Does any government agency have the right to forbid tabloid newspapers from publishing pure fabrications as news? Should the government be allowed to ban what it considers to be false stories in newspapers, or just on radio and television? Should hoaxes be banned in all of the media? When does a broadcast dramatization—a fictitious work— become a hoax and therefore illegal on the air?

Payola. *Payola*, the practice of record labels, promoters, and others secretly paying radio deejays for putting certain songs on the air, was controversial more than 50 years ago. The FCC eventually rewrote the rules to outlaw such paid exposure unless it is disclosed. But in the 2000s, the issue reappeared and triggered a new crackdown in New York.

CBS Radio agreed in 2006 to donate $2 million to nonprofit New York music programs to end an investigation; there was evidence that CBS Radio employees accepted gifts from music labels to play songs that wouldn't otherwise have been aired. In 2007, four broadcast groups (Clear Channel, CBS Radio, Entercom Communications, and Citadel Broadcasting) signed an FCC consent decree agreeing to pay $12.5 million in fines. While admitting no wrongdoing, the four promised that their 1,600-plus radio stations would not accept compensation for airing music without disclosing it and agreed to provide more airtime for independent and local artists.

Lotteries. Another kind of content that has been restricted is advertising and other programming that promotes gambling. The advertising of gambling is restricted both by FCC regulations and by various state laws. However, government-run lotteries may advertise on local stations in their areas, and charitable lotteries are generally exempt from these restrictions, as are promotions and drawings by non-casinos. Under the Charity Games Advertising Clarification Act of 1988, only casinos and others whose gambling is an end in itself are forbidden to advertise *by federal law*. However, the 1988 act left the states free to restrict or ban lottery advertising even if the advertising would be legal under federal law.

What constitutes a lottery? A lottery exists any time the three *elements of a lottery* are present. They are: (1) a valuable prize; (2) determining the winner at least partly by chance; and (3) requiring participants to pay some "consideration" to enter the contest. To get around these rules, many businesses set up drawings with the disclaimer "no purchase necessary" to eliminate the consideration element and make their drawings legal to advertise. In many states, that is no longer necessary for businesses not primarily engaged in gambling. Chapter Thirteen contains discussions of several cases (in particular, *U.S. v. Edge Broad.*, 1993, and *Greater New Orleans Broad. Ass'n v. U.S.*, 1999) that implicate gambling advertising.

In the *Greater New Orleans* decision, the Court ruled that the federal government may not ban broadcast advertising for private casino gambling. After that case, the FCC issued a statement saying that broadcasters are indeed free to carry gambling ads anywhere that gambling is legal—but hedged about the rights of broadcasters in states that prohibit gambling. Nevertheless, the FCC stopped enforcing the lottery rule, leaving broadcasters free to carry advertising for out-of-state casinos if their state does not forbid gambling advertising. However, this does not supersede the *Edge* decision, which refused to legalize lottery advertising by broadcasters licensed to a state that has no state lottery and prohibits lottery advertising.

Other rules. Broadcasters are subject to many other laws that govern advertising in general. For instance, the federal Truth-in-Lending Act requires the full disclosure of all credit terms if any of the terms of a loan are mentioned in an ad. Almost no one would quarrel with the wisdom of having laws requiring credit advertising to be truthful and complete. However, the required disclosures are sometimes so detailed that they cannot all be squeezed into a short broadcast advertisement.

As for serving "the public interest," the FCC, Congress, and media advocacy groups continue to debate what that should mean. Is it in the public interest for the government to require broadcasters to provide free airtime to political candidates? If so, should only major-party candidates get free airtime? Should cable and satellite TV channels be held to the same standard? Who should decide what is in the public interest—Congress, the FCC, broadcasters? If government makes these decisions and tells broadcasters what to put on the air, where does the First Amendment fit into the equation?

■ CABLE TELEVISION REGULATION

Just as radio was the growth medium in the 1920s and television boomed in the 1950s, cable and cable-like technologies were the mass communications growth leaders in the 2000s. In 1980, about a quarter of all American homes were served by cable. And by 2008, a whopping 85–90% were served by cable, satellite, or other subscription television services. The rise of on-demand video services with bingeable programming, coupled with rising cable costs and "cut the cord" movements, though, caused a nosedive. By 2020, only 45% of U.S. households said they had active cable subscriptions (still millions of homes).

"Community TV." Cable began in the 1950s as something called "community antenna television" or CATV. In its early days, it was literally what its name implied: an elaborate antenna system serving a whole community. Because it offered little more than improved television reception, CATV first developed in rural areas far from the nearest television transmitters. By pooling their resources, the people of a community could afford a large antenna system and signal boosters to receive the weak signals from distant television stations. Each home was connected to this central receiving system via coaxial cable, a special kind of wire that will efficiently carry television signals a considerable distance.

When cable television got its start in the countryside, it had little appeal in big cities where reception was good. However, in the 1960s that began to change because of two trends. First, a growing number of people were forbidden to put up TV antennas at condominiums, apartment complexes, and even some tracts of single-family homes. Instead, they were offered cable hookups for a fee. But even more important, cable systems began offering a lot more than clear television reception: they began providing many additional channels of programming, including out-of-town "superstations," original made-for-cable programming, and such special attractions as music videos, recent movies, and sports events.

Early history of cable regulation: not much. Because cable systems do not actually transmit an over-the-air signal, they are not treated as users of the radio spectrum, and they don't need an FCC license to operate (although cable systems do receive programming via satellites that use the airwaves). Cable also has other advantages. For instance, the number of channels offered via cable is limited mainly by the number of channels a television receiver or cable converter can cover. A local cable system can put programming on every one of those channels without interfering with other cable systems or over-the-air broadcasters.

Because of these factors, cable television was able to develop without much federal regulation—at first. However, by the late 1960s, broadcasters became alarmed at the growth of cable television systems. So did the producers of TV programming, which cable operators picked up off the air at no charge—and then delivered to their subscribers for a fee. Two Supreme Court decisions held that cable operators didn't have to pay copyright royalties for the material carried over their systems, since the Court viewed CATV as nothing more than an adjunct of the TV receiving function (see Chapter Six on *Fortnightly* and *Teleprompter*). The owners of copyrighted programming felt they were being deprived of a fair profit by these decisions, and Congress enacted the 1976 Copyright Act in part to remedy that. Cable systems now pay royalties for the copyrighted programming on non-local stations they carry. Also, under the Cable Act of 1992 (discussed below), they must pay, or at least obtain broadcasters' consent, to carry some local stations but not others, for reasons explained later.

As cable systems expanded and began carrying distant signals, broadcasters became alarmed about this new medium. If a cable system imported distant signals, that could mean economic losses for local broadcasters. At least some of the cable subscribers would watch distant stations instead of local ones, especially if a cable system offered subscribers high-budget stations based in large cities along with nearby low-budget stations. Also, of course, the added non-broadcast programming represented new competition for broadcasters, siphoning off part of their audience.

Given the embryonic status of CATV in the 1950s, the FCC had refused to assume jurisdiction over cable because CATV didn't involve a use of the spectrum, and the commission had no specific statutory authority to regulate it. But by 1966 the FCC had changed its mind. To protect broadcasters and program producers, the agency issued regulations for cable television systems. The new regulations had many technical provisions, but one of the most important was a strict limit on distant signal importation. For instance, cable systems were required to carry the nearest station affiliated with each network rather than more distant ones. The rules also spelled out the relationship between cable systems and local governments, which had been granting franchises (in effect, government-sanctioned monopolies) to CATV operators. The FCC claimed the authority to make these rules by arguing that cable affected over-the-air broadcasters, and that regulation was necessary to carry out the commission's regulatory responsibilities to broadcasters. Legally, this is called *ancillary jurisdiction,* and this will become an important concept in net neutrality regulation later on.

The FCC's cable rules were quickly challenged in court, and in 1968, the Supreme Court affirmed the FCC's authority to regulate cable television in *U.S. v. Southwestern Cable Co.*

(392 U.S. 157). The high court found authority for the FCC's regulation of cable not only in the concept of ancillary jurisdiction but also in a provision of the Communications Act that places wire and telecommunications in general under FCC control.

Cable Regulation, Deregulation, and Reregulation, in Brief

Over the decades, the FCC has expanded its cable rules, placing restrictions on cable systems, then rescinded some of these rules, and then reimplemented some of them. Many cable operators felt these rules were intended to protect the FCC's major clientele, the over-the-air broadcasters, not to promote the public interest. The Supreme Court in 1972 gave the FCC authority to implement programming origination rules on cable (*U.S. v. Midwest Video Corp.*, 406 U.S. 649) as "reasonably ancillary" to its regulation of broadcasters, but it handed the commission a loss a few years later, asking the FCC to get Congressional mandate for rules it had promulgated for public access common carriage on cable (*FCC v. Midwest Video*, 440 U.S. 689, 1979). Congress provided that in 1984 (the Cable Act of 1984).

Syndex. The *Syndicated Exclusivity Rule* (or "Syndex") rule required cable systems to black out syndicated programs shown by distant stations (including "superstations") when a local station had an exclusive agreement to show the program. In 1980, the FCC deleted it, but only temporarily; it returned in 1988 in a new form: it now permitted superstations to negotiate exclusive national syndication rights contracts. Under such a contract, only the superstation could carry a certain show, and no local station could obtain rights to that show.

This new Syndex rule took effect in 1990. Several cable system owners and superstations challenged the new Syndex rule in court, but in *United Video v. FCC* (890 F.2d 1173), the U.S. Court of Appeals held that the FCC had the legal authority to reimpose this rule.

Federal law preemption. In 1984, the Supreme Court ruled on another of the FCC's cable regulations, sharply curtailing the power of local governments to regulate cable content when the local rules conflict with the FCC's rules. In *Capital Cities Cable Inc. v. Crisp* (467 U.S. 691), the Court overturned an Oklahoma law that prohibited cable systems from carrying advertising for wine and hard liquor, even if the advertising in question was legal where it originated. Although the Oklahoma law banned wine and hard liquor advertising on that state's TV stations, stations in several nearby states were allowed to carry it.

The Oklahoma law directly conflicted with the federal must-carry rules then in effect, which required cable systems to carry nearby television stations without altering the content of their broadcasts. Several cable systems near other states' borders were required by FCC regulations to carry television signals from out of state, including their alcoholic beverage advertising. As a result, Oklahoma cable operators were in a classic Catch-22 situation. If they obeyed the federal must-carry rules and carried alcoholic beverage advertising, they faced prosecution under Oklahoma law. If they obeyed the state law and blacked out such ads, they risked punishment for violating federal regulations. The high court resolved this conflict by ruling decisively in favor of the federal rules.

In 1988, the Supreme Court ruled on another aspect of the right of the FCC—and local governments—to regulate cable. The Court held in *City of New York v. FCC* (486 U.S. 57) that local governments could not impose stricter technical requirements on cable systems than those from the FCC. The FCC had adopted standards for such things as signal quality and had prohibited local governments from setting different standards. The idea was to allow the cable industry to operate under uniform national standards rather than standards that might vary from town to town. The Court ruled that the FCC had the right to set uniform national standards and to prevent any city from establishing different standards.

In 2010, the FCC extended for five years a prohibition against exclusive contracts between cable operators and cable networks. Several cable companies petitioned for a review of the statute. In *Cablevision Sys. Corp. v. FCC* (597 F.3d 1306) the D.C. Circuit denied their petition, saying that the FCC did not exceed its authority in extending the prohibition, and the decision to do so was not arbitrary and capricious. The companies' First Amendment claims also failed, the court said, as the FCC met the intermediate scrutiny standard applied by the court (a statute is upheld if "it furthers an important or substantial governmental interest; if the governmental interest is unrelated to the suppression of free expression; and if the incidental restriction on alleged First Amendment freedoms is no greater than is essential to the furtherance of that interest").

Cable Television Legislation

Even before *Capital Cities,* local governments and cable operators were lobbying in Congress, seeking a clarification of the roles of federal, state, and local governments in regulating cable. As local governments saw their right to regulate cable being eroded by the Supreme Court and the FCC, their leaders decided they needed cable legislation from Congress—even if it wasn't exactly the kind of legislation they had originally hoped for. They worked out a compromise with the cable industry; the two rival groups jointly endorsed an amended version of a cable bill that had been bogged down in Congress for two years.

The 1984 Cable Act. The Cable Communications Policy Act of 1984 further curtailed the right of local governments to regulate cable. The law deregulated many cable subscription fees after a two-year transition period wherever cable systems had "effective competition," which meant merely that there had to be three local television stations that viewers could watch without cable, if they had a good antenna. In addition, the 1984 law barred local governments from charging franchise fees in excess of 5% of a cable system's gross revenues. In return for this rate deregulation, the law authorized many local governments to require public access, government, and educational channels

The Cable Act of 1984 affirmed the right of local governments to award franchises, but it also protected cable operators from arbitrary franchise nonrenewals. The law also prohibited TV stations from owning cable systems in their service areas (although the FCC can grant waivers). And it required cable operators to wire their entire franchise service areas, not just the most affluent neighborhoods where the potential for profit might be greatest.

The 1984 act left the cable industry free to grow with minimal government regulation. However, the FCC, Congress, and local governments began hearing many complaints about poor service and skyrocketing rates charged by cable systems under deregulation.

Focus on...
Cable à la carte

Imagine being able to pick exact channels—and individual programs—for a cable lineup. No paying for unwatched stuff (167 channels on average); no clutter.

Called *à la carte programming,* it's the holy grail for consumers. But cable companies want to bundle channels, grouping popular channels with untried or less popular ones, for their advertisers.

Maine passed a cable à la carte law in 2019—the first state to do so. Cable providers challenged it on First Amendment grounds. A federal court and the First Circuit supported a preliminary injunction (*Comcast of Me./N.H. v. Mills,* 988 F.3d 607, 2021).

But this wasn't a full cable win. The First Circuit said the First Amendment applied, and Maine admitted it hadn't provided the evidence to survive strict scrutiny. So the case was remanded for a trial on the merits. Stay tuned.

Critics began calling cable an "unregulated monopoly," because in most areas there was only one cable system, leaving consumers with no real choice if they wanted any of the non-broadcast programming that became available. Without either competition or government regulation of their rates, many cable systems were free to do just about whatever they wanted, and consumers were the losers, critics charged.

The 1992 Cable Act. By 1992, the complaints about cable's rates and service were so widespread that Congress reregulated the industry, enacting the Cable Television Consumer Protection and Competition Act of 1992. The bill was passed just before the 1992 election, and President George H.W. Bush vetoed it. Congress mustered a two-thirds majority to override the veto, something that had never before happened during his presidency. Perhaps that indicated the degree to which Congress was hearing from angry constituents about the cable industry's alleged misdeeds. The law made sweeping changes in cable regulation—and in the relationship between the broadcast and cable industries. The era of cable deregulation was over—for the moment, at least. Some highlights of the 1992 Cable Act:

Rate regulation—Local governments were empowered to reregulate basic cable rates everywhere except where there is "effective competition," which was defined as 50% of the households in an area having a choice between two cable or cable-like services, with the smaller of the two having a 15% or higher market share.

Rate rollbacks—The FCC was directed to adopt rules to reduce cable rates substantially. In 1993, the FCC adopted rules intended to reduce most cable systems' rates by about 10%, but the rules were so complex and voluminous (more than 500 pages) that virtually everyone was confused. The rollbacks were expected to save consumers about $1.5 billion per year, but in some communities rates actually went up, not down. In 1994, the FCC adopted extensive amendments to its rate rollback rules. The result was additional reductions that averaged about 7%, although the actual reduction still varied widely among communities. Very small cable systems were exempt from some regulations. Many of these rate regulations were repealed in early 1999 under provisions of the 1996 Telecommunications Act.

Proportional rates—Cable systems were directed to charge rates that were proportional to their costs for various kinds of programming, and to fairly apportion the cost of the system itself among the various basic and premium channels.

Service standards—The FCC was directed to establish minimum service standards. Cable systems were told to have someone on duty to answer the telephone and respond to customers' complaints about poor reception, for example.

Nondiscriminatory program access for cable's competitors—The FCC was directed to adopt rules under which wireless and other non-cable video delivery systems would have fair access to the popular cable networks at a reasonable price.

Channel repositioning—Cable systems were ordered not to reposition television stations that select the must-carry option to a different channel than their on-air channel without the station's consent. In addition to their on-air channel, stations were given the right to choose a channel they occupied on the cable system as of certain earlier dates. (One of broadcasters' major complaints had been that it was impossible to advertise their programming and urge viewers to watch "channel two," for instance, if their signal was moved to various other channels by cable systems in their service area.)

Must-carry/retransmission consent—In perhaps the most important single aspect of the 1992 Act, each television station was given the right to choose either "must-carry" or "retransmission consent." If a station selected "must-carry," all cable systems in its service area were then required to carry that station (although no cable system was to be required to set aside more than one-third of its channel capacity for commercial television stations). However, the station would receive no payment for the mandatory carriage of its signal by cable systems. On the other hand, each station could also choose "retransmission consent." Then local cable systems were not allowed to carry that station's signal without obtaining permission and, presumably, some form of payment to the station.

All stations were required to notify their local cable systems of their choice by mid-1993, and most large stations opted for retransmission consent. Then the serious negotiations began, with both sides well aware that if a station and a local cable system could not agree on a price, the cable system would be free to drop the station. In the end, virtually all television stations agreed to accept some form of non-cash compensation for carriage of their signals by cable systems. For the most part, the cable industry simply refused to pay for broadcast signals, and broadcasters found that they lacked sufficient bargaining power to win major concessions from cable companies. What broadcasters got in lieu of cash payments from cable systems was a variety of other kinds of compensation for the right to retransmit broadcasters' signals. Several major networks and broadcast station groups gained new cable channels. ABC, NBC, and Fox got cable channels in this way. Some stations and smaller groups got free advertising or promotional time on the cable. CBS held out for cash payments for retransmission consent—and got nothing in the 1993 negotiations, although it did in later rounds (retransmission consent agreements have to be renegotiated every few years). By the mid-2000s, more broadcasters were successful in negotiating for cash payments from cable systems for retransmission consent.

Litigating "must-carry." Faced with the prospect of such a massive reregulation, the cable industry filed numerous different lawsuits in an attempt to keep the 1992 law from going into effect. However, most of these lawsuits were not successful. By far, the most important court test of the 1992 Cable Act came in *Turner Broadcasting System v. FCC*, a case that produced two Supreme Court decisions, one in 1994 (512 U.S. 622) and another in 1997 (520 U.S. 180). In the 1994 ruling, the high court voted 5-4 to uphold the authority of Congress to authorize the FCC to impose must-carry requirements on cable systems. In so ruling, the Court chose not to follow several earlier decisions of lower federal courts that had said previous must-carry rules violated the First Amendment rights of cable operators.

The Supreme Court noted that cable operators often have a monopoly of the primary television delivery system in a community. If a cable system with monopoly power should drop a television station, that could deny the station access to the majority of the viewers it is licensed by the FCC to serve. The high court said that the government's goal of fostering universal, over-the-air television service for the entire public was sufficiently important to justify requiring cable operators to carry local TV stations, even if it meant deleting other, made-for-cable programming.

In the 1994 case, the Court sent the case back to a lower court to reconsider whether cable systems that drop local TV stations really do threaten their ability to serve the public.

The Supreme Court reconsidered the *Turner Broadcasting* case in 1997 and again voted 5-4 to uphold the must-carry rules. In the meantime, a lower court had amassed considerable evidence that without must-carry, many local stations would indeed lose up to two-thirds of their potential audience. And some stations would probably go bankrupt as a result.

ROBOCALLS, TEXTS AND SPOOFING

ROBOCALLS AND TEXTS CAN BE ANNOYING, FRUSTRATING AND EVEN WORSE - FRAUDULENT.

FIG. 98. FCC spoofing brochure.

Source: Federal Communications Commission

Focus on...
Spoofing and robocalling (mostly illegal)

Ever answered a call that caller ID said was someone you knew—and then been hit with a recorded sales message? Scammers have figured out ways to change their caller ID information to make it seem that a friend or trusted entity is calling so you'll be more likely to pick up (a practice called *spoofing*). They've also developed ways to deliver prerecorded sales messages if you do answer (*robocalling*). These related practices are not only annoying but, if the robocaller is trying to sell you something without your consent, also illegal. In recent years, Congress and the FCC (as well as other agencies) have focused more regulatory attention to fraudulent uses of telephone technology.

Recent legislation in this area continues government's penchant for acronyms. The framework under which caller ID is to be authenticated is named *STIR/SHAKEN* (STIR for "Secure Telephony Identity Revisited" and SHAKEN for "Secure Handling of Asserted information using toKENs"). Use of this framework is mandated by the *TRACED (Telephone Robocall Abuse Criminal Enforcement and Deterrence) Act,* passed in 2019 and in effect as of June 30, 2021, under which the FCC must require phone companies to implement caller ID verification.

The FCC means business: in March 2021, the agency used a 2009 caller ID law to assess a $225 million fine—the largest fine in its history—against Rising Eagle, a Texas health insurance tele-marketer, for making *one billion robocalls,* many of them spoofed. These short-term insurance plans were portrayed as originating from trusted companies like Blue Cross Blue Shield.

Certain robocalls are permissible under TRACED. These include political calls, purely informational messages (like an airline notifying you of a flight cancellation), some health care calls, calls from charities (but only if you've given to that charity before), and calls from debt collectors. Certain caller ID changes are also okay. Domestic violence shelters can alter their IDs to protect their clients, and, as you know if you've ever gotten a call that appears non-local from a food delivery or ridesharing service (like Uber), these changes in caller ID are also permitted to protect driver privacy. Think you've been scammed by a spoofed call? You can report the incident to the FCC (consumercomplaints.fcc.gov), the FTC (reportfraud.ftc.gov), or your state's consumer protection offices (find out where at usa.gov/state-consumer).

On this basis, the high court's majority concluded that must-carry was necessary to fulfill the government's objectives of ensuring the survival of free local broadcast television and fostering competition in the TV programming marketplace. On the other hand, the burden this imposed on most cable operators was found to be minimal. Thus, the must-carry requirement was not an undue restriction on cable operators' First Amendment freedoms, the Court held in its 1997 ruling.

As a result of the *Turner Broadcasting* decision, the must-carry provision of the 1992 Cable Act remains in effect, requiring all but the smallest cable systems to carry local TV stations.

The must-carry provision was in the courts again in 2009 in *Cablevision Sys. Corp. v. FCC* (570 F.3d 83) (not the same case as the exclusive contracts or digital recording cases we'll discuss elsewhere, although they share a name). The case arose out of a dispute between a broadcast television station and a cable system. The FCC ruled that Cablevision could not exclude WRNN, a station licensed in Kingston, New York, from its Long Island cable systems. Cablevision appealed, and the Second Circuit upheld the FCC's order. Cablevision appealed to the Supreme Court, asking the Court to reconsider whether the must-carry provision was still necessary in this media environment's increased competition, creating a stir among both consumer advocates and the cable companies and stations. However, the Court declined to hear the appeal, leaving the must-carry rule in place—for now.

Meanwhile, many other lawsuits challenging various other provisions of the 1992 Cable Act were combined, and in an important decision in 1995, the D.C. Circuit rejected most of the cable industry's claims. In *Time Warner Entm't v. FCC* (56 F.3d 151), the court upheld the FCC's rate rollbacks, which averaged 17% over two years.

The appellate court also upheld the FCC's authority under the Cable Act to regulate rates in both the basic tier of service (which usually includes local TV stations) plus the "enhanced basic" tier (which often includes such channels as CNN, ESPN, and MTV). The court said it was reasonable for the FCC to regulate both to prevent cable systems from moving popular programming from tier to tier to escape rate regulation. Perhaps most important, the appellate court rejected the cable industry's basic argument: that many of these rules violate cable operators' First Amendment rights.

Another controversial issue was largely resolved in 1993 when several leading cable program providers settled antitrust lawsuits by agreeing to sell their programming to non-cable video services such as direct broadcast satellite (DBS) systems.

Can the FCC make rules to limit anti-competitive practices in cable under the Cable Act of 1992? Yes, in some cases, said the D.C. Circuit in 2011 in yet another Cablevision case (*Cablevision Sys. Corp. v. FCC*, 649 F.3d 695). The FCC had created new rules to extend anti-competitive programming restrictions applied to satellite programming to cable programming, and cable companies objected. The court said that the Cable Act gave the FCC authority to promote public interest and increased competition, and that the new regulations were reasonable exercises of the act's goals. The court also rejected the claim that the rules violated the First Amendment by burdening the speech of cable companies. In applying intermediate scrutiny, the court said that the FCC "has no obligation to establish that vertically integrated cable companies retain a stranglehold on competition nationally or that all withholding of terrestrially delivered programming negatively affects competition."

Cable First Amendment Issues

Cable has been the subject of several First Amendment challenges. One involves the cable franchising process, in which local governments authorize a cable system to wire a community, crossing public streets in the process. Another is whether a private corporation that operates a city's public access channels should be considered a state actor and thus subject to the First Amendment.

Franchising. In *City of Los Angeles v. Preferred Commc'ns* (476 U.S. 488, 1986), the Supreme Court partially upheld a Ninth Circuit ruling that the local government franchising process may violate the First Amendment rights of cable operators as "electronic publishers." In so ruling, the Court finally accepted an argument cable operators had been making for years—that their First Amendment rights cannot be arbitrarily abridged by local governments.

In an opinion by Justice William Rehnquist, the Court agreed that cable systems "plainly implicate First Amendment interests." Rehnquist said cable's rights had to be balanced against "competing social interests," perhaps including a city's desire to award exclusive franchises. The Court sent the *Preferred* case back to a trial court to reconsider.

Public access channel operators as state actors. In 2019, the high court said that a private nonprofit corporation operating public access channels in Manhattan wasn't a state actor subject to the First Amendment—and it didn't take the opportunity to expound on social media's state actor standing.

As do many states, New York mandates that cable companies designate some channels for use by the public (public access channels, sometimes known as PEG—public, educational, or governmental—stations). The case of *Manhattan Cmty. Access Corp. v. Halleck* (139 S. Ct. 1921) arose when two employees of Manhattan Neighborhood Network (MNN), the organization that runs the Time Warner (now Charter) public access channels, were denied access to the organization's premises and channels after producing and broadcasting a documentary (*The 1% Visit El Barrio*) critical of MNN. They sued, saying their First Amendment rights were violated because MNN censored their speech.

Some commentators watched the case with excitement, thinking it an ideal vehicle for the justices to explain the relationship between the First Amendment and social media companies. Indeed, MNN lawyers suggested that the justices could do what the *Packingham* Court (see Chapter Ten) did not: determine whether social media companies are state actors bound by the First Amendment—and thus unable to regulate content on their platforms.

But the Court declined that invitation. Instead, Justice Brett Kavanaugh, writing for a 5-4 majority, rejected the Second Circuit's holding to the contrary. Using a test from previous state-action cases, he said that "to qualify as a traditional, exclusive public function … the government must have traditionally and exclusively performed the function" under consideration. Few functions qualify: Kavanaugh said that managing voting and running a company town are among them. Simply providing a forum for speech, as MNN has done, doesn't transform a private entity into a state actor, he added.

Justice Sonia Sotomayor, joined in dissent by Justices Ruth Bader Ginsburg, Stephen Breyer, and Elena Kagan, dryly remarked that the majority "tells a very reasonable story about a case that is not before us." The question should focus, she said, on the agency relationship between MNN and the city of New York. Sotomayor added that "because the City (1) had a duty to provide that public forum once it granted a cable franchise and (2) had a duty to abide by the First Amendment once it provided that forum, those obligations did not evaporate when the City delegated the administration of that forum to a private entity." MNN became a state actor when it accepted the delegation of power for administering the channels from the city, she said.

Indecency on Cable

The cable industry won several First Amendment victories in lawsuits challenging government attempts to ban indecent but non-obscene adult programming on cable channels. In 1987, the Supreme Court ruled that cable systems cannot be forbidden to carry indecent programming by state or local governments. In *Wilkinson v. Jones* (480 U.S. 926), the Supreme Court upheld a lower court ruling that Utah's state Cable Decency Act is unconstitutional. The high court did not issue its own opinion or even hold oral arguments. But by affirming a lower appellate court's decision, the Court gave this case the weight of a Supreme Court decision.

The invalidated Utah law had forbidden nudity or sex acts on cable systems except between midnight and 7 a.m. In overturning the law, the Court of Appeals had said, "The scope of the language (in the Utah law) is so uncertain as to chill legitimate expression in a way that the (Constitution's) overbreadth doctrine forbids."

In 1996, the Supreme Court again addressed the question of sexually oriented programming on cable in *Denver Area Educ. Telecommc'ns Consortium v. FCC*, 518 U.S. 727). In this case, the Court ruled on the constitutionality of three provisions of the 1992 Cable Act concerning "patently offensive" sexually oriented programming on cable access channels. The high court upheld Section 10(a) of the 1992 Act, which said cable operators may ban patently offensive material on commercial leased access channels if they choose to do so. The Court said this provision does not violate the First Amendment; it leaves cable operators free to carry such programs or reject them, just as cable operators have a First Amendment right to carry or reject other cable programming.

However, the Court overturned Section 10(b) and Section 10(c) of the 1992 Cable Act, ruling that both violate the First Amendment. Section 10(b) required cable operators who choose to carry patently offensive material on a leased access channel to segregate it on a single channel and block that channel to everyone except subscribers who specifically ask to receive it 30 days in advance. The Court said this was an excessive burden on First Amendment freedoms: it would not allow a viewer to decide spontaneously to watch a specific program; nor would it protect subscribers who feared having their names appear on a list of persons who had requested to receive a "sex channel."

The justices also ruled that cable operators cannot censor sexually oriented programming on public access, educational, and government (PEG) channels, as Section 10(c) of the 1992 law required. These channels have traditionally been a public forum, not subject to censorship. But the majority stopped short of ruling one way or another on whether private

Focus on...
"FrankenFM" broadcast stations

A TV station that acts ... like a radio? Well, yes. As of 2021, about two dozen of these low-power analog "television" stations continue to broadcast in the United States Although they're eventually supposed to transition to digital (like other, larger broadcasters did in 2009), the FCC has thrown at least one of them a lifeline to continue operating as it has been—for a little while.

These stations, dubbed "FrankenFMs" due to their odd hybrid of TV and radio, exist because of a quirk in the spectrum. They transmit on VHF channel 6, which sits right on the border between the FM and analog TV bands. So, if you tune your radio to 87.7 (or 87.8 on some units) on the FM dial, a spot below the lowest official standard FM band at 88.1, you might be able to pick up one of these analog stations.

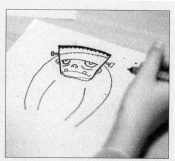

FIG. 99. Drawing of Frankenstein's monster.

freestocks, Oct. 25, 2017, via Unsplash.

How? Under the earliest broadcast standards, the audio and video portions of a broadcast were transmitted separately. When the 2009 digital transition happened, some small LPTV stations dropped their video signals and started broadcasting on 87.7 FM as just radio stations. The channel 6 FrankenFM stations were exempt from 2009 digital transition deadlines and were supposed to make that transition by July 13, 2021. But in June 2021, the FCC issued a temporary grant allowing one of them six more months of operation as a sort of experiment. There's also a petition at the FCC to make the hybrid digital TV/analog radio setup permanent. Stay tuned.

nonprofit operators of PEG channels are state actors for purposes of the First Amendment; the Court finally answered that question in the negative in 2019 in *Halleck*, discussed above.

"Signal bleed." The Communications Decency Act, which is a section of the 1996 Telecommunications Act, went further in regulating adult programming on cable, requiring cable systems that carry sexually explicit adult channels either to scramble them completely or carry them only between 10 p.m. and 6 a.m. But complete scrambling is not technically feasible for some older cable systems because of "signal bleed" (which allows some non-subscribers to see a fuzzy picture or hear muffled audio in spite of the scrambling). That meant adult channels could only broadcast during the late-night hours under this law. Playboy Entertainment sued, alleging a First Amendment violation. A three-judge federal court ruled that the scrambling requirement violates the First Amendment.

The federal government appealed, leading to another Supreme Court decision and another decisive First Amendment victory for cable in 2000: *U.S. v. Playboy Entertainment Group* (529 U.S. 803). The high court voted 5-4 to allow adult cable programming in the daytime even if a cable system cannot prevent all signal bleed. The Court's 5-4 majority said the provision allowing any subscriber who wants it to request an additional blocking device is sufficient to enable parents to keep their children from watching adult programming on a fuzzy, partially scrambled screen. The Court noted that fewer than 1% of cable subscribers had requested the additional device, despite the widespread mailing of notices of its availability, indicating minimal parental concern about signal bleed.

The majority said it was a violation of the First Amendment for government to deny non-obscene adult programming to millions of daytime viewers who want it when the extra blocking device is a less-restrictive alternative to government censorship for those who do not want even a fuzzy, partially scrambled picture arriving in their homes. Writing for the Court, Justice Anthony Kennedy said, "This case involves speech alone; and even where speech is indecent and enters the home, the objective of shielding children does not suffice to support a blanket ban if the protection can be accomplished by a less restrictive alternative." Kennedy also said parents reacted to this problem "with a collective yawn."

Meanwhile, many cable systems offered new "family tiers" that excluded channels carrying programs not considered suitable for young children. Another controversial idea was to require cable systems to offer *à la carte* pricing. That would allow subscribers to choose only those channels they actually want instead of packages of channels.

Consumers have long wanted the ability to purchase individual cable channels instead of the bundles traditionally offered by cable companies. But is such bundling unlawful? The Ninth Circuit said no, at least not under antitrust law. The court rejected consumer allegations that cable companies' bundling of multi-channel packages was a violation of Section 1 of the Sherman Antitrust Act (*Brantley v. NBC Universal*, discussed in Chapter Twelve).

Cable and Digital Recording

When programming is "transmitted" "to the public," copyright law requires that cable and other companies must obtain licenses to do it. In the 2000s and 2010s, courts were asked whether a remote-storage digital video recorder (RS-DVR) system, a cross between DVRs and video-on-demand services which stores programs on drives maintained not by consumers but by a cable company for retrieval on demand, violates the Copyright Act by infringing copyright holders' exclusive rights of reproduction and public performance.

The *Cablevision* recording case. The Second Circuit said no infringement in what has become an important holding in yet another Cablevision case (*Cartoon Network v. CSC*

Holdings and Cablevision Sys Corp., 536 F.3d 121). While the *Sony* Betamax case discussed in Chapter Six addressed the time-shifting issue from the perspective of consumers using their own equipment to save programming, this case dealt with cable companies themselves storing copyrighted content. Cablevision's system splits the delivery of a cable program into two streams when it comes in: one is delivered to the consumer immediately, and a second stream with a buffer evaluates whether any customer has asked to record the program. If yes, the data is sent to that customer's hard disk. If no, the buffer is discarded.

The Second Circuit said that making a "copy" has two elements: "the work must be embodied in a medium, i.e., placed in a medium such that it can be perceived, reproduced, etc., from that medium (the 'embodiment requirement'), and it must remain thus embodied 'for a period of more than transitory duration' (the 'duration requirement')."

The court said that the buffer, which could hold no more than 1.2 seconds of programming at a time before being overwritten, was sufficiently transitory (short) so as not to fulfill the "duration element" of the test. The Supreme Court declined to hear an appeal.

The rise of MVPDs. What will be the definition of a cable company? Broadcasters and cable companies are watching internet start-ups closely, as these companies have the potential to significantly impact how television is delivered to American consumers. The FCC is reviewing *multi-channel video programming distributors* (MVPDs), which may affect the ways in which online programming is regulated, particularly regarding retransmission rights. These MVPDs often operate without the restrictions or rights accorded to cable or satellite.

And Congress has gotten in on the MVPD regulatory action, too; in 2019, as part of an omnibus spending bill, it passed the *Television Viewer Protection Act.* This law places broad restrictions on how MVPDs advertise and bill for video and broadband services. For example, these providers must tell consumers when they agree to subscribe the "total monthly charge" they can expect to pay for those services—including fees, equipment rentals, and taxes. The act also mandates new disclosures for electronic bills, such as the ending date of any video promotional discounts. It went into effect (after a pandemic delay) in Dec. 2020. Consumers advocates responded with joy; *Consumer Reports* said it received thousands of consumer complaints about unexpected cable and satellite fees which could add, on average, $37 a month (nearly $450 per year) to their bills.

Courts are being asked to consider whether companies like ivi and Aereo are cable companies. ivi retransmits over-the-air broadcasts from channels like ABC and Fox but without paying retransmission fees. It claims to be operating legally because of a loophole under which cable and satellite companies can retransmit this programming as long as they pay copyright fees as mandated by Section 111 of the Copyright Act—which ivi has applied to do. A federal district court refused to consider ivi a cable company. The Second Circuit agreed (*WPIX, Inc. v. ivi, Inc.*, 691 F.3d 275): ivi is not a cable system. Congress' goal in passing Section 111 was to "support localized—rather than nationwide—systems that use cable or optical fibers to transmit signals through 'a physical, point-to-point connection between a transmission facility and the television sets of individual subscribers'"—and not to internet subscribers. The court said that "ivi's actions—streaming copyrighted works without permission—would drastically change the industry, to plaintiffs' detriment." The Supreme Court denied *cert*, and ivi.tv appears in 2021 to be targeting primarily Russian audiences.

Aereo, on the other hand, used tiny antennae, the size of a dime, to bring local over-the-air broadcasting to customers for a monthly fee. It argued that it focused on local consumers,

V-chip:
mandatory technology
that allows parents to
program their TVs to
block objectionable
content, like sex or
violence, based on
ratings assigned by the
networks.

Prime Time Access Rule:
repealed FCC rule that
restricted the amount
of network program-
ming that local TV
stations owned by,
or affiliated with,
a network may air
during the evening.

"Fin-Syn" Rule:
short for *Financial
Interest and Syndica-
tion Rule*, a defunct
rule that prohibited
networks to have a
financial interest in
the TV programs they
aired and to create
in-house syndication.

Syndex Rule:
syndicated exclusivity,
intended to protect
a local TV station's
rights to air syndicated
programs by grant-
ing exclusive rights to
that station for that
program in its local
market.

Video news release:
a video version of a
press release, created
by public relations or
advertising profession-
als to try to influence
public opinion.

as opposed to ivi's national reach, making free local broadcasts available (legally) via individual antennae. Aereo beat broadcasters in several battles in the courts. One federal district judge threw out an unfair competition claim as preempted by the Copyright Act. Another federal district court tossed an injunction against Aereo, claiming that the networks' attempts to distinguish the Second Circuit *Cablevision* recording case didn't work. In fact, the judge said, Aereo's system is identical to that in *Cablevision*, and as she thought that the Cablevision service was probably lawful, she couldn't disregard the harms Aereo would suffer from an injunction, so she denied it.

The Second Circuit agreed. Combining the cases in *WNET, Thirteen v. Aereo, Inc.* (712 F.3d 676), the court identified the main question as whether Aereo infringed the networks' public performance rights in the Copyright Act. Despite a number of arguments advanced by the networks, a 2-1 divided panel said it did not. Claiming that "unanticipated technological developments" resulted in conflicts between Congress and the Copyright Act, the panel said that the Aereo transmissions "are not 'public performances' of the Plaintiffs' copyrighted works under *Cablevision*." Calling the platform a "sham," dissenting judge Denny Chin blasted Aereo for trying to circumvent the law. "[T]he system is a Rube Goldberg-like contrivance, over-engineered in an attempt to avoid the reach of the Copyright Act and to take advantage of a perceived loophole in the law," he complained.

The *Aereo* decision. The U.S. Supreme Court agreed with the dissent in 2014, saying in *ABC, Inc. v. Aereo, Inc.* (573 U.S. 431) that Aereo *was* indeed infringing the networks' copyrights because it "performs petitioners' works publicly within the meaning of the Transmit Clause" of the Copyright Act. Justice Stephen Breyer wrote for a 6-3 majority that lower courts' interpretations were incorrect; those courts had said that because each Aereo customer account has its own antenna which was only activated upon the customer's request, and no other customer could access that antenna, Aereo was not "publicly" broadcasting. But Breyer disagreed, noting Aereo's similarity to cable: "But the many similarities between Aereo and cable companies ... convince us that this difference is not critical here. We conclude that Aereo is not just an equipment supplier and that Aereo 'perform[s].'"

In dissent, Justice Antonin Scalia, joined by Justices Clarence Thomas and Samuel Alito, said essentially that the lower courts had it right. Calling the majority's opinion a "looks-like-cable-TV" model, Scalia offered one of his famous analogies, this one to a photocopy shop and its customers' uses of that shop: "One customer might copy his 10-year-old's drawings—a perfectly lawful thing to do—while another might duplicate a famous artist's copyrighted photographs—a use clearly prohibited by [the Copyright Act]. Either way, the customer chooses the content and activates the copying function; the photocopier does nothing except in response to the customer's commands." The case was remanded to the lower court. Digital recording company TiVo acquired Aereo in 2015.

■ ELECTRONIC MEDIA TECHNOLOGIES

A number of promising new electronic communications technologies have appeared in recent years. Some seem destined to fundamentally alter media consumption patterns. Others have failed to win consumer acceptance, becoming boondoggles that produced nothing but billion-dollar losses for investors.

Cable, of course, is hardly a new technology. But its emergence as the fastest growing video delivery system of the 1980s contributed to disappointing early failures of direct broadcast satellites (DBS) and some other new technologies. By the 2000s and beyond, though, a new generation of satellite television services became viable competitors to cable while other new technologies such as the internet and digital television (DTV) gained prominence.

Digital and High-Definition Television

After years of research, planning, and debate, in 1997 the FCC authorized the transition to digital television (DTV) in the United States. Under the FCC's rules, each existing full-power television station was assigned a new channel for DTV. The FCC ordered network-owned and network-affiliated stations in the largest markets to begin digital broadcasting in 1999, with stations in smaller markets required to go digital in 2000 and 2001. For various reasons, many stations were unable to meet those deadlines. By 2005, though, most television stations had launched their DTV channels, although only about 15% of American households owned digital television receivers by then.

That posed a major problem. The federal government needed to retrieve some old analog TV channels and sell them to new users, including police and fire authorities who desperately need more channels. Wireless broadband internet service providers also need some of those channels if they are to provide a viable alternative to cable and telephone company–based internet service. Recognizing these needs, Congress decreed that broadcasters must go all-digital, shutting off their analog broadcasts on Feb. 18, 2009.

2009 analog shutdown. Cable and satellite systems provided digital converter boxes to subscribers who owned only analog TV sets—for a fee. However, an estimated 70 million analog TV sets are not hooked to a cable or satellite service. That includes second or third TV sets in many homes with subscription TV service. Nearly 20% of American homes have no cable or satellite service at all. Without converters or new digital TV sets, those households would lose their TV service in 2009. Congress allocated $1.5 billion to subsidize the purchase of digital converter boxes for those homes.

Meanwhile, the FCC adopted rules requiring TV manufacturers to include digital capability in all new TV sets starting in March 2007. TV sets had to have built-in digital tuners and not merely be "digital ready" (only able to receive digital programming with an external converter). The converter boxes don't allow the reception of true high-definition television (HDTV) signals on analog TV sets. These signals are converted back to standard definition.

The digital transition was postponed from February 18 to June 12, 2009, as high demand for coupons to defray the costs of digital converters saw millions on waiting lists and funding exhausted. How smoothly did it go? The FCC in a June 13, 2009, press release, the day after 971 stations' analog signals "went dark," reported almost 700,000 calls to its helpline, which was staffed by 4,000 agents. And a law allowed about 120 full-power stations in 87 markets to maintain analog "nightlight" service for 30 days to provide emergency service and information about the analog shutdown. (See discussions elsewhere in this chapter regarding the transitions status of low-power television and "FrankenFM" broadcast stations.)

Under the FCC's rules for digital TV, each station may broadcast *high-definition television* (HDTV) on its digital channel or instead deliver four or five lower quality programs simultaneously on subchannels within the digital channel. Many broadcasters carry multiple signals most of the broadcast day, providing more programming choices than ever before, but without the long-promised picture quality of HDTV. Some broadcasters lease some of their subchannels or use them to broadcast radio programming instead of TV. The FCC also adopted a rule requiring cable systems to carry the full digital signal of each local TV station, even if that consists of several standard-definition subchannels instead of one HDTV channel. During a transition period, cable systems were also required to carry many TV stations in an analog format for viewers unable to receive digital signals.

Telecom Convergence

Perhaps no part of the Telecommunications Act of 1996 had a greater long-range impact on the American way of life than the provisions designed to open all of the communications industries to new competition. Among other things, this law allows telephone companies and cable systems to *converge:* to enter each others' businesses, preempting any state and local regulations in the way.

Even before the 1996 law was enacted, a number of states had taken steps toward allowing cable companies to offer telephone service, and vice versa. The FCC had also taken some preliminary steps in that direction, too. But Congress declared that wide-open competition is to be the norm. This means:

- Local phone companies are allowed to offer video programming, even in their own telephone service areas.
- Local phone companies may offer internet access and TV programming.
- Local phone companies may offer long-distance telephone service.
- Cable systems may offer local telephone service and broadband (high-speed) internet access.
- Local phone companies are free to manufacture telephone equipment, something they were largely prevented from doing under the court order that broke up the nationwide AT&T monopoly.

To facilitate all of these changes in the communications business, the 1996 act overruled a variety of federal, state, and local regulations and industry practices that might stand in the way. In 2002 the Supreme Court upheld the rules giving cable systems access to utility poles at low cost, even if the cable system is using the poles to deliver high-speed internet access instead of television (*Nat'l Cable & Telecomm. Ass'n v. Gulf Power Co.*, 534 U.S. 327).

In addition to all of these provisions, the 1996 act included a vast array of provisions designed to foster competition and prevent anticompetitive business practices. The various companies are not allowed to "cross-subsidize" their new businesses with revenue from their established businesses in which they enjoy a near monopoly. And technical standards must not be set up by entities such as the research arm of the local phone companies in a manner that gives the phone companies a competitive advantage.

By the 2000s, millions of American households had dropped traditional telephone service for VOIP (voice over internet protocol) service from cable companies or over the internet. Telephone companies were meanwhile setting up their own broadband delivery systems to make their internet services competitive with those offered by cable companies.

Direct Broadcast Satellites

The number-one high-tech disappointment of the 1980s was the direct broadcast satellite (DBS) business. A decade later, DBS had become a dramatic success story—boosted by government regulators as a needed source of competition for cable.

Billed in the early 1980s as the television technology of the future, DBS at first was a dismal failure. All of the original DBS companies bailed out, victims of technical, financial, and marketing problems that began almost as soon as DBS was first proposed as a serious medium of mass communication. All of the firms that were originally awarded licenses for direct satellite broadcasting dropped their plans in the face of prohibitive costs and serious questions about the economic potential of the service. Several would-be satellite program providers were forced to absorb multimillion dollar losses in the process. It was not until much later that DBS became a viable medium.

The concept underlying DBS is fairly simple, although the technology to accomplish it is complex and expensive. A number of satellites are positioned above the equator at an altitude of 22,300 miles. At that altitude each satellite would orbit the earth at a speed that exactly matches the Earth's rotation speed. The result: each satellite appears to remain stationary over one point on the Earth's surface, not moving at all. Such a satellite is said to be *geosynchronous*. This allows receiving dish antennas to be locked in position, permanently pointed at a satellite. If communications satellites were not geosynchronous, very costly tracking hardware and software would have to be used to keep every dish antenna pointed at a satellite that appeared to be moving around the sky.

Once a geosynchronous satellite is in orbit, transmitting stations on the ground send up signals on an "uplink" frequency. The satellite receives these signals and retransmits them back to earth on a "downlink," which is usually a different frequency.

Geosynchronous communications satellites are not new. Virtually all major cable systems, broadcasters, wire services, and newspapers used these satellites for years to relay programming or information. However, early communications satellites operated with such low transmitter power that a very sensitive (and therefore large) dish antenna was required to receive the signal. Perhaps one reason the DBS ventures of the early 1980s failed is because consumers had to have large dish antennas in their yards or on their roofs to receive the signals. Early dishes were typically 10 feet in diameter (and ugly, in the opinion of homeowners' associations, local governments, and neighbors; new dish antennas are far smaller).

While the DBS ventures of the 1980s all failed, several major players in the communications business launched new DBS systems in the 1990s; the DBS industry had a combined total of more than 20 million subscribers by 2008—enough to have a major impact on the fortunes of cable companies. DirecTV and EchoStar, the leading DBS providers, gained many new subscribers in 1999 and 2000 after Congress passed the Satellite Television Home Viewers Act, allowing satellite systems to carry local television stations, including those offering network programming. Before then, DBS providers were barred from carrying the major broadcast networks except in "white areas" far enough from any city to be out of range of over-the-air TV stations. This law amended the Copyright Act to allow this; it is discussed in Chapter Six. Under the 1996 Telecommunications Act, the FCC took other steps to help DBS systems provide viable competition to cable. For instance, the FCC overruled local zoning and deed restrictions that prohibited the small dish antennas needed for DBS. The FCC adopted rules requiring local governments, homeowners' associations, and landlords to allow not only dish antennas but also TV antennas for those who wanted to receive free TV broadcasts over the air. The FCC rule governing apartments allows tenants to put antennas on balconies and other private areas but not on roofs or outside walls.

Other Technologies

Perhaps the new video delivery technology that has captured the public imagination more than any other is internet, iPad, and other tablet- and cell phone-based television broadcasting. Many TV broadcasters are moving aggressively to add streaming to their existing websites so they can do full-blown broadcasting using these new technologies. They are well aware that other industries (including newspaper publishers, among others) are also moving rapidly toward video streaming on the internet. More and more consumers are getting video programming via the internet and cell phones. This kind of convergence may force policy-makers to rewrite all of their definitions of broadcasting and publishing. Broadcasters and newspaper or magazine publishers are becoming direct competitors on the internet, all offering interactive (two-way) broadcasting and video on demand. The major networks offer programming directly to iPad and other tablet viewers, an arrangement that could short-circuit local broadcasters and undercut their audience (and advertising) base.

But there are other technologies that are less well known than the ubiquitous tablet or cell phone. These technologies, some old, some new, have the potential to bring hyperlocal content to neighborhoods or remote locations in ways that national corporations are ill-equipped to understand or manage.

Low-power radio. While large corporations were buying more and more stations during the 1990s, the FCC approved a plan to foster grassroots ownership of local radio stations. In 1998, FCC Chair William Kennard called for a study of a proposal to allow *microradio* stations, extremely low power locally owned stations that would serve a small community or a small area of a larger city. The proposal was seen as a response to the growing popularity of "pirate" radio stations that were simply going on the air without a license.

At a time when some companies own hundreds of radio stations, it's not easy for an individual to get a radio license: the few new licenses that are available are auctioned off at high prices, and existing stations also sell for enormous sums of money. In recent years, more and more people who feel they have something to say and nowhere to say it have built bootleg radio stations to broadcast a few hours a day—until being caught by the FCC. FCC officials said they shut down nearly 100 pirate radio stations during 1997 alone. In 2006, the number busted by the FCC was closer to 200.

A driving force behind the pirate radio movement was a station calling itself "Free Radio Berkeley" in California. When the FCC sought a court order to shut that station down, the station's lawyer argued that the lack of any provision for low-power radio broadcasting violated the First Amendment. A federal court at first refused to order Free Radio Berkeley off the air; it took the FCC two years to persuade the court to issue a permanent injunction. By the time the court finally did so in mid-1998, Free Radio Berkeley was legendary: imitators were springing up all over the country, with the help of free advice—and transmitter "kits"—from

Free Radio Berkeley's founder, Stephen Dunifer. He runs workshops to teach unlicensed broadcasters how to set up their stations and get on the air (freeradio.org).

Apparently believing that this indicated a need for low-power, minimally regulated radio stations to serve local communities, Kennard said the FCC would consider licensing such stations. Despite concerns from commercial and public broadcasters, in 2000 the FCC created the low-power FM radio service. To open up the airwaves to local community groups who are largely excluded from corporate-owned broadcasting, the FCC approved two classes of low-power FM (LPFM) radio stations with maximum power levels of 10 watts and 100 watts. The new 10-watt and 100-watt stations can be heard well over a radius of 1 to 2 miles and 3.5 miles, respectively.

LPFM stations must be noncommercial. Owners of existing radio and television stations, cable systems and newspapers are not eligible for these licenses. The licenses are granted only to local residents. The FCC's intent is for these stations to have some production facilities and staff present in the community. To make room for LPFM stations, the FCC relaxed the mileage separation rules that protect broadcasters from interference. However, amidst an outcry from existing broadcasters, Congress intervened, attaching a provision to a large federal spending bill that restricted the new low-power FM radio stations mainly to smaller markets where they can operate without violating the FCC's original mileage separation rules. Congress later relaxed the restrictions on LPFM licensing a little.

However, the FCC in 2003 had opened an application window for FM *translator* stations, and 13,000 applications were submitted. Translators are low-power stations originally intended to rebroadcast a nearby station into a local community where it cannot be received well, often due to mountainous terrain. But translators and LPFM stations share the same frequencies. If these translator applications were to be granted, there would be no room left for LPFM stations in large cities. In 2005, the FCC stopped issuing new translator licenses after local broadcasting advocacy groups pointed out that three organizations in one town in Idaho had been granted about 100 translator licenses for communities all over the country and resold them to religious broadcasters who intended to build new national networks instead of doing local programming in each community.

By 2006, of the initial 255 LPFM stations authorized in 2000, only a handful were on the air with regular programming, raising questions about the viability of LPFM as a form of local broadcasting in an era when unlicensed web- and podcasting are booming. Yet by 2012 over 800 LPFM licenses had been issued. The Local Community Radio Act of 2010 provided governmental support for small, low-power stations as important to their communities.

The last time that an LPFM application could be submitted was in 2013. No new filing windows are open, but acting FCC chair Jessica Rosenworcel suggested in May 2021 that the agency was considering a new window as part of its commitment to supporting local radio voices. And in 2020 the FCC adjusted the LPFM rules "to improve reception and increase flexibility in transmitter siting while maintaining interference protection and the core LPFM goals of diversity and localism." Stay tuned.

LPTV stations. A technology that is sometimes labeled as "new" is *low-power television (LPTV)*. LPTV is really nothing more than a new kind of conventional television broadcasting that was introduced during the 1980s. The FCC acted in 1982 to allow "mini-stations" to serve small towns and localized areas in larger cities. The idea was that these stations would transmit with low power and would operate efficiently with low overhead and bring TV service to communities that had little or no local service. To help them do that, the FCC freed LPTV stations of many regulations that apply to full-power stations. LPTV stations are

CATV:
"community antenna television," an antenna system serving a whole community.

geosynchronous orbit:
an orbit by which a satellite can stay in synch with the Earth's orbit, thus permitting satellite dishes to remain fixed.

high-definition television:
a digitally broadcast system with higher resolution than traditional television systems; the use of digital video compression means that less bandwidth is used than for analog broadcasts.

must-carry rule:
a Cable Act provision that required cable systems to carry local broadcast channels, held to be content-neutral and necessary for the survival of over-the-air broadcast stations.

net neutrality:
a policy that prevents restrictions on the delivery of online content or websites, under the idea that all traffic that flows through the internet should be treated the same.

authorized to serve a radius of 10–15 miles from their transmitter sites.

By 2000, LPTV faced a threat from digital television: new interference from high-power digital stations. In some communities LPTV stations had to change to less desirable channels, accept new interference, or even curtail their operations to avoid causing interference to new digital television stations, which have legal priority over LPTV stations. Eventually, LPTV stations were given some protection from new DTV stations, but only LPTV stations that were broadcasting at least 18 hours a day, with three hours of local programming, were given this protection—standards only about 400 of the 2,200 LPTV stations met.

LPTV stations were permitted to stay on-air after the 2009 digital transition and given more time to make that transition. All digital transition is supposed to be completed by July 13, 2021. However, as discussed in a "Focus On..." box elsewhere in this chapter, so-called "FrankenFM" stations received a six-month reprieve from this deadline in June 2021.

Digital audio broadcasting. Another new-ish communications technology is digital audio broadcasting. In 2008, the FCC approved a proposal by Sirius and XM to merge into a single entity. The merger was approved earlier by the Justice Department, but it was vehemently opposed by local radio broadcasters and consumer groups, partly because the original FCC authorization of digital satellite radio included a ban on the two companies ever merging.

Hoping to compete with the new satellite-delivered digital radio services, over-the-air radio broadcasters in 2002 won FCC permission to launch "in-band on-channel" (IBOC) digital broadcasting. This allows AM and FM broadcasters to offer digital sound to those equipped to receive it. By 2006, about 600 radio stations were broadcasting digital multi-channel programming, but the least expensive radios that could receive the digital signals were still selling for about $200.

AM radio. Perhaps the oldest "new" technology of all is AM radio broadcasting. Long dismissed as an outdated technology that could not deliver good sound quality, old-fashioned analog AM radio may make a comeback, with the backing of the broadcast industry and the FCC. The FCC allocated 10 new channels for AM radio just above 1600 kHz, where the AM band ended almost from the beginning of AM broadcasting.

In addition, the commission set a higher standard for audio quality on the new channels, and set up a priority system for awarding frequencies to existing stations, with a preference for a few daytime-only stations in large cities so they could broadcast full time and for stations that had interference problems on their previous channels.

◼ NET NEUTRALITY

Most of the time, unless you're gaming, streaming video, or downloading something large, you probably don't think about how fast your internet service is. But if you're a heavy user of Netflix, Overwatch, Destiny 2, or any of dozens of bandwidth-hogging services or games, you've probably heard of net neutrality, even if you only learned about it recently.

Net neutrality, the concept that all traffic that passes through the internet should be treated equally, became a hot political and social topic in the late 2000s. Under net neutrality, all websites are delivered at an equal speed, based on the speed of your online service; if you go to Amazon.com, your webpage is delivered just as fast as if you go to the White House's website (whitehouse.gov) or the *New York Times* (nytimes.com) or a social networking site like Facebook or Snapchat—or if you're streaming a binge-watch of *Game of Thrones.*

Concerns arose when internet service providers began considering methods of service wherein they could charge more for faster access to certain sites or types of data, in effect creating a two- (or more) tiered internet, or where they might either cut consumers off when they hit certain data caps or start charging more for hitting those caps. Critics alleged that circumventing net neutrality was just a way for internet providers to make more money by selling premier services.

Many people had never heard of net neutrality before 2014 or 2015. Perhaps that's because it was taken for granted that all online traffic was treated the same. A person may have a faster or a slower connection, but the idea may not have occurred that there could be another way. Of course, cynics might suggest that where money is involved, there are always other ways—aimed at moving dollars around. Regardless, net neutrality has its roots in the 1934 Communications Act, as amended by the Telecommunications Act of 1996. A couple of parts of that act, Title I and Title II, are at the bottom of the brouhaha.

Title I, Title II—what does that even mean? Congress created Titles I and II for different services. Title I enhanced "information services" are subject to fewer regulations, while Title II "common carrier" services are subject to more.

What's a "common carrier"? Sometimes also called a "public utility," a common carrier provides the same service to everyone who is willing to pay, for the same fee and without regard to who they are or for what reason they want the service. An easy example is the telephone: when someone calls, no matter if it's your mom, your bestie, a bill collector, or a creeper, the phone company puts the call through—it doesn't ask who's calling before it connects you. (It's like being a distributor under Section 230, from Chapter Four.)

Remember that the original Communications Act was passed in the 1930s, even before TV was common. Title II was primarily intended to regulate phone companies (or POTS—which stands for "plain old telephone service"), to try to rein in their monopolistic tendencies. Companies under this common carriage rule tend to be heavily regulated. Title I, on the other hand, says that wire and wireless communications are lightly regulated; the actual language states that Title I applies "to all interstate and foreign communication by wire or radio and all interstate and foreign transmission of energy by radio, which originates and/or is received within the United States, and to all persons engaged within the United States in such communication or such transmission of energy by radio." As the language indicates, it's far from clear what industries might fall under this vague definition—hence the FCC's classification, reclassification, and re-reclassification of broadband that's taken place over the past few years, not to mention the resulting public outcry and federal lawsuits.

As an aside, in December 2018, the FCC classified text messaging services under Title I, saying that putting them under the regulation-heavy Title II umbrella would prevent companies "from helping consumers by incorporating robotext-blocking, anti-spoofing measures, and other anti-spam features into their offerings." It's possible that, under a Biden administration and its expected return to net neutrality, these services will get reclassified.

In essence, these titles determine who gets regulated more and less by the FCC. So, being under Title II might seem counterproductive for technology dealing with information acquisition. Less regulation is better for the First Amendment, right? Not when you think about how net neutrality works. Under Title II, the FCC retains more regulatory power, so it can (under administrations that want to) enforce rules that prevent internet service providers from creating systems that financially benefit them at the expense of consumers—such as throttling and blocking certain kinds of online traffic or charging more for websites with services that they think people will be willing to pay more to keep receiving (like Netflix). It's complicated, but sometimes more government regulation is a good thing.

Beginnings of the Net Neutrality Saga

As mentioned above, the Telecommunications Act of 1996 defines two titles under which communications technologies can be regulated; one gets more regulation, and one gets less. In the early internet days, when most people got online using either phone lines or DSL, the FCC classified DSL, the transmitter of data, under Title II (common carrier), and the applications running over DSL as Title I (information services). This made sense, and it was similar to how phones worked (regular phones are common carriers, while an enhanced information service could be something like a for-pay 1-900 line that you might call for, say, a psychic reading late on a Saturday night at a set price per minute).

2002: Broadband is Title I, info service. The Telecom Act's categories, as broad as they are, did not specify where broadband should fit. In 2002, when cable companies first started offering internet services, the FCC was in a deregulatory mood. So it classified cable internet as a Title I service. This move freed cable from many FCC burdens (like having to work with the agency to establish "reasonable" pricing), and it made cable companies very happy.

As might be expected, a number of challenges to this ruling ensued. In 2005, the U.S. Supreme Court said that the FCC's categorization of broadband under Title I was an acceptable interpretation of the 1934 act in *Nat'l Cable & Telecomm. Ass'n v. Brand X Internet Serv.* (545 U.S. 967). In a 6-3 decision, written by Justice Clarence Thomas, the majority said that since the Telecom Act's language was unclear regarding broadband, *Chevron's* test allowed the FCC's reasonable interpretation to govern. Thomas also said that the FCC should be permitted, with its expertise, to make these calls.

Scalia dissents—with pizza. The dissenters, led by Justice Antonin Scalia, who was joined in part by Justices Ruth Bader Ginsburg and David Souter, focused on the concept of "stand-alone" services as part of the FCC's definition of "offering." The majority said that "offering" can be read to mean "a 'stand-alone' offering of telecommunications." Scalia offered this memorable illustration of the majority's incongruous result:

> If ... I call up a pizzeria and ask whether they offer delivery, both common sense and common "usage" would prevent them from answering: "No, we do not offer delivery—but if you order a pizza from us, we'll bake it for you and then bring it to your house." The logical response to this would be something on the order of, "so, you *do* offer delivery." But our pizza-man may continue to deny the obvious

and explain, paraphrasing the FCC and the Court: "No, even though we bring the pizza to your house, we are not actually 'offering' you delivery, because the delivery that we provide to our end users is 'part and parcel' of our pizzeria-pizza-at-home service and is 'integral to its other capabilities.'"

This construction is nonsense, Scalia said, and it's not always true that something that's part of a joint offering is offered merely because it isn't offered on a stand-alone basis. Still, the cable companies had their win. But as administrations and FCC members change, so do interpretations and enforcement actions.

The Net Neutrality Debate Heats Up

With the *Brand X* decision in hand, cable companies started doing business. In 2008, the FCC, under chair Kevin Martin, fined Comcast for blocking or throttling (delaying) traffic from BitTorrent sites, which take up a lot of bandwidth, arguing that such measures were necessary to manage network capacity. The FCC claimed that Comcast's actions contravened federal broadband policy. Comcast had already stopped these actions but filed suit anyway, alleging that the FCC had no authority to regulate in this area.

Ancillary (versus express) jurisdiction. The FCC under chair Julius Genachowski (who replaced Martin in 2009) supported net neutrality and had acted as though it had the authority to mandate it. But the *Comcast* case raised the question of whether the internet itself fell under the commission's *ancillary jurisdiction*—general powers not specifically defined within a statute (here, the Communications Act of 1934 amended by the Telecom Act of 1996). The FCC said it did, relying on the Supreme Court's 2005 decision in *Brand X*: "The Commission has jurisdiction to impose additional regulatory obligations under its Title I ancillary jurisdiction to regulate interstate and foreign communications."

However, in 2010 the D.C. Circuit said that not only was there no *express* authority for the FCC to regulate net neutrality, there was no authority in the agency's *ancillary* powers granted by the Communications Act of 1934, either, and it overturned the FCC's order against Comcast. This was a huge setback for the FCC—and a significant win for ISPs—and the agency would face the ancillary/express authority issue again in 2019.

In overturning the order, the D.C. Circuit said that the FCC had "failed to tie its assertion of ancillary authority over Comcast's internet service to any 'statutorily mandated responsibility'" (*Comcast Corp. v. FCC*, 600 F.3d 642). The agency must justify any ancillary jurisdiction independently, and it had stretched the meaning of *Brand X* too far. Rejecting the many legislative and judicial precedents the FCC gave to justify its jurisdiction, the judges said that "the allowance of wide latitude in the exercise of delegated powers is not the equivalent of untrammeled freedom to regulate activities over which the statute fails to confer ... Commission authority." In other words, even though Congress allows for great leeway for agencies like the FCC to interpret their mandates, that leeway isn't limitless.

In response, FCC chair Genachowski issued a statement called "The Third Way" in which he proposed a hybrid structure for broadband which he said would give the FCC enough power to regulate net neutrality without overreaching. Under this approach, the FCC would "recognize the transmission component of broadband access service—and only this component—as a telecommunications service" and "apply only a handful of provisions of Title II [common carriers] that, prior to the Comcast decision, were widely believed to be within the Commission's purview for broadband."

2010 rules. The FCC in 2010 adopted new rules, called "Preserving the Free and Open Internet," that required more transparency from internet service providers, forbade internet service providers like telephone and cable companies ("fixed-line" providers) from preventing access to competitors or to certain websites, and mandated more relaxed rules for wireless providers. Consumers who are heavy users can be charged more. When the rules went into effect in 2011, Verizon and other companies promptly filed suit; the D.C. Circuit consolidated the cases into one case

Then in 2012 the CEO of movie streaming company Netflix accused Comcast of violating net neutrality principles when it exempted its own Xfinity app (video streaming over Xbox 360) data use from its 250GB monthly data cap—making it far more attractive for Comcast users to use its service rather than Hulu or Netflix, whose data usage would count against the monthly cap. But Comcast was off the hook: the FCC said that Comcast was in the clear because Xfinity does not stream over the open internet.

Classification matters. The FCC was dealt another blow in its pursuit of net neutrality regulatory power in 2014 (*Verizon v. FCC*, 740 F.3d 623) when the D.C. Circuit struck down parts of the 2010 "Preserving the Free and Open Internet" rules. The court agreed with Verizon that because the FCC had previously classified broadband internet as an "information service," not a "telecommunications service," broadband carriers were not considered to be common carriers—and thus not bound by the 2010 rules.

FCC chair Tom Wheeler proposed a new set of rules following the decision, but because they allowed for broadband providers to charge for faster delivery of content, there was a huge backlash. In May 2014, the commission issued a new report, "Protecting and Promoting the Open Internet," in which Wheeler backed down somewhat from the first draft.

2015: Broadband is Title II, common carrier, and the rules are clear. In 2015, the FCC released its newest rules in a document entitled "Protecting and Promoting the Open Internet." The agency took the step that some had long hoped for of reclassifying high-speed internet as a telecommunications service rather than an information service. This brought internet service providers (ISPs) under Title II of the Communications Act as common carriers and allows the FCC to regulate discriminatory practices in online traffic.

The rules included *prohibitions on blocking, throttling and paid prioritizing of online traffic.* The language was clear (condensed for brevity here):

> **No Blocking.** ... this Order adopts a straightforward ban:
>> *A person engaged in the provision of broadband Internet access service ... shall not block lawful content, applications, services, or nonharmful devices...*
>
> **No Throttling.** ...This Order creates a separate rule to guard against [bandwidth] degradation targeted at specific uses of a customer's broadband connection:
>> *A person engaged in the provision of broadband Internet access service ... shall not impair or degrade lawful Internet traffic on the basis of Internet content, application, or service, or use of a non-harmful device ...*
>
> **No Paid Prioritization.** ... To protect against "fast lanes," this Order adopts a rule that establishes that:
>> *A person engaged in the provision of broadband Internet access service ... shall not engage in paid prioritization. "Paid prioritization" refers to the management of a broadband provider's network to directly or indirectly favor some traffic over other*

Focus on...
Net neutrality: a timeline of key developments

It's hard to keep track of what's happened in the net neutrality (NN) saga. Here's a summary of some key events (as of June 2021).

Feb. 1996: Telecommunications Act gives FCC authority over broadband providers.

March 2002: FCC classifies broadband as a Title I information service (with fewer regulations).

June 2003: Law professor Tim Wu coins the term "net neutrality" in a journal article.

June 2005: Supreme Court in *Nat'l Cable & Telecomm. Ass'n v. Brand X Internet Serv.* upholds FCC's authority and Title I broadband classification.

Aug. 2008: FCC under Martin issues order against Comcast for throttling BitTorrent traffic.

April 2010: DC Circuit rules in *Comcast v. FCC* that FCC can't regulate how ISPs handle content/traffic under either express or ancillary authority.

Dec. 2010: FCC under Genachowski adopts "Open Internet Order," making NN official.

Jan. 2014: DC Circuit strikes down *Open Internet Order* in *Verizon v. FCC*, citing FCC's Title I classification of broadband in 2002 and saying it has no authority to regulate NN.

May 2014: FCC under Wheeler proposes "Protecting and Promoting the Open Internet," new NN rules; Title II classification as well as "fast lane" options met with public protest.

Nov. 2014: President Barack Obama asks FCC to reclassify ISPs as common carriers under Title II. Donald Trump calls NN "the Fairness Doctrine," and says it "will target conservative media."

Feb. 2015: FCC adopts "Protecting and Promoting the Open Internet" on partisan 3-2 vote, reclassifies broadband as common carrier under Title II.

June 2016: DC Circuit rejects ISPs' First Amendment challenge to "Protecting and Promoting the Open Internet" and upholds NN in *U.S. Telecomm'ns Ass'n v. FCC.*

Aug. 2016: Ninth Circuit holds in *FTC v. AT&T Mobility LLC* that "common carrier" is determined by status, denying FTC jurisdiction over common carriers, and preventing FTC from suing AT&T for data throttling. FTC gets *en banc* rehearing.

Jan. 2017: Trump is sworn in as president and promotes FCC commissioner Ajit Pai to chair.

April 2017: Pai announces plans to revise 2015 NN rules and asks for public comments.

May 2017: DC Circuit denies *en banc* rehearing of *U.S. Telecomm'ns Ass'n* (future Justice Kavanaugh dissents). Telecomms appeal.

FIG. 100. Tim Wu, law professor who coined the term "net neutrality" in 2003.

Timothy Vollmer, "Tim Wu at Free Press Changing Media Summit, Newseum," May 13, 2009 via Flickr, Creative Commons attribution license.

Nov. 2017: FCC releases "Restoring Internet Freedom," returning broadband to its original Title I information service classification.

Dec. 2017: On partisan 3-2 vote, FCC adopts "Restoring Internet Freedom," eliminating NN. State attorneys general announce plans to sue for reversal.

Jan. 2018: State attorneys general sue FCC at the DC Circuit, challenging agency's preemption of NN.

Feb. 2018: Ninth Circuit *en banc* overturns three-judge panel in *AT&T Mobility LLC* and establishes that "common carrier" under FTC Act is defined by activity, not status, allowing FTC throttling suit against AT&T to go forward.

May 2018: AT&T says it won't challenge *en banc* Ninth Circuit *Mobility* decision, will settle with FTC.

June 2018: "Restoring Internet Freedom" takes effect.

Aug. 2018: Internet companies and state attorneys general file suit challenging FCC preemption.

Sept. 2018: Calif. NN passed but not implemented.

Oct. 2018: ISPs file suit against Vermont law.

Nov. 2018: Supreme Court denies *cert* in *U.S. Telecomm'ns Ass'n*, DC Circuit opinion left in place.

Feb. 2019: DC Circuit rules in *Mozilla v. FCC* that FCC can't preempt state NN laws but upholds most of "Restoring Internet Freedom."

Feb. 2020: DC Circuit won't review *Mozilla en banc.*

Aug. 2020: Justice Dep't and ISPs join in suit to stop implementation of Calif. NN law.

Jan. 2021: Joe Biden takes office, Pai leaves FCC; Jessica Rosenworcel appointed acting chair.

Feb. 2021: Biden Justice Dep't drops out of suit against Calif. NN law, but ISPs continue suit. Fed. judge refuses to enjoin the state law.

April 2021: ISPs appeal to the Ninth Cir. to overturn Calif. law.

May 2021: ISPs and Vermont agree to delay suit until Calif. law is litigated.

traffic ... either (a) in exchange for consideration (monetary or otherwise) from a third party, or (b) to benefit an affiliated entity.

In addition, the FCC had the power to decide questions on a case-by-case basis. Wheeler said, "We have created a playing field where there are known rules, and the FCC will sit there as a referee and will throw the flag." These rules were hailed by many as a welcome strengthening of the FCC's formerly flabby stance, and even President Barack Obama trumpeted them in White House statements, touting them as Americans speaking up for a strong net neutrality policy. As expected, several telecommunications companies filed suit.

The 2015 rules are upheld. The FCC finally scored a win in 2016 for the "Protecting and Promoting the Open Internet" net neutrality policy. In *U.S. Telecomm'ns Ass'n v. FCC* (825 F. 3d 674), a panel of the D.C. Circuit by a 2-1 vote agreed with the FCC's position that broadband internet access should be treated like a utility (like water, basic phone service, and electricity) rather than as a luxury item.

The majority, in an opinion written by two judges (one the same judge who had written the *Verizon* opinion striking down the FCC's 2010 rules two years before), rejected the telecommunication companies' argument that the FCC lacked authority to reclassify broadband as a telecommunications service, saying that the commission acted in accordance with prior law. "[T]he proper classification of broadband turns 'on the factual particulars of how Internet technology works and how it is provided,'" questions that are properly within the scope of the FCC's purview.

In addressing why the FCC took so long to reclassify broadband from an information service (and thus not a common carrier) to a telecommunications service, the majority said that the commission did not believe it could have adopted rules without that reclassification. The FCC, said the court, "found it necessary to establish three bright-line rules, the anti-blocking, anti-throttling, and anti-paid-prioritization rules, all of which impose *per se* common carrier obligations by requiring broadband providers to offer indiscriminate service to edge providers." And, the judges said, *Chevron* gives agencies broad deference for their own (reasonable) interpretations. The dissenting judge called the majority decision an "unreasoned patchwork" and an invitation to monopoly.

Many consumer groups and online company representatives lauded the decision as a huge win for the American public. FCC chair Wheeler said in a statement, "After a decade of debate and legal battles, today's ruling affirms the commission's ability to enforce the strongest possible internet protections—both on fixed and mobile networks—that will ensure the internet remains open, now and in the future." However, a senior AT&T executive told the *New York Times*, "We have always expected this issue to be decided by the Supreme Court and we look forward to participating in that appeal."

And the telecom companies did appeal. First, they asked the D.C. Circuit for a rehearing *en banc*, so all judges could participate. The court said no, but at least one judge clearly stated in dissent from that denial what he thought of net neutrality: "The net neutrality rule is unlawful and must be vacated, however, for two alternative and independent reasons."

A future justice speaks. The first reason, this judge said, was that Congress never authorized the FCC to regulate net neutrality. Second, he claimed that the Court in the *Turner* cases in 1993 and 1997 said that "the First Amendment bars the Government from restricting the editorial discretion of internet service providers, absent a showing that an internet service provider possesses market power in a relevant geographic market. Here, however, the FCC has not even tried to make a market power showing." In addition, he said that the *Chevron* test for agency deference only applied to "ordinary" agency rules, not "major" rules like net neutrality. Why should we care? The judge who wrote this dissent is Brett Kavanaugh—now a Supreme Court justice, occupying Kennedy's vacated seat.

The telecomms also appealed to the Supreme Court after the D.C. Circuit's denial of an *en banc* rehearing. In November 2018, the justices denied *cert* (with Kavanaugh and Chief Justice John Roberts both recusing). As the 2015 rules under consideration in the case had by then been replaced by the 2018 FCC rules eliminating net neutrality, the case would have focused on the precedential value of the appellate court's opinion—which the Court allowed to stand instead of deciding it had been erroneously decided.

A quick interlude: Net neutrality privacy implications, or "two cops" on the broadband "beat." As we learned in Chapter Five, the Federal Trade Commission is the government agency with primary responsibility for privacy regulation. But what happens when privacy concerns meet telecommunications (a not uncommon event) under FCC watch? Closing a gap in privacy regulation, an *en banc* Ninth Circuit in 2018 unanimously said that the FTC *could* regulate non-telephone privacy activities of telecommunication providers. The suit arose in 2016 when the FTC accused AT&T of throttling data speeds of customers with unlimited data plans. The agency alleged that when customers hit a ceiling arbitrarily set by AT&T, their data speed slowed—regardless of whether network congestion required it— so that web-browsing or streaming video was impossible. But AT&T claimed that only the FCC had jurisdiction to sue it, and in 2016 a panel of the Ninth Circuit agreed, saying that because AT&T had "status" as a common carrier, it was shielded from FTC enforcement actions—barring the throttling case. Privacy expert Daniel Solove called the outcome "an awful decision for consumers" because most telecomm companies don't fall neatly into one category or another anymore. The ruling, if left untouched, would leave a regulatory gap that companies could exploit to consumers' detriment, he said.

Solove's fears were shortlived; the FTC won an *en banc* review. Calling the case "one of agency jurisdiction and statutory construction," in 2018 a full complement of 11 Ninth Circuit judges unanimously overturned the panel's decision and affirmed the district court's denial of AT&T's motion to dismiss (*FTC v. AT&T Mobility LLC*, 883 F.3d 848). The judges held that "the phrase 'common carriers subject to the acts to regulate commerce' thus provides immunity from FTC regulation only to the extent that a common carrier is engaging in common-carrier services." In other words, AT&T could not use the common-carrier exemption as a blanket exemption to engage in throttling.

The judges also took notice of the urgings of both the FCC and FTC to adopt an activity-based definition for common carriage. In addition, the agencies had in 2015 drafted a memo in which the two commissions said they believed that "the scope of the common carrier exemption in the FTC Act does not preclude the FTC from addressing non-common carrier activities engaged in by common carriers." The court commented approvingly (and with a sly wink), "This Memorandum reflects a classic example of concurrent jurisdiction with two agencies sharing regulatory oversight. In the administrative context, two cops on the beat is nothing unusual." The decision meant that the FTC could resume its suit against AT&T for data throttling, and in May 2018, AT&T announced that it would not challenge the ruling and would instead work with the FTC toward a fair resolution.

2018: Broadband is Title I, info service (again), and the rule is "light-touch." On Dec. 14, 2017, the FCC, on a partisan 3-2 vote, the FCC formally ended net neutrality with an order entitled "Restoring Internet Freedom." This order accomplished several important things. First, it returned broadband's classification to Title I information service status, returning it to, as the press release under FCC chair Pai puts it, the "longstanding, bipartisan light-touch regulatory framework that has fostered rapid internet growth, openness, and freedom for nearly 20 years." Second, it gave the FTC regulatory power over consumer protection issues (such as when a broadband provider engages in an unfair or deceptive act or practice). Finally, it acknowledged that the three major things called for in the 2015 order—no throttling, blocking, or paid prioritization—were beneficial to consumers but costly. Transparency, then, when providers engage in these activities, coupled with consumers' abilities to choose their own providers, would accomplish the same benefits but at a lower cost. (Most ISPs have said that they would not engage in blocking or throttling, as those actions are very unpopular with consumers.) Moreover, the commission said it was committed to eliminating unnecessary regulations so broadband innovation and growth could flourish. On June 11, 2018, the rules became official.

The states jump in—and lose, kind of. The 2018 FCC rules claimed to preempt state law. At the time, Vermont, Oregon, and Washington had net neutrality laws already on the books (governors in six other states had signed executive orders supporting it, and many cities had also passed or were considering local rules). The FCC wanted these laws invalidated, and it argued that under the "impossibility exception to state jurisdiction," where an agency can "preempt state law when (1) it is impossible or impracticable to regulate the intrastate aspects of a service without affecting interstate communications and (2) the Commission determines that such regulation would interfere with federal regulatory objectives," that could happen. But 22 state attorneys general argued the point: in January 2018, they joined with internet companies and nonprofit organizations in a case against the FCC in the D.C. Circuit. The FCC's 2018 rules were "arbitrary, capricious, and an abuse of discretion within the meaning of the Administrative Procedures Act," among other violations, they claimed. Before the case was decided, California passed its own state net neutrality law but agreed not to enforce it until the D.C. Circuit had its say. In October 2018, broadband companies challenged the Vermont law; the state followed California's lead in pausing its enforcement.

The appeals court issued its ruling on Oct. 1, 2019, in *Mozilla Corp. v. FCC* (940 F.3d 1). Although the outcome was a mixed bag, it was mostly a win for the FCC. The 186-page *per curiam* (unsigned) opinion supported the FCC's rollback of the 2015 rules as well as the rest of the 2018 rules, including broadband's Title I classification. The court also remanded three parts of the 2018 rules for FCC consideration and revision (public safety, pole attachments, and a program to support broadband for low-income consumers).

But the states' big win was the court's ruling on preemption: to preempt the states, the FCC must have either express or ancillary authority, and it had neither. The court pointed out that the agency had actually defined itself out of express authority: "By reclassifying broadband as an information service, the Commission placed broadband *outside* of its Title II jurisdiction." What about ancillary authority? The court noted that the Title I classification mattered here, too. Ancillary authority here can be derived from Title II and several other titles—but not from Title I. Yes, the court said, the FCC has the right to classify broadband under either Title I or Title II, but that choice "does not carry with it the option to mix and match its favorite parts of both." In other words, the agency can't have its cake and eat it too.

The court concluded that the FCC "lacked the legal authority to categorically abolish all fifty States' statutorily conferred authority to regulate intrastate communications." However, nothing in the decision would prevent the FCC from taking on state net neutrality laws one at a time, something the court said was due to the "fact-intensive inquiries" necessary to determine each state preemption. The D.C. Circuit declined to review the case *en banc* in February 2020, and neither party appealed to the high court.

State net neutrality in the courts. In August 2020, the Trump Department of Justice joined the major ISPs in asking for a preliminary injunction against the California law; the Biden DoJ dropped out of the case, but the ISPs still wanted a stop on the law. A federal judge said no on Feb. 23, 2021, saying he thought that the ISPs weren't likely to succeed at trial (*Am. Cable Ass'n v. Becerra*, No 2:18-cv-02684; Xavier Becerra was tapped to serve as Biden's secretary for health and human services and will be replaced by California AG Rob Bonta). The ISPs have appealed to the Ninth Circuit. And the Vermont case? The parties have agreed to stand down until the California situation resolves. Stay tuned.

Bottom line. As of June 2021, the National Council on State Legislatures reports seven states (California, Colorado, Maine, New Jersey, Oregon, Vermont, and Washington) have passed laws regulating net neutrality, as have some cities. Battles over net neutrality will probably move to the states: once a full Biden FCC is in place, the commissioners are likely to start dismantling Pai's "light-touch" Title I regime, moving broadband back under Title II and implementing net neutrality rules. How to avoid this see-saw effect? Congress could step in and pass a law that establishes where broadband should live, once and for all. Is it better to have one federal regulation or 50 state laws? Even ISPs might lean toward a (limited) federal net neutrality rule if faced with a patchwork of inconsistent state laws. While net neutrality isn't quite the hot-button topic it was a few years back, the fight's not over.

◼ OTHER DIGITAL TECHNOLOGIES AND CHALLENGES

In the 2000s and beyond, it has become increasing clear how essential internet access is to all sectors of society. As a result, state and federal government sought to expand access to (and exercise control over) internet services, and businesses saw huge money-making opportunities. The FCC offered a plan to attempt to ensure that Americans have access to high-speed internet access at affordable prices, and several court cases interpreted laws that had, in some cases, been on the books for decades. Finally, an executive order from a former president pushed questions of the FCC's authority to regulate social media into the public eye but didn't result in many answers.

Broadband

President Barack Obama promised access to fast, affordable broadband (high-speed internet access) as part of his campaign. The FCC in 2005 summarized its Broadcast Policy Statement in four maxims: Internet consumers are entitled to "any lawful content, any lawful application, any lawful device, any provider." Congress in 2009 directed the FCC to come up with a broadband plan to ensure that all Americans have access to broadband capabilities. In 2010, the FCC did so—its 376-page plan, called "Connecting America: The National Broadband Plan" (fcc.gov/general/national-broadband-plan) notes that nearly 100 million Americans do not have broadband at home and lays out an ambitious plan to remedy that.

The plan is four-fold: establishing policies for competition; ensuring efficient allocation and use of government resources; creating incentives for adopting broadband; and setting standards to maximize use. The major long-term goal in the plan was that "At least

100 million U.S. homes should have affordable access to actual download speeds of at least 100 megabits per second and actual upload speeds of at least 50 megabits per second." (For context, in 2010, there were 117.5 million U.S. households, so a goal of 100 million with fast, cheap broadband was ambitious; it's still not bad even with the 2020 estimate of 128.5 million American households.) Other goals include leading the world in broadband innovation, assisting with affordability, ensuring faster speeds for public institutions like schools and hospitals, and making certain that first responders have access to a fast, interoperable national network.

Who will pay for this bonanza? No one, the FCC says; it will be paid for by spectrum auctions: "Given the plan's goal of freeing 500 megahertz of spectrum, future wireless auctions mean the overall plan will be revenue neutral, if not revenue positive." The plan generated controversy when it was released; the *New York Times* reported that telecom agencies, television stations, and rural internet providers were expressing concern. All agreed that the goals were laudable but, as one analyst put it, "the devil is always in the details."

Computer Fraud and Abuse Act (CFAA)

The Computer Fraud and Abuse Act, passed in 1986, has been the subject of much litigation regarding unauthorized access to computer data (and the use of that data once gotten). The act says that whoever "intentionally accesses a computer without authorization or exceeds authorized access" can be criminally punished.

Many lawsuits focused on the words "exceeds authorized access," disagreeing on whether that language dealt at all with the actual use of the data obtained. A circuit split developed, with the Second, Fourth, Sixth, and Ninth Circuits opting for narrow interpretations and the First, Fifth, Seventh, and Eleventh saying the law should be broadly construed. For example, in 2012, the *en banc* Ninth Circuit in *U.S. v. Nosal* (676 F.3d 854) limited the CFAA's reach, saying that it theoretically could be used to prosecute many Americans who engage in harmless but unauthorized computer use at work. David Nosal, who worked for executive search firm Korn/Ferry, asked several colleagues to help him start a competing firm; those colleagues used their passwords to log into a confidential source database and gave Nosal that data. The court ruled the language of the CFAA was focused on *access* to that material, which Nosal's colleagues were permitted, not its *use*. The quotable former chief judge of the Ninth Circuit, Alex Kozinski, said that to interpret the law broadly would open up harmless activities to criminal prosecution: "Employees can sneak in the sports section of the *New York Times* to read at work, but they'd better not visit ESPN.com. And sudoku enthusiasts should stick to the printed puzzles, because visiting www.dailysudoku.com from their work computers might give them more than enough time to hone their sudoku skills behind bars." The dissenters pointedly noted that the case wasn't about sudoku or ESPN, but rather "stealing an employer's valuable information to set up a competing business."

On the other hand, the Fifth Circuit chose a broader reading. In *U.S. v. John* (597 F. 3d 263, 2010), that court upheld the conviction of Citigroup account manager Dimetriace Eva-Lavon John for giving customer account data to her half-brother that enabled him to engage in fraud. John exceeded her authorized access under CFAA because she exceeded "the purposes for which access has been given." John's access to that data was "confined," the court reasoned, because she knew that she was "not authorized to access a computer and information obtainable from that access in furtherance of or to perpetrate a crime." Cases similar to this one and *Nosal* created a circuit split ripe for the Supreme Court's review.

The high court steps in. In its first serious interpretation of the CFAA in 2021, the Supreme Court resolved that split, siding with the Ninth and its companion circuits. The justices on a 6-3 vote came down in *Van Buren v. U.S.* (No. 19–783) on the side of a narrow reading of "exceeds authorized access." The case involved Georgia police officer Nathan Van Buren's conviction and 18-month prison sentence under the CFAA for taking a bribe to run a license plate number through a police database he was only authorized to use for law enforcement purposes. The Court overturned both the trial court's conviction and the Eleventh Circuit's upholding of the conviction.

Rejecting the government's broad view that users "exceed authorized access" under CFAA whenever they get and use computer information for unapproved reasons, Justice Amy Coney Barrett said that it was the *act* of retrieving, not the *use* of the retrieved data, that is key. The CFAA, she said, prohibits someone from obtaining "information one is not allowed to obtain *by using a computer that he* [sic] *is authorized to access.*" She gave an example of this "gates up or down" interpretation: someone with access to information stored in "Folder Y" on a computer doesn't violate the law by getting that information from Folder Y, regardless of the reason. But, she said, "if the information is instead located in prohibited 'Folder X,' to which the person lacks access, he [sic] violates the CFAA by obtaining such information." Some commentators said this was the correct approach. As the Electronic Frontier Foundation put it, the decision kept online services from using the law "to enforce limitations on how or why you use their service, including for purposes such as collecting evidence of discrimination or identifying security vulnerabilities."

The dissenters (Justice Clarence Thomas, joined by Chief Justice John Roberts and Justice Samuel Alito) said the majority's position that the CFAA only applies "when a person is 'not entitled [*under any possible circumstance*] so to obtain' information" is flawed. Thomas proffered real-world examples as illustrations: for example, a valet can "access" a car to park and retrieve it but not to take a joyride. And he offered another "awkward" result: an employee would not be liable under CFAA for deleting all computer files that the person could "access" just before resigning, but another employee would face criminal penalties for playing solitaire on a work computer if that person's employer forbade all access to the Windows "games" folder to combat losses of productivity.

Cyberbullying and academic articles. The CFAA was also used to prosecute Lori Drew in the Megan Meier cyberbullying case discussed elsewhere in this chapter (*U.S. v. Drew*, 259 F.R.D. 449, 2009) and in a case againg internet activist Aaron Swartz (one of the creators of Creative Commons, Reddit, and the Really Simple Syndication protocol). Swartz used his Massachusetts Institute of Technology school account to download and make available, free to the public, millions of academic articles from JSTOR, an online academic paper archive. He committed suicide in 2013 after failing to come to an agreement with prosecutors over 13 felony counts of hacking and wire fraud under the CFAA.

Telephone Consumer Protection Act (TCPA)

In the span of just three years, the Supreme Court issued three opinions interpreting the Telephone Consumer Protection Act, a 1991 law that many people had never heard of. The three cases, one each year from 2019 to 2021, dealt with a variety of issues. But before getting into the details, let's set the stage for understanding this area of law.

A little history. Telephone technology has been around for over a century. The first landline was established in April 1877, connecting Boston and Somerville, Massachusetts.

According to one estimate, by 1920, 35% of U.S. households had a phone, a number that steadily climbed over the decades to a high of 98.2% in 2008. Cell phones didn't appear until 1984, when the first "brick" mobile phone, the Motorola DynaTAC, debuted. The DynaTAC was a giant 9-inch blocky unit weighing two and a half pounds with 30 minutes of battery time–and sold for $3,995. It's the phone made famous by corporate villain Gordon Gekko (played by Michael Douglas) in the 1987 movie *Wall Street*.

Why TCPA? Congress passed TCPA in response to what one court called "voluminous consumer complaints about abuses of telephone technology." These complaints included concerns about increases in unsolicited telephone marketing calls and faxes as well as automated dialing systems and prerecorded ads. TCPA restricts unsolicited marketing over phone or fax; it also forbids the falsification of caller identification for fraudulent purposes. Cases can be brought in either federal or state court.

Requirements. Telemarketers have both mandates and prohibitions under TCPA. They must honor the National Do Not Call Registry (managed by the FTC at donotcall. gov) and provide their own names as well as the name of the entity they represent and a way to contact that entity. Telemarketers can't call before 8:00 a.m. or after 9:00 p.m. local time; use recordings or artificial voices; employ automated dialers to call emergency lines (911), hospitals, doctors' offices, cell phones, or any service that charges for call receipt; or send unsolicited advertising faxes. Victims of a TCPA violation can sue (up to $500 for each violation, or actual damages), seek an injunction against the advertiser, or both. Willful violations can result in treble damages.

The rise of cell phones. Cable isn't the only place where consumers are cutting cords. The Centers for Disease Control and Prevention, which has been tracking phone ownership in national health surveys since 2004, found that in 2020, only 36.7% of all U.S. households have an operational landline. A 2021 report from Pew Research Centers notes that 97% of Americans own a cell phone, and 85% of those are smartphones.

When TCPA was passed in 1991, 95% of American households relied on landlines, and only 3% had mobile phones. The next year, 1992, saw the sending of the first text message (in the United Kingdom, the message "Merry Christmas" was sent from a computer to a mobile phone), and in 2019, Americans sent 2.1 trillion text messages–52 billion more than the year before, according to wireless trade association CTIA.

Not surprisingly, the dramatic shift in the way "telephone" services are used in the United States since 1991 resulted in criticism of the TCPA and calls for its modernization. The act has in fact been amended several times, and one of those amendments resulted in one of the lawsuits heard by the high court between 2019 and 2021. So, let's turn to the cases.

TCPA and the Hobbs Act. The Court first took on *PDR Network, LLC v. Carlton & Harris Chiropractic Inc.* (139 S. Ct. 2051), a case more about agency deference than TCPA, in 2019. The FCC issued an order in 2006 which said that TCPA's ban on "unsolicited ads" included even faxes for free goods or services but not purely informational faxes. PDR Network, the producer of the popular *Physicians' Desk Reference* containing information about prescription drugs and their interactions, sent a fax to Carlton & Harris Chiropractic offering a free e-book copy of the reference (PDR charges drug companies to be listed in the reference book and distributes it to health care providers for free). The chiropractors sued PDR for the unsolicited advertising fax. A federal district court said that the PDR fax wasn't an "unsolicited ad" as it contained no commercial offers, and moreover, the FCC's order saying otherwise didn't bind it. But the Fourth Circuit disagreed, holding the order binding on the district court under the Hobbs Act (also called the Administrative Orders Review Act). This act allows the federal appeals court to modify "final orders" of certain agencies.

The Supreme Court took the case but didn't resolve the issue. Justice Stephen Breyer, writing for a Court unanimous in the outcome, admitted, "We have found it difficult to answer this question"—so he remanded the case to the appellate court to answer two questions: first, whether the 2006 FCC order is a "legislative rule" (has the force of law) or an "interpretive rule" (merely advisory), and second, whether PDR had a "prior and adequate" chance under Hobbs (60 days) to review and challenge the FCC's order—even if the order is considered "legislative." Stay tuned.

Collecting government debt. The Court in 2020 decided *Barr v. Am. Ass'n of Political Consultants Inc.* (140 S. Ct. 2335), a case dealing with a 2015 amendment to TCPA that exempted robocalls (recorded messages) trying to collect government debt. The plaintiffs, organizations wanting to make political robocalls (banned under TCPA), alleged that the amendment violated their First Amendment rights by treating their calls differently from government-debt calls—and they asked for the whole TCPA robocall restriction to be overturned. A federal district court agreed that the 2015 amendment was a content-based restriction on speech subject to strict scrutiny. But, it said, the government's interest in collecting its debts was sufficient to allow the law to stand. The Fourth Circuit, although agreeing that strict scrutiny should apply, thought that the government hadn't made a good enough case to allow the amendment to stand.

Justice Brett Kavanaugh wrote for a 7-2 Court agreeing with both lower courts that the amendment was indeed content based, but he saw no need to invalidate the whole TCPA robocall ban. Pointing out that "the Court's remedial preference after finding a provision of a federal law unconstitutional has been to salvage rather than destroy the rest of the law," Kavanaugh did just that: he invalidated the government-debt exemption and left the rest of TCPA intact. This meant, he said, that "plaintiffs still may not make political robocalls to cell phones, but their speech is now treated equally with debt-collection speech."

Justice Sonia Sotomayor concurred in the judgment, saying that the exemption would fail even intermediate scrutiny as insufficiently narrowly tailored. Justice Stephen Breyer, joined by Justices Ruth Bader Ginsburg and Elena Kagan, thought that the government-debt exemption was constitutional and would have used intermediate scrutiny to find it so. He also agreed that the TCPA should be subject to severability. Justice Neil Gorsuch, joined by Justice Clarence Thomas, felt the opposite. He agreed that the exemption was a content-based rule that couldn't survive strict scrutiny but said that severing it from the TCPA—leaving the rest of the robocall rules in place—"leads to the unlikely result that not a single person will be allowed to speak more freely and, instead, more speech will be banned."

"Automatic dialing." The last of the trio of cases decided by the Court, in 2021, dealt with what counts as an "automatic telephone dialing system" under TCPA (*Facebook v. Duguid*, No. 19-511). Facebook sent out automated text messages to Noah Duguid, who had never used Facebook, containing security alerts for a non-existent account. Duguid asked Facebook to stop sending these messages but they kept coming, and he finally sued. Facebook argued that their system didn't count as an autodialer because it didn't use a "random or sequential number generator." The district court dismissed Duguid's complaint on a narrow definition, saying that Duguid claimed that Facebook sent targeted texts, not texts to randomly generated numbers. But the Ninth Circuit reversed: a system doesn't have to use a random generator to be an autodialer—it just must be able to store phone numbers and dial them automatically.

Justice Sonia Sotomayor, writing for a Court unanimous in the outcome, phrased the question as whether the TCPA definition of an automatic telephone dialing system "encompasses equipment that can 'store' and dial telephone numbers, even if the device does not 'us[e] a random or sequential number generator.'" She reversed the Ninth Circuit, answering simply, "It does not." Basing her analysis on canons of statutory interpretation, she said that Facebook's system failed to meet TCPA's definition of an autodialer, which "requires that in all cases, whether storing or producing numbers to be called, the equipment in question must use a random or sequential number generator."

These cases aren't the last word on TCPA, even in this book. As Americans continue to increase their reliance on cell phones and the FCC continues to battle fraudulent use of this technology, other parts of the law will likely be challenged in future years.

Section 230 and the FCC

As you've probably guessed by now, Section 230 of the Telecom Act has broad implications for several areas of media law. As was discussed in Chapter Two, after the Capitol insurrection that took place on Jan. 6, 2021—and social media's banning of former president Donald Trump—loud cries for changes to Section 230 erupted all over. The question on everyone's minds seemed to be whether social media companies, held privately and by few individuals, should be allowed to exercise as much power over public communication as they have done over the past few years.

Executive order. Questions about the appropriate role of the FCC in regulating social media and interpreting Section 230 arose in the summer of 2020 when Twitter added labels to several of then-President Donald Trump's tweets. In those tweets, sent on May 26, 2020, Trump had said that the planned expansion of the mail-in ballot system in many states for the 2020 elections in response to the COVID-19 pandemic would be "substantially fraudulent." He further accused Democratic California governor Gavin Newsom of "sending Ballots to millions of people" who have never voted with directions on who to vote for. Studies have shown no evidence of voter fraud as a result of mail-in ballots, and the Federal Elections Commission was quick to refute the president's claims, with one commissioner retorting, "There's simply no basis for the conspiracy theory that voting by mail causes fraud. None."

But the Twitter labels infuriated Trump, who soon issued an executive order targeting Section 230. Alleging that social media companies engage in "selective censorship that is hurting our national discourse," the president ordered the FCC to "expeditiously propose regulations" that ensure Section 230 protection isn't given to, for example, actions taken in bad faith or deceptive or pretextual actions.

Does the FCC have any power to do any of that? Brendan Carr, a Republican appointee, clearly thought so (his public statements had titles bordering on rhapsodic: "Carr Applauds Chairman Pai's Announcement on Section 230"). Another Republican member of the commission, Michael O'Rielly, wasn't so sure. He expressed his doubts in several speeches, including one on C-SPAN, but said he would consult with others before deciding. "I have deep reservations that [Congress] provided [the FCC] any intentional authority for this matter but I want to listen to people," he said. O'Rielly wouldn't get to pick a side: not long after he gave those speeches, Trump declined to renominate him to the FCC (commissioners are appointed for five-year terms unless filling a vacancy and can be reappointed).

FIG. 101.
Syncom, the first
geosynchronous
satellite, 1963.

NASA.

Chair Ajit Pai said that the FCC's lawyers advised him he had the authority, and a statement from a FCC staff attorney stated it concisely: "Simply put, the FCC has the authority to interpret all provisions of the Communications Act, including amendments such as Section 230." But the analysis rested on a grant of power that fell under Title II of the Communications Act (Section 201(b), giving the FCC power to "prescribe such rules and regulations as may be necessary in the public interest to carry out this Act")— yes, the very Title II from which Pai had taken such pains to distance broadband. In the end, it didn't matter: Pai left the FCC when Biden took office without having taken any action on the matter.

Repercussions of the order. But the order had sparked other initiatives. Facebook created an Oversight Board intended to evaluate its decisions: one of its earliest 2021 actions was to evaluate the decision to ban Trump. The board said that it was the right decision, but the ban shouldn't be indefinite. Members of Congress rolled out at least a dozen bills that ran the range of alterations to Section 230 from complete elimination (Stop Shielding Culpable Platforms Act) to revisions requiring platform accountability for enabling harassment and discrimination (Safeguarding Against Fraud, Exploitation, Threats, Extremism and Consumer Harms [SAFE TECH] Act). Will any pass? Stay tuned.

And, perhaps most interestingly, in May 2021 Florida governor Ron DeSantis signed a state law intended to prevent large social media platforms (more than $100 million in revenues or at least 100 million monthly subscribers) from banning political candidates. The law included a requirement that users be permitted to opt out of algorithmic sorting systems and what some called an "eyebrow-raising" exemption for theme parks. It came as no surprise to most legal scholars when a federal district judge blocked the law just a month later. Pointing out that the governor's signing statements and those of other members of his administration "show rather clearly that the legislation is viewpoint-based," the judge said that the law "come(s) nowhere close" to surviving strict scrutiny (*NetChoice, LLC v. Moody*, 2021 WL 2690876). And, as he put it, "Balancing the exchange of ideas among private speakers is not a legitimate governmental interest."

■ AN OVERVIEW OF MAJOR ISSUES

The electronic media face enormous legal, economic, and policy questions today. We may be in the midst of a communications revolution even more far-reaching than the one that brought us television 60 years ago. With cable or satellite TV losing their grip on American homes to streaming, television, satellite radio, and podcasting, many of the old rules of broadcast law and economics are obsolete. The day when three major television networks could dominate home entertainment in America is past. In 1979, ABC, CBS, and NBC commanded 91% of the prime time television audience. By 2008, the original "Big Three" networks' share of the prime time audience was usually far below 50% and steadily declining. Fox, a latecomer to network broadcasting, often had a larger audience than any of the "Big Three." Cable and satellite networks also were winning a large share of the audience. Recognizing these trends, the Federal Communications Commission has tried several different approaches to broadcast regulation. Some would say the FCC has moved in fits and starts, taking a zig-zag route toward no discernable destination.

In the early years of television, the FCC attempted to promote the public interest by adopting the Fairness Doctrine and other content controls. Then an FCC chair started calling the old rules "regulatory debris" and launched a broad deregulation of electronic communications. The FCC looked mainly to the marketplace for answers, while attempting to provide a "level playing field" for broadcasters, cable, and other audio and video delivery systems. Then starting in the 1990s, the FCC adopted or considered a series of new content controls, raising new questions about the degree to which the First Amendment should protect the electronic media.

Perhaps the most fundamental question is this: should the federal government regulate broadcast content—not to mention other forms of video news and entertainment? When then-FCC Chair Newton Minow called network television a "vast wasteland" in 1961, he clearly believed the government had the power—and the obligation—to regulate content to improve it (based on his and other government officials' views of what content was good and bad for the American public). By the 1980s, another FCC chair said TV is merely "a toaster with pictures," and not in need of much federal regulation.

Is either of these views right in a country with a First Amendment as well as a tradition of requiring broadcasters to serve the public interest, as that is defined by the government?

Are the FCC's rules, new and old, really "regulatory debris"? Is deregulation a good idea? What about abolishing a rule like the Fairness Doctrine? Should broadcasters be as free as newspaper publishers are to cover the news as they see it? Should the government even decide what is in the public interest?

Should television be "friendly to kids," as another FCC chair suggested? Does the federal government know what is best for the nation's children—or adults, for that matter? If so, is it right for over-the-air broadcasting to be singled out for government controls that do not apply to other media? And do these content controls really work? Should Congress authorize the FCC to restrict TV violence? Would such regulations violate the First Amendment?

Should there be different indecency rules for over-the-air television than there are for satellite and cable channels? Do most viewers really know when they have clicked from an over-the-air channel to a cable channel? Does it make sense to protect children by banning words that are routinely used at most schools and in most neighborhoods?

Cable has seen regulation, deregulation, reregulation—and then more deregulation. During the 1990s, the FCC adopted the most complex regulatory scheme cable has ever faced in America. The question that remains, of course, is whether the public really won or lost under this regulatory regimen. The cable industry said that with the rate rollbacks, retransmission consent fees, and other new costs, there would be little money left for new programming and technology. Broadcasters and public interest groups, on the other hand, pointed to a litany of alleged abuses by cable systems during the cable industry's "unregulated monopoly" era. "They had it coming," some said of the tough rules cable faced.

In all of this, has anybody really answered the big question: will all of the new audio and video services and proposals for content regulation really give us better programming or just another "vast wasteland"? Is programming to address the perceived need of community leaders for new infrastructure really "better" than *American Idol* or live sports coverage?

Where does the internet fit into this equation? Old laws (CFAA, 1986 and TCPA, 1991) are being interpreted in ways their drafters probably never dreamed of. The internet's broad First Amendment protection may lead to new questions—and new absurdities. Is it okay to have a four-letter word or an explicit depiction of sex on television if it arrived via the internet but not okay if it arrived via over-the-air TV (or cable, if Congress bans indecency on cable)? What if children view or hear programs containing four-letter words on their phones or tablets? And what about KidVid? With so much available (at least to some households) programming, what rules make sense, and who should be bound by them?

It is clear that one of the federal government's goals in the 2010s and beyond is to help Americans get online. How should this goal be accomplished? Should the FCC have the authority to regulate the internet, including how online traffic is managed, or should there be a new agency created—or no regulator at all? In all the confusion over Title I and Title II designations, what's best for consumers may have gotten lost. As of this writing, net neutrality is still not in place, although President Biden is expected to support its return. What new (and maybe better) arguments will arise to fight the FCC's claims of (de)regulatory power? And what new challenges will social media face in a post-January 6 world? One justice suggested several ways to bring social media under government regulation.

Through online audio and video streaming, anyone can be a "broadcaster" now—no government license needed. Is the scarcity rationale still viable? Should *Red Lion* go, as at least one sitting justice on the Supreme Court would prefer?

WHAT SHOULD I KNOW ABOUT MY STATE?

- Much of this law is federal law.
- How are my local broadcast stations complying with localism reporting standards?
- What cable franchises are in my area? What arrangements do they have with the cities?

SUMMARY

A SUMMARY OF ELECTRONIC MEDIA REGULATION

Why Do Broadcasters Have Special Laws to Follow?

Broadcasters do not own their frequencies; spectrum is a valuable and limited resource; Congress declared that those given the privilege of using it must serve *the public interest, convenience, and necessity.* Broadcasters obtain licenses from the Federal Communications Commission, the agency charged with regulating the electronic media. License renewal challenges by citizens' groups and others have become more commonplace than they once were, but non-renewals are still rare.

What Are the Major Rules Governing Broadcast Content?

The *Fairness Doctrine* was an FCC policy that for nearly 40 years required broadcasters to provide overall balance in their programming. It was abolished in 1987, to the dismay of Congress and some public interest groups but to the delight of broadcasters who objected to government officials second-guessing their judgments. Despite calls to bring the Fairness Doctrine back, current FCC commissioners and chairs oppose it. The *Equal Time Rule,* on the other hand, is a provision of the Communications Act that requires broadcasters to sell comparable airtime to political candidates at similar rates; it has not been abolished. Television stations are also required to carry three hours per week of children's educational programming, and broadcasters are required to serve the public interest, as that is defined by the FCC, in various other ways.

What Is Indecency?

Indecency is a standard of law applied to sexual content broadcast on over-the-air television or radio (not cable or satellite TV or radio). The FCC may regulate indecent content that is broadcast during the hours of 6:00 a.m. and 10:00 p.m., when children are most likely to be in the audience. The agency may punish "fleeting expletives" if they take place during that time.

How Is Cable Television Regulated?

Cable television systems need no FCC license, since they do not broadcast over the air. However, they are subject to many FCC rules because their operations affect on-the-air broadcasting. Cable was deregulated during the 1980s, but in 1992 Congress reregulated cable. The 1992 law mandated subscription rate reductions and must-carry or retransmission consent requirements to protect local television stations. Cable systems also must have *franchise agreements,* which give cities and counties some control over cable systems. The 1996 Telecommunications Act has repealed some rate reductions and other rules established by the 1992 law.

12 *Antitrust and Media Ownership Issues*

Does it matter who owns America's media? Does the public win or lose when one corporation owns many newspapers, magazines, movie and television studios, internet services, radio stations, television stations, networks, and cable systems—or a combination? Ever since William Randolph Hearst and the Scripps family built the nation's first newspaper chains more than a century ago, these have been controversial questions.

Media critics often regard the ongoing trend toward centralized ownership of the media as a threat to the public interest. Regardless of how well intentioned the management of a large media conglomerate may be, central ownership deprives the media of the independence that is so vital in a democracy, critics say. But others note the growing concentration of ownership of the traditional media is inevitable if they are to survive in the highly competitive new media marketplace, in which traditional media—newspapers and over-the-air broadcasters alike—are losing readers, listeners, viewers, and advertisers to new, largely unregulated competitors. Media companies can achieve *economies of scale* by combining operations. For example, a company that owns eight radio stations in one city can sell advertising, do programming, and handle station engineering more efficiently than eight individually owned stations. Some industry analysts say older media must cut costs or risk being silenced by economic realities.

But even defenders of multimedia ownership concede that abuses have occurred, and government agencies have sometimes tried to correct these abuses. The Antitrust Division of the U.S. Justice Department, for instance, has often acted against anticompetitive business practices in the media. And at times the Federal Communications Commission has limited both chain ownership in broadcasting and cross-ownership of print and broadcast media. At other times, however, both Justice and the FCC have acquiesced when large multimedia conglomerates merged with other equally large corporations. And Congress relaxed many media ownership restrictions in the Telecommunications Act of 1996, adopting the philosophy that companies should be free to grow and compete with other growing companies, all of whom are free to enter each other's areas of business. The 1996 law not only abolished many ownership restrictions, it also directed the FCC to review the remaining restrictions every few years to determine which ones can be eliminated.

Never have questions of media ownership and business practices been more controversial than they are now, with almost daily news accounts of mergers, ownership rule changes, and antitrust lawsuits. This chapter examines some of the results.

Chapter Objectives:

- Describe the history of antitrust actions from early Sherman Act trustbusting to JOAs to today's giant media mergers.
- Summarize the FCC's current media ownership rules and how they got where they are.
- Constrast American and European Union antitrust actions and claims.

Essential Questions:

- The FCC's broadcast ownership rules have been increasingly loosened over the years to allow more stations to be owned by fewer companies. Is this the right decision? Has the agency over- or underestimated the importance of digital media?
- To what extent should government act against companies they suspect of engaging in restraint of trade? Is innovation tied to bigness?
- In the 1980s, antitrust policy changed focus from companies to consumers. Is this the correct way to view the problem? Why or why not?

◼ AN OVERVIEW OF ANTITRUST LAW

Serious government regulation of monopolistic business practices in America began with the *Sherman Antitrust Act*, enacted in 1890 to combat rampant abuses in the post–Civil War era of industrialization. The act is the nation's pioneering antitrust law; it forbids a wide variety of "contracts, combinations ...or conspiracies in restraint of trade or commerce."

In 1914, the *Clayton Act* was adopted, forbidding certain other business practices and expanding the federal government's antitrust enforcement powers. This law was strengthened in 1950 by the addition of the *Celler-Kefauver Act*, which prohibits one company from buying out a competitor where the result is more monopoly and less competition. Thus, business ownership as well as business practices have come under federal regulation.

Definitions. Of the many business practices banned by these antitrust laws, a few should be specifically noted. For instance, *price fixing* and *profit pooling* are prohibited. That means it is generally unlawful for competing companies to enter an agreement either to charge non-competitive prices or share profits. Rival companies are supposed to keep each others' prices low by competing. They're not supposed to conspire to avoid price competition.

In addition, many *mergers, tying arrangements,* and *boycotts* are illegal. A merger is an arrangement in which two businesses combine. Mergers are illegal when they substantially reduce competition to the detriment of consumers or other businesses. Before a merger of large companies can occur, federal officials must review and approve the transaction.

A tying arrangement forces customers to buy something they may not want to get something they do want and cannot readily get elsewhere. Boycotts take many forms, but one common type is a refusal to do business with a person or a company as a means of coercing that person (or company) to do something he or she wouldn't otherwise be willing to do.

These business practices may or may not violate the law, depending on the specific facts of a particular case. In some antitrust cases, the courts apply the *rule of reason*, weighing the specific facts to determine whether a violation has occurred. This may involve a very complex economic analysis, often involving close judgment calls. In other cases, the *per se rule* applies: some business practices are so egregiously unlawful as to be *per se* antitrust violations.

Federal law. Federal antitrust laws establish three different kinds of legal actions to be used against businesses that engage in anti-competitive practices: (1) criminal prosecutions by the U.S. government to punish wrongdoers; (2) civil actions by the U.S. government to halt monopolistic business practices; and (3) civil actions for treble damages by private individuals or businesses allegedly injured by these practices. Treble damages, three times the actual losses, is a very strong remedy intended to discourage antitrust violations.

State law. All of these are provisions of *federal* antitrust laws. They apply to businesses engaged in interstate commerce and to local businesses whose activities in some way affect interstate commerce, and the U.S. Justice Department's Antitrust Division is primarily responsible for enforcing them.

However, where purely local businesses are involved, the jurisdiction over antitrust matters falls to the 50 states, all of which have at least some laws prohibiting monopolistic business practices within their borders. Also, *state* officials may sue to enforce the *federal* antitrust laws. For example, in 1990 the Supreme Court held that a state may sue to halt a merger between competing companies, even if the merger was already approved by the federal government (*California v. American Stores*, 495 U.S. 271).

Antitrust cartoons.

(L) FIG. 102. Standard oil trust trampling "common people" and police, 1901.

Rhyme: "O is the Oil Trust, a modern Bill Sikes; he defies the police, and does just as he likes."

(Bill Sikes is a criminal from Charles Dickens' 1838 novel *Oliver Twist*.)

Library of Congress Prints and Photographs Division, [LC-USZ62-63122]

Library of Congress.

FIG. 103. Theodore Roosevelt wrestling "railroad trust" bull, a reference to TR's use of the Sherman Antitrust Act to break up the Northern Securities railroad trust. (Charles Lewis Bartholomew, 1903).

Should public and private entities be treated differently under antitrust law? For example, should public government bodies be exempt from antitrust laws that govern private companies? No, the Supreme Court said unanimously in 2013 (*FTC v. Phoebe Putney Health System, Inc.*, 568 U.S. 216). In an opinion written by Justice Sonia Sotomayor, the Court said that a 1941 Georgia law that allowed hospital authorities to acquire other hospitals did not exempt the state from federal antitrust laws. The law "does not clearly articulate and affirmatively express a state policy empowering the [hospital authority] to make acquisitions of existing hospitals that will substantially lessen competition," Justice Sotomayor said, adding that "nothing in the [1941] Law or any other provision of Georgia law clearly articulates a state policy to allow authorities to exercise their general corporate powers, including their acquisition power, without regard to negative effects on competition."

International law. In recent years, as we'll see, many American companies have also learned that antitrust enforcement isn't just a matter of satisfying federal and state regulators in the United States. The European Union has a policy-making commission with the power to overrule mergers and acquisitions that will have an adverse effect on competition in Europe. More than one merger that won U.S. regulatory approval has been rejected by European authorities. With the globalization of trade, no large American company can ignore European regulators and complete a merger or acquisition that has been disapproved in Europe.

■ THE FIRST AMENDMENT AND ANTITRUST LAW

For about 150 years, Congress and the Department of Justice assumed that they had no right to regulate the business practices of the media because of the First Amendment, but that changed in the New Deal era. The economic depression of the 1930s, the formation of a labor union for journalists, and the Roosevelt administration's willingness to challenge business practices that earlier administrations ignored all contributed to new scrutiny of the media. By 1945, the U.S. Supreme Court had twice ruled that the business practices of the media were very much within the government's purview. Both of these pioneering cases involved the Associated Press, the nation's largest news wire service.

Supreme Court rulings: no special media exception. The U.S. Supreme Court ruled that the First Amendment does not exempt the media from regulations that apply to other industries in a 1937 case involving labor laws, *Assoc. Press v. Nat'l Labor Relations Bd.* (301 U.S. 130). The case arose when an Associated Press writer was fired for engaging in union organizing activities on behalf of the American Newspaper Guild. The guild complained to the NLRB, which found the AP guilty of an unfair labor practice. The wire service appealed the NLRB ruling, and the Court affirmed it, brushing aside the AP's argument that union activity was a threat to the agency's editorial freedom. The Court said the National Labor Relations Act "permits a discharge for any reason other than union activity or agitation for collective bargaining with employees." Later in the opinion, the Court added:

> The business of the Associated Press is not immune from regulation because it is an agency of the press. The publisher of a newspaper has no special immunity from the application of general laws. He has no special privilege to invade the rights and liberties of others.

A few years later, the Court again ruled against the AP's claims of a First Amendment exemption from government regulation in a landmark case involving antitrust law, *Assoc. Press v. U.S.* (326 U.S. 1, 1945). This case arose when the *Chicago Sun's* application for AP membership was vetoed by its primary competitor, the *Chicago Tribune*. Under the AP's bylaws, each member was given what amounted to blackball privileges to prevent competitors from joining the wire service and gaining access to its worldwide news coverage. This policy had been in effect for nearly 100 years, but when it was used by such a prominent newspaper to blackball a well-known competitor, it invited government scrutiny.

The U.S. Justice Department said the exclusion of the *Sun* from AP membership was a violation of federal antitrust laws, pointing out that it was very easy for papers that didn't directly compete with an AP member to join. But any potential competitor of an AP member was forced not only to get past the competitor's veto but also pay a very large fee to join. Without joining the organization, a paper could not get AP news, since it was also against the bylaws to provide AP news to a non-member.

The Supreme Court ruled that these bylaw provisions indeed violated antitrust law. The First Amendment does not exempt the media from obeying laws regulating business practices, the Court said, adding, "The fact that the publisher handles news while others (engaged in business) handle goods does not...afford the publisher a peculiar constitutional sanctuary in which he [sic] can with impunity violate laws regarding his [sic] business practices."

One other case worth mentioning is *U.S. v. Paramount Pictures* (334 U.S. 131, 1948). The Court said that the *vertical integration* of the motion picture industry (where a studio owned everything from directors and actors to production facilities and distribution) violated the antitrust laws. The resulting Paramount Decrees mandated the breakup of such arrangements, and these rules lasted for over seven decades. But in 2020, the decrees were terminated and will be entirely gone after two years of sunset.

■ NEWSPAPER ANTITRUST AND JOINT OPERATING AGREEMENTS

Two antitrust cases involving newspapers reached the Supreme Court during the 1950s and several others were decided by lower federal courts. The first of these involved a newspaper refusing to accept advertising from anyone who also advertised on a local radio station. The case, *Lorain Journal Co. v. U.S.* (342 U.S. 143, 1951), resulted in a unanimous Supreme Court ruling in favor of the government and against the publisher. Because the paper reached almost every home in its market area, its threat to refuse advertising from those who advertised on the radio station was a viable one: many merchants at the time needed to advertise in the paper because there was no other way to reach a lot of their customers.

Defending its policies in court, the newspaper cited not only the First Amendment but also the well-recognized principle that a publisher has a right to refuse advertising. The Court dismissed these arguments, pointing out that antitrust law creates an exception to the publisher's right to refuse advertising. When the refusal to accept advertising is based on a desire to monopolize commerce, that right must give way to the right of other businesses to be free of monopolistic competition, the Court said. A lower court injunction against the paper's business practices was affirmed, as was an unusual and slightly humiliating order that the newspaper publish a notice of the ruling every week for six months.

However, a newspaper publisher fared better in another antitrust lawsuit that reached the Supreme Court in the 1950s, *Times-Picayune v. U.S.* (345 U.S. 594, 1953). In that case, the Justice Department challenged a tying arrangement in which an advertiser had to buy space in an evening paper, the *New Orleans States*, to get space in the same company's morning paper, the *New Orleans Times-Picayune*. A competing evening paper, the *New Orleans Item*, was the alleged victim in this tying arrangement.

When the case reached the Supreme Court, the justices voted 5-4 in the *Times-Picayune's* favor. The majority agreed with the Justice Department's contention that this was a tying arrangement. However, the court said there was insufficient evidence of injury to the other paper to justify an antitrust action in this instance. This was true because the *Item* was profitable, gaining in ad revenue and actually carrying more advertising than its evening competitor, the Times-Picayune Company's *States*. The Court majority refused to view the *Times-Picayune* as a sufficiently "dominant" product for the tying arrangement to be unlawful; in short, the Justice Department didn't prove its case. A few years later the *Item* fell on hard times and was taken over by the Times-Picayune Company, forming the *New Orleans States-Item*.

No overlapping newspaper markets. Antitrust law is clear: it's perfectly legal to buy newspapers in various markets all over America, but it isn't legal to buy nearby newspapers in *overlapping* markets. The fact that a management close to home may be better able to meet community needs than one thousands of miles away complicates the ethical issues, but it doesn't change the law. On the other hand, the Justice Department has a lot of discretion in these matters, sometimes approving media takeovers, mergers, and buyouts that would appear to be violations of antitrust law.

Joint operating agreements. The late 1960s produced another Supreme Court decision on antitrust law that disturbed many publishers. The case, *Citizen Publ'g Co. v. U.S.* (394 U.S. 131, 1969), stemmed from a *joint operating agreement* (JOA), a kind of cooperative arrangement between once-competing newspapers that had become commonplace in practice. Under a JOA, two newspaper publishers in the same town merge many of their business and

FIG. 104.
Las Vegas news-
papers in a joint
operating agreement.
The *Las Vegas Sun* is
delivered as an insert
inside its competitor,
the *Las Vegas Review-
Journal*. Note the "In
the Sun" banner at
the top of the *Review-
Journal*.

Author's collection.

printing operations but maintain separate editorial staffs so the two papers retain separate identities. The objective, of course, is to cut costs by only maintaining one expensive newspaper printing plant, for instance, instead of two. Obviously, the arrangement works best if one of the papers is a morning paper and the other an afternoon paper, so scheduling conflicts can be minimized. These arrangements often also include joint advertising sales, with advertisers offered a package deal and a discount if they place ads in both papers.

Such an agreement had existed between the *Tucson Daily Citizen* and the *Arizona Daily Star* since 1940. Not only did it involve a merger of production, advertising, and circulation operations of the two papers, but it also involved profit pooling. In the mid-1960s, the *Star* appeared to be in financial difficulty, but a purchase offer from a large newspaper chain was rejected. Shortly later, the owners of the *Citizen* organized a new company and bought the *Star*. As a result of this series of events, the once-independent editorial staff of the *Star* found itself working for the owners of the *Citizen*.

Newspaper Preservation Act. The American Newspaper Publishers Association, the major trade organization for the industry, went to work lobbying for a change in antitrust laws to legalize joint operating agreements. Congress obliged in 1970 with the *Newspaper Preservation Act*. Basically, this law legalized the 22 existing JOAs. In effect, Congress revised the law to overrule the Supreme Court's interpretation of it. In addition to protecting the existing JOAs, the Newspaper Preservation Act authorized the Justice Department to approve new agreements when it could be shown that at least one of the newspapers involved would fail without a JOA. The Act was opposed by Justice, which contended it would allow publishers to enter anti-competitive arrangements even when they could survive on their own. Publishers of small newspapers also opposed it, fearing that large papers in their area would offer joint advertising packages so attractive the smaller papers would be squeezed out of the marketplace. Also, labor unions opposed the act because it authorized consolidations that would certainly eliminate jobs. Nevertheless, the act quickly moved through Congress and was signed by President Nixon.

Once enacted, the Newspaper Preservation Act was challenged on constitutional grounds by a small San Francisco newspaper, the *Bay Guardian*. This muckraking alternative paper contended that the joint operating agreement between the *San Francisco Chronicle* and

San Francisco Examiner resulted in an unconstitutional infringement of its First Amendment rights by encouraging a monopoly that made it difficult for other papers to operate. But the act was upheld in 1972 when a federal district judge rejected the *Guardian*'s arguments, affirming its constitutionality (*Bay Guardian Co. v. Chronicle Publishing Co.*, 344 F.Supp. 1155). Ironically, almost 30 years later Hearst sold the *Examiner*, purchased the rival *Chronicle*, and won an antitrust lawsuit challenging that transaction.

Newspaper closures equal fewer JOAs. In the years since its enactment, the Newspaper Preservation Act didn't exactly produce an avalanche of applications for new joint operating agreements. And by the early 2000s, the idea that joint operating agreements could save "failing" newspapers was widely questioned. While these agreements undoubtedly have saved some newspapers from oblivion (or at least postponed their demise), it was becoming clear that metropolitan daily newspapers are an endangered species, with or without JOAs.

By 2020, there had been fewer than 30 total approved JOAs, most of them dissolved due to newspaper closures. For example, the JOA between the the *Denver Post* and the *Rocky Mountain News*, rivals for more than 100 years, dissolved when the the *Rocky Mountain News* closed in 2009.

Only three JOAs remain in 2021. In Detroit, the *Detroit Free Press*, a Gannett paper, and the *Detroit News*, owned by MediaNews Group (and formerly by Gannett), maintain an agreement begun in 1988 that could end as soon as 2025. In Las Vegas, the JOA combination led to a bizarre only-in-Vegas deal in 2005: the prosperous Libertarian-leaning *Review-Journal* agreed to place the politically liberal, advertising-poor *Sun* inside its own newspaper—as an insert, an arrangement that will expire in 2040. So subscribers get one newspaper wrapped around its competitor. Finally, York, Pennsylvania, hosts two papers joined in a 1990 JOA: the *York Daily Record* and the *York Dispatch*, a deal that is set to last until 2090.

■ BROADCAST MEDIA OWNERSHIP ISSUES

Few aspects of communications law have been as historically volatile as the ownership and control of the electronic media. Congress, the FCC, the Justice Department, and the courts have devoted endless hours to these issues over the years. Since its inception, the FCC (and the Federal Radio Commission before it) has encouraged ownership diversity, and the Supreme Court in the 1945 *Assoc. Press* case discussed earlier endorsed it, saying that "the widest possible dissemination of information from diverse and antagonistic sources is essential to the welfare of the public."

The FCC looks for four types of diversity: viewpoint, programming, independently owned outlets, and minority/female ownership of broadcast media. But how did the FCC get into ownership regulation at all? Answering that will require going back a bit in time.

A Brief History of Broadcast Ownership Regulation

Broadcast ownership has been controversial almost from the beginning of broadcasting. Just before the U.S. Justice Department challenged the Associated Press' exclusionary practices in 1945, the FCC was taking a tough look at the way the networks (especially NBC) dominated radio broadcasting in America. Originally, the FCC had little authority over antitrust matters, but as part of its licensing process the commission has always been empowered to consider all factors that affect the "public interest, convenience and necessity." Thus, the FCC can scrutinize the business practices and ownership patterns of broadcast licensees.

antitrust:
prohibitions of agreements or practices that restrict trade and competition between companies, and bans on anti-competitive practices that lead to a company's dominant position.

joint operating agreement (JOA):
two or more companies combine some operations to share costs and reduce expenses; in newspapers, the companies combine their advertising and business departments and operate separate editorial departments.

broadcast (or media) ownership rules:
FCC rules, evaluated and revised every four years as required by the Telecom Act of 1996, that regulate corporate ownership of media organizations to encourage a variety of broadcast voices and viewpoints in each market.

By the late 1930s, the FCC didn't like what it saw in radio broadcasting. About 97% of all night-time transmitter wattage was controlled by three networks, with the vast majority of the most powerful stations affiliated with either the National Broadcasting Company or the Columbia Broadcasting System (CBS). In fact, NBC operated two different networks, known as "Red" and "Blue," both of which had affiliates in many major cities.

Even more disturbing, the networks imposed strict contractual controls on their affiliates. For instance, network affiliates were not permitted to carry any programming from another network. Moreover, affiliates were locked into five-year contracts with the networks—something the FCC found alarming in view of the fact that broadcasters were then issued licenses for only three years at a time. And the networks tied up virtually all of their affiliates' prime time programming. In addition, affiliates' rights to reject network programs were limited.

To end these abuses, the FCC issued a set of rules known as the Chain Broadcasting Regulations in 1941. These rules prohibited many of the questionable network practices. One provision was intended to force NBC to sell one of its two networks. NBC quickly took the FCC to court, charging that these new rules exceeded the FCC's authority and violated the First Amendment. In *NBC v. U.S.* (319 U.S. 190), an important 1943 case that foreshadowed the 1945 *Assoc. Press v. U.S.* decision, the Supreme Court ruled against NBC on all grounds. The Court said the First Amendment does not exempt broadcasters from government regulation of their business practices. Moreover, the justices said, the FCC could issue rules to curb monopolistic network policies, despite the fact that enforcement of antitrust laws is beyond the commission's authority.

After this decision NBC had no choice but to sell one of its networks, so the "Blue" network—considered by NBC executives as the weaker of the two—was sold later in 1943. That network became known as the American Broadcasting Company, or ABC, two years later, joining CBS and NBC to form the "big three" of broadcasting that dominated the industry for decades. The other radio network of the 1930s, the Mutual Broadcasting System, included a large number of affiliates, most of them in smaller markets. Mutual remained only a minor force in broadcasting.

Broadcast Ownership Restrictions

The Telecommunications Act of 1996 requires that the FCC conduct a review of its media ownership rules every four years, called the *quadrennial review*. The agency is on its seventh such round of reviews, the 2018 edition—and those rules have been mired in controversy and litigation almost since the start.

The FCC has adopted a variety of restrictions on broadcast ownership over the years to prevent monopoly control of the airwaves. All of these rules have been intended to supplement antitrust laws, which also forbid anti-competitive business practices by broadcasters. However, the commission's philosophy about this has varied greatly, and litigation has resulted.

A quick note on the Prometheus cases. Prometheus Radio Project appears in a lot of litigation over media ownership. Formed in 1998 "by activists working within social change movements such as housing, environmentalism, health care, anti-war, and criminal justice reform," the organization fights against ownership rules that aggregate radio ownership in large corporate hands. As the mission statement puts it, "We believe in participatory radio because it is a proven tool for movement-building and cultural expression."

Prometheus appears in four major Third Circuit court cases fighting for ownership rules that loosen corporate control over radio, and it appeared before the Supreme Court as well in 2021. The circuit cases are numbered to help you trace the litigation.

Early rules. For many years no individual or company could own more than seven television stations, seven AM radio stations, and seven FM radio stations nationwide. That rule was sometimes called the *Rule of Sevens*. In 1984, the FCC changed the number to 12 of each, thus creating the *Rule of Twelves*. The FCC liberalized the radio station ownership rules again in 1992, increasing the limit to 18 AM and 18 FM stations under one ownership. That limit was increased to 20 AM and 20 FM stations in 1994, with minority-controlled companies permitted to own up to 23 AM and 23 FM stations. The TV station limit was left at 12 in 1992.

Telecom Act. In the Telecommunications Act of 1996, Congress ordered the FCC to liberalize some of these broadcast ownership rules. The 1996 law also directed the FCC to conduct comprehensive reviews of its remaining ownership restrictions every two years (later every four years) and to eliminate rules no longer needed. Those reviews, plus several court decisions overturning other rules, led to the 2003 and 2007 FCC deregulation actions.

The Telecommunications Act abolished some limits, leaving *no* limit on the number of radio or television stations one company may own nationwide. However, the law did retain a limit on the percent of the nation's TV households one company's stations could reach, but that limit was also liberalized. Under the rules in effect between 1984 and 1996, one company could own stations that reached no more than 25% of the nation's television households. The limit was increased to 35% by the 1996 act. In its 2003 deregulation, the FCC further liberalized the limit, allowing any one company to own stations that reach up to 45% of the nation's television households. In 2004, Congress responded to a public outcry over the FCC's 45% cap, substituting a 39% ceiling in its place—a cap still in place.

Note that this 39% cap adopted by Congress in 2004 applies only to stations owned by a company; the limits do not apply to *affiliates*. Each of the major networks has affiliates that reach virtually *all* television households. Each network also has *network-owned and operated stations*, most of them in large cities. The limits apply only to these network-owned stations and to large groups of stations owned by other companies.

2003 deregulation. The FCC first adopted tough restrictions on the number of stations one individual or company could own—and then abandoned many of those rules, little by little. The FCC in 2003 abolished or liberalized many long-standing ownership restrictions on a controversial 3-2 vote. By 2004, Congress had vetoed a portion of the FCC's ownership deregulation and a federal appeals court had halted implementation of many other aspects of the deregulation, ordering the FCC to reconsider many of the actions it took a year earlier (*Prometheus Radio Project v. FCC*, 373 F.3d 372, *Prometheus I*). After the Supreme Court declined to review that decision, the FCC in 2007 announced a scaled-back liberalization of its ownership rules, prompting more lawsuits.

Although there is no nationwide limit on the number of radio stations that one company may own, there are still local limits, and the FCC did not further liberalize them in 2003. The system is tiered: for example, in metropolitan areas having 45 or more radio stations (counting both AM and FM stations), one company may own up to eight stations, although no more than five of them may be AM stations or FM stations. (This rule prevents any one company from owning eight FM or eight AM stations in one market.) In markets having 30 to 44 stations, the limit is seven stations with no more than four of them either AM or FM, and so on. There is an exception for markets with three stations: one company may own two of them if the two are an AM-FM combination.

The FCC made minor changes in the local radio ownership rules in 2003. The definition of a local market was rewritten to close a loophole that allowed a single company to own all of the radio stations in a relatively small city. In some cases an FCC-defined market included enough surrounding towns with radio stations that one company could own all of the stations in a given city without violating the ownership formula. In an attempt to close that loophole, the FCC decided to use market definitions developed by the Arbitron rating service in place of its former definitions based on signal coverage areas. Another issue was that the old rules did not count stations in Canada and Mexico, even if they could be heard well in U.S. cities near the border. A company could get around the limits by taking control of foreign stations in addition to buying as many stations as the law allows in a U.S. border city. The 2003 rules largely closed that loophole.

The FCC's 2003 deregulation was especially controversial because the 1996 Telecommunication Act's liberalization of local radio ownership restrictions (and its elimination of the nationwide radio ownership limit) led to major changes in radio broadcasting. Several large radio station groups quickly expanded, buying many stations—and driving up the selling price of radio stations in the process. By the late 2000s, Clear Channel Communications had grown from a small Texas company with a handful of radio stations to a giant national corporation with more than 1,200 stations (about 10% of all American radio stations).

Many new owners of station groups combined various aspects of their stations' operations. For example, it became commonplace for station groups to program several stations jointly, manage them jointly, and sell advertising for them jointly. A company can now purchase several small stations surrounding a big city and do regional programming, including some simulcasting on the various stations. This allows a company to buy inexpensive small stations and compete with the giant metropolitan stations, encouraging listeners to tune in to whichever of the jointly programmed stations is loudest in their area. Critics say that something is lost in this equation, though: there is less local service to the small suburban towns that the individual stations once served exclusively.

Critics also charged that something else is lost when a large company buys up local media outlets: news programming. The FCC itself conducted a study that reached this conclusion in 2004, but the study was not released publicly until whistleblowers revealed its existence two years later. The study showed that locally owned stations, on average, had more local news programming than stations owned by large outside corporations.

The FCC's ownership rules also address another phenomenon in broadcasting: the use of time brokerage or *local marketing agreements (LMAs)* in which a station owner gives someone else the right to program the station. Like owning multiple stations in the same market,

LMAs are attractive to station owners because of the cost savings possible if one station's staff can program and sell advertising for two or more stations. The ownership rules say that a station operated under an LMA is treated as if the person or firm in control of the station actually owns it. Therefore, a company that programs stations under an LMA in a given city may not be allowed to own as many stations there. The FCC did not rewrite this rule in 2003.

Cross-ownership rules (now gone). Over the years the FCC also adopted a variety of rules restricting cross-ownerships. *Cross-ownership* is a situation in which one individual or company owns more than one kind of communications medium, usually in one market. The most notable of these rules is the newspaper-broadcast cross-ownership rule.

The FCC adopted the *newspaper-broadcast cross-ownership rule* in 1975. It banned new cross-ownerships between newspapers and television stations in the same market. The FCC allowed a number of companies that already owned both a newspaper and a television station in the same market to keep both until one or the other is sold.

From the beginning, this rule stirred criticism from all sides. Both broadcasters and newspaper publishers attacked the ban on new cross-media combinations. Consumer groups, meanwhile, attacked the FCC for not insisting on the breakup of more existing cross-ownerships. When the resulting case, *FCC v. Nat'l Citizens Comm. for Broad.* (436 U.S. 775, 1978), reached the Supreme Court, the court unanimously affirmed the FCC's cross-ownership rule, thus satisfying neither group of critics. The court said the FCC had acted within its authority and had based its rule on appropriate grounds.

Since 1975, the FCC granted only a few waivers to let multimedia owners get around the rule and acquire both a newspaper and a TV station in the same market.

2007 deregulation. In 2007, the FCC approved a plan to deregulate the long-controversial newspaper-TV cross-ownership rules. On a partisan 3-2 majority, the FCC modified the rules to allow one company to acquire both a newspaper and a TV station in the nation's 20 largest markets, provided the station is not one of the top four in the market in revenue and also provided there are still eight different media "voices" (TV stations or newspapers) after the merger. The 2007 rules, written and pushed through the commission by FCC chair Kevin Martin, would allow newspaper-broadcast combinations in smaller markets if the merger involves a failing newspaper or would result in at least seven hours per week of local news programming on a station that was not previously airing local news. Martin justified the liberalized rules by pointing to the widespread financial woes of the newspaper industry. Many local TV stations have also seen viewership decline in recent years, a reality that led the FCC to liberalize its Duopoly Rule to allow one company to own more than one TV station in larger metropolitan areas.

The 2007 deregulation granted the Tribune Corporation a permanent waiver in Chicago because the company owned both WGN-TV and the *Chicago Tribune* long before cross-ownership was banned in 1975. It had acquired both newspapers and TV stations in other markets under previous waivers or loopholes in the ownership restrictions. The 2007 deregulation granted Tribune new (but temporary) waivers in New York, Los Angeles, Hartford, and South Florida.

Beyond 2007. In 2011, in the second installment of the *Prometheus* cases, the Third Circuit again rejected the rule relaxations on newspaper-broadcast combinations, and it upheld other local broadcasting ownership restrictions retained by the FCC. But the FCC had not given appropriate notice for comments on the change in rules as required by the Administrative Procedures Act, the court added, and the procedures followed by the commission in this rule change were "highly irregular." Moreover, the court said, the agency "referenced *no* data on television ownership by minorities or women and *no* data regarding commercial radio ownership by women."

Thus, the court said, "we have little choice but to conclude that the FCC did not ... fulfill its 'obligation to make its views known to the public in a concrete and focused form so as to make criticism or formulation of alternatives possible'" (*Prometheus Radio Project v. FCC*, 652 F.3d 431, *Prometheus II*). The court also told the FCC to do a better job evaluating its rules for their impact on diversity in media ownership. Public interest groups hailed the win—a spokesperson for advocacy group Media Access Project called it "a vindication of the public's right to have a diverse media environment." The Supreme Court declined to review the case.

Demonstrating what can be done to cut costs when one company owns both a newspaper and a television station in the same market, in 2008 Tribune combined the offices of WSFL-TV, its Miami TV station, and the *South Florida Sun Sentinel*, merging advertising, business, and content-producing operations of the jointly owned newspaper and TV station. In a way, Tribune was coming full circle by doing this. During the 1920s, the *Chicago Tribune* sponsored a pioneering radio station, WGN (the call sign was derived from the *Tribune's* slogan, "World's Greatest Newspaper") with heavy involvement of newspaper staffers and financial subsidies from the newspaper of more than $1 million during WGN's first 15 years on the air. Like many early radio station owners, the Tribune company did not see radio as a commercially viable business but wanted a high-profile radio station for other reasons.

Combining the offices of two TV stations in the same market, as opposed to combining a newspaper and a TV station, has become commonplace since the FCC legalized owning two TV stations in the same market by amending its television *Duopoly Rule* in 1999. In 2003, the agency further liberalized its TV Duopoly Rule to allow one company to own up to three stations in the largest markets instead of two, and to own two stations in some smaller markets where no company could own more than one station under the previous rules. But in *Sinclair Broad. Group v. FCC* (284 F.3d 148, 2002), the D.C. Circuit rejected the FCC's

Focus on...
The Sherman Antitrust Act of 1890

The Sherman Act was passed in 1890 to permit the federal government to act against *trusts*, or arrangements that consolidate industry power under one controlling board. The law was President Theodore Roosevelt's main tool for "busting trusts" at the turn of the twentieth century, starting with a railroad trust created by New York financier J.P. Morgan. Named for Sen. John Sherman (R-Ohio), the act has two sections. The first section focuses on the means of attempting to gain a monopoly, and the second examines the end results of potential monopolies.

FIG. 105. Sen. John Sherman, between 1865 and 1880.

Library of Congress Prints and Photographs Division, [LC-DIG-cwpbh-04797]

Section One has three parts:
    (1) an agreement
    (2) that unreasonably restrains competition and
    (3) that affects interstate commerce.

Section Two has two parts:
    (1) the possession of monopoly power and
    (2) the willful acquisition or maintenance of that power other than by having a superior
       product or good business sense, or by accident (innocent monopolies are legal).

justification for the Duopoly Rule. The rewritten rule allowed one company to own two television stations in the same market if there were eight competing "voices," which the FCC defined as television stations under eight different ownerships even after one company buys a second station. The court rejected this definition of "voices" as arbitrary and capricious because it ignored other media outlets such as newspapers, radio stations, and cable television. In response, the FCC's 2003 rules would allow a company to own three TV stations in any market with 18 or more stations, or two in any market with five or more stations.

Most of the 2003 ownership rule changes (but not the Congressionally imposed 39% limit on the number of TV households one company may serve) were questioned by the Third Circuit in its 2004 *Prometheus I* decision. The court's 2-1 majority did not actually overturn many of the rules, but it did tell the FCC either to rescind the liberalized rules or better justify them. The FCC then reconsidered and adopted its 2007 deregulation, but it did not authorize a single company to own three TV stations in the same market this time. And the agency dragged its feet in acting on the court's later requirements, resulting in another suit by Prometheus (*Prometheus Radio Project v. FCC*, 824 F.3d 33, *Prometheus III*). The Third Circuit unanimously agreed that the delay "was 'agency action unlawfully withheld or unreasonably delayed'" in violation of the Administrative Procedures Act. The FCC's response, however, didn't please Prometheus.

In 2016, the FCC issued an order that left the ownership rules mostly unchanged, claiming that the public interest was best served by those rules. In particular, the agency said that its rules promoted the race/gender ownership diversity it claimed to have long supported. As a result, in 2019, in another Prometheus action (*Prometheus Radio Project v. FCC*, 939 F. 3d 567, *Prometheus IV*), the Third Circuit threw out the rules due to insufficient justification. The court, sighing "Here we are again," accused the agency of an analysis "so insubstantial that we cannot say it provides a reliable foundation" for its rules.

The court agreed with the FCC that the rules it eliminated or changed (the newspaper-broadcast and radio/TV cross-ownership rules were tossed and the local TV ownership rule modified) didn't serve other FCC goals, those fostering competition, localism, and viewpoint diversity. But that didn't mean that the FCC was in the clear. Because of a lack of evidence assessing the impact of the rules on women and minorities, the court accused the commission of inadequately considering "the effect its sweeping rule changes will have on ownership of broadcast media by women and racial minorities." The rules were invalidated.

FCC leadership did not take the loss well. "It's become quite clear that there is no evidence or reasoning—newspapers going out of business, broadcast radio struggling, broadcast TV facing stiffer competition than ever—that will persuade [the Third Circuit judges] to change their minds," snapped chair Ajit Pai. The FCC appealed, and the Supreme Court agreed to take the case.

The high court steps in. The question before the Court was whether the FCC's 2017 decision to repeal the ownership rules was "arbitrary or capricious" under the Administrative Procedures Act. In April 2021, the justices unanimously said that it wasn't (*FCC v. Prometheus Radio Project*, No. 19-1231), reversing the Third Circuit. Justice Brett Kavanaugh agreed that the agency "did not have perfect empirical or statistical data" on the effects of its rules on minority/female ownership. But that's not unusual in most agency decision-making. "The APA imposes no general obligation on agencies to conduct or commission their own empirical or statistical studies," he said. And the FCC did ask for commenters to provide the evidence it didn't itself have, he pointed out, and no one "produced such evidence indicating that changing the rules was likely to harm minority and female owner-ship." Absent that, Kavanaugh said, the FCC's rules were reasonable based on the data it had.

Justice Clarence Thomas concurred, adding a reason to overturn the Third Circuit's decision. That court, he said, "improperly imposed nonstatutory procedural requirements on the FCC by forcing it to consider ownership diversity in the first place." And because there is no statutory requirement for the FCC to consider women or minority ownership, the agency need not do so in the future, either.

As expected, reactions to the decision were mixed. Acting FCC chair Jessica Rosenworcel expressed her disappointment, but her colleague Brendan Carr was jubilant, saying, "The FCC must now embrace the modern approach to media regulation vindicated by the Court and, in the context of our current quadrennial review proceeding, ensure that our remain-ing broadcast ownership rules reflect the realities of the marketplace." Advocacy group Free Press called on the FCC and Congress to "recognize that hedge-fund and Wall Street-driven consolidation harms local communities, and only decimates what's left of competition and diversity." Many seemed pleased, however, that the Court deferred to the FCC's judgment and expressed hopes that a Biden FCC would make things better.

Ownership Rules Today

So after years of litigation, where do the rules stand now? The FCC has been particu-larly interested in five ownership issues: (1) the Local Television Multiple Ownership Cap, limiting owners to two stations in markets with at least eight competitors (the "Eight Voices" rule); (2) the Local Radio Ownership Cap, limiting owners to eight stations in the largest markets; (3) the Newspaper-Broadcast Cross-Ownership Rule, forbidding cross-ownership of broadcast stations and newspapers without a waiver; (4) the Radio-Television Cross-Owner-ship Rule, limiting the number of radio and television stations owned by a single company in one market; and (5) the Dual Network Rule, prohibiting common ownership of any of the top four TV stations. The FCC also seeks comment on structural analysis and other issues, particularly the impact of digital technologies, in pursuit of its policy goals of local-ism, competition, and diversity.

Here are these five (and a few more) rules as they stand in 2021:

Local television multiple ownership (Duopoly Rule). One company can own two TV stations in the same area as long as one isn't in the top four rated stations in that area. The FCC's "Eight Voices" rule was eliminated in favor of this one, what the agency calls the "Top-Four Prohibition." A waiver could circumvent this restriction.

Local radio ownership cap. Tiered based on market size:

Number of stations in area	Ownership cap	AM/FM service limitation
45 or more	Up to eight stations	No more than five in same service
30–44	Up to seven stations	No more than four in same service
15–29	Up to six stations	No more than four in same service
14 or fewer	Up to five stations	No more than three in the same service (as long as the entity doesn't own more than half of all radio stations in the market)

No change to this rule. Waivers are likely in the New York and Washington, D.C., markets.

Newspaper-broadcast cross-ownership rule. Gone. The FCC called the rule antiquated due to, as the agency put it, "the explosive growth of the number and variety of sources of local news and information in the modern marketplace."

Radio-TV cross-ownership rule. Gone. Saying local TV and radio ownership rules already control the number of stations an entity can own in a market, the FCC abolished this rule.

Dual network rule. No two large networks (ABC, NBC, Fox, CBS) can merge. The agency left this rule unchanged.

National TV station ownership. There is no limit on the number of stations an entity may own nationally as long as those stations reach no more than 39% of all U.S. TV households. (Unlike the others, this rule is no longer subject to the FCC's quadrennial review.)

Incubator. In addition, the FCC announced that it would call for comments on an incubator program to help develop diversity ownership in broadcast. The program, the agency said, would "seek to encourage new and diverse broadcast station owners by drawing on the technical expertise and/or financial assistance of existing broadcasters."

No "main studio" required. Finally, as part of the 2017 deregulatory bonanza, the FCC (on a 3-2 partisan vote) also did away with the "Main Studio Rule," a mandate from 1939 requiring a radio or TV broadcaster to have a main studio in or near its community of license. Broadcasters still must have a local toll-free phone number, and they have to keep the paper parts of their public files (anything not online) in a publicly accessible location within their community of license. The elimination of this rule also wasn't without controversy: Republicans called it a relic and said that the money spent keeping a local studio open in the digital age could be better spent, while Democrats thought that closing local studios would break the relationship between the studio and its community. Jessica Rosenworcel, then a commissioner, said that the agency should have granted waivers to those wishing to eliminate their studios rather than eradicating the rule altogether.

Cable Antitrust

As many listeners switch to largely unregulated web-based or satellite radio services and viewers opt for cable, satellite, and Web-based television, the larger question the FCC and the traditional media themselves must address is how to compete. But cable is not immune from antitrust actions.

In another case that implicated the Administrative Procedure Act (the same one discussed in Chapter Eleven and elsewhere), a federal appeals court in 2009 said that there would be no exclusive cable rights for cable companies in apartment buildings they wire—ending exclusive agreements allowing companies to get exclusive rights to provide service to all residents in a complex by wiring multi-unit buildings. The D.C. Circuit upheld the FCC's banning of these deals and said preexisting deals like them could not be enforced, and said that the FCC did not violate the APA, and in fact had appropriately "balanced benefits against harms and expressly determined that applying the rule to existing contracts was worth its costs" (*Nat'l Cable & Telecomm. Ass'n v. FCC*, 567 F.3d 659).

What about cable channel "grouping"? Not an antitrust violation. In *Brantley v. NBC Universal* (675 F.3d 1192, 2012), the Ninth Circuit said that cable companies' grouping popular channels with less popular ones into packages didn't violate Section 1 of the Sherman Antitrust Act. While "tying" of products together may have antitrust implications, particularly if the tying "impose[s] restraints on competition in the market for a tied product," such tying must actually injure competition. But, said the court, "plaintiffs here have not alleged in their complaint how competition (rather than consumers) is injured" by this practice.

In 2013, the U.S. Supreme Court handed down a decision reviewing the Third Circuit's ruling on whether cable customers could file suit as a class against alleged antitrust violations in Comcast's pricing schemes in Philadelphia (*Comcast Corp. v. Behrend*, 569 U.S. 27), and said that the customers could not be considered a class. A deeply divided Court said that "common answers" are necessary to certify a group as a class for purposes of antitrust litigation: "Questions of individual damage calculations will inevitably overwhelm questions common to the class," Justice Antonin Scalia wrote. The dissent, however, focused on the need for "common questions" in that group: Justice Ruth Bader Ginsburg retorted that the model the defendants used "simply shows *that* Comcast's conduct brought about higher prices" rather than how it did so, which is sufficient. There is no need to have the answers, the dissent said, for the defendants to be considered a class.

■ MASS MEDIA MERGERS AND ANTITRUST LAW

Media critics often regard the ongoing trend toward centralized ownership of the media as a threat to journalistic freedom—and the public interest. The last several decades have been times of unprecedented corporate mergers and acquisitions. With federal regulators clearly taking a relaxed attitude toward antitrust enforcement during much of this period, corporate America became engulfed in high-stakes consolidations. There were numerous takeovers and buyouts of media corporations, often raising antitrust questions that might have led to enforcement actions by the federal government in an earlier time. All three of the oldest television networks have been purchased or merged. General Electric took control of NBC, Westinghouse purchased CBS, and Walt Disney Co. purchased Capital Cities/ABC. The Westinghouse-CBS combination also merged with Infinity Broadcasting to create one of the nation's largest and most powerful radio groups (second in size only to the radio empire created by Clear Channel).

Marriage and divorce in the media world. It's not uncommon to see companies merge, divest, and then merge again. For example, in 1999 CBS announced that it would join up with Viacom in a merger under the Viacom name, bringing together CBS, Westinghouse, Infinity, Paramount Pictures, MTV, Nickelodeon, 35 television stations, 163 radio stations, Blockbuster, several major production companies, two broadcast networks (CBS and UPN), and several other cable networks—all under single ownership. The FCC modified its rules to allow the two networks to be operated jointly under common ownership and completed that action in 2001, allowing each of the largest networks to own a smaller network.

Then in 2005 Viacom was spun off from what became CBS Corporation. The "new" Viacom took several cable networks including MTV plus Paramount Pictures, leaving CBS with the broadcast networks, radio and TV stations, and Paramount's television production company, among other assets. But by 2019, the former partners paired up again, in a $15.9 billion deal that created ViacomCBS, a deal that closed that December.

Cable is *not* a telecom service. The FCC by then had declared that cable systems are not "telecommunications services" and therefore do *not* have to open their broadband networks to competitors. In 2005, the U.S. Supreme Court upheld that FCC ruling in *Nat'l Cable & Telecomm. Ass'n v. Brand X Internet Serv.* (also discussed in Chapter Eleven), allowing cable systems to exclude competitors from their networks. Consumer groups and non-cable internet service providers argued that giving cable a monopoly would drive up prices. They said broadband internet service is much more expensive and less prevalent in the United States than in other countries. The Court's 6-3 majority ruled as it did in part on the rationale that cable companies invested heavily in broadband and should be able to profit from that. The net neutrality impact of *Brand X* is discussed in Chapter Eleven.

Effect of antitrust laws. How do the antitrust laws affect all of these big-ticket mergers and buyouts? The Hart-Scott-Rodino Antitrust Improvements Act of 1976 requires prior government approval for all large corporate mergers and acquisitions. Both the Justice Department and the Federal Trade Commission must be notified. And when a merger involves broadcast properties, FCC approval of license transfers is required as well.

For the most part, these mergers drew few protests from the antitrust lawyers at the Justice Department, and the FCC routinely issued waivers of some cross-ownership rules, allowing many deals to go through. Eventually, many of the merged companies had to sell some of their newly acquired properties to comply with the rules. And in some cases the Justice Department has refused to approve mergers that fully complied with the FCC's rules and the Telecommunications Act.

Other big mergers stirred controversy during the 2000s. In 2004, GE, the parent of NBC, won government permission to merge with Vivendi Universal, creating a conglomerate with two television networks, numerous cable channels, theme parks, studios, and television stations as well as GE's vast worldwide network of non-media businesses that range from financial services to jet aircraft engine manufacturing.

In one of the most controversial moves, News Corp., parent company of the Fox Television Network, the 20th Century Fox movie studio, 35 TV stations, MySpace.com, and many other media properties, took control of Dow Jones & Co., publisher of the *Wall Street Journal*. Although the deal included a provision guaranteeing the editorial independence of the *Journal*, it troubled critics of consolidation more than most mergers because of the paper's long-cultivated national reputation for excellence.

In 2011, the FCC and the Department of Justice approved the merger of Comcast with NBCUniversal, creating a $30 billion company. The FCC announced that Comcast had committed to "increase local news coverage to viewers; expand children's programming; enhance the diversity of programming available to Spanish-speaking viewers; offer broadband services to low-income Americans at reduced monthly prices; and provide high-speed broadband to schools, libraries and underserved communities, among other public benefits." While the FCC and Justice officials said the merger would serve the public interest, critics allege that it gives the new company unprecedented consolidated media power.

Nor were FCC commissioners unanimous in their endorsement. Michael Copps, a Democrat, dissented, saying, "Comcast's acquisition of NBCUniversal is a transaction like no other that has come before this commission—ever. It reaches into virtually every corner of our media and digital landscapes ... And it confers too much power in one company's hands." Perhaps Copps was prescient in his concern: in 2012, Comcast paid an $800,000 settlement to the FCC regarding a probe into its compliance with the merger rules set forth by the agency during a probationary period, although it admitted no wrongdoing.

Mergers Past and Present

Although it's unlikely that any combinations on the horizon will break the record set by the America Online/Time Warner merger of 2000 ($182 billion in stock and debt), current players are no slouches when it comes to money changing hands. The late 2010s have seen mega-mergers proposed by telecom giants like ABC, AT&T, Time Warner, Disney, and others. The deregulatory mood that has prevailed in the last decade is evident here too. There are too many to cover in depth, but here are a few to watch—and a few that failed.

Succeeded then spun off: AT&T/Time Warner becomes WarnerMedia/Discovery. In 2016, AT&T agreed to buy Time Warner Inc. for $85.4 billion. The companies told the *Wall Street Journal* that they wanted to be the first wireless company to compete nationally with cable by offering an online video bundle that would resemble a pay-TV package.

But not everyone was happy about that. In 2017, the Department of Justice filed suit to stop the merger from going through. The complaint alleged that the merger violated Section 7 of the Clayton Antitrust Act by lessening competition.

It took the companies three years and two lawsuits, but they finally won in 2019 (*U.S. v. AT&T Inc.*, 916 F. 3d 1029). A federal judge and the D.C. Circuit both rejected the government's arguments. The appellate court, in granting the win to the companies, handed the Justice Department a loss in its first court challenge to a vertical merger since the 1970s.

Then, in 2021, AT&T announced it would merge its hard-won WarnerMedia company with Discovery, Inc., creating Warner Bros. Discovery, with AT&T getting $43 billion and access to the Discovery "unscripted" reality TV and other media products. The new Warner Bros. Discovery company, when complete, is expected to be the second-largest media company in the world (after Disney). Commentators saw the merger as an attempt by AT&T to compete with streaming giant Netflix. The deal is expected to close in mid-2022.

Failure: Sinclair/Tribune. Sinclair Broadcast announced in 2017 that it would buy Tribune Media for $3.9 billion, a deal which would have added 42 TV stations in 33 markets as well as a number of cable and other properties. The FCC review dragged on for a year as Sinclair revised and re-revised the deal in attempts to comply with antitrust concerns by divesting itself of properties.

Finally, in mid-2018, FCC chair Ajit Pai had enough: announcing his "serious concerns" about the merger, he required a review by an administrative law judge. This is something that the FCC does when companies cannot persuade it that a merger, even with divestitures and other conditions met, would be in the public interest. Because this review takes so long, it's often a death knell for the merger under investigation. In this case, the FCC was concerned that the divestitures were shams—instead of being sold to other independent companies, the agency thought that these divested properties were going to entities closely related to Sinclair. And indeed the merger fell apart later that year: Tribune pulled out and sued Sinclair for $1 billion for breach of contract. The suit was settled in 2020, with Sinclair paying Nexstar Media Group (who had acquired Tribune in the interim) $60 million.

Success: Disney/Fox Entertainment. In "one of the most intriguing global media battles in decades," as one commentator put it, Disney beat out Comcast in 2019 to buy the Fox entertainment portfolio—which houses franchises like *The Simpsons, American Dad!,* and some X-Men properties (including Wolverine and Deadpool) in a $71.3 billion deal. Critics feared that this entertainment conglomerate could seriously harm competition. But, as one commentator put it, this isn't particularly new, as Disney has always played merger hardball: "Disney is not a corporation that pushes the bounds of artistic and technological possibility but a corporation that pushes the bounds of legal possibility under a radical pro-consolidation framework that has existed since the 1990s."

One to watch. In May 2021, Amazon announced plans to acquire MGM in a $9 billion deal. But soon thereafter, the FTC announced it would be investigating the deal, expressing concerns about Amazon's market power. Some view this case as a test for Biden's FTC and its chair, Lina Khan, on how the administration will handle mergers. Amazon is clearly nervous, however, as it requested that Khan recuse herself from the investigation due to her past advocacy work on antitrust. Stay tuned.

New merger Guidelines. In 2010, the FTC and the Department of Justice issued new joint Guidelines for *horizontal mergers*—mergers of companies that are actual or potential competitors. These guidelines are still in use. The basic message of the Guidelines, the agencies said, "is that mergers should not be permitted to create, enhance, or entrench market power or to facilitate its exercise." The document provided a blueprint on how the agencies will evaluate mergers to determine whether market power is affected, outlined types and sources of evidence that will be examined, and supplied hypothetical cases and their outcomes. The agencies also committed to "avoiding unnecessary interference with mergers that are either competitively beneficial or neutral."

The FTC further elaborated on its evaluation process in remarks to the House Subcommittee on Courts and Competition Policy in 2010: "[W]e ask: will this merger reduce competition in the future, or will new or existing competitors emerge to challenge the merged firm so that customers will receive the benefits of competition going forward?"

Perhaps the bottom line with all of these mergers and takeovers is that the FCC, the FTC, and the Justice Department all have broad discretion in deciding when to let two big companies join forces and when to play hardball with them.

■ ANTITRUST AND DIGITAL MEDIA

Given how much mass media has moved to both digital formats and online, it is no surprise that many recent antitrust battles have focused on this industry's competition and commerce. Big names like Microsoft, Google, Amazon, and Apple, as well as social media sites like Twitter and Facebook, regularly appear before Congress and the courts to defend their business models and trade practices against antitrust claims.

An Early Digital Antitrust Case: Microsoft

Public attention was focused on antitrust law in the 2000s more than at almost any time in recent history because of the *U.S. v. Microsoft Corp.* case. The U.S. Justice Department and 18 states jointly sued Microsoft, alleging a variety of unlawful business practices.

Judge Thomas Penfield Jackson, who presided at the original trial, first determined that Microsoft in fact had a monopoly of personal computer operating systems with Windows. He then ruled that, as a matter of law, many of Microsoft's business practices were antitrust violations. For example, he said that Microsoft engaged in unlawful *tying arrangements,* improperly tying the Windows operating system with its internet browser, Internet Explorer, to the detriment of Netscape, a competing browser.

Judge Jackson then ordered Microsoft broken up into two companies, one to develop and market Windows and another to do everything else (called "Baby Bills" by some wags in homage to Bill Gates). He also ordered Microsoft to sell the Windows operating system to all large computer makers for the same price, among other things. But in 2001, the D.C. Circuit unanimously overturned Jackson's proposed remedies, including the breakup. The court also disqualified Jackson from the case because he made inflammatory statements to the media. However, the appellate court agreed that "the company behaved anti-competitively... and that those actions contributed to the maintenance of its monopoly power" and broke the law in other ways (*U.S. v. Microsoft Corp.*, 253 F.3d 34).

The case was remanded to the trial court to reconsider several issues, including remedies for Microsoft's antitrust violations, but with a different judge, Colleen Kollar-Kotelly. Before she could rule, the Justice Department and nine of the 18 states agreed to settle. Judge Kollar-Kotelly then ordered a 60-day public comment period, as required in antitrust cases (resulting in 30,000 written comments, mostly objecting to the settlement). The nine states that didn't join in the settlement asked for added sanctions. Judge Kollar-Kotelly eventually approved the settlement, granting only a few of the holdout states' demands—most notably ordering Microsoft to disclose some sensitive technologies to its rivals much earlier than the company and the Justice Department had proposed.

Seven of the nine holdout states did not appeal, but Massachusetts pursued the case. (West Virginia at first joined Massachusetts but then settled with Microsoft in mid-2003, accepting about $20 million in hardware and software for its schools in return for dropping out.) In mid-2004, the D.C. Circuit ruled against Massachusetts and upheld the settlement in *Commonwealth of Massachusetts v. Microsoft Corp.* (373 F.3d 1199). The unanimous six-judge panel praised the settlement as "well done," declaring it to be in the public interest.

Judge Kollar-Kotelly retained jurisdiction until 2011 to monitor Microsoft's compliance with the settlement and made it clear there would be ongoing judicial scrutiny of the company's business practices. But she granted only a small part of what the nine states sought in addition to the changes in Microsoft's business practices covered by the settlement. In May 2011, this Microsoft saga in the United States finally ended with the expiration of the consent decree. The company said in a press release, "Our experience has changed us and shaped how we view our responsibility to the industry."

Other Microsoft antitrust suits, in the United States and abroad. Meanwhile, Microsoft agreed to settle a group of private antitrust lawsuits by promising to give about $1 billion worth of software and refurbished hardware to schools in low-income areas, a proposal that drew criticism because the cost to Microsoft for making extra copies of its software and giving away out-of-date hardware would be minimal—and hardly an adequate sanction for Microsoft's monopolistic behavior toward its competitors. A federal judge rejected this settlement as inadequate, a move that forced Microsoft to renegotiate the deal. In 2004, Microsoft agreed to pay $1.1 billion in California to settle antitrust claims from an estimated 14 million customers. Microsoft also settled an antitrust lawsuit filed in Minnesota for about $175 million, an Iowa lawsuit for $180 million, and one filed in Vermont for $9.7 million. In other states, Microsoft settled for large but often undisclosed sums.

In the mid-2000s Microsoft settled several other large antitrust lawsuits with private companies. The company agreed to pay AOL Time Warner $750 million to drop a lawsuit alleging that unlawful business practices by Microsoft led to the demise of Netscape as a rival to Microsoft's Internet Explorer web browser. Then the company paid about $2 billion to settle lawsuits with Sun Microsystems, $761 million to settle with RealNetworks, $536 million to settle with Novell Inc., and $425 million to settle a lawsuit filed by a Silicon Valley high-tech security firm. Microsoft also struck a deal with the Computer & Communications Industry Association in which the association pledged not to appeal Microsoft's settlement with the federal government to the Supreme Court.

While Microsoft was fighting multiple antitrust battles in U.S. courts, it was also fighting antitrust litigation in the European Union (EU). In 2004, the European Commission, a regulatory arm of the EU, found Microsoft guilty of anti-competitive and monopolistic business practices in Europe, fining the company about $600 million and ordering changes in the way Windows is packaged and sold there. The EU forced Microsoft to stop bundling the Windows operating system with its media player to allow other media software producers to compete more effectively. When Microsoft then launched the unbundled version of Windows as "Windows XP Reduced Media Edition," EU regulators acted quickly to halt the use of that name. In 2005, EU regulators also told Microsoft to make more information available to competing makers of networking software.

In 2008, the European Commission fined Microsoft an additional $1.39 billion for failing to comply with its earlier antitrust orders, bringing to $2.63 billion the total fines imposed on Microsoft by European regulators. Microsoft once again appealed, further extending this protracted legal battle with astronomical financial consequences.

Microsoft continued to have antitrust troubles with the European Union in 2009. The company decided that Windows 7 would be shipped to the EU market in fall 2009 without Internet Explorer 8 to avoid EU charges that it was unlawfully tying the browser to the operating system. But in March 2013, the European Union fined Microsoft $732 million for failure to comply with some of its settlement rules. Oddly, the regulators placed some of the non-compliance blame on themselves, saying that they had been too naïve in believing that the software company would self-monitor, and pledging to be more vigilant in its own monitoring—a warning to Google and others that the EU will not stand idly by in any settlement agreements. As we will see, the EU has kept its word.

Social Media and Search Engine Antitrust in the United States and Abroad

It's not surprising that people's increased reliance on digital tools like search engines and social media platforms—and the enormous power the companies that provide these services wield—makes governments nervous. Both the United States and the European Union have undertaken investigations into the market and monopoly power of these companies.

Google: U.S. antitrust investigations. One of the earliest of these investigations started in 2011 when several government bodies began antitrust investigations against Google. A Senate antitrust panel held hearings into allegations that Google's search results favor its own commercial ventures over others. Jeffrey Katz, the CEO of shopping site Nextag, testified, "When you search for 'running shoes' or 'digital camera,' Google transforms itself from an independent search engine to a commerce site. But that is not what happens when you type in a search for, say, 'kidney dialysis.'"

But Google prevailed. In 2013, FTC chair Jon Leibowitz announced that it had settled all its competition-related issues with Google. One element of the settlement was a patent settlement in which Google agreed "to stop seeking to exclude competitors using essential patents that Motorola, which Google later purchased, had first promised, but then refused, to license on fair and reasonable terms."

The FTC also announced that they were dropping concerns about Google biasing its search results to harm its competition, finding that there was no evidence to support that allegation. However, the commission did say that "Google has also committed to stop the most troubling of its business practices related to internet search and search advertising. Google will stop misappropriating—or 'scraping'—the content of its rivals for use in its own specialized search results."

Google versus the government: four 2020-21 U.S. lawsuits. In 2020 and 2021, Google was back in the courts fending off a whopping four new antitrust attacks from the government as well as from private companies. In October 2020, after a year-long investigation, the Department of Justice, joined by 11 Republican state attorneys general, filed a suit against the company accusing it of monopolies in search and search advertising. The government accused Google of abusing its market dominance to force manufacturers to preload its software on cell phones and to set its apps as the default. "Google's exclusionary agreements cover just under 60 percent of all general search queries," the Justice lawsuit said, adding, "Google in recent years has accounted for nearly 90 percent of all general-search-engine queries in the United States, and almost 95 percent of queries on mobile devices." The trial has been initially set for June 2023.

Then, in December 2020, the Texas attorney general, joined by colleagues in nine other states, sued Google, alleging that the company engaged in deceptive acts in running its buy-and-sell auction system for digital ads. Alleging both monopolization and attempted monopolization, the attorneys general also listed Facebook as a co-conspirator due to an agreement (code-named "Jedi Blue") between the companies to manipulate advertising auctions. A day later, a group of 38 states, led by Colorado, sued Google to stop the company "from unlawfully restraining trade and maintaining monopolies in markets that include general search services, general search text advertising, and general search advertising." What did Google say? In a blog post, the company claimed that redesigning its search results would be harmful to consumers; the company told consumers that the lawsuit "suggests we shouldn't have worked to make Search better and that we should, in fact, be less useful to you."

Finally, just as this book was going to press, Google was hit with a fourth government antitrust suit. In July 2021, 36 states sued the company for antitrust violations connected to its app store, Google Play Store, from which over 90% of all Android apps in the United States are distributed. The attorneys general, led by Utah, brought suit when Google announced it would more vigorously enforce its requirement that developers process payments through the Play Store's billing system—including in-app purchases. While most app developers already use the system, companies like Spotify and Netflix, who had managed their billing directly, complained that the policy would cost them millions if they had to pay Google's 30% commission. As the lawsuit put it, "By imposing this unduly restrictive and anticompetitive tie, Google can indefinitely collect supracompetitive commissions from consumers who purchase in-app digital content."

The company had announced that it was lowering the commissions it would take from Play Store app sellers from 30% to 15% on the first million dollars earned each year. Its response to the suit was to label it without merit and to suggest that the state attorneys general should be targeting other companies (i.e., Apple). Google public policy director Wilson White wrote, "This lawsuit isn't about helping the little guy or protecting consumers. It's about boosting a handful of major app developers who want the benefits of Google Play without paying for it."

Google versus private companies. Google is also facing suits from private companies. *Fortnite* developer Epic Games sued the company (and Apple, discussed elsewhere) in August 2020 for the same Play Store billing reasons targeted by the state attorneys general in July 2021; Google dropped *Fortnite* from the Play Store. In its complaint, Epic alleged that "Twenty-two years [after its 1998 start], Google has relegated its motto ["Don't Be Evil"] to nearly an afterthought and is using its size to do evil upon competitors, innovators, customers, and users in a slew of markets it has grown to monopolize."

And in December 2020, several online publishing companies (including Genius Media Group and The Nation) sued the search engine for allegedly inhibiting advertising competition. "Through its campaign of anticompetitive conduct, Google has achieved and maintained a monopoly or near-monopoly in (the) marketplace by erecting a toll bridge between publishers and advertisers and charging an unlawfully high price for passage," the suit claimed. Stay tuned for developments in all these cases.

Google: EU antitrust investigations. The company is faring little better abroad. In 2015, the European Union, spearheaded by 30 companies (some of them American), brought suit against Google on antitrust grounds, alleging that the search engine favors its own shopping sites ("Google Shopping") over others, privileging itself over other online shopping venues. The EU also alleged Google's anticompetitive use of the Android operating system.

In 2017, in what many thought the most significant antitrust ruling in Europe since the 2004 Microsoft case, the European Commission (the EU's antitrust enforcer) found that Google acted unlawfully: the company systematically gave prominence to its own comparison shopping service over others in search results and in so doing, demoted rival shopping

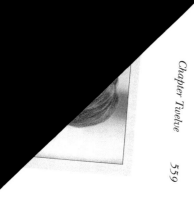

in the results. The commission fined Google €2.42 billion
..., telling five judges at the General Court in Luxembourg
... ot require Google to hold back innovation or compromise
..."

...ean Commission announced it was opening investigations
...ke those under attack in the Texas case. The commission
...violated EU competition rules by favouring its own online
...ervices in the so called 'ad tech' supply chain, to the detri-
...of advertising technology services, advertisers and online
...d it will focus on whether Google restricts access to user data
...anies as well as on allegations that it excluded competitors
...Tube (which Google owns). Stay tuned.

Apple antitrust. ... ... with facts mirroring those against Google regarding its Play
Store, Epic Games, creator of battle royale game *Fortnite*, sued Apple in 2020 for forcing
in-app purchases to use ApplePay and its App Store (and taking a 30% cut). Epic intentionally made changes in *Fortnite* to bypass the App Store, causing Apple to drop the game from
the store. Epic also develops and licenses the Unreal Engine, software used in many videogames as well as in TV and film (including Disney's TV hit *The Mandalorian*). Apple filed a
countersuit alleging that Epic breached its contract when it changed *Fortnite* to circumvent
the App Store. The case went to trial in May 2021. Some antitrust experts predict a split
decision; as one lawyer put it, ""I tend to think that the judge may support Apple's ability to
manage their App Store, but find for Epic on forced use of ApplePay." A case in Australia has
also been cleared to proceed. Stay tuned.

Facebook antitrust. Facebook, however, beat two antitrust allegations, one brought by
48 states and districts (*New York v. Facebook, Inc.*, No. 20-3589) and the second by the federal
government in 2021 (*FTC v. Facebook, Inc.*, No. 20-3590). The judge said the FTC's claim
was "legally insufficient"—the agency "failed to plead enough facts to plausibly establish ...
that Facebook has monopoly power in the market for Personal Social Networking (PSN)
Services." As for the states' claim—central to which was a demand that Facebook divest
itself of Instagram and WhatsApp—the judge said they had waited too long to sue. Citing
the laches doctrine (discussed in Chapter Six), he said that Facebook had acquired
Instagram in 2012 and WhatsApp in 2014, and the states provided no legal rationale for
the delay. Nor did Facebook have to provide interoperability with other apps, another
allegation by the states.
But the company is facing antitrust allegations from both Great Britain and the European Union. The organizations announced in June 2021 that they would be investigating
Facebook Marketplace, an auction site, and British authorities will also examine Facebook
Dating, a service similar to Match.com and Tinder. Stay tuned.

The tip of the iceberg. These Facebook investigations are just a few of many filed
nationally and internationally against big tech companies. Facebook, Google, Apple, and
other companies face a number of challenges to their business practices in China, India,
and Australia, among others. Tech companies also see the looming possibility of stronger
regulation in the United States: the House Judiciary Committee approved a six-part
package of legislation aimed at reforming antitrust in June 2021, and President Joe Biden
is expected to issue executive orders in the same vein. This area of law is going to heat up
in coming years.

Other Antitrust Issues

While giant companies like Google, Apple, and Facebook tend to dominate media attention when they get sued, other antitrust actions can and do arise.

Domain names. A consumers' group won the right to pursue antitrust claims against Verisign, a major domain name registrar, for its actions in the .com domain name market. In *Coalition for ICANN Transparency Inc. v. Verisign* (567 F.3d 1084), the Ninth Circuit in 2009 reversed a district court's dismissal of antitrust claims against Verisign. The court said the coalition had successfully argued that Verisign may be engaging in predatory pricing in the .com top-level domain and trying to monopolize the market for expiring domain names.

Since 2001, Verisign managed the databases of registered .com and .net domain names, contracting with the Internet Corporation for Assigned Names and Numbers (ICANN) to do so. The court said that "Verisign and ICANN had the intent to impose terms for pricing and price increases that restrained trade," thus violating Section 1 of the Sherman Act. Verisign also violated Section Two of the Sherman Act, the court said, by trying "to control ICANN's operations in its own favor." The case was remanded to the district court.

A federal judge allowed a suit to proceed against ICANN regarding its handling of .xxx domain names. ICANN signed a deal with another registry that allowed companies and individuals to pay $150 to prevent their names from being registered as domains with an .xxx at the end. ICANN is not-for-profit, and it argued against Luxembourg-based porn company Manwin Licensing that it is a charitable, not commercial, organization, serving to help oversee the domain name registration process. In *Manwin Licensing Internat'l S.A.R.L. v. ICM Registry, LLC* (2012-2 Trade Cas. (CCH) P78,009), the judge disagreed, saying that ICANN is subject to antitrust laws in this area, and ICANN failed in its argument that "the payment of contractually agreed upon fees is not commercial activity within the Sherman Act."

Online music. What about agreements on how much to charge for music online? The Second Circuit vacated a district court's dismissal in 2010 of an antitrust case alleging that major recording companies, including Sony and Vivendi, conspired to fix the prices and terms under which their music would be sold over the internet (*Starr v. Sony BMG Music*, 592 F.3d 314). The court said the antitrust claim did not fail to meet the Sherman Act's requirements. Plaintiffs argued that there was evidence of illegal conspiracy, including the charging of "unreasonably high prices" for music and the similarity of the companies' copyright restriction plans. The court remanded the case to determine if there was a Sherman Antitrust Act violation.

Apple price fixing for electronic books. The Justice Department brought an antitrust case against Apple and several book publishers accused of electronic book ("e-book") price-fixing. The 2012 suit said that Apple had worked with five publishers (HarperCollins, Simon & Schuster, Hachette, Macmillan, and Penguin Group) to set e-book prices in concert and limit competition as early as 2010—a violation of the Sherman Act.

All five publishers subsequently settled their case with Justice, leaving Apple the sole defendant. In Apple's 2013 case before Judge Cote, as reported by CNN Money, the sides could have been arguing different cases. The government, said Justice's attorney Mark Ryan, saw this case as just the final step in the entire price-fixing scheme—capturing the "ringmaster." Orin Snyder, Apple's lead attorney, argued that Apple was just doing what all businesses new to an industry do, and all parties to the case were acting independently, not in concert.

Judge Cote agreed with the government (*U.S. v. Apple Inc.*, 952 F. Supp. 2d 638). She said that Apple played a key role in coordinating the e-book price fixing agreements, and without that, the conspiracy would have failed. She put it bluntly: "The Plaintiffs [Justice and 33 states] have shown that the Publisher Defendants conspired with each other to eliminate retail price competition in order to raise e-book prices, and that Apple played a central role in facilitating and executing that conspiracy."

Evidence also included declarations and emails from Steve Jobs, former Apple chief executive. Judge Cote said that, despite Apple's valiant attempts to recast them in a non-collusive way, Jobs' statements "acknowledged his understanding that the Publisher Defendants would now wrest control of pricing from Amazon and raise e-book prices, and that Apple would not have to face any competition from Amazon on price."

In June 2015, a divided Second Circuit panel agreed, upholding the $450 million judgment. In another lengthy (157-page) opinion, the court traced the meetings and email correspondences among Apple and the other publishers and determined that Apple was indeed conspiring with them in violation of the Sherman Act (*U.S. v. Apple Inc.*, 791 F.3d 290). "Apple's benign portrayal of its Contracts with the Publisher Defendants is not persuasive—not because those Contracts themselves were independently unlawful, but because, in context, they provide strong evidence that Apple consciously orchestrated a conspiracy among the Publisher Defendants," Judge Debra Ann Livingston said.

In dissent, Judge Dennis Jacobs said that Apple was not guilty of collusion with the other publishers. "Collusion among competitors does not describe Apple's conduct or account for its motive," he wrote. The Supreme Court denied *cert.*

■ AN OVERVIEW OF MAJOR ISSUES

At a time when the nation's giant media corporations are maneuvering for bigger shares of the communications marketplace, there are major unresolved issues in media ownership and antitrust law. Recent times have seen massive media consolidation without much intervention by the Justice Department, which is supposed to act under the antitrust laws to prevent mergers and consolidations that lessen competition. At other times, relatively small mergers have received considerable scrutiny at the Justice Department.

Just what sort of merger is "anti-competitive" rather than "pro-competitive"? Does it really lessen competition when one company owns program production facilities, hundreds of broadcast stations, cable systems, television networks, national magazines, and newspapers? What about foreign ownership of American communications companies? The FCC has rules limiting foreign ownership of broadcast stations, but not Hollywood production companies. Does foreign ownership in Hollywood have any implications for the public interest? Should the limits on foreign ownership of radio and television stations be liberalized?

What about private equity investment firms—money managers with billions of dollars from pension funds and wealthy individuals to invest—buying media companies that were once publicly owned? For companies that once had their stock traded on Wall Street, with all of the public disclosure requirements that entails, this was a return to the days of doing business behind closed doors. In 2007 alone four of the largest station groups (Tribune, Clear Channel, Univision, and Ion) announced plans to be acquired by private equity investors. Is that in the public interest?

Now that the FCC has eliminated several of its ownership regulations and opened the field to even more potential media consolidation, what is likely to happen? Given Congress' mandate to the FCC to conduct quadriennial reviews of media ownership regulations, and given earlier court decisions overturning various restrictions, did the FCC have a choice? What does the latest *Prometheus* decision, upholding the FCC's most recent ownership rules, tell us?

Do the traditional ownership restrictions make sense in a marketplace that offers so many new choices in home entertainment programming? Are there lessons to be learned from what happened after the national radio ownership limits were eliminated by the 1996 Telecommunications Act? Are low-power radio stations catering to local needs and demographics an answer?

The internet has created new questions about monopolization and collusion. In the 2005 *Brand X* decision, cable systems won the Supreme Court's authorization to exclude competitors from broadband cable networks. Telephone companies are seeking the same regulatory treatment so they can exclude competitors from their DSL systems. Other would-be broadband competitors face serious obstacles, leaving U.S. consumers with limited choices and high prices for broadband service compared to consumers in many other countries. Because cable and the telcos have invested heavily to set up broadband services, their investors expect the highest return possible, but where does that leave consumers?

The influence of investors has also raised other issues. Wall Street likes profitability and the potential for growth. The 2006 dismantling of Knight Ridder, once the second largest newspaper chain in America, was largely the result of stockholder pressure. Like other newspaper companies, Knight Ridder didn't offer strong growth prospects even though the company remained profitable in the 2000s.

Wall Street analysts thought—perhaps correctly—that individual newspapers might be worth more than the company as a whole. Similar considerations may have played a role in the split of CBS and Viacom. The combined company had seen its stock price stagnate, and the spinoff created a company expected to grow rapidly (the new Viacom) and a company composed of older, slower-growth businesses (CBS). The re-merger might put the lie to this notion, but does Wall Street have too much influence on the media? Is ownership by private equity firms better?

We now know that it's almost commonplace to see news reports about huge mega-mergers, like 2014's Comcast and Time Warner proposed deal, worth $45 billion. Despite their assertions to the contrary, there are significant public, consumer, business, and government concerns regarding this giant proposal. The Department of Justice and the FTC will have their hands full. Should such enormous deals be permitted to go through?

Questions like these will affect all of our lives. Fortunes may be made and lost, and the public interest may be served or disserved, as private industry and government regulators struggle to find answers.

WHAT SHOULD I KNOW ABOUT MY STATE?	• What are my state's applications of federal antitrust laws? • What antitrust laws does my state have? • Are any of the newspapers in my area in a joint operating agreement? What are the terms? • Who owns the media organizations in my city or county?

SUMMARY

A SUMMARY
OF
OWNERSHIP
ISSUES

Do Antitrust Laws Apply to the Media?

Yes. For many years, publishers argued that the First Amendment exempted them from antitrust laws, but the Supreme Court ruled otherwise in 1945. Antitrust laws forbid price fixing, profit pooling, tying arrangements, boycotts, and certain other coercive business practices. Also, mergers that substantially reduce competition are unlawful.

What Is a Joint Operating Agreement, or JOA?

Under a JOA, two competing newspapers merge their business, advertising, and printing operations while maintaining separate editorial staffs. Some publishers say they could not stay in business without such arrangements. The Supreme Court once ruled that a joint operating agreement violated antitrust laws, but then Congress passed the Newspaper Preservation Act, legalizing existing agreements and setting up a procedure for the approval of new ones.

What Is Cross-Ownership?

Cross-ownership occurs when one party owns a combination of newspapers, broadcast properties, and/or cable systems in the same metropolitan market area. Under FCC rules that were upheld by the Supreme Court, new newspaper-broadcast cross-ownerships were forbidden for many years. In 2003, the FCC dropped many of these restrictions; a federal appellate court ordered the FCC to reconsider in 2004, and the agency released new rules in 2007.

What Are the Broadcast Ownership Restrictions?

Under the Telecommunications Act of 1996, there is no limit to the number of radio or television stations one company may own nationally. However, no company may own more than two television stations or eight radio stations in a large metropolitan area. In smaller markets the number of stations a company may own is correspondingly lower. No company may own television stations that reach more than 39% of the nation's television households under a 2004 act of Congress.

How Will the New Technologies Affect Media Ownership?

As new technologies such as fiber optics, satellite communication, digital television, and high-speed internet access develop, the print and electronic media are converging, and the corporations behind these technologies are merging, with each seeking to offer as many communication services as possible.

13   *Advertising and the Law*

Like broadcasting, the advertising industry has specialized legal problems not shared by other mass communications industries. In addition to the legal problems other communicators face, advertisers—like broadcasters—have a federal agency assigned to look after them: advertisers have to get along with the Federal Trade Commission. Advertisers must also deal with other federal agencies and state-level advertising regulators, sometimes including officials of multiple states or multiple federal agencies working together.

Marketing and advertising cases are becoming increasingly expensive in current years; in 2009, the *New York Times* reported that Pfizer, a pharmaceutical company, agreed to pay $2.3 *billion* in a civil and criminal settlement with the Department of Justice over its marketing of the painkiller Bextra. It was the largest health care fraud settlement and the largest criminal fine ever, said the *Times.* "The whole culture of Pfizer is driven by sales, and if you didn't sell drugs illegally, you were not seen as a team player," said a former Pfizer sales representative, whose whistleblowing complaints drove the investigation.

The COVID-19 pandemic also brought a host of FTC actions against companies advertising that their products would cure the virus. In 2020, the agency sent letters to nearly 50 companies touting everything from herbal remedies to a nasal spray claiming to reduce the COVID-19 virus to "an undetectable amount," citing regulations that forbid ad claims that "a product or service can prevent, treat, or cure human disease" without "competent and reliable scientific evidence."

"Off-label marketing" is also under attack. In 2012, the Justice Department fined Merck nearly $322 million for a marketing campaign involving the painkiller Vioxx. Merck had marketed Vioxx for rheumatoid arthritis before the Food and Drug Administration had approved it for such use. This off-label marketing is a violation of the Food, Drug, and Cosmetic Act, which states that a drug cannot be marketed for a use before the FDA says it's safe and effective for that use.

Advertisers have fought many legal battles in recent years and have even won a few, including several U.S. Supreme Court decisions that extended substantial First Amendment protection to commercial speech.

■ THE FIRST AMENDMENT AND ADVERTISING

For many years, the prevailing rule was that advertising had no First Amendment protection. If a particular expression of fact or

Chapter Objectives:

- Define the commercial speech doctrine and trace its development through American history.
- Apply the elements of the *Central Hudson* test to regulations on advertising.
- Explain the roles of the various government agencies in regulating advertising, particularly regarding so-called "vice" products such as tobacco and liquor.

Essential Questions:

- The *Central Hudson* test has been key to determining the constitutionality of regulations on advertising since 1980, but some justices don't approve of it. What do you think?
- Should advertising for legal products like alcohol, gambling, and tobacco get regulated more heavily than other advertising? Why or why not?
- How has the rise of online advertising changed the face of commercial speech regulation?

opinion could be dismissed as *commercial speech,* it could be arbitrarily suppressed by law. The *Commercial Speech Doctrine,* as it came to be known, simply said advertisers were at the mercy of every arm of government, without the guarantees of freedom the Constitution afforded to most other kinds of speech and publishing.

That has all changed, starting in 1975. The U.S. Supreme Court handed down a series of decisions between 1975 and 1980 that established substantial First Amendment protection for commercial speech. During the 1980s, the Supreme Court wavered at times, sometimes upholding government restrictions on advertising in decisions that seemed inconsistent with the cases from the 1970s. But in the 1990s and beyond, the Court again strongly reaffirmed the First Amendment protection of commercial speech. In fact, in 1996, the justices handed down a decision on liquor price advertising so broad that it appeared to give commercial speech *almost* the same First Amendment protection as noncommercial speech. This line of cases is one of the best examples of American law growing through judicial precedent to be found anywhere in the mass communications field.

Early advertising law. The starting point for this summary is a 1942 Supreme Court decision that denied First Amendment protection to commercial speech, a landmark ruling that stood for many years. That case is *Valentine v. Chrestensen* (316 U.S. 52). It stemmed from a bizarre situation. Just before World War II, F.J. Chrestensen acquired a surplus U.S. Navy submarine and tried to dock it at a city-owned wharf in New York City. City authorities wouldn't let him, so he had to arrange for other dock facilities. Next, he started advertising guided tours of the submarine, but city officials wouldn't let him distribute his handbills on city streets because an anti-litter ordinance banned all but political leaflets. So he added a note criticizing city officials for refusing him dockage to the back of the handbill. Then he sued the city for denying his right to distribute literature. The Supreme Court had just ruled in favor of that right in the first of the Jehovah's Witness cases (see Chapter Three).

When his case reached the high court, Chrestensen was in for a surprise. The high court said his back-of-the-handbill political statement was really a ruse to justify a purely commercial advertisement. And that was different from the Jehovah's Witness cases. Where purely commercial advertising is involved, the First Amendment does not apply, the Court ruled. For many years, *Valentine* was regarded as the prevailing precedent on commercial speech. In fact, when the landmark *New York Times v. Sullivan* libel decision was announced in 1964,

FIG. 108.
The Federal Trade Commission building (formerly called the Apex Building) in Washington, D.C.

Author's collection.

the Court went to some trouble to explain why the *Valentine* rule didn't apply (the *Sullivan* libel suit was based on an advertisement). The Court said the ad involved in the *Sullivan* case was an idea ad supporting the civil rights movement, not an ad for a purely commercial product or service as in *Valentine*. Thus, the *Valentine* rule still denied First Amendment protection to commercial advertising for another decade, despite *New York Times v. Sullivan*.

Discrimination in advertising. In 1973, the Supreme Court again denied First Amendment protection to commercial advertising, this time in a case involving the "help wanted" ads in a large newspaper. In *Pittsburgh Press v. Pittsburgh Commission on Human Relations* (413 U.S. 376), the Human Relations Commission ordered the newspaper to stop classifying its employment ads as "Jobs—Male Interest" and "Jobs—Female Interest." The newspaper contended that there were editorial judgments inherent in the decision to classify job openings that way, and that those judgments were protected by the First Amendment.

The Court disagreed, ruling that the classified ads are not only commercial speech but commercial speech promoting an illegal form of discrimination as well. The court had no difficulty in ruling that whatever First Amendment considerations might be involved were secondary to the city's right to outlaw advertising for an illegal commercial activity.

An interesting follow-up note to this case is that in 1979 the Pennsylvania Supreme Court ruled against the Human Relations Commission when it tried to stop the *Pittsburgh Press* from accepting "help wanted" ads from individuals who wished to indicate their age, sex, race, or religion in the ad. The commission objected to such language as "salesman age 30," "born-again Christian seeks work in Christian business," or "white woman seeks domestic work." The state high court said the job seeker had a First Amendment right to communicate such information as this, even though an employer isn't supposed to consider these factors. The U.S. Supreme Court declined to review this second *Pittsburgh Press* decision. Despite this decision, most federal and state laws governing housing and employment discrimination forbid advertising that expresses a preference for applicants of a particular race, gender, family status, or sexual orientation.

Early Victories for Commercial Speech

Only two years after the original *Pittsburgh Press* decision, the Supreme Court handed down the first of its major decisions extending First Amendment protection to commercial speech (*Bigelow v. Virginia*, 421 U.S. 809, 1975). The case began in 1971 when Jeffrey Bigelow published an ad in *The Virginia Weekly* for an abortion service in New York, where abortions had just been legalized. The Supreme Court's *Roe v. Wade* decision, which held that abortions could not be banned in any state, did not occur until 1973. But both abortions and abortion advertising were illegal in Virginia in 1971.

Bigelow was prosecuted for violating the Virginia law. He appealed his conviction; the U.S. Supreme Court used his case to rewrite the Commercial Speech Doctrine. The high court emphasized that the service in question was not illegal where it was offered, and said the readers had a First Amendment right to receive this information. The court distinguished this case from *Pittsburgh Press* by pointing out that the commercial activity in question in the *Pittsburgh* case was illegal. But above all, the Supreme Court in *Bigelow* declared that this message did not lose the First Amendment protection it would otherwise enjoy merely because it appeared in the form of an advertisement. The high court said that in the future there would have to be a *compelling state interest* to justify laws prohibiting any form of commercial speech that has a legitimate purpose.

A year later the Supreme Court took another giant step toward protecting commercial speech under the First Amendment. In *Virginia State Board of Pharmacy v. Virginia Citizens Consumer Council* (425 U.S. 748, 1976), the Supreme Court overturned Virginia's state law against advertising drug prices. Many other states had similar prohibitions on drug price advertising, but the justices emphasized the First Amendment right of consumers to receive information as they overturned the state regulations. An interesting footnote expounded on the lasting power of ads: "Also, commercial speech may be more durable than other kinds. Since advertising is the *sine qua non* of commercial profits, there is little likelihood of its being chilled by proper regulation and forgone entirely."

Again, the Court said the information was protected by the First Amendment despite being used to sell a product. At that point, it seemed clear that the old *Valentine* doctrine was dead: commercial speech *did* have constitutional protection. However, while the Court recognized the importance of price advertising to free enterprise, it also emphasized that this ruling did not affect the right of governments to control false and misleading advertising.

More ad-positive cases. In 1977, the Supreme Court handed down several more decisions strengthening the First Amendment protection of commercial speech. First, in *Linmark Assoc. v. Willingboro* (431 U.S. 85), the Court said homeowners have a First Amendment right to place "for sale" signs in front of their homes. The town of Willingboro, New Jersey, outlawed "for sale" signs to discourage "white flight" at a time when the area's racial composition was changing. Officials wanted to discourage panic selling by white homeowners, and they thought one way to do this was to keep it from appearing that entire neighborhoods were for sale. A real estate firm challenged the constitutionality of the ordinance and the Supreme Court ruled against the city. Justice Thurgood Marshall wrote for the majority that the city could not constitutionally deprive its residents of the information that a "for sale" sign offers. "If the dissemination of this information can be restricted, then every locality in the country can suppress any facts that reflect poorly on the locality," Marshall wrote.

Although the *Linmark* decision held that homeowners have a First Amendment right to put up "for sale" signs, many cities continued to restrict real estate signs. For example, some towns allowed "for sale" signs but banned "sold" signs on the theory that the presence of a lot of "sold" signs would also send the message that many homeowners are leaving.

In addition to *Linmark*, in 1977 the Supreme Court handed down a commercial speech decision that was not at all surprising in view of its earlier ruling in *Bigelow v. Virginia*. In *Carey v. Population Serv. Int'l* (431 U.S. 678, 1977), the Court overturned a variety of New York laws that restricted advertising of contraceptive devices. Even though these devices were legal in New York, state laws prohibited advertising, in-store displays and even sales of these products except by licensed pharmacists. The Court found First Amendment violations in these laws and said there was no compelling state interest to justify them, as required in *Bigelow*.

■ THE CENTRAL HUDSON TEST

In 1980, the Supreme Court established a new legal test that has been used ever since then to determine the validity of government restrictions on commercial speech. That happened in the case of *Central Hudson Gas & Elec. v. Public Serv. Comm'n of New York* (447 U.S. 557). The *Central Hudson* case challenged rules adopted by the New York Public Service Commission in 1977 in an effort to promote conservation and discourage energy use. Among other things, the commission prohibited advertising by utilities that might encourage consumption of utility services rather than conservation. The Central Hudson Gas and Electric Company challenged this wide-ranging regulation of its advertising. The company lost in the New York Court of Appeals, which ruled that the ban was justified because the need to conserve energy outweighed the slight free speech issue involved.

The U.S. Supreme Court reversed the New York court, holding that the ban on promotional advertising would have only a "highly speculative" effect on energy consumption or utility rates, and that a total ban on such advertising was going too far. If there was any doubt by this time, the court said commercial speech is constitutionally protected if it concerns "lawful activity" and is not misleading or fraudulent.

If commercial speech is constitutionally protected, how can the courts determine if a particular government restriction is proper under the First Amendment? In the *Central Hudson* case the Supreme Court said courts should evaluate government restrictions on advertising under these four criteria:

1. whether the expression is *protected by the First Amendment* (if it involves deception or unlawful activities, it is not protected by the First Amendment and may be banned without considering the rest of this test);
2. whether the *governmental interest that justifies the restrictions is substantial;*
3. whether the regulation *directly advances the governmental interest* in question;
4. whether the regulation is *more broad than needed* to fulfill the governmental interest.

This test has been cited in hundreds of cases since it was handed down in 1980 as both state and federal courts have had to rule on a variety of government restrictions on advertising. At the same time as its *Central Hudson* decision, the high court ruled on a separate case involving *noncommercial corporate speech,* as opposed to commercial speech. The justices established a different test for judging the constitutionality of government restrictions on that type of speech. This topic is discussed later in the chapter.

Applying Central Hudson: *Early Cases*

The 1980 *Central Hudson* test for advertising regulation resulted in rulings on commercial speech rights in many contexts—with mixed results. In 1981, the Supreme Court ruled on the right of local governments to outlaw roadside billboards in *Metromedia v. San Diego* (453 U.S. 490). The justices overturned a San Diego city ordinance banning both political and commercial billboard messages. The Court was deeply divided, and Justice William Rehnquist called the decision a "virtual Tower of Babel from which no definitive principles can be drawn." Nevertheless, a majority of the justices agreed that San Diego's billboard ban was too broad because it banned all billboards containing political messages as well as purely commercial ones. The Court left open the possibility that a narrower ordinance forbidding only commercial but not political billboards would be constitutionally permissible. But beyond that, the justices issued five different opinions that shed more confusion than light.

The Ninth Circuit used the *Metromedia* case as precedent in a 2009 decision that upheld a Los Angeles ordinance restricting billboards but allowing bus shelter advertising. The facts in *Metro Lights v. Los Angeles* (551 F.3d 898) were "virtually identical" to those in the *Metromedia* case, said the court, and the same outcome was "compelled" by *Metromedia*. Metro Lights had asked the court to distinguish the *Metromedia* case by suggesting that the billboard ordinance was content based, but the judges were not convinced. Both cases featured a ban on billboards except for bus shelters and transit stops "to promote traffic safety and aesthetics."

In 1984, the Supreme Court again addressed the constitutionality of a local ordinance restricting political signs, but this time the justices upheld it. In *Members of the Los Angeles City Council v. Taxpayers for Vincent* (466 U.S. 789), the Court said the city of Los Angeles has the right to ban political posters on public property. The justices ruled that forbidding posters on city-owned utility poles and buildings was not an excessive restriction on First Amendment freedoms. The Court said this decision was not inconsistent with the *Metromedia* decision, in which a ban on all billboards (including on private property with owner consent) was overturned. In contrast, the Los Angeles ordinance only prohibited attaching posters to public property, not placing signs and billboards on private property. In upholding the ordinance, the Court said a city has the right to prevent the "visual assault on the citizens... presented by an accumulation of signs posted on public property."

What about political signs on private property rather than public property? As we saw in Chapter Three, the Supreme Court has ruled that a city may not ban all signs on private property conveying political messages (*City of Ladue v. Gilleo*).

In view of the earlier commercial speech rulings, the Supreme Court surprised no one when it decided *Bolger v. Youngs Drug Products Corp.* (463 U.S. 60) in 1983. The Court overturned a U.S. Post Office ban on mailing unsolicited ads for contraceptive devices. The Court said such a ban denies consumers access to important information that the public has a constitutional right to receive. In the majority opinion, Justice Thurgood Marshall emphasized the importance of family planning and the prevention of venereal disease as social issues, and said the post office had not adequately justified the ban on mailing this material.

The high court is nothing if not unpredictable. In 1986, there was a surprise awaiting those who thought they understood the commercial speech doctrine. In *Posadas de Puerto Rico Assoc. v. Tourism Co. of Puerto Rico* (478 U.S. 328, 1986), the Court announced a highly controversial decision on commercial speech *upholding* Puerto Rico's Games of Chance Act of 1948, which legalized casino gambling on the island and casino advertising aimed at tourists but barred casinos from advertising locally.

The law was challenged by Posadas, a Texas-based partnership. The Tourism Company, a public corporation responsible for enforcing the island's gambling law, twice fined Posadas for advertising locally, and the casino operator eventually challenged the constitutionality of the Puerto Rican law. The local "advertising" included such things as matchbook covers and elevator signs that used the forbidden word "casino."

Justice William Rehnquist's majority opinion not only affirmed the Puerto Rican law but also mentioned alcoholic beverages and cigarettes as products whose advertising could be further restricted without violating the First Amendment. The Court said, in essence, that advertising of anything "deemed harmful" enjoys less First Amendment protection than other advertising, even if the product itself is legal. (Ironically, as we'll see, a decade later the Supreme Court would reconsider that idea and hand down a series of decisions *upholding* the First Amendment rights of alcohol, gambling, and tobacco advertisers—again illustrating the uncertainties in this area of law.)

In defending their law restricting gambling ads, Puerto Rican officials said the law was designed to attract tourist dollars while minimizing the harmful effects of gambling ("the disruption of moral and cultural patterns, the increase in local crime, the fostering of prostitution, the development of corruption and the infiltration of organized crime") on Puerto Ricans. The Court's 5-4 majority agreed that these were substantial government purposes—enough to justify restrictions on commercial speech. The ruling attracted strenuous dissents from four justices, including William Brennan, who said the Puerto Rican law was intended to "suppress the dissemination of truthful information about entirely lawful activity merely to keep its residents ignorant." It was a setback for media industries, all of whom filed briefs urging the Court to overturn the law.

The Court followed up the *Posadas* decision with another ruling that upheld restrictions on commercial speech in 1989, *State University of New York v. Fox* (492 U.S. 469). In this case, the court upheld the SUNY system's rules restricting commercial activities on campus. The rules forbid using campus facilities for many types of selling; a cookware salesperson was arrested for refusing to leave a dormitory on the SUNY Cortland campus where she was conducting a Tupperware party in violation of the rules.

The Court not only upheld the SUNY rules but also used the case to declare that governments need not use the "least restrictive means" to regulate commercial speech. If political speech is involved, the least restrictive means test still applies, but the Court's 6-3 majority held that governments have more leeway in regulating commercial speech under the First Amendment. The majority said that the *Central Hudson* test is satisfied if there is a "reasonable fit" between a government's purpose and the restrictions on commercial speech that are adopted to help achieve that purpose.

The *SUNY* decision continued the Court's movement away from upholding commercial speech rights in close cases. During the late 1980s, the high court retreated from the sweeping protection extended to commercial speech in the 1970s. But the 1990s changed that.

Applying Central Hudson: *The 1990s and Beyond—Expanding Commercial Speech Rights*

Bucking the *Posadas* trend, the Supreme Court expanded the constitutional protection of commercial speech during the 1990s, beginning with a 1993 case involving advertising circulars. By 1996, there could be no doubt that truthful commercial speech about lawful activities enjoys substantial protection from government censorship.

In the 1993 case, *Cincinnati v. Discovery Network* (507 U.S. 410), the Court said the city of Cincinnati could not flatly ban newsracks for advertising flyers while allowing newspaper vending machines. As explained in the section on newsrack ordinances in Chapter Three, city officials had ordered publishers of free magazines that were predominantly advertising to remove 62 newsracks from city property while allowing about 2,000 newspaper stands to remain in place. In a 6-3 ruling, the justices said the city had not provided a reasonable basis for this action. Citing the *SUNY* case, the Court emphasized that, even though commercial speech does not enjoy the same level of protection as noncommercial speech, it cannot be arbitrarily banned. The justices again said a government entity that bans commercial speech must show a "reasonable fit" between a legitimate government purpose (such as safety or aesthetics) and the ban. The majority was clearly troubled when the city tried to defend its action by talking about visual blight and litter—at a time when it was acting against only 62 newsracks for free magazines, not 2,000 newspaper stands. The city, the justices chided, had seriously underestimated the value of commercial speech under the First Amendment.

While the *Discovery* case was a strong affirmation of First Amendment rights of commercial speech, the majority stopped short of giving it *full* protection. The Court reaffirmed that a government may restrict commercial speech when there is a "reasonable fit" between the restriction and the government's legitimate goals. This is a far lower standard than government must meet to justify censoring noncommercial speech on the basis of its content.

1990s gambling advertising cases. Shortly after *Cincinnati,* the Court *upheld* another gambling ad restriction in *U.S. v. Edge Broad.* (509 U.S. 418, 1993). Here the justices said that laws that prohibited a North Carolina radio station from advertising Virginia's state-sponsored lottery, even though more than 90% of the station's listeners were in Virginia, were acceptable. North Carolina had a legitimate governmental interest in discouraging its citizens from gambling, and the state's ban on lottery advertising advanced that interest, even though it also prevented many listeners in Virginia from hearing ads for their own state's government-sponsored lottery.

However, in 1999 the Court ruled that the ban on broadcast advertising of gambling *cannot* be enforced against broadcasters in states where gambling is legal. The high court unanimously overturned the ban on First Amendment grounds in *Greater New Orleans Broad. Assoc. v. U.S.* (527 U.S. 173). The Court reversed a lower court decision upholding the ban against New Orleans broadcasters who wanted to carry advertising for local casinos.

Writing for the Court, Justice John Paul Stevens said the federal law in question fails to meet two parts of the commercial speech test set forth in the *Central Hudson* case. Noting that there are exceptions to the ban on gambling advertising for Indian-owned casinos and state-run lotteries, Stevens said the law has so many loopholes that it does not materially advance the government's claimed interest in reducing compulsive gambling: "The operation of Section 1304 (the ban on casino advertising) and its attendant regulatory regime is so pierced by exemptions and inconsistencies that the government cannot hope to exonerate it." Stevens said the government "cannot overcome the presumption that the speaker and the audience, not the government, should be left to assess the value of accurate and nonmisleading information about lawful conduct. Had the government adopted a more coherent policy, or accommodated the rights of speakers in states that have legalized the underlying conduct, this might be a different case," he concluded.

Two years earlier, the Ninth Circuit ruled in a Nevada case that the ban on gambling advertising violates the First Amendment (*Valley Broad. v. U.S.*, 107 F.3d 1328). That decision left broadcasters free to carry gambling ads in the western states in the Ninth Circuit. Now broadcasters in other parts of the country are free to carry casino gambling ads. The language of the *Greater New Orleans* Supreme Court decision suggested that even broadcasters in non-gambling states may carry casino gambling ads as long as there is no state law that forbids gambling advertising. In fact, after this Supreme Court decision, the FCC stopped enforcing its restrictions on gambling except in the situation that led to the *Edge Broadcasting* decision: a radio or television station in a non-lottery state still cannot advertise another state's lottery in violation of the law in the state where it is licensed.

Drinking, smoking, sex: (almost) no "vice exceptions." The Court continued its permissive stance toward commercial speech in the 1990s even in so-called "vice" advertising. To the amazement of those who remember the language in *Posadas de Puerto Rico* about the low status of advertising for products and services "deemed harmful," the Court decisively upheld not only gambling advertising but also tobacco and alcoholic beverage advertising.

Alcohol advertising. In 1995, the Supreme Court overturned the beer labeling rules enforced by the Bureau of Alcohol, Tobacco and Firearms (ATF) in the Treasury Department. In *Rubin v. Coors Brewing Co.* (514 U.S. 476), the Court unanimously ruled that there is a First Amendment right to disclose the alcohol content of beer on the label, something that federal law and ATF policies prohibited. Writing for the Court, Justice Clarence Thomas acknowledged that the government had a substantial interest in curbing beer "strength wars."

However, he said the ban was overly broad because there are other ways the government could prevent brewers from promoting their products by emphasizing high alcohol strength. Explaining the Court's decision, Thomas said, "Here (Coors) seeks to disclose only truthful, verifiable and nonmisleading factual information concerning alcohol content."

If the *Coors Brewing* case in 1995 was a victory for those who engage in commercial speech and a defeat for government regulators, the Supreme Court went even further in affirming the First Amendment protection of commercial speech in a 1996 ruling that also involved alcoholic beverages: *44 Liquormart v. Rhode Island* (517 U.S. 484).

In a case hailed by many in the advertising industry as a decisive victory, the Court unanimously ruled that Rhode Island cannot ban liquor price advertising. All nine justices agreed that even the Twenty-First Amendment, which repealed nationwide Prohibition but allowed individual states to ban alcoholic beverages, does not allow the states to legalize alcoholic beverages and then ban their advertising (contrary to what was suggested in *Posadas*). The Twenty-First Amendment, the Court held, does not override the First Amendment.

Although all nine justices voted to overturn Rhode Island's ban on liquor price advertising, they were divided in their reasoning. There was no single majority opinion of the Court. But the conclusion was clear enough. At least seven of the nine justices either disavowed the *Posadas* decision or "distinguished" it (which means they said it does not apply to this situation while not voting to overturn it). Justice John Paul Stevens wrote the plurality opinion. When a government bans a type of advertising instead of just regulating it, he wrote, courts must exercise "special care" in applying the *Central Hudson* test. Stevens and the three other justices who joined in all or part of his opinion wanted to extend broad First Amendment protection to commercial speech—perhaps protection as broad as that afforded to noncommercial speech.

Justice Clarence Thomas went even further: he said the *Central Hudson* criteria need not be considered because restrictions on commercial speech such as these are *per se* unconstitutional. Thomas added, "All attempts to dissuade legal choices by citizens by keeping them ignorant are impermissible." Justice Stevens' plurality opinion was only a bit more restrained: "The First Amendment directs us to be especially skeptical of regulations that seek to keep people in the dark for what the government perceives to be their own good."

Four justices joined an opinion by Sandra Day O'Connor which agreed that the Rhode Island ban on liquor price advertising was unconstitutional, but only because the ban failed to satisfy the *Central Hudson* test. O'Connor said there was no "reasonable fit" between the ban and the state's stated goal: discouraging alcohol consumption by keeping liquor prices high. Given the four different opinions, *44 Liquormart* was not as clear an affirmation of the First Amendment status of commercial speech as it might have been. Nonetheless, commercial speech has come a long way since 1942—when the Supreme Court said it had no First Amendment protection at all.

Tobacco advertising. In 2001, the Court ruled that the regulation of cigarette advertising is federally preempted under the Federal Cigarette Labeling and Advertising Act, thereby invalidating hundreds of state and local laws banning or restricting tobacco ads. In *Lorillard Tobacco Co. v. Reilly* (533 U.S. 525), a case challenging restrictions on tobacco advertising in Massachusetts, the Court ruled by a 5-4 vote that many of the state's regulations violated the First Amendment as well as being federally preempted.

This case marked the second time in a year that the Supreme Court overturned a government attempt to regulate cigarette advertising or marketing. In 2000, the Court said the Food and Drug Administration lacked the authority to curb cigarette marketing by regulating tobacco as a drug (in *FDA v. Brown & Williamson Tobacco*, which is discussed later).

The *Lorillard* case was a challenge to Massachusetts regulations forbidding tobacco ads within 1,000 feet of any school, park, or public playground and requiring retailers to post point-of-sale advertising at least five feet off the floor, out of the immediate sight of young children. The Court overturned those rules, and in the process swept away state and local restrictions on cigarette ads in many other states by holding that the regulation of cigarette advertising is *federally preempted.*

Writing for the Court, Justice Sandra Day O'Connor said the states may not single out cigarette advertising for special restrictions. She said the states may still use their zoning powers to regulate all advertising, but they cannot target cigarette advertising without intruding into a federally preempted area.

The Court also ruled that Massachusetts' restrictions on outdoor and point-of-sale advertising for cigars and smokeless tobacco, which are *not* federally preempted, are invalid because they violate the First Amendment. As the justices did in overturning Rhode Island's ban on alcoholic beverage price advertising in *44 Liquormart* and the federal ban on broadcast ads for casino gambling in *Greater New Orleans Broadcasting*, they once again refused to allow a "vice exception" to the First Amendment—abandoning the rationale used to justify Puerto Rico's ban on local advertising by casinos in the *Posadas de Puerto Rico* case.

In a concurring opinion joined by Justices Antonin Scalia and Anthony Kennedy, Justice Clarence Thomas was again the Court's most outspoken defender of "vice advertising." "Harmful products, (like) harmful ideas, are protected by the First Amendment," he wrote. He objected to the Court's "uncertain course" on commercial speech, with "much of the uncertainty being generated by the malleability of the four-part balancing test of *Central Hudson.*" Justice O'Connor's majority opinion was more reserved, but it also said Massachusetts was violating the First Amendment as well as federal labeling law because the rules were overly broad: the 1,000-foot buffer zone meant tobacco ads were banned virtually

Historic advertising when the rule was "caveat emptor."

(L) FIG. 109. Patent medicine ad for Merchant's Gargling Oil, about 1873.

(R) FIG. 110. Package label for Genuine Havana Cigars, 1868.

Library of Congress Prints and Photographs Division Washington, LC-USZ62-48534

Library of Congress Prints and Photographs Division Washington, D.C [LC-USZ62-78340]

everywhere in the major cities. She cited *Reno v. ACLU*, the case in which the high court rejected a ban on indecency on the internet because it denied adults their First Amendment rights in the name of protecting children (see Chapter Ten), and said the same principle applies to tobacco advertising. "Protecting children from harmful materials...does not justify an unnecessarily broad suppression of speech addressed to adults," she wrote.

The result: unless anti-smoking groups can persuade Congress to end the federal preemption, tobacco advertising will be governed by federal law—and by the industry's 1998 settlement of a massive lawsuit by 46 states. In the $206 billion settlement, the industry voluntarily agreed to discontinue billboard advertising, stop using cartoon characters or otherwise targeting underage smokers, and to bankroll an anti-smoking billboard campaign.

The Federal Cigarette Labeling and Advertising Act forbids only broadcast advertising of cigarettes while requiring health warnings in ads and on cigarette packages. If the federal law or FTC regulations were to be expanded to further curtail tobacco advertising, that, too, could raise First Amendment issues, given the Court's recent rulings on "vice" advertising. Taken together, the *Greater New Orleans* case on gambling, the *Coors* and *44 Liquormart* cases on alcoholic beverages and the *Lorillard Tobacco* decision on cigarette advertising illustrate just how far the Court has come since its *Posadas de Puerto Rico* decision in 1986.

The U.S. Supreme Court in 2007 allowed the states to entertain some lawsuits involving tobacco marketing. In *Watson v. Philip Morris* (551 U.S. 142), the Court allowed consumer groups to pursue class action lawsuits in state courts to litigate their claims that tobacco companies falsely marketed "light" cigarettes as safer than other cigarettes. Philip Morris had argued that these cases could only be heard in federal courts because tobacco companies were testing cigarettes using methods approved by the FTC—and using those testing methods made the companies federal agents. The justices didn't buy that argument.

Nevertheless, most state regulation of tobacco advertising is now federally preempted. The California Supreme Court emphasized that point in a 2007 decision dismissing class-action lawsuits by smokers who said they took up the habit as minors because of the tobacco industry's marketing. The court unanimously rejected the smokers' lawsuits because they couldn't prove that any particular ads were misleading and targeted exclusively to children, factors that might have allowed them to sue under various state laws and avoid the federal preemption problem (*In re Tobacco Cases II*, 41 C.4th 1257). The state high court relied on the U.S. Supreme Court's *Lorillard Tobacco* decision in reaching this conclusion. And, as we'll see, other federal agencies are joining the FTC in regulating tobacco advertising.

Two Providence, Rhode Island, tobacco ordinances intended to reduce smoking in children were upheld by the First Circuit in 2013 (*Nat'l Ass'n of Tobacco Outlets, Inc. v. City of Providence*, 731 F.3d 71). The two ordinances, the "Price Ordinance," which restricted sellers from reducing prices on tobacco products with coupons or multipack pricing, and the "Flavor Ordinance," which restricted sales of flavored tobacco products other than cigarettes, were challenged by a national tobacco association as violations of the First Amendment. In rejecting the association's claims, the First Circuit said that the "Pricing Ordinance" did not implicate the First Amendment's commercial speech doctrine because it did not affect advertising, only pricing. And the "Flavor Ordinance" was not preempted by the federal Family Smoking Prevention and Tobacco Control Act (discussed later in this chapter): "It is not a blanket prohibition because it allows the sale of flavored tobacco products in smoking bars. Rather, it is a regulation 'relating to' sales specifically allowed by the [FSPTCA]..." Nor did either ordinance violate the Rhode Island Constitution regulating tobacco licensing.

Advertising prostitution (and prostitution as a product?). In one of the few (maybe only) court decisions to address the issue, the Ninth Circuit in 2010 reversed a district court's decision that Nevada's regulations on prostitution advertising violated the First Amendment (*Coyote Publ'g Inc. v. Miller*, 598 F.3d 592). The court applied *Central Hudson* and found that the state has a substantial interest in limiting "the commodification of human sexuality." The restrictions on advertising advanced that interest as "[i]ncreased advertising of commercial sex throughout the state of Nevada would increase the extent to which sex is presented to the public as a commodity for sale." Finally, the court said that the regulations did not burden more speech than necessary; they were regionally tailored to match the places in Nevada where prostitution is legal. The Supreme Court denied *cert.*

Could being a prostitute count as "selling a product" and thus be protected under the commercial speech doctrine? Three prostitutes, a potential client, and an advocacy group decided to try out that argument in California in *Erotic Serv. Provider Legal Educ. & Research Proj. v. Gascon* (880 F.3d 450, 2018). The Ninth Circuit, not surprisingly, said no. Applying *Central Hudson*, the court said that illegal commercial speech gets no protection under the first prong of the test, and that ends the analysis. But, the court continued, in addition, the state does have substantial interests in controlling prostitution (protection of women, reduction of illicit drug use, and other interests), limiting demand for prostitution advances those interests, and the state tailored the law appropriately. The court also rejected plaintiffs' attempts to use *Lawrence v. Texas*, discussed in Chapter Five, to suggest that there was a relationship between a prostitute and the hirer, saying that *Lawrence* "has not previously been interpreted as creating a liberty interest that invalidates laws criminalizing prostitution."

Lawyers' Advertising as Commercial Speech

The Supreme Court has repeatedly addressed the First Amendment rights of lawyers and other professionals who advertise—and who are subject to special rules restricting their right to do so. The Court first dealt with lawyer advertising in 1977, handing down one of its most far-reaching commercial speech decisions: *Bates v. Arizona State Bar* (433 U.S. 350).

That case overturned Arizona's ban on advertising by lawyers, a rule similar to those found in nearly every other state. The case involved a legal clinic run by two young lawyers disciplined by the State Bar for advertising the prices of routine legal services, prices that were far below the "going rate" charged by other lawyers. In ruling against the state bar, the Supreme Court again emphasized the First Amendment right of consumers to receive commercial information. The Court said advertising by lawyers (and presumably other professionals) could not be prohibited unless it was misleading or fraudulent. However, the justices expressed reservations about ads that say something about the quality of the services offered ("we're the best lawyers in town") because such ads could well be misleading.

That warning about misleading advertising by professionals foreshadowed two more Supreme Court rulings, *Ohralik v. Ohio State Bar Ass'n* (436 U.S. 447, 1978) and *Friedman v. Rogers* (440 U.S. 1, 1979). In *Ohralik*, the Supreme Court affirmed sanctions against a lawyer for soliciting new clients in a manner sometimes called "ambulance chasing." The Court said the First Amendment does not prevent a state bar association from adopting rules against that sort of conduct. In *Friedman*, the Court went a step further, upholding a Texas ban on the use of trade names by optometrists. The Court said a trade name could be mislead-ing and that it did not provide consumers important information—as did the commercial advertising in question in earlier cases—and it could be misleading because there could be a change of optometrists (and thus a change in the quality of service offered) without the name changing. Therefore, a state is not violating the First Amendment when it requires an optometrist to practice under his own name rather than a trade name, the Court ruled. Critics pointed out that it was customary and completely legal for law firms, for instance, to continue to use the names of the founding partners long after their deaths. Isn't such a name really a trade name at some point? The Court didn't address that issue.

The Supreme Court has decided a number of other commercial speech cases involving advertising by attorneys (between 1985 and 1995 the justices handed down at least five, two of which we'll examine). Perhaps the fact that the Court has handed down so many rulings on lawyer advertising not only illustrates how deeply divided the legal community is on this issue, but also that lawyers tend to file lawsuits.

Arguably the most important of these cases, *Zauderer v. Office of Disciplinary Counsel* (471 U.S. 626, 1985), began when Philip Zauderer, a Columbus, Ohio, lawyer, was disciplined for publishing newspaper ads that contained a drawing of the Dalkon Shield contraceptive (which has been linked to miscarriages, injuries, and possibly cancer). Zauderer's ads said that he was representing numerous women in lawsuits against the manufacturer of the Dalkon Shield and would be willing to take more cases involving the device on a contingent-fee basis, where instead of paying hourly rates, his clients would pay him a percentage of any awards they received—but he omitted the fact that these clients would still be liable for court and other fees if they lost. Ohio's rules mandated that this information be disclosed.

The Supreme Court voted 5-3 to strike down Ohio's ban on the use of illustrations in lawyers' advertising. The Court said, in essence, that bar associations could require lawyers' ads to be truthful and little more. As it had in earlier commercial speech cases, the Court said in *Zauderer* that consumers had a right to receive the message that local authorities wanted to suppress, and that the advertiser had a right to communicate it. The Court did uphold Ohio's right to discipline Zauderer for aspects of his advertising.

Perhaps more importantly, though, the justices said a lower level of scrutiny than *Central Hudson* could be applied to certain compelled advertising cases: the justices said that Ohio's rules mandating the disclosure of fee calculations in ads offering contingent-fee rates were acceptable, as they compelled only "factual and uncontroversial information about the terms under which ... services will be available." As will be discussed elsewhere, this element of the *Zauderer* case has become important in other compelled advertising cases.

In 1994, the Court ruled that a state board could not prevent accountants who are also lawyers from advertising that fact. In *Ibanez v. Florida Dep't of Prof'l & Bus. Regulation* (512 U.S. 136, 1994) the Court held that Silvia Ibanez, who was a certified financial planner as well as a lawyer and an accountant, could advertise these credentials on her business cards and other public advertisements. To deny her that right would be an improper restriction on commercial speech, the Court held.

Lower court decisions. Lawyers' ads have fared less well at the circuit court level. Appeals courts in recent years have upheld several state rules about attorney advertising: a Wisconsin state bar rule on the use of bar association fees to fund public image campaigns (*Kingstad v. State Bar of Wis.*, 622 F.3d 708, 2010, in the Seventh Circuit), a Texas state law that prohibits solicitation for legal services to accident victims for 30 days after the accident under the *Central Hudson* test (*McKinley v. Abbott*, 643 F.3d 403, 2011, in the Fifth Circuit), and, also using *Central Hudson*, parts of the Louisiana Rules of Professional Conduct that forbid attorneys from promising results, using pictures of non-clients and depicting them as clients, and using "a nickname, moniker, motto or trade name that states or implies an ability to obtain results in a matter" (*Public Citizen v. La. Attorney Discipline Bd.*, 632 F.3d 212, 2010, also in the Fifth Circuit; the court upheld parts of the rules that forbid testimonials to past success and portrayals of judges or juries, and that regulate font size and other formatting on ads).

Compelled Generic Advertising and the First Amendment

Still another advertising issue involving First Amendment rights was addressed in three U.S. Supreme Court decisions and several lower court cases in the 1990s and 2000s: mandatory assessments imposed on growers to pay for generic advertising of farm products. Some growers object to state and federal laws that force them to pay for advertising campaigns to which they object, preferring instead to advertise the unique qualities of their own products.

The U.S. Supreme Court in 2005 upheld *government-sponsored* advertising and marketing programs for which farmers and ranchers must pay. Ruling in *Johanns v. Livestock Mktg. Ass'n* (544 U.S. 550), a 6-3 majority said that a beef advertising program created by an act of Congress does not violate the First Amendment. Beef producers are assessed $1 per head of cattle to pay for advertising. Writing for the Court, Justice Antonin Scalia said, "Compelled support of government—even those programs of government one does not approve—is of course perfectly constitutional, as every taxpayer must attest."

The key to the *Johanns* decision is that the program was government-sponsored. It may resolve other challenges to mandatory advertising programs that were making their way through the courts. These challenges were encouraged when the Supreme Court earlier overturned a mandatory advertising program for mushrooms.

Regulatory marketing schemes. Ruling in 2001, the Supreme Court held that the mushroom advertising program violated the First Amendment. Ruling in *U.S. v. United Foods Inc.* (533 U.S. 405), the Court overturned a federal program (not actually run by a government agency) that required all mushroom growers to pay for generic advertising. United Foods, a Tennessee mushroom grower, objected, preferring to do its own advertising that emphasized the quality of its mushrooms as opposed to those grown elsewhere.

Writing for the Court, Justice Anthony Kennedy said that the advertising assessments constituted "compelled speech." He traced the history of prior cases involving such issues as government agencies forcing all workers to pay union dues used for political purposes in concluding that coerced speech is just as unconstitutional as a government ban on speech.

The *United Foods* decision was surprising to some because four years earlier, in 1997, the Supreme Court had *upheld* a California state program that required all growers to pay for generic product advertising (*Glickman v. Wileman Brothers & Elliot Inc.*, 521 U.S. 457). Justice Kennedy distinguished the 2001 decision from *Glickman* by pointing out that the growers in the earlier case were part of an association that had a *government-sponsored regulatory marketing scheme.* "In *Glickman*, the mandated assessments for speech were ancillary to a more comprehensive program restricting marketing autonomy. Here [for mushroom growers], for all practical purposes, the advertising itself, far from being ancillary, is the principal object of the regulatory scheme," Kennedy pointed out. So when can generic advertising be compelled? The *Glickman* and *United Foods* cases seem to suggest that such advertising is acceptable if it's one part of a larger regulatory marketing scheme, but not if it's the sole reason for the assessment of fees by a regulating body.

The Ninth Circuit found that a requirement that grape growers pay assessments levied by a California commission for generic advertising did not violate the First Amendment (*Delano*

Farms v. California Table Grape Commission, 586 F.3d 1219, 2009). Several growers alleged that the law "harmfully equate[d] all table grapes, by virtue of the 'generic' advertisements." The court relied on *Johanns* and found that the ads were government speech outside the First Amendment: "Because the Commission's activities are effectively controlled by the State of California, also rendering them government speech...the Commission's advertising activities are government speech and thus beyond the restraints of the First Amendment."

***Central Hudson* or *Zauderer*?** Two cases can guide a court's reasoning in compelled commercial speech cases: *Zauderer* (the attorney advertising case discussed earlier) and *Central Hudson.* In *Zauderer,* the high court did not apply the stringent *Central Hudson* test to a purely factual ad, and that case is often thought to be the primary precedent in compelled speech advertising cases. But courts may still sometimes select between the two tests.

The D.C. Circuit court said in 2014 that a Department of Agriculture rule mandating that meat be labeled with its country of origin violated the First Amendment. The country of origin label (COOL) "passport" requirement was challenged by American Meat Institution, a group of trade associations, alleging that the statute would fail under a *Central Hudson* analysis. A three-judge panel said the appropriate governing case was *Zauderer* because the COOL law "applies only to requirements that a commercial actor disclose factual and non-controversial information." Upholding the law, the panel said that it advances government goals in allowing consumers to make informed decision for meat purchases. However, the full circuit court reheard the case en banc, vacating the panel's decision and focusing on the question of whether *Central Hudson* or *Zauderer* should rule here (*Am. Meat Inst. v. Dep't of Agric.,* 760 F.3d 18). Agreeing that *Zauderer* was the appropriate case here, the full court said that *Zauderer* would indeed uphold the COOL law. Citing a long history of the appropriateness of COOL laws, the court said, "Simply because the agency believes it has other, superior means to protect food safety doesn't delegitimize a congressional decision to empower consumers to take possible country-specific differences in safety practices into account."

In another case questioning whether *Zauderer* or *Central Hudson* provided the appropriate test, *Safelite Group v. Jepsen* (764 F.3d 258, 2014), the Second Circuit invalidated a district court's use of *Zauderer* and instead applied *Central Hudson* to invalidate a Connecticut automotive glass work statute that forbade the mention by an insurance company of its affiliated repair shops unless it also named a competitor. This mandate raised the level of review, the court said, to a *Central Hudson* analysis. In fact, the court said, the law "prevents the speaker from making such disclosure by requiring advertisements for a competitor and thereby deters helpful disclosure to consumers. ...[T]he speech requirement here does more to inhibit First Amendment values than to advance them."

■ CORPORATE FREEDOM OF SPEECH

While the Supreme Court was extending some First Amendment protection to commercial speech, it also began to protect another kind of speech: *noncommercial corporate speech.*

A strong caseline. The Court took a major step in this direction in 1978, ruling that corporations also have First Amendment rights. In *First Nat'l Bank v. Bellotti* (435 U.S. 765), the Court overturned a Massachusetts law that forbade corporate advertising for or against ballot measures except when such a measure might "materially affect" a company's business. In reaching this conclusion, the Court emphasized the importance of a free flow of information, even when some information comes from corporations rather than individuals.

Massachusetts tried to defend its ban on corporate political advertising by arguing that corporations have so much money they could drown out other viewpoints if allowed to advertise. However, there was no evidence presented to prove that, and the court wasn't persuaded. Another problem with the Massachusetts law was that it allowed corporations engaged in mass communications (newspapers, television stations, etc.) to say anything they pleased on political issues, but that freedom was denied to other corporations. The Supreme Court said that, if anything, banks and other financial institutions might be better informed on economic issues than the media.

Thus, *Bellotti* was a major victory for corporate advertising. It didn't guarantee corporations any special right of access when the media refuse to accept their issue-oriented advertising (a problem discussed later in this chapter), but it did say that, where the media are willing to accept advertising from corporations, a state cannot prohibit it just because it comes from a company instead of an individual or a campaign committee.

As explained earlier, when the Supreme Court decided the *Central Hudson* case in 1980 (affirming the right of utility companies to advertise, even if the advertising might encourage energy use rather than conservation) the Court also handed down an important decision on noncommercial corporate speech: *Consolidated Edison v. Public Service Comm'n of New York* (447 U.S. 530). In that case, the Court said the New York Public Service Commission could not prevent utility companies from sending inserts with their bills that discussed "political matters" or "controversial issues of public policy."

Like the *Central Hudson* case, *Consolidated Edison* challenged rules adopted by the New York Public Service Commission in 1977. In this case, New York's highest court had held that the ban on inserts with bills was a reasonable regulation of the time, place, and manner of speech. The U.S. Supreme Court reversed the New York court on that point, ruling that the ban on bill inserts was an excessive restriction of corporations' First Amendment rights.

This was a major victory for corporate First Amendment rights. Unlike *Bellotti*, which came on a narrow 5-4 vote, this case was decided by a 7-2 majority—seven justices voted to uphold the right of corporations to speak out on the issues of the day. In addition, the Court set forth guidelines to determine whether future restrictions on corporate speech are valid.

Noncommercial corporate speech test. The Court noted the distinction between commercial advertising, in which a company seeks to promote sales of a product or service, and noncommercial corporate speech, in which a company expresses its views on controversial issues. When a government attempts to restrict noncommercial corporate speech, the Supreme Court established a more stringent test than the one applied to the regulation of commercial speech in the *Central Hudson* case. When noncommercial corporate speech is involved, government restrictions are justified only if *one* of these three conditions is met: (1) the restriction in question is a "precisely drawn means of serving a compelling state interest"; (2) the restriction is required to fulfill a "significant government interest" and just regulates time, place and manner, leaving open "ample alternate channels for communication"; or (3) there is a narrowly drawn restriction on speech under a few circumstances where disruption of government activities must be avoided, such as a military base.

In 1986, the Court again reaffirmed that corporations have First Amendment rights in *Pacific Gas & Electric Co. v. Public Utilities Comm'n of California* (475 U.S. 1). In this case, the Public Utilities Commission (PUC) had ordered PG&E, a large utility company, to insert a utility watchdog group's materials with consumers' utility bills in place of the company's own newsletter four times a year. The court held that the PUC order violated the First Amendment rights of the utility company. Four justices joined in a plurality opinion that said the company's newsletter "receives the full protection of the First Amendment." They said forcing the company to insert an outside group's material in place of its own is unconstitutional.

A fifth justice (Thurgood Marshall) agreed that the PUC could not force a utility company to insert notices from outside groups with utility bills, but he also said that corporate communications should *not* enjoy full First Amendment protection. And three other justices dissented, saying they would have allowed the PUC to require utility companies to insert the materials with utility bills.

This was, in short, a mixed victory for corporate First Amendment rights, delivered by a deeply divided Supreme Court. And corporate speech rights fared no better in a 1990 Supreme Court decision, *Austin v. Michigan Chamber of Commerce* (494 U.S. 652). Here, the Court affirmed a Michigan law that prohibited contributions to political candidates from the general treasury of a company or private association, while allowing contributions from special-purpose funds. The majority declared that this type of restriction on corporate speech does not violate the First Amendment, at least in part because it does allow corporations to endorse or oppose candidates through separate funds or political action committees. However, it is no longer good law; the Court explicitly overruled it in the 2010 *Citizens United* case that will be discussed later.

Public relations. The distinction between commercial speech and noncommercial corporate speech may have been blurred in a case the Supreme Court agreed to hear and then dismissed in 2003, *Nike v. Kasky* (539 U.S. 654). In that case, Nike, a manufacturer of shoes and athletic apparel, responded to criticism of working conditions at its overseas factories by issuing press releases, letters to the editor, and other corporate messages addressing the charges.

Nike was then sued by consumer activist Marc Kasky under California's false advertising law, disputing the truthfulness of the company's statements on this issue. A California appellate court held that Nike's statements were protected by the First Amendment and were not commercial speech. The California Supreme Court reversed that ruling and held that Nike's messages really were commercial speech because they were aimed in part at consumers who might buy more of the company's products if they believed the company's statements about working conditions at its factories. In *Kasky v. Nike Inc.* (27 C.4th 939, 2002), a 4-3 majority of the state supreme court ruled that the company's statements were not entitled to First Amendment protection and were instead subject to the false advertising law. Thus, Kasky would have a right to take his claims to trial.

The Supreme Court agreed to hear the *Nike* case but then dismissed it on the final day of the 2002-2003 term, apparently because a majority of justices decided the case should go to trial before being considered by the high court. That led to a dissent by Justice Stephen Breyer, joined by Sandra Day O'Connor, arguing that even postponing a ruling on this case would have a chilling effect on the First Amendment rights of other corporations that wish to speak out on controversial issues. Eventually Nike settled with Kasky, agreeing to pay about $1.5 million to a workers' rights group to monitor conditions in overseas factories.

Credit card "swipe fees." If a customer pays for something with a credit card, the merchant usually pays the credit card company for the service. These charges are called "swipe fees," and their costs are passed on to consumers. Several state laws said that companies couldn't tell consumers about the surcharges they were paying—but they could offer customers who pay cash a discount. The New York and Florida laws were challenged, and the circuits split:

commercial speech doctrine:
a limited level of First Amendment protection awarded to advertisements or speech that is intended to sell goods or services.

corporate speech doctrine:
corporations are considered entities entitled to some First Amendment protection; restrictions on that speech are acceptable only if one of the following are met: (1) the restriction is a "precisely drawn means of serving a compelling state interest"; (2) the restriction is required to fulfill a "significant government interest" and regulates only time, place, and manner, leaving open "ample alternate channels for communication"; or (3) the restriction is narrowly drawn and only applies to speech under a few special circumstances where disruption of government activities must be avoided.

quid pro quo:
Latin for "this for that"; often used in campaign finance law with "corruption" to indicate an unlawful exchange of money for privileges or favor.

the Eleventh Circuit said the Florida law unconstitutionally restricted speech about price information, while the Second Circuit said that the New York law only regulated commerce, not speech. The high court took the case to resolve the split.

In *Expressions Hair Design v. Schneiderman* (137 S. Ct. 1144, 2017), the Court said that the New York law regulated speech as well as commerce. Chief Justice John Roberts, writing for a unanimous Court, said the New York law regulates "how sellers may communicate their prices." And that was that: Roberts didn't bother to apply a test to the law; he remanded the case to the Second Circuit to determine the test and the constitutionality, noting that the Supreme Court is "a court of review, not of first view."

Justice Stephen Breyer concurred in the judgment but added that "virtually all government regulation affects speech" and that courts should steer away from a "speech or conduct" inquiry, relying instead on "whether and how a statute or rule affects a protected First Amendment interest." Justice Sonia Sotomayor, joined by Justice Samuel Alito, also concurred in the judgment, but she scolded the Court for its "quarter-loaf outcome," adding that the Second Circuit should have *certified the question* of how the law actually works to the New York Court of Appeals (the state's highest court)—specifically, she would have asked the state high court to answer the question "What pricing schemes or pricing displays does [the law] prohibit?"

What does this mean? There is still a hierarchy of First Amendment protection, depending on the nature and source of the message. Commercial advertising still enjoys less constitutional protection than idea-oriented or "editorial" advertising and similar forms of noncommercial corporate speech. But even noncommercial corporate speech enjoys something less than complete First Amendment protection, and the distinction between commercial speech and noncommercial speech is becoming less clear in the 2000s and beyond.

■ POLITICAL ADVERTISING LAW

The year 2010 saw a significant shakeup in campaign finance law. But the Court's decision in the controversial *Citizens United v. FEC* case did not arise in a vacuum. The Supreme Court has been considering campaign funding issues for decades.

Exacting scrutiny. Before getting into the Court's campaign finance cases, it's worth noting that the justices often use a slightly different type of judicial scrutiny for these cases. Called *exacting scrutiny*, it's been described by one legal scholar as "something like a substantial relationship between the challenged government regulation and a government interest that is somehow judged to be of sufficient importance."

How is that different from other levels of scrutiny? As discussed in earlier chapters, to get past strict scrutiny, the law must further a *compelling* governmental interest and must be *narrowly tailored* to achieve that interest. On the other hand, under intermediate (or heightened) scrutiny, the government's interest must be *important*, and the law must *be substantially related* to that interest. Relaxed or ordinary scrutiny (also known as rational basis) requires merely that the government have a *legitimate* interest that the law is *rationally related* to advancing. So exacting scrutiny falls somewhere between strict and intermediate scrutiny. Some have suggested that it falls closer to strict scrutiny; others say it's synonymous with strict. As we'll see, the Court provided an updated definition in 2021.

Campaign finance at the start. The Court's first serious foray into campaign finance regulation was in 1976, in *Buckley v. Valeo* (424 U.S. 1). Here, the justices held certain parts of the Federal Election Campaign Act of 1971 (FECA) unconstitutional, throwing out limits on the expenditure of a candidate's personal funds and on spending by independent entities. The justices also used exacting scrutiny for the first time: the *per curiam* (unsigned) opinion said that FECA should be judged on "whether the governmental interests advanced in its support satisfy the exacting scrutiny applicable to limitations on core First Amendment rights of political expression."

The First Amendment protection of corporate speech was a key factor in a 2007 Supreme Court decision that upheld the right of corporations, labor unions, and other entities to do issue advertising on television mentioning a candidate by name, free of campaign spending limits. In *FEC v. Wisconsin Right to Life* (551 U.S. 449), the Court overturned a portion of the Bipartisan Campaign Reform Act (BCRA, and popularly called the McCain-Feingold Act, replacing FECA) that prohibited issue advertising mentioning a federal candidate by name within 30 days of a primary election or within 60 days of a general election.

Congress enacted the McCain-Feingold Act in 2002 to curb abuses of "soft money" (unlimited, unregulated contributions by wealthy individuals, corporations, unions, and other entities to political parties as opposed to specific candidates). One provision was a ban on the use of soft money to fund "issue advertising" that may be heavily partisan and aimed at specific candidates. Earlier federal laws and similar laws in most states already limited the amount of money any individual or any entity may donate to a specific candidate.

Litigating McCain-Feingold. Under McCain-Feingold, money spent on television advertising referring to a "clearly identified candidate" is treated as a campaign contribution, subject to those limits. However, those restrictions do not apply to more general issue ads that don't refer to candidates, and in the 2004 election large contributions flowed into the coffers of independent organizations that were skirting the law by bankrolling advertising that didn't name any candidate. In 2003, the Supreme Court had upheld much of the McCain-Feingold Act, including key provisions affecting political advertising on television (*McConnell v. FEC*, 540 U.S. 93). The Court said then that the act was not unconstitutional on its face. Parts of *McConnell* were overturned in *Citizens United*, discussed below.

However, in 2007 a new 5-4 majority on the Supreme Court overturned the restriction on issue advertising that names candidates in *FEC v. Wisconsin Right to Life*. The Court held that entities spending this unregulated money have a First Amendment right to mention candidates in their issue advertising, even late in a campaign. The Court's lead opinion by Chief Justice John G. Roberts made a distinction between legitimate issue ads that mention a candidate and other ads that are "susceptible of no reasonable interpretation other than as an appeal to vote for or against a specific candidate." The latter fall within the McCain-Feingold Act's restrictions on "electioneering communications." Applying the test from the *Bellotti* case to this kind of issue advertising, the justices said corporate funding of ads that are really campaign ads can still be restricted, while the funding of ads that address an issue but mention a candidate is protected by the First Amendment.

What's the difference between *issue advertising* and *electioneering communications?* In the *Wisconsin Right to Life* case, the right-to-life group wanted to air ads urging citizens to contact the state's two U.S. senators and ask them to allow a Senate vote on several nominees for federal judgeships. One of the senators, Russell Feingold (who co-sponsored the McCain-Feingold Act), was running for re-election. The ads didn't specifically urge voters to support or oppose Feingold, but a lower court said the ads could be banned as electioneering communications. The Supreme Court majority disagreed and said such ads are constitutionally protected, even during an election campaign. The decision did not affect the other major provision of the McCain-Feingold Act, its limit on fund-raising for campaign advertising by political parties and political action committees. That part of the law is still valid.

In 2008, the Court voted 5-4 to overturn another feature of McCain-Feingold: a "millionaires' amendment" that allowed those running against a wealthy candidate spending a lot of personal funds to exceed normal contribution limits. The majority said this amendment violated the First Amendment right of candidates to use their personal funds by burdening them with otherwise unlawful excess gifts to opponents (*Davis v. FEC*, 554 U.S. 724).

The Federal Election Commission, which enforces the McCain-Feingold Act, issued regulations in 2006 that treat the internet far differently than broadcasting, largely exempting many internet postings from campaign advertising rules. In general, the FEC only regulates messages on the internet if they are actually paid advertising or paid fund-raising messages for a candidate. Other messages such as YouTube videos can be posted anonymously without even their production cost being treated as a campaign contribution.

The *Citizens United* case. In a landmark case with significant and far-reaching implications for campaign finance, the Supreme Court, in considering whether a film should be considered an "electioneering communication" in 2010, took the opportunity to eliminate restrictions on corporate campaign donations. At issue in *Citizens United v. FEC* (558 U.S. 310) was a film entitled *Hillary: The Movie*, a critical examination of then-Democratic presidential hopeful Sen. Hillary Rodham Clinton, made and distributed by Citizens United, a conservative Virginia nonprofit group. Citizens United wanted to show the film and ads promoting it, which included interviews and footage of Clinton at public appearances, during the election season. The group argued that the film was not "electioneering communication" because it didn't expressly recommend a vote against Clinton, but the district court said the film couldn't be interpreted as anything other than an encouragement to vote against her.

In a rare and surprising move, the Court did not issue an opinion in the *Citizens United* case in the 2008 term in which it heard oral arguments; instead, it reheard the case in September 2009, a month before the new term started. In one of the most eagerly awaited speech cases of the year, the Court shifted its perspective on campaign finance speech and regulation. It overturned two of its own precedents (parts of *McConnell* and all of *Austin v. Michigan Chamber of Commerce*, discussed earlier) and ruled that limits on corporate spending for political advertisements violated basic First Amendment principles that supply citizens and corporations with a fundamental right to engage in political speech.

Justice Anthony Kennedy, writing for the Court, said that the movie could *only* be considered to be corporately funded "electioneering communications" prohibited by a provision in McCain-Feingold. However, that provision was an unconstitutional infringement of the First Amendment rights that corporations share with citizens. In declining to decide the case narrowly without affecting McCain-Feingold, Kennedy wrote:

> We decline to adopt an interpretation that requires intricate case-by-case determinations to verify whether political speech is banned, especially if we are convinced that, in the end, this corporation has a constitutional right to speak on this subject. ...[T]he Court cannot resolve this case on a narrower ground without chilling political speech, speech that is central to the meaning and purpose of the First Amendment.

In a bitter dissent read from the bench, Justice John Paul Stevens soundly rejected the notion that corporations should have the same speech rights as people. "Corporations," he said, "have no consciences, no beliefs, no feelings, no thoughts, no desires." Speech funded by corporations has a great potential to drown out speech by citizens, he said, adding that citizens who believe that their government is controlled by corporations are unlikely to be engaged in the civic process:

> When citizens turn on their televisions and radios before an election and hear only corporate electioneering, they may lose faith in their capacity, as citizens, to influence public policy. A Government captured by corporate interests, they may come to believe, will be neither responsive to their needs nor willing to give their views a fair hearing. The predictable result is cynicism and disenchantment: an increased perception that large spenders "'call the tune'" and a reduced "willingness of voters to take part in democratic governance."

The justices left in place reporting and disclaimer requirements for independent expenditures and electioneering communications.

Impact of *Citizens United*. The *Citizens United* case has had significant repercussions in campaign finance law. The whole legal area is in flux as cities and states try to figure out whether their existing regulations are constitutional in the wake of the Court's holding.

There have been many cases heard in many courts since *Citizens United* was handed down in early 2010. For example, in a Washington case, the Ninth Circuit said that, based on *Citizens United*, the state's disclosure law, which "enables the public to 'follow the money' with respect to campaigns and lobbying," did not violate the First Amendment (*Human Life of Wash. v. Brumsickle*, 624 F.3d 990, 2010). The Ninth Circuit said that the City of Long Beach's anti-corruption rule that was intended to "reduce the influence of large contributors with a specific financial stake in matters before the City Council" had been narrowed by *Citizens United* to cover "*quid pro quo* corruption only, as opposed to money spent to obtain 'influence over or access to elected officials'" (*Long Beach Area Chamber of Commerce v. City of Long Beach*, 603 F.3d 684, 2010). The Ninth Circuit also upheld an injunction on San Diego's campaign finance regulations that restricted fund-raising and spending of independent political committees under *Citizens United* and *Buckley v. Valeo*; the court noted, almost with a sigh, that "the district court properly applied the applicable preliminary injunction standard in the context of the presently discernible rules governing campaign finance

FIG. 111.
Former Secretary
of State Hillary
Rodham Clinton
talking to President
Barack Obama,
aboard Air Force
One, April 2009.

*Official White House
Photo by Pete Souza,
April 28, 2009 via
Flickr.*

restrictions" (*Thalheimer v. City of San Diego*, 645 F.3d 1109, 2011). But the Eighth Circuit *upheld* a Minnesota law that prohibited direct contributions to candidates and their affiliated entities (*Minn. Citizens Concerned for Life v. Swanson*, 640 F.3d 304, 2011).

The Colorado Supreme Court struck down a state constitutional amendment limiting labor unions' abilities to contribute to political candidates. Amendment 54, which passed by a narrow margin, had made it illegal for companies or unions with government contracts that total more than $100,000 to contribute to candidates for state or local office (*Dallman v. Ritter*, 225 P.3d 610, 2010).

Citizens United continues to have a significant impact on the campaign finance world. In 2011 and 2012, no fewer than six circuits decided cases that turned on the Court's decision in *Citizens United*. An example: the Seventh Circuit in *Wisconsin Right to Life Political Action Committee v. Barland* (664 F.3d 139, 2011) overturned a Wisconsin law limiting the amount that individuals could contribute to state and local candidates, political parties, and political committees to $10,000 a year, writing, "*Citizens United* held that independent expenditures do not pose a threat of actual or apparent *quid pro quo* corruption, which is the only governmental interest strong enough to justify restrictions on political speech. Accordingly, applying the $10,000 aggregate annual cap to contributions made to organizations engaged only in independent spending for political speech violates the First Amendment."

The number of campaign finance challenges in the wake of *Citizens United* continues to grow. A few examples from 2012 and 2013: In the First Circuit, several unions challenged as unconstitutional Puerto Rican campaign finance laws amended after *Citizens United* (*Sindicato Puertorriqueño de Trabajadores v. Fortuño*, 699 F.3d 1, 2012). A district court denied the unions' request for an injunction; the appellate court said that the "burdensome" regulations placed on unions in the amendments would not survive strict scrutiny.

The Sixth Circuit rebuffed a challenge to Missouri's law limiting individual campaign contributions per election cycle. In *McNeilly v. Land* (684 F.3d 611, 2012), Greg McNeilly wanted to contribute more. He said that the government's interest in preventing *quid pro quo* corruption was important but that the rules for determining corruption had changed in *Citizens United*. The court disagreed: "However, while the Supreme Court in *Citizens United* held that the government has no anti-corruption interest in limiting independent expenditures, it left intact the government's interest in limiting *individual contributions* in order to prevent *quid pro quo* corruption or the appearance of such corruption."

In one district case of note, a federal district court found that a campaign consultant who produced an anonymous political website and was fined under Maine campaign finance laws had violated them (*Bailey v. Maine Comm'n on Gov'tal Ethics & Election Practices*, 900 F. Supp. 2d 75, 2013). Dennis Bailey, "well known" in state politics, created a website hostile to a gubernatorial candidate. He spent $91.38 on the site, just below the $100 state law threshold for reporting requirements. Bailey argued that the site was equivalent to the press, and thus exempt, and the judge disagreed, calling it more like "more like a negative campaign flyer": "The website was established for the sole purpose of advocating the defeat of a single candidate for election … by an individual working for an opposing candidate."

The Iowa post–*Citizens United* amendments fared somewhat better in the Eighth Circuit in *Iowa Right to Life Comm. v. Tooker* (717 F.3d 576, 2013). The court considered four arguments made by Iowa Right to Life (IRTL). Of particular note was the finding that one section, that bans direct corporate contributions to a candidate, a candidate's committee or a political committee, did not violate the First Amendment. IRTL argued that Iowa's interests in stopping *quid pro quo* corruption would justify limits, not bans, on these contributions, but the court said no, citing a 2003 Supreme Court case that "upheld a federal law banning direct corporate campaign contributions." This decision stood, the court said, post–*Citizens United*.

An amendment to the federal elections act, the DISCLOSE ("Democracy is Strengthened by Casting Light on Spending in Elections") Act, passed the House in 2010. The act, proposed to combat what some members of Congress saw as the dangerous ramifications of *Citizens United*, would require the head of the organization funding a political advertisement to appear on-camera (a "stand by your ad" requirement) and would require all corporations and advocacy groups to create campaign accounts to which donations of over $1,000 and all expenditures would be reported to the FEC. The bill failed to advance in the Senate and has been reintroduced several times, including in 2021. As watchdog organizations like the Sunlight Foundation put it, there must be enough political will to get DISCLOSE passed.

Supreme Court cases since *Citizens United*. But the U.S. Supreme Court was not through with campaign finance. In its first such decision since *Citizens United*, a divided Supreme Court overturned the Ninth Circuit and struck down an Arizona law providing escalating matching funds to candidates who accept public financing. In *Ariz. Free Enterprise Club's Freedom Club PAC v. Bennett* (564 U.S. 721, 2011), the Court reversed the Ninth Circuit's holding that the matching funds system was only a minimal burden and justified based on the desire to reduce *quid pro quo* corruption.

The Arizona matching funds law allowed candidates for state office who accept public financing to receive additional funds from the state—roughly dollar-for-dollar for those spent by opposing privately financed candidates, and dollar-for-dollar for those spent by independent groups supporting privately funded candidates. Relying on *Davis v. FEC*, the Court said that the state's justification of leveling the playing field was not sufficient to justify the matching scheme. Writing for the majority, Chief Justice John Roberts said, "'Leveling the playing field' can sound like a good thing. But in a democracy, campaigning for office is not a game. It is a critically important form of speech. The First Amendment embodies our choice as a Nation that, when it comes to such speech, the guiding principle is freedom—the 'unfettered interchange of ideas'—not whatever the State may view as fair."

Justice Elena Kagan, joined by Justices Ruth Bader Ginsburg, Stephen Breyer, and Sonia Sotomayor, dissented: "The First Amendment's core purpose is to foster a healthy, vibrant political system full of robust discussion and debate," she wrote, adding that "the

Act promotes the values underlying both the First Amendment and our entire Constitution by enhancing the 'opportunity for free political discussion...'" Rejecting the majority's claim that the matching scheme restricts speech, she added, "What the law does—all the law does—is fund more speech."

Critics continue to allege that the ruling was an open invitation for corruption and huge expenditures by corporations, but the Court signaled in 2012 that it wasn't yet ready to revisit the case. A divided Montana Supreme Court in *Western Trad. P'ship, Inc. v. Attorney General of Montana* (363 Mont. 220) said that *Citizens United* didn't apply to a 1912 state law that restricted spending on campaigns. Calling *Citizens United* a "crabbed view of corruption," the state supreme court said that the Montana law wasn't affected by the opinion because of the state's history and the differences between Montana's law and McCain-Feingold. Even one dissenter said that *Citizens United* was "smoke and mirrors" but believed that the court was bound to follow the dictates of a constitutional ruling by the high court.

The U.S. Supreme Court issued a one-page *per curiam* (unsigned) opinion without oral argument in 2012, *American Trad. P'ship, Inc. v. Bullock* (567 U.S. 516), stating that *Citizens United* did indeed apply to the Montana law, and the state had not advanced any meaningful distinctions to demonstrate why it should not. Four justices dissented. Justice Breyer, joined by Justices Ginsburg, Sotomayor, and Kagan, wrote, "Montana's experience, like considerable experience elsewhere since the Court's decision in *Citizens United*, casts grave doubt on the Court's supposition that independent expenditures do not corrupt or appear to do so."

The Supreme Court revisited campaign finance reform in 2014. In *McCutcheon v. FEC* (572 U.S. 185), the justices, led by Chief Justice John Roberts, struck down aggregate limits for individual donors. These aggregate limits were $46,200 per two-year cycle for candidates and $70,800 per two-year cycle for parties and PACs. Pointing out that the Court has recognized limits on campaign finance "to protect against corruption or the appearance of corruption," Roberts said that attempting to increase influence of and access to political actors and campaigns is "a central feature of democracy—that constituents support candidates who share their beliefs and interests, and candidates who are elected can be expected to be responsive to those concerns" and is not a form of corruption. Base limits, on the other hand, the maximum that any one person can contribute to a candidate, party, or PAC, are what Congress believed appropriate to combat corruption or its appearance.

Moreover, the chief justice added: "To put it in the simplest terms, the aggregate limits prohibit an individual from fully contributing to the primary and general election campaigns of ten or more candidates, even if all contributions fall within the base limits Congress views as adequate to protect against corruption." Then Roberts went on to suggest that First Amendment analysis should focus on the individual, rather than an aggregated public good recommended by the dissenters:

> [O]ur established First Amendment analysis already takes account of any "collective" interest that may justify restrictions on individual speech. ... [S]uch restrictions are measured against the asserted public interest (usually framed as an important or compelling governmental interest). ...[W]e do not doubt the compelling nature of the "collective" interest in preventing corruption in the electoral process. But we permit Congress to pursue that interest only so long as it does not unnecessarily infringe an individual's right to freedom of speech; we do not truncate this tailoring test at the outset.

Justice Clarence Thomas concurred only in the judgment, saying that he would rather override *Buckley* and subject BCRA's limits to strict scrutiny, which they would fail. In dissent, Justice Stephen Breyer, joined by Justices Ruth Bader Ginsburg, Sonia Sotomayor, and Elena Kagan, feared the creation of a loophole under which wealthy individuals could contribute millions, and he lamented, "Taken together with *Citizens United v. FEC*, today's decision eviscerates our Nation's campaign finance laws, leaving a remnant incapable of dealing with the grave problems of democratic legitimacy that those laws were intended to resolve." Corruption, said Breyer, is not just a *quid pro quo* problem. He also touted the importance of a First Amendment that protects not only individual speech but also collective speech, noting that it "advances not only the individual's right to engage in political speech, but also the public's interest in preserving a democratic order in which collective speech *matters.*"

Citizens United appeared again in court in 2014, questioning whether a film it made that included references to Colorado political candidates was exempt from Colorado campaign finance disclosure law (*Citizens United v. Gessler*, 773 F.3d 200). The film, entitled *Rocky Mountain Heist*, alleged negative impact on Colorado politics by various interest groups. A divided panel of the Tenth Circuit overturned a district court's holding that would have applied the state campaign finance disclosure laws and forced disclosures. The appellate court interpreted the state requirements to apply in this way: "[I]f *Rocky Mountain Heist* attacks or supports Colorado candidates, the production costs of the film must be disclosed, but a donation must be disclosed only if it was directed to be used solely to attack or support Colorado candidates. Money donated to Citizens United for general use need not be disclosed, nor would Citizens United be required to report a donation to be used, at Citizen United's discretion, for films attacking or supporting candidates in states including (but not limited to) Colorado."

However, the court did not exempt Citizens United from the laws in its advertising of *Rocky Mountain Heist*, saying that the film was no different than other media in this regard. The dissent alleged that the majority "makes a leap: it says that because Citizens United has the attributes of traditional media, Colorado must not have an important government interest in requiring disclosure from Citizens United."

The Supreme Court continues to take on political advertising and campaign finance cases. In a 2019 case involving an Alaskan law on political contribution limits, the justices said in *Thompson v. Hebdon* (140 S. Ct. 348) that the law may well be too strict, as it limited individual contributions to political candidates and to election groups other than political parties to $500 a year.

Both the district and Ninth Circuit upheld the limits as narrowly tailored to meet the state's desired goals. But the Court said that in some cases, states can set contribution limits too low, and that violates the First Amendment. Relying on a 2006 decision invalidating a similar Vermont law (*Randall v. Sorrell*, 548 U.S. 230, where the law set annual limits at $400 to a candidate for governor, lieutenant governor, or other state office, $300 to a state senatorial candidate, and $200 to a state representative candidate), the Court noted that "contribution limits that are too low can ... harm the electoral process by preventing challengers from mounting effective campaigns against incumbent officeholders, thereby reducing democratic accountability." The Ninth Circuit hadn't used Randall in its determination in this particular case, which involved even more stringent caps, said the justices, and remanded the case for a reevaluation under the 2006 precedent.

indemnification clause:
a clause in a contract that says that one party will hold the other harmless for any damages incurred.

Wheeler-Lea Amendment:
a 1938 amendment to the Federal Trade Commission Act authorizing the FTC to act against "unfair or deceptive acts or practices" that might mislead consumers.

Magnuson-Moss Act:
the 1975 federal law that covers product warranties and allows the FTC to act against fraudulent practices wherever they occur.

exacting scrutiny:
a level of judicial scrutiny, somewhat below strict but not well defined, usually used in campaign finance cases requiring a substantial relationship between a government regulation and a government interest of sufficient importance.

The uncertain state of disclosure laws. The 2010 *Citizens United* decision left state disclosure laws in place; as the Court put it, "Disclaimer and disclosure requirements may burden the ability to speak, but they 'impose no ceiling on campaign-related activities,' and 'do not prevent anyone from speaking.'" But these laws might no longer get such protection. In a 2021 decision (*Americans for Prosperity Found v. Bonta*, No. 19-251) with potentially significant consequences for state campaign donor disclosure laws, the justices struck down a California law requiring that nonprofit organizations give the names and addresses of their largest donors to the state attorney general by turning over Schedule B of its Form 990, information that must be filed by all nonprofits to the IRS.

The case was an aggregation of two cases brought by conservative groups Americans for Prosperity Foundation and the Thomas More Law Center—an organization that bills itself as a defender of "America's Judeo-Christian heritage and moral values." The groups refused to hand over their donors' information, citing concerns about privacy and safety. A district court found for the groups and enjoined the law, but the Ninth Circuit remanded for a bench trial. The district court again said the law was invalid—it wasn't being used to investigate fraud, as the state argued, and it burdened donors' association rights. The Ninth Circuit again disagreed, saying that the law survived a strict scrutiny examination because it was narrowly tailored to promote efficiency and didn't meaningfully burden the association rights of donors.

But the Supreme Court disagreed. A 6-3 majority said that the state simply didn't use the information the way it said it did. Writing for the Court, Chief Justice John Roberts said, "Given the amount and sensitivity of this information harvested by the State, one would expect Schedule B collection to form an integral part of California's fraud detection efforts. It does not. To the contrary, the record amply supports the District Court's finding that there was not 'a single, concrete instance in which pre-investigation collection of a Schedule B did anything to advance the Attorney General's investigative, regulatory or enforcement efforts.'" Finding that the state's use of the law was for administrative, rather than investigative, purposes, Roberts said that this use wasn't a good enough justification for the burden placed on donors' association rights. Rather, it was overbroad, and thus invalid. Nor did the Court provide a clear definition for exacting scrutiny; threading a line between the parties' arguments about what exacting scrutiny means, Roberts said, "While exacting scrutiny does not require that disclosure regimes be the least restrictive means of achieving their ends, it does require that they be narrowly tailored to the government's asserted interest."

The decision, as might be expected, drew a host of additional opinions that fell along ideological lines. Justice Clarence Thomas agreed with the outcome but questioned the Court's overbreadth doctrine in general, claiming that "the Court has no power to enjoin the lawful application of a statute just because that statute might be unlawful as-applied in other circumstances." Justice Samuel Alito, joined by Justice Neil Gorsuch, wouldn't have bothered to reach the scrutiny issue, as he thought the law failed under either exacting or strict scrutiny.

Justice Sonia Sotomayor dissented, joined by Justices Stephen Breyer and Elena Kagan. Saying that the majority opinion "marks reporting and disclosure requirements with a bull's-eye," she pointed out that the Court set aside its previous test for disclosure laws: the standard had been that to invalidate such laws, plaintiffs had to "prove that disclosure will likely expose them to objective harms, such as threats, harassment, or reprisals." But here, the plaintiffs offered no allegations of any harm. Rather, Sotomayor said, nonprofits can simply claim vague privacy concerns rather than offer evidence of real harm. The "narrowly tailored" requirement the majority imposed for disclosure laws was, she said, insufficiently flexible (in earlier cases, this standard was defined as "a 'substantial relation' between the disclosure requirement and a 'sufficiently important' governmental interest"). Sotomayor also pointed out what she saw as a disconnect between the types of individuals whose privacy the Court sought to protect. "The same scrutiny the Court applied when NAACP members in the Jim Crow South did not want to disclose their membership for fear of reprisals and violence now applies equally in the case of donors only too happy to publicize their names across the websites and walls of the organizations they support," she wrote.

Critics expressed fear that the decision laid the groundwork for all state disclosure laws to be invalidated. One commenter, writing for *Vox*, called the decision "a disaster for anyone hoping to know how wealthy donors influence American politics." But, as a representative for Independent Sector, a nonprofit organization with a focus on racial equity, put it, "The ruling protects diverse voices in our democracy, but also poses a significant challenge for preserving public trust in the nonprofit sector," adding that the decision didn't mean that donor data couldn't or shouldn't be collected. Disclosure laws must simply balance transparency, privacy, and First Amendment values differently.

■ ADVERTISING AND MEDIA ACCESS

Is there a constitutional right to place an ad in the media? Or may an advertiser buy space (or time, in the case of broadcasting) only if those who control the media are willing to accept the ad? To put it another way, is there any right of access to newspapers or radio and TV stations?

Different media, different access. The answer to these questions has traditionally been straightforward: there is *no* right of access to the print media for advertising purposes, and only a *limited* right of access to the broadcast media, mainly for political advertising. Even so, under certain circumstances, a right to advertise may exist—particularly if the rejected advertiser can show that the refusal to place the material fell within a pattern of unfair or monopolistic business practices. Also, under certain circumstances government-sponsored media cannot deny public access.

Courts have repeatedly ruled that newspapers have no obligation to carry anyone's commercial advertising. Several appellate decisions were setbacks for advocates of public access to the press, but an even greater defeat came in 1974, when the U.S. Supreme Court handed down its landmark decision on access to the print media. The decision, *Miami Herald v. Tornillo* (418 U.S. 241), overturned a Florida state law creating a limited right of access.

The case arose when Pat Tornillo, a Miami teacher's union leader, ran for the state legislature. The *Miami Herald* twice editorially attacked Tornillo. Tornillo demanded space for a reply. The law seemed to be on his side when he made this demand: Florida had a right-of-reply law requiring newspapers to publish replies when they editorially attacked candidates for office. The *Herald* turned Tornillo down and he sued, invoking the Florida law. The state supreme court ruled in his favor, and the newspaper appealed to the U.S. Supreme Court. The Supreme Court unanimously reversed the Florida ruling, affirming the newspaper's First Amendment right to control its content without government interference. Thus, the Court invalidated Florida's right-of-reply law.

Writing for the Court, Chief Justice Warren Burger said, "A responsible press is an undoubtedly desirable goal, but press responsibility is not mandated by the Constitution and like many other virtues it cannot be legislated." The First Amendment simply does not permit a government to tell a newspaper publisher what to print and what not to print, he noted. This case involved a state's attempt to dictate editorial content rather than advertising, but it affirmed the publisher's right to control the content of the entire publication; the ruling was not limited to the news side. In the years since *Tornillo*, courts have continued to reject any right of access to the editorial and advertising columns of newspapers and magazines except when there was evidence of unfair or monopolistic business practices.

What sort of monopolistic business practices would cause a court to force a newspaper to accept unwanted advertising? A good example is provided by a series of lawsuits challenging the classified advertising policies of the *Providence Journal* and *Providence Evening Bulletin*. These papers did not accept ads from rental referral services, a policy they defended as necessary to prevent fraud (*Home Placement Service v. Providence Journal*, 682 F.2d 274, 1982).

In a complex series of lawsuits, several rental referral services challenged this policy. They claimed it violated federal antitrust laws because the Providence papers enjoyed a virtual monopoly in their market and were, in fact, competitors of the rental services (both newspaper ads and rental referral services help people find housing). At first the federal courts upheld the Providence papers' policies as reasonable anti-fraud measures: they said the referral service challenging the policies was guilty of deceptive practices. However, in 1983 a federal appellate court ruled that the papers were violating antitrust laws by denying advertising space to this would-be competitor.

The point: a newspaper that enjoys a virtual monopoly in its service area (as many papers do) risks an antitrust lawsuit if it denies advertising space to someone whose business might be viewed as being in competition with the paper. However, aside from potential antitrust situations, both print and broadcast media are generally free to reject advertising if they wish. As Chapter Eleven explains, however, there are circumstances when broadcasters must accept advertising that the print media are free to reject. For example, broadcasters must accept political advertising in federal elections under Section 312(a)(7) of the Communications Act. Newspapers and magazines, on the other hand, may turn down all political ads or even accept ads for one candidate and not others.

Access to Government-Sponsored Media

Another exception to the rule that there is no mandatory access to the media involves government-run communications media. Under some circumstances, government-sponsored media have an obligation to be *viewpoint-neutral*, and that may involve accepting advertising that the staff might prefer to reject.

Starting in the 1960s, several state and federal courts recognized a limited right to advertise on city buses. When state action is involved, as it is here, courts sometimes ruled that authorities were constitutionally required to accept controversial advertising. For example, a federal New York court and a California state court both prohibited public transportation systems from denying space to advertisers whose ideas they disliked (*Kissinger v. New York City Transit Auth.*, 274 F.Supp. 438, and *Wirta v. Alameda-Contra Costa Transit District*, 68 C.2d 51.)

Supreme Court steps in. However, the idea that there should be any general right of access to state-run media was dealt a severe blow by a U.S. Supreme Court ruling, *Lehman v. Shaker Heights* (418 U.S. 298). In that 1974 decision, handed down the same day as *Tornillo*, the Court denied a political candidate's appeal for access to the ad space on a city bus line. The bus line's policy was to accept only commercial ads, not political ads, and the Supreme Court denied that the First Amendment creates any right to advertise even on government-run media such as this. Although the Supreme Court has repeatedly said city streets and parks, for instance, are "public forums" protected by the First Amendment, it refused to rule that ad space on city-run buses is automatically a public forum.

On the other hand, if a state-run communications medium rejects one candidate's ads while accepting others, the person whose ads are rejected may still have a case under the Fourteenth Amendment's "equal protection" clause, the court said. But in the *Lehman* case, all political ads were rejected; there was no discrimination, and the advertising acceptance policies were *viewpoint-neutral.*

Public forum? However, the problem of public access to a state-run communications medium sometimes takes a different perspective when the management creates a public forum by accepting some political and social issue ads while rejecting ads from those whose ideas it dislikes. A federal appellate court so ruled in a case involving the Washington, D.C., public transit system. In *Lebron v. Washington Metro. Area Transit Auth.* (749 F.2d 893, 1984), the court held that transit officials could not reject a photo montage critical of the Reagan administration by artist Michael Lebron after accepting a variety of other political ads.

In 1998, a federal appellate court reached the same conclusion when a public transit system rejected anti-abortion ads after accepting other ads concerning sex and family planning. In *Christ's Bride Ministries v. SE Pennsylvania Transp. Auth.* (148 F.3d 242), the court held that the transit system had created a public forum by its ad acceptance policies. Therefore, the court ruled that the transit system violated the First Amendment by rejecting an ad in which an anti-abortion group wanted to say, "Women Who Choose Abortion Suffer More & Deadlier Breast Cancer."

Focus on...
Miami Herald v. Tornillo, 418 U.S. 241 (1974)

Jerome Barron, who argued for access in the *Tornillo* case, claimed that media had become so large and monopolistic that it was difficult to access them.

The Court was not unsympathetic. Chief Justice Burger quoted Justice William O. Douglas on the dangers of monopoly ownership: "Where one paper has a monopoly in an area, it seldom presents two sides of an issue. It too often hammers away on one ideological or political line, using its monopoly position not to educate people, not to promote debate, but to inculcate in its readers one philosophy, one attitude—and to make money."

But that wasn't enough. Noting its sensitivity to "whether a restriction or requirement constituted the compulsion exerted by government on a newspaper to print that which it would not otherwise print," the Court rejected Barron's position.

On the other hand, if a government medium consistently accepts only commercial advertising and does not create a public forum for political and social issue ads, it can reject such ads. In *Children of the Rosary v. City of Phoenix* (154 F.3d 972), another 1998 decision, a federal appellate court upheld the right of a city-run bus system in Phoenix, Arizona, to reject anti-abortion advertising because the buses consistently carried *only* commercial advertising.

Similarly, the Sixth Circuit said that preventing a nonprofit organization from placing ads on the sides of city buses was *not* a First Amendment violation. In *Am. Freedom Def. Initiative v. Suburban Mobility Auth. for Regional Transp.* (698 F.3d 885), the organization AFDI wanted to put signs on buses that said, "Fatwa on your head? Is your family or community threatening you? Leaving Islam? Got Questions? Get Answers! RefugefromIslam.com." In finding that the decision by the transportation authority to refuse those ads was constitutional, the court said that the sides of buses were not public fora because the authority exercised "tight control over the advertising space and [had] multiple rules governing advertising content."

It is not easy to reconcile all of the varying court decisions involving the right to advertise in state-run media, but the prevailing rule since *Lehman* seems to be that there is no such right unless an agency of government accepts some ads of a certain type and then arbitrarily rejects other similar ads.

In 1995, the Supreme Court called new attention to this issue by ruling that Amtrak is a government agency for First Amendment purposes in *Lebron v. Nat'l Railroad Passenger Corp.* (513 U.S. 374)—another case involving artist Michael Lebron. Thus, when Amtrak rejected Lebron's proposal to purchase space for a political ad on "The Spectacular," a large billboard in New York City's Penn Station (controlled by Amtrak), that raised a First Amendment issue. The Court remanded the case to a lower court to conduct a First Amendment analysis and determine whether Amtrak as a government agency had any obligation to accept the billboard display. A federal appellate court reconsidered the case and said Amtrak's status as a government agency didn't change anything. In a brief opinion, the court concluded that the First Amendment was not violated because Amtrak had never accepted *any* political advertising for The Spectacular—and had no obligation to do so in the future. Therefore, Amtrak had the right to reject Lebron's display (*Lebron v. Nat'l Railroad Passenger Corp.*, 74 F.3d 371, 1995). As noted earlier, the Court ruled in *Lehman v. Shaker Heights* that even government-run media can reject political advertising as long as they do so consistently.

Billboards

Two billboard regulations were before the courts in 2010, and both were upheld. New York has billboard zoning regulations that prohibit the placement of billboards that do not advertise an on-premise business within 200 feet and within sight of major roads. Clear Channel Outdoor challenged those rules as an unconstitutional restriction on commercial speech. The Second Circuit applied the *Central Hudson* test and found that the regulation advanced the state's interest in public safety and aesthetics without burdening too much speech (*Clear Channel Outdoor, Inc. v. City of New York*, 594 F.3d 94, 2010).

Los Angeles' regulations similarly ban billboards located within 2,000 feet of and viewed primarily from freeways or on-/off-ramps; the rules also prohibit "supergraphics," multi-story vinyl ads that span across buildings. A supergraphics company brought suit, alleging that the regulations were unconstitutional (*World Wide Rush, LLC v. City of Los Angeles*, 606 F.3d 676, 2010), especially since the city bent its rules to allow signs at some locations. The court said the exceptions were intended to advance the city's interests in safety and beauty, and it has authority to create both regulations and exceptions, noting, "The First Amendment is not implicated by the City Council's exercise of legislative judgment in these circumstances."

Are advertisements for news products given the same protection as the news product itself? No, said the Ninth Circuit in *Charles v. City of Los Angeles* (697 F.3d 1146, 2012). A request by appellants to install a temporary sign advertising "E! News" without a permit was denied. The city ordinance requiring a permit was for temporary signs that don't have "a political, ideological or other noncommercial message." The Ninth Circuit agreed with the lower court, which said the sign was purely commercial.

Can a city ban billboards altogether? Maybe. A full ban on commercial billboards by a city may be justified if it is narrowly enough tailored and advances a substantial interest in traffic safety and aesthetics, said the Third Circuit (*Interstate Outdoor Adver. v. Zoning Bd. of the Twp. of Mt. Laurel*, 706 F.3d 527, 2013).

The high court will also take on a billboard case in its October 2021 term, *City of Austin v. Reagan Nat'l Advertising of Texas* (No. 20-1029). The justices will consider the constitutionality of an Austin ordinance that permits businesses to use digital billboards on their premises but not off-premises. Stay tuned.

■ FEDERAL ADVERTISING REGULATION

Beyond the issues of advertising access and commercial speech, advertising law is a field dominated by the Federal Trade Commission and, to an increasing degree, other federal agencies as well as state and local regulatory agencies.

FTC advertising regulation. Unquestionably, the FTC is the most important single regulatory agency for advertisers. Created by the Federal Trade Commission Act in 1914, this

Focus on...
Hillary: The Movie

The *Citizens United* case turned on whether federal campaign finance laws applied to a critical feature-length film about Sen. Hillary Clinton by a conservative nonprofit organization intended to be shown in theaters and on-demand to cable subscribers. The Supreme Court ultimately overruled some of its earlier jurisprudence and held that there could be no limits on independent political spending by corporations. The decision brought firestorms of controversy over whether the speech of ordinary citizens would be diluted by huge expenditures by large companies, or whether instead this was a huge win for free speech.

But what about the movie itself? Clinton appears in archive footage, and conservative commentators like Ann Coulter, Bay Buchanan, and Newt Gingrich were featured. Justice Anthony Kennedy, who wrote the majority opinion in *Citizens United*, summed it up best: "The movie, in essence, is a feature-length negative advertisement that urges viewers to vote against Senator Clinton for President. In light of historical footage, interviews with persons critical of her, and voiceover narration, the film would be understood by most viewers as an extended criticism of Senator Clinton's character and her fitness for the office of the Presidency."

FIG. 112. *Hillary: The Movie* DVD.
Author's collection.

independent federal agency is responsible for overseeing many kinds of business activities in America. The 1914 act said: "Unfair methods of competition in commerce are hereby declared unlawful; the Commission is hereby empowered and directed to prevent persons, partnerships, or corporations from using unfair methods of competition in commerce."

The FTC's initial mandate was to prevent unfair business practices—but only to protect other businesses. It was not at first given the job of protecting *consumers* from fraudulent business practices. Perhaps this was because of an old tradition in American advertising: *caveat emptor* (roughly translated "let the buyer beware").

For several centuries, that meant advertisers were free to flagrantly exaggerate the merits of their products. Newspapers in the 1800s were full of fraudulent advertising, most notably ads for patent medicine (an image of one appears in this chapter). These medicines were trumpeted as cures for everything from colds to cancer, although many had no medicinal value at all. The consumer who was deceived by this false advertising had few legal remedies under the common law; the only remedies available involved complicated lawsuits that were difficult to win. Most victims of advertising fraud had no choice but to accept their losses and vow not to be fooled again. But the FTC quickly made false advertising a main concern.

Early Supreme Court cases. By the 1920s, the majority of FTC enforcement actions involved advertising. The agency contended that false advertising was unfair to other businesses. For instance, in a famous case that went all the way to the Supreme Court, the FTC challenged a company that advertised clothing as "natural wool" when it was really only 10% wool. In *FTC v. Winsted Hosiery Co.* (258 U.S. 483, 1922), the Court agreed that false advertising is a form of unfair competition, since it diverts customers from honest merchants' products to those of dishonest competitors.

However, a few years later the Supreme Court curtailed the FTC's crusade against false advertising by ruling that the agency had no authority to act on behalf of consumers in the absence of evidence that the false advertising was unfair to a competing business. That happened in 1931, in *FTC v. Raladam* (283 U.S. 643). As a result, the FTC's powers were sharply reduced, but only temporarily. In two other cases during the 1930s, the Supreme Court upheld FTC actions against deceptive selling tactics (*FTC v. R.F. Keppel & Brother*, 291 U.S. 304, and *FTC v. Standard Education Society*, 302 U.S. 112). And in 1938, Congress enacted the *Wheeler-Lea Amendment*, authorizing the FTC to act against "unfair or deceptive acts or practices" that might mislead the consumer. Wheeler-Lea also expanded the FTC's enforcement powers.

The FTC operated under this enabling legislation until 1975, when its powers were again expanded by the *Magnuson-Moss Act*. That law specifically empowered the commission to act against fraudulent practices all the way down to the local level. No longer would it be limited to practices involving interstate commerce as it had been; instead, the FTC could pursue businesses that merely "affected" interstate commerce. In addition, Magnuson-Moss authorized the FTC to issue "Trade Regulation Rules," orders carrying the force of law that govern business practices in entire industries.

Under these broad new powers, the commission entered an unprecedented period of activism in the late 1970s, but some of its actions so angered many business leaders that they prevailed upon Congress to hold up the FTC's budget until the agency changed its policies. As a result, in 1980 the agency briefly had to lock its doors and cease all operations. Finally, it was given an operating budget, but with severe restrictions on its authority, in the Federal Trade Commission Improvements Act of 1980. The 1980s saw a much tamer

FTC in action, pursuing advertising fraud with far less enthusiasm than was true a decade earlier. By the 2000s, though, the FTC returned to a more aggressive posture in enforcing advertising rules.

FTC Procedures and Enforcement Tools

The Federal Trade Commission, like the Federal Communications Commission, is an independent regulatory agency. It is governed by a five-member commission, with an administrative staff of more than 1,000 persons. The five commissioners are appointed by the president with Senate ratification.

FTC deceptive ad analysis. How does the FTC go about the task of enforcing the rules against deceptive advertising? First, the FTC uses a three-part analysis to determine if a particular advertisement is deceptive: 1) Identify each affirmative claim or material omission and ask the advertiser to document what the ad says; 2) determine whether the claim could mislead a typical consumer acting reasonably; and 3) determine whether the claim is "material" (i.e., is it likely to affect purchasing decisions?). In deciding this, the FTC looks at the "net impression" created by an advertisement.

How does the FTC even locate advertising messages that may be deceptive? In addition to relying on complaints from consumers and competitors, the FTC does a lot of its own monitoring of the traditional media and, increasingly, the internet. Once what appears to be a widespread problem is identified, the FTC may conduct a *sweep*: a simultaneous law enforcement action targeting numerous businesses of a certain kind in a particular region. Often the FTC staff works closely with a state's attorney general in these actions. Investigators may "test shop" many businesses—or systematically surf the internet for a particular type of advertising that is under investigation. These sweeps often yield dramatic results—and send a message to others that the FTC is out there looking for false or misleading advertising.

Once the FTC decides an advertising message is unlawful and that formal action is warranted, the commission may use a variety of enforcement tools. Although most involve legal actions, the FTC's most effective means of controlling fraudulent advertising is often publicity. Since an advertiser's purpose is to persuade a segment of the public to buy or believe something, one of the worst things that can happen to an advertiser is to have the same media that carry the ads also publish news stories reporting that a government agency thinks the ads are false.

Enforcement powers. But beyond the clout of its press releases, the FTC has a variety of enforcement powers. The agency often acts on the basis of complaints from consumers or other businesses, but whatever the source of a complaint, the first step in an enforcement action is usually for the FTC to notify an advertiser that it considers his or her ads deceptive or misleading. The advertiser may be provided a copy of a proposed *cease and desist order*, along with supporting documents. Rather than face the lengthy and costly proceedings that lead to the issuance of such a decree, the advertiser may well choose to sign a *consent agreement*, agreeing to discontinue the challenged advertising without admitting any wrongdoing.

Even though this is an informal way to settle an FTC complaint, the consent agreement is placed in the public record. There is usually a 60-day period for public comment on it, after which the FTC may issue a *consent order*, which carries the force of law.

In some cases, the FTC is willing to let an advertiser merely sign an affidavit called an *assurance of voluntary compliance*. But under either this procedure or the more official consent order, the FTC usually negotiates with the advertiser to reach a settlement. The agency prefers to avoid its more formal proceedings when possible, not only to save staff time but also to halt the misleading advertising quickly enough to protect the public. A typical advertising campaign runs for only a few months; the entire campaign may be over long before the FTC can complete its formal proceedings.

However, if the advertiser refuses to sign a consent order, the agency may initiate formal proceedings. Those proceedings involve bringing the advertiser before an administrative law judge, who will hear both the commission's and the advertiser's arguments and issue a ruling. The commission has the right to review the judge's decision, and may issue a formal cease and desist order, which the advertiser may then appeal to a federal appellate court. Because these are civil proceedings, the defending advertiser isn't afforded the full rights available in criminal trials. For instance, an administrative law judge may decide the FTC is wrong and the challenged ads are perfectly legal. In a criminal trial, that would be an acquittal and would end the proceeding. But here, the FTC can rule that the ads are illegal and issue a decree anyway, ignoring the judge's findings. The advertiser has no recourse then, except to appeal the FTC decision to a federal appellate court.

Once a consent order or cease and desist order is in effect, the advertiser faces large civil penalties—sometimes $10,000 a day or more—for violating its terms.

In addition to these enforcement tools, the FTC uses several other procedures. For example, the FTC can bring a legal action against an advertiser in a federal district court, avoiding the delays inherent in the handling of cease and desist orders.

But the FTC can't always get money from companies who break the rules. In 2021, the Supreme Court unanimously said that the FTC Act did not allow the agency to ask for (or a court to award) monetary relief in cases where the agency bypassed administrative proceedings against a party and went right to court. The only remedies are temporary restraining orders or injunctions, wrote Justice Stephen Breyer for a unanimous Court (*AMG Capital Mgmt., LLC v. FTC*, No. 19–508). The FTC Act has two routes for proceeding against alleged violators: an administrative route (§45(b-c)) that allows for the recovery of money and a judicial route (§13(b)) that does not. Breyer looked at the text of §13(b) and said that taken as a whole, the language didn't offer the option of money. To read it otherwise, he said, "would allow a small statutory tail to wag a very large dog."

Advisory *Guides*, *Opinions*, and TRRs. Another option is for the FTC to publish purely advisory *Guides*. These pamphlets tell advertisers how the FTC interprets the law on a given point, such as the use of testimonials in advertising or product pricing. Violating a *Guide* is not a violation of law, but *Guides* are valuable to advertisers because they provide insight into the FTC's current thinking on various advertising practices. Another similar FTC action is to issue *Advisory Opinions*. Like *Guides*, they are voluntary, but they differ in that they are issued in response to inquiries from advertisers rather than on the commission's own initiative.

A similar policy guideline—but carrying the force of law—is called a *Trade Regulation Rule* (TRR). These rules generally apply to an entire industry, requiring specific advertising practices and forbidding others. The liberal use of TRRs was largely responsible for Congress' action to limit the FTC's authority in 1980.

During the 1970s, the FTC also launched another major effort to control ad fraud, this one through an *Advertising Substantiation Program*. In this program, the FTC required certain industries to document all claims in their ads, something that produced voluminous and technical reports in some cases.

FIG. 113.

Ad for Sperry &
Hutchinson Green
Trading Stamps, *Ariz.
Republic*, Apr. 27, 1910.

Fun facts from the *Sperry*
Court: In 1964, S&H had
40% of the trading stamp
business which issued
400 billion stamps in
over 200,000 stores in
connection with $400 billion
in sales, and over 60% of all
U.S. consumers saved S&H
Green Stamps.

Library of Congress.

Corrective ads and affirmative disclosures. Two of the FTC's more controversial approaches to enforcement have been *Affirmative Disclosure Orders* and *corrective advertising*. Affirmative disclosure involves requiring the advertiser to reveal the negative as well as the positive aspects of a product. In a pioneering case of this sort, a federal appellate court upheld an FTC order aimed at the makers of Geritol. Geritol was advertised as a "tired blood" cure for the elderly, and the manufacturer was ordered to reveal that it did little to help people with certain kinds of anemia (*J.B. Williams Co. v. FTC*, 381 F.2d 884, 1967). The FTC required hundreds of advertisers to reveal similarly negative facts about their products after this decision. Many advertisers found these requirements onerous and embarrassing, but corrective advertising angered the business community even more. Probably the most famous FTC corrective advertising order was one aimed at Warner-Lambert Company, maker of Listerine mouthwash. For nearly a century, Listerine had been advertised as a cure for colds and sore throats, a claim that medical research did not support.

The FTC ordered Warner-Lambert not only to spend $10 million on advertisements admitting that Listerine would not cure sore throats but also to preface the correction with the phrase, "Contrary to prior advertising." Warner-Lambert appealed the FTC ruling, but the federal appellate court affirmed the corrective order—although it did agree that saying "contrary to prior advertising" was too much penance. Warner-Lambert was allowed to run its corrective ads without that confession of past sins (*Warner-Lambert Co. v. FTC*, 562 F.2d 749, 1977). The Supreme Court denied *cert.*

The FTC has issued a number of other corrective advertising orders, including one that required the makers of STP oil additive to publish ads telling the public its claims that STP would reduce auto oil consumption were based on unreliable road tests.

The FTC required a petroleum company to do corrective advertising in 1997. The Exxon Corporation settled a complaint by agreeing to run TV ads informing consumers that its most expensive premium grade of gasoline does not keep engines cleaner or reduce maintenance costs. Exxon had aired ads claiming its Exxon 93 Supreme gas "has the power to drive down maintenance costs" and "keeps your engine cleaner." In fact, all grades of Exxon gas contained the same engine-cleaning additives, which are similar to those in many other brands of gas, the FTC noted. While agreeing to do corrective advertising in 18 major markets, Exxon did not admit any wrongdoing in connection with its previous advertising.

The FTC ordered corrective advertising in another field in 1999, directing the manufacturer of Doan's back-pain medicine to spend $8 million on ads including the words, "Although Doan's is an effective pain reliever, there is no evidence that Doan's is more effective than other pain relievers for back pain." The FTC took this action because Doan's manufacturer, Novartis, and its predecessor, Ciba-Geigy Corp., spent about $65 million over a 20-year period on advertising claiming that Doan's was better for back pain than other pain relievers—a claim that could not be substantiated.

In 2000, the Bayer Corporation agreed to spend $1 million on consumer education to settle FTC charges that it made unsubstantiated claims in its aspirin ads. Bayer ads said that aspirin will prevent heart attacks and strokes without explaining that some persons may not benefit or may actually be harmed by an aspirin regimen. Bayer agreed to give free brochures to consumers to correct its advertising, and to do print ads to tell consumers of the availability of these brochures.

Other Examples of Enforcement Actions

In addition to cases involving various forms of penance by advertisers, the FTC has acted against thousands of advertising campaigns that the agency considered to be false, misleading, or deceptive. A few examples illustrate the FTC's approach to advertising regulation.

Mockups. Perhaps the best-known FTC case for many years, in part because it produced a U.S. Supreme Court decision, was the "sandpaper shave case," *FTC v. Colgate-Palmolive Co.* (380 U.S. 374, 1965). In one of the most famous television ads of the era, Colgate-Palmolive Rapid Shave was shown shaving the sand off sandpaper. The only problem was that what the viewer really saw was sand being scraped off a transparent plastic sheet. The FTC contended that this was deceptive and ordered the ads halted. Colgate-Palmolive chose to fight the order and set out to prove that the sand really could be shaved off a sheet of sandpaper. The company did it, but it took a little longer in real life than in the ads: about 90 minutes.

The Supreme Court eventually upheld the FTC's conclusion that the ad was deceptive. In so ruling, the Court did not say that *all* TV mockups are deceptive. But, the Court said, mockups that are central to the point of the ad or enhance the product are deceptive. A common industry practice was to use mashed potatoes in place of ice cream because of the heat generated by television lighting. The Court used that mockup to explain its point. Perhaps showing actors eating ice cream that was really mashed potatoes would not be deceptive if the point of the ad was to promote something else, but it would be deceptive if the point was to sell the ice cream by showing its rich texture and full color, the Court said.

In the years since *Colgate-Palmolive*, the FTC has acted against a variety of advertising practices. The FTC has gone after advertisers who used a number of other mockups, mockups that hardly seem as deceptive as the Rapid Shave commercial. In one Lever Brothers commercial for All detergent, an actor was shown standing in a huge washing machine with a stain on his shirt. The water rose to his neck and then receded—and the stain vanished. The FTC said it was deceptive, since the whole process couldn't really happen that fast.

Often the FTC has based its complaints on ads that were literally true but nonetheless deceiving. As early as 1950 the commission acted against a cigarette manufacturer for advertising that a study found its brand lower in tar and nicotine than others tested. That was true, but the study also concluded that all brands tested were dangerously high in tar and nicotine. The ads were literally true but still misleading, the FTC said.

Testimonials. The FTC has also expressed interest in misleading testimonials, requiring that celebrities who endorse products actually use them, and that "experts" who give endorsements must really be experts. Moreover, the claims users make in endorsements must in fact be verifiably true. A grass-roots or "plain folks" ad cannot have someone saying he gets 50 miles per gallon from his Guzzlemobile Diesel when tests indicate it won't deliver over 40. In fact, an ad in which "Mrs. Holly Hollingsworth" of "Guzzle Gulch, Nevada" endorses a product must actually show Mrs. Hollingsworth, not an actress portraying her.

In 1978, the commission acted against entertainer Pat Boone for what the FTC considered to be a misleading endorsement of a skin-care product. The FTC accused the manufacturer, the advertising agency, and Boone of participating in false and misleading advertising. The FTC charged that the product would not cure acne as the ad implied it would. The commission sought a $5,000 penalty from Boone, and he signed a consent order agreeing to pay the $5,000 into a fund to compensate customers who were misled by the ad.

This action, the first to hold a celebrity accountable for a misleading endorsement, was a major shock to other celebrities who endorse products. After the Boone incident, virtually all celebrities demanded *indemnification clauses* in their endorsement contracts. (Indemnification means the advertiser must pay any penalty the celebrity may incur because of the ad.)

If a celebrity is not aware of the falsity of an endorsement, he or she may escape liability. The FTC launched an enforcement action against former baseball star Steve Garvey and Enforma Natural Products for false weight-loss claims in infomercials and other advertising. Enforma had income of at least $100 million from sales of its products between 1998 and 2000, and Enforma eventually paid $10 million in penalties for making false claims about its products. However, a federal court rejected the FTC's action against Garvey, ruling that because he and his wife had tried the products and actually lost weight, he was unaware of the falsity of the scripts he read. In 2004, the FTC appealed that decision and the Ninth Circuit upheld the ruling in Garvey's favor (*FTC v. Garvey*, 383 F.3d 891).

Comparison ads. Like testimonials, comparison advertising has attracted the FTC's attention. Traditionally, advertisers have hesitated to criticize each other's products, partly out of fear of lawsuits and partly because industry self-regulation codes discouraged the practice. But in 1979, the FTC issued a policy statement demanding that the advertising industry and broadcasters drop their restrictions on comparative ads and calling on advertisers to compare their products "objectively" against competing brands by name.

"Unfairness Doctrine." The FTC's definition of what it considers *unfair advertising* was summarized in a 1994 policy statement. An advertisement is unfair if it: (1) causes or is likely to cause substantial consumer injury; (2) which is not reasonably avoidable by consumers themselves; and (3) is not outweighed by countervailing benefits to consumers or competition. The FTC's authority to act against ads that are "unfair" was affirmed by the U.S. Supreme Court in 1972 in *FTC v. Sperry & Hutchinson Co.* (405 U.S. 233). The Court said the FTC has the power to act against "business practices which have an unfair impact on consumers, regardless of whether the practice is deceptive...or anti-competitive in the traditional sense." Sperry & Hutchinson (S&H) issued S&H Green Stamps from 1896 until the 1980s which could be collected through purchases from participating stores and pasted into booklets, which could then be redeemed for products from an S&H store or catalog. The FTC said that S&H violated Section 5 of the Federal Trade Commission Act by suppressing trading stamp exchanges. S&H responded by asserting that the FTC Act didn't give the agency the power to regulate it that way; the FTC could only regulate practices that were "in violation of the antitrust laws, deceptive, or repugnant to public morals."

The FTC lost the battle but won the war: the Court said that S&H wasn't engaging in any illegal activity, but, more importantly, Section 5 of the FTC Act did allow the agency to regulate unfair and deceptive acts and practices. Congress, the Court explained, when drafting the FTC Act, "explicitly considered, and rejected, the notion that it reduce the ambiguity of the phrase 'unfair methods of competition' by tying the concept of unfairness to a common-law or statutory standard or by enumerating the particular practices to which it was intended to apply." Thus, the justices said, the phrase could be widely applicable.

The FTC also used its authority during this era to issue Trade Regulation Rules to ban allegedly unfair practices in various industries. These campaigns stirred bitter opposition among businesses and eventually in Congress. For example, in 1978 the agency initiated a controversial proposal to severely restrict TV advertising aimed at children. The proposed restrictions would have completely banned advertising aimed at young children and prohibited ads for sugared food products targeted to older children.

In addition, the FTC proposed rules forcing funeral directors to list all their prices and service options, as well as rules requiring used car dealers to inspect the cars they sell and post a list of mechanical problems on each car. On other occasions, the commission acted to break up Sunkist Growers, an agricultural cooperative, and launched campaigns against various trademarks, seeking to take them from their owners and have them declared generic words. The FTC also issued rules requiring trade and vocational schools to provide a great deal of information to incoming students and let them withdraw with a prorated tuition refund during their programs.

The FTC's policy on corrective advertising angered the advertising profession. The extensive use of the Unfairness Doctrine against advertisers intensified that feeling, as did the move to ban children's television advertising. Pertschuk's public pronouncements further united the business community. Finally, the rules aimed at morticians, used car dealers, the Sunkist cooperative, and trade schools were the FTC's undoing.

FTC Improvements Act. Responding to nationwide protests about the FTC's regulatory zeal, Congress refused to appropriate a budget for the agency in 1980 and then enacted the restrictive *Federal Trade Commission Improvements Act.* This law extended the FTC's funding for three more years, but at a high price. It temporarily prohibited the FTC from acting against advertising that is only "unfair" but not deceptive or misleading. Responding to the industry's complaints and to the Court's rulings extending First Amendment protection to advertising, Congress declared that FTC actions should not be aimed at truthful advertising.

In addition, the 1980 act halted the FTC proceeding on children's television until the commission published a new specific proposal aimed only at "deceptive" advertising, and ordered the FTC to publish the text of every proposed new rule at the start of the rule making proceeding. The FTC eventually terminated its study of advertising aimed at children in 1981 without taking any action.

The 1980 act specifically set aside the FTC's actions involving morticians and agricultural cooperatives such as Sunkist Growers (although the FTC later adopted extensive regulations concerning advertising by morticians). Moreover, the agency was ordered to give Congress advance notice of new proposed rules. The 1980 law also declared that Congress would have the power to veto future FTC regulations. Finally, the FTC was ordered to reduce the paperwork burden on businesses and to stop trying to invalidate businesses' trademarks.

FIG. 114.
Cover of the 2019 "Disclosures 101" brochure from the Federal Trade Commission.

This document provides FTC guidance on how and when to disclose endorsement relationships. If you review products and have special relationships or arrangements with companies to get products to review, you need to inform people of those relationships.

Federal Trade Commission (downloadable from ftc.gov/influencers).

Taken as a whole, these revisions constituted a substantial curtailment of the FTC's power. Business interests lobbied heavily in Congress to harness the FTC; their campaign happened to fit in with the mood of the times. Certainly, popular distaste for government regulation was a factor in Ronald Reagan's decisive victory in the 1980 presidential election. In the years that followed, Congress repeatedly debated the merits of the Unfairness Doctrine—and eventually allowed the FTC to act against unfair advertising again.

Congress exercised its power to veto FTC regulations in 1982, overturning the FTC's long-awaited rules requiring auto dealers to disclose known defects in used cars. However, later that year a federal appellate court ruled that Congress did not have the right to give itself this veto power. In 1983, the Supreme Court agreed, ruling in an unrelated case: *Immigration & Naturalization Service v. Chadha* (462 U.S. 919). With that one ruling, the high court invalidated some 200 different laws that gave Congress the power to veto actions taken by agencies in the executive branch of the federal government.

The Appropriate Role of the FTC

The proper role of the Federal Trade Commission has long been a subject of ongoing Congressional debate. By the early 1990s, the FTC had abandoned the non-regulatory posture it assumed during the 1980s, and Janet Steiger, the FTC chair in the first Bush administration, declared that henceforth the FTC would take a more aggressive posture in enforcing the advertising laws. She said the FTC wanted to eliminate the public perception that the agency was no longer interested in fighting false and misleading advertising.

The agency followed through. By 2000, the FTC was nearly as aggressive as it had been in the 1970s, launching hundreds of regulatory actions against advertisers every year. The agency was especially targeting advertisers who made questionable environmental claims and false, misleading, or unfair advertising that might appear on the internet.

By the 1990s, the FTC was again aggressively pursuing advertisers who were allegedly guilty of misleading consumers. For example, in 1993 the commission launched a highly publicized effort to stop five of the nation's largest commercial diet programs from engaging in deceptive advertising. The FTC said the weight-loss firms had to include in their advertising disclaimers such as: "For many dieters, weight loss is temporary," or "This result is not typical. You may be less successful."

Three of the five firms signed consent decrees agreeing to comply with the FTC's demands. The other two, Jenny Craig and Weight Watchers, engaged in protracted legal battles against the FTC. Weight Watchers won a minor victory against the FTC in 1994 when a federal appellate court ruled that the company could sue the FTC to challenge the agency's enforcement policies for the weight-loss industry. Weight Watchers charged the FTC with changing its rules governing weight-loss advertising on a case-by-case basis instead of conducting a formal rule making proceeding (*Weight Watchers Internat'l v. FTC*, 47 F.3d 990).

At almost the same time as its actions against weight-loss programs and the Eskimo Pie Corp., the FTC sought a $2.4 million civil penalty against General Nutrition Inc., the operator of about 1,500 GNC stores. GNC was accused of violating previous consent orders by making unsubstantiated claims about various health-oriented products. GNC eventually signed a consent decree in which it agreed to pay the $2.4 million penalty and stop making unsubstantiated health claims for its products.

Weight-loss claims. In 2002, the FTC launched a new initiative against misleading weight-loss claims. This time, it called on the media to reject both conventional advertising and infomercials that include implausible claims of miracle weight loss. The FTC released guidelines for the media to follow in evaluating such claims. That caused several media and First Amendment lawyers to protest, citing the right of the media to publish advertising without first evaluating the accuracy of each ad. In 2007, the commission fined the makers of four other weight-loss products a total of $25 million. The FTC accused the four, Xenadrine EFX, CortiSlim, One-A-Day WeightSmart, and TrimSpa, of false and misleading advertising.

The FTC continues to be concerned about false weight-loss claims. In 2011, the agency upheld a $37.6 million award against Kevin Trudeau for disobeying settlement agreements on advertising the content of his book, *The Weight Loss Cure "They" Don't Want You to Know About*. Trudeau argued that the fine should not be calculated against the amount of consumer loss, but the Seventh Circuit disagreed. Moreover, the court added, "The government is not impotent to protect consumers—nor is the court powerless to enforce its orders—by imposing narrowly tailored restrictions on commercial speech" (*Trudeau v. FTC*, 662 F.3d 947). The FTC may not be able to catch every phony weight-loss advertiser, but established advertisers may face costly penalties even for advertising that could be misleading but isn't false. In 1999, the Mazda Corporation agreed to pay $5.25 million in fines and civil penalties alleged violations of an earlier FTC order requiring the car maker to disclose the terms of its car and truck leases in its print and television advertising. Among other things, the FTC concluded that the disclosures were in small and unreadable print, offset by distracting images and sounds, and on screen for too short a time.

The FTC has taken other initiatives in the area of obesity and weight loss. The agency issued a report in 2006 urging the food industry to better address the problem of childhood obesity. Although voluntary, the guidelines could lead to new regulations. Among other things, the FTC urged advertisers to make sure foods advertised to children meet minimum nutritional standards. The FTC also called for marketing that better educates consumers about nutrition and fitness.

There have also been FTC actions in health care. For example, POM Wonderful markets pomegranate juice, and many of its ads made claims about its health benefits. An administrative judge said that without substantiation, POM cannot claim that its juice cures *anything*. The judge wrote a 345-page decision saying POM ads would result in some consumers believing that drinking POM "treats, prevents or reduces the risk of heart disease," or treats prostate cancer or erectile dysfunction (*In the Matter of POM Wonderful LLC*, No. 9344, 2012)— when there is no data to suggest that. The FTC issued a final order in 2013, saying that POM could not "make any representation ... that such product is effective in the diagnosis, cure, mitigation, treatment, or prevention of any disease." (But POM won at the Supreme Court; see POM's Lanham Act win later in this chapter.)

The FTC is also cracking down on mobile apps claiming health benefits. For example, in 2012 the agency said that claims that apps "AcneApp" and "Acne Pwner," which its owners claimed would cure acne with pulses of light from a smart phone, would actually cure acne were unsubstantiated. The FTC fined the companies, marking the first time that the agency targeted health claims in the mobile app market.

The agency also provides a website to help consumers navigate the sometimes-complex world of health and weight-loss products and services, among others. (Check out www.consumer.ftc.gov/articles/0061-weighing-claims-diet-ads.) The FTC also offers a media reference guide called "Gut Check" to help determine when a weight-loss ad is making deceptive claims. Included in the list of seven statements are "causes weight loss of two pounds or more a week for a month or more without dieting or exercise" and blocks the absorption of fat or calories to enable consumers to lose substantial weight." The FTC encourages media companies: "If one of these seven claims crosses your desk, do a gut check" before running the ad. The guide can be found on the FTC's website (www.ftc.gov/tips-advice/business-center/guidance/gut-check-reference-guide-media-spotting-false-weight-loss).

The FTC released industry-wide regulations to prevent false or misleading "green" or environmental advertising claims. Among other things, the new rules require those who claim a product has "recycled content" to document the amount that really is made from recycled materials. The rules also prohibit the use of terms such as "ozone safe" or "ozone friendly" if the product contains any ozone-depleting chemical, and they ban the use of terms such as "biodegradable" to describe products that will not degrade quickly when buried in a landfill.

What about claims that consumers can save "up to" a percent or a dollar figure if they do as the ad suggests? In 2012, the FTC released a study that suggested that consumers don't really read the "up to" part of the ad. Between 36 and 45.6% of consumers who saw an ad containing the words "Proven to Save Up to 47% on Your Heating and Cooling Bills" thought that this meant that they would actually save 47% on their bills. The agency said that this means that advertisers who use "up to" claims need to demonstrate that most of the time, consumers will get to that number.

The FTC, "Joe Camel," and Cigarette Advertising

One of the most controversial advertising campaigns in American history involved "Joe Camel," R.J. Reynolds' cartoon character used to promote the Camel cigarette brand. "Old Joe," or "Smokin' Joe," as his fans sometimes called him, first appeared in European advertising for Camel cigarettes during the 1970s. A massive "Old Joe Camel" campaign was launched in the United States in 1988—and drew immediate fire from critics of the tobacco industry. Their main claim: "Old Joe" unfairly targeted underage smokers.

Before the controversy ended, the entire tobacco industry was fighting new restrictions on cigarette advertising from coast to coast—restrictions that ultimately led to a Supreme Court decision overturning state and local laws regulating cigarette ads: *Lorillard Tobacco Co. v. Reilly* (discussed earlier).

During the mid-1990s, the FTC spent several years trying to decide how to deal with cigarette advertising, and particularly how to handle "Old Joe Camel." In 1994, the FTC voted 3-2 not to pursue an unfair advertising complaint against "Old Joe." But three years later, the FTC voted 3-2 to reverse itself and bring legal action to halt the "Old Joe" campaign.

This strange case began after the attorneys general of 27 states jointly asked the FTC to halt the ads, contending that the "Old Joe" campaign resulted in a huge increase in smoking among teenagers. They argued that this cartoon camel—this "debonair dromedary"—was enormously appealing to teenagers. In refusing to halt the "Old Joe" ad campaign in 1994, a deeply divided FTC decided that R.J. Reynolds was targeting young adults rather than teenagers and that, in any case, the company had a First Amendment right to use this cartoon character. In reaching that conclusion, the FTC's 3-2 majority rejected the recommendation of its own staff, which contended that "Old Joe" did encourage underage smoking.

By 1997, however, the public mood had changed. Cigarette manufacturers were on the defensive everywhere. And there was far more evidence that cigarette makers had indeed set out to target teenagers. The FTC then reconsidered the "Old Joe" issue and voted 3-2 (with two new commissioners in the majority) to launch a legal action designed to banish "Old Joe" as an unfair advertising image that improperly targeted underage smokers. The FTC not only voted to ban "Old Joe" but to order R.J. Reynolds to run a corrective advertising campaign to combat underage smoking.

The FTC ultimately dropped its civil lawsuit against R.J. Reynolds after the tobacco industry reached its landmark $206 billion settlement with 46 states. The industry agreed to end billboard advertising, to stop using cartoon characters, and to refrain from targeting underage smokers. The industry also agreed to compensate the states for some health costs associated with cigarette smoking. (The other four states—Mississippi, Texas, Florida, and Minnesota—reached a separate $40 billion settlement with the tobacco industry earlier.)

In 2003, a global anti-tobacco-advertising treaty backed by the World Health Organization was approved in Geneva, Switzerland, by delegates from 40 nations. By 2005, 57 nations had ratified the treaty, but not the United States. Under this treaty, all signing countries are required to ban tobacco advertising and event sponsorships within five years.

The Supreme Court said in 2008 (*Altria Group v. Good*, 555 U.S. 70) that the Federal Cigarette Labeling and Advertising Act doesn't preempt state law deceptive practice claims in connection with the advertising of cigarettes as "light" or containing "lower tar and nicotine." Neither the act nor the FTC's actions in this field preempt a state-law fraud claim. But the Second Circuit struck down a New York City Board of Health's mandate that tobacco sellers must display graphic anti-smoking signs, saying this area of law *is* federally preempted by the act (*23-34 94th St. Grocery v. N.Y.C. Bd. of Health*, 685 F.3d 174, 2012).

Other Federal Regulators

Although the Federal Trade Commission has primary responsibility for regulating advertising on the federal level, other federal agencies also have responsibilities in this area.

The FDA: Food and drugs. Under the Food, Drug, and Cosmetic Act of 1938, the Food and Drug Administration is responsible for ensuring the purity and safety of foods, drugs, and cosmetics. One of the FDA's major duties is to act against false and fraudulent packaging and labeling practices. In this respect, its duties overlap those of the FTC, which is empowered to act against false food, drug, and cosmetic advertising. The two agencies cooperate in sharing their regulatory responsibilities. (Product labeling or ads that raise environmental issues may also be regulated by the Environmental Protection Agency.) In 1994, the FDA and FTC agreed to use the same definitions in evaluating claims made in food advertising.

The FDA plays an important role in regulating prescription drug advertising. In 1997 the FDA issued new guidelines that made it easier for drug makers to target the general public with their advertising. Until then, prescription drug advertising mainly targeted medical professionals. After 1997, prescription drug advertising became the fastest-growing kind of consumer advertising. Prescription drug ads must be submitted to the FDA for review when they appear in the media but not beforehand. Critics charged that drug makers were too heavily promoting the advantages of their products without adequately emphasizing risks and side effects. Congress later considered but did not pass legislation that would have forbidden direct-to-consumer drug advertising during a waiting period after a drug receives FDA approval, giving drug makers more time to discover unexpected side effects.

The U.S. Supreme Court in 2002 overturned a federal law prohibiting the advertising of *compounded prescription drugs.* In *Thompson v. Western States Medical Center* (535 U.S. 357), the Court voted 5-4 to invalidate a provision of the 1997 Food and Drug Administration Modernization Act that banned compounded drug advertising. Compounded drugs are combinations of prescription drugs prepared by pharmacists to meet special needs of patients at the request of doctors. Under federal law, drugs may be compounded without the normal testing that is required of new drugs as long as the compounded drug is not advertised.

Explaining the Court's rejection of this law as unconstitutional, Justice Sandra Day O'Connor wrote, "If the First Amendment means anything, it means that regulating speech must be a last—not first—resort. Yet here it seems to have been the first strategy the government thought to try." In making this observation, Justice O'Connor was evaluating the ban on

Sample front   Sample back

FIG. 115.
Sample graphic warning labels from the FDA's 2020 rules. Such labels are required by the Family Smoking Prevention and Tobacco Control Act but are being challenged in court by tobacco companies as First Amendment violations.

Food & Drug Administration.

compounded drug advertising under the classic *Central Hudson* test of the validity of government restrictions on commercial speech. She pointed out that there are several ways the federal government could achieve its stated goal—to prevent the mass production and widespread sale of compounded drugs that have not undergone the normal testing required of new drugs—without banning advertising. Thus, she wrote, this ban on advertising failed to meet the final part of the *Central Hudson* test: the ban was more extensive than necessary to achieve the government's goal.

Voluntary drug ad guidelines. Responding to criticism of direct-to-consumer drug advertising, the Pharmaceuticals Research and Manufacturers Association adopted voluntary advertising guidelines that went into effect in 2006. The guidelines say that all new direct-to-consumer television advertising should be submitted to the FDA before it is aired, and that ads should provide a balanced presentation of benefits and risks associated with each drug.

Off-label ads. What about speech that promotes an *off-label drug use?* Off-label uses are uses that are not approved by the Food and Drug Administration but that physicians sometimes prescribe because they are shown to help. An off-label prescription by a doctor is not punishable by the FDA, but is speech promoting an off-label use by a drug sales representative? No, said the Second Circuit in 2012 (*U.S. v. Caronia*, 703 F.3d 149). Alfred Caronia, a pharmaceutical sales rep, promoted the drug Xyrem for uses other than FDA-approved uses. The court pointed out that the Food, Drug, and Cosmetic Act does not "criminaliz[e] the simple promotion of a drug's off-label use because such a construction would raise First Amendment concerns." Calling the law "paternalistic," the court said penalizing dissemination of information about a drug could be harmful to the public.

The HHS: mandatory drug price ad rules fail. In May 2019, the U.S. Department of Health & Human Services (HHS) promulgated a rule under the Social Security Act that would require drug manufacturers to disclose pricing information in all their TV advertising. This disclosure requirement mandated text describing "the current list price for a typical 30-day regimen or for a typical course of treatment" unless that price was less than $35 for a month. Pharmaceutical companies challenged the rule, and a district court vacated it, saying that HHS had no authority to require such disclosures. In 2020, on appeal, the D.C. Circuit agreed (*Merck & Co. v. HHS*, 962 F.3d 531). The court pointed out that agency rules must either be "necessary to the efficient administration of the [agency's] functions," or "necessary to carry out the administration of the [Medicare] insurance programs"—and the disclosure rule was neither. While the decision didn't ban all price disclosure rules, some commentators thought that it called similar future rules into question.

The FDA: tobacco. The FDA has also taken steps to regulate tobacco as a drug—and to severely restrict cigarette advertising. The FDA adopted rules in the 1990s, backed by the Clinton administration, to limit cigarette advertising on billboards and in most magazines to plain black type, without illustrations, and to stop them sponsoring sporting events and concerts in the name of their tobacco brands (although they could still sponsor events using their corporate names). In addition, the FDA acted to ban cigarette vending machines and to require the tobacco industry to fund a $150 million educational campaign to discourage teenagers from smoking. The campaign was to include heavy TV use. Most of these tobacco rules never went into effect: they were immediately challenged in federal court. In 2000, the U.S. Supreme Court ruled that the Food and Drug Administration lacked the statutory authority to regulate tobacco as a drug. In *FDA v. Brown & Williamson Tobacco* (529 U.S. 120), the Court overturned a number of the FDA's restrictions on cigarette marketing.

The Court did not rule out the possibility of future Congressional action to give the FDA this authority. Instead, it merely said the FDA had no authority under existing federal law. The 5-4 majority traced the legislative history of the acts of Congress governing the FDA and concluded that Congress never intended to authorize the FDA to regulate tobacco as a drug. In fact, the FDA itself denied that it had the authority to regulate tobacco for many years before it announced the new restrictions on tobacco marketing in 1996.

This Supreme Court decision did not affect the voluntary agreement of the tobacco industry to curtail its advertising as part of its settlement of lawsuits filed by the states: that agreement still stands. Nor did this case affect the Federal Trade Commission's authority to regulate cigarette advertising. In fact, this Supreme Court decision didn't even directly affect most of the FDA's restrictions on cigarette advertising, as opposed to other aspects of cigarette marketing. In a separate action, a federal court earlier overturned the advertising portions of the FDA's rules. In *Beahm v. FDA* (966 F.Supp. 1374, 1997), a judge ruled that those rules exceeded the FDA's statutory authority.

First Amendment challenges to graphic warnings. In 2009, Congress passed the Family Smoking Prevention and Tobacco Control Act (usually called the Tobacco Control Act or TCA), granting the FDA the authority to regulate tobacco advertising and creating a tobacco control center within the agency. The act banned flavored cigarettes (except for menthol). It also limited advertising aimed toward young smokers and regulated the use of terms like "light," "mild," or "low." The TCA also amended a 1965 federal cigarette labeling act to require every cigarette package and ad to bear warnings about tobacco's health risks.

The TCA was challenged on First Amendment grounds in 2010 by five tobacco companies in *Commonwealth Brands, Inc. v. U.S.* (678 F. Supp. 2d 512), targeting label size and package design requirements. A federal district court agreed in part, calling the design requirements problematic, and saying the tobacco companies "are clearly right when they say that images of packages of their products, simple brand symbols, and some uses of color communicate important commercial information about their products, i.e., what the product is and who makes it." The government did not explain how restricting those symbols or colors would achieve its goals. But the tobacco companies lost their warning label challenge.

The FDA then announced in 2011 that new cigarette packaging laws would be imposed, mandating "color graphic images depicting the negative health consequences of smoking; these images were proposed to accompany the nine new textual warning statements" outlined in the TCA. These warnings include such statements as "WARNING: Tobacco smoke can harm your children." The agency said that this change was in response to studies demonstrating that larger warnings would confer greater health benefits than existing ones.

In 2012, the Sixth Circuit in *Discount Tobacco City & Lottery v. U.S.* (674 F.3d 509) upheld most of the Act, including provisions that placed restrictions on the marketing of some tobacco products, bans on event sponsorship, branding of non-tobacco merchandise and free samples, and the packaging space allotment, as well as the color graphic label requirements. "Ample evidence establishes that current warnings do not effectively inform consumers of the health risks of tobacco use and that consumers do not understand these risks," said the court, and thus the Act was an appropriate use of government power to combat consumer deception. But a federal judge overturned the graphic labels as unconstitutional, and the D.C. Circuit affirmed (*R.J. Reynolds Tobacco Co. v. FDA*, 696 F.3d 1205, 2012). A divided court said that under *Central Hudson*, the government had not met the burden under the Administrative Procedure Act (APA) to show substantial evidence that the warnings would advance its interest in reducing the number of smokers. In fact, the court said, "FDA has not provided a shred of evidence—much less the 'substantial evidence' required by the APA—showing that the graphic warnings will 'directly advance' its interest in reducing the number of Americans who smoke. FDA ... offers no evidence showing that such warnings have *directly caused* a material decrease in smoking rates in any of the countries that now require them." The FDA didn't appeal but said it would do more research to make better rules that comply with both the APA and the Tobacco Control Act.

Finally, the rules... But the agency dragged its feet—and advocacy groups got tired of waiting. In 2016, a group of public health organizations sued the FDA for failing to start rule making on the graphic warnings, despite more than four years' time to do so. These organizations also pointed out that the FDA has no discretion here; it must make rules for these warnings. In September 2018, a district court agreed, scolding the agency for its "extraordinary delay" and putting it on an expedited schedule to get the rules in place. A month later, the FDA proposed a May 2021 date for the warnings that the organizations rejected as too slow, and the court agreed, insisting on a March 2020 date (*Am. Acad. of Pediatrics v. FDA*, 399 F. Supp. 3d 479, 2019). The FDA appealed that decision, but in the meantime, it published final rules on March 17, 2020 that contained 13 (not nine) sample warnings (examples appear elsewhere in this chapter).

... And the challenges. Then, in April 2020, R.J. Reynolds challenged the FDA's 2020 final rules in Texas district court, saying that they were "unprecedented." The companies claimed that the warnings were unconstitutional because they were a form of compelled speech: "Never before in the United States have producers of a lawful product been required to use their own packages and advertising to convey an emotionally charged government message urging adult consumers to shun their product." On the heels of the Reynolds complaint, tobacco companies owned by Altria Group also sued the FDA in D.C. district court in May 2020, offering complaints very similar to those raised by R.J. Reynolds. The Altria complaint contains many of the same arguments raised by R.J. Reynolds, including claims that the FDA's 2020 rule violates the First Amendment and the Administrative Procedures Act. The cases were postponed due to the COVID-19 pandemic, so the FDA's rules won't be implemented until October 2021—barring any court decisions to the contrary. Stay tuned.

The FDA: E-cigarettes, too. In 2016, the FDA took what some called the monumental step of adding e-cigarettes to the Tobacco Control Act. The FDA can regulate "electronic nicotine delivery systems" (ENDS, "including e-cigarettes, e-hookah, e-cigars, vape pens, advanced refillable personal vaporizers, and electronic pipes") and their "components" (such as atomizers, batteries, cartridges, flavors, and the like for e-cigarettes) by banning their sale to those under 18 and requiring proof of age for sale to those under 26. Items deemed to be "accessories," like ashtrays, hookah tongs, and cigar humidors, are not regulated because they don't add to the public health risk.

E-cigarette and vaping companies challenged the act, claiming that the FDA didn't have the authority to regulate e-cigarettes, and in doing so, the agency violated the First and Fifth Amendments and the Administrative Procedures Act. In 2017, a federal district court found for the FDA, and on appeal in 2019 the D.C. Circuit agreed (*Nicopure Labs, LLC v. FDA*, 944 F.3d 267). Most commentators summarized the opinion as a win for the FDA and a suggestion that e-cigarette and vaping companies take their complaints to Congress. The court upheld the FDA's pre-market review requirement for new e-cigarette products (calling it "entirely rational and nonarbitrary") as well as its authority to ban ads that claim e-cigarettes are safer than traditional tobacco—an unproven claim. No Supreme Court appeal was filed.

Both public and health provider opinions on vaping are divided—some think it is a gateway to cigarettes, while others think it could help smokers eventually quit. The American Vaping Association, an industry trade group, put the price tag of getting one product approved at more than 1,700 hours and more than $1 million. These kinds of figures, if true, would mean that only the largest ENDS businesses could afford to stay afloat—including the traditional leaf tobacco companies who have also gotten into vaping.

Other FDA concerns. The legal battles over tobacco have overshadowed other regulatory actions by the Food and Drug Administration—actions that may be on firmer legal footing. For years, the FDA has refused to let the makers of dietary supplements claim that their products will cure or even treat the symptoms of diseases. These products, used by millions of Americans and sold almost everywhere, represent a $6 billion business. Medications designed to treat specific illnesses must undergo rigorous testing; these dietary supplements are usually sold without any government-supervised testing to prove their effectiveness. In 2000, the FDA loosened its restrictions on dietary supplements, announcing that they can claim to treat symptoms of "common conditions" that are considered "passages of life" such as morning sickness in pregnancy or memory loss. These products still cannot be advertised as treatments for specific diseases without full testing and documentation, the FDA said.

The FCC. Other federal agencies have the authority to regulate various aspects of advertising. The Federal Communications Commission has some authority in the advertising area, although much of it is indirect, derived from the FCC's licensing powers. For many years the FCC had specific guidelines that limited the amount of advertising a broadcaster could carry without risking special scrutiny at license renewal time. Those guidelines were eventually deleted as part of a comprehensive deregulation package. The FCC still has the right to consider the quantity and quality of advertising when it renews broadcast licenses, but there are no longer any specific quotas for broadcasters to follow except in the case of advertising in children's programs. In practice, most broadcasters carry less advertising than the old FCC guidelines permitted, anyway.

The FCC also has several other rules that affect broadcast advertising, perhaps the most notable being regulations requiring sponsorship identification. And Congress got into the regulatory act with the FCC in 2011 with the passage of the Commercial Advertisement Loudness Mitigation Act, or CALM Act, which requires the FCC to make compliance with the document "Recommended Practice: Techniques for Establishing and Maintaining Audio Loudness for Digital Television" mandatory—to ensure that commercials aren't louder than regular television. The CALM Act went into effect in December 2012.

In April 2021, the FCC received a letter from the act's author, asking the agency to investigate complaints of increased ad volumes. The FCC wasted no time reacting, calling for comments to determine whether the CALM Act should be revised. Stay tuned.

The SEC. Another federal agency with authority over some advertising is the Securities and Exchange Commission. The SEC is responsible for preventing the release of incomplete or fraudulent information about corporations whose stock is publicly traded. Thus, the SEC has responsibility for advertising regarding offerings of stock and certain other investment advertising. The agency exercises its authority by acting mainly against the corporation whose advertising is judged false, often by canceling stock offerings. It requires those who advertise stock offerings to make it clear that a media ad is neither an offer to sell nor a solicitation of an offer to buy, since media ads don't lend themselves to the highly detailed reporting of corporate information that is required. That information is provided in a prospectus.

The ATF. Still another federal agency with authority over advertising is the Bureau of Alcohol, Tobacco and Firearms, which regulates alcoholic beverage labeling and advertising, among other things. The bureau has stirred controversy in recent years by sometimes refusing to allow winemakers to make health claims (even claims they could document) or to use reproductions of paintings by noted artists that included nudity in wine labels or advertising. Although the bureau has the authority to ban "obscene and indecent" wine ads, critics have accused its staff of acting arbitrarily in some of these situations.

The U.S. Post Office: marijuana ads. As more states either legalize marijuana for medicinal purposes or decriminalize it altogether, the nation has become a patchwork of different pot laws. As of May 2021, 18 states plus Washington, D.C., and Guam have legalized marijuana for recreational use for adults over age 21, and 36 states plus Washington, D.C., Guam, Puerto Rico, and the Virgin Islands permit medical marijuana. And U.S. support for it is growing—according to a 2021 Pew Research report, a whopping 91% of Americans favor either legalization of recreational and medical marijuana (60%) or just medical marijuana (31%). But what about advertising marijuana? Not through the federal mail.

Several members of Congress in Oregon, which has legalized the drug, received notice in 2015 that newspapers containing ads for pot could not be sent through the U.S. mail, which is a federal service and bound by federal law. They wrote to the Postal Service for clarification and got a response from the United States Postal Service (USPS) general counsel and executive vice president Thomas Marshall: the federal Controlled Substances Act forbids using the mail system to transmit advertising for the sale or purchase of marijuana, even if it is allowed under state law (federal law also prohibits placing advertising in newspapers and magazines for its sale and use). The USPS determines whether an item may be mailed based on federal, not state, law, so state laws allowing marijuana use don't affect whether the U.S. mail will carry those ads. In 2016, it was reported that no mail had yet been stopped, and no inspection service had been notified of a cannabis advertisement mailing.

However, it's unclear who can police newspapers for non-complying ads (postal officials must accept mailings but are allowed to notify postmasters for additional action) and how the law will affect the newspapers—can they be prosecuted under the Controlled Substances Act? This area will continue to be problematic as states consider whether to legalize pot.

Federal Lawsuits for Damages

Still another sanction for false advertising was created by Section 43(a) of the federal trademark law, the Lanham Act (discussed in Chapter Six). Under the Lanham Act's advertising fraud provisions, companies may file civil lawsuits against competitors whose advertising is false and detrimental to their business. Significantly, the Lanham Act now permits courts to award *treble damages* (i.e., three times the actual monetary damages) in these private false-advertising lawsuits. And the victims of false advertising may also win injunctions—court orders to halt the advertising.

Suits under the Lanham Act. A number of courts have awarded damages in federal false advertising lawsuits under the Lanham Act. A large advertising fraud judgment—$40 million—was affirmed by the U.S. Court of Appeals in *U-Haul Int'l v. Jartran* (793 F.2d 1034, 1986). In that case, Jartran entered the move-yourself market with an aggressive advertising campaign, and U-Haul (Jartran's main competitor) sued. The court held that some of Jartran's claims were false and detrimental to U-Haul's business. The huge damage award was based on a projection of U-Haul's lost profits ($20 million) plus the amount of money Jartran spent on false advertising (another $20 million).

The Lanham Act allows substantial damage awards not only against advertisers but also against *advertising agencies*, according to a 1992 federal court decision. In *The Gillette Co. v. Wilkinson Sword Inc.* (795 F. Supp. 662), an unpublished decision of a New York federal district court, the Friedman Benjamin ad agency was ordered to pay almost $1 million in damages to Gillette for ads that falsely claimed Wilkinson's shaving system provided a shave six times smoother than Gillette's.

Puffery is protected. Few advertising fraud cases filed under the Lanham Act have drawn more media attention than the "pizza wars" case, *Pizza Hut Inc. v. Papa John's Int'l Inc.* (227 F.3d 489, 2000). Papa John's ran an advertising campaign with the theme "Better Ingredients, Better Pizza" and follow-up ads comparing specific ingredients in its pizza and competitors' pizzas. Pizza Hut sued, alleging that Papa John's ads were deceptive and intended to mislead customers. After a trial jury ruled in Pizza Hut's favor, Papa John's appealed. A federal appellate court overturned the verdict, ruling that Pizza Hut failed to prove that consumers were actually deceived sufficiently that their purchasing decisions were affected by Papa John's advertising claims, which the Court called "typical puffery." Proof not only that consumers were deceived, but also that the deception affected their purchasing decisions, is an element of a Lanham Act advertising fraud case. The Supreme Court denied *cert.* What is *puffery*? Puffery includes exaggerated claims that a reasonable consumer would not rely on or claims of product superiority so vague or subjective that consumers will generally recognize the claim as an exaggeration.

There are limitations to the Lanham Act's power, however. The "advertising" statements must actually *be* commercial speech, not just *next to* it. In 2017, a case brought by one doctor for posts on another doctor's blog criticizing his practice could not support a false advertising claim under the Lanham Act, even though the posts appeared on a website that generated revenue from advertising and subscriptions. In this case, *Edward Lewis Tobinick, MD v. Novella* (848 F.3d 935), Dr. Edward Tobinick, a dermatologist and internal medicine doctor who practices in California and Florida, sued Connecticut neurologist Dr. Steven Novella for posts written on the Science-Based Medicine blog. Dr. Novella's posts criticized Dr. Tobinick's uses of certain medications to treat strokes and Alzheimer's disease that are not FDA-approved for those uses ("off-label" uses). The posts also reported that Dr. Tobinick had been investigated by the Medical Board of California for his claims about the alleged effectiveness of the treatments with those off-label uses, placed on probation, and ordered to take remedial classes in medication prescribing. A federal district court in Florida granted summary judgment to Dr. Novella, saying that the posts were not commercial in nature, and the Eleventh Circuit agreed.

In rejecting the false advertising claim, the Eleventh Circuit said that to qualify as advertising, the statements at issue had to propose a commercial transaction. The statements also failed several other tests for commercial speech: for example, they did not appear to be advertising, and the author had no economic motivation for distributing them. And the fact that the posts appeared near ads and subscription information did not transform them into ads themselves; as the court noted, "magazines and newspapers often have commercial purposes, but those purposes do not convert the individual articles within these editorial sources into commercial speech subject to Lanham Act liability."

And the Seventh Circuit said in 2010 in *Stayart v. Yahoo* (623 F.3d 436) that users cannot use the Lanham Act to sue search engines just because their names happen to pop up next to sponsored ads for objectionable products when typed in as searches. Beverly Stayart filed a Lanham Act challenge in the Seventh Circuit, alleging that the search engines should be liable for linking her name randomly to products of which she doesn't approve.

The court said Stayart did not have standing to sue because she didn't have a commercial interest in her name, a standard required by the Lanham Act. The act "is a private remedy for a commercial plaintiff who meets the burden of proving that its commercial interests have been harmed by a competitor," said the court.

The Lanham Act continues to be litigated and interpreted. For example, in 2014 the Fifth Circuit took on the question of whether the act covers "non-actionable scientific opinions rather than actionable statements of fact" and answered in the affirmative (*Eastman Chem. Co. v. Plastipure, Inc.*, 775 F.3d 230). Eastman Chemical filed suit against Plastipure for its advertising in which Plastipure alleged that Tritan, an Eastman resin product, contained elements that could cause estrogenic activity (perhaps resulting in cancer and reproductive abnormalities). Eastman said that this was false information, but Plastipure alleged that the information was purely scientific and thus not covered by the Lanham Act, and a jury had erred in finding that information false. Pointing out that ads "do not become immune from Lanham Act scrutiny simply because their claims are open to scientific or public debate," the judges said that a jury could have determined the truth or falsity of the statements.

The Supreme Court on Lanham. The Supreme Court decided two Lanham cases in 2014. In *Lexmark Int'l, Inc. v. Static Control Components, Inc.* (572 U.S. 118), the Court said that Static Control, a refurbisher and reseller of Lexmark toner cartridges, had sufficiently pled a case for a Lanham Act cause of action for false advertising. To compete against "remanufacturers" like Static Control, Lexmark had created a microchip that would prevent reuse unless the cartridge was returned to Lexmark. Not to be outdone, Static Control created a competing microchip for remanufacturers, for which Lexmark sued for copyright infringement. In return, Static Control countersued for false advertising, alleging that Lexmark misled consumers into thinking that they were legally required to return the cartridges to Lexmark after one use, and that Lexmark had written to remanufacturers, telling them that it was illegal to refurbish its cartridges and to use Static Control's chip in doing so.

Justice Antonin Scalia, writing for a unanimous Court in finding that Static Control had a Lanham Act case, said, "We thus hold that to come within the zone of interests in a suit for false advertising under [Lanham Act] §1125(a), a plaintiff must allege an injury to a commercial interest in reputation or sales." Consumers do not have this protection. Scalia went on, "We thus hold that a plaintiff suing under §1125(a) ordinarily must show economic or reputational injury flowing directly from the deception wrought by the defendant's advertising; and that that occurs when deception of consumers causes them to withhold trade from the plaintiff." Having found that Static Control met both of these elements, Scalia then gave Static Control the go-ahead to plead damages under the Lanham Act. This decision creates one standard (as opposed to different ones in different circuits, encouraging plaintiffs to go forum-shopping), and it simplified the test to two parts: the zone of interests, an injury in sales or reputation, and the proximate harm, "flowing directly from the deception" and causing loss of sales.

In the second case, the Court addressed the question of whether a private party could bring a Lanham Act claim challenging a product label under the Food, Drug, and Cosmetic Act (FDCA). In *POM Wonderful LLC. v. Coca-Cola Co.* (573 U.S. 102), a unanimous Court said yes. POM, a pomegranate juice company, objected to Coke's Minute Maid brand of juice, labeled "POMEGRANATE BLUEBERRY" (in all caps) that is 0.3% pomegranate juice, 0.2% blueberry juice, and the rest mostly apple and grape juice. POM said that the label is misleading and harmed POM's sales. In finding for POM, Justice Anthony Kennedy said, "Competitors, in their own interest, may bring Lanham Act claims like POM's that challenge food and beverage labels that are regulated by the FDCA." Pointing out that the Lanham

Focus on...
"An almond doesn't lactate"—so should it be "almond juice"?

The FDA struggles with labeling plant-based beverages (including those made of soy, almonds, and oats) "milk." The agency in 2018 proposed a rule that would forbid the use of "milk" on a product label unless that product was a "lacteal secretion...obtained by the complete milking of one or more healthy cows." (Not particularly appetizing.)

Dairy producers, of course, support this perspective; one organization called for the beverage to be called "almond juice," since "almond milk" is "definitely not a milk under the definition in the Oxford dictionary." And FTC commissioner Scott Gottlieb added fuel to the fire when he said in 2018, "An almond doesn't lactate." But shouldn't labels help consumers understand what's in the products they're buying? One federal appeals court said that consumers aren't confused by the "milk" label on almond beverages into thinking that they contain dairy (*Painter v. Blue Diamond Growers*, 2018 BL 472638, 2018). This finding was supported in a 2019 study of FDA comments in which 76% of commenters said they supported the use of dairy terms by plant-based foods.

FIG. 116. Almond milk.

Sandi Benedicta, Sept. 29, 2020, via Unsplash.

The "lacteal secretion" definition for milk is still in use by the FDA as of Apr. 2020. Don't expect dairy farmers to back down—and producers of plant-based beverages are ready with their First Amendment arguments against being forced to call their products by (non-milk) names like "almond juice."

Act and the FDCA complement each other, Kennedy noted, "Congress did not intend the FDCA to preclude Lanham Act suits like POM's. The position Coca-Cola takes in this Court that because food and beverage labeling is involved it has no Lanham Act liability here for practices that allegedly mislead and trick consumers, all to the injury of competitors, finds no support in precedent or the statutes."

■ STATE ADVERTISING REGULATION

Virtually all states also have laws empowering their officials to act against advertising fraud. At least 45 states have adopted various versions of what has been known as the "Printer's Ink Statute," an advertising fraud law first proposed in *Printer's Ink* magazine in 1911. The statute makes advertising fraud a crime, giving state and local prosecutors the responsibility for enforcement. Because it is a criminal law that must be enforced by officials who often feel they have more serious crimes to worry about, enforcement has traditionally been lax. Recognizing the shortcomings of this law, most of the states have enacted other laws giving consumers and competitors civil remedies in instances of advertising fraud: victims of false advertising generally may sue for damages under state law as well as the federal Lanham Act. In addition, some states have given local and state prosecutors civil enforcement responsibilities much like those the FTC Act gave to the Federal Trade Commission. In a few other states, separate agencies have enforcement responsibilities.

Other Recent State Regulations on Advertising

Both the Supreme Court and appellate courts have recently decided other cases that involve state regulations on advertising. The topics run the gamut; a few are discussed here.

At the Supreme Court. In a win for data mining companies, states may not regulate how doctors' prescribing data is used without meeting heightened scrutiny, said the Supreme Court in 2011. Several states had laws that banned using information gathered from pharmacies about doctors' prescribing history for the purposes of increasing drug sales. The practice, called "detailing," has pharmaceutical sales representatives meet individually with physicians to promote their wares, armed with data from pharmacies about prescribing histories. The First Circuit upheld these laws in New Hampshire law and Maine, but the Second Circuit overturned the Vermont law. The Supreme Court granted *cert* in the Vermont case. In *Sorrell v. IMS Health* (564 U.S. 552), the Court said by a 6-3 vote that pharmaceutical marketing speech was protected by the First Amendment, and laws that regulate this speech must undergo heightened scrutiny—which the Vermont law failed to meet.

Justice Anthony Kennedy noted that Vermont had not alleged that the detailing information was false or misleading, so the law was simply premised on "a difference of opinion." He wrote for the Court, "'The commercial marketplace, like other spheres of our social and cultural life, provides a forum where ideas and information flourish. Some of the ideas and information are vital, some of slight worth. But the general rule is that the speaker and the audience, not the government, assess the value of the information presented.'" The dissenters would have found that the regulation of detailing was connected to an important government interest in regulating commercial speech and would have upheld the Vermont law, which would have survived a *Central Hudson* analysis.

In *Nat'l Inst. of Family & Life Advocates v. Becerra* (138 S. Ct. 2361), the Supreme Court in 2018 ruled that a California law requiring pro-life "crisis pregnancy" centers to post advertisements about the state's abortion services is likely unconstitutional. The state law required the posting of information about abortion services in part because it feared women who visited the centers were getting inaccurate information about their options. The centers argued that the law violated their First Amendment rights by requiring compelled speech that undermined their anti-abortion beliefs.

In a decision by Justice Clarence Thomas, a 5-4 Court ruled that the law was likely not able to meet strict scrutiny standards nor even a lower level of scrutiny because it is "wildly underinclusive." He pointed out that California has over 1,000 community clinics serving more than 5.6 million patients, and the law as written would exclude most of them because it "applies only to clinics that have a 'primary purpose' of 'providing family planning or pregnancy-related services' and that provide two of six categories of specific services." The dissenters, led by Justice Stephen Breyer, asked why, if the state can require a doctor to tell a woman seeking an abortion that adoption is an alternative, can't it require that a pregnancy center tell a woman about abortion options?

At the circuit courts. In *Int'l Dairy Foods Assoc. v. Boggs* (622 F.3d 628, 2010), the Sixth Circuit determined that Ohio's law prohibiting the labeling of milk from cows not treated with rBST (*recombinant bovine somatotropin*, also known as recombinant bovine growth hormone [rbGH]) with labels like "rbST free," "antibiotic-free," and "pesticide-free" was unconstitutional. The two kinds of milk were different, the court said, disagreeing with the FDA on the issue. After first finding that the labeling was not misleading, the court looked at the other parts of the *Central Hudson* test and noted that the Ohio law does not directly advance the state's interest and is more extensive than necessary.

The Ninth Circuit held in 2012 that the Yellow Pages were protected speech (*Dex Media West, Inc. v. City of Seattle*, 696 F.3d 952), striking down an ordinance regulating yellow pages directories. The court said that the ordinance, which imposed fees and regulations on yellow pages directories, was unconstitutional because they contained both commercial and noncommercial speech. Drawing an analogy to newspapers, the court said, "To treat yellow pages directories as lesser-protected commercial speech because commercial content is published alongside noncommercial content, we would have to draw a distinction between the phone books and other publications that combine commercial and noncommercial speech with different underlying speakers, such as newspapers and magazines."

In 2017, the Eleventh Circuit overturned a Florida labeling law under a *Central Hudson* analysis. Ocheesee Creamery wanted to sell its all-natural skim milk without adding back anything lost during the skimming process, but Florida law required that if any Vitamin A lost from a product during skimming isn't replaced, the product must be labeled and sold as "imitation skim milk." Ocheesee refused to add Vitamin A, and it also objected to the "imitation" label because, as it noted, the only ingredient in its product was skim milk.

A district court ruled for the state, but the Eleventh Circuit overturned (*Ocheesee Creamery LLC v. Putnam*, 851 F.3d 1228). Applying *Central Hudson*, the court said that the labeling wasn't misleading, as the product was in fact skim milk. While both parties agreed that the state did have a substantial interest in ensuring nutritional standards are clear, the court sided with Ocheesee on the third and fourth prongs, saying the law was far more restrictive than it needed to be. The court offered one example of a workable solution: "allowing skim milk to be called what it is and merely requiring a disclosure that it lacks vitamin A."

■ SELF-REGULATION

Another important influence on the content of advertising is self-regulation, the voluntary methods the advertising industry and the media have developed to prevent the release of false and distasteful advertising.

NARC. In 1971, four major advertising and business groups united to form an organization known as the National Advertising Review Council (NARC). The council is a cooperative venture of the American Association of Advertising Agencies, the American Advertising Federation, the Association of National Advertisers, and the Council of Better Business Bureaus. NARC is housed at the Council of Better Business Bureaus, which has a staff-level National Advertising Division and a Children's Advertising Review Unit to do much of the administrative work of handling truth-in-advertising issues. Decisions may be appealed to a voluntary appeals body, the National Advertising Review Board.

With representation from national advertisers and advertising agencies as well as non-industry or public representatives, NARC accepts complaints about advertising and asks advertisers to substantiate their ad claims. The council asks advertisers to change their ads if they cannot be substantiated. If they refuse, the council is authorized to present its findings to a suitable government enforcement agency, but that is almost never necessary.

Although NARC's main tools are persuasion and peer pressure, it has dealt with hundreds of questionable advertisements and represents an excellent example of an industry endeavoring to keep its own house in order without government involvement.

NAB. For many years, the National Association of Broadcasters maintained similar voluntary codes for radio and television advertising and programming practices. Broadcasters who subscribed to these codes were allowed to display a "seal of good practice." At one time about 4,500 television and radio broadcasters were code subscribers.

The NAB codes set limits on the number of commercials broadcasters were to carry and also set standards for the content of both advertising and non-advertising materials. The NAB "Code Authority" and "Code Board" enforced these rules, although their only real enforcement power was to prevent violators from using the "seal of good practice."

However, in 1979 the U.S. Justice Department filed an antitrust lawsuit against the NAB, charging that the codes constituted a restraint of trade. By placing limits on the number of commercials and the amount of commercial time that would be permitted, the NAB codes artificially forced up ad rates, the government contended.

After losing the case in federal district court, the NAB signed a consent decree in 1982, agreeing to drop many of the provisions of the television code. To avoid any further potential antitrust liability, the NAB then decided to eliminate its codes altogether and to disband the Code Authority and Code Board. Thus, the broadcast industry's first major attempt at self-regulation fell victim to a government antitrust lawsuit. In the mid-2000s, the NAB was developing a new voluntary code.

In the print media, there is no industry-wide code of advertising practices. Various organizations have adopted codes of ethics, but they generally deal with editorial matters, not advertising. However, many major newspapers have their own policies on advertising acceptability, and these policies are very influential. The *New York Times* not only has an advertising acceptability policy but also a department that reviews ads prior to publication. That department independently checks advertising claims and bars future ads from those found to have violated the company's standards. The *New York Times* prohibits ads considered in bad taste and attacks on individuals or competing products, among others.

In 2011, the FTC announced that it would again review the voluntary rules (for the fourth time in 12 years) that alcoholic beverage advertisers use, and it is likely that social media advertising will be among the areas on which the agency will focus its attention. It got comments in 2013 but has yet to act on them.

■ ADVERTISING ON THE INTERNET

The explosive growth of internet advertising led to a variety of government initiatives to regulate that advertising, as well as questions about how both traditional and new advertising laws should apply to online ads. For example, what if an online service that carries thousands or millions of ads fails to screen out every ad that could promote illegal discrimination—or doesn't do any screening at all? Is the online service liable, or only the advertiser? In 2008, two federal appeals courts ruled on that issue and reached *opposite* conclusions—in cases involving famous online services: Craigslist.org and Roommates.com.

The Craigslist case. Craigslist regularly ranks in the top 20 most visited websites in the United States (a May 2021 estimate says that it gets more than 561 million visits per month). And it's big on ads; in 2017, the company reported that U.S. users posted 80 million ads per month. Invariably some of these ads are problematic. Is Craigslist responsible?

The Seventh Circuit ruled that Craigslist.org is *not* the publisher of the ads posted on its site and therefore cannot be held accountable for their content; that is, Craigslist is not comparable to a newspaper that publishes classified ads. Ruling in *Chicago Lawyers' Committee for Civil Rights Under Law v. Craigslist* (519 F.3d 666), the court said Section 230 of the Communications Decency Act (see Chapter Four) exempts Craigslist from liability for ads posted by others. Although the court did not say internet providers have complete protection from all liability for materials on their sites, it did say internet providers are exempt from liability for posting unscreened third-party content.

The court said the lawyers' group that brought the case is free to sue individuals who post illegal ads—or to urge federal prosecutors to go after those whose Craigslist ads violate the Fair Housing Act or other laws. But Craigslist itself is protected by Section 230. The court said, in essence, that Craigslist cannot be expected to review millions of ads every month to spot ads that advocate an illegal act any more than a telephone company can screen every call. As anyone who has surfed Craigslist for long knows, there are not only ads that could promote housing discrimination but also ads offering all sorts of services that may not be legal (even after the takedowns discussed below). Craigslist has taken many steps to curb such ads. But if an illegal message is posted in spite of all that, the company is not responsible for its content, according to this Seventh Circuit decision.

But Craigslist responded to pressure from several states' attorneys general when a masseuse was killed in Boston in 2009 after being lured to a hotel by a medical student who found her on Craigslist (one of the earliest of many "Craigslist killers"). The alleged killer met his victim when she had advertised in Craigslist's "erotic services" category. Craigslist complied with a request by the attorneys general to remove the ads, eliminating its "erotic services" category and creating a new "adult services" category. But that change fared no better; in response to another letter from the attorneys general in 2010, Craigslist also closed down the new adult section. In 2017, the company also voluntarily closed down its "personals" section after the passage of FOSTA (*Fight Online Sex Trafficking Act*). As discussed in Chapters Four and Ten, this law eliminates Section 230 protection for sites that knowingly host information and ads for sex trafficking. Craigslist, out of an abundance of caution, chose to shutter its personals section rather than risk losing Section 230 protection—*despite* the 2008 Seventh Circuit holding of 230 immunity.

The Roommates case. However, soon after *Craigslist*, an 11-judge *en banc* panel of the Ninth Circuit reached a different conclusion in a case involving Roommates.com. Ruling in *Fair Housing Council of San Fernando Valley v. Roommates.com* (521 F.3d 1157, 2008), the court said Roommates crossed the line and *lost* Section 230 immunity because it requires those who want to place ads to create a "profile" by answering specific questions about their gender, family status, and sexual orientation. Doing that screening makes Roommates an "information content provider" and not a mere conduit for content created by others. The 8-3 majority in this hotly contested case said Roommates' profile questions made this case different and caused Roommates to lose its Section 230 immunity. The majority opinion said Roommates would not lose its immunity if all it did was to allow advertisers to post a message in a comment box without any structuring by the service.

The dissenting judges in *Roommates* pointed out that no court had yet determined any of the profiles to be actual advocacy of unlawful housing discrimination. Most fair housing laws exempt individuals' choices of roommates from discrimination complaints. It's not usually illegal to rule out prospective roommates who would share your residence based on their age, gender, family status, or sexual orientation. A single, 21-year-old female can choose to share her home only with other young women who have no children, as opposed to older men who want to move in with their children, for example. Even private individuals who rent out up to three single-family homes are exempt from most fair housing laws. So the question raised in the *Roommates* case comes down to whether it is right to penalize an internet provider for allowing ads that may or may not promote illegal housing discrimination.

Given two federal appeals court decisions that reached opposite conclusions about the liability of internet services for possible fair housing violations by their users, perhaps the Supreme Court will someday rule on this issue. Or perhaps the case against FOSTA will clarify the issue. Stay tuned.

Spam. One major regulatory effort began in response to a public outcry: Congress passed a law to curb "spam," or unsolicited advertising by bulk email—which was itself controversial. The technology of email makes it easy to build a huge mailing list—and send a deluge of messages to everyone on that list. An advertiser can send messages to millions of email addresses almost instantly and at virtually no cost. It was inevitable that such a powerful technology would be abused.

The federal *CAN-SPAM Act* (another Congressional acronym, "Controlling the Assault of Non-Solicited Pornography and Marketing" Act) went into effect in 2004 and banned unsolicited commercial email, preempting state anti-spam laws that were sometimes stricter than the federal law. The Act forbids sending unsolicited email after any recipient has asked a spammer to discontinue it. It requires commercial email to include a valid postal address, opt-out information, and a reply mechanism. Spammers are required to remove opt-outs from their lists within 10 days. Violators may face both criminal and civil penalties.

The problem, of course, is that most spammers conceal their identity and provide no valid sender's address that would facilitate consumer opt-outs. Recognizing this problem, the federal CAN-SPAM Act forbids "spoofing," the practice of concealing a message's origin by using someone else's email address (discussions of caller ID spoofing appear in Chapter Eleven). Like the ban on spam itself, the ban on email spoofing has proven almost impossible to enforce. Unfortunately for consumers, for every spammer that the FTC manages to catch, there are dozens of others who escape detection. In 2005, a year after the federal CAN-SPAM Act went into effect, Microsoft estimated that about 80% of all email is spam, up from 50 to 60% before the law went into effect.

Questions were immediately raised about the constitutionality of the federal CAN-SPAM Act. However, courts have generally upheld state anti-spam laws. In 2001, the Washington Supreme Court upheld that state's anti-spam law in a case where a bulk emailer had been sending up to one million pieces of unsolicited email a week promoting a $40 package he called, "How to profit from the Internet." The court declared that the Washington anti-spam law did not violate either the First Amendment or the interstate commerce clause of the U.S. Constitution (*Washington v. Heckel*, 24 P.3d 404). In 2002, an appellate court also upheld California's anti-spam law (*Ferguson v. Friendfinders*, 94 C.A.4th 1255).

In 2010, Florida announced a $2.9 million settlement with ModernAd Media, LLC, after finding it in violation of the federal CAN-SPAM Act, which also prohibits misleading headers. ModernAd Media must now "disclose and prominently display all necessary information on internet-based advertisements necessary so consumers can make informed decisions before they agree to purchase products or participate in trial offers," according to the Florida attorney general's press release.

CAN-SPAM is not without its enemies. Some, playing on the law's name, relabel it the "YOU-CAN-SPAM Act," claiming that not only doesn't the law work to curb spam, it actually makes it easier to spam. CAN-SPAM doesn't require that a spammer get permission to send junk emails. And because the federal law preempts state laws, stronger protections are impossible to achieve. One critic bluntly called the act "a travesty that was foisted upon the American people by a small handful of powerful companies, most notably AOL and Microsoft, and by their obedient lackeys in Congress."

Text message spam. The Ninth Circuit also dealt a blow to text message spam in 2009 in *Satterfield v. Simon & Schuster* (569 F.3d 946). Laci Satterfield sued Simon & Schuster for sending an unsolicited text message ad for a new Stephen King book to her son's cell phone. She claimed the message violated the Telephone Consumer Protection Act (TCPA, discussed at length in Chapter Eleven) because it was sent through an automatic dialing system; Simon & Schuster said that there was no auto-dial system, no "calls" as defined by the law actually took place, and Satterfield agreed to the ads when she joined a ringtone download service. The Ninth Circuit disagreed. The court said it was unclear whether an auto-dial system was used, a text message could reasonably be considered a call under FCC rules ("to communicate with or try to get into communication with a person by telephone"), and that no permission was given. The case was remanded.

In 2013, Papa John's Pizza paid $16.5 million to settle a complaint that it spammed text messages containing advertising under the TCPA. Customers complained of getting 15 or more texts a night after ordering from Papa John's, without having agreed to them.

Also in 2013, new amendments to the TCPA went into effect. These include a definition of "prior express written consent" to telemarketing that means just that: a written agreement that the person receiving the messages agrees to receive them, as well as several methods to obtain that agreement. The amendments also eliminate the "established business relationship" exception that allowed prerecorded telemarketing calls from businesses who had established a relationship with a consumer.

Online advertising. Consumer advocates have also been concerned about outright fraud in advertising on websites. The FTC has launched a series of sweeps that targeted fraudulent e-commerce. One of the FTC's chief concerns was false, misleading or unfair health claims on the internet: by 1999, the FTC had notified the owners of several hundred sites that their health claims could violate federal law. In a 1999 announcement, the FTC said about one-fourth of the sites that received such notices over a two-year period removed the questionable claims or shut down their websites altogether without any further federal enforcement action. The FTC said it was considering various options to deal with the others, including legal actions to halt false or misleading advertising.

In 2001, the FTC responded to Sept. 11 by going after websites that were exploiting the fear of terrorism by making false claims about cures for various diseases. The FTC warned operators of about 40 websites to remove claims that dietary supplements can cure anthrax or smallpox and also went after operators of websites claiming that products such as zinc mineral oil can cure anthrax. Sites offering gas masks, protective suits, mail sterilizers, and products to detect the presence of anthrax also were warned to drop deceptive claims. As mentioned earlier, similar issues faced the agency during the COVID-19 pandemic in 2020.

"Dot Com Disclosures." The Federal Trade Commission also took another step to combat false and misleading internet advertising: the agency added a section to its own website (www.ftc.gov) addressing the issue. The report has links to examples and mock ads that illustrate the FTC's suggestions for internet advertising. While the information available on this site is only the FTC's opinion and is not legally binding, it is dangerous for any advertiser to ignore the FTC's published guidelines. In fact, the FTC's report, entitled "Dot Com Disclosures," also has links to many FTC's advisory *Guides* concerning advertising of various types of products and services.

The FTC updated "Dot Com Disclosures" most recently in 2013. Among its recommendations: remember that consumer protection laws apply online as well as offline, and to all platforms; advertisers should "incorporate relevant limitations and qualifying information into the underlying claim, rather than having a separate disclosure qualifying the claim;" disclosures should be clear, conspicuous, and as close as possible to the claim itself; and "If a disclosure is necessary to prevent an advertisement from being deceptive, unfair, or otherwise violative of a Commission rule, and it is not possible to make the disclosure clearly and conspicuously, then that ad should not be disseminated."

Online behavioral advertising. A 2009 report from the FTC entitled "Self-Regulatory Principles For Online Behavioral Advertising" caused some to believe that the FTC was planning to increase its scrutiny of *online behavioral advertising*—defined by the FTC as "the practice of tracking an individual's online activities in order to deliver advertising tailored to the individual's interests." The FTC offered four principles that the advertising industry should evaluate in crafting a self-regulatory plan for online behavioral advertising that look similar to those proposed for data privacy: transparency: "meaningful disclosures to consumers about the practice and choice about whether to allow the practice"; security: "reasonable data security measures so that behavioral data does not fall into the wrong hands, and ... retain data only as long as necessary for legitimate business or law enforcement needs"; consent: "before a company uses behavioral data in a manner that is materially different from promises made when the company collected the data"; and affirmative express consent for sensitive data: "for example, data about children, health, or finances...." It is clear that the FTC is interested in *opt-in* strategies, where consumers must *actively agree* to events before they occur, rather than *opt-out* ones, in which they must tell companies to *stop* doing something.

In essence, the FTC's position is that all of the consumer safeguards that apply in other kinds of advertising also apply online. That means all of the normal rules concerning deceptive and unfair practices must be observed by internet advertisers. Internet advertisers must be prepared to substantiate their claims. And advertisers must make "clear and conspicuous" affirmative disclosures in many instances.

Endorsements. Also in 2009, the FTC said it would start evaluating bloggers and their endorsements and advertisements. The FTC's *Guides for the Use of Endorsements and Testimonials in Advertising* allow the agency to pursue both bloggers and companies that give them freebies or otherwise compensate them for reviews for false claims or failure to disclose conflicts of interest. What counts as an "endorsement"? The FTC defines endorsements as "any advertising message…that consumers are likely to believe reflects the opinions, beliefs, findings, or experiences of a party other than the sponsoring advertiser, even if the views expressed by that party are identical to those of the sponsoring advertiser."

The *Guides* raised several concerns. Critics expressed fears that the FTC may start investigating bloggers who do reviews without any compensation or freebies. They also pointed out the likely futility of trying to monitor hundreds of thousands of blogs, with new ones appearing daily. The FTC said it was primarily concerned about those who receive money for blogging positive reviews or who have an undisclosed marketing arrangement with a company. Google's sale of trademarks as keyword search terms also implicates Lanham Act concerns, as discussed in Chapter Six (*Rescuecom v. Google* and *Rosetta Stone v. Google*).

The first fine leveled under the endorsement rules came in 2011 when the FTC fined a company that sold guitar lesson materials online $250,000 for deceptively advertising its products through online affiliates who posed as ordinary customers or independent reviewers. Legacy Learning Systems Inc., based in Nashville, did not reveal, as the *Guides* mandate, that the online affiliates "received in exchange for substantial commissions on the sale of each product resulting from referrals"—sales of more than $5 million for Legacy.

In November 2019, the FTC provided an updated "plain language" version of the endorsement guidelines in a brochure entitled "Disclosures 101 for Social Media Influencers." This explainer, available at ftc.gov/influencers, gives straightforward advice to endorsers (an example: "Disclose when you have any financial, employment, personal, or family relationship with a brand") and reminds endorsers that they can't endorse things they haven't tried, or lie about a product or service (if they didn't like it, they should say so).

A law protecting honest reviews. Imagine you're staying at a hotel for a weekend. At the front desk, you initial the standard forms and hand over your credit card to receive the key to your room, and when you get inside, it's … just nasty. Perhaps it has filthy carpets or smells like mold, or it's close to a noisy highway, or the staff gives you attitude when you request more towels—you're upset enough to write a review on Yelp about your experiences and the poor rating you believe the hotel deserves. Later, you're checking your credit card bills, and there's an extra $500 charge from the hotel—a fine for that negative Yelp review. When you call to demand that the charge be removed, you're told that the forms you signed at the front desk contained a clause assessing a $500 penalty for every negative review posted. Unconscionable, right? (According to a 2014 *Forbes* article, a New York hotel actually did something very much like this to its guests.)

Congress agreed and passed the *Consumer Review Fairness Act* in 2016 to protect against companies' attempts to squelch negative customer reviews by inserting insidious terms into their standard contracts. This act protects honest customer reviews of company products or services, as well as employee conduct with those customers, in written, oral, or pictorial forms, including on social media. It forbids companies from inserting terms into their contracts that restrict a signer's ability to review a company's products, services, or customer service; assign a fee or fine against someone who reviews the company; or force the author of a review to give up intellectual property rights in that review. The act does not cover contracts between employers and independent contractors

Companies aren't completely at the mercy of customers. A company can remove a review (or have it removed) if it contains confidential information, like financial or medical records or corporate trade secrets. Reviews that are libelous, obscene, vulgar, racist, sexist, homophobic, or otherwise offensive or inappropriate may also be taken down, as can reviews that are unrelated to the company's products or services or are clearly false or misleading. The FTC and state attorneys general have enforcement powers for the act, violations of which can result in the same punishments against a company as if it had engaged in unfair or deceptive acts or practices—generally, a fine.

FTC guidance on native advertising. *Native advertising* is a hot trend in the advertising business. The FTC defines it as "content that bears a similarity to the news, feature articles, product reviews, entertainment, and other material that surrounds it online." Is it legal? There have been cases in which consumers have been fooled into thinking advertising content is real news or is unsolicited, "grass-roots" consumer recommendation—which runs afoul of the FTC Act's prohibition of unfair and deceptive advertising.

In 2015, the FTC issued two important documents: one entitled *Native Advertising: A Guide for Businesses* and one named *Enforcement Policy Statement on Deceptively Formatted Advertisements.* These documents outline and explain the FTC's regulatory stance on native advertising. The FTC wants advertisers to remember that although the native advertising trend may be new, the rules governing unfair and deceptive advertising are not—and apply just as much to new kinds of advertising as they do to more traditional models.

The Policy Statement makes clear the rules "regarding advertising and promotional messages integrated into and presented as non-commercial content." The *Guide* provides 17 hypothetical native ads, along with suggestions of the legal issues each ad raises and the advertiser's disclosure requirements. Here's an example: "A video game immerses a player in a virtual world. While exploring part of the virtual world, a player sees billboards advertising actual products. The marketers of the advertised products paid the game designers to include the ads in the game. That billboards are advertisements is apparent to consumers. To the extent that the billboards are for actual products, consumers are likely to attribute the ads to the sponsoring advertisers and no disclosure is necessary. However, the sponsoring advertisers would be liable for any deceptive product claims on the billboards."

The FTC's publication of these documents signals that the commission will be watching native advertising closely and will pursue advertisers not in compliance. In 2016, for example, the FTC settled with clothing retailer Lord & Taylor over a native advertising campaign that used Instagram in such a way that consumers didn't know that the content was sponsored by Lord & Taylor and not just random fashionistas expressing delight over a dress.

■ AN OVERVIEW OF MAJOR ISSUES

As America undergoes a new revolution in communications technology, major questions about advertising and media economics are unanswered. In view of cable and satellite TV, plus the declining market share of free, advertiser-supported broadcasting, is it certain that advertising will remain the dominant source of revenue for the media? What will happen if it isn't? Millions of people now devote a lot of their television-viewing time to advertising-free video programming such as movies on DVDs or DVRs. New technology makes it easier than ever for consumers to "zap" commercials (see Chapter Eleven) that cost advertisers millions of dollars to put on the air. Will advertisers always be willing to pay the bills?

Criticism of cigarette advertising has been intense, but should there be an across-the-board ban on this advertising? There have been many government efforts to regulate or forbid cigarette advertising. Does this really violate the First Amendment rights of tobacco companies? Are restrictions on graphic cigarette ads an appropriate response to the problem of teen smoking? How will cases challenging those packaging rules play out? And how about the developing rules on e-cigarettes?

What role should Congress and the courts play in advertising regulation? Will the courts continue the trend, begun in 1975, toward protection for commercial speech? Or will they again say a message is protected only if its creator is in the business of selling ideas, not products and services? Do the *44 Liquormart*, *Greater New Orleans*, and *Lorillard Tobacco* decisions mark a new era of protection for commercial speech, even speech promoting a "vice"?

What of the FTC's varying zeal in enforcing the law? If the FTC fails to aggressively enforce its rules forbidding false and misleading advertising, should other bodies step in? Will Congress step in and forbid advertising for some "harmful" products or services? Also, what role will self-regulation play in the future of advertising?

What of the trend toward enormous damage awards in false advertising lawsuits under the Lanham Act? Should the threat of *treble damages* for advertising fraud change the way advertising claims are verified before a campaign begins?

And what about political advertising and campaign finance regulations? In the wake of the highly controversial and far-reaching *Citizens United* case, the Supreme Court has cast doubt on the constitutionality of many state and local regulations on campaign finance. And what exactly is "exacting scrutiny"? Is it really just strict scrutiny by another name? More importantly, how will it play out in the challenges that will inevitably be leveled against state donor disclosure laws in the wake of the Court's 2021 *Americans for Prosperity Found.* case?

In short, are we moving into an era of new freedom for advertisers, or, perhaps, a new era of heavy government regulation of advertising?

WHAT SHOULD I KNOW ABOUT MY STATE?

- What are my state's advertising fraud and consumer protection laws?
- How have those laws been interpreted to regulate advertising in my state?
- What are my state's campaign finance laws? Have they been amended? How will they fare under *Citizens United* and related campaign finance cases?

SUMMARY

A SUMMARY OF ADVERTISING AND THE LAW

Is Advertising Protected by the First Amendment?

Until 1975, *commercial speech* was not generally protected by the First Amendment. However, since then the Supreme Court has extended some constitutional protection to commercial speech and greater protection to noncommercial corporate speech. While advertising has its own body of law, the general rules of media law, like libel and copyright, also apply to advertising.

Do Advertisers Have a Right of Access to the Media?

Generally, there is no right of access to the media. A publisher or broadcaster may accept or reject advertising at will, unless the acceptances and rejections fall into a pattern of unfair or monopolistic business practices. However, broadcasters (but not other media) must sell advertising to federal election candidates, and sometimes state-owned media are required to grant advertising access.

Who Regulates Advertising Content and Why?

The primary federal agency that regulates advertising is the Federal Trade Commission. To protect the public from false and misleading advertising, the FTC has a Congressional mandate to monitor advertising and act against practices it considers improper. The FTC's authority extends to all U.S. media, including online. It has several enforcement tools, including informal letters of compliance, consent decrees, and formal cease and desist orders. The FTC may require substantiation of an advertising claim, and it may order corrective advertising if an ad has been particularly false or misleading. It issues formal trade regulation rules and advisory guides addressing specific advertising content.

Does Anyone Else Regulate Advertising?

Other federal agencies have authority over certain kinds of advertising. All 50 states have statutory laws prohibiting fraudulent business practices; some states vigorously enforce them against false advertisers, but some are less diligent. The National Association of Attorneys General has coordinated multistate legal actions against allegedly fraudulent advertising.

Does the Advertising Industry Self-Regulate?

The advertising industry has an elaborate system of self-regulation. The National Advertising Division (NAD), part of the Better Business Bureau, works with national advertisers to ensure that advertising meets regulatory standards and is fair. Decisions of the NAD can be appealed to the National Advertising Review Board.

14 *Freedom of the Student Press*

Almost all student media—no matter how well edited or produced—eventually face the wrath of administrators who don't like something in print, online or on the air. Official reactions vary from telephone calls or irate memos to outright censorship. Although the student press has been censored for as long as there have been student newspapers, instances of censorship appear to rise and decline in cycles. Until the 1960s, administrative censorship seemed almost routine on many high school and college campuses. And when it happened, the staffs and their faculty advisers could do little about it.

The student protest era of the late 1960s changed that—for a while. Students in that period were unwilling to limit their expression to editorials bemoaning the lack of school spirit or urging students to keep the campus clean. Instead, many high school and college newspapers focused on issues such as war and peace, civil rights and later drug use, sexual orientation, and other sensitive issues. Amazingly, many of them got away with it, creating a legacy of First Amendment protection that stood up in court for many years. However, the trend was clearly away from campus press freedom by the 1980s into the 2000s—at least at the high school level. Many student editors were less concerned about the great issues of the day than their predecessors had been.

But in the 2020s, is the pendulum swinging back to an activist student body? The doubling of "New Voices" state laws suggests that students, in pursuit of their speech and press rights, are willing to partner with advocates to gain specific legal protections for their media products—and that at least some state legislatures listened.

The Supreme Court first extended First Amendment protection to students in 1969; hundreds of decisions have followed that precedent, overruling administrative censorship of student publications and other campus expression. Whenever an instance of censorship involved state action (i.e., an act by a government employee such as a public school principal or college dean), the courts have often (but not always) held that the First Amendment and other constitutional safeguards applied. At private institutions, though, school officials are not government officials; the courts have rarely found state action in their conduct.

There are many confrontations between administrators and student journalists every year. Although many of these incidents involve blatant prior restraint that may not be legal today, these acts of censorship often go unchallenged because no one has the money, the inclination, or the legal resources to haul campus officials into court. This chapter discusses cases that *did* make it to court and produced legal precedents.

Chapter Objectives:

- Describe the history of student speech regulation, from *Tinker* to *Mahanoy*, and how it has evolved over time.
- Apply the tests developed by the Supreme Court in those cases.
- Explain the differences between the regulatory power of officials at public and private institutions as determined by whether they are state actors.

Essential Questions:

- Early cases focused on "analog" expression, like armbands and print papers. How has digital communication—which can happen anytime and anywhere—changed how the law deals with student expression? Should the communication mode matter? Why?
- Should the *Hazelwood* standard for middle/high school student speech be applied to colleges? What should the standard be there?
- When should administrators be able to claim qualified immunity for their actions?

■ EARLY SUPREME COURT DECISIONS

In many areas of media law, the basic principles can be traced to a few landmark Supreme Court decisions, and student press freedom is one of those areas.

The *Tinker* case, a big win for student press at the high court. In 1969, the Court ruled on the case of *Tinker v. Des Moines Independent Community School District* (393 U.S. 503), often called the "black armbands case." The case arose when John and Mary Beth Tinker, ages 15 and 13, and a 16-year-old friend were suspended for wearing black armbands at school as a symbolic protest of the Vietnam War. The Des Moines school principals had heard of the pending protest and hurriedly adopted a rule against wearing armbands on campus.

The suspension was challenged on First Amendment grounds. Two lower courts upheld the school officials' action, but the Supreme Court reversed, declaring the act symbolic speech protected by the First Amendment. Justice Abe Fortas, writing for the Court, famously said, "It can hardly be argued that either students or teachers shed their constitutional rights to freedom of speech or expression at the schoolhouse gate."

The Court noted that the three students did nothing to disrupt the educational process. Justice Fortas noted, "In our system, state-operated schools may not be enclaves of totalitarianism. School officials do not possess absolute authority over their students." However, the Court did make it clear that the rights of students were not "co-extensive" with those of adults off-campus. Student speech could be suppressed when its interferes with the rights of others or "would materially and substantially interfere with the requirements of appropriate discipline in the operation of the school" (the "substantial disruption" test).

***Healy* and *Papish*.** During the 1970s, the Supreme Court addressed the First Amendment status of college students twice, both times expanding students' rights on campus. In the first case, a chapter of Students for a Democratic Society, a national organization known for its militancy, was denied recognition as a campus group at Central Connecticut State College. Without that status, the group could not use campus facilities. The group sued, and in *Healy v. James* (408 U.S. 169, 1972), the Court said the local group couldn't be denied campus privileges merely because of the national organization's reputation. Public colleges "are not enclaves immune from the sweep of the First Amendment," the Court famously said.

A year later, in *Papish v. Univ. of Missouri Curators* (410 U.S. 670, 1973), the high court overruled the expulsion of Barbara Papish, a graduate student and editor of the *Free Press*. Papish previously angered university officials by distributing her paper when high school students and their parents were on campus, but when she published an issue they regarded as particularly indecent, they took action. That edition featured a political cartoon depicting a policeman raping the Statue of Liberty and the Goddess of Justice, and a profane headline. The Court ruled that neither the cartoon nor the headline was obscene. Nor did Papish's activities "materially and substantially" interfere with campus order.

■ THE SUPREME COURT CHANGES THE RULES

By the late 1980s it was clear that the mood of the country had changed. The student protest era was over, and most school officials were determined to reassert their authority. The Supreme Court decided it was time to help the authorities do precisely that.

In its first rulings on the First Amendment rights of students since the heyday of the student protest movement, the justices sharply curtailed students' constitutional rights. Even before the landmark *Hazelwood* decision, the Court was chipping away at students' First Amendment rights.

The *Fraser* case. Ruling in 1986 in the case of *Bethel Sch. Dist. v. Fraser* (478 U.S. 675), the Supreme Court held that a Washington state high school student could be disciplined for delivering a speech containing sexual innuendoes, even though the speech contained no four-letter words, wasn't clearly obscene in a legal sense, and didn't threaten to disrupt the educational process. The *Fraser* case began in 1983 when Matthew Fraser gave a speech at a Bethel High School assembly to endorse a friend's candidacy for a student body office. A state champion public speaker, Fraser avoided obscenity in the nominating speech, but he thoroughly amused those students who understood his innuendoes.

However, school administrators didn't think it was funny: they suspended Fraser for two days and removed his name from a list of candidates in a student election to select a graduation speaker. Fraser won the graduation speaker election on a write-in vote and school officials permitted him to speak at his graduation—but only after he filed suit.

Lower courts ruled that school officials had violated Fraser's First Amendment rights by suspending him, but the Supreme Court disagreed. Writing for a 7-2 majority, Chief Justice Warren Burger said, "The schools, as instruments of the state, may determine that the essential lessons of civil, mature conduct cannot be conveyed in a school that tolerates lewd, indecent, or offensive speech and conduct such as that indulged in by this confused boy." Burger took pains to distinguish this case from the *Tinker* decision, in which the Supreme Court had strongly affirmed the First Amendment rights of students nearly 20 years earlier. Burger said this case was different because "the penalties imposed in this case were unrelated to any political viewpoint." (In *Tinker*, students wore black armbands to protest the Vietnam War.)

It does not follow, Burger added, "that simply because the use of an offensive form of expression may not be prohibited to adults making what the speaker considers a political point, that the same latitude must be permitted to children in a public school." Significantly, the Court declined to use a *Tinker* analysis, which would have asked whether Fraser's speech was disruptive or violated others' rights—the two grounds for speech censorship in *Tinker.*

The *Hazelwood* case. Having ruled against Matthew Fraser, the Supreme Court had little difficulty disposing of the *Hazelwood Sch. Dist. v. Kuhlmeier* case (484 U.S. 260, 1988) two years later. The Court ruled against the editors of *The Spectrum*, the student newspaper at Hazelwood East High School in Missouri. Their principal censored two articles they planned to publish: a story about teenage pregnancy that quoted students who had become pregnant,

Focus on...
§1983 claims and qualified immunity

Student speech plaintiffs sometimes charge administrators with civil rights violations under 42 U.S.C. §1983, a federal law allowing government officials to be personally sued for damages. Officials usually claim *qualified immunity*, arguing they didn't know they were violating the law since it wasn't "clearly established." This defense is wildly successful, particularly for police, even though it doesn't appear in §1983.

Courts often let qualified immunity shield school officials (e.g., *Morse, Doninger, Hosty*). Why? Judges simply accept their claims that the law isn't "clearly established." Critics say that's hard to fix; as one notes, "If courts refuse to resolve legal claims because the law was not clearly established, then the law will never become clearly established."

Still, don't expect to see a decline in the use of qualified immunity. It just works too well.

and an article in which students explained how their parents' divorces had affected them. None of the students' real names were used in the stories.

The Supreme Court held in a 5-3 decision that the principal was entitled to censor the articles even though they neither violated the rights of other students nor threatened to cause a campus disruption (again, the landmark *Tinker* ruling had permitted campus censorship for only these two reasons). Writing for the Court, Justice Byron White said, "We hold that educators do not offend the First Amendment by exercising editorial control over the style and content of student speech in school-sponsored expressive activities so long as their actions are reasonably related to legitimate pedagogical concerns."

White said school officials never intended for this student newspaper to be an open forum for student opinion like the "underground" and off-campus newspapers involved in so many earlier decisions that upheld students' rights. Instead, White concluded, school officials "reserved the forum [the school newspaper] for its intended purpose, as a supervised learning experience for journalism students. Accordingly, school officials were entitled to regulate the contents of *Spectrum* in any reasonable manner." White added, "A school need not tolerate student speech that is inconsistent with its basic educational mission, even though the government could not censor similar speech outside the school...."

How can *Hazelwood* be reconciled with the Court's strong affirmation of student rights in the *Tinker* decision? White explained: "The question whether the First Amendment requires a school to tolerate particular student speech...is different from the question whether the First Amendment requires a school affirmatively to promote particular student speech." Thus, White viewed the curricular *Spectrum* newspaper as a promotional or official tool.

Justice William Brennan wrote a dissenting opinion in which he and two other justices (Thurgood Marshall and Harry Blackmun) condemned the majority's message to students: "The young men and women of Hazelwood East expected a civics lesson, but not the one the Court teaches them today.... Such unthinking contempt for individual rights is ... particularly insidious from one to whom the public entrusts the task of inculcating in its youth an appreciation for the cherished democratic liberties that our Constitution guarantees."

Nevertheless, the precedent from the *Hazelwood* case is clear: the First Amendment does not ordinarily protect official student newspapers (and other school-sponsored activities, such as drama productions) from administrative control. However, this does not necessarily mean that school newspapers have no protection at all from administrative censorship: the Supreme Court ruling did not invalidate state laws and local policies that protect the free-press rights of student journalists. All the Court really said was that, in the absence of any other rules barring administrative censorship, the First Amendment does not protect student newspapers from such censorship.

While the *Hazelwood* decision applies only to official school-sponsored activities, students who express controversial views in unofficial newspapers or in other ways may be punished by methods that do not involve direct prior restraint—as Matthew Fraser was, with the Supreme Court's blessing. Students who feel strongly enough about an issue to go to the trouble of publishing an unofficial newspaper or tract often end up including offensive language as well as political rhetoric. Under the *Fraser* precedent, school officials may justify punishing them on the basis of the language alone.

Under the *Tinker* rule, school officials were allowed to abridge students' First Amendment rights only when the exercise of those rights might disrupt the orderly educational process or violate the rights of others. Under the *Hazelwood* rule, no threat of a disruption

FIG. 117.
The original "Bong
Hits" banner at
the Newseum,
Washington, D.C.

Author's collection.

is needed to justify censorship. Instead, the First Amendment no longer prevents school officials from restricting students' rights whenever there is a violation of what school officials consider to be the proper standards of good taste and decency for students.

The *Morse* decision. That point was underscored in a 2007 U.S. Supreme Court decision that upheld a high school principal's seizure of a banner with the slogan "BONG HiTS 4 JESUS." Ruling in *Morse v. Frederick* (551 U.S. 393), a 5-4 decision, the Court said because the message on the banner could be interpreted as advocating illegal drug use, it was not protected by the First Amendment. In an opinion by Chief Justice John Roberts, the Court again declined to apply *Tinker*. Although there was no disruption of the educational process and no violation of others' rights (the two circumstances when *Tinker* allows student speech to be suppressed), the apparent advocacy of drug use was enough to justify censorship.

Joseph Frederick, then a student at Juneau-Douglas (Ala.) High School, was suspended for 10 days for displaying his "Bong Hits" banner across the street from the school as the Olympic Torch Relay, an event leading up to the 2002 Winter Olympics, was passing—in what he said was an attempt to get on national TV. Principal Deborah Morse crossed the street, confronted Frederick, crumpled the banner and suspended him. He sued, alleging a violation of his First Amendment rights and seeking money damages from Morse in what's known as a §1983 claim (targeting a government official's *personal* liability for civil rights violations). School officials did not argue that displaying the banner disrupted the torch relay or school activities, but they said it interfered with the school's goal of promoting a drug-free environment.

Reversing a ruling of the Ninth Circuit, the Supreme Court said Frederick's "Bong Hits" message had no First Amendment protection. The Court conceded that Frederick would have the right to display that banner off campus, but this event wasn't "off campus"—it was a school "social event or class trip" across the street from the school during school hours.

Emphasizing the decisions's limited scope, Justices Samuel Alito and Anthony Kennedy-filed a concurring opinion in which they said they voted with Roberts only because the issue was drug use. They emphasized that the decision would not allow any restriction on political or social advocacy by students. Justice Clarence Thomas also concurred, agreeing with the outcome but adding his belief that *Tinker* should be overturned: historically, he wrote, "teachers taught, and students listened. Teachers commanded, and students obeyed. Teachers ... relied on discipline to maintain order."

Justice Stephen Breyer said he would limit the decision to simply barring §1983 damages against Morse; he thought she shouldn't face monetary damages for a spur-of-the-moment decision. Justice Clarence Thomas also concurred, agreeing with the outcome but adding his belief that *Tinker* should be overturned: historically, he wrote, "teachers taught, and

FIG. 118.
Brandi Levy's profane Snap from 2017, resulting in her suspension from the cheerleading team at her Pennsylvania high school. The Supreme Court vindicated her in 2021, saying her First Amendment rights were violated by that suspension.

From court documents.

students listened. Teachers commanded, and students obeyed. Teachers ... relied on discipline to maintain order." The dissenters, though, said that Frederick's banner *should* get First Amendment protection. "Most students, however, do not shed their brains at the school-house gate... The notion that the message on this banner would actually persuade either the average student or even the dumbest one to change his or her behavior is most implausible," Justice John Paul Stevens scoffed.

The *Mahanoy* decision. High school sophomore and junior varsity cheerleader Brandi Levy, upset that she'd failed to make the varsity cheerleading squad at her Mahanoy City, Pennsylvania, high school, vented her anger over Snapchat, sending a profane Snap to her 250 followers from a convenience store on a Saturday in 2017. One recipient captured the Snap (which would have ordinarily disappeared within a day) and shared it with cheerleading coaches—who suspended Levy from the cheerleading squad altogether for violating policy against disparaging the team. She sued, and both a district court and the Third Circuit said that her First Amendment rights had been violated. But the appellate court made it clear that *Tinker* didn't apply to off-campus speech, and so the school could not punish Levy for the Snap she created and sent off-campus on a weekend, saying that "the First Amendment protects students engaging in off-campus speech to the same extent it protects speech by citizens in the community at large." In *Mahanoy Area Sch. Dist. v. B.L.* (No. 20–255, 2021), the Supreme Court agreed with the Third Circuit's outcome but not its reasoning.

Justice Stephen Breyer, writing for an 8-1 Court, declined to go as far as the Third Circuit. "[W]e do not believe the special characteristics that give schools additional license to regulate student speech always disappear when a school regulates speech that takes place off campus," he wrote, noting that schools might be able to extend their reach in situations like targeted bullying, threats, or breaches of school security. But, although Breyer declined to offer a rule for when schools could regulate off-campus student expression, he did say that it should be rare. "[A] school, in relation to off-campus speech, will rarely stand *in loco parentis*" ("in the place of a parent," a status that schools have for on-campus students), he wrote. Justice Samuel Alito, joined by Justice Neil Gorsuch, concurred. Enrollment in a public school "cannot be treated as a complete transfer of parental authority over a student's speech," Alito said.

The sole dissenter, Justice Clarence Thomas, repeated his perspective from *Morse*. Calling it "well settled that [schools] still could discipline students for off-campus speech or conduct that had a proximate tendency to harm the school environment," he claimed the majority ignored "the 150 years of history supporting the coach." And, he complained, the majority "fails to address the historical contours of [*in loco parentis*], whether the doctrine applies to off-campus speech, or why the Court has abandoned it." He said that maybe the qualities of social media should give schools *more*, not less, power to regulate student expression there. Finally, Thomas said, the majority didn't question Levy's assertion that her speech qualified as "off campus," calling it "a much trickier question" than the majority made it.

New Voices. In 2017, the American Bar Association, the professional organization for attorneys, issued a resolution urging all states to pass laws to protect student media organizations against censorship. This call came in the wake of a number of new "New Voices" laws—an initiative begun in 2015 by the Student Press Law Center (SPLC) in Washington, D.C., a nonprofit organization dedicated to protecting student speech and press legal rights.

As of 2021, 15 states have New Voices laws that protect student media in various capacities. These are, in order of passage: California (1977), Massachusetts (1988), Iowa (1989), Colorado (1990), Kansas (1992), Arkansas (1995), Oregon (2007), North Dakota (2015), Maryland (2016), Illinois (2016), Vermont (2017), Nevada (2017), Rhode Island (2017), Washington (2018), and New Jersey (2021). The New Jersey bill was sent at the end of June 2021 to the governor, who had 45 days to sign or allow it to become law without his signature. The SPLC said at least 10 states had also introduced bills as of March 2021 (among them Hawaii, Missouri, New York, Iowa, West Virginia, and Texas). Several of these bills are still working through the legislative process. The SPLC is continuing this initiative.

■ COLLEGE STUDENT SPEECH CASES AND ISSUES

The Court's post-*Tinker* cases had far-reaching implications for the legal rights of students, implications that extended well beyond a student's right to publish news stories about divorce and pregnancy or to give a speech containing a few sexual innuendoes. *Hazelwood's* impact has been felt even at the college level. While a footnote in *Hazelwood* said the Court was not ruling on the status of college student publications, a U.S. Supreme Court decision such as that one inevitably has an impact on courts ruling on First Amendment freedoms on college campuses. Several federal appeals courts have held that *Hazelwood* does apply to college students, although other courts have disagreed.

Federal courts. In the 2000s, federal courts ruled both ways on this issue. In 2001, the Sixth Circuit supported the First Amendment rights of the college media in *Kincaid v. Gibson* (236 F.3d 342). The court, ruling *en banc*, held that Kentucky State University (KSU) officials violated the First Amendment by impounding all copies of the KSU yearbook in 1994. A three-judge panel had said that KSU administrators didn't violate the First Amendment because the yearbook was not a public forum protected by the First Amendment. Campus officials objected to the yearbook for several reasons, including its color (purple), the lack of captions for many of the photographs, and the inclusion of considerable off-campus material.

In the *en banc* ruling, the judges held that the KSU *Thorobred* yearbook was a limited public forum and couldn't be arbitrarily censored. Significantly, the court ruled that the U.S. Supreme Court's *Hazelwood* decision does not apply to student publications at the college level, at least in this particular instance. The eight-judge majority even said campus media that are nonpublic forums cannot be censored if the censorship is not *viewpoint-neutral*. To reach its conclusion that the yearbook was a limited forum entitled to First Amendment protection, the majority analyzed KSU's written policy governing the yearbook, the actual practice of the university in overseeing it, the nature of the yearbook as an expressive activity, and the campus context. After the *en banc* decision, KSU officials settled the case by agreeing to pay damages and attorney's fees and to release the impounded yearbooks and attempt to distribute them to students who were entitled to receive them seven years earlier.

Hosty: a near miss? On the other hand, in 2005 the Seventh Circuit rejected the Sixth Circuit's reasoning and applied *Hazelwood* to college students in *Hosty v. Carter* (412 F.3d 731). In another *en banc* decision, the court voted 7-4 to overturn an earlier decision by a three-judge panel and limit the First Amendment rights of student journalists in that circuit (Illinois, Indiana, and Wisconsin). Patricia Carter, dean of student affairs at Governors State University near Chicago, ordered the printer of the student paper, *The Innovator*, not to print future issues until she reviewed and approved the copy. Margaret Hosty and other staffers sued, alleging that this prior review violated the First Amendment. Initially, the three-judge panel agreed, holding that the *Hazelwood* principle did not apply at the college level. The court also ruled that the law on this point is so clear that Carter's qualified immunity defense failed: she could be held personally liable and forced to pay damages.

Then the three-judge panel's decision was withdrawn and the *en banc* panel ruled that Carter had qualified immunity from being personally liable because the law does not clearly support the students' position. In fact, the majority said that student freedom must be analyzed under *Hazelwood*: "We hold, therefore, that *Hazelwood* framework applies to subsidized student newspapers at colleges as well as elementary and secondary schools." Under that standard, administrative censorship is not barred by the First Amendment. The majority opinion, written by Judge Frank Easterbrook, also said, "There is no sharp difference between high school and college newspapers," alluding to the fact that some are financially subsidized or produced by journalism classes, or both. *The Innovator* was subsidized but not produced by a class. But Judge Easterbrook also said that a student newspaper could be a "designated public forum." If it is, it would be protected by the First Amendment. In 2006, the U.S. Supreme Court denied *cert*.

The *Hosty* case prompted strong reactions across the country. It was widely condemned by journalism educators and First Amendment advocates. While federal circuit court decisions are binding only within the particular circuit, such rulings carry considerable legal weight in other circuits. Many earlier federal appellate court decisions upholding student press freedom have been widely cited outside the particular circuits in which they originated.

Christine Helwick, general counsel for the 400,000-student California State University system, issued a memo to campus presidents in 2005 that addressed the impact of *Hosty* in California. She said the case suggested "more latitude than previously believed to censor the content of subsidized student newspapers." That may have been true, but not for long. In 2006, the state legislature enacted a law forbidding administrative censorship of student newspapers at California public colleges and universities: "Nothing in this section shall be construed to authorize any prior restraint of student speech or the student press."

The Illinois legislature passed a similar law, the College Campus Press Act, in 2007—taking direct aim at *Hosty* in the state where the case arose. The Illinois law declares that all campus media at public colleges and universities are public forums. Then it says: "Campus media, whether campus-sponsored or noncampus-sponsored, is not subject to prior review by public officials of a state-sponsored institution of higher learning… A collegiate media adviser must not be terminated, transferred, removed, otherwise disciplined or retaliated against for refusing to suppress protected free expression rights of collegiate student journalists and of collegiate student editors…" The Illinois law also protects public colleges from lawsuits based on the content of student media (and as of 2016, high schools, too).

California also adopted the Journalism Teacher Protection Act in 2008, which applies to both high school and college advisers. It amends several sections of the Education Code, saying that "an employee shall not be dismissed, suspended, disciplined, reassigned, transferred, or otherwise retaliated against" for protecting students doing journalism.

Can you "steal" a free paper? Many college newspapers have had to deal with large-scale newspaper thefts that in some cases were condoned if not encouraged by campus administrators. By 2006, there had been incidents on at least 200 campuses in which someone or some group systematically removed the entire press run of a newspaper from the newsracks. Sometimes the act was a protest against a specific story or the newspaper's editorial policies in general, but on other occasions there was no discernible reason for the theft. In some cases, campus police acted to halt newspaper thefts and to apprehend those who cleaned out the newsracks. But on other campuses, administrators ordered the police *not* to act and openly sided with the thieves. Since most campus papers are free for the taking, some administrators refused to accept that taking the entire press run was a wrongful act, despite the fact that the cost of printing replacements can be hundreds or thousands of dollars. The Student Press Law Center suggested that campus newspapers include a statement saying individual copies are free, but multiple copies carry a substantial charge. This at least makes it more clear that taking the entire press run is theft. However, even that has not worked on some campuses: some administrators decreed that such a statement would constitute the imposition of an illegal new student fee.

On many college campuses, administrators are well aware that they cannot directly censor the student media without risking a lawsuit and a lot of bad publicity. But with a wink and a nod, they can certainly encourage someone else to do the dirty work for them by rounding up all the copies of an offending newspaper. In 2007, the California legislature passed the California Newspaper Theft Law, making it a misdemeanor to take more than 25 copies of a free paper with the intent of recycling or selling the papers, stopping others from reading it, or harming a business competitor.

Concerns about "professionalism." Some universities have policies that punish behavior deemed "unprofessional"—policies that often include restrictions on speech. The Eighth Circuit in 2016 relied on both *Hazelwood* and concerns about professionalism when it upheld a student's dismissal from a nursing program for hostile Facebook posts about his classmates. In *Keefe v. Adams* (840 F.3d 523), Craig Keefe challenged his removal, which was based on posts such as "Glad group projects are group projects. I give her a big fat F for changing the group power point [sic] at eleven last night and resubmitting. Not enough whiskey to control that anger." His classmate expressed fear about working with him. Administration cited his lack of professionalism and remorse for the posts' effects.

In upholding the lower court's dismissal of Keefe's First Amendment claim (and upholding his removal), the Eighth Circuit used the standard from *Hazelwood*: "speech reflecting non-compliance with [the Nurses Association Code of Ethics] that is related to academic activities 'materially disrupts' the Program's 'legitimate pedagogical concerns.'" Moreover, nursing students in that program consented in writing to be bound by that national code of ethics and other policies concerning professional behavior and boundaries.

And in 2019, the Tenth Circuit said that the University of New Mexico was within its rights to order a grad student to engage in a "professionalism enhancement prescription" after posting profane political speech on Facebook (*Hunt. v. Bd. of Regents*, 792 F. App'x 595). Calling online student expression "a developing area of constitutional law," the court said that because of that uncertainty, the university was within its rights in "requiring a graduate student to meet standards of professionalism that would be expected of him." The Supreme Court declined to hear appeals in both cases.

Campus Advertising and the First Amendment

Another troubling question on some campuses is whether the campus media have the right to accept controversial advertising: what happens if the administration or state officials order a campus newspaper to reject alcoholic beverage advertising, for example? Alternately, what happens if the staff decides on its own not to accept a certain kind of advertising?

This question has been litigated for 50 years. In the 1960s, federal courts in New York and Wisconsin overturned state-supported school and college administrators' efforts to keep student newspapers from accepting ads that espoused controversial ideas. The same issues were raised in the 1970s when a federal appellate court rejected an appeal for access to the ad columns of the Mississippi State University newspaper in *Mississippi Gay Alliance v. Goudelock* (536 F.2d 1073, 1976). The Gay Alliance wanted to place an announcement of its services and was turned down. The court said this case was different from previous cases because here the staff, as opposed to the administration, rejected the ad. Hence, there was no state action in this decision to reject advertising from a gay organization. But in addition, the court said previous court decisions had given the editors final say over the content.

Focus on...
"Boobies" in school

You may have seen them on the street or on campus: brightly colored silicone bracelet with slogans, made popular by Lance Armstrong's "LiveStrong" campaign for cancer research.

The Keep A Breast organization (keep-a-breast. org) created a series of bracelets to support breast health and cancer prevention and early detection. These bracelets were emblazoned with the phrases "I ♥ Boobies" and "Keep A Breast." They became popular with students

FIG. 119. "I ♥ Boobies" bracelets.

Author's collection.

at all levels, from colleges to grade schools, sometimes running afoul of dress codes that forbid sexual references. Some students fought back—with mixed results.

A federal judge in Wisconsin agreed with the ban: "It is reasonable for school officials to conclude that this phrase is vulgar and inconsistent with their goal of fostering respectful discourse..." (*K.J. v. Sauk Center Sch. Dist.*, 3:11-cv-00622-bbc, 2012). But in Pennsylvania, the *en banc* Third Circuit held that the bracelets couldn't be banned under the Supreme Court's student-speech tests (*B.H. v. Easton Sch. Dist.*, 725 F.3d 293, 2013). Because the bracelets were not plainly lewd (that is, they had several meanings) and no school disruptions resulted, the court admonished, "Just because letting in one idea might invite even more difficult judgment calls about other ideas cannot justify suppressing speech of genuine social value." The Supreme Court denied *cert.*

The Third Circuit ultimately overturned a Pennsylvania law banning alcoholic beverage advertising in campus media as a violation of the First Amendment. In 2004, the court ruled in favor of *The Pitt News,* the student newspaper at the University of Pittsburgh (*Pitt News v. Pappert,* 379 F.3d 96). In a decision written by Samuel Alito, now a Supreme Court justice, the appellate court noted that *The Pitt News,* a financially independent, ad-supported newspaper, derived a significant part of its revenue from alcoholic beverage advertising before the state barred alcoholic beverage advertisers from placing ads in campus media in 1996. After that, several off-campus publications distributed on campus continued to carry alcohol ads, but not *The Pitt News.* Because of the obvious financial implications of this state law, *The Pitt News* challenged its constitutionality. At first, the courts sided with the state, but *The Pitt News* eventually prevailed when the Third Circuit accepted the argument that because the policy financially burdened the campus newspaper while benefiting off-campus competitors, it singled out one medium of communication as opposed to others for disfavored treatment. Citing classic Supreme Court decisions on newspaper taxation such as *Grosjean* and *Minneapolis Star & Tribune* (discussed in Chapter Three), Alito wrote: "If the government were free to suppress disfavored speech by preventing potential speakers from being paid, there would not be much left of the First Amendment."

Following a similar path, the Fourth Circuit upheld in 2010—and then reversed in 2013—a state ban on some kinds of alcohol advertising in college newspapers. In the 2013 case, the court ultimately overturned the regulation as overbroad. In *Educ. Media Co. at Va. Tech, Inc. v. Insley* (731 F.3d 291), the court said that despite the laudable government goal of reducing underage drinking, the ban failed "because it prohibits large numbers of adults who are 21 years of age or older from receiving truthful information about a product that they are legally allowed to consume."

Campus Fees, Campus Groups, and Student Freedom

In 1995, the U.S. Supreme Court ruled on another aspect of student press freedom: the right of a religious student group to receive university printing subsidies if other groups receive them. In *Rosenberger v. Rector & Visitors of the Univ. of Virginia* (515 U.S. 819), the high court ruled that the University of Virginia had to pay for the printing of a Christian student newspaper from its Student Activities Fund if it paid for the printing of other student groups' newspapers. In so ruling, the 5-4 majority held that the First Amendment's *establishment clause* (which has been interpreted to forbid government sponsorship of religious activities such as prayers in public schools) does *not* require a public university to withhold support from a religious student newspaper when it supports other publications produced by student organizations.

Writing for the majority, Justice Anthony Kennedy said the university was engaged in *viewpoint discrimination* in violation of the free expression provisions of the First Amendment because it favored student newspapers expressing certain viewpoints over others. The viewpoint discrimination in the university's action was "a denial of the right of free speech and would risk fostering a pervasive bias or hostility to religion, which could undermine the very neutrality (toward religion) the Establishment Clause requires," Kennedy wrote.

Viewpoint neutrality. The Supreme Court ruled on a related case concerning university student fees in 2000. The justices said that a public university may grant money derived from mandatory student fees to controversial organizations as long as the money is available to various groups on a *viewpoint-neutral* basis. Ruling in *Board of Regents v. Southworth* (529 U.S. 217), the Court rejected a challenge by conservative students to the University of Wisconsin's practice of awarding fee money to groups with which these students disagreed.

Writing for a unanimous Court, Justice Kennedy said that it does not violate the First Amendment for student fee monies to be given to groups that espouse controversial viewpoints. Although this does force students to pay fees that go to groups with which they disagree, Kennedy said this is not unconstitutional as long as the fee-granting process is open to a variety of organizations with divergent viewpoints. This is different from a situation where students (or government employees) must pay fees to support only one specific viewpoint, Kennedy said. Here, the mandatory student fee money was given to many groups with varying viewpoints—not just to a group representing one viewpoint.

The Supreme Court ordered a lower court to make sure that the fee-granting system at Wisconsin really is viewpoint-neutral before reaching a final decision on this case. This case differs from the *Rosenberger* case in that the student-fee-awarding policy there was *not* viewpoint-neutral: student fee money was denied to campus publications produced by religious groups while being awarded to groups producing non-religious publications.

In 2010, the Supreme Court supported a public law school's decision to deny a religious student organization official status. The organization's bylaws did not comply with the university's non-discrimination policy, which included a provision that students could not be denied membership in organizations based on religion or sexual orientation (*Christian Legal Society v. Martinez*, 561 U.S. 661). The Christian Legal Society required its members to sign a "Statement of Faith" and agree to adhere to other religious tenets. This violated Hastings Law School's "all-comers" policy that allows open eligibility for student group membership.

The Ninth Circuit upheld the law school's decision, and the Court agreed. Writing for a 5-4 Court, Justice Ruth Bader Ginsburg said that "[c]ompliance with Hastings' all-comers policy...is a reasonable, viewpoint-neutral condition on access to the student-organization forum." The policy was reasonable and content-/viewpoint-neutral: "It is, after all, hard to imagine a more viewpoint-neutral policy than one requiring *all* student groups to accept *all* comers," she wrote. Dissenters said the policy was not viewpoint-neutral: "Brushing aside inconvenient precedent, the Court arms public educational institutions with a handy weapon for suppressing the speech of unpopular groups," wrote Justice Samuel Alito.

Other College First Amendment Questions

By the early 2000s, a number of courts had upheld the First Amendment rights of students and others on college campuses in several other contexts. For example, in 2001 the Seventh Circuit upheld the right of students to present a controversial play at the Fort Wayne campus of Indiana University-Purdue University in *Linnemeir v. Board of Trustees of Purdue University* (260 F.3d 757). The play, *Corpus Christi*, depicts a Christ-like figure as a gay man and has language that is offensive to many Christians. A group of residents sued to halt the student performance, contending that by allowing a presentation of anti-Christian material, the university was violating the First Amendment's establishment of religion clause, which requires separation of church and state. The appellate court rejected that argument and allowed the play to be presented. "The contention that the First Amendment forbids a state university to provide a venue for the expression of views antagonistic to conventional Christian beliefs is absurd," wrote the court.

But the Ninth Circuit ruled in 2001 that a college violated the First Amendment by prohibiting the expression of Christian beliefs on campus. In *Orin v. Barclay* (272 F.3d 1207), the court said Olympic Community College in Bremerton, Washington, violated the free speech and free exercise of religion rights of anti-abortion demonstrators by forbidding them to discuss the religious basis for their beliefs. Officials imposed conditions on anti-abortion protesters, including a ban on "religious worship or instruction." The judge said, "Having created a forum for the demonstrators' expression, [the dean of students] could not, consistent with the dictates of the First Amendment, limit their expression to secular content."

Advisers. The First Amendment also doesn't necessarily protect faculty advisers of student media. Nor does it necessarily give students standing to sue on behalf of a reassigned or terminated adviser. In 2007, the Tenth Circuit so ruled in dismissing as moot an appeal by former student editors after their faculty adviser was reassigned to other duties at Kansas State University. In *Lane v. Simon* (495 F.3d 1182), the court said the case had to be dismissed because the plaintiffs, former editors of the KSU *Collegian*, had graduated. In a brief opinion that focused on the mootness issue, the three-judge panel cited two earlier cases in which a student's graduation rendered her/his constitutional rights claims moot.

Former *Collegian* editors Katie Lane and Sarah Rice alleged that the reassignment of their faculty adviser, Ron Johnson, violated their First Amendment rights. Johnson was initially a party to the lawsuit, but his case was dismissed by a district court judge and he did not appeal. The district judge ruled that Johnson's First Amendment rights were not violated because he didn't engage in any activities protected by the First Amendment, such as editing the news. Like many advisers, he exercised no control over the newspaper's content.

The two student editors appealed, but the court said the entire case should be dismissed because the students had graduated: "Plaintiffs have not formally sued in a representative capacity, and there has been no effort on anyone's part to substitute current editors as parties. ...*Amici* urge us to confer third-party standing to plaintiffs on behalf of current and future *Collegian* editors. Given that Johnson did not appeal, and neither the publisher nor the present editors have joined in this litigation, we cannot countenance this type of end-run around the general requirement that parties raise their own claims..."

Although this ruling makes it more difficult for students to litigate cases like this one, at least in the Tenth Circuit, the editors faced difficult hurdles to begin with. In this appeal two former editors were claiming that the reassignment of their adviser violated their rights even after they graduated. But they served out their terms as editors without any incidents of administrative censorship, they faced no disciplinary action, and they graduated as planned.

Off-campus speech regulation. Lack of clarity in the law regarding university regulation of off-campus speech resulted in the Tenth Circuit in 2018 affirming a University of Kansas (KU) student's expulsion for derogatory Twitter comments about his ex-girlfriend. The case took a lengthy path through both state and federal courts. After Navid Yeasin was expelled for violating a KU no-contact order obtained by his ex-girlfriend, both a Kansas trial and appeals court said that the university student code used in the determination governed only nonacademic misconduct "while on University premises or at University-sponsored or supervised events." Yeasin's tweets couldn't be proven to have originated on-campus. So KU readmitted Yeasin, who then brought a §1983 claim in federal court against vice provost Tammara Durham, saying she was personally responsible for violating his rights. Durham claimed qualified immunity: she couldn't be held liable because the law governing off-campus student speech regulation wasn't clear. A federal district court agreed with Durham, and Yeasin appealed. The Tenth Circuit (*Yeasin v. Durham*, 719 F. App'x 844) held that Yeasin couldn't prove that Durham actually knew she was violating his rights (as required by §1983) "At the intersection of university speech and social media, First Amendment doctrine is unsettled," the court said, upholding Durham's claim of qualified immunity. KU has since revised its code to include off-campus speech.

Free speech zones. Many colleges have areas set aside for protests, often established during the Vietnam era. But not all "free speech zones" are acceptable. One example: The University of Cincinnati had a zone that was only 0.1% of its campus and required 10 days' notice before its use. Students attempting to gather signatures for a petition were unable to do so effectively because of the low traffic near the small area. A federal judge said that other areas of campus were considered to be public fora, and the 10-day notice requirement was overbroad. Moreover, she wrote, the school gave no good reason for "restricting all demonstrations, rallies, and protests from all but one designated public forum on campus" (*Univ. of Cincinnati Chapter of Young Am. for Liberty v. Williams*, 2012 U.S. Dist. LEXIS 80967).

Speech codes. While college speech codes have gone in and out of fashion since the 1970s, recent years have seen a spate of such codes both considered and adopted. Perhaps most currently controversial is the code adopted in October 2017 and later revised by the University of Wisconsin for its 18 public schools.

The UW code, defended by one regent as intended to promote listening ("I don't consider drowning out another speaker as freedom of speech"), contains this language: "Protests and demonstrations that materially and substantially disrupt the rights of others to engage in or listen to expressive activity shall not be permitted and shall be subject to sanction." Punishments are meted out on a three-strike basis (a hearing, followed by a semester suspension, and finally expulsion). Opponents say the code is also too vague to allow understanding of what is and isn't allowed, and that the very existence of such a code chills free speech. FIRE, the Foundation for Individual Rights in Education (thefire.org), keeps an online list of speech codes at universities and publishes news items on developments in the area.

■ LOWER COURT CASES AFTER HAZELWOOD

At the high school level, the *Hazelwood* decision clearly opened the way for widespread administrative censorship where no local law or policy forbids it.

Official student media. In 1989, a federal appellate court held that administrators may also control the content of the advertising in high school newspapers, yearbooks, and athletic event programs. In *Planned Parenthood v. Clark Co. Sch. Dist.* (887 F.2d 935), the court upheld a decision by school officials to forbid advertising by Planned Parenthood clinics in Las Vegas school publications. However, if school officials choose not to control advertising in school publications but instead leave decisions about advertising entirely up to the student staff, there is no state action involved in a school newspaper or yearbook's rejection of a controversial ad. The students are then free to accept or reject advertising, as a federal appellate court ruled in *Yeo v. Town of Lexington* (141 F.3d 241, 1997). The First Circuit ruled that student editors at Lexington High School in Massachusetts could reject advocacy advertising, in this case an ad from a group advocating sexual abstinence because there was a clear record that the students and not school officials were in complete control of the school newspaper and yearbook, and that they made the decision to reject the ad on their own.

Even the broad sweep of the *Hazelwood* decision has limits: there are still circumstances under which school officials may violate the First Amendment by censoring a student newspaper.

In 1994, the New Jersey Supreme Court overruled an act of administrative censorship of an official school newspaper at a *junior high school*—on First Amendment grounds. In *Desilets v. Clearview Reg'l Bd. of Educ.* (647 A.2d 150), the state supreme court held that the principal of Clearview Junior High School did not have sufficient grounds to censor two movie reviews that were written by Brien Desilets, then an eighth grader, for publication in the *Pioneer Press*, the school's official student newspaper. The reviews concerned *Mississippi Burning* and *Rain Man*, both R-rated films. Although the principal conceded he had no objection to the content of either review, he removed them from the school paper because school officials did not want to encourage junior high students to see R-rated movies.

In the lawsuit that followed, the Appellate Division of the Superior Court of New Jersey held that this act of administrative censorship violated the First Amendment *in spite of the Hazelwood precedent*, and the New Jersey Supreme Court ultimately agreed. The principal and superintendent attempted to justify the censorship under the school board's policy on school publications by arguing that reviews of R-rated movies fell within the category of "material which advocated the use or advertised the availability of any substance believed to constitute a danger to student health." But nothing in either review said anything about any "substance" that could affect "student health." Nor is either movie about such subjects.

The state high court emphasized that the school officials involved in this case had no adequate policy governing issues such as the content of the school newspaper. The court chastised the state commissioner of education for failing to ensure that the schools had clear policies on such matters. Given the lack of a policy, school officials did not have a valid basis for censoring this particular newspaper, the court said.

Unofficial and off-campus speech. Years before Brandi Levy sent her profane Snap in 2017, courts struggled with regulating student speech on social media. The *Mahanoy* case makes it clear that such administrative actions should be rare, but it doesn't shut that door entirely, and the Court didn't provide a legal test. As several justices pointed out, the censorship of off-campus student speech acts, such as those on social network sites, accompanied by on-campus disciplinary action against students, raises serious First Amendment questions.

Early cases relied on the fact that online content could be accessed on school grounds. For example, in 2002, the Pennsylvania Supreme Court upheld disciplinary action against an eighth-grade boy for an off-campus website that contained "derogatory, profane, offensive and threatening comments" about a teacher and the principal. The court said there was

FIG. 120.
Mary Beth Tinker
at the Kansas
Scholastic Press
Association
conference, Sept.
2017.

*Photo by
Lauren Payne Muth.
Used with permission.*

a connection to the school because students viewed the website on campus computers and it created an actual, substantial disruption (*J.S. v. Bethlehem Area Sch. Dist.*, 807 A.2d 847).

Federal appellate courts started to hear these cases in the 2010s, with mixed results. In *Doninger v. Niehoff* (642 F.3d 334, 2011), the Second Circuit addressed both on- and off-campus speech acts. Avery Doninger, a high school student in Burlington, Connecticut, wrote a blog post expressing her anger that a battle-of-the-bands event called Jamfest would not be held in the school auditorium on the planned date because the person who operated the sound equipment could not be there (the event could be moved or rescheduled). Upset, Doninger sent a mass email from a parent's official school account encouraging people to contact the school to get Jamfest back on schedule in the auditorium, in violation of school policy regarding the use of such email accounts. The next day, principal Karissa Niehoff said that the superintendent was so upset by the emails she got that Jamfest would be cancelled. That night Doninger wrote on her public LiveJournal blog site, calling the administrators "douchebags" and encouraging more Jamfest support. Then, when Doninger went into the administrative office to accept her nomination for senior class secretary, the principal told her that she could not run for the position because of the blog post.

The Second Circuit held that it was not clearly legally established that punishing Doninger for her blog and making students remove "Team Avery" T-shirts would violate the First Amendment. Based on the facts, it was "reasonably foreseeable that Doninger's post would reach school property and have disruptive consequences there." But the court didn't address whether the speech *should* have been protected—it only supported administrators' qualified immunity defense, saying they weren't personally liable. As for the T-shirts, the court said the same thing: the law is unsettled, so administrators could not have known they were violating Doninger's rights—adding that *if* the principal made a mistake, it was a reasonable one, hardly a ringing endorsement of student free expression rights.

The Third Circuit in 2011 clarified its position on off-campus expression in two *en banc* opinions resolving prior opposing decisions. In both cases, students created fake profiles of their high school principals on the social network MySpace, and earlier panels at the Third Circuit had come to different conclusions. The *en banc* opinions resolved the panels' different outcomes, which resulted mainly from differences in campus disruption.

In *Layshock v. Hermitage Sch. Dist.* (650 F.3d 205), both a district court and a three-judge panel of the Third Circuit had ruled in favor of student Justin Layshock, who had used his grandmother's computer to create the fake profile. The court said that its decision was based on the fact that Layshock created the profile off-campus, and the profile did not disrupt the school—even though it suggested that the principal did drugs and shoplifted. "It would be an unseemly and dangerous precedent to allow the state, in the guise of school authorities, to reach into a child's home," said the court.

However, a different set of facts were at issue in *J.S. v. Blue Mountain Sch. Dist.* (650 F.3d 915; not the same J.S. as in the *Bethlehem* case), where an eighth-grade girl created a fake profile for her middle-school principal alleging that he was a sex addict and pedophile. Both a district court and a three-judge appellate panel found for the school, using *Fraser* as justification to punish "vulgar and offensive" speech and claiming an "effect" from the profile on school discipline. But the Third Circuit *en banc* reversed: there was no disruption in school from the fake profile, and students couldn't even see the page in school because school computers blocked the MySpace website. In addition, the profile was so juvenile and outrageous that no one would take it seriously (it said things like "it's your oh so wonderful, hairy, expressionless, sex addict, fagass ... PRINCIPAL"), and the student did not identify the principal by name and made the profile private so that only she and her friends could see it. Six dissenting judges said that the majority leaves officials powerless to punish offenders.

Unprotected social media speech. Justice Breyer in *Mahanoy* said there are some occasions where administrators can punish off-campus speech, particularly when it's students targeting other students. For example, in 2011, Kara Kowalski, a senior at Musselman High School in Berkeley County, West Virginia, was suspended from school for five days for creating a MySpace page called "S.A.S.H.," which she said stood for "Students Against Sluts Herpes" and was targeted against another student. In ruling that Kowalski could be disciplined, the Fourth Circuit said that she "used the Internet to orchestrate a targeted attack on a classmate, and did so in a manner that was sufficiently connected to the school environment as to implicate the School District's recognized authority to discipline speech" (*Kowalski v. Berkeley County Schools*, 652 F.3d 565).

In another unprotected off-campus speech act, twin brothers Steven and Sean Wilson created a website entitled "NorthPress," in which they wrote about issues at Lee's Summit (Missouri) North High School. A third student also posted racist comments and sexually degrading remarks about some female students on the blog. The Eighth Circuit reversed a lower court's support of the brothers (*SJW v. Lee's Summit R-7 School Dist.*, 696 F.3d 771, 2013). School officials testified that NorthPress "caused considerable disturbance and disruption," and thus under *Tinker*, even though the speech was made at least partially off-campus (although the parties could not agree on how much), it could be suppressed.

What about instant messages that focus on guns and violence? In *Wynar v. Douglas County Sch. Dist.* (728 F.3d 1062, 2013), the Ninth Circuit said that high school sophomore Landon Wynar's expulsion did not violate the First Amendment. Wynar's instant messages over MySpace bragged about his gun collection, invoked Hitler and his 4/20 birthdate, and threatened violence against other students. Concerned classmates turned him in, and he was expelled for 90 days. Wynar said he was only joking, but the Ninth Circuit said that Douglas High School was justified in taking him seriously. "Landon's messages threatened the student body as a whole and targeted specific students by name. They represent the quintessential harm to the rights of other students to be secure," wrote the court.

Bottom line. Given the high court's unwillingness in *Mahanoy* to extend schools' ability to punish even profane off-campus online student speech, courts may be willing to rein in overeager administrators. But because there's no test to guide lower courts, such cases will continue to arise. Those that involve a mix of on-campus and off-campus expression, like Avery Doninger's, will probably be the most challenging to resolve.

Social controversies. Contentious religious and social issues often give rise to student speech issues, as the Vietnam War did for Mary Beth Tinker. Black armbands made a return to the courts in 2008, and in the circuit in which *Tinker* originated. In *Lowry v. Watson Chapel Sch. Dist.* (540 F.3d 752), the Eighth Circuit upheld students' rights to wear protest armbands. Arkansas student Chris Lowry and others wore black armbands to protest a school dress code and were disciplined. The facts in *Lowry* were nearly identical to those in the *Tinker* case, but administrators tried to distinguish by saying that the issue was not the Vietnam war but merely a dress code. The court was not convinced: "In both cases, a school district punished students based on their non-disruptive protest of a government policy."

Several cases in 2013 demonstrate the clash between students and administration in two very contentious areas, with mixed results: gay rights and abortion. A student won his case against a teacher who ejected him from class for saying "I don't accept gays" in *Glowacki v. Howell Pub. Sch. Dist.* (2013 U.S. Dist. LEXIS 85960). Daniel Glowacki and his teacher, Jay McDowell, had an exchange on a school-sponsored anti-bullying day in which Glowacki said that accepting gay people conflicted with his Catholic religion. McDowell threw Glowacki out of class, and Glowacki filed suit. The court found for the student, saying that even though McDowell was concerned about the feelings of students in the class he suspected were gay, "[t]he Court does not believe that Daniel's comments, addressed as they were to McDowell during a classroom discussion initiated by McDowell, impinged upon the rights of any individual student." There was no serious disruption, and therefore, Glowacki's speech was protected under *Tinker*. The Sixth Circuit later affirmed this outcome.

But *Tinker* could not protect students handing out rubber dolls shaped like fetuses (*Taylor v. Roswell Indep. Sch. Dist.*, 713 F.3d 25, 2013). Seth Taylor and other students, members of a religious group, distributed the dolls at their high schools with a tag containing a Bible

Focus on...
When just doing journalism gets you in trouble

In fall 2020, Jared Nally, an enrolled member of the Miami Tribe of Oklahoma and editor-in-chief of Haskell Indian Nations (Kansas) University's award-winning campus newspaper *The Indian Leader*, got a "directive" from university president Ronald Graham. In his investigatory work, Nally engaged in traditional newsgathering activities: recording a university official without her knowledge (as Kansas is a "one-party consent" state, that's legal), talking to police as a representative of the paper about a deceased university employee (legal), and writing critical letters to university personnel (also

FIG. 121. Jared Nally, *The Indian Leader*.

Gary Rohman / FIRE.

legal). But Graham told Nally those activities "brought yourself, *The Indian Leader*, Haskell, and me unwarranted attention" and demanded that Nally act with "appropriate respect"—threatening disciplinary action if disobeyed. He also didn't recognize *The Indian Leader* as a student organization, so staff couldn't access the paper's bank account—in retaliation, Nally said, for his activities.

This wasn't the first time Haskell administration clashed with its student media: an earlier conflict produced a 1989 settlement between administrators and the newspaper that made it clear that students have editorial control over the *Leader* and that Haskell officials couldn't "censor, edit, or modify the contents" of student publications. The Foundation for Individual Rights in Education (FIRE) sent a complaint on Nally's behalf to the Department of the Interior, under which the Bureau of Indian Education (BIE) is housed, asking for an investigation into Graham's behavior. Graham eventually backed down—but didn't tell Nally that he'd withdrawn the directive until January 2021, three months after he allegedly decided to do so, leaving Nally and *Leader* staff under a chilling effect. Graham didn't last long afterwards; in May 2021, after targeting employees' speech rights (prohibiting "derogatory opinions" about his decisions and ordering them not to speak to the media or post online identifying themselves with Haskell without permission) and receiving a unanimous no-confidence vote from the faculty, he was removed as president by the BIE after less than a year in the position.

Haskell is one of only two universities directly operated by the BIE; the other is Southwest Indian Polytechnic Institute in Albuquerque. Through the Indian Civil Rights Act of 1968, the Bill of Rights (including the First Amendment) applies in full force to Native nations.

passage and other information. Some students caused chaos with the dolls: dismembering them, throwing the heads against the walls like rubber balls, using them to plug toilets—a "disaster," as one school employee put it. Principals at both schools confiscated the remaining dolls. The Tenth Circuit said that the policy was a content-neutral one, applied equally. And, as the court put it, a rubber doll, because it can be torn apart and used in disruptive and destructive ways, "carries more potential for disruption than the passive, silent act of wearing a t-shirt or a black armband."

Student activism reached a zenith in 2018 after the February shooting at at Marjory Stoneman Douglas High School in Parkland, Florida, which left 17 students and staff dead. At the March 24 "March for Our Lives," students and others all over the world marched to protest the National Rifle Association's gun advocacy. Over 1.2 million people participated in more than 450 events just in the United States. Following the march, an April 20 "National School Walkout" was organized to mark the anniversary of the Columbine High School mass shooting and demand an end to gun violence. That event was to start at 10:00 a.m. across time zones (when the Columbine shooting started) and last for 13 seconds of silence to honor the 13 killed at Columbine. These events—organized and attended by students—were important stories for student media to cover. But that didn't mean that administration wanted that to happen. In the days following, stories emerged about administrative clashes with students about everything from attendance to coverage of the events. One Houston principal threatened a three-day suspension for participation and even sent letters home to parents saying that their notes excusing their students would not prevent suspensions, asserting that students "are here for an education and not a political protest."

Other Issues

Student dress codes and other forms of communication, like violent essays, have also been challenged in court. And other laws have recently been implicated in some cases.

Dress codes. Dress codes, often passed in elementary and high schools to avoid issues like gang affiliation or classroom distraction and to promote safety and harmony, are increasingly the subject of lawsuits. A recent example: In an Eighth Circuit case, *B.W.A. v. Farmington R-7 Sch. Dist.* (554 F.3d 734, 2009), B.W.A., a minor, wore clothing to school featuring the Confederate flag and was suspended. He said that his First Amendment rights had been violated. The Eighth Circuit said that "schools may act proactively to prohibit race-related violence." The court, in dismissing the student's case against the Missouri school district, added that "the school's ban on the flag was reasonably related to a substantial disruption, did not amount to viewpoint discrimination, and did not violate the First Amendment."

Another example comes from the Fifth Circuit in *Palmer v. Waxahachie Indep. Sch. Dist.* (579 F.3d 502). Paul Palmer, a Texas high school student, wore a t-shirt to school supporting John Edwards for president in 2008. He was ordered to remove it because it contained printed words which did not support the school, its instructional goals, or school spirit. The district revamped its dress code, and Palmer submitted three shirts for approval: the original Edwards t-shirt plus a polo shirt with the same message and a t-shirt that contained "Freedom of Speech" on the front and the text of the First Amendment on the back—all rejected.

The court said the rule was content-neutral because it did not target any particular kind of speech even though the code allowed certain expression, saying, "The District was in no way attempting to suppress any student's expression through its dress code—a critical fact based on earlier cases—so the dress code is content-neutral." The court then applied intermediate scrutiny, under which the code passed. The circuits are split on the level of scrutiny for student speech cases, but the Supreme Court declined to hear an appeal.

Relying on *Tinker*, the Fourth Circuit in 2013 found that a school's punishing a student's wearing of Confederate flag shirts was appropriate. Candice Hardwick said her First Amendment rights were violated, but the court said long-running racial tensions in the Latta, South Carolina, schools she attended made the theme of the Confederate flag shirts Hardwick wore run afoul of the schools' codes prohibiting offensive dress. Even though Hardwick's shirts never caused a problem, the court agreed with administrators that it was reasonable to foresee they would: "[T]he potential for such vastly different views among students about the meaning of the Confederate flag provide a sufficient basis to justify the school officials' conclusion that [they] would cause a substantial disruption" (*Hardwick v. Heyward*, 711 F.3d 426).

In an interesting, and for some, troubling, case, students wearing American flag t-shirts during Cinco de Mayo (Fifth of May, a national Mexican day of celebration) events at a California public school were told to remove them, and this was not considered to be a First Amendment violation (*Dariano v. Morgan Hill Unified Sch. Dist.*, 767 F.3d 764, 2014). A three-judge panel of the Ninth Circuit said that under *Tinker*, it is not necessary to wait for violence to take place to act. In prior years, there had been violence when students displayed the American flag on Cinco de Mayo, and the court reasoned that "school officials could 'curtail the exercise of First Amendment rights when they c[ould] reasonably forecast material interference or substantial disruption,' but could not discipline the student without 'show[ing] justification for their action.'" The students petitioned for an *en banc* rehearing, but that was denied, and the Supreme Court also denied *cert.* Some commentators were disturbed by this case because the court sided not with student speakers but instead with those exercising "heckler's vetoes"—actions intended to shut down speech.

Title IX. In a different—and successful—approach to challenging a North Carolina private charter school's dress code, plaintiffs in *Peltier v. Charter Day Sch., Inc.* (384 F. Supp. 3d 579, 2019) invoked both the Fourteenth Amendment's equal protection clause and Title IX, a 1972 law originally intended to ensure gender equality in scholastic sports. Expanded to cover sexual assault and harassment during the Obama administration and amended in the Trump administration, Title IX's focus remained gender-based discrimination. Charter Day School's dress code required girls to wear "skirts, skorts, or jumpers" and boys to wear shorts or pants. Some girls objected to the code, saying that skirts were not only less warm and comfortable but restricted their physical movement. The girls' parents sued, citing not the First Amendment but Title IX and the Fourteenth Amendment's equal protection clause.

A federal district judge agreed with the parents. Title IX doesn't apply, said the judge, since the federal Department of Education interprets Title IX to leave dress code issues at the local level. Still, this private school is a state actor: not only does North Carolina law classify charter schools as public, the free public education provided by Charter Day is "an historical, exclusive and traditional state function." Since "the skirts requirement causes the girls to suffer a burden the boys do not, simply because they are female," the judge wrote, it violates equal protection. The case has been appealed to the Fourth Circuit, which heard oral arguments in March 2021. Stay tuned.

Violent content. Courts have been supportive of administrative censorial decisions that involve students making violent comments, writing violent essays or notes, or wishing violence upon others. An example from many in recent years: in *Cuff v. Valley Cent. Sch. Dist.* (677 F.3d 109, 2012), a fifth-grade student drew a picture of an astronaut and expressed a desire to blow up the school with teachers inside. Another student saw the drawing and brought it to a teacher's attention; the fifth-grader was suspended. In upholding the suspension, the Second Circuit said that the student's history of violence, as well as concerns of his teachers, suggested that there might be disruption to school activities as a result of this drawing, and that *Tinker* only required a showing of "facts which might reasonably have led school authorities to forecast substantial disruption of or material interference with school activities," not that such disruption actually occurred.

A 2-1 Fifth Circuit panel, supported by an *en banc* decision, found a student's violent rap song published off-campus to be unprotected expression. Taylor Bell's song contained, among others, the phrase "looking down girls' shirts / drool running down your mouth / messing with wrong one / going to get a pistol down your mouth." The district court said the lyrics were threatening and offensive and could reasonably be expected to cause a material disruption. A Fifth Circuit panel agreed, as did the *en banc* Fifth Circuit (*Bell v. Itawamba Cty. Sch. Bd.*, 799 F.3d 379, 2015). Quoting the *Doninger* case from the Second Circuit, the majority said that "*Tinker* applies to speech originating off-campus if it 'would foreseeably create a risk of substantial disruption within the school environment, at least when it was similarly foreseeable that the off-campus expression might also reach campus.'" The majority added, "[W]hen a student intentionally directs at the school community speech reasonably understood by school officials to threaten, harass, and intimidate a teacher, even when such speech originated, and was disseminated, off-campus without the use of school resources," *Tinker* would apply and would leave such speech unprotected. Dissenters viewed the majority opinion as too broad in scope.

■ FREEDOM AT PRIVATE SCHOOLS

This chapter has been devoted to freedom of expression at public schools and colleges. What about private institutions? At private schools, the general rule is that freedom only exists if school officials find it in their interest to grant it: in the absence of *state action*, the First Amendment does not apply. There are exceptions; the *Peltier* case discussed earlier is one, where the combination of state law and school function combined to make a private school a state actor. But this isn't common. When a private university newspaper is censored or its editors are fired, normally the worst the administration need fear is bad public relations. The school may face condemnation by professional media and journalistic organizations, but there is usually little chance for the aggrieved students to win a lawsuit.

This problem was well illustrated by a 1980 incident at Baylor University, a Baptist church-related institution in Waco, Texas. *Playboy* magazine was doing a photo feature on "Girls of the Southwest Conference," and a *Playboy* photographer was coming to town. The university president warned that any Baylor student who posed nude for *Playboy* would be punished (and presumably expelled). The Baylor newspaper, the *Lariat*, editorially said that Baylor students should be free to make up their own minds about whether to pose. Then the president told the *Lariat* editors not to cover the growing *Playboy* controversy. The editors rejected that demand, and several were fired. Shortly, more staff members and two journalism professors resigned in protest. One faculty member who resigned was abruptly ordered to leave Baylor mid-semester. Before it was over, the Baylor incident had stirred a national controversy, but the *Lariat* staff had no legal recourse. They were out.

Although the issues that provoke censorship aren't often as spectacular as the one at Baylor, "censorship" incidents aren't unusual at private universities. During the era of student activism, many lawsuits were filed alleging constitutional violations by private institutions, but courts consistently ruled in favor of school officials—except in a very few cases where state action could be shown. To establish state action, it must be shown that a government is deeply involved not only in funding the institution but also in its management. In separate cases (neither involving student press freedom), state action was shown at two major private universities in Pennsylvania: Pittsburgh and Temple. In both instances Pennsylvania had entered agreements with school officials in which the state provided major funding in return for substantial reductions in tuition for Pennsylvania residents. Moreover, the state was given the power to appoint one-third of each institution's governing board. (See *Isaacs v. Temple Univ.*, 385 F.Supp. 473, 1974; and *Braden v. Pittsburgh Univ.*, 552 F.2d 948, 1977.)

Aside from these two Pennsylvania cases and the *Peltier* case discussed above, decisions establishing state action at private schools are hard to find. In 1982, the Supreme Court did address the question of state action at private institutions, in *Rendell-Baker v. Kohn* (457 U.S. 830), ruling that state action was not present at a private high school for students with special problems, even though the school received 90% of its revenue from government funds. In a 7-2 ruling, the justices made it highly unlikely that state action can be shown at a private school or college. Thus, the conclusion seems clear: in the absence of an arrangement like those at Temple and Pittsburgh, or of state laws like North Carolina's, there's no state action, and private school administrators may therefore ignore the First Amendment.

There is, however, one other possible recourse. Some scholars have suggested that the common law principles of private association law be applied to student rights cases. A private association must operate in accordance with its own bylaws. When it fails to do that, its members may turn to the courts for help. That principle has not often been used by students, but it could be, given a university policy that guarantees freedom of the press and a clear violation of that policy. Perhaps in an appropriate case a court would follow this reasoning and recognize that private university students have some rights, at least when the institution has adopted a policy that says they do.

Workarounds for private schools: using the front-page fold. But that doesn't mean that there aren't workarounds for students at private schools. Journalists at a private college dealt with censorship by administrators in a very creative way in 2011. When told they couldn't publish a story about a professor who had allegedly used exotic dancers at an off-campus symposium on the front page "above the fold" where it could be seen in campus newsracks, the editors decided to leave the top half of the front page totally blank except for the words "See below the fold" in small type—where, of course, the full story ran. The editors at the LaSalle University *Collegian* ran an editorial explaining why they did what they did.

■ PRACTICAL CONSIDERATIONS

So far, we've talked about student press freedom mostly in terms of lawsuits and the First Amendment. Because this chapter will certainly be read for guidance by students facing threats of censorship, a few practical observations are in order.

First, it should be emphasized that it is sometimes necessary to fight for constitutional rights—in court, if necessary. School administrators often ignore the First Amendment until forced to recognize that it exists. Student newspapers are censored every year without anyone doing anything about it.

It is unfortunate but true that winning one's constitutional rights can be expensive and time-consuming. If you are censored, you may have some tough choices to make. Ask yourself some questions. Is the censorship really unlawful? High school administrators now have wide latitude to control the content of official student newspapers unless there is a state law or local policy forbidding censorship. College administrators have less latitude in controlling the student press, although that could change as a result of recent court decisions.

Also, how important is the item you've been told you can't publish? How would a judge react to it? Justice Oliver Wendell Holmes' legal maxim "hard cases make bad law" applies here. Don't pursue a case that invites a bad legal precedent, one that could be used to deny freedom to students elsewhere. A well-documented story about malfeasance by the college administration is one thing; a column that uses four-letter words gratuitously is another.

After weighing these questions, there are some specific steps to take if you have a case worth pursuing. First, go through all available channels. Consult your faculty adviser if you have one. If there is a publications policy board, take the case there. Only if all internal remedies fail is it time to consider a lawsuit.

But if you reach that point, weigh your options again. Is there a local attorney willing to represent you on a low-cost basis? The American Civil Liberties Union has represented students in numerous First Amendment cases. The Student Press Law Center in Washington may also be able to offer advice—or help you find an attorney. If legal help isn't available, compromise may again be in order. But if, on the other hand, you really have a good case and a good lawyer, perhaps your name will someday appear in law books like this one.

■ AN OVERVIEW OF MAJOR ISSUES

The question of student press freedom is a miniature version of many other questions addressed in this book. In trying to address it, the Supreme Court and federal appellate courts extended First Amendment rights to students at public high schools and colleges—and then began to curtail those rights. Online student speech muddies the waters.

Underlying these legal principles, there are questions on which there is little consensus. To what extent should students be protected by the First Amendment? When are prior restraints justified at a public school or college? Should the rules differ at high schools and colleges? Why should the rules be different for private schools? Should "underground" media productions—whether physical or online—be treated differently than official ones?

If the rationale for extending First Amendment rights to students is the concept of state action, doesn't that run afoul of the idea that the *taxpayers* should have the final say about what goes on at a public school? Isn't the school principal the school board's surrogate, charged with doing *the public's* bidding? In effect, the Supreme Court ruled in *Hazelwood* that the principal has the powers of a publisher, to exercise control at will, at least in expression that takes places on the school campus. Yet much student expression now takes place off-campus and online. Justice Breyer may have suggested that schools should be "nurseries of democracy" in *Mahanoy*, but it's clear that the case was intended to be limited.

In the end, perhaps the most basic question in student press law is this: should the schools be a microcosm of society at large, or should they be insulated places with stricter rules and fewer constitutional safeguards?

WHAT SHOULD I KNOW ABOUT MY STATE?

SUMMARY

A SUMMARY
OF STUDENT
PRESS LAW

- Does my state have any protections for student speech and press? Are they statutes, common law, or both, and what do they say? (Check out the Student Press Law Center's website at www.splc.org for help or support.)
- What does my school or campus policy say about student speech and press rights? Is there a "free speech zone"?
- How has my federal circuit handled student free speech and press issues?

Does the First Amendment Apply to Students?

In *Tinker v. Des Moines Ind. School District*, the Supreme Court extended First Amendment protection to students attending public schools. But the Court said high school students' freedom of expression may be limited when necessary to protect the rights of others and to maintain an orderly educational process. The courts have generally extended somewhat broader First Amendment rights to college students.

Are Student Publications Constitutionally Protected?

Federal courts have consistently held that unofficial or "underground" high school publications are protected by the First Amendment and may not be arbitrarily censored by school administrators. But be careful, as courts have differed on the standing for online unofficial publications.

Where Do High School Journalists Stand Now?

In *Hazelwood School District v. Kuhlmeier* the Court said the First Amendment does not prevent administrators from censoring official high school newspapers. The Court said there is a difference between the free speech activities that public school officials must *tolerate* (as in *Tinker*) and the kind of speech the First Amendment requires them to sponsor by permitting it in official publications or at school activities. Some states have "New Voices" laws to offer protection to student expression.

Are Private Schools Treated Differently?

The First Amendment prohibits the denial of free expression rights by governments, not by private entities. Unless a private school official's conduct constitutes state action (which it rarely does), the First Amendment is inapplicable.

What About Social Media?

The Court in *Mahanoy Sch. Dist. v. B.L.* said that administrators should be able to censor online off-campus student speech only rarely, but it didn't give a definitive test to determine when such punishment might be acceptable.

Selected Excerpts from the Law

The First Amendment

Congress shall make no law respecting an establishment of religion, or prohibiting the free exercise thereof; or *abridging the freedom of speech or of the press*; or the right of the people peaceably to assemble, and to petition the Government for a redress of grievances. (1791)

The Fourth Amendment

The right of the people to be secure in their persons, houses, papers, and effects, against unreasonable searches and seizures, shall not be violated, and no Warrants shall issue, but upon probable cause, supported by Oath or affirmation, and particularly describing the place to be searched, and the persons or things to be seized. (1791)

The Sixth Amendment

In all criminal prosecutions, the accused shall enjoy the right to a speedy and public trial, *by an impartial jury* of the State and district wherein the crime shall have been committed... (1791)

The Fourteenth Amendment

...No state shall make or enforce any law which shall abridge the privileges or immunities of citizens of the United States; *nor shall any state deprive any person of life, liberty or property, without due process of law*; nor deny to any person within its jurisdiction the equal protection of the laws.... (1868)

Section 230 of the Telecommunications Act

No provider or user of an interactive computer service shall be treated as the publisher or speaker of any information provided by another information content provider. (1996)

Section 326 of the Communications Act

Nothing in this Act shall be understood or construed to give the (Federal Communications) Commission the power of censorship over the radio communications or signals transmitted by any radio station, and no regulation or condition shall be promulgated or fixed by the Commission which shall interfere with the right of free speech by means of radio communication. (1934)

Section 1464 of the U.S. Criminal Code

Whoever utters any obscene, indecent, or profane language by means of radio communication shall be fined under this title or imprisoned not more than two years, or both. (1948)

Index